Lecture Notes in Computer Science 4833

Commenced Publication in 1973
Founding and Former Series Editors:
Gerhard Goos, Juris Hartmanis, and Jan van Leeuwen

Kaoru Kurosawa (Ed.)

Advances in Cryptology – ASIACRYPT 2007

13th International Conference on the Theory
and Application of Cryptology and Information Security
Kuching, Malaysia, December 2-6, 2007
Proceedings

 Springer

Volume Editor

Kaoru Kurosawa
Ibaraki University
Department of Computer and Information Sciences
4-12-1 Nakanarusawa
Hitachi, Ibaraki 316-8511, Japan
E-mail: kurosawa@mx.ibaraki.ac.jp

Library of Congress Control Number: 2007939450

CR Subject Classification (1998): E.3, D.4.6, F.2.1-2, K.6.5, C.2, J.1, G.2

LNCS Sublibrary: SL 4 – Security and Cryptology

ISSN   0302-9743
ISBN-10   3-540-76899-8 Springer Berlin Heidelberg New York
ISBN-13   978-3-540-76899-9 Springer Berlin Heidelberg New York

Springer is a part of Springer Science+Business Media

springer.com

©International Association for Cryptology Research 2007

Typesetting: Camera-ready by author, data conversion by Scientific Publishing Services, Chennai, India
Printed on acid-free paper   SPIN: 12194407   06/3180   5 4 3 2 1 0

Preface

ASIACRYPT 2007 was held in Kuching, Sarawak, Malaysia, during December 2–6, 2007. This was the 13th ASIACRYPT conference, and was sponsored by the International Association for Cryptologic Research (IACR), in cooperation with the Information Security Research (iSECURES) Lab of Swinburne University of Technology (Sarawak Campus) and the Sarawak Development Institute (SDI), and was financially supported by the Sarawak Government. The General Chair was Raphael Phan and I had the privilege of serving as the Program Chair.

The conference received 223 submissions (from which one submission was withdrawn). Each paper was reviewed by at least three members of the Program Committee, while submissions co-authored by a Program Committee member were reviewed by at least five members. (Each PC member could submit at most one paper.) Many high-quality papers were submitted, but due to the relatively small number which could be accepted, many very good papers had to be rejected. After 11 weeks of reviewing, the Program Committee selected 33 papers for presentation (two papers were merged). The proceedings contain the revised versions of the accepted papers. These revised papers were not subject to editorial review and the authors bear full responsibility for their contents.

The Committee selected the following two papers as the best papers: "Cryptanalysis of Grindahl" by Thomas Peyrin; and "Faster Addition and Doubling on Elliptic Curves" by Daniel J. Bernstein and Tanja Lange. The authors of these two papers were invited to submit the full version of their paper to the *Journal of Cryptology*. The author of the first paper, Thomas Peyrin, received the Best Paper Award.

The conference featured invited lectures by Ran Canetti and Tatsuaki Okamoto. Ran Canetti's paper "Treading the Impossible: A Tour of Set-Up Assumptions for Obtaining Universally Composable Security" and Tatsuaki Okamoto's paper "Authenticated Key Exchange and Key Encapsulation in the Standard Model" have been included in this volume.

There are many people who contributed to the success of ASIACRYPT 2007. I would like to thank many authors from around the world for submitting their papers. I am deeply grateful to the Program Committee for their hard work to ensure that each paper received a thorough and fair review. I gratefully acknowledge the external reviewers listed on the following pages. I am also grateful to Arjen Lenstra, Bart Preneel, and Andy Clark for their advice as the directors of IACR. Finally, I would like to thank the General Chair, Raphael Phan, for organizing the conference and Shai Halevi for developing and maintaining his very nice Web Submission and Review System.

September 2007   Kaoru Kurosawa

Asiacrypt 2007

December 2–6, 2007, Kuching, Sarawak, Malaysia

Sponsored by
the International Association for Cryptologic Research (IACR)

in cooperation with
the Information Security Research (iSECURES) Lab
of Swinburne University of Technology (Sarawak Campus)

and
the Sarawak Development Institute (SDI)

and
financially supported by the Sarawak Government

General Chair

Raphael C.-W. Phan, EPFL, Switzerland

Program Chair

Kaoru Kurosawa, Ibaraki University, Japan

Program Commitee

Masayuki Abe	NTT, Japan
Alex Biryukov	University of Luxembourg, Luxembourg
Alexandra Boldyreva	Georgia Institute of Technology, USA
Jung Hee Cheon	Seoul National University, Korea
Jean-Sebastien Coron	University of Luxembourg, Luxembourg
Joan Daemen	STMicroelectronics, Belgium
Serge Fehr	CWI, Netherlands
Steven Galbraith	Royal Holloway University of London, UK
Craig Gentry	Stanford University, USA
Henri Gilbert	France Telecom, France
Shai Halevi	IBM T.J. Watson Research Center, USA
Helena Handschuh	Spansion, France
Tetsu Iwata	Nagoya University, Japan
Thomas Johansson	Lund University, Sweden
Marc Joye	Thomson R&D France, France
Jonathan Katz	University of Maryland, USA
Lars R. Knudsen	Technical University of Denmark, Denmark

Hugo Krawczyk	IBM T.J. Watson Research Center, USA
Kaoru Kurosawa	Ibaraki University, Japan
Xuejia Lai	Shanghai Jiaotong University, China
Arjen K. Lenstra	EPFL IC LACAL, Switzerland
Stefan Lucks	Bauhaus University Weimar, Germany
Anna Lysyanskaya	Brown University, USA
Alexander May	Technische Universität Darmstadt, Germany
Jesper Buus Nielsen	University of Aarhus, Denmark
Elisabeth Oswald	University of Bristol, UK
Josef Pieprzyk	Macquarie University, Australia
Bart Preneel	Katholieke Universiteit Leuven, Belgium
Pandu Rangan	Indian Institute of Technology, India
Palash Sarkar	Indian Statistical Institute, India
Nigel Smart	Bristol University, UK
Tsuyoshi Takagi	Future University-Hakodate, Japan
Serge Vaudenay	EPFL, Switzerland
Brent Waters	SRI International, USA
Stefan Wolf	ETH Zurich, Switzerland

External Reviewers

Jesus Almansa	Claus Diem	Stuart Haber
Frederik Armknecht	Yevgeniy Dodis	Sang Geun Hahn
Gilles Van Assche	Orr Dunkelman	Safuat Hamdy
Georges Baatz	Håkan Englund	Daewan Han
Thomas Baignéres	Pooya Farshim	Wei Han
Boaz Barak	Martin Feldhofer	Goichiro Hanaoka
Mira Belenkiy	Marc Fischlin	Martin Hell
Waldyr Benits	Matthias Fitzi	Dennis Hofheinz
Kamel Bentahar	Ewan Fleischmann	Xuan Hong
Come Berbain	Eiichiro Fujisaki	Nick Howgrave-Graham
Dan Bernstein	Jun Furukawa	Jim Hughes
Guido Bertoni	Philippe Gaborit	Sebastiaan Indesteeghe
Olivier Billet	Nicolas Gama	Tetsuya Izu
Andrey Bogdanov	Pierrick Gaudry	Markus Jakobsson
Arnaud Boscher	Rosario Gennaro	Stas Jarecki
Xavier Boyen	Ralf Gerkmann	Ellen Jochemsz
Ran Canetti	Zheng Gong	Pascal Junod
Christophe De Cannière	Vipul Goyal	Alexandre Karlov
Zhenfu Cao	Rob Granger	Ulrich Kühn
Chris Charnes	Johann Großchädl	Marcelo Kaihara
Sanjit Chatterjee	Gaurav Gupta	Yael Kalai
Scott Contini	Frank Gurkaynak	Alexandre Karlov
Yang Cui	Kil-Chan Ha	Dmitry Khovratovich
Alexander Dent	Robbert de Haan	Eike Kiltz

Vlastimal Klima
Markulf Kohlweiss
Yuichi Komano
Chiu-Yuen Koo
Ranjit Kumaresan
Taekyoung Kwon
Tanja Lange
Jooyoung Lee
Mun-Kyu Lee
Frédéric Lefèbvre
Hoon Wei Lim
Yehuda Lindell
Joseph Liu
Yu Long
Xianhui Lu
Changshe Ma
Subhamoy Maitra
Keith Martin
Krystian Matusiewicz
Florian Mendel
Daniele Micciancio
Wil Michiels
Lorenz Minder
Andrew Moss
Siguna Mueller
Toru Nakanishi
Arvind Narayanan
Gregory Neven
Phong Nguyen
Svetla Nikova
Ryo Nishimaki
Adam O'Neill
Miyako Ohkubo
Katsuyuki Okeya

Dag Arne Osvik
Khaled Ouafi
Dan Page
Pascal Paillier
Sylvain Pasini
Rafael Pass
Vijayakrishnan
  Pasupathinathan
Kenny Paterson
Maura Paterson
Thomas Peyrin
Duong Hieu Phan
Krzysztof Pietrzak
Norbert Pramstaller
Deike Priemuth-Schmid
Prashant Punya
Wenfeng Qi
Tal Rabin
Dominik Raub
Christian Rechberger
Tom Ristenpart
Maike Ritzenhofen
Matthieu Rivain
Panagiotis Rizomiliotis
Matthew Robshaw
Kazuo Sakiyama
Joern-Marc Schmidt
Yannick Seurin
Runting Shi
Masaaki Shirase
Igor Shparlinski
Tom Shrimpton
Ben Smith
Martijn Stam

Ron Steinfeld
Marc Stevens
Koutarou Suzuki
Christophe Tartary
Emin Islam Tatli
Isamu Teranishi
Soren Thomsen
Stefan Tillich
Frederik Vercauteren
Martin Vuagnoux
Camille Vuillaume
Zhongmei Wan
Huaxiong Wang
Bogdan Warinschi
Hoeteck Wee
Benne de Weger
Ralf-Philipp Weinmann
Mi Wen
William Whyte
Christopher Wolf
Duncan Wong
Hongjun Wu
Juerg Wullschleger
Go Yamamoto
Bo-Yin Yang
Jin Yuan
Aaram Yun
Erik Zenner
Xianmo Zhang
Yunlei Zhao
Jinmin Zhong

Table of Contents

MAC and Implementation

Multiparty Computation I

Block Ciphers

Multiparty Computation II

Foundation

Invited Talk II

Public Key Encryption

Cryptanalysis

A Kilobit Special Number Field Sieve Factorization

Kazumaro Aoki[1], Jens Franke[2], Thorsten Kleinjung[2],
Arjen K. Lenstra[3,4], and Dag Arne Osvik[3]

[1] NTT, 3-9-11 Midori-cho, Musashino-shi, Tokyo, 180-8585 Japan
[2] University of Bonn, Department of Mathematics,
Beringstraße 1, D-53115 Bonn, Germany
[3] EPFL IC LACAL, INJ 330, Station 14, 1015-Lausanne, Switzerland
[4] Alcatel-Lucent Bell Laboratories, Murray Hill, NJ, USA

Abstract. We describe how we reached a new factoring milestone by completing the first special number field sieve factorization of a number having more than 1024 bits, namely the Mersenne number $2^{1039} - 1$. Although this factorization is orders of magnitude 'easier' than a factorization of a 1024-bit RSA modulus is believed to be, the methods we used to obtain our result shed new light on the feasibility of the latter computation.

1 Introduction

Proper RSA security evaluation is one of the key tasks of practitioning cryptologists. This evaluation includes tracking progress in integer factorization. In this note we present a long awaited factoring milestone. More importantly, we consider to what extent the methods we have developed to obtain our result, and which are under constant refinement, may be expected to enable us or others to push factoring capabilities even further.

We have determined the complete factorization of the Mersenne number $2^{1039} - 1$ using the special number field sieve integer factorization method (SNFS). The factor 5080711 was already known, so we obtained the new factorization of the composite 1017-bit number $(2^{1039} - 1)/5080711$. The SNFS, however, cannot take advantage of the factor 5080711. Therefore, the difficulty of our SNFS factoring effort is equivalent to the difficulty of the effort that would be required for a 1039-bit number that is very close to a power of two. This makes our factorization the first SNFS factorization that reaches the 1024-bit milestone. The previous SNFS record was the complete factorization of the 913-bit number $6^{353} - 1$ (cf. [1]).

Factoring an RSA modulus of comparable size would be several orders of magnitude harder. Simply put, this is because RSA moduli require usage of the general number field sieve algorithm (NFS), which runs much slower than the SNFS on numbers of comparable size. It is even the case that factoring a 768-bit RSA modulus would be substantially harder than a 1024-bit 'special' one. For

K. Kurosawa (Ed.): ASIACRYPT 2007, LNCS 4833, pp. 1–12, 2007.

that reason we chose to first attempt a 1024-bit SNFS factorization, as presented in this paper, before embarking on a much harder 768-bit RSA modulus using NFS. We point out that a 768-bit NFS factorization will prove to be more helpful than our present 1039-bit SNFS factorization to assess the difficulty of factoring a 1024-bit RSA modulus.

The aspects of our effort where we made most progress, and where our effort distinguishes itself most from previous factoring work such as the previous (913-bit) SNFS record, apply equally well to NFS as they apply to SNFS. They will therefore also have an effect on the assessment of feasibility of NFS-based factorizations such as those of RSA moduli. This need for re-assessment is the main reason that we feel that our result should be reported in the cryptologic literature. For more information on this point see below under '**Matrix**'.

Descriptions of the SNFS and NFS catering to almost all levels of understanding are scattered all over the literature and the web (cf. [16]). There is no need to duplicate any of these previous efforts for the purposes of the present paper. Although familiarity with sieving methods is helpful to fully appreciate all details, for an adequate understanding of the main points it suffices to know that both SNFS and NFS consist of the following major steps (cf. [10]).

Polynomial selection. Decide on polynomials to sieve with. For SNFS this does not require any computational effort, for NFS it pays off to spend a considerable effort to find 'good' polynomials. Since we factored $2^{1039} - 1$ using the SNFS our choice was easy and is reported in Section 3.

Sieving. For appropriately chosen parameters, perform the sieving step to find sufficiently many *relations*. Though finding enough relations is the major computational task, it can be done in embarrassingly parallel fashion. All relevant data for our effort are reported in Section 3.

Filtering. Filter the relations to produce a matrix. See Section 4 for the effort involved in our case.

Matrix. Find linear dependencies modulo 2 among the rows of the matrix. In theory, and asymptotically, this requires an effort comparable to the sieving step. For numbers in our current range of interest, however, the amount of computing time required for the matrix step is a fraction of the time required for the sieving step. Nevertheless, and to some possibly surprisingly, the matrix step normally constitutes the bottleneck of large factorization efforts. This is caused by the fact that it does not seem to allow the same level of parallelization as the sieving step. So far, the matrix step has, by necessity, been carried out at a single location and requires many weeks, if not months, of dedicated computing time on a tightly coupled full cluster (typically consisting of on the order of a hundred compute nodes). Consequently, our matrix-handling capabilities were limited by accessibility and availability of large single clusters.

The major point where our effort distinguishes itself from previous work is that we did the matrix step in parallel as four *independent* jobs on different clusters at various locations. This was made possible by using Coppersmith's block Wiedemann algorithm [7] instead of the block Lanczos method [6].

Further work and fine-tuning in this area can have a major impact on what can realistically be achieved, matrix-wise, and therefore factoring-wise: as implied by what was mentioned before, the effort required for the sieving step is not what practically limited our factoring capabilities, it was limited by the matrix step. The details of the new matrix step are reported in Section 5.

Square root. For each dependency in turn a square root calculation in a certain number field is performed, until the factorization is found (which happens for each dependency with probability $\geq 1/2$, independent of the other dependencies). The details, and the resulting factorization, are reported in Section 6.

Sections 3 through 6, with contents related to our factorization of $2^{1039} - 1$ as indicated above, are followed by a discussion of the wider consequences of our approach in Section 7. Furthermore, in Section 2 we describe how the number $2^{1039} - 1$ was selected as the target number for our kilobit SNFS attempt.

Throughout this paper M and G denote 10^6 and 10^9, respectively, and logarithms are natural.

2   Selecting a Kilobit SNFS Target Number

Once the decision had been reached to attempt a kilobit SNFS factorization by a joint effort, it remained to find a suitable target number to factor. In this section we describe the process that led to our choice of $2^{1039} - 1$.

Regular RSA moduli were ruled out, since in general they will not have the special form required for SNFS. Special form numbers, however, are not especially concocted to have two factors of approximately the same size, and have factors of a priori unknown sizes. In particular, they may have factors that could relatively easily be found using factoring methods different from SNFS, such as Pollard's $p - 1$ or ρ method, or the elliptic curve method (ECM, cf. [12]). Thus, for all kilobit special form numbers under consideration, we first spent a considerable ECM effort to increase our confidence that the number we would eventually settle for would not turn out to have an undesirably small factor, i.e., a factor that could have been found easier using, for instance, ECM.

Of the candidates that we tried, a 304-digit factor of $10^{371} - 1$ turned out to have a 50-digit prime factor (found by ECM after 2,652 curves with first phase bound $43M$), for a 306-digit factor of the number known as 2,2062M a 47-digit factor was found (by ECM, after 4,094 curves with the same bound), for a 307-digit factor of 2,2038M a 49-digit factor was found (ECM with 5,490 curves and same bound), and $10^{311} - 1$ was similarly ruled out after ECM found a 64-digit factor (11,214 curves with $850M$ as first phase bound and corresponding GMP-ECM 6.0 default second phase bound $12,530G$, cf. [2]).

The 307-digit number $(2^{1039} - 1)/5080711$ withstood all our ECM efforts: 1,472 curves with first and second phase bounds $850M$ and $12,530G$, respectively, and 256,599 curves with bounds $1,100M$ and $2,480G$, failed to turn up a factor. This calculation was carried out on idle PCs at NTT. It would have required more than 125 years on a single Opteron 2.2GHz with 4GB RAM. Based on the number of curves and the bounds used, it is estimated that a 65-digit factor would be missed with probability about 3.4%, a 70-digit one with probability 53.2%, and an 80-digit factor with probability 98.2%. Given the ECM failure and the substantial effort spent on it, we settled for the 307-digit factor of $2^{1039} - 1$ for our kilobit SNFS factorization attempt.

The software used for the ECM attempt was GMP-ECM 6.0 [19] and Prime95 24.14 [17] on a variety of platforms.

3   Parameter Selection and Sieving

In this section we present the polynomials that we used for the SNFS factorization of $2^{1039} - 1$ and give a superficial description of the sieving step.

With $1039 = 1 + 6 \cdot 173$ it follows that the polynomials $g(X) = X - 2^{173}$ and $f(X) = 2X^6 - 1$ have the root 2^{173} in common modulo $2^{1039} - 1$. As customary, everything related to $g(X)$ is referred to as the 'rational side', as opposed to the 'algebraic side' for $f(X)$. In the sieving step we find sufficiently many relations: coprime integers a, b with $b \geq 0$ such that both norms $bg(a/b) = a - 2^{173}b$ and $b^6 f(a/b) = 2a^6 - b^6$ have only small prime factors. Here 'sufficiently many' depends on the meaning of 'small'. What we deem to be 'small' depends in the first place on the memory sizes of the machines used for sieving and on the matrix size that we should be aiming for given what matrix size we think we can handle. This means that 'small' cannot be too large. In the second place, the expected time until we have enough relations should be acceptable too, which implies that 'small' cannot be too small either. The choice made always involves this trade-off and is given below. The theoretical justification, and parameter choice, can be found in the NFS literature (cf. [10]).

To find relations we used so-called special q's on the rational side combined with lattice sieving: primes q dividing $bg(a/b)$, such that each q leads to an index q sublattice L_q of $\mathbb{Z}^2$. Most of the $40M$ special q's between $123M$ and $911M$ were used (though the results of some small regions of q's were for organizational reasons not included in the later steps). For most special q's the rectangular region of size $2^{16} \times 2^{15}$ in the upper half plane of L_q was sieved via lattice sieving. For the special q's smaller than $300M$ this was done with factor bases consisting of all (prime, root) pairs for all primes up to $300M$ on the algebraic side and all primes $\leq 0.9q$ on the rational side, but up to $300M$ on both sides for the special q's larger than $300M$. Running our lattice siever with these parameters required approximately 1GB RAM, which was available on most machines we were using. A small fraction of the special q's was used on machines with smaller amounts of memory with factor base bounds of $120M$ on both sides. Large primes (i.e., factors beyond the factor base bounds) up to 2^{38} were accepted on both sides, without trying hard to find anything larger than 2^{36} and casting aside cofactors larger than 2^{105}. Also, cofactor pairs were not considered for which the quotient of the probability of obtaining a relation and the time spent on factoring was below a certain threshold, as described in [9].

After a period of about 6 months, at first using PCs and clusters at NTT and the University of Bonn, but later joined by clusters at EPFL, we had collected $16,570,808,010$ relations. Of these relations, 84.1% were found at NTT, 8.3% at EPFL, and 7.6% at the University of Bonn. The total CPU time would be 95 years when scaled to a 3GHz (dual core) Pentium D, or about 100 years on a 2.2GHz Athlon64/Opteron. This boils to 190 Pentium D core years and to about 2.5 relations per seconds per core. The relations required more than a terabyte of diskspace, with copies held at NTT, EPFL, and the University of Bonn.

We used the sieving software from [8].

4 Filtering

Because of the special q's the raw data as produced by the sieving step will contain a considerable number of duplicates. Before doing the complete sieving step we had estimated the number of duplicates as follows. We did lattice sieving for a tiny fraction, say $\frac{1}{t}$, of special q's, uniformly distributed over the special q range that we roughly expected to process. For each relation r (corresponding to (a,b)) obtained in this way, we computed how often it will be generated in the sieving step. Denote this number by $\mu(r)$. In an ideal situation $\mu(r)$ can be calculated as follows. First, one checks for each prime in the factorization of $bg(\frac{a}{b})$ whether it is in the special q range, i.e., whether it is a potential special q producing this relation. Secondly, for each such potential special q one checks whether the point (a,b) would be in the sieving region for this special q, and if it passed this test, whether the cofactor bounds are kept. Since a lot of approximations are made in the sieving process, the true $\mu(r)$ might be a bit smaller.

The expected number of relations for the complete special q range is $t\sum_r 1$, and the estimated number of unique relations is $t\sum_r \frac{1}{\mu(r)}$. Note that by possibly overestimating $\mu(r)$ we underestimate the number of unique relations. Doing this calculation for 99 of the special q's and the sieving parameters that we actually used, we expected that slightly more than one sixth (16.73%) of the relations found would be duplicates. It turned out that just a little less than one sixth of the relations (namely $2,748,064,961$ for 16.58%) were identified as duplicates. This resulted in a uniqued set of $13,822,743,049$ relations. Identifying and removing the duplicates took less than ten days on two 2GHz Opterons with 4GB RAM each.

Next the singletons were removed: these are relations in which a prime or (prime, root) pair occurs that does not occur in any other relation. This step is combined with the search for cliques, i.e., combinations of the relations where the large primes match up, as fully described in [4]. This took less than 4 days on single cores of 113 3GHz Pentium D processors. Finally, the same hardware was used for 69 hours for a final filtering step that produced a $66,718,354 \times 66,718,154$ matrix of total weight $9,538,688,635$.

Overall the CPU time required to produce the matrix from the raw relations was less than 2 years on a 3GHz Pentium D. It was completed in less than a week, since most of the uniqueing was done during the sieving.

As usual we did some 'over-sieving', i.e., a smaller number of relations sufficed to produce an over-square, but harder to solve, matrix. More specifically, at $14.32G$ relations (of which $12.34G$ were unique) we found an $82,848,491 \times 82,848,291$ matrix of weight $10,003,376,265$, but this matrix was obtained using suboptimal settings and the relations involving 38-bit primes were not used. At $15.61G$ relations ($13.22G$ unique), using better settings and all relations found, we obtained a $71,573,531 \times 71,773,331$ matrix of weight $9,681,804,348$. We do not know at which point precisely we had enough relations to build a matrix. But from our figures it follows that, since $2 * 2^{38} / \log(2^{38}) \approx 20.9G$, finding $0.68 * 2 * \pi(2^{38})$ (non-uniqued) relations sufficed to construct a matrix. This low value 0.68 compared to previous efforts is due to the relatively large bound 2^{38} on the large primes.

5   The Matrix Step

In the matrix step linear dependencies modulo 2 among the rows of the $66,718,354 \times 66,718,154$ matrix were sought. This was done using the block Wiedemann algorithm with block length 4 times 64. The details of this algorithm are described in Section 5.1 below. It resulted in 50 dependencies which gave, after quadratic characters tests, 47 useful solutions. A partial explanation of why we got only 50 dependencies as opposed to the expected 200 ones can be found in Section 5.2.

The major part of the calculation (the matrix×vector multiplies, cf. steps 2 and 4 in Section 5.1 below) was carried out in parallel on a cluster of 110 3GHz Pentium D processors (with 2 cores per processor) at NTT and a cluster of 96 2.66 GHz Dual Core2Duo processors (with 4 cores per node) at EPFL. On the latter cluster one or two jobs were run on a varying number of the 96 processors. Scaled to the processors involved, the entire computation would have required 59 days on the Pentium cluster, which is 35 Pentium D core years, or 162 days on 32 nodes of the other cluster, i.e., 56 Dual Core2Duo core years. It should be noted that each of two parallel jobs running on the Pentium D cluster ran about 1.5 times slower than a single job, whereas the load was about 1. This seems to indicate that the same wall-clock time can be achieved on a cluster of 110 single core 3GHz Pentium Prescott processors on a similar network. The relatively poor performance of the cluster at EPFL is probably caused by the fact that the four cores per Dual Core2Duo node share a single network connection. The cluster at NTT has torus topology and the nodes are connected with gigabit ethernet. Transferring intermediate data between NTT and EPFL took about half a day over the Internet.

The computation took place over a period of 69 days, due to several periods of inactivity caused by a variety of circumstances. In principle it could have been done in less than 59 days: if we would have done everything at NTT under ideal conditions (no inactivity), it would take 59 days, but if we would have used both clusters under ideal conditions it should take less time. The software we used for the matrix step was written by the second and third author.

A relatively minor step of the calculation (the Berlekamp-Massey step, cf. step 3 in Section 5.1 below) took 8 hours on 64 cores at the University of Bonn. On 72 cores at EPFL it took a bit less than 7 hours.

5.1   The Block Wiedemann Algorithm

We give a brief description of the block Wiedemann algorithm (see [7], and for the Berlekamp-Massey algorithm [18]). Let B be a $d \times d$ matrix over $\mathbb{F}_2$. The block Wiedemann algorithm depends on two parameters $m, n \in \mathbb{N}$ and heuristically finds n solutions of $Bv = 0$. For our matrix $d = 66,178,354$ and we used $m = 512 = 64 \cdot 8$ and $n = 256 = 64 \cdot 4$. It consists of the following five steps (suppressing some technical details):

1. Random vectors $x_1, \ldots, x_m$ and $z_1, \ldots, z_n$ are chosen and $y_l = Bz_l$ for $l = 1, \ldots, n$ are computed. It is possible to choose x_i as unit vectors to simplify the next step.
2. For $i = 1, \ldots, \frac{d}{m} + \frac{d}{n} + O(1)$ the scalar products $a_{lk}^{(i)} = \langle x_k, B^i y_l \rangle$ are computed. We used $i \leq 393,216$. Denote the polynomial

$$\sum_i a_{lk}^{(i)} t^i$$

   of $n \times m$ matrices over $\mathbb{F}_2$ by A.
3. (Berlekamp-Massey step) In this step a polynomial F of $n \times n$ matrices is constructed such that

$$FA = G + t^c E$$

   holds with $\deg(F), \deg(G) \leq \frac{d}{n} + O(1)$ and $c = \frac{d}{m} + \frac{d}{n} + O(1)$. For us the values were approximately $\deg(F) = \deg(G) = 260,600$ and $c = 391,000$. Writing $F = \sum_{j=0}^{\deg(F)} f_{lk}^{(j)} t^j$ this is equivalent to the orthogonality of the n vectors

$$\sum_{j,k} f_{lk}^{(j)} B^{\deg(F)-j} y_k \qquad (1 \leq l \leq n)$$

   to the vectors $(B^T)^i x_k$, $0 \leq i \leq \frac{d}{m}$, $1 \leq k \leq m$.
4. For $k, l = 1, \ldots, n$ the vectors $v_{lk} = \sum_j f_{lk}^{(j)} B^{\deg(F)-j} z_k$ are computed.
5. With high probability $B \cdot \sum_k v_{lk} = 0$ holds for $l = 1, \ldots, n$. The vectors $v_l = \sum_k v_{lk}$ for which this holds are output as solutions.

For the complexity analysis the first and the last step can be neglected. The second and the fourth step require $(1 + \frac{n}{m})d + O(1)$ resp. $d + O(1)$ matrix vector multiplications. If the vectors x_i are chosen as unit vectors the scalar product calculations in the second step become trivial. In the fourth step additional computations are required, equivalent to $n^2 d$ additions in $\mathbb{F}_2$. These can be neglected as long as n is much smaller than the square root of the weight of B (which we can assume). In both steps we have to store the matrix B and two auxiliary vectors for doing the multiplications. Additionally, in step four n vectors need to be stored.

For the Berlekamp-Massey step we used the sub-quadratic algorithm from [18] with FFT for polynomial multiplication. Its complexity is $O(\frac{(m+n)^3}{n}d^{1+o(1)})$ and its space requirement is $O(\frac{(m+n)^2}{n}d)$.

For small m and n most of the time is spent in steps 2 and 4. The total number of matrix vector multiplications, namely $(2 + \frac{n}{m})d$, will be minimal for $m \to \infty$. So, n being chosen, m should be chosen as large as possible such that the Berlekamp-Massey step does not dominate the run time resp. space requirements.

The computations in steps 2 and 4 can be parallelized in several ways. First, the calculation of $B^i y_l$ can be done simultaneously for different l. These computations are completely independent. Notice that for current computers there is almost no difference in doing one or, e.g., 64 such computations. So, we might set $n = 64n'$ and do the computations on n' independent computers or clusters thereof. We used $n' = 4$ and ran the 4 computations on two clusters, sometimes 2 jobs in parallel per cluster. This ability to spread the computation across different clusters is the crucial difference between our block Wiedemann approach and many previous factoring efforts that relied on the block Lanczos method [6,13]. Unlike block Wiedemann, block Lanczos does not allow this type of independent distribution, roughly speaking because it requires the inversion of an $n \times n$ matrix modulo 2 per iteration, which would obviously lead to considerable communication and synchronization issues when run at different locations.

Second, the calculation of Bv for a vector v can be parallelized. As opposed to the above, this requires a lot of communication. More precisely, for a cluster with $n_1 \times n_2$ nodes in a torus topology the communication required for one multiplication is approximately $\frac{d}{n_1} + \frac{d}{n_2}$ per node. When n_1 and n_2 are chosen approximately equal, the communication costs deteriorate as the square root $\sqrt{n_1 n_2}$ of the number of participating nodes. At NTT we mostly used $n_1 = 11$ and $n_2 = 10$. At EPFL we used 8×8 on 64 cores (sometimes two simultaneous jobs totalling 128 cores, i.e., 32 processors), 10×8 on 80 cores, and 12×12 on 144. Lower numbers of cores were noticeably more efficient per core: when going from 64 to 144 cores we did not get a speed-up of more than 100% (as one would hope for when increasing the number of cores by more than 100%), but only a speed-up of approximately 50%. Roughly, in steps 2 and 4, a third of the time was spend on computation and two-thirds on communication.

A wider collaboration would lead to a larger n' and thus larger n and m. Given currently available hardware and the fact that we used a little more than 128GB of memory to run the Berlekamp-Massey step with our parameters, it might be possible to increase m and n by a factor 4. This would increase the run time by a factor 16. Given our 8 hours on 64 cores, this would result in slightly more than 5 days on existing hardware, which is feasible. Unless a much bigger cluster is used, increasing m and n by larger amounts seems to be difficult at the moment.

Finally, we mention a promising idea that we have experimented with. If approximately the same amounts of time are spent on computation and communication, it is possible to run two different jobs simultaneously on a single cluster, in such a way that one job is computing while the other is communicating, and vice versa. If run as independent—but intertwined—jobs (as we did), this approach requires the matrix to be stored twice. Combining the two chunks in a single job in such a way that they have non-overlapping computational and communication needs would require the matrix to be stored just once.

5.2 Only 50 Dependencies

As mentioned above, we expected to find 200 dependencies but found only 50. Two independent oversights contributed to this phenomenon, but as far as we currently understand still fail to fully explain it.

In the first place an error was uncovered in the selection of the z_l vectors (cf. Step 1 of the algorithm in Section 5.1) that has a large effect on the number of solutions one may expect to find and that depends on the cluster configuration one is using. In our case this led to a reduction of the dimension of the solution space from 200 to about 34.

Secondly, after close inspection of the input matrix it was found that it contains 37 duplicate rows. Due to the peculiar way their arrangement interacts with the other error, this leads to 54 expected dependencies. Both these problems are easily avoided during future computations.

6   The Square Root Step

Each independent solution has a chance of at least 50% to lead to a factorization. The main calculation per solution involves the computation of a square root of a huge algebraic number that factors into small prime ideals whose norms are known. To calculate this square root we used Montgomery's square root method [14] as described in [15] and implemented by Friedrich Bahr as part of his diploma thesis (cf. [3]). The first three solutions all led to the trivial factorization, the fourth one produced the following 80-digit prime factor

55853666619936291260749204658315944968646527018488637648010052346319853288374753

with prime 227-digit cofactor

20758181946442382764570481370359469516293970800739520988120838703792729090324679
38234314388414483488253405334476911222302815832769652537609141018910524199389933
4109711624358962065972167481161749004803659735573409253205425523689

thereby completing the factorization of $2^{1039} - 1$.

Preparing the data for 4 solutions simultaneously took 2 hours, and processing thereafter took 1.8 hours per solution, all run times on a 2.2GHz Opteron.

Note that our attempt to select a special number with a large smallest factor was only partially successful: with more luck we would have found the 80-digit factor using ECM. To some this result is somewhat disappointing, because an 80-digit factor is considered to be 'small' given the size of the 307-digit composite $(2^{1039} - 1)/5080711$ that we factored. Note, however, that the factor-size is irrelevant for our result. Also, as may be infered from the figures presented in

Section 2, one may expect to spend much more computing time to find this factor using ECM than we spent on SNFS: we estimate it would require about a million curves with first phase bound $8G$, at a cost of several thousand CPU years and ignoring the very substantial memory demands for the second phase (much more than 4GB RAM). If $(2^{1039} - 1)/5080711$ would have had a 70-digit factor, we would have been quite unlucky, a 60-digit factor we should have caught with ECM and we would most likely have selected another 'special' number to factor.

7 Discussion

As far as we are aware our factorization is the first kilobit factorization achieved using the special number field sieve. It must be stressed, and was already pointed out in the introduction, that our work does not imply that 1024-bit RSA moduli can now be factored by a comparable effort. Quite on the contrary, according to all information available to us, and as far as we know to anyone else in the open community, factoring a 1024-bit RSA modulus is still beyond the capabilities of anyone with resources a few orders of magnitude larger than ours. We estimate that the effort we spent would suffice to factor a 700-bit RSA modulus.

Nevertheless, our work showed that one major hurdle is not as unsurmountable as some thought it would be: unlike previous efforts we managed to distribute the major computation of the matrix step into 4 chunks whose completion did not require any interaction. It required a huge data exchange among our three locations. This was enabled by the advancement of the Internet, allowing relatively efficient, economical, and convenient communication among geographically dispersed locations at speeds up to about 100megabits per second. It remains a subject of further research how the adverse effects of wider parallelization can be addressed and how substantially larger chunks could be handled per location. But, the beginning is there, and without any doubt our work will inspire further work in this area and lead to more and better results.

Until our work there were two major factoring milestones on our way to 1024-bit RSA moduli. One of these milestones, a kilobit SNFS factorization, is now behind us. The next one, and the only remaining major milestone before we would face 1024-bit RSA moduli, is the factorization of a 768-bit RSA modulus. We have no doubt that 768-bit RSA moduli are firmly within our reach, both as far as sieving effort and size of the matrix problem are concerned. If it would indeed be reached, as is now safe to predict, factoring a 1024-bit RSA modulus would begin to dawn on the horizon of what is practically possible for the open community.

It is unclear how long it will take to get there. But given the progress we keep making, and given that we consistently keep reaching our factoring milestones, it would be unwise to have much faith in the security of 1024-bit RSA moduli for more than a few years to come. To illustrate, substantiate, and quantify this remark, note that the first published factorization of a 512-bit RSA modulus is less than a decade ago (cf. [5]) and that

$$\frac{T(1024)}{T(768)} < \frac{1}{5} \times \frac{T(768)}{T(512)},$$

where

$$T(b) = \exp(1.923 \ln(2^b)^{1/3} (\ln(\ln(2^b)))^{2/3})$$

is a rough growth rate estimate for the run time of NFS when applied to a b-bit RSA modulus (cf. [11]). A more precise estimate, involving the $o(1)$ which we omitted in $T(b)$, would result in a value that is even smaller than $\frac{1}{5}$. This means that by the time we manage to factor a 768-bit RSA modulus—something we are convinced we are able to pull off—the relative effort of factoring a 1024-bit RSA modulus will look at least 5 times easier than the relative effort of factoring a 768-bit RSA modulus compared to a 512-bit one. As a final remark we note that since 1989 we have seen no major progress in factoring algorithms that can be run on existing hardware, but just a constant stream of refinements. There is every reason to expect that this type of progress will continue.

References

1. Aoki, K., Kida, Y., Shimoyama, T., Ueda, H.: http://www.crypto-world.com/announcements/SNFS274.txt
2. Aoki, K., Shimoyama, T.: R311 is factored by ECM, Proceedings of SCIS 2004, no.2E1-1, Hiroshima, Japan, Technical Group on Information Security (IEICE) (in Japanese)
3. Bahr, F.: Liniensieben und Quadratwurzelberechnung für das Zahlkörpersieb, University of Bonn (2005)
4. Cavallar, S.: Strategies for filtering in the number field sieve. In: Bosma, W. (ed.) ANTS IV. LNCS, vol. 1838, pp. 209–231. Springer, Heidelberg (2000)
5. Cavallar, S., Dodson, B., Lenstra, A.K., Leyland, P., Montgomery, P.L., Murphy, B., te Riele, H., Zimmermann, P., et al.: Factoring a 512-bit RSA modulus. In: Preneel, B. (ed.) EUROCRYPT 2000. LNCS, vol. 1807, pp. 1–18. Springer, Heidelberg (2000)
6. Coppersmith, D.: Solving linear equations over GF(2): block Lanczos algorithm. Linear algebra and its applications 192, 33–60 (1993)
7. Coppersmith, D.: Solving homogeneous linear equations over GF(2) via block Wiedemann algorithm. Math. of Comp. 62, 333–350 (1994)
8. Franke, J., Kleinjung, T.: Continued fractions and lattice sieving. In: Proceedings SHARCS 2005, http://www.ruhr-uni-bochum.de/itsc/tanja/SHARCS/talks/FrankeKleinjung.pdf
9. Kleinjung, T.: Cofactorisation strategies for the number field sieve and an estimate for the sieving step for factoring 1024-bit integers. In: Proceedings SHARCS 2006, http://www.hyperelliptic.org/tanja/SHARCS/talks06/thorsten.pdf.
10. Lenstra, A.K., Lenstra, H.W.: The development of the number field sieve. LNM, vol. 1554. Springer, Heidelberg (1993)
11. Lenstra, A.K., Verheul, E.R.: Selecting cryptographic key sizes, J. of Cryptology 14, 255–293 (2001)
12. Lenstra, H.W.: Factoring integers with elliptic curves, Ann. of Math. 126, 649–673 (1987)
13. Montgomery, P.L.: A block Lanczos algorithm for finding dependencies over GF(2). In: Guillou, L.C., Quisquater, J.-J. (eds.) EUROCRYPT 1995. LNCS, vol. 921, pp. 106–120. Springer, Heidelberg (1995)

14. Montgomery, P.L.: Square roots of products of algebraic numbers,
    `http://ftp.cwi.nl/pub/pmontgom/sqrt.ps.gz`
15. Nguyen, P.: A Montgomery-like square root for the number field sieve. In: Buhler,
    J.P. (ed.) ANTS III. LNCS, vol. 1423, pp. 151–168. Springer, Heidelberg (1998)
16. Pomerance, C.: A tale of two sieves,
    `http://www.ams.org/notices/199612/pomerance.pdf`
17. Prime95, `http://www.mersenne.org/freesoft.htm`
18. Thomé, E.: Subquadratic computation of vector generating polynomials and im-
    provement of the block Wiedemann algorithm. Journal of symbolic computation 33,
    757–775 (2002)
19. Zimmermann, P.: `http://gforge.inria.fr/projects/ecm/`

When e-th Roots Become Easier Than Factoring

Antoine Joux[1,*], David Naccache[2], and Emmanuel Thomé[3]

[1] DGA and Université de Versailles, UVSQ PRISM 45 avenue des États-Unis,
F-78035 Versailles CEDEX, France
antoine.joux@m4x.org
[2] École normale supérieure, Équipe de cryptographie, 45 rue d'Ulm,
F-75230 Paris CEDEX 05, France
david.naccache@ens.fr
[3] INRIA Lorraine, LORIA, CACAO – bâtiment A, 615 rue du Jardin botanique,
F-54602 Villiers-lès-Nancy CEDEX, France
emmanuel.thome@normalesup.org

Abstract. We show that computing e-th roots modulo n is easier than factoring n with currently known methods, given subexponential access to an oracle outputting the roots of numbers of the form $x_i + c$.

Here c is fixed and x_i denotes small integers of the attacker's choosing. The attack comes in two flavors:

- A first version is illustrated here by producing selective roots of the form $x_i + c$ in $L_n(\frac{1}{3}, \sqrt[3]{\frac{32}{9}})$. This matches the *special* number field sieve's (SNFS) complexity.
- A second variant computes *arbitrary* e-th roots in $L_n(\frac{1}{3}, \gamma)$ after a subexponential number of oracle queries. The constant γ depends on the type of oracle used.

  This addresses in particular the One More RSA Inversion problem, where the e-th root oracle is not restricted to numbers of a special form. The aforementioned constant γ is then $\sqrt[3]{\frac{32}{9}}$.

  Constraining the oracle to roots of the form $\sqrt[e]{x_i + c} \bmod n$ increases γ.

Both methods are faster than factoring n using the GNFS $(L_n(\frac{1}{3}, \sqrt[3]{\frac{64}{9}}))$.

This sheds additional light on RSA's malleability in general and on RSA's resistance to affine forgeries in particular – a problem known to be polynomial for $x_i > \sqrt[3]{n}$, but for which no algorithm faster than factoring was known before this work.

Keywords: RSA, factoring, NFS, roots.

1 Introduction

The RSA cryptosystem [17] is commonly used for providing privacy and authenticity of digital data. A very common *historical* practice for signing with RSA

---

* Work partially supported by DGA research grant 05.34.058.

was to first hash the message, add a padding pattern c and then raise the result to the power of the decryption exponent. This paradigm is the basis of numerous standards such as PKCS#1 v1.5 [18].

Let n and e denote usual RSA public parameters (with $\lceil \log_2 n \rceil = N$)[1].

In this paper we explore RSA signatures with a fixed c but without the hash function, *i.e.* modular roots of the form:

$$\sqrt[e]{c + x} \bmod n$$

We call such numbers *affine modular roots* (AMRs).

A thread of publications [15,7,10,14,4,13] stretching over a decade progressively established that given access to an AMR-oracle, new AMRs could be forged in polynomial complexity for $x > \sqrt[3]{n}$.

No strategies faster than factoring n are known for $x < \sqrt[3]{n}$ – a case tackled here at the cost of subexponential complexity. The main novelty in this paper is that, while subexponential, our method forges new AMRs for *arbitrarily small* x (down to $x < \sqrt[\epsilon]{n}, \forall \epsilon > 0$) *faster than factoring* n.

Moreover, we show that access to an e-th root oracle (in particular, an AMR-oracle) even allows to compute *arbitrary e-th roots faster than factoring* n. Here, the arbitrary e-th root to be computed is not known before all oracle queries have been completed.

We achieve this by tweaking the quadratic sieve (QS) and the number field sieve (NFS) factoring algorithms.

The Results. Denoting $L_n(\alpha, c) = \exp\left(c\,(1 + o(1))\,(\log n)^\alpha\,(\log \log n)^{1-\alpha}\right)$, we show that:

- Using a QS-like algorithm, new AMRs can be computed in $L_{\frac{n}{x}}(\frac{1}{2}, 1)$ instead of the $L_n(\frac{1}{2}, 1)$ required for QS-factoring n.
- Using an NFS-like approach, we selectively produce new AMRs in $L_n(\frac{1}{3}, \sqrt[3]{\frac{32}{9}})$.

  This matches the *special* number field sieve's (SNFS) complexity which is substantially lower than the $L_n(\frac{1}{3}, \sqrt[3]{\frac{64}{9}})$ required to GNFS-factor n.

  Our experimental results for $N = 512$ and a recent SNFS-factoring record[2], clearly underline the insecurity of affine-padding RSA.

- We present a procedure for computing *arbitrary e-th roots* in $L_n(\frac{1}{3}, \sqrt[3]{\frac{32}{9}} \simeq 1.53)$, requiring a general (not only AMR) e-th root oracle.

  A more practical variant with a slightly higher complexity $L_n(\frac{1}{3}, 1.58)$ was used in the experiments reported in this paper.

- Finally, a last variant allows the computation of *arbitrary e-th roots* given access to an AMR-oracle with complexity $L_n(\frac{1}{3}, \sqrt[3]{6})$. To date, we could not make this variant practical.

---

[1] Throughout this paper, we will frequently denote by $|x|$ the bitlength of x.

[2] [1], factoring a 1039-bit number using $\simeq$ 95 Pentium-D-years at 3 GHz.

Our algorithms rely on an extension of Montgomery's square root algorithm for the number field sieve [16]. If one avoids this algorithm, alternative variants exist with claim a higher complexity $(L_n(\frac{1}{3}, \sqrt[3]{\frac{9}{2}}))$.

2   The Strategy – A General Outline

For the sake of simplicity assume that $|x| = \frac{N}{4}$ (generalization to smaller x sizes is straightforward). We start by writing c, as a modular ratio[3]:

$$c = \frac{a}{b} \bmod n \quad \text{where} \quad |a| = (1 - s)N \quad \text{and} \quad |b| = sN$$

for some $0 < s < 1$ that will be determined later.

Noting that $c + x = \frac{a + xb}{b} \bmod n$, it is easy to derive an index calculus attack[4] as in [6][5] on numbers of the form $a + xb$, that we expect to be smooth with respect to some factor base $\mathcal{B}$. We can ascertain that $a + xb$ is partially smooth by applying a special-q strategy. Two options are possible: Either choose different partial products of size $\frac{N}{4}$ of primes belonging to $\mathcal{B}$ (denote these partial products u_i) and sieve on x_i values such that $x_i = -c \bmod u_i$ or, select as special-q primes of size $\frac{N}{4}$ and use them as the u_i in the first option. From an asymptotic standpoint, the two approaches are equivalent. In practice, the first approach can produce any given equation more than once and thus require extra bookkeeping. As for the second approach, each special-q requires one extra equation to cancel out, thereby resulting in a larger system of equations.

It remains to optimize s. To maximize the smoothness odds of $a + xb$ we require that $|a| = |xb|$ hence:

$$(1 - s)N = |a| = |xb| = |x| + |b| = \frac{N}{4} + |b| = \frac{N}{4} + sN \quad \Rightarrow \quad s = \frac{3}{8}$$

In other words, we need to find multiplicative relations between numbers of size $\frac{5N}{8}$ divisible, *by construction*, by smooth factors of size $\frac{N}{4}$. All in all this amounts to chasing smooth numbers of size $\frac{3N}{8}$ which is easier than QS-factoring n (identical task for numbers of size $\frac{N}{2} = \frac{4N}{8}$).

More generally, when x is an $\frac{N}{t}$ bit number, the job boils-down to finding smooth numbers of size $\frac{N(t-1)}{2t}$ i.e. QS-factoring $\frac{N(t-1)}{t}$ bit RSA moduli.

Hence, the presented strategy approaches the QS's complexity as t grows, while remaining below the QS's complexity curve[6].

---

[3] E.g. Using a continued fraction algorithm.

[4] Treat b as an extra element of the factor base, together with the primes in the basis to account for the denominator in the equations.

[5] In [6] the signing oracle is used to compute e-th roots whose combination allows to compute new e-th roots of factor-base elements.

[6] To sieve, it suffices to set $x_i = -c \bmod u_i$ and consider successively $a(x_i + ju_i) + b$ for $j = 1, 2, \ldots$ (note that this will pollute a logarithmic number of bits in c).

Given that the quadratic-sieve is *not* the fastest factoring strategy for usual-size RSA moduli, the extension of the above strategy to the NFS is a natural question (that this paper answers positively).

NFS algorithms work by exhibiting relations between objects in two different "worlds". In some cases, we have a single number field and consider relations between integers and elements in that field. In other cases, there are two number fields. Nonetheless, with both approaches, there are two sides to consider. In this paper, the AMR-oracle is going to replace one of the two sides. Consequently, our setting is that of a single-sided NFS. This turns out to greatly improve the smoothness probability and hence the algorithm's efficiency.

We start by selecting a parameter d and finding a polynomial f of degree d having sufficiently small coefficients such that $f(c) \equiv 0 \bmod n$. Without loss of generality, we may assume that f is irreducible over $\mathbb{Q}$. Indeed, if $f = f_1 \times f_2$, either $\gcd(f_1(c), n)$ is a non-trivial factor of n, or we can use the (smaller) polynomial f_1 instead of f.

Once f is chosen, we construct the number field $K = \mathbb{Q}[\alpha]$ where α is a root of f over $\mathbb{Q}$. We now proceed as in the NFS and given integers x, we construct elements $\alpha + x \in \mathbb{Q}[\alpha]$ with smooth norm over some factor base $\mathcal{B}$. We recall that the norm of $\alpha + x$ is the absolute value of $f(-x)$. Note a major difference with NFS-factoring: indeed, we only need to smooth a *single* $\alpha + x$ for each candidate x as there is no second (or rational) side to smooth in addition. Instead, the second side is given for free by the AMR-oracle for the number corresponding to $\alpha + x$, i.e. for $c + x$. When the norm is smooth, we can decompose $\alpha + x$ into a product of ideals of small norm in the ring of integers $\mathcal{O}_K$ of $K = \mathbb{Q}[\alpha]$.

Once enough smooth elements are found, we write them down as rows in a matrix where each row contains the valuation of the corresponding $\alpha + x$ at each prime ideal occurring in its decomposition. We also add to each row enough character maps in order to account for the existence of units in the number field.

Then, using a sparse linear algebra algorithm, we find a linear combination of rows equal to zero modulo e. This allows us to write an e-th power in $\mathbb{Q}[\alpha]$ as a product of $\alpha + x_i$.

The final step computes the actual e-th root of this e-th power. This yields a multiplicative relation between AMRs corresponding to the $\alpha + x_i$ used in the relation. Thus, querying all these values but one yields a new AMR for the missing value. The e-th root can be computed in a way very similar to the NFS' square root computation phase.

Alternatively, the final step can be replaced by a more involved strategy. Namely, combining the e-th root computation with a descent procedure very similar to the individual logarithm step of discrete logarithm computations with the NFS. This enables the calculation of e-th roots of *arbitrary* values, i.e. not restricted to the form $c + x$, by making a small number of additional queries of the restricted form $c + x$. This option is presented in Section 4.

3   A Detailed Step-by-Step Description

3.1   Polynomial Construction

Given a target degree d we first need to construct a polynomial f irreducible over $\mathbb{Q}$. f will then be used to define the number field $K = \mathbb{Q}[\alpha]$. The two important constraints on f are that its coefficients should be small and that we must have $f(c) = 0 \bmod n$. Since we want to minimize the average norm $f(-x)$ of numbers $\alpha + x$, it is a good idea to use a skewed polynomial. More precisely, assume that B bounds the absolute value of x, then we want to choose a bound C such that the coefficient of degree i in f has absolute value smaller than $\frac{C}{B^i}$. Assuming[7] that $B^{d(d+1)} < n$, we choose $C = \sqrt[d+1]{n}B^{d/2}$ and the polynomial f can be constructed by reducing the lattice generated by the columns of the $(d+1) \times (d+1)$ matrix

$$L = \begin{pmatrix} \Lambda & \cdots & \Lambda c^d & \Lambda n \\ 1 & & 0 & 0 \\ & \ddots & & \vdots \\ 0 & & B^d & 0 \end{pmatrix}$$

where Λ is a sufficiently large constant to guarantee that any short vector in the lattice has zero in its first coordinate. Such a short vector can be easily interpreted as a polynomial by reading the coefficient of x^i in row $i + 2$ (the coefficient should be re-normalized by a division by B^i). This polynomial clearly has c as a root modulo n. Moreover, when evaluating the polynomial at x smaller than B (in absolute value) we see that each term is bounded by the corresponding value in the initial short vector.

Since the determinant of L is $nB^{d(d+1)/2}$, we expect short-vector coefficients to be of size

$$C = \sqrt[d+1]{n}B^{\frac{d}{2}}2^{\frac{d}{4}}$$

3.2   Sieving

From a sieving standpoint, there is an essential difference between our algorithm and the NFS. Indeed, our sieving has a single degree of freedom instead of two. More precisely, instead of scanning numbers of the form $a\alpha + b$ for a fixed α and arbitrary pairs of small $\{a, b\}$, we need to examine numbers of the form $\alpha + x$.

Luckily, the bound on x is large enough to compensate the absence of the second degree of freedom but this restricts our sieving technique options. Indeed, we cannot use a lattice sieve strategy and have to rely instead on a straightforward sieve-by-line algorithm. To avoid using large numbers while sieving over x, we used a special-q approach: for each special-q prime ideal $\langle q, \alpha - r \rangle$, we considered the algebraic integers $\alpha + (qx - r)$, with $x \in [-\frac{S}{q}, +\frac{S}{q}]$.

---

[7] This is necessary to avoid finding zero for high degree coefficients; of course, where necessary, we can always lower B in this construction and sieve over a smaller x range (as long as enough equations are found.).

3.3   Linear Algebra and Characters

Depending on the size of e, one may either use Lanczos/Wiedeman or block Lanczos/Wiedeman approach. If e is large enough, no self-orthogonal vector appears (unless we are extremely unlucky) and the simple approach succeeds. For smaller e, a block approach is required (the block size $2 \leq z \leq 32$ varies with e and is a bit lesser when $e = 3$).

When linear algebra is performed directly on the sieving phase's output, the method yields a multiplicative relation between ideals of the form:

$$\prod_i \langle \alpha + x_i \rangle^{\mu_i} = \left(\prod_j \mathfrak{p}_j^{\nu_j} \right)^e$$

Such a relation, however, is insufficient to ensure that the product $\prod_i (\alpha + x_i)^{\mu_i}$ is an e-th power in K. Obstructions may arise from the e-part of the ideal class group of $\mathcal{O}_K$, as well as from the quotient of the unit group $\mathcal{O}_K^* / (\mathcal{O}_K^*)^e$. To annihilate these obstructions we have to add characters. We require that:

$$\chi \left(\prod_i (\alpha + x_i)^{\mu_i} \right) = \sum_i \mu_i \chi(\alpha + x_i)$$

vanishes, for several (additive) character maps $\chi : K^* \to \mathbb{F}_e$. We have the following choices for character maps:

- In [19], an approximation of the e-adic logarithm is used. Such characters are easy to compute but might fail to account for the full obstruction, as they cover at most the obstruction stemming from the unit group. Should e ramify in $\mathcal{O}_K$, or $e\mathcal{O}_K$ be divisible by a prime ideal belonging to the factor base, technicalities occur but do not prevent from using these characters.
- It is also possible to follow the classical approach used for NFS-factoring [3] i.e. test for powers modulo primes congruent to 1 mod e. The number of characters accessible thereby is infinite. To map these multiplicative characters to additive ones, a discrete logarithm modulo e must be solved, which is trivial for small e. For larger e values (where this might be a problem) heuristic arguments indicate that characters of the first kind would suffice anyway [19].

A typical drawback of characters is that they add a dense part to the relation matrix, which might cause a slight performance penalty. In the particular case we are interested in (just as in NFS-factoring) it is possible to perform the linear algebra *without* the character columns, produce several row dependencies and do a second reduction to recombine these dependencies into dependencies with vanishing characters.

If we elect to adopt the latter idea it becomes particularly advisable to use block algorithms for the linear algebra, since these algorithms output several vectors of the null-space simultaneously.

The linear algebra step also gives us the opportunity to check that K's class number is co-prime to e (to avoid possible technical problems *infra*). We do so by checking that the rank of the relation matrix is not abnormally low modulo e. This extra check is achieved in the same complexity and is therefore ignored hereafter. Moreover, when e is a large prime, we do not need to test anything, since the probability that e divides the class number is negligible.

3.4 Root Extraction

The linear algebra stage yields a product of algebraic integers $\pi = \prod(\alpha + x_i)^{\mu_i}$ which is known to be an e-th power in K since $\chi(\pi) = 0$ for satisfyingly many characters χ. This allows us to compute an e-th root in $\mathbb{Z}_n$ for any $c + x_{i'}$, as long as the corresponding exponent $\mu_{i'} \neq 0 \bmod e$. To do so, we first have to raise π to the power of $\mu_{i'}^{-1} \bmod e$. In other words, we can assume without loss of generality that $\mu_{i'} = 1$.

When e is small, the computation of the e-th root of π can be done using a straightforward generalization of Montgomery's square root algorithm [16].

Once the e-th root $R(\alpha)$ is computed, we have:

$$(c + x_{i'}) \prod_{i \neq i'} (c + x_i)^{\mu_i} = R(c)^e \bmod n,$$

$$\textit{i.e.:} \qquad (c + x_{i'})^d = R(c) \prod_{i \neq i'} (c + x_i)^{-\mu_i} \bmod n.$$

One might question the applicability of Montgomery's algorithm to very large values of e. Our computations in appendix A indicate that $e = 65,537$ is achievable with no difficulty and tests up to $e \simeq 10^{15}$ were conducted successfully. These results lead us to infer that this approach is practical at least for our range of interest.

However, should this strategy become difficult for larger e, a different (more expensive) approach might be used: replace the sparse linear algebra modulo e by exact Gaussian elimination or Hermite normal form and find relations expressing each ideal as a product (quotient) of smooth elements. This associates to each ideal a projection[8] in $\mathbb{Z}_n$ and also its e-th root. The drawbacks are higher memory requirements and a higher exponent in the linear algebra's complexity.

3.5 Complexity Analysis

Our complexity analysis closely follows the NFS's one. Let w denote the linear algebra's exponent. We write the degree d, the sieving range $[-S, +S]$ and the factor base bound B as:

$$d = \delta \times \sqrt[3]{\frac{\log n}{\log \log n}}, \quad S = L_n(\tfrac{1}{3}, w\beta) \quad \text{and} \quad B = L_n(\tfrac{1}{3}, \beta).$$

---

[8] In theory, such a projection can be defined rigorously using the Hilbert class field of the number field used. Indeed, in the Hilbert class field, all ideals are principal and sending a generator to $\mathbb{Z}_n$ is easy; however, since the degree of the Hilbert class field is extremely large, it cannot be used in practice.

This particular choice of S and B ensures that the sieving step (which costs S) and the linear algebra step (which costs B^w) are balanced.

Using the lattice-based construction, the coefficients of f have average size $A = \sqrt[4]{n} = L_n(\frac{2}{3}, \frac{1}{5})$. By choosing a skewed f, we find that the size of $f(x)$ for $x \in [-S, +S]$ is:

$$A \times S^{d/2} = L_n\left(\frac{2}{3}, \frac{1}{5} + \frac{w}{2}\delta\beta\right)$$

The probability that $f(x)$ is B-smooth is $L_n(\frac{1}{3}, -\pi)$ with $\pi = \frac{1}{3}(\frac{1}{5\beta} + \frac{w}{2}\delta)$. To get enough smooth relations, we need to ensure that $w\beta - \pi = \beta$.

For $w = 2$, these equations lead to the choice $\{\delta = \sqrt[3]{\frac{2}{3}}, \beta = \sqrt[3]{\frac{4}{9}}\}$. As a consequence, the complexity of the sieving and linear algebra steps put together is $L_n(\frac{1}{3}, 2\beta) = L_n(\frac{1}{3}, \sqrt[3]{\frac{32}{9}})$. This is equal to the complexity the SNFS factoring algorithm which applies to a restricted class of numbers [12].

Another very important parameter is the number of AMR-oracle queries, which is subexponential but significatively smaller than the algorithm's runtime. This number of queries is $L_n(\frac{1}{3}, \beta) = L_n(\frac{1}{3}, \sqrt[3]{\frac{4}{9}})$.

The alternative using integer linear algebra mentioned above yields a complexity of:

$$L_n\left(\frac{1}{3}, \sqrt[3]{\frac{2w^4}{9(w-1)^2}}\right)$$

The case $w = 3$ gives $L_n(\frac{1}{3}, \sqrt[3]{\frac{9}{2}} \simeq 1.65)$. Note that according to [8,9], the integer linear algebra can be done with exponent $w = 2.5$, which yields $L_n(\frac{1}{3}, \sqrt[3]{\frac{625}{162}} \simeq 1.57)$. However this approach requires asymptotically fast matrix multiplication techniques which might prove too cumbersome for cryptographic applications.

As our algorithms are subexponential, the assessment of their *experimental* behavior is essential. We hence implemented them and actually forged a 512-bit AMR. Details are given in Appendix A.

Open Problem – Potential Improvements: When the number of fixed pad bits is small enough, the possible sieving range of x when sieving over $c + x$ (or $\alpha + x$) may be too large[9].

Under such circumstances, we get some additional freedom when constructing f. Indeed, we may replace c by some $c' \simeq c$, thereby reducing the sieving range. Clearly, amongst all possible c' values some yield f'-s whose coefficients are smaller than average.

We could not find any efficient way of taking advantage of this extra freedom to build better polynomials and further reduce the attack's complexity.

---

[9] *Cf.* To the related footnote in section 3.1.

4   Attacking the One More RSA Inversion Problem

Up to now, we have obtained either an AMR-forgery or an adaptive chosen cipher-text attack (CCA2) on plain RSA. In this section, we extend the attack to obtain a non adaptive chosen ciphertext attack (CCA1) on plain RSA. Equivalently, we attack the One More RSA Inversion Problem, proposed by Bellare et al., in [2]. Again, while subexponential, this attack is faster than GNFS-factoring n. In the context of the One More RSA Problem it is not really meaningful to assume that the initial RSA queries have a special form, thus we grant the attacker access to an unlimited e-th root oracle during the first phase of the attack.

Once the restriction on oracle queries is lifted, we are no longer constrained to use polynomials with a prescribed root P. Moreover, we are no longer limited to a single dimensional sieve, but can use a classical NFS sieve with two degrees of freedom, using a *lattice sieving* technique. This does not change the asymptotic complexity but allows us to reuse existing fast sieving code more easily. Not being restricted to a prescribed root, we may use any polynomial of our choice. Despite this clear gain, to solve the One More RSA Inversion Problem and become non-adaptive, we need to devise an algorithm allowing us to compute the e-th root of an arbitrary number without any additional oracle queries. This requires a new descent procedure since the technique sketched at the end of Section 2 requires additional oracle queries. Looking at similar problems arising in the individual discrete logarithm phase of discrete logarithms computations, we see that such a non adaptive descent can be done by alternating between two NFS sides. Thus, we need to introduce a second side into our algorithm. While, at a first glance, this seems to void our single-sided NFS complexity improvement, it turns out that this intuitive perception is false since we can initially do the single sided NFS separately for both sides.

The addition of a second side entails a complication for the descent, however. To achieve the announced complexity, the initial factor base bound is set to $L_n(\frac{1}{3}, \sqrt[3]{\frac{4}{9}})$. This is well below the $L_n(\frac{1}{3}, \sqrt[3]{\frac{8}{9}})$ encountered when computing dis-crete logarithms. This implies that the descent procedure has to descend *below* what is done for computing discrete logarithms. While the impact on the overall complexity is not visible, this is a clear practical concern. To compensate for this fact, we add an intermediate phase in our algorithm in order to enlarge the factor base from $L_n(\frac{1}{3}, \sqrt[3]{\frac{4}{9}})$ to $L_n(\frac{1}{3}, \sqrt[3]{\frac{8}{9}})$.

4.1   The Inversion Algorithm

Step 0 – Setup. We first set up on the *algebraic side* a number field $K = \mathbb{Q}(\alpha)$ defined by a polynomial equation $f(\alpha) = 0$. The easiest (though not unique) choice for the second side is a *rational side* given by a polynomial g such that f and g share a common root P modulo n. The classical *base-m* technique can be used for this purpose.

We denote by ρ the rational root of g (we have $\rho = m$ if g is monic).

Step 1 – Precomputation. The factor base $\mathcal{F}$ on the algebraic side consists of ideals of norm bounded by $B \simeq L_n(\frac{1}{3}, \sqrt[3]{\frac{4}{9}})$. By sieving, we obtain coefficient pairs $\{x, y\}$ yielding relations of the form:

$$(x - y\alpha) = \prod_{\mathfrak{p} \in \mathcal{F}} \mathfrak{p}^{m_\mathfrak{p}}, \quad \text{and} \quad \chi(x - y\alpha) = (\lambda_k)_{k=1,\dots,c}$$

where χ is a character map onto $\mathbb{F}_\ell^c$, for some arbitrary dimension c. We concatenate the coefficients $(m_\mathfrak{p})$ and λ_k to form the rows of a matrix M.

Step 2 – Factor Base Extension. The extended factor base $\mathcal{F}'$ consists of ideals of norm bounded by $B' \simeq L_n(\frac{1}{3}, \sqrt[3]{\frac{8}{9}})$. We sieve on the algebraic side only, using each additional prime ideal that we want to add as a special-q. We ask for a single relation between this prime ideal and the smaller ones.

Step 3 – Oracle Queries. We query the oracle for the e-th root of the numbers $x - yP$ for each integers pair $\{x, y\}$ encountered in steps 1 and 2. We also query for the e-th root of all prime numbers below B'.

Step 4 – Descent Initialization. In our game, it is only at this point that the attacker learns the challenge number t whose e-th root he must compute.

The descent mimics individual discrete logarithm computations. The descent is initialized by picking a random mask m and two integers u and v such that $\frac{u}{v} \equiv m^e t \bmod n$, and which factor simultaneously into primes bounded by $L_n(\frac{2}{3}, \bullet)$.

Step 5 – Descent. We maintain a set $\{(\sigma, \epsilon)\}$ of polynomials σ and exponents ϵ such that $S = \prod \sigma^\epsilon$ satisfies:

$$(S(\alpha)) = \prod_{\mathfrak{p} \in \mathcal{F}'} \mathfrak{p}^{\mu_\mathfrak{p}} \cdot I_1 \quad \text{(algebraic side)},$$

$$\text{and} \quad \frac{u}{v} S(\rho) = \prod_{p < B'} p^{\nu_p} \cdot I_2 \quad \text{(rational side)}.$$

Initially $S = 1$, and the exponents ν_p mark the prime numbers appearing in the factorization of u and v.

The remaining terms I_1 and I_2 factor into ideals (or primes) outside the factor base. The descent procedure aims at eliminating these ideals. For this purpose, we iteratively use special-q sieving to trade these ideals for ideals of smaller norm.

Using the relations obtained from the factor base extension step, we form another rational fraction T such that the ideal $(S(\alpha)T(\alpha))$ factors into ideals belonging to the smaller factor base $\mathcal{F}$.

Step 6 – Linear Algebra. Once we have reached the point where $I_1 = (1)$ and $I_2 = (1)$, we seek a linear combination of the rows of the matrix M which equals the valuations and character values corresponding to the algebraic number $S(\alpha)T(\alpha)$.

This inhomogeneous linear system amounts to exhibiting an algebraic number $U(\alpha)$ obtained as a combination of the numbers $x - y\alpha$ found in step 1, and such that $S(\alpha)T(\alpha)U(\alpha)$ is an e-th power in K.

Step 7 – End. We use Montgomery's e-th root algorithm to write the previous number explicitly as an e-th power of an algebraic number $r(\alpha)^e$.

By construction, the e-th roots of $T(P)$ and $U(P)$ are known by the oracle queries. Using the rational side product form and the corresponding oracle queries, the e-th root of $\frac{u}{v}S(P)$ is known as well. We infer:

$$\sqrt[e]{t} = \frac{1}{m} \cdot \frac{\sqrt[e]{\frac{u}{v}S(P)}}{r(P)} \sqrt[e]{T(P)} \sqrt[e]{U(P)}.$$

4.2 Complexity Analysis

Using the same parameters as in Section 3, all steps except steps 2 to 5 are achieved with complexity $L_n(\frac{1}{3}, \sqrt[3]{\frac{32}{9}})$.

The complexity of step 2 depends of course on the choice of β'. The summation from $B = L_n(\frac{1}{3}, \beta)$ to $B' = L_n(\frac{1}{3}, \beta')$ yields a complexity $L_n(\frac{1}{3}, \theta)$ where θ ranges from $\sqrt[3]{\frac{32}{9}}$ when β' is chosen close to β, up to 1.577 with the suggested value $\beta' = \sqrt[3]{\frac{8}{9}}$ (the detailed calculations, omitted for brevity, will be included in the IACR ePrint version of this paper).

The number of oracle queries (step 3) is $L_n(\frac{1}{3}, \beta' = \sqrt[3]{\frac{8}{9}})$.

The descent (steps 4 and 5) is analyzed in [5], and found to have complexity $L_n(\frac{1}{3}, \sqrt[3]{3})$.

We highlight, however, the complexity of the last descent steps, where ideals of norm just above $B' = L_n(\frac{1}{3}, \beta')$ have to be canceled. For each such ideal, one relation is sought. Using special-q sieving, we can form $L_n(\frac{1}{3}, 2\alpha)$ candidates whose algebraic (resp. rational) norm is bounded by $L_n\left(\frac{2}{3}, \frac{1}{\delta} + \delta\left(\alpha + \frac{\beta'}{2}\right)\right)$ (resp. $L_n\left(\frac{2}{3}, \frac{1}{\delta}\right)$). One relation is expected when α satisfies:

$$2\alpha - \frac{1}{3}\left(\frac{1}{\delta\beta'} + \frac{\delta}{\beta'}\left(\alpha + \frac{\beta'}{2}\right) + \frac{1}{\delta\beta'}\right) = 0.$$

Substituting $\beta' = \sqrt[3]{\frac{8}{9}}$ above, we obtain that the last descent steps are achieved in complexity $L_n(\frac{1}{3}, 0.99)$, which is not dominating. Using $\beta' = \beta$ (thereby skipping the factor base extension), this cost would be $L_n(\frac{1}{3}, 1.27)$ which is not dominating either.

This implies that we have some flexibility in the tuning of the factor base extension. In order to match previously completed discrete logarithm computations, we chose to extend to $\beta' = \sqrt[3]{\frac{8}{9}}$, but this choice should be regarded as unconstrained.

We conclude that the asymptotic complexity of the arbitrary e-th root computation is either $L_n(\frac{1}{3}, \sqrt[3]{\frac{32}{9}})$ or $L_n(\frac{1}{3}, 1.58)$. We believe the latter to be more practical, as is illustrated by our experiments (Appendix B).

4.3 Computing e-th Roots with an AMR-Oracle

While we have presented and implemented the arbitrary e-th root computation algorithm using access to a general e-th root oracle, the same can also be achieved using an AMR-oracle only. In this case, the common root P is prescribed, and it is not possible to use a rational side. Nonetheless, the above approach works using two algebraic sides; steps 1, 2, 6, and 7 have to be done separately on both sides. Step 4, however, turns out to have a higher complexity requirement $L_n(\frac{1}{3}, \sqrt[3]{6})$, and the individual descent steps in step 5 are more expensive. We could not demonstrate the practicality of such a setting.

Acknowledgements

The authors would like to thank P. Zimmermann who provided early experimental input for the quadratic sieve version.

References

1. Aoki, K., Franke, J., Kleinjung, T., Lenstra, A., Osvik, D.: Electronic newsgroup posting announcing the factorization of the 1039-th Mersenne number by the snfs (May 21, 2007), http://www.loria.fr/zimmerma/records/21039-
2. Bellare, M., Namprempre, C., Pointcheval, D., Semanko, M.: The One-More-RSA-Inversion Problems and the Security of Chaum's Blind Signature Scheme. Journal of Cryptology 16(3), 185–215 (2003)
3. Buhler, J.P., Lenstra, A.K., Pollard, J.M.: Factoring integers with the number field sieve. In: Lenstra, A.K., Lenstra Jr., H.W. (eds.) The development of the number field sieve. LMN, vol. 1554, pp. 50–94. Springer, Heidelberg (1993)
4. Brier, É., Clavier, C., Coron, J.-S., Naccache, D.: Cryptanalysis of RSA signatures with fixed-pattern padding. In: Kilian, J. (ed.) CRYPTO 2001. LNCS, vol. 2139, pp. 433–439. Springer, Heidelberg (2001)
5. Commeine, A., Semaev, I.: An algorithm to solve the discrete logarithm problem with the number field sieve. In: Yung, M., Dodis, Y., Kiayias, A., Malkin, T.G. (eds.) PKC 2006. LNCS, vol. 3958, pp. 174–190. Springer, Heidelberg (2006)
6. Coron, J.-S., Naccache, D., Stern, J.P.: On the Security of RSA padding. In: Wiener, M.J. (ed.) CRYPTO 1999. LNCS, vol. 1666, pp. 1–18. Springer, Heidelberg (1999)
7. De Jonge, W., Chaum, D.: Attacks on some RSA signatures. In: Williams, H.C. (ed.) CRYPTO 1985. LNCS, vol. 218, pp. 18–27. Springer, Heidelberg (1986)

8. Eberly, W., Giesbrecht, M., Giorgi, P., Storjohann, A., Villard, G.: Solving sparse rational linear systems. In: Trager, B.M. (ed.) ISSAC 2006, pp. 63–70. ACM Press, New York (2006)

9. Eberly, W., Giesbrecht, M., Giorgi, P., Storjohann, A., Villard, G.: Faster inversion and other black box matrix computations using efficient block projections. In: Brown, C.W. (ed.) ISSAC 2007, pp. 143–150. ACM Press, New York (2007)

10. Girault, M., Misarksy, J.-F.: Selective forgery of RSA signatures using redundancy. In: Fumy, W. (ed.) EUROCRYPT 1997. LNCS, vol. 1233, pp. 495–507. Springer, Heidelberg (1997)

11. Joux, A., Lercier, R.: Improvements to the general number field sieve for discrete logarithms in prime fields. A comparison with the gaussian integer method. Mathematics of Computation 242(72), 953–967 (2003)

12. Lenstra, A.K., Lenstra Jr., H.W., Manasse, M.S., Pollard, J.M.: The number field sieve. In: Lenstra, A.K., Lenstra Jr., H.W. (eds.) AMCP 1998. LNM, vol. 1554, pp. 11–42. Springer, Heidelberg (1993)

13. Lenstra, A.K., Shparlinski, I.: Selective forgery of RSA signatures with fixed-pattern padding. In: Proceedings of the 5-th International Workshop on Practice and Theory in Public Key Cryptosystems: Public Key Cryptography. LNCS, vol. 2274, pp. 228–236. Springer, Heidelberg (2002)

14. Misarsky, J.-F.: A multiplicative attack using LLL algorithm on RSA signatures with redundancy. In: Proceedings of Crypto 1997. LNCS, vol. 1294, pp. 221–234. Springer, Heidelberg (1997)

15. Misarsky, J.-F.: How (not) to design RSA signature schemes. In: Imai, H., Zheng, Y. (eds.) PKC 1998. LNCS, vol. 1431, pp. 14–28. Springer, Heidelberg (1998)

16. Montgomery, P.L.: Square roots of products of algebraic numbers. In: W. Gautschi, Ed., Mathematics of Computation 1943–1993: A Half-Century of Computational Mathematics, vol. 48 of Proc. Sympos. Appl. Math., pp. 567–571. AMS (1994)

17. Rivest, R., Shamir, A., Adleman, L.: A method for obtaining digital signatures and public key cryptosystems. CACM 21 (1978)

18. RSA Laboratories, pkcs #1 : RSA cryptography specifications, version 2.0 (September 1998)

19. Schirokauer, O.: Discrete logarithms and local units. Philos. Trans. Roy. Soc. London Ser. a 345(1676), 409–423 (1993)

A   Implementation Details

As our algorithms are subexponential, the assessment of their *experimental* behavior is essential. We hence implemented them and actually computed a 512-bit AMR.

We wrote our software chain in C and C++, relying upon the computer algebra systems PARI-GP and MAGMA for a handful of specific tasks. The attacked instance was $c = 10^{154}$, $e = 65,537$ and $n = $ RSA-155 (RSA Laboratories 512-bit challenge modulus).

The polynomial selection (section 3.1) was implemented in MAGMA. To obtain a satisfactory relation yield, we have set $B = 2^{22}$ (*i.e* a factor base comprising *circa* 300,000 prime ideals). For $S = 2^{50}$, the polynomial selection program returned the quartic candidate[10] $f(x) = \sum_{i=0}^{4} a_i x^i$ where:

$a_4 = \quad 8$

$a_3 = \quad 5451802006688119$

$a_2 = - \ 7344893341388732622814165470437$

$a_1 = \quad 8330506303515765255845075245428410906703868803$

$a_0 = - \ 806909024332519991161585163300207022921904012239943504 45959$

We worked in $K = \mathbb{Q}[x]/f$ and counted 295,842 prime ideals of degree one (or dividing the leading coefficient) in K's integer ring.

The sieving process was run on a heterogeneous set of CPUs: AMD Opteron 250 at 2.4 GHz and Intel Core-2 at various clock speeds.

For each special-q ideal written as $\langle q, \alpha - r \rangle$, we isolated the integers $x \in [-2^{28}, 2^{28}]$ such that the added contribution of factor base ideals to the norm of the ideal $(r + qx - \alpha)$ exceeded 2^{145} (out of an order of magnitude just below 2^{200}). This selection process isolated instantaneously[11] *circa* 100 candidates of which around nineteen yielded relations. Considering the largest 20,000 ideals in the factor base as special-q ideals, we obtained 380,000 relations. The sieving step was distributed over twenty CPUs and claimed a couple of hours. We stress that we did not use any "large prime" variation.

After pruning the columns corresponding to ideals never encountered in the factorizations, we were left with a row dependency to be obtained on a 283,355×283,355 matrix. We included four readily computed character columns in the matrix, to ensure that the computed dependency corresponds to an e-th power. The dependency was obtained using the block Wiedemann algorithm, with a "blocking factor" of $m = n = 8$. This took four CPU[12] hours distributed on four machines to produce one row dependency.

The e-th root computation was done in MAGMA.

We started with a product formula π whose numerator and denominator had a norm $\approx e^{7.6 \times 10^5}$ and with a moderate unit contribution, since the logarithms of the complex embeddings were approximately:

$$(\lambda + 45, \lambda + 45, \lambda - 155, \lambda + 65) \quad \text{where} \quad \lambda = \frac{1}{d} \log \text{Norm}(\pi) \simeq 6710$$

Here λ is the normalizing term. This is quite small since a unit with logarithms of complex embeddings equal to $(45, 45, -155, 65)$ would correspond to an algebraic integer with coefficients of about twenty decimal digits. The first four reduction steps sufficed to eliminate this unit contribution (*i.e.* equalling the logarithms of the complex embeddings with their average). After 2,000 reduction steps, we obtained a complete product formula for the root, the remaining e-th power being -1. It took five minutes to compute this e-th root.

---

[10] Best amongst a set of 1,000 candidates.

[11] 2.667 GHz Intel Core-2 CPU.

[12] 2.667 GHz Intel Core-2.

The corresponding final multiplicative dependency involved $242,700$ integers of the form $c + x_i \bmod n$.

B   Example of an e-th Root Computation

As an experimental illustration of the arbitrary e-th root computation, we used once again $n = $ RSA-155. For a public exponent $e = 65,537$, we detail the computation of an arbitrary e-th root given access to a preliminary e-th root oracle (the attacker is given the challenge only once all oracle queries have been performed).

We have chosen a setup resembling a typical NFS factoring experiment or a computation of discrete logarithms. The polynomials $f_1 = \sum a_i x^i$ and $f_2 = \sum b_i x^i$ are given by the following coefficients, the polynomial f_2 corresponding to a rational side:

$$a_5 = 28200000$$
$$a_4 = -7229989539851$$
$$a_3 = -24220733860168568962$$
$$a_2 = -6401736489600175386662132$$
$$a_1 = 4117850270472750057831223534880$$
$$a_0 = 7474745811455763707762443469909292200$$

$$b_1 = 14507315380338583$$
$$b_0 = -207858336487818193824240150287$$

These two polynomials are easily seen to share a common root P modulo n.

The sieving stage has been performed only on the number field side. We chose as a *small* factor base the set of prime ideals of norm below $B = 4 \times 10^6$ (*i.e.* 283,042 ideals). For the sieving, we have used the lattice sieving program lasieve4 of J. Franke and T. Kleinjung included in the ggnfs software suite. The program was modified to sieve only on one side. Using a double large prime variation, the sieving step has been completed in two CPU hours on a 2.4GHz AMD Opteron.

We then extended the factor base to the larger bound $B' = 2^{32}$. After 44 CPU hours, we were able to relate 37% of the ideals of this larger factor base to ideals of the smaller factor base (the larger factor base comprises approximately 2×10^8 ideals).

Counting oracle queries related to both sides, we need to perform 4×10^8 queries before being able to compute arbitrary e-th roots.

We have implemented the descent procedure using MAGMA, as well as the lasieve4 program, modified in order to account for very large *special q's* as used in the descent process. The factorization of the numerous sieve residues produced was handled by the GMP-ECM program.

The descent was initialized on the rational side. We obtained integers u and v which factored into primes with at most 35 decimal digits. Each step of the descent procedure involved a lasieve4 call, in order to select several candidate polynomials. Amongst the possible polynomials, our strategy selected the one leading to the fewest ideals outside the factor base (taking into account the large ideals coming from the factor base extension). After 42 descent steps, we obtained a product formula involving 594 prime numbers and ideals below $B' = 2^{32}$. Some (19) ideals in this product formula belonged to the set of "missed" ideals from the larger factor base. With 21 extra descent steps, these ideals were eliminated. The descent procedure took roughly one hour.

The schedule time for solving the resulting inhomogeneous linear system and computing the algebraic e-th root compares in every respect to the data given for the previous example (Appendix A).

Faster Addition and Doubling on Elliptic Curves

Daniel J. Bernstein[1] and Tanja Lange[2,*]

[1] Department of Mathematics, Statistics, and Computer Science (M/C 249)
University of Illinois at Chicago, Chicago, IL 60607–7045, USA
djb@cr.yp.to
[2] Department of Mathematics and Computer Science
Technische Universiteit Eindhoven, P.O. Box 513, 5600 MB Eindhoven, Netherlands
tanja@hyperelliptic.org

Abstract. Edwards recently introduced a new normal form for elliptic curves. Every elliptic curve over a non-binary field is birationally equivalent to a curve in Edwards form over an extension of the field, and in many cases over the original field.

This paper presents fast explicit formulas (and register allocations) for group operations on an Edwards curve. The algorithm for doubling uses only $3M + 4S$, i.e., 3 field multiplications and 4 field squarings. If curve parameters are chosen to be small then the algorithm for mixed addition uses only $9M + 1S$ and the algorithm for non-mixed addition uses only $10M + 1S$. Arbitrary Edwards curves can be handled at the cost of just one extra multiplication by a curve parameter.

For comparison, the fastest algorithms known for the popular "$a_4 = -3$ Jacobian" form use $3M + 5S$ for doubling; use $7M + 4S$ for mixed addition; use $11M + 5S$ for non-mixed addition; and use $10M + 4S$ for non-mixed addition when one input has been added before.

The explicit formulas for non-mixed addition on an Edwards curve can be used for doublings at no extra cost, simplifying protection against side-channel attacks. Even better, many elliptic curves (approximately 1/4 of all isomorphism classes of elliptic curves over a non-binary finite field) are birationally equivalent—over the original field—to Edwards curves where this addition algorithm works for *all* pairs of curve points, including inverses, the neutral element, etc.

This paper contains an extensive comparison of different forms of elliptic curves and different coordinate systems for the basic group operations (doubling, mixed addition, non-mixed addition, and unified addition) as well as higher-level operations such as multi-scalar multiplication.

Keywords: Elliptic curves, addition, doubling, explicit formulas, register allocation, scalar multiplication, multi-scalar multiplication, side-channel countermeasures, unified addition formulas, complete addition formulas, efficient implementation, performance evaluation.

* Permanent ID of this document: **95616567a6ba20f575c5f25e7cebaf83**. Date of this document: 2007.09.28. This work has been supported in part by the European Commission through the IST Programme under Contract IST–2002–507932 ECRYPT. This work was carried out while the first author was visiting Technische Universiteit Eindhoven.

1 Introduction

The core operations in elliptic-curve cryptography are single-scalar multiplication $(m, P \mapsto mP)$, double-scalar multiplication $(m, n, P, Q \mapsto mP + nQ)$, etc. Miller, in his Crypto '85 paper introducing elliptic-curve cryptography, proposed carrying out these operations on points represented in Jacobian form: "Each point is represented by the triple (x, y, z) which corresponds to the point $(x/z^2, y/z^3)$" on a curve $y^2 = x^3 + a_4 x + a_6$. See [37, page 424]. One can add two points using 16 field multiplications, specifically $11\mathbf{M} + 5\mathbf{S}$, with the fastest algorithms known today; here we keep separate tallies of squarings $\mathbf{S}$ and general multiplications $\mathbf{M}$. A mixed addition — this means that one input has $z = 1$ — takes only $7\mathbf{M} + 4\mathbf{S}$. A doubling takes $1\mathbf{M} + 8\mathbf{S} + 1\mathbf{D}$, where $\mathbf{D}$ denotes the cost of multiplying by a_4; a doubling takes $3\mathbf{M} + 5\mathbf{S}$ in the special case $a_4 = -3$.

Several subsequent papers analyzed the performance of other forms of elliptic curves proposed in the mathematical literature. See, e.g., [18] for the speed of several dialects of the Weierstrass form, [34] for the speed of Jacobi intersections, [28] for the speed of Hessians, and [9] for the speed of Jacobi quartics; see also [38] and [23], which introduced the Montgomery and Doche/Icart/Kohel forms and analyzed their speed. These alternate forms attracted some interest — in particular, many of them simplify protection against side-channel attacks, and the speed records in [7] for single-scalar multiplication were set with the Montgomery form — but the Jacobian form remained the overall speed leader for multi-scalar multiplication.

A new form for elliptic curves was added to the mathematical literature a few months ago: Edwards showed in [25] that all elliptic curves over number fields could be transformed to the shape $x^2 + y^2 = c^2(1 + x^2 y^2)$, with $(0, c)$ as neutral element and with the surprisingly simple and symmetric addition law

$$(x_1, y_1), (x_2, y_2) \mapsto \left(\frac{x_1 y_2 + y_1 x_2}{c(1 + x_1 x_2 y_1 y_2)}, \frac{y_1 y_2 - x_1 x_2}{c(1 - x_1 x_2 y_1 y_2)} \right).$$

Similarly, all elliptic curves over non-binary finite fields can be transformed to Edwards form. Some elliptic curves require a field extension for the transformation, but some elliptic curves have transformations defined over the original number field or finite field.

To capture a larger class of elliptic curves over the original field, we expand the notion of Edwards form to include all curves $x^2 + y^2 = c^2(1 + dx^2 y^2)$ where $cd(1 - dc^4) \neq 0$. More than $1/4$ of all isomorphism classes of elliptic curves over a finite field — for example, the curve "Curve25519" previously used to set speed records for single-scalar multiplication — can be transformed to Edwards curves over the same field. See §2 and §3 of this paper for further background on Edwards curves.

Our main goal in this paper is to analyze the impact of Edwards curves upon cryptographic applications. Our main conclusions are that the Edwards form (1) breaks solidly through the Jacobian speed barrier, (2) is competitive with the Montgomery form for single-scalar multiplication, and (3) is the new speed leader for multi-scalar multiplication. Specifically, we present explicit formulas (i.e., sequences of additions, subtractions, and multiplications) that

- compute an addition $(X_1 : Y_1 : Z_1), (X_2 : Y_2 : Z_2) \mapsto (X_1 : Y_1 : Z_1) + (X_2 : Y_2 : Z_2)$ using $10\mathbf{M} + 1\mathbf{S} + 1\mathbf{D}$ — here $\mathbf{D}$ is the cost of multiplying by a selectable curve parameter;
- compute a mixed addition $(X_1 : Y_1 : Z_1), (X_2 : Y_2 : 1) \mapsto (X_1 : Y_1 : Z_1) + (X_2 : Y_2 : 1)$ using $9\mathbf{M} + 1\mathbf{S} + 1\mathbf{D}$; and
- compute a doubling $(X_1 : Y_1 : Z_1) \mapsto 2(X_1 : Y_1 : Z_1)$ using $3\mathbf{M} + 4\mathbf{S}$.

See §4 for details of these computations; §5 for a comparison of these speeds to the speeds of explicit formulas for Jacobian, Hessian, etc.; §6 and §7 for an analysis of the resulting speeds of single-scalar multiplication and general multi-scalar multiplication; and §8 for a discussion of side-channel attacks.

An Edwards curve with a unique point of order 2 has the extra feature that the addition formulas are *complete*. This means that the formulas work for *all* pairs of input points on the curve, with no exceptions for doubling, no exceptions for the neutral element, no exceptions for negatives, etc. Some previous addition formulas have been advertised as *unified* formulas that can handle generic doublings, simplifying protection against side-channel attacks; our addition formulas are faster than previous unified formulas and have the stronger property of completeness. See §3, §5, and §8 for further discussion.

Acknowledgments. We thank Harold M. Edwards for his comments and encouragement, and of course for finding the Edwards addition law in the first place. We thank Marc Joye for suggesting using the curve equation to accelerate the computation of the x-coordinate of $2P$; see §4.

2 Transformation to Edwards Form

Fix a field k of characteristic different from 2. Let E be an elliptic curve over k having a point of order 4. This section shows that some quadratic twist of E is birationally equivalent over k to an Edwards curve: specifically, a curve of the form $x^2 + y^2 = 1 + dx^2y^2$ with $d \notin \{0, 1\}$. (Perhaps this twist is E itself; perhaps not.) §3 shows that the Edwards addition law on the Edwards curve corresponds to the standard elliptic-curve addition law.

If E has a unique point of order 2 then some quadratic twist of E is birationally equivalent over k to an Edwards curve having non-square d. If k is finite and E has a unique point of order 2 then the twist can be removed: E is birationally equivalent over k to an Edwards curve having non-square d. §3 shows that the Edwards addition law is complete in this case.

All of these equivalences can be computed efficiently. The proof of Theorem 2.1 explicitly constructs d given a Weierstrass-form elliptic curve, and explicitly maps points between the Weierstrass curve and the Edwards curve.

As an example, consider the elliptic curve published in [7] for fast scalar multiplication in Montgomery form, namely the elliptic curve $v^2 = u^3 + 486662u^2 + u$ modulo $p = 2^{255} - 19$. This curve "Curve25519" is birationally equivalent over

$\mathbb{Z}/p$ to the Edwards curve $x^2 + y^2 = 1 + (121665/121666)x^2y^2$. The transformation is easy: simply define $x = \sqrt{486664}u/v$ and $y = (u-1)/(u+1)$; note that 486664 is a square modulo p. The inverse transformation is just as easy: simply define $u = (1+y)/(1-y)$ and $v = \sqrt{486664}u/x$.

Every Edwards curve has a point of order 4; see §3. So it is natural to consider elliptic curves having points of order 4. What about elliptic curves that do not have points of order 4 — for example, the NIST curves over prime fields? Construct an extension field k' of k such that $E(k')$, the group of points of E defined over k', has an element of order 4. Then replace k by k' in Theorem 2.1 to see that some twist of E is birationally equivalent over k' to an Edwards curve defined over k'.

Theorem 2.1. *Let k be a field in which $2 \neq 0$. Let E be an elliptic curve over k such that the group $E(k)$ has an element of order 4. Then*

(1) *there exists $d \in k - \{0,1\}$ such that the curve $x^2 + y^2 = 1 + dx^2y^2$ is birationally equivalent over k to a quadratic twist of E;*

(2) *if $E(k)$ has a unique element of order 2 then there is a nonsquare $d \in k$ such that the curve $x^2 + y^2 = 1 + dx^2y^2$ is birationally equivalent over k to a quadratic twist of E; and*

(3) *if k is finite and $E(k)$ has a unique element of order 2 then there is a nonsquare $d \in k$ such that the curve $x^2 + y^2 = 1 + dx^2y^2$ is birationally equivalent over k to E.*

Proof. Write E in long Weierstrass form $s^2 + a_1rs + a_3s = r^3 + a_2r^2 + a_4r + a_6$. Assume without loss of generality that $a_1 = 0$ and $a_3 = 0$; to handle the general case, define $\bar{s} = s + (a_1r + a_3)/2$.

Write P for the hypothesized point of order 4 on E. Assume without loss of generality that $2P = (0,0)$ and thus $a_6 = 0$; to handle the general case, define $\bar{r} = r - r_2$ where $2P = (r_2, s_2)$.

The elliptic curve E now has the form $s^2 = r^3 + a_2r^2 + a_4r$. Write P as (r_1, s_1). The next step is to express a_2 and a_4 in terms of r_1 and s_1.

Note that $s_1 \neq 0$, as otherwise P has order 2. Consequently $r_1 \neq 0$. The equation $2P = (0,0)$ means that the tangent line to E at P passes through $(0,0)$, i.e., that $s_1 - 0 = (r_1 - 0)\lambda$ where λ is the tangent slope $(3r_1^2 + 2a_2r_1 + a_4)/2s_1$. Thus $3r_1^3 + 2a_2r_1^2 + a_4r_1 = 2s_1^2$. Also $2s_1^2 = 2r_1^3 + 2a_2r_1^2 + 2a_4r_1$ since P is on the curve. Subtract to see that $r_1^3 = a_4r_1$, i.e., $r_1^2 = a_4$. Furthermore $a_2 = (s_1^2 - r_1^3 - a_4r_1)/r_1^2 = s_1^2/r_1^2 - 2r_1$. Putting $d = 1 - 4r_1^3/s_1^2$ we obtain $a_2 = 2((1+d)/(1-d))r_1$.

Note that $d \neq 1$ since $r_1 \neq 0$. Note also that $d \neq 0$: otherwise the right hand side of E's equation would be $r^3 + a_2r^2 + a_4r = r^3 + 2r_1r^2 + r_1^2r = r(r + r_1)^2$, contradicting the hypothesis that E is elliptic. Note also that if d is a square then there is another point of order 2 in $E(k)$, namely $(r_1(\sqrt{d}+1)/(\sqrt{d}-1), 0)$.

Consider two quadratic twists of E, namely the elliptic curves E' and E'' defined by $(r_1/(1-d))s^2 = r^3 + a_2r^2 + a_4r$ and $(dr_1/(1-d))s^2 = r^3 + a_2r^2 + a_4r$.

If k is finite and d is nonsquare then either $r_1/(1-d)$ or $dr_1/(1-d)$ is a square in k so E is isomorphic to either E' or E''.

Substitute $u = r/r_1$ and $v = s/r_1$ to see that E' is isomorphic to the elliptic curve $(1/(1-d))v^2 = u^3 + 2((1+d)/(1-d))u^2 + u$ and that E'' is isomorphic to $(d/(1-d))v^2 = u^3 + 2((1+d)/(1-d))u^2 + u$.

We now show that the curve $x^2 + y^2 = 1 + dx^2y^2$ is birationally equivalent to $(1/(1-d))v^2 = u^3 + 2((1+d)/(1-d))u^2 + u$, and therefore to E'. The rational map $(u,v) \mapsto (x,y)$ is defined by $x = 2u/v$ and $y = (u-1)/(u+1)$; there are only finitely many exceptional points with $v(u+1) = 0$. The inverse rational map $(x,y) \mapsto (u,v)$ is defined by $u = (1+y)/(1-y)$ and $v = 2(1+y)/(1-y)x$; there are only finitely many exceptional points with $(1-y)x = 0$. A straightforward calculation, included in [8], shows that the inverse rational map produces (u,v) satisfying $(1/(1-d))v^2 = u^3 + 2((1+d)/(1-d))u^2 + u$.

Substitute $1/d$ for d and $-u$ for u to see that $x^2 + y^2 = 1 + (1/d)x^2y^2$ is birationally equivalent to the curve $(1/(1-1/d))v^2 = (-u)^3 + 2((1+1/d)/(1-1/d))(-u)^2 + (-u)$, i.e., to $(d/(1-d))v^2 = u^3 + 2((1+d)/(1-d))u^2 + u$, and therefore to E''.

To summarize: (1) The curve $x^2 + y^2 = 1 + dx^2y^2$ is equivalent to a quadratic twist E' of E. (2) If E has a unique point of order 2 then d is a nonsquare and $x^2 + y^2 = 1 + dx^2y^2$ is equivalent to a quadratic twist E' of E. (3) If k is finite and E has a unique point of order 2 then d is a nonsquare so E is isomorphic to E' or to E''; thus E is birationally equivalent to $x^2 + y^2 = 1 + dx^2y^2$ or to $x^2 + y^2 = 1 + (1/d)x^2y^2$. $\square$

Notes on Isomorphisms. If $d = \bar{d}\bar{c}^4$ then the curve $x^2 + y^2 = 1 + dx^2y^2$ is isomorphic to the curve $\bar{x}^2 + \bar{y}^2 = \bar{c}^2(1 + \bar{d}\bar{x}^2\bar{y}^2)$: simply define $\bar{x} = \bar{c}x$ and $\bar{y} = \bar{c}y$. In particular, if k is a finite field, then at least $1/4$ of the nonzero elements of k are 4th powers, so $d/\bar{d}$ is a 4th power for at least $1/4$ of the choices of $\bar{d} \in k - \{0\}$; the smallest qualifying $\bar{d}$ is typically extremely small. But for computational purposes we do not recommend minimizing $\bar{d}$ as a general strategy: a small $\bar{c}$ is more valuable than a small $\bar{d}$. See §4.

3   The Edwards Addition Law

This section presents the Edwards addition law for an Edwards curve $x^2 + y^2 = c^2(1 + dx^2y^2)$. We show (1) that the Edwards addition law produces points on the curve, (2) that the Edwards addition law corresponds to the standard addition law on a birationally equivalent elliptic curve, and (3) that the Edwards addition law is complete when d is not a square. Proofs appear at the end of the section.

Fix a field k of characteristic different from 2. Fix $c, d \in k$ such that $c \neq 0$, $d \neq 0$, and $dc^4 \neq 1$. Consider the *Edwards addition law*

$$(x_1, y_1), (x_2, y_2) \mapsto \left(\frac{x_1y_2 + y_1x_2}{c(1 + dx_1x_2y_1y_2)}, \frac{y_1y_2 - x_1x_2}{c(1 - dx_1x_2y_1y_2)} \right)$$

on the Edwards curve $x^2 + y^2 = c^2(1 + dx^2y^2)$ over k.

Examples: for each point $P = (x_1, y_1)$ on the curve, P is the sum of $(0,c)$ and P, so $(0,c)$ is a neutral element of the addition law; the only neutral element is $(0, c)$; $(0, c)$ is the sum of P and $-P = (-x_1, y_1)$; in particular, $(0, -c)$ has order 2; $(c, 0)$ and $(-c, 0)$ have order 4.

The next theorem states that the output of the Edwards addition law is on the curve when the output is defined, i.e., when $dx_1 x_2 y_1 y_2 \notin \{-1, 1\}$.

Theorem 3.1. *Let k be a field in which $2 \neq 0$. Let c, d be nonzero elements of k with $dc^4 \neq 1$. Let x_1, y_1, x_2, y_2 be elements of k such that $x_1^2 + y_1^2 = c^2(1 + dx_1^2 y_1^2)$ and $x_2^2 + y_2^2 = c^2(1 + dx_2^2 y_2^2)$. Assume that $dx_1 x_2 y_1 y_2 \notin \{-1, 1\}$. Define $x_3 = (x_1 y_2 + y_1 x_2)/c(1 + dx_1 x_2 y_1 y_2)$ and $y_3 = (y_1 y_2 - x_1 x_2)/c(1 - dx_1 x_2 y_1 y_2)$. Then $x_3^2 + y_3^2 = c^2(1 + dx_3^2 y_3^2)$.*

The next theorem states that the output of the Edwards addition law corresponds to the output of the standard addition law on a birationally equivalent elliptic curve E. One can therefore perform group operations on E (or on any other birationally equivalent elliptic curve) by performing the corresponding group operations on the Edwards curve, at the expense of evaluating and inverting the correspondence once for each series of computations.

Theorem 3.2. *In the situation of Theorem 3.1, let $e = 1 - dc^4$ and let E be the elliptic curve $(1/e)v^2 = u^3 + (4/e - 2)u^2 + u$. For each $i \in \{1, 2, 3\}$ define P_i as follows: $P_i = \infty$ if $(x_i, y_i) = (0, c)$; $P_i = (0, 0)$ if $(x_i, y_i) = (0, -c)$; and $P_i = (u_i, v_i)$ if $x_i \neq 0$, where $u_i = (c + y_i)/(c - y_i)$ and $v_i = 2c(c + y_i)/(c - y_i)x_i$. Then $P_i \in E(k)$ and $P_1 + P_2 = P_3$.*

Here $P_1 + P_2$ means the sum of P_1 and P_2 in the standard addition law on $E(k)$. Note that $x_i \neq 0$ implies $y_i \neq c$.

The group operations could encounter exceptional points where the Edwards addition law is not defined. One can, in many applications, rely on randomization to avoid the exceptional points, or one can switch from the Edwards curve back to E when exceptional points occur.

The next theorem states that, when d is not a square, there are no exceptional points: the denominators in the Edwards addition law cannot be zero. In other words, when d is not a square, the Edwards addition law is *complete*: it is defined for *all* pairs of input points on the Edwards curve over k. The set $E(k)$, with the standard addition law, is isomorphic as a group to the set of points $(x_1, y_1) \in k \times k$ on the Edwards curve, with the Edwards addition law. The Edwards addition law can carry out any sequence of group operations, without risk of failure.

Theorem 3.3. *Let k be a field in which $2 \neq 0$. Let c, d, e be nonzero elements of k with $e = 1 - dc^4$. Assume that d is not a square in k. Let x_1, y_1, x_2, y_2 be elements of k such that $x_1^2 + y_1^2 = c^2(1 + dx_1^2 y_1^2)$ and $x_2^2 + y_2^2 = c^2(1 + dx_2^2 y_2^2)$. Then $dx_1 x_2 y_1 y_2 \neq 1$ and $dx_1 x_2 y_1 y_2 \neq -1$.*

Example: $d = 121665/121666$ is not a square in the field $k = \mathbf{Z}/(2^{255} - 19)$. The Edwards addition law is defined for all $(x_1, y_1), (x_2, y_2)$ on the Edwards curve $x^2 + y^2 = 1 + dx^2 y^2$ over k, and corresponds to the standard addition law on "Curve25519," the elliptic curve $v^2 = u^3 + 486662u^2 + u$ over k. The point at ∞ on Curve25519 corresponds to the point $(0, 1)$ on the Edwards curve;

the point $(0,0)$ on Curve25519 corresponds to $(0,-1)$; any other point (u,v) on Curve25519 corresponds to $(\sqrt{486664}u/v,(u-1)/(u+1))$; a sum of points on Curve25519 corresponds to a sum of points on the Edwards curve. One can therefore perform a sequence of group operations on points of the elliptic curve $v^2 = u^3 + 486662u^2 + u$ by performing the same sequence of group operations on the corresponding points of the Edwards curve.

The reader might wonder why [11, Theorem 1] ("The smallest cardinality of a complete system of addition laws on E equals two") does not force exceptional cases in the addition law for the curve $x^2 + y^2 = c^2(1 + dx^2y^2)$. The simplest answer is that [11, Theorem 1] is concerned with exceptional cases in the algebraic closure of k, whereas we are concerned with exceptional cases in k itself.

The reader might also wonder why we ignore the two projective points $(0:1:0)$ and $(1:0:0)$ on the Edwards curve. The answer is that, although these points might at first glance appear to be defined over k, they are actually singularities of the curve, and resolving the singularities produces four points that are defined over $k(\sqrt{d})$, not over k.

Proof (of Theorem 3.1). The special case $d = 1$ is equivalent to [25, Theorem 8.1]. We could deduce the general case from the special case, but to keep this paper self-contained we instead give a direct proof.

The first ingredient in the proof is a mechanically verifiable polynomial identity. Define $T = (x_1y_2+y_1x_2)^2(1-dx_1x_2y_1y_2)^2+(y_1y_2-x_1x_2)^2(1+dx_1x_2y_1y_2)^2-d(x_1y_2+y_1x_2)^2(y_1y_2-x_1x_2)^2$. The identity says that $T = (x_1^2 + y_1^2 - (x_2^2 + y_2^2)dx_1^2y_1^2)(x_2^2 + y_2^2 - (x_1^2 + y_1^2)dx_2^2y_2^2)$.

The second ingredient is the curve equation, i.e., the hypotheses on (x_1,y_1) and (x_2,y_2). Subtract the equation $(x_2^2 + y_2^2)dx_1^2y_1^2 = c^2(1 + dx_2^2y_2^2)dx_1^2y_1^2$ from the equation $x_1^2 + y_1^2 = c^2(1 + dx_1^2y_1^2)$ to see that $x_1^2 + y_1^2 - (x_2^2 + y_2^2)dx_1^2y_1^2 = c^2(1 - d^2x_1^2x_2^2y_1^2y_2^2)$. Similarly $x_2^2 + y_2^2 - (x_1^2 + y_1^2)dx_2^2y_2^2 = c^2(1 - d^2x_1^2x_2^2y_1^2y_2^2)$. Thus $T = c^4(1 - d^2x_1^2x_2^2y_1^2y_2^2)^2$.

The third ingredient is the Edwards addition law, i.e., the definition of (x_3,y_3) in terms of x_1,x_2,y_1,y_2. We have $x_3^2+y_3^2-c^2dx_3^2y_3^2 = \frac{(x_1y_2+y_1x_2)^2}{c^2(1+dx_1x_2y_1y_2)^2} + \frac{(y_1y_2-x_1x_2)^2}{c^2(1-dx_1x_2y_1y_2)^2} - \frac{c^2d(x_1y_2+y_1x_2)^2(y_1y_2-x_1x_2)^2}{c^4(1+dx_1x_2y_1y_2)^2(1-dx_1x_2y_1y_2)^2} = \frac{T}{c^2(1+dx_1x_2y_1y_2)^2(1-dx_1x_2y_1y_2)^2} = \frac{T}{c^2(1-d^2x_1^2x_2^2y_1^2y_2^2)^2} = c^2$. Thus $x_3^2 + y_3^2 = c^2(1 + dx_3^2y_3^2)$ as claimed. $\square$

Proof (of Theorem 3.2). First we show that each P_i is in $E(k)$. If $(x_i,y_i) = (0,c)$ then $P_i = \infty \in E(k)$. If $(x_i,y_i) = (0,-c)$ then $P_i = (0,0) \in E(k)$. Otherwise $P_i = (u_i,v_i) \in E(k)$ by essentially the same calculations as in Theorem 2.1, omitted here.

All that remains is to show that $P_1 + P_2 = P_3$. There are several cases in the standard addition law for $E(k)$; the proof thus splits into several cases.

If $(x_1,y_1) = (0,c)$ then $(x_3,y_3) = (x_2,y_2)$. Now P_1 is the point at infinity and $P_2 = P_3$, so $P_1 + P_2 = \infty + P_2 = P_2 = P_3$. Similar comments apply if $(x_2,y_2) = (0,c)$. Assume from now on that $(x_1,y_1) \neq (0,c)$ and $(x_2,y_2) \neq (0,c)$.

If $(x_3,y_3) = (0,c)$ then $(x_2,y_2) = (-x_1,y_1)$. If $(x_1,y_1) = (0,-c)$ then also $(x_2,y_2) = (0,-c)$ and $P_1 = (0,0) = P_2$; otherwise x_1,x_2 are nonzero so $u_1 =$

$(c + y_1)/(c - y_1) = u_2$ and $v_1 = 2cu_1/x_1 = -2cu_2/x_2 = -v_2$ so $P_1 = -P_2$. In both cases $P_1 + P_2 = \infty = P_3$. Assume from now on that $(x_3, y_3) \neq (0, c)$.

If $(x_1, y_1) = (0, -c)$ then $(x_3, y_3) = (-x_2, -y_2)$. Now $(x_2, y_2) \neq (0, -c)$ (since otherwise $(x_3, y_3) = (0, c)$) and $(x_2, y_2) \neq (0, c)$ so $x_2 \neq 0$. Thus $P_1 = (0, 0)$ and $P_2 = (u_2, v_2)$ with $u_2 = (c+y_2)/(c-y_2)$ and $v_2 = 2cu_2/x_2$. The standard addition law says that $(0, 0) + (u_2, v_2) = (r_3, s_3)$ where $r_3 = (1/e)(v_2/u_2)^2 - (4/e - 2) - u_2 = 1/u_2$ and $s_3 = (v_2/u_2)(-r_3) = -v_2/u_2^2$. Furthermore $P_3 = (u_3, v_3)$ with $u_3 = (c + y_3)/(c - y_3) = (c - y_2)/(c + y_2) = 1/u_2 = r_3$ and $v_3 = 2cu_3/x_3 = -2c/u_2x_2 = -v_2/u_2^2 = s_3$. Thus $P_1 + P_2 = P_3$. Similar comments apply if $(x_2, y_2) = (0, -c)$.

Assume from now on that $x_1 \neq 0$ and $x_2 \neq 0$. Then $P_1 = (u_1, v_1)$ with $u_1 = (c+y_1)/(c-y_1)$ and $v_1 = 2cu_1/x_1$, and $P_2 = (u_2, v_2)$ with $u_2 = (c+y_2)/(c-y_2)$ and $v_2 = 2cu_2/x_2$.

If $(x_3, y_3) = (0, -c)$ then $(x_1, y_1) = (x_2, -y_2)$ so $u_1 = (c + y_1)/(c - y_1) = (c - y_2)/(c + y_2) = 1/u_2$ and $v_1 = 2cu_1/x_1 = v_2/u_2^2$. Furthermore $P_3 = (0, 0)$ so the standard addition law says as above that $-P_3 + P_2 = (0, 0) + P_2 = (1/u_2, -v_2/u_2^2) = (u_1, -v_1) = -P_1$, i.e., $P_1 + P_2 = P_3$.

Assume from now on that $x_3 \neq 0$. Then $P_3 = (u_3, v_3)$ with $u_3 = (c+y_3)/(c-y_3)$ and $v_3 = 2cu_3/x_3$.

If $P_2 = -P_1$ then $u_2 = u_1$ and $v_2 = -v_1$, so $x_2 = -x_1$ and $y_2 = c(u_2 - 1)/(u_2 + 1) = c(u_1 - 1)/(u_1 + 1) = y_1$, so $(x_3, y_3) = (0, c)$, which is already handled above. Assume from now on that $P_2 \neq -P_1$.

If $u_2 = u_1$ and $v_2 \neq -v_1$ then the standard addition law says that $(u_1, v_1) + (u_2, v_2) = (r_3, s_3)$ where $\lambda = (3u_1^2 + 2(4/e - 2)u_1 + 1)/((2/e)v_1)$, $r_3 = (1/e)\lambda^2 - (4/e - 2) - 2u_1$, and $s_3 = \lambda(u_1 - r_3) - v_1$. A straightforward calculation, included in [8], shows that $(r_3, s_3) = (u_3, v_3)$.

The only remaining case is that $u_2 \neq u_1$. The standard addition law says that $(u_1, v_1) + (u_2, v_2) = (r_3, s_3)$ where $\lambda = (v_2 - v_1)/(u_2 - u_1)$, $r_3 = (1/e)\lambda^2 - (4/e - 2) - u_1 - u_2$, and $s_3 = \lambda(u_1 - r_3) - v_1$. Another straightforward calculation, included in [8], shows that $(r_3, s_3) = (u_3, v_3)$.

Conclusion: $P_3 = P_1 + P_2$ in every case. □

Proof (of Theorem 3.3). Write $\epsilon = dx_1x_2y_1y_2$. Suppose that $\epsilon \in \{-1, 1\}$. Then $x_1, x_2, y_1, y_2 \neq 0$. Furthermore $dx_1^2y_1^2(x_2^2 + y_2^2) = c^2(dx_1^2y_1^2 + d^2x_1^2y_1^2x_2^2y_2^2) = c^2(dx_1^2y_1^2 + \epsilon^2) = c^2(1 + dx_1^2y_1^2) = x_1^2 + y_1^2$ so

$$(x_1 + \epsilon y_1)^2 = x_1^2 + y_1^2 + 2\epsilon x_1y_1 = dx_1^2y_1^2(x_2^2 + y_2^2) + 2x_1y_1dx_1x_2y_1y_2$$
$$= dx_1^2y_1^2(x_2^2 + 2x_2y_2 + y_2^2) = dx_1^2y_1^2(x_2 + y_2)^2.$$

If $x_2 + y_2 \neq 0$ then $d = ((x_1 + \epsilon y_1)/x_1y_1(x_2 + y_2))^2$ so d is a square, contradiction. Similarly, if $x_2 - y_2 \neq 0$ then $d = ((x_1 - \epsilon y_1)/x_1y_1(x_2 - y_2))^2$ so d is a square, contradiction. If both $x_2 + y_2$ and $x_2 - y_2$ are 0 then $x_2 = 0$ and $y_2 = 0$, contradiction. □

4   Efficient Group Operations in Edwards Form

This section presents fast explicit formulas and register allocations for doubling, mixed addition, etc. on Edwards curves with arbitrary parameters c, d.

As usual we count the number of operations in the underlying field. We keep separate tallies of the number of general multiplications (each costing $\mathbf{M}$), squarings (each costing $\mathbf{S}$), multiplications by c (each costing $\mathbf{C}$), multiplications by d (each costing $\mathbf{D}$), and additions/subtractions (each costing $\mathbf{a}$). The costs $\mathbf{M}, \mathbf{S}, \mathbf{C}, \mathbf{D}, \mathbf{a}$ depend on the choice of platform, on the choice of finite field, and on the choice of c and d.

Every Edwards curve can easily be transformed to an isomorphic Edwards curve over the same field having $c = 1$ and thus $\mathbf{C} = 0$; see "Notes on isomorphisms" in §2. In subsequent sections we assume that $c = 1$. However, we can imagine applications in which $c \neq 1$ (for example, a curve with a fairly small c and with $d = 1$ could have smaller $\mathbf{C} + \mathbf{D}$ than an isomorphic curve with $\bar{c} = 1$ and $\bar{d} = c^4$), so we allow arbitrary (c, d) in our explicit formulas.

Addition. To avoid the inversions in the original Edwards addition formulas, we homogenize the curve equation to $(X^2 + Y^2)Z^2 = c^2(Z^4 + dX^2Y^2)$. A point $(X_1 : Y_1 : Z_1)$ satisfying $(X_1^2 + Y_1^2)Z_1^2 = c^2(Z_1^4 + dX_1^2Y_1^2)$ and $Z_1 \neq 0$ corresponds to the affine point $(X_1/Z_1, Y_1/Z_1)$. The neutral element is $(0 : c : 1)$, and the inverse of $(X_1 : Y_1 : Z_1)$ is $(-X_1 : Y_1 : Z_1)$.

The following formulas, given $(X_1 : Y_1 : Z_1)$ and $(X_2 : Y_2 : Z_2)$, compute the sum $(X_3 : Y_3 : Z_3) = (X_1 : Y_1 : Z_1) + (X_2 : Y_2 : Z_2)$:

$$A = Z_1 \cdot Z_2;\; B = A^2;\; C = X_1 \cdot X_2;\; D = Y_1 \cdot Y_2;\; E = d \cdot C \cdot D;$$
$$F = B - E;\; G = B + E;\; X_3 = A \cdot F \cdot ((X_1 + Y_1) \cdot (X_2 + Y_2) - C - D);$$
$$Y_3 = A \cdot G \cdot (D - C);\; Z_3 = c \cdot F \cdot G.$$

One readily counts $10\mathbf{M} + 1\mathbf{S} + 1\mathbf{C} + 1\mathbf{D} + 7\mathbf{a}$. We have saved operations here by rewriting $x_1y_2 + x_2y_1$ as $(x_1 + y_1)(x_2 + y_2) - x_1x_2 - y_1y_2$ and by exploiting common subexpressions.

The following specific sequence of operations starts with registers R_1, R_2, R_3 containing X_1, Y_1, Z_1 and registers R_4, R_5, R_6 containing X_2, Y_2, Z_2, uses just two temporary registers R_7, R_8 and constants c, d, ends with registers R_1, R_2, R_3 containing X_3, Y_3, Z_3 and untouched registers R_4, R_5, R_6 containing X_2, Y_2, Z_2, and uses $10\mathbf{M} + 1\mathbf{S} + 1\mathbf{C} + 1\mathbf{D} + 7\mathbf{a}$:

$$R_3 \leftarrow R_3 \cdot R_6;\; R_7 \leftarrow R_1 + R_2;\; R_8 \leftarrow R_4 + R_5;\; R_1 \leftarrow R_1 \cdot R_4;\; R_2 \leftarrow R_2 \cdot R_5;$$
$$R_7 \leftarrow R_7 \cdot R_8;\; R_7 \leftarrow R_7 - R_1;\; R_7 \leftarrow R_7 - R_2;\; R_7 \leftarrow R_7 \cdot R_3;\; R_8 \leftarrow R_1 \cdot R_2;$$
$$R_8 \leftarrow d \cdot R_8;\; R_2 \leftarrow R_2 - R_1;\; R_2 \leftarrow R_2 \cdot R_3;\; R_3 \leftarrow R_3^2;\; R_1 \leftarrow R_3 - R_8;$$
$$R_3 \leftarrow R_3 + R_8;\; R_2 \leftarrow R_2 \cdot R_3;\; R_3 \leftarrow R_3 \cdot R_1;\; R_1 \leftarrow R_1 \cdot R_7;\; R_3 \leftarrow c \cdot R_3.$$

We emphasize that these formulas work whether or not $(X_1 : Y_1 : Z_1) = (X_2 : Y_2 : Z_2)$. There is no need to go to extra effort to unify the addition formulas with separate doubling formulas; the addition formulas are already unified. If d is not a square then the addition law works for *all* pairs of input points. See §3 for further discussion of the scope of validity of the addition formulas.

As an alternative, one can obtain $A(B-E)$ and $A(B+E)$ and $(B-E)(B+E)$ as linear combinations of $A^2, B^2, E^2, (A+B)^2, (A+E)^2$. This change replaces $10M+1S$ by $7M+5S$, presumably saving time on platforms where $S/M < 0.75$. Note that $S/M \approx 0.67$ in [7].

Mixed Addition. "Mixed addition" refers to the case that Z_2 is known to be 1. In this case the multiplication $A = Z_1 \cdot Z_2$ can be eliminated, reducing the total costs to $9M + 1S + 1C + 1D + 7a$.

Doubling. "Doubling" refers to the case that $(X_1 : Y_1 : Z_1)$ and $(X_2 : Y_2 : Z_2)$ are known to be equal. In this case we rewrite $c(1 + dx_1^2 y_1^2)$ as $(x_1^2 + y_1^2)/c$ using the curve equation, and we rewrite $c(1 - dx_1^2 y_1^2)$ as $(2c^2 - (x_1^2 + y_1^2))/c$:

$$2(x_1, y_1) = \left(\frac{2x_1 y_1}{c(1 + dx_1^2 y_1^2)}, \frac{y_1^2 - x_1^2}{c(1 - dx_1^2 y_1^2)} \right) = \left(\frac{2x_1 y_1 c}{x_1^2 + y_1^2}, \frac{(y_1^2 - x_1^2)c}{2c^2 - (x_1^2 + y_1^2)} \right).$$

We thank Marc Joye for suggesting rewriting $c(1 + dx_1^2 y_1^2)$ as $(x_1^2 + y_1^2)/c$. We save further operations by rewriting $2x_1 y_1$ as $(x_1 + y_1)^2 - x_1^2 - y_1^2$ and by exploiting common subexpressions. The resulting formulas (with $2H$ computed as $H + H$) use only $3M + 4S + 3C + 6a$:

$$B = (X_1 + Y_1)^2; \quad C = X_1^2; \quad D = Y_1^2; \quad E = C + D; \quad H = (c \cdot Z_1)^2;$$
$$J = E - 2H; \quad X_3 = c \cdot (B - E) \cdot J; \quad Y_3 = c \cdot E \cdot (C - D); \quad Z_3 = E \cdot J.$$

The following specific sequence of operations, starting with X_1, Y_1, Z_1 in registers R_1, R_2, R_3, changes registers R_1, R_2, R_3 to contain X_3, Y_3, Z_3, using $3M + 4S + 3C + 6a$ and using just two temporary registers R_4, R_5:

$$R_4 \leftarrow R_1 + R_2; \quad R_3 \leftarrow c \cdot R_3; \quad R_1 \leftarrow R_1^2; \quad R_2 \leftarrow R_2^2; \quad R_3 \leftarrow R_3^2; \quad R_4 \leftarrow R_4^2;$$
$$R_3 \leftarrow R_3 + R_3; \quad R_5 \leftarrow R_1 + R_2; \quad R_2 \leftarrow R_1 - R_2; \quad R_4 \leftarrow R_4 - R_5; \quad R_3 \leftarrow R_5 - R_3;$$
$$R_1 \leftarrow R_3 \cdot R_4; \quad R_3 \leftarrow R_3 \cdot R_5; \quad R_2 \leftarrow R_2 \cdot R_5; \quad R_1 \leftarrow c \cdot R_1; \quad R_2 \leftarrow c \cdot R_2.$$

The following alternate sequence of operations uses one more addition, totalling $3M + 4S + 3C + 7a$, but uses just one additional register R_4:

$$R_3 \leftarrow c \cdot R_3; \quad R_4 \leftarrow R_1^2; \quad R_1 \leftarrow R_1 + R_2; \quad R_1 \leftarrow R_1^2; \quad R_2 \leftarrow R_2^2; \quad R_3 \leftarrow R_3^2; \quad R_3 \leftarrow 2R_3;$$
$$R_4 \leftarrow R_2 + R_4; \quad R_2 \leftarrow 2R_2; \quad R_2 \leftarrow R_4 - R_2; \quad R_1 \leftarrow R_1 - R_4; \quad R_2 \leftarrow R_2 \cdot R_4;$$
$$R_3 \leftarrow R_4 - R_3; \quad R_1 \leftarrow R_1 \cdot R_3; \quad R_3 \leftarrow R_3 \cdot R_4; \quad R_1 \leftarrow c \cdot R_1; \quad R_2 \leftarrow c \cdot R_2.$$

Another option is to scale $(X_3 : Y_3 : Z_3)$ to $(X_3/c : Y_3/c : Z_3/c)$, replacing two multiplications by c with one multiplication by $1/c$; typically $1/c$ can be precomputed. Of course, all three multiplications by c can be skipped if $c = 1$.

Compression. Given x one can easily recover $\pm y = \sqrt{(c^2 - x^2)/(1 - c^2 dx^2)}$.

5   Comparison to Previous Addition Speeds

This section compares the speeds of the algorithms in §4 to the speeds of previous algorithms for elliptic-curve doubling, elliptic-curve mixed addition, etc. The next three sections perform similar comparisons for higher-level elliptic-curve operations relevant to various cryptographic applications.

Level of Detail of the Comparison. We follow most of the literature in ignoring the costs of additions, subtractions, and multiplications by small constants. We recognize that these costs (and the costs of non-arithmetic operations) can be quite noticeable in practice, and we plan a more detailed cost evaluation of the Edwards form along the lines of [7], but for this paper we ignore the costs.

Consider, for example, the usual doubling algorithm for Jacobian coordinates in the case $a_4 = -3$: there are 4 squarings, 4 general multiplications, 5 additions and subtractions, and 5 multiplications by the small constants $2, 3, 4, 8, 8$. We summarize these costs as $4\mathbf{M} + 4\mathbf{S}$.

Some algorithms involve multiplications by curve parameters, such as the parameter d in Edwards curves. Some applications can take advantage of multiplying by a constant d, and some applications can choose curves where d is small, but other applications cannot. To cover both situations we separately tally the cost $\mathbf{D}$ of multiplying by a curve parameter; the reader can substitute $\mathbf{D} = 0$, $\mathbf{D} = \mathbf{M}$, or anything in between.

Each of our tables includes a column "(1, 1)" that substitutes $(\mathbf{S}, \mathbf{D}) \approx (\mathbf{M}, \mathbf{M})$, a column "(0.8, 0.5)" that substitutes $(\mathbf{S}, \mathbf{D}) \approx (0.8\mathbf{M}, 0.5\mathbf{M})$, and a column "(0.8, 0)" that substitutes $(\mathbf{S}, \mathbf{D}) \approx (0.8\mathbf{M}, 0\mathbf{M})$. We sort each table using the standard, but debatable, approximations $(\mathbf{S}, \mathbf{D}) \approx (0.8\mathbf{M}, 0\mathbf{M})$. We do not claim that these approximations are valid for most applications. The order of entries in our tables can easily be affected by small changes in the $\mathbf{S}/\mathbf{M}$ ratio, the $\mathbf{D}/\mathbf{M}$ ratio, etc.

Algorithms in the Literature. We have built an "Explicit-Formulas Database" [8] containing, in computer-readable format, various algorithms for operations on elliptic curves. EFD currently consists of 123 scripts for the Magma computer-algebra system checking the correctness of algorithms for elliptic curves in the following forms:

- **Projective:** A point (x, y) on an elliptic curve $y^2 = x^3 + ax + b$, with neutral element at infinity, is represented as $(X : Y : Z)$ satisfying $Y^2 Z = X^3 + aXZ^2 + bZ^3$. Here $(X : Y : Z) = (\lambda X : \lambda Y : \lambda Z)$ for all nonzero λ.
- **Jacobian:** A point (x, y) on an elliptic curve $y^2 = x^3 + ax + b$, with neutral element at infinity, is represented as $(X : Y : Z)$ satisfying $Y^2 = X^3 + aXZ^4 + bZ^6$. Here $(X : Y : Z) = (\lambda^2 X : \lambda^3 Y : \lambda Z)$ for all nonzero λ.
- **Jacobi quartic** (with leading and trailing coefficients 1): A point (x, y) on an elliptic curve $y^2 = x^4 + 2ax^2 + 1$, with neutral element $(0, 1)$, is represented as $(X : Y : Z)$ satisfying $Y^2 = X^4 + 2aX^2Z^2 + Z^4$. Here $(X : Y : Z) = (\lambda X : \lambda^2 Y : \lambda Z)$ for all nonzero λ.
- **Jacobi intersection:** A point (s, c, d) on an elliptic curve $s^2 + c^2 = 1$, $as^2 + d^2 = 1$, with neutral element $(0, 1, 1)$, is represented as $(S : C : D : Z)$ satisfying $S^2 + C^2 = Z^2$, $aS^2 + D^2 = Z^2$. Here $(S : C : D : Z) = (\lambda S : \lambda C : \lambda D : \lambda Z)$ for all nonzero λ.
- **Hessian:** A point (x, y) on an elliptic curve $x^3 + y^3 + 1 = 3axy$, with neutral element at infinity, is represented as $(X : Y : Z)$ satisfying $X^3 + Y^3 + Z^3 = 3aXYZ$. Here $(X : Y : Z) = (\lambda X : \lambda Y : \lambda Z)$ for all nonzero λ.

- **Doubling-oriented Doche/Icart/Kohel:** A point (x, y) on an elliptic curve $y^2 = x^3 + ax^2 + 16ax$, with neutral element at infinity, is represented as $(X : Y : Z : Z^2)$ satisfying $Y^2 = ZX^3 + aZ^2X^2 + 16aZ^3X$. Here $(X : Y : Z : Z^2) = (\lambda X : \lambda^2 Y : \lambda Z : \lambda^2 Z^2)$ for all nonzero λ.
- **Tripling-oriented Doche/Icart/Kohel:** A point (x, y) on an elliptic curve $y^2 = x^3 + 3a(x + 1)^2$, with neutral element at infinity, is represented as $(X : Y : Z : Z^2)$ satisfying $Y^2 = X^3 + 3aZ^2(X + Z^2)^2$. Here $(X : Y : Z : Z^2) = (\lambda^2 X : \lambda^3 Y : \lambda Z : \lambda^2 Z^2)$ for all nonzero λ.
- **Edwards** (with $c = 1$): A point (x, y) on an elliptic curve $x^2 + y^2 = 1 + dx^2y^2$, with neutral element $(0, 1)$, is represented as $(X : Y : Z)$ satisfying $(X^2 + Y^2)Z^2 = Z^4 + dX^2Y^2$. Here $(X : Y : Z) = (\lambda X : \lambda Y : \lambda Z)$ for all nonzero λ.

We copied formulas from several sources in the literature; see [24] for an overview. One particularly noteworthy source is the 1986 paper [16] by Chudnovsky and Chudnovsky, containing formulas and operation counts for several forms of elliptic curves: projective, Jacobian, Jacobi quartic, Jacobi intersection, and Hessian. Liardet and Smart in [34] presented faster algorithms for Jacobi intersections. Billet and Joye in [9] presented faster algorithms for Jacobi quartics. Joye and Quisquater in [28] pointed out that the Hessian addition formulas (dating back to Sylvester) could also be used for doublings after a permutation of input coordinates, providing a weak form of unification: specifically, $2(X_1 : Y_1 : Z_1) = (Z_1 : X_1 : Y_1) + (Y_1 : Z_1 : X_1)$. Brier and Joye in [13] presented unified addition formulas for projective (and affine) coordinates; see also [12]. Of course, we also include our own algorithms for Edwards curves.

Chudnovsky and Chudnovsky also pointed out, in the case of Jacobian coordinates, that *readdition* of a point is less expensive than the first addition. The addition formulas for $(X_1 : Y_1 : Z_1) + (X_2 : Y_2 : Z_2)$ use $1\mathbf{M} + 1\mathbf{S}$ to compute Z_2^2 and Z_2^3; by caching Z_2^2 and Z_2^3 one can save $1\mathbf{M} + 1\mathbf{S}$ in computing any $(X' : Y' : Z') + (X_2 : Y_2 : Z_2)$. We comment that similar savings are possible for Jacobi intersections and Jacobi quartics.

(Rather than distinguishing readditions from initial additions, Chudnovsky and Chudnovsky reported speeds for addition and doubling of points represented as $(X : Y : Z : Z^2 : Z^3)$. But this representation is wasteful, as pointed out by Cohen, Miyaji, and Ono in [18]: if $(X_1 : Y_1 : Z_1)$ is used only for a doubling and not for a general addition then there is no need to compute Z_1^3. Sometimes coordinates $(X : Y : Z : Z^2 : Z^3)$ are called "Chudnovsky coordinates" or "Chudnovsky-Jacobian coordinates," and computing Z^2 and Z^3 only when they are needed is called "mixing Chudnovsky coordinates with Jacobian coordinates." We prefer to describe the same speedup using the simpler concept of readditions).

Our operation counts for previous systems are often better than the operation counts reported in the literature. One reason is that a multiplication can often be replaced with a squaring, saving $\mathbf{M} - \mathbf{S}$. For example, as pointed out in

[5, pages 16–17], Jacobian doubling with $a = -3$ uses $3M + 5S$ rather than the usual $4M + 4S$. As another example, Doche/Icart/Kohel doubling uses $2M + 5S + 2D$ rather than $3M + 4S + 2D$. The Explicit-Formulas Database contains full justification for each of our operation counts.

Comparison Charts. The following table reports speeds for addition of two points:

System	ADD	$(1,1)$	$(0.8, 0.5)$	$(0.8, 0)$
Doche/Icart/Kohel 2	$12M + 5S + 1D$	18M	16.5M	16M
Doche/Icart/Kohel 3	$11M + 6S + 1D$	18M	16.3M	15.8M
Jacobian	$11M + 5S$	16M	15M	15M
Jacobi intersection	$13M + 2S + 1D$	16M	15.1M	14.6M
Projective	$12M + 2S$	14M	13.6M	13.6M
Jacobi quartic	$10M + 3S + 1D$	14M	12.9M	12.4M
Hessian	$12M$	12M	12M	12M
Edwards	$10M + 1S + 1D$	12M	11.3M	10.8M

Readdition of a point already used in an addition:

System	reADD	$(1,1)$	$(0.8, 0.5)$	$(0.8, 0)$
Doche/Icart/Kohel 2	$12M + 5S + 1D$	18M	16.5M	16M
Doche/Icart/Kohel 3	$10M + 6S + 1D$	17M	15.3M	14.8M
Projective	$12M + 2S$	14M	13.6M	13.6M
Jacobian	$10M + 4S$	14M	13.2M	13.2M
Jacobi intersection	$11M + 2S + 1D$	14M	13.1M	12.6M
Hessian	$12M$	12M	12M	12M
Jacobi quartic	$9M + 3S + 1D$	13M	11.9M	11.4M
Edwards	$10M + 1S + 1D$	12M	11.3M	10.8M

Mixed addition (i.e., addition assuming that $Z_2 = 1$):

System	mADD	$(1,1)$	$(0.8, 0.5)$	$(0.8, 0)$
Jacobi intersection	$11M + 2S + 1D$	14M	13.1M	12.6M
Doche/Icart/Kohel 2	$8M + 4S + 1D$	13M	11.7M	11.2M
Projective	$9M + 2S$	11M	10.6M	10.6M
Jacobi quartic	$8M + 3S + 1D$	12M	10.9M	10.4M
Doche/Icart/Kohel 3	$7M + 4S + 1D$	12M	10.7M	10.2M
Jacobian	$7M + 4S$	11M	10.2M	10.2M
Hessian	$10M$	10M	10M	10M
Edwards	$9M + 1S + 1D$	11M	10.3M	9.8M

Doubling:

System	DBL	$(1,1)$	$(0.8, 0.5)$	$(0.8, 0)$
Projective	$5M + 6S + 1D$	12M	10.3M	9.8M
Projective if $a = -3$	$7M + 3S$	10M	9.4M	9.4M
Hessian	$7M + 1S$	8M	7.8M	7.8M
Doche/Icart/Kohel 3	$2M + 7S + 2D$	11M	8.6M	7.6M
Jacobian	$1M + 8S + 1D$	10M	7.9M	7.4M
Jacobian if $a = -3$	$3M + 5S$	8M	7M	7M
Jacobi quartic	$2M + 6S + 2D$	10M	7.8M	6.8M
Jacobi intersection	$3M + 4S$	7M	6.2M	6.2M
Edwards	$3M + 4S$	7M	6.2M	6.2M
Doche/Icart/Kohel 2	$2M + 5S + 2D$	9M	7M	6M

Unified addition:

System	UNI	$(1,1)$	$(0.8, 0.5)$	$(0.8, 0)$
Projective	$11M + 6S + 1D$	18M	16.3M	15.8M
Projective if $a = -1$	$13M + 3S$	16M	15.4M	15.4M
Jacobi intersection	$13M + 2S + 1D$	16M	15.1M	14.6M
Jacobi quartic	$10M + 3S + 1D$	14M	12.9M	12.4M
Hessian	$12M$	12M	12M	12M
Edwards	$10M + 1S + 1D$	12M	11.3M	10.8M

Most of the addition formulas in this last table are *strongly unified*: they work without change for doublings. The Hessian addition algorithm is an exception: it works for doublings only after a permutation of input coordinates. As mentioned earlier, the addition algorithm for Edwards curves with non-square d has the stronger feature of being *complete*: it works without change for *all* inputs.

6   Single-Scalar Variable-Point Multiplication

This section compares Edwards curves to previous curve forms for single-scalar variable-point multiplication: computing nP given an integer n and a curve point P. This is one of the critical computations in elliptic-curve cryptography; for example, if n is a secret key and P is another user's public key then nP is a Diffie-Hellman secret shared between the two users. The next section considers variations of the same problem: fixed points P (allowing precomputation of, e.g., $2^{128}P$), more scalars and points, etc.

See [2] and [22] for surveys of the classic algorithms for scalar multiplication. We focus on "signed sliding window" algorithms, specifically with "window width 1" (also known as "non-adjacent form" or "NAF") or "window width 4." We also discuss the "Montgomery ladder."

We make the standard assumption that the input point P has $Z = 1$. All additions of P can thus be computed as mixed additions. By scaling other points to have $Z = 1$ one can create more mixed additions at the expense of extra field inversions; for the sake of simplicity we ignore this option in our comparison.

The NAF algorithm, for an average b-bit scalar n, uses approximately b doublings and approximately $(1/3)b$ mixed additions. So we tally the cost of 1 doubling and 1/3 mixed additions:

System	1 DBL, 1/3 mADD	$(1,1)$	$(0.8, 0.5)$	$(0.8, 0)$
Projective	8M + 6.67S + 1D	15.7M	13.8M	13.3M
Projective if $a = -3$	10M + 3.67S	13.7M	12.9M	12.9M
Hessian	10.3M + 1S	11.3M	11.1M	11.1M
Doche/Icart/Kohel 3	4.33M + 8.33S + 2.33D	15M	12.2M	11M
Jacobian	3.33M + 9.33S + 1D	13.7M	11.3M	10.8M
Jacobian if $a = -3$	5.33M + 6.33S	11.7M	10.4M	10.4M
Jacobi intersection	6.67M + 4.67S + 0.333D	11.7M	10.6M	10.4M
Jacobi quartic	4.67M + 7S + 2.33D	14M	11.4M	10.3M
Doche/Icart/Kohel 2	4.67M + 6.33S + 2.33D	13.3M	10.9M	9.73M
Edwards	6M + 4.33S + 0.333D	10.7M	9.63M	9.47M

The "signed width-4 sliding windows" algorithm involves, on average, approximately $b - 4.5$ doublings, $7b/48 + 5.2$ readditions, $b/48 + 0.9$ mixed additions, and 0.9 non-mixed additions; e.g., approximately 251.5 doublings, 42.5 readditions, 6.3 mixed additions, and 0.9 non-mixed additions for $b = 256$. (Different variants of the algorithm have slightly different costs; we chose one variant and measured it for 10000 uniform random 256-bit integers n.) So we tally the cost of $251.5/256 \approx 0.98$ doublings, $42.5/256 \approx 0.17$ readditions, $6.3/256 \approx 0.025$ mixed additions, and $0.9/256 \approx 0.0035$ non-mixed additions:

System	0.98 DBL, 0.17 reADD, etc.	$(1,1)$	$(0.8, 0.5)$	$(0.8, 0)$
Projective	7.17M + 6.28S + 0.982D	14.4M	12.7M	12.2M
Projective if $a = -3$	9.13M + 3.34S	12.5M	11.8M	11.8M
Doche/Icart/Kohel 3	3.84M + 7.99S + 2.16D	14M	11.3M	10.2M
Hessian	9.16M + 0.982S	10.1M	9.94M	9.94M
Jacobian	2.85M + 8.64S + 0.982D	12.5M	10.3M	9.77M
Jacobian if $a = -3$	4.82M + 5.69S	10.5M	9.37M	9.37M
Doche/Icart/Kohel 2	4.2M + 5.86S + 2.16D	12.2M	9.96M	8.88M
Jacobi quartic	3.69M + 6.48S + 2.16D	12.3M	9.95M	8.87M
Jacobi intersection	5.09M + 4.32S + 0.194D	9.6M	8.64M	8.54M
Edwards	4.86M + 4.12S + 0.194D	9.18M	8.26M	8.16M

Another approach to high-speed single-scalar multiplication is Montgomery's algorithm in [38] for x-coordinate operations on curves in Montgomery form $y^2 = x^3 + ax^2 + x$. This algorithm does not support fast addition $P, Q \mapsto P + Q$, does not support arbitrary addition chains, and does not fit into our previous tables; but it does support fast "differential addition" $P - Q, P, Q \mapsto P + Q$, and therefore fast computation of "differential addition-subtraction chains."

In particular, the "Montgomery ladder" uses $5\mathbf{M} + 4\mathbf{S} + 1\mathbf{D}$ per bit of n to compute $P \mapsto nP$. For comparison, the NAF algorithm for Edwards curves with our formulas takes $6\mathbf{M} + 4.33\mathbf{S} + 0.333\mathbf{D}$ per bit of n, clearly slower than $5\mathbf{M} + 4\mathbf{S} + 1\mathbf{D}$ per bit. But signed width-4 sliding windows take only $4.86\mathbf{M} + 4.12\mathbf{S} + 0.194\mathbf{D}$ per bit for $b = 256$, saving $0.14\mathbf{M} - 0.12\mathbf{S} + 0.806\mathbf{D}$ per bit. Note that Edwards form is less sensitive to a large $\mathbf{D}$ than Montgomery form. Larger b's favor larger window widths, reducing the number of additions per bit and making Edwards curves even more attractive.

7   Multiple Scalars, Fixed Points, etc.

General multi-scalar multiplication means computing $\sum n_i P_i$ given integers n_i and curve points P_i. Specific tasks are obtained by specifying the number of points, by specifying which points are known in advance, by specifying which integers are known in advance, etc. See generally [2] and [22].

We focus on four specific algorithms: the popular "joint sparse form" ("JSF") algorithm for computing $n_1 P_1 + n_2 P_2$, given b-bit integers n_1, n_2 and curve points P_1, P_2; the accelerated ECDSA verification algorithm in [1, page 9]; batch verification of elliptic-curve signatures, using the "Small Exponents Test" from [4, §3.3] and the multi-scalar multiplication algorithm that de Rooij in [20, §4] credits to Bos and Coster; and computation of nP for a fixed point P, using a standard "comb" table containing 90 precomputed multiples of P, essentially $2^{\{0,1,2,3,4,5\}b/6}(\{0,1\}P + \{0,1\}2^{b/24}P + \{0,1\}2^{2b/24}P + \{0,1\}2^{3b/24}P)$, normalized to have $Z = 1$.

The JSF algorithm uses about b doublings, about $(1/4)b$ mixed additions (for average n_1, n_2), and about $(1/4)b$ readditions. So we tally the cost of 1 doubling, $1/4$ mixed additions, and $1/4$ readditions:

System	1 DBL, 1/4 mADD, 1/4 reADD	(1,1)	(0.8, 0.5)	(0.8, 0)
Projective	$10.2\mathbf{M} + 7\mathbf{S} + 1\mathbf{D}$	18.2M	16.4M	15.8M
Projective if $a = -3$	$12.2\mathbf{M} + 4\mathbf{S}$	16.2M	15.4M	15.4M
Doche/Icart/Kohel 3	$6.25\mathbf{M} + 9.5\mathbf{S} + 2.5\mathbf{D}$	18.2M	15.1M	13.8M
Hessian	$12.5\mathbf{M} + 1\mathbf{S}$	13.5M	13.3M	13.3M
Jacobian	$5.25\mathbf{M} + 10\mathbf{S} + 1\mathbf{D}$	16.2M	13.8M	13.2M
Jacobian if $a = -3$	$7.25\mathbf{M} + 7\mathbf{S}$	14.2M	12.8M	12.8M
Doche/Icart/Kohel 2	$7\mathbf{M} + 7.25\mathbf{S} + 2.5\mathbf{D}$	16.8M	14.1M	12.8M
Jacobi intersection	$8.5\mathbf{M} + 5\mathbf{S} + 0.5\mathbf{D}$	14M	12.8M	12.5M
Jacobi quartic	$6.25\mathbf{M} + 7.5\mathbf{S} + 2.5\mathbf{D}$	16.2M	13.5M	12.2M
Edwards	$7.75\mathbf{M} + 4.5\mathbf{S} + 0.5\mathbf{D}$	12.8M	11.6M	11.3M

The accelerated ECDSA verification algorithm uses about $(1/3)b$ doublings, about $(1/4)b$ mixed additions, and about $(1/4)b$ readditions. So we tally the cost of $1/3$ doublings, $1/4$ mixed additions, and $1/4$ readditions:

System	1/3 DBL, 1/4 mADD, 1/4 reADD	$(1,1)$	$(0.8, 0.5)$	$(0.8, 0)$
Projective	$6.92M + 3S + 0.333D$	10.2M	9.48M	9.32M
Projective if $a = -3$	$7.58M + 2S$	9.58M	9.18M	9.18M
Doche/Icart/Kohel 2	$5.67M + 3.92S + 1.17D$	10.7M	9.38M	8.8M
Doche/Icart/Kohel 3	$4.92M + 4.83S + 1.17D$	10.9M	9.37M	8.78M
Jacobi intersection	$6.5M + 2.33S + 0.5D$	9.33M	8.62M	8.37M
Jacobian	$4.58M + 4.67S + 0.333D$	9.58M	8.48M	8.32M
Jacobian if $a = -3$	$5.25M + 3.67S$	8.92M	8.18M	8.18M
Hessian	$7.83M + 0.333S$	8.17M	8.1M	8.1M
Jacobi quartic	$4.92M + 3.5S + 1.17D$	9.58M	8.3M	7.72M
Edwards	$5.75M + 1.83S + 0.5D$	8.08M	7.47M	7.22M

The batch-verification algorithm is not as well known as it should be, so we summarize it here for one variant of the ElGamal signature system. Fix a hash function H and a base point B on an elliptic curve over a 256-bit field. Define (R, s) as a signature of a message m under a public key K if R, K are curve points, s is a 256-bit integer, and $sB = H(R, m)R + K$. The batch-verification algorithm is given (e.g.) 100 alleged signatures (R_i, s_i) of 100 messages m_i under 100 keys K_i. The algorithm checks the equations $s_i B = H(R_i, m_i)R_i + K_i$ by choosing random 128-bit integers v_i and checking that the combination $(\sum_i v_i s_i)B - \sum_i v_i H(R_i m_i)R_i - \sum_i v_i K_i$ is zero. Computing this combination — a 201-scalar multiplication with 101 256-bit scalars and 100 128-bit scalars — takes about $0.8 \cdot 256$ mixed additions and about $24.4 \cdot 256$ readditions with the Bos-Coster algorithm. So we tally the cost of 0.8 mixed additions and 24.4 readditions:

System	0.8 mADD, 24.4 reADD	$(1,1)$	$(0.8, 0.5)$	$(0.8, 0)$
Doche/Icart/Kohel 2	$299M + 125S + 25.2D$	450M	412M	399M
Doche/Icart/Kohel 3	$250M + 150S + 25.2D$	424M	382M	369M
Projective	$300M + 50.4S$	350M	340M	340M
Jacobian	$250M + 101S$	350M	330M	330M
Jacobi intersection	$277M + 50.4S + 25.2D$	353M	330M	318M
Hessian	$301M$	301M	301M	301M
Jacobi quartic	$226M + 75.6S + 25.2D$	327M	299M	286M
Edwards	$251M + 25.2S + 25.2D$	302M	284M	271M

The 90-point-comb algorithm computes a b-bit fixed-point single-scalar multiplication as a 24-scalar multiplication with about $b/24$ doublings and about $15b/64 = 5.625(b/24)$ mixed additions. So we tally the cost of 1/24 doublings and 15/64 mixed additions:

System	1/24 DBL, 15/64 mADD	$(1,1)$	$(0.8, 0.5)$	$(0.8, 0)$
Jacobi intersection	$2.7M + 0.635S + 0.234D$	3.57M	3.33M	3.21M
Projective	$2.32M + 0.719S + 0.0417D$	3.08M	2.91M	2.89M
Projective if $a = -3$	$2.4M + 0.594S$	2.99M	2.88M	2.88M
Doche/Icart/Kohel 2	$1.96M + 1.15S + 0.318D$	3.42M	3.03M	2.88M
Jacobi quartic	$1.96M + 0.953S + 0.318D$	3.23M	2.88M	2.72M
Doche/Icart/Kohel 3	$1.72M + 1.23S + 0.318D$	3.27M	2.87M	2.71M
Jacobian	$1.68M + 1.27S + 0.0417D$	2.99M	2.72M	2.7M
Jacobian if $a = -3$	$1.77M + 1.15S$	2.91M	2.68M	2.68M
Hessian	$2.64M + 0.0417S$	2.68M	2.67M	2.67M
Edwards	$2.23M + 0.401S + 0.234D$	2.87M	2.67M	2.56M

Montgomery's x-coordinate algorithm in [38] can also be used for multi-scalar multiplication, but does not seem to provide competitive performance as the number of scalars increases, despite recent differential-addition-chain improvements in [6] and [14].

8   Countermeasures Against Side-Channel Attacks

The scalar-multiplication algorithms discussed in §6 and §7 are often unacceptable for cryptographic hardware and embedded systems. Many secret bits of the integers n_i are leaked, through the pattern of doublings and mixed additions and non-mixed additions, to side-channel attacks such as simple power analysis. See generally [27], [33], and [36].

One response is to use a fixed pattern of doublings, mixed additions, etc., independent of the integers n_i. Another response is to hide the pattern of doublings, mixed additions, etc. Some of these responses still leak the Hamming weight in the single-scalar case, and the total number of operations in the general case, but this information can be shielded at low cost in other ways. Of course, at a lower level, field operations must be individually shielded. In particular, an operation counted as **M** must be carried out by a multiplication unit whose time, power consumption, etc. do not depend on the inputs. Even if the inputs happen to be the same, and even if a faster squaring unit is available, the multiplication must not be carried out by the squaring unit. An operation counted as **S** can be carried out by a faster squaring unit whose time, power consumption, etc. do not depend on the input.

We focus on four specific side-channel countermeasures: non-sliding windows with digits $\{1, 2, 3, 4, 5, 6, 7, 8\}$; signed width-4 sliding windows with unified addition-or-doubling formulas; width-4 sliding windows with atomic blocks; and the Montgomery ladder. For concreteness we consider two examples of primitives: first single-scalar multiplication and then triple-scalar multiplication. Extra scalars produce extra additions, reducing the importance of doublings, as in §7; in particular, extra scalars make unified formulas more attractive.

We also discuss differential attacks at the end of the section.

Single-Scalar Multiplication. Non-sliding windows with digits $\{1, 2, 3, \ldots, 8\}$ use, on average, approximately $b - 1.9$ doublings and $b/3 + 6$ readditions for single-scalar multiplication: e.g., 254.1 doublings and 91.4 readditions for $b = 256$. So we tally the cost of $254.1/256 \approx 0.99$ doublings and $91.4/256 \approx 0.36$ readditions:

System	0.99 DBL, 0.36 reADD	(1,1)	(0.8, 0.5)	(0.8, 0)
Projective	9.27M + 6.66S + 0.99D	16.9M	15.1M	14.6M
Projective if $a = -3$	11.2M + 3.69S	14.9M	14.2M	14.2M
Doche/Icart/Kohel 3	5.58M + 9.09S + 2.34D	17M	14M	12.9M
Jacobian	4.59M + 9.36S + 0.99D	14.9M	12.6M	12.1M
Hessian	11.2M + 0.99S	12.2M	12M	12M
Doche/Icart/Kohel 2	6.3M + 6.75S + 2.34D	15.4M	12.9M	11.7M
Jacobian if $a = -3$	6.57M + 6.39S	13M	11.7M	11.7M
Jacobi quartic	5.22M + 7.02S + 2.34D	14.6M	12M	10.8M
Jacobi intersection	6.93M + 4.68S + 0.36D	12M	10.9M	10.7M
Edwards	6.57M + 4.32S + 0.36D	11.2M	10.2M	10M

Signed width-4 sliding windows with unified addition-or-doubling formulas use, on average, $7b/6 + 2.5$ unified operations for single-scalar multiplication: e.g., 301.2 unified operations for $b = 256$. So we tally the cost of $301.2/256 \approx 1.18$ unified operations:

System	1.18 UNI	(1,1)	(0.8, 0.5)	(0.8, 0)
Projective	13M + 7.08S + 1.18D	21.2M	19.2M	18.6M
Projective if $a = -1$	15.3M + 3.54S	18.9M	18.2M	18.2M
Jacobi intersection	15.3M + 2.36S + 1.18D	18.9M	17.8M	17.2M
Jacobi quartic	11.8M + 3.54S + 1.18D	16.5M	15.2M	14.6M
Hessian	14.2M	14.2M	14.2M	14.2M
Edwards	11.8M + 1.18S + 1.18D	14.2M	13.3M	12.7M

Next we consider signed width-4 sliding windows with atomic blocks. In [15], Chevallier-Mames, Ciet, and Joye presented Jacobian-coordinate formulas using 10 atomic blocks for doubling and 16 atomic blocks for addition. Each block costs 1M and consists of one field multiplication, one field addition, one field negation, and another field addition; many of the additions and negations are dummy operations. Barbosa and Page in [3] presented automatic tools that turn arbitrary explicit formulas using mM + sS into formulas using $m + s$ atomic blocks, each consisting of one field multiplication and some number of field additions and negations, thus costing 1M. So we tally the cost of 0.98 doublings, 0.17 readditions, 0.025 mixed additions, and 0.0035 non-mixed additions, as in §6, except that we insist on S = M:

System	0.98 DBL, 0.17 reADD, etc., S = M	$(1,1)$	$(1,0)$
Projective	13.5M + 0.982D	14.4M	13.5M
Projective if $a = -3$	12.5M	12.5M	12.5M
Doche/Icart/Kohel 3	11.8M + 2.16D	14M	11.8M
Jacobian	11.5M + 0.982D	12.5M	11.5M
Jacobian if $a = -3$	10.5M	10.5M	10.5M
Jacobi quartic	10.2M + 2.16D	12.3M	10.2M
Hessian	10.1M	10.1M	10.1M
Doche/Icart/Kohel 2	10.1M + 2.16D	12.2M	10.1M
Jacobi intersection	9.41M + 0.194D	9.6M	9.41M
Edwards	8.99M + 0.194D	9.18M	8.99M

The Montgomery ladder for single-scalar multiplication naturally uses a fixed double-add pattern costing only 5M + 4S + 1D per bit. This combination of side-channel resistance and high speed has already attracted interest; see, e.g., [13, §4], [29], and [7].

We comment that, in some situations, the dummy operations in atomic blocks can be detected by fault attacks. Non-sliding windows (with nonzero digits), unified formulas, and the Montgomery ladder have the virtue of avoiding dummy operations.

Triple-Scalar Multiplication. Non-sliding windows with digits $\{1, 2, 3, \ldots, 8\}$ use approximately 0.99 doublings and 1.08 readditions per bit for triple-scalar multiplication:

System	0.99 DBL, 1.08 reADD	$(1,1)$	$(0.8, 0.5)$	$(0.8, 0)$
Projective	17.9M + 8.1S + 0.99D	27M	24.9M	24.4M
Projective if $a = -3$	19.9M + 5.13S	25M	24M	24M
Doche/Icart/Kohel 3	12.8M + 13.4S + 3.06D	29.2M	25M	23.5M
Doche/Icart/Kohel 2	14.9M + 10.3S + 3.06D	28.4M	24.8M	23.2M
Jacobian	11.8M + 12.2S + 0.99D	25M	22.1M	21.6M
Jacobian if $a = -3$	13.8M + 9.27S	23M	21.2M	21.2M
Hessian	19.9M + 0.99S	20.9M	20.7M	20.7M
Jacobi intersection	14.9M + 6.12S + 1.08D	22.1M	20.3M	19.7M
Jacobi quartic	11.7M + 9.18S + 3.06D	23.9M	20.6M	19M
Edwards	13.8M + 5.04S + 1.08D	19.9M	18.3M	17.8M

Signed width-4 sliding windows with unified addition-or-doubling formulas use approximately 1.54 unified operations per bit:

System	1.54 UNI	$(1,1)$	$(0.8, 0.5)$	$(0.8, 0)$
Projective	16.9M + 9.24S + 1.54D	27.7M	25.1M	24.3M
Projective if $a = -1$	20M + 4.62S	24.6M	23.7M	23.7M
Jacobi intersection	20M + 3.08S + 1.54D	24.6M	23.3M	22.5M
Jacobi quartic	15.4M + 4.62S + 1.54D	21.6M	19.9M	19.1M
Hessian	18.5M	18.5M	18.5M	18.5M
Edwards	15.4M + 1.54S + 1.54D	18.5M	17.4M	16.6M

Signed width-4 sliding windows with atomic blocks use approximately 0.98 doublings and 0.56 readditions per bit:

System	0.98 DBL, 0.56 reADD, $\mathbf{S} = \mathbf{M}$	$(1,1)$	$(1,0)$
Projective	18.6M + 0.98D	19.6M	18.6M
Doche/Icart/Kohel 3	17.8M + 2.52D	20.3M	17.8M
Projective if $a = -3$	17.6M	17.6M	17.6M
Jacobian	16.7M + 0.98D	17.6M	16.7M
Doche/Icart/Kohel 2	16.4M + 2.52D	18.9M	16.4M
Jacobian if $a = -3$	15.7M	15.7M	15.7M
Jacobi quartic	14.6M + 2.52D	17.1M	14.6M
Hessian	14.6M	14.6M	14.6M
Jacobi intersection	14.1M + 0.56D	14.7M	14.1M
Edwards	13M + 0.56D	13.6M	13M

The Montgomery ladder can be generalized to a multi-scalar multiplication method using a fixed pattern of doublings and additions, as discussed in [6] and [14], but the performance of the generalization degrades rapidly as the number of scalars increases, as mentioned in §7.

Countermeasures Against Differential and Correlation Side-Channel Attacks. Curves in Edwards form are compatible with countermeasures against differential and correlation side-channel attacks:

- Randomized representations of scalars as addition-subtraction chains; see, e.g., [42] and [34, §4]. Our point representation supports arbitrary additions and subtractions.
- Randomized scalars; see, e.g., [19, §5.1].
- Randomized coordinates; see, e.g., [19, §5.3]. Our point representation is redundant and can be scaled freely: $(X_1 : Y_1 : Z_1) = (\lambda X_1 : \lambda Y_1 : \lambda Z_1)$ for any $\lambda \neq 0$.
- Randomized points, for example computing nP as $n(P + Q) - nQ$; see, e.g., [19, §5.2]. Our point representation supports arbitrary additions and subtractions.
- Randomized curves; see, e.g., [33, §29.2]. Using the generalized addition law involving c and d one can easily transfer the computation to an isomorphic curve with $\bar{c}$ and $\bar{d}$ satisfying $dc^4 = \bar{d}\bar{c}^4$. As another example, one can perform computations on a 3-isogenous curve.

We suggest using a combination of these countermeasures. In particular, point randomization or scalar randomization appears to be vital to counteract Goubin-type attacks.

Curves in Edwards form are also compatible with countermeasures to other types of attacks discussed in [36].

References

1. Antipa, A., Brown, D.R.L., Gallant, R.P., Lambert, R.J., Struik, R., Vanstone, S.A.: Accelerated verification of ECDSA signatures, in [43], pp. 307–318 (2006). MR 2007d:94044, www.cacr.math.uwaterloo.ca/techreports/2005/tech_reports2005.html (Cited in §7)

2. Avanzi, R.M.: The complexity of certain multi-exponentiation techniques in cryptography. Journal of Cryptology 18, 357–373 (2005). MR 2007f:94027, www.eprint.iacr.org/2002/154 (Cited in §6, §7)

3. Barbosa, M., Page, D.: On the automatic construction of indistinguishable operations (2005), www.eprint.iacr.org/2005/174 (Cited in §8)

4. Bellare, M., Garay, J.A., Rabin, T.: Batch verification with applications to cryptography and checking, in [35], pp. 170–191 (1998). MR 99h:94043. (Cited in §7)

5. Bernstein, D.J.: A software implementation of NIST P-224 (2001), www.cr.yp.to/talks.html#2001.10.29 (Cited in §5)

6. Bernstein, D.J.: Differential addition chains (2006), www.cr.yp.to/papers.html#diffchain (Cited in §7, §8)

7. Bernstein, D.J.: Curve25519: new Diffie-Hellman speed records, in [45], pp. 207–228 (2006), www.cr.yp.to/papers.html#curve25519 (Cited in §1, §2,§4, §5, §8)

8. Bernstein, D.J., Lange, T.: Explicit-formulas database (2007), www.hyperelliptic.org/EFD (Cited in §2, §3, §3,§5)

9. Billet, O., Joye, M.: The Jacobi model of an elliptic curve and side-channel analysis, in [26], pp. 34–42 (2003). MR 2005c:94045, www.eprint.iacr.org/2002/125 (Cited in §1, §5)

10. Blake, I.F., Seroussi, G., Smart, N.P. (eds.): Advances in elliptic curve cryptography. London Mathematical Society Lecture Note Series, 317. Cambridge University Press, Cambridge (2005), MR 2007g:94001. See [27]

11. Bosma, W., Lenstra Jr., H.W.: Complete systems of two addition laws for elliptic curves. Journal of Number Theory 53, 229–240 (1995), MR 96f:11079. (Cited in §3, §3)

12. Brier, É., Déchène, I., Joye, M.: Unified point addition formulae for elliptic curve cryptosystems, in [40], pp. 247–256 (2004) (Cited in §5)

13. Brier, É., Joye, M.: Weierstrass elliptic curves and side-channel attacks, in [39], pp. 335–345 (2002), www.geocities.com/MarcJoye/publications.html (Cited in §5, §8)

14. Brown, D.R.L.: Multi-dimensional Montgomery ladders for elliptic curves (2006), www.eprint.iacr.org/2006/220 (Cited in §7, §8)

15. Chevallier-Mames, B., Ciet, M., Joye, M.: Low-cost solutions for preventing simple side-channel analysis: side-channel atomicity. IEEE Transactions on Computers 53, 760–768 (2004), www.bcm.crypto.free.fr/pdf/CCJ04.pdf (Cited in §8)

16. Chudnovsky, D.V., Chudnovsky, G.V.: Sequences of numbers generated by addition in formal groups and new primality and factorization tests. Advances in Applied Mathematics 7, 385–434 (1986), MR 88h:11094. (Cited in §5)

17. Cohen, H., Frey, G. (eds.): Handbook of elliptic and hyperelliptic curve cryptography. CRC Press, Boca Raton (2005), MR 2007f:14020. See [22], [24], [33]

18. Cohen, H., Miyaji, A., Ono, T.: Efficient elliptic curve exponentiation using mixed coordinates, in [41], pp. 51–65 (1998), MR 1726152, www.math.u-bordeaux.fr/~cohen/asiacrypt98.dvi (Cited in §1, §5)

19. Coron, J.-S.: Resistance against differential power analysis for elliptic curve cryptosystems, in [32], pp. 292–302 (1999) (Cited in §8, §8, §8)

20. de Rooij, P.: Efficient exponentiation using precomputation and vector addition chains, in [21], pp. 389–399 (1995), MR 1479665. (Cited in §7)

21. De Santis, A. (ed.): Advances in cryptology: EUROCRYPT 1994. LNCS, vol. 950. Springer, Heidelberg (1995), MR 98h:94001. See [20]

22. Doche, C.: Exponentiation, in [17], pp. 145–168 (2005) MR 2162725. (Cited in §6, §7)

23. Doche, C., Icart, T., Kohel, D.R.: Efficient scalar multiplication by isogeny decompositions, in [45], pp. 191–206 (2006) (Cited in §1)
24. Doche, C., Lange, T.: Arithmetic of elliptic curves, in [17], pp. 267–302 (2005), MR 2162729. (Cited in §5)
25. Edwards, H.M.: A normal form for elliptic curves. Bulletin of the American Mathematical Society 44, 393–422 (2007), www.ams.org/bull/2007-44-03/S0273-0979-07-01153-6/home.html (Cited in §1, §3)
26. Fossorier, M.P.C., Høholdt, T., Poli, A. (eds.): Applied Algebra, Algebraic Algorithms and Error-Correcting Codes. LNCS, vol. 2643. Springer, Heidelberg (2003). ISBN 3-540-40111-3. MR 2004j:94001. (Sec [9])
27. Joye, M.: Defences against side-channel analysis, in [10], pp. 87–100 (2005) (Cited in §8)
28. Joye, M., Quisquater, J.-J.: Hessian elliptic curves and side-channel attacks, in [31], pp. 402–410 (2001). MR 2003k:94032, www.geocities.com/MarcJoye/publications.html (Cited in §1, §5)
29. Joye, M., Yen, S.-M.: The Montgomery powering ladder, in [30], pp. 291–302 (2003), www.gemplus.com/smart/rd/publications/pdf/JY03mont.pdf (Cited in §8)
30. Kaliski Jr., B.S., Koç, Ç.K., Paar, C. (eds.): Cryptographic hardware and embedded systems-CHES 2002. LNCS, vol. 2523. Springer, Heidelberg (2003). ISBN 3-540-42521-7. See [29]
31. Koç, Ç.K., Naccache, D., Paar, C. (eds.): Cryptographic hardware and embedded systems-CHES 2001. LNCS, vol. 2162. Springer, Heidelberg (2001). ISBN 3-540-42521-7. MR 2003g:94002. See [28], [34], [42]
32. Koç, Ç.K., Paar, C. (eds.): Cryptographic hardware and embedded systems. In: first international workshop CHES 1999. LNCS, vol. 1717. Springer, Heidelberg (1999). ISBN 3-540-66646-X. See [19]
33. Lange, T.: Mathematical countermeasures against side-channel attacks, in [17], pp. 687–714 (2005), MR 2163785. (Cited in §8, §8)
34. Liardet, P.-Y., Smart, N.P.: Preventing SPA/DPA in ECC systems using the Jacobi form, in [31], pp. 391–401 (2001), MR 2003k:94033. (Cited in §1, §5, §8)
35. Lucchesi, C.L., Moura, A.V. (eds.): LATIN 1998: theoretical informatic. LNCS, vol. 1380. Springer, Heidelberg (1998). ISBN 3-540-64275-7. MR 99d:68007. See [4]
36. Mangard, S., Oswald, E., Popp, T.: Power analysis attacks: revealing the secrets of smart cards. Springer, Heidelberg (2007) (Cited in §8, §8)
37. Miller, V.S.: Use of elliptic curves in cryptography, in [44], pp. 417–426 (1986) MR 88b:68040. (Cited in §1)
38. Montgomery, P.L.: Speeding the Pollard and elliptic curve methods of factorization. Mathematics of Computation 48, 243–264 (1987) MR 88e:11130, www.links.jstor.org/sici?sici=0025-5718(198701)48:177<243:STPAEC>2.0.CO;2-3 (Cited in §1, §6, §7)
39. Naccache, D., Paillier, P. (eds.): Public key cryptography. In: PKC 2002. LNCS, vol. 2274. Springer, Heidelberg (2002). ISBN 3-540-43168-3. MR 2005b:94044. See [13]
40. Nedjah, N., de Macedo Mourelle, L. (eds.): Embedded Cryptographic Hardware: Methodologies & Architectures, Nova Science Publishers (2004) ISBN 1-59454-012-8. See [12]
41. Ohta, K., Pei, D. (eds.): Advances in cryptology-ASIACRYPT 1998. LNCS, vol. 1514. Springer, Berlin (1998). ISBN 3-540-65109-8. MR 2000h:94002. See [18]
42. Oswald, E., Aigner, M.: Randomized addition-subtraction chains as a countermeasure against power attack, in [31], pp. 39–50 (2001) MR 2003m:94068. (Cited in §8)

43. Preneel, B., Tavares, S.E. (eds.): Selected Areas in Cryptography. In: SAC 2005. LNCS, vol. 3897, Springer, Heidelberg (2006). ISBN3-540-33108-5. MR 2007b:94002. See [1]
44. Williams, H.C. (ed.): CRYPTO 1985. LNCS, vol. 218. Springer, Berlin (1986). ISBN 3-540-16463-4. MR 87d:94002. See [37]
45. Yung, M., Dodis, Y., Kiayias, A., Malkin, T. (eds.): 9th international conference on theory and practice in public-key cryptography. LNCS, vol. 3958. Springer, Heidelberg (2006). ISBN 978-3-540-33851-2. See [7], [23]

A Non-interactive Shuffle with Pairing Based Verifiability*

Jens Groth[1],[**] and Steve Lu[2],[***]

[1] University College London
j.groth@ucl.ac.uk
[2] University of California, Los Angeles
stevelu@math.ucla.edu

Abstract. A shuffle is a permutation and re-encryption of a set of ciphertexts. Shuffles are for instance used in mix-nets for anonymous broadcast and voting. One way to make a shuffle verifiable is to give a zero-knowledge proof of correctness. All currently known practical zero-knowledge proofs for correctness of a shuffle rely on interaction. We give the first efficient non-interactive zero-knowledge proof for correctness of a shuffle.

Keywords: Shuffle, mix-net, non-interactive zero-knowledge, bilinear group.

1 Introduction

A shuffle is a permutation and re-encryption of a set of ciphertexts. Shuffles are used for instance in mix-nets [Cha81], which in turn are used in protocols for anonymous broadcast and electronic voting. In a typical construction of a mix-net, the users encrypt messages that they want to publish anonymously. They send the encrypted messages to a set of mix-net servers that will anonymize the messages. The first server permutes and re-encrypts the incoming set of messages, i.e., it carries out a shuffle. The next server takes the output from the first server and shuffles these ciphertexts. The protocol continues like this until all servers have permuted and re-encrypted the ciphertexts. After the mixing is complete, the mix-servers may now perform a threshold decryption operation to get out the permuted set of messages. The idea is that if just one mix-server is honest, the messages will be randomly permuted and because of the re-encryption step nobody will know the permutation. The messages therefore appear in random order and cannot be traced back to the senders.

The mix-net protocol we just described is not secure if one of the mix-servers is dishonest. A dishonest mix-server could for instance discard some of the ciphertexts and inject new ciphertexts of its own choosing. It is therefore desirable to make the shuffle verifiable. An obvious way to make the mix-net verifiable is to ask each mix-server to

* Work initiated while participating in Securing Cyberspace: Applications and Foundations of Cryptography and Computer Security, Institute of Pure and Applied Mathematics, UCLA, 2006.
** Work done while at UCLA supported by NSF ITR/Cybertrust grant No. 0456717.
*** Supported by NSF Cybertrust grant No. 0430254.

K. Kurosawa (Ed.): ASIACRYPT 2007, LNCS 4833, pp. 51–67, 2007.

provide a zero-knowledge proof of its shuffle being correct. The zero-knowledge proof guarantees that the shuffle is correct, yet reveals nothing about the permutation or the re-encryption and therefore preserves the privacy of the mix-net.

Much research has already been done on making shuffles verifiable by providing interactive proofs of correctness [SK95, Abe99, AH01, Nef01, FS01, Gro03, NSNK06, NSNK05, Fur05, Wik05, GL07]. The proofs in these papers are all interactive and rely on the verifier choosing random challenges. Using the Fiat-Shamir heuristic, where the verifier's challenges are computed through the use of a cryptographic hash-function, it is possible to make these proofs non-interactive. As a heuristic argument for the security of these non-interactive proofs, one can prove them secure in the random oracle model [BR93], where the cryptographic hash-function is viewed as a random oracle that outputs a random string. However, Goldwasser and Kalai [GK03] demonstrate that the Fiat-Shamir heuristic sometimes yields insecure non-interactive proofs. Other works casting doubt on the Fiat-Shamir heuristic are [CGH98, Nie02, BBP04, CGH04].

It is still an open problem to construct efficient non-interactive zero-knowledge (NIZK) proofs or arguments for the correctness of a shuffle that do not rely on the random oracle model in the security proof. Such NIZK arguments can be used to reduce the round-complexity of protocols relying on verifiable shuffles. Moreover, interactive zero-knowledge proofs are usually deniable [Pas03]; a transcript of an interactive proof can only convince somebody who knows that the challenges were chosen correctly. NIZK arguments on the other hand are transferable. They consist of a single message that can be distributed and convince anybody that the shuffle is correct.

Obviously, one can apply general NIZK proof techniques to demonstrate the correctness of a shuffle. However, reducing the shuffle proof to a general NP statement and applying a general NIZK to it is very inefficient. Using NIZK techniques developed by Groth, Ostrovsky and Sahai [GOS06b, GOS06a, Gro06, GS07] one can get better performance. Some existing interactive zero-knowledge arguments for correctness of a shuffle naturally fit this framework. For example, it is possible to achieve non-interactive shuffle proofs of size $O(n \log n)$ group elements for a shuffle of n ciphertexts by using Abe and Hoshino's scheme [AH01]. This kind of efficiency still falls short of what can be achieved using interactive techniques and the interactive proofs or arguments that grow linearly in the size of the shuffle do not seem easy to make non-interactive using the techniques of Groth, Ostrovsky and Sahai.

OUR CONTRIBUTION. We offer the first (efficient) non-interactive zero-knowledge argument for correctness of a shuffle. The NIZK argument is in the common reference string model and has perfect zero-knowledge. The security proof of our scheme does not rely on the random oracle model. Instead we make use of recently developed techniques for making non-interactive witness-indistinguishable proofs for bilinear groups by Groth and Sahai [GS07], which draws on earlier work by Groth, Ostrovsky and Sahai [GOS06b, GOS06a, Gro06].

The NIZK argument we suggest is for the correctness of a shuffle of BBS ciphertexts. This cryptosystem, suggested by Boneh, Boyen and Shacham [BBS04], has ciphertexts that consist of 3 group elements for each group element that they encrypt. We consider statements consisting of n input ciphertexts and n output ciphertexts and the claim that the output ciphertexts are a shuffle of the input ciphertexts. Our NIZK arguments consist of $15n$ group elements, which is reasonable in comparison with the statement size, which is $6n$ group elements.

2   Preliminaries and Notation

In this paper, we work over prime order bilinear groups. In other words, we assume there is probabilistic polynomial time algorithm $\mathcal{G}$ that takes a security parameter k as input and outputs (p, G, G_T, e, g), where:

1. p is a prime
2. G and G_T are cyclic groups of order p
3. g is a random generator of G
4. $e : G \times G \to G_T$ is a map with the following properties
   - Bilinearity: $e(g^a, g^b) = e(g, g)^{ab}$ for all $a, b \in \mathbb{Z}_p$
   - Non-degeneracy: $e(g, g)$ generates G_T
5. Group operations and the bilinear map are efficiently computable and group membership is efficiently decidable.

We will for notational simplicity assume that group membership always is checked when appropriate without writing this explicitly.

2.1   BBS Encryption

The BBS cryptosystem was introduced by Boneh, Boyen and Shacham [BBS04]. We work in a bilinear group (p, G, G_T, e, g). The public key is of the form $(f = g^x, h = g^y)$. The secret key is $(x, y) \in (\mathbb{Z}_p^*)^2$. To encrypt $m \in G$, we choose random $s, t \in \mathbb{Z}_p$ and let the ciphertext be

$$(u, v, w) := (f^s, h^t, g^{s+t}m).$$

To decrypt a ciphertext $(u, v, w) \in G^3$, we compute

$$m = u^{-1/x} v^{-1/y} w.$$

The BBS cryptosystem is semantically secure under chosen plaintext attack if the Decisional Linear Problem is hard in the bilinear group. We refer to Section 3.1 for a formal definition of this assumption.

2.2   Shuffling BBS Ciphertexts

The BBS cryptosystem is homomorphic in the sense that entrywise multiplication of two ciphertexts yields an encryption of the product of the plaintexts. We have:

$$(f^s, h^t, g^{s+t}m) \cdot (f^S, h^T, g^{S+T}M) = (f^{s+S}, h^{t+T}, g^{s+S+t+T}mM).$$

It is easy to make a random shuffle of BBS ciphertexts. Given n input ciphertexts, we permute them randomly and then re-encrypt them by multiplying them with random encryptions of 1. Multiplication with encryptions of 1 preserves the plaintexts by the homomorphic property, but the plaintexts now appear in permuted order. If the Decisional Linear Assumption holds, the BBS cryptosystem is semantically secure and thus the permutation is hidden. For notational purposes, we will let $\{x_i\}$ denote $\{x_i\}_{i=1}^n$.

Definition 1. *A shuffle of* n *BBS ciphertexts* $\{(u_i, v_i, w_i)\}$ *is a list of output ciphertexts* $\{(U_i, V_i, W_i)\}$ *such that there exists some permutation* $\pi \in S_n$ *and randomizers* $\{(S_i, T_i)\}$ *so:*

$$(\forall i) \qquad U_i = u_{\pi(i)} f^{S_i} \quad \wedge \quad V_i = v_{\pi(i)} h^{T_i} \quad \wedge \quad W_i = w_{\pi(i)} g^{S_i + T_i}.$$

2.3 Non-interactive Zero-Knowledge Arguments

We will construct non-interactive zero-knowledge (NIZK) arguments for correctness of a shuffle of n BBS ciphertexts. Informally, such an argument will demonstrate that the shuffle is correct, but will not reveal anything else, in particular the permutation will remain secret. We will now define NIZK arguments with perfect completeness, perfect zero-knowledge and R_{co}-soundness. The notion of co-soundness in NIZK arguments for NP-languages was introduced in the full paper of [GOS06b, GOS06a]. Since it is quite new we will give some further intuition after the formal definitions.

An NIZK argument for R with R_{co}-soundness consists of six probabilistic polynomial time algorithms: a setup algorithm $\mathcal{G}$, a CRS generation algorithm K, a prover P, a verifier V and simulators (S_1, S_2). The setup algorithm $\mathcal{G}$ outputs some initial information gk. The CRS generation algorithm produces a common reference string σ corresponding to the setup. The prover takes as input (gk, σ, x, w) and produces a proof ψ. The verifier takes as input (gk, σ, x, ψ) and outputs 1 if the proof is acceptable and 0 if the proof is rejected. The simulator S_1 takes as input gk and outputs a simulated common reference string σ as well as a simulation trapdoor τ. S_2 takes as input gk, σ, τ, x and simulates a proof ψ.

Definition 2. *We call* $(\mathcal{G}, K, P, V, S_1, S_2)$ *an NIZK argument for* R *with* R_{co}-*soundness if for all non-uniform adversaries* $\mathcal{A}$ *we have completeness, soundness and zero-knowledge as described below.*

Perfect completeness:

$$\Pr \Big[gk \leftarrow \mathcal{G}(1^k)\,;\; \sigma \leftarrow K(gk)\,;\; (x, w) \leftarrow \mathcal{A}(gk, \sigma)\,;$$
$$\psi \leftarrow P(gk, \sigma, x, w)\,:\; (gk, x, w) \notin R \,\vee\, V(gk, \sigma, x, \psi) = 1 \Big] = 1.$$

Computational R_{co}-soundness:

$$\Pr \Big[gk \leftarrow \mathcal{G}(1^k)\,;\; \sigma \leftarrow K(gk)\,;\; (x, \psi, w_{co}) \leftarrow \mathcal{A}(gk, \sigma)\,:$$
$$V(gk, \sigma, x, \psi) = 1 \,\wedge\, (gk, x, w_{co}) \in R_{co} \Big] \approx 0.$$

Perfect zero-knowledge:

$$\Pr \Big[gk \leftarrow \mathcal{G}(1^k)\,;\; \sigma \leftarrow K(gk)\,;\; (\mathrm{St}, x, w) \leftarrow \mathcal{A}(gk, \sigma)\,;$$
$$\psi \leftarrow P(gk, \sigma, x, w)\,:\; (gk, x, w) \in R \,\wedge\, \mathcal{A}(\mathrm{St}, \psi) = 1 \Big]$$
$$= \Pr \Big[gk \leftarrow \mathcal{G}(1^k)\,;\; (\sigma, \tau) \leftarrow S_1(gk)\,;\; (\mathrm{St}, x, w) \leftarrow \mathcal{A}(gk, \sigma)\,;$$
$$\psi \leftarrow S_2(gk, \sigma, \tau, x)\,:\; (gk, x, w) \in R \,\wedge\, \mathcal{A}(\mathrm{St}, \psi) = 1 \Big].$$

We remark that if R ignores gk then R defines a language in NP. The definition given here generalizes the notion of NIZK arguments by allowing R to depend on a setup. The setup we have in mind in this paper, is to let gk be a description of a bilinear group. Given gk describing a bilinear group, the relation R defines a *group-dependent* language L. It is common in the cryptographic literature to assume an appropriate finite group or bilinear group has already been chosen and build protocols in this setting, so it is natural to consider NIZK arguments for setup-dependent languages as we do here.

Our definition also differs in the definition of soundness, where we let R_{co} be a relation that specifies what it means to break soundness. Informally, computational R_{co}-soundness can be interpreted as it being infeasible for the adversary to prove $x \in L$ if it knows $x \in L_{co}$. We remark that the standard definition of soundness is a special type of R_{co}-soundness. If R ignores gk and R_{co} ignores gk, w_{co} and contains all $x \notin L$, then the definition given above corresponds to saying that it is infeasible to construct a valid proof for $x \notin L$.

Let us explain further, why it is worthwhile to consider R_{co}-soundness in the context of non-interactive arguments with perfect zero-knowledge instead of just using the standard definition of soundness. The problem with the standard definition appears when the adversary produces a statement x and a valid NIZK argument without knowing whether $x \in L$ or $x \notin L$. In these cases it may not be possible to reduce the adversary's output to a breach of some underlying (polynomial) cryptographic hardness assumption. Abe and Fehr [AF07] give a more formal argument for this. They consider NIZK arguments with direct black-box reductions to a cryptographic hardness assumption and show that only languages in P/poly can have direct black-box NIZK arguments with perfect zero-knowledge. Since all known constructions of NIZK arguments rely on direct black-box reductions this indicates that the "natural" definition of soundness is not the right definition of soundness for perfect NIZK arguments. We note that for NIZK *proofs* there is no such problem since they are not perfect zero-knowledge except for trivial languages; and in the case of interactive arguments with perfect zero-knowledge this problem does not appear either because the security proofs rely on rewinding techniques which make it possible to extract a witness for the statement being proven.

The generalization to R_{co}-soundness makes it possible to get around the problem we described above. The adversary only breaks R_{co}-soundness when it knows a witness w_{co} for $x \in L_{co}$. By choosing R_{co} the right way, this witness can make it possible to reduce a successful R_{co}-soundness attack to a breach of a standard polynomial cryptographic complexity assumption.

At this point, one may wonder whether it is natural to consider a soundness definition where we require the adversary to supply some w_{co}. It turns out that many cryptographic schemes assume a setup where such a w_{co} is given automatically. One example is shuffling that we consider in this paper: when setting up a mix-net using a homomorphic threshold cryptosystem, the threshold decryption keys can be used to decrypt the ciphertexts and check whether indeed they do constitute a shuffle or not.

In our paper, the setup algorithm will be $\mathcal{G}$ that outputs a description of a bilinear group. The relation R will consist of statements that contain a public key for the BBS cryptosystem using the bilinear group and a shuffle of n ciphertexts. The witness will be the permutation used in the shuffle as well as the randomness used for re-randomizing the ciphertexts. In other words:

$$R = \Big\{ \Big((p, G, G_T, e, g) , (f, h, \{(u_i, v_i, w_i)\}, \{(U_i, V_i, W_i)\}) , (\pi, \{(S_i, T_i)\}) \Big) \Big|$$
$$\pi \in S_n \ \wedge \ \forall i : U_i = u_{\pi(i)} f^{S_i} \ \wedge \ V_i = v_{\pi(i)} h^{T_i} \ \wedge \ W_i = w_{\pi(i)} g^{S_i + T_i} \Big\}.$$

The relation R_{co} will consist of non-shuffles. The witness w_{co} will be the decryption key, which makes it easy to decrypt and check that there is no permutation matching the input plaintexts with the output plaintexts. As we remarked above, NIZK arguments for correctness of a shuffle are usually deployed in a context where such a decryption key can be found. It is for instance common in mix-nets that the mix-servers have a threshold secret sharing of the decryption key for the cryptosystem used in the shuffle. NIZK arguments with R_{co}-soundness for correctness of a shuffle therefore give us exactly the guarantee we need for the shuffle being correct.

$$R_{co} = \Big\{ \Big((p, G, G_T, e, g) , (f, h, \{(u_i, v_i, w_i)\}, \{(U_i, V_i, W_i)\}) , (x, y) \Big) \Big|$$
$$x, y \in \mathbb{Z}_p^* \ \wedge \ f = g^x \ \wedge \ h = g^y \ \wedge$$
$$\forall \pi \in S_n \exists i : W_i U_i^{-1/x} V_i^{-1/y} \neq w_{\pi(i)} u_{\pi(i)}^{-1/x} v_{\pi(i)}^{-1/y} \Big\}.$$

2.4 Non-interactive Witness-Indistinguishable Proofs for Bilinear Groups

We will employ the non-interactive proof techniques of Groth and Sahai [GS07]. They allow a prover to give short proofs for the existence of group elements which satisfy a list of so-called pairing product equations. With their techniques, one can prove that there exists $x_1, \ldots, x_n \in G$ and $\phi_1, \ldots, \phi_n \in \mathbb{Z}_p$ such that they simultaneously satisfy a set of pairing product equations, for instance $\prod_{i=1}^{n} e(a_i, x_i) = 1$ and $\prod_{i=1}^{n} x_i^{\phi_i} = 1$. One instantiation of their scheme works over bilinear groups where the Decisional Linear Assumption holds.

Their scheme has the following properties. It has a key generation algorithm that outputs a common reference string consisting of 8 group elements. These 8 group elements specify the public key for two commitment schemes: one for group elements in G and one for exponents in $\mathbb{Z}_p$. In their proof, the prover commits to the witness by committing to the group elements $x_1, \ldots, x_n \in G$ and the exponents $\phi_1, \ldots, \phi_n \in \mathbb{Z}_p$. After that the prover makes non-interactive proofs that the committed elements satisfy all the pairing product equations.

There are two ways of setting up the commitment schemes. One can choose the common reference string such that both commitment schemes are perfectly binding, in which case the proof has perfect completeness and perfect soundness. With a perfect binding key, the commitments to group elements are BBS ciphertexts, so we can decrypt the commitments to learn $x_1, \ldots, x_n$.

Another way to choose the common reference string is to have perfectly hiding commitment schemes. In this case, we can set up the commitment to the exponents

$\phi_1, \ldots, \phi_n$ as a perfect trapdoor commitment scheme. We can create a commitment and two different openings to respectively 0 and 1 for instance. When we have perfectly hiding keys in the common reference string, the non-interactive proof has perfect completeness and perfect witness-indistinguishability. In other words, an adversary that sees a proof for a statement for which two or more witnesses exist, gets no information whatsoever as to whether one witness or the other was used in the non-interactive proof.

We write $(\sigma_{\text{binding}}, \xi_{\text{extraction}}) \leftarrow K_{\text{binding}}(p, G, G_T, e, g)$, when creating a perfectly binding common reference string with extraction key $\xi_{\text{extraction}}$ for the commitments to group elements in G. We write $(\sigma_{\text{hiding}}, \tau_{\text{trapdoor}}) \leftarrow K_{\text{hiding}}(p, G, G_T, e, g)$ when creating a perfect hiding common reference string with trapdoor τ_{trapdoor} for the commitments to exponents in $\mathbb{Z}_p$. Perfect binding common reference strings and perfect hiding common reference strings are computationally indistinguishable if the Decisional Linear Assumption holds for the bilinear group we are working over.

3 Cryptographic Assumptions

The security of our NIZK argument for correctness of a shuffle will be based on three assumptions: the Decisional Linear Assumption, the Permutation Pairing Assumption and the Simultaneous Pairing Assumption. The BBS cryptosystem and the non-interactive proofs of Groth and Sahai rely on the Decisional Linear Assumption. The other two assumptions are needed for the NIZK argument for correctness of a shuffle. We will now formally define these assumptions and for the two new assumptions give heuristic reasons for believing them by showing that they hold in the generic group model.

3.1 Decisional Linear Assumption

We first recap the Decisional Linear Problem introduced by Boneh, Boyen and Shacham [BBS04]: Given $gk = (p, G, G_T, e, g)$ and $f, h, g, f^s, h^t, g^z \in G$, decide if $z = s + t$.

Definition 3. *The Decisional Linear Assumption holds for $\mathcal{G}$ if for all non-uniform polynomial time adversaries A we have:*

$$\Pr \left[gk := (p, G, G_T, e, g) \leftarrow \mathcal{G}(1^k) \; ; \; f, h \stackrel{R}{\leftarrow} G \; ; \right.$$
$$\left. s, t \stackrel{R}{\leftarrow} \mathbb{Z}_p \; : \; A(gk, f, h, f^s, h^t, g^{s+t}) = 1 \right]$$
$$\approx \Pr \left[gk := (p, G, G_T, e, g) \leftarrow \mathcal{G}(1^k) \; ; \; f, h \stackrel{R}{\leftarrow} G \; ; \right.$$
$$\left. s, t, z \stackrel{R}{\leftarrow} \mathbb{Z}_p \; : \; A(gk, f, h, f^s, h^t, g^z) = 1 \right].$$

3.2 Permutation Pairing Assumption

The Permutation Pairing Problem is: Given (p, G, G_T, e, g) and $g_1 := g^{x_1}, \ldots, g_n := g^{x_n}, \gamma_1 := g^{x_1^2}, \ldots, \gamma_n := g^{x_n^2}$ for random $x_1, \ldots, x_n \in \mathbb{Z}_p$ find elements $a_1, \ldots, a_n, b_1, \ldots, b_n \in G$ such that the following holds:

$$\prod_{i=1}^{n} a_i = \prod_{i=1}^{n} g_i$$

$$\prod_{i=1}^{n} b_i = \prod_{i=1}^{n} \gamma_i$$

$$e(a_i, a_i) = e(g, b_i) \text{ for } i = 1 \ldots n$$

$$\{a_i\} \quad \text{is not a permutation of } \{g_i\}$$

Note that if $\{a_i\}$ is a permutation of $\{g_i\}$, then by the third equation $\{b_i\}$ is $\{\gamma_i\}$ permuted in the same way.

Observe that permutations trivially satisfy the first three conditions and not the fourth, but one could imagine some particular choice of the $\{a_i\}$ and $\{b_i\}$ would satisfy all four conditions. The *Permutation Pairing Assumption* holds if finding such a clever choice is computationally infeasible.

Definition 4. *The Permutation Pairing Assumption holds if for all non-uniform polynomial time adversaries $\mathcal{A}$ we have:*

$$\Pr\left[gk := (p, G, G_T, e, g) \leftarrow \mathcal{G}(1^k) ; \ x_1, \ldots, x_n \overset{R}{\leftarrow} \mathbb{Z}_p ; \right.$$

$$\{g_i\} := \{g^{x_i}\} ; \ \{\gamma_i\} := \{g^{x_i^2}\} ; \ (\{a_i\}, \{b_i\}) \leftarrow \mathcal{A}(gk, \{g_i\}, \{\gamma_i\}) :$$

$$\prod_{i=1}^{n} a_i g_i^{-1} = 1 \ \wedge \ \prod_{i=1}^{n} b_i \gamma_i^{-1} = 1 \ \wedge \ (\forall i) \, e(a_i, a_i) = e(g, b_i) \ \wedge$$

$$\left. \{a_i\} \text{ is not a permutation of } \{g_i\} \right] \approx 0$$

3.3 Simultaneous Pairing Assumption

The Simultaneous Pairing Problem is: Given (p, G, G_T, e, g) and $g_1 := g^{x_1}, \ldots, g_n := g^{x_n}, \gamma_1 := g^{x_1^2}, \ldots, \gamma_n := g^{x_n^2}$ for random $x_1, \ldots, x_n \in \mathbb{Z}_p$ find a non-trivial set of elements $\mu_1, \ldots, \mu_n \in G$ such that the following holds:

$$\prod_{i=1}^{n} e(\mu_i, g_i) = 1 \qquad \wedge \qquad \prod_{i=1}^{n} e(\mu_i, \gamma_i) = 1.$$

The intuition behind this problem is that it may be hard to find a set of non-trivial elements to simultaneously satisfy two pairing products of "independent" sets of elements. The *Simultaneous Pairing Assumption* holds if this problem is hard.

Definition 5. *The Simultaneous Pairing Assumption holds if for all non-uniform polynomial time adversaries $\mathcal{A}$ we have:*

$$\Pr\left[gk := (p, G, G_T, e, g) \leftarrow \mathcal{G}(1^k) ; \ x_1, \ldots, x_n \overset{R}{\leftarrow} \mathbb{Z}_p ; \ \{g_i\} := \{g^{x_i}\} ; \right.$$

$$\{\gamma_i\} := \{g^{x_i^2}\} ; \ \{\mu_i\} \leftarrow \mathcal{A}(gk, \{g_i\}, \{\gamma_i\}) :$$

$$\left. \prod_{i=1}^{n} e(\mu_i, g_i) = 1 \ \wedge \ \prod_{i=1}^{n} e(\mu_i, \gamma_i) = 1 \ \wedge \ \exists i : \mu_i \neq 1 \right] \approx 0$$

3.4 Our Assumptions in the Generic Group Model

We will provide heuristic evidence for our new assumptions by showing that they hold in the generic group model [Sho97]. In this model the adversary is restricted to using only generic bilinear group operations and evaluating equality of group elements.

We accomplish this restriction of the adversary by using a model of the bilinear group where we encode the group elements (or equivalently we encode their discrete logarithms) as unique random strings and letting the adversary see only this representation of the group elements. We then provide the adversary with a bilinear group operation oracle such that it can still perform group operations.

Let us give a few more details. We start by picking a random bilinear group $(p, G, G_T, e, g) \leftarrow \mathcal{G}(1^k)$, which the adversary gets as input. We also pick random bijections $[\cdot] : \mathbb{Z}_p \rightarrow G$ and $[[\cdot]] : \mathbb{Z}_p \rightarrow G_T$. We give the adversary access to an oracle that operates as follows:

- On input $(\mathbf{exp}, a)$ return $[a]$.
- On input $(\mathbf{mult}, [a], [b])$ return $[a + b]$.
- On input $(\mathbf{mult}, [[a]], [[b]])$ return $[[a + b]]$.
- On input $(\mathbf{map}, [a], [b])$ return $[[ab]]$.

This oracle corresponds to the effect exponentiations, group operations and using the bilinear map have on the discrete logarithms of group elements. Please note that other operations such as inversion of a group element for instance can be easily computed using these group operations since the group order p is known to the adversary.

Theorem 1. *The Permutation Pairing Assumption holds in the generic group model.*

Proof. Let us first formulate the Permutation Pairing Assumption in the generic group model. We generate $(p, G, G_T, e, g) \leftarrow \mathcal{G}(1^k)$. We pick $[\cdot] : \mathbb{Z}_p \rightarrow G$ and $[[\cdot]] : \mathbb{Z}_p \rightarrow G_T$ as random bijective functions. We pick $x_1, \ldots, x_n \leftarrow \mathbb{Z}_p$. We now give the adversary $\mathcal{A}$ the following input: $(p, G, G_T, e, g, \{[x_i]\}, \{[x_i^2]\})$ and access to the bilinear group operation oracle. $\mathcal{A}$ is computationally unbounded but can only make a polymomial number of queries to the bilinear group operation oracle. The challenge for $\mathcal{A}$ is to find $\{([a_i], [b_i])\}$ so:

$$\sum_{i=1}^{n} a_i = \sum_{i=1}^{n} x_i \quad \wedge \quad \sum_{i=1}^{n} b_i = \sum_{i=1}^{n} x_i^2 \quad \wedge \quad \forall i : a_i^2 = b_i \quad \wedge \quad \forall \pi \exists i : a_i \neq x_{\pi(i)}.$$

In the generic group model we can without loss of generality assume the adversary computes $[a_i], [b_i]$ via repeated calls to the group operation oracle. This means we have

$$a_i = \sum_{j=1}^{n} x_j a_{ij} + \sum_{j=1}^{n} x_j^2 \alpha_{ij} + r_i, \qquad b_i = \sum_{j=1}^{n} x_j b_{ij} + \sum_{j=1}^{n} x_j^2 \beta_{ij} + s_i$$

for values $\{a_{ij}\}, \{\alpha_{ij}\}, \{r_i\}, \{b_{ij}\}, \{\beta_{ij}\}, \{s_i\}$ that can be deduced from the calls to the group operation oracle.

Consider now the first conditions on the adversary being successful:

$$\sum_{i=1}^{n} a_i - \sum_{i=1}^{n} x_i = 0 \quad \wedge \quad \sum_{i=1}^{n} b_i - \sum_{i=1}^{n} x_i^2 = 0 \quad \wedge \quad \forall i : a_i^2 = b_i.$$

These are polynomials over unknowns $x_1, \ldots, x_n$ that are randomly chosen. The adversary only has indirect access to them by using the bilinear group operation oracle. The adversary can choose two strategies for satisfying the equations. It can pick the values $a_{ij}, \alpha_{ij}, r_i, b_{ij}, \beta_{ij}, s_i$ so the polynomials are identical zero in $\mathbb{Z}_p[x_1, \ldots, x_n]$ or it can hope to be lucky that the polynomials evaluate to zero on the random choice of $x_1, \ldots, x_n \leftarrow \mathbb{Z}_p$. The Schwartz-Sippel theorem tells us that a guess according to the latter strategy has only negligible probability of being successful. Since the adversary can access the bilinear group operation oracle only a polynomial number of times, it can only verify a polynomial number of guesses, so the latter strategy has negligible success probability.

Let us now see what happens if the adversary follows the first strategy. The first equation gives us:

$$\sum_{i=1}^{n} \left(\sum_{j=1}^{n} x_j a_{ij} + \sum_{j=1}^{n} x_j^2 \alpha_{ij} + r_i \right) - \sum_{i=1}^{n} x_i = 0.$$

Viewed as a multivariate polynomial equation over vairables $x_1, \ldots, x_n$ we must have for all j, $\sum_{i=1}^{n} a_{ij} = 1$ and $\sum_{i=1}^{n} \alpha_{ij} = 0$ and $\sum_{i=1}^{n} r_i = 0$.

Next, if $\prod_{i=1}^{n} b_i = \sum_{i=1}^{n} x_i^2$ then it must be the case that

$$\sum_{i=1}^{n} \left(\sum_{j=1}^{n} x_j b_{ij} + \sum_{j=1}^{n} x_j^2 \beta_{ij} + s_i \right) - \sum_{i=1}^{n} x_i^2 = 0.$$

When viewed as a polynomial in $x_1, \ldots, x_n$, we see that we must have for all j, $\sum_{i=1}^{n} b_{ij} = 0$ and $\sum_{i=1}^{n} \beta_{ij} = 1$ and $\sum_{i=1}^{n} s_i = 0$.

Finally, if $(\forall i)\ a_i^2 = b_i$ then it must be the case that

$$\sum_{j=1}^{n}\sum_{k=1}^{n} x_j x_k a_{ij} a_{ik} + \sum_{j=1}^{n}\sum_{k=1}^{n} x_j^2 x_k^2 \alpha_{ij} \alpha_{ik} + r_i^2$$

$$+ 2\sum_{j=1}^{n}\sum_{k=1}^{n} x_j x_k^2 a_{ij}\alpha_{ik} + 2\sum_{j=1}^{n} x_j a_{ij} r_i + 2\sum_{j=1}^{n} x_j^2 \alpha_{ij} r_i$$

$$= \sum_{j=1}^{n} x_j b_{ij} + \sum_{j=1}^{n} x_j^2 \beta_{ij} + s_i$$

Once again by viewing this as a polynomial equation, for all i we must have that $a_{ij}\alpha_{ik} = 0$. Also $a_{ij}a_{ik} = 0$ when $j \neq k$, $r_i^2 = s_i$, $b_{ij} = 2a_{ij}r_i$, $\beta_{ij} = a_{ij}^2 + 2\alpha_{ij}r_i$.

We now consider what the matrix $A = (a_{ij})$ must be. Each row A has at most one non-zero entry by the fact that $a_{ij}a_{ik} = 0$ when $j \neq k$. Also, each column must sum to 1 by $\sum_{i=1}^{n} a_{ij} = 1$. These two facts combined implies A to have exactly one 1 in each column and each row, thus A is a permutation matrix. Since permutation matrices are invertible, from the equations $\sum_{i=1}^{n} a_{ij}\alpha_{ik} = \sum_{i=1}^{n} 0 = 0$, $\sum_{i=1}^{n} a_{ij}r_i = \frac{1}{2}\sum_{i=1}^{n} b_{ij} = 0$, we obtain that $\alpha_{ik} = 0$ and $r_i = 0$. Therefore, the $\{a_i\}$ are a permutation of the $\{x_i\}$.   □

Theorem 2. *The Simultaneous Pairing Assumption holds in the generic group model.*

Proof. Let us first formulate the Simulatenous Pairing Assumption in the generic group model. We generate $(p, G, G_T, e, g) \leftarrow \mathcal{G}(1^k)$. We pick $[\cdot] : \mathbb{Z}_p \rightarrow G$ and $[[\cdot]] : \mathbb{Z}_p \rightarrow G_T$ as random bijective functions. We pick $x_1, \ldots, x_n \leftarrow \mathbb{Z}_p$. We now give the adversary $\mathcal{A}$ the following input: $(p, G, G_T, e, g, \{[x_i]\}, \{[x_i^2]\})$ and access to the bilinear group operation oracle. $\mathcal{A}$ is computationally unbounded but can only make a polymomial number of queries to the bilinear group operation oracle. The challenge for $\mathcal{A}$ is to find non-trivial $\{[m u_i]\}$ so $\sum_{i=1}^{n} \mu_i x_i = 0$ and $\sum_{i=1}^{n} \mu_i x_i^2 = 0$. The Simultaneous Pairing Assumption in the generic model says that any adversary $\mathcal{A}$ has negligible probability of succeeding in this game.

Without loss of generality we can think of $\mathcal{A}$ as being restricted to computing $\{[\mu_i]\}$ using the bilinear group operation oracle only. This means it chooses

$$\mu_i = \sum_{j=1}^{n} x_j a_{ij} + \sum_{j=1}^{n} x_j^2 \alpha_{ij} + r_i$$

for known a_{ij}, α_{ij} and r_i.

A successful adversary chooses these values so both of these equations are satisfied:

$$\sum_{i=1}^{n} \left(\sum_{j=1}^{n} x_j a_{ij} + \sum_{j=1}^{n} x_j^2 \alpha_{ij} + r_i \right) x_i = 0$$

$$\sum_{i=1}^{n} \left(\sum_{j=1}^{n} x_j a_{ij} + \sum_{j=1}^{n} x_j^2 \alpha_{ij} + r_i \right) x_i^2 = 0$$

We can view them as multi-variate polynomials in $x_1, \ldots, x_n$ which are chosen at random. The adversary never sees $x_1, \ldots, x_n$, it only has indirect access to them through the group operation oracle. There are two strategies the adversary can use: It can select a_{ij}, α_{ij}, r_i so the two polynomials have zero-coefficients or it can hope to be lucky that the random choice of $x_1, \ldots, x_n$ actually evaluates zero. The Schwartz-Sippel theorem tells us that a guess has negligible chance of being correct when $x_1, \ldots, x_n$ are chosen at random from $\mathbb{Z}_p$. Since the adversary can access the bilinear group operations oracle only a polynomial number of times, it can only verify the correctness of a polynomial number of guesses. The latter strategy therefore has negligible success-probability.

Let us now consider the former strategy, where the adversary chooses the coefficients of the polynomials in $\mathbb{Z}_p[x_1, \ldots, x_n]$ so they are the zero-polynomials. Looking at the coefficients for the first polynomial we see that we must have $r_i = 0$ and $\alpha_{ij} = 0$. Looking at the coefficients of the second polynomial we see that $a_{ij} = 0$. The adversary can therefore only find the trivial solution $\mu_1 = \ldots = \mu_n = 0$.   □

4   NIZK Argument for Correctness of a Shuffle

We will now present an NIZK argument for correctness of a shuffle of BBS ciphertexts. The common reference string contains $2n$ elements $\{g_i := g^{x_i}\}$ and $\{\gamma_i := g^{x_i^2}\}$ for random $x_1, \ldots, x_n \in \mathbb{Z}_p$. The statement contains a public key (f, h) and a set of n input ciphertexts $\{(u_i, v_i, w_i)\}$ and a set of output ciphertexts $\{(U_i, V_i, W_i)\}$ that may be a shuffle of the input ciphertexts.

The first part of the NIZK argument consists of setting up pairing product equations that can only be satisfied if indeed we are dealing with a shuffle. The prover will use a set of variables $\{a_i\}$ and $\{b_i\}$ in these pairing product equations. She will set up a Permutation Pairing Problem over these variables to guarantee that $\{(a_i, b_i)\}$ are a permutation of $\{(g_i, \gamma_i)\}$.

Assume now that $\{(a_i, b_i)\}$ are a permutation of $\{(g_i, \gamma_i)\}$. Let $\{m_i\}$ be the plaintexts of $\{(u_i, v_i, w_i)\}$ and $\{M_i\}$ be the plaintexts of $\{(U_i, V_i, W_i)\}$. The prover also sets up equations such that $\prod_{i=1}^n e(a_i, M_i) = \prod_{i=1}^n e(g_i, m_i)$ and $\prod_{i=1}^n e(b_i, M_i) = \prod_{i=1}^n e(\gamma_i, m_i)$. Since $\{(a_i, b_i)\}$ are a permutation of $\{(g_i, \gamma_i)\}$, then there exists a permutation $\pi \in S_n$ so

$$\prod_{i=1}^n e(g_i, M_{\pi^{-1}(i)} m_i^{-1}) = 1 \quad \wedge \quad \prod_{i=1}^n e(\gamma_i, M_{\pi^{-1}(i)} m_i^{-1}) = 1.$$

This is a Simultaneous Pairing Problem, and assuming the hardness of this problem we will have $M_{\pi^{-1}(i)} = m_i$ for all i.

To give further intuition of the construction, consider a naïve protocol where the prover sends the permutation directly to the verifier. Denote $a_i := g_{\pi(i)}$ and $b_i := \gamma_{\pi(i)}$. With $U_i = u_{\pi(i)} f^{S_i}, V_i = v_{\pi(i)} h^{T_i}, W_i = w_{\pi(i)} g^{S_i + T_i}$ we have:

$$\prod_{i=1}^n e(a_i, u_{\pi(i)} f^{S_i}) = e(\prod_{i=1}^n a_i^{S_i}, f) \prod_{i=1}^n e(g_{\pi(i)}, u_{\pi(i)}) = e(c_u, f) \prod_{i=1}^n e(g_i, u_i)$$

$$\prod_{i=1}^n e(a_i, v_{\pi(i)} h^{T_i}) = e(\prod_{i=1}^n a_i^{S_i}, h) \prod_{i=1}^n e(g_{\pi(i)}, v_{\pi(i)}) = e(c_v, h) \prod_{i=1}^n e(g_i, v_i)$$

$$\prod_{i=1}^n e(a_i, w_{\pi(i)} g^{S_i + T_i}) = e(\prod_{i=1}^n a_i^{S_i}, g) \prod_{i=1}^n e(g_{\pi(i)}, w_{\pi(i)}) = e(c_w, g) \prod_{i=1}^n e(g_i, w_i),$$

where $c_u = \prod_{i=1}^n a_i^{S_i}, c_v = \prod_{i=1}^n a_i^{T_i}$ and $c_w = \prod_{i=1}^n a_i^{S_i + T_i}$. By construction, $c_w = c_u c_v$. In addition, we may look at the equations by pairing the $\{b_i\}$ with the U_i, V_i, and W_i. From this we obtain another three equations, and we define new elements $c_u' = \prod_{i=1}^n b_i^{S_i}, c_v' = \prod_{i=1}^n b_i^{T_i}, c_w' = c_u' c_v'$. In total we have six equations:

$$\prod_{i=1}^n e(a_i, U_i) = e(c_u, f) \prod_{i=1}^n e(g_i, u_i) \qquad \prod_{i=1}^n e(b_i, U_i) = e(c_u', f) \prod_{i=1}^n e(\gamma_i, u_i)$$
$$\prod_{i=1}^n e(a_i, V_i) = e(c_v, h) \prod_{i=1}^n e(g_i, v_i) \qquad \prod_{i=1}^n e(b_i, V_i) = e(c_v', h) \prod_{i=1}^n e(\gamma_i, v_i)$$
$$\prod_{i=1}^n e(a_i, W_i) = e(c_u c_v, g) \prod_{i=1}^n e(g_i, w_i) \quad \prod_{i=1}^n e(b_i, W_i) = e(c_u' c_v', g) \prod_{i=1}^n e(\gamma_i, w_i)$$

A naïve non-interactive argument would be to let the prover sends $\pi, c_u, c_v, c_u', c_v'$ to the verifier. The verifier can check the six above equations himself for the verification step.

The naive protocol described is complete by observation. We also have the following lemma:

Lemma 1. *The naïve protocol is R_{co}-sound.*

Proof. The idea behind R_{co}-soundness is to look at the underlying messages. If a dishonest prover were to convince a verifier with a non-shuffle as well as produce a witness (decryption key) $w_{co} = (x, y)$, we can "decrypt" the equations checked by the verifier. Namely, if we let $m_i = u_i^{-1/x} v_i^{-1/y} w_i$ and $M_i = U_i^{-1/x} V_i^{-1/y} W_i$, then by applying the same algebraic manipulations to the equations, we obtain:

$$\left[\prod_{i=1}^n e(a_i, U_i)\right]^{-1/x} \cdot \left[\prod_{i=1}^n e(a_i, V_i)\right]^{-1/y} \cdot \left[\prod_{i=1}^n e(a_i, W_i)\right]$$
$$= \left[e(c_u, f)\prod_{i=1}^n e(g_i, u_i)\right]^{-1/x} \cdot \left[e(c_v, h)\prod_{i=1}^n e(g_i, v_i)\right]^{-1/y} \cdot \left[e(c_u c_v, g)\prod_{i=1}^n e(g_i, w_i)\right].$$

This gives us $\prod_{i=1}^n e(a_i, M_i) = e(c_u^{-1}, g)e(c_v^{-1}, g)e(c_u c_v, g)\prod_{i=1}^n e(g_i, m_i) = \prod_{i=1}^n e(g_i, m_i)$.

In a similar way we can show that $\prod_{i=1}^n e(b_i, M_i) = \prod_{i=1}^n e(\gamma_i, m_i)$. Observe that the equations may be rearranged to be $\prod_{i=1}^n e(\mu_i, g_i) = 1$ and $\prod_{i=1}^n e(\mu_i, \gamma_i) = 1$ where $\mu_i = m_i/M_{\pi^{-1}(i)}$. By the Simultaneous Pairing Assumption, it it is infeasible for the prover to find non-trivial μ_i satisfying these two equations and thus we reach a contradiction. □

The downfall of the naïve protocol is that it completely reveals the permutation. In the actual NIZK argument, we will instead argue that there exist elements $\{a_i\}$ and $\{b_i\}$ that satisfy the equations above rather than revealing them directly. We accomplish this by making a GS proof for the set of pairing product equations given earlier. Our NIZK argument is described in Figure 1.

Theorem 3. *The protocol in Figure 1 is a non-interactive perfectly complete, computationally R_{co}-sound, perfect zero-knowledge argument of a correct shuffle of BBS ciphertexts under the Decisional Linear Assumption, Permutation Pairing Assumption, and Simultaneous Pairing Assumption.*

Proof. As we see in the protocol, the prover can generate the witness for the GS proof herself. Perfect completeness follows from the perfect completeness of the GS proofs.

We will now prove that we have perfect zero-knowledge. The simulator $S = (S_1, S_2)$ will generate a transcript as described in Figure 2. By construction, the common reference strings are generated in the same way. The only difference between a real proof and a simulated proof is the witness given to the GS proof. By the perfect witness-indistinguishability of the GS proof, real proofs and simulated proofs are perfectly indistinguishable.

It remains to prove that we have computational R_{co}-soundness. The adversary is trying to output a public key (f, h) and a non-shuffle of n input ciphertexts and n output ciphertexts, a convincing NIZK argument ψ of it being a shuffle, and a decryption key

---

Setup: Generate a bilinear group $gk := (p, G, G_T, e, g) \leftarrow \mathcal{G}(1^k)$.

Common reference string: Generate a perfectly hiding common reference string
$(\sigma_{\text{hiding}}, \tau_{\text{trapdoor}}) \leftarrow K_{\text{hiding}}(p, G, G_T, e, g)$ to get perfectly
witness-indistinguishable GS proofs. Pick random $x_1, \ldots, x_n \leftarrow \mathbb{Z}_p$ and compute
$\forall i: g_i := g^{x_i}, \gamma_i := g^{x_i^2}$.
The common reference string is $\sigma := (\sigma_{\text{hiding}}, \{g_i\}, \{\gamma_i\})$.

Shuffle statement: Public key (f, h) for the BBS cryptosystem. Input ciphertexts
$\{(u_i, v_i, w_i)\}$ and output ciphertexts $\{(U_i, V_i, W_i)\}$.

Prover's input: Permutation $\pi \in S_n$ and randomizers $\{(S_i, T_i)\}$ so
$U_i = u_{\pi(i)} f^{S_i}$, $V_i = v_{\pi(i)} h^{T_i}$ and $W_i = w_{\pi(i)} g^{S_i+T_i}$ for all i.

Proof: The prover sets up the following pairing product equations:

$$\phi = 1 \bmod p, \quad d_u^\phi = 1, \quad d_v^\phi = 1, \quad d_w^\phi = 1, \quad (d_u')^\phi = 1, \quad (d_v')^\phi = 1, \quad (d_w')^\phi = 1,$$

$$\prod_{i=1}^n a_i^\phi g_i^{-\phi} = 1, \qquad \prod_{i=1}^n b_i^\phi \gamma_i^{-\phi} = 1, \qquad (\forall i)\ e(a_i, a_i) = e(g, b_i)$$

$$e(d_u, g) \prod e(a_i, U_i) = e(c_u, f) \prod e(g_i, u_i) \qquad e(d_u', g) \prod e(b_i, U_i) = e(c_u', f) \prod e(\gamma_i, u_i)$$
$$e(d_v, g) \prod e(a_i, V_i) = e(c_v, h) \prod e(g_i, v_i) \qquad e(d_v', g) \prod e(b_i, V_i) = e(c_v', h) \prod e(\gamma_i, v_i)$$
$$e(d_w, g) \prod e(a_i, W_i) = e(c_u c_v, g) \prod e(g_i, w_i)$$
$$e(d_w', g) \prod e(b_i, W_i) = e(c_u' c_v', g) \prod e(\gamma_i, w_i)$$

A witness for satisfiability of the equations can be computed as:

$$\phi := 1, \qquad c_u := \prod_{i=1}^n a_i^{S_i}, \qquad c_v := \prod_{i=1}^n a_i^{T_i}, \qquad c_u' := \prod_{i=1}^n b_i^{S_i}, \qquad c_v' := \prod_{i=1}^n b_i^{T_i},$$

$$\forall i: \quad a_i := g_{\pi(i)}, \qquad b_i := \gamma_{\pi(i)},$$

and setting the remaining variables to 1. The prover generates a GS proof ψ that there
exists an exponent $\phi \in \mathbb{Z}_p$ and group elements
$\{a_i\}, \{b_i\}, c_u, c_v, c_u', c_v', d_u, d_v, d_w, d_u', d_v', d_w'$ that satisfy the equations.

Verification: The verifier accepts the non-interactive argument if and only if the GS proof
ψ is valid.

Fig. 1. NIZK Argument for Correct Shuffle of BBS Ciphertexts

(x, y). The relation R_{co} is a polynomial time decidable relation that tests that (x, y) is
the decryption key for (f, h) and that indeed we do have a non-shuffle.

We will change the way we construct the common reference string for the NIZK
argument. Instead of generating $\sigma = (\sigma_{\text{hiding}}, \{g_i\}, \{\gamma_i\})$ as in the scheme, we return
$\sigma := (\sigma_{\text{binding}}, \{g_i\}, \{\gamma_i\})$ where $(\sigma_{\text{binding}}, \xi_{\text{extraction}}) \leftarrow K_{\text{binding}}(p, G, G_T, e, g)$.
By the Decisional Linear Assumption, perfect binding and perfect hiding common reference strings for the GS proofs are computationally indistinguishable, so the adversary's success probability only changes negligibly.

The commitment with trivial randomness is now a perfectly binding commitment
to the exponent $\phi = 1$. The GS proof is a perfect proof of knowledge of variables
$c_u, c_v, c_u', c_v', d_u, d_v, d_w, d_u', d_v', d_w', \{a_i\}, \{b_i\}$ satisfying the equations, which can be
extracted using $\xi_{\text{extraction}}$. Since $\phi = 1$, the equations demonstrate that $d_u = d_v = $

$d_w = d'_u = d'_v = d'_w = 1$. The elements $\{a_i\}, \{b_i\}$ satisfy a Permutation Pairing problem and the hardness of this problem tells us that with overwhelming probability they are a permutation of $\{(g_i, \gamma_i)\}$. Lemma 1 now gives us that there is negligible probability of $c_u, c_v, c'_u, c'_v, \{a_i\}, \{b_i\}$ satisfying the equations and at the same time the input and output ciphertexts not being a shuffle. □

Simulated common reference string: The simulator S_1 runs the common reference string generation protocol. It sets $\tau := (\tau_{\text{trapdoor}}, x_1, \ldots, x_n)$ and outputs (σ, τ).

Shuffle statement: Public key (f, h) for the BBS cryptosystem. Input ciphertexts $\{(u_i, v_i, w_i)\}$ and output ciphertexts $\{(U_i, V_i, W_i)\}$.

Simulator's input: The simulator S_2 receives the shuffle statement and (σ, τ).

Simulated proof: Create a trapdoor commitment with double opening to $\phi = 0$ and $\phi = 1$.
Compute

$$d_u := \prod_{i=1}^{n} u_i^{x_i}, \qquad d_v := \prod_{i=1}^{n} v_i^{x_i}, \qquad d_w := \prod_{i=1}^{n} w_i^{x_i},$$

$$d'_u := \prod_{i=1}^{n} u_i^{x_i^2}, \qquad d'_v := \prod_{i=1}^{n} v_i^{x_i^2}, \qquad d'_w := \prod_{i=1}^{n} w_i^{x_i^2}.$$

Set the remaining variables to 1 and create a perfect witness indistinguishable GS proof ψ that there exists an exponent $\phi \in \mathbb{Z}_p$ and group elements $\{a_i\}, \{b_i\}, c_u, c_v, c'_u, c'_v, d_u, d_v, d_w, d'_u, d'_v, d'_w$ that satisfy the required equations.

Fig. 2. Simulated Argument for Correct Shuffle of BBS Ciphertexts

SIZE OF THE NIZK ARGUMENT. To commit to $\phi = 1$ we can use trivial randomness, so the commitment to ϕ does not have to be included in the proof – the verifier can compute it himself. There are $2n + 10$ variables in G and it takes 3 group elements for each commitment, so the commitments contribute a total of $6n + 30$ group elements towards the proof size.

The first 6 equalities cost 9 group elements each for a total of 54 group elements. The next two multi-exponentiation equations cost 9 group elements each for a total of 18 group elements. We then have n pairing product equations of the form $e(a_i, a_i) = e(g, b_i)$ which cost a total of $9n$ group elements. Finally, we have 6 pairing product equations, where one side of the pairings is publicly known and one side is committed. They each cost 3 group elements for a total of 18 group elements.

The total size of the proof is $15n + 120$ group elements. The size of the common reference string is $2n + 8$ group elements.[1]

We remark that the cost of shuffling multiple sets of ciphertexts with the same permutation may be amortized to a constant number of group elements. The first set of ciphertexts costs $15n + 120$ group elements. But we only need to commit to a_i, b_i and prove $e(a_i, a_i) = e(g, b_i)$ once. Regardless of n, the subsequent shuffles under the same permutation only cost 120 group elements each.

---

[1] One could wish for a common reference string that has only a constant number of group elements, but currently even all known 3-move zero-knowledge arguments have common reference strings of size $\Omega(n)$.

5   Remark on Shuffling BGN Ciphertexts

Another homomorphic cryptosystem over bilinear groups was introduced by Boneh, Goh and Nissim [BGN05]. This cryptosystem is based on the Subgroup Decision Assumption over composite order bilinear groups. The ciphertexts consist of one group element each, so with n input ciphertexts and n outputs ciphertexts, the shuffle statement contains $2n$ group elements and another group elements to describe the public key. The techniques we have presented in this paper can also be used to shuffle BGN ciphertexts. Assuming the Subgroup Decision Assumption holds and assuming suitable variants of the Permutation Pairing and the Simultaneous Pairing Assumptions hold, we can make an NIZK argument for correctness of a shuffle consisting of $3n + O(1)$ group elements. Since the Subgroup Decision Assumption only holds when factoring the group order is hard, the group elements in this scheme are quite large though.

While this scheme may have applications, we note that there is one subtle issue that one must be careful about. The GS proofs can be instantiated with bilinear groups of composite order where the Subgroup Decision Problem is hard, but they are only secure if the factorization of the composite group is unknown. The decryption key for the cryptosystem is the factorization of the group order. The R_{co}-soundness of the scheme therefore only holds as long as the adversary does not know the decryption key for the cryptosystem. The NIZK argument is therefore not R_{co}-sound as defined in this paper, albeit it will satisfy a suitably weakened R_{co}-soundness definition.

References

[Abe99]   Abe, M.: Mix-networks on permutation networks. In: Lam, K.-Y., Okamoto, E., Xing, C. (eds.) ASIACRYPT 1999. LNCS, vol. 1716, pp. 258–273. Springer, Heidelberg (1999)

[AF07]   Abe, M., Fehr, S.: Perfect nizk with adaptive soundness. In: Vadhan, S.P. (ed.) TCC 2007. LNCS, vol. 4392, pp. 118–136. Springer, Heidelberg (2007)

[AH01]   Abe, M., Hoshino, F.: Remarks on mix-network based on permutation networks. In: Kim, K.-c. (ed.) PKC 2001. LNCS, vol. 1992, pp. 317–324. Springer, Heidelberg (2001)

[BBP04]   Bellare, M., Boldyreva, A., Palacio, A.: An uninstantiable random-oracle-model scheme for a hybrid encryption problem. In: Cachin, C., Camenisch, J.L. (eds.) EUROCRYPT 2004. LNCS, vol. 3027, pp. 171–188. Springer, Heidelberg (2004), Full paper available at http://eprint.iacr.org/2003/077

[BBS04]   Boneh, D., Boyen, X., Shacham, H.: Short group signatures. In: Franklin, M. (ed.) CRYPTO 2004. LNCS, vol. 3152, pp. 41–55. Springer, Heidelberg (2004)

[BGN05]   Boneh, D., Goh, E.-J., Nissim, K.: Evaluating 2-DNF formulas on ciphertexts. In: Kilian, J. (ed.) TCC 2005. LNCS, vol. 3378, pp. 325–341. Springer, Heidelberg (2005)

[BR93]   Bellare, M., Rogaway, P.: Random oracles are practical: A paradigm for designing efficient protocols. In: ACM CCS 1993, pp. 62–73. ACM Press, New York (1993)

[CGH98]   Canetti, R., Goldreich, O., Halevi, S.: The random oracle methodology, revisited. In: Proceedings of STOC 1998, pp. 209–218 (1998)

[CGH04]   Canetti, R., Goldreich, O., Halevi, S.: On the random-oracle methodology as applied to length-restricted signature schemes. In: Naor, M. (ed.) TCC 2004. LNCS, vol. 2951, pp. 40–57. Springer, Heidelberg (2004)

[Cha81]   Chaum, D.: Untraceable electronic mail, return addresses, and digital pseudonyms. Communications of the ACM 24(2), 84–88 (1981)

[FS01]   Furukawa, J., Sako, K.: An efficient scheme for proving a shuffle. In: Kilian, J. (ed.) CRYPTO 2001. LNCS, vol. 2139, pp. 368–387. Springer, Heidelberg (2001)

[Fur05]   Furukawa, J.: Efficient and verifiable shuffling and shuffle-decryption. IEICE Trans. Fundam. Electron. Commun. Comput. Sci. 88-A(1), 172–188 (2005)

[GK03]   Goldwasser, S., Kalai, Y.T.: On the (in)security of the Fiat-Shamir paradigm. In: proceedings of FOCS 2003, pp. 102–113 (2003), Full paper available at http://eprint.iacr.org/2003/034

[GL07]   Groth, J., Lu, S.: Verifiable shuffle of large size ciphertexts. In: PKC 2007. Proceedings of Practice and Theory in Public Key Cryptography, vol. 4450, pp. 377–392. Springer, Heidelberg (2007)

[GOS06a]   Groth, J., Ostrovsky, R., Sahai, A.: Non-interactive zaps and new techniques for nizk. In: Dwork, C. (ed.) CRYPTO 2006. LNCS, vol. 4117, pp. 97–111. Springer, Heidelberg (2006)

[GOS06b]   Groth, J., Ostrovsky, R., Sahai, A.: Perfect non-interactive zero-knowledge for NP. In: Vaudenay, S. (ed.) EUROCRYPT 2006. LNCS, vol. 4004, pp. 339–358. Springer, Heidelberg (2006)

[Gro03]   Groth, J.: A verifiable secret shuffle of homomorphic encryptions. In: Desmedt, Y.G. (ed.) PKC 2003. LNCS, vol. 2567, pp. 145–160. Springer, Heidelberg (2002)

[Gro06]   Groth, J.: Simulation-sound nizk proofs for a practical language and constant size group signatures. In: Lai, X., Chen, K. (eds.) ASIACRYPT 2006. LNCS, vol. 4284, Springer, Heidelberg (2006),
            http://www.brics.dk/~jg/NIZKGroupSignFull.pdf

[GS07]   Groth, J., Sahai, A.: Efficient non-interactive proof systems for bilinear groups. Cryptology ePrint Archive, Report 2007/155 (2007), available at http://eprint.iacr.org/2007/155

[Nef01]   Neff, C.A.: A verifiable secret shuffle and its application to e-voting. In: Proceedings of ACM CCS 2001, pp. 116–125. ACM Press, New York (2001)

[Nie02]   Nielsen, J.B.: Separating random oracle proofs from complexity theoretic proofs: The non-committing encryption case. In: Yung, M. (ed.) CRYPTO 2002. LNCS, vol. 2442, pp. 111–126. Springer, Heidelberg (2002)

[NSNK05]   Nguyen, L., Safavi-Naini, R., Kurosawa, K.: A provably secure and effcient verifiable shuffle based on a variant of the paillier cryptosystem. Journal of Universal Computer Science 11(6), 986–1010 (2005)

[NSNK06]   Nguyen, L., Safavi-Naini, R., Kurosawa, K.: Verifiable shuffles: a formal model and a paillier-based three-round construction with provable security. International Journal of Informations Security 5(4), 241–255 (2006)

[Pas03]   Pass, R.: On deniability in the common reference string and random oracle model. In: Boneh, D. (ed.) CRYPTO 2003. LNCS, vol. 2729, pp. 316–337. Springer, Heidelberg (2003)

[Sho97]   Shoup, V.: Lower bounds for discrete logarithms and related problems. In: Fumy, W. (ed.) EUROCRYPT 1997. LNCS, vol. 1233, pp. 256–266. Springer, Heidelberg (1997)

[SK95]   Sako, K., Kilian, J.: Receipt-free mix-type voting scheme - a practical solution to the implementation of a voting booth. In: Guillou, L.C., Quisquater, J.-J. (eds.) EUROCRYPT 1995. LNCS, vol. 921, pp. 393–403. Springer, Heidelberg (1995)

[Wik05]   Wikström, D.: A sender verifiable mix-net and a new proof of a shuffle. In: Roy, B. (ed.) ASIACRYPT 2005. LNCS, vol. 3788, pp. 273–292. Springer, Heidelberg (2005)

On Privacy Models for RFID

Serge Vaudenay

EPFL, CH-1015 Lausanne, Switzerland
http://lasecwww.epfl.ch

Abstract. We provide a formal model for identification schemes. Under this model, we give strong definitions for security and privacy. Our model captures the notion of a powerful adversary who can monitor all communications, trace tags within a limited period of time, corrupt tags, and get side channel information on the reader output. Adversaries who do not have access to this side channel are called narrow adversaries. Depending on restrictions on corruption, adversaries are called strong, destructive, forward, or weak adversaries. We derive some separation results: strong privacy is impossible. Narrow-strong privacy implies key agreement. We also prove some constructions: narrow-strong and forward privacy based on a public-key cryptosystem, narrow-destructive privacy based on a random oracle, and weak privacy based on a pseudorandom function.

1 The Privacy Issue in RFID Schemes

RFID protocols are used to identify cheap tags through wireless channels. However, putting tags in wearable items leads to privacy concerns. Although several privacy models exist so far, all have their own limitations, and finally, the classes of protocols that achieve privacy for one model or the other are not always comparable. A widely accepted flexible model permitting to establish a common measure of the performance of identification protocol is still under construction. We aim at contributing to this effort. To do so, we propose formal definitions of RFID schemes and adversaries and consider a twofold characterization of a scheme in terms of *security* and *privacy*. The former assesses the soundness of tag authentication. The latter property is for the ability to resist to adversaries aiming at identifying, tracing, or linking tags.

In a nutshell, we formalize several types of privacy and study inherent limitations for RFID applications. We discuss which restrictions we can assume regarding tag corruption and availability of side channels. We show how to achieve those levels of privacy and what must be used in terms of conventional vs. public-key cryptography or stateless vs. rewritable tags. We show that the strongest possible level of privacy implies key agreement, thus mandating the use of some public-key cryptography techniques. We present a simple protocol for that.

We assume a *powerful adversary* who can control all communications and interfere with the system. Cheap tags are not tamper-resistant so we analyze the ability to assure privacy and security even when an adversary is allowed to *corrupt* tags and retrieve the internal state. One novelty of our models is that they provide some kind of "exposure slots". Namely, adversaries can trace a tag within a limited time period during which this tag remains at the vicinity of the adversary. During this period, they can refer to the tag by using a temporary identity. In practice, this temporary identity can be the 32-bit number that is used in ISO/IEC 14443-3 norm [22] in singulation protocols for collision avoidance [4]. It can also be some tag named from its radiation pattern signature [21]. Exposure time periods are indeed unavoidable.

We consider several types of restrictions regarding tag corruption. The weakest model does not allow corruption. The relevant model for the so-called *forward privacy* allows corruption, but only at the end of the attack so that no further active action happens after corruption.[1] One less restrictive (thus stronger) model tolerates corruption at any time, but assumes that opening a tag destroys it so that it no longer circulates in nature. This model is called *destructive*. Our strongest model allows corruption at any time and even to put the tag back to nature so that tracing it is still considered as a threat. Although the purpose for distinguishing those two latter models is not clear, we prove that they separate.

Another question, as studied in Juels-Weis [24], is whether the adversary has access to the protocol partial output or not. Namely, can we consider that the adversary knows whether a reader succeeded to identify a legitimate tag or not? We call *narrow* adversaries those who do not have access to this information while "wider" adversaries can get it from side channels (e.g. the question whether a door opens or not). It is well known that security or privacy can collapse in such a case (e.g. for the HB+ protocol [17,23,25] or the OSK protocol [24,30]). It happens to be quite orthogonal to the corruption variants so that we obtain an array of $4 \times 2 = 8$ adversarial models. We prove that those privacy models are pairwise different.

Related Work. Many simple challenge-response protocols have been proposed without addressing corruption [14,28,39]. The Ohkubo-Suzuki-Kinoshita protocol (OSK) [30,31] (see also [3,12,32]) made forward privacy possible. A few attempts have been made to really formalize privacy in RFID protocols. One of the first attempts was made by Avoine-Dysli-Oechslin [3], later extended in the Thesis of Avoine [2]. Following their model, privacy is formalized by the ability to distinguish two known tags. The model excludes the availability of side-channel information such as whether a protocol instance on the reader did succeed. Juels and Weis [24] extended this model using side-channel information and making the two target tags chosen by the adversary. Another model was proposed by Burmester, van Le, and de Medeiros [8,26]. In all these models, corrupted tags cannot be the target of privacy adversaries. Another approach by Damgård-Østergaard [10] studies RFID schemes "with symmetric cryptography only" to focus on the tradeoffs between complexity and security.

Our Contribution. In this paper we present a complete formalism for defining RFID schemes, their security, and build a hierarchy of privacy models. Our definition for security is equivalent to Damgård-Østergaard [10]. We prove that security against strong adversaries can be easily achieved using a pseudorandom

---

[1] Note that some authors call this notion *backward privacy* [27]. Their notion of *forward privacy* is included in our notion of strong privacy.

function family. We prove that strong privacy is impossible. We show that an RFID scheme that achieves narrow-strong privacy can efficiently be transformed into a key agreement protocol, meaning that this type of privacy essentially needs public-key cryptography techniques. On the other hand, we show that a public-key cryptosystem that resists to adaptively chosen ciphertext attacks can be used to define a simple narrow-strong private and forward private protocol. We further prove the narrow-destructive privacy of an OSK-like protocol [31] in the random oracle model and the weak privacy of a classical challenge-response protocol based on a pseudorandom function. This work follows up some joint work during the Thesis of Bocchetti [7].

2   Definitions

In the sequel, a function in terms of a security parameter s is said *polynomial* if there exists a constant n such that it is $\mathcal{O}(s^n)$. Similarly, a function is said *negligible* if there exists a constant $x > 0$ such that it is $\mathcal{O}(x^{-s})$. For the sake of readability we concentrate on asymptotic complexities and security although all our results can be written with more precise bounds.

The tag is a passive transponder identified by a unique ID. We typically focus on a cheap tag which is *passive*: it has no batteries, it can operate just when interrogated by a reader and only for a short time. It has *limited memory*: each tag has only a few Kbit of memory on board. It has *limited computational abilities*. Each tag can perform only basic cryptographic calculations: hash calculations [15], pseudorandom generation [35], symmetric encryption [14]. Some elliptic-curve arithmetic [5] and zero-knowledge identification [9,18,19] may fit, as well as public-key cryptography [1,16,38], but remain expensive so far. It is *not tamper proof*. It communicates at up to a limited *distance*: the communication Tag→Reader is limited to a few meters (if not centimeters).

The reader is a device composed by one or more transceivers and a backend processing subsystem. Security issues within the reader are not addressed in this work, moreover we focus on single backend readers. Note however that sometimes in literature "reader" denotes the transceiver alone. The purpose of the reader is to interact with tags so that it can tell legitimate tags (i.e. tags which are registered in the database) and unknown tags apart, and further identify (i.e. infer their ID) legitimate tags.

Definition 1 (RFID Scheme). *An RFID scheme is composed by*

- *a setup scheme* SetupReader(1^s) *which generates a private/public key pair* (K_S, K_P) *for the reader depending on a security parameter s. The key K_S is to be stored in the reader backend. The key K_P is publicly released. Throughout this paper we assume that s is implicitly specified in K_P so that there is no need to mention s any longer.*
- *a polynomial-time algorithm* SetupTag$_{K_P}$(ID) *which returns (K, S): the tag specific secret K and the initial state S of the tag. The pair (ID, K) is to be stored in the reader backend when the tag is legitimate.*

 - *a polynomial-time interactive protocol between a reader and a tag in which the reader ends with a tape* Output.

An RFID scheme is such that the output is correct except with a negligible probability for any polynomial-time experiment which can be described as follows.

1: set up the reader
2: create many tags including a subject one named ID
3: execute a complete protocol between reader and tag ID

The output is correct if and only if Output $=\perp$ *and tag* ID *is not legitimate, or* Output $=$ ID *and* ID *is legitimate.*

When Output $=\perp$ but tag ID is legitimate, we have a *false negative*. When Output $\neq\perp$ but tag ID is not legitimate, we have a *false positive*. When Output $\notin \{ID, \perp\}$ and tag ID is legitimate, we have an *incorrect identification*.

The RFID scheme is *stateless* if the tag state S is not allowed to change in time. Note that we do not a priori assume that tags know their ID nor their secret K: this is up to the protocol specification to make them extractable from S. We assume that a reader can run several concurrent instances of a protocol but that tags cannot. In this paper, we do not consider reader authentication so we do not consider any output on the side of the tag.[2]

In practice, some information about Output may leak from a side channel (e.g. by observing a door opening at a tag transit and deducing that authentication was successful). Having access to such an information could allow an adversary to gather information about tag identities. For simplicity, we focus here on passive tags which are exempt of side channel except by full corruption.

2.1 Adversaries

The characterization of the adversary is essentially done by specifying the actions that she is allowed to perform (i.e. the *oracles* she can query), the goal of her attack (i.e. the *game* she plays) and the way in which she can interact with the system (i.e. the *rules* of the game). We consider that, at every time, a tag can either be a *free tag* or a *drawn tag*. Drawn tags are the ones within "visual contact" to the adversary so that she can communicate while being able to link communications. Free tags are all the other tags. Two oracles are defined below to draw or free tags. We call *virtual tag* a unique reference (e.g. using a drawing sequence number or a nonce) to the action of drawing a tag. This plays the same role as a *temporary identity*. Note that two different virtual tags may refer to the same tag that has been drawn, freed, and drawn again.

Definition 2 (Adversary). *An adversary is an algorithm which takes a public key K_P as input and runs by using the eight following oracles.*

 - CREATETAG^b(ID): *creates a free tag, either legitimate ($b = 1$) or not ($b = 0$), with unique identifier* ID. *This oracle uses* SetupTag$_{K_P}$ *algorithm to set up the tag and (for $b = 1$ only) to update the system database. By convention, b is implicitly 1 when omitted.*

---

[2] This model was extended for mutual authentication in the Thesis of Paise [33].

- DRAWTAG(distr) → $(\text{vtag}_1, b_1, \ldots, \text{vtag}_n, b_n)$: *moves from the set of free tags to the set of drawn tags a tuple of tags at random following the probability distribution* distr *(which is specified by a polynomially bounded sampling algorithm). The oracle returns a vector of fresh identifiers* $(\text{vtag}_1, \ldots, \text{vtag}_n)$ *which allows to anonymously designate these tags. Drawing tags already drawn or not existing provoke the oracle to return* ⊥ *in place of the respective virtual tag. We further assume that this oracle returns bits* $(b_1, \ldots, b_n)$ *telling whether the drawn tags are legitimate or not.[3] This oracle keeps a hidden table* T *such that* $T(\text{vtag})$ *is the ID of* vtag.
- FREE(vtag): *moves the virtual tag* vtag *back to the set of the free tags. This makes* vtag *unreachable. (That is, using* vtag *in oracle calls is no longer allowed.)*
- LAUNCH → π: *makes the reader launch a new protocol instance* π.
- SENDREADER(m, π) → m' *(resp.* SENDTAG(m, vtag) → m'): *sends a message* m *to a protocol instance* π *for the reader (resp. to virtual tag* vtag) *and receives the answer* m' *(that is meant to be sent to the counterpart). By convention we write* EXECUTE(vtag) → $(\pi, \text{transcript})$ *to group one* LAUNCH *query and successive use of* SENDREADER *and* SENDTAG *to execute a complete protocol between the reader and the tag* vtag. *It returns the transcript of the protocol, i.e. the list of successive protocol messages.*
- RESULT(π) → x: *when* π *is complete, returns 1 if* Output $\neq \perp$ *and 0 otherwise.*
- CORRUPT(vtag) → S: *returns the current state* S *of the tag. If* vtag *is no longer used after this oracle call, we say that* vtag *is* destroyed.

The adversary plays a game which starts by setting up the RFID system and feeding the adversary with the public key. The adversary uses the oracle following some rules of the game and produces an output. Depending on the rules, the adversary wins or looses.

Definition 3 (Strong, destructive, forward, weak, and narrow adversary). *We consider polynomial-time adversaries. Let* STRONG *be the class of adversaries who have access to the above oracles. Let* DESTRUCTIVE *be the class of adversaries who never use* vtag *again after a* CORRUPT(vtag) *query (i.e. who destroy it). Let* FORWARD *be the class of adversaries in which* CORRUPT *queries can only be followed by other* CORRUPT *queries. Let* WEAK *be the class of adversaries who do no* CORRUPT *query. Let* NARROW *be the class of adversaries who do no* RESULT *query.*

Clearly, we have WEAK ⊆ FORWARD ⊆ DESTRUCTIVE ⊆ STRONG.

2.2 Security of RFID Schemes

Definition 4 (Security). *We consider any adversary in the class* STRONG. *We say the adversary wins if at least one protocol instance* π *on the reader identified an uncorrupted legitimate tag* ID *but* π *and* ID *did not have any matching*

---

[3] Namely, we assume that adversaries always have means to deduce whether a tag is legitimate or not by side channels.

conversation, i.e. they exchanged well interleaved and faithfully (but maybe with some time delay) transmitted messages until π completed. We call ID *a target tag and π a target instance. We say that the RFID scheme is secure if the success probability of any such adversary is negligible.*

All protocols that we study here are two-pass protocols in which the reader starts by sending a random challenge a and the tag produces a response c depending on a. This way, attacks leading to matching protocol transcripts but badly interleaved messages have negligible probability of success.

We use the following lemma to prove security of RFID schemes in our paper.

Lemma 5 (Simple security for special RFID scheme). *We consider an RFID scheme for which the reader protocol satisfies the following structure. First, the communication messages from the reader do not depend on the database. Second, there is a predicate R and a sampling algorithm S such that the output is computed by running S on the set $\mathcal{E}$ of all* ID *corresponding to a database entry* (ID, K) *verifying $R(\text{ID}, K; \tau)$, where τ is the protocol transcript. We assume that R and S do not use the database (but may use the secret key K_S). Third, the selected database entry may be updated by an extra algorithm not depending on other database entries or K_S. The algorithm S is such that*

- *if $\mathcal{E} = \emptyset$ then $S(\mathcal{E}) = \perp$*
- *if $\mathcal{E} \neq \emptyset$ then $S(\mathcal{E})$ outputs an element of $\mathcal{E}$.*

Finally, we assume that there exists an easily computable predicate R' such that if a tag ID *and the reader have a matching conversation with transcript τ and if* (ID, K) *is a database entry then $R(\text{ID}, K; \tau) \iff R'(n)$ where n is the number of previously completed protocol executions on the tag* ID *side since the last succeeded one. (A protocol execution with* ID *is called succeeded if it has a matching conversation with the reader with output* ID.*) We consider adversaries who*

- *create (and draw) a single tag* ID
- *use* LAUNCH, SENDREADER, SENDTAG
- *use an oracle who checks the predicate R on inputs different from* ID
- *use an oracle simulating S*
- *end on a final* SENDREADER *to an instance π.*

The adversary wins if the protocol instance π on the reader identified tag ID *but has no matching conversation. We say that the scheme is simply secure if the success probability of any such adversary is negligible. If the scheme is simply secure, then it is secure.*

Proof (Sketch). Let $\mathcal{A}$ be a strong adversary playing the security game. We can simulate DRAWTAG and FREE queries and reduce to adversaries who draw tags once for all upon creation. Next, we can reduce to an adversary who guesses the first target tag ID upon creation, as well as the first target instance π. (The success probability is divided by a polynomially bounded factor.) Then, we can simulate all tags except ID so that only tag ID is really created. We show by induction that Output can be generated with same distribution (except on π) when the adversary knows all database entries except (ID, K). To compute $R(\text{ID}, K; \tau)$ without knowing K, if τ is non-matching then R is not satisfied, otherwise R' can be used. We can thus simulate the reader and RESULT queries. One trick is not to send the last message to a reader instance if the simulated output is not ID and to send it otherwise so that the database entry can be updated. By using the simple security we deduce that $\mathcal{A}$ has negligible success probability. The scheme is thus secure.   □

2.3   Privacy of RFID Schemes

RFID schemes are given three cryptographic properties: correctness, security, and privacy. Depending on the application, not all properties may be required. Correctness is part of the definition of RFID schemes and is implicitly assumed. Security (i.e. soundness of tag identification) is defined in Section 2.2. We define privacy in terms of ability to infer non-trivial ID relations from protocol messages. This generalizes the notion of *anonymity* (for which the ID of tags cannot be inferred) and *untraceability* (for which the equality of two tags cannot be inferred).

Definition 6 (Privacy). *We consider adversaries who start with an attack phase allowing oracle queries then pursuing an analysis phase with no oracle query. In between phases, the adversary receives the hidden table T of the* DRAWTAG *oracle then outputs either* true *or* false. *The adversary wins if the output is* true. *We say that the RFID scheme is P-private if all such adversaries which belong to class P are trivial following Def. 7.*

Definition 7 (Blinder, trivial adversary). *A Blinder B for an adversary $\mathcal{A}$ is a polynomial-time algorithm which sees the same messages as $\mathcal{A}$ and simulates the* LAUNCH, SENDREADER, SENDTAG, *and* RESULT *oracles to $\mathcal{A}$. The blinder does not have access to the reader tapes so does not know the secret key nor the database. A blinded adversary $\mathcal{A}^B$ is itself an adversary who does not use the* LAUNCH, SENDREADER, SENDTAG, *and* RESULT *oracles. An adversary $\mathcal{A}$ is trivial if there exists a B such that $|\Pr[\mathcal{A} \text{ wins}] - \Pr[\mathcal{A}^B \text{ wins}]|$ is negligible.*

Informally, an adversary is trivial if it makes no effective use of protocol messages. Namely, these messages can be simulated without significantly affecting the success probability of the adversary. We stress that our privacy notion measures the privacy loss in the wireless link but not through tag corruption (since CORRUPT queries are not blinded). In other words, we assume that corrupting a tag always compromise privacy and we only focus on wireless leakage.

Clearly, we have the following links between privacy notions.

strong	$\Rightarrow$	destructive	$\Rightarrow$	forward	$\Rightarrow$	weak
$\Downarrow$		$\Downarrow$		$\Downarrow$		$\Downarrow$
narrow-strong	$\Rightarrow$	narrow-destructive	$\Rightarrow$	narrow-forward	$\Rightarrow$	narrow-weak

We will show separation between all those notions. We summarize below the non-implications with a reference to the appropriate notes.

		Note 10		Note 14	
strong	destructive	$\not\Leftarrow$	forward	$\not\Leftarrow$	weak
$\not\Uparrow$ Note 10	$\not\Uparrow$ Note 18		$\not\Uparrow$ Note 18		$\not\Uparrow$ Note 18

	Note 16		Note 17		Note 14	
narrow-strong	$\not\Leftarrow$	narrow-destructive	$\not\Leftarrow$	narrow-forward	$\not\Leftarrow$	narrow-weak

Some non-implication results may assume the existence of standard primitives such as IND-CCA public-key cryptosystems, random oracles, or pseudorandom functions. The non-implication of destructive privacy to strong privacy is equivalent to the feasibility of destructive privacy which is open so far.

In this model, corrupted tags can be the victims of tracing attacks, contrarily to the model of Juels-Weis [24] and Burmester-van Le-de Medeiros [8]. For instance, the protocol O-TRAP provides privacy in the sense of [8]. In this protocol, the reader sends a r_{sys}^t challenge to the tag and the tag answers with some random r_i and $h_{K_i}(r_{sys}^t, r_i)$ where h is a keyed hash function and K_i is a key which is permanently stored in the tag state. Clearly, corrupting the tag reveals K_i that was used in former protocols and enables to identified the tag in previous sessions. Hence, O-TRAP is not narrow-forward private.

We provide a useful lemma to get rid of RESULT queries.

Lemma 8. *We consider an RFID scheme with the property that whenever a legitimate tag and the reader have some matching conversation, the reader does not output $\bot$. If the scheme is secure, then narrow-forward (resp. narrow-weak) privacy implies forward (resp. weak) privacy.*

Proof (Sketch). Let $\mathcal{A}$ be a forward (resp. weak) adversary for privacy. W.l.o.g. we can assume that there is no RESULT query related to an instance that has a matching conversation with a legitimate tag (in such a case the answers is 1, due to the hypothesis). Since corruption (if any) are lately done, remaining RESULT queries are most likely to yield 0 due to security. Let B be a partial blinder for $\mathcal{A}$ who blinds all RESULT queries: for all such queries, the simulated answer 0 is returned. We further define an adversary $\mathcal{A}'$ playing the security game by simulating $\mathcal{A}$ and ending before the CORRUPT queries. Let E be the event that one of the RESULT queries in $\mathcal{A}$ would answer 1. When E does not occur, $\mathcal{A}$ and $\mathcal{A}^B$ produce the same result. Since the scheme is secure, E occurs with negligible probability. We obtain that $\mathcal{A}$ is as effective as the narrow-forward (resp. narrow-weak) adversary $\mathcal{A}^B$. By blinding $\mathcal{A}^B$ due to the privacy hypothesis, we obtain that $\mathcal{A}$ is as effective as $\mathcal{A}^C$ for some blinder C. $\square$

3 Separation Results

3.1 Strong Privacy Is Impossible

Theorem 9. *A destructive-private RFID scheme is not narrow-strong private.*

Namely, no RFID scheme can achieve privacy with respect to the class

$$\text{DESTRUCTIVE} \cup (\text{NARROW} \cap \text{STRONG}).$$

Note 10. As a consequence, strong privacy cannot be achieved. As another consequence, narrow-strong privacy (which is achieved by the scheme of Th. 19) does not imply strong privacy. Similarly, forward privacy (which is achieved by the same scheme) does not imply destructive privacy.

Proof. Let us consider the following destructive adversary $\mathcal{A}$ who simulates to the reader a tag with state S_b which is either forged (S_0) or the one of a corrupted legitimate tag (S_1). The adversary yields true if and only if the reader recognizes the right case (from RESULT).

1: $(\cdot, S_0) \leftarrow \mathsf{SetupTag}_{K_P}(\mathsf{ID}_0)$
2: CREATETAG(ID_1)
3: $(\mathsf{vtag}_1, \cdot) \leftarrow \mathrm{DRAWTAG}(\mathsf{ID}_1)$
4: $S_1 \leftarrow \mathrm{CORRUPT}(\mathsf{vtag}_1)$ (destroy it)
5: flip a coin $b \in \{0, 1\}$

6: $\pi \leftarrow$ LAUNCH
7: simulate tag of state S_b with π
8: $x \leftarrow \mathrm{RESULT}(\pi)$
9: output whether $x = b$

The complexity of this adversary is polynomial. Clearly, if the protocol execution is correct, the adversary succeeds. Thus, $1 - \Pr[\mathcal{A} \text{ wins}]$ is negligible. Hence, if we have destructive privacy, there must exist a blinder B such that $1 - \Pr[\mathcal{A}^B \text{ wins}]$ is negligible as well. If we now look at a privacy game from the blinder perspective, it works as follows:

- blinder receives a public key K_P
- blinder gets one tag state S_1 (by looking at the answer from CORRUPT)
- blinder impersonates a reader to a tag whose state is either S_1 or some unknown S_0 depending on some unknown bit b
- with high probability, blinder guesses b

Indeed, a blinder is a distinguisher who never uses the secret key of the reader between a tag with known state and a random one. This means that for a destructive-private scheme, it must be possible to identify tags whose states are known a priori. We can use this blinder to construct the following narrow-strong adversary. Basically, the adversary creates and corrupt two legitimate tags, feeds the previous distinguisher with one of the tag states, and makes one of the two tags interact with it. If the distinguisher distinguishes well, the output is true.

1: create tag ID_0 and tag ID_1
2: draw both tags
3: corrupt both tags and get their states S_0 and S_1
4: free both tags
5: draw a random tag: $(\mathsf{vtag}, \cdot) \leftarrow \mathrm{DRAWTAG}(\Pr[\mathsf{ID}_0] = \Pr[\mathsf{ID}_1] = \frac{1}{2})$
6: simulate B with input K_P, S_1, and interacting with vtag and get bit x
7: get $\mathcal{T}$ and output whether $\mathcal{T}(\mathsf{vtag}) = \mathsf{ID}_x$

This adversary $\mathcal{A}'$ has polynomial complexity and $1 - \Pr[\mathcal{A}' \text{ wins}]$ is negligible. Clearly, for any blinder B' we have $\Pr[\mathcal{A}'^{B'} \text{ wins}] = \frac{1}{2}$. Hence the scheme is not narrow-strong private. $\square$

3.2   Narrow-Strong Privacy Requires Key Agreement

A key agreement protocol [11] is an interactive protocol between two participants Alice and Bob with common public input set to the security parameter s which ends with a common output bit (the *key*), except with negligible probability. We assume that Alice initiates the protocol and that Bob responds. The protocol is secure (against passive adversary) if the probability that any polynomial-time algorithm that is fed with the common input and the protocol transcript has a negligible advantage over $\frac{1}{2}$ to guess the key bit.

We recall that a 2-round key agreement protocol can define a public-key cryptosystem. Rudich [36] proved a separation between key agreement in $k+1$ rounds and key agreement in k rounds, for any k. That is, a separation exists between key agreement in k rounds (for $k \neq 2$) and a public-key cryptosystem. Nevertheless, we do not know any efficient key agreement protocol based on conventional cryptography only. We use this fact to show that RFID schemes which achieve narrow-strong privacy need more than conventional cryptography techniques.

Theorem 11. *A narrow-strong private RFID scheme can be transformed (in polynomial time) into a secure key agreement protocol with same number of rounds in which Alice simulates* SETUPTAG *and the reader and Bob simulates the tag.*

This means that any RFID scheme based on a pseudorandom function or a digital signature scheme only is unlikely to be narrow-strong private. Indeed, the tag workload should be at least the same as a responder Bob in a key agreement protocol of same number of rounds. For two-round protocols, this is equivalent to a public-key encryption algorithm (the reader does the decryption).

Proof. We construct a protocol that securely sends a key bit b from Bob to Alice. Intuitively, Alice first creates two legitimate tags and sends their initial states to Bob. Then, Alice simulates the reader and Bob simulates either tag depending on the key bit. By identifying the tag, Alice gets b.

1: Alice: $(K_P, K_S) \leftarrow$ SetupReader(1^s)
2: Alice: $(K_0, S_0) \leftarrow$ SetupTag$_{K_P}(\mathsf{ID}_0)$, $(K_1, S_1) \leftarrow$ SetupTag$_{K_P}(\mathsf{ID}_1)$
3: Alice sends (K_P, S_0, S_1) to Bob and simulates the reader protocol with database $\{(\mathsf{ID}_0, K_0), (\mathsf{ID}_1, K_1)\}$
4: Bob simulates the tag protocol with state S_b and interact with Alice
5: Alice sets a such that $\mathsf{ID}_a =$ Output

If the instance of the protocol is correct, Alice obtains $a = b$. This proves the correctness of the key agreement. Note that the number of message rounds is the same as in the RFID protocol. An adversary is an algorithm $\mathcal{P}$ which takes (K_P, S_0, S_1) and the transcript τ of the RFID protocol and returns a bit $\mathcal{P}(K_P, S_0, S_1, \tau)$. We can now define an adversary $\mathcal{A}$ against the RFID scheme.

1: create tag ID_0 and tag ID_1, draw them, corrupt them, get their states S_0 and S_1, and free them
2: draw a random tag $(\mathsf{vtag}, \cdot) \leftarrow$ DRAWTAG$(\Pr[\mathsf{ID}_0] = \Pr[\mathsf{ID}_1] = \frac{1}{2})$

3: $(\cdot, \tau) \leftarrow$ EXECUTE(vtag)
4: set $a = \mathcal{P}(K_P, S_0, S_1, \tau)$
5: get $\mathcal{T}$ and output whether $\mathcal{T}(\text{vtag}) = \text{ID}_a$

Clearly, this is a narrow-strong adversary such that $\Pr[\mathcal{A} \text{ wins}] = \Pr[\mathcal{P} \text{ wins}]$. There must exist a blinder B such that $\Pr[\mathcal{A} \text{ wins}] - \Pr[\mathcal{A}^B \text{ wins}]$ is negligible. Clearly, $\mathcal{A}^B$ gets no information on whether ID_0 or ID_1 is drawn, so $\Pr[\mathcal{A}^B \text{ wins}] = \frac{1}{2}$. Hence, $\Pr[\mathcal{P} \text{ wins}] - \frac{1}{2}$ is negligible: the key agreement protocol is secure.   □

We can similarly prove the following result.

Theorem 12. *A narrow-forward private stateless RFID scheme can be transformed into a secure key agreement with same number of rounds.*

This is why protocols like OSK [30] require tags to update their states.

Proof. We proceed as before and use the following adversary $\mathcal{A}$.
1: create tag ID_0 and tag ID_1
2: draw one tag at random $(\text{vtag}, \cdot) \leftarrow$ GETTAG($\Pr[\text{ID}_0] = \Pr[\text{ID}_1] = \frac{1}{2}$)
3: $(\cdot, \tau) \leftarrow$ EXECUTE(vtag)
4: FREE(vtag)
5: draw tag ID_0 and tag ID_1, corrupt them, get their states S_0 and S_1
6: set $a = \mathcal{P}(K_P, S_0, S_1, \tau)$
7: get $\mathcal{T}$ and output whether $\mathcal{T}(\text{vtag}) = \text{ID}_a$
We observe that EXECUTE does not modify the state of vtag.   □

4   Case Studies

4.1   Weak Privacy Based on a Pseudorandom Function

We first construct a weak-private and secure protocol based on a pseudorandom function family (PRF). Let $(F_{s,K})_{K \in \{0,1\}^{k(s)}}$ be a family of functions from $\{0,1\}^{\delta(s)}$ to $\{0,1\}^{\gamma(s)}$. We say it is a PRF if k, δ, γ are polynomially bounded, if $2^{-\delta(s)}$, and $2^{-\gamma(s)}$ are negligible, if $F_{s,K}(x)$ is computable in polynomial time, and if any distinguisher with polynomial complexity has a negligible advantage for distinguishing an oracle simulating $F_{s,K}$ initialized with a random K from an oracle initialized with a truly random function. For more readability we omit the parameter s.

We construct an RFID scheme as depicted on Fig. 1 with $\alpha = \beta = \frac{\delta}{2}$. The algorithm SetupTag(ID) simply picks a random k-bit key K and sets $S = K$.

1. Reader picks a random α-bit string a and sends it to tag.
2. Tag with state S sends a random β-bit string b and $c = F_S(a, b)$ to reader.
3. Reader looks for (ID, K) in the database such that $c = F_K(a, b)$ and gets ID.

This protocol is essentially equivalent to the ISO/IEC 9798-2 3-pass mutual authentication protocol that is used in [14] and to the CR building block of [28],

Tag		**System**
state: S $(S = K)$		$\{\ldots, (\text{ID}, K), \ldots\}$
pick $b \in \{0,1\}^\beta$ $\xleftarrow{ a }$		pick $a \in \{0,1\}^\alpha$
$c = F_S(a,b)$ $\xrightarrow{ b,c }$		find (ID, K) s.t. $c = F_K(a,b)$
		output: ID or $\bot$ if not found

Fig. 1. A Weak-Private RFID Scheme based on PRF

both without their third pass (the reader authentication pass). The randomized Hash-Lock identification scheme [39] is this one with no a. But this opens the door to delay attacks where the reader protocol is launched after the tag protocol completed (so conversation are no longer matching). ISO/IEC 9798-2 2-pass unilateral authentication is this protocol with no b [14]. But this opens the door to privacy threats by replaying a.

Theorem 13. *If F is a PRF, the above RFID scheme is secure and weak private.*

Note 14. The scheme is clearly not narrow-forward private since afterward corruption makes it possible to link tags. So, as corollary of this theorem, weak privacy does not imply forward privacy and narrow-weak privacy does not imply narrow-forward privacy.

Proof. Correctness. No false negative is possible here. False positives and incorrect identifications are possible when given the selected tag key K and (a,b) values, there exists $K' \neq K$ in the database such that $F_K(a,b) = F_{K'}(a,b)$. Let us assume that we have n legitimate tags in addition to a subject tag. We construct a distinguisher that simulates the creation of the n tags and simulates a protocol between the subject tag and the reader. To compute F_K on a given input with the subject tag, $\mathcal{A}$ sends the input to an oracle which returns the output. If the subject tag is correctly identified in the simulation, $\mathcal{A}$ answers 1, otherwise it answers 0. This is a distinguisher for F, so it has a negligible advantage. When the oracle implements a random function, the probability of incorrect identification is bounded by $n2^{-\gamma}$ which is negligible. Hence, the probability of incorrect identification with the right oracle is also negligible.

Security. We first note that the protocol suits the special form in Lemma 5 where $R(\text{ID}, K; a, b, c) \iff F_K(a,b) = c$ and R' is always true. We can thus prove simple security and apply Lemma 5.

Let $\mathcal{A}$ be an adversary for simple security with a single tag ID. W.l.o.g. we assume that $\mathcal{A}$ does not call R since R can be simulated. Since database entries are never modified we can reduce to the case where only the target π is launched and others are simulated. $\mathcal{A}$ calls SENDREADER$(\pi) \to \hat{a}$ at time t and ends by SENDREADER$((\hat{b}, \hat{c}), \pi)$. $\mathcal{A}$ further calls SENDTAG$(a_i, \text{ID}) \to (b_i, c_i)$ at time t'_i. $\mathcal{A}$ wins if $\hat{c} = F_K(\hat{a}, \hat{b})$ and for every i such that $t < t'_i$ we have $(a_i, b_i, c_i) \neq (\hat{a}, \hat{b}, \hat{c})$ (namely: conversations are not matching). As for correctness, let $\mathcal{A}'$ be an algorithm who simulates $\mathcal{A}$ and all oracles then looks whether the attack succeeded.

To simulate $\text{SENDTAG}(a_i, \text{ID})$, $\mathcal{A}'$ simply picks a random b_i and queries an oracle F with (a_i, b_i) to get c_i and returns (b_i, c_i). To determine whether the attack succeeded, $\mathcal{A}'$ queries the oracle F again. Clearly, $\mathcal{A}$ and $\mathcal{A}'$ interacting with an oracle simulating F_K have the same success probability. $\mathcal{A}'$ can be considered as a distinguisher between F and a truly random function. Since F is pseudorandom, the distinguisher has negligible advantage, so $\mathcal{A}'$ interacting with an oracle simulating a random function has similar success probability as $\mathcal{A}$. If $t_i' < t$, $\Pr[\hat{a} = a_i]$ is negligible. If now $t < t_i'$, wining cases are for $(a_i, b_i, c_i) \neq (\hat{a}, \hat{b}, \hat{c})$, $c_i = F(a_i, b_i)$, $\hat{c} = F(\hat{a}, \hat{b})$, thus $(a_i, b_i) \neq (\hat{a}, \hat{b})$. However, if $(a_i, b_i) \neq (\hat{a}, \hat{b})$, the value for $F(\hat{a}, \hat{b})$ before the final query is free so $\Pr[\hat{c} = F(\hat{a}, \hat{b})] = 2^{-k}$, which is negligible. Therefore, $\mathcal{A}$ succeeds with negligible probability. This proves simple security. Lemma 5 concludes.

Weak Privacy. Thanks to Lemma 8, we only have to prove narrow-weak privacy. We want to prove that, for any narrow-weak adversary $\mathcal{A}$, there exists a blinder B such that $\mathcal{A}$ has no significant advantage over $\mathcal{A}^B$. Let B be the blinder who simulates $\text{SENDTAG}(a, \text{vtag})$ by answering with a random (b, c).

Clearly, all LAUNCH and SENDREADER queries can be perfectly simulated so we assume w.l.o.g. that these oracles are no longer used. We use the proof methodology of Shoup [37]. Let $\text{game}_0 = \text{game}_1(0)$ be the privacy game.

Let $\text{game}_1(i)$ be the same game as $\text{game}_1(i-1)$ in which the ith created tag is simulated using an ad-hoc random oracle F_i from $\{0,1\}^{\alpha+\beta}$ to $\{0,1\}^{\gamma}$ to compute $F_{K_i}(a, b) = F_i(a, b)$. Clearly, $|\Pr[\mathcal{A} \text{ wins } \text{game}_1(i)] - \Pr[\mathcal{A} \text{ wins } \text{game}_1(i-1)]|$ can be expressed as a distinguisher advantage for F so it is negligible. Let $\text{game}_1 = \text{game}_1(n)$ where n is the number of tags. Since n is polynomial, $|\Pr[\mathcal{A} \text{ wins } \text{game}_1] - \Pr[\mathcal{A} \text{ wins } \text{game}_0]|$ is negligible.

Let game_2 be the same game as game_1 in which the adversary wins when SENDTAG never picked a duplicate b. This duplication happens with probability bounded by $q^2 \cdot 2^{-\beta}$ where q is the number of SENDTAG queries. Clearly, this probability is negligible. Hence $|\Pr[\mathcal{A} \text{ wins } \text{game}_2] - \Pr[\mathcal{A} \text{ wins } \text{game}_0]|$ is negligible.

Using B, $|\Pr[\mathcal{A}^B \text{ wins } \text{game}_2] - \Pr[\mathcal{A}^B \text{ wins } \text{game}_0]|$ is negligible as well. Clearly, the B simulation is perfect when there is no duplicate b. This leads us to $|\Pr[\mathcal{A}^B \text{ wins } \text{game}_2] - \Pr[\mathcal{A} \text{ wins } \text{game}_2]|$ being negligible. Finally, we obtain that $|\Pr[\mathcal{A}^B \text{ wins } \text{game}_0] - \Pr[\mathcal{A} \text{ wins } \text{game}_0]|$ is negligible. Hence, $\mathcal{A}$ is a trivial adversary. □

4.2   Narrow-Destructive Privacy in the Random Oracle Model

We now consider a new scheme based on two oracles F and G running random functions from $\{0,1\}^{\alpha+k}$ and $\{0,1\}^k$ to $\{0,1\}^k$, respectively. The tag generation algorithm $\text{SetupTag}(\text{ID})$ picks a random k-bit key K and sets the initial state to $S = K$. The protocol works as depicted on Fig. 2.

1. Reader picks a random α-bit string a and sends it to tag.
2. Tag with state S sends $c = F(S, a)$ then refreshes its state S with $G(S)$.
3. Reader looks for (ID, K) in the database such that $c = F(G^i(K), a)$ with $i < t$, gets ID, and replaces (ID, K) by $(\text{ID}, G^i(K))$ in the database.

Note that after t iterations without the reader a tag can no longer be identified. Thus, this scheme does not satisfy the hypothesis of Lemma 8. (See also Note 18.) As opposed to the previous construction, F and G cannot be just PRFs since the adversary can get the code of F and G by corrupting a tag.

Tag		**System**
state: S	$(S = K)$	$\{\ldots,(\text{ID}, K),\ldots\}$
	$\xleftarrow{\qquad a \qquad}$	pick $a \in \{0,1\}^\alpha$
$c = F(S, a)$	$\xrightarrow{\qquad c \qquad}$	find (ID, K) and i s.t.
replace S by $G(S)$		$c = F(G^i(K), a)$ and $i < t$
		replace K by $G^i(K)$
		output: ID or $\perp$ if not found

Fig. 2. A Narrow-Destructive-Private RFID Scheme based on a Random Oracle

The OSK protocol [30,31] uses no a, so delay attacks can be made. Avoine et al. [3] proposed to add a random a and use $c = F(S \oplus a)$. Dimitriou [12] proposed to add a (useless) b and to send $F(S)$ and b in addition to $c = F(S, a, b)$.[4]

Theorem 15. *Assuming that k and t are polynomially bounded and that 2^{-k} is negligible, the above scheme is a secure and narrow-destructive private RFID scheme in the random oracle model.*

Note 16. This is not narrow-strong private since early corruption enables to link tags. So, narrow-destructive privacy does not imply narrow-strong privacy.

Note 17. We can artificially tweak the protocol of Th. 15 to get narrow-forward privacy but not narrow-destructive privacy, which separates the two models. To do so, we add in all tag states a common secret K_s such that when a tag receives $a = K_s$ it outputs $c = S$. Readers should not select $a = K_s$ but narrow-destructive adversaries could do so after a tag is sacrificed to leak K_s. Obviously, the scheme is no longer narrow-destructive private. Nevertheless, it is still narrow-forward private since corruption output cannot be used in interaction.

Note 18. As pointed out in Juels-Weis [24], a weak adversary against the scheme of Fig. 2 could run a sort of denial of service. The adversary proceeds as follows.

1: CREATETAG(ID_0), CREATETAG(ID_1)
2: $\text{vtag}_0 \leftarrow$ DRAWTAG(ID_0)
3: **for** $i = 1$ to $t + 1$ **do**
4:    pick a random x
5:    SENDTAG(x, vtag_0)
6: **end for**
7: FREE(vtag_0)

---

[4] Sending $F(S)$ is used to decrease the workload in optimistic cases.

8: $(\mathsf{vtag}, \cdot) \leftarrow \mathrm{DRAWTAG}(\Pr[\mathsf{ID}_0] = \Pr[\mathsf{ID}_1] = \frac{1}{2})$
9: $(\pi, \cdot) \leftarrow \mathrm{EXECUTE}(\mathsf{vtag})$
10: $x \leftarrow \mathrm{RESULT}(\pi)$
11: get $\mathcal{T}$ and output whether $\mathcal{T}(\mathsf{vtag}) = \mathsf{ID}_x$

Clearly, $\Pr[\mathcal{A} \text{ wins}] = 1$, but for any blinder B, we have $\Pr[\mathcal{A}^B \text{ wins}] = \frac{1}{2}$. So this weak adversary is not trivial. Hence, narrow-destructive privacy does not imply weak privacy.

Proof. Correctness. False negatives are not possible. False positives and wrong identifications are possible when given K, a, b, and i, there exist K' and $j < t$ such that $K' \neq K$ and $F(G^i(K), a, b) = F(G^j(K'), a, b)$. In the random oracle model, the probability of such event is at most $nt^2 2^{-k}$, which is negligible.

Security. We apply Lemma 5 where oracle $R(\mathsf{ID}, K; a, c)$ simply checks that there exists $i < t$ such that $F(G^i(K), a) = c$ and $R'(n) \Longleftrightarrow n < t$. By using standard random oracle techniques, we can assume that $\mathcal{A}$ never queries F with $G^i(K)$ for $i = 0, \ldots, t + n - 1$ and n is the number of SENDTAG queries.

We proceed as in the proof of Th. 13 with same notations. If $t'_i < t$, $\Pr[\hat{a} = a_i]$ is negligible. If $t < t'_i$, wining cases are for $(a_i, c_i) \neq (\hat{a}, \hat{c})$ and $\hat{c} = F(G^j(K), \hat{a})$ for some j smaller than t. Since $\mathcal{A}$ never queried F with any $G^j(K)$ and the tag did not query it with any $(G^j(K), \hat{a})$, the values of $F(G^j(K), \hat{a})$ are free so $\Pr[\hat{c} = F(G^j(K), \hat{a}); j < t] = t2^{-k}$, which is negligible.

Narrow-Destructive Privacy. Clearly, all LAUNCH and SENDREADER queries are trivial to simulate since no RESULT query is allowed. So, we assume w.l.o.g. that no such query is made. We want to prove that, for any adversary $\mathcal{A}$ there exists a blinder B such that $\mathcal{A}$ has no significant advantage over $\mathcal{A}^B$.

Let E (resp. E') be the event that at least one of the queries by $\mathcal{A}$ to the F or the G oracles equals one query made (resp. that should have been made if it was not blinded) by some SENDTAG(a, vtag) query.

SENDTAG queries are simulated by B by returning a random c. Note that there is no SENDTAG query to corrupted tags since adversaries are destructive. This simulation is perfect (in the sense that the adversary and the blinded adversary recover the same information about the virtual tag from the protocol transcript) when the event E does not occur. Namely, $\Pr[\mathcal{A} \text{ wins}|\neg E] = \Pr[\mathcal{A}^B \text{ wins}|\neg E']$ and $\Pr[E] = \Pr[E']$.

Hence, $|\Pr[\mathcal{A} \text{ wins}] - \Pr[\mathcal{A}^B \text{ wins}]| \leq \Pr[E]$. If q queries to F and G were made by $\mathcal{A}$, in the worst case $\mathcal{A}$ knows that all $G^i(K)$'s are in a set of $2^k - q$ values. Note that no CORRUPT query gives information on any $G^i(K)$ that can be used by any SENDTAG query. The probability to pick one is at most $\frac{tn}{2^k - q}$ where n is the number of tags. Hence, E occurs with probability at most $\frac{tnq}{2^k - q}$, which is negligible. $\qquad\square$

4.3   Narrow-Strong and Forward Privacy Based on a PKC

We now achieve narrow-strong and forward privacy using public-key cryptography. We use the standard definitions of public-key cryptosystems (PKC),

IND-CPA and IND-CCA security [6,13,20,29,34]. A PKC consists of a key generator, a probabilistic encryption algorithm, and a deterministic decryption algorithm. It must be correct in the sense that the decryption of the encryption of any x is always x. The scheme is IND-CPA-secure (resp. IND-CCA-secure) if all polynomial-time adversaries win the IND-CPA (resp. IND-CCA) with negligible advantage. In the IND-CPA game, the adversary receives a public key, submits two plaintexts, receives the encryption of one of the two, and tries to guess which plaintext was encrypted. In the IND-CCA game, the adversary can query a decryption oracle, except on the received ciphertext.

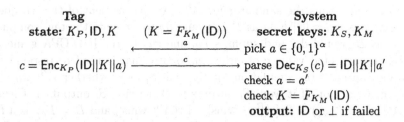

Fig. 3. A Narrow-Strong and Forward -Private RFID Scheme based on a PKC

We initialize the scheme by generating a private/public key pair (K_S, K_P) for the Enc/Dec PKC. The tag generation algorithm SetupTag(ID) picks a random k-bit key K and sets the initial state to $S = (K_P, \mathsf{ID}, K)$. We assume that k and α are polynomial. The protocol works as depicted on Fig. 3.

1. Reader sends an identification request with an α-bit random a.
2. Tag calculates $c = \mathsf{Enc}_{K_P}(\mathsf{ID}||K||a)$ and sends c to the reader.
3. Reader gets $\mathsf{ID}||K||a = \mathsf{Dec}_{K_S}(c)$ and checks that a is correct and that (ID, K) is in database.[5]

Theorem 19. *If the public-key cryptosystem is IND-CPA-secure then the above RFID scheme is narrow-strong private. If the cryptosystem is IND-CCA-secure and 2^{-k} is negligible, the RFID scheme is further secure and forward private.*

Namely, with an IND-CCA PKC, this RFID scheme achieves privacy with respect to the class

FORWARD ∪ (NARROW ∩ STRONG).

Due to Th. 9, this scheme is not strong private so narrow-strong privacy does not imply strong privacy and forward privacy does not imply strong privacy.

Proof. Correctness. This comes from the correctness of the cryptosystem.

Narrow-Strong Privacy. We prove that for any narrow-strong adversary $\mathcal{A}$ there exists a blinder B such that $\mathcal{A}$ has no significant advantage over $\mathcal{A}^B$. Since the

---

[5] Using $K = F_{K_M}(\mathsf{ID})$ as depicted on Fig. 3 given a PRF F and a master secret K_M does not modify our result. The same simplification could apply to the scheme of Fig. 1 as well, in order to shrink the database.

reader just sends random a and no RESULT query is allowed, every LAUNCH and SENDREADER query can be simulated in a trivial way so we can assume without loss of generality that no such query is done. We construct the blinder by using standard hybrid arguments. We consider the hybrid blinder B_i which works as follows: any of the i first SENDTAG queries with input a, returns the encryption c of a random r of same length as ID$||K||a$. Other SENDTAG queries by $\mathcal{A}$ are forwarded to the SENDTAG oracle.

The adversary, hybrid blinders, and tags can be simulated without using K_S. Let S_i be a simulator for the $\mathcal{A}^{B_i}$ attack except for the ith SENDTAG query which is indeed released. We use S_i to play the IND-CPA game. At the beginning, S_i receives K_P and runs the simulator for $\mathcal{A}^{B_i}$. At the moment of the ith query a, S_i computes $m_0 = $ ID$||K||a$ as B_{i-1} would do to simulate the tag, computes $m_1 = r$ as B_i would do, and submits m_0 and m_1 to the IND-CPA game. S_i receives an encrypted value c of either m_0 or m_1 that is used to respond the query and continues the simulation. At the end, S_i looks whether $\mathcal{A}^{B_i}$ won the privacy game or not. If it won, S_i outputs 0. Otherwise, S_i outputs 1. Clearly $\mathcal{A} = \mathcal{A}^{B_0}$, $\mathsf{Adv}^{\mathsf{IND}}(S_i) = \Pr[\mathcal{A}^{B_{i-1}}$ wins$] - \Pr[\mathcal{A}^{B_i}$ wins$]$, and $B = B_{q_T}$ is a full blinder where q_T is the number of SENDTAG queries. The complexity of S_i is polynomial. Due to IND-CPA security, $|\Pr[\mathcal{A}$ wins$] - Pr[\mathcal{A}^B$ wins$]|$ is negligible.

Security. The protocol suits the special form in Lemma 5 where $R(\mathsf{ID}, K; a, c)$ means $\mathsf{Dec}_{K_S}(c) = \mathsf{ID}||K||a$ and R' is always true. We can thus prove simple security and apply Lemma 5.

Let $\mathcal{A}$ be an adversary for the simple security game with a single tag ID and a single instance π (others are simulated). W.l.o.g. $\mathcal{A}$ does not query $R(\cdot; \cdot, c)$ when there is a protocol transcript $(\cdot, c)$. (The first input of R queries cannot be ID thus R cannot be satisfied.) $\mathcal{A}$ queries SENDREADER$(\pi) \rightarrow \hat{a}$ at time t, SENDTAG$(a_i, \mathsf{ID}) \rightarrow c_i$ at time t'_i, and ends by SENDREADER$(\hat{c}, \pi)$. If $t'_i < t$, $\Pr[a_i = \hat{a}]$ is negligible. If $t < t'_i$, wining cases are for $(\hat{a}, \hat{c}) \neq (a_i, c_i)$, $\mathsf{Dec}_{K_S}(\hat{c}) = \mathsf{ID}||K||\hat{a}$, and $\mathsf{Dec}_{K_S}(c_i) = \mathsf{ID}||K||a_i$. Hence, w.l.o.g. we can assume that $\hat{c} \neq c_i$ for all i.

We construct a partial blinder B_i as before. We construct a simulator S_i for $\mathcal{A}^{B_i}$ playing the IND-CCA game as before. S_i terminates by determining whether $\mathcal{A}$ succeeded by calling $\hat{c}$ to a decryption oracle. Finally, by using the IND-CCA security, we obtain a blinded adversary $\mathcal{A}^B$ such that $|\Pr[\mathcal{A}$ wins$] - Pr[\mathcal{A}^B$ wins$]|$ is negligible. Clearly, if the tag is no longer used and the reader leaks no information, making it identify the tag reduces to guessing the tag key K which can only happen with probability 2^{-k}, which is negligible.

Forward Privacy. Narrow-forward privacy implies forward privacy thanks to Lemma 8.   □

5   Conclusion

We have proven that public-key cryptography can assure the highest level of feasible privacy in RFID: narrow-strong and forward privacy, even with stateless protocols. We have shown narrow-destructive privacy for an OSK-like protocol in the random oracle model. Finally, we have proven weak privacy for a simple challenge-response protocol. The problem of achieving destructive privacy or forward privacy without public-key techniques are left open.

Acknowledgment. I thank Gildas Avoine for providing many useful references.

References

1. Aumasson, J.-Ph., Finiasz, M., Meier, W., Vaudenay, S.: TCHo: a Hardware-Oriented Trapdoor Cipher. In: Information Security and Privacy (ACISP 2007), Townsville, Australia. LNCS, vol. 4586, pp. 184–199. Springer, Heidelberg (2007)
2. Avoine, G.: Cryptography in Radio Frequency Identification and Fair Exchange Protocols. PhD Thesis no. 3407, EPFL (2005), http://library.epfl.ch/theses/?nr=3407
3. Avoine, G., Dysli, E., Oechslin, P.: Reducing Time Complexity in RFID Systems. In: Preneel, B., Tavares, S. (eds.) SAC 2005. LNCS, vol. 3897, pp. 291–306. Springer, Heidelberg (2006)
4. Avoine, G., Oechslin, P.: RFID Traceability: A Multilayer Problem. In: Patrick, A.S., Yung, M. (eds.) FC 2005. LNCS, vol. 3570, pp. 125–140. Springer, Heidelberg (2005)
5. Batina, L., Mentens, N., Sakiyama, K., Preneel, B., Verbauwhede, I.: Security and Privacy in Ad-Hoc and Sensor Networks. In: Buttyán, L., Gligor, V., Westhoff, D. (eds.) ESAS 2006. LNCS, vol. 4357, Springer, Heidelberg (2006)
6. Bellare, M., Desai, A., Pointcheval, D., Rogaway, P.: Relations Among Notions of Security for Public-Key Encryption Schemes. In: Krawczyk, H. (ed.) CRYPTO 1998. LNCS, vol. 1462, Springer, Heidelberg (1998)
7. Bocchetti, S.: Security and Privacy in RFID Protocols. Master Thesis (2006)
8. Burmester, M., van Le, T., de Medeiros, B.: Provably Secure Ubiquitous Systems: Universally Composable RFID Authentication Protocols. In: SecureComm 2006. Conference on Security and Privacy for Emerging Areas in Communication Networks, Baltimore, MA, USA, IEEE, Los Alamitos (2006)
9. Calmels, B., Canard, S., Girault, M., Sibert, H.: Low-Cost Cryptography for Privacy in RFID Systems. In: Domingo-Ferrer, J., Posegga, J., Schreckling, D. (eds.) CARDIS 2006. LNCS, vol. 3928, pp. 237–251. Springer, Heidelberg (2006)
10. Damgård, I., Østergaard, M.: RFID Security: Tradeoffs between Security and Efficiency. Technical report 2006/234, IACR (2006), http://eprint.iacr.org/2006/234
11. Diffie, W., Hellman, M.E.: New Directions in Cryptography. IEEE Transactions on Information Theory IT-22, 644–654 (1976)
12. Dimitriou, T.: A Lightweight RFID Protocol to Protect against Traceability and Cloning Attacks. In: SecureComm 2005. Conference on Security and Privacy for Emerging Areas in Communication Networks, Athens, Greece, IEEE, Los Alamitos (2005), http://ieeexplore.ieee.org/iel5/10695/33755/01607559.pdf?arnumber=1607559
13. Dolev, D., Dwork, C., Naor, M.: Non-Malleable Cryptography. In: Proceedings of the 23rd ACM Symposium on Theory of Computing, New Orleans, Louisiana, U.S.A, pp. 542–552. ACM Press, New York (1991)

14. Feldhofer, M., Dominikus, S., Wolkerstorfer, J.: Strong Authentication for RFID Systems using the AES Algorithm. In: Joye, M., Quisquater, J.-J. (eds.) CHES 2004. LNCS, vol. 3156, pp. 357–370. Springer, Heidelberg (2004)
15. Feldhofer, M., Rechberger, C.: A Case against Currently used Hash Functions in RFID Protocols. In: Meersman, R., Tari, Z., Herrero, P. (eds.) On the Move to Meaningful Internet Systems 2006: OTM 2006 Workshops. LNCS, vol. 4277, pp. 372–381. Springer, Heidelberg (2006)
16. Finiasz, M., Vaudenay, S.: When Stream Cipher Analysis Meets Public-Key Cryptography (Invited Talk.). In: Proceedings of SAC 2006. LNCS, Springer, Heidelberg (2006)
17. Gilbert, H., Robshaw, M., Sibert, H.: An Active Attack Against HB+: A Provably Secure Lightweight Authentication Protocol. IEE Electronic Letters 41, 1169–1170 (2005)
18. Girault, M., Lefranc, D.: Public Key Authentication with One (Online) Single Addition. In: Joye, M., Quisquater, J.-J. (eds.) CHES 2004. LNCS, vol. 3156, pp. 413–427. Springer, Heidelberg (2004)
19. Girault, M., Poupard, G., Stern, J.: On the Fly Authentication and Signature Schemes Based on Groups of Unknown Order. Journal of Cryptology 19, 463–487 (2006)
20. Goldwasser, S., Micali, S.: Probabilistic Encryption. Journal of Computer and System Sciences 28(2), 270–299 (1984)
21. Hall, J., Barbeau, M., Kranakis, E.: Detecting Rogue Devices in Bluetooth Networks using Radio Frequency Fingerprinting. In: Proceedings of the Third IASTED International Conference on Communications and Computer Networks (CCN 2006), Lima, Peru, pp. 108–113. IASTED/ACTA Press (2006)
22. ISO/IEC 14443-3. Identification Cards — Contactless Integrated Circuit(s) Cards — Proximity Cards. Part 3: Initialization and Anticollision. ISO (2001)
23. Juels, A., Weis, S.: Authenticating Pervasive Devices with human Protocols. In: Shoup, V. (ed.) CRYPTO 2005. LNCS, vol. 3621, pp. 293–308. Springer, Heidelberg (2005)
24. Juels, A., Weis, S.: Defining Strong Privacy for RFID. Technical report 2006/137, IACR (2006), http://eprint.iacr.org/2006/137
25. Katz, J., Shin, J.S.: Parallel and Concurrent Security of the HB and HB+ Protocols. In: Vaudenay, S. (ed.) EUROCRYPT 2006. LNCS, vol. 4004, pp. 73–87. Springer, Heidelberg (2006)
26. van Le, T., Burmester, M., de Medeiros, B.: Universally Composable and Forward Secure RFID Authentication and Authenticated Key Exchange. In: ASIACCS 2007. Proceedings of the 2007 ACM Symposium on Information, Computer and Communications Security, Singapore, pp. 242–252. ACM, New York (2007)
27. Lim, C.H., Kwon, T.: Strong and Robust RFID Authentication Enabling Perfect Ownership Transfer. In: Ning, P., Qing, S., Li, N. (eds.) ICICS 2006. LNCS, vol. 4307, pp. 1–20. Springer, Heidelberg (2006)
28. Molnar, D., Wagner, D.: Privacy and Security in Library RFID: Issues, Practices, and Architectures. In: 11th ACM Conference on Computer and Communications Security, Washington, DC, USA, pp. 210–219. ACM Press, New York (2004)
29. Naor, M., Yung, M.: Public-Key Cryptosystems Provably Secure against Chosen Ciphertext Attacks. In: Proceedings of the 22nd ACM Symposium on Theory of Computing, Baltimore, Maryland, U.S.A, pp. 427–437. ACM Press, New York (1990)
30. Ohkubo, M., Suzuki, K., Kinoshita, S.: Cryptographic Approach to a Privacy Friendly Tag. In: Presented at the RFID Privacy Workshop, MIT, USA (2003)

31. Ohkubo, M., Suzuki, K., Kinoshita, S.: Efficient Hash-Chain based RFID Privacy Protection Scheme. In: Davies, N., Mynatt, E.D., Siio, I. (eds.) UbiComp 2004. LNCS, vol. 3205, Springer, Heidelberg (2004)

32. Ohkubo, M., Suzuki, K.: RFID Privacy Issues and Technical Challenges. Communications of the ACM 48, 66–71 (2005)

33. Paise, R.I.: A Privacy Model for Mutual Authentication in Radio Frequency Systems. Master Thesis (2007)

34. Rackoff, C., Simon, D.: Non-Interactive Zero-Knowledge Proof of Knowledge and Chosen Ciphertext Attack. In: Feigenbaum, J. (ed.) CRYPTO 1991. LNCS, vol. 576, Springer, Heidelberg (1992)

35. Robshaw, M.J.B.: Searching for Compact Algorithms: CGEN. In: Nguyen, P.Q. (ed.) VIETCRYPT 2006. LNCS, vol. 4341, pp. 37–49. Springer, Heidelberg (2006)

36. Rudich, S.: The Use of Interaction in Public Cryptosystems. In: Feigenbaum, J. (ed.) CRYPTO 1991. LNCS, vol. 576, pp. 242–251. Springer, Heidelberg (1992)

37. Shoup, V.: Sequences of Games: A Tool for Taming Complexity in Security Proofs. Technical report 2004/332, IACR (2004), http://eprint.iacr.org/2004/332

38. Vaudenay, S.: RFID Privacy based on Public-Key Cryptography (Invited Talk). In: Rhee, M.S., Lee, B. (eds.) ICISC 2006. LNCS, vol. 4296, pp. 1–6. Springer, Heidelberg (2006)

39. Weis, S., Sarma, S., Rivest, R., Engels, D.: Security and Privacy Aspects of Low-Cost Radio Frequency Identification Systems. In: Hutter, D., Müller, G., Stephan, W., Ullmann, M. (eds.) Security in Pervasive Computing. LNCS, vol. 2802, pp. 454–469. Springer, Heidelberg (2004)

Obtaining Universally Compoable Security: Towards the Bare Bones of Trust*

Ran Canetti

IBM T.J. Watson Research Center

Abstract. A desirable goal for cryptographic protocols is to guarantee security when the protocol is composed with other protocol instances. Universally Composable (UC) security provides this guarantee in a strong sense: A UC-secure protocol maintains its security properties even when composed concurrently with an unbounded number of instances of arbitrary protocols. However, many interesting cryptographic tasks are provably impossible to realize with UC security, unless some trusted set-up is assumed. Impossibility holds even if ideally authenticated communication channels are provided.

This survey examines and compares a number of set-up assumptions (models) that were recently demonstrated to suffice for constructing UC-secure protocols that realize practically any cryptographic task. We start with the common reference string (CRS) and key registration (KR) models. We then proceed to the "sunspot" models, which allow for some adversarial control over the set-up, a number of models which better captures set-up that is globally available in the system, and a timing assumption. Finally, we briefly touch upon set-up models for obtaining authenticated communication.

1 Introduction

Designing protocols that guarantee security in open, multi-protocol, multi-party execution environments is a challenging task. In such environments a protocol instance is executed concurrently with an unknown number of instances of the protocol, as well as arbitrary other protocols. Indeed, it has been demonstrated time and again that adversarially-coordinated interactions between different protocol instances can compromise the security of protocols that were demonstrated to be secure when run in isolation (see, e.g., [GK89, DDN00, KSW97, DNS98, KLR06, CAN06]). A natural way for guaranteeing security of protocols in such complex execution environments is to require that protocols satisfy a notion of security that provides a general *secure composability* guarantee. That is, it should be guaranteed that a secure protocol

---

* This survey complements a talk given by the author at this conference. Work supported by NSF grants CT-0430450 and CFF-0635297, and US-Israel Binational Science Foundation Grant 2006317.

maintains its security even when composed with (i.e., runs alongside) arbitrary other protocols. Such a general notion of security is provided by the universally composable (UC) security framework [C01], which provides a very general composability property: A UC secure protocol is guaranteed to maintain its security (in the sense of emulating an ideally trusted and secure service) even when run concurrently with multiple copies of itself, plus arbitrary network activity.

Which cryptographic tasks are realizable by protocols that guarantee UC security? Are existing protocols, which are known to be secure in a stand-alone setting, UC secure? When the majority of the parties are honest (i.e., they are guaranteed to follow the protocol), the general feasibility results for stand-alone secure computations can be extended to the case of UC security. In fact, some known protocols for general secure function evaluation turn out to be UC secure. For instance, the [BGW88] protocol (both with and without the simplification of [GRR98]), together with encrypting each message using non-committing encryption [CFGN96], is universally composable as long as less than a third of the parties are corrupted, and authenticated and synchronous communication is available. Using [RB89], any corrupted minority is tolerable. Asynchronous communication can be handled using the techniques of [BCG93, BKR94]. Note that here some of the participants may be "helpers" (e.g., dedicated servers) that have no local inputs or outputs; they only participate in order to let other parties obtain their outputs in a secure way.

However, things are different when honest majority of the parties is not guaranteed, and in particular in the case where only two parties participate in the protocol and either one of the parties may be corrupted: It turns out that many interesting tasks are impossible to realize in the "bare" model of computation. Impossibility holds even if ideally authenticated communication is guaranteed. (In keeping with common terminology, we use the terms plain protocols and protocols in the plain model to denote protocols that assume ideally authenticated communication but no other set-up.) For instance, basic cryptographic tasks such as Bit Commitment, Coin-Tossing, Zero-Knowledge, or Oblivious Transfer cannot be realized by plain protocols, when naturally translated to the UC framework. Impossibility also extends to many other tasks [CF01, C01, CKL03, DDMRS06], including multi-party extensions of these primitives, whenever the honest parties are not in majority.

One potential approach for circumventing these impossibility results is to come up with relaxed notions of security that would still guarantee meaningful composable security, and at the same time would be realizable by plain protocols. It turns out, however, that such an approach will necessarily result in notions of security that either do not provide general composability guarantees, or alternatively are too weak to guarantee even stand-alone security as in, say, [C00] (see e.g. [L03, L04, CAN06]). Still, some meaningful such relaxations exist, see e.g. [PS04, BS05, MMY06].

Another approach is to stick with UC security, but consider protocols that rely on some trusted set-up assumption on the system. Here the meaningfulness of the security guarantee hinges on the "reasonability" of the set-up assumption, or in other words on the ability to realize the assumed set-up in actual systems.

This survey studies some set-up assumptions (or, models) that were recently proposed and shown to suffice for realizing essentially any cryptographic task in a universally composable way. The various set-up models are compared to each other, and the relative strengths and weaknesses are discussed.

The survey is organized as follows. Section 2 provides a brief review of the UC security framework. Section 3 reviews the basic impossibility result for obtaining UC commitment in the plain model. Section 4 reviews the common reference string (CRS) set-up. Section 5 reviews the key registration (KR) set-up. Section 6 reviews the adversarially controlled CRS (Sunspot) set-up. Section 7 reviews the augmented CRS (ACRS) set-up. Section 8 reviews the first set-up assumption, which relates to the delays on message delivery. Section 9 briefly discusses st-up assumptions for the purpose of obtaining authenticated communication. Section 10 concludes and discussed some open problems.

2   UC Security: A Brief Review

This section briefly reviews the UC framework. As in many other frameworks (e.g., [GL90, MR91, B91, C00, PW00, PW01]), the security of protocols with respect to a given task is defined via the "trusted party paradigm" [GMW87], where the protocol execution is compared with an ideal process where the outputs are computed by a trusted party that sees all the inputs. That is, a protocol is said to securely carry out a given task if running the protocol with a realistic adversary amounts to "emulating" the ideal process with the appropriate trusted party. We call the algorithm run by the trusted party an ideal functionality.

The UC framework substantiates this approach as follows. First, the process of executing a protocol in the presence of an adversary and in a given computational environment is substantiated. Next, the "ideal process" for carrying out the task is substantiated. Finally, one defines what it means for an execution of the protocol to "mimic" the ideal process. We sketch these three steps.

The Model of Protocol Execution. The model for executing an multiparty protocol π consists of a system of computing elements (modeled as interactive Turing machines, or ITMs) $(\mathcal{Z}, \mathcal{A}, M_1, M_2, ...)$ where $\mathcal{Z}$ and $\mathcal{A}$ are adversarial entities called the environment and adversary, respectively, and the machines $M_1, M_2, ...$ represent parties that run an "extended instance" of π. (An *instance* of protocol π is a set of ITMs that run π and in addition have a common identifier, called the *session ID*. The number of parties in an instance may vary from instance to instance, as well as during the lifetime of an instance.) Intuitively, the environment represents all the other protocols running in the system, including the protocols that provide inputs to, and obtain outputs from, the protocol instance under consideration. The adversary represents adversarial activities that are directly aimed at the protocol execution under consideration, including attacks on protocol messages and corruption of protocol participants.

An execution of the system consists of a sequence of activations of the individual elements, where the environment is activated first, and in each activation the active element determines the next element to be active, by sending information to it. This information may be labeled as either input, output, or protocol message. We impose the following restrictions on the way in which the above system runs. The environment $\mathcal{Z}$ is allowed to provide only *inputs* to other machines. A party of π may send messages to $\mathcal{A}$, or give inputs to the environment. The adversary $\mathcal{A}$ may give output to $\mathcal{Z}$ or send messages to other parties.

Let $\text{EXEC}_{\pi,\mathcal{A},\mathcal{Z}}(z)$ denote the random variable (over the local random choices of all the involved machines) describing the output of environment $\mathcal{Z}$ when interacting with adversary $\mathcal{A}$ and parties running protocol π on input z as described above. Let $\text{EXEC}_{\pi,\mathcal{A},\mathcal{Z}}$ denote the ensemble $\{\text{EXEC}_{\pi,\mathcal{A},\mathcal{Z}}(z)\}_{z\in\{0,1\}^*}$. We restrict attention to the case where the environment outputs only a single bit; namely, the ensemble $\text{EXEC}_{\pi,\mathcal{A},\mathcal{Z}}$ is an ensemble of distributions over $\{0,1\}$.

Subroutines. For the purpose of formulating the ideal process and the notion of protocol composition it will be convenient to allow designating an ITM as a *subroutine* of another ITM. If an ITM M is a subroutine of M' then M' can give input to M and M can give output to M'. Note that M and M may have different session ID and run different codes. The above model of protocol execution is then extended in the natural way to protocols where the parties have subroutines, with the important restriction that the environment only provides inputs to and receives outputs from the parties of a single instance of π. In particular, it does not directly communicate with any subroutine of a party of that single instance.

Ideal Functionalities and Ideal Protocols. Security of protocols is defined via comparing the protocol execution to an *ideal process* for carrying out the task at hand. For convenience of presentation, we formulate the ideal process for a task as a special protocol within the above model of protocol execution. (This avoids formulating an ideal process from scratch.) A key ingredient in this special protocol, called the ideal protocol, is an ideal functionality that captures the desired functionality, or the specification, of the task by way of a set of instructions for a "trusted party".

That is, let $\mathcal{F}$ be an ideal functionality (i.e., an algorithm for the trusted party). Then an instance of the ideal protocol IDEAL$_{\mathcal{F}}$ consists of dummy parties, plus a party $\mathcal{F}$ that's a subroutine of all the main parties. Upon receiving an input v, each dummy party forwards v as input to the subroutine $\mathcal{F}$. Any subroutine output coming from $\mathcal{F}$ is forwarded by the dummy party as subroutine output for the environment. We note that $\mathcal{F}$ can model reactive computation, in the sense that it can maintain local state and its outputs may depend on all the inputs received and all random choices so far. In addition, $\mathcal{F}$ may receive messages directly from the adversary $\mathcal{A}$, and may contain instructions to send messages to $\mathcal{A}$. This "back-door channel" of direct communication between $\mathcal{F}$ and $\mathcal{A}$ provides a way to *relax* the security guarantees provided $\mathcal{F}$. Specifically, by letting $\mathcal{F}$ take into account information received from $\mathcal{A}$, it is possible to capture the "allowed influence" of the adversary on the outputs of the parties, in terms of both contents and timing. By letting $\mathcal{F}$ provide information directly to $\mathcal{A}$ it is possible to capture the "allowed leakage" of information on the inputs and outputs of the parties.

Protocol Emulation. It remains to define what it means for a protocol to "mimic" or "emulate" the ideal process for some task. As a step towards this goal, we first formulate a more general notion of emulation, which applies to any two protocols. Informally, protocol π emulates protocol ϕ if, from the point of view of any environment, protocol π is "just as good" as ϕ, in the sense that no environment can tell whether it is interacting with π and some (known) adversary, or with ϕ and some other adversary. More precisely:

Definition (protocol emulation): *Protocol π UC-emulates protocol ϕ if for any adversary $\mathcal{A}$ there exists an adversary $\mathcal{S}$ such that, for any environment $\mathcal{Z}$ the ensembles $\text{EXEC}_{\pi,\mathcal{A},\mathcal{Z}}$ and $\text{EXEC}_{\phi,\mathcal{S},\mathcal{Z}}$ are indistinguishable. That is, on any input, the probability that $\mathcal{Z}$ outputs 1 after interacting with $\mathcal{A}$ and parties running π differs by at most a negligible amount from the probability that $\mathcal{Z}$ outputs 1 after interacting with $\mathcal{S}$ and ϕ.*

Once the general notion of protocol emulation is defined, the notion of realizing an ideal functionality is immediate:

Definition (realizing functionalities): *Protocol π UC-realizes an ideal functionality $\mathcal{F}$ if π emulates $\text{IDEAL}_{\mathcal{F}}$, the ideal protocol for $\mathcal{F}$.*

2.1   The Universal Composition Theorem

As in the case of protocol emulation, we present the composition operation and theorem in the more general context of composing two arbitrary protocols. The case of composing ideal protocols follows as a special case.

The Universal Composition Operation. The universal composition operation is a natural generalization of the "subroutine substitution" operation for sequential algorithms to the case of distributed protocols. That is, let ρ be a protocol that contains instructions to call protocol protocol ϕ as a subroutine, and let π be a protocol that UC-emulates ϕ. The composed protocol, denoted $\rho^{\pi/\phi}$, is the protocol that is identical to ρ, except that each instruction to call protocol ϕ is replaced with an instruction to call protocol π *with the same parameters an inputs*. Similarly, any output from a party running π is treated as an input form a party running ϕ. In particular, if some party running ρ calls multiple instances of ϕ, differentiated via their session IDs, then the corresponding instance of $\pi^{\rho/\phi}$ will use multiple instances of ρ.

The Composition Theorem. In its general form, the composition theorem says that if protocol π UC-emulates protocol ϕ then, for any protocol ρ, the composed protocol $\rho^{\pi/\phi}$ emulates ρ. This can be interpreted as asserting that replacing calls to ϕ with calls to π does not affect the behavior of ρ in any distinguishable way.

There is one caveat: For this result to hold we need that protocols π and ρ are "nice" in that only the main parties of the protocol have I/O with the outside world. More precisely, say that a protocol π is *subroutine respecting* if only the main parties of any instance of π receive input from external parties and send output to external parties. In particular, subroutines of the main parties, and subroutines thereof, do not directly get inputs from or send outputs to an external party. Then:

Theorem (universal composition): *Let ρ, ϕ, π be subroutine respecting protocols such that ρ uses ϕ as subroutine and π UC-emulates ϕ. Then protocol $\rho^{\pi/\phi}$ UC-emulates ρ. In particular, if ρ UC-realizes an ideal functionality $\mathcal{G}$ then so does $\rho^{\pi/\phi}$.*

A first, immediate corollary of the general theorem states that if protocol π UC-realizes an ideal functionality $\mathcal{F}$, and π uses as subroutine protocol IDEAL$_\mathcal{F}$, the ideal protocol for $\mathcal{F}$, then the composed protocol $\rho^{\pi/\phi^\mathcal{F}}$ UC-emulates ρ.[1] Another corollary states that if π UC-realizes an ideal functionality $\mathcal{G}$, then so does $\rho^{\pi/\phi}$.

Remark: On the Universality of Universal Composition. Many different ways of "composing together" protocols into larger systems are considered in the literature. Examples include sequential, parallel, and concurrent composition, of varying number of protocol instances, where the composed instances are run either by the same set of parties or by different sets of parties, use either the same program or different programs, and have either the same input or different inputs. A more detailed discussion appears in [CAN06].

We observe that all of these composition methods can be captured as special cases of universal composition. That is, any such method for composing together protocol instances can be captured by an appropriate "calling protocol" ρ that uses the appropriate number of protocol instances as subroutines, provides them with appropriately chosen inputs, and arranges for the appropriate synchronization in message delivery among the various subroutine instances. Consequently, it is guaranteed that a protocol that UC-realizes an ideal functionality $\mathcal{F}$ continues to UC-realize $\mathcal{F}$ even when composed with other protocols using any of the composition operations considered in the literature.

2.2   Generalized UC Security

In the UC framework the UC theorem holds only for protocols which are subroutine respecting. This simplifies the model and the analysis of protocols within it, but it does not allow to guarantee security in interesting cases where the same computational entity is used as a subroutine within multiple protocol instances.

---

[1] We say that an instance of protocol ρ uses an instance of protocol ϕ as a subroutine if each party in the instance of ϕ is a subroutine of some party of the instances of ρ.

To get around this limitation, the generalized UC (GUC) framework [CDPW07] modifies the model of protocol execution by allowing the environment to create and interact with other entities, in addition to the adversary and the parties of a single instance of the analyzed protocol, π. These additional entities may in turn provide inputs to and get outputs from participants in π. Say that protocol π GUC-emulates protocol ϕ if π UC-emulates ϕ with the modified protocol execution model. Now it can be seen that, within the GUC framework, the UC theorem holds even with respect to protocols that are not subroutine respecting:

Theorem (generalized universal composition): *Let ρ, ϕ, π be protocols such that ρ uses ϕ as subroutine and π GUC-emulates ϕ. Then protocol $\rho^{\pi/\phi}$ UC-emulates ρ. In particular, if ρ GUC-realizes an ideal functionality $\mathcal{G}$ then so does $\rho^{\pi/\phi}$.*

Two results surveyed here use this generalized model, for different purposes. One is the modeling of the augmented CRS model in [CDPW07], with the purpose of modeling set-up that's available to more than one protocol instance. The other is the modeling of adversarially controlled reference strings in [CPS07].

3   Prologue: Impossibility of UC Commitment

We recall some basic results regarding realizability of functionalities in the UC framework. These results motivate and shape the search for better set-up assumptions.

In a nutshell, the natural formulations of Commitment, Zero-Knowledge, Coin Tossing, or Oblivious Transfer as ideal functionalities within the UC framework turn out to be "complete" for UC realizability. That is, UC-realizing any one of these functionalities is necessary and sufficient for obtaining general realizability results for practically any ideal functionality.

In other words, there exist ideal functionalities, $\mathcal{F}_{\text{COM}}$, $\mathcal{F}_{\text{ZK}}$, $\mathcal{F}_{\text{COIN}}, \mathcal{F}_{\text{OT}}$, that naturally capture the security requirements from the corresponding primitives, and such that it is possible to UC-realize any one of these ideal functionalities by protocols that make use of any one of these ideal functionalities as a subroutine (see [C01] for more details). Furthermore, there exist constructions for UC-realizing any "well-formed" ideal functionality via protocols that use, say, $\mathcal{F}_{\text{ZK}}$ as subroutine (see e.g. [CLOS02]).

Furthermore, it is impossible to UC-realize any one of these functionalities via two-party plain protocols.

Here we briefly recall the impossibility result for UC-realizing the ideal commitment functionality, $\mathcal{F}_{\text{COM}}$. Impossibility for the other primitives follow similar lines. First, however, let us recall the formulation of $\mathcal{F}_{\text{COM}}$.

The Ideal Commitment Functionality. The ideal commitment functionality, $\mathcal{F}_{\text{COM}}$, formalizes the "sealed envelope" intuition in a straightforward way. That is, when receiving from the committer C an input requesting to commit to value x to a receiver R, $\mathcal{F}_{\text{COM}}$ records (x, R) and notifies R and the adversary that C has committed to some value. (Notifying the adversary means that the fact that a commitment took place need not be hidden.) The opening phase is initiated by the committer inputting a request to open the recorded value. In response, $\mathcal{F}_{\text{COM}}$ outputs x to R and the adversary. (Giving x to the adversary means that the opened value can be publicly available).

In order to correctly handle adaptive corruption of the committer during the course of the execution, $\mathcal{F}_{\text{COM}}$ responds to a request by the adversary to corrupt C by first outputting a corruption output to C, and then revealing the recorded value x to the adversary. In addition, if the Receipt value was not yet delivered to R, then $\mathcal{F}_{\text{COM}}$ allows the adversary to modify the committed value. This last stipulation captures the fact that the committed value is fixed only at the end of the commit phase, thus if the committer is corrupted during that phase then the adversary might still be able to modify the committed value. (Corruption of the receiver does not require any move).

$\mathcal{F}_{\text{COM}}$ is described in Figure 1. For brevity, we use the following terminology: The instruction "send a delayed output x to party P" should be interpreted as "send (x, P) to the adversary; when receiving ok from the adversary, output x to P."

Functionality $\mathcal{F}_{\text{COM}}$

1. Upon receiving an input (Commit, x) from party C, record (C, R, x) and generate a delayed output (Receipt) to R. Ignore any subsequent (Commit...) inputs.
2. Upon receiving an input (Open) from C, do: If there is a recorded value x then generate a delayed output (Open, x) to R. Otherwise, do nothing.
3. Upon receiving a message (Corrupt, C) from the adversary, output a Corrupted value to C, and send x to the adversary. Furthermore, if the adversary now provides a value x', and the (Receipt) output was not yet written on R's tape, then change the recorded value to x'.

Fig. 1. The Ideal Commitment functionality, $\mathcal{F}_{\text{COM}}$

Impossibility of Realizing $\mathcal{F}_{\text{COM}}$ in the Plain Model. Roughly speaking, the requirements from a protocol that UC-realizes $\mathcal{F}_{\text{COM}}$ boil down to the following two requirements from the ideal-process adversary (simulator) $\mathcal{S}$. (a). When the committer is corrupted (i.e., controlled by the adversary), $\mathcal{S}$ must be able to "extract" the committed value from the commitment. That is, $\mathcal{S}$ has to come up with a value x such that the committer will almost never be able to successfully decommit to any $x' \neq x$. This is so since in the ideal process $\mathcal{S}$ has to explicitly provide $\mathcal{F}_{\text{COM}}$ with a committed value. (b). When the receiver is uncorrupted, $\mathcal{S}$ has to be able to generate a "simulated commitment" c that looks like a real commitment and yet can be "opened" to any value, to be determined at the time of opening. This is so since $\mathcal{S}$ has to provide adversary $\mathcal{A}$ and environment

$\mathcal{Z}$ with the simulated commitment c before the value committed to is known. All this needs to be done *without rewinding the environment* $\mathcal{Z}$.

Intuitively, these requirements look impossible to meet: A simulator that has the above abilities can be used by a dishonest receiver to "extract" the committed value from an honest committer. This intuition can indeed be formalized to show that in the plain model it is impossible to UC-realize $\mathcal{F}_{\text{COM}}$ by a two-party protocol. Essentially, the proof proceeds as follows. Let π be a protocol that UC-realizes $\mathcal{F}_{\text{COM}}$. Consider an execution of π by an adversarially controlled committer C and an honest receiver R, and assume that the adversary merely sends messages that are generated by the environment, and delivers to the environment any message received from R. The environment, $\mathcal{Z}_C$, secretly picks a random bit b at the beginning and generates the messages for C by running the protocol of the honest committer for b and R's answers. Once $\mathcal{Z}_C$ received a "receipt" output from R, it starts running the honest opening protocol in the name of C. Finally, $\mathcal{Z}_C$ outputs 1 iff the b' that R outputs equals the secret bit b. We know that the in an execution of π with honest receiver and committer, in the opening stage the receiver always outputs the bit committed to by the committer. However, since π UC-realizes $\mathcal{F}_{\text{COM}}$, there should exist an ideal-model adversary $\mathcal{S}$ that interacts with $\mathcal{F}_{\text{COM}}$ and generates a view for $\mathcal{Z}_C$ that is indistinguishable from a real execution with π. In particular, it must also be the case that $b = b'$ almost always even in the ideal process. For this to hold, it must be that $\mathcal{S}$ must have given to $\mathcal{F}_{\text{COM}}$ the correct bit b at the commitment stage. Now, given $\mathcal{S}$, we can construct another environment, $\mathcal{Z}_R$, and a corrupted receiver $\mathcal{A}_R$, such that $\mathcal{Z}_R$ successfully distinguishes between an execution of π and an interaction with $\mathcal{F}_{\text{COM}}$ and *any* adversary $\mathcal{S}_R$. $\mathcal{Z}_R$ and $\mathcal{A}_R$ proceed as follows: $\mathcal{Z}_R$ chooses a random bit b and hands b as input to the honest committer C. It then waits to receive a bit b' from $\mathcal{A}_R$ (which controls the receiver). $\mathcal{Z}_R$ outputs 1 iff $b = b'$. $\mathcal{A}_R$ proceeds as follows: Recall that $\mathcal{S}$ can "extract" the committed bit b via simple interaction with the committers messages, without rewinding or any additional information. Therefore, $\mathcal{A}_R$ can simply run $\mathcal{S}$ and guess b almost always. In contrast, when $\mathcal{Z}_R$ interacts with $\mathcal{F}_{\text{COM}}$, the adversary's view is independent of b, and thus $b = b'$ with probability exactly one half.

4   The Common Reference String Model

The common reference string model, first proposed in [BFM88] and used extensively since, assumes that the parties have access to a common string that is guaranteed to come from a pre-specified distribution. Furthermore, it is guaranteed that the string was chosen in an "opaque" way, namely that no information related to the process of choosing this string is available to any party. A very natural distribution for the common string, advocated in [BFM88], is the uniform distribution over the strings of some length. Still, it is often useful to consider reference strings that are taken from other distributions.

In the Zero-Knowledge context of [BFM88], the fact that the reference string comes from an external source that is unrelated to the actual computation is

captured by allowing the simulator to choose the reference string as it wishes —
as long as the adversary cannot distinguish this "simulated string" from a "real
string" taken from the prescribed distribution. Indeed, it is this extra freedom
given to the simulator which makes this model powerful.

Within the present framework, the CRS model can be captured in a natural
way by modeling the reference string as coming from an appropriate ideal functionality. More specifically, we formulate functionality $\mathcal{F}_{\text{CRS}}$, presented in Figure
2 below. The functionality is parameterized by a distribution D and a set $\mathcal{P}$ of
recipients of the reference string. Upon invocation, it first draws a value r from
distribution D. Next, on input from a party $P \in \mathcal{P}$, $\mathcal{F}_{\text{CRS}}^{D}$ returns r to P.

Letting the adversary know r models the fact that r is public, and cannot be
assumed secret. Prohibiting parties not in $\mathcal{P}$ from obtaining r directly from $\mathcal{F}_{\text{CRS}}$
models the fact that r is treated as local to a specific protocol instance, and is
intended to be used only within this protocol instance. (This point is elaborated
on in Section 7.) Other protocol instances should use different "draws" from
distribution D. This restriction on the use of the reference string limits the
applicability of the CRS model: To realize $\mathcal{F}_{\text{CRS}}$ in reality, the participants of
each protocol execution need to somehow "get together" and obtain a reference
string that they all trust to be taken from the specified distribution. The next
sections discuss set-up assumptions that are aimed at mitigating this limitations
in a number of different ways.

Functionality $\mathcal{F}_{\text{CRS}}^{D,\mathcal{P}}$

1. When receiving input (CRS,sid) from party P, first verify that $P \in$
   $\mathcal{P}$; else ignore the input. Next, if there is no value r recorded then
   choose and record a value $r \xleftarrow{\text{R}} D$. Finally, send a public delayed output
   (CRS,sid,r) to P.

Fig. 2. The Common Reference String functionality

From $\mathcal{F}_{\text{CRS}}$ to $\mathcal{F}_{\text{COM}}$. Several protocols that UC-realize $\mathcal{F}_{\text{COM}}$ given access to
$\mathcal{F}_{\text{CRS}}$ are known. Here we briefly sketch the protocol of [CF01]. What "saves" the
simulator in the CRS model from the above impossibility result is the following
observation, which parallels the original CRS model of [BFM88]: When interacting with a commitment protocol that used $\mathcal{F}_{\text{CRS}}$, the environment learns about
the value of the reference string only from the adversary. This means that, the
ideal process for $\mathcal{F}_{\text{COM}}$, the simulator can choose the reference string on its own.
Consequently, the simulator can know some "trapdoor information" associated
with the reference string, and even change its distribution slightly.

The [CF01] commitment protocol uses this observation as follows. The reference string will consist of a public key e of an encryption scheme and a
claw-free pair of permutations f_0, f_1 with trapdoor. (That is, given only the
description f_0, f_1 it is infeasible to find x_0, x_1 such that $f_0(x_0) = f_1(x_1)$, but
given a trapdoor t one can efficiently invert, say, f_0.) Now, to commit to bit

b, the committer chooses a random value r and sends the commitment message $(f_b(r), E_e(r_0, id), E_e(r_1, id))$ where $r_b = r$, $r_{1-b} = 0$, and id is an identifier for the session. (Typically, id would include the identities of the committer and receiver, plus additional commitment-specific information.) To open to bit b, the committer sends r and the randomness used for encrypting r; this is the first or second encryption, depending on b.[2] Now, in a standard execution of the protocol the commitment is committing (due to the claw-freeness of f_0, f_1), and hiding (due to the security of the encryption scheme). However, in a simulated execution the simulator can know both t and the decryption key associated with e. It can thus easily generate commitment strings that can be opened both ways, and at the same time it can easily extract the hidden value committed in an honestly generated commitment. When the encryption scheme is secure against chosen ciphertext attacks, it can be shown that the simulator can successfully extract the hidden value even when the commitment string is chosen adversarially. This ideas are at the basis of the proof of security of the protocol.

We note that the above protocol can generate multiple commitments using a single reference string. In other words, it actually realizes a "multi-session version" of $\mathcal{F}_{\text{COM}}$, where a single instance allows multiple parties can commit and open multiple commitments. (This multi-session version is called $\mathcal{F}_{\text{MCOM}}$ in the literature.) This somewhat alleviates the need to agree on a different reference string for each protocol instance, since a single instance of the above protocol suffices for generating commitments for an entire system. However, the solution is far from satisfying: First, strictly speaking, all protocol instances that use the same commitment protocol now have some joint state and can no longer be analyzed separately and be composed later. Second, no security guarantee is given with respect to other protocols that use the same reference string in other ways than via that global instance of the commitment protocol. The first issue is handled by the Universal Composition with Joint State (JUC) theorem of [CR03]. The second issue is more subtle and is addressed in Section 7.

5   The Key Set-Up Model

The CRS set-up assumption has the advantage that it only requires knowledge of a single short string. In particular, it does not require parties to identify themselves or to go through a registration process before participating in a protocol. Thus, in settings where it is reasonable to assume existence of trusted reference string, this assumption is very attractive. However, when the reference string is being generated by a computational entity that may be corrupted or subverted, the CRS modeling is somewhat unsatisfactory, in that it puts complete trust in a single entity. In fact, this entity, if subverted, can completely undermine the security of the protocol by choosing the reference string from a different distribution, or alternatively by leaking to some parties some secret information related to the string. Furthermore, it can do so without being detected.

---

[2] The actual protocol is slightly different, to account for adaptive corruptions.

The key set-up functionality, $\mathcal{F}_{KS}$, formulated in [BCNP04] and presented in Figure 3, is written in a way that can be realized by real-world mechanisms that do not require all participants to put full trust in a single string. At the same time, it can be realized even in the CRS model itself. We first describe the functionality and its use, and then discuss how it can be realized.

$\mathcal{F}_{KS}$ is parameterized by a set $\mathcal{P}$ of parties and a deterministic function $f : \{0,1\}^* \rightarrow \{0,1\}^*$, that represents a method for computing a public key given a secret (and supposedly random) key. The functionality allows parties to register their identities together with an associated "public key". However, $\mathcal{F}_{KS}$ provides only relatively weak guarantees regarding this public key, giving the adversary considerable freedom in determining this key. (This freedom is what makes $\mathcal{F}_{KS}$ so relaxed.) Specifically, the "public key" to be associated with a party upon registration is determined as follows. The functionality keeps a set R of "good public keys". Upon receiving a registration request from party $P \in \mathcal{P}$, the functionality first notifies the adversary that a request was made and gives the adversary the option to set the registered key to some key p that is already in R. If the adversary declines to set the registered key, then the functionality determines the key on its own, by choosing a random secret r from a given domain (say, $\{0,1\}^k$ for a security parameter k) and letting $p = f(r)$. Once the registered key p is chosen, the functionality records (P,p) and returns p to P and to the adversary. Finally, if p was chosen by the functionality itself then p is added to R. If the registering party is corrupted, then the adversary can also specify, if it chooses, an arbitrary "secret key" r. In this case, P is registered with the value $f(r)$ (but r is not added to R).

A retrieval request, made by a party in $\mathcal{P}$, for the public key of party P is answered with either an error message $\perp$ or one of the registered public keys of P, where the adversary chooses which registered public key, if any, is returned. (That is, the adversary can prevent a party from retrieving any of the registered keys of another party).

Notice that the uncorrupted parties do not obtain any secret keys associated with their public keys, whereas the corrupted parties may know the secret keys of their public keys. Furthermore, $\mathcal{F}_{KS}$ gives the adversary a fair amount of freedom in choosing the registered keys. It can set the keys associated with corrupted parties to be any arbitrary value (as long as the functionality received the corresponding private key). The adversary can also cause the keys of both corrupted and uncorrupted parties to be identical to the keys of other (either corrupted or uncorrupted) parties. Still, $\mathcal{F}_{KS}$ guarantees two basic properties: (a) the public keys of good parties are "safe" (in the sense that their secret keys were chosen at random and kept secret from the adversary), and (b) the public keys of the corrupted parties are "well-formed", in the sense that the functionality received the corresponding private keys.

In [BCNP04] it is shown how to UC-realize $\mathcal{F}_{MCOM}$ given access to $\mathcal{F}_{KS}$. A non-interactive protocol for realizing $\mathcal{F}_{ZK}$ given access to KS is also shown. The protocol for realizing $\mathcal{F}_{MCOM}$ is essentially identical to the [CF01] protocol described above; the only difference is that the claw-free pair f_0, f_1 is now the public key of the

---

Functionality $\mathcal{F}_{\mathrm{KS}}^{\mathcal{P},f}$

$\mathcal{F}_{\mathrm{KS}}^{f}$ proceeds as follows, given set $\mathcal{P}$ of identities, function f and security parameter k. At the first activation a set R of strings is initialized to be empty.

Registration: When receiving input (Register, sid) from a party P, verify that that $P \in \mathcal{P}$; else ignore the input. Next, send (Register, sid, P) to the adversary, and receive a value p' from the adversary. Then, if $p' \in R$ then let $p \leftarrow p'$. Else, choose $r \xleftarrow{\text{R}} \{0,1\}^k$, let $p \leftarrow f(r)$, and add p to R. Finally, record (P,p) and return (sid,p) to P and to the adversary.

Registration by a corrupted party: When receiving input (Register, sid, r) from a corrupted party $P \in \mathcal{P}$, record $(P,f(r))$. In this case, $f(r)$ is *not* added to R.

Retrieval: When receiving a message (Retrieve, sid, P) from party $P' \in \mathcal{P}$, send (Retrieve, sid, P, P') to the adversary and obtain a value p in return. If (P,p) is recorded then return (sid, P, p) to P'. Else, return $(sid, P, \bot)$ to P'.

Fig. 3. The Key Registration functionality

receiver, whereas the encryption key e is now the public key of the committer. Intuitively, this works since the committer is only concerned that the secret decryption key associated with e remains unknown, whereas the receiver is only concerned that the trapdoor t of f_0, f_1 remains unknown. We note, however, that this protocol remains secure only for non-adaptive party corruption.

Realizing $\mathcal{F}_{\mathrm{KS}}$. $\mathcal{F}_{\mathrm{KS}}$ can be realized in a number of different ways. First, we observe that $\mathcal{F}_{\mathrm{KS}}^{\mathcal{P},f}$ can be realized in the $\mathcal{F}_{\mathrm{CRS}}^{\mathcal{P},D}$-hybrid model, where $D = D_k$ is the distribution of $f(r)$ for r that is uniform in $\{0,1\}^k$. The protocol is straightforward: On input either (Register, sid) or (Retrieve, sid, P), party P sends (CRS, sid) to $\mathcal{F}_{\mathrm{CRS}}$ and returns the obtained value.

Realizing $\mathcal{F}_{\mathrm{KS}}$ Given a Distributed Registration Service. Consider a setting where the parties have access to registration servers where parties can register and obtain public keys that were chosen at random according to a given distribution (i.e., the public key is $f(r)$ for an $r \xleftarrow{\text{R}} \{0,1\}^k$). Alternatively, parties can choose their keys themselves and provide them to the server. Note that here each party needs to put full trust (to keep its key secret) only in the server it registers with. The trust put in other servers is much lower - it only needs to be trusted that the public keys obtained from these servers are "well formed".

Realizing $\mathcal{F}_{\mathrm{KS}}$ Using Traditional Proofs of Knowledge. Finally, it is possible to realize $\mathcal{F}_{\mathrm{KRK}}^{f}$ (and thus also $\mathcal{F}_{\mathrm{KS}}^{f}$) via traditional (non-UC) proofs of knowledge of the private key, under the assumption that the proofs of knowledge occur when there is no related network activity. (Intuitively, in this case it is ok to "rewind" the environment, as necessary to prove security of the traditional proof of knowledge.

6   Adversarially Controlled Set-Up

The common reference string model provides the guarantee that the reference string is drawn from a pre-specified distribution. This is a very convenient abstraction for the purpose of designing protocols. Indeed, all existing protocols use this guarantee in a crucial sense: Security analyses quickly fall apart as soon as distribution of the reference string is changed even slightly.

This property is quite limiting. In particular, it seems to rule out "physical implementations" where the reference string is taken to be the result of joint measurement of some physical phenomenon such as astronomic measurements, fluctuations of the stock market, or even network delays across the Internet. Indeed, while it is reasonable to believe that such phenomena are largely unpredictable and uncontrollable, namely they have "high entropy", it is a stretch of the imagination to believe that they are taken from a distribution that is known to and useful for the protocol designer.

Can composable security be obtained if we only have an *imperfect* reference strings, or alternatively a reference string that are adversarially controlled to some extent? More specifically, are there protocols that UC-realize, say, $\mathcal{F}_{\text{COM}}$ in such a setting?

A first indication that this might not be an easy task is the result of Dodis et al. [DOPS04] that demonstrates the impossibility of NIZK in a relaxed variant of the CRS model in which the distribution of the reference string can be arbitrary subject to having some minimal min-entropy. However, this result does not rule rule out composable protocols; more importantly, it does not consider the case where the reference string is guaranteed to be taken from an efficiently samplable distribution. Indeed, for such distributions deterministic extractors are known to exist (under computational assumptions) [TV00]. Thus, one might expect it to be possible to "compile" any protocol in the CRS model (or at least protocols that can do with a uniformly distributed reference string) into a protocol that uses a reference string that is taken from any efficiently samplable distribution that has sufficient min-entropy: First have the parties use a deterministic extractor to transform the reference string into a string that is almost uniformly distributed. Next, run the original protocol. Since the extracted string is almost uniform, one might expect the original analysis to work in the same way.

However, deterministic extractability turns out to be insufficient for this purpose. In fact, it turns out that if one relaxes $\mathcal{F}_{\text{CRS}}$ so as to allow the distribution to be adversarially determined, then UC-realizing $\mathcal{F}_{\text{COM}}$ becomes impossible [CPS07]. Impossibility holds even if the chosen distribution is guaranteed to have full min-entropy minus a polynomially vanishing fraction, even if the distribution is guaranteed to be sampled via an *algorithmic* process, namely via a sampling process that has a relatively succinct description, and even when this process is guaranteed to be computationally efficient.

As a recourse, one may restrict attention to the case where the algorithm for sampling the reference string is known to the adversaries involved. (Still, it is of course unknown to the protocol.) Here it turns out to be possible to UC-realize $\mathcal{F}_{\text{COM}}$, as long as the reference string is taken from a distribution that is guaranteed to have a polynomial time sampling algorithm, a short description, and super-logarithmic min-entropy. Furthermore, all three conditions are simultaneously necessary, in the sense that impossibility holds as soon as any one of the conditions is relaxed [CPS07].

Discussion. It may appear over-optimistic to assume that the physical (or man-made) phenomena used to generate the reference string are governed by distributions where the sampling algorithm is computable in polynomial time. Indeed, why should Nature be governed by succinct and efficient algorithms? However, beyond the technical fact that these restrictions are necessary, one can view our analysis as a proof that any successful attack against the proposed protocols demonstrates that either the underlying hardness assumptions are violated, *or else that the process for choosing the reference string is not efficiently computable, or has long description.* This might be an interesting revelation in itself. Alternatively, the positive result may be interpreted as addressing situations where the process of choosing the reference string is influenced by an actual attacker. Here the guarantee that the distribution has some min-entropy represents the fact that the attacker's influence on the sampling process is limited.

The [CPS07] Results in More Detail. Three relaxations of $\mathcal{F}_{\text{CRS}}^{P,D}$ are formulated. The first relaxation, called $\mathcal{F}_{\text{BBSUN}}$, proceeds as follows. (Here sun stands for "sunspots", which is the term used in the first works that propose the CRS model when referring to astronomic observations [BFM88, F88] and bb stands for "black-box"). Instead of treating the distribution D as a fixed, public parameter, let the environment determine the distribution by providing a description of a sampling algorithm for D. Then, $\mathcal{F}_{\text{BBSUN}}$ chooses a sufficiently long random string ρ and computes the reference string $r = D(\rho)$. In addition, $\mathcal{F}_{\text{BBSUN}}$ lets the adversary (and simulator) obtain additional independent samples from the distribution "on the side". These samples are not seen by the environment or the parties running the protocol.

Three parameters of $\mathcal{F}_{\text{BBSUN}}$ turn out to be salient. First is the min-entropy, or "amount of randomness" of the reference string (measured over the random choices of both the environment and the sunspot functionality). Next is the runtime, or computational complexity of the sampling algorithm D. Last is the description-size of D (namely, the number of bits in its representation as a string); this quantity essentially measures the amount of randomness in the reference string that comes from the random choices of the environment. All quantities are measured as a function of the length n of the reference string; that is, we treat n as the security parameter.

Theorem: There exist no two-party protocols that UC-realize $\mathcal{F}_{\text{COM}}$ when given access to of $\mathcal{F}_{\text{BBSUN}}$. This holds even if the distribution of the reference string is guaranteed to have min-entropy greater than $n - n^\epsilon$, and even if both the description size and the computational complexity of the provided sampling algorithm are guaranteed to be at most n^ϵ, for any $\epsilon > 0$.

Next a more restricted setting is considered, where the adversary has access to the "code", or description of the sampling algorithm D. This is modeled by having the set-up functionality explicitly send the description of D to the adversary. (Note that this relaxation is meaningful only for sampling algorithms that can be described in $poly(n)$ bits, else the adversary cannot read the description.) Call this functionality $\mathcal{F}_{\mathrm{GBSUN}}$ (for "gray box"). The third variant, called $\mathcal{F}_{\mathrm{SUN}}$, gives to the adversary also the local random choices used to generate the reference string. It turns out that this variant provides an incomparable setup guarantee to that of $\mathcal{F}_{\mathrm{GBSUN}}$. (This is so since the setup functionality is invoked directly by the environment. Consequently, the functionality exists both in the real-life and in the ideal models).

Theorem: There exist no two-party protocols that UC-realize $\mathcal{F}_{\mathrm{COM}}$ when given access to either $\mathcal{F}_{\mathrm{GBSUN}}$ or $\mathcal{F}_{\mathrm{SUN}}$. This holds even if either one of the following holds

1. The computational complexity of the sampling algorithm can be super-polynomial in n, as long as the distribution of the reference string is guaranteed to have min-entropy $n - \mathrm{poly}\log n$, and the description size of the provided sampling algorithm is guaranteed to be at most $\mathrm{poly}\log n$ (assuming one-way functions with sub-exponential hardness).
2. The description size of the sampling algorithm is at least $\mu(n) - \log n$, as long as the distribution of the reference string is guaranteed to have min-entropy $\mu(n) = n$ and the computational complexity is guaranteed to be at most $O(n)$.
3. The distribution of the reference string has min-entropy at most $\log n$, as long as the description length is $O(1)$ and the computational complexity is $O(n)$.

On the other hand, we have:

Theorem: Assume there exist collision-resistant hash functions, dense cryptosystems and one-way functions with sub-exponential hardness. Then there exists a two-party protocol that UC-realizes $\mathcal{F}_{\mathrm{MCOM}}$, when given access to $O(1)$ instances of either $\mathcal{F}_{\mathrm{GBSUN}}$ or $\mathcal{F}_{\mathrm{SUN}}$, as long as it is guaranteed that the min-entropy of the reference string is at least $\mu(n) = \mathrm{poly}\log n$ the computational complexity of the provided sampling algorithm is at most $poly(n)$ and its description size is at most $\mu(n) - \mathrm{poly}\log n$.

Furthermore, the protocol from Theorem 3 withstands even adaptive party corruptions, with no data erasure, whereas Theorems 1 and 2 apply even to protocols that only withstand static corruptions.

In other words, under computational assumptions, Theorem 2 and 3 provide an essentially tight characterization of the feasibility of UC protocols, in terms of the min-entropy, computational complexity and description length of the reference string. Informally,

> *UC-security of non-trivial tasks is possible if and only if the reference string has min-entropy at least $\mu(n) = \text{poly}\log n$, and is generated by a computationally-efficient sampling algorithm with description length at most $\mu(n) - \text{poly}\log n$.*

Techniques for the Impossibility Results. The impossibility results combine the [CF01] proof of impossibility of UC-realizing $\mathcal{F}_{\text{COM}}$ in the plain model with techniques from [GK89]. Recall that the model does not let the environment see the reference string directly, which in principle allows the simulator to present the environment with any string of its choosing and claim that this is the reference string chosen in the execution. To mitigate this freedom, the environment chooses a special distribution D that makes sure that the string presented by the simulator as the actual reference string can only be one of the strings that the simulator received as "extra samples" from the set-up functionality. Since the simulator can only ask for a polynomial number of such samples, it can be seen that a dishonest verifier can still use the simulator to extract the committed bit from an honest committer, much as in the proof of [CF01], and with only polynomial degradation in success probability. All impossibility results use this idea, with different techniques or choosing the distribution D so as to obtain the desired effect.

Protocol Techniques. To explain the main idea behind the protocol, it is useful to first sketch a simpler protocol that is only secure with respect to static corruptions. Also, the protocol aims to realize the zero-knowledge functionality, $\mathcal{F}_{\text{ZK}}$, rather than $\mathcal{F}_{\text{MCOM}}$. The idea is to use a variation on Barak's protocol [B01]: Let L be an NP language and assume that a prover P wishes to prove to a verifier V that $x \in L$, having access to a reference string r that is taken from an unknown distribution with min-entropy at least $\mu = n^\epsilon$. Then, P and V will engage in a witness-indistinguishable proof that *"either $x \in L$ or the reference string r has a description of size $\mu/2$"*. (As in Barak's protocol, the description size is measured in terms of the Kolmogorov complexity, namely existence of a Turing machine M with description size $\mu/2$ that outputs r on empty input. Also, in order to guarantee that the protocol is simulatable in polynomial-time M should be polynomial time.) Soundness holds because in a real execution of the protocol, r is taken from a distribution with min-entropy at least μ, so the second part of the "or" statement is false with high probability. To demonstrate zero-knowledge, the simulator generates a simulated reference string $\tilde{r}$ by running the sampling algorithm D for the distribution on a *pseudo*random random-input. That is, the simulator chooses a random string $\tilde{\rho}$ of length, say, $\mu/2 - |D|$ (where $|D|$ denotes the description size of D) and computes $\tilde{r} = D(G(\tilde{\rho}))$, where G is some length-tripling pseudo-random generator. Now, $\tilde{r}$ indeed has description of size $\mu/2$ (namely, $\tilde{\rho}$ plus $|D|$ plus the constant-size description of G); furthermore, the simulator knows this description. Also, since both D and the environment are polynomial time, the simulated string $\tilde{r}$ is indistinguishable from the real string r.

The above protocol allows for straight-line simulation. It is not yet straight-line extractable, but it can be modified to be so using the techniques of [BL04]. Still, it is only secure against *static* corruptions of parties. In order to come up with a protocol that withstands *adaptive* corruptions a somewhat different technique is used, which combines the above idea with techniques from [CDPW07]. First, they move to realizing $\mathcal{F}_{\text{MCOM}}$. They then proceed in several steps: The first step is to construct a commitment scheme that is *equivocal* and adaptively secure. This is done using Feige and Shamir's technique [FS89] for constructing equivocal commitments from Zero-Knowledge protocols such as the one described above. Next, the constructed equivocal commitment scheme is used in a special type of a coin-tossing protocol, and use the obtained coin tosses as a reference string for a standard UC commitment protocol such as [CF01].

The protocol allows *two* parties to perform *multiple* commitment and decommitment operations between them, using only *two* reference strings —one for the commitments by each party. This means that in a multi-party setting it is possible to realize any ideal functionality using one reference string for each (ordered) pair of parties, regardless of the number of commitments and decommitment performed. Furthermore, each reference string needs to be trusted only by the two parties who use it.

7 Globally Available Set-Up

All the set-up models considered so far model the set-up information as information that's available only to the participants of a single protocol instance. This means that, in order to implement such a model, one has to generate a fresh reference string (or fresh public keys) for each instance of a protocol that uses it. Furthermore, this has to be done in a way that makes the reference string available only to the protocol participants. While such implementations are possible (say, via joint measurements of physical phenomena at the onset of an execution), this is a severe limitation. In particular, this modeling stands in contrast with the prevalent intuitive perception of the reference string (or public key infrastructure) as a "global" construct that is chosen in advance and made available to all throughout the lifetime of the system.

Furthermore, this limitation turns out to be not only "academic". For instance, all existing protocols designed in the CRS model turn out to be *insecure* in a setting where the reference string can be used by multiple, arbitrary protocols. In fact, as shown in [CDPW07], this limitation is inherent: No set-up assumption that only gives out public set-up information can suffice for realizing, say, $\mathcal{F}_{\text{COM}}$, if the same set-up information can be used by all protocols in the system.

To exemplify this point, consider the "non-transferability" (or, "deniability") concern, namely allowing party A to interact with party B in a way that prevents B from later "convincing" a third party, C, that the interaction took place.

Indeed, if A and B interact via an idealized "trusted party" that communicates only with A and B then deniability is guaranteed in a perfect, idealized way. Thus, intuitively, if A and B interact via a protocol that emulates the trusted party, then deniability should hold just the same. When the protocol in question uses no set-up, or alternatively set-up that's local to each protocol instance, this intuition works, in the sense that UC-realizing such a trusted party automatically implies non-transferability. However, when a global set-up is used, this is no longer the case: There are protocols that emulate such a trusted party but do *not* guarantee non-transferability.

For instance, consider the case of Zero-Knowledge protocols, namely protocol that emulate the trusted party for the "Zero-Knowledge functionality": Zero-Knowledge protocols in the plain model are inherently deniable, but all existing Zero-Knowledge protocols in the CRS model are completely *un*deniable whenever the reference string is public knowledge (see [P03]).

Non-transferability is not the only concern that remains un-captured in the present formulation of security in the CRS model. For instance, the protocol in [CF01] for realizing the single-instance commitment functionality becomes malleable as soon as *two* instances use the same reference string; indeed, to avoid this weakness a more involved protocol was developed, where multiple commitments can explicitly use the same reference string in a specific way. Other demonstrations of this point are given in [YYZ07A].

The Global CRS Model. Taking a second look at the way we modeled set-up so far, the main reason for the inability to capture such global set-up is the fact that so far the set-up was modeled as an ideal functionality that interacts only with the parties of a given protocol execution. In particular, the set-up does not explicitly take part in the ideal process. A natural way to capture global set-up is thus to model the set-up as an ideal functionality that interacts not only with the parties running the protocol, but also with other parties (or, in other words, with the external environment). This in particular means that the set-up functionality exists not only as part of the protocol execution, but also in the *ideal process,* where the protocol is replaced by the trusted party.

More precisely, modify the CRS functionality, $\mathcal{F}_{\mathrm{CRS}}$, as follows: Instead of giving the reference string only to the adversary and the parties running the actual protocol instance, the new "global CRS" functionality, $\mathcal{F}_{\mathrm{GCRS}}$, will give the reference string to all parties and in particular to the environment. (Technically, in order to model $\mathcal{F}_{\mathrm{GCRS}}$ one has to use the generalized UC security notion, as sketched in Section 2.2. Indeed, it is for this reason that the generalized model was first formulated).

Technically, the effect of this modeling is that now the simulator (namely, the adversary in the ideal process) cannot choose the reference string or know related trapdoor information. In a way, proofs of security in the new modeling, even with set-up, are reminiscent of the proofs of security without set-up, in the sense that the only freedom enjoyed by the simulator is to control the local random choices of the uncorrupted parties. Indeed, as mentioned above, in [CDPW07] the argument of [CF01] is extended to show that no two-party protocol can

UC-realize $\mathcal{F}_{\text{COM}}$. The proof extends to rule out any set-up functionality that makes all of its inputs and outputs available to the environment.

New Set-Up Assumptions and Constructions. It turns out, however, that it is possible to come up with global set-up functionalities that lend to reasonable implementation and are still sufficient for UC-realizing $\mathcal{F}_{\text{COM}}$. We briefly sketch three such functionalities.

The first functionality is reminiscent of the key set-up functionality from Section 5, $\mathcal{F}_{\text{KS}}$, with the exception that here the registration is done once per party throughout the lifetime of the system, and the public key can be used in all instances of all the protocols that the party might run. In particular, public keys are directly accessible by the environment, even in the ideal process. It turns out that one of the [BCNP04] protocols for UC-realizing $\mathcal{F}_{\text{COM}}$ given $\mathcal{F}_{\text{KS}}$ continues to work even when $\mathcal{F}_{\text{KS}}$ is replaced by the global variant, $\mathcal{F}_{\text{GKS}}$, as long as party corruptions are *non-adaptive*. However, when party corruptions can be adaptive, and the adversary can observe the past internal data of corrupted parties, this protocol becomes insecure. To address this concern, a more sophisticated protocol is constructed in [CDPW07].

A second functionality, called $\mathcal{F}_{\text{ACRS}}$ for "augmented CRS (ACRS)", is reminiscent of the CRS set-up, but is somewhat augmented so as to circumvent the impossibility result for plain CRS. That is, as in the case of $\mathcal{F}_{\text{GCRS}}$, all parties and the environment have access to a short reference string that is taken from a pre-determined distribution. In addition, the ACRS set-up allows corrupted parties to obtain "personalized" secret keys that are derived from the reference string, their public identities, and some "global secret" that's related to the public string and remains unknown. It is stressed that in the formal model *only corrupted parties* may obtain their secret keys. This effect of this modeling is that protocol may not include instructions that require knowledge of the secret keys, and yet corrupted parties are assumed to have access to their secret keys. A protocol for UC-realizing $\mathcal{F}_{\text{COM}}$ (in fact, $\mathcal{F}_{\text{MCOM}}$) given $\mathcal{F}_{\text{ACRS}}$ is constructed in [CDPW07]. The main additional technique on top of the protocol using $\mathcal{F}_{\text{GKS}}$ is a new *identity-based trapdoor commitment (IBTC)* protocol. (IBTC protocols in the Random Oracle model appear in [ZSS03, AM04]).

"Real world implementations" of $\mathcal{F}_{\text{GKS}}$ and $\mathcal{F}_{\text{ACRS}}$ can involve a trusted entity (say, a "post office") that only publicizes the public value. The trusted entity will also agree to provide the secret keys to the corresponding parties upon request, with the understanding that once a party gets hold of its key then it alone is responsible to safeguard it and use it appropriately (much as in the case of standard PKI). In light of the impossibility of a completely non-interactive set-up (CRS), this seems to be a minimal "interactiveness" requirement from the trusted entity.

Another global set-up assumption, formulated in Hofheinz et al. [HMU06], provides each party p with a public "verification key" V_p (chosen by the functionality). Next, the functionality provides p with unforgeable signatures on messages of p's choice, where the signatures can be publicly verified using V_p. It is stressed that the signing keys are not made available to the parties, even to corrupted ones. A protocol for realizing $\mathcal{F}_{\mathrm{COM}}$ given access to this functionality, for non-adaptive corruptions, is given in [HMU06]. This functionality is much more interactive than $\mathcal{F}_{\mathrm{ACRS}}$ or $\mathcal{F}_{\mathrm{GKS}}$. Still, as suggested in [HMU06], in reality it can be implemented by a tamper-proof signing device such as a smart-card.

8   A Timing Assumption

Last but not least, we consider an alternative approach for making assumptions on the the system in order to guarantee composable security. Specifically, rather than assuming that parties have access to some trusted information, some minimal assumptions are made regarding the synchrony of the system at some point in its execution. More precisely, it is assumed that all messages sent are eventually delivered unmodified within some time bound, and in addition there is a bound on the amount of relative "drift" between local clocks of parties in the system. In [LPT04] it is shown how to UC-realize $\mathcal{F}_{\mathrm{CRS}}$ and $\mathcal{F}_{\mathrm{COM}}$ in such a setting.

The fact that a timing assumption suffices for UC-realizing, say, $\mathcal{F}_{\mathrm{CRS}}$, is not surprising in of itself: Assume for instance that the network is completely synchronous, and furthermore no party (not even corrupted ones) receives messages sent in round i before the last chance to send out its messages for round i. Then a simple, unconditionally secure two-party protocol for UC-realizing $\mathcal{F}_{\mathrm{CRS}}$ would be to simply have each of the two parties send a random string of the appropriate length at a certain round, and then let the reference string be the bitwise xor of the two strings. In [LPT04] it is shown, via a sophisticated protocol and under standard hardness assumptions, how to obtain a similar effect while making (much) weaker synchronization assumptions on the system.

It is interesting to note that the timing assumptions have to hold only during the execution of the protocol for UC-realizing $\mathcal{F}_{\mathrm{CRS}}$. Once the reference string is fixed, no timing assumptions are needed. Also, since there is no trusted piece of information to be passed around, this approach bypasses the "transferability" issues of the other set-up assumptions and provides complete deniability.

9   Realizing Authenticated Communication

The treatment of Sections 3 through 8 concentrates on the case of ideally authenticated networks, where messages are not modified en route and arrive with an authentic sender identity. More precisely, the parties are assumed to have access to multiple copies of an ideal functionality, $\mathcal{F}_{\mathrm{AUTH}}$, that, roughly, takes input (sid, B, m) from party A, and provides output (sid, A, m) to B, where sid is a session identifier.

It is interesting to note that the above ideal authentication guarantee implicitly carries with it a non-transferability guarantee: The above ideally authenticated communication setting does not provide the recipient of a message sent by party A with any means to convince a third party that a message was indeed sent by A. $\mathcal{F}_{\mathrm{AUTH}}$ provides a similar guarantee. This means that communication via $\mathcal{F}_{\mathrm{AUTH}}$ is in effect "non-transferable", or in other words "deniable".

As observed in [C04], it is impossible to UC-realize $\mathcal{F}_{\text{AUTH}}$ in the "bare" model with no set-up assumptions. Still, $\mathcal{F}_{\text{AUTH}}$ can be UC-realized, via standard authentication mechanisms, when given access to an ideal functionality that allows parties to register public values associated with their identities [C04]. It is stressed that this functionality, $\mathcal{F}_{\text{REG}}$, does not verify knowledge of any secret information associated with the registered value; it merely provides a registration (or, "bulletin-board") service.

However, akin to the formulation of the traditional CRS model, the formulation of $\mathcal{F}_{\text{REG}}$ in [C04] is that of a "local" set-up that is available only to the parties that run the specific protocol instance. Implementing $\mathcal{F}_{\text{REG}}$ is thus susceptible to the same limitations that apply to implementing $\mathcal{F}_{\text{CRS}}$ (see Section 7): Essentially, a new instance of the registration service is needed for each new protocol instance. In particular, similarly to the case of $\mathcal{F}_{\text{CRS}}$, when the [C04] protocol for UC-realizing $\mathcal{F}_{\text{AUTH}}$ uses a "global" registration service that's available to arbitrary protocols, authentication becomes "transferable". (In fact, a publicly verifiable signature by the sender on the transmitted information becomes available).

Modeling authenticated communication in the presence of global set-up is an interesting challenge. One direction is to model the security guarantees provided by standard authentication mechanisms (such as the simple signature-based mechanism studied in [C04]) in the presence of global set-up. These guarantees are naturally described by means of an ideal authentication functionality that allows for transferability *even in ideal process*. Another direction is to study protocols that UC-realize the original, non-transferable version of $\mathcal{F}_{\text{AUTH}}$ even when given only globally available set-up. This is an interesting venue for current and future research.

10   Conclusion and Open Problems

We have exemplified the need for trusted set-up models in order to obtain composable security, and have studied a variety of set-up models. These models have very different characteristics, both from the point of view of the guarantees provided to protocols designed in these models, and from the point of view of the requirements from practical implementations of the models.

While some progress has been made in the past few years towards understanding how to formulate models that allow bypassing the strong impossibility results regarding composable security, how to develop protocols in these models, and how to implement such models in practice, much remains to be understood. Some specific challenges and questions include:

1. Finding protocols that use current set-up models more efficiently. Finding easier and more secure ways to implement existing set-up models in practice. Finding new set-up models that allow for more efficient protocols and/or easier implementations.
2. Finding a characterization of the set-up models that allow for UC-realizing, say, $\mathcal{F}_{\text{COM}}$ (or any other ideal functionality that allows for UC-realizing general ideal functionalities). We've seen that set-up functionalities can have

very different flavors and characteristics. Are there some salient properties that are common to all and are necessary and/or sufficient for UC-realizing $\mathcal{F}_{\text{COM}}$?

3. More specifically, are there *global* set-up models that allow for adversarial control over the set-up information akin to $\mathcal{F}_{\text{SUN}}$, and still allow for UC-realizing $\mathcal{F}_{\text{COM}}$? Are there set-up models that allow for adversarial control over the set-up information, and at the same time allow for UC-realizing authenticated communication?

4. Are there general relationships between set-up models that allow for UC-realizing authenticated communication and set-up models that allow for UC-realizing $\mathcal{F}_{\text{COM}}$?

5. More generally, how can we better model the information shared between protocol instances in arbitrary systems? Is global set-up information the only information that can be shared, or are there other ways to share state and information? How to capture these? An indication that in some situations protocols indeliberately (but inevitably) share more information than just the set-up is given in [YYZ07B].

References

[AM04]   Ateniese, G., de Medeiros, B.: Identity-based Chameleon Hash and Applications. In: Proc. of Financial Cryptography (2004), available at http://eprint.iacr.org/2003/167/

[B01]   Barak, B.: How to go Beyond the Black-Box Simulation Barrier. In: 42nd FOCS, pp. 106–115 (2001)

[BCNP04]   Barak, B., Canetti, R., Nielsen, J.B., Pass, R.: Universally Composable Protocols with Relaxed Set-Up Assumptions. In: 45th FOCS, pp. 186–195 (2004)

[BL04]   Barak, B., Lindell, Y.: Strict polynomial-time in simulation and extraction. SIAM J. Comput 33(4), 738–818 (2004)

[BS05]   Barak, B., Sahai, A.: How To Play Almost Any Mental Game Over the Net - Concurrent Composition via Super-Polynomial Simulation. In: 46th FOCS (2005)

[B91]   Beaver, D.: Secure Multi-party Protocols and Zero-Knowledge Proof Systems Tolerating a Faulty Minority. J. Cryptology 4, 75–122 (1991)

[BCG93]   Ben-Or, M., Canetti, R., Goldreich, O.: Asynchronous Secure Computation. In: 25th Symposium on Theory of Computing (STOC), 1993, pp. 52–61. Longer version appears in TR #755, CS dept., Technion (1992)

[BGW88]   Ben-Or, M., Goldwasser, S., Wigderson, A.: Completeness Theorems for Non-Cryptographic Fault-Tolerant Distributed Computation. In: STOC. 20th Symposium on Theory of Computing, pp. 1–10. ACM, New York (1988)

[BKR94]   Ben-Or, M., Kelmer, B., Rabin, T.: Asynchronous Secure Computations with Optimal Resilience. In: 13th PODC, pp. 183–192 (1994)

[BFM88]   Blum, M., Feldman, P., Micali, S.: Non-interactive zero-knowledge and its applications. In: STOC 1988, pp. 103–112 (1988)

[C00]   Canetti, R.: Security and composition of multi-party cryptographic protocols. J. Cryptology 13(1) (2000)

[C01]   Canetti, R.: Universally composable security: A new paradigm for crypto-
           graphic protocols. Extended abstract in 42nd FOCS, 2001. A revised ver-
           sion is available at IACR Eprint Archive, eprint.iacr.org/2000/067/ and at
           the ECCC archive (2005),
           http://eccc.uni-trier.de/eccc-reports/2001/TR01-016/

[C04]   Canetti, R.: Universally Composable Signature, Certification, and Au-
           thentication. In: 17th Computer Security Foundations Workshop (CSFW),
           Long version at eprint.iacr.org/2003/239 (2004)

[CAN06]   Canetti, R.: Security and composition of cryptographic protocols: A tuto-
           rial. SIGACT News, vol. 37(3 & 4), Available also at the Cryptology ePrint
           Archive, Report 2006/465 (2006)

[CDPW07]   Canetti, R., Dodis, Y., Pass, R., Walfish, S.: Universally Composable Se-
           curity with Pre-Existing Setup. In: 4th theory of Cryptology Conference
           (TCC) (2007)

[CFGN96]   Canetti, R., Feige, U., Goldreich, O., Naor, M.: Adaptively Secure Compu-
           tation. In: STOC. 28th Symposium on Theory of Computing, ACM, New
           York (1996) (Fuller version in MIT-LCS-TR 682, 1996)

[CF01]   Canetti, R., Fischlin, M.: Universally Composable Commitments. In: Kil-
           ian, J. (ed.) CRYPTO 2001. LNCS, vol. 2139, Springer, Heidelberg (2001)

[CKL03]   Canetti, R., Kushilevitz, E., Lindell, Y.: On the Limitations of Univer-
           sally Composable Two-Party Computation without Set-up Assumptions.
           In: Biham, E. (ed.) Advances in Cryptology – EUROCRPYT 2003. LNCS,
           vol. 2656, pp. 68–86. Springer, Heidelberg (2003)

[CLOS02]   Canetti, R., Lindell, Y., Ostrovsky, R., Sahai, A.: Universally composable
           two-party and multi-party secure computation. In: 34th STOC, pp. 494–
           503 (2002)

[CPS07]   Canetti, R., Pass, R., shelat, A.: Cryptography from sunspots: How to use
           an imperfect reference string. In: STOC. 39th Symposium on Theory of
           Computing, ACM, New York (2007)

[CR03]   Canetti, R., Rabin, T.: Universal Composition with Joint State. In: Boneh,
           D. (ed.) CRYPTO 2003. LNCS, vol. 2729, Springer, Heidelberg (2003)

[DDMRS06] Datta, A., Derek, A., Mitchell, J.C., Ramanathan, A., Scedrov, A.: Games
           and the Impossibility of Realizable Ideal Functionality. In: 3rd theory of
           Cryptology Conference (TCC) (2006)

[DOPS04]   Dodis, Y., Ong, S., Prabhakaran, M., Sahai, A.: On the (im)possibility
           of cryptography with imperfect randomness. In: FOCS 2004, pp. 196–205
           (2004)

[DDN00]   Dolev, D., Dwork, C., Naor, M.: Non-malleable cryptography. SIAM. J.
           Computing. vol. 30(2), pp. 391-437 (2000). Preliminary version in 23rd
           Symposium on Theory of Computing (STOC) (1991)

[DNS98]   Dwork, C., Naor, M., Sahai, A.: Concurrent Zero-Knowledge. In: 30th
           STOC, pp. 409–418 (1998)

[FS89]   Feige, U., Shamir, A.: Zero knowledge proofs of knowledge in two rounds.
           In: Brassard, G. (ed.) CRYPTO 1989. LNCS, vol. 435, pp. 526–544.
           Springer, Heidelberg (1990)

[F88]   Forges, F.: Can sunspots replace a mediator? J. of Math. Ec. 17(4), 347–368
           (1988)

[GRR98]   Gennaro, R., Rabin, M., Rabin, T.: Simplified VSS and Fast-track Mul-
           tiparty Computations with Applications to Threshold Cryptography. In:
           17th PODC, pp. 101–112 (1998)

112   R. Canetti

[GK89]   Goldreich, O., Krawczyk, H.: On the Composition of Zero-Knowledge Proof Systems. SIAM. J. Computing 25(1) (1996)

[GMW87]   Goldreich, O., Micali, S., Wigderson, A.: How to Play any Mental Game. In: 19th Symposium on Theory of Computing (STOC), pp. 218–229 (1987)

[GL90]   Goldwasser, S., Levin, L.: Fair Computation of General Functions in Presence of Immoral Majority. In: Menezes, A.J., Vanstone, S.A. (eds.) CRYPTO 1990. LNCS, vol. 537, Springer, Heidelberg (1991)

[HMU06]   Hofheinz, D., Muller-Quade, J., Unruh, D.: Universally Composable Zero-Knowledge Arguments and Commitments from Signature Cards. Tatra Mountains Mathematical Publications (2005)

[KSW97]   Kelsey, J., Schneier, B., Wagner, D.: Protocol Interactions and the Chosen Protocol Attack. In: Security Protocols Workshop, pp. 91–104 (1997)

[KLR06]   Kushilevitz, E., Lindell, Y., Rabin, T.: Information-Theoretically Secure Protocols and Security Under Composition. In: 38th STOC, pp. 109–118 (2006)

[L03]   Lindell, Y.: General Composition and Universal Composability in Secure Multi-Party Computation. In: 43rd FOCS, pp. 394–403 (2003)

[L04]   Lindell, Y.: Lower Bounds for Concurrent Self Composition. In: 1st Theory of Cryptology Conference (TCC), pp. 203–222 (2004)

[LPT04]   Lindell, Y., Prabhakaran, M., Tauman, Y.: Concurrent General Composition of Secure Protocols in the Timing Model. Manuscript (2004)

[MMY06]   Malkin, T., Moriarty, R., Yakovenko, N.: Generalized Environmental Security from Number Theoretic Assumptions. In: 3rd Theory of Cryptology Conference (TCC), pp. 343–359 (2006)

[MR91]   Micali, S., Rogaway, P.: Secure Computation. In: Feigenbaum, J. (ed.) CRYPTO 1991. LNCS, vol. 576, Springer, Heidelberg (1992)

[P03]   Pass, R.: On Deniabililty in the Common Reference String and Random Oracle Model. In: Boneh, D. (ed.) CRYPTO 2003. LNCS, vol. 2729, pp. 216–337. Springer, Heidelberg (2003)

[PW00]   Pfitzmann, B., Waidner, M.: Composition and integrity preservation of secure reactive systems. In: 7th ACM Conf. on Computer and Communication Security (CCS), pp. 245–254 (2000)

[PW01]   Pfitzmann, B., Waidner, M.: A model for asynchronous reactive systems and its application to secure message transmission. IEEE Symposium on Security and Privacy, May 2001, IBM Research, Zurich (December 2000), Preliminary version in and IBM Research Report RZ 3304 (#93350) http://eprint.iacr.org/2000/066

[PS04]   Prabhakaran, M., Sahai, A.: New notions of security: achieving universal composability without trusted setup. In: 36th STOC, pp. 242–251 (2004)

[RB89]   Rabin, T., Ben-Or, M.: Verifiable Secret Sharing and Multi-party Protocols with Honest Majority. In: 21st Symposium on Theory of Computing (STOC), pp. 73–85 (1989)

[TV00]   Trevisan, L., Vadhan, S.: Extracting randomness from samplable distributions. In: FOCS 2000, pp. 32–42 (2000)

[YYZ07A]   Yao, A., Yao, F.F., Zhao, Y.: A Note on Universal Composable Zero Knowledge in Common Reference String Model. In: TAMC 2007, pp. 462–473 (2007)

[YYZ07B]   Yao, A., Yao, F.F., Zhao, Y.: A Note on the Feasibility of Generalized Universal Composability. In: TAMC 2007, pp. 474–485 (2007)

[ZSS03]   Zhang, F., Safavi-Naini, R., Susilo, W.: ID-Based Chameleon Hashes from Bilinear Pairings. available at http://eprint.iacr.org/2003/208/

A Simple Variant of the Merkle-Damgård Scheme with a Permutation

Shoichi Hirose[1], Je Hong Park[2], and Aaram Yun[2]

[1] Graduate School of Engineering, The University of Fukui
hirose@fuee.fukui-u.ac.jp
[2] ETRI Network & Communication Security Division
jhpark@etri.re.kr, aaramyun@gmail.com

Abstract. We propose a new composition scheme for hash functions. It is a variant of the Merkle-Damgård construction with a permutation applied right before the processing of the last message block. We analyze the security of this scheme using the indifferentiability formalism, which was first adopted by Coron et al. to the analysis of hash functions. And we study the security of simple MAC constructions out of this scheme. Finally, we also discuss the random oracle indifferentiability of this scheme with a double-block-length compression function or the Davies-Meyer compression function composed of a block cipher.

1 Introduction

Background. Merkle-Damgård [19,12] is an iterative hash function construction. Given a fixed-input-length (FIL) compression function, it combines the output of the compression function in a serial fashion to produce a hash function that can process strings of arbitrary length.[1] While it is a clean design with proven collision resistance, it suffers the extension property; one can compute $H(M_1 \| M_2)$ from $H(M_1)$ even without the knowledge of M_1.

Suppose that we try to use a Merkle-Damgård (MD) hash function for message authentication. There are many proposals for hash-based MACs, but currently the most popular hash-based MAC is definitely HMAC [3,2]. It has a simple structure, and also it has rigorous security proofs. But, given a hash function $H(\cdot)$, one of the best ways to make a MAC out of H is the prefix construction [22]:

$$M_K(x) \stackrel{\text{def}}{=} H(K \| x).$$

Indeed, the efficiency of the above construction would be almost twice than that of the HMAC, for short messages, and we know that if $H(\cdot)$ is a random oracle, rather than a concrete hash algorithm, then the construction gives a secure MAC. Unfortunately, due to the extension property, the prefix construction is not secure when the underlying hash function is an MD hash function; given a

---

[1] Or up to some large number (2^{64} in case of SHA-1, for example) depending on the padding and other specific details.

K. Kurosawa (Ed.): ASIACRYPT 2007, LNCS 4833, pp. 113–129, 2007.

message x and its MAC $M_K(x) = H(K\|x)$, the attacker can easily forge another message x', which has x as its prefix, and compute the MAC $M_K(x')$.

The goal of HMAC was to design an efficient MAC with security proofs, out of already widely deployed MD hash functions. Therefore the designers of HMAC had to 'fix' the extension property of the underlying MD hash function, at the upper MAC construction level.

But then we may consider another way, namely, to start freshly with a hash function design without such structural flaws like the extension property. Then perhaps we may use much simpler hash-based MACs such as the prefix construction $H(K\|M)$. Indeed, after Wang's attacks on many popular hash functions, there are renewed interests in the design of hash functions. So this would be a good opportunity to consider an alternative to the MD scheme.

In CRYPTO 2005, Coron et al. introduced new methodology for assessing generic, structural properties of hash function constructions [11]. They applied the notion of indifferentiability, which was first introduced by Maurer et al. [16], to the analysis of hash functions. Coron et al. analyzed the structural property of hash function constructions by first swapping the underlying compression function with a FIL random oracle, then comparing the resulting hash function with a true random oracle. If no efficient distinguisher can tell the two objects apart, then the construction is considered secure, i.e., it has no structural flaws. The notion of indifferentiability is an appropriate framework to express these ideas rigorously. In fact, Coron et al. showed that the MD scheme is *not* indifferentiable from a random oracle, and suggested a few modifications for the MD scheme so that all of these are indifferentiable from a random oracle.

Hence, we now have a rigorous methodology for assessing the structural flaws of a hash function, such as the extension property of MD scheme, which was the main obstacle for adopting the simple constructions like the prefix construction instead of HMAC. Now all we need is an actual design for hash function composition scheme which is efficient and structurally sound (in the sense of random oracle indifferentiability), and which admits a direct and efficient usage as a MAC. Then in the future hash function design, we may adopt such a construction as an alternative to the MD scheme.

Our Contribution. We propose a simple and efficient hash composition scheme. We call it Merkle-Damgård with a permutation (MDP). It is almost identical to the plain Merkle-Damgård scheme, but just before the last message block is processed, a permutation π is applied: for a message $M = M_1 M_2 \cdots M_k$,

$$H(M) = F(\pi(F(\cdots F(F(IV, M_1), M_2) \cdots, M_{k-1})), M_k).$$

In this paper, we describe the MDP composition scheme, and prove that it satisfies many desirable security properties:

- It is collision resistant if the underlying compression function is.
- It is indifferentiable from a random oracle when a FIL random oracle is used as the compression function.

- It is also a PRF when keyed via the IV if the compression function is a PRF, secure against a (very mild) related-key attack when keyed via the chaining variable. In addition, if the compression function is also a PRF when keyed via the input message block, then MDP yields a PRF when key is prepended to the message: $M \mapsto H(K\|M)$ for a secret key K.
- It is unforgeable if the underlying compression function is an unforgeable FIL MAC with a dedicated key input.

Despite the miniscule modification MDP makes to the original MD scheme, we see that it has many benefits. MDP loses essentially none of the efficiency of the MD scheme. As categorized above, MDP preserves collision resistance, random oracle and unforgeability. Furthermore it 'almost' preserves PRF property, with a weak related-key assumption. So not only it gives a strong hash function, as a PRF it also gives a secure MAC mechanism which is twice as fast as HMAC for short messages.

We also study the random oracle indifferentiability of MDP when the underlying compression function has some structure; we consider MDP with two specific type of compression functions. The one is a double-block-length (DBL) compression function of the form $F(s\|x) = f(s\|x)\|f(p(s)\|x)$, where f is a smaller compression function and p is a permutation. The other is the Davies-Meyer compression function. We show that MDP emulates a VIL random oracle if

- f is a random oracle and π and p are chosen appropriately in the DBL compression function F; or
- F is the Davies-Meyer compression function in the ideal cipher model.

Related Works. A hash function composition scheme very similar to MDP was suggested before; in a public comment to a FIPS 180-2 draft, Kelsey [14] proposed a simple enhancement to SHA-2 hash functions, which was originally suggested by Ferguson. Their scheme is a special case of MDP, when the permutation π is equal to $\pi(x) = x \oplus C$, where C is a fixed, non-zero offset. Their motivation was to eliminate the extension property of MD hash functions with least modification. But, as far as the authors know, the security of this proposal was never rigorously proven before.

While proposing indifferentiability from a random oracle as an important security goal for a hash function, Coron et al. also proposed four constructions which satisfy indifferentiability from a random oracle [11], thereby proving that such schemes exist. Also, Bellare and Ristenpart proposed the EMD construction [6]. Probably it is the first paper that succeeded in finding a serious practical alternative to the MD scheme which meets the raised security goals (like, indifferentiability to a random oracle, among others). Similar to MDP, EMD is also a variant of the MD scheme. Also, EMD achieves essentially the same goals as MDP, but there are a few differences:

- The structure of MDP is simpler than that of EMD; this is reflected in the fact that MDP is slightly more efficient than EMD, especially for short messages.

- When used as a MAC by key-via-IV strategy, MDP needs slightly stronger assumption than in the case of EMD; assuming that the compression function is secure as PRF under a very weak related-key attack, we prove that the keyed MDP is secure as a PRF. Therefore, at least for PRFness, MDP is *not* a 'multi-property-preserving' transform like EMD.
- On the other hand, MDP needs only one key in the above situation, while EMD needs two separate keys, while achieving the security of only one key due to the divide-and-conquer attack. One may consider a one-key version of EMD by employing some key derivation function similar to the case of HMAC, but then one would need additional assumption on the compression function, namely PRF-security under some related-key attacks, which is essentially the same type of assumption needed for MDP.
- Given an MDP hash function H, one can use H as a black-box to obtain a secure MAC, by prefix construction $H(K\|M)$. This seems to be difficult in the case of EMD.

Chang et al. [9] further discussed the indifferentiability from the random oracle for the MD scheme with prefix-free encoding. They considered compression functions consisting of a block cipher [21] and DBL compression functions of the same form we considered. Nandi [20] introduced this formalization of a class of DBL compression functions and discussed the collision-resistance of hash functions composed of them.

In studying MAC properties of MDP, we follow two directions. First, we show that MDP gives a very efficient MAC by showing its pseudorandomness under the assumption that the compression function is a PRF-security against a mild form of related-key attacks. For this, we use a restricted version of the notion of PRF-security against related-key attacks formalized and studied by Bellare and Kohno [5]. Essentially, the proof can be considered as a related-key version of the proof for prefix-free PRF security of the cascade construction given in [4].

We are also interested in seeing whether security of MDP as MAC can be proved under weaker assumptions, similar to the security of HMAC under a weaker-than-PRF assumption on the compression function [2]. After An and Bellare [1] initiated such investigations, Maurer and Sjödin [17] provided several transforms as well as a general security proof technique. As stated in [6], these works consider the setting where compression functions and hash functions are families indexed by a dedicated key, and only focus on MAC preservation when the underlying compression function is a MAC itself, namely, that it is an unforgeable FIL MAC.

Recently, Bellare and Ristenpart [7] further considered several hash function constructions in the dedicated-key setting, and provided a multi-property-preservation oriented treatment of them.

Organization of the Paper. In Section 2, we provide basic definitions of PRFs, RKA-secure PRFs, indifferentiability, and unforgeability. We also fix notational conventions in this section. In Section 3, we formally define the MDP construction. In Section 4, we analyze the security of MDP. Section 4 consists of three parts; first, we prove that MDP is indifferentiable from a random oracle, and then prove that MDP gives a secure PRF under necessary assumptions. And we prove that MDP yields a secure MAC under a weaker-than-PRF assumption. In Section 5, we focus on the indifferentiability of MDP based on two specific types of compression function: one is a DBL compression function and the other is the Davies-Meyer compression function composed of a block cipher. Detailed proofs for several lemmas and theorems in Section 4 are described in the full version of this paper [13].

2   Definitions

Pseudorandom Functions. Let $F : \mathcal{K} \times \mathcal{D} \to \mathcal{R}$ be a function family from $\mathcal{D}$ to $\mathcal{R}$ indexed by keys $K \in \mathcal{K}$. Usually we'll use $F_K(x)$ as shorthand for $F(K, x)$. Let $\mathsf{Maps}(\mathcal{D}, \mathcal{R})$ denote the set of all functions $f : \mathcal{D} \to \mathcal{R}$. Given an adversary $A(g)$ with access to an oracle $g(\cdot)$, we define its PRF-advantage over F as

$$\mathrm{Adv}_F^{\mathrm{prf}}(A) = \Pr\left[A(F_K) \Rightarrow 1 \mid K \xleftarrow{\$} \mathcal{K}\right] - \Pr\left[A(\rho) \Rightarrow 1 \mid \rho \xleftarrow{\$} \mathsf{Maps}(\mathcal{D}, \mathcal{R})\right]$$

Informally, we say that F is a PRF when no efficient adversary A can have any significant PRF-advantage over F.

RKA-Secure PRFs. Related-key attacks were considered in cryptanalysis of block ciphers, and many modern block ciphers are designed against such attacks. Bellare and Kohno [5] first gave a formal definition to related-key attacks and provided a theoretical treatment. They extended the formal definition of PRFs to PRFs secure against related-key attacks (RKA-secure PRFs).

According to the definition given by Bellare and Kohno, they consider a set Φ of related-key-deriving (RKD) functions $\phi : \mathcal{K} \to \mathcal{K}$. As in the case of the plain PRFs, an adversary cannot access the given secret key K directly, but she can query the PRF with respect to other keys $\phi(K)$ by selecting a RKD function ϕ from Φ. The set Φ is a parameter of the definition, and it formalizes the varying capabilities of related-key adversaries on different situations.

In this paper, we need only a very weak adversary in terms of related-key attacks: the RKD function set Φ consists of only two functions: $\Phi = \{id, \pi\}$, where $id : \mathcal{K} \to \mathcal{K}$ is the identity function, and $\pi : \mathcal{K} \to \mathcal{K}$ is a permutation. We'll refer this type of related-key attacks as the π-related-key attacks and formalize in the following way. Given an adversary $A(g, g')$ with access to a pair of oracles $g(\cdot)$ and $g'(\cdot)$, we define its PRF-advantage over F with respect to π-related-key attacks as

$$\mathrm{Adv}_{\pi,F}^{\mathrm{prf\text{-}rka}}(A) =$$
$$\Pr\left[A(F_K, F_{\pi(K)}) \Rightarrow 1 \mid K \xleftarrow{\$} \mathcal{K}\right] - \Pr\left[A(\rho, \rho') \Rightarrow 1 \mid \rho, \rho' \xleftarrow{\$} \mathsf{Maps}(\mathcal{D}, \mathcal{R})\right].$$

Note that this formalism is equivalent to that of Bellare and Kohno, when $\Phi = \{id, \pi\}$ is used.

Again informally, we say that F is a π-RKA-secure PRF when no efficient adversary A can have any significant advantage over F. Since π-related-key attack is the only kind of related-key attacks that we consider in this paper, sometimes we'll abuse the terminology and call F simply as a RKA-secure PRF.

Indifferentiability. We use the indifferentiability framework [16,11] to assess the security of the MDP. Consider a cryptosystem $C = C(\mathcal{F})$ with oracle access to an ideal primitive $\mathcal{F}$. Also consider an ideal primitive $\mathcal{H}$ and a simulator $S = S(\mathcal{H})$ which has oracle access to $\mathcal{H}$. C is supposed to be a 'construction' involving $\mathcal{F}$. For example, $\mathcal{F}$ could be a FIL random oracle, and C then could be the MD hash function using $\mathcal{F}$ as the compression function. The goal of the simulator $S(\mathcal{H})$ is to mimic $\mathcal{F}$ in order to convince an adversary that $\mathcal{H}$ is C. Let A be an adversary with access to two oracles. We define the differentiability advantage of A against C with respect to S as:

$$\mathrm{Adv}_{C,S}^{\mathrm{diff}}(A) = \Pr\left[A(C(\mathcal{F}),\mathcal{F}) \Rightarrow 1\right] - \Pr\left[A(\mathcal{H},S(\mathcal{H})) \Rightarrow 1\right].$$

Informally, we say that $C(\mathcal{F})$ is indifferentiable from $\mathcal{H}$ if there exists a simulator $S(\mathcal{H})$ so that no efficient adversary A can have any significant differentiability advantage against C with respect to S.

Unforgeability. A MAC is a family of functions $F : \mathcal{K} \times \mathcal{M} \rightarrow \mathcal{C}$. The security of a MAC is measured via its resistance to existential forgery under an adaptive chosen-message attack. The MAC-advantage of a forger A over F is

$$\mathrm{Adv}_F^{\mathrm{mac}}(A) = \Pr\left[A(F_K, \mathrm{Vf}_{F_K}) \text{ forges} \mid K \xleftarrow{\$} \mathcal{K}\right].$$

A forger A queries to the oracle $F_K(\cdot)$ for adaptively chosen messages and learns the corresponding tag values. It then returns a forgery (M,τ). The forger A is considered successful if it makes a verification query (M,τ) to the oracle $\mathrm{Vf}_{F_K}(\cdot,\cdot)$, and confirms that $F_K(M) = \tau$ but M was not queried to $F_K(\cdot)$. We refer to a forger A of this kind as a (t,q,l,ϵ)-forger if $\mathrm{Adv}_F^{\mathrm{mac}}(A) \geq \epsilon$, where t, q and l are upper bounds on the running time, the number of messages, and the maximal length (in bits) of each oracle query including the forgery message M, respectively. Informally, a MAC is considered secure against existential forgery under an adaptive chosen-message attack, if there is no (t,q,l,ϵ)-forger, even for very high values of t, q and l, and very small values of ϵ.

Notation. Let b be the size of the message blocks, and c the size of the chaining variables. As usually is in popular hash functions, we assume that $c \leq b$. Then the compression function $F(s,x)$ has the following form:

$$F : \{0,1\}^c \times \{0,1\}^b \rightarrow \{0,1\}^c.$$

Let $\mathcal{C} = \{0,1\}^c$ and $\mathcal{B} = \{0,1\}^b$ to abbreviate the above as $F : \mathcal{C} \times \mathcal{B} \rightarrow \mathcal{C}$.

We denote by $M_1\|M_2$ the concatenation of bitstrings M_1 and M_2. We will often abbreviate $M_1\|M_2\|\cdots\|M_k$ simply as $M_1 M_2 \cdots M_k$. Let $\mathcal{B}^i$ be the set of all messages of form $M_1 M_2 \cdots M_i$, where $M_j \in \mathcal{B}$ for all $j = 1, \ldots, i$. Clearly, $\mathcal{B}^0 = \{\epsilon\}$, where ϵ means the null bitstring, the bitstring of length 0. Let's define $\mathcal{B}^* = \cup_{i=0}^{\infty}\mathcal{B}^i$, $\mathcal{B}^+ = \cup_{i=1}^{\infty}\mathcal{B}^i$, and $\mathcal{B}^{\leq k} = \cup_{i=1}^{k}\mathcal{B}^i$.

We will process messages block by block. The notation $M_1 M_2 \cdots M_k \leftarrow$ parse(M) will mean that $M = M_1\|M_2\|\cdots\|M_k$ and $|M_i| = b$ for all $i = 1, \ldots, k - 1$, and $|M_k| \leq b$. We denote by $s \xleftarrow{\$} S$ the operation of selecting a random element from S (the uniform probability distribution over S is assumed).

We sometimes use the O-notation. This is not about asymptotics, but we use this notation to hide unimportant small constants which are dependent on specific machine formalisms, and whose values can be determined from the proof.

3   The MDP Construction

Given $F : \mathcal{C} \times \mathcal{B} \to \mathcal{C}$, we define $F^* : \mathcal{C} \times \mathcal{B}^* \to \mathcal{C}$ as follows:

$$F^*(s, M) \stackrel{\text{def}}{=} \begin{cases} s & \text{if } k = 0, \text{ i.e., } M = \epsilon, \\ F(F^*(s, M_1 M_2 \cdots M_{k-1}), M_k) & \text{otherwise,} \end{cases}$$

for $M = M_1 M_2 \cdots M_k$ ($M_i \in \mathcal{B}$ for all i). This is the plain Merkle-Damgård iteration of F. Now we define $F_\pi^\circ : \mathcal{C} \times \mathcal{B}^+ \to \mathcal{C}$ as follows:

$$F_\pi^\circ(s, M_1 M_2 \cdots M_k) \stackrel{\text{def}}{=} F(\pi(F^*(s, M_1 \cdots M_{k-1})), M_k).$$

where π is a permutation applied right before the last iteration. π is a fixed permutation given as a parameter of the definition. We require both π and π^{-1} to be efficiently computable. Often we omit π from the notation F_π° and simply write F°.

The domain of F° is $\mathcal{B}^+ = \cup_{i=1}^{\infty}\mathcal{B}^i = \cup_{i=1}^{\infty}\{0,1\}^{bi}$. In order to let MDP process messages of arbitrary lengths (up to 2^l, for some large number l satisfying $0 < l \leq b$), we have to use a padding function pad $: \cup_{i=0}^{2^l}\{0,1\}^i \to \mathcal{B}^+$ with the following property: the last block of pad(M) encodes the l-bit representation of the length $|M|$ of M. For example, the SHA-1's padding rule could be used.

Finally, given a compression function $F : \mathcal{C} \times \mathcal{B} \to \mathcal{C}$, a padding function pad, a permutation π, and a fixed IV $IV \in \mathcal{C}$, we formally define the MDP (Merkle-Damgård with a Permutation) hash function as

$$\text{MDP}(M) \stackrel{\text{def}}{=} F_\pi^\circ(IV, \text{pad}(M)).$$

When we want to emphasize the dependency of MDP(M) to F and π, we sometimes use the notation MDP$[F, \pi](M)$.

Figure 1 illustrates the structure of MDP. One can consider the MDP construction as a minor variant of the MD scheme with the MD strengthening. Therefore the efficiency of the MDP is exactly the same as the Strengthened MD (SMD).

More precisely, let's write the number of compression function invocations needed to compute the hash value of an ℓ-bit string as $N(\ell)$. Suppose that we

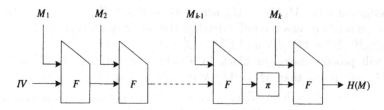

Fig. 1. The structure of MDP

use the padding function similar to the padding function of SHA-1: given a message M of length ℓ, append the bit '1' to the end of the message, followed by k zero bits, where k is the smallest non-negative solution to the equation $\ell + 1 + k \equiv b - l \pmod{b}$. Then append the l-bit representation of the number ℓ. In case of SHA-1, we have $b = 512$, and $l = 64$. Then for MDP (and SMD), the following holds:

$$N(\ell) = \begin{cases} \lceil \frac{\ell}{b} \rceil & \text{if } \ell \bmod b < b - l, \\ \lceil \frac{\ell}{b} \rceil + 1 & \text{otherwise.} \end{cases}$$

For comparison, this is slightly better than the efficiency of EMD; for EMD the following holds:

$$N(\ell) = \begin{cases} \lceil \frac{\ell}{b} \rceil & \text{if } \ell \bmod b < b - c - l, \\ \lceil \frac{\ell}{b} \rceil + 1 & \text{otherwise} \end{cases}$$

Concretely, if we take the parameters of SHA-1, that is, $b = 512$, $c = 160$, and $l = 64$, then for messages of length between 288 and 447, EMD needs one more invocation than MDP. On the average, EMD needs c/b more invocations of the compression function than MDP. Again with the parameters of SHA-1, $c/b \approx 0.31$.

4   Security of MDP

In this section, we study the security of MDP and prove that MDP indeed meets all the security goals that we wanted.

4.1   Collision Resistance

First, MDP is collision-resistant. Given a collision-resistant compression function F, MDP construction from F is also collision-resistant. The proof is trivial; since the structure of MDP is very similar to the MD scheme, we may follow the proof of collision resistance of the MD almost verbatim.

4.2   Indifferentiability from Random Oracle

We show that MDP is indifferentiable from a random oracle $\mathcal{H}$, when a FIL random oracle $\mathcal{F}$ is used as the compression function. Therefore we need a simulator

```
Initialize:
    V ← S ← {IV}

Interface F(s, x):
100:  V ← V ∪ {s}
101:  if F(s, x) = ⊥ then
102:      if s ∈ S then
103:          t ←$ C \ (V ∪ π(S) ∪ π⁻¹(V) ∪ Pπ)
104:          S ← S ∪ {t}
105:          F(s, x) ← t
106:      else if π⁻¹(s) ∈ S then
107:          F(s, x) ← H(M‖x), where F*(IV, M) = π⁻¹(s)
108:      else
109:          F(s, x) ←$ C
110:      V ← V ∪ {F(s, x)}
111:  return F(s, x)
```

Fig. 2. Pseudocode for the simulator $S_{\mathcal{F}}$

$S_{\mathcal{F}}$ so that no efficient adversary can distinguish (or rather, differentiate) the pair $(\mathrm{MDP}[\mathcal{F}, \pi], \mathcal{F})$ from the pair $(\mathcal{H}, S_{\mathcal{F}})$. We will use the simulator illustrated in Figure 2.

$S_{\mathcal{F}}$ maintains a structure $F(s, x)$ where it stores previously selected value of the query $S_{\mathcal{F}}(s, x)$. Initially $F(s, x) = \bot$ for all s and x, where $\bot$ means undefined. $S_{\mathcal{F}}$ also maintains two sets $\mathcal{V}$ and $\mathcal{S}$. Both are initially set to the singleton set $\{IV\}$. As more queries are inquired, new elements are added to the sets. Note that elements never leave the sets.

When queried $S_{\mathcal{F}}(s, x)$, if $F(s, x) = \bot$, $S_{\mathcal{F}}$ will choose a value t randomly depending on the algorithm in Figure 2, and define $F(s, x) \leftarrow t$. If we consider the labeled directed graph G whose edges are $s \xrightarrow{x} F(s, x)$ for all $F(s, x) \neq \bot$, then we can see that $\mathcal{V}$ denotes the set of all vertices of G. On the other hand, $\mathcal{S}$ is then the set of all vertices that can be reached by following a path from the vertex IV. In order to prove the indifferentiability of MDP, we need a few lemmas about the simulator $S_{\mathcal{F}}$:

Lemma 1. *At any time during the execution of the simulator $S_{\mathcal{F}}$, if $s \in \mathcal{S}$ for some s, then $F*(IV, M) = s$ for some M. Conversely, if $F*(IV, M) \neq \bot$, then $F*(IV, M) \in \mathcal{S}$.*

Lemma 2. *Suppose that both $F*(IV, M)$ and $F*(IV, M')$ are defined. Then, $F*(IV, M) = F*(IV, M')$ if and only if $M = M'$.*

Lemma 3. *Suppose that both $F*(IV, M)$ and $F*(IV, M')$ are defined. Then, $F*(IV, M) \neq \pi(F*(IV, M'))$ and $F*(IV, M) \neq \pi^{-1}(F*(IV, M'))$.*

Lemmas 1 and 2 essentially say that the subgraph $\mathcal{S}$ of $\mathcal{V}$ is in fact a rooted tree with IV as the root. Note that, because these three lemmas are only about the subgraph S, as long as the lines 102 to 105 are intact, the lines 106 to 109 do not change the validity of the lemmas. Also, due to Lemma 1 and 2, the line 107 in the pseudocode in Figure 2 works correctly. We will omit the proofs of the three lemmas since they are straightforward.

The basic intuition involved in the pseudocode of $S_{\mathcal{F}}$ is this: the permutation π disrupts the extension property of the MD scheme if it has only a small number of fixed points and IV is not a fixed point. Now, the best strategy of an adversary seems to be computing $F^*(IV, M)$ for various messages M (by querying the FIL oracle), until one of the following happens:

- The adversary finds two distinct messages M, M' such that $F^*(IV, M) = F^*(IV, M')$: in this case, we have $H(M\|P) = H(M'\|P)$ for any message block P, if H is the MDP. But the probability of this equality is very low, if H is a true random oracle.
- The adversary finds two distinct messages M, M' such that $F^*(IV, M) = \pi(F^*(IV, M'))$: in this case, we have $H(M\|P\|Q) = F(\pi(H(M'\|P)), Q)$ for any message block P and Q, if H is the MDP. But similarly the probability of this equality is very low, if H is a true random oracle, because the simulator which selects the value $F(\pi(H(M'\|P)), Q)$ has information about Q, but it doesn't have access to the adversarial choice of P.

Other minor strategy is to find a message M such that $F^*(IV, M)$ is a fixed point of π or a part of a previous query to F.

The simulator $S_{\mathcal{F}}$ is designed so that Lemmas 1, 2, and 3 hold, which delays the above failing situations as late as possible. This is achieved by careful expansion of the tree S at line 103. Note that by birthday attack, the attacker can eventually find the message pair M, M' satisfying $F^*(IV, M)$ equals $F^*(IV, M')$ or $\pi(F^*(IV, M'))$. Therefore, MDP can be indifferentiable from a random oracle only up to the birthday bound.[2]

Now, the indifferentiability of MDP is expressed in the next theorem.

Theorem 1. *Let A be an adversary distinguishing the pairs $(\mathsf{MDP}[\mathcal{F}, \pi], \mathcal{F})$ and $(\mathcal{H}, S_{\mathcal{F}})$, where the simulator $S_{\mathcal{F}}$ is defined in Fig. 2. Let π be a permutation on $\mathcal{C}$ and P_π be the set of its fixed points such that $IV \notin P_\pi$. Then,*

$$\mathrm{Adv}^{\mathrm{diff}}_{\mathsf{MDP}[\mathcal{F}, \pi], S_{\mathcal{F}}}(A) \leq \frac{5(lq_V + q_F)(3lq_V + q_F + 1)}{2^{c+1}} + \frac{lq_V q_F}{2^c} + \frac{|P_\pi|(2lq_V + q_F)}{2^c},$$

where q_F is the number of queries to the FIL oracle, and q_V the number of queries to the VIL oracle. l is the maximum number of message blocks for each VIL query. c is the size of the chaining variables. Moreover, $S_{\mathcal{F}}$ makes at most q_F queries and runs in time $O(q_F{}^2)$.

---

[2] MDP, being random-oracle indifferentiable, prevents the extension property. But once a colliding message pair due to an internal MD collision is found, for example by birthday attack, or by insecurity of the compression function, any common suffix can be added to the message pair. This serious effect of extension attacks is not resolved by MDP (nor by other similarly proposed composition schemes).

4.3 MDP Yields Secure PRFs

In this section, we show that when the compression function F is a PRF secure against π-related-key attack, then MDP yields a secure PRF. This construction could be used as an alternative to HMAC or NMAC.

In order to use MDP as a PRF, we need to provide a keying strategy to MDP. We may consider at least two straightforward such approaches[3].

- Keyed-MDP: We may use a secret key $K \xleftarrow{\$} \mathcal{C}$ instead of the fixed IV, and define a MAC scheme out of MDP by $\mathsf{KMDP}_K(M) = F^\circ(K, \mathsf{pad}(M))$.
- Prefix-MDP: Given a message M and a key $K \xleftarrow{\$} \mathcal{B}$, we define $\mathsf{PMDP}_K(M) = \mathsf{MDP}(K\|M)$, i.e., the secret prefix construction. Note that $\mathsf{PMDP}_K(M) = \mathsf{KMDP}_{F(IV,K)}(M)$. Although less efficient than Keyed-MDP, this has a benefit that it may use the underlying hash function as a black-box.

Remark 1. If $\mathsf{KMDP}_K(M)$ were a secure PRF whenever F is a secure PRF, then we may say that MDP preserves the PRF property, in the sense of Bellare and Ristenpart [6]. Unfortunately this is not the case; if, for example, F satisfies $F_K(x) = F_{\pi(K)}(x)$ for any K and x, then the MDP construction reduces to the plain Merkle-Damgård scheme, which is vulnerable to the extension attack.

Related-Key Multi-oracles. In order to prove the security of the two MAC schemes, first we need to introduce the notion of multi-oracle distinguishers. This was first given in [4] in order to prove that, if the MD scheme is keyed via IV, then the resulting iterated construction is PRF with respect to prefix-free adversaries. What we actually need is not this notion itself, but an extension of it, which we call the related-key multi-oracle distinguisher.

Given a π-RKA-secure PRF F, consider the problem of distinguishing a $2m$-tuple of instances of F, from a $2m$-tuple of independent random functions. But, for the $2m$-tuple of F, we choose m of the keys $K_1, \ldots K_m$ randomly and independently, and use $\pi(K_1), \ldots, \pi(K_m)$ as the other m keys. That is, we would like to distinguish the distribution of the following $2m$-tuple of functions:

$$(F_{K_1}, F_{\pi(K_1)}, \ldots, F_{K_m}, F_{\pi(K_m)})$$

from that of $2m$-tuple of independent random functions.

We define the advantage of a distinguisher $A(g_1, g_1', \ldots, g_m, g_m')$ with access to $2m$ oracles $g_1, g_1', g_2, g_2', \ldots, g_m, g_m'$ as follows:

$$\mathrm{Adv}_{\pi,F}^{m\text{-prf-rka}}(A) = \Pr\left[A(F_{K_1}, F_{\pi(K_1)}, \ldots, F_{K_m}, F_{\pi(K_m)}) \Rightarrow 1 \mid K_1, \ldots, K_m \xleftarrow{\$} \mathcal{C}\right]$$
$$- \Pr\left[A(\rho_1, \rho_1', \ldots, \rho_m, \rho_m') \Rightarrow 1 \mid \rho_1, \rho_1', \ldots, \rho_m, \rho_m' \xleftarrow{\$} \mathsf{Maps}(\mathcal{B}, \mathcal{C})\right]$$

---

[3] We may consider Keyed-MDP as analogous to NMAC, and Prefix-MDP as analogous to HMAC.

Lemma 4 (Related-Key Multi-oracle Lemma). *Suppose that A is a distinguisher with access to $2m$ oracles $g_1, g_1', \ldots, g_m, g_m'$ as above, and suppose that A has time-complexity at most t, and makes at most q queries. Then we can construct an adversary $B(g, g')$ attacking the π-RKA-security of F such that*

$$\mathrm{Adv}_{\pi, F}^{m\text{-prf-rka}}(A) = m \cdot \mathrm{Adv}_{\pi, F}^{\mathrm{prf\text{-}rka}}(B).$$

B makes at most q queries. And the running time of B is bounded by

$$t + O(q \cdot \mathrm{Time}(F) + qb \log q + qc).$$

Security of Keyed-MDP. Now that we have Lemma 4, we prove the following lemma which connects the PRF-security of the Keyed-MDP with the related-key multi-oracles:

Lemma 5 (Reduction to the Related-Key Multi-oracle). *Let A be a PRF-adversary against KMDP. Suppose that A has time-complexity at most t, and makes at most q queries, and each query has the length at most l. Then we can construct a related-key multi-oracle distinguisher $B(g_1, g_1', \ldots, g_q, g_q')$ with access to $2q$ oracles so that the following holds:*

$$\mathrm{Adv}_{\mathsf{KMDP}}^{\mathrm{prf}}(A) = l \cdot \mathrm{Adv}_{\pi, F}^{q\text{-prf-rka}}(B).$$

B makes at most q queries, and the running time of B is bounded by

$$t + O(q((l-1)(b \log q + \mathrm{Time}(F)) + c)).$$

Combining Lemma 4 and 5, we obtain the following theorem:

Theorem 2 (PRF-Security of Keyed-MDP). *Let A be a PRF-adversary against KMDP. Suppose that A has time-complexity at most t, and makes at most q queries, and each query has the length at most l. Then we can construct an adversary $B(g, g')$ against the π-RKA-secure PRF F such that*

$$\mathrm{Adv}_{\mathsf{KMDP}}^{\mathrm{prf}}(A) = lq \cdot \mathrm{Adv}_{\pi, F}^{\mathrm{prf\text{-}rka}}(B).$$

B makes at most q queries, and the running time of B is bounded by

$$t + O(lq(b \log q + \mathrm{Time}(F) + c)).$$

Security of Prefix-MDP. We prove the security of the Prefix-MDP scheme by lifting the security proof for the Keyed-MDP. Remember that

$$\mathsf{PMDP}_K(M) = \mathsf{MDP}(K \| M) = \mathsf{KMDP}_{F(IV, K)}(M).$$

Hence, here we have to regard $F(s, x)$ as a function family indexed by the data input x. We express this formally by defining a dual function family $\bar{F} : \mathcal{B} \times \mathcal{C} \to \mathcal{C}$ of F:

$$\bar{F}(K, x) \overset{\mathrm{def}}{=} F(x, K).$$

In order to prove the security of the Prefix-MDP, in addition to the previous assumption that F is a π-RKA-secure PRF, we also need to assume that F is a PRF when keyed by its data input, i.e., $\bar{F}$ is a PRF. Then we have:

Lemma 6. *Let A be a PRF-adversary against* PMDP *that has time-complexity at most t. Then we can construct a PRF-adversary $B_{\bar{F}}(g)$ against the dual PRF $\bar{F}$ such that*

$$\mathrm{Adv}^{\mathrm{prf}}_{\mathsf{PMDP}}(A) = \mathrm{Adv}^{\mathrm{prf}}_{\mathsf{KMDP}}(A) + \mathrm{Adv}^{\mathrm{prf}}_{\bar{F}}(B_{\bar{F}}).$$

Furthermore, $B_{\bar{F}}$ has time complexity at most t, and makes only 1 oracle query.

Theorem 3 (PRF-Security of Prefix-MDP). *Let A be a PRF-adversary against* PMDP*. Suppose that A has time-complexity at most t, and makes at most q queries, and each query has the length at most l. Then we can construct an adversary $B_F(g, g')$ against the π-RKA-secure PRF F, and a PRF-adversary $B_{\bar{F}}(g)$ against the dual PRF $\bar{F}$ so that*

$$\mathrm{Adv}^{\mathrm{prf}}_{\mathsf{PMDP}}(A) = lq \cdot \mathrm{Adv}^{\mathrm{prf\text{-}rka}}_{\pi,F}(B_F) + \mathrm{Adv}^{\mathrm{prf}}_{\bar{F}}(B_{\bar{F}}).$$

Furthermore, $B_{\bar{F}}$ has time complexity at most t, and makes only 1 oracle query.

Remark 2. Even if F is a secure PRF, it could be vulnerable to a π-related-key attack. For example, Contini and Yin [10] exhibited a related-key distinguishing attack on the keyed MD5 compression function using pseudo-collisions of MD5 [8]. This attack shows that the keyed MD5 compression function is not a good π-RKA-secure PRF, when $\pi(x) = x \oplus \Delta$.

Remark 3. Kim et al. [15], and also Contini and Yin [10], showed how to construct various attacks on HMAC and NMAC using weakness of keyed compression functions like MD4. The same attacks will work against PMDP under the same keyed compression functions.

4.4 Unforgeability Preservation

We may use MDP as a MAC under a different keying strategy from the above section. Now, we consider MDP in the dedicated-key setting, where a compression function is a MAC $F : \mathcal{K} \times \mathcal{C} \times \mathcal{B} \to \mathcal{C}$ with a dedicated key input.

Theorem 4. *Let π be a permutation on $\mathcal{C}$ with no fixed point. Let A be a (t, q, l, ϵ)-forger of* MDP$[F, \pi]$. *Then we can construct a (t', q', l', ϵ')-forger B attacking the FIL MAC F, where $q' = qN(l) + N(l) - 1$, $l' = b + c$, and $\epsilon' = 2\epsilon/(3q'^2 + 3q' + 2)$. Also, the running time t' is essentially that of A with some small overhead that is obvious from the construction of B [17].*

5 Further Results on Indifferentiability

5.1 MDP with a Double-Block-Length Compression Function

A compression function F is called double-block-length (DBL) if it is composed of a smaller compression function f and the output length of F is twice as large as that of f. We consider a DBL compression function of the form defined in the following definition.

Definition 1. *Let c be an even integer, and $f : C \times B \to \{0,1\}^{c/2}$. $F : C \times B \to C$ is a DBL compression function such that $F(s,x) = f(s,x) \| f(p(s),x)$, where $s \in C$, $x \in B$, and p is an involution on C with no fixed points.*

The following theorem states that $\mathsf{MDP}[F,\pi]$ is indifferentiable from a VIL random oracle if f is a FIL random oracle and π is chosen appropriately.

Theorem 5. *Let F be a DBL compression function defined in Definition 1. Let π be a permutation on C and $P_{\pi,p} = \{u \mid u \in C, \text{ and } \pi(u) = u \text{ or } p(u)\}$. Let A be an adversary distinguishing the pairs $(\mathsf{MDP}[F,\pi], \mathcal{F})$ and $(\mathcal{H}, S_{\mathcal{F}})$, where the simulator $S_{\mathcal{F}}$ is defined in Fig. 3. Suppose that $IV \notin P_{\pi,p}$. Then,*

$$\mathbf{Adv}^{\mathrm{diff}}_{\mathsf{MDP}[\mathcal{F},\pi],S_{\mathcal{F}}}(A) \leq \frac{7(lq_V + q_F)(3lq_V + q_F + 1) + lq_V q_F + |P_{\pi,p}|(2lq_V + q_F)}{2^c},$$

where q_F is the number of queries to the FIL oracle, and q_V the number of queries to the VIL oracle. l is the maximum number of message blocks for each

---

Initialize:

 $\mathcal{V} \leftarrow \mathcal{S} \leftarrow \{IV\}$

Interface $\mathcal{F}(s,x)$:

100: $\mathcal{V} \leftarrow \mathcal{V} \cup \{s, p(s)\}$
101: if $F(s,x) = \perp$ then
102:   if $s \in \mathcal{S}$ then
103:    $t \xleftarrow{\$} C \setminus (\mathcal{V} \cup \pi(\mathcal{S}) \cup \pi^{-1}(\mathcal{V}) \cup p(\mathcal{V}) \cup p(\pi(\mathcal{S})) \cup \pi^{-1}(p(\mathcal{V})) \cup P_{\pi,p})$
104:    $\mathcal{S} \leftarrow \mathcal{S} \cup \{t\}$
105:    $F(s,x) \leftarrow t$
106:    $F(p(s),x) \leftarrow \mathsf{swap}(t)$
107:   else if $p(s) \in \mathcal{S}$ then
108:    $t \xleftarrow{\$} C \setminus (\mathcal{V} \cup \pi(\mathcal{S}) \cup \pi^{-1}(\mathcal{V}) \cup p(\mathcal{V}) \cup p(\pi(\mathcal{S})) \cup \pi^{-1}(p(\mathcal{V})) \cup P_{\pi,p})$
109:    $\mathcal{S} \leftarrow \mathcal{S} \cup \{t\}$
110:    $F(p(s),x) \leftarrow t$
111:    $F(s,x) \leftarrow \mathsf{swap}(t)$
112:   else if $\pi^{-1}(s) \in \mathcal{S}$ then
113:    $F(s,x) \leftarrow \mathcal{H}(M\|x)$, where $F^*(IV, M) = \pi^{-1}(s)$
114:    $F(p(s),x) \leftarrow \mathsf{swap}(F(s,x))$
115:   else if $\pi^{-1}(p(s)) \in \mathcal{S}$ then
116:    $F(p(s),x) \leftarrow \mathcal{H}(M\|x)$, where $F^*(IV, M) = \pi^{-1}(p(s))$
117:    $F(s,x) \leftarrow \mathsf{swap}(F(p(s),x))$
118:   else
119:    $F(s,x) \xleftarrow{\$} C$
120:    $F(p(s),x) \leftarrow \mathsf{swap}(F(s,x))$
121:   $\mathcal{V} \leftarrow \mathcal{V} \cup \{F(s,x), F(p(s),x)\}$
122: return $F(s,x)$

Fig. 3. Pseudocode for the simulator $S_{\mathcal{F}}$. $\mathsf{swap}(t_1\|t_2) = t_2\|t_1$ for every $t_1, t_2 \in \{0,1\}^{c/2}$.

VIL query. c is the size of the chaining variables. $S_{\mathcal{F}}$ makes at most q_F queries and runs in time $O(q_F{}^2)$.

In Theorem 5, a simulator is prepared for F instead of f. Let $\hat{p}$ be a permutation on $\mathcal{C} \times \mathcal{B}$ such that $\hat{p}(s, x) = (p(s), x)$. Since p has no fixed points and $p \circ p$ is an identity permutation, so does $\hat{p}$. Since $\hat{p} \circ \hat{p}$ is an identity permutation, $f(s, x)$ and $f(\hat{p}(s, x))$ are only used for $F(s, x)$ and $F(\hat{p}(s, x))$ for every $(s, x) \in \mathcal{C} \times \mathcal{B}$. Thus, $F(s, x)$ and $F(s', x')$ are random and independent of each other if $(s', x') \neq \hat{p}(s, x)$, since f is a random oracle. Moreover, since $\hat{p}$ has no fixed points and $F(s, x) = f(s, x) \| f(\hat{p}(s, x))$, the first half and the second half of $F(s, x)$ are also random and independent of each other. Thus, as is shown in Fig. 3, $S_{\mathcal{F}}$ can randomly select an output of F for each query.

5.2   MDP with the Davies-Meyer Compression Function

In this section, we consider the case that F is the Davies-Meyer compression function [18] composed of a block cipher. We show that MDP$[\mathcal{F}, \pi]$ is indifferentiable from a VIL random oracle if the underlying block cipher is ideal.

Initialize:

   $\mathcal{V} \leftarrow \mathcal{S} \leftarrow \{IV\}$
   $\mathcal{P}(x) \leftarrow \mathcal{Q}(x) \leftarrow \mathcal{C}$

Interface $\mathcal{E}(x, s)$:

100: $\mathcal{V} \leftarrow \mathcal{V} \cup \{s\}$
101: if $E_x(s) = \bot$ then
102:     if $s \in \mathcal{S}$ then
103:         $E_x(s) \xleftarrow{\$} \mathcal{Q}(x) \setminus \mathbf{S}_{\text{bad}}$
104:         $\mathcal{S} \leftarrow \mathcal{S} \cup \{E_x(s) \oplus s\}$
105:     else if $\pi^{-1}(s) \in \mathcal{S}$ then
106:         $u \leftarrow \mathcal{H}(M\|x) \oplus s$, where $F^*(IV, M) = \pi^{-1}(s)$
107:         if $u \notin \mathcal{Q}(x)$ then
108:             return fail
109:         else
110:             $E_x(s) \leftarrow u$
111:     else
112:         $E_x(s) \xleftarrow{\$} \mathcal{Q}(x)$
113:     $\mathcal{V} \leftarrow \mathcal{V} \cup \{E_x(s) \oplus s\}$
114:     $\mathcal{P}(x) \leftarrow \mathcal{P}(x) \setminus \{s\}$
115:     $\mathcal{Q}(x) \leftarrow \mathcal{Q}(x) \setminus \{E_x(s)\}$
116: return $E_x(s)$

Interface $\mathcal{D}(x, u)$:

200: if $D_x(u) = \bot$ then
201:     for every $s \in \mathcal{S}$ do
202:         if $u \oplus H(M\|x) = \pi(s)$ then
203:             $\mathbf{N} \leftarrow \mathbf{N} \cup \{s\}$, where $F^*(IV, M) = s$
204:     if $|\mathbf{N}| \geq 2$ then
205:         return fail
206:     else if $|\mathbf{N}| = 1$ then
207:         if $\pi(s) \notin \mathcal{P}(x)$ then
208:             return fail
209:         else
210:             $D_x(u) \leftarrow \pi(s)$
211:     else
212:         $D_x(u) \xleftarrow{\$} \mathcal{P}(x) \setminus (\mathcal{S} \cup \pi(\mathcal{S}))$
213:     $\mathcal{V} \leftarrow \mathcal{V} \cup \{D_x(u), D_x(u) \oplus u\}$
214:     $\mathcal{P}(x) \leftarrow \mathcal{P}(x) \setminus \{D_x(u)\}$
215:     $\mathcal{Q}(x) \leftarrow \mathcal{Q}(x) \setminus \{u\}$
216: return $D_x(u)$

Fig. 4. Pseudocode for the simulator $S_{\mathcal{E}}$ and $S_{\mathcal{D}}$. $\mathbf{S}_{\text{bad}} = \{u \oplus s \mid u \in \mathcal{V} \cup \pi(\mathcal{S}) \cup \pi^{-1}(\mathcal{V}) \cup P_{\pi}\}$.

A block cipher with the block length c and the key length b is called a (c, b) block cipher. Let $E : \mathcal{B} \times \mathcal{C} \to \mathcal{C}$ be a (c, b) block cipher. Then, $E(K, \cdot) = E_K(\cdot)$ is a permutation for every $K \in \mathcal{B}$, and $D(K, \cdot) = D_K(\cdot) = E_K^{-1}(\cdot)$. E is called an ideal cipher if E_K is a truly random permutation for every $K \in \mathcal{B}$.

Theorem 6. *Let $F : \mathcal{C} \times \mathcal{B} \to \mathcal{C}$ be the Davies-Meyer compression function with an ideal (c, b) block cipher E, that is, $F(s, x) = E_x(s) \oplus s$. Let A be an adversary that asks at most q_V queries to the VIL oracle, q_{F_0} queries to the FIL encryption oracle and q_{F_1} queries to the FIL decryption oracle. Let l be the maximum number of message blocks for each VIL query. Suppose that $lq_V + q_{F_0} + q_{F_1} \leq 2^{c-1}$. Then,*

$$\mathbf{Adv}_{\mathrm{MDP}[\mathcal{F},\pi],S_\mathcal{E},S_\mathcal{D}}^{\mathrm{diff}}(A) \leq \frac{13(lq_V + q_{F_0} + q_{F_1})(2lq_V + q_{F_0} + q_{F_1}) + |P_\pi|(3lq_V + q_{F_0})}{2^{c+1}},$$

where the simulators $S_\mathcal{E}$ and $S_\mathcal{D}$ are given in Fig. 4. $S_\mathcal{E}$ is a simulator for the encryption oracle, and $S_\mathcal{D}$ for the decryption oracle. $S_\mathcal{E}$ makes at most q_{F_0} queries and runs in time $O(q_{F_0}(q_{F_0} + q_{F_1}))$. $S_\mathcal{D}$ makes at most $q_{F_0} \cdot q_{F_1}$ queries and runs in time $O(q_{F_1}(q_{F_0} + q_{F_1}))$.

Acknowledgements

We would like to thank the anonymous reviewers for their valuable comments. The first author was supported in part by International Communications Foundation (ICF).

References

1. An, J.H., Bellare, M.: Constructing VIL-MACs from FIL-MACs: Message authentication under weakened assumptions. In: Wiener, M.J. (ed.) CRYPTO 1999. LNCS, vol. 1666, pp. 252–269. Springer, Heidelberg (1999)
2. Bellare, M.: New proofs for NMAC and HMAC: Security without collision-resistance. In: Dwork, C. (ed.) CRYPTO 2006. LNCS, vol. 4117, pp. 602–619. Springer, Heidelberg (2006)
3. Bellare, M., Canetti, R., Krawczyk, H.: Keying hash functions for message authentication. In: Koblitz, N. (ed.) CRYPTO 1996. LNCS, vol. 1109, pp. 1–15. Springer, Heidelberg (1996)
4. Bellare, M., Canetti, R., Krawczyk, H.: Pseudorandom functions revisited: The cascade construction and its concrete security. In: Proc. of FOCS 1996, pp. 514–523 (1996)
5. Bellare, M., Kohno, T.: A theoretical treatment of related-key attacks: RKA-PRPs, RKA-PRFs, and applications. In: Biham, E. (ed.) Advances in Cryptology – EUROCRPYT 2003. LNCS, vol. 2656, pp. 491–506. Springer, Heidelberg (2003)
6. Bellare, M., Ristenpart, T.: Multi-property-preserving hash domain extension and the EMD transform. In: Lai, X., Chen, K. (eds.) ASIACRYPT 2006. LNCS, vol. 4284, pp. 299–314. Springer, Heidelberg (2006)

7. Bellare, M., Ristenpart, T.: Hash functions in the dedicated-key setting: Design choices and MPP transforms. In: Automata, Languages and Programming - ICALP 2007. LNCS, vol. 4596, pp. 399–410. Springer, Heidelberg (2007)

8. den Boer, B., Mosselaers, A.: Collisions for the compression function of MD5. In: Helleseth, T. (ed.) EUROCRYPT 1993. LNCS, vol. 765, pp. 293–304. Springer, Heidelberg (1994)

9. Chang, D., Lee, S., Nandi, M., Yung, M.: Indifferentiable security analysis of popular hash function with prefix-free padding. In: Lai, X., Chen, K. (eds.) ASIACRYPT 2006. LNCS, vol. 4284, pp. 283–298. Springer, Heidelberg (2006)

10. Contini, S., Yin, Y.L.: Forgery and partial key-recovery attacks on HMAC and NMAC using hash collisions. In: Lai, X., Chen, K. (eds.) ASIACRYPT 2006. LNCS, vol. 4284, pp. 37–53. Springer, Heidelberg (2006)

11. Coron, J.-S., Dodis, Y., Malinaud, C., Puniya, P.: Merkle-Damgård revisited: How to construct a hash function. In: Shoup, V. (ed.) CRYPTO 2005. LNCS, vol. 3621, pp. 430–448. Springer, Heidelberg (2005)

12. Damgård, I.: A design principle for hash functions. In: Brassard, G. (ed.) CRYPTO 1989. LNCS, vol. 435, pp. 416–427. Springer, Heidelberg (1990)

13. Hirose, S., Park, J.H., Yun, A.: A simple variant of the Merkle-Damgård scheme with a permutation. Full version of this paper

14. Kelsey, J.: Public Comments on the Draft Federal Information Processing Standard (FIPS) Draft FIPS 180-2, Secure Hash Standard (SHS) (2001), http://csrc.nist.gov/CryptoToolkit/shs/dfips-180-2-comments1.pdf

15. Kim, J., Biryukov, A., Preneel, B., Lee, S.: On the Security of HMAC and NMAC Based on HAVAL, MD4, MD5, SHA-0 and SHA-1. In: De Prisco, R., Yung, M. (eds.) SCN 2006. LNCS, vol. 4116, Springer, Heidelberg (2006), available at http://eprint.iacr.org/2006/187

16. Maurer, U.M., Renner, R., Holenstein, C.: Indifferentiability, impossibility results on reductions, and applications to the random oracle methodology. In: Naor, M. (ed.) TCC 2004. LNCS, vol. 2951, pp. 21–39. Springer, Heidelberg (2004)

17. Maurer, U., Sjödin, J.: Single-key AIL-MACs from any FIL-MAC. In: Caires, L., Italiano, G.F., Monteiro, L., Palamidessi, C., Yung, M. (eds.) ICALP 2005. LNCS, vol. 3580, pp. 472–484. Springer, Heidelberg (2005)

18. Menezes, A.J., van Oorschot, P.C., Vanstone, S.A.: Handbook of Applied Cryptography. CRC Press (1996)

19. Merkle, R.: One way hash functions and DES. In: Brassard, G. (ed.) CRYPTO 1989. LNCS, vol. 435, pp. 428–446. Springer, Heidelberg (1990)

20. Nandi, M.: Towards optimal double-length hash functions. In: Maitra, S., Madhavan, C.E.V., Venkatesan, R. (eds.) INDOCRYPT 2005. LNCS, vol. 3797, pp. 77–89. Springer, Heidelberg (2005)

21. Preneel, B., Govaerts, R., Vandewalle, J.: Hash functions based on block ciphers: A synthetic approach. In: Stinson, D.R. (ed.) CRYPTO 1993. LNCS, vol. 773, pp. 368–378. Springer, Heidelberg (1994)

22. Tsudik, G.: Message authentication with one-way hash functions. ACM Computer Communications Review 22(5), 29–38 (1992)

Seven-Property-Preserving Iterated Hashing: ROX*

Elena Andreeva[1], Gregory Neven[1,2], Bart Preneel[1], and Thomas Shrimpton[3,4]

[1] SCD-COSIC, Dept. of Electrical Engineering, Katholieke Universiteit Leuven
{Elena.Andreeva,Gregory.Neven,Bart.Preneel}@esat.kuleuven.be
[2] Département d'Informatique, Ecole Normale Supérieure
[3] Dept. of Computer Science, Portland State University
teshrim@cs.pdx.edu
[4] Faculty of Informatics, University of Lugano

Abstract. Nearly all modern hash functions are constructed by iterating a compression function. At FSE'04, Rogaway and Shrimpton [28] formalized seven security notions for hash functions: collision resistance (Coll) and three variants of second-preimage resistance (Sec, aSec, eSec) and preimage resistance (Pre, aPre, ePre). The main contribution of this paper is in determining, by proof or counterexample, which of these seven notions is preserved by each of eleven existing iterations. Our study points out that none of them preserves more than three notions from [28]. As a second contribution, we propose the new Random-Oracle XOR (ROX) iteration that is the first to provably preserve all seven notions, but that, quite controversially, uses a random oracle in the iteration. The compression function itself is *not* modeled as a random oracle though. Rather, ROX uses an auxiliary small-input random oracle (typically 170 bits) that is called only a logarithmic number of times.

1 Introduction

Cryptographic hash functions, publicly computable maps from inputs of arbitrary length to (short) fixed-length strings, have become a ubiquitous building block in cryptography. Almost all cryptographic hash functions are iterative: given a compression function F that takes $(n + b)$ bits of input and produces n bits of output, they process an arbitrary length input by dividing it into b-bit blocks and iterating F appropriately. The widely used Strengthened Merkle-Damgård (SMD) construction [21,11] is known to yield a collision-resistant iterated hash function if the underlying compression function is collision resistant; in other words, SMD *preserves* collision resistance of the compression function.

Unfortunately, designing collision resistant compression functions seems quite hard: witness the recent collision attacks on several popular hash functions by Wang et al. [33,32]. One way out is to aim for a weaker security notion for the compression function, but not so weak as to make the resulting hash function useless in practice. A natural question to ask is whether these weaker proper-

---

* Extended abstract; we refer to the full version [1] for more details and proofs.

K. Kurosawa (Ed.): ASIACRYPT 2007, LNCS 4833, pp. 130–146, 2007.

ties are also preserved by SMD. For example, does it preserve second-preimage resistance? One may think so, because SMD preserves collision resistance, and collision resistance can be shown to imply second-preimage resistance, but this says *nothing* about what happens if you *start* with a compression function that is only second-preimage resistant. Lai and Massey [16] claimed that finding second preimages for an iterated hash is equally as hard as finding second preimages for the compression function, but this was found to be incorrect by Dean [12] and Kelsey and Schneier [15], who show that (for the case of SMD) efficient collision-finding attacks immediately give rise to second-preimage attacks that beat the anticipated security bound.

CONTRIBUTIONS. We took as a starting point a paper by Rogaway and Shrimpton [28] that provides a unifying framework of seven security notions for hash functions and the relations among them. Our work explores in detail which of the seven properties of [28] are preserved by several published hash constructions. Of the eleven schemes we consider (see Table 1), we found that in fact none preserved all seven. This raises the question whether it is possible at all to preserve all seven properties. We answer this question in the affirmative, in the random oracle model [6], by presenting a construction that builds on previous work by Bellare, Rogaway, Shoup and Mironov [7,30,23]. Our construction iterates a *real-world* compression function but, in the iteration, makes a logarithmic (in the message length) number of calls to an auxiliary small-input random oracle; we will say more in a moment to justify this choice. The existence of seven-property-preserving iterations in the standard model is left as an open problem.

RELEVANCE OF THE SEVEN PROPERTIES. Apart from collision-resistance, Rogaway and Shrimpton consider three variants of second-preimage resistance (Sec) and preimage resistance (Pre). The standard variants of Sec and Pre are restricted to randomly chosen preimages, and have important applications like the Cramer-Shoup cryptosystem [10] for Sec and Unix-like password storage [18,31] for Pre. The stronger *everywhere* variants (eSec, ePre) consider adversarially chosen preimages. The notion of eSec is equivalent to the universal one-way hash functions of Naor and Yung [25] and to the target collision resistance of Bellare and Rogaway [7]. Bellare and Rogaway show that eSec is sufficient to extend the message space of signature schemes that are defined for small messages only.

Following the standard convention established by Damgård [11], and Bellare and Rogaway [7], these notions were formalized for hash function families, indexed by a (publicly known) key K. Current practical hash functions however do not have explicit keys. In fact, it is not even clear what the family is that they belong to, so it is rather contrived to regard SHA-256 as a randomly drawn member of such a family. Instead, the always-notions aSec and aPre capture the intuition that a hash function ought to be (second-)preimage resistant for *all* members of the family, so that it doesn't matter which one is actually used. Alternatively, one could see the aSec and aPre notions as the the natural extensions to (second-)preimage resistance of Rogaway's human-ignorance approach to collision-resistant hashing with unkeyed compression functions [27]. (See [2] for a subsequent work on property preservation for iterations of unkeyed compression

Table 1. Overview of constructions and the properties they preserve. Each row in the table represents a hash function construction, each column a security notion of [28]. The symbol "Y" means that the notion is provably preserved by the construction; "N" means that it is not preserved, in the sense that we come up with a counterexample; "?" means that neither proof nor counterexample are known. Underlined entries were known, all other results are new.

Scheme	Coll	Sec	aSec	eSec	Pre	aPre	ePre
Strengthened MD [22,11]	Y	N	N	N	N	N	Y
Linear [7]	N	N	N	N	N	N	Y
XOR-Linear [7]	Y	N	N	Y	N	N	Y
Shoup's [30]	Y	N	N	Y	N	N	Y
Prefix-free MD [9]	N	N	N	N	N	N	Y
Randomized [13]	Y	N	N	N	N	N	Y
HAIFA [8]	Y	N	N	N	N	N	Y
Enveloped MD [4]	Y	N	N	N	N	N	Y
Strengthened Merkle Tree [20]	Y	N	N	N	N	N	Y
Tree Hash [7]	N	N	N	N	N	N	Y
XOR Tree [7]	?	?	N	?	Y	N	Y
ROX	Y	Y	Y	Y	Y	Y	Y

functions.) In this sense, the aSec and aPre notions strengthen the standard notions of second-preimage resistance and preimage resistance, respectively, in the way needed to say that a fixed function such as SHA-256 is Sec and Pre secure. They therefore inherit the practical applications of Sec and Pre security, and are thus the right notions to consider when instantiating Cramer-Shoup encryption or Unix-like password storage with a fixed function like SHA-256. The formal definitions of all seven notions are recalled in Section 2.

EXISTING CONSTRUCTIONS. Let us now take a closer look at a number of existing constructions to see which of the seven notions of [28] they preserve. Our findings are summarized in Table 1, which we see as the main research contribution of our paper. Except for the few entries in the table with question marks, we come up with either proofs or counterexamples in support of our claims. We found for example that the ubiquitous SMD construction preserves Coll and ePre security, but surprisingly fails to preserve any of the other notions. Of the eleven schemes in the table, none preserves all seven notions. In fact, the best-performing constructions in terms of property preservation are the XOR Linear hash and Shoup's hash, which still preserve only three of the seven notions (Coll, eSec, and ePre). The XOR Tree hash is the only iteration to preserve Pre, and none of the schemes preserve Sec, aSec or aPre. Remember that the latter two are particularly relevant for the security of practical hash functions because they do not rely on the compression functions being chosen at random from a family.

PRESERVING ALL PROPERTIES: THE ROX CONSTRUCTION. This rather poor state of affairs may leave one wondering whether preserving all seven notions is possible at all. We answer this question in the affirmative, but, quite controversially, were only able to do so in the random oracle model. We explicitly do *not* model the compression function itself as a random oracle however. While we view the main interest of our construction to be a feasibility result for seven-property-preserving hashing, we do have reasons to believe that our construction makes very "reasonable" use of the random oracle. Allow us to explain.

Our Random-Oracle-XOR (ROX) construction draws largely on the XOR-linear hash [7] and Shoup's hash [30]. The latter is an extension of SMD where a logarithmic (in the message length) number of masks are XORed into the chaining value. We take the same approach, but have the masks generated by applying a random oracle to 170-bit inputs, for a security level of 80 bits. To hash an ℓ-block message, we query the random oracle on a number of domain points that is logarithmic in ℓ. This limited use of the random oracle has the important practical ramification that the function instantiating it need not be as efficient as the compression function, and can therefore be made with large security margins. We'll come back to candidate instantiations in Section 4.

The idea of generating the masks through a random oracle is not new; in fact, it was explicitly suggested at two separate occasions by Mironov [23,24]. The idea was discarded in [23] for trivializing the problem, but was revisited in [24] as a viable way to obtain shorter keys for eSec-secure hashing. Indeed, if one assumes the existence of random oracles with very large domains, then one can simply use the random oracle to do the hashing. The ROX construction, on the other hand, still uses a real compression function in the chaining, and uses a small-domain random oracle to preserve all seven notions of [28] using a very short key, including the important aSec and aPre notions.[1] Moreover, we do so without changing the syntax of the compression function [8] or doubling its output size [19], both of which can come at a considerable performance penalty.

WHAT ABOUT OTHER PROPERTIES? The seven security notions formalized by [28] are certainly not the only ones that are of interest. Kelsey and Kohno [14] suggest chosen-target forced-prefix security, which can be seen as a special form of multi-collision resistance, as the right goal to stop Nostradamus attacks. Bellare and Ristenpart [4], following previous work by Coron et al. [9] and Bellare et al. [3], formalize pseudorandom oracle preservation (PRO-Pr) and pseudorandom function preservation (PRF-Pr) as goals. Their EMD construction is shown to be PRO-Pr, PRF-Pr and to preserve collision resistance. More recently, and independently of this work, Bellare and Ristenpart [5] study the Coll, eSec, PRO, PRF, and MAC (unforgeability) preservation of various iterations, including the SMD, Prefix-free MD, Shoup, and EMD iterations that we study. Their work does not cover the five other notions of [28], while our work does not cover the PRO, PRF, and MAC properties. We leave the study of the preservation of these properties by our $\mathcal{ROX}$ construction to future work.

---

[1] While ROX itself is an explicitly keyed construction, its preservation of aSec/aPre implies that the instantiating compression function need not be. Indeed, when instantiated with a fixed aSec/aPre-secure compression function like SHA-256, then the resulting iterated hash is aSec/aPre-secure and therefore also Sec/Pre-secure. ROX thereby provides a secure way of iterating unkeyed (second-)preimage resistant compression functions.

2   Security Definitions

In this section, we explain the security notions for hash functions of [28]. Let us begin by establishing some notation. Let $\mathbb{N} = \{0, 1, \ldots\}$ be the set of natural numbers and $\{0,1\}^*$ be the set of all bit strings. If $k \in \mathbb{N}$, then $\{0,1\}^k$ denotes the set of all k-bit strings and $\{0,1\}^{k \times *}$ denotes the set of all bit strings of length an integer multiple of k. The empty string is denoted ε. If b is a bit then $\bar{b}$ denotes its complement. If x is a string and $i \in \mathbb{N}$, then $x^{(i)}$ is the i-th bit of x and x^i is the concatenation of i copies of x. If x, y are strings, then $x\|y$ is the concatenation of x and y. If $k, l \in \mathbb{N}$ then $\langle k \rangle_l$ is the encoding of k as an l-bit string. We occasionally write $\langle k \rangle$ when the length is clear from the context. If S is a set, then $x \xleftarrow{\$} S$ denotes the uniformly random selection of an element from S. We let $y \leftarrow \mathsf{A}(x)$ and $y \xleftarrow{\$} \mathsf{A}(x)$ be the assignment to y of the output of a deterministic and randomized algorithm A, respectively, when run on input x.

An *adversary* is an algorithm, possibly with access to oracles. To avoid trivial lookup attacks, it will be our convention to include in the time complexity of an adversary A its running time and its code size (relative to some fixed model of computation).

SECURITY NOTIONS FOR KEYED HASH FUNCTIONS. Formally, a *hash function family* is a function $\mathsf{H} : \mathcal{K} \times \mathcal{M} \to \mathcal{Y}$ where the key space $\mathcal{K}$ and the target space $\mathcal{Y}$ are finite sets of bit strings. The message space $\mathcal{M}$ could be infinitely large; we only assume that there exists at least one $\lambda \in \mathbb{N}$ such that $\{0,1\}^\lambda \subseteq \mathcal{M}$. We treat (fixed input length) compression functions and (variable input length) hash functions just the same, the former being simply a special case of the latter.

The seven security notions from [28] are the standard three of *collision resistance* (Coll), *preimage resistance* (Pre), and *second-preimage resistance* (Sec), and the *always-* and *everywhere*-variants of (second-)preimage resistance (aPre, aSec, ePre, and eSec). The advantage of an adversary A in breaking H under security notion atk is given by $\mathbf{Adv}_{\mathsf{H}}^{\mathrm{atk}}(\mathsf{A}) = \Pr[\mathrm{Exp}_{\mathrm{atk}} : M \neq M'$ and $\mathsf{H}(K, M) = \mathsf{H}(K, M')]$ if atk $\in \{\mathrm{Coll}, \mathrm{Sec}[\lambda], \mathrm{eSec}, \mathrm{aSec}[\lambda]\}$, and by $\mathbf{Adv}_{\mathsf{H}}^{\mathrm{atk}}(\mathsf{A}) = \Pr[\mathrm{Exp}_{\mathrm{atk}} : \mathsf{H}(K, M') = Y]$ if atk $\in \{\mathrm{Pre}[\lambda], \mathrm{ePre}, \mathrm{aPre}[\lambda]\}$, where the experiments $\mathrm{Exp}_{\mathrm{atk}}$ are given below.

atk	$\mathrm{Exp}_{\mathrm{atk}}$
Coll	$K \xleftarrow{\$} \mathcal{K}\,;\; (M, M') \xleftarrow{\$} \mathsf{A}(K)$
Sec[λ]	$K \xleftarrow{\$} \mathcal{K}\,;\; M \xleftarrow{\$} \{0,1\}^\lambda\,;\; M' \xleftarrow{\$} \mathsf{A}(K, M)$
eSec	$(M, St) \xleftarrow{\$} \mathsf{A}\,;\; K \xleftarrow{\$} \mathcal{K}\,;\; M' \xleftarrow{\$} \mathsf{A}(K, St)$
aSec[λ]	$(K, St) \xleftarrow{\$} \mathsf{A}\,;\; M \xleftarrow{\$} \{0,1\}^\lambda\,;\; M' \xleftarrow{\$} \mathsf{A}(M, St)$
Pre[λ]	$K \xleftarrow{\$} \mathcal{K}\,;\; M \xleftarrow{\$} \{0,1\}^\lambda\,;\; Y \leftarrow \mathsf{H}(K, M)\,;\; M' \xleftarrow{\$} \mathsf{A}(K, Y)$
ePre	$(Y, St) \xleftarrow{\$} \mathsf{A}\,;\; K \xleftarrow{\$} \mathcal{K}\,;\; M' \xleftarrow{\$} \mathsf{A}(K, St)$
aPre[λ]	$(K, St) \xleftarrow{\$} \mathsf{A}\,;\; M \xleftarrow{\$} \{0,1\}^\lambda\,;\; Y \leftarrow \mathsf{H}(K, M)\,;\; M' \xleftarrow{\$} \mathsf{A}(Y, St)$

We say that A is (t, ϵ) atk-secure if no adversary running in time at most t has advantage more than ϵ. When giving results in the random oracle model, we will talk about (t, q_{RO}, ϵ) atk-secure schemes, where q_{RO} is the total number of queries that A makes to its random oracles.

Note that the security notions above do not insist that the colliding message M' be of length λ. It is our conscious choice to focus on arbitrary-length security here, meaning that adversaries may find collisions between messages of varying lengths. In practice, the whole purpose of hash iterations is to extend the domain of a compression function to arbitrary lengths, so it makes perfect sense to require that the hash function withstands attacks using messages of different lengths.

3   Properties Preserved by Existing Constructions

In this section we take a closer look at eleven hash iterations that previously appeared in the literature, and check which of the seven security properties from [28] they preserve. The algorithms are described in Fig. 1, the results of our analysis are summarized in Table 1.

As mentioned in the previous section, we focus on arbitrary-length security in this paper. Allowing for arbitrary-length message attacks invariably seems to require some sort of message padding (unstrengthened MD does not preserve collision resistance), but care must be taken when deciding on the padding method: one method does not fit all. This was already observed by Bellare and Rogaway [7], who proposed an alternative form of strengthening where a final block containing the message length is appended and processed with a different key than the rest of the iteration. This works fine in theory, but since current compression functions are not keyed, it is not clear how this construction should be instantiated in practice. In absence of a practical generic solution, we chose to add standard one-zeroes padding and length strengthening to all chaining iterations that were originally proposed without strengthening. For tree iterations we use one-zeroes padding for the message input at the leaves, and at the root make one extra call to the compression function on input the accumulated hash value concatenated with the message length. (Standard length strengthening at the leaves fails to preserve even collision resistance here.) These strengthening methods sometimes help but never harm for property preservation.

STRENGTHENED MERKLE-DAMGÅRD. The *Strengthened Merkle-Damgård* (*SMD*) construction is known to preserve collision resistance [11] and to not preserve eSec security [7]. In the following two theorems we prove that it also preserves ePre security, but does not preserve Sec, aSec, Pre, and aPre security. τ_F is the time required for an evaluation of F and $\ell = \lceil (\lambda + 2n)/b \rceil$ where $\lambda = |M|$.

Theorem 1. *If* F *is* (t', ϵ') ePre-*secure, then* SMD_F *is* (t, ϵ) ePre-*secure for* $\epsilon = \epsilon'$ *and* $t = t' - \ell \cdot \tau_F$.

Proof. Given an ePre-adversary A against SMD_F, consider the following ePre-adversary B against F. B runs A to obtain the target value Y and outputs the same string Y. When it gets a random key K it runs A on the same key to obtain

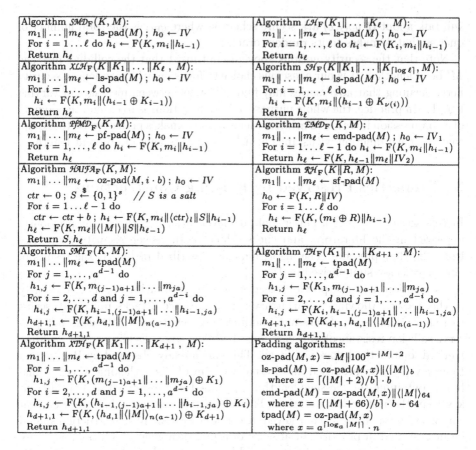

Fig. 1. Some existing iterative hash constructions. Chaining iterations SMD, LH, XLH, SH, PfMD, RH, and EMD use a compression function $F : \{0,1\}^k \times \{0,1\}^{b+n} \rightarrow \{0,1\}^n$; HAIFA uses a compression function $F : \{0,1\}^k \times \{0,1\}^{b+l+s+n} \rightarrow \{0,1\}^n$. Tree iterations SMT, TH, and XTH use a compression function $F : \{0,1\}^k \times \{0,1\}^{an} \rightarrow \{0,1\}^n$. Strings $IV, IV_1, IV_2 \in \{0,1\}^n$ are fixed initialization vectors. Padding algorithms are given on the bottom right; pf-pad(M) and sf-pad(M) are any prefix-free padding and suffix-free padding algorithms, respectively. The function $\nu(i)$ is the largest integer j such that $2^j | i$.

a preimage message M'. Let $m'_1 \| \ldots \| m'_\ell \leftarrow$ ls-pad(M') and let $h'_{\ell-1}$ be the one-but-last chaining value computed in an execution of $\mathit{SMD}_F(K, M')$. Algorithm B outputs $m'_\ell \| h'_{\ell-1}$ as its own preimage.

While at first sight the above proof may seem to go through for Pre and aPre security as well, this is not the case. The target point Y in a Pre attack on F is distributed as $F(K, m \| h)$ for a random $m \| h \xleftarrow{\$} \{0,1\}^{b+n}$. But the target point for the iterated structure SMD_F is generated as $\mathit{SMD}_F(K, M)$ for a random $M \xleftarrow{\$} \{0,1\}^\lambda$. These two distributions can actually be very different, as is illustrated by the following counterexample.

Theorem 2. *For* atk $\in \{\text{Sec}, \text{aSec}, \text{Pre}, \text{aPre}\}$, *if there exists a* (t, ϵ) atk-*secure compression function* $G : \mathcal{K} \times \{0,1\}^{b+n} \rightarrow \{0,1\}^{n-1}$, *then there exists a* $(t, \epsilon - 1/2^n)$ atk-*secure compression function* $CE_1 : \mathcal{K} \times \{0,1\}^{b+n} \rightarrow \{0,1\}^n$ *and an adversary* A *running in one time step with* atk$[\lambda]$-*advantage one in breaking* $\mathcal{SMD}_{CE_1}$.

Proof. For any compression function G, consider CE_1 given by

$$CE_1(K, m\|h) = IV \qquad\qquad \text{if } h = IV$$
$$= G(K, m\|h) \parallel \overline{IV}^{(n)} \quad \text{otherwise}.$$

If G is (t, ϵ) atk secure, then CE_1 is $(t, \epsilon - 1/2^n)$ atk secure; we refer to the full version [1] for the proof. From the construction of CE_1, it is clear that $\mathcal{SMD}_{CE_1}(K, M) = IV$ for all $M \in \{0,1\}^*$. Hence, the adversary can output any message M' as its (second) preimage.

LINEAR HASH. The *Linear Hash* ($\mathcal{LH}$) [7] uses ℓ different keys for ℓ-block messages, because it calls the compression function on a different key at every iteration. The Linear Hash is known to preserve eSec-security for same-length messages, but Bellare and Rogaway claim [7] that length-strengthening does not suffice to preserve eSec for different-length messages. The following theorem confirms their claim, and also shows that $\mathcal{LH}$ does not preserve Coll. The counterexample CE_1 of Theorem 2 can be used to disprove the preservation of Sec, aSec, Pre and aPre-security. A proof similar to that of Theorem 1 can be used to show that $\mathcal{LH}$ does preserve ePre-security.

Theorem 3. *For any* atk $\in \{\text{Coll}, \text{eSec}\}$, *if there exists a* (t, ϵ) atk-*secure compression function* $G : \{0,1\}^k \times \{0,1\}^{b+n} \rightarrow \{0,1\}^{n-2}$, *then there exists a* (t, ϵ) atk-*secure compression function* $CE_2 : \{0,1\}^k \times \{0,1\}^{b+n} \rightarrow \{0,1\}^n$ *and an adversary* A *running in one step time with* atk-*advantage* $1/4$ *in breaking* $\mathcal{LH}_{CE_2}$.

Proof. For any compression function G, consider CE_2 given by

$$CE_2(K, m\|h) = IV \qquad\qquad\qquad\qquad \text{if } m\|h = 010^{b-2}\|IV$$
$$= 0^{n-1} \parallel \overline{IV}^{(n)} \qquad\qquad \text{if } (K^{(1)} = 0 \text{ and } m\|h = \langle 1 \rangle_b\|IV)$$
$$\qquad\qquad\qquad\qquad\qquad \text{or } (K^{(1)} = 1 \text{ and } m\|h = \langle b+1 \rangle_b\|IV)$$
$$= G(K, m\|h) \parallel 1 \parallel \overline{IV}^{(n)} \quad \text{otherwise},$$

In the full version [1] we prove that if G is (t, ϵ) atk-secure for atk $\in \{\text{Coll}, \text{eSec}\}$, then CE_2 is (t, ϵ) atk-secure. When iterating CE_2 through $\mathcal{LH}_{CE_2}$ with independent keys $K_1\|K_2\|K_3$, one can easily see that if $K_2^{(1)} = 0$ and $K_3^{(1)} = 1$, then messsages $M = 0$ and $M' = 010^{b-1}$ both hash to $0^{n-1}\|\overline{IV}^{(n)}$. Since in the Coll and eSec games this case happens with probability $1/4$, we have attacks satisfying the claim in the theorem.

XOR-LINEAR HASH. The *XOR-Linear Hash* ($\mathcal{XLH}$) [7] uses keys that consist of a compression function key K and ℓ masking keys $K_1, \ldots, K_\ell \in \{0,1\}^n$. It is known to preserve eSec security [7]. It can also be seen to preserve Coll and ePre by similar arguments as used for $\mathcal{SMD}$ and $\mathcal{LH}$. Counterexample CE_1 can be used to show that aSec and aPre are not preserved: the adversary gets to choose the key in these notions, so it can choose $K_1 = \ldots = K_\ell = 0^n$ so that $\mathcal{XLH}$ boils down to $\mathcal{SMD}$. In the following we show that the $\mathcal{XLH}$ construction does not preserve Sec or Pre security either.

Theorem 4. *For any* atk $\in \{\text{Sec}, \text{Pre}\}$, *if there exists a* (t, ϵ) atk*-secure compression function* $G : \mathcal{K} \times \{0,1\}^{b+n} \to \{0,1\}^{n-1}$, *then there exists a* $(t, \epsilon + 1/2^b)$ atk*-secure compression function* $CE_3 : \mathcal{K} \times \{0,1\}^{b+n} \to \{0,1\}^n$ *and an adversary* A *running in one step time with* atk$[\lambda]$*-advantage one in breaking* $\mathcal{XLH}_{CE_3}$.

Proof. For any $\lambda \leq 2^b$ and compression function G, consider CE_3 given by

$$CE_3(K, m\|h) = 0^n \qquad \text{if } m = \langle \lambda \rangle_b$$
$$= G(K, m\|h)\|1 \text{ otherwise .}$$

In the full version [1] we prove that if G is (t, ϵ) Sec or Pre-secure, then CE_3 is $(t, \epsilon + 1/2^b)$ Sec or Pre-secure. It is easy to see that, when iterated through $\mathcal{XLH}_{CE_3}$, the hash of any λ-bit message is 0^n. A Pre$[\lambda]$ adversary can therefore simply output any $M' \in \{0,1\}^\lambda$, a Sec$[\lambda]$ adversary can output any $M' \neq M \in \{0,1\}^\lambda$.

SHOUP'S HASH. The iteration due to Shoup ($\mathcal{SH}$) [30] is similar to the XOR-Linear hash but uses a different key scheduling that reduces the key length to logarithmic in the message length, rather than linear. Shoup's hash is known to preserve eSec-security [30], and it can be shown to preserve Coll and ePre-security as well. The proofs are very similar to the case of SMD, and hence omitted. Counterexample CE_1 disproves preservation of aSec and aPre-security, and counterexample CE_3 disproves preservation of Sec and Pre.

PREFIX-FREE MERKLE-DAMGÅRD. Bellare and Ristenpart showed [4] that the *prefix-free Merkle-Damgård* construction ($\mathcal{PfMD}$) [9] does not preserve Coll security. The counterexample of [7] can also be used to show that it does not preserve eSec, and counterexample CE_1 can be used to disprove the preservation of Sec, aSec, Pre and aPre. Finally, using a proof similar to that for $\mathcal{SMD}$, one can show that ePre-security is preserved.

Another variant of $\mathcal{PfMD}$ by [9] prepends the message length encoding to the message in advance. The security results of this scheme easily follow from the ones for the $\mathcal{SMD}$ construction.

RANDOMIZED HASH. The *Randomized Hash* ($\mathcal{RH}$) [13] XORs each message block with a random value $R \in \{0,1\}^b$. The construction was originally proved to be eSec secure by making stronger assumptions on the underlying compression function. Its pure security preservation characteristics (i.e., assuming only the eSec security of the compression function) were never studied. In our security analysis of $\mathcal{RH}$ treating the value R as either randomness per message or fixed long term key yields identical results with respect to seven property preservation.

By arguments similar to the case of $\mathcal{SMD}$, one can show that $\mathcal{RH}$ preserves Coll and ePre security, but none of the other notions are preserved. Counterexample

CE_1 can be used to contradict preservation of Sec, aSec, Pre, and ePre, and the counterexample of [7] can be used to contradict preservation of eSec.

HAIFA. While the newly proposed *HAsh Iterative FrAmework* ($\mathcal{HAIFA}$) [8] does preclude a number of specific attacks [12,15,14] to which $\mathcal{SMD}$ admits, they perform exactly the same in terms of preservation of our security notions. Similar proofs as for $\mathcal{SMD}$ can be used to show that $\mathcal{HAIFA}$ preserves Coll and ePre-security, counterexample CE_1 can be used to contradict the preservation of Sec, aSec, Pre, and aPre, and the counterexample of [7] applies to contradict preservation of eSec.

ENVELOPED MERKLE-DAMGÅRD. The *enveloped Merkle-Damgård* ($\mathcal{EMD}$) construction [4] is known to preserve collision resistance, pseudo-random-oracle, and pseudo-random function behavior. For the seven security notions that we consider, however, it does not perform better than $\mathcal{SMD}$. Counterexample CE_1 of Theorem 2 can be used (setting $IV = IV_2$) to show that neither of Sec, aSec, Pre, or aPre are preserved. An adaptation of the counterexample of [7] shows that eSec is not preserved either. Preservation of ePre on the other hand can be proved in a similar way as done in Theorem 1.

STRENGTHENED MERKLE TREE. We consider here the strengthened Merkle tree [20], the Tree Hash [7], and the XOR Tree Hash [7]. For conciseness we do not cover other tree iterations that have appeared in the literature (e.g. [17,29]). The Merkle tree [20] in its most basic form (i.e., without length strengthening) suffers from a similar anomaly as basic Merkle-Damgård in that it does not preserve Coll for arbitrary-length messages. We therefore consider the strengthened variant $\mathcal{SMT}$ here, depicted in Fig. 1. We believe $\mathcal{SMT}$ is commonly known to preserve Coll, but we reprove this in the full version [2] for completeness. The notion of ePre is easily seen to be preserved as well. It can be seen not to preserve eSec by a counterexample similar to that of [7] given in the full version [2]. $\mathcal{SMT}$ also fails to preserve Sec, aSec, Pre, and aPre however, as shown in the following theorem.

Theorem 5. *For any* atk $\in$ {Sec, aSec, Pre, aPre}, *if there exists a* (t', ϵ') *atk-secure compression function* G $: \mathcal{K} \times \{0,1\}^{an} \to \{0,1\}^{n-2}$, *then there exists a* (t, ϵ) *atk-secure compression function* $CE_4 : \mathcal{K} \times \{0,1\}^{an} \to \{0,1\}^n$ *for* $\epsilon = \epsilon' + 1/2^{n-1}$, $t = t'$, *and an adversary* A *running in one step time with* atk$[\lambda]$ *advantage 1 in breaking* $\mathcal{SMT}_{CE_4}$.

Proof. For any compression function G, consider CE_4 given by

$$CE_4(K, m_1\| \ldots \|m_a) = 0^n \qquad \qquad \text{if } m_a = 0^n$$
$$= 1^n \qquad \qquad \text{if } m_{a-1} = 0^n \text{ and } m_a \neq 0^n$$
$$= G(K, m_1\| \ldots \|m_a) \| 10 \text{ otherwise .}$$

We prove in the full version [1] that the bounds mentioned above hold for the atk security of CE_4. It is easy to see that, due to the one-zeroes padding to a^d bits, any message of length $a^{d-1} - 1 \leq \lambda \leq a^d - 1$ hashes to 1^n, leading to trivial constant-time attacks for any such length λ.

TREE HASH. The unstrengthened Tree Hash ($\mathcal{TH}$) was proposed in [7] for same-length messages; we consider the strengthened variant here. It is a variant of $\mathcal{SMT}$ where at each level i of the tree the compression functions use an independent key K_i. It can be seen to preserve ePre for the same reasons as the $\mathcal{SMT}$ construction. Our counterexample CE_4 can be used to exhibit the non-preservation of Sec, aSec, Pre and aPre security. The case of Coll and eSec are a bit more subtle, but the counterexample below shows that $\mathcal{TH}$ does not preserve these either.

Theorem 6. *For any* atk $\in \{\text{Coll}, \text{eSec}\}$, *if there exists a* (t', ϵ') atk-*secure compression function* G $: \{0,1\}^k \times \{0,1\}^{an} \rightarrow \{0,1\}^{n-1}$, *then there exists a* (t, ϵ) atk-*secure compression function* $CE_5 : \{0,1\}^k \times \{0,1\}^{an} \rightarrow \{0,1\}^n$ *for* $\epsilon = \epsilon'$, $t = t'$, *such that there exists an* eSec-*adversary breaking the* eSec *security of* $\mathcal{TH}_{CE_5}$ *in constant time with advantage* $1/4$.

Proof. For any compression function G, consider CE_5 given by

$$
\begin{aligned}
CE_5(K, M) &= 10^{n-1} && \text{if } M = (10^{n-1})^a \\
&= 1^n && \text{if } \left(K^{(1)} = 0 \text{ and } M = (10^{n-1})^{a-1} \| \langle (a-1)n \rangle_n \right) \\
&&& \text{or } \left(K^{(1)} = 1 \text{ and } M = (10^{n-1})^{a-1} \| \langle (a^2 - 1)n \rangle_n \right) \\
&= 0 \, \| \, G(K, M) && \text{otherwise} .
\end{aligned}
\tag{1}
$$

We prove in the full version [2] that CE_5 is (t, ϵ) atk-secure whenever G is (t, ϵ) atk-secure, for atk $\in \{\text{Coll}, \text{eSec}\}$.

Let $M = (10^{n-1})^{a-1}$ and $M' = (10^{n-1})^{a^2-1}$. Note that $\text{tpad}(M) = (10^{n-1})^a$ and $\text{tpad}(M') = (10^{n-1})^{a^2}$, where tpad is the tree padding algorithm of Fig. 1. If $\mathcal{TH}_{CE_5}$ is instantiated with keys $K_1\|K_2\|K_3$ such that $K_2^{(1)} = 0$ and $K_3^{(1)} = 1$, then one can verify that $\mathcal{TH}_{CE_5}(K_1\|K_2\|K_3, M') = \mathcal{TH}_{CE_5}(K_1\|K_2\|K_3, M) = 1^n$. Hence, the adversary that outputs M and M' as colliding message pair has advantage $1/4$ in winning the Coll and eSec games.

XOR TREE. The unstrengthened XOR Tree ($\mathcal{XTH}$) was proposed in [7] for fixed-length messages; we consider the strengthened variant here. It is again a variant of the Merkle tree, where the inputs to the compression functions on level i are XORed with a key $K_i \in \{0,1\}^{an}$. As for all other iterations, it is straightforward to see that $\mathcal{XTH}$ preserves ePre; we omit the proof. Quite remarkably, the masking of the entire input to the compression function makes it the only iteration in the literature that preserves Pre, while at the same time it seems to stand in the way of even proving preservation of Coll. It does not preserve aSec or aPre because the adversary can choose $K_i = 0^{an}$ and apply counterexample CE_4. We were unable to come up with either proof or counterexample for Coll, Sec, and eSec, leaving these as an open question. The proof of preservation of Pre is given in the full version [1].

4   The ROX Construction

We are now ready to present in detail our Random-Oracle-XOR (ROX) construction. Let F $: \{0,1\}^k \times \{0,1\}^{b+n} \rightarrow \{0,1\}^n$ be a fixed-length compression function.

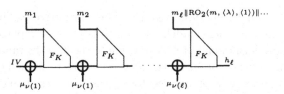

Fig. 2. The ROX Construction. The message is padded with bits generated by $RO_2(K, \mathfrak{m}, \langle\lambda\rangle, \langle i\rangle)$, where $\mathfrak{m}$ are the first k bits of M. The last block must contain at least $2n$ padding bits, otherwise an extra padding block is added. In the picture above, IV is the initialization vector, $\nu(i)$ is the largest integer j such that $2^j | i$, and the masks $\mu_i \leftarrow RO_1(K, \mathfrak{m}, \langle i\rangle)$.

Let 2^l be the maximum message length in bits; typically one would use $k = 80$ and $l = 64$. The construction uses two random oracles $RO_1 : \{0,1\}^k \times \{0,1\}^k \times \{0,1\}^{\lceil \log l \rceil} \to \{0,1\}^n$ and $RO_2 : \{0,1\}^k \times \{0,1\}^l \times \{0,1\}^{\lceil \log b \rceil} \to \{0,1\}^{2n}$. These random oracles can be built from a single one by adding an extra bit to the input that distinguishes calls to RO_1 and RO_2. Our construction can be thought of as a variant of Shoup's hash, but with the masks being generated by RO_1 and the padding being generated by RO_2. More precisely, on input a message M, our padding function rox-pad outputs a sequence of b-bit message blocks

$$m_1 \| \ldots \| m_\ell = M \| RO_2(\mathfrak{m}, \langle\lambda\rangle, \langle 1\rangle) \| RO_2(\mathfrak{m}, \langle\lambda\rangle, \langle 2\rangle) \| \ldots,$$

where $\mathfrak{m}$ are the first k bits of M and $\lambda = |M|$. The padding adds a number of bits generated by RO_2 such that the final block m_ℓ contains at least $2n$ bits generated by RO_2, possibly resulting in an extra block consisting solely of padding. It is worth noting though that we do not have a separate length strengthening block. We assume that $\lambda \geq k$ because aPre security, and therefore seven-property-preservation as a whole, do not make sense for short messages. Indeed, the adversary can always exhaustively try the entire message space. To hash shorter messages, one should add a random salt to the message.

Let $\nu(i)$ be the largest integer j such that 2^j divides i, let $IV \in \{0,1\}^n$ be an initialization vector, and let $\mathfrak{m}$ be the first k bits of the message M. Our construction is described in pseudocode below; a graphical representation is given in Fig. 2.

> Algorithm $\mathcal{ROX}_F^{RO_1, RO_2}(K, M)$:
> $m_1 \| \ldots \| m_\ell \leftarrow$ rox-pad$^{RO_2}(M)$; $h_0 \leftarrow IV$
> For $i = 0, \ldots, \lfloor \log_2(\ell) \rfloor$ do $\mu_i \leftarrow RO_1(K, \mathfrak{m}, \langle i\rangle)$
> For $i = 1 \ldots \ell$ do $g_i \leftarrow h_{i-1} \oplus \mu_{\nu(i)}$; $h_i \leftarrow F(K, m_i \| g_i)$
> Return h_ℓ .

We want to stress that that the ROX construction does not require that the compression function accept an additional input that might be influenced by the attacker (such as a salt or a counter). We see this as an important advantage, since imposing additional requirements on the compression function may make compression functions even harder to design or less efficient.

It is quite standard in cryptography for new primitives to first find instantiations in the random oracle model, only much later to be replaced with constructions in the standard model. It is interesting to see how the random oracles in the ROX construction can be instantiated if one were to implement it in practice. For an 80-bit security level, our results suggest that we should take $k = 80$ and $n = 160$. This means that we need a random oracle that reduces about 170 bits to 160 bits. A first suggestion might be to re-use the compression function with, say, three times as many rounds as normal, and with some different values of the constants. This approach violates good cryptographic hygiene, however, by having the design of the random oracle depend on that of the surrounding scheme. Perhaps a better solution would be to use one or more calls to a blockcipher like AES that was designed independently of the compression function.

5   Properties Preserved by the ROX Construction

The following theorem states that the ROX construction preserves all seven security properties that we consider here. We give a proof sketch for the preservation of Coll and a full proof for aSec below; the other proofs can be found in the full version [2]. We only note that the proofs for Sec, aSec and eSec are in the programmable random oracle model [26]; that for the case of Pre and aPre non-programmable random oracles suffice; and that Coll and ePre are preserved in the standard model.

Theorem 7. *For atk $\in \{$Coll, Sec, eSec, aSec, Pre, ePre, aPre$\}$, if the compression function F $: \{0,1\}^k \times \{0,1\}^{b+n} \to \{0,1\}^n$ is (t', ϵ') atk-secure, then the iterated function $\mathcal{ROX}_F$ is (t, q_{RO}, ϵ) atk-secure in the random oracle for*

$$\epsilon = \epsilon' + \frac{q_{RO}^2}{2^{2n}}, \qquad t = t' - 2\ell \cdot \tau_F \quad \text{for atk} = \text{Coll} \qquad (2)$$

$$\epsilon = \ell \cdot \epsilon' + \frac{q_{RO}}{2^{2n}}, \qquad t = t' - 2\ell \cdot \tau_F \quad \text{for atk} = \text{Sec} \qquad (3)$$

$$\epsilon = \ell \cdot \epsilon' + \frac{q_{RO}}{2^k} + \frac{q_{RO}^2}{2^{2n}}, \qquad t = t' - 2\ell \cdot \tau_F \quad \text{for atk} = \text{eSec} \qquad (4)$$

$$\epsilon = \ell \cdot \epsilon' + \frac{q_{RO}}{2^k} + \frac{q_{RO}}{2^{2n}}, \qquad t = t' - 2\ell \cdot \tau_F \quad \text{for atk} = \text{aSec} \qquad (5)$$

$$\epsilon = \epsilon', \qquad t = t' - \ell \cdot \tau_F \quad \text{for atk} \in \{\text{Pre}, \text{ePre}\} \qquad (6)$$

$$\epsilon = \epsilon' + \frac{q_{RO}}{2^k}, \qquad t = t' - \ell \cdot \tau_F \quad \text{for atk} = \text{aPre} \qquad (7)$$

Here, τ_F is the time required for an evaluation of F and $\ell = \lceil(\lambda + 2n)/b\rceil$ where $\lambda = |M|$.

We repeat that above we do not model the compression function as a random oracle, but it is worth considering what the equations tell us if we do. Assuming for simplicity that $\tau_F = 1$, we know that a collision adversary running in $t' = 2^{n/2}$ steps has probability about $1/2$ to find collisions in F, due to the birthday paradox, but only has probability $\epsilon' = 2^{-n/2}$ to find preimages or second preimages. Nevertheless, existing iterations cannot guarantee (second) preimage resistance against $2^{n/2}$-time adversaries, because they merely inherit their (second) preimage resistance by implication from collision resistance.[2] The ROX construction, on the other hand, can. Assuming that queries to RO_1, RO_2 take unit time and taking $k = n$, Equations (2), (3), (6) imply that an adversary running in time $t = 2^{n/2} - 2\ell \approx 2^{n/2}$ steps has probability at most $\epsilon = \ell \cdot 2^{-n/2} + 2^{n/2-k} + 2^{-n} \approx (\ell + 1) \cdot 2^{-n/2}$ to find second preimages, and has probability at most $\epsilon' = 2^{-n/2} + 2^{n/2-n} \approx 2^{-n/2+1}$ to find preimages.

Proof (Equation (2) (Sketch)). If M, M' is a pair of colliding messages, then consider the two chains of compression function calls in the computation of $\mathcal{ROX}_F(K, M) = \mathcal{ROX}_F(K, M')$. If the inputs to the final call to F are different for M and M', then these inputs form a collision on F and we're done. If they are the same, then remember that at least $2n$ bits of these inputs are the output of $RO_2(\mathfrak{m}, \langle\lambda\rangle, \langle i \rangle)$ and $RO_2(\mathfrak{m}', \langle\lambda'\rangle, \langle j \rangle)$, respectively. If these are different queries to RO_2, yet their outputs are the same, then the adversary must have found a collision on RO_2; the odds of it doing so are bounded by $q_{RO}^2 / 2^{2n}$. If these queries are the same, however, then we have that $\mathfrak{m} = \mathfrak{m}'$ and $\lambda = \lambda'$, and therefore that the masks in both chains $\mu_i = \mu_i' = RO_1(K, \mathfrak{m}, \langle i \rangle)$. Identical chaining inputs to ℓ-th call to F must therefore be caused by identical outputs of the $(\ell - 1)$-st call to F. If the inputs to the $(\ell - 1)$-st call are different then we have a collision on F here, otherwise we repeat the argument to the $(\ell - 2)$-nd call, and so on. A collision on F will be found unless $M = M'$. We refer to the full version [2] for a more detailed proof.

Proof (Equation (5)). Given an $\text{aSec}[\lambda]$ adversary A against $\mathcal{ROX}_F$ for any $\lambda \in \mathbb{N}$, we will construct an aSec adversary B against F. The overall strategy will be that B "embeds" his own challenge message at a random point in the chain, and hopes that A's output yields a second preimage at exactly the point in the chain where B has embedded his challenge.

Algorithm B runs A to obtain a key $K \in \{0, 1\}^k$, responding to its random oracle queries by maintaining associative arrays $T_1[\cdot], T_2[\cdot]$. B outputs the same key K and is then given as input a random challenge message $m\|g \in \{0, 1\}^{b+n}$. It chooses a random index $i^* \xleftarrow{\$} \{1, \ldots, \ell = \lceil(\lambda + 2n)/b\rceil\}$. We first explain how B can construct a message M of length λ so that $m_{i^*} = m$ in $m_1\|\ldots\|m_\ell \leftarrow \text{rox-pad}^{RO_2}(M)$; the rest of the message blocks are randomly generated. After that, we will show how g can be embedded into the chain such that $g_{i^*} = g$. If $i^* = 1$ then B sets $\mathfrak{m}$ to the first k bits of m, otherwise it chooses $\mathfrak{m} \xleftarrow{\$} \{0, 1\}^k$ and sets the first k bits of M to $\mathfrak{m}$. We distinguish between Type-I message blocks that only contain bits of M, Type-II message blocks of which the first $\lambda_b = (\lambda \bmod b)$ bits are the last λ_b bits of M and the remaining bits are generated by RO_2, and Type-III message blocks that consist entirely of bits generated by RO_2. Embedding m in a Type-I message block can simply be done by setting b

---

[2] For the Prefix-free MD [9] and EMD [4] iterations this is a bit paradoxical, because they were designed to preserve "random oracle behavior". Surely, (second) preimage resistance should fall under any reasonable definition of "random oracle behavior"? The caveat here is that the proof [4, Theorem 5.2] bounds the distinguishing probability to $O(q_{RO}^2/2^n)$, so that the theorem statement becomes moot for $q_{RO} = 2^{n/2}$.

bits of M to $\mathfrak{m}$ starting at bit position $(i^* - 1)b + 1$. To embed $\mathfrak{m}$ in a Type-II message block, B sets the last λ_b bits of M to the first λ_b bits of $\mathfrak{m}$, and programs the first $(b - \lambda_b)$ bits of $T_2[\mathfrak{m}, \langle \lambda \rangle, \langle 1 \rangle] \parallel T_2[\mathfrak{m}, \langle \lambda \rangle, \langle 2 \rangle] \parallel \ldots$ to be the last $(b - \lambda_b)$ bits of $\mathfrak{m}$. For Type-III blocks, B chooses M completely at random and sets b bits of $T_2[\mathfrak{m}, \langle \lambda \rangle, \langle 1 \rangle] \parallel T_2[\mathfrak{m}, \langle \lambda \rangle, \langle 2 \rangle] \parallel \ldots$ to $\mathfrak{m}$, starting at the $(b - \lambda_b + 1)$-st bit position. Bits of M and $T_2[\mathfrak{m}, \cdot]$ that are still undefined are chosen at random. If any of these table entries were already defined during A's first run, then B aborts. Notice however that A's view during the first run is independent of $\mathfrak{m}$, so its probability of making such a query is at most $q_{\mathrm{RO}}/2^k$.

To enforce that $g_{i^*} = g$ in the computation of $\mathcal{ROX}_{\mathsf{F}}^{\mathrm{RO}_1,\mathrm{RO}_2}(K, M)$, algorithm B runs the reconstruction algorithm of [30,23] that, given message blocks $m_1, \ldots, m_{i^*}$ and chaining value g_{i^*}, outputs random mask values $\mu_0, \ldots, \mu_t$ such that the chaining input to the i^*-th compression function call is g_{i^*}. B's goal is to program these masks into RO_1 by setting $T_1[K, \mathfrak{m}, \langle i \rangle] \leftarrow \mu_i$ for $0 \leq i \leq t$, such that it is possible to check that the value for g_{i^*} obtained during the h_i computation is indeed g. However, if any of the hash table entries $T_1[K, \mathfrak{m}, \langle i \rangle]$ for $0 \leq i \leq t$ has already been defined, then B aborts. This can only occur when A asked a query $\mathrm{RO}_1(K, \mathfrak{m}, \langle i \rangle)$ during its first phase, but again, the probability of it doing so is at most $q_{\mathrm{RO}}/2^k$ because its view is independent of $\mathfrak{m}$.

Algorithm B then runs A again on input target message M, responding to its random oracle queries as before, until it outputs a second preimage M'. Let $m_0' \parallel \ldots \parallel m_{\ell'}' \leftarrow \text{rox-pad}^{\mathrm{RO}_2}(M')$ be the parsed messages. For the same arguments as in the proof of Equation (2) above, there must exist an index $I > 0$ such that $h_I = h_I'$ but $m_I \parallel g_I \neq m_I' \parallel g_I'$, unless A found a collision in the random oracle RO_2. If $i^* = I$, then B outputs $m_I' \parallel g_I'$.

B wins the game whenever A does and $i^* = I$, unless A succeeded in causing a collision in RO_2 or any of the values that are programmed in $\mathrm{RO}_1, \mathrm{RO}_2$ were already queried. Let E_1 be the event that at least one of the preprogrammed values is queried by A on a different input and E_2 be the event that A manages to find at least one collision in RO_2. Let ABORT be the event that B aborts, then

$$\Pr[\text{ABORT}] = \Pr[E_1] + \Pr[E_2 : \overline{E_1}] \leq \Pr[E_1] + \Pr[E_2].$$

Since B perfectly simulates A's environment, the advantage of B is given by

$$\epsilon' \geq \Pr[\text{A wins} \wedge i^* = I : \overline{\text{ABORT}}] \cdot \Pr[\overline{\text{ABORT}}]$$
$$\geq \frac{\epsilon}{\ell}\left(1 - \left(\frac{q_{\mathrm{RO}}}{2^k} + \frac{q_{\mathrm{RO}}^2}{2^{2n}}\right)\right) \geq \frac{1}{\ell}\left(\epsilon - \frac{q_{\mathrm{RO}}}{2^k} - \frac{q_{\mathrm{RO}}^2}{2^{2n}}\right).$$

The running time of B is that of A plus at most 2ℓ evaluations of F. Equation (5) follows.

POSSIBLE TWEAKS. The scheme can be simplified not all seven properties need to be preserved. For example, if the key K is dropped from the input to RO_1, the $\mathcal{ROX}$ construction fails to preserve eSec and ePre, but still preserves all other notions. Dropping the message bits $\mathfrak{m}$ from the input of either RO_1 or RO_2 destroys the preservation of aSec and aPre, but leaves the preservation of other notions unharmed.

Acknowledgements

We would like to thank David Cash and the anonymous referees for their useful feedback. This work was supported in part by the European Commission through the IST Programme under Contract IST-2002-507932 ECRYPT, and in part by the IAP Programme P6/26 BCRYPT of the Belgian State (Belgian Science Policy). The first author is supported by a Ph.D. Fellowship and the second by a Postdoctoral Fellowship from the Flemish Research Foundation (FWO - Vlaanderen). The fourth author was supported by NSF CNS-0627752.

References

1. Andreeva, E., Neven, G., Preneel, B., Shrimpton, T.: Seven-property-preserving iterated hashing: ROX. Cryptology ePrint Archive, Report 2007/176 (2007)
2. Andreeva, E., Neven, G., Preneel, B., Shrimpton, T.: Three-property preserving iterations of keyless compression functions. In: ECRYPT Hash Workshop (2007)
3. Bellare, M., Canetti, R., Krawczyk, H.: Keying hash functions for message authentication. In: Koblitz, N. (ed.) CRYPTO 1996. LNCS, vol. 1109, Springer, Heidelberg (1996)
4. Bellare, M., Ristenpart, T.: Multi-property-preserving hash domain extension: The EMD transform. In: Lai, X., Chen, K. (eds.) ASIACRYPT 2006. LNCS, vol. 4284, pp. 299–314. Springer, Heidelberg (2006)
5. Bellare, M., Ristenpart, T.: Hash functions in the dedicated-key setting: Design choices and MPP transforms. In: Arge, L., Cachin, C., Tarlecki, A. (eds.) ICALP 2007. 34th International Colloquium on Automata, Languages and Programming. LNCS, vol. 4596, Springer, Heidelberg (2007)
6. Bellare, M., Rogaway, P.: Random oracles are practical: A paradigm for designing efficient protocols. In: ACM CCS 1993, pp. 62–73. ACM Press, New York (1993)
7. Bellare, M., Rogaway, P.: Collision-resistant hashing: Towards making UOWHFs practical. In: Kaliski Jr., B.S. (ed.) CRYPTO 1997. LNCS, vol. 1294, Springer, Heidelberg (1997)
8. Biham, E., Dunkelman, O.: A framework for iterative hash functions – HAIFA. Second NIST Cryptographic Hash Workshop (2006)
9. Coron, J.-S., Dodis, Y., Malinaud, C., Puniya, P.: Merkle-Damgård revisited: How to construct a hash function. In: Shoup, V. (ed.) CRYPTO 2005. LNCS, vol. 3621, pp. 430–448. Springer, Heidelberg (2005)
10. Cramer, R., Shoup, V.: Design and analysis of practical public-key encryption schemes secure against adaptive chosen ciphertext attack. SIAM Journal on Computing 33(1), 167–226 (2003)
11. Damgård, I.: A design principle for hash functions. In: Brassard, G. (ed.) CRYPTO 1989. LNCS, vol. 435, pp. 416–427. Springer, Heidelberg (1990)
12. Dean, R.D.: Formal Aspects of Mobile Code Security. PhD thesis, Princeton University (1999)
13. Halevi, S., Krawczyk, H.: Strengthening digital signatures via randomized hashing. In: Dwork, C. (ed.) CRYPTO 2006. LNCS, vol. 4117, pp. 41–59. Springer, Heidelberg (2006)
14. Kelsey, J., Kohno, T.: Herding hash functions and the Nostradamus attack. In: Vaudenay, S. (ed.) EUROCRYPT 2006. LNCS, vol. 4004, pp. 183–200. Springer, Heidelberg (2006), from http://eprint.iacr.org/2005/281

15. Kelsey, J., Schneier, B.: Second preimages on n-bit hash functions for much less than 2^n work. In: Cramer, R.J.F. (ed.) EUROCRYPT 2005. LNCS, vol. 3494, pp. 474–490. Springer, Heidelberg (2005)

16. Lai, X., Massey, J.L.: Hash functions based on block ciphers. In: Rueppel, R.A. (ed.) EUROCRYPT 1992. LNCS, vol. 658, pp. 55–70. Springer, Heidelberg (1993)

17. Lee, W., Chang, D., Lee, S., Sung, S.H., Nandi, M.: New parallel domain extenders for UOWHF. In: Laih, C.-S. (ed.) ASIACRYPT 2003. LNCS, vol. 2894, pp. 208–227. Springer, Heidelberg (2003)

18. Luby, M., Rackoff, C.: A study of password security. Journal of Cryptology 1(3), 151–158 (1989)

19. Lucks, S.: A failure-friendly design principle for hash functions. In: Roy, B. (ed.) ASIACRYPT 2005. LNCS, vol. 3788, pp. 474–494. Springer, Heidelberg (2005)

20. Merkle, R.C.: Protocols for public key cryptosystems. In: IEEE Symposium on Security and Privacy, pp. 122–134. IEEE Computer Society Press, Los Alamitos (1980)

21. Merkle, R.C.: A certified digital signature. In: Brassard, G. (ed.) CRYPTO 1989. LNCS, vol. 435, pp. 218–238. Springer, Heidelberg (1990)

22. Merkle, R.C.: One way hash functions and DES. In: Brassard, G. (ed.) CRYPTO 1989. LNCS, vol. 435, pp. 428–446. Springer, Heidelberg (1990)

23. Mironov, I.: Hash functions: From Merkle-Damgård to Shoup. In: Pfitzmann, B. (ed.) EUROCRYPT 2001. LNCS, vol. 2045, pp. 166–181. Springer, Heidelberg (2001)

24. Mironov, I.: Collision-resistant no more: Hash-and-sign paradigm revisited. In: PKC 2006. LNCS, pp. 140–156. Springer, Heidelberg (2006)

25. Naor, M., Yung, M.: Universal one-way hash functions and their cryptographic applications. In: 21st ACM STOC, pp. 33–43. ACM Press, New York (1989)

26. Nielsen, J.B.: Separating random oracle proofs from complexity theoretic proofs: The non-committing encryption case. In: Yung, M. (ed.) CRYPTO 2002. LNCS, vol. 2442, pp. 111–126. Springer, Heidelberg (2002)

27. Rogaway, P.: Formalizing human ignorance: Collision-resistant hashing without the keys. In: Nguyen, P.Q. (ed.) VIETCRYPT 2006. LNCS, vol. 4341, Springer, Heidelberg (2006)

28. Rogaway, P., Shrimpton, T.: Cryptographic hash-function basics: Definitions, implications, and separations for preimage resistance, second-preimage resistance, and collision resistance. In: Roy, B., Meier, W. (eds.) FSE 2004. LNCS, vol. 3017, pp. 371–388. Springer, Heidelberg (2004)

29. Sarkar, P.: Masking-based domain extenders for UOWHFs: bounds and constructions. IEEE Transactions on Information Theory 51(12), 4299–4311 (2005)

30. Shoup, V.: A composition theorem for universal one-way hash functions. In: Preneel, B. (ed.) EUROCRYPT 2000. LNCS, vol. 1807, pp. 445–452. Springer, Heidelberg (2000)

31. Wagner, D., Goldberg, I.: Proofs of security for the Unix password hashing algorithm. In: Okamoto, T. (ed.) ASIACRYPT 2000. LNCS, vol. 1976, Springer, Heidelberg (2000)

32. Wang, X., Yin, Y.L., Yu, H.: Finding collisions in the full SHA-1. In: Shoup, V. (ed.) CRYPTO 2005. LNCS, vol. 3621, pp. 17–36. Springer, Heidelberg (2005)

33. Wang, X., Yu, H.: How to break MD5 and other hash functions. In: Cramer, R.J.F. (ed.) EUROCRYPT 2005. LNCS, vol. 3494, pp. 19–35. Springer, Heidelberg (2005)

How to Build a Hash Function
from Any Collision-Resistant Function

Thomas Ristenpart[1] and Thomas Shrimpton[2,3]

[1] Dept. of Computer Science & Engineering, University of California San Diego
9500 Gilman Drive, La Jolla, CA 92093-0404, USA
tristenp@cs.ucsd.edu
http://www-cse.ucsd.edu/users/tristenp
[2] Dept. of Computer Science, Portland State University
Room 120, Forth Avenue Building, 1900 SW 4th Avenue, Portland OR 97201 USA
teshrim@cs.pdx.edu
http://www.cs.pdx.edu/~teshrim
[3] Faculty of Informatics, University of Lugano
Via Buffi 13, CH-6900 Lugano, Switzerland
thomas.shrimpton@unisi.ch
http://www.inf.unisi.ch/

Abstract. Recent collision-finding attacks against hash functions such as MD5 and SHA-1 motivate the use of *provably* collision-resistant (CR) functions in their place. Finding a collision in a provably CR function implies the ability to solve some hard problem (e.g., factoring). Unfortunately, existing provably CR functions make poor replacements for hash functions as they fail to deliver behaviors demanded by practical use. In particular, they are easily distinguished from a random oracle. We initiate an investigation into building hash functions from provably CR functions. As a method for achieving this, we present the Mix-Compress-Mix (**MCM**) construction; it envelopes any provably CR function H (with suitable regularity properties) between two injective "mixing" stages. The MCM construction simultaneously enjoys (1) provable collision-resistance in the standard model, and (2) indifferentiability from a monolithic random oracle when the mixing stages themselves are indifferentiable from a random oracle that observes injectivity. We instantiate our new design approach by specifying a blockcipher-based construction that appropriately realizes the mixing stages.

1 Introduction

BACKGROUND. SHA-1, a Merkle-Damgård style [24, 15] iterated function, is provably collision resistant under the *assumption* that its underlying compression function is collision resistant. But the recent collision-finding attacks against SHA-1 (and related hash functions) [37, 38] have made clear the point that assumptions of collision resistance are often unfounded in practice.

Rather than assuming collision resistance outright, several works [12, 22, 26, 33, 14] build functions for which the guarantee of collision resistance rests, in a

K. Kurosawa (Ed.): ASIACRYPT 2007, LNCS 4833, pp. 147–163, 2007.

provable way, on the hardness of some well-studied computational problem. As a simple example, consider the function $H(m) = x^m \mod n$ where x is some fixed base and n is a (supposedly) hard-to-factor composite [26,33]. This function is (what we shall call) *provably* CR since there exists a formal reduction showing that the ability to find collisions in H implies the ability to efficiently factor n.

But such a collision-resistant function is not a *hash function*, at least not when one attempts to define a hash function by its myriad uses in practice[1]. For example, hash functions are frequently used as a way to compress and 'mix-up' strings of bits in an 'unpredictable' way; here it seems clear that the intent is for the hash function to mimic a random oracle, a publicly available random function with a large domain. Unfortunately, the provably CR function H is a poor real-world instantiation of a random oracle. Note, for example, that $H(2m) \equiv H(m)^2$ (mod n), which would be true with exceedingly small probability if H were instead a random oracle. The very structure that gives H and other provably CR functions their collision-resistance thus renders them useless for many practical applications of hash functions [12,36].

On the other hand, recent results [13,2,11] offer constructions that 'behave' as random oracles (and are called pseudorandom oracles, or PROs) when the underlying primitives are themselves idealized objects, like fixed-input length random oracles or ideal ciphers. In theory then, a PRO is a secure hash functions in a very broad sense. But the security guarantees offered by a PRO only hold in an idealized model. When one steps outside of the ideal model in which the security proofs take place, the actual security guarantees are much less clear. As an example, Bellare and Ristenpart [2] have pointed out that the PRO constructions from [13] fail to be collision resistant when the underlying compression function is only assumed to be CR (rather than being a fixed-input-length random oracle).

THIS PAPER. We begin an investigation into methods for building functions that are *both* provably CR in the standard model and provably pseudorandom oracles in idealized models. In particular, we offer a generic construction that we call Mix-Compress-Mix, or MCM; See Figure 1. Essentially MCM is a way to encapsulate a provably CR function in such a way that the resulting object is a PRO when the encapsulation steps behave ideally, and yet remains provably collision resistant in the standard model (i.e., when the encapsulation steps are only complexity theoretic objects).

The construction is simple: first apply an injective "mixing" step $\mathcal{E}_1$ to the input message, then compress the result using a provably CR function H, and finally apply a second injective "mixing" step $\mathcal{E}_2$ to produce the output. Here H and $\mathcal{E}_1$ can accept variable-input-lengths. Note that since MCM is building a hash function, the mixing steps $\mathcal{E}_1$ and $\mathcal{E}_2$ are necessarily deterministic and publically computable functions. By demanding that they also be injective, we have immediately that collisions against MCM imply collisions against H. We stress that *no* cryptographic assumptions about the mixing steps are needed to prove collision resistance of MCM.

---

[1] This viewpoint is not ours alone. One of the designers of VSH [12], Arjen Lenstra, once publicly stated "VSH is not a hash function."

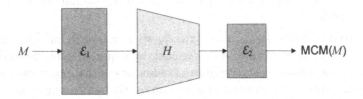

Fig. 1. The MCM construction: H is a collision resistant hash function, and $\mathcal{E}_1, \mathcal{E}_2$ are mixing functions. All three components of MCM must be deterministic and publically computable.

At the same time, MCM behaves like a random oracle when $\mathcal{E}_1, \mathcal{E}_2$ are PROs, and the CR hash function is close to regular (i.e., the preimage set of any particular output isn't too large). In fact, we will actually construct $\mathcal{E}_1, \mathcal{E}_2$ to be *pseudorandom injective oracles*, or PRIOs; we'll say more about these in a moment. To make precise our use of the word "behaves" above, we use the indifferentiability framework of Maurer et al. [23]. We'll prove that MCM is indifferentiable from a monolithic random oracle when the mixing steps $\mathcal{E}_1$ and $\mathcal{E}_2$ are indifferentiable from random oracles (that observe injectivity). While the formal results are quite technical, the practical intuition behind the security of MCM is straightforward: the mixing steps obfuscate input-output relationships of the underlying compressing step. Recall our provably CR example $H(m) = x^m \bmod n$ and the associated attack that distinguished it from a random oracle. Adapting that attack for use against $\mathcal{H}(M) = \mathcal{E}_2(H(\mathcal{E}_1(M)))$ requires that the adversary determine non-trivial input-output relationships across both $\mathcal{E}_1$ and $\mathcal{E}_2$, too.

One might be tempted to think a construction even simpler than MCM meets our goals. In Section 4 we discuss natural simplifications of MCM (e.g., dropping $\mathcal{E}_1$ or lifting our stringent injectivity requirements), showing that these fall short in one way or another. Moreover, we review in more detail why existing approaches for building hash functions also fail.

Although we have just described MCM in the variable-input-length setting, we note that it also works for building a dual-property compression function (i.e., a fixed-input-length function) from any CR compression function. The result could be then be used inside a multi-property-preserving domain extension transform such as EMD [2].

A NEW APPROACH TO HASH FUNCTION DESIGN. By generically composing appropriate mixing and compressing stages, MCM allows the following separation of design tasks. First, design a function with strong guarantees of collision-resistance, inducing whatever structure is necessary. Second, design an injective function that destroys any structure present in its input. This approach is a significant departure from traditional hash function designs, in which one typically constructs a compression function that must necessarily (and simultaneously) be secure in various ways. With MCM, we instead build a hash function by designing components to achieve specific security goals. The benefits of such specialized components are immediate: MCM allows building a single hash function that has very strong CR guarantees while simultaneously being suitable for instantiating a random oracle.

SECURE MIXING STEPS. Remaining is the question of how to build mixing steps sufficient for the goals of MCM. As we've said, we require the mixing steps to be both injective *and* indifferentiable from a random oracle that observes injectivity. At first glance these requirements might seem overly burdensome. Can't the requirement simply be for the mixing steps to realize pseudorandom oracles, which we already know (via [13, 11, 2]) how to build? No: while a PRO would satisfy the second constraint, albiet with some additive birthday-bound loss in concrete security, it would not at the same time suffice for MCM's crucial standard-model CR guarantee. This is because a PRO provides no guarantees of collision-resistance outside of an idealized model. In fact, simultaneously satisfying both requirements, injectivity and indifferentiability, is technically challenging.

To our knowledge, building a PRIO has never been considered before. Dodis and Puniya [17, 16] consider a similar goal, that of building random permutations from random functions, but these are invertible by construction, whereas PRIOs are not. Moreover, their proofs of security only hold for honest-but-curious adversaries. We therefore present the Tag-and-Encipher (TE) construction for realizing a PRIO (see Section 5). It is a blockcipher mode of operation (which also employs a single trapdoor one-way permutation call) that is injective by construction. In the ideal cipher model and under the assumption of trusted setup of the trapdoor permutation, the TE construction is indifferentiable from an injective random oracle. While not particularly efficient, we view the TE construction as a proof-of-concept, and hope it fosters future efforts to build these novel primitives.

NOTES ON INDIFFERENTIABILITY AND COMPOSABILITY. In order to accomplish our task of building a hash function with both strong standard model and ideal model guarantees, we exercise the indifferentiability framework in novel ways. First, both MCM and TE are a combination of complexity-theoretic objects (the CR function H and the trapdoor permutation) and information-theoretic objects (the idealized components). Previous indifferentiability results have been solely information-theoretic. Second, our model allows the simulator to choose the trapdoor permutation utilized in TE. These two facts imply limitations on the generic composability of our schemes. Composability refers to the guarantee that *any* cryptographic scheme proven secure using an ideal object remains secure when this object is replaced by a construction that is indifferentiable from it. In practice the limited composability of our constructions means that they might not be suitable for all applications of random (injective) oracles. We discuss this matter in more detail, and pose some interesting open questions raised by it, in Section 6.

2 Preliminaries

BASICS. Let $X, Y \in \{0, 1\}^*$. We denote the concatenation of X and Y by $X \parallel Y$ or simply XY. The ith bit of X is $X[i]$ and so $X = X[1]X[2] \cdots X[|X|]$. We write $X|_n$ (resp. $X|^n$) to represent the substring consisting of the last (resp. first) n bits of X for any $n \leq |X|$. For a set S we often write $S \overset{\cup}{\leftarrow} x$, which means $S \leftarrow S \cup \{x\}$. We define $\mathsf{Time}_f(\mu)$ as the worst-case time to compute f on a message of length at most μ.

Following [8, 13] we utilize Interactive Turing Machines (ITM) for our computational model. Cryptographic primitives, schemes, and adversaries are all interactive Turing machines.

RANDOM FUNCTIONS AND INJECTIONS. Let Dom and Rng be sets. Recall that a function $f: Dom \rightarrow Rng$ is injective if $f(X) = f(X')$ implies that $X = X'$. (Necessarily for an injection $|Dom| \leq |Rng|$.) For simplicity, we only consider injections with constant stretch τ. Particularly if $X \in Dom$ then $|f(X)| = |X| + \tau$. The following algorithms implement a *random function* and a *random injection*.

Algorithm $\mathsf{RF}_{Dom,Rng}(X)$:
If $\mathsf{R}[X] \neq \perp$ then Ret $\mathsf{R}[X]$
Ret $\mathsf{R}[X] \overset{\$}{\leftarrow} Rng$

Algorithm $\mathsf{RI}_{Dom,Rng}(X)$:
$\ell \leftarrow |X| + \tau$
If $\mathsf{I}[X] \neq \perp$ then Ret $\mathsf{I}[X]$
$\mathsf{I}[X] \overset{\$}{\leftarrow} \{0,1\}^\ell \backslash \mathcal{R}_\ell$
$\mathcal{R}_\ell \overset{\cup}{\leftarrow} \mathsf{I}[X]$
Ret $\mathsf{I}[X]$

The tables R and I are initially everywhere set to $\perp$ and the set $\mathcal{R}_\ell$ is initially empty for every ℓ. We write $f = \mathsf{RF}_{Dom,Rng}$ to signify that f is an ITM mapping points from Dom to Rng according to the algorithm specified above. We write $\mathsf{RF}_{d,r}$ if $Dom = \{0,1\}^d$ and $Rng = \{0,1\}^r$ for some numbers d, r. We write $\mathcal{I} = \mathsf{RI}_{Dom,Rng}$ for an ITM mapping points from Dom to Rng as per the algorithm specified above. (The other notational conventions lift to RI in the obvious ways.) A random oracle is a random function that is publically accessible by all parties. Similarly an random (or ideal) injection is a publically-accessible random function that respects injectivity.

IDEAL CIPHERS. For integers $k, n > 0$, a blockcipher $E: \{0,1\}^k \times \{0,1\}^n \rightarrow \{0,1\}^n$ is a function for which $E(K, \cdot) = E_K(\cdot)$ is a permutation for every $K \in \{0,1\}^k$. The inverse of E is D and is defined such that $D(K, Y) = M$ iff $E(K, M) = Y$. An ideal cipher is a blockcipher uniformly selected from $\mathrm{BC}(k, n)$, the space of all blockciphers with k-bit keys and n-bit blocksize. In the ideal cipher model, both an ideal cipher E and its inverse are given to all parties as oracles.

SECURITY NOTIONS. Let $f: \mathcal{K} \times Dom \rightarrow Rng$ be a function family indexed by a non-empty key space $\mathcal{K}$. Then we define the collision-finding advantage of an adversary $\mathcal{A}$ against f as

$$\mathbf{Adv}_f^{\mathrm{cr}}(\mathcal{A}) = \Pr\left[f_K(X) = f_K(X') \ : \ K \overset{\$}{\leftarrow} \mathcal{K}; (X, X') \overset{\$}{\leftarrow} \mathcal{A}(K) \right]$$

where the probability is over the random choice of K and the random coins utilized by $\mathcal{A}$.

A function $f: Dom \rightarrow \{0,1\}^n$ is *regular* if each image has an equal number of preimages. A function family $f: \mathcal{K} \times Dom \rightarrow \{0,1\}^n$ is regular if f_K is regular for each $K \in \mathcal{K}$. Associated to a function family f is the set $\mathsf{Prelm}(K, \ell, Y)$ that, for each $K \in \mathcal{K}$, ℓ such that $\{0, 1\}^{\ell} \subseteq Dom$, and $Y \in \{0, 1\}^{\eta}$, is the set of preimages (under K) of Y that are of length ℓ. That is, $\mathsf{Prelm}(K, \ell, Y) = \{X : X \in Dom \wedge |X| = \ell \wedge f_K(X) = Y\}$. We also define the following function related to f

$$\delta(K, \ell, Y) = \frac{|\mathsf{Prelm}(K, \ell, Y)| - 2^{\ell - \eta}}{2^{\ell}}.$$

The δ function measures how much bigger (or smaller) a particular preimage set is than it would be if f_K were regular. We define $\Delta_K = \max\{\delta(K, \ell, Y)\}$, where the maximum is taken over all choices of ℓ and Y, and we say a function family f is Δ-regular if

$$\frac{\sum_{K \in \mathcal{K}} \Delta_K}{|\mathcal{K}|} \leq \Delta.$$

Intuitively, this measures on average (over keys) how far f is from regular.

Let $\mathbb{F}$ be a *trapdoor permutation generator*: on input 1^k it outputs a trapdoor permutation pair (f, f^{-1}) where $f: \{0, 1\}^k \to \{0, 1\}^k$ and $f^{-1}(f(X)) = X$. The one-way advantage of an adversary $\mathcal{A}$ against $\mathbb{F}$ for security parameter k is defined by

$$\mathbf{Adv}_{\mathbb{F}}^{\mathrm{owf}}(\mathcal{A}) = \Pr\left[f(X) = f(X') : \begin{array}{l} (f, f^{-1}) \xleftarrow{\$} \mathbb{F}(1^k); X \xleftarrow{\$} \{0, 1\}^k; \\ Y \leftarrow f(X); X' \xleftarrow{\$} \mathcal{A}(f, Y) \end{array} \right].$$

The RSA and Rabin function families are conjectured to allow generation of secure trapdoor permutations [32, 28, 29].

PROs AND PRIOs. The notion of indifferentiability [23] is a generalization of conventional indistinguishability [18].] It facilitates reasoning about the ability of constructions to emulate some idealized functionality (e.g., a random oracle) in settings where the construction itself utilizes public, idealized components (e.g., an ideal cipher or fixed-input-length (FIL) random oracle). We follow the formalization of indifferentiability from [13, 2] to define security for pseudorandom oracles and pseudorandom injective oracles. First, a *simulator* $\mathcal{S} = (\mathcal{S}_1, \ldots, \mathcal{S}_l)$ is an interactive Turing machine with l interfaces $\mathcal{S}_1, \ldots, \mathcal{S}_l$. The interfaces share common state, i.e. all variables defined in one interface are available to all other interfaces. Let C be some cryptographic scheme utilizing primitives $f_1, \ldots, f_l$ and let Dom and Rng be non-empty sets. We define the pro and prio advantage of an adversary $\mathcal{A}$ against C with respect to simulator $\mathcal{S}$ as

$$\mathbf{Adv}_{C, \mathcal{S}}^{\mathrm{pro}}(\mathcal{A}) = \Pr\left[\mathcal{A}^{C^{f_1, \ldots, f_l}, f_1, \ldots, f_l} \Rightarrow 1 \right] - \Pr\left[\mathcal{A}^{\mathcal{F}, \mathcal{S}^{\mathcal{F}}} \Rightarrow 1 \right]$$

$$\mathbf{Adv}_{C, \mathcal{S}}^{\mathrm{prio}}(\mathcal{A}) = \Pr\left[\mathcal{A}^{C^{f_1, \ldots, f_l}, f_1, \ldots, f_l} \Rightarrow 1 \right] - \Pr\left[\mathcal{A}^{\mathcal{I}, \mathcal{S}^{\mathcal{I}}} \Rightarrow 1 \right]$$

where $\mathcal{F} = \mathrm{RF}_{Dom, Rng}$ and $\mathcal{I} = \mathrm{RI}_{Dom, Rng}$ and the probabilities are over the random coins used by the appropriate objects. We emphasize that the simulator has oracle access to the idealized object ($\mathcal{F}$ or $\mathcal{I}$), but does not see the queries $\mathcal{A}$

makes to it. In the case that the construction uses publically-keyed components (e.g., the key for a CR function), all three entities (C, S, A) have access to the key. We disallow A from making *pointless* queries, which in this setting means querying an oracle twice.

Informally we call a cryptographic scheme C a pseudorandom oracle (PRO), or say it is indifferentiable from a random oracle, if there exists an "efficient" simulator against which all adversaries have "small" pro advantage. Likewise we call a cryptographic scheme C a pseudorandom injective oracle (PRIO) if there exists an "efficient" simulator against which all adversaries have "small" prio advantage. We do not formalize "efficient" or "small", giving concrete running times and bounds, instead.

We formalize trusted setup of a trapdoor permutation generator $\mathbb{F}$ via an interactive Turing machine TGen that behaves as follows. When called, it computes $(f, f^{-1}) \xleftarrow{\$} \mathbb{F}(1^k)$ and returns f. Subsequent calls return the same f. Constructions that utilize a trapdoor permutation are given oracle access to TGen, for example in the pro and prio definitions $f_i = $ TGen for some $i \in [1..l]$. We also allow the simulator to run the oracle corresponding to TGen. This means, in particular, that the simulator knows the trapdoor f^{-1}, while the adversary does not. See Section 6 for a discussion of the repercussions of this modeling decision.

3   The MCM Construction

Fix numbers η and τ. Let $H: \mathcal{K} \times \mathcal{M}_H \to \{0,1\}^\eta$ be a function family with key space $\mathcal{K}$ and domain $\mathcal{M}_H = \{0,1\}^{\leq L}$ for some large number L (e.g., 2^{64}). Let $\mathcal{E}_1: \mathcal{M} \to \mathcal{M}_H$ be an injective function where $\mathcal{M} = \{0,1\}^{\leq L'}$ for $L' = L - \tau$. For any $X \in \mathcal{M}$ we have that $|\mathcal{E}_1(X)| = |X| + \tau$, hence τ is the *stretch* of $\mathcal{E}_1$. Finally let $\mathcal{E}_2: \{0,1\}^\eta \to \{0,1\}^{\eta+\tau}$ be an injective function. Then we define the hash function $\mathcal{H} = $ MCM$[\mathcal{E}_1, H, \mathcal{E}_2]$ with key space $\mathcal{K}$, domain $\mathcal{M}$, and range $\{0,1\}^{\eta+\tau}$ by $\mathcal{H}_K(M) = \mathcal{H}(K, M) = \mathcal{E}_2(H_K(\mathcal{E}_1(M)))$. Overloading our notation, if $\mathcal{I}_1 = $ RI$_{\mathcal{M},\mathcal{M}_H}$ and $\mathcal{I}_2 = $ RI$_{\eta,\eta+\tau}$ then we write $\mathcal{H} = $ MCM$[\mathcal{I}_1, H, \mathcal{I}_2]$ where now $\mathcal{H}$ is itself an ITM using oracle access to $\mathcal{I}_1$ and $\mathcal{I}_2$ to calculate $\mathcal{H}_K(M) = \mathcal{I}_2(H_K(\mathcal{I}_1(M)))$.

Here τ is also the stretch of $\mathcal{H}$ — it's the number of bits beyond η needed to hold a hash value. Ideally $\tau = 0$, in which case $\mathcal{E}_1$ and $\mathcal{E}_2$ would be a permutations. We have the following theorem, which states that $\mathcal{H}$ inherits the collision-resistance of H.

Theorem 1. *Fix $\eta > 0$ and $\tau \geq 0$. Let $H: \mathcal{K} \times \mathcal{M}_H \to \{0,1\}^\eta$ be a function and $\mathcal{E}_1: \mathcal{M} \to \mathcal{M}_H$ and $\mathcal{E}_2: \{0,1\}^\eta \to \{0,1\}^{\eta+\tau}$ be injections. Let $\mathcal{H} = $ MCM$[\mathcal{E}_1, H, \mathcal{E}_2]$. Let A be an adversary that runs in time t and outputs messages each of length at most μ. Then there exists an adversary B such that*

$$\mathbf{Adv}^{cr}_{\mathcal{H}}(A) = \mathbf{Adv}^{cr}_{H}(B)$$

where B runs in time $t' \leq t + 2(c\mu + $ Time$_{\mathcal{E}_1}(\mu))$ for an absolute constant c. $\square$

Proof. Let $\mathcal{B}$ be the adversary that behaves as follows. On input key K It runs $\mathcal{A}(K)$, which eventually outputs (X, X'). Then $\mathcal{B}$ outputs $(\mathcal{E}_1(X), \mathcal{E}_1(X'))$. We have that if $\mathcal{H}_K(X) = \mathcal{H}_K(X')$ then because $\mathcal{E}_1$ and $\mathcal{E}_2$ are injections, necessarily $H_K(\mathcal{E}_1(X)) = H_K(\mathcal{E}_1(X'))$. Adversary $\mathcal{B}$ runs in time $t' \leq t + 2(c\mu + \mathsf{Time}_{\mathcal{E}_1}(\mu))$ where c is an absolute constant. ∎

We point out that similar theorems can be given for several other hash function properties, including target collision-resistance (TCR, or eSec), preimage resistance, and always preimage resistance (aPre) [34][2]. The next theorem captures that MCM is a PRO if both $\mathcal{E}_1$ and $\mathcal{E}_2$ are modeled as random injections.

Theorem 2. *Fix $\eta > 0$ and $\tau \geq 0$. Let $H: \mathcal{K} \times \mathcal{M}_H \to \{0,1\}^\eta$ be a Δ-regular function, $\mathcal{I}_1 = \mathsf{RI}_{\mathcal{M}, \mathcal{M}_H}$, and $\mathcal{I}_2 = \mathsf{RI}_{\eta, \eta+\tau}$. Let $\mathcal{H} = MCM[\mathcal{I}_1, H, \mathcal{I}_2]$. Let ν be the minimal message length of $\mathcal{H}$. Let $\mathcal{A}$ be an adversary that runs in time t and making at most (q_1, q_2, q_3) queries with the combined length of all queries being at most μ. Then there exists an adversary $\mathcal{B}$ such that*

$$\mathbf{Adv}^{\mathrm{pro}}_{\mathcal{H}, S}(\mathcal{A}) \leq \mathbf{Adv}^{\mathrm{cr}}_H(\mathcal{B}) + \frac{(q_1 + q_3)^2}{2^{\eta+\tau}} + \frac{(q_1 + q_2)^2}{2^{\nu+\tau}} + (q_1 + q_2)q_3 \left(\frac{1}{2^\eta} + \Delta \right)$$

where the simulator S, specified below, runs in time $t_S \leq c\mu(q_1 + q_1q_3)$ for some absolute constant c and makes at most $\min\{q_2, q_3\}$ oracle queries. Adversary $\mathcal{B}$ runs in time at most $t_\mathcal{B} \leq t + t_S + c'\mu$ for some absolute constant c'. □

The proof of this theorem is given in the full version of the paper [31], though below we give a sketch highlighting the main aspects of the proof. First, we discuss the theorem statement. As long as $\mathcal{E}_1$ and $\mathcal{E}_2$ are PRIOs we can securely replace them by actual random injections (as per the composition theorem of [23]). Then, Theorem 2 states that no adversary can differentiate between a real random oracle and the construction unless it is given sufficient time to break the collision-resistance of H or allowed to make approximately $2^{(\tau+\min\{\eta,\nu\})/2}$ queries. Here ν could in fact be small, since this is the minimal message length in the domain of our hash function (and we'd certainly want to include short messages). However, in practice, H will have some minimal message length ν_H (e.g., the blocksize of an underlying compression function) to which short messages would necessarily be padded anyway. Thus, $\mathcal{H}$ can 'aggressively' pad short strings to a minimal length $\nu = \nu_H - \tau$, recovering our security guarantee.

Proof (Sketch). We first fix a simulator $S = (S_1, S_2)$, which has access to the random oracle $\mathcal{R}$. The first interface S_1 implements a random injection $\hat{\mathcal{I}}_1 = \mathsf{RI}_{\mathcal{M}, \mathcal{M}_H}$ without ever using its access to $\mathcal{R}$. The second interface works as described below (recall that it has access to all of the values defined for $\hat{\mathcal{I}}_1$):

---

[2] Although it is unclear how one would prove that MCM preserves the other notions from [34], specifically everywhere preimage resistance (ePre), second-preimage resistance (Sec) and always second-preimage resistance (aSec).

procedure $\mathcal{S}_2(Y)$

If $\exists M$ s.t. $Y = H_K(\hat{\mathcal{I}}_1(M))$ then
   Ret $\mathcal{R}(M)$
Ret $C \xleftarrow{\$} \{0,1\}^n$

This interface checks if $\hat{\mathcal{I}}_1$ already maps a string M to a preimage under H_K of the queried value Y. In the case that multiple such M exist, then the lexicographically first is used. If such an M exists, then the simulator queries $\mathcal{R}$ on M and the output of $\mathcal{S}_2(Y)$ is "programmed" to match this value.

Now we argue that no adversary $\mathcal{A}$, given K, can differentiate between oracles $(\mathcal{H}, \mathcal{I}_1, \mathcal{I}_2)$ and $(\mathcal{R}, \mathcal{S}_1, \mathcal{S}_2)$. Let $\mathcal{O}_1, \mathcal{O}_2, \mathcal{O}_3$ be the oracles given to $\mathcal{A}$. By the construction of the simulator, the adversary gains no advantage by querying messages in the order of the construction, i.e. a query $X \leftarrow \mathcal{O}_2(M)$ and then $\mathcal{O}_3(H_K(X))$. On the other hand, there do exist sequences of queries that can cause the simulator to fail (with high probability) to respond in a manner consistent with the responses of $(\mathcal{H}, \mathcal{I}_1, \mathcal{I}_2)$. We argue that these "bad" sequences are hard for any adversary to generate.

The first is if two messages M and M' are queried to $\mathcal{S}_1$ and the returned values are such that $H_K(\hat{\mathcal{I}}_1(M)) = H_K(\hat{\mathcal{I}}_1(M')) = Y$. In this case the adversary can query Y to $\mathcal{S}_2$ and the simulator can at best guess whether to return $\mathcal{R}(M)$ or $\mathcal{R}(M')$ (which are distinct with high probability). But note that since $\hat{\mathcal{I}}$ is an injection, this actually implies that $\mathcal{A}$ has found a collision against H_K. This reflects the first term in the bound of the theorem statement.

The second "bad" sequence occurs if $\mathcal{A}$ queries $\mathcal{S}_2(Y)$, forcing the simulator to commit to a return value Z, and then later queries $\mathcal{S}_1(M)$ which returns a value X such that $H_K(X) = Y$. Since the probability is low that $\mathcal{R}(M) = Z$, there exists little chance that $\mathcal{S}$ answered the original query consistently. But the probability that $\mathcal{S}_1(M)$ returns Y is in fact the probability of choosing a random domain point X such that $H_K(X) = Y$. Indeed the Δ-regularity of H gives that this can only happen with low probability. This accounts for the last term in the bound.

The remaining two unexplained terms correspond to birthday-bounds for moving between random injections and random functions. For a complete proof see the full version of the paper [31]. ∎

4   Insecurity of Other Approaches

Here we give just a brief investigation of several alternative approaches to MCM. In all cases, either the resulting object is not provably collision-resistant in the standard model or not provably a PRO in an ideal model.

USING EXISTING BLOCKCIPHER-BASED HASH FUNCTIONS. Let $E: \{0,1\}^n \times \{0,1\}^n \to \{0,1\}^n$ be a blockcipher, modeled as ideal. Let f be a $2n$-bit to n-bit compression function. Fix some suitable domain extension transform, for example Merkle-Damgård with a prefix-free encoding. That is $\mathcal{H}(M) = f^+(g(M))$, where $f^+(M_1 \cdots M_m)$ is equal to Y_m defined recursively by $Y_0 = IV$ (some constant) and $Y_i = f(Y_{i-1}, M_i)$, and $g: \{0,1\}^* \to (\{0,1\}^n)^+$ is a prefix-free padding function. For simplicity let $g(M)$ simply split M into blocks of $n-1$ bits (M having been appropriately padded), and then appending a zero to each block except the last and appending a one to the last block. If f is one of the twenty group-1/2 schemes from [5], then $\mathcal{H}$ is collision-resistant in the ideal cipher model. Moreover, a recent paper by Chang et al. [11] shows that sixteen of these twenty yield a PRO $\mathcal{H}$.

However as soon as one leaves the ideal cipher model, $\mathcal{H}$ is *not* provably CR. For example let E' be the blockcipher defined as follows:

$$E'(K, M) = \begin{cases} M & \text{if } K = 0^k \\ E(K, M) & \text{otherwise} \end{cases}.$$

where, now, E is no longer ideal. Let $f(Y_{i-1}, M_i) = E'(M_i, Y_{i-1}) \oplus Y_{i-1}$. We can see that an adversary can trivially find collisions against $\mathcal{H}$ built using E'. This is true even though E' is a good pseudorandom permutation (the usual standard model security property of blockciphers) whenever E is also.[3]

REMOVING INJECTIVITY REQUIREMENTS. If either $\mathcal{E}_1$ or $\mathcal{E}_2$ are not injective, then the MCM construction looses its provable collision-resistance. Assuming they are built from using blockciphers (as we suggest), then one can, in spirit similar to the counter-example above, construct a collision resistant function H' and a good PRP E' that, when utilized in MCM, would lead to a trivial collisions.

Note that one might imagine replacing $\mathcal{E}_1$ and $\mathcal{E}_2$ with objects that are not injective, yet have some other standard model guarantees to ensure provable collision-resistance in MCM. Short of establishing their collision-resistance, its not clear what properties could achieve this goal. Additionally, this approach would seem to violate the separation of design tasks intrinsic to the MCM approach.

OMITTING $\mathcal{E}_1$ FROM MCM. If one omits the first "mixing" step $\mathcal{E}_1$ of MCM, then the construction no longer results in a PRO. This result is essentially equivalent to the Coron et al. insecurity result regarding the composition of a CR and one-way function H with a random oracle [13], but we state a version of it here for completeness. Let $\mathcal{H} = \mathsf{CM}[H, \mathcal{I}_2]$ be this modified construction for $\mathcal{I}_2 = \mathsf{RI}_{\eta, \eta+\tau}$, i.e. $\mathcal{H}(M) = \mathcal{I}_2(H(M))$. Now we show that $\mathcal{H}$ is easily differentiable from a true random oracle $\mathcal{R} = \mathsf{RF}_{\mathcal{M}_H, \eta+\tau}$. Let $\mathcal{A}$ be an adversary that queries it's first oracle on a uniformly selected message of length $M \in \mathcal{M}_H$ of some length ℓ. Let the returned value be C. Now the adversary queries its second oracle (representing either $\mathcal{I}_2$ or a simulator) on $H_K(C)$. Let the returned value be C'. If $C = C'$ then $\mathcal{A}$ returns one, guessing that it's interacting with the construction. Otherwise it returns zero, guessing that it's interacting with the true random oracle. We have that $\Pr\left[\mathcal{A}^{\mathcal{H}, \mathcal{I}_2} \Rightarrow 1\right] = 1$. On the other hand, $\Pr\left[\mathcal{A}^{\mathcal{R}, \mathcal{S}} \Rightarrow 1\right]$ is bounded by the advantage of a related adversary in breaking the one-wayness of H.

ALLOWING $\mathcal{E}_1, \mathcal{E}_2$ TO BE INVERTIBLE. Our formalization of PRIOs ensure that constructions meeting the goal are *not* invertible. Thus, objects that are invert-

---

[3] Hopwood and Wagner noted (in postings on sci.crypt) that one could exhibit good PRPs that would make finding collisions in the twenty [5] functions trivial.

ible do not meet the goal. It remains an open question whether MCM is, in fact, secure under easy-to-invert mixing steps.

5   Secure Mixing Steps: The TE Construction

PSEUDORANDOM INJECTIVE ORACLES. We now turn to showing the feasibility of instantiating the mixing steps $\mathcal{E}_1$ and $\mathcal{E}_2$ starting from blockciphers. We note that our eventual construction also works starting from a suitable fixed-input-length random oracle. This would have slight theoretical benefits because of a lack of implication between the ROM and ICM [17]. However, one might want to utilize blockciphers and the proofs are only rendered more complex when considering invertible components, thus we stick to the former.

We specify a construction that is a PRIO, i.e. indifferentiable from a random injection. Under the composability guarantees of the indifferentiability framework [23] (though see Section 6), the security of schemes (e.g., MCM) proven secure while modeling components as ideal injections remains when these objects are replaced by PRIOs.

At first glance the notion of a PRIO might appear to be essentially equivalent to that of a pseudorandom oracle. The distinction is analogous to the difference between PRPs and PRFs. Indeed, random injections and random functions behave similarly up to a birthday-bound, which implies that any PRIO is a good PRO and vice versa. But the more important (and subtle) concern is that the closeness of the definitions might lead one to the conclusion that there are trivial constructions for our mixing steps, utilizing any PRO. However, this would be entirely insufficient for our application because, while a PRO appears injective with high probability, it is *not* necessarily injective by construction. Once we step outside of idealized models we would then have a standard model object that *does not* suffice for the collision-resistance guarantee of Section 3. So for clarity of exposition and analysis, we found it useful to draw a distinction between the two objects.

Building a PRIO that is injective by construction from a blockcipher (modeled as ideal) proves a challenging task. Our object must be publically computable, so no secret keys are allowed. A minimum intuitive security requirement for the object is that the outputs resulting from applying it to two messages that differ in a single bit must appear to have been chosen independently at random, even when adversaries have direct access to the underlying blockcipher. This rules out the straightforward use of existing blockcipher modes of operation, such as CBC, with a public key and fixed IV or even the more complex variable-length enciphering schemes (e.g. [21, 20, 30, 19]).

THE TE CONSTRUCTION. Our construction utilizes two blockciphers and a trapdoor one-way permutation. Note that in the ideal cipher model one can easily derive two ciphers from a single cipher $\hat{E}$ at the cost of one bit of keying material: $E(K, M) \equiv \hat{E}(1 \parallel K, M)$ and $E'(K, M) \equiv \hat{E}(0 \parallel K, M)$. For simplicity then we assume access to two ciphers E: $\{0,1\}^k \times \{0,1\}^n \to \{0,1\}^n$ and E': $\{0,1\}^k \times \{0,1\}^n \to \{0,1\}^n$. The cipher E will be used in a blockcipher mode

Algorithm $\mathcal{E}(M)$:	Algorithm $\mathcal{F}(M)$:
$T \leftarrow \mathcal{F}(M)$	$M_1 M_2 \cdots M_l \xleftarrow{n} \mathsf{PadPF}(M)$
$M_1 M_2 \cdots M_m \xleftarrow{n} M$	$X_0 \leftarrow IV1$
For $i = 1$ to m do	For $i = 1$ to l do
$\quad Y_i \leftarrow E(T, i) \oplus M_i$	$\quad X_i \leftarrow E'(M_i, X_{i-1}) \oplus X_{i-1}$
$Y_0 \leftarrow f(T)$	Ret X_l
Ret $Y_0 \| Y_1 \| \cdots \| Y_m$	

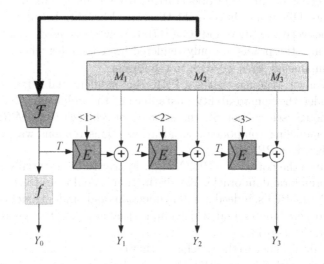

Fig. 2. (Left) Algorithm $\mathcal{E} = \mathsf{TE}[E, \mathcal{F}, f]$ and the description of function $\mathcal{F}$. (Right) A diagram of $\mathcal{E}$ applied to a message M for which $|M| = 3n$.

much like CTR mode encryption. The cipher E' will be utilized to build a function $\mathcal{F}$ for generating *tags* that will be (with high probability) unique to each input message. A message's tag then serves as the key for the CTR-mode-like enciphering step. In fact our function $\mathcal{F}$ will realize a blockcipher-based construction of a pseudorandom oracle, originally suggested in [13] and proven secure in [11]. Finally, a trapdoor one-way permutation f is applied to the tag value, the result being the first portion of the output. This step ensures the injectivity of the construction, while the one-wayness "hides" the tag. We will require the trapdoor property in the proof.

Formally, we define the injection $\mathcal{E} = \mathsf{TE}[E, \mathcal{F}, f]$ by the algorithms in Figure 2. The padding function $\mathsf{PadPF}: \{0,1\}^* \rightarrow (\{0,1\}^n)^+$ is any prefix-free encoding function: for any two messages $M, M' \in \{0,1\}^*$ with $|M| \neq |M'|$ the string $\mathsf{PadPF}(M)$ is not a prefix of $\mathsf{PadPF}(M')$. (Such functions are simple, one example is to unambiguously pad M to sequence of $n-1$ bit blocks. Then append a zero to all the blocks except the last, to which a one is appended.) The domain of $\mathcal{E}$ is $\mathcal{M} = \{0,1\}^{\leq L'}$ where $L' = n \cdot 2^{128}$. It maps a string X to a string of length $|X| + k$.

THE SECURITY OF TE. To analyze the security of TE, we start by treating the function $\mathcal{F}$ as a random oracle. This is justified by the proof that $\mathcal{F}$ is a PRO, found in [11], and the composability guarantees of the indifferentiability framework established in [23]. Thus from now on $\mathcal{F} = \mathsf{RF}_{\mathcal{M},n}$. We overload our notation to define TE in terms of idealized components. Let E be an ideal cipher, i.e. $E \xleftarrow{\$} \mathsf{BC}(k,n)$, let $\mathcal{F} = \mathsf{RF}_{\mathcal{M},n}$, and let TGen be the trusted setup oracle described in Section 2. Now let $\mathcal{E} = \mathsf{TE}[E, \mathcal{F}, \mathsf{TGen}]$ be the ITM that follows Algorithm $\mathcal{E}$ of Figure 2 except it utilizes TGen to get f initially and queries E and $\mathcal{F}$ oracles where appropriate. The next theorem captures the main result of this section.

Theorem 3. *Let* $E\colon \{0,1\}^k \times \{0,1\}^n \to \{0,1\}^n$ *be an ideal cipher,* $\mathcal{F} = \mathsf{RF}_{\mathcal{M},k}$, *and* TGen *be the oracle described above. Let* $\mathcal{E} = \mathsf{TE}[E, \mathcal{F}, \mathsf{TGen}]$. *Let* $\mathcal{A}$ *be an adversary that asks at most* $(q_1, q_2, q_3, q_4, 1)$ *oracle queries, each of length at most* μ *bits, and runs in time at most* t. *Then there exists an adversary* $\mathcal{C}$ *such that*

$$\mathbf{Adv}^{\mathrm{prio}}_{\mathcal{E},\mathcal{S}}(\mathcal{A}) \leq q_1 \mathbf{Adv}^{\mathrm{owf}}_{\mathbb{F}}(\mathcal{C}) + \frac{(q_1\sigma + q_2 + q_3)^2}{2^n} + \frac{q_1^2 - q_1}{2^{k+1}}$$

where $\sigma = \lceil \mu/n \rceil$ *and* $\mathcal{S}$, *the simulator defined in Figure 3, runs in time at most* $t_{\mathcal{S}} \leq c(\mu + q_2 q_4)$ *for some absolute constant* c *and makes* $q_{\mathcal{S}} = q_4$ *queries. Adversary* $\mathcal{C}$ *runs in time* $t' \leq t + t_{\mathcal{S}} + (q_2 + q_4)\mathsf{Time}_f + (q_1 + q_2 + q_4)\log(q_1 + q_2 + q_4) + c'\mu$ *for some absolute constant* c'. ∎

A proof of the theorem is provided in the full version of the paper [31], here we just provide a brief proof sketch. An adversary is given either the oracles $(\mathcal{E}, E, D, \mathcal{F}, \mathsf{TGen})$ or the oracles $(\mathcal{I}, \mathcal{S}_E, \mathcal{S}_D, \mathcal{S}_{\mathcal{F}}, \mathcal{S}_{\mathsf{TGen}})$. Recall that D is the oracle implementing the inverse of E. Intuitively the structure of TE ensures that an adversary, attempting to discover information about the tag and via it the random pad created for some message M, must reveal M to the simulator (by querying the fourth oracle). Knowing M, the simulator can 'program' the random pad to be consistent with output of the ideal injection $\mathcal{I}$.

The simulator will fail if either of two events occurs. The first event corresponds to when two tags collide in the course of simulating the construction. If this happens the CTR mode must generate the same pad, and no longer hides relationships between input and output bits. Such an event will occur with low probability because $\mathcal{F}$ is a RO. The second kind of event is if the adversary infers a tag value without utilizing its fourth oracle ($\mathcal{F}$ or $\mathcal{S}_{\mathcal{F}}$). If it can do so, then it can compute the pad using the second oracle (E or $\mathcal{S}_E$) before the simulator knows the message the tag corresponds to. This event should happen with low probability because it requires the adversary inverts f on some image returned as the first k bits of a query to the first oracle. We can bound the probability of $\mathcal{A}$ inverting f on some point in terms of its ability to invert on a particular point (hence the $q_1 \mathbf{Adv}^{\mathrm{owf}}_{\mathbb{F}}(\mathcal{C})$ term). Since neither event occurs with high probability, we achieve a bound on the adversary's ability to differentiate the two sets of oracles.

DISCUSSION. One might wonder if we can dispense with the one way permutation. In fact it is requisite: omitting it would result in a construction easily differentiable

procedure $\mathcal{S}_E(K, C)$: If $\exists j$ s.t. $\Gamma^j = K$ and $C \leq |M^j|/n$ then $\quad$ Ret $M_C^j \oplus Y_{C+1}^j$ Ret $Y \xleftarrow{\$} \{0,1\}^n$	**procedure** $\mathcal{S}_\mathcal{F}(M)$ $j \leftarrow j+1; \; M^j \leftarrow M$ $Y_0^j \parallel \tilde{Y}^j \leftarrow \mathcal{I}(M^j)$ $\Gamma^j \leftarrow f^{-1}(Y_0^j)$ Ret Γ^j
procedure $\mathcal{S}_D(K, Y)$ Return $D \xleftarrow{\$} \{0,1\}^n$	**procedure** $\mathcal{S}_{\mathsf{TGen}}()$ $(f, f^{-1}) \xleftarrow{\$} \mathbb{F}(1^k)$ Return f

Fig. 3. The simulator $\mathcal{S}$ used in proof of Theorem 3. Initially $j = 0$.

from a random injective oracle. An adversary could simply query its first oracle on a random message M_1, receiving $T \parallel Y_1$. Then the adversary could query its third oracle (either D or $\mathcal{S}_D$) on (T, Y_1). At this point the simulator has no knowledge about M_1 and will therefore only respond correctly with low probability.

The TE construction is a proof-of-concept: it is the first object to achieve our new goal of being simultaneously constructively injective and indifferentiable from a random injection. On the other hand it has several drawbacks when considering it for practical use. It is length-increasing (outputs are larger than the inputs by at least the number of key bits of the underlying blockcipher). This means that when utilized in MCM the output hash values will be larger compared to the outputs of the provably CR function H. Further, the construction requires two passes over the data and the application of a trapdoor permutation. In settings where speed is not essential (e.g., contract signing), the extra expense of using TE over that already incurred by hashing with a standard-model, provably collision-resistant function H might not be prohibitive. All this said, the TE construction *does* show that the MCM approach is feasible. We hope that future research will surface improvements.

6   Composability Limitations and Open Problems

Recall that the key benefit of indifferentiability results is the guarantee of composability, as discussed in depth in [23]. For example, a cryptographic scheme $\mathcal{E}$ proven secure when utilizing a (monolithic) random oracle $\mathcal{R}$ remains secure if the random oracle is replaced by a PRO construction C. When we say "remains secure" we mean that the existence of an adversary breaking the security of $\mathcal{E}^\mathcal{R}$ implies the existence of an adversary that breaks the security of $\mathcal{E}^C$. This means we can safely argue about the security of $\mathcal{E}^C$ in two steps: show that C is indifferentiable from $\mathcal{R}$ and then that $\mathcal{E}^\mathcal{R}$ is secure. Enabling this approach is a significant benefit of simulation-based definitions (the UC framework is another example [8]). Our results also allow for secure composition, but with important (and perhaps subtle) qualifications.

First, we note that both Theorem 2 and Theorem 3 differ from previous indifferentiability results because they are complexity-theoretic in nature. Specifically, the indifferentiability of MCM from a random oracle (Theorem 2) relies on an adversary's inability to find collisions under H. The indifferentiability of TE from a random injection (Theorem 3) relies on an adversary's inability to invert the trapdoor permutation f. We must bound the computational power of the adversary in both results, since an unbounded adversary can *always* find collisions against H or invert f. This means that $\mathcal{E}^{\mathsf{MCM}}$, for example, is secure *only* against computationally-bounded adversaries, even if $\mathcal{E}^{\mathcal{R}}$ is information-theoretically secure. This is a problem for random-oracle-based constructions $\mathcal{E}$ that require information-theoretic security (see, e.g. [7]).

Second, Theorem 3 relies on a simulator that knows the trapdoor of the one-way permutation (i.e., it gets to control generation of the permutation). Effectively then, instantiating TE requires a trusted party to publish a description of f, which can be considered a common reference string (CRS). We allow the simulator to choose the CRS in the proof. Recent results by Pass and Canetti et al. [6,9] call into question the (wide) use of such powerful simulators, in that composability of some security properties might be lost. For example, Pass discusses how deniability of non-interactive zero-knowledge proofs (the prover can assert that he never even proved a statement) does not hold if the proof relies on the zero-knowledge simulator choosing the CRS [6]. Indeed interpreting the composability theorem for the indifferentiability framework [23, Thm. 1] in the context of TGen implies that some security properties (e.g., deniability) of constructions using TE will not hold in settings where other parties are allowed to know f.

These subtle nuances of our results lead to a host of provocative open questions. What other properties, beyond deniability, are compromised by the weak composability guarantees of TE? Is it (im)possible to build PRIOs without relying on such strong simulators? Can we strengthen the MCM security result, or find other constructions, that simultaneously are provably CR and yet have information-theoretic indifferentiability from a RO?

Acknowledgments

The authors thank Yevgeniy Dodis for illuminating discussions regarding composability and deniability and the anonymous reviewers for their valuable comments. The first author is supported in part by Mihir Bellare's NSF grant CNS 0524765 and his gift from Intel Corporation. The second author is supported by NSF grant CNS 0627752.

References

1. Bellare, M., Boldyreva, A., Palacio, A.: An Uninstantiable Random-Oracle-Model Scheme for a Hybrid-Encryption Problem. In: Cachin, C., Camenisch, J.L. (eds.) EUROCRYPT 2004. LNCS, vol. 3027, pp. 171–188. Springer, Heidelberg (2004)

2. Bellare, M., Ristenpart, T.: Multi-property-preserving Hash Domain Extension and the EMD Transform. In: Lai, X., Chen, K. (eds.) ASIACRYPT 2006. LNCS, vol. 4284, pp. 299–314. Springer, Heidelberg (2006)

3. Bellare, M., Ristenpart, T.: Hash Functions in the Dedicated-key Setting: Design Choices and MPP Transforms. In: ICALP 2007. International Colloquim on Automata, Languages, and Programming. LNCS, vol. 4596, pp. 399–410. Springer, Heidelberg (2007)

4. Bellare, M., Rogaway, P.: The Security of Triple Encryption and a Framework for Code-Based Game-Playing Proofs. In: Vaudenay, S. (ed.) EUROCRYPT 2006. LNCS, vol. 4004, pp. 409–426. Springer, Heidelberg (2006)

5. Black, J., Rogaway, P., Shrimpton, T.: Black-Box Analysis of the Block-Cipher-Based Hash-Function Constructions from PGV. In: Yung, M. (ed.) CRYPTO 2002. LNCS, vol. 2442, pp. 320–325. Springer, Heidelberg (2002)

6. Pass, R.: On deniability in the common reference String and Random Oracle model. In: Boneh, D. (ed.) CRYPTO 2003. LNCS, vol. 2729, pp. 316–337. Springer, Heidelberg (2003)

7. Boyen, X., Dodis, Y., Katz, J., Ostrovsky, R., Smith, A.: Secure Remote Authentication Using Biometric Data. In: Cramer, R.J.F. (ed.) EUROCRYPT 2005. LNCS, vol. 3494, pp. 147–163. Springer, Heidelberg (2005)

8. Canetti, R.: Universally Composable Security: A New Paradigm for Cryptographic Protocols. In: FOCS 2001. Symposium on Foundations of Computer Science, pp. 136–145. IEEE Computer Society, Los Alamitos (2001)

9. Canetti, R., Dodis, Y., Pass, R., Walfish, S.: Universally Composable Protocols with Global Set-up. In: Vadhan, S.P. (ed.) TCC 2007. LNCS, vol. 4392, pp. 61–85. Springer, Heidelberg (2007)

10. Canetti, R., Goldreich, O., Halevi, S.: The random oracle methodology, revisited. J. ACM 51(4), 557–594 (2004)

11. Chang, D., Lee, S., Nandi, M., Yung, M.: Indifferentiable Security Analysis of Popular Hash Functions with Prefix-Free Padding. In: Lai, X., Chen, K. (eds.) ASIACRYPT 2006. LNCS, vol. 4284, pp. 283–298. Springer, Heidelberg (2006)

12. Contini, S., Lenstra, A., Steinfeld, R.: VSH, an Efficient and Provable Collision-Resistant Hash Function. In: Vaudenay, S. (ed.) EUROCRYPT 2006. LNCS, vol. 4004, pp. 165–182. Springer, Heidelberg (2006)

13. Coron, J.S., Dodis, Y., Malinaud, C., Puniya, P.: Merkle-Damgard Revisited: How to Construct a Hash Function. In: Shoup, V. (ed.) CRYPTO 2005. LNCS, vol. 3621, pp. 21–39. Springer, Heidelberg (2005)

14. Damgård, I.: hash functions and public key signature schemes. In: Price, W.L., Chaum, D. (eds.) EUROCRYPT 1987. LNCS, vol. 304, pp. 416–427. Springer, Heidelberg (1988)

15. Damgård, I.: A design principle for hash functions. In: Brassard, G. (ed.) CRYPTO 1989. LNCS, vol. 435, pp. 416–427. Springer, Heidelberg (1990)

16. Dodis, Y., Puniya, P.: Feistel networks made public, and applications. In: Advances in Cryptology– EUROCRYPT 2007. LNCS, vol. 4515, pp. 534–554. Springer, Heidelberg (2007)

17. Dodis, Y., Puniya, P.: On the relation between the ideal cipher and random oracle models. In: Halevi, S., Rabin, T. (eds.) TCC 2006. LNCS, vol. 3876, pp. 184–206. Springer, Heidelberg (2006)

18. Goldwasser, S., Micali, S.: Probabilistic Encryption. Journal of Computer and System Sciences 28, 270–299 (1984)

19. Halevi, S.: EME*: Extending EME to handle arbitrary-length messages with associated data. In: Canteaut, A., Viswanathan, K. (eds.) INDOCRYPT 2004. LNCS, vol. 3348, pp. 315–327. Springer, Heidelberg (2004)
20. Halevi, S., Rogaway, P.: A parallelizable enciphering mode. In: Okamoto, T. (ed.) CT-RSA 2004. LNCS, vol. 2964, pp. 292–304. Springer, Heidelberg (2004)
21. Halevi, S., Rogaway, P.: A tweakable enciphering mode. In: Boneh, D. (ed.) CRYPTO 2003. LNCS, vol. 2729, pp. 482–499. Springer, Heidelberg (2003)
22. Lyubashevsky, V., Micciancio, D., Peikert, C., Rosen, A.: Provably secure FFT hashing. In: NIST 2nd Cryptographic Hash Function Workshop (2006)
23. Maurer, U., Renner, R., Holenstein, C.: Indifferentiability, Impossibility Results on Reductions, and Applications to the Random Oracle Methodology. In: Naor, M. (ed.) TCC 2004. LNCS, vol. 2951, pp. 21–39. Springer, Heidelberg (2004)
24. Merkle, R.: One way hash functions and DES. In: Brassard, G. (ed.) CRYPTO 1989. LNCS, vol. 435, pp. 428–446. Springer, Heidelberg (1990)
25. National Institute of Standards and Technology.FIPS PUB 180-1: Secure Hash Standard. Supersedes FIPS PUB 180 1993 May 11(1995)
26. Pointcheval, D.: The Composite Discrete Logarithm and Secure Authentication. In: Imai, H., Zheng, Y. (eds.) PKC 2000. LNCS, vol. 1751, pp. 113–128. Springer, Heidelberg (2000)
27. Preneel, B., Govaerts, R., Vandewalle, J.: Hash functions based on block ciphers: A synthetic approach. In: Stinson, D.R. (ed.) CRYPTO 1993. LNCS, vol. 773, pp. 368–378. Springer, Heidelberg (1994)
28. Rabin, M.: Digital signatures. In: Millo, R.A., et al. (eds.) Foundations of secure computation, Academic Press, London (1978)
29. Rabin, M.: Digital signatures and public key functions as intractable as factorization. MIT Laboratory for Computer Science Report TR-212 (January 1979)
30. Ristenpart, T., Rogaway, P.: How to Enrich the Message Space of a Cipher. In: Fast Software Encryption– FSE 2007. LNCS, vol. 4593, pp. 101–118. Springer, Heidelberg (2007)
31. Ristenpart, T., Shrimpton, T.: How to Build a Hash Function from any Collision-Resistant Function (full version of this paper), http://www.cse.ucsd.edu/users/tristenp/
32. Rivest, R., Shamir, A., Adleman, L.: A Method for Obtaining Digital Signatures and Public-Key Cryptosystems. Communications of the ACM 21(2), 120–126 (1978)
33. Rivest, R., Tauman, Y.: Improved online/offline signature schemes. In: Kilian, J. (ed.) CRYPTO 2001. LNCS, vol. 2139, pp. 355–367. Springer, Heidelberg (2001)
34. Rogaway, P., Shrimpton, T.: Cryptographic Hash-Function Basics: Definitions, Implications, and Separations for Preimage Resistance, Second-Preimage Resistance, and Collision Resistance. In: Roy, B., Meier, W. (eds.) FSE 2004. LNCS, vol. 3017, pp. 371–388. Springer, Heidelberg (2004)
35. RSA Laboratories, RSA PKCS #1 v2.1: RSA Cryptography Standards (2002)
36. Saarinen, M.: Security of VSH in the Real World. In: Barua, R., Lange, T. (eds.) INDOCRYPT 2006. LNCS, vol. 4329, pp. 95–103. Springer, Heidelberg (2006)
37. Wang, X., Yin, Y.L., Yu, H.: Finding Collisions in the Full SHA-1. In: Shoup, V. (ed.) CRYPTO 2005. LNCS, vol. 3621, pp. 17–36. Springer, Heidelberg (2005)
38. Wang, X., Yu, H.: How to Break MD5 and Other Hash Functions. In: Cramer, R.J.F. (ed.) EUROCRYPT 2005. LNCS, vol. 3494, pp. 19–35. Springer, Heidelberg (2005)
39. Whitfield, D., Hellman, M.: Privacy and Authentication: An Introduction to Cryptography. Proceedings of the IEEE 67, 397–427 (1979)

Fully Anonymous Group Signatures Without Random Oracles

Jens Groth*

University College London, United Kingdom
jgroth@adastral.ucl.ac.uk

Abstract. We construct a new group signature scheme using bilinear groups. The group signature scheme is practical, both keys and group signatures consist of a constant number of group elements, and the scheme permits dynamic enrollment of new members. The scheme satisfies strong security requirements, in particular providing protection against key exposures and not relying on random oracles in the security proof.

Keywords: Group signatures, certified signatures, bilinear groups.

1 Introduction

Group signatures make it possible for a member of a group to sign messages anonymously so that outsiders and other group members cannot see which member signed the message. The group is controlled by a group manager that handles enrollment of members and also has the ability to identify the signer of a message. Group signatures are useful in contexts where it is desirable to preserve the signer's privacy, yet in case of abuse we want some authorities to have the means of identifying her.

Group signatures were introduced by Chaum and van Heyst [CvH91] and have been the subject of much research. Most of the proposed group signatures have been proven secure in the random oracle model [BR93] and now quite efficient schemes exist in the random oracle model [ACJT00, BBS04, CL04, CG04, FI05, KY05]. The random oracle model has been the subject of criticism though. Canetti, Goldreich and Halevi [CGH98] demonstrated the existence of an insecure signature scheme that has a security proof in the random oracle model. Other works showing weaknesses of the random oracle model are [Nie02, GK03, BBP04, CGH04].

There are a few group signature schemes that avoid the random oracle model. Bellare, Micciancio and Warinschi [BMW03] suggested security definitions for group signatures and offered a construction based on trapdoor permutations. Their security model assumed the group was static and all members were given their honestly generated keys right away. Bellare, Shi and Zhang [BSZ05] strengthened the security model to include dynamic enrollment of members. This security model also separated the group manager's role into two parts: issuer and opener. The issuer is responsible for enrolling members, but cannot trace who has signed a group signature. The opener on the other

---

* Work done while at UCLA supported by NSF ITR/Cybertrust grant No. 0456717.

K. Kurosawa (Ed.): ASIACRYPT 2007, LNCS 4833, pp. 164–180, 2007.

hand cannot enroll members, but can open a group signature to see who signed it. More-over, it was required that this opener should be able to prove that said member made the group signature to avoid false accusations of members. [BSZ05] demonstrated that trapdoor permutations suffice also for constructing group signatures in this model. Both of these schemes use general and complicated primitives and are very inefficient. Groth [Gro06] used bilinear groups to construct a group signature scheme in the BSZ-model, with nice asymptotic performance, where each group signature consists of a constant number of group elements. Still the constant is enormous and a group signature consists of thousands or perhaps even millions of group elements.

There are also a few practical group signature schemes with security proofs in the standard model. Ateniese, Camenisch, Hohenberger and de Medeiros [ACHdM05] give a highly efficient group signature scheme, where each group signature consists of 8 group elements in prime order bilinear groups. This scheme is secure against a non-adaptive adversary that never gets to see private keys of honest members. If a member's key is exposed, however, it is easy to identify all group signatures she has made, so their scheme is not secure in the BMW/BSZ-models.

Boyen and Waters [BW06, BW07] suggest group signatures that are secure against key exposure attacks. Their constructions are secure in a restricted version of the BMW-model where the anonymity of the members relies on the adversary not being able to see any openings of group signatures. In the latter scheme [BW07], the group signatures consist of 6 group elements in a composite order bilinear group. The public key in [BW07] grows logarithmically in the size of the message space though and will for practical purposes typically contain a couple of hundred group elements.

OUR CONTRIBUTION. We propose a new group signature scheme based on prime order bilinear groups. All parts of the group signature scheme, including the group public key and the group signatures, consist of a constant number of group elements. The constants are reasonable for practical purposes; for instance using 256-bit prime order bilinear groups, a group public key would be less than 1kB and a group signature less than 2kB.

We prove under some well-known assumptions, the strong Diffie-Hellman assump-tion [BB04] and the decisional linear assumption [BBS04], as well as a new assumption that the scheme is secure in the BSZ-model. This means the scheme permits dynamic enrollment of members, preserves anonymity of a group signature even if the adversary can see arbitrary key exposures or arbitrary openings of other group signatures, and separates the role of the issuer and opener such that they can operate independently.

TECHNIQUE. We use in our group signature scheme a certified signature scheme. Cer-tified signatures, the notion stemming from Boldyreva, Fischlin, Palacio and Warinschi, allow a user to pick keys for a signature scheme and use them to sign messages. The user can ask a certification authority to certify her public verification key for the sig-nature scheme. The verification algorithm checks both the certificate and the signature and accepts if both of them are acceptable. A trivial way to build a certified signature schemes is just to let the certification authority output a standard signature on the user's public verification key. Non-trivial solutions such as for instance using an aggregate signature scheme [BGLS03] also exist. Certified signature schemes may be more effi-cient though since the certificate does not have to be unforgeable. In a certified signature scheme, the requirement is just that it is infeasible to forge a certificate together with a valid signature. We refer to Section 3 for a formal definition.

In our group signature scheme, enrolling members will create a key for a signature scheme and ask the issuer to issue a certificate on their verification key. To make a group signature, the member will make a certified signature. To be anonymous she will encrypt the certified signature and use non-interactive witness-indistinguishable and non-interactive zero-knowledge proofs to demonstrate that the ciphertext contains a valid certified signature.

In order to have efficient non-interactive proofs, it is essential to preserve as much of the bilinear group structure of the encrypted certified signature as possible. In particular, using cryptographic hash-functions or using group elements from one part of the certified signature as exponents in other parts of the certified signature does not work. We will combine the signature scheme of Boneh and Boyen [BB04] with the signature scheme of Zhou and Lin [ZL06] to get a certified signature scheme that is both efficient and relies only on generic group operations.

2 Setup

Let $\mathcal{G}$ be a probabilistic polynomial time algorithm that generates $(p, G, G_T, e, g) \leftarrow \mathcal{G}(1^k)$ such that:

- p is a k-bit prime.
- G, G_T are groups of order p.
- g is a randomly chosen generator of G.
- e is a non-degenerate bilinear map, i.e., $e(g, g)$ is a generator of G_T and for all $a, b \in \mathbb{Z}_p$ we have $e(g^a, g^b) = e(g, g)^{ab}$.
- Group operations, evaluation of the bilinear map, and membership of G, G_T are all efficiently computable.

We will now present some of the security assumptions that will be used in the paper.

DLIN ASSUMPTION. The decisional linear assumption was introduced by Boneh, Boyen and Shacham [BBS04]. The DLIN assumption holds for $\mathcal{G}$, when it is hard to distinguish for randomly chosen group elements and exponents (f, g, h, f^r, g^s, h^t) whether $t = r + s$ or t is random.

q-SDH ASSUMPTION. The strong Diffie-Hellman assumption was introduced by Boneh and Boyen [BB04]. The q-SDH assumption holds for $\mathcal{G}$, when it is hard to find a pair $(m, g^{\frac{1}{1+x}}) \in \mathbb{Z}_p \times G$ when given $g, g^x, g^{x^2}, \ldots, g^{x^{q(k)}}$ as input. In the paper, it suffices to have q being a polynomial.

q-U ASSUMPTION. We will now define the unfakeability assumption. The q-U assumption holds for $\mathcal{G}$ if for any non-uniform polynomial time adversary $\mathcal{A}$ we have:

$$\Pr\Big[(p, G, G_T, e, g) \leftarrow \mathcal{G}(1^k) \, ; \, x_1, r_1, \ldots, x_{q(k)}, r_{q(k)} \leftarrow \mathbb{Z}_p \, ;$$
$$f, h, z \leftarrow G \, ; \, T := e(f, z) \, ; \, a_i := f^{r_i} \, ; \, b_i := h^{r_i} g^{x_i r_i} z \, ;$$
$$(V, A, B, m, S) \leftarrow \mathcal{A}(p, G, G_T, e, g, f, h, T, x_1, a_1, b_1, \ldots, x_{q(k)}, a_{q(k)}, b_{q(k)}) :$$
$$V \notin \{g^{x_1}, \ldots, g^{x_{q(k)}}\} \wedge e(A, hV)e(f, B) = T \wedge e(S, Vg^m) = e(g, g)\Big] \approx 0.$$

The q-U assumption is implied by a stronger assumption from Zhou and Lin [ZL06] that is similar in nature. A heuristic argument for the assumption is that it holds in the generic group model; see the full paper for a proof.

3 Certified Signatures

Typically, using a signature in a public key infrastructure works like this: A user that wants to set up a signature scheme, generates a public verification key vk and a secret signing key sk. She takes the public key to a certification authority that signs vk and possibly some auxiliary information such as name, e-mail address, etc. We call this the certificate. Whenever the user wants to sign a message, she sends both the certificate and the signature to the verifier. The verifier checks that the certification authority has certified that the user has the public key vk and also checks the user's signature on the message.

In the standard way of certifying verification keys described above, the process of issuing certificates and verifying certificates is separate from the process of signing messages and verifying signatures. Boldyreva, Fischlin, Palacio and Warinschi [BFPW07] show that combining the two processes into one can improve efficiency. As they observe, we do not need to worry about forgeries of the certificate itself, we only need to prevent the *joint* forgery of both the certificate and the signature.

A certified signature scheme [BFPW07], is a combined scheme for signing messages and producing certificates for the verification keys. We will give a formal definition that is tailored to our purposes and slightly simpler than the more general definition given by Boldyreva, Fischlin, Palacio and Warinschi. Formally, a certified signature scheme consists of the following probabilistic polynomial time algorithms.

Setup: $\mathcal{G}$ takes a security parameter as input and outputs a description gk of our setup.
Certification key: CertKey on input gk outputs a pair (ak, ck), respectively a public authority key and a secret certification key.
Key registration: This is an interactive protocol $\langle \text{User}, \text{Issuer} \rangle$ that generates keys for the user together with a certificate. User takes gk, ak as input, whereas Issuer takes gk, ck as input. If successful User outputs a triple $(vk, sk, cert)$, whereas Issuer outputs $(vk, cert)$. We write $((vk, sk, cert), (vk, cert)) \leftarrow \langle \text{User}(gk, ak), \text{Issuer}(gk, ck) \rangle$ for this process. We call vk the verification key, sk the signing key and $cert$ the certificate. Either party outputs $\perp$ if the other party deviates from the key registration protocol.
Signature: Sign gets a signing key and a message m as input. It outputs a signature σ.
Verification: Ver takes as input $gk, ak, vk, cert, m, \sigma$ and outputs 1 if accepting the certificate and the signature on m. Otherwise it outputs 0.

The certified signature scheme must be correct, unfakeable and unforgeable as defined below.

Perfect correctness: For all messages m we have

$$\Pr\left[gk \leftarrow \mathcal{G}(1^k) \, ; \, (ak, ck) \leftarrow \text{CertKey}(gk) \, ; \right.$$

$$((vk, sk, cert), (vk, cert)) \leftarrow \langle \text{User}(gk, ak), \text{Issuer}(gk, ck) \rangle \ ;$$

$$\sigma \leftarrow \text{Sign}_{sk}(m) : \text{Ver}(gk, ak, vk, cert, m, \sigma) = 1 \Big] = 1.$$

Unfakeability: We want it to be hard to create a signature with a faked certificate. Only if the verification key has been generated correctly and been certified by the certification authority should it be possible to make a certified signature on a message. For all non-uniform polynomial time adversaries $\mathcal{A}$ we require:

$$\Pr\Big[gk \leftarrow \mathcal{G}(1^k); (ak, ck) \leftarrow \text{CertKey}(gk); (vk, cert, m, \sigma) \leftarrow \mathcal{A}^{\text{KeyReg}}(gk, ak) :$$

$$vk \notin Q \text{ and } \text{Ver}(gk, ak, vk, cert, m, \sigma) = 1\Big] \approx 0,$$

where KeyReg is an oracle that allows $\mathcal{A}$ to sequentially start up new key registration sessions and lets $\mathcal{A}$ act as the user. That is in session i we run $(*, (vk_i, cert_i)) \leftarrow \langle \mathcal{A}, \text{Issuer}(gk, ck) \rangle \ ; \ Q := Q \cup \{vk_i\}$ forwarding all messages to and from $\mathcal{A}$ through the oracle.

Existential M-unforgeability: Let M be a stateful non-uniform polynomial time algorithm. We say the certified signature scheme is existentially M-unforgeable if for all non-uniform polynomial time adversaries $\mathcal{A}$ we have:

$$\Pr\Big[gk \leftarrow \mathcal{G}(1^k) \ ; \ (\text{St}_1, ak) \leftarrow \mathcal{A}(gk) \ ;$$

$$((vk, sk, cert), \text{St}_2) \leftarrow \langle \text{User}(gk, ak), \mathcal{A}(\text{St}_1) \rangle \ ;$$

$$(cert', m, \sigma) \leftarrow \mathcal{A}^{\text{MessageSign}(\cdot)}(\text{St}_2) :$$

$$m \notin Q \text{ and } \text{Ver}(gk, ak, vk, cert', m, \sigma) = 1\Big] \approx 0,$$

where MessageSign$(\cdot)$ is an oracle that on input a_i runs $(m_i, h_i) \leftarrow M(gk, a_i) \ ; \ \sigma_i \leftarrow \text{Sign}_{sk}(m_i) \ ; \ Q := Q \cup \{m_i\}$ and returns (m_i, h_i, σ_i).

Adaptive chosen message attack corresponds to letting M be an algorithm that on input m_i outputs (m_i, ε). On the other hand, letting M be an algorithm that ignores $\mathcal{A}$'s inputs corresponds to a weak chosen message attack, where messages to be signed by the oracle are chosen without knowledge of vk. In a weak chosen message attack, the h_i's may contain a history of how the messages were selected. In this paper, we only need security against weak chosen message attack.

4   A Certified Signature Scheme

We will construct a certified signature scheme from bilinear groups that is existentially unforgeable under weak chosen message attack. There are two parts of the scheme: certification and signing. For signing, we will use the Boneh-Boyen signature scheme that is secure under weak chosen message attack. In their scheme the public key is $v := g^x$ and the secret signing key is x. A signature on message $m \in \mathbb{Z}_p \setminus \{x\}$ is $\sigma = g^{\frac{1}{x+m}}$. It can be verified by checking $e(\sigma, vg^m) = e(g, g)$. Boneh and Boyen [BB04] proved that this signature scheme is secure against weak chosen message attack under the q-SDH assumption. The existential unforgeability of our certified signature scheme under weak chosen message attack will follow directly from the security of the Boneh-Boyen signature scheme under weak chosen message attack.

What remains is to specify how to generate the verification key v and how to certify it. This is a 2-step process, where we first generate a random $v = g^x$ such that the issuer learns v but only the user learns x. In Section 4.1 we describe in detail the properties we need this key generation protocol to have. In the second step, we use a variation of the signature scheme of Zhou and Lin [ZL06] to certify v.[1]

To set up the certified signature scheme, the certification authority picks random group elements $f, h, z \in G$. The authority key is (f, h, T) and the secret certification key is z so $T = e(g, z)$. To certify a Boneh-Boyen key v the authority picks $r \leftarrow \mathbb{Z}_p$ and sets $(a, b) := (f^{-r}, (hv)^r z)$. The certificate is verified by checking $e(a, hv)e(f, b) = T$. We remark that this is not a good signature scheme, since given v, a, b it is easy to create a certificate for $v' := v^2 h$ as $(a', b') := (a^{\frac{1}{2}}, b)$. For certified signatures it works fine though since we cannot use the faked verification keys to actually sign any messages. The nice part about the certified signature scheme we have suggested here is that a certificate consists of only two group elements and is created through the use of generic group operations. These two properties of the certified signature scheme are what enable us to construct a practical group signature scheme on top of it.

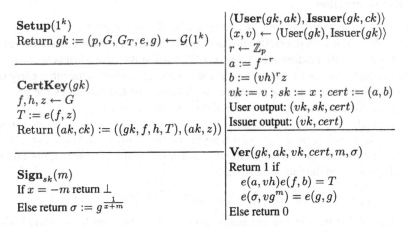

Fig. 1. The certified signature scheme

Theorem 1. *The scheme in Figure 1 is a certified signature scheme with perfect correctness for messages in $\mathbb{Z}_p \setminus \{x\}$. It is unfakeable under the q-U assumption and is existentially unforgeable under weak chosen message attack under the q-SDH assumption.*

---

[1] The signature scheme of Zhou and Lin [ZL06] can be used to sign exponents. As they observe, however, it is sufficient to know $v = g^x$ to sign x. In our notation, their scheme computes a signature on x by setting $v = g^x$ and computing the signature (a, b) as $a := f^r, b := (hv)^r z$, where $z = h^{\log_f g}$ so $T = e(g, h)$.

Sketch of proof. Perfect correctness follows from the perfect correctness of the key generation protocol.

We will now argue that the certified signature scheme is unfakeable. Part of the key registration protocol is the interactive key generation protocol. We can black-box simulate the view of the adversarial user in each of these key generation protocols. We can therefore pick $x_1, \ldots, x_{q(k)}$ in advance and simulate the key generation such that the adversarial user i get the signing key x_i (or gets no key at all in case it deviates from the protocol). With this modified key registration, $\mathcal{A}$ only sees certificates on $v_1 := g^{x_1}, \ldots, v_{q(k)} := g^{x_{q(k)}}$. These certificates are of the form $a_i := f^{-r_i}$ and $b_i := h^{r_i} g^{x_i r_i} z$. It therefore follows directly from the q-U assumption that it is hard to come up with a certified signature using a new public verification key.

We will now ague that the certified signature scheme is existentially unforgeable under weak chosen message attack. By definition th key generation protocol has the property that it is possible to choose $v := g^x$ in advance and black-box simulate the malicious issuer's view in a protocol that gives it v as output. Now we are in a situation, where v is an honestly chosen Boneh-Boyen verification key and $\mathcal{A}$ only has access to a weak chosen message attack. Existential unforgeability of the certified signature scheme therefore follows from the existential unforgeability of Boneh-Boyen signatures under weak chosen message attack.   □

4.1 Key Generation

In the certified signature scheme, we require that the user generates her signing key honestly. We will use an interactive protocol between the user and the issuer that gives the user a uniformly random secret key $x \in \mathbb{Z}_p$, while the issuer learns $v := g^x$. In case either party does not follow the protocol or halts prematurely, the other party will output $\perp$. We will now give a more precise definition of the properties the protocol should have. For notational convenience, define $g^{\perp} = \perp$.

Write $(x, v) \leftarrow \langle \text{User}(gk), \text{Issuer}(gk) \rangle$ for running the key generation protocol between two probabilistic polynomial time interactive Turing machines User, Issuer on common input gk giving User output x and Issuer output v. We require that the protocol is correct in the following sense:

$$\Pr \left[gk \leftarrow \mathcal{G}(1^k) ; (x, v) \leftarrow \langle \text{User}(gk), \text{Issuer}(gk) \rangle : v = g^x \right] = 1.$$

We require that the view of the issuer, even if malicious, can be simulated. More precisely, for any $\delta > 0$ and polynomial time Issuer* there exists a polynomial time (in k and the size of the input to Issuer*) black-box simulator S_I, such that for all non-uniform polynomial time adversaries $\mathcal{A}$ we have:

$$\Pr \left[gk \leftarrow \mathcal{G}(1^k) ; y \leftarrow \mathcal{A}(gk) ; x \leftarrow \mathbb{Z}_p ; v := g^x ; (g^u, i) \leftarrow S_I^{\text{Issuer}^*(y)}(gk, v) : \right.$$

$$\left. \mathcal{A}(u, i) = 1 \right]$$

$$- \Pr \left[gk \leftarrow \mathcal{G}(1^k) ; y \leftarrow \mathcal{A}(gk) ; (x, i) \leftarrow \langle \text{User}(gk), \text{Issuer}^*(y) \rangle : \right.$$

$$\left. \mathcal{A}(u, i) = 1 \right] < k^{-\delta},$$

where S_I outputs g^u so $u \in \{\perp, x\}$.

We also require that the view of the user, even if malicious, can be simulated. For any $\delta > 0$ and any polynomial time User* there exists a polynomial time (in k and the size of the input to User*) black-box simulator S_U, such that for all non-uniform polynomial time adversaries $\mathcal{A}$ we have:

$$\Pr\left[gk \leftarrow \mathcal{G}(1^k)\,;\, y \leftarrow \mathcal{A}(gk)\,;\, x \leftarrow \mathbb{Z}_p\,;\, v := g^x\,;\, (u, i) \leftarrow S_U^{\mathrm{User}^*(y)}(gk, x)\,:\right.$$
$$\left.\mathcal{A}(u, i) = 1\right]$$
$$-\Pr\left[gk \leftarrow \mathcal{G}(1^k)\,;\, y \leftarrow \mathcal{A}(gk)\,;\, (u, i) \leftarrow \langle \mathrm{User}^*(y), \mathrm{Issuer}(gk)\rangle\,:\right.$$
$$\left.\mathcal{A}(u, i) = 1\right] < k^{-\delta},$$

where S_U outputs $i \in \{\bot, v\}$.

There are many ways in which one can construct a key generation protocol with these properties. One example of a simple 5-move key generation protocol is given in the full paper.

5 Defining Group Signatures

In a group signature scheme there is a group manager that decides who can join the group. Once in the group, members can sign messages on behalf of the group. Members' signatures are anonymous, except to the group manager who can open a signature and see who signed the message. In some scenarios it is of interest to separate the group manager into two entities, an issuer who enrolls members and an opener who traces signers.

We imagine that enrolled member's when joining have some identifying information added to a registry reg. This registry may or may not be publicly accessible. The specifics of how the registry works are not important, we just require that $reg[i]$ only contains content both the issuer and user i agrees on. One option could be that the issuer maintains the registry, but the user has to sign the content of $reg[i]$ for it to be considered a valid entry. User i stores her corresponding secret key in $gsk[i]$. The number i we associate with the user is simply a way to distinguish the users. Without loss of generality, we will assume users are numbered $1, \ldots, n$ according to the time they joined or attempted to join.

Key generation: GKg generates (gpk, ik, ok). Here gpk is a group public key, while ik and ok are respectively the issuer's and the opener's secret key.

Join/Issue: This is an interactive protocol between a user and the issuer. If successful, the user and issuer register a public key vk_i in $reg[i]$ and the user stores some corresponding secret signing key information in $gsk[i]$.

[BSZ05] specify that communication between the user and the issuer in this protocol should be secret. The Join/Issue protocol in our scheme works when all messages are sent in clear though. In our scheme, we will assume the issuer joins users in a sequential manner, but depending on the setup assumptions one is willing to make, it is easy to substitute the Join/Issue protocol for a concurrent protocol.

Sign: Group member i can sign a message m as $\Sigma \leftarrow \text{Gsig}(gpk, gsk[i], m)$.

Verify: To verify a signature Σ on message m we run $\text{GVf}(gpk, m, \Sigma)$. The signature is valid if and only if the verification algorithm outputs 1.

Open: The opener has read-access to the registration table reg. We have $(i, \tau) \leftarrow \text{Open}(gpk, ok, reg, m, \Sigma)$ gives an opening of a valid signature Σ on message m pointing to user i. In case the signature points to no member, the opener will assume the issuer forged the signature and set $i := 0$. The role of τ is to accompany $i \neq 0$ with a proof that user i did indeed sign the message.

Judge: This algorithm is used to verify that openings are correct. We say the opening is correct if $\text{Judge}(gpk, i, reg[i], m, \Sigma, \tau) = 1$.

[BSZ05] define four properties that the group signature must satisfy: correctness, anonymity, traceability and non-frameability. We will here give a quick informal description of the properties. We refer to [BSZ05] for details and a discussion of how these security definitions cover and strengthen other security definitions that have appeared in the literature.

Non-frameability: Non-frameability protects the user against being falsely accused of making a group signature, even if both the issuer and the opener are corrupt.

Traceability: When the issuer is honest and the opening algorithm is applied correctly, albeit the opener's key may be exposed, traceability guarantees that a group signature always can be traced back to a member who made it.

Anonymity: An opener knows who made a particular group signature, but provided the opener is honest and the opener's key is kept secret, nobody else should be able to identify the member. Anonymity gives this guarantee even in an environment where all users' keys are exposed and the issuer is corrupt. In the definition, the adversary is also permitted to ask the opener to open group signatures, except the group signature where it is trying to guess who signed it.

A weaker variant of anonymity called CPA-anonymity does not permit the adversary to see openings of other group signatures. The difference between full anonymity and CPA-anonymity is analogous to the difference between security under chosen ciphertext attack and chosen plaintext attack for public-key encryption.

6   Tools

To construct our group signature scheme, we will use the certified signature scheme from Section 4. We will also use several other tools in our construction, namely collision-free hash functions, non-interactive proofs for bilinear groups, strong one-time signatures secure against weak chosen message attack and selective-tag weak CCA-secure cryptosystems.

6.1   Collision-Free Hash-Functions

$\mathcal{H}$ is a generator of collision free hash-functions $\text{Hash} : \{0, 1\}^* \rightarrow \{0, 1\}^{\ell(k)}$ if for all non-uniform polynomial time adversaries $\mathcal{A}$ we have:

$$\Pr\left[\text{Hash} \leftarrow \mathcal{H}(1^k) \, ; \, x, y \leftarrow \mathcal{A}(\text{Hash}) : \text{Hash}(x) = \text{Hash}(y)\right] \approx 0.$$

We will use a collision-free hash-function to compress messages before signing them. For this purpose we will require that we can hash down to $\mathbb{Z}_p$, so we want to have $2^{\ell(k)} < p$. We remark that collision-free hash-functions can be constructed assuming the discrete logarithm problem is hard, so the existence of collision-free hash-functions follows from our assumptions on the bilinear group.

6.2 Strong One-Time Signatures

We will use a one-time signature scheme that is secure against an adversary that has access to a single weak chosen message attack. We say the one-time signature scheme is strong, if the adversary can neither forge a signature on a different message nor create a different signature on the chosen message she already got signed. An obvious candidate for such a scheme is the Boneh-Boyen signature scheme [BB04], since this signature scheme is deterministic and hence automatically has the strongness property.

6.3 Non-interactive Proofs for Bilinear Groups

Groth and Sahai [GS07] suggest non-interactive proofs that capture relations for bilinear groups. They look at sets of equations in our bilinear group (p, G, G_T, e, g) over variables in G and $\mathbb{Z}_p$ such as pairing product equations, e.g. $e(x_1, x_2)e(x_3, x_4) = 1$, or multi-exponentiation equations, e.g. $x_1^{\delta_1} x_2^{\delta_2} = 1$. They suggest non-interactive proofs for demonstrating that a set of equations of the form described above has a solution $x_1, \ldots, x_I \in G, \delta_1, \ldots, \delta_J \in \mathbb{Z}_p$ so all equations are simultaneously satisfied. Their proofs are in the common reference string model. There are two types of common reference strings that yield respectively perfect soundness and perfect witness indistinguishability/perfect zero-knowledge. The two types of common reference strings are computationally indistinguishable and they both give perfect completeness. We now give some further details.

[GS07] show that there exists four probabilistic polynomial time algorithms (K, P, V, X), which we call respectively the key generator, the prover, the verifier and the extractor. The key generator takes (p, G, G_T, e, g) as input and outputs a common reference string $crs = (F, H, U, V, W, U', V', W') \in G^8$ as well as an extraction key xk. Given a set of equations, the prover takes crs and a witness $x_1, \ldots, x_I, \delta_1, \ldots, \delta_J$ as input and outputs a proof π. The verifier given crs, a set of equations and π outputs 1 if the proof is valid and else it outputs 0. Finally, the extractor on a valid proof π will extract $x_1, \ldots, x_I \in G$, in other words it will extract part of the witness.

The proofs of [GS07] have perfect completeness: on a correctly generated CRS and a correct witness, the prover always outputs a valid proof. They have perfect soundness: on a correctly generated CRS it is impossible to create a valid proof unless the equations are simultaneously satisfiable. Further, they have perfect partial knowledge: given xk the algorithm X can extract $x_1, \ldots, x_I$ from the proof, such that there exists a solution for the equations that use these $x_1, \ldots, x_I$.

There exists a simulator S_1 that outputs a simulated common reference string crs and a simulation trapdoor key tk. These simulated common reference strings are computationally indistinguishable from the common reference strings produced by K assuming the DLIN problem is hard. On a simulated common reference string, the proofs created by the prover are perfectly witness-indistinguishable: if there are many possible witnesses for the equations being satisfiable, the proof π does not reveal anything about which witness was used by the prover when creating the proof. Further, let us call a set of equations tractable, if it is possible to find a solution, where $x_1, \ldots, x_I$ are the same in all equations, but $\delta_1, \ldots, \delta_J$ are allowed to vary from equation to equation. Tractable equations have perfect zero-knowledge proofs on simulated reference strings: there exists a simulator S_2 that on a simulated reference string crs and a simulation trapdoor key tk produces a simulated proof π for the tractable equations being satisfiable. If the equations are satisfiable, then simulated proofs are perfectly indistinguishable from the proofs a real prover with a witness would form on a simulated reference string.

It will be useful later in the paper to know some technical details of the construction. The values F, H, U, V, W will be used to commit to the variables x as $(c_1, c_2, c_3) := (F^r U^t, H^s V^t, g^{r+s} W^t x)$ for randomly chosen $r, s, t \in \mathbb{Z}_p$. On a real common reference string, they are set up so $U = F^R, V = H^S, W = g^{R+S}$ so the commitment can be rewritten as $(F^{r+Rt}, H^{s+St}, g^{r+s+(R+S)t} x)$. The extraction key is $xk := (\phi, \eta)$ so $F = g^\phi, H = g^\eta$. This permits decryption of the commitment as $x = c_3 c_1^{-\phi} c_2^{-\eta}$. On the other hand, on a simulation reference string, we use $U = F^R, V = H^S, W = g^T$ with $T \neq R + S$, which makes the commitment perfectly hiding.

To commit to a variable $\delta \in \mathbb{Z}_p$ using randomness r, s we use the commitment $(d_1, d_2, d_3) := (F^r (U')^\delta, H^s (V')^\delta, g^{r+s} (W')^\delta)$. On a normal common reference string, we pick $U' = F^R, V' = H^S, W' = g^T$ for $T \neq R + S$. This makes the commitment perfectly binding. On a simulated common reference string, on the other hand, we pick $U' = F^R, V' = H^S, W' = g^{R+S}$. The simulation trapdoor key is $tk := (R, S)$, which permits us to trapdoor open a commitment to 0 to any value δ since $(F^r, H^s, g^{r+s}) = (F^{r-R\delta} (U')^\delta, H^{s-S\delta} (V')^\delta, g^{r+s-(R+S)\delta} (W')^\delta)$.

6.4 Selective-Tag Weakly CCA-Secure Encryption

We will use a tag-based cryptosystem [MRY04] due to Kiltz [Kil06]. The public key consists of random non-trivial elements $pk = (F, H, K, L) \in G^4$ and the secret key is $sk = (\phi, \eta)$ so $F = g^\phi, H = g^\eta$. We encrypt $m \in G$ using tag $t \in \mathbb{Z}_p$ and randomness $r, s \in \mathbb{Z}_p$ as $(y_1, \ldots, y_5) := (F^r, H^s, g^{r+s} m, (g^t K)^r, (g^t L)^s)$. The validity of the ciphertext is publicly verifiable, since valid ciphertexts have $e(F, y_4) = e(y_1, g^t K)$ and $e(H, y_5) = e(y_2, g^t L)$. Decryption can be done by computing $m = y_3 y_1^{-\phi} y_2^{-\eta}$. In the group signature scheme, we will set up the cryptosystem with the same F, H as in the common reference string of the non-interactive proofs.

[Kil06] shows that under the DLIN assumption this cryptosystem is selective-tag weakly CCA-secure. By this we mean that it is indistinguishable which message we encrypted under a tag t, even when we have access to a decryption oracle that decrypts ciphertexts under any other tag. Formally, for all non-uniform polynomial time adversaries $\mathcal{A}$ we have:

$$\Pr\Big[gk \leftarrow \mathcal{G}(1^k) \,;\, t \leftarrow \mathcal{A}(gk) \,;\, (pk, sk) \leftarrow K(gk) \,;\, (m_0, m_1) \leftarrow \mathcal{A}^{D_{sk}(\cdot, \cdot)}(pk) \,;$$

$$y \leftarrow E_{pk}(t, m_0) \,:\, \mathcal{A}^{D_{sk}(\cdot, \cdot)}(y) = 1 \Big]$$

$$\approx \Pr \left[gk \leftarrow \mathcal{G}(1^k) \;;\; t \leftarrow \mathcal{A}(gk) \;;\; (pk, sk) \leftarrow K(gk) \;;\; (m_0, m_1) \leftarrow \mathcal{A}^{D_{sk}(\cdot,\cdot)}(pk) \;; \right.$$

$$\left. y \leftarrow E_{pk}(t, m_1) \;:\; \mathcal{A}^{D_{sk}(\cdot,\cdot)}(y) = 1 \right],$$

where the oracle returns $D_{sk}(t_i, y_i)$ if $t_i \neq t$.

7 The Group Signature Scheme

The core of our group signature scheme is the certified signature scheme from Section 4. The issuer acts as a certification authority and whenever a new member i wants to enroll, she needs to create a verification key v_i for the Boneh-Boyen signature scheme and get a certificate from the issuer. In the group signature scheme, the verification key and the corresponding secret key is generated with an interactive key generation protocol as defined in Section 4.1. This way both user and issuer know that v_i is selected with the correct distribution and that the user holds the corresponding secret key x_i.

When making a group signature, the member will generate a key pair $(vk_{\text{sots}}, sk_{\text{sots}})$ for a strong one-time signature that is secure under weak chosen message attack. She will sign the message using sk_{sots} and use x_i to sign vk_{sots}. The combination of certified signatures and strong one-time signatures is what makes it hard to forge group signatures.

Group signatures have to be anonymous and therefore we cannot reveal the certified signature. Instead, a group signature will include a non-interactive witness-indistinguishable (NIWI) proof of knowledge of a certified signature on vk_{sots}. Witness-indistinguishability implies that a group signature does not reveal which group member has signed the message. The opener will hold the extraction key for the NIWI proof of knowledge and will be able to extract the certified signature. Whenever an opening is called for, she extracts the signature on vk_{sots}, which points to the member who signed the message. In case no member has certified signed vk_{sots}, the opener points to the issuer since the certified signature has a valid certificate.

The ideas above suffice to construct a CPA-anonymous group signature scheme. To get anonymity even when the adversary has access to the Open oracle, we will encrypt the signature on vk_{sots} with Kiltz' cryptosystem using vk_{sots} as a tag. We will also give an NIZK proof that the encrypted signature is the same as the one used in the NIWI proof of knowledge.

We present the full group signature scheme in Figure 2. Let us explain the non-interactive proofs further. The NIWI proof of knowledge, will demonstrate that there exists a certified signature (a, b, v, σ) on vk_{sots} so

$$e(a, hv)e(f, b) = T \;\wedge\; e(\sigma, vg^{\text{Hash}(vk_{\text{sots}})}) = e(g, g).$$

In the terminology of [GS07], these are two pairing product equations over three variables b, v, σ. The last element a will be public, since we can rerandomize the certificate such that a does not identify the member. [GS07] gives us an NIWI proof of knowledge for these two equations being simultaneously satisfiable that consists of 27 group elements. This proof consists of three commitments to respectively b, v, σ, which consist of 3 group elements each, and two proofs for the committed values satisfying the two equations consisting of 9 group elements each.

In the NIZK proof we have a ciphertext y under tag $\text{Hash}(vk_{\text{sots}})$ and a commitment c to σ from the NIWI proof of knowledge. We wish to prove that the plaintext of y and the committed value in c are the same. The ciphertext is of the form $(y_1, \ldots, y_5) = (F^{r_y}, H^{s_y}, g^{r_y+s_y}\sigma, (g^{\text{Hash}(vk_{\text{sots}})}K)^{r_y}, (g^{\text{Hash}(vk_{\text{sots}})}L)^{s_y})$ and the commitment is of the form $(c_1, c_2, c_3) = (F^{r_c}U^t, H^{s_c}V^t, g^{r_c+s_c}W^t\sigma)$. Setting $r := r_c - r_y, s := s_c - s_y$ we have $(c_1 y_1^{-1}, c_2 y_2^{-1}, c_3 y_3^{-1}) = (F^r U^t, H^s V^t, g^{r+s} W^t)$. On the other hand, if the plaintext and the committed value are different, then no such r, s, t exist. Proving that the plaintext and the committed value are the same, therefore corresponds to proving the simultaneous satisfiability of the following equations over $\phi, r, s, t \in \mathbb{Z}_p$:

$$\phi = 1 \ \wedge \ (c_1^{-1}y_1)^\phi F^r U^t = 1 \ \wedge \ (c_2^{-1}y_2)^\phi H^s V^t = 1 \ \wedge \ (c_3^{-1}y_3)^\phi g^{r+s} W^t.$$

This set is tractable, i.e., if we allow ϕ to take different values in the equations, then there is a trivial solution $\phi = 1$ in the first equation and $\phi = r = s = t = 0$ in the other three equations. Since the set of equations is tractable, there is an NIZK proof for the 4 equations being simultaneously satisfiable. The proof consists of commitments to ϕ, r, s, t, but since the first equation is straightforward we can simply use (U', V', W') as the commitment to ϕ, which makes it easy to verify that the first equation holds. The three commitments to r, s, t each consist of 3 group elements. The three last equations are multi-exponentiations of constants and using the proof of [GS07] each equation costs 2 group elements to prove. The NIZK proof therefore costs a total of 15 group elements.

Theorem 2. *The scheme in Figure 2 is a group signature scheme with perfect correctness. Under the DLIN, q-SDH and q-U assumption and assuming the strong one-time signature scheme is secure against weak chosen message attack and the hash-function is collision resistant, the group signature has anonymity, traceability and non-frameability.*

Sketch of proof. Perfect correctness follows by inspection and the fact that the constituent protocols have perfect correctness and perfect completeness. We will sketch a proof that the group signature is secure, we refer to the full paper for more details.

To argue anonymity we consider a situation where the issuer may be corrupt and the members' keys are exposed. Since the adversary controls the issuer, she can let both corrupt users and honest users join the group. She can also ask the opener to open arbitrary valid group signatures. At some point she will choose two honest members and a message and get a group signature from one of the members. We want to show that she cannot tell which of the honest members made the group signature, as long as she does not ask the opener to open the challenge group signature.

The NIZK proof implies that the ciphertext y contains the same Boneh-Boyen signature σ as the NIWI proof of knowledge. The opener can therefore use the decryption key for the tag-based cryptosystem to track down the user instead of extracting it from the NIWI proof of knowledge. This means we do not need the extraction key for the NIWI proof, so we can switch to using a common reference string that gives perfect witness-indistinguishability. The only information about the member now resides in the

$\mathbf{GKg}(1^k)$
$gk \leftarrow \mathcal{G}(1^k)$; Hash $\leftarrow \mathcal{H}(1^k)$
$((f, h, T), z) \leftarrow \text{CertKey}(gk)$
$(crs, xk) \leftarrow K_{\text{NI}}(gk)$; $K, L \leftarrow G$
$(F, H, \text{the rest}) \leftarrow \text{Parse}(crs)$; $pk := (F, H, K, L)$
$(gpk, ik, ok) := ((gk, \text{Hash}, f, h, T, crs, pk), z, xk)$

$\mathbf{Join/Issue}(\text{User } i : gpk, \text{ Issuer} : gpk, ik)$
$((v_i, x_i, a_i, b_i), (v_i, a_i, b_i)) \leftarrow \langle \text{User}, \text{Issuer} \rangle$
User: If $e(a_i, hv_i)e(f, b_i) = T$ set
$\quad reg[i] := v_i$; $gsk[i] := (x_i, a_i, b_i)$

$\mathbf{GSig}(gpk, gsk[i], m)$
$(vk_{\text{sots}}, sk_{\text{sots}}) \leftarrow \text{KeyGen}_{\text{sots}}(1^k)$
$\quad (\text{Repeat until } \text{Hash}(vk_{\text{sots}}) \neq -x_i)$
$\rho \leftarrow \mathbb{Z}_n$; $a := a_i f^{-\rho}$; $b := b_i(hv_i)^\rho$
$\sigma := g^{\frac{1}{x_i + \text{Hash}(vk_{\text{sots}})}}$
$\pi \leftarrow P_{\text{NIWI}}(crs, (gpk, a, \text{Hash}(vk_{\text{sots}})), (b, v_i, \sigma))$
$y \leftarrow E_{pk}(\text{Hash}(vk_{\text{sots}}), v_i)$
$\psi \leftarrow P_{\text{NIZK}}(crs, (gpk, y, \pi), (r, s, t))$
$\sigma_{\text{sots}} \leftarrow \text{Sign}_{sk_{\text{sots}}}(vk_{\text{sots}}, m, a, \pi, y, \psi)$
Return $\Sigma := (vk_{\text{sots}}, a, \pi, y, \psi, \sigma_{\text{sots}})$

$\mathbf{GVf}(gpk, m, \Sigma)$
Return 1 if these verifications pass:
$\text{Ver}_{vk_{\text{sots}}}((vk_{\text{sots}}, m, a, \pi, y, \psi), \sigma_{\text{sots}})$
$V_{\text{NIWI}}(crs, (gpk, a, \text{Hash}(vk_{\text{sots}})), \pi)$
$V_{\text{NIZK}}(crs, (gpk, \pi, y), \psi)$
ValidCiphertext$(pk, \text{Hash}(vk_{\text{sots}}), y)$
Else return 0

$\mathbf{Open}(gpk, ok, m, \Sigma)$
$(b, v, \sigma) \leftarrow X_{xk}(crs,$
$\quad\quad (gpk, a, \text{Hash}(vk_{\text{sots}})), \pi)$
Return (i, σ) if there is i so $v = v_i$
Else return $(0, \sigma)$

$\mathbf{Judge}(gpk, i, reg[i], m, \Sigma, \sigma)$
Return 1 if
$i \neq 0 \wedge e(\sigma, v_i g^{\text{Hash}(vk_{\text{sots}})}) = e(g, g)$
Else return 0

Fig. 2. The group signature scheme

ciphertext. The existential unforgeability of the one-time signature under weak chosen message attack and the collision-freeness of the hash-function make it infeasible for the adversary to query the opener with a valid group signature that recycles vk_{sots} from the challenge or that collides with $\text{Hash}(vk_{\text{sots}})$. Since $\text{Hash}(vk_{\text{sots}})$ is the tag for the cryptosystem and is never recycled in a query to the opener, the ciphertext does not reveal which member made the group signature.

We have to argue that a user cannot be framed. We consider an unfriendly environment where both the issuer and the opener are corrupt. They are trying to come up with a proof that the user signed a message, a proof that consists of a Boneh-Boyen signature. When joining the group, the user and the issuer engage in a key registration protocol. This protocol gives the user a uniformly random x and a Boneh-Boyen verification key $v = g^x$, without the issuer learning x. Even if the user makes group signatures on arbitrary messages, this just corresponds to signing randomly chosen verification keys for the strong one-time signature scheme. The weak chosen message attack security of the Boneh-Boyen signature scheme is therefore sufficient to guarantee that the adversary cannot falsely accuse the user of having signed a message that she did not sign.

Finally, we consider an honest issuer that keeps her issuer key secret and an honest opener with an exposed opener key. We have to argue that a valid group signature can always be traced back to a member of the group. By the perfect extractability of the

NIWI proof of knowledge, we can extract a valid certified signature on $\text{Hash}(vk_{\text{sots}})$ from the NIWI proof π. The key registration protocol guarantees that all members have correctly generated signing keys. The unfakeability of the certified signature scheme therefore implies that a member has made the group signature. The Boneh-Boyen signature σ is sufficient to trace this member, since it matches a unique verification key v_i. $\square$

EFFICIENCY. If we instantiate the strong one-time signature with the Boneh-Boyen signature scheme a verification key is one group element and a one-time signature is also one group element. We make the element a public. The NIWI proof of knowledge consists of 27 group elements. The ciphertext consists of 5 group elements. The NIZK proof consists of 15 group elements. The total size of a group signature is therefore 50 group elements in G. This is of course much better than the many thousand elements required for a group signature in [Gro06].

In case CPA-anonymity is sufficient, we can consider a lighter version of our group signature, where we omit the ciphertext y and the NIZK proof ψ. This CPA-anonymous group signature scheme would consist of 30 group elements. We observe that regular anonymity implies that the group signature is strong, i.e., even when seeing a message m and a group signature Σ on it, it is not possible to create a different group signature Σ' on m such that it still points to the same member. In CPA-anonymity, however, we do not give the adversary access to an opening oracle and thus mauling signatures is no longer a problem. If we do not care about the group signature being strong, we do not need the strong one-time signature key and we can simply sign $\text{Hash}(m)$ instead of $\text{Hash}(vk_{\text{sots}})$. This reduces the size of the group signatures further to 28 group elements. In comparison, the CPA-anonymous group signature scheme of [BW07] consists of 6 group elements in a composite order group. Since composite order groups rely on the hardness of factoring, these groups are very large and our CPA-anonymous group signatures are therefore comparable in size for practical parameters, perhaps even a bit smaller. However, our CPA-anonymous group signature scheme still supports dynamic enrollment of members and has a group public key gpk consisting of a constant number of group elements.

KEY GENERATION. Since the [BSZ05]-model assumes a trusted key generator it is worth considering how the key generation should be carried out in practice. The trust in our scheme relies on the bilinear group (p, G, G_T, e, g) being generated so the cryptographic assumptions hold and it relies on the hash-function being collision-free. We remark that an advantage of our scheme is that we work over prime order bilinear groups, so it may be possible to use a uniform random string to set up (p, G, G_T, e, g). Also, since the trust is based on a very elementary setup, a bilinear group and a hash-function, it is possible that suitable public standards can be found. One could for instance use SHA-256 as the hash-function.

The non-frameability of the user relies only on the collision-freeness of the hash-function and the cryptographic assumptions in (p, G, G_T, e, g). The rest of the group public key gpk can be generated jointly by the issuer and the opener. The issuer generates the authority key for the certified signature scheme. The opener generates crs and pk, anonymity follows from the opener generating these keys correctly. Since the opener can break anonymity anyway, it is quite reasonable to trust the opener with protecting anonymity. The opener will have to make a zero-knowledge proof of knowledge of the corresponding extraction key to the issuer, since the security proof for traceability relies on the opener being able to actually extract a signature from the NIWI proof of knowledge.

References

[ACHdM05] Ateniese, G., Camenisch, J., Hohenberger, S., de Medeiros, B.: Practical group signatures without random oracles. Cryptology ePrint Archive, Report 2005/385 (2005), http://eprint.iacr.org/2005/385.

[ACJT00] Ateniese, G., Camenisch, J., Joye, M., Tsudik, G.: A practical and provably secure group signature scheme. In: Bellare, M. (ed.) CRYPTO 2000. LNCS, vol. 1880, pp. 255–270. Springer, Heidelberg (2000)

[BB04] Boneh, D., Boyen, X.: Short signatures without random oracles. In: Cachin, C., Camenisch, J.L. (eds.) EUROCRYPT 2004. LNCS, vol. 3027, pp. 56–73. Springer, Heidelberg (2004)

[BBP04] Bellare, M., Boldyreva, A., Palacio, A.: An uninstantiable random-oracle-model scheme for a hybrid encryption problem. In: Cachin, C., Camenisch, J.L. (eds.) EUROCRYPT 2004. LNCS, vol. 3027, pp. 171–188. Springer, Heidelberg (2004), Full paper available at http://eprint.iacr.org/2003/077

[BBS04] Boneh, D., Boyen, X., Shacham, H.: Short group signatures. In: Franklin, M. (ed.) CRYPTO 2004. LNCS, vol. 3152, pp. 41–55. Springer, Heidelberg (2004)

[BFPW07] Boldyreva, A., Fischlin, M., Palacio, A., Warinschi, B.: A closer look at pki: Security and efficiency. In: Proceedings of PKC 2007. LNCS, vol. 4450, pp. 458–475. Springer, Heidelberg (2007)

[BGLS03] Boneh, D., Gentry, C., Lynn, B., Shacham, H.: Aggregate and verifiably encrypted signatures from bilinear maps. In: Biham, E. (ed.) Advances in Cryptology – EUROCRPYT 2003. LNCS, vol. 2656, pp. 416–432. Springer, Heidelberg (2003)

[BMW03] Bellare, M., Micciancio, D., Warinschi, B.: Foundations of group signatures: Formal definitions, simplified requirements, and a construction based on general assumptions. In: Biham, E. (ed.) Advances in Cryptology – EUROCRPYT 2003. LNCS, vol. 2656, pp. 614–629. Springer, Heidelberg (2003)

[BR93] Bellare, M., Rogaway, P.: Random oracles are practical: A paradigm for designing efficient protocols. In: ACM CCS 1993, pp. 62–73. ACM Press, New York (1993)

[BSZ05] Bellare, M., Shi, H., Zhang, C.: Foundations of group signatures: The case of dynamic groups. In: Menezes, A.J. (ed.) CT-RSA 2005. LNCS, vol. 3376, pp. 136–153. Springer, Heidelberg (2005)

[BW06] Boyen, X., Waters, B.: Compact group signatures without random oracles. In: Vaudenay, S. (ed.) EUROCRYPT 2006. LNCS, vol. 4004, pp. 427–444. Springer, Heidelberg (2006)

[BW07] Boyen, X., Waters, B.: Full-domain subgroup hiding and constant-size group signatures. In: Proceedings of PKC 2007. LNCS, vol. 4450, pp. 1–15. Springer, Heidelberg (2007), http://www.cs.stanford.edu/~xb/pkc07/

[CG04] Camenisch, J., Groth, J.: Group signatures: Better efficiency and new theoretical aspects. In: Blundo, C., Cimato, S. (eds.) SCN 2004. LNCS, vol. 3352, pp. 120–133. Springer, Heidelberg (2005), Full paper available at http://www.brics.dk/~jg/GroupSignFull.pdf

[CGH98]   Canetti, R., Goldreich, O., Halevi, S.: The random oracle methodology, revisited. In: Proceedings of STOC 1998, pp. 209–218 (1998)

[CGH04]   Canetti, R., Goldreich, O., Halevi, S.: On the random-oracle methodology as applied to length-restricted signature schemes. In: Naor, M. (ed.) TCC 2004. LNCS, vol. 2951, pp. 40–57. Springer, Heidelberg (2004)

[CL04]   Camenisch, J., Lysyanskaya, A.: Signature schemes and anonymous credentials from bilinear maps. In: Franklin, M. (ed.) CRYPTO 2004. LNCS, vol. 3152, pp. 56–72. Springer, Heidelberg (2004)

[CvH91]   Chaum, D., van Heyst, E.: Group signatures. In: Davies, D.W. (ed.) EURO-CRYPT 1991. LNCS, vol. 547, pp. 257–265. Springer, Heidelberg (1991)

[FI05]   Furukawa, J., Imai, H.: An efficient group signature scheme from bilinear maps. In: Boyd, C., González Nieto, J.M. (eds.) ACISP 2005. LNCS, vol. 3574, pp. 455–467. Springer, Heidelberg (2005)

[GK03]   Goldwasser, S., Kalai, Y.T.: On the (in)security of the Fiat-Shamir paradigm. In: Proceedings of FOCS 2003, pp. 102–113 (2003), Full paper available at http://eprint.iacr.org/2003/034

[Gro06]   Groth, J.: Simulation-sound nizk proofs for a practical language and constant size group signatures. In: Lai, X., Chen, K. (eds.) ASIACRYPT 2006. LNCS, vol. 4284, Springer, Heidelberg (2006), Full paper available at http://www.brics.dk/~jg/NIZKGroupSignFull.pdf

[GS07]   Groth, J., Sahai, A.: Efficient non-interactive proof systems for bilinear groups. Cryptology ePrint Archive, Report 2007/155 (2007), available at http://eprint.iacr.org/2007/155

[Kil06]   Kiltz, E.: Chosen-ciphertext security from tag-based encryption. In: Halevi, S., Rabin, T. (eds.) TCC 2006. LNCS, vol. 3876, pp. 581–600. Springer, Heidelberg (2006)

[KY05]   Kiayias, A., Yung, M.: Group signatures with efficient concurrent join. In: Cramer, R.J.F. (ed.) EUROCRYPT 2005. LNCS, vol. 3494, pp. 198–214. Springer, Heidelberg (2005), Full paper available at http://eprint.iacr.org/345

[MRY04]   MacKenzie, P.D., Reiter, M.K., Yang, K.: Alternatives to non-malleability: Definitions, constructions, and applications. In: Naor, M. (ed.) TCC 2004. LNCS, vol. 2951, pp. 171–190. Springer, Heidelberg (2004)

[Nie02]   Nielsen, J.B.: Separating random oracle proofs from complexity theoretic proofs: The non-committing encryption case. In: Yung, M. (ed.) CRYPTO 2002. LNCS, vol. 2442, pp. 111–126. Springer, Heidelberg (2002)

[ZL06]   Zhou, S., Lin, D.: Shorter verifier-local revocation group signatures from bilinear maps. In: Pointcheval, D., Mu, Y., Chen, K. (eds.) CANS 2006. LNCS, vol. 4301, pp. 126–143. Springer, Heidelberg (2006)

Group Encryption

Aggelos Kiayias[1], Yiannis Tsiounis[2], and Moti Yung[3]

[1] Computer Science and Engineering, University of Connecticut
Storrs, CT, USA
aggelos@cse.uconn.edu
[2] BQuotes, New York, NY, USA
yiannis@bquotes.com
[3] Google and Computer Science, Columbia University
New York, NY, USA
moti@cs.columbia.edu

Abstract. We present group encryption, a new cryptographic primitive which is the encryption analogue of a group signature. It possesses similar verifiability, security and privacy properties, but whereas a group signature is useful whenever we need to conceal the source (signer) within a group of legitimate users, a group encryption is useful whenever we need to conceal a recipient (decryptor) within a group of legitimate receivers.

We introduce and model the new primitive and present sufficient as well as necessary conditions for its generic implementation. We then develop an efficient novel number theoretic construction for group encryption of discrete logarithms whose complexity is independent of the group size. As part of achieving this we construct a new public-key encryption for discrete logarithms that satisfies CCA2-key-privacy and CCA2-security in the standard model (this gives the first Pailler-based system with the above two properties proven in the standard model).

Applications of group encryption include settings where a user wishes to hide her preferred trusted third party or even impose a hidden hierarchy of trusted parties while being required to assure well-formed ciphertexts, as well as oblivious storage settings where the set of retrievers need to be verifiable but the storage distribution should be oblivious to the server.

1 Introduction

Group signatures were introduced in [22] and further developed in a line of works, e.g., [23,20,17,18,11,36,4,3,14,6,33,8,16,7,34,2,43,9,35,30]. In a nutshell a group signature allows a registered member of a PKI (a.k.a. a group of registered users) to issue a signature on behalf of the group so that the issuer's identity is assured to be valid but is hidden from the verifier. After its introduction, the primitive has found numerous applications.

In this work we introduce a novel cryptographic primitive that is the encryption analogue of a group signature; we call it *group encryption* (not to be confused with group-oriented cryptography as in [26,12], which is essentially threshold cryptosystems). A group encryption scheme allows a sender to prepare a ciphertext and convince a verifier that it can be decrypted by a member

K. Kurosawa (Ed.): ASIACRYPT 2007, LNCS 4833, pp. 181–199, 2007.

of a given PKI group. As in group signature, in a group encryption there can be an opening authority that can, reveal the identity of the group member who is the recipient of the ciphertext when the appropriate circumstances are triggered. Note that group encryption provides "receiver anonymity" in the same way that group signature provides "sender anonymity." Nevertheless, this primitive was never considered in the group-signature literature before, even though public-key encryption and signatures are typically dual primitives that have been developed in parallel in many other settings.

A Motivating Typical Scenario: In many protocols that attempt to maintain privacy/ anonymity and employ trusted parties, it has been often naturally advocated as a flexible service to allow a user to choose its recipient trustee (e.g., a trusted third party for conditionally opening the ciphertext) among a set of available authorized parties. However, the choice of a third party, while increasing flexibility, might also reveal some preference of the user, thus reducing privacy. Group encryption is motivated by such applications. As observed by Chaum [21] the fact that the trustee is hidden within a large set of trusted parties makes attempts to bribe officials harder, thus contributing to secrecy of individuals as well.

Let us investigate whether it is possible to implement the above typical scenario by employing existing primitives. The notion of key-privacy was introduced in [5] (also [31]) who showed that there exist encryption schemes where it is impossible for an adversary to distinguish what public-key has been used for the message encryption. If we attempt to use these encryption schemes, a user may make his own trustee's public key (without even publishing this public key) and use that one for encryption, thus faking an encryption to a trustee. Note that this amounts to attacking the application, since this user's encryption cannot be opened by any valid trustee. Key privacy for users who encrypt with their own key was given in [13], but this means that the user has to be his own trustee, which, again, is insufficient for the application above. Finally, the notion of verifiable encryption allows the sender to prove certain properties of the encrypted message (cf. e.g., [1,12,44,19]). If we employ verifiable encryption for the above application, it only assures verifiability when the public key employed is known to the verifier. Knowledge of the public key employed, in turn, is an attack on the anonymity of the trustee in the above application.

Our Major Contributions. In this work, motivated by the above examples, we first contribute the definition, formalization and generic feasibility of group encryption. We then construct an efficient concrete implementation and investigate its related number theoretic properties.

– *Definition and Model.* The group encryption primitive (GE) involves a public-key encryption scheme with special properties, a group joining protocol (involving public-key certification) and a message space that may have a required structure. Besides correctness, there are three security properties that pertain to GE schemes. The first two of these properties, called *Security* and *Anonymity* protect the sender from a hostile environment that tries to either extract information about the message (security) or to extract information about who the recipient is (anonymity). We require both properties to have the strongest notion of immunity to attack, namely CCA2 [27,41]. The third property, that we call *Soundness* protects the verifier from a hostile environment in which the sender, the group manager and the recipients collude against him, so that he accepts a ciphertext (e.g., an encrypted record to be stored) that either does not have the required structure or cannot be decrypted by a registered group member.

– *Necessary and Sufficient Conditions and Generic Design.* We identify the necessary cryptographic components of a GE scheme that include: a digital signature with adaptive chosen message security, a public-key encryption scheme that satisfies both CCA2-key-privacy and CCA2-security, and zero-knowledge proofs for NP statements. Using such components we demonstrate how a generic GE scheme can be implemented and how, in turn, the scheme implies these components (where encryption is derived directly with a relatively tight reduction).

– *Efficient Design.* We design a GE scheme for the discrete logarithm relation, which is one of the most useful relations in cryptography. To this end we employ the modular design as a guide. However, in order to get an efficient scheme, we need to design, exploit and combine primitives that algebraically suit the primitive's structure so that the ciphertext and the interaction associated with it has size independent of the size of the group of potential receivers. Given the large multitude of strong security requirements the model possesses, we found the task of designing and proving the properties to be quite challenging.

– *Efficient Encryption of Discrete Logarithm with CCA2-Security and CCA2-key-privacy.* As our first step in the overall group encryption design, we point out that no existing public-key encryption scheme is suitable for designing a GE for discrete logarithm relations, since the compound set of the requirements that include verifiability, CCA2-security and CCA2-key-privacy for anonymity has not been achieved before and requires special attention. We then design a public-key encryption with CCA2 key-privacy suitable for CCA2 secure verifiable encryption of discrete-logarithms. The security of the scheme is based on the *Decisional Composite Residuosity* (DCR) assumption of [40] (and its design is motivated by earlier works of [24,28,19,10]). We note that our encryption is the first Paillier-based scheme proven to satisfy key-privacy, a fact which may be of independent interest.

– *Algebraic Structure and Intractability Assumption.* A new intractability assumption is required for proving the key-privacy property of our encryption scheme: *Decisional Diffie Hellman assumption for the subgroup of square (quadratic) n-th residues* (DDH$_{SQNR}$). We explain why this is a natural variation of DDH over a cyclic subgroup of $\mathbb{Z}_{n^2}^*$ that has order without small prime divisors and moreover, to strengthen the claim of intractability, we prove that the DCR (which is needed for arguing the security of the scheme anyway) implies the computational Diffie Hellman (CDH) assumption in this subgroup. Note that we know of no arithmetic cyclic group without a partial discrete-log trapdoor, where CDH holds but where DDH does not and thus the assumption seems reasonable.

Applications of Group Encryption. The combination of CCA2 security of ciphertexts, CCA2 anonymity of receivers and verifiability is a strong one and supports some enhanced properties of known constructions as well as opens the door for new applications.

- **Anonymous Trusted Third Party Applications.** Many protocols such as Fair Encryption, Escrow Encryption, Group Signatures, Fair Exchange, etc. employ a trustee, namely a trusted third party who is off-line during the protocol and gets invoked in case something goes wrong. For these primitives it is expected and has been advocated that there will be a multitude of these trustees. In this case the identity of a chosen trustee may reveal certain aspects of the user, whereas the user prefers to retain her privacy. For example, imagine an "International Key Escrow" scenario where a user wants to deposit (decrypt) a key with her own national trusted representative (and needs to do this in a verifiable way). However, such a choice, if made public, may reveal the user's nationality (in violation of privacy). The new group encryption primitive enables the user to trust her own representative, but without revealing its identity, yet to assure others that indeed a designated trustee has been chosen (and not a "faked trustee"). We believe this enhanced privacy while allowing flexibility of choice of trustee is an important step forward in privacy primitives. In this new setting two models are possible for taking keys off escrow: In the first one, each trustee tries to retrieve all the keys from the available ciphertext repository, and will be successful only when the ciphertext is his to open. In the second model, there is an opening authority which can open the identity of the trustee (but not the encrypted key, due to separation of duties). The opening authority, in turn, directs the ciphertext to the chosen trustee to be decrypted. Our primitive supports both opening models. Another scenario that is similar to the above, is proxy voting where users deposit their votes encrypted under the public-key of a proxy of their choice. A proxy is a designated trustee in this case and each user may prefer (or even be required due to legislation) to hide her choice when depositing her vote. In this manner, the proxies can be called upon later, in the tallying phase, to recover the votes entrusted to them. Recall that, as motivated above when contrasting the notion of group encryption with mere key privacy or verifiable encryption, if any of the security properties of group encryption is missing, the application loses its effectiveness, and only the combination of provability (soundness), CCA2 security and CCA2 key privacy delivers the desired effect on the overall escrow system.

- **Ad-Hoc Access Structure Group Signature.** We may implement the opening authority in group encryption as a multitude of trustees and use it to encrypt a signing credential. In this way we can build a group signature where signers can organize the set of trustees to open their signature by acting on it in a predetermined order following an ad-hoc structure that is only partially revealed to the verifier (e.g., a tree or other graph). This can be achieved by cascading the group encryption primitive so that a sequence of hops (identity discoveries and transfers) will be required to recover the identity of the signer in the signature opening step. This notion generalizes "hierarchical group signatures" a primitive introduced in [43] where the trustee access structure was determined as a fixed tree. This application demonstrates the power of our primitive in organizing hidden structures of decrypting parties with CCA2 hiding and securing properties.

– **Secure Oblivious Retriever Storage.** In the area of ubiquitous computing, secure and anonymous credentials may move between computing elements (computer, mobile unit, embedded device, etc.). A user may want to pass a credential secretly and anonymously between devices (either between her own devices, or devices of her peers, all belonging to the same group). Asynchronous transfer that does not require all devices to be present at the same time requires a storage server (similar to a mail server). We can employ group encryption in implementing such a storage server safely, where it is guaranteed that (1) the server only stores valid credentials (i.e., well formed ones that can be delivered to a legitimate retriever and avoid being tricked into storing garbage); (2) the credentials are encrypted and thus the server (or anyone who may compromise it) cannot employ them; and (3) the identity of retrievers of credentials is hidden (even under active attacks, i.e. CCA2 security conditions are needed). A device reading the storage can recover its credentials by scanning the storage sequentially and being successful in decrypting the credentials directed to it (with or without the aid of an opening authority).

We note that group encryption is naturally related to the notion of "custodian-hiding verifiable encryption" that was investigated in [38,37] and may apply in similar application scenarios. From the construction point of view, the focus of the present work is in attaining constant complexity in the group size as opposed to linear that was the case in this previous work.

2   Group Encryption: Model and Definitions

The parties involved in a GE scheme are the sender, the verifier, a group manager (GM) that manages the group of receivers and an opening authority (OA) that is capable of discovering the identity of the receiver. Formally, a GE scheme that is verifiable for a public-relation $\mathcal{R}$ is a collection of procedures and protocols that are denoted as: SETUP, JOIN, $\langle \mathcal{G}_r, \mathcal{R}, \mathsf{sample}_{\mathcal{R}} \rangle$, ENC, DEC, OPEN, $\langle \mathcal{P}, \mathcal{V}, \mathsf{recon} \rangle$
The functionality of the above procedures is as follows: the SETUP is a set of intialization procedures for the system, one for the GM, one for the OA and one to produce public-parameters (denoted by $\mathsf{SETUP_{GM}}, \mathsf{SETUP_{OA}}, \mathsf{SETUP_{init}}$ respectively). Using their respective setup procedures, the GM and the OA will produce their public/secret-key pairs $\langle \mathsf{pk_{GM}}, \mathsf{sk_{GM}} \rangle$ and $\langle \mathsf{pk_{OA}}, \mathsf{sk_{OA}} \rangle$; JOIN $= \langle \mathsf{J_{user}}, \mathsf{J_{GM}} \rangle$ is a protocol between a prospective group member and the GM. After an execution of a JOIN protocol the group member will output his public/secret-key pair $(\mathsf{pk}, \mathsf{sk})$; the new member's public-key pk along with a certificate cert will be published in the public directory database by the GM. We will denote by $\mathcal{L}_{pk}^{\mathsf{param}}$ the language of all valid public-keys where param is a public parameter produced by the $\mathsf{SETUP_{init}}$ procedure.

To employ GE in a transaction, it is assumed that the sender (call her Alice) has obtained a pair (x, w) that is sampled according to the procedure $\mathsf{sample}_{\mathcal{R}}(\mathsf{pk}_{\mathcal{R}}, \mathsf{sk}_{\mathcal{R}})$, where $\mathsf{pk}_{\mathcal{R}}, \mathsf{sk}_{\mathcal{R}}$ are produced by the generation procedure $\mathcal{G}_r(1^{\nu})$ that samples the public/secret parameters for the relation $\mathcal{R}$. We remark that the secret-parameter $\mathsf{sk}_{\mathcal{R}}$ may be empty depending on the relation (e.g., in the case of discrete logarithm the relation is typically publicly samplable, hence $\mathsf{sk}_{\mathcal{R}}$ is empty – but this is not be the case in general). The polynomial-time testing procedure $\mathcal{R}(x, w)$ returns true iff (x, w) belongs to the relation based on the public-parameter $\mathsf{pk}_{\mathcal{R}}$. We note that given the relation $\mathcal{R}(\cdot, \cdot)$ it will be useful that it is hard to extract a "witness" w given an instance x; however this need not be included in the formal requirements for a GE scheme. Note that if verifiability is not desired from the GE, the relation $\mathcal{R}$ will be set to be the trivial relation that includes any string of a fixed size as a witness (and in such case x will be simply equal to $1^{|w|}$).

Alice possessing the pair (x, w), she wishes to encrypt w for her chosen receiver, call him Bob. She obtains Bob's certified public-key $\langle \mathsf{pk}, \mathsf{cert} \rangle$ from database, and employing the public-keys $\mathsf{pk}_{\mathsf{GM}}$ and $\mathsf{pk}_{\mathsf{OA}}$ she encrypts w as $\mathsf{ENC}(\mathsf{pk}_{\mathsf{GM}}, \mathsf{pk}_{\mathsf{OA}}, \mathsf{pk}, w, L)$ to obtain the ciphertext ψ with a certain label L (L is a public string bound to the ciphertext that may contain some transaction related data or be empty; we call it the "context" of ψ). Alice will give x, ψ, L to the verifier. Subsequently, Alice and the verifier will engage in the proof of knowledge $\langle \mathcal{P}, \mathcal{V} \rangle$ that will ensure the following regarding the ciphertext ψ and label L: there exists a group member whose key is registered in the database (i.e., Bob in this case) that is capable of decrypting ψ in context L and obtaining a value w' for which it holds that if $w \leftarrow \mathsf{recon}(w')$ we have that $(x, w) \in \mathcal{R}$. Note that, for $\mathcal{P}, \mathcal{V}$, the input to the verifier will be the values $\mathsf{param}, \mathsf{pk}_{\mathsf{GM}}, \mathsf{pk}_{\mathsf{OA}}, \mathsf{pk}_{\mathcal{R}}, x, \psi, L$, whereas the prover (Alice) will have as additional input the values $\mathsf{pk}, \mathsf{cert}, w$ as well as the coin tosses used for the formation of ψ. The function $\mathsf{recon}(\cdot)$ reconstructs a witness based on the decryption of ψ and may be the identity function.

In the remaining of the section we give four definitions, correctness and the three security related properties of GE, security, anonymity, and soundness. For simulating two-party protocols we use the following notation: $\langle \mathsf{output}_A \mid \mathsf{output}_B \rangle \leftarrow \langle A(\mathsf{input}_A), B(\mathsf{input}_B) \rangle (\mathsf{common\_input})$.

Definition 1. (Correctness) *A* GE *scheme is correct if the following "correctness game" returns 1 with overwhelming probability.*

1. $\mathsf{param} \leftarrow \mathsf{SETUP}_{\mathsf{init}}(1^{\nu})$; $\langle \mathsf{pk}_{\mathcal{R}}, \mathsf{sk}_{\mathcal{R}} \rangle \leftarrow \mathcal{G}_r(1^{\nu})$; $(x, w) \leftarrow \mathsf{sample}_{\mathcal{R}}(\mathsf{pk}_{\mathcal{R}}, \mathsf{sk}_{\mathcal{R}})$.
2. $\langle \mathsf{pk}_{\mathsf{GM}}, \mathsf{sk}_{\mathsf{GM}} \rangle \leftarrow \mathsf{SETUP}_{\mathsf{GM}}(\mathsf{param})$; $\langle \mathsf{pk}_{\mathsf{OA}}, \mathsf{sk}_{\mathsf{OA}} \rangle \leftarrow \mathsf{SETUP}_{\mathsf{OA}}(\mathsf{param})$;
3. $\langle \mathsf{pk}, \mathsf{sk}, \mathsf{cert} \mid \mathsf{pk}, \mathsf{cert} \rangle \leftarrow \langle \mathsf{J}_{\mathsf{user}}, \mathsf{J}_{\mathsf{GM}}(\mathsf{sk}_{\mathsf{GM}}) \rangle (\mathsf{pk}_{\mathsf{GM}})$. If $\mathsf{pk} \notin \mathcal{L}_{\mathsf{pk}}^{\mathsf{param}}$ then abort;
4. $\psi \leftarrow \mathsf{ENC}(\mathsf{pk}_{\mathsf{GM}}, \mathsf{pk}_{\mathsf{OA}}, \mathsf{pk}, \mathsf{cert}, w, L)$.
5. $\mathsf{out}_1 \leftarrow w \overset{?}{=} \mathsf{recon}(\mathsf{DEC}(\mathsf{sk}, \psi, L))$.
6. $\mathsf{out}_2 \leftarrow \mathsf{pk} \overset{?}{=} \mathsf{OPEN}(\mathsf{sk}_{\mathsf{OA}}, [\psi]_{\mathsf{oa}}, L)$.
7. $\langle \mathsf{done} \mid \mathsf{out}_3 \rangle \leftarrow \langle \mathcal{P}(w, \psi, \mathit{coins}_{\psi}), \mathcal{V} \rangle (\mathsf{param}, \mathsf{pk}_{\mathsf{GM}}, \mathsf{pk}_{\mathsf{OA}}, \mathsf{pk}_{\mathcal{R}}, x, \psi, L)$.
8. if $(\mathsf{out}_1 = \mathsf{out}_2 = \mathsf{out}_3 = \mathsf{true})$ return 1.

As shown above the opening procedure OPEN may not operate on the ciphertext ψ but on a substring of the ciphertext ψ that is denoted by $[\psi]_{oa}$; we make the distinction explicit as it is relevant in terms of chosen ciphertext security.

There are three "security notions" for GE schemes: security, anonymity and soundness (that includes verifiability). Security and anonymity are properties that protect Alice (the prover) against a system that acts against her.

Formulation of the Security Property. In our definitions we use a number of traditional oracles that express the nature of the interaction of the adversary and the system. Accordingly, we employ oracles that are stateless (those that maintain no state across queries) and those that are stateful. Next, we introduce the decryption oracle, the challenge procedures and the prover simulator oracle.

DEC(sk, ·): This is a decryption oracle for the GE decryption function DEC. The value sk is a secret-key that will be clarified from the context. If ψ is some "forbidden" ciphertext with label L that the oracle must reject we will write $\text{DEC}^{\neg \langle \psi, L \rangle}(\text{sk}, \cdot)$.

$\text{CH}^{b}_{\text{ror}}(1^{\nu}, \text{pk}, w, L)$: This a real-or-random challenge procedure for the GE encryption scheme. It returns two values denoted as $\langle \psi, coins_{\psi} \rangle$ so that if $b = 1$ then $\psi \leftarrow \text{ENC}(\text{pk}_{\text{GM}}, \text{pk}_{\text{OA}}, \text{pk}, \text{cert}, w, L)$, whereas if $b = 0$, $\psi \leftarrow \text{ENC}(\text{pk}_{\text{GM}}, \text{pk}_{\text{OA}}, \text{pk}, \text{cert}, w', L)$ where w' is a plaintext sampled at random from the space of all possible plaintexts of length 1^{ν} for the encryption function (it is assumed at least two plaintexts exist). In either case $coins_{\psi}$ are the random coin tosses that are used for the computation of ψ.

$\text{PROVE}^{b}_{\mathcal{P}, \mathcal{P}'}(\text{pk}_{\text{GM}}, \text{pk}_{\text{OA}}, \text{pk}, \text{cert}, \text{pk}_{\mathcal{R}}, x, w, \psi, L, coins_{\psi})$: This is an oracle that if $b = 1$, it simulates an execution of the prover procedure of $\mathcal{P}$ of the GE scheme (i.e., Alice), on $\text{pk}_{\text{GM}}, \text{pk}_{\text{OA}}, \text{pk}, \text{cert}, \text{pk}_{\mathcal{R}}, x, w, \psi, L, coins_{\psi}$. On the other hand, if $b = 0$, it simulates the protocol $\mathcal{P}'$ that takes the same input as $\mathcal{P}$ with the exception of the values of w and $coins_{\psi}$ (the design of $\mathcal{P}'$ is part of proving the security property).

Based on the above three procedures we are ready to give the security definition, which is reminiscent of a real-or-random attack on the underlying encryption scheme. In the game below the adversary controls the GM and OA and all group members except the member that Alice chooses as her recipient, i.e., Bob. In fact, the adversary is the entity that introduces Bob into the group and issues a certificate for his public-key. Moreover, the adversary has CCA2 access to Bob's secret-key. The adversary also selects some public relation $\mathcal{R}$ based on $\text{pk}_{\mathcal{R}}$ as well as a pair (x, w). Subsequently a coin is tossed and the adversary either receives the encryption of w and engages with Alice in the proof of ciphertext validity or the adversary receives an encryption of a random plaintext and engages in a simulated proof of validity. A GE would satisfy security if the adversary is unable to tell the difference. More formally (note that $\text{negl}(\nu)$ is a function that for any c, is less than ν^{-c} for sufficiently large ν):

Definition 2. *A GE scheme satisfies* security *if there exists a protocol $\mathcal{P}'$ s.t. the "security game" below when instantiated by any PPT $\mathcal{A}$, returns 1 with probability less or equal to $1/2 + \mathsf{negl}(\nu)$.*

1. $\mathsf{param} \leftarrow \mathsf{SETUP}_{\mathsf{init}}(1^\nu); \langle \mathsf{aux}, \mathsf{pk}_{\mathsf{GM}}, \mathsf{pk}_{\mathsf{OA}} \rangle \leftarrow \mathcal{A}(\mathsf{param});$
2. $\langle \mathsf{pk}, \mathsf{sk}, \mathsf{cert} \mid \mathsf{aux} \rangle \leftarrow \langle \mathsf{J}_{\mathsf{user}}, \mathcal{A}(\mathsf{aux}) \rangle (\mathsf{pk}_{\mathsf{GM}});$
3. $\langle \mathsf{aux}, x, w, L, \mathsf{pk}_{\mathcal{R}} \rangle \leftarrow \mathcal{A}^{\mathsf{DEC}(\mathsf{sk}, \cdot)}(\mathsf{aux});$ *if* $(x, w) \notin \mathcal{R}$ *then abort;*
4. $b \xleftarrow{r} \{0, 1\}; \langle \psi, \mathit{coins}_\psi \rangle \leftarrow \mathsf{CH}_{\mathsf{ror}}^b(1^\nu, \mathsf{pk}, w, L);$
5. $b^* \leftarrow \mathcal{A}^{\mathsf{PROVE}_{\mathcal{P}, \mathcal{P}'}^b(\mathsf{pk}_{\mathsf{GM}}, \mathsf{pk}_{\mathsf{OA}}, \mathsf{pk}, \mathsf{cert}, \mathsf{pk}_{\mathcal{R}}, x, w, \psi, L, \mathit{coins}_\psi), \mathsf{DEC}^{\neg\langle \psi, L \rangle}(\mathsf{sk}, \cdot)}(\mathsf{aux}, \psi)$
6. *if* $b = b^*$ *return 1 else 0.*

Formulation of the Anonymity Property. In the anonymity attack the adversary controls the system except the opening authority. Anonymity can be thought of as a CCA2 attack against the encryption system of the OA. The adversary registers the two possible recipients into the PKI database and provides the relation and the witness to Alice. Alice will encrypt the same witness always as provided by the adversary but will use the key of one of the two recipients at random. The adversary, who has CCA2 decryption access to both recipients as well as the OA, will have to guess which one of the two is Alice's choice. We define the following procedures:

$\mathsf{CH}_{\mathsf{anon}}^b(\mathsf{pk}_{\mathsf{GM}}, \mathsf{pk}_{\mathsf{OA}}, \mathsf{pk}_0, \mathsf{pk}_1, w, L)$: The challenge procedure receives a plaintext w and two public-keys $\mathsf{pk}_0, \mathsf{pk}_1$, and returns two values, $\langle \psi, \mathit{coins}_\psi \rangle$ so that $\psi \leftarrow \mathsf{ENC}(\mathsf{pk}_{\mathsf{GM}}, \mathsf{pk}_{\mathsf{OA}}, \mathsf{pk}_b, \mathsf{cert}_b, w, L)$ and coins_ψ are the random coin tosses that are used for the computation of ψ.

$\mathsf{USER}(\mathsf{pk}_{\mathsf{GM}})$: This is an oracle that simulates two instantiations of $\mathsf{J}_{\mathsf{user}}$, i.e., it is given $\mathsf{pk}_{\mathsf{GM}}$ and simulates two users that wish to become members of the group; the oracle has access to a string denoted by keys in which USER will write the output of the two $\mathsf{J}_{\mathsf{user}}$ instances.

$\mathsf{OPEN}(\mathsf{sk}_{\mathsf{OA}}, \cdot)$: This is an oracle that simulates the OPEN operation of the opening authority; recall that OPEN may not operate on the whole ciphertext ψ but rather on substring of it that will be denoted by $[\psi]_{\mathsf{oa}}$.

Definition 3. *A GE scheme satisfies* anonymity *if the following game instantiated for any PPT $\mathcal{A}$, it returns 1 with probability less or equal $1/2 + \mathsf{negl}(\nu)$.*

1. $\mathsf{param} \leftarrow \mathsf{SETUP}_{\mathsf{init}}(1^\nu); \langle \mathsf{pk}_{\mathsf{OA}}, \mathsf{sk}_{\mathsf{OA}} \rangle \leftarrow \mathsf{SETUP}_{\mathsf{OA}}(\mathsf{param});$
2. $\langle \mathsf{pk}_{\mathsf{GM}}, \mathsf{sk}_{\mathsf{GM}} \rangle \leftarrow \mathsf{SETUP}_{\mathsf{GM}}(\mathsf{param}); \mathsf{aux} \leftarrow \mathcal{A}^{\mathsf{USER}(\mathsf{pk}_{\mathsf{GM}}), \mathsf{OPEN}(\mathsf{sk}_{\mathsf{OA}}, \cdot)}(\mathsf{sk}_{\mathsf{GM}});$
3. *if* $\mathsf{keys} \neq \langle \mathsf{pk}_0, \mathsf{sk}_0, \mathsf{cert}_0, \mathsf{pk}_1, \mathsf{sk}_1, \mathsf{cert}_1 \rangle$ *then abort;*
4. $\langle \mathsf{aux}, x, w, L, \mathsf{pk}_{\mathcal{R}} \rangle \leftarrow \mathcal{A}^{\mathsf{OPEN}(\mathsf{sk}_{\mathsf{OA}}, \cdot), \mathsf{DEC}(\mathsf{sk}_0, \cdot), \mathsf{DEC}(\mathsf{sk}_1, \cdot)}(\mathsf{aux});$
5. *if* $(x, w) \notin \mathcal{R}$ *then abort;* $b \xleftarrow{r} \{0, 1\};$
6. $\langle \psi, \mathit{coins}_\psi \rangle \leftarrow \mathsf{CH}_{\mathsf{anon}}^b(\mathsf{pk}_{\mathsf{GM}}, \mathsf{pk}_{\mathsf{OA}}, \mathsf{pk}_0, \mathsf{pk}_1, w, L);$
7. $t_b \leftarrow \langle \mathsf{pk}_{\mathsf{GM}}, \mathsf{pk}_{\mathsf{OA}}, \mathsf{pk}_{\mathcal{R}}, \mathsf{pk}_b, \mathsf{cert}_b, x, w, \psi, L, \mathit{coins}_\psi \rangle;$
8. $b^* \leftarrow \mathcal{A}^{\mathcal{P}(t_b), \mathsf{OPEN}^{\neg\langle [\psi]_{\mathsf{oa}}, L \rangle}(\mathsf{sk}_{\mathsf{OA}}, \cdot), \mathsf{DEC}^{\neg\langle \psi, L \rangle}(\mathsf{sk}_0, \cdot), \mathsf{DEC}^{\neg\langle \psi, L \rangle}(\mathsf{sk}_1, \cdot)}(\mathsf{aux}, \psi);$
9. *if* $b = b^*$ *return 1 else 0;*

respect to multiplication with -1 (cf. the decryption test below). To summarize, encryption works as follows:

$$r \leftarrow_R \left[\frac{n}{4}\right] \quad : \quad u_1 \leftarrow g_1^r \quad u_2 \leftarrow g_2^r \quad e \leftarrow y^r h^m \quad v \leftarrow ||c^r d^{r\mathcal{H}(u_1, u_2, e, L)}||$$

Decryption. The decryption function $\mathcal{D}$ given a ciphertext (u_1, u_2, e, v) and a label L it performs the following checks:

$$v \stackrel{?}{=} ||v|| \quad \wedge \quad v^2 \stackrel{?}{=} (u_1^{x_1} u_2^{x_2})^2 (u_1^{y_1} u_2^{y_2})^{2\mathcal{H}(u_1, u_2, e, L)}$$

if all tests pass it computes $m' = e^2 u_1^{-2z} - 1 (\bmod n^2)$ and returns $(m' \cdot 2^{-1} \bmod n)/n$, otherwise it returns $\bot$.

This completes the description of the cryptosystem. Observe that the cryptosystem is correct, i.e., encryption inverts decryption: indeed, assuming that $\langle u_1, u_2, e, v \rangle \leftarrow \mathcal{E}(\mathsf{pk}, w, L)$, we have that $m' = e^2 u_1^{-2z} - 1 \equiv_{n^2} h^{2w} - 1$ and due to the fact that $h^x \equiv_{n^2} 1 + xn$ for all $x \in \mathbb{Z}_n$ we have that $w' \equiv_{n^2} (2m \bmod n) \cdot n$. It follows that $(w' \cdot 2^{-1} \bmod n)/n = w$.

We will next argue about the security of the cryptosystem. We note that the above cryptosystem has a "double trapdoor" property: for each public-key, c, d, y, based on parameters $n, g_1, g_2, \mathrm{desc}\mathcal{H}$, one trapdoor is the discrete-logarithm of y base g_1, whereas the the other trapdoor is the factorization of n. Indeed given the factorization of n, one can easily decrypt any ciphertext $\langle u_1, u_2, e, v \rangle$ by computing $e^{p'q'} \equiv_{n^2} h^{p'q'm}$. Subsequently m can be computed easily similarly to the regular decryption function. In GE the global trapdoor will not be used and the factorization of n will be assumed unknown by all parties. The intractability assumption that will be employed is the following:

Definition 5. *The* Decisional Composite Residuosity DCR *assumption [40]: It is computationally hard to distinguish between: (i) tuples of the form $(n, u^n \bmod n^2)$ where n is a composite RSA modulus and $u \leftarrow_R \mathbb{Z}_{n^2}^*$, and (ii) tuples of the form (n, v) where $v \leftarrow_R \mathbb{Z}_{n^2}^*$.*

Next, we prove IND-CCA2 security under the DCR.

Theorem 2. *The cryptosystem $\langle \mathcal{Z}_e, \mathcal{G}_e, \mathcal{E}, \mathcal{D} \rangle$ defined above satisfies CCA2 security under the DCR assumption and the target collision resistance of the employed UOWH family.*

Interestingly, it is not clear whether the DCR can be used for proving the key-privacy of the cryptosystem. To see why this is the case consider the following: Consider the CPA version of the cryptosystem using only a single generator over $\mathcal{X}_{n^2}$: in the CPA case the cryptosystem is similar to ElGamal, with ciphertexts pairs of the form $\langle g^r \bmod n^2, y^r h^m \bmod n^2 \rangle$. Note that IND-CPA security can be easily shown under the DCR assumption. On the other hand, to show CPA-key-privacy one has to (essentially) establish the indistinguishability of the distributions $\langle g, y_0, y_1, g^r, y_0^r h^m \rangle$ and $\langle g, y_0, y_1, g^r, y_1^r h^m \rangle$. It is not apparent how to apply DCR to prove this indistinguishability; ultimately this is because the message m is the same in both of these distributions and its randomization (easily provided by DCR) appears to be immaterial to the indistinguishability of the two distributions. It should be noted that since the adversary is not interested in the h^m portion of the ciphertext he can easily cancel it out by raising everything to n. For this reason the power of DCR seems of little use in this case, and a Diffie-Hellman-like assumption in $\mathcal{X}_{n^2}$ would seem more appropriate.

Based on the above we employ the Decisional Diffie Hellman assumption over the group $\mathcal{X}_{n^2}$, denoted as DDH$_{\mathsf{SQNR}}$. Regarding the relationship between Diffie Hellman type of problems and the DCR we show the following theorem:

Theorem 3. DCR $\Longrightarrow$ CDH$_{\mathsf{SQNR}}$

Based on the above we formulate our key-privacy theorem for the cryptosystem:

Theorem 4. *The cryptosystem $\langle \mathcal{Z}, \mathcal{G}_e, \mathcal{E}, \mathcal{D} \rangle$ defined above satisfies CCA2-key-privacy under the DDH$_{\mathsf{SQNR}}$ assumption and the target collision resistance of the employed UOWH family.*

Proof of Public-Key Validity. We will employ the public-key encryption scheme above to build the public-key **database** of the GE scheme. When a user joins the group he will be allowed to generate a public-key and he will be required to show that the public-key is valid. For our new cryptosystem the language of valid public-keys is $\mathcal{L}_{pk}^{\mathsf{param}} = \{\langle c, d, y \rangle \mid c, d, y \in \mathcal{X}_{n^2}\}$ where $\mathsf{param} = \langle n, g_1, g_2, \mathcal{H} \rangle$. It follows that joining will require three instances of a proof of language membership to the subgroup $\mathcal{X}_{n^2}$ of $\mathbb{Z}_{n^2}^*$. The validity of an element y can be performed by executing the following steps where $k_0, k_1 \in \mathbb{N}$ are parameters that affect the soundness and zero-knowledge properties of the proof of language membership below:

1. [User:] Select $t \xleftarrow{r} \{0,1\}^{k_0}$ and transmit $a \leftarrow g^t \bmod n^2$.
2. [GM:] Select $c \xleftarrow{r} \{0,1\}^{k_1}$ and transmit c.
3. [User:] Compute $s \leftarrow t - cz \in \mathbb{Z}$ and transmit s.
4. [GM:] Verify $a^2 \equiv_{n^2} (g_1^2)^s y^{2c}$.

It is easy to verify that given any prover that produces a value y and then executes the proof above, it must be the case that $y^2 \in \mathcal{X}_{n^2}$ with probability $1 - 2^{-k_1}$. Note that this still allows for a slight misbehavior on the part of the user as he can multiply y with an element of order 2 inside $\mathbb{Z}_{n^2}^*$; while it is easy to add an additional step in the above proof to avoid this slight misbehavior we will not do so as we will show the security properties of our GE scheme without such guarantee.

Construction of GE of Discrete-logarithms. We proceed to the description of the GE scheme SETUP, JOIN, $\langle \mathcal{G}_{\mathsf{dl}}, \mathcal{R}_{\mathsf{dl}}, \mathsf{sample}_{\mathsf{dl}} \rangle$, ENC, DEC, OPEN, $\langle \mathcal{P}, \mathcal{V}, \mathsf{recon} \rangle$. First recall that from the discrete-logarithm relation, $\mathcal{G}_{\mathsf{dl}}$ given 1^ν samples a description of a cyclic group of ν-bits order and a generator γ of that group; $\mathcal{R}_{\mathsf{dl}}$ contains pairs of the form (x, w) where $x = \gamma^w$. Finally $\mathsf{sample}_{\mathsf{dl}}$ on input $\mathsf{pk}_{\mathcal{R}} = \langle \mathsf{desc}(G), \gamma \rangle$ selects a witness w and returns the pair $(x = \gamma^w, w)$.

Parameter Selection. The procedure SETUP selects the following parameters:

o Integer values k_0, k_1.
o A safe composite n of ℓ_n bits and generators $g, \breve{g}, g_1, g_2$ of the group $\mathcal{X}_{n^2}$.
o The description of a hash function $\mathcal{H}$ drawn at random from a UOWH family.
o A prime number Q of the form $\lambda \cdot n^2 + 1$ and F, H generators of the order n^2 subgroup of $\mathbb{Z}_Q^*$.
o A safe composite $\hat{n}$ of ℓ_N bits and two generators $\hat{g}, \hat{y}$ of the group $\mathcal{X}_{\hat{n}^2}$.
o A sequence of integers $G, Y_1, Y_2, Y_3 \in \mathbb{N}$ of length ℓ_N.

We stress that the above parameters are part of the trusted setup of the system (also referred to as the common reference string, and no participant of the system, including the GM, OA, or any user will know any private information about these values).

SETUP$_{OA}$. The procedure selects $x_1, x_2, y_1, y_2, z \leftarrow_R [\frac{n^2}{4}]$ and set $pk_{OA} = \langle \breve{y}, \breve{c}, \breve{d} \rangle = \langle g^z, g^{x_1} \breve{g}^{x_2}, g^{y_1} \breve{g}^{y_2} \rangle$.

SETUP$_{GM}$. The GM will employ a digital signature $\langle \mathcal{G}_s, \mathcal{S}, \mathcal{V}_s \rangle$ that must satisfy adaptive chosen message security and be suitable for engaging in proofs of knowledge of signed messages when the signature is committed. In our design will employ the block signature of Camenisch and Lysyanskaya [15] as the underlying digital signature scheme (hence referred to as CL-signature). The choice of the digital signature is not unique to our design and other signature schemes can be employed as well. The key-generation procedure $\mathcal{G}_s$ (that will be used by GM in SETUP$_{GM}$) samples a pair $\langle sk_{GM}, pk_{GM} \rangle$ where $pk_{GM} = \langle A_0, A_{1,c}, A_{1,d}, A_{1,y}, A_2, N \rangle$ with N a safe composite of ℓ_N bits and $A_0, A_{1,c}, A_{1,d}, A_{1,y}, A_2 \in \mathbb{Z}_N^*$ are random quadratic residues in $\mathcal{Q}_N$. The signing key sk_{GM} is the factorization of N. In addition to ℓ_N we have the parameters ℓ_m where $[0, 2^{\ell_m}) \times [0, 2^{\ell_m}) \times [0, 2^{\ell_m})$ will be the message space for the signature such that $n^2 < 2^{\ell_m}$ (this is because we want to use the signature to sign public-keys of the encryption scheme).

JOIN. The prospective group member submits c, d, y as generated by the encryption system $\langle \mathcal{G}_e, \mathcal{E}, \mathcal{D} \rangle$ given in the beginning of the section. In particular, recall that $\langle c, d, y \rangle$ is defined as $c \leftarrow g_1^{x_1} g_2^{x_2} \bmod n^2, d \leftarrow g_1^{y_1} g_2^{y_2} \bmod n^2$, $y \leftarrow g_1^z$ and $x_1, x_2, y_1, y_2, z \leftarrow_R [\frac{n^2}{4}]$. The secret key of the user is set to the values x_1, x_2, y_1, y_2, z. The user engages with the GM in a proof of membership for the validity of c, d, y. Upon acceptance the GM will use the signing procedure $\mathcal{S}$ for CL-signatures that is as follows: given the message $M = \langle c, d, y \rangle$, the GM will sample $R \leftarrow [0, 2^{\ell_N + \ell_m + \ell})$ where ℓ is a security parameter and a random prime $E > 2^{\ell_m + 1}$ of length $\ell_m + 2$ bits; then it will compute $A = (A_0 A_{1,c}^c A_{1,d}^d A_{1,y}^y A_2^R)^{1/E} (\bmod N)$ (recall that the factorization of N is the signing key). Finally the signature to M is the triple $\langle A, E, R \rangle$.

Finally, the GM will enter $\langle c, d, y \rangle$ into the public **database** followed by the signature. Note that the GM should not allow a user to enter into **database** a key $\langle c, d, y \rangle$ such that there is some $\langle c_i, d_i, y_i \rangle$ in the database already for which it holds that $c^2 = c_i^2$, or $d^2 = d_i^2$ or $y^2 = y_i^2$. Recall that the verification algorithm $\mathcal{V}_s$ given a message $M = \langle c, d, y \rangle$ and a signature $\langle A, E, R \rangle$ on it, checks whether it holds that $A^E = A_0 A_{1,c}^c A_{1,d}^d A_{1,y}^y A_2^R \bmod N$ and verifies all the range constraints on c, d, y, E, R as stated above.

ENC, DEC and recon. Following our modular design methodology of section 3 the GE encryption function consists of the encryption of the witness w under a recipient's public-key $\langle c, d, y \rangle$ and a sequence of commitments to the public-key used and commitments to the certificate of this public-key. More specifically when Alice wants to encrypt her witness w for her public-value $x = \gamma^w$ under label L she computes the following:

1. Commitment to Certificate of Public-key. The commitment to the certificate of the public-key of the recipient that Alice selected is formed as follows: for the certificate $\langle A, E, R \rangle$ the following values are computed $\tilde{B} = G^{2u} \bmod N$, $\tilde{A} = Y_1^{2u} A \bmod N$, $\tilde{E} = Y_2^{2u} G^{2E} \bmod N$, $\tilde{R} = Y_3^{2u} G^{2R} \bmod N$.

2. Bridge Commitments. The "bridge commitments" will assist in the efficient proof of ciphertext validity. In particular Alice includes the commitments $\hat{E} = \check{g}^E (l_1)^{\hat{n}} \bmod \hat{n}^2$, $\hat{R} = \check{g}^R (l_2)^{\hat{n}} \bmod \hat{n}^2$ and $l_j \xleftarrow{r} \mathbb{Z}_n$ for $j = 1, 2$. Moreover she includes the commitments $\tilde{y} = H_y^{u'} F^y \bmod Q$, $\tilde{c} = H_c^{u'} F^c \bmod Q$, $\tilde{d} = H_d^{u'} F^d \bmod Q$.

3. Encryption of the recipient's public-key. Encryption of the public-key that Alice selected is formed as three ciphertexts: $\langle f_c, \check{f}_c, \ddot{f}_c, \ddot{f}_c \rangle$, $\langle f_d, \check{f}_d, \dot{f}_d, \ddot{f}_d \rangle$, $\langle f_y, \check{f}_y, \dot{f}_y, \ddot{f}_y \rangle$, where each is selected as $\langle g^{u_a}, \check{g}^{u_a}, \ddot{y}^{u_a} a, \check{c}^{u_a} \check{d}^{u_a \mathcal{H}(L'_a)} \rangle$ where $u_a \xleftarrow{r} [\frac{n}{4}]$, a $\in \{y, c, d\}$, $a \in \{y, c, d\}$ and $L'_a = \langle f_a, \check{f}_a, \dot{f}_a, \ddot{f}_a, L \rangle$.

4. Encryption of the witness. The encryption of witness w is as follows: $\langle u_1, u_2, e, v \rangle \leftarrow \langle g_1^r, g_2^r, y^r h^w, \|c^r d^{r \mathcal{H}(u_1, u_2, e, L'_c, L'_d, L'_y)}\| \rangle$.

DEC is the decryption process as defined in the beginning of the section for the new encryption scheme. recon is simply the identity function.

OPEN. The opening procedure applies to the three ciphertext excluding the witness ciphertext (item 4, above). In particular, it returns $\langle c, d, y \rangle = \langle f_c \check{f}_c^{-z}, \dot{f}_d \ddot{f}_d^{-z}, \dot{f}_y \ddot{f}_y^{-z} \rangle$ or $\perp$ depending on the outcome of the tests $f_a^{x_1 + y_1} \check{f}_a^{(x_2 + y_2) \mathcal{H}(L')} \overset{?}{=} \dot{f}_a$ for $a \in \{y, c, d\}$. The owner of the public-key is identified by comparing $\langle c^2, d^2, y^2 \rangle$ to all entries $\langle c_i^2, d_i^2, y_i^2 \rangle$ that are inside the database **database**.

The proof of validity $\langle \mathcal{P}, \mathcal{V} \rangle$. This protocol will be constructed as an AND composition of four sub-protocols that due to lack of space presented in the full version [32]. These protocols belong to a class of efficient proofs for discrete log relations that are very common in the design of cryptographic primitives and their concrete and efficient instantiation has become quite standard in the literature. An exception perhaps is protocol # 2 which is a more complex protocol and is related to the "double-decker" proof of knowledge for discrete-logarithms [42,20]. This protocol is the least efficient as it requires parallel repetition for decreasing the knowledge-error. Still, we stress that the overall communication is independent of the size of the group and well within practical limits.

Based on the above, the theorem below follows as a corollary of theorem 1:

Theorem 5. *The* GE *scheme for discrete-logarithms defined above satisfies (i)* Correctness; *(ii)* Anonymity *and (iii)* Security, *under the* DDH$_{\mathsf{SQNR}}$, DDH *over* $\mathcal{Q}_N$, DCR *and the collision resistance of the* UOWH *family; (iv)* Soundness, *under the Strong-RSA and the DLOG assumptions.*

References

1. Asokan, N., Shoup, V., Waidner, M.: Optimistic fair exchange of digital signatures (extended abstract). In: EUROCRYPT, pp. 591–606 (1998)
2. Ateniese, G., Camenisch, J., Hohenberger, S., de Medeiros, B.: Practical group signatures without random oracles. Cryptology ePrint Archive, Report 2005/385 (2005), http://eprint.iacr.org/
3. Ateniese, G., Camenisch, J., Joye, M., Tsudik, G.: A practical and provably secure coalition-resistant group signature scheme. In: Bellare, M. (ed.) CRYPTO 2000. LNCS, vol. 1880, Springer, Heidelberg (2000)
4. Ateniese, G., Tsudik, G.: Some open issues and new directions in group signatures. In: Franklin, M.K. (ed.) FC 1999. LNCS, vol. 1648, pp. 196–211. Springer, Heidelberg (1999)
5. Bellare, M., Boldyreva, A., Desai, A., Pointcheval, D.: Key-privacy in public-key encryption. In: Boyd, C. (ed.) ASIACRYPT 2001. LNCS, vol. 2248, pp. 566–582. Springer, Heidelberg (2001)
6. Bellare, M., Micciancio, D., Warinschi, B.: Foundations of group signatures: Formal definitions, simplified requirements, and a construction based on general assumptions. In: Biham, E. (ed.) Advances in Cryptology – EUROCRPYT 2003. LNCS, vol. 2656, Springer, Heidelberg (2003)
7. Bellare, M., Shi, H., Zhang, C.: Foundations of group signatures: The case of dynamic groups. In: Menezes, A.J. (ed.) CT-RSA 2005. LNCS, vol. 3376, pp. 136–153. Springer, Heidelberg (2005)
8. Boneh, D., Boyen, X., Shacham, H.: Short group signatures. In: Franklin, M. (ed.) CRYPTO 2004. LNCS, vol. 3152, pp. 41–55. Springer, Heidelberg (2004)
9. Boyen, X., Waters, B.: Compact group signatures without random oracles. In: Vaudenay, S. (ed.) EUROCRYPT 2006. LNCS, vol. 4004, pp. 427–444. Springer, Heidelberg (2006)
10. Bresson, E., Catalano, D., Pointcheval, D.: A simple public-key cryptosystem with a double trapdoor decryption mechanism and its applications. In: Laih, C.-S. (ed.) ASIACRYPT 2003. LNCS, vol. 2894, pp. 37–54. Springer, Heidelberg (2003)
11. Camenisch, J.: Efficient and generalized group signatures. In: Fumy, W. (ed.) Advances in Cryptology - EUROCRYPT 1997, International Association for Cryptologic Research. International Conference on the Theory and Application of Cryptographic Techniques. LNCS, pp. 465–479. Springer, Heidelberg (1997)
12. Camenisch, J., Damgård, I.: Verifiable encryption, group encryption, and their applications to separable group signatures and signature sharing schemes. In: Okamoto, T. (ed.) ASIACRYPT 2000. LNCS, vol. 1976, pp. 331–345. Springer, Heidelberg (2000)
13. Camenisch, J., Lysyanskaya, A.: An efficient system for non-transferable anonymous credentials with optional anonymity revocation. In: Pfitzmann, B. (ed.) EUROCRYPT 2001. LNCS, vol. 2045, pp. 93–118. Springer, Heidelberg (2001)

14. Camenisch, J., Lysyanskaya, A.: An identity escrow scheme with appointed verifiers. In: Kilian, J. (ed.) CRYPTO 2001. LNCS, vol. 2139, pp. 388–407. Springer-Verlag, Berlin Germany (2001)
15. Camenisch, J., Lysyanskaya, A.: A signature scheme with efficient protocols. In: Cimato, S., Galdi, C., Persiano, G. (eds.) SCN 2002. LNCS, vol. 2576, pp. 268–289. Springer, Heidelberg (2003)
16. Camenisch, J., Lysyanskaya, A.: Signature schemes and anonymous credentials from bilinear maps. In: Franklin, M.K. (ed.) CRYPTO 2004. LNCS, vol. 3152, pp. 56–72. Springer, Heidelberg (2004)
17. Camenisch, J., Michels, M.: A group signature scheme with improved efficiency. In: Ohta, K., Pei, D. (eds.) ASIACRYPT 1998. LNCS, vol. 1514, pp. 160–174. Springer, Heidelberg (1998)
18. Camenisch, J., Michels, M.: Separability and efficiency for generic group signature schemes (extended abstract). In: Wiener, M.J. (ed.) CRYPTO 1999. LNCS, vol. 1666, pp. 413–430. Springer, Heidelberg (1999)
19. Camenisch, J., Shoup, V.: Practical verifiable encryption and decryption of discrete logarithms. In: Boneh, D. (ed.) CRYPTO 2003. LNCS, vol. 2729, Springer, Heidelberg (2003)
20. Camenisch, J., Stadler, M.: Efficient group signature schemes for large groups. In: Kaliski Jr., B.S. (ed.) CRYPTO 1997. LNCS, vol. 1294, pp. 410–424. Springer, Heidelberg (1997)
21. Chaum, D.: Private communication (2006)
22. Chaum, D., van Heyst, E.: Group signatures. In: Davies, D.W. (ed.) EUROCRYPT 1991. LNCS, vol. 547, pp. 257–265. Springer, Heidelberg (1991)
23. Chen, L., Pedersen, T.P.: New group signature schemes (extended abstract). In: De Santis, A. (ed.) EUROCRYPT 1994. LNCS, vol. 950, pp. 171–181. Springer, Heidelberg (1995)
24. Cramer, R., Shoup, V.: A practical public key cryptosystem provably secure against adaptive chosen ciphertext attack. In: Krawczyk, H. (ed.) CRYPTO 1998. LNCS, vol. 1462, pp. 13–25. Springer, Heidelberg (1998)
25. Damgård, I.: Efficient concurrent zero-knowledge in the auxiliary string model. In: EUROCRYPT, pp. 418–430 (2000)
26. Desmedt, Y.: Society and group oriented cryptography: A new concept. In: Pomerance, C. (ed.) CRYPTO 1987. LNCS, vol. 293, pp. 120–127. Springer, Heidelberg (1988)
27. Dolev, D., Dwork, C., Naor, M.: Non-malleable cryptography (extended abstract). In: Proceedings of the Twenty Third Annual ACM Symposium on Theory of Computing, New Orleans, Louisiana, May 6–8, 1991, pp. 542–552. ACM Press, New York (1991)
28. Gennaro, R., Lindell, Y.: A framework for password-based authenticated key exchange. In: Biham, E. (ed.) Advances in Cryptology – EUROCRPYT 2003. LNCS, vol. 2656, Springer, Heidelberg (2003)
29. Goldreich, O.: The Foundations of Cryptography, vol. 1. Cambridge University Press, Cambridge (2004)
30. Groth, J.: Simulation-sound nizk proofs for a practical language and constant size group signatures. In: Lai, X., Chen, K. (eds.) ASIACRYPT 2006. LNCS, vol. 4284, pp. 444–459. Springer, Heidelberg (2006)
31. Halevi, S.: Sufficient condition for key privacy. Cryptology ePrint Archive, Report 2005/005 (2005), http://eprint.iacr.org/
32. Kiayias, A., Tsiounis, Y., Yung, M.: Group encryption. Cryptology ePrint Archive, Report 2007/015 (2007), http://eprint.iacr.org/

33. Kiayias, A., Yung, M.: Extracting group signatures from traitor tracing schemes. In: Biham, E. (ed.) Advances in Cryptology – EUROCRPYT 2003. LNCS, vol. 2656, pp. 630–648. Springer, Heidelberg (2003)

34. Kiayias, A., Yung, M.: Group signatures with efficient concurrent join. In: Cramer, R.J.F. (ed.) EUROCRYPT 2005. LNCS, vol. 3494, pp. 198–214. Springer, Heidelberg (2005)

35. Kiayias, A., Yung, M.: Secure scalable group signature with dynamic joins and separable authorities. Int. J. Security and Networks 1(1/2), 24–45 (2006)

36. Kilian, J., Petrank, E.: Identity escrow. In: Krawczyk, H. (ed.) CRYPTO 1998. LNCS, vol. 1462, pp. 169–185. Springer, Heidelberg (1998)

37. Liu, J.K., Tsang, P.P., Wong, D.S., Zhu, R.W.: Universal custodian-hiding verifiable encryption for discrete logarithms. In: Won, D.H., Kim, S. (eds.) ICISC 2005. LNCS, vol. 3935, pp. 389–409. Springer, Heidelberg (2006)

38. Liu, J.K., Wei, V.K., Wong, D.S.: Custodian-hiding verifiable encryption. In: Lim, C.H., Yung, M. (eds.) WISA 2004. LNCS, vol. 3325, pp. 51–64. Springer, Heidelberg (2005)

39. Naor, M., Yung, M.: Universal one-way hash functions and their cryptographic applications. In: STOC, pp. 33–43. ACM, New York (1989)

40. Paillier, P.: Public-key cryptosystems based on composite degree residuosity classes. In: Stern, J. (ed.) EUROCRYPT 1999. LNCS, vol. 1592, pp. 223–238. Springer, Heidelberg (1999)

41. Rackoff, C., Simon, D.R.: Non-interactive zero-knowledge proof of knowledge and chosen ciphertext attack. In: Feigenbaum, J. (ed.) CRYPTO 1991. LNCS, vol. 576, pp. 433–444. Springer, Heidelberg (1992)

42. Stadler, M.: Publicly verifiable secret sharing. In: Maurer, U.M. (ed.) EUROCRYPT 1996. LNCS, vol. 1070, pp. 190–199. Springer, Heidelberg (1996)

43. Trolin, M., Wikström, D.: Hierarchical group signatures. In: Caires, L., Italiano, G.F., Monteiro, L., Palamidessi, C., Yung, M. (eds.) ICALP 2005. LNCS, vol. 3580, pp. 446–458. Springer, Heidelberg (2005)

44. Young, A., Yung, M.: A pvss as hard as discrete log and shareholder separability. In: Kim, K.-c. (ed.) PKC 2001. LNCS, vol. 1992, pp. 287–299. Springer, Heidelberg (2001)

Identity-Based Broadcast Encryption with Constant Size Ciphertexts and Private Keys

Cécile Delerablée[1,2]

[1] Orange Labs - Caen, France
[2] ENS - Paris, France
cecile.delerablee@orange-ftgroup.com

Abstract. This paper describes the first identity-based broadcast encryption scheme (IBBE) with constant size ciphertexts and private keys. In our scheme, the public key is of size linear in the maximal size m of the set of receivers, which is smaller than the number of possible users (identities) in the system. Compared with a recent broadcast encryption system introduced by Boneh, Gentry and Waters (BGW), our system has comparable properties, but with a better efficiency: the public key is shorter than in BGW. Moreover, the total number of possible users in the system does not have to be fixed in the setup.

1 Introduction

Broadcast Encryption. The concept of Broadcast Encryption (BE) was introduced by Fiat and Naor in [16]. In BE schemes, a broadcaster encrypts messages and transmits them to a group of users who are listening to a broadcast channel and use their private keys to decrypt transmissions. At encryption time, the broadcaster can choose the set $\mathcal{S}$ of identities that will be able to decrypt messages. A BE scheme is said to be fully collusion resistant when, even if all users that are not in $\mathcal{S}$ collude, they can by no means infer information about the broadcast message.

Many BE systems have been proposed [23,20,19,10,15]. The best known fully collusion systems are the schemes of Boneh, Gentry and Waters [10] which achieve $O(\sqrt{n})$-size ciphertexts and public key, or constant size ciphertexts, $O(n)$-size public key and constant size private keys in a construction that we denote by $\mathsf{BGW_1}$ in the following. A lot of systems make use of the hybrid (KEM-DEM) encryption paradigm where the broadcast ciphertext only encrypts a symmetric key used to encrypt the broadcast contents. We will adopt this methodology in the following.

Dynamic Broadcast Encryption. The concept of Dynamic Broadcast Encryption (DBE) was introduced by Delerablée, Paillier and Pointcheval in [15]. A DBE scheme is a BE in which the total number of users is not fixed in the setup, with the property that any new user can decrypt all previously distributed messages. Thus a DBE scheme is suitable for some applications, like DVD encryption.

K. Kurosawa (Ed.): ASIACRYPT 2007, LNCS 4833, pp. 200–215, 2007.

Nevertheless, some applications like Video on Demand (VOD) need forward secrecy. This paper address this problem, in the identity-based setting.

ID-based Encryption. In 1984, Shamir [24] asked for a public key encryption scheme in which the public key can be an arbitrary string.

Since the problem was posed in 1984, there have been several proposals for Identity-Based Encryption (IBE) schemes. However, we can considerer that the first practical IBE scheme was introduced by Boneh and Franklin in 2001 [9]. Since 2001, several schemes have been introduced [14,26,12,8,7,6,17]. Concerning the security, there are mainly two definitions:

1. Full security, which means that the attacker can choose adaptively the identity he wants to attack (after having seen the parameters);
2. Selective-ID security, which means that the attacker must choose the identity he wants to attack at the beginning, before seeing the parameters. The Selective-ID security is thus weaker than full security.

Since the scheme in [9] is proved secure in the random oracle model, several papers have proposed systems secure without random oracles. In [6], one of the systems has short parameters and tight security reduction, in the standard model (proved secure against selective-ID adversaries). In [17], Gentry proposed the first IBE system that is fully secure without random oracles, has short public parameters and has a tight security reduction.

Multi-receiver ID-based Key Encapsulation (mID-KEM). A multi-receiver key encapsulation scheme (mKEM) is an efficient key encapsulation mechanism for multiple parties. This notion was introduced in [25]. Note that this notion is different from multi-recipient public key encryption [4,5,22], where the sender wants to send one (different) message to each receiver.

Later, in [2] and [3], the notion of mKEM was extended to multi-receiver identity-based key encapsulation (mID-KEM), i.e. mKEM in the identity-based setting. In [2] and [3], the ciphertext size grows with the number of receivers. In [13], Chatterjee and Sarkar achieved a controllable trade-off between the ciphertext size and the private key size: ciphertexts are of size $|\mathcal{S}|/N$, and private keys are of size N where $\mathcal{S}$ is the set of receivers and N a parameter of the protocol (which also represents, in the security reduction, the maximum number of identities that the adversary is allowed to target). Thus they introduced the first mID-KEM protocols to achieve sub-linear ciphertext sizes. Very recently, Abdalla et al. proposed in [1] a generic construction that achieves ciphertexts of constant size, but private keys of size $O(n_{max}^2)$.

In the following, we do not employ the term "mID-KEM" anymore, but we talk about "identity-based broadcast encryption" (IBBE), to emphasize that this notion is close to broadcast encryption and ID-based encryption. We consider IBBE as a natural generalization of IBE. Indeed, in IBE schemes, one public key can be used to encrypt a message to any possible identity. In an IBBE scheme, one public key can be used to encrypt a message to any possible group of s identities. Consequently, if we set $s = 1$, the resulting IBBE scheme is an IBE scheme. The trivial solution to construct an IBBE scheme would be to use an IBE scheme to encrypt the message once for each identity. The resulting ciphertext would be of size linear in s. We also see IBBE as a way to make broadcast encryption more practical.

Motivations. We focus on schemes with ciphertexts of constant size. In BGW_1, as we said before, the public key is linear in the total number of decryption keys that can be distributed. Moreover, this number is fixed in the setup. Thus one of our motivations is to introduce a system in which the number of possible decryption keys is not fixed in the setup, and thus does not have any impact on the size of the public key. In [13] and [1], the trade-off between the ciphertext size and the private key size implies that if we want to have short ciphertexts, the private keys cannot be of constant size. Thus we would like to have both ciphertexts and private keys of constant size (as in BGW_1). Note that in some systems like the HIBE scheme in [8], the size of the public key can be reduced by using a hash function, viewed as a random oracle in the security proof, but this is not the case in BGW_1, because all the elements of the public depend on a single value.

Our contributions. In this paper, we propose the first identity-based broadcast encryption scheme with constant size ciphertexts *and* private keys. Our construction is a Key Encapsulation Mechanism (KEM), thus long messages can be encrypted under a short symmetric key. In our solution, ciphertexts and private keys are of constant size, and the public key is linear in the maximal value of s. Moreover, in our scheme, the Private Key Generator ($\mathcal{PKG}$) can dynamically add new members without altering previously distributed information (as in IBE schemes). We also note that there is no hierarchy between identities, contrary to HIBE (Hierarchical IBE [21,18,8]). No organization of the users is needed to have short ciphertexts. Note that the public key is linear in the maximal size of $\mathcal{S}$, and not in the number of decryption keys that can be distributed, which is the number of possible identities. The following framework is an example to show the benefits of our solution: The $\mathcal{PKG}$ can send short term decryption keys. Then sending a new decryption key could be conditional (each month, if the user pays his bill for example), without affecting the performances of the system. Indeed, there is no need to revoke previous keys, because the encryption takes into account the set of users who can decrypt. We can compare our scheme with BGW_1 in such a situation: if we consider that the number of users who can decrypt is s, and that each user receives a new key at the end of each time period, then the size of the public key in BGW_1 would be $\lambda_{PK} = s \cdot t$ with t the number of time periods for example. In our scheme, we have $\lambda_{PK} = s$. Thus one can note that BGW_1 is not really suited to such an situation (the public key would grow linearly with the number of time periods). In other words, in BGW_1, the public key is linear in the number of private keys that can be distributed, whereas in our construction, the public key is linear in the maximal number of receivers of a ciphertext, which is independent of the number of private keys that can be distributed. Indeed, in our case, the number of possible private keys is the number of possible identities. Note that if there are n receivers and it happens that $n > m$, we can just concatenate several encryptions together and get n/m size ciphertexts (as in [13]), still with constant size private keys. Moreover, in our construction, ciphertext size is deterministic whereas [13] makes probabilistic efficiency claims.

2   Preliminaries

We propose a formal definition of an identity-based broadcast encryption scheme and security notions that we associate to it. We basically include an Extract procedure in the definition of Broadcast Encryption given in [10]. Our formal model can also be viewed as a generalization of classical IBE systems. Concerning the security, we follow the definition of the classical security notions for BE (security against static adversaries) [10], which is close to the notion of selective-ID security, used in [6,11].

2.1   Identity-Based Broadcast Encryption (IBBE)

An IBBE scheme involves an authority: the Private Key Generator ($\mathcal{PKG}$). The $\mathcal{PKG}$ grants new members capability of decrypting messages by providing each new member (with identity ID_i) a decryption key $\mathsf{sk}_{\mathsf{ID}i}$. The generation of $\mathsf{sk}_{\mathsf{ID}i}$ is performed using a master secret key MSK. The broadcaster encrypts messages and transmits these to the group of users via the broadcast channel. In a (public-key) IBBE encryption scheme, the broadcaster does not hold any private information and encryption is performed with the help of a public key PK and identities of the receivers. Following the KEM-DEM methodology, broadcast encryption is viewed as the combination of a specific key encapsulation mechanism (a Broadcast-KEM) with a symmetric encryption (DEM) that shall remain implicit throughout the paper. More formally, an identity-based broadcast encryption scheme $\mathcal{IBBE}$ with security parameter λ and maximal size m of the target set, is a tuple of algorithms $\mathcal{IBBE} = (\mathsf{Setup}, \mathsf{Extract}, \mathsf{Encrypt}, \mathsf{Decrypt})$ described as follows:

$\mathsf{Setup}(\lambda, m)$. Takes as input the security parameter λ and m the maximal size of the set of receivers for one encryption, and outputs a master secret key MSK and a public key PK. The $\mathcal{PKG}$ is given MSK, and PK is made public.

$\mathsf{Extract}(\mathsf{MSK}, \mathsf{ID}_i)$. Takes as input the master secret key MSK and a user identity ID_i. Extract generates a user private key $\mathsf{sk}_{\mathsf{ID}i}$.

$\mathsf{Encrypt}(\mathcal{S}, \mathsf{PK})$. Takes as input the public key PK and a set of included identities $\mathcal{S} = \{\mathsf{ID}_1, \ldots, \mathsf{ID}_s\}$ with $s \leq m$, and outputs a pair (Hdr, K), where Hdr is called the header and $K \in \mathcal{K}$ and $\mathcal{K}$ is the set of keys for the symmetric encryption scheme.

When a message $M \in \{0,1\}^*$ is to be broadcast to users in $\mathcal{S}$, the broadcaster generates $(\mathsf{Hdr}, K) \leftarrow \mathsf{Encrypt}(\mathcal{S}, \mathsf{PK})$, computes the encryption C_M of M under the symmetric key $K \in \mathcal{K}$ and broadcasts $(\mathsf{Hdr}, \mathcal{S}, C_M)$. We will refer to Hdr as the header or broadcast ciphertext, $(\mathsf{Hdr}, \mathcal{S})$ as the full header, K as the message encryption key and C_M as the broadcast body.

$\mathsf{Decrypt}(\mathcal{S}, \mathsf{ID}, \mathsf{sk_{ID}}, \mathsf{Hdr}, \mathsf{PK})$. Takes as input a subset $\mathcal{S} = \{\mathsf{ID}_1, \ldots, \mathsf{ID}_s\}$ (with $s \leq m$), an identity ID and the corresponding private key $\mathsf{sk_{ID}}$, a header Hdr, and the public key PK. If $\mathsf{ID} \in \mathcal{S}$, the algorithm outputs the message encryption key K which is then used to decrypt the broadcast body C_M and recover M.

Remark. This model defines, when $m = 1$, an IBE system.

2.2 Security Notions for IBBE

The standard notion for BE schemes is Chosen Ciphertext Security against Static Adversaries. For IBE, one standard notion is selective-ID security (weaker than full security), where the adversary must choose at the beginning of the game the set of identities he wants to attack.

Remark. Note that for $m = 1$ the following security model fits with IND-sID-CCA security for IBE schemes, that is used in [6] for example.

IND-sID-CCA Security. We define IND-sID-CCA security of an IBBE system. Security is defined using the following game between an adversary $\mathcal{A}$ and a challenger. We basically refine the definition of [10], by adding extraction queries. Both the adversary and the challenger are given as input m, the maximal size of a set of receivers $\mathcal{S}$.

Init: The adversary $\mathcal{A}$ first outputs a set $\mathcal{S}^* = \{\mathsf{ID}_1^*, \ldots, \mathsf{ID}_s^*\}$ of identities that he wants to attack (with $s \leq m$).

Setup: The challenger runs $\mathsf{Setup}(\lambda, m)$ to obtain a public key PK. He gives $\mathcal{A}$ the public key PK.

Query phase 1: The adversary $\mathcal{A}$ adaptively issues queries $q_1, \ldots, q_{s_0}$, where q_i is one of the following:
  - Extraction query (ID_i) with the constraint that $\mathsf{ID}_i \notin \mathcal{S}^*$: The challenger runs $\mathsf{Extract}$ on ID_i and forwards the resulting private key to the adversary.
  - Decryption query, which consists of a triple $(\mathsf{ID}_i, \mathcal{S}, \mathsf{Hdr})$ with $\mathcal{S} \subseteq \mathcal{S}^*$ and $\mathsf{ID}_i \in \mathcal{S}$. The challenger responds with $\mathsf{Decrypt}(\mathcal{S}, \mathsf{ID}_i, \mathsf{sk_{ID_i}}, \mathsf{Hdr}, \mathsf{PK})$.

Challenge: When $\mathcal{A}$ decides that phase 1 is over, the challenger runs $\mathsf{Encrypt}$ algorithm to obtain $(\mathsf{Hdr}^*, K) = \mathsf{Encrypt}(\mathcal{S}^*, \mathsf{PK})$ where $K \in \mathcal{K}$. The challenger then randomly selects $b \leftarrow \{0,1\}$, sets $K_b = K$, and sets K_{1-b} to a random value in $\mathcal{K}$. The challenger returns $(\mathsf{Hdr}^*, K_0, K_1)$ to $\mathcal{A}$.

Query phase 2: The adversary continues to issue queries $q_{s_0+1}, \ldots, q_s$ where q_i is one of the following:

- Extraction query (ID_i), as in phase 1.
- Decryption query, as in phase 1, but with the constraint that $\mathsf{Hdr} \neq \mathsf{Hdr}^*$. The challenger responds as in phase 1.

Guess: Finally, the adversary $\mathcal{A}$ outputs a guess $b' \in \{0, 1\}$ and wins the game if $b = b'$.

We denote by q_D the total number of Decryption queries and by t the total number of extraction queries that can be issued by the adversary during the game. Viewing t, m, q_D as attack parameters, we denote by $\mathsf{Adv}^{\mathsf{ind}}_{\mathcal{IBBE}}(t, m, q_D, \mathcal{A})$ the advantage of $\mathcal{A}$ in winning the game:

$$\mathsf{Adv}^{\mathsf{ind}}_{\mathcal{IBBE}}(t, m, q_D, \mathcal{A}) = |2 \times \Pr[b' = b] - 1| = |\Pr[b' = 1 | b = 1] - \Pr[b' = 1 | b = 0]|$$

where the probability is taken over the random coins of $\mathcal{A}$, the challenger and all probabilistic algorithms run by the challenger.

Definition 1. *Let* $\mathsf{Adv}^{\mathsf{ind}}_{\mathcal{IBBE}}(t, m, q_D) = \max_{\mathcal{A}} \mathsf{Adv}^{\mathsf{ind}}_{\mathcal{IBBE}}(t, m, q_D, \mathcal{A})$ *where the maximum is taken over all probabilistic algorithms* $\mathcal{A}$ *running in time* $\mathsf{poly}(\lambda)$. *An identity-based broadcast encryption scheme* $\mathcal{IBBE}$ *is said to be* (t, m, q_D)-*IND-sID-CCA secure if* $\mathsf{Adv}^{\mathsf{ind}}_{\mathcal{IBBE}}(t, m, q_D) = \mathsf{negl}(\lambda)$.

IND-sID-CPA. Analogously to [10], we define semantic security for an IBBE scheme by preventing the attacker from issuing decryption queries.

Definition 2. *We say that an identity-based broadcast encryption system is* (t, m)-*IND-sID-CPA secure if it is* $(t, m, 0)$-*IND-sID-CCA secure.*

Remark. In [10], the choice of $\mathcal{S}^*$ implies a choice of corrupted users, because the total number of users is fixed in the setup. In the model we described before, the corrupted users are not chosen at the beginning but adaptively. We describe below a modification of our model which does not allow adaptive corruptions, as in [10].

Definition 3. (t, m, q_D)-*IND-na-sID-CCA security (non adaptive sID): at initialization time, the attacker outputs a set* $\mathcal{S}^* = \{\mathsf{ID}_1^*, \ldots, \mathsf{ID}_s^*\}$ *of identities that he wants to attack, and a set* $\mathcal{C} = \{\bar{\mathsf{ID}}_1, \ldots, \bar{\mathsf{ID}}_t\}$ *of identities that he wants to corrupt (i.e. to obtain the corresponding private key). Thus the attacker issues* t *extraction queries only at the beginning of the game.*

Definition 4. *We say that an identity-based broadcast encryption system is* (t, m)-*IND-na-sID-CPA secure if it is* $(t, m, 0)$-*IND-na-sID-CCA secure.*

Full collusion resistance. In an IBBE system, the number of possible users (identities) does not have to be fixed at the beginning, thus we cannot really talk about full collusion resistance. If the number n of possible users was fixed, as in [10] for example, our construction would be fully collusion resistant.

2.3 Bilinear Maps

We briefly review the necessary facts about bilinear maps. Let $\mathbb{G}_1$, $\mathbb{G}_2$ and $\mathbb{G}_T$ be three cyclic groups of prime order p. A bilinear map $e\,(\cdot,\cdot)$ is a map $\mathbb{G}_1 \times \mathbb{G}_2 \to \mathbb{G}_T$ such that for any generators $g_1 \in \mathbb{G}_1$, $g_2 \in \mathbb{G}_2$ and $a, b \in \mathbb{Z}_p$,

- $e\left(g_1{}^a, g_2{}^b\right) = e\left(g_1, g_2\right)^{ab}$ (Bilinearity)
- $e\left(g_1, g_2\right) \neq 1$ (Non-degeneracy).

A bilinear map group system $\mathcal{B}$ is a tuple $\mathcal{B} = (p, \mathbb{G}_1, \mathbb{G}_2, \mathbb{G}_T, e\,(\cdot,\cdot))$, composed of objects as described above. $\mathcal{B}$ may also include group generators in its description. We impose all group operations as well as the bilinear map $e\,(\cdot,\cdot)$ to be efficiently computable, i.e. in time $\mathsf{poly}(|p|)$.

As seen later, we make use of an arbitrary bilinear map group system in our constructions. In particular, we do not need $\mathbb{G}_1$ and $\mathbb{G}_2$ to be distinct or equal. Neither do we require the existence of an efficient isomorphism going either way between $\mathbb{G}_1$ and $\mathbb{G}_2$, as it is the case for some pairing-based systems.

2.4 The General Diffie-Hellman Exponent Assumption

As in [15], we make use of the generalization of the Diffie-Hellman exponent assumption due to Boneh, Boyen and Goh [8]. They introduced a class of assumptions which includes a lot of assumptions that appeared with new pairing-based schemes. It includes for example DDH (in $\mathbb{G}_T$), BDH, q−BDHI, and q−BDHE assumptions.

We give an overview in the symmetric case. Let then $\mathcal{B} = (p, \mathbb{G}_1, \mathbb{G}_2, \mathbb{G}_T, e\,(\cdot,\cdot))$ be a bilinear map group system such that $\mathbb{G}_1 = \mathbb{G}_2 = \mathbb{G}$. Let $g_0 \in \mathbb{G}$ be a generator of $\mathbb{G}$, and set $g = e\,(g_0, g_0) \in \mathbb{G}_T$. Let s, n be positive integers and $P, Q \in \mathbb{F}_p[X_1, \ldots, X_n]^s$ be two s-tuples of n-variate polynomials over $\mathbb{F}_p$. Thus, P and Q are just two lists containing s multivariate polynomials each. We write $P = (p_1, p_2, \ldots, p_s)$ and $Q = (q_1, q_2, \ldots, q_s)$ and impose that $p_1 = q_1 = 1$. For any function $h : \mathbb{F}_p \to \Omega$ and vector $(x_1, \ldots, x_n) \in \mathbb{F}_p^n$, $h(P(x_1, \ldots, x_n))$ stands for $(h(p_1(x_1, \ldots, x_n)), \ldots, h(p_s(x_1, \ldots, x_n))) \in \Omega^s$. We use a similar notation for the s-tuple Q. Let $f \in \mathbb{F}_p[X_1, \ldots, X_n]$. It is said that f depends on (P, Q), which we denote by $f \in \langle P, Q \rangle$, when there exists a linear decomposition

$$f = \sum_{1 \leq i,j \leq s} a_{i,j} \cdot p_i \cdot p_j + \sum_{1 \leq i \leq s} b_i \cdot q_i\,, \qquad a_{i,j}, b_i \in \mathbb{Z}_p\,.$$

Let P, Q be as above and $f \in \mathbb{F}_p[X_1, \ldots, X_n]$. The (P, Q, f)-General Diffie-Hellman Exponent problems are defined as follows.

Definition 5 $((P, Q, f)$-GDHE$)$. *Given the tuple*

$$H(x_1, \ldots, x_n) = \left(g_0^{P(x_1,\ldots,x_n)}, g^{Q(x_1,\ldots,x_n)}\right) \in \mathbb{G}^s \times \mathbb{G}_T^s\,,$$

compute $g^{f(x_1,\ldots,x_n)}$.

Definition 6 $((P,Q,f)$-**GDDHE**$)$. *Given* $H(x_1,\ldots,x_n) \in \mathbb{G}^s \times \mathbb{G}_T^s$ *as above and* $T \in \mathbb{G}_T$, *decide whether* $T = g^{f(x_1,\ldots,x_n)}$.

We refer to [8] for a proof that (P,Q,f)-GDHE and (P,Q,f)-GDDHE have generic security when $f \notin \langle P,Q \rangle$. We will prove our constructions are secure based on the assumption that (P,Q,f)-GDDHE is intractable for any $f \notin \langle P,Q \rangle$ and polynomial parameters $s,n = \mathsf{poly}(\lambda)$. We just have to determine P, Q and f, such that we can perform our simulation, and then proving the condition on the polynomials will prove the intractability of our problem (because as seen before, the (P,Q,f)-GDDHE problem is hard for any choice of P, Q and f which satisfy the aforementioned condition).

3   Our Construction

3.1   Description

In this section, we present our new IBBE, with constant size ciphertexts and private keys.

Setup(λ, m). Given the security parameter λ and an integer m, a bilinear map group system $\mathcal{B} = (p, \mathbb{G}_1, \mathbb{G}_2, \mathbb{G}_T, e(\cdot,\cdot))$ is constructed such that $|p| = \lambda$. Also, two generators $g \in \mathbb{G}_1$ and $h \in \mathbb{G}_2$ are randomly selected as well as a secret value $\gamma \in \mathbb{Z}_p^\star$. Choose a cryptographic hash function $\mathcal{H} : \{0,1\}^\star \to \mathbb{Z}_p^\star$. The security analysis will view $\mathcal{H}$ as a random oracle. $\mathcal{B}$ and $\mathcal{H}$ constitute system public parameters. The master secret key is defined as $\mathsf{MSK} = (g, \gamma)$. The public key is $\mathsf{PK} = \left(w, v, h, h^\gamma, \ldots, h^{\gamma^m}\right)$ where $w = g^\gamma$, and $v = e(g, h)$.

Extract$(\mathsf{MSK}, \mathsf{ID})$. Given $\mathsf{MSK} = (g, \gamma)$ and the identity ID, it outputs

$$\mathsf{sk}_{\mathsf{ID}} = g^{\frac{1}{\gamma + \mathcal{H}(\mathsf{ID})}}$$

Encrypt$(\mathcal{S}, \mathsf{PK})$. Assume for notational simplicity that $\mathcal{S} = \{\mathsf{ID}_j\}_{j=1}^s$, with $s \le m$. Given $\mathsf{PK} = \left(w, v, h, h^\gamma, \ldots, h^{\gamma^m}\right)$, the broadcaster randomly picks $k \leftarrow \mathbb{Z}_p^\star$ and computes $\mathsf{Hdr} = (C_1, C_2)$ and K where

$$C_1 = w^{-k}, \qquad C_2 = h^{k \cdot \prod_{i=1}^s (\gamma + \mathcal{H}(\mathsf{ID}_i))}, \qquad K = v^k.$$

Encrypt outputs (Hdr, K). (Then K is used to encrypt the message)

Decrypt$(\mathcal{S}, \mathsf{ID}_i, \mathsf{sk}_{\mathsf{ID}_i}, \mathsf{Hdr}, \mathsf{PK})$. In order to retrieve the message encryption key K encapsulated in the header $\mathsf{Hdr} = (C_1, C_2)$, user with identity ID_i and the corresponding private key $\mathsf{sk}_{\mathsf{ID}_i} = g^{\frac{1}{\gamma + \mathcal{H}(\mathsf{ID}_i)}}$ (with $\mathsf{ID}_i \in \mathcal{S}$) computes

$$K = \left(e\left(C_1, h^{p_{i,s}(\gamma)}\right) \cdot e\left(\mathsf{sk}_{\mathsf{ID}_i}, C_2\right)\right)^{\frac{1}{\prod_{j=1, j\neq i}^s \mathcal{H}(\mathsf{ID}_j)}}$$

with

$$p_{i,\mathcal{S}}(\gamma) = \frac{1}{\gamma} \cdot \left(\prod_{j=1, j\neq i}^s (\gamma + \mathcal{H}(\mathsf{ID}_j)) - \prod_{j=1, j\neq i}^s \mathcal{H}(\mathsf{ID}_j)\right)$$

Correctness: Assuming C is well-formed for $\mathcal{S}$:

$$K' := e\left(C_1, h^{p_i, s(\gamma)}\right) \cdot e\left(\mathsf{sk}_{\mathsf{ID}_i}, C_2\right)$$

$$= e\left(g^{-k \cdot \gamma}, h^{p_i, s(\gamma)}\right) \cdot e\left(g^{\frac{1}{\gamma + \mathcal{H}(\mathsf{ID}_i)}}, h^{k \cdot \prod_{j=1}^{s}(\gamma + \mathcal{H}(\mathsf{ID}_j))}\right)$$

$$= e\left(g, h\right)^{-k \cdot \left(\prod_{j=1, j \neq i}^{s}(\gamma + \mathcal{H}(\mathsf{ID}_j)) - \prod_{j=1, j \neq i}^{s} \mathcal{H}(\mathsf{ID}_j)\right)} \cdot e\left(g, h\right)^{k \cdot \prod_{j=1, j \neq i}^{s}(\gamma + \mathcal{H}(\mathsf{ID}_j))}$$

$$= e\left(g, h\right)^{k \prod_{j=1, j \neq i}^{s} \mathcal{H}(\mathsf{ID}_j)}$$

$$= K^{\prod_{j=1, j \neq i}^{s} \mathcal{H}(\mathsf{ID}_j)}$$

Thus $K'^{\frac{1}{\prod_{j=1, j \neq i}^{s} \mathcal{H}(\mathsf{ID}_j)}} = K$.

Efficiency. Our construction achieves $O(1)$-size ciphertexts, $O(m)$-size public keys and constant size private keys. Note that public key is linear in the maximal size of $\mathcal{S}$, and not in the number of decryption keys that can be distributed. If we would like to fix the total number n of users, and set $m = n$, then we would reduce the public key size by a factor of two from BGW. Note also that as we said before, the broadcaster has to send the set $\mathcal{S}$ of identities that are included in the ciphertext. This set is needed to decrypt, as in previous schemes, thus it is counted in the full header, but not in the header.

3.2 Security Analysis

We prove the IND-sID-CPA security of our system by using the GDDHE framework of [8]. We start by defining the following intermediate decisional problem.

Definition 7 $((f, g, F)$-GDDHE$)$. *Let $\mathcal{B} = (p, \mathbb{G}_1, \mathbb{G}_2, \mathbb{G}_T, e(\cdot, \cdot))$ be a bilinear map group system and let f and g be two coprime polynomials with pairwise distinct roots, of respective orders t and n. Let g_0 be a generator of $\mathbb{G}_1$ and h_0 a generator of $\mathbb{G}_2$. Solving the (f, g, F)-GDDHE problem consists, given*

$$g_0, g_0^{\gamma}, \ldots, g_0^{\gamma^{t-1}}, \qquad g_0^{\gamma \cdot f(\gamma)}, \qquad g_0^{k \cdot \gamma \cdot f(\gamma)},$$
$$h_0, h_0^{\gamma}, \ldots, h_0^{\gamma^{2n}}, \qquad h_0^{k \cdot g(\gamma)},$$

and $T \in \mathbb{G}_T$, in deciding whether T is equal to $e(g_0, h_0)^{k \cdot f(\gamma)}$ or to some random element of $\mathbb{G}_T$.

We denote by $\mathsf{Adv}^{\mathsf{gddhe}}(f, g, F, \mathcal{A})$ the advantage of an algorithm $\mathcal{A}$ in distinguishing the two distributions and set $\mathsf{Adv}^{\mathsf{gddhe}}(f, g, F) = \max_{\mathcal{A}} \mathsf{Adv}^{\mathsf{gddhe}}(f, g, F, \mathcal{A})$ over poly($|p|$)-time $\mathcal{A}$'s.

The following statement is a corollary of Theorem 2 which can be found in Appendix A. This corollary concerns the case where the polynomials are of the form described above (see the reformulation of the problem in Appendix A).

Corollary 1 (Generic security of (f, g, F)-GDDHE). *For any probabilistic algorithm $\mathcal{A}$ that totalizes of at most q queries to the oracles performing the group operations in $\mathbb{G}_1, \mathbb{G}_2, \mathbb{G}_T$ and the bilinear map $e(\cdot, \cdot)$,*

$$\mathsf{Adv}^{\mathsf{gddhe}}(f, g, F, \mathcal{A}) \leq \frac{(q + 2(n + t + 4) + 2)^2 \cdot d}{2p}$$

with $d = 2 \cdot \max(n, t + 1)$.

IND-sID-CPA Security. Let $\mathcal{IBBE}$ denote our construction as per Section 3. We state:

Theorem 1. *For any n, t, we have $\mathsf{Adv}^{\mathsf{ind}}_{\mathcal{IBBE}}(t, n) \leq 2 \cdot \mathsf{Adv}^{\mathsf{gddhe}}(f, g, F)$.*

The rest of this section is dedicated to proving Theorem 1. To establish the semantic security of $\mathcal{IBBE}$ against static adversaries, we assume to be given an adversary $\mathcal{A}$ breaking it under a (t, n)-collusion and we build a reduction algorithm $\mathcal{R}$ that distinguishes the two distributions of the (f, g, F)-GDDHE problem.

Both the adversary and the challenger are given as input n, the maximal size of a set of included users $\mathcal{S}$, and t the total number of extraction queries and random oracle queries that can be issued by the adversary.

Algorithm $\mathcal{R}$ is given as input a group system $\mathcal{B} = (p, \mathbb{G}_1, \mathbb{G}_2, \mathbb{G}_T, e(\cdot, \cdot))$, and a (f, g, F)-GDDHE instance in $\mathcal{B}$ (as described in Definition 7). We thus have f and g two coprime polynomials with pairwise distinct roots, of respective orders t and n, and $\mathcal{R}$ is given

$$g_0, g_0^\gamma, \ldots, g_0^{\gamma^{t-1}}, \qquad g_0^{\gamma \cdot f(\gamma)}, \qquad g_0^{k \cdot \gamma \cdot f(\gamma)},$$
$$h_0, h_0^\gamma, \ldots, h_0^{\gamma^{2n}}, \qquad\qquad\qquad h_0^{k \cdot g(\gamma)},$$

as well as $T \in \mathbb{G}_T$ which is either equal to $e(g_0, h_0)^{k \cdot f(\gamma)}$ or to some random element of $\mathbb{G}_T$.

For simplicity, we state that f and g are unitary polynomials, but this is not a mandatory requirement.

Notations

- $f(X) = \prod_{i=1}^{t}(X + x_i)$, $g(X) = \prod_{i=t+1}^{t+n}(X + x_i)$
- $f_i(x) = \frac{f(x)}{x + x_i}$ for $i \in [1, t]$, which is a polynomial of degree $t - 1$
- $g_i(x) = \frac{g(x)}{x + x_i}$ for $i \in [t + 1, t + n]$, which is a polynomial of degree $n - 1$

Init: The adversary $\mathcal{A}$ outputs a set $\mathcal{S}^* = \{\mathsf{ID}_1^*, \ldots, \mathsf{ID}_{s^*}^*\}$ of identities that he wants to attack (with $s^* \leq n$).

Setup: To generate the system parameters, $\mathcal{R}$ formally sets $g = g_0^{f(\gamma)}$ (i.e. without computing it) and sets

$$h = h_0^{\prod_{i=t+s^*+1}^{t+n}(\gamma+x_i)} , \qquad w = g_0^{\gamma \cdot f(\gamma)} = g^\gamma ,$$

$$v = e(g_0, h_0)^{f(\gamma) \cdot \prod_{i=t+s^*+1}^{t+n}(\gamma+x_i)} = e(g, h) .$$

$\mathcal{R}$ then defines the public key as $\mathsf{PK} = (w, v, h, h^\gamma, \ldots, h^{\gamma^n})$. Note that $\mathcal{R}$ can by no means compute the value of g. $\mathcal{R}$ runs $\mathcal{A}$ on the system parameters $(\mathcal{B}, \mathcal{H})$ and PK, with $\mathcal{H}$ a random oracle controlled by $\mathcal{R}$ described below.

Hash Queries: At any time the adversary $\mathcal{A}$ can query the random oracle on any identity ID_i (at most $t - q_E$ times, with q_E the number of extraction queries). To respond to these queries, $\mathcal{R}$ maintains a list $\mathcal{L}_\mathcal{H}$ of tuples $(\mathsf{ID}_i, x_i, \mathsf{sk}_{\mathsf{ID}_i})$ that contains at the beginning:

$$\{(*, x_i, *)\}_{i=1}^t , \quad \{(\mathsf{ID}_i, x_i, *)\}_{i=t+1}^{t+s^*}$$

(we choose to note "$*$" an empty entry in $\mathcal{L}_\mathcal{H}$). When the adversary issues a hash query on identity ID_i,

1. If ID_i already appears in the list $\mathcal{L}_\mathcal{H}$, $\mathcal{R}$ responds with the corresponding x_i.
2. Otherwise, $\mathcal{R}$ sets $\mathcal{H}(\mathsf{ID}_i) = x_i$, and completes the list with $(\mathsf{ID}_i, x_i, *)$.

Query phase 1: The adversary $\mathcal{A}$ adaptively issues queries $q_1, \ldots, q_m$, where q_i is an Extraction query (ID_i): The challenger runs Extract on $\mathsf{ID}_i \notin \mathcal{S}^*$ and forwards the resulting private key to the adversary. To generate the keys,

- if $\mathcal{A}$ has already issued an extraction query on ID_i, $\mathcal{R}$ responds with the corresponding $\mathsf{sk}_{\mathsf{ID}_i}$ in the list $\mathcal{L}_\mathcal{H}$.
- else, if $\mathcal{A}$ has already issued a hash query on ID_i, then $\mathcal{R}$ uses the corresponding x_i to compute

$$\mathsf{sk}_{\mathsf{ID}_i} = g_0^{f_i(\gamma)} = g^{\frac{1}{\gamma + \mathcal{H}(\mathsf{ID}_i)}}$$

One can verify that $\mathsf{sk}_{\mathsf{ID}_i}$ is a valid private key. $\mathcal{R}$ then completes the list $\mathcal{L}_\mathcal{H}$ with $\mathsf{sk}_{\mathsf{ID}_i}$ for ID_i.

1. Otherwise, $\mathcal{R}$ sets $\mathcal{H}(\mathsf{ID}_i) = x_i$, computes the corresponding $\mathsf{sk}_{\mathsf{ID}_i}$ exactly as above, and completes the list $\mathcal{L}_\mathcal{H}$ for ID_i.

Challenge: When $\mathcal{A}$ decides that phase 1 is over, algorithm $\mathcal{R}$ computes Encrypt to obtain $(\mathsf{Hdr}^*, K) = \mathsf{Encrypt}(\mathcal{S}^*, \mathsf{PK})$

$$C_1 = g_0^{-k \cdot \gamma \cdot f(\gamma)} , \quad C_2 = h_0^{k \cdot g(\gamma)} , \quad K = T^{\prod_{i=t+s^*+1}^{t+n} x_i} \cdot e\left(g_0^{k \cdot \gamma \cdot f(\gamma)}, h_0^{q(\gamma)}\right)$$

with $q(\gamma) = \frac{1}{\gamma} \cdot \left(\prod_{i=t+s^*+1}^{t+n}(\gamma + x_i) - \prod_{i=t+s^*+1}^{t+n} x_i\right)$.

One can verify that:

$$C_1 = w^{-k} , \quad C_2 = h_0^{k \cdot \prod_{i=t+s^*+1}^{t+n}(\gamma+x_i) \cdot \prod_{i=t+1}^{t+s^*}(\gamma+x_i)} = h^{k \cdot \prod_{i=t+1}^{t+s^*}(\gamma+\mathcal{H}(\mathsf{ID}_i^*))} .$$

Note that if $T = e(g_0, h_0)^{k \cdot f(\gamma)}$, then $K = v^k$.

The challenger then randomly selects $b \leftarrow \{0, 1\}$, sets $K_b = K$, and sets K_{1-b} to a random value in $\mathcal{K}$. The challenger returns $(\mathsf{Hdr}^*, K_0, K_1)$ to $\mathcal{A}$.

Query phase 2: The adversary continues to issue queries $q_{m+1}, \ldots, q_E$ where q_i is an extraction query (ID_i) with the constraint that $\mathsf{ID}_i \notin \mathcal{S}^*$ (identical to phase 1).

Guess: Finally, the adversary $\mathcal{A}$ outputs a guess $b' \in \{0, 1\}$ and wins the game if $b = b'$.

One has

$$\mathsf{Adv}^{\mathsf{gddhe}}(f, g, F, \mathcal{R}) = \Pr[b' = b \mid \mathsf{real}] - \Pr[b' = b \mid \mathsf{rand}]$$
$$= \frac{1}{2} \times (\Pr[b' = 1 \mid b = 1 \wedge \mathsf{real}] - \Pr[b' = 1 \mid b = 0 \wedge \mathsf{real}])$$
$$- \frac{1}{2} \times (\Pr[b' = 1 \mid b = 1 \wedge \mathsf{rand}] + \Pr[b' = 1 \mid b = 0 \wedge \mathsf{rand}]) .$$

Now in the random case, the distribution of b is independent from the adversary's view wherefrom

$$\Pr[b' = 1 \mid b = 1 \wedge \mathsf{rand}] = \Pr[b' = 1 \mid b = 0 \wedge \mathsf{rand}] .$$

In the real case however, the distributions of all variables defined by $\mathcal{R}$ perfectly comply with the semantic security game since all simulations are perfect. Therefore

$$\mathsf{Adv}^{\mathsf{ind}}_{\mathcal{IBBE}}(t, n, \mathcal{A}) = \Pr[b' = 1 \mid b = 1 \wedge \mathsf{real}] - \Pr[b' = 1 \mid b = 0 \wedge \mathsf{real}] .$$

Putting it altogether, we get that $\mathsf{Adv}^{\mathsf{gddhe}}(f, g, F, \mathcal{R}) = \frac{1}{2} \cdot \mathsf{Adv}^{\mathsf{ind}}_{\mathcal{IBBE}}(t, n, \mathcal{A})$.

Remark. Note that if the attacker makes less key derivation queries than random oracle queries, we generate keys that we never give out, but this is not a problem.

About chosen-ciphertext attacks. The Cannetti, Halevi, and Katz [12] result applies here. Just making one of the identities that we broadcast to derive from a verification key of a strong signature scheme. Then it can be used to sign the ciphertext.

Removing the Random Oracle Model. One way to remove the random oracle model could be to randomize the private key extraction as follows: For an identity ID_i, $\mathsf{sk}_{\mathsf{ID}_i} = g^{\frac{1}{\gamma + \mathsf{ID}_i}}$ could be replaced by $A_i = g^{\frac{1}{\gamma + \mathsf{ID}_i + r_i \cdot \alpha}}$, with α an element of MSK and r_i chosen by the $\mathcal{PKG}$. Note that this randomization has already been employed in [6].

Note also that we could easily obtain IND-na-sID-CPA *without* random oracles by using an assumption which is not fully non-interactive. Indeed, during the setup, if the algorithm is given a (f, g, F)-GDDHE instance, with g that corresponds to the target set and f to the corrupted set (chosen by the attacker at initialization), then the rest of the proof can be done without any oracle.

4 Conclusion

We introduced the first identity-based broadcast encryption (IBBE) scheme with constant size ciphertexts and private keys. One interesting open problem would be to construct an IBBE system with constant size ciphertexts and private keys that is secure under a more standard assumption, or which achieves a stronger security notion, equivalent to full security in IBE schemes.

Acknowledgements

The author would like to thank David Pointcheval, Pascal Paillier and Brent Waters for helpful discussions, and anonymous referees for helpful comments.

References

1. Abdalla, M., Kiltz, E., Neven, G.: Generalized key delegation for hierarchical identity-based encryption. In: ESORICS 2007. LNCS, vol. 4734, pp. 139–154. Springer, Berlin, Germany (2005)
2. Baek, J., Safavi-Naini, R., Susilo, W.: Efficient multi-receiver identity-based encryption and its application to broadcast encryption. In: Vaudenay, S. (ed.) PKC 2005. LNCS, vol. 3386, pp. 380–397. Springer, Heidelberg (2005)
3. Barbosa, M., Farshim, P.: Efficient identity-based key encapsulation to multiple parties. In: Smart, N.P. (ed.) Cryptography and Coding. LNCS, vol. 3796, pp. 428–441. Springer, Heidelberg (2005)
4. Bellare, M., Boldyreva, A., Micali, S.: Public-key encryption in a multi-user setting: Security proofs and improvements. In: Preneel, B. (ed.) EUROCRYPT 2000. LNCS, vol. 1807, pp. 259–274. Springer, Berlin, Germany (2000)
5. Bellare, M., Boldyreva, A., Staddon, J.: Randomness re-use in multi-recipient encryption schemeas. In: Desmedt, Y.G. (ed.) PKC 2003. LNCS, vol. 2567, pp. 85–99. Springer, Heidelberg (2002)
6. Boneh, D., Boyen, X.: Efficient selective-ID secure identity based encryption without random oracles. In: Cachin, C., Camenisch, J.L. (eds.) EUROCRYPT 2004. LNCS, vol. 3027, pp. 223–238. Springer, Berlin, Germany (2004)
7. Boneh, D., Boyen, X.: Sécure identity based encryption without random oracles. In: Franklin, M. (ed.) CRYPTO 2004. LNCS, vol. 3152, Springer, Berlin, Germany (2004)
8. Boneh, D., Boyen, X., Goh, E.-J.: Hierarchical identity based encryption with constant size ciphertext. In: Cramer, R.J.F. (ed.) EUROCRYPT 2005. LNCS, vol. 3494, pp. 440–456. Springer, Heidelberg (2005), available at http://eprint.iacr.org/2005/015
9. Boneh, D., Franklin, M.: Identity-based encryption from the Weil pairing. In: Kilian, J. (ed.) CRYPTO 2001. LNCS, vol. 2139, pp. 213–229. Springer, Berlin, Germany (2001)

10. Boneh, D., Gentry, C., Waters, B.: Collusion resistant broadcast encryption with short ciphertexts and private keys. In: Shoup, V. (ed.) CRYPTO 2005. LNCS, vol. 3621, pp. 258–275. Springer, Berlin, Germany (2005)
11. Canetti, R., Halevi, S., Katz, J.: A forward-secure public-key encryption scheme. In: Biham, E. (ed.) Advances in Cryptology – EUROCRPYT 2003. LNCS, vol. 2656, pp. 255–271. Springer, Berlin, Germany (2003)
12. Canetti, R., Halevi, S., Katz, J.: Chosen-ciphertext security from identity-based encryption. In: Cachin, C., Camenisch, J.L. (eds.) EUROCRYPT 2004. LNCS, vol. 3027, pp. 207–222. Springer, Berlin, Germany (2004)
13. Chatterjee, S., Sarkar, P.: Multi-receiver identity-based key encapsulation with shortened ciphertext. In: Barua, R., Lange, T. (eds.) INDOCRYPT 2006. LNCS, vol. 4329, pp. 394–408. Springer, Heidelberg (2006)
14. Cocks, C.: An identity based encryption scheme based on quadratic residues. In: Honary, B. (ed.) Cryptography and Coding. LNCS, vol. 2260, pp. 360–363. Springer, Berlin, Germany (2001)
15. Delerablée, C., Paillier, P., Pointcheval, D.: Fully collusion secure dynamic broadcast encryption with constant-size ciphertexts or decryption keys. In: Takagi, T., et al. (eds.) PAIRING 2007. LNCS, vol. 4575, pp. 39–59. Springer, Berlin, Germany (2007)
16. Fiat, A., Naor, M.: Broadcast encryption. In: Stinson, D.R. (ed.) CRYPTO 1993. LNCS, vol. 773, pp. 480–491. Springer, Heidelberg (1994)
17. Gentry, C.: Practical identity-based encryption without random oracles. In: Vaudenay, S. (ed.) EUROCRYPT 2006. LNCS, vol. 4004, pp. 445–464. Springer, Berlin, Germany (2006)
18. Gentry, C., Silverberg, A.: Hierarchical ID-based cryptography. In: Zheng, Y. (ed.) ASIACRYPT 2002. LNCS, vol. 2501, pp. 548–566. Springer, Berlin, Germany (2002)
19. Goodrich, M.T., Sun, J.Z., Tamassia, R.: Efficient tree-based revocation in groups of low-state devices. In: Franklin, M. (ed.) CRYPTO 2004. LNCS, vol. 3152, pp. 511–527. Springer, Heidelberg (2004)
20. Halevy, D., Shamir, A.: The LSD broadcast encryption scheme. In: Yung, M. (ed.) CRYPTO 2002. LNCS, vol. 2442, pp. 47–60. Springer, Heidelberg (2002)
21. Horwitz, J., Lynn, B.: Toward hierarchical identity-based encryption. In: Knudsen, L.R. (ed.) EUROCRYPT 2002. LNCS, vol. 2332, pp. 466–481. Springer, Heidelberg (2002)
22. Kurosawa, K.: Multi-recipient public-key encryption with shortened ciphertext. In: Naccache, D., Paillier, P. (eds.) PKC 2002. LNCS, vol. 2274, pp. 48–63. Springer, Heidelberg (2002)
23. Naor, D., Naor, M., Lotspiech, J.: Revocation and tracing schemes for stateless receivers. In: Kilian, J. (ed.) CRYPTO 2001. LNCS, vol. 2139, pp. 41–62. Springer, Berlin, Germany (2001)
24. Shamir, A.: Identity-based cryptosystems and signature schemes. In: Blakely, G.R., Chaum, D. (eds.) CRYPTO 1984. LNCS, vol. 196, pp. 47–53. Springer, Heidelberg (1985)
25. Smart, N.P.: Efficient key encapsulation to multiple parties. In: Blundo, C., Cimato, S. (eds.) SCN 2004. LNCS, vol. 3352, pp. 208–219. Springer, Heidelberg (2005)
26. Brent, R.: Efficient identity-based encryption without random oracles. In: Cramer, R.J.F. (ed.) EUROCRYPT 2005. LNCS, vol. 3494, pp. 114–127. Springer, Berlin, Germany (2005)

A   Intractability of (f, g, F)-GDDHE

In this section, we prove the intractability of distinguishing the two distributions involved in the (f, g, F)-GDDHE problem (cf. Corollary 1, section 3.2). We first review some results on the General Diffie-Hellman Exponent Problem, from [8]. In order to be the most general, we assume the easiest case for the adversary: when $\mathbb{G}_1 = \mathbb{G}_2$, or at least that an isomorphism that can be easily computed in either one or both ways is available.

Theorem 2 ([8]). *Let $P, Q \in \mathbb{F}_p[X_1, \ldots, X_m]$ be two s-tuples of m-variate polynomials over $\mathbb{F}_p$ and let $F \in \mathbb{F}_p[X_1, \ldots, X_m]$. Let d_P (resp. d_Q, d_F) denote the maximal degree of elements of P (resp. of Q, F) and pose $d = \max(2d_P, d_Q, d_F)$. If $F \notin \langle P, Q \rangle$ then for any generic-model adversary $\mathcal{A}$ totalizing at most q queries to the oracles (group operations in $\mathbb{G}, \mathbb{G}_T$ and evaluations of e) which is given $H(x_1, \ldots, x_m)$ as input and tries to distinguish $g^{F(x_1, \ldots, x_m)}$ from a random value in $\mathbb{G}_T$, one has*

$$\mathsf{Adv}(\mathcal{A}) \leq \frac{(q + 2s + 2)^2 \cdot d}{2p}.$$

Proof (of Corollary 1). In order to conclude with Corollary 1, we need to prove that the (f, g, F)-GDDHE problem lies in the scope of Theorem 2. As already said, we consider the weakest case $\mathbb{G}_1 = \mathbb{G}_2 = \mathbb{G}$ and thus pose $h_0 = g_0^\beta$. Our problem can be reformulated as (P, Q, F)-GDHE where

$$P = \begin{pmatrix} 1, \gamma, \gamma^2, \ldots, \gamma^{t-1}, & \gamma \cdot f(\gamma), k \cdot \gamma \cdot f(\gamma) \\ \beta, \beta \cdot \gamma, \beta \cdot \gamma^2, \ldots, \beta \cdot \gamma^{2n}, & k \cdot \beta \cdot g(\gamma) \end{pmatrix}$$

$$Q = 1$$

$$F = k \cdot \beta \cdot f(\gamma),$$

and thus $m = 3$ and $s = t + n + 4$. We have to show that F is independent of (P, Q), i.e. that no coefficients $\{a_{i,j}\}_{i,j=1}^{s}$ and b_1 exist such that $F = \sum_{i,j=1}^{s} a_{i,j} p_i p_j + \sum_{k=1}^{2} b_1 q_1$ where the polynomials p_i and q_1 are the one listed in P and Q above. By making all possible products of two polynomials from P which are multiples of $k \cdot \beta$, we want to prove that no linear combination among the polynomials from the list R below leads to F:

$$R = \begin{pmatrix} k \cdot \beta \cdot \gamma \cdot f(\gamma), \ k \cdot \beta \cdot \gamma^2 \cdot f(\gamma), \ldots, \ k \cdot \beta \cdot \gamma^{n+1} \cdot f(\gamma), \\ k \cdot \beta \cdot g(\gamma), \ k \cdot \beta \cdot \gamma \cdot g(\gamma), \ldots, \ k \cdot \beta \cdot \gamma^{t-1} \cdot g(\gamma) \\ k \cdot \beta \cdot \gamma \cdot f(\gamma) g(\gamma) \end{pmatrix}.$$

Note that the last polynomial can be written as $k \cdot \beta \cdot \gamma \cdot f(\gamma) g(\gamma) = \sum_{i=0}^{i=n} \nu_i \cdot k \cdot \beta \cdot \gamma^{i+1} \cdot f(\gamma)$, and thus as a linear combination of the polynomials from the first line. We therefore simplify the task to refuting a linear combination of elements of the list R' below which leads to $f(\gamma)$:

$$R' = \begin{pmatrix} \gamma \cdot f(\gamma), \ \gamma^2 \cdot f(\gamma), \ldots, \ \gamma^{n+1} \cdot f(\gamma), \\ g(\gamma), \ \gamma \cdot g(\gamma), \ldots, \ \gamma^{t-1} \cdot g(\gamma) \end{pmatrix}.$$

Any such linear combination can be written as

$$f(\gamma) = A(\gamma) \cdot f(\gamma) + B(\gamma) \cdot g(\gamma)$$

where A and B are polynomials such that $A(0) = 0$, $\deg A \leq n + 1$ and $\deg B \leq t - 1$. Since f and g are coprime by assumption, we must have $f \mid B$. Since $\deg f = t$ and $\deg B \leq t - 1$ this implies $B = 0$. Hence $A = 1$ which contradicts $A(0) = 0$. $\square$

Boosting Merkle-Damgård Hashing
for Message Authentication

Kan Yasuda

NTT Information Sharing Platform Laboratories, NTT Corporation
3-9-11 Midoricho Musashino-shi, Tokyo 180-8585 Japan
yasuda.kan@lab.ntt.co.jp

Abstract. This paper presents a novel mode of operation of compression functions, intended for dedicated use as a message authentication code (MAC.) The new approach is faster than the well-known Merkle-Damgård iteration; more precisely, it is $(1 + c/b)$-times as fast as the classical Merkle-Damgård hashing when applied to a compression function $h : \{0,1\}^{c+b} \rightarrow \{0,1\}^c$. Our construction provides a single-key MAC with provable security; we show that the proposed scheme yields a PRF(pseudo-random function)-based MAC on the assumption that the underlying compression function h satisfies certain PRF properties. Thus our method offers a way to process data more efficiently than the conventional HMAC without losing formal proofs of security. Our design also takes into account usage with prospective compression functions; that is, those compression functions h with relatively weighty load and relatively large c (i.e., "wide-pipe") greatly benefit from the improved performance by our mode of operation.

Keywords: Merkle-Damgård, pseudo-random function, related-key attack, message authentication code, hash function, compression function, mode of operation, NMAC, HMAC.

1 Introduction

The Merkle-Damgård iteration [16,10] is a popular and classical mode of operation for cryptographic hash functions. It is widely used not only for keyless hash functions but also for randomized hash functions, message authentication codes (MACs) and pseudo-random functions (PRFs.) It is popular, widespread and successful in some respects, but nowadays some problems are becoming more and more evident, which initiates investigation into better modes of operation [14,9].

Inspired by this trend, in this paper we free ourselves from the traditional Merkle-Damgård iteration and devise a novel mode of operation that can be used exclusively as a secure, single-keyed MAC. Our method is the first of its kind that can process a message more efficiently than the conventional Merkle-Damgård iteration and that can be provided with formal proofs of security. More precisely, the proposed scheme is $(1 + c/b)$-times faster than the conservative

K. Kurosawa (Ed.): ASIACRYPT 2007, LNCS 4833, pp. 216–231, 2007.

Merkle-Damgård hashing (and hence HMAC [2]), when applied to a compression function $h : \{0,1\}^{c+b} \rightarrow \{0,1\}^c$. For example, with the compression function sha256 : $\{0,1\}^{256+512} \rightarrow \{0,1\}^{256}$ the new method yields a 50% increase in performance as compared to HMAC. As to the security of our new scheme, we obtain results that are similar to the recent ones of NMAC and HMAC [2]; namely, we prove that the proposed mode of operation results in a PRF-based MAC whose security relies on the pseudo-randomness properties of the underlying compression function.

Brief Outline of Our Construction and Its Security. Our construction can be regarded as a derivative of NMAC. Recall that NMAC is based on a nested structure consisting of an inner part of hashing and an outer part of encryption. In our construction we boost up the performance of the inner hashing by introducing a novel method of iteration, where each invocation to the underlying compression function $h : \{0,1\}^{c+b} \rightarrow \{0,1\}^c$ processes more input bits. It takes $c + b$ bits of a message, rather than just b bits as in the conventional Merkle-Damgård iteration.

The inner hashing should satisfy a certain form of collision resistance, in order for the nested MAC to be secure. NMAC fulfills this requirement by assuming that the underlying compression function is a PRF [3,2]. On the other hand, in our construction it turns out that we need to impose an extra condition on the underlying compression function in order to ensure the desired property of the inner hashing. The additional condition is a type of pseudo-randomness in a mild form of related-key setting; in fact, our proofs of security can be viewed as a related-key version of those in [3].

Backgrounds. A motive for this work originates from the recent degradation of existing hash functions such as MD5 and SHA-1. These algorithms are first shown to be vulnerable to collision attacks as keyless hash functions, but the techniques are then extended to forgery and key-recovery attacks against NMAC/HMAC constructed of these hash functions [8,13]. These attacks tell us that it is high time to move toward new compression functions. In fact, NIST announces ending its support for SHA-1 and recommends migrating to SHA-2 family by the year 2010 [17,18]. Since SHA-2 family are slower than SHA-1, the replacement would result in lowering performance and losing an advantage of hash-based MACs (as compared to MACs of other types, say block-cipher-based or universal-hash-based ones.) One way to overcome this problem is to use a more efficient mode of operation, absorbing the decrease in performance caused by the new compression function.

Another reason to propose the new mode comes from a security principle of iterated functions that the size c of a chaining variable be relatively large. This requirement is particularly evident for MACs, due to the birthday attack [20] showing that half the size of c of the chaining variable corresponds to a security parameter. Having a large size c of a chaining variable is a good design principle also in the context of keyless hash functions, as illustrated by the "wide-pipe" argument [14]. Such design with large c, unfortunately, results in a performance disadvantage of the traditional Merkle-Damgård iteration. On the other hand, in our approach the size c is irrelevant in terms of efficiency, and indeed large c is welcomed; such large c increases relative performance of our scheme as compared to the conventional Merkle-Damgård iteration.

Organization of This Paper. In the following section we review some of the previous results concerning modes of operation of compression functions and identify the position of this work among them. Section 3 introduces design principles of our approach and a two-key prototype of our MAC construction. In Sect. 4 and 5 we define security notions utilized in this paper and discuss some aspects of them. Section 6 is devoted to security proofs of the two-key construction. In Sect. 7 and 8 we show techniques of constructing a single-key version and those of using a shorter key, respectively. Section 9 summarizes this paper.

2 Related Work

Merkle-Damgård. The Merkle-Damgård iteration gives a way to extend the domain of a compression function, having an attractive property that collision resistance of the compression function extends to the entire hash function (in either a keyless or keyed context) [16,10]. Owing to standardization and lack of regulation on export control, hash functions such as MD5 and SHA-1 are widely available in software libraries today. The widespread use of these keyless hash functions implemented with the Merkle-Damgård iteration also influences design principles for randomized hash functions and hash-based MACs/PRFs.

Randomized Hash Functions. The question of domain extension of target-collision-resistant (TCR) functions is intensively studied [7,21], where several modes of operation are suggested, which extend a TCR compression function to TCR hash functions. The common problem of these schemes is that the key size grows as a message length does. This obstacle is resolved in [12], where proposed is a mode of operation that runs as efficiently as the Merkle-Damgård iteration and that requires only a constant-size key. The trick is that its security is based on the assumption that the compression function satisfies new (but reasonable) properties, which are different from the notion of TCR.

MACs and PRFs. The NI and CS constructs [1,15] provide domain extension of MACs. The problem is that these modes are slower than the Merkle-Damgård iteration. This drawback is absent from HMAC, which achieves the same efficiency as the Merkle-Damgård iteration. This is a natural outcome since HMAC gives domain extension of PRFs, not MACs.[1]

In this paper we push ahead with this idea in order to obtain a PRF via a mode of operation that is even more efficient than HMAC. The trick is that

---

[1] Recall that a PRF is a secure MAC. There is another construct based on a PRF, called XOR-MAC [4]. XOR-MAC is capable of parallel processing, yet without it XOR-MAC is in general slower than the Merkle-Damgård iteration.

Table 1. Comparison of modes of operation for MAC/PRF

	Performance	Goal	Assumptions[2]	Reference
NI / CS	< Merkle-Damgård	MAC	MAC	[1,15]
NMAC / HMAC	= Merkle-Damgård	MAC	pp-MAC, 2PRF	[3,2]
		PRF	PRF	
Proposed	> Merkle-Damgård	MAC	pp-MAC, Δ-2PRF	—
construction		PRF	PRF, Δ-2PRF	

our security result is based on the assumption that the underlying compression function satisfies, in addition to the usual PRF, a new (but reasonable) PRF property (which we call Δ-2PRF).

Our construction is dedicated to MAC/PRF use. In return, our approach accomplishes higher performance than the Merkle-Damgård iteration, which seems to be hard to realize in the context of keyless or randomized hash functions — we may consider the circumstances as evidence that our mode of operation fully takes advantage of the presence of a "secret" key in the MAC/PRF situation. See Table 1 for comparison of these MAC/PRF modes.

Multi-property Preservation. EMD [5] and ESh [6] are modes of operation that preserve multiple properties (e.g., collision resistance, pseudo-randomness, etc..) These are integrative approaches, taking the converse point of view to the problem of domain extension; our goal is to construct a mode of operation that is specific to MAC/PRF property. While EMD or ESh offers a single program that can be used for multiple purposes (and hence a small source code, less confusion and a safety net), it may not perform the best with respect to a specific property (e.g., pseudo-randomness.) It should be noted that the code size of our mode of operation is much smaller than that of the compression function: The description of our construction requires only a loop, an XOR and a concatenation.

ENMAC. ENMAC [19] is an improvement over NMAC/HMAC, which is efficient particularly with short messages. This technique is also orthogonal to our approach, but it is so in a compatible way. That is, both ENMAC and our MAC in principle conform to the nested construction of NMAC (Recall that NMAC consists of outer encryption and inner hashing.) While ENMAC is an improvement on the outer function of NMAC, our construction is an improvement on the inner function. Hence ENMAC and our approach can coexist, but throughout the paper we base our construction upon the conventional NMAC for the sake of simplicity.[3]

---

[2] "pp-MAC" stands for privacy-preserving MAC, and "2PRF" for PRF against just two oracle queries.

[3] Intuitively, ENMAC improves performance mainly for short messages while our construction does so mainly for long messages. To a greater or lesser degree, each scheme alone improves performance essentially for all messages.

3   Design Principles

Merkle-Damgård. Figure 1 depicts the traditional Merkle-Damgård iteration using a compression function $h : \{0, 1\}^{c+b} \to \{0, 1\}^c$. In this classical hashing, a message M is divided into b-bit blocks as $M = m_1 \| m_2 \| \cdots$, and it is processed via the iteration $x_i \stackrel{\text{def}}{=} h(x_{i-1} \| m_i)$. Note that each invocation to h processes b-bits of M in this conservative mode of operation.

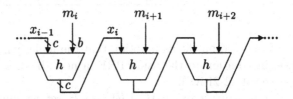

Fig. 1. Usual Merkle-Damgård iteration

Boosting. We start by trying to "maximize" the efficiency of each invocation to the compression function h. Note that h has $(c + b)$-bit input; we devise a mode of iteration we call "hyper-Merkle-Damgård," in which each invocation to h disposes of $c + b$ bits of a message M. We do this by XOR-ing the chaining variable x_i and the next c bits of M on each input. This is illustrated in Fig. 2. In the hyper-Merkle-Damgård iteration, a message M is divided as $M = m_1 \| m_2 \| \cdots$ so that $|m_1| = |m_3| = \cdots = c$ and $|m_2| = |m_4| = \cdots = b$. We refer to the $(c + b)$-bit segment $m_{2i-1} \| m_{2i}$ as a "chunk." The iteration works as $x_i \stackrel{\text{def}}{=} h\big((x_{i-1} \oplus m_{2i-1}) \| m_{2i}\big)$. Thus, the hyper-Merkle-Damgård iteration is c/b as fast again as the usual Merkle-Damgård.

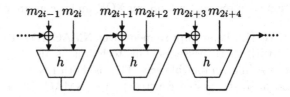

Fig. 2. Hyper-Merkle-Damgård iteration

Keying. We adopt the popular approach of keying a compression function h via its chaining variable. Namely, we obtain $h_K : \{0, 1\}^b \to \{0, 1\}^c$ by defining $h_K(\cdot) \stackrel{\text{def}}{=} h(K \| \cdot)$ where $K \stackrel{\$}{\leftarrow} \{0, 1\}^c$. Also, let $\{0, 1\}^{(c+b)*}$ denote the set of bit strings whose lengths are multiples of $c + b$ bits and define $H_K : \{0, 1\}^{(c+b)*} \to \{0, 1\}^c$ as $x_1 \leftarrow h_{K \oplus m_1}(m_2)$, $x_i \leftarrow h_{x_{i-1} \oplus m_{2i-1}}(m_{2i})$, $H_K(M) \stackrel{\text{def}}{=} x_n$, for an n-chunk message $M = m_1 \| \cdots \| m_{2n}$.

Nesting. The keyed function H_K constructed above as it is cannot be used as a secure MAC/PRF. In order to turn it into secure construction, we employ the "nested approach" of the NI and NMAC construction. Namely, define $\mathsf{BNMAC}_{K,K'} : \{0,1\}^{(c+b)*} \to \{0,1\}^c$ via $\mathsf{BNMAC}_{K,K'}(\cdot) \overset{\mathrm{def}}{=} h_{K'}\big(H_K(\cdot)\|1^{b-c}\big).$[4] See Fig. 3 for a pictorial definition of our BNMAC construction. As already pointed out in [2], the conventional NMAC construction can be viewed as a computational version of the Carter-Wegman paradigm. Similarly, our result can be viewed as a related-key version of the result for the conventional NMAC. Since our assumptions concerning the function h include a related-key, non-standard one, we try to base the assumption upon as weak a condition as possible. We successfully do this; the condition only allows an adversary to make just two (related-key) oracle queries in a non-adaptive way.

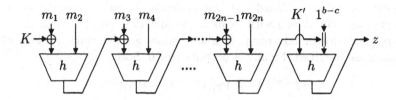

Fig. 3. Proposed MAC construction, double-key version (BNMAC)

Padding. The above $\mathsf{BNMAC}_{K,K'}(\cdot)$ accepts only messages whose lengths are multiples of $c + b$ bits. In order for the scheme to process a message of arbitrary length, the message M needs to be somehow padded. It turns out that any (one-to-one) padding $\{0,1\}^* \to \{0,1\}^{(c+b)*}$ works with our BNMAC construction, so hereafter we assume that a message always has a length multiple of $c + b$ bits (As an example of padding, just append $10\cdots0$).

4 Definitions

Notation. The concatenation $x\|y$ of strings x and y is sometimes written simply xy. We say that a string x is a prefix of another string y and write $x \sqsubset y$ if there exists a string e such that $xe = y$. We write $x \xleftarrow{\$} X$ to denote the operation of choosing an element uniformly at random from a set X and assigning its value to a variable x. An adversary A is a probabilistic machine that may have access to an oracle $\mathcal{O}$. The notation $A^{\mathcal{O}} \Rightarrow x$ indicates the event that, when run with the oracle $\mathcal{O}$, the adversary A outputs x. An oracle $\mathcal{O}$ is often defined by a game $\mathcal{G}$. In such a case we write $A^{\mathcal{G}}$ in place of $A^{\mathcal{O}}$. We also write $A \Leftarrow x$ to denote the operation of inputting the value x into A.

---

[4] Here we assume that $b \geq c$. Although we could get around this requirement by extending the outer function via Merkle-Damgård iteration [22], yet for simplicity we assume this condition throughout the paper.

Notion of PRF. Let $\{f_K : \mathcal{M} \to X\}$ be a family of functions with $K \in \{0,1\}^k$. A prf-adversary A tries to distinguish between two oracles, the "real" oracle being $f_K(\cdot)$, $K \xleftarrow{\$} \{0,1\}^k$ and the "random" oracle being $f(\cdot)$, $f \xleftarrow{\$} \{f : \mathcal{M} \to X\}$ (Fixing K fixes the real oracle, and fixing f fixes the random oracle.) Succinctly, define the advantage function of A as

$$\mathrm{Adv}_f^{\mathrm{prf}}(A) \overset{\mathrm{def}}{=} \Pr[A^f \Rightarrow 1] - \Pr[A^{\$} \Rightarrow 1],$$

where by f we denote the real oracle and by $\$$ the random oracle. The first probability is defined over the coins of A and $K \xleftarrow{\$} \{0,1\}^k$, and the second probability over the coins of A and $f \xleftarrow{\$} \{f : \mathcal{M} \to X\}$.

New Notion of Δ-2PRF. Let $\{f_K : \mathcal{M} \to X\}$ be a family of functions with $K \in \{0,1\}^k$. A Δ-2prf adversary A tries to distinguish between two games, as defined in Table 2. Namely, at the beginning of each game the adversary A queries once (m, Δ, m') with $m, m' \in \mathcal{M}$ and $\Delta \in \{0,1\}^k$. Then the oracle answers (x, x') to the adversary A, whose values are determined differently in each game as described. Finally A outputs 1 or 0. Succinctly define

$$\mathrm{Adv}_f^{\Delta\text{-}2\mathrm{prf}}(A) \overset{\mathrm{def}}{=} \Pr[A^f \Rightarrow 1] - \Pr[A^{\$} \Rightarrow 1],$$

where again by f we denote the real oracle and by $\$$ the random oracle.

Table 2. Real and random games for Δ-2PRF

Real	Random
$A \Rightarrow (m, \Delta, m')$	$A \Rightarrow (m, \Delta, m')$
$K \xleftarrow{\$} \{0,1\}^k$	$x, x' \xleftarrow{\$} X$
$x \leftarrow h_K(m); \ x' \leftarrow h_{K \oplus \Delta}(m')$	If $\Delta = 0$ and $m = m'$ then $x' \leftarrow x$ EndIf
$A \Leftarrow (x, x')$	$A \Leftarrow (x, x')$

Resource Parameters. An adversary A's resources are quantified with respect to its time complexity t, the number q of oracle queries and the length ℓ (in chunks, if applicable) of each query. We adopt the convention that the time complexity t includes the total execution time of an overlying game (the maximum of each game) plus the code size of A. Define

$$\mathrm{Adv}_f^{\mathrm{goal}}(t, q, \ell) \overset{\mathrm{def}}{=} \max_A \mathrm{Adv}_f^{\mathrm{goal}}(A),$$

where max is taken over adversaries A, each having time complexity at most t and making at most q oracle queries, each query being at most ℓ chunks. Often one or two of t, q, ℓ are inappropriate to be quantified, in which case they are omitted from the notation. Here, "goal" indicates the property in question, e.g., "prf." We write $T_f(\ell)$ to denote the time complexity that takes to compute a function f on a input whose length is ℓ chunks (and again, ℓ may be omitted).

5 Discussion on Δ-2PRF Property

Since we introduce the new notion Δ-2PRF on which our proofs of security are based, in this section we take a closer look at this requirement on the underlying compression function h. Intuitively, we can view the Δ-2PRF condition as a form of pseudo-randomness under a related-key attack. Yet, it is so in one of the weakest forms possible; namely, in Δ-2PRF, an adversary is limited to ask only two queries, and these queries must be performed non-adaptively. In other words, he must submit his entire queries (two messages m, m' and a relation Δ) together at the beginning of the game.

So the notion of Δ-2PRF itself is not a demanding requirement, though it cannot be deduced from the standard PRF (against q queries) assumption. We remark that the condition that h be a Δ-2PRF and the condition that h be a PRF (against q queries) are independent; neither one implies the other.

To get the feel of handling the notion of Δ-2PRF, we give an example of MD5. Let $\mathsf{md5} : \{0,1\}^{128+512} \to \{0,1\}^{128}$ be the compression function of MD5. It is known [11] that $\mathsf{md5}$ is vulnerable to so called a "pseudo-collision" attack. That is, for $\Delta \overset{\text{def}}{=}$ 8000 0000 8000 0000 8000 0000 8000 0000 the condition $\mathsf{md5}_K(m) = \mathsf{md5}_{K \oplus \Delta}(m)$ $(K \overset{\$}{\leftarrow} \{0,1\}^{128}, m \overset{\$}{\leftarrow} \{0,1\}^{512})$ holds with a probability of about $1/2^{46} \gg 1/2^{128}$. Using this technique, an adversary A can attack $\mathsf{md5}$ in the Δ-2PRF sense: A queries (m, Δ, m) $(m \overset{\$}{\leftarrow} \{0,1\}^{512})$ and receives (x, x'); if $x = x'$, then A outputs 1; otherwise, A outputs 0. Such an A has advantage $\mathrm{Adv}_{\mathsf{md5}}^{\Delta\text{-2prf}}(A) \approx 1/2^{46} - 1/2^{128}$. Thus, $\mathsf{md5}$ does not satisfy the Δ-2PRF property.

This characteristic of $\mathsf{md5}$ is rather critical in its architecture. We expect that this sort of attack be precluded by structural designs of forthcoming compression functions, and certainly we would hope for designs without such a flaw in more "matured" compression functions such as $\mathsf{sha256}$.

At the end of this discussion, we emphasize the point that breaking Δ-2PRF is easier than finding pseudo-collisions. Our proofs of security require that h be a Δ-2PRF, and h just being resistant to pseudo-collisions would not suffice for our purpose according to the current reduction.

6 Security Proofs (Double-Key Version)

This section proves the following:

Theorem 1. *Let* BNMAC *be the two-key construction as defined in Sec. 3. If the underlying compression function h is a PRF and a Δ-2PRF, then* BNMAC *is a PRF. More concretely, we have*

$$\mathrm{Adv}_{\mathsf{BNMAC}}^{\mathrm{prf}}(t, q, \ell) \le \mathrm{Adv}_h^{\mathrm{prf}}(t, q) + \binom{q}{2} \cdot \left(2(\ell+1) \cdot \mathrm{Adv}_h^{\Delta\text{-2prf}}(t') + \frac{1}{2^c} \right),$$

where $t' = (4\ell + 1) \cdot T_h$.

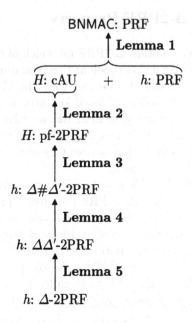

Fig. 4. A proof map

The reduction in the above theorem is essentially tight, due to the birthday attack [20]. For more discussion on the gap from the exactly tight bound, see [2].

In order to prove this theorem, we need the following five lemmas. The five lemmas sequentially reduce the PRF condition on the BNMAC scheme to the PRF and Δ-2PRF conditions on the underlying compression function. Along the proofs, we need several intermediate security notions, which are defined when they first appear. See Fig. 4 for a guide map.

For stating the first lemma, we need to define the notion of cAU (computational almost-universality.) An au-adversary A against a keyed function $H_K : \{0,1\}^{(c+b)*} \rightarrow \{0,1\}^c$ (with $K \in \{0,1\}^c$) simply outputs a pair of messages (M, M') with $M, M' \in \{0,1\}^{(c+b)*}$; define

$$\text{Adv}_H^{\text{au}}(A) \overset{\text{def}}{=} \Pr\left[H_K(M) = H_K(M') \wedge M \neq M' \mid A \Rightarrow (M, M'), K \overset{\$}{\leftarrow} \{0,1\}^c\right].$$

Here note that such an adversary is non-adaptive. It also means that we can disregard the time complexity of au-adversaries (and often it is set to $2 \cdot T_H(\ell)$).

Lemma 1. *Let* $H_K : \{0,1\}^{(c+b)*} \rightarrow \{0,1\}^c$ *and* $h_{K'} : \{0,1\}^b \rightarrow \{0,1\}^c$ *be keyed functions with* $K, K' \in \{0,1\}^c$. *If* H_K *is cAU and* $h_{K'}$ *a PRF, then the composition* $h \circ H_{(K',K)}$ *defined by* $h_{K'}(H_K(M)\|1^{b-c})$ *is a PRF. More concretely written, the following holds:*

$$\text{Adv}_{h \circ H}^{\text{prf}}(t, q, \ell) \leq \text{Adv}_h^{\text{prf}}(t, q) + \binom{q}{2} \cdot \text{Adv}_H^{\text{au}}(t', \ell),$$

where $t' = 2 \cdot T_H(\ell)$.

Table 3. Real and random games for 2PRF

Real	Random
$A \Rightarrow (M, M')$	$A \Rightarrow (M, M')$
$K \xleftarrow{\$} \{0,1\}^c$	$x, x' \xleftarrow{\$} \{0,1\}^c$
$x \leftarrow H_K(M); \; x' \leftarrow H_K(M')$	If $M = M'$ then $x' \leftarrow x$ EndIf
$A \Leftarrow (x, x')$	$A \Leftarrow (x, x')$

Table 4. Real and random games for $\Delta \# \Delta'$-2PRF

Real	Random
$A \Rightarrow (\Delta, m, \#, \Delta', m')$	$A \Rightarrow (\Delta, m, \#, \Delta', m')$
$K, K' \xleftarrow{\$} \{0,1\}^c$	$x, x' \xleftarrow{\$} \{0,1\}^c$
If $\# = 1$ then	If $\# = 1$ and
$\quad x \leftarrow h_{K \oplus \Delta}(m); \; x' \leftarrow h_{K \oplus \Delta'}(m')$	$(\Delta, m) = (\Delta', m')$ then
Else (i.e., $\# = 2$)	$\quad x' \leftarrow x$
$\quad x \leftarrow h_{K \oplus \Delta}(m); \; x' \leftarrow h_{K' \oplus \Delta'}(m')$	EndIf
EndIf; $A \Leftarrow (x, x')$	$A \Leftarrow (x, x')$

Proof. This lemma (along with its pp-MAC version) is proved in [2].   □

The next lemma relates cAU to pseudo-randomness property, utilizing the iterative structure of the hyper-Merkle-Damgård. See Table 3 for the notion of 2PRF. We say that a 2prf-adversary A is "prefix-free" (pf-2prf) if $M \not\subset M'$ and $M \not\supset M'$, where (M, M') is the query output by A. Note that in particular, prefix-freeness implies $M, M' \neq \varepsilon$ (null) and $M \neq M'$.

Lemma 2. *Let* $h : \{0,1\}^{c+b} \to \{0,1\}^c$ *be a compression function and* $H_K : \{0,1\}^{(c+b)*} \to \{0,1\}^c$ *the hyper-Merkle-Damgård iteration constructed of* h, *keyed via its initial chaining variable. If* H_K *is prefix-free 2PRF, then it is cAU. More concretely,*

$$\text{Adv}_H^{\text{au}}(t, \ell) \leq \text{Adv}_H^{\text{pf-2prf}}(t, \ell + 1) + \frac{1}{2^c}.$$

Proof. This can be easily proven by using the well-known "extension trick" [2].   □

Now we reduce the condition that H be a prefix-free 2PRF to the condition that h be a $\Delta \# \Delta'$-2PRF, whose definition can be found in Table 4.

Lemma 3. *If* h *is a* $\Delta \# \Delta'$-*2PRF, then its hyper-Merkle-Damgård iteration* H *is a prefix-free PRF. More concretely, we have*

$$\text{Adv}_H^{\text{pf-2prf}}(t, \ell) \leq \ell \cdot \text{Adv}_h^{\Delta \# \Delta'\text{-2prf}}(t'),$$

where $t' = t + 2 \cdot T_H(\ell)$.

Game $\mathcal{G}_i$	**Adversary** B_i
$A \Rightarrow (M, M')$	$A \Rightarrow (M, M')$
	If $m_1 \cdots m_{2i} = m'_1 \cdots m'_{2i}$ then
	$\quad (x, x') \leftarrow \mathcal{O}(m_{2i+1}, m_{2i+2}, 1, m'_{2i+1}, m'_{2i+2})$
$x, x' \xleftarrow{\$} \{0, 1\}^c$	Else (i.e., $m_1 \cdots m_{2i} \neq m'_1 \cdots m'_{2i}$)
	$\quad (x, x') \leftarrow \mathcal{O}(m_{2i+1}, m_{2i+2}, 2, m'_{2i+1}, m'_{2i+2})$
	EndIf
Define (y, y') as in Table 5	Define (y, y') as in Table 6
$A \Leftarrow (y, y')$	$A \Leftarrow (y, y')$
	Output whatever A outputs

Fig. 5. Intermediate games $\mathcal{G}_i$ and adversaries B_i

Table 5. Definition of (y, y') in game $\mathcal{G}_i$

	$n' \leq i$	$n' \geq i + 1$
$n \leq i$	$y \leftarrow x$	$y \leftarrow x$
	$y' \leftarrow x'$	$y' \leftarrow H_{x'}(m'_{2i+1} \cdots m'_{2n'})$
$n \geq i + 1$	$y \leftarrow H_x(m_{2i+1} \cdots m_{2n})$	If $m_1 \cdots m_{2i} = m'_1 \cdots m'_{2i}$ then
	$y' \leftarrow x'$	$\quad y \leftarrow H_x(m_{2i+1} \cdots m_{2n})$
		$\quad y' \leftarrow H_x(m'_{2i+1} \cdots m'_{2n'})$
		Else (i.e., $m_1 \cdots m_{2i} \neq m'_1 \cdots m'_{2i}$)
		$\quad y \leftarrow H_x(m_{2i+1} \cdots m_{2n})$
		$\quad y' \leftarrow H_{x'}(m'_{2i+1} \cdots m'_{2n'})$

Proof. Let A be a pf-2prf adversary attacking H, having time complexity at most t and querying messages each of at most ℓ chunks. We would like to bound the advantage $\text{Adv}_H^{\text{pf-2prf}}(A)$. Let (M, M') denote the pair of messages that A outputs, and write $M = m_1 \cdots m_{2n}$ (n chunks) and $M' = m'_1 \cdots m'_{2n'}$ (n' chunks). Note that $n, n' \leq \ell$. Consider the intermediate games $\mathcal{G}_i$ defined in Fig. 5 for $i = 0, \cdots, \ell$. Note that running $A^{\mathcal{G}_0}$ can be identified with running A^H, treating the condition $m_1 \cdots m_{2i} = m'_1 \cdots m'_{2i}$ to be true when $i = 0$. Also, running $A^{\mathcal{G}_\ell}$ coincides with the random game for A. Hence

$$\text{Adv}_H^{\text{pf-2prf}}(A) = \Pr[A^H \Rightarrow 1] - \Pr[A^\$ \Rightarrow 1]$$
$$= P_0 - P_\ell$$
$$= \sum_{i=0}^{\ell-1} (P_i - P_{i+1}),$$

where $P_i \overset{\text{def}}{=} \Pr[A^{\mathcal{G}_i} \Rightarrow 1]$ for $i \in \{0, \ldots, \ell\}$.

Now for each $i = 0, \ldots, \ell - 1$ we define an adversary B_i that uses A as a subroutine and attacks h in the $\Delta \# \Delta'$-2PRF sense, as described in Fig. 5. It

Table 6. Definition of (y, y') in adversary B_i

	$n' \leq i$	$n' \geq i+1$
$n \leq i$	$y \leftarrow x$ $y' \leftarrow x'$	$y \leftarrow x$ $y' \leftarrow H_{x'}(m'_{2i+3} \cdots m'_{2n'})$
$n \geq i+1$	$y \leftarrow H_x(m_{2i+3} \cdots m_{2n})$ $y' \leftarrow x'$	$y \leftarrow H_x(m_{2i+3} \cdots m_{2n})$ $y' \leftarrow H_{x'}(m'_{2i+3} \cdots m'_{2n'})$

Table 7. Real and random games for $\Delta\Delta'$-2PRF

Real	Random
$A \Rightarrow (\Delta, m, \Delta', m')$	$A \Rightarrow (\Delta, m, \Delta', m')$
$K \xleftarrow{\$} \{0,1\}^c$	$x, x' \xleftarrow{\$} \{0,1\}^c$
$x \leftarrow h_{K \oplus \Delta}(m)$	If $(\Delta, m) = (\Delta', m')$ then
$x' \leftarrow h_{K \oplus \Delta'}(m')$	$x' \leftarrow x$ EndIf
$A \Leftarrow (x, x')$	$A \Leftarrow (x, x')$

can be directly verified that $\Pr\left[B_i^h \Rightarrow 1\right] = \Pr\left[A^{\mathcal{G}_i} \Rightarrow 1\right] = P_i$ and $\Pr\left[B_i^\$ \Rightarrow 1\right]$ $= \Pr\left[A^{\mathcal{G}_{i+1}} \Rightarrow 1\right] = P_{i+1}$. Hence

$$
\begin{aligned}
\mathrm{Adv}_H^{\mathrm{pf\text{-}2prf}}(A) &= \sum_{i=0}^{\ell-1} (P_i - P_{i+1}) \\
&= \sum_{i=0}^{\ell-1} \left(\Pr\left[B_i^h \Rightarrow 1\right] - \Pr\left[B_i^\$ \Rightarrow 1\right] \right) \\
&= \sum_{i=0}^{\ell-1} \mathrm{Adv}_h^{\Delta\#\Delta'\text{-}2prf}(B_i) \\
&\leq \sum_{i=0}^{\ell-1} \mathrm{Adv}_h^{\Delta\#\Delta'\text{-}2prf}(t') \\
&= \ell \cdot \mathrm{Adv}_h^{\Delta\#\Delta'\text{-}2prf}(t').
\end{aligned}
$$
□

Next we reduce the condition that h be a $\Delta\#\Delta'$-2PRF to the condition that h be a $\Delta\Delta'$-2PRF, whose definition can be found in Table 7. The notion of $\Delta\Delta'$-2PRF is simpler than that of $\Delta\#\Delta'$-2PRF, and it is also closer to that of Δ-2PRF.

Lemma 4. *If a compression function h is $\Delta\Delta'$-2PRF, then it is $\Delta\#\Delta'$-2PRF. More concretely, we have*

$$
\mathrm{Adv}_h^{\Delta\#\Delta'\text{-}2prf}(t) \leq 2 \cdot \mathrm{Adv}_h^{\Delta\Delta'\text{-}2prf}(t'),
$$

where $t' = t + T_h$.

Adversary C	**Adversary** C'
$B \Rightarrow (\Delta, m, \#, \Delta', m')$	$B \Rightarrow (\Delta, m, \#, \Delta', m')$
If $\# = 1$ then	$K \xleftarrow{\$} \{0,1\}^c$; $x \leftarrow h_{K \oplus \Delta}(m)$
$\quad (x, x') \leftarrow \mathcal{O}(\Delta, m, \Delta', m')$	If $\# = 1$ then
Else (i.e., $\# = 2$)	$\quad x' \leftarrow h_{K \oplus \Delta'}(m')$
$\quad (x, x) \leftarrow \mathcal{O}(\Delta, m, \Delta, m)$	Else (i.e., $\# = 2$)
$\quad x' \xleftarrow{\$} \{0,1\}^c$ EndIf	$\quad (x', x') \leftarrow \mathcal{O}(\Delta', m', \Delta', m')$ EndIf
$B \Leftarrow (x, x')$	$B \Leftarrow (x, x')$
Output whatever B outputs	Output whatever B outputs

Fig. 6. Adversaries C, C'

Proof. Let B be a $\Delta\#\Delta'$-2prf adversary against h having time complexity at most t. We create $\Delta\Delta'$-2prf adversaries C and C', each using B as its subroutine, as described in Fig. 6. It can be directly verified that $\Pr[C^h \Rightarrow 1] = \Pr[C'^{\$} \Rightarrow 1]$, $\Pr[C^{\$} \Rightarrow 1] = \Pr[B^{\$} \Rightarrow 1]$ and $\Pr[C'^h \Rightarrow 1] = \Pr[B^h \Rightarrow 1]$. Therefore

$$
\begin{aligned}
\mathrm{Adv}_h^{\Delta\#\Delta'\text{-2prf}}(B) &= \Pr[B^h \Rightarrow 1] - \Pr[B^{\$} \Rightarrow 1] \\
&= \Pr[C'^h \Rightarrow 1] - \Pr[C'^{\$} \Rightarrow 1] + \Pr[C^h \Rightarrow 1] - \Pr[C^{\$} \Rightarrow 1] \\
&= \mathrm{Adv}_h^{\Delta\Delta'\text{-2prf}}(C') + \mathrm{Adv}_h^{\Delta\Delta'\text{-2prf}}(C) \\
&\leq 2 \cdot \mathrm{Adv}_h^{\Delta\Delta'\text{-2prf}}(t').
\end{aligned}
$$
□

Finally, we are ready to reach the condition of Δ-2PRF. The last lemma gives us straight-forward reduction of $\Delta\Delta'$-2PRF to Δ-2PRF:

Lemma 5. *If a compression function h is Δ-2PRF, then it is $\Delta\Delta'$-2PRF. More concretely, we have*

$$
\mathrm{Adv}_h^{\Delta\Delta'\text{-2prf}}(t) \leq \mathrm{Adv}_h^{\Delta\text{-2prf}}(t).
$$

Proof. Let C be a $\Delta\Delta'$-2prf adversary against h having time complexity at most t. We construct a Δ-2prf adversary D against h that uses C as its subroutine, as follows.

D runs C and obtains the query (Δ, m, Δ', m'). Then D asks its oracle a query and receives $(x, x') \leftarrow \mathcal{O}(m, \Delta \oplus \Delta', m')$. D forwards (x, x') to C and outputs whatever C outputs.

Here observe that $\Pr[D^h \Rightarrow 1] = \Pr[C^h \Rightarrow 1]$ and that $\Pr[D^{\$} \Rightarrow 1] = \Pr[C^{\$} \Rightarrow 1]$. Hence we have

$$
\begin{aligned}
\mathrm{Adv}_h^{\Delta\Delta'\text{-2prf}}(C) &= \mathrm{Adv}_h^{\Delta\text{-2prf}}(D) \\
&\leq \mathrm{Adv}_h^{\Delta\text{-2prf}}(t),
\end{aligned}
$$

neglecting the increase in D's time complexity.
□

The above five lemmas prove Theorem 1. Recall that, without loss of generality we can estimate the time complexity of a cAU adversary to be $2 \cdot T_H(\ell)$. So for the time complexity t' in Theorem 1 we get $t' = 2 \cdot T_H(\ell) + 2 \cdot T_H(\ell) + T_h = (4\ell+1) \cdot T_h$.

7 Single-Key Versions

Our BNMAC construction so far requires two independent keys $K, K' \in \{0,1\}^c$, which may be an undesirable feature in some cases in practice. However, this problem is easily resolved through the pseudo-randomness of h. We show two solutions.

The first method is a trivial way of deriving two keys. Let $K^* \in \{0,1\}^c$ be a master key. From K^* derive two keys as $K \leftarrow h_{K^*}(0^b)$ and $K' \leftarrow h_{K^*}(1^b)$. We then use these two keys in place of $K, K' \in \{0,1\}^c$ in the BNMAC construction. See Fig. 7 for a pictorial description. The only difference between the original double-key version and this single-key variant lies in the way how the two keys K and K' are produced (in the former $K, K' \xleftarrow{\$} \{0,1\}^c$, whereas in the latter these keys are derived via h from $K^* \xleftarrow{\$} \{0,1\}^c$.) Hence distinguishing between the two versions amounts to breaking the pseudo-randomness of h (with two constant queries 0^b and 1^b to the oracle.) It should be noted that if we replace the PRF assumption with that of pp-MAC in Lemma 1, then the pp-MAC version of Theorem 1 still holds for this single-key variant. This is because the 2PRF requirement on h for key derivation is absorbed into Δ-2PRF of h, not PRF (against q queries).

The second method takes the idea from [22]. See Fig. 8 for the description of this variant. While this version saves one extra block of invocation to the compression function, there are two points to be attended to. One is that now

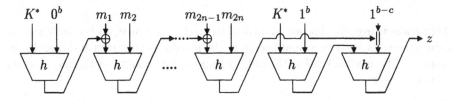

Fig. 7. Single-key version 1

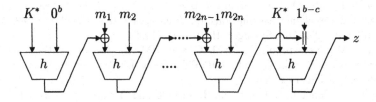

Fig. 8. Single-key version 2

we need the condition $b \geq c + 1$ (rather than $b \geq c$.) The other is that the pp-MAC version appears to be infeasible in this case.

8   Using a Shorter Key

Recall that the size c of a chaining variable may be larger than one's desired security parameter, depending on a choice of compression functions. This means that in practice the desired size k of the master key K^* may be smaller than c, disabling the above single-key construction.

This difficulty can be settled in several ways. One is to use only the first k bits of c in the above single-key variant (and the remaining $c - k$ bits may be padded with zeros.) Another is to fill out the c bits by multiple copies of a k-bit key, as $K^* \| K^* \| \cdots$. In either example, note that we still do not lose our formal proofs of security with the first version of the single-key construction, assuming additionally that the newly keyed function is a 2PRF against corresponding two oracle queries.

9   Summary

This paper proposes a novel mode of operation of compression functions, called hyper-Merkle-Damgård, which can process a message faster than the conventional Merkle-Damgård iteration and can be used exclusively as a MAC/PRF. The proofs of security are based on the assumption that the underlying compression function satisfies some PRF properties. These PRF properties include a new notion which we call Δ-2PRF. We carefully take a look at this property and identify it as not a demanding condition. We first give proofs of security of a double-key version, called BNMAC, and then show that single-key versions can be easily derived, along with flexibility of the key size.

Acknowledgments. The author would like to thank ASIACRYPT 2007 anonymous reviewers for their valuable comments, insightful questions and useful suggestions. The feedback helps the author improve the quality of the paper in its various aspects.

References

1. An, J.H., Bellare, M.: Constructing VIL-MACs from FIL-MACs: Message authentication under weakened assumptions. In: Wiener, M.J. (ed.) CRYPTO 1999. LNCS, vol. 1666, pp. 252–269. Springer, Heidelberg (1999)
2. Bellare, M.: New proofs for NMAC and HMAC: Security without collision-resistance. In: Dwork, C. (ed.) CRYPTO 2006. LNCS, vol. 4117, pp. 602–619. Springer, Heidelberg (2006)
3. Bellare, M., Canetti, R., Krawczyk, H.: Pseudorandom functions revisited: The cascade construction and its concrete security. In: IEEE Symposium on Foundations of Computer Science, pp. 514–523 (1996)

4. Bellare, M., Guérin, R., Rogaway, P.: XOR MACs: New methods for message authentication using finite pseudorandom functions. In: Coppersmith, D. (ed.) CRYPTO 1995. LNCS, vol. 963, pp. 15–28. Springer, Heidelberg (1995)
5. Bellare, M., Ristenpart, T.: Multi-property-preserving hash domain extension and the EMD transform. In: Lai, X., Chen, K. (eds.) ASIACRYPT 2006. LNCS, vol. 4284, pp. 299–314. Springer, Heidelberg (2006)
6. Bellare, M., Ristenpart, T.: Hash functions in the dedicated-key setting: Design choices and MPP transforms. In: Arge, L., Cachin, C., Jurdzinski, T., Tarlecki, A. (eds.) ICALP 2007. LNCS, vol. 4596, pp. 399–410. Springer, Heidelberg (2007)
7. Bellare, M., Rogaway, P.: Collision-resistant hashing: Towards making UOWHFs practical. In: Kaliski Jr., B.S. (ed.) CRYPTO 1997. LNCS, vol. 1294, pp. 470–484. Springer, Heidelberg (1997)
8. Contini, S., Yin, Y.L.: Forgery and partial key-recovery attacks on HMAC and NMAC using hash collisions. In: Lai, X., Chen, K. (eds.) ASIACRYPT 2006. LNCS, vol. 4284, pp. 37–53. Springer, Heidelberg (2006)
9. Coron, J.S., Dodis, Y., Malinaud, C., Puniya, P.: Merkle-Damgård revisited: How to construct a hash function. In: Shoup, V. (ed.) CRYPTO 2005. LNCS, vol. 3621, pp. 430–448. Springer, Heidelberg (2005)
10. Damgård, I.: A design principle for hash functions. In: Brassard, G. (ed.) CRYPTO 1989. LNCS, vol. 435, pp. 416–427. Springer, Heidelberg (1990)
11. den Boer, B., Bosselaers, A.: Collisions for the compressin function of MD5. In: Helleseth, T. (ed.) EUROCRYPT 1993. LNCS, vol. 765, pp. 293–304. Springer, Heidelberg (1994)
12. Halevi, S., Krawcyzk, H.: Strengthening digital signatures via randomized hashing. In: Dwork, C. (ed.) CRYPTO 2006. LNCS, vol. 4117, pp. 41–59. Springer, Heidelberg (2006)
13. Kim, J., Biryukov, A., Preneel, B., Hong, S.: On the security of HMAC and NMAC based on HAVAL, MD4, MD5, SHA-0 and SHA-1. In: De Prisco, R., Yung, M. (eds.) SCN 2006. LNCS, vol. 4116, pp. 242–256. Springer, Heidelberg (2006)
14. Lucks, S.: A failure-friendly design principle for hash functions. In: Roy, B. (ed.) ASIACRYPT 2005. LNCS, vol. 3788, pp. 474–494. Springer, Heidelberg (2005)
15. Maurer, U.M., Sjödin, J.: Single-key AIL-MACs from any FIL-MAC. In: Caires, L., Italiano, G.F., Monteiro, L., Palamidessi, C., Yung, M. (eds.) ICALP 2005. LNCS, vol. 3580, pp. 472–484. Springer, Heidelberg (2005)
16. Merkle, R.C.: One way hash functions and DES. In: Brassard, G. (ed.) CRYPTO 1989. LNCS, vol. 435, pp. 428–446. Springer, Heidelberg (1990)
17. NIST: NIST brief comments on recent cryptanalytic attacks on secure hashing functions and the continued security provided by SHA-1 (2004)
18. NIST: NIST brief comments on recent cryptanalytic attacks on SHA-1 (2004)
19. Patel, S.: An efficient MAC for short messages. In: Nyberg, K., Heys, H.M. (eds.) SAC 2002. LNCS, vol. 2595, pp. 353–368. Springer, Heidelberg (2003)
20. Preneel, B., van Oorschot, P.C.: On the security of iterated message authentication codes. IEEE Transactions on Information Theory 45(1), 188–199 (1999)
21. Shoup, V.: A composition theorem for universal one-way hash functions. In: Preneel, B. (ed.) EUROCRYPT 2000. LNCS, vol. 1807, pp. 445–452. Springer, Heidelberg (2000)
22. Yasuda, K.: "Sandwich" is indeed secure: How to authenticate a message with just one hashing. In: Pieprzyk, J., Ghodosi, H., Dawson, E. (eds.) ACISP 2007. LNCS, vol. 4586, pp. 355–369. Springer, Heidelberg (2007)

On Efficient Message Authentication Via Block Cipher Design Techniques

G. Jakimoski and K.P. Subbalakshmi*

Department of Electrical and Computer Engineering
Stevens Institute of Technology, Hoboken, NJ 07030, USA
goce.jakimoski@stevens.edu, ksubbala@stevens.edu

Abstract. In an effort to design a MAC scheme that is built using block cipher components and runs faster than the modes of operation for message authentication, Daemen and Rijmen have proposed a generic MAC construction ALRED and a concrete ALRED instance Pelican. The Pelican MAC uses four rounds of AES as a building block to compute the authentication tag in a CBC-like manner. It is about 2.5 times faster than a CBC-MAC with AES, but it is not proven secure. Minematsu and Tsunoo observed that one can build almost universal (AU_2) hash functions using differentially uniform permutations (e.g., four AES rounds with independent keys), and hence, provably secure MAC schemes as well. They proposed two MAC schemes MT-MAC and PC-MAC. MT-MAC hashes the message using a Wegman-Carter binary tree. Its speedup for long messages approaches 2.5, but it is not very memory efficient. PC-MAC hashes the message in a CBC-like manner. It is more memory efficient. However, its speedup over the message authentication modes is about 1.4.

We notice that using a non-linear permutation as a building block, one can construct almost XOR universal (AXU_2) hash functions whose security is close to the maximum differential probability of the underlying non-linear permutation. Hence, using four AES rounds as a building block will lead to efficient Wegman-Carter MAC schemes that offer much better security than the modes of operation for message authentication. If the target security is that of the message authentication modes with AES, then one can use non-linear permutations defined on 64-bit blocks and achieve greater speedup and better key agility. For instance, the ideally achievable speedup when using the 64-bit components we suggest is 3.3 to 5.0 as opposed to the 2.5 speedup when using four AES rounds.

Keywords: Message authentication, Wegman-Carter construction, universal hash functions, block ciphers, maximum differential probability.

1 Introduction

Message Authentication. Message authentication is one of the basic information security goals, and it addresses the issues of source corroboration and

---

* This work was funded in part by NSF CT grant number: 0627688 and US Army ARDEC/Picattiny Arsenal.

improper or unauthorized modification of data. The message authentication model usually involves three participants: a sender, a receiver and an adversary. The sender and the receiver have agreed on a secret key. Prior to sending a message, the sender uses a signing algorithm that given the message and the secret key outputs an authentication tag (or MAC). The sender sends the tag along with the message to the receiver. On receipt, the receiver uses a verification algorithm that given the secret key, the message and the tag returns 1 if the MAC is valid, or returns 0 otherwise. The goal of the adversary is to trick the receiver into accepting a message that was not sent by the sender.

Message authentication has been heavily addressed in the literature. We briefly overview some of the results. There are three common approaches to message authentication. One approach involves using cryptographic hash functions. The first such schemes were proposed by Tsudik [49] and Kaliski and Robshaw [29], and later analyzed by Preneel and Van Oorschot [44,45]. A popular hash function based MAC is the HMAC construction of Bellare, Canetti and Krawczyk [3,5].

Another approach to message authentication involves secure block ciphers modeled as pseudorandom permutations. The CBC MAC [20,25] is probably the most studied MAC construction based on block ciphers. Bellare, Kilian and Rogaway proved its security for fixed-length messages [2]. Petrank and Rackoff [43] (another proof was provided by Vaudenay [50]) showed that EMAC [6], a CBC MAC variant using additional encryption, is secure when the message length is a multiple of the block size. Black and Rogaway [13] proposed a solution for arbitrary message lengths that uses three keys and only one key scheduling of the underlying block cipher. Jaulmes, Joux and Valette proposed RMAC [27], which is an extension of EMAC using two keys and a randomness. Iwata and Kurosawa provided solutions that use only two [37] and one key [27]. There are also block cipher based MAC constructions that do not follow the CBC paradigm (e.g., the PMAC construction of Black and Rogaway [14]).

The third approach is the universal hash function approach. Wegman and Carter were the first to propose the notion of universal hash functions [16] and their use in message authentication [51]. The construction proposed by Wegman and Carter provides unconditional security. A computationally secure scheme can be obtained if the random keys are replaced by pseudorandom keys. This approach was first studied by Brassard [15]. The topics related to universal hash functions and unconditional message authentication have been studied a lot in the past years. Some of the results include the following. Unconditional message authentication was first considered by Gilbert, Williams and Sloane [22]. Simmons [47] developed the theory of unconditional authentication and derived some lower bounds on the deception probability. The use of universal hashing to construct unconditionally secure authentication codes has also been studied by Stinson [48] and by Bierbrauer et al.[9]. The notion of almost XOR universal hash functions is due to Krawczyk [29]. A bucket hashing technique for constructing an AXU_2 families of universal hash functions and their use to construct computationally secure MACs were proposed by Rogaway [46]. Afanassiev, Gehrmann and Smeets [1] proposed an efficient procedure for polynomial evaluation that can be used for fast message authentication. MMH, proposed by Halevi and Krawczyk [23], and SquareHash, proposed by Etzel, Patel and Ramzan [19], are examples of fast universal hash functions. An efficient universal hash function family NH and a message authentication code UMAC based on NH were also proposed by Black et al.[12]. Another fast message authentication scheme and stronger bounds for Wegman-Carter-Shoup authenticators were recently provided by Bernstein [8,7].

Differential Probability Bounds. Since the publication of the differential cryptanalysis attacks on DES (Biham and Shamir [10]), differential cryptanalysis has become one of the most studied general attacks on block ciphers, and the resistance to differential cryptanalysis has become one of the basic block cipher design criteria. The round keys used by block ciphers are derived from a single key using a key scheduling algorithm. However, in order to augment the belief that certain block cipher structures are secure against differential cryptanalysis, some researchers have provided security proofs assuming random and independent round keys. The provable security against differential cryptanalysis of some Feistel structures has been studied by Matsui [38]. Hong et al. [24] proved an upper bound on the maximum differential probability for 2 rounds of a substitution permutation network with highly diffusive linear transformation. Kang et al. [30] provided a bound for any value of the branch number of the linear transformation. Keliher, Meijer and Tavares [31,32] proposed a new method for finding the upper bound on the maximum average linear hull probability for substitution permutation networks (SPN) and applied their method to AES. Park et al. proved that the maximum differential probability of four rounds of AES is upper bounded by 1.06×2^{-96} [41], and later proved a better bound 1.144×2^{-111} in [42]. A slightly better bound (2^{-113}) was provided by Keliher and Sui [33].

Closely Related Work. Daemen and Rijmen [17] have recently proposed a new heuristic MAC construction ALRED, and a concrete MAC scheme Pelican [18]. The Pelican MAC uses four rounds of AES as a building block to compute the authentication tag in a CBC-like manner, and it is about 2.5 times faster than a CBC-MAC with AES. However, it is not proven secure. Minematsu and Tsunoo [40] observe that one can obtain provably secure almost universal hash functions (AU_2) by using differentially uniform permutations such as four rounds of AES with independent keys in a Wegman-Carter binary tree. They also propose a message authentication scheme MT-MAC that makes use of the proposed AU_2 hash function. However, they note that such construction is not memory efficient, and suggest a CBC-like AU_2 hash PCH (Periodic CBC Hash) and a proven secure MAC scheme PC-MAC based on PCH. The speedup of PC-MAC over the modes with AES is 1.4.

Our Contribution. We propose a CBC-like AXU_2 hash UHC (Universal Hash Chaining) and a variant of a Wegman-Carter binary tree AXU_2 hash (the MACH hash). Both constructions use a non-linear invertible transformation as a building block. Their proven security is somewhat smaller than the maximum differential probability of the underlying non-linear permutation, and it does not change with the message length as in the polynomial constructions or PCH. Hence, if one uses four rounds of AES with independent keys as a building block one can obtain a message authentication scheme that is more time efficient and offers significantly greater security compared to the message authentication modes with AES. If the target security is that of the message authentication modes with AES, then one can use non-linear permutations defined on 64-bit strings (blocks). This allows for greater speedup and better key agility. For instance, the non-linear transformations that we suggest use 128- and 192-bit keys as opposed to the 512-bit key required by four rounds of AES. If these components are used in a Wegman-Carter single-binary-tree hash, then the achievable speedup for lengthy messages approaches 4.5 on 8-bit architectures, 3.3 on 32-bit architectures and 5 on 64-bit architectures with relatively large L1 cache as opposed to the 2.5 speedup achievable when the non-linear permutation is four rounds of AES. In order to improve the memory efficiency, MACH, the message authentication scheme we propose, uses the modified Wegman-Carter tree AXU_2 hash function (the MACH hash) instead of a single tree. The estimated speedup of the resulting scheme is somewhat smaller, but still significant (see Section 4.3 for more details).

2   Basic Building Blocks

In this section, we propose some basic AXU_2 and AU_2 hash functions. We use these functions as building blocks to construct efficient message authentication schemes.

2.1 AXU_2 Hash Functions Based on Block Cipher Design Techniques

Given a (keyed) non-linear function F, one can construct an AXU_2 hash function as follows. To hash a message x, two keys K and K_r are chosen randomly. The hash of x is $F(K, x \oplus K_r)$. If F is not a keyed transformation, then the hash of x is $F(x \oplus K_r)$. The role of the key K_r is to randomize the input of F since the maximum differential probability is defined for a randomly selected input and a constant input difference. The AXU_2 definition on the other hand requires both the input and the input difference to be constant. A more formal analysis is given below.

Lemma 1. *Let $F : \{0,1\}^k \times \{0,1\}^m \to \{0,1\}^n$ be a mapping that maps a pair of a k-bit key and a message (block) of length m into an n-bit string. The family of hash functions $\mathcal{H} = \{h_{K,K_r} : \{0,1\}^m \to \{0,1\}^n | K \in \{0,1\}^k, K_r \in \{0,1\}^m, h_{K,K_r}(x) = F(K, x \oplus K_r)\}$ is ϵ-AXU$_2$, where ϵ is equal to the maximum (expected) differential probability of F*

$$\mathrm{DP}_F = \max_{\Delta x \neq 0, \Delta y} \frac{\#\{(K, x) \in \{0,1\}^k \times \{0,1\}^m | F(K, x \oplus \Delta x) \oplus F(K, x) = \Delta y\}}{2^{m+k}}.$$

The non-linear function defined by four rounds of AES is a good candidate for constructing AXU hash functions. To hash a 128-bit block x, one selects four uniformly random keys and "encrypts" x using the four keys as round keys. Here, we assume that the key addition is at the beginning of the rounds, not at the end of the rounds. We also assume that the fourth round is a final AES round. It was shown in [33] that the maximum differential probability of four rounds of AES is at most about 2^{-113} when the round keys are independent. Hence, the hash function family $\mathcal{H}_{AES}$ consisting of the transformations defined by four rounds of AES for all possible values of the round keys is ϵ-AXU$_2$, where $\epsilon \approx 2^{-113}$. We propose two additional constructions.

The first AXU$_2$ family of hash functions that we suggest is defined by the Feistel structure depicted in Fig. 1. The 64-bit input is transformed into a 64-bit hash using three Feistel rounds. Each round uses a new 64-bit key. The round function is depicted in Fig. 1(b). It is constructed using AES components. That is, the S-box and the mixing transformation used in the round function are same as those used in AES. Each key defines a hash function that maps a 64-bit string (message) into a 64-bit hash, and we denote by $\mathcal{H}_{FES}$ the family of hash functions defined by the 2^{192} possible keys.

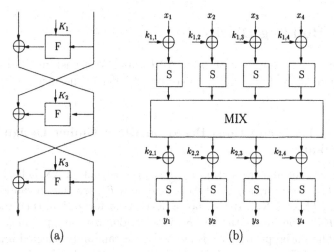

Fig. 1. A Feistel AXU construction: (a) the 64-bit message is hashed using three Feistel rounds with independent keys, (b) The round function is an SPN structure. The S-box and the mixing transformation are those used in AES.

The security of $\mathcal{H}_{FES}$ is provided by the following lemma.

Lemma 2. *The $\mathcal{H}_{FES}$ family of hash functions is ϵ-AXU$_2$, where $\epsilon = 1.52 \times 2^{-56}$.*

The second AXU$_2$ family of hash functions that we suggest is defined by the keyed nonlinear transformation shown in Fig. 2. It is a two-round SPN structure that transforms a 64-bit input into a 64-bit output. The S-box that is used in the construction is same as the one used in AES. The mixing transformation is given by the circulating-like MDS matrix proposed in [28] (p. 167). The multiplication and addition are over GF(256) modulo the irreducible polynomial $x^8 + x^4 + x^3 + x^2 + 1$ over GF(2). The coefficients are given by the following polynomials over GF(2): $a = x + 1$, $b = x^3 + 1$, $c = x^3 + x^2$, $d = x$, $e = x^2$ and $f = x^4$. Each key defines a hash function that maps a 64-bit message into a 64-bit hash, and we denote by $\mathcal{H}_{F64}$ the family of 2^{128} hash functions whose members are determined by the possible key values.

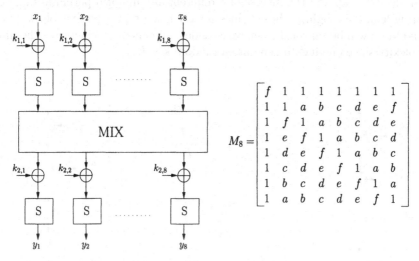

Fig. 2. An SPN AXU construction: (a) The global structure, (b) The 8×8 matrix used in the linear mixing layer. The multiplication and addition are over GF(256) modulo $x^8 + x^4 + x^3 + x^2 + 1$ over GF(2). The coefficients are $a = x + 1$, $b = x^3 + 1$, $c = x^3 + x^2$, $d = x$, $e = x^2$ and $f = x^4$.

The following lemma establishes the security of $\mathcal{H}_{F64}$.

Lemma 3. *The $\mathcal{H}_{F64}$ family of hash functions is ϵ-AXU$_2$, where $\epsilon = 1.25 \times 2^{-54}$.*

2.2 The AU$_2$ Hash Functions

Given a keyed non-linear function that can be represented as a composition of two non-linear transformations whose keys[1] are independent (see Fig. 3(a)), one can construct an AU hash function (see Fig. 3(b)) as follows.

Lemma 4 (Twisting Lemma). *Let $F(K, x)$ be defined as $F(K, x) = F_2(K_2, F_1(K_1, x) \oplus K_s)$, where $K = K_1 | K_s | K_2$, $F_1 : \{0, 1\}^{k_1} \times \{0, 1\}^l \to \{0, 1\}^n$, and $F_2 : \{\{0, 1\}^{k_2} \times \{0, 1\}^n \to \{0, 1\}^n\}$ is a bijection for any key value K_2.*

---

[1] We consider a more general case. However, F_1 and F_2 does not have to be keyed transformations (i.e., the lengths of the keys K_1 and K_2 can be zero as well).

Then, the family of hash functions $\mathcal{H} = \{h_{K_1,K_{r1},K_2,K_{r2}} : \{0,1\}^l \times \{0,1\}^n \rightarrow \{0,1\}^n | h_{K_1,K_{r1},K_2,K_{r2}}(x_1, x_2) = F_1(K_1, x_1 \oplus K_{r1}) \oplus F_2^{-1}(K_2, x_2 \oplus K_{r2})\}$ is an ϵ-AU_2, where $K_1 \in \{0,1\}^{k_1}$; $K_2 \in \{0,1\}^{k_2}$; $x_1, K_{r1} \in \{0,1\}^l$; $x_2, K_{r2} \in \{0,1\}^n$, and $\epsilon = \mathrm{DP}_F$.

The structure of the function F depicted in Fig. 3(a) can be found in almost any block cipher and allows for a variety of AU_2 hash function constructions by "twisting" block ciphers. One such example is the construction proposed in [40], which is depicted in Fig. 3(c). The function F in this case is a composition of an identity map and the inverse of a differentially uniform permutation. The twisting lemma is slightly abused since no key is added to the first block. Such key addition will be canceled when we consider differences and increases the time complexity since one has to generate a random key K_{r1}.

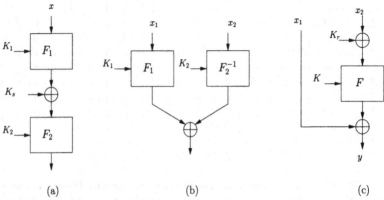

(a)   (b)   (c)

Fig. 3. AU_2 construction by "twisting" block ciphers: (a) the original non-linear transformation F, (b) the non-linear transformation F' obtained by "twisting" F, (c) AU_2 construction proposed in [40]

The general construction of Lemma 4 offers a somewhat greater level of parallelism than the one of Fig. 3(c) (one can evaluate F_1 and F_2 in parallel). However, the overall impact on the schemes proposed in this paper is not significant, and we use a variant of Fig. 3(c) which is derived by extending its domain to include messages of length 0 and 1 blocks:

$$g_F(x_1, x_2) = \begin{cases} \lambda & \text{if } x_1 = x_2 = \lambda \\ x_1 & \text{if } x_1 \neq \lambda, x_2 = \lambda \\ x_1 \oplus F(K, x_2 \oplus K_r) & \text{if } x_1 \neq \lambda, x_2 \neq \lambda \end{cases}$$

where λ is the empty string, $x_1, x_2 \in \{0,1\}^n \bigcup \{\lambda\}$, $K_r \in \{0,1\}^n$ and F is a (keyed) non-linear permutation on $\{0,1\}^n$.

Let $\mathcal{G}_F$ be the family of the hash functions defined as above. We have the following lemma.

Lemma 5. *The family of hash functions $\mathcal{G}_F$ is ϵ-AU_2, where $\epsilon = \mathrm{DP}_F$.*

The AU_2 families that we use are obtained when the AXU_2 hash function $F(K, K_r \oplus x)$ is realized using the transformations discussed in Section 2.1. We denote by $\mathcal{G}_{AES}$, $\mathcal{G}_{FES}$ and $\mathcal{G}_{F64}$ the families of hash functions when $F(K, K_r \oplus x)$ is realized using four AES rounds, the Feistel structure of Fig. 1 and the SPN structure of Fig. 2 respectively. According to the previous discussion, $\mathcal{G}_{AES}$, $\mathcal{G}_{FES}$ and $\mathcal{G}_{F64}$ are ϵ-AU_2 with ϵ being 2^{-113}, 1.52×2^{-56} and 1.25×2^{-54} correspondingly.

3 AXU_2 Hash Functions Defined for Arbitrary-Length Messages

The universal hash functions introduced in the previous section operate on message blocks. In this section, we consider some techniques for extending the domains to include arbitrary-length messages. The proposed constructions use a large number of keys. However, these keys are derived from a single 128-bit key in the message authentication scheme we propose in Section 4.

3.1 A CBC-Like Construction

CBC is a popular approach to MAC design. The Pelican MAC of [18] and the PCH (Periodic CBC Hash) of [40] resemble CBC as well. Here, we present another CBC-like family of hash functions $\mathcal{H}_{UHC}$ (Universal Hash Chaining). The advantage of UHC over the Pelican construction is that it is proven secure. Its advantage over PCH is that the security does not decrease with the message length. Assuming small differential probabilities, the provided upper bound on the collision probability of PCH is roughly $l^2/2^n$, where l is the message length and n is the block length. If the message length is about 2^{40}, this results in about 2^{-50} proven security when using four rounds of AES as a building block. The proven security of UHC in this case will be about 2^{-112}.

$\mathcal{H}_{UHC}$ is depicted in Fig. 4. We assume that F is a permutation on the set of n-bit strings for a given key. To hash a message consisting of l segments of m blocks, we select randomly $m - 2$ randomization keys $K_3^r, \ldots, K_m^r$ and $m - 1$ keys $K_2, K_3, \ldots, K_m$ for the non-linear map F. These keys are used for all segments of the message. In addition, two fresh randomization keys $K_{i,1}^r, K_{i,2}^r$ and a fresh key $K_{i,1}$ for the non-linear map are selected anew for each segment of the message. The message is "digested" in a CBC-like manner using these keys as depicted in Fig. 4. The resulting family of hash functions is AXU_2.

Lemma 6. $\mathcal{H}_{UHC}$ is ϵ-AXU_2, where $\epsilon = 2\mathrm{DP}_F$.

3.2 A Modified Wegman-Carter Binary Tree Construction

MACH, the MAC scheme that we propose, uses the following variant of the Wegman-Carter binary tree hash.

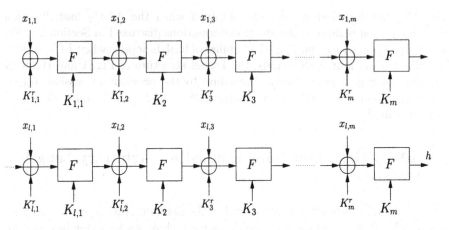

Fig. 4. A CBC-like AXU construction. Fresh keys are used only for the first two blocks of each segment.

To hash a message M consisting of l blocks[2], we first "append" λ-"blocks" [3] so that the number of blocks in the message is a multiple of 2^N. The resulting λ-padded message is partitioned into segments consisting of 2^N blocks. Each segment is hashed using the same secret member of $\mathcal{G}_F$ in a binary hash tree of height N. Recall that that the members of $\mathcal{G}_F$ were defined as $g_F(x_1, x_2) = x_1 \oplus F(K, K_r \oplus x_2)$ if x_2 is not λ, $g_F(x_1, \lambda) = x_1$, and $g_F(\lambda, \lambda) = \lambda$, where F is a (keyed) non-linear permutation on n-bit strings. The output of each binary tree is hashed using F as in Lemma 1, and the resulting n-bit blocks are xored to give the final hash value. The keys used in the last step are generated independently for different segments of the message. We use $\mathcal{H}_{MACH}^F(N)$ to denote the family of hash functions described above. An example when $N = 2$ is given in Fig.5.

The time complexity of the MACH hash is determined by the time to generate the required keys, and the time to hash the message. Assuming that the keys are already generated, the time to hash the message is one F evaluation per n-bit block of the message, and it is same as that of UHC. The same levels of the binary trees in the MACH hash use the same key. So, one has to generate and memorize N keys that will be used by the binary trees. In addition, one has to generate one potentially large key per segment for the last step of the hashing procedure. Since the length of the segments is 2^N blocks, the MACH hash is advantageous over the UHC hash where one has to generate fresh keys every N blocks.

Using a single binary tree will lead to greater speedup for long messages. However, one will have to memorize a large number of keys to allow hashing of lengthy messages. In the MACH hash, the fresh keys can be "thrown away"

---

[2] We assume that the message length is a multiple of the block length.

[3] The sole purpose of the λ padding is to simplify our description and analysis. In practice, the λ padding will be omitted.

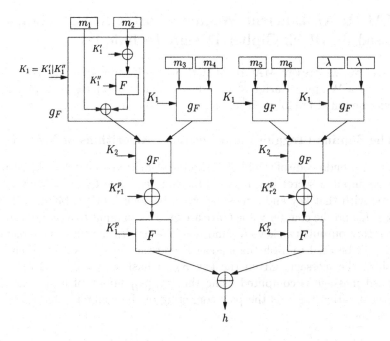

Fig. 5. An AXU_2 construction using a modification of the Wegman-Carter binary tree $(N = 2)$

after their use. So, by carefully selecting the value of N, one can achieve close to a single-binary-tree speed while significantly improving the key agility and memory efficiency compared to the single-binary-tree construction.

$\mathcal{H}^F_{MACH}(N)$ is basically a composition of an AU_2 hash function (the binary trees in parallel) and an AXU_2 hash function (the xor of the AXU_2 hash functions). As it was case with the $\mathcal{H}_{UHC}$, the security of $\mathcal{H}^F_{MACH}(N)$ does not decrease with the message length.

Lemma 7. $\mathcal{H}^F_{MACH}(N)$ *is an* ϵ-AXU_2 *family of hash functions, where* $\epsilon = (N + 1) \times DP_F$.

The message authentication schemes that we propose in this paper use the $\mathcal{H}^{AES}_{MACH}(5)$, $\mathcal{H}^{FES}_{MACH}(7)$ and $\mathcal{H}^{F64}_{MACH}(7)$ hash function families. Here, $\mathcal{H}^{AES}_{MACH}(5)$ is the MACH hash functions where the binary trees are of height 5, the AU hash function family used in the binary trees is $\mathcal{G}_{AES}$ of Section 2.2, and the AXU hash function family used in the last step is the $\mathcal{H}_{AES}$ hash function family described in Section 2.1. Similarly, $\mathcal{H}^{FES}_{MACH}(7)$ (resp., $\mathcal{H}^{F64}_{MACH}(7)$) is the MACH hash function family that uses binary trees of height 7, and whose non-linear function F is implemented using the Feistel (resp., SPN) structure of Fig. 1 (resp., Fig. 2).

4 MACH: An Efficient Wegman-Carter MAC Scheme Based on Block Cipher Design Techniques

In this section, we present MACH. MACH, where H stands for the use of hash functions, is a Wegman-Carter MAC scheme that is obtained by applying the technique presented in [46] to $\mathcal{H}_{MACH}^F$.

4.1 The Signing (Tagging) and Verifying Algorithms of MACH

Signing. A pseudo-code of the MACH signing algorithm is given in Algorithm 1. It takes as input a secret key K, a 64-bit counter value $Cntr <$ MAX_CNTR associated with that key and a message M of bit length $|M| <$ MAX_LEN. The secret key K and the counter value $Cntr$ are used as an input to a pseudorandom generator that outputs two keys K_h and K_T. The key K_h specifies which member $\mathcal{H}_{MACH}^F$ will be used to hash the messages, and the key K_T is used to encrypt the hash of the message. Given the key K_h, a hash $h = h_{K_h}(M|10^i)$ of the 10^i padded message is computed using the $\mathcal{H}_{MACH}^F$ family of hash functions. The authentication tag τ is the pair consisting of the counter value $Cntr$ and $h_\tau = h \oplus K_T$.

Algorithm 1. MACH.Sign(K,$Cntr$,M)

Input: A (128-bit) secret key K, a 64-bit counter value $Cntr$ and a message M.
Output: An authentication tag τ.

$Cntr + +$
len $\leftarrow |M|$ // len is the bit length of the message M.
$K_h, K_T \leftarrow$ Gen($Cntr, K$)

$i \leftarrow (n - ((\text{len} + 1) \bmod n)) \bmod n$
$h \leftarrow h_{K_h}(M|10^i)$
$h_\tau \leftarrow h \oplus K_T$

return $\tau \equiv (Cntr, h_\tau)$

The keys K_h and K_T can be generated using a pseudorandom generator (i.e., a stream cipher). The key generation in this case will be faster than using a block cipher, and the resulting scheme will be more competitive for small message lengths. However, there are some practical advantages of generating the keys using a block cipher in a counter-like mode. So, we suggest the keys to be generated using AES as follows. The key K_T is computed as $K_T = \text{trun}(AES_K(1|0^{63}|Cntr))$, where $Cntr$ is a 64-bit counter value, and $\text{trun}(\cdot)$ selects the first $|h|$ bits of $AES_K(1|0^{63}|Cntr)$. The words of the key K_h are computed as $K_h[i] = AES_K(0^{64}|\langle i \rangle)$, where $\langle i \rangle$ is a 64-bit representation of i. If the length of K_h is not a multiple of 128, then the last "word" $K_h[\text{K\_BLCKS}]$ of K_h is derived by selecting the first $|K_h[\text{K\_BLCKS}]|$ bits of $AES_K(0^{64}|\langle \text{K\_BLCKS} \rangle)$. Here, K_BLCKS is the number of blocks in K_h, and it is determined by the length of the key material we need to hash a message of length MAX_LEN.

Remark. To simplify our description and security analysis, we have assumed that the key K_h is generated at the beginning, and that it is long enough to hash messages of maximum length. Clearly, such implementation is not practical at all. In practice, to avoid expensive key setup and increase the memory efficiency of the scheme, the keys will be generated on the fly, and only a small portion of the keys (e.g., the keys used by the binary trees) will be memorized when computing the hash of the message.

Verifying. Given a message M, an authentication tag $\tau = (Cntr, h_\tau)$ associated with the message and the secret key K, the verifier computes the keys K_h, K_T, and recomputes the authentication tag using these keys. If the recomputed tag $(Cntr, K_T \oplus h_{K_h}(M|10^i))$ is equal to the one that was sent, then the verifier accepts the message M as authentic. Otherwise, the verifier rejects the message M.

4.2 Security of MACH

The security of MACH is established by the following theorem.

Theorem 1. *The advantage of any forger of MACH that runs in at most t time and makes at most q_v forgery attempts is upper bounded by*

$$\mathbf{Adv}_{MACH}^{\mathrm{wuf-cma}}(t, q_v) \leq \mathbf{Adv}_{AES}^{\mathrm{prp}}(c_1 t + c_2, Q_e) + q_v (1 - \frac{Q_e - 1}{2^{128}})^{-Q_e/2}(N+1)\mathrm{DP}_F,$$

where c_1 and c_2 are small implementation dependent constant, $Q_e = $ K_BLCKS$+$ MAX_CNTR, N is the height of the binary trees used by the hash function, DP_F is the maximum differential probability of the nonlinear permutation F used by the hash function, and $\mathbf{Adv}_{AES}^{\mathrm{prp}}(c_1 t + c_2, Q_e)$ is the advantage of distinguishing AES from a random permutation when running in at most $c_1 t + c_2$ time and querying an encryption oracle at Q_e distinct message blocks.

4.3 MACH Variants, Security and Performance Comparison

We suggest three MACH variants MACH-AES, MACH-FES and MACH-F64. As their names suggest, the proposed MACH variants are obtained when the messages are hashed using $\mathcal{H}_{MACH}^{AES}(5)$, $\mathcal{H}_{MACH}^{FES}(7)$ and $\mathcal{H}_{MACH}^{F64}(7)$ respectively (see Section 3.2 for a description of these hash functions). In the following, we briefly discuss the security and performance of these schemes.

Security. A comparison of the proposed variants in terms of their security and the speedup over the modes for message authentication that use AES as a building block is given in Table 1. The security expressions are derived using Theorem 1. We assume that both K_BLCKS and MAX_CNTR are 2^{64}. The number of encryption queries in this case will be $Q_e = 2^{65}$, and δ is the advantage of distinguishing AES from a random permutation given Q_e pairs of plaintext/ciphertext blocks.

Table 1. Security and performance comparison of the MACH variants

Scheme	Speedup over message authentication modes						Security
	8-bit c.a.		32-bit c.a.		64-bit c.a.		
	1 KB	∞	1 KB	∞	1 KB	∞	
MACH-AES	1.25	2.10	1.19	1.90	1.19	1.90	$\delta + q_v \times 1.28 \times 2^{-110}$
MACH-FES	2.37	3.76	1.99	2.88	1.99	2.88	$\delta + q_v \times 1.30 \times 2^{-52}$
MACH-F64	1.85	2.10	1.51	1.86	2.10 – 2.94	2.81 – 4.64	$\delta + q_v \times 1.07 \times 2^{-50}$

The tag length and the security of MACH-FES and MACH-F64 are comparable to those of the modes of operation for message authentication using AES as a building block. Note that the security of MACH-FES and MACH-F64 is determined by the number of forgery attempts. If the application allows the verifier to limit the number of forgery attempts, then one can achieve good security for a large number of very long messages. For example, assume that the verifier keeps a track of the number of invalid message/tag pairs. If this number exceeds 2^{20}, then the verifier assumes it is under attack and rejects any subsequent message. Under these circumstances, we can use MACH-FES and MACH-F64 to authenticate 2^{64} messages of length $\gtrsim 2^{64}$ blocks with $\approx 2^{-30}$ forgery probability. However, using 2^{64} signing queries and a single forgery attempt, one can easily break most of the existing modes of operation for message authentication. If the maximum allowed message length is relatively large, then the security of MACH-FES and MACH-F64 is comparable or better than that of the polynomial-based constructions too. For example, if one allows messages of length $> 2^{52}$ blocks, then the proven security of Poly1305-AES becomes smaller than that of MACH-FES and MACH-F64.

Assuming that the advantage of distinguishing AES from a random permutation given 2^{65} plaintext/ciphertext pairs is small, MACH-AES provides significantly better security than MACH-FES and MACH-F64. The tag length (including the counter) of MACH-AES is 192 bits, and it is larger than that of the modes of operations for message authentication.

Performance. Performance evaluation of a given message authentication scheme is not an easy task since it depends on the specific platform, the implementation of the algorithms and the message length distribution. The speedup estimates given in Table 1 are computed by making the following assumption: the algorithms are implemented using basic arithmetic and memory reference instructions available on RISC computer architectures. The speedup is computed by dividing the time needed to compute the tag using AES in a message authentication mode and the time needed to compute the tag using the proposed schemes. The execution time on the other hand is estimated based on the number of arithmetic and memory reference instructions required to compute the tag.

We have considered two cases. In the first case, which is denoted 1 KB, the message length is 1024 bytes as in [7]. The speedup in this case approximates the speedup when the message length distribution follows the IP packet size distribution on the Internet. The time to compute the tag in this case includes the time needed to generate all the keys that are required to hash the message. In the second case, which is denoted ∞, we assume that the keys used by the binary trees of the hash function are already generated and memorized. The time to compute the tag includes the time needed to generate the fresh keys used for the different segments of the message, but it does not include the time to generate the keys used by the binary trees in the MACH hash. The speedup in the second case approximates the speedup when authenticating a single long message or authenticating a relatively long sequence of short messages (e.g., stream authentication, authenticating the packets exchanged between two routers in a VPN, authenticating the packets exchanged during a single communication session, etc.).

MACH-AES and MACH-FES use AES components as building blocks. Hence, the estimation of their speedups is easier. The key generation cost is one AES encryption per 128 bits of the key material. Given the keys, the cost of hashing per 128-bit block is about 4 AES rounds for MACH-AES and 3 AES rounds for MACH-FES on 32-bit and 64-bit architectures. The AES matrix multiplication is relatively costly on 8-bit architectures (about 40 arithmetic operations). The mixing transformation is omitted in the fourth round of the non-linear function used by MACH-AES. Thus, on 8-bit architectures, the cost of hashing is about 3.5 AES rounds per 128-bit block when using MACH-AES. For similar reasons, the cost of hashing is about 2.2 AES rounds per 128-bit block on 8-bit architectures when using MACH-FES.

MACH-F64 uses an 8×8 multiplication matrix which is not a component of AES. Hence, the computation of the speedup is more complicated. A detailed discussion on implementing this matrix multiplication on various platforms can be found in [28]. We will only note that the largest speedup values on 64-bit architectures are computed assuming that the non-linear transformation of MACH-F64 is implemented using 8 look-up tables each one containing 256 64-bit entries. The memory required to store these tables is 16 KB, which is a relatively small portion of the L1 cache of many processors. For example, AMD Athlon, Ultra-Sparc III and Alpha 21264 have 64 KB L1 cache, PowerPC G4 and G5 have 32 KB L1 cache, etc.

Summary. MACH-AES is less time and memory efficient than MACH-FES and MACH-F64. However, it provides much better security, and the achievable speedup over the message authentication modes is significant in some settings. MACH-F64 and MACH-FES provide security and tag lengths that are comparable to those of the message authentication modes. The target computer architecture of the MACH-F64 design was a 64-bit architecture with large L1 cache, and it is extremely efficient on these architectures. MACH-FES on the other hand is very efficient on 8-bit architectures, and achieves a significant speedup on 32- and 64-bit architectures as well. Both MACH-AES and MACH-FES are built using AES components. So, they have the advantage of reusing AES software and hardware.

References

1. Afanassiev, V., Gehrmann, C., Smeets, B.: Fast message authentication using efficient polynomial evaluation. In: Biham, E. (ed.) FSE 1997. LNCS, vol. 1267, pp. 190–204. Springer, Heidelberg (1997)
2. Bellare, M., Kilian, J., Rogaway, P.: The security of the cipher block chaining message authentication code, JCSS 61(3), 2000. In: Desmedt, Y.G. (ed.) CRYPTO 1994. LNCS, vol. 839, pp. 341–358. Springer, Heidelberg (1994)
3. Bellare, M., Canetti, R., Krawczyk, H.: Keying hash functions for message authentication. In: Koblitz, N. (ed.) CRYPTO 1996. LNCS, vol. 1109, p. 1. Springer, Heidelberg (1996)
4. Bellare, M., Namprempre, C.: Authenticated encryption: relations among notions and analysis of the generic composition paradigm. In: Okamoto, T. (ed.) ASIACRYPT 2000. LNCS, vol. 1976, Springer, Heidelberg (2000)
5. Bellare, M.: New Proofs for NMAC and HMAC: Security without Collision-Resistance. In: Dwork, C. (ed.) CRYPTO 2006. LNCS, vol. 4117, Springer, Heidelberg (2006)
6. Berendschot, A., den Boer, B., Boly, J.P., Bosselaers, A., Brandt, J., Chaum, D., Damgard, I., Dichtl, M., Fumy, W., van der Ham, M., Jansen, C.J.A., Landrock, P., Preneel, B., Roelofsen, G., de Rooij, P., Vandewalle, J.: Final Report of RACE Integrity Primitives. In: Bosselaers, A., Preneel, B. (eds.) Integrity Primitives for Secure Information Systems. LNCS, vol. 1007, Springer, Heidelberg (1995)
7. Bernstein, D.: Stronger security bounds for Wegman-Carter-Shoup authenticators. In: Cramer, R.J.F. (ed.) EUROCRYPT 2005. LNCS, vol. 3494, pp. 164–180. Springer, Heidelberg (2005)
8. Bernstein, D.: The Poly1305-AES message authentication code. In: Gilbert, H., Handschuh, H. (eds.) FSE 2005. LNCS, vol. 3557, pp. 32–49. Springer, Heidelberg (2005)
9. Bierbrauer, J., Johansson, T., Kabatianskii, G., Smeets, B.: On families of hash functions via geometric codes and concatenation. In: Proceedings of CRYPTO 1993. LNCS, pp. 331–342. Springer, Heidelberg (1993)
10. Biham, E., Shamir, A.: Differential cryptanalysis of DES-like cryptosystems. Journal of Cryptology 4(1), 3–72 (1991)
11. Biham, E., Dunkelman, O., Keller, N.: Related-key impossible differential attacks on 8-round AES-192. In: Pointcheval, D. (ed.) CT-RSA 2006. LNCS, vol. 3860, pp. 21–33. Springer, Heidelberg (2006)
12. Black, J., Halevi, S., Krawczyk, H., Krovetz, T., Rogaway, P.: UMAC: Fast and secure message authentication. In: Advances in Cryptology - CRYPTO 1999. LNCS, pp. 216–233. Springer, Heidelberg (1999)
13. Black, J., Rogaway, P.: CBC MACs for arbitrary-length messages: The three key constructions. In: Bellare, M. (ed.) CRYPTO 2000. LNCS, vol. 1880, pp. 197–215. Springer, Heidelberg (2000)
14. Black, J., Rogaway, P.: A block-cipher mode of operation for parallelizable message authentication. In: Knudsen, L.R. (ed.) EUROCRYPT 2002. LNCS, vol. 2332, pp. 384–397. Springer, Heidelberg (2002)
15. Brassard, G.: On computationally secure authentication tags requiring short secret shared keys. In: Advances in Cryptology - CRYPTO 1982. LNCS, pp. 79–86. Springer, Heidelberg (1982)
16. Carter, L., Wegman, M.: Universal classes of hash functions. JCSS 22, 265–279 (1981)

17. Daemen, J., Rijmen, V.: A New MAC Construction ALRED and a Specific Instance ALPHA-MAC. In: Gilbert, H., Handschuh, H. (eds.) FSE 2005. LNCS, vol. 3557, pp. 1–17. Springer, Heidelberg (2005)
18. Daemen, J., Rijmen, V.: The Pelican MAC Function, IACR ePrint Archive, 2005/088
19. Etzel, M., Patel, S., Ramzan, Z.: Square Hash: Fast message authentication via optimized universal hash functions. In: Wiener, M.J. (ed.) CRYPTO 1999. LNCS, vol. 1666, Springer, Heidelberg (1999)
20. FIPS 113. Computer data authentication. Federal Information Processing Standards Publication 113, U. S. Department of Commerce / National Bureau of Standards, National Technical Information Service, Springfield, Virginia (1994)
21. Advanced Encryption Standard (AES), FIPS Publication 197 (November 26, 2001), available at http://csrc.nist.gov/encryption/aes
22. Gilbert, E., Williams, F.M., Sloane, N.: Codes which detect deception. Bell System Technical Journal 53(3), 405–424 (1974)
23. Halevi, S., Krawczyk, H.: MMH: Message authentication in software in the gbit/second rates. In: Proceedings of the 4th FSE Workshop. LNCS, Springer, Heidelberg (1997)
24. Hong, S., Lee, S., Lim, J., Sung, J., Cheon, D., Cho, I.: Provable security against differential and linear cryptanalysis for the SPN structure. In: Schneier, B. (ed.) FSE 2000. LNCS, vol. 1978, pp. 273–283. Springer, Heidelberg (2001)
25. ISO/IEC 9797-1. Information technology - security techniques - data integrity mechanism using a cryptographic check function employing a block cipher algorithm. International Organization for Standards, Geneva, Switzerland, Second edn. (1999)
26. Iwata, T., Kurosawa, K.: OMAC: One-Key CBC MAC. In: Johansson, T. (ed.) FSE 2003. LNCS, vol. 2887, pp. 129–153. Springer, Heidelberg (2003)
27. Jaulmes, É., Joux, A., Valette, F.: On the security of randomized CBC-MAC beyond the birthday paradox limit: A new construction. In: Daemen, J., Rijmen, V. (eds.) FSE 2002. LNCS, vol. 2365, pp. 237–251. Springer, Heidelberg (2002)
28. Junod, P.: Statistical Cryptanalysis of Block Ciphers, PhD Thesis, EPF, Switzerland
29. Kaliski, B., Robshaw, M.: Message authentication with MD5. Technical newsletter of RSA Laboratories (1995)
30. Kang, J.-S., Hong, S., Lee, S., Yi, O., Park, C., Lim, J.: Practical and provable security against differential and linear cryptanalysis for substitution-permutation networks. ETRI Journal 23(4), 158–167 (2001)
31. Keliher, L., Meijer, H., Tavares, S.: New method for upper bounding the maximum average linear hull probability for SPNs. In: Pfitzmann, B. (ed.) EUROCRYPT 2001. LNCS, vol. 2045, pp. 420–436. Springer, Heidelberg (2001)
32. Keliher, L., Meijer, H., Tavares, S.: Improving the upper bound on the maximum average linear hull probability for Rijndael. In: Vaudenay, S., Youssef, A.M. (eds.) SAC 2001. LNCS, vol. 2259, pp. 112–128. Springer, Heidelberg (2001)
33. Keliher, L., Sui, J.: Exact Maximum Expected Differential and Linear Probability for 2-Round Advanced Encryption Standard (AES), IACR ePrint Archive, 2005/321
34. Kelsey, J., Schneier, B., Wagner, D.: Related-key cryptanalysis of 3-WAY, Biham-DES, CAST, DES-X, NewDES, RC2 and TEA. In: Han, Y., Quing, S. (eds.) ICICS 1997. LNCS, vol. 1334, pp. 233–246. Springer, Heidelberg (1997)
35. Krawczyk, H.: LFSR-Based Hashing and Authentication. In: Desmedt, Y.G. (ed.) CRYPTO 1994. LNCS, vol. 839, pp. 129–139. Springer, Heidelberg (1994)

36. Krovetz, T., Rogaway, P.: Fast universal hashing with small keys and no preprocessing: The PolyR construction. In: Proceedings of ICICS 2000, pp. 73–89. Springer, Heidelberg (2000)
37. Kurosawa, K., Iwata, T.: TMAC: Two-Key CBC MAC, Cryptology ePrint Archive, Report 2002/092, http://eprint.iacr.org/
38. Matsui, M.: New Structure of Block Ciphers with Provable Security against Differential and Linear Cryptanalysis. In: Gollmann, D. (ed.) Fast Software Encryption. LNCS, vol. 1039, Springer, Heidelberg (1996)
39. Matsui, M.: New block encryption algorithm MISTY. In: Biham, E. (ed.) FSE 1997. LNCS, vol. 1267, pp. 53–67. Springer, Heidelberg (1997)
40. Minematsu, K., Tsunoo, Y.: Provably Secure MACs from Differentially-Uniform Permutations and AES-Based Implementations. In: Robshaw, M. (ed.) FSE 2006. LNCS, vol. 4047, pp. 226–241. Springer, Heidelberg (2006)
41. Park, S., Sung, S.H., Chee, S., Yoon, E.-J., Lim, J.: On the security of Rijndael-like structures against differential and linear cryptanalysis. In: Zheng, Y. (ed.) ASIACRYPT 2002. LNCS, vol. 2501, pp. 176–191. Springer, Heidelberg (2002)
42. Park, S., Sung, S.H., Lee, S., Lim, J.: Improving the upper bound on the maximum differential and the maximum linear hull probability for SPN structures and AES. In: Johansson, T. (ed.) FSE 2003. LNCS, vol. 2887, pp. 247–260. Springer, Heidelberg (2003)
43. Petrank, E., Rackoff, C.: CBC MAC for real-time data sources. J.Cryptology 13(3), 315–338 (2000)
44. Preneel, B., van Oorschot, P.: MDx-MAC and building fast MACs from hash functions. In: Coppersmith, D. (ed.) CRYPTO 1995. LNCS, vol. 963, pp. 1–14. Springer, Heidelberg (1995)
45. Preneel, B., van Oorschot, P.: On the security of two MAC algorithms. In: Maurer, U.M. (ed.) EUROCRYPT 1996. LNCS, vol. 1070, pp. 19–32. Springer, Heidelberg (1996)
46. Rogaway, P.: Bucket hashing and its application to fast message authentication. In: Coppersmith, D. (ed.) CRYPTO 1995. LNCS, vol. 963, pp. 29–42. Springer, Heidelberg (1995)
47. Simmons, G.J.: Authentication theory Coding theory. In: Advances of Cryptology - CRYPTO 1984. LNCS, pp. 411–432. Springer, Heidelberg (1984)
48. Stinson, D.: Universal hashing and authentication codes. Designs, Codes and Cryptography 4, 369–380 (1994)
49. Tsudik, G.: Message authentication with one-way hash functions. In: Proceedings of Infocom 1992, IEEE Press, Los Alamitos (1992)
50. Vaudenay, S.: Decorrelation over infinite domains: The encrypted CBC-MAC case. Communications in Information and Systems (CIS) 1, 75–85
51. Wegman, M., Carter, L.: New hash functions and their use in authentication and set equality. JCSS 22, 265–279 (1981)

Symmetric Key Cryptography on Modern Graphics Hardware

Jason Yang and James Goodman

Advanced Micro Devices, Inc.
Graphics Product Group
{jasonc.yang,jim.goodman}@amd.com

Abstract. GPUs offer a tremendous amount of computational bandwidth that was until now largely unusable for cryptographic computations due to a lack of integer arithmetic and user-friendly programming APIs that provided direct access to the GPU's computing resources. The latest generation of GPUs, which introduces integer/binary arithmetic, has been leveraged to create several implementations of the AES and DES symmetric key algorithms. Both conventional and bitsliced implementations are described that achieve data rates on the order of 3-30 Gbps from a single AMD HD 2900 XT graphics card, yielding speedups of 6-60x over equivalent implementations on high-performance CPUs.

1 Introduction

In recent years, there has been significant interest from both academia and industry in applying commodity graphics processing units (GPUs) toward general computing problems [1]. This trend toward *general-purpose computation on GPUs* (GPGPU) is spurred by the large number of arithmetic units and the high memory bandwidth available in today's GPUs. In certain applications, where there is a high compute to memory bandwidth ratio (a.k.a., arithmetic intensity) the GPU has the potential to be orders of magnitude faster than conventional CPUs due to the parallel nature of GPUs versus CPUs, which are inherently optimized for sequential code. In addition, the computational power of GPUs is growing at a faster rate than what Moore's Law predicts for CPUs (Figure 1).

With the introduction of native integer and binary operations in the latest generation of GPUs, we believe that bulk encryption and its related applications (e.g., key searching) are ideally suited to the GPGPU programming model. In this paper we demonstrate the viability of the GPGPU programming model for implementing symmetric key ciphers on GPUs. We examine high-efficiency bitsliced implementations of the AES and DES algorithms, as well as compare conventional block-based implementations of AES on previous/current generation GPUs. We demonstrate AES and DES running on an AMD HD 2900 XT GPU to be up to 16 and 60 times faster respectively than high end CPUs.

The following section describes previous work related to implementing symmetric cryptographic algorithms on GPUs and vector-based processors. Next we describe GPU hardware architecture and programming APIs to provide context

K. Kurosawa (Ed.): ASIACRYPT 2007, LNCS 4833, pp. 249–264, 2007.

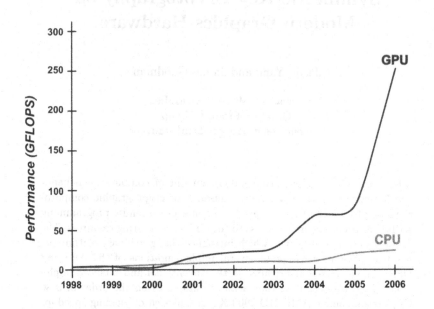

Fig. 1. GPU vs. CPU GFLOPS performance over time

for the GPGPU programming model. Bitsliced implementations of DES and AES are then described in the context of high-performance GPGPU-accelerated key searching applications that demonstrate the potential speedup of GPUs over conventional CPUs in certain classes of problems. Lastly, a comparison of a conventional block-based implementation of AES on both the current and previous generations of GPUs is presented to illustrate the computational advantages of the latest generation of GPUs.

2   Previous Work

Cook et al. [2] were the first to investigate the feasibility of using GPUs for symmetric key encryption. Using OpenGL they implemented AES on various previous-generation GPUs. Unfortunately, the limited capability of the graphics programming model they used limited their performance and prevented them from exploiting some of the programmable features of their hardware. Instead they were forced to use a fixed-function pipeline, rely on color maps to transform bytes, and exploit a hardware XOR unit in the output-merger stage. A complete execution of AES required multiple passes through the pipeline, which significantly impacted their performance. Their experiments found that the GPU could only perform at about 2.3% of the CPU rate when both were running code optimized for their individual instruction sets. A recent OpenGL implementation [3] on a NVIDIA Geforce 8800 GTS achieves rates of almost 3 Gbps.

Vector processors have been considered for implementation of symmetric algorithms such as DES [4], and cryptography in general [5], which yielded some performance increase. Recently, Costigan and Scott [6] implemented RSA using the vector units of the Cell processor. They were able to achieve rates up to 7× faster using 6 vector units (SPU) over the onboard PowerPC unit (PPU).

3   GPGPU Programming Model

The latest generation of GPUs (e.g., Nvidia's 8000 series or AMD's HD 2000 series) has adopted the unified shader programming model pioneered by AMD in the Xbox 360's GPU [7]. In the unified shader model, all graphics functions are executed on programmable ALUs that can handle the different types of programs (i.e., shader programs) that need to be run by the different stages of the conventional graphics pipeline. The programmable nature of these ALUs can be exploited to implement non-graphics functions using a virtualized SIMD processing programming model that operates on streams of data. In this programming model, arrays of input data elements stored in memory are mapped one-to-one onto the virtualized SIMD array, which executes a shader program to generate one or more outputs that are then written back to output arrays in memory. Each instance of a shader program running on a virtualized SIMD array element is called a thread. The GPU and its components map the array of threads onto a finite pool of physical shader processors (SPs) by scheduling the available resources in the GPU such that each element of the virtual SIMD array is eventually processed, at which point additional shader programs can also be executed until the application has completed. A simplified view of the GPGPU programming model and mapping of threads to the GPUs processing resources is shown in Figure 2.

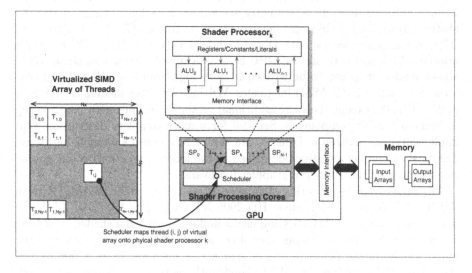

Fig. 2. Simplified view of the GPGPU programming model and thread mapping

Table 1. GPU characteristics

	X1950 XTX	HD 2900 XT
# of SP Units	48	64
# of ALU Units	192	320
# of Memory Fetch Units	16	16
SP Frequency	650 MHz	750 MHz
Memory Frequency	1 GHz	825 MHz
Memory Bandwidth	64 GB/s	105.60 GB/s
Local Memory Size	1 GB	1 GB

Modern GPUs are designed to be very efficient at running large numbers of threads (e.g., thousands/millions) in a manner that is transparent to the application/user. The GPU uses the large number of threads to hide memory access latencies by having the resource scheduler switch the active thread in a given SP whenever the current thread finds itself stalled waiting for a memory access to complete. Time multiplexing is also used in the SPs' ALUs to execute multiple threads concurrently and hide the latency of ALU operations via pipelining. Both of these techniques require that a thread contains a large number of calculations to improve the ability of the resource scheduler to hide the aforementioned latencies. When that condition is satisfied, the entire computational bandwidth of the GPU can be utilized to help GPGPU applications achieve performance increases on the order of $10 - 100\times$ over conventional CPUs.

DirectX [8] and OpenGL [9] are the standard programming APIs for GPUs and provide high-level languages for writing shader programs (e.g., HLSL and GLSL). However, these APIs are optimized for graphics and are difficult to use for non-graphics developers. Recently several projects have begun to try and abstract away the graphics-specific aspects of traditional GPU APIs ([10], [11], [12]). In this paper we use both DirectX and CTM [13], AMD's GPU hardware interface API, which treats the GPU as a data parallel virtual machine. CTM allows shader programs to be written in both high-level (e.g., HLSL) and low-level (e.g., native GPU ASM) languages. Writing high-level shaders is similar to writing C code, except there are additional vector data types with multiple (up to four) accessible components. See [14] for a more complete description. Our implementations written in DirectX can run on any DirectX capable hardware. The bitsliced implementations described in the following sections could also be implemented on most modern graphics hardware.

All of the experiments in this work were conducted on either an AMD Radeon X1950 XTX or an AMD Radeon HD 2900 XT GPU. The HD 2900 XT is the latest generation of AMD GPUs and uses a unified, superscalar shader processing architecture. Shader processors also share a limited number of memory fetch units, which are the physical devices that access memory. Table 1 summarizes the relevant GPU feature sets. With significantly more ALUs than memory fetch units, GPUs perform better on applications with high arithmetic intensity.

4   High-Performance Bitsliced DES Key Searching Application

Bitslicing was first suggested by Biham in [15] as a means of exploiting large word widths in conventional CPUs to increase the bandwidth of software implementations of symmetric algorithms. The HD 2900 XT can be utilized in a variety of configurations due to its flexible superscalar architecture. For this application we utilized it as a $2 \times 64-$bit wide processor with 64 individual processing cores to implement a bitsliced implementation of DES [16] for use in a key search application implemented using AMD's CTM GPGPU programming infrastructure. The full width of the GPU (160-bits) was not used as the resulting register requirements to store the entire cipher state and key vector would limit the number of threads executing at any given time, reducing overall program performance.

The key search application partitions the key space of size 2^{56} into 2^{22} independent jobs that each check 2^{34} keys. Each job is composed of 2^{12} (64×64) individual program invocations (threads), each of which is run on a shader processor using an optimized bitsliced DES shader program written in the GPUs native assembly language. Each shader program computes 64 DES calculations in parallel, and iterates a total of 2^{16} times, for a total of 2^{22} key checks per thread. In general such a brute force searching application is of limited use, but combined with a directed, template-based approach, such as that used in popular password recovery utilities, or in conjunction with side channel techniques that are used to find a subset of the secret key bytes, it can prove to be a very potent tool capable of operating substantially faster than conventional CPU implementations.

The bitsliced DES shader program utilizes the XOR, AND, OR, and NOT instructions of the GPU to implement the necessary functions, which are primarily the eight DES S-boxes. Matthew Kwan's optimized DES S-box implementations [17] were utilized as the basis for our implementation. Modifications were made to both the data format and S-box functions to enable two S-boxes to be computed concurrently (e.g., sbox15 = sbox1 and sbox5) as a means of reducing the execution time by almost a factor of 2. Table 2 compares the performance of the conventional and parallelized S-box implementations. The even/odd round distinction is required due to the alternating write-back of the left and right cipher states in the even/odd rounds when you leave the cipher state in place to eliminate DES' right/left state swapping. The difference in instruction counts between the even/odd versions is due to the insertion of NOPs to avoid write conflicts within the ALU/register interface.

S-box parallelization, combined with a reduction in the number of registers needed by the shader program, more than offset the fact that we are only able to use less than half of the full 160-bit width available in the shader processor for bitslicing. The net effect is approximately 2.5× increase in overall performance using the 64-bit solution with S-box parallelization compared to a full-width (i.e., 128-bit) bitsliced solution.

The resulting bitsliced implementation is shown graphically in Figure 3. The main loop consists of 16 rounds of S-box applications, along with short setup functions that mix in the necessary key bits for each round. The InitCipherState

Table 2. Comparison of DES S-box instruction counts

S-box	Odd Round Instruction Count	Even Round Instruction Count	S-box	Instruction Count
sbox15	69	72	sbox1	67
sbox26	65	64	sbox2	60
sbox37	63	63	sbox3	61
sbox48	61	61	sbox4	46
Total	**258**	**260**	sbox5	66
			sbox6	61
			sbox7	61
			sbox8	58
			Total	**480**

function loads IP-permuted plaintext(s) into the GPU using constants as they don't change during the shader program's execution. The CheckResult function compares the pre-IP^{-1} permuted output to a similarly formatted reference ciphertext, generating a 64-bit bitmask of each bitsliced calculation where a "1" indicates a match was found (i.e., the reference plaintext encrypted with the key corresponding to that slice generated the reference ciphertext). Note that multiple plaintexts and ciphertexts can be utilized as those values are passed in as simple parameters. When a match is found the necessary information required to reconstruct the corresponding key is written to the output array where it can be scanned by the application running on the CPU while the next job is being processed by the GPU, thereby incurring no overall result-checking performance penalty. The IncrementKey function increments the bitsliced key vector stored within the GPU using a simple bitsliced bit-serial addition on the 16 key bits that track the iteration number.

The theoretical peak bandwidth of the GPU for the bitsliced DES calculation can be determined by computing the maximum rate that can be achieved by all 64 SPs operating at their peak rate, ignoring any degradation in performance due to memory accesses and overhead:

$$PeakRate = \frac{64\ SPs \times 750\ Minstructions/s \times 64\ blocks/iteration}{4691\ instructions/iteration}$$

$$= 654.9\ Mblocks/s$$

The execution time of the shader program is key-invariant. The performance measured on HD 2900 XT hardware is shown in Figure 4. All measurements were based on timing the program across multiple iterations for several minutes of real time execution. The implementation achieves a maximum device utilization of 83% for a maximum key checking rate of 545 Mkeys/s (i.e., encrypting 545M DES blocks per second, or 34.9 Gbps of data, though memory read/write bandwidth limitations may constrain this general case). The remaining 17% of the available

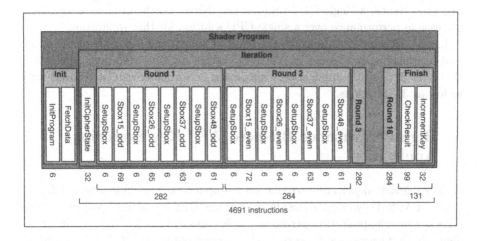

Fig. 3. Bitsliced DES implementation instruction count

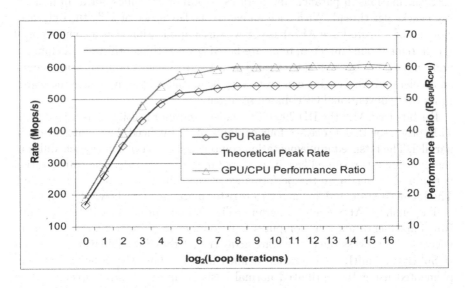

Fig. 4. Measured bitsliced DES performance

performance is lost to the overhead associated with the scheduling and execution of the shader program on the GPU, along with the costs of reading/writing memory during execution.

Figure 4 also shows the performance advantage of using the HD 2900 XT compared to a comparable bitsliced DES key search program using Matthew Kwan's optimized S-boxes executing on a dual-core AMD 2.8 GHz Athlon FX-62 system. The CPU-based solution had a measured key checking rate of 9

Mkeys/s. Hence, a single-GPU solution can deliver on the order of a $19 - 60\times$ increase in performance over a single-CPU solution for this application.

Lastly, Figure 4 demonstrates the effect of amortizing a portion of the fixed-cost overhead of processing on the GPU across multiple iterations, indicating that over 87% of the application's maximum performance can be realized with as few as 32 iterations.

5   High-Performance Bitsliced AES Key Searching Application

A more relevant algorithmic exploration was undertaken to implement an efficient bitsliced AES [18] version of the aforementioned DES key search application. The AES key search application partitions the key space of size 2^{128} into 2^{95} independent jobs that each check 2^{33} keys. Each job is composed of 2^{12} (64×64) individual threads, each of which executes an optimized bitsliced AES shader program written in the GPU's native assembly language. Each shader program computes 32 AES calculations in parallel, and iterates a total of 2^{16} times, for a total of 2^{21} key checks per thread. With such an enormous key space of 2^{128}, the only realistic use of a brute-force AES-based key search application is as a component of the aforementioned directed, template-based key searching utilities, or helping to find missing key bytes in side channel attacks. In this sort of application having an accelerated AES engine can prove very beneficial to greatly reduce the search times over conventional CPU-based solutions.

For bitsliced AES the HD 2900 XT shader processor is utilized as a $4 \times 32-$bit wide processor that processes four columns of 32 bitsliced AES state arrays in parallel. The bitsliced implementation computes the encryption key schedule on-the-fly using a transposed key array stored in the register file. The transposition is required to maximize the performance of the round key generation function. The bitsliced state and key array to register mappings are shown in Figure 5.

The bitsliced AES shader program utilizes an optimized AES ByteSub/Shift-Row implementation that computes four columns in parallel, requiring four invocations to process the entire state array (i.e., 4 ByteSub/ShiftRow operations = SubBytes/ShiftRows operation defined in [18]). The AES S-boxes were implemented using the optimized normal basis composite S-box implementation described in [19] and shown in Figure 6. Additional optimizations to eliminate redundant calculations/storage were used to yield a final implementation requiring 126 instructions, which is substantially less than previously reported bitsliced AES S-box solutions (e.g., 205 instructions in [20]).

The round key update function (Figure 7) exploits the transposed key array and optimized ByteSub/ShiftWord function to yield a 160 instruction operation. The transposition of the key array is undone when the round key is XORed into the state array using a transposed XOR operation that has no performance penalty since the transposition is done via register addressing.

The resulting bitsliced AES implementation is summarized graphically in Figure 8. The main loop adds some additional initialization as both state and

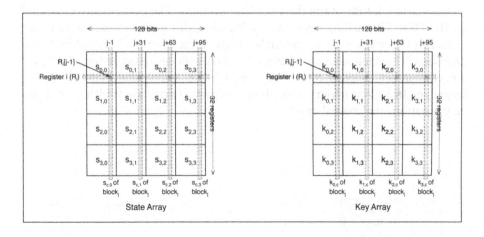

Fig. 5. Bitsliced AES register mapping of state and key arrays

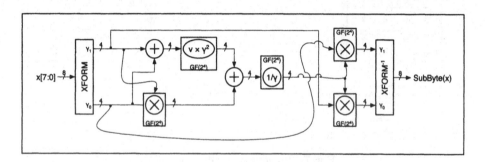

Fig. 6. Composite normal basis S-box implementation

key arrays need to be reset. The ByteSub/ShiftRow, UpdateRoundKey, and AddRoundKey functions have already been discussed. The MixColumns function processes all four columns in parallel, in-place, and in a single invocation. The CheckResult and IncrementKey functions are functionally equivalent to previously described bitsliced DES functions. As in the case of DES, arbitrary plaintexts and ciphertexts can be used, and, as previously mentioned, the key schedule is computed on-the-fly. With pre-generated keys, the performance could be increased by 23%.

The theoretical peak bandwidth of the GPU for bitsliced AES calculations can be computed as with DES using the formula:

$$PeakRate = \frac{64\ SPs \times 750\ Minstructions/s \times 32\ blocks/iteration}{8560\ instructions/iteration}$$

$$= 179.4\ Mblocks/s\ (w/key\ generation)$$

The execution time of the shader is key-invariant. The performance measured on HD 2900 XT hardware is shown in Figure 9. All measurements were based on timing the program across multiple iterations for several minutes of real time execution. The implementation achieves a maximum device utilization of 81% for a maximum key checking rate of 145 Mkeys/s (i.e., encrypting 145M blocks per second, or 18.5 Gbps of data, though memory read/write bandwidth limitations may constrain the general case).

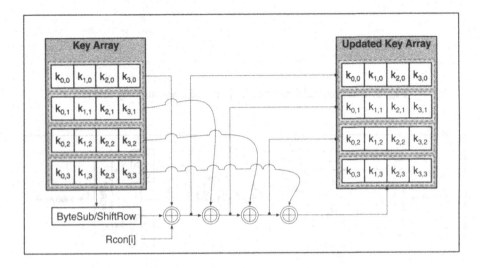

Fig. 7. Round key update function

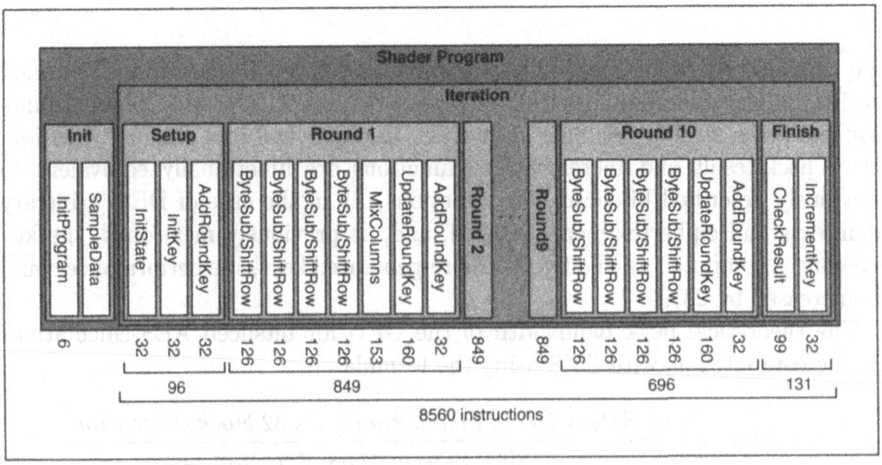

Fig. 8. Bitsliced AES implementation instruction count

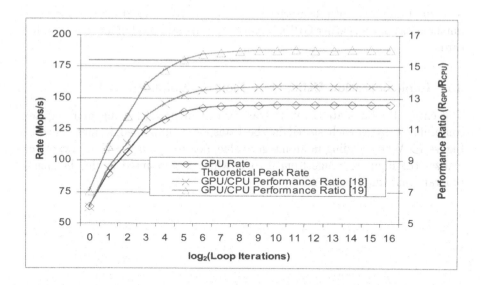

Fig. 9. Measured bitsliced AES performance

Figure 9 also compares the performance on the GPU to two previously reported software implementations ([20], [21]). The authors of [20] describe a non-bitsliced implementation on an AMD Athlon 64 3500+ CPU running @ 2.2 GHz at a rate of 2200 MHz / 170 cycles/block ∼ 13 Mblocks/s. The authors of [21] describe a non-bitsliced implementation on an AMD Opteron 64 CPU running @ 2.4 GHz at a rate of 2400 MHz / 254 cycles/block ∼ 9 Mblocks/s. Unfortunately, simple comparisons to our work aren't possible as neither implementation generates their key schedule on the fly, which is required in a key searching application. Figure 9 attempts to normalize the key generation process out of the equation by removing the key generation portion of our implementation since we don't have the necessary information to derate the results of [20] and [21]. Hence Figure 9 shows GPU implementation's results prorated by the aforementioned 23% attributed to round key generation. Hence, a single-GPU solution can deliver on the order of 6 − 16× increase in performance over a single-CPU solution for this application.

As with the bitsliced DES implementation, Figure 9 demonstrates the amortization effect of running multiple loop iterations, indicating that over 85% of the application's maximum performance can be realized with as few as 8 iterations.

6   Conventional Block-Based AES Implementation

In this section, we describe the implementation of a conventional block-based AES decryption implementation on both the previous-generation X1950 XTX GPU, which only has floating point ALU units, and the current HD 2900 XT GPU that features an enhanced instruction set with full integer support. Even with the availability of full integer support, it is still important to understand implementations on earlier GPUs because they are still used in low-cost graphics cards.

6.1   Implementation Using Only Floating Point Hardware

The entire 128-bit state array is transformed in parallel using four registers containing 4 bytes each stored in the transposed, unpacked format shown in Figure 10. When reading in an integer value, floating point GPU hardware normalizes the input to range from 0 to 1, which is accounted for in the shader program that implements AES.

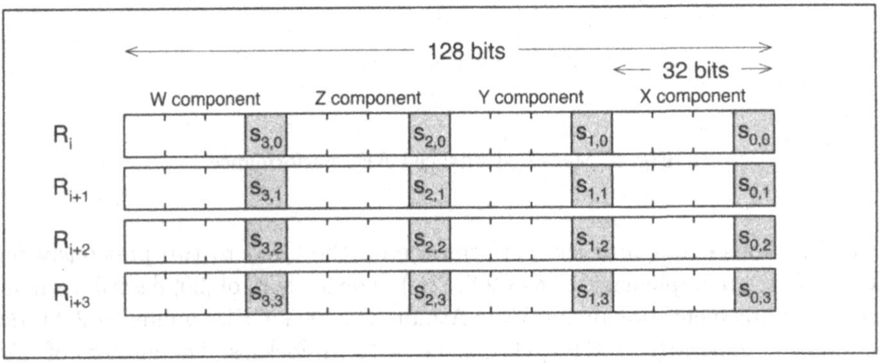

Fig. 10. AES state array register storage mapping

The internal floating-point representation introduces complications with the required XOR operation. [2] proposed using XORs in the output stage which incurs a steep penalty due to the overhead involved with issuing multiple passes through the GPU's pipeline. One alternative is to use the GPU's native instruction set to implement a XOR function at the cost of 20 instructions per 4×8−bit row of the state array. A more economical solution is to utilize a 256×256 table-lookup in local memory to implement each 8-bit XOR operation in a single instruction. The cost of this approach is the memory latency associated with performing the lookup, but GPUs are optimized to hide these latencies by efficiently switching to other threads whenever a stall occurs due to fetching data from memory. However, a 256×256 (64 KB) lookup table is actually quite large, so a hybrid approach can also be used that processes the 8-bit XOR as two 4-bit XORs through a combination of a 16×16 (256 bytes) lookup table or ALU instructions. Table 3 compares the performance of the different XOR alternatives; however, actual performance in the full AES implementation will depend on shader instruction ordering.

Table 3. Performance of 8-bit XOR operations on the X1950 XTX

Shader Type	XORs per sec
ALU Only	6307 M
256x256 Table	778 M
16x16 Table	2980 M
Hybrid	4877 M

The GPU-based AES implementation is performed using the T-box approach described in the original Rijndael submission [22] to the AES contest:

$$T_{round}[x] \qquad T_{round}[x] \qquad T_{round}[x] \qquad T_{round}[x]$$
$$s'_{0,c} = (0E \cdot Sbox[s_{0,c}]) \wedge (0B \cdot Sbox[s_{1,c}]) \wedge (0D \cdot Sbox[s_{2,c}]) \wedge (09 \cdot Sbox[s_{3,c}])$$
$$s'_{1,c} = (09 \cdot Sbox[s_{0,c}]) \wedge (0E \cdot Sbox[s_{1,c}]) \wedge (0B \cdot Sbox[s_{2,c}]) \wedge (0D \cdot Sbox[s_{3,c}])$$
$$s'_{2,c} = (0D \cdot Sbox[s_{0,c}]) \wedge (09 \cdot Sbox[s_{1,c}]) \wedge (0E \cdot Sbox[s_{2,c}]) \wedge (0B \cdot Sbox[s_{3,c}])$$
$$s'_{3,c} = (0B \cdot Sbox[s_{0,c}]) \wedge (0D \cdot Sbox[s_{1,c}]) \wedge (09 \cdot Sbox[s_{2,c}]) \wedge (0E \cdot Sbox[s_{3,c}])$$

Using the above implementation, each column of the state array would require 4 lookups to compute the $GF(2^8)$ multiplications (each fetch can return 4×8-bit values simultaneously) and 12 lookups for computing the 8-bit XORs, assuming 1 fetch per XOR, for a total of 64 lookups per round. The number of lookups can be reduced to 24 by combining two $GF(2^8)$ multiplications and XORs into a single lookup table. Hence, every lookup of $T_{round}[x, y]$ would return a 4-tuple containing $[0E \cdot x \wedge 0B \cdot y, 09 \cdot x \wedge 0E \cdot y, 0D \cdot x \wedge 09 \cdot y, 0B \cdot x \wedge 0D \cdot y]$ which reduces each state array column update to 6 lookups (2 for the multiplications and 4 for the XORs), or 24 MixColumns lookups per round. With swizzling, the ability for hardware to arbitrarily access register components, only one table is required.

AddRoundKey is implemented using a similar lookup based technique that requires us to pre-process the key expansion table and XOR it with the range of 8-bit values forming a 2D lookup table that can be accessed using 16 lookups. Every byte in every round maps to a specific entry in the key expansion, so every table access is of the form $T_{keyadd}[byte\_value, key\_entry]$. For the last round, which has no MixColumns operation, the S-Box transform is also included.

The following shader program pseudo-code processes one complete column of the round function:

```
float4 a, b, t, c0;
a = Tround[r0.w, r3.z];
b = Tround[r2.y, r1.x];
t = XOR(a, b);
c0.w = Tkeyadd[t.x, round_offset];
c0.z = Tkeyadd[t.y, round_offset + 1];
c0.y = Tkeyadd[t.z, round_offset + 2];
c0.x = Tkeyadd[t.w, round_offset + 3];
```

Assuming a single lookup per 8-bit XOR, the complete round function is 40 lookups.

When the shader program has processed all 10 rounds the 128-bit state array is written out to memory. The hardware can write four outputs simultaneously, which is used to write back the state as four, 4×8-bit values, each representing a row in the transposed state array (e.g., $s_{c,0}$, $s_{c,1}$, $s_{c,2}$, or $s_{c,3}$ in Figure 10).

The measured performance of this straightforward implementation is approximately 315 Mbps on a X1950 XTX and 380 Mbps on a HD 2900 XT. This assumes all input blocks use the same key and does not include the key expansion which can be computed on the CPU in parallel with previous GPU computations such that it can be effectively hidden in a well-balanced implementation. The performance is limited due to the number of lookups, which can be a penalty if there are not enough threads and ALU instructions to hide the associated memory access latencies. This is why performance does not scale by the number of ALU units, because both GPUs have the same number of memory fetch units. In addition, the random nature of the fetches due to the mixing properties of the AES algorithm impacts the ability of the GPU to use caching to minimize the memory access latencies of the lookups.

One possible optimization replaces the 2D round processing lookup tables with a 3D table that incorporates three $GF(2^8)$ multiplies and two XORs, as well as a 2D table that incorporates the fourth $GF(2^8)$ multiply and round key XOR. This reduces the entire round function to 24 lookups. In this mode, performance increases to 770 Mbps. However, the memory requirements are greatly increased as we now need a $256 \times 256 \times 256$ (16 MB) lookup table.

Taking advantage of latency hiding, a fully optimized shader using hybrid XORs performs at 840 Mbps on a X1950 XTX and 990 Mbps on a HD 2900 XT.

6.2   Implementation on the HD 2900 XT

AMD's HD 2900 XT allows for native integer operations and data types, as well as the ability to access data structures in memory (i.e., lookup tables) using integer values. XORs can be computed using the native XOR instruction of the GPU, so all 256×256 byte lookup tables with precomputed XORs from the previous section can be replaced with much smaller 256×4 byte tables (similar to CPU implementations) and their results summed using explicit XOR operations. Hence, the round operation shader code can be greatly simplified:

```
float4 c0, r0;
c0 = txMCol[r0.w].wzyx ∧ txMCol[r3.z].xwzy ∧
    txMCol[r2.y].yxwz ∧ txMCol[r1.x].zyxw;
r0 = c0 ∧ T_keyadd[round_offset];
```

With swizzling, only a single table is needed to represent an entire state array column update (e.g., four S-Box transforms and four $GF(2^8)$ multiplies) in one lookup.

The AddRoundKey step requires the key expansion to be stored as a separate lookup table and the XOR is performed in the shader. In the very last round, SubBytes must be performed without the MixColumns. Previously we would have to precompute this into a dedicated lookup table, but now we perform separate lookups for all the S-Box transform values and then a final AddRoundKey.

With these changes, we can achieve rates of 3.5 Gbps on the HD 2900 XT compared to an optimized bitsliced implementation on a CPU running at 1.6 Gbps [20] and the floating point versions on X1950 XTX and HD 2900 XT GPUs running at 840 Mbps and 990 Mbps respectively. This is about 2× faster than a CPU and 3.5× faster than the floating point implementation. This is also comparable to the performance achieved by [3] using OpenGL on a NVIDIA Geforce 8800. Although the floating point implementation runs at half the rate of the CPU, this is still considerably better than 2.3% found by [2].

7   Conclusion and Future Work

In this work we have demonstrated both that GPUs can execute symmetric key ciphers, and that that they can perform significantly faster than CPUs in certain applications. Bitsliced DES on a single HD 2900 XT was shown to operate up to 60 times faster than on a CPU, and bitsliced AES was shown to run up to 16 times faster.

We also demonstrated the advantages of the latest generation of GPUs over the previous generation. A block-based GPU implementation of AES runs 4× faster on the latest generation of GPUs versus the previous generation and 2× faster than a CPU version.

It should be noted that the GPU is optimized for algorithms that are parallel in nature with high arithmetic intensity. Hence, when programs must be executed serially, such as when there are dependencies between threads, then CPUs will outperform GPUs. This will be the case for certain block cipher operating modes such as CBC encryption due to the dependencies between successive blocks, unless there are a sufficient number of streams that can be processed in parallel to provide the large number of independent threads required to extract the performance in the GPU.

We believe that the entire gamut of cryptography is waiting to be explored with current and future GPU hardware. Algorithmic exploration awaits on the symmetric algorithm front with investigations of efficient implementations of other block/stream ciphers, particularly those amenable to bitsliced implementations that can leverage the large datapath width inherent in modern GPUs. In addition, the word-level integer support should be exploitable in conventional hashing algorithms to achieve significant performance increases over conventional CPUs. One particularly interesting area of potential research is finding efficient mappings of the integer support on the latest generation of GPUs to DH/RSA/ECC, and other generic integer arithmetic algorithms. With processor design trending towards multi-core, and combining CPU(s) and GPU(s) on a single die, the GPU would appear to be a good research platform for future algorithm development.

Acknowledgements

We would like to thank Justin Hensley for typesetting and proofreading. Thanks also to Arcot Preetham and Avi Bleiweiss for proofreading.

References

1. Owens, J.D., Luebke, D., Govindaraju, N., Harris, M., Krüger, J., Lefohn, A.E., Purcell, T.J.: A survey of general-purpose computation on graphics hardware. Computer Graphics Forum 26(1), 80–113 (2007)
2. Cook, D., Keromytis, A.: CryptoGraphics: Exploiting Graphics Cards For Security (Advances in Information Security). Springer-Verlag New York, Inc., Secaucus (2006)
3. Yamanouchi, T.: AES Encryption and Decryption on the GPU. In: GPU Gems 3, Addison-Wesley Professional, Reading (2007)
4. Seidel, E.: Preparing tomorrow's cryptography: Parallel computation via multiple processors, vector processing, and multi-cored chips. (Senior Honors Project, Lawrence University)
5. Fournier, J.J.A., Moore, S.W.: A vector approach to cryptography implementation. In: Safavi-Naini, R., Yung, M. (eds.) DRMTICS 2005. LNCS, vol. 3919, pp. 277–297. Springer, Heidelberg (2006)
6. Costigan, N., Scott, M.: Accelerating ssl using the vector processors in ibm's cell broadband engine for sony's playstation 3. Cryptology ePrint Archive, Report 2007/061(2007), http://eprint.iacr.org/
7. Doggett, M.: Xenos: Xbox 360 gpu. In: Game Developers Conference - Europe (2005), http://ati.amd.com/developer/eg05-xenos-doggett-final.pdf
8. Blythe, D.: The direct3d 10 system. In: SIGGRAPH 2006: ACM SIGGRAPH 2006 Papers, pp. 724–734. ACM Press, New York (2006)
9. Segal, M., Akeley, K.: Opengl 2.1 specification. Technical report, Silicon Graphics Computer Systems, Mountain View, CA, USA (2006)
10. McCool, M., Toit, S.D.: Metaprogramming GPUs with Sh. AK Peters Ltd (2004)
11. Buck, I., Foley, T., Horn, D., Sugerman, J., Fatahalian, K., Houston, M., Hanrahan, P.: Brook for gpus: stream computing on graphics hardware. In: SIGGRAPH 2004: ACM SIGGRAPH 2004 Papers, pp. 777–786. ACM Press, New York (2004)
12. NVIDIA Corporation: NVIDIA CUDA Programming Guide (2007)
13. Advanced Micro Devices: ATI CTM Technical Reference Manual (2006)
14. Microsoft Corporation: The DirectX Software Development Kit (2007)
15. Biham, E.: A fast new DES implementation in software. In: Biham, E. (ed.) FSE 1997. LNCS, vol. 1267, pp. 260–272. Springer, Heidelberg (1997)
16. National Institute of Standards and Technology: Data Encryption Standard (DES). U.S. Department of Commerce, FIPS pub. 46 (1977)
17. Kwan, M.: Bitsliced des s-box source code, http://www.darkside.com.au/bitslice/index.html
18. National Institute of Standards and Technology: Advanced Encryption Standard (AES). U.S. Department of Commerce, FIPS pub. 197 (2001)
19. Canright, D.: A very compact rijndael s-box. Technical Report NPS-MA-04-001, (Naval Postgraduate School)
20. Matsui, M.: How far can we go on the x64 processors? In: Robshaw, M. (ed.) FSE 2006. LNCS, vol. 4047, pp. 341–358. Springer, Heidelberg (2006)
21. Dai, W.: Crypto++ benchmarks for amd64 processor, http://www.cryptopp.com/benchmarks-amd64.html
22. Daemen, J., Rijmen, V.: The Design of Rijndael. Springer-Verlag New York, Inc., Secaucus (2002)

Blind Identity-Based Encryption and Simulatable Oblivious Transfer[*]

Matthew Green and Susan Hohenberger

The Johns Hopkins University
Information Security Institute
3400 N. Charles Street; Baltimore, MD 21218, USA
{mgreen,susan}@cs.jhu.edu

Abstract. In an identity-based encryption (IBE) scheme, there is a *key extraction* protocol where a user submits an identity string to a master authority who then returns the corresponding secret key for that identity. In this work, we describe how this protocol can be performed efficiently and in a *blind* fashion for several known IBE schemes; that is, a user can obtain a secret key for an identity without the master authority learning anything about this identity.

We formalize this notion as *blind IBE* and discuss its many practical applications. In particular, we build upon the recent work of Camenisch, Neven, and shelat [12] to construct oblivious transfer (OT) schemes which achieve full simulatability for both sender and receiver. OT constructions with comparable efficiency prior to Camenisch *et al.* were proven secure in the weaker half-simulation model. Our OT schemes are constructed from the blind IBE schemes we propose, which require only static complexity assumptions (*e.g.*, DBDH) whereas prior comparable schemes require dynamic assumptions (*e.g.*, q-PDDH).

1 Introduction

In an oblivious transfer (OT^N_k) protocol, introduced by Rabin [41] and generalized by Even, Goldreich and Lempel [25] and Brassard, Crépeau and Robert [10], a Sender with messages $M_1, \ldots, M_N$ and a Receiver with indices $\sigma_1, \ldots, \sigma_k \in [1, N]$ interact in such a way that at the end the Receiver obtains $M_{\sigma_1}, \ldots, M_{\sigma_k}$ without learning anything about the other messages and the Sender does not learn anything about $\sigma_1, \ldots, \sigma_k$. Naor and Pinkas were the first to consider an *adaptive* setting, $\mathsf{OT}^N_{k \times 1}$, where the sender may obtain $M_{\sigma_{i-1}}$ before deciding on σ_i [36]. Oblivious transfer is a useful, interesting primitive in its own right, but it has even greater significance as OT^4_1 is a key building block for secure multi-party computation [46,28,32]. Realizing efficient protocols under modest complexity assumptions is therefore an important goal.

The definition of security for oblivious transfer has been evolving. Informally, security is defined with respect to an ideal-world experiment in which the Sender

---

[*] This work was supported in part by the NSF under grant CT-0716142.

K. Kurosawa (Ed.): ASIACRYPT 2007, LNCS 4833, pp. 265–282, 2007.

and Receiver exchange messages via a trusted party. An OT protocol is secure if, for every real-world cheating Sender (resp., Receiver) we can describe an ideal-world counterpart who gains as much information from the ideal-world interaction as from the real protocol. Bellare and Micali [1] presented the first practical OT_1^2 protocol to satisfy this intuition in the honest-but-curious model. This was followed by practical OT protocols due to Naor and Pinkas [35,36,37] in the "half-simulation" model where the simulation-based model (described above) is used only to show Sender security and Receiver security is defined by a simpler game-based definition. Almost all efficient OT protocols are proven secure with respect to the half-simulation model, e.g., [36,35,37,24,38,31]. Unfortunately, Naor and Pinkas demonstrated that this model permits *selective-failure* attacks, in which a malicious Sender can induce transfer failures that are dependent on the message that the Receiver requests [36].

Recently, Camenisch, Neven, and shelat [12] proposed practical $OT_{k\times 1}^N$ protocols that are secure in the "full-simulation" model, where the security of both the Sender and Receiver are simulation-based. These simulatable OT protocols are particularly nice because they can be used to construct other cryptographic protocols in a simulatable fashion. More specifically, Camenisch et al. [12] provide two distinct results. First, they show how to efficiently construct $OT_{k\times 1}^N$ generically from any unique blind signature scheme in the random oracle model. The two known efficient unique blind signature schemes due to Chaum [19] and Boldyreva [2] both require *interactive* complexity assumptions: one-more-inversion RSA and chosen-target CDH, respectively. (Interestingly, when instantiated with Chaum signatures, this construction coincides with a prior one of Ogata and Kurosawa [38] that was analyzed in the half-simulation model.) Second, they provide a clever $OT_{k\times 1}^N$ construction in the standard model based on dynamic complexity assumptions, namely the q-Power Decisional Diffie-Hellman (*i.e.*, in a bilinear setting $e : \mathbb{G} \times \mathbb{G} \to \mathbb{G}_T$, given $(g, g^x, g^{x^2}, \ldots, g^{x^q}, H)$ where $g \leftarrow \mathbb{G}$ and $H \leftarrow \mathbb{G}_T$, distinguish $(H^x, H^{x^2}, \ldots, H^{x^q})$ from random values) and q-Strong Diffie-Hellman (q-SDH) assumptions. (Unfortunately, Cheon showed that q-SDH requires larger than commonly used security parameters [21]). These dynamic (including interactive) assumptions seem significantly stronger than those, such as DDH and quadratic residuosity, used to construct efficient OT schemes in the half-simulation model. Thus, a well-motivated problem is to find efficient, fully-simulatable OT schemes under weaker complexity assumptions.

Our Contributions. In this work, we provide, to our knowledge, the first efficient and fully-simulatable OT_k^N and $OT_{k\times 1}^N$ schemes secure under *static* complexity assumptions (*e.g.*, DBDH, where given (g, g^a, g^b, g^c), it is hard to distinguish $e(g, g)^{abc}$ from random). We summarize our results as follows.

First, we introduce a building block, which is of independent interest. In identity-based encryption (IBE) [43], there is an *extraction* protocol where a user submits an identity string to a master authority who then returns the corresponding decryption key for that identity. We formalize the notion of *blindly* executing this protocol, in a strong sense; where the authority does not learn the identity nor can she cause failures dependent on the identity, and the user learns nothing beyond the normal extraction protocol. This concept has similarities to recent work by Goyal [29], in which a user wishes to hide certain characteristics of an extracted IBE key from the authority. In §3.1, we describe efficient *blind extraction* protocols satisfying this definition for the IBE schemes due to Boneh and Boyen [3] and Waters [44] (using a generalization proposed independently by Naccache [34] and Chatterjee and Sarkar [17]). The latter protocol is similar to a blind signature scheme proposed by Okamoto [39]. We call IBE schemes supporting efficient blind extraction protocols: *blind IBE*, for short.

Second, we present an efficient and fully-simulatable OT^N_k protocol constructed from any of the proposed blind IBE schemes (without requiring additional assumptions), and thus our constructions are secure under only DBDH. Intuitively, consider the following OT^N_k construction. The Sender runs the IBE setup algorithm and sends the corresponding public parameters to the Receiver. Next, for $i = 1$ to N, the Sender encrypts M_i under identity "i" and sends this ciphertext to the Receiver. To obtain k messages, the Receiver blindly extracts k decryption keys for identities of his choice and uses these keys to decrypt and recover the corresponding messages. While this simple protocol does not appear to be simulatable, we are able to appropriately modify it. (Indeed, one must also be cautious of possibly malformed ciphertexts, as we discuss later.) Our constructions from blind IBE are inspired by the Camenisch et al. [12] generic construction from unique blind signatures. Indeed, recall that the secret keys sk_{id} of any fully-secure IBE can be viewed as signatures by the authority on the message id [6]. Camenisch et al. [12] require *unique* blind signatures, whereas we do not; however, where they require unforgeability, we require that our "blind key extraction" protocol does not jeopardize the semantic security of the IBE.

Third, we present an efficient and fully-simulatable $OT^N_{k \times 1}$ protocol constructed from our proposed blind IBE schemes in the random oracle model. We discuss how to remove these oracles at an additional cost. This improves on the complexity assumptions required by the comparable random-oracle scheme in Camenisch et al. [12], although we leave the same improvement for their adaptive construction without random oracles as an open problem. Finally, in §5, we discuss the independent usefulness of blind IBE to other applications, such as blind signatures, anonymous email, and encrypted keyword search.

2   Technical Preliminaries

Let BMsetup be an algorithm that, on input the security parameter 1^κ, outputs the parameters for a bilinear mapping as $\gamma = (q, g, \mathbb{G}, \mathbb{G}_T, e)$, where g generates $\mathbb{G}$, both $\mathbb{G}$ and $\mathbb{G}_T$ have prime order q, and $e : \mathbb{G} \times \mathbb{G} \to \mathbb{G}_T$. In our schemes, we will require that the correctness of these parameters be publicly verifiable (Chen et al. [20] describe efficient techniques for verifying these parameters in a typical instantiation). We will refer to the following complexity assumption made in these groups.

Decisional Bilinear Diffie-Hellman (DBDH) [6]: Let $\mathsf{BMsetup}(1^\kappa) \to (q, g, \mathbb{G}, \mathbb{G}_T, e)$. For all p.p.t. adversaries Adv, the following probability is strictly less than $1/2 + 1/\text{poly}(\kappa)$: $\Pr[a, b, c, d \leftarrow \mathbb{Z}_q; \ x_0 \leftarrow e(g, g)^{abc}; \ x_1 \leftarrow e(g, g)^d; \ z \leftarrow \{0, 1\}; \ z' \leftarrow \text{Adv}(g, g^a, g^b, g^c, x_z) : z = z']$.

Known Discrete-Logarithm-Based, Zero-Knowledge Proofs. We use known techniques for proving statements about discrete logarithms, such as (1) proof of knowledge of a discrete logarithm modulo a prime [42], (2) proof that a committed value lies in a given integer interval [16,11,8], and also (3) proof of the disjunction or conjunction of any two of the previous [23]. These protocols are secure under the discrete logarithm assumption, although some implementations of (2) require the Strong RSA assumption.

When referring to the proofs above, we will use the notation of Camenisch and Stadler [13]. For instance, $PoK\{(x, r) : y = g^x h^r \wedge (1 \leq x \leq n)\}$ denotes a zero-knowledge proof of knowledge of integers x and r such that $y = g^x h^r$ holds and $1 \leq x \leq n$. All values not in enclosed in ()'s are assumed to be known to the verifier. We can apply the Fiat-Shamir heuristic [26] to make such proofs non-interactive in the random oracle model.

Commitments. Let (CSetup, Commit, Decommit) be a commitment scheme where CSetup generates public parameters ρ; on input a message M, Commit(ρ, M) outputs a pair $(\mathcal{C}, \mathcal{D})$; and Decommit($\rho, M, \mathcal{C}, \mathcal{D}$) outputs 1 if $\mathcal{D}$ decommits $\mathcal{C}$ to M, or 0 otherwise. Our subsequent constructions require an efficient protocol for proving knowledge of a decommitment $\mathcal{D}$ with respect to $(\rho, M, \mathcal{C})$. We recommend using the Pedersen commitment scheme [40] based on the discrete logarithm assumption, in which the public parameters are a group of prime order q, and random generators $(g_0, \ldots, g_m)$. In order to commit to the values $(v_1, \ldots, v_m) \in \mathbb{Z}_q^m$, pick a random $r \in \mathbb{Z}_q$ and set $\mathcal{C} = g_0^r \prod_{i=1}^m g_i^{v_i}$ and $\mathcal{D} = r$. Schnorr's technique [42] is used to efficiently prove knowledge of the value $\mathcal{D} = r$.

3   Blind Identity-Based Encryption

An identity-based encryption (IBE) scheme supports two types of players: a single master authority and multiple users; together with the algorithms Setup, Encrypt, Decrypt and the protocol Extract. Let us provide some input/output specification for these protocols with intuition for what they do.

Notation: Let $\mathcal{I}$ be the identity space and $\mathcal{M}$ be the message space. We write $P(\mathcal{A}(a), \mathcal{B}(b)) \to (c, d)$ to indicate that protocol P is between parties $\mathcal{A}$ and $\mathcal{B}$, where a is $\mathcal{A}$'s input, c is $\mathcal{A}$'s output, b is $\mathcal{B}$'s input and d is $\mathcal{B}$'s output.

- In the Setup($1^\kappa, c(\kappa)$) algorithm, on input a security parameter 1^κ and a description of an the identity space $|\mathcal{I}| \leq 2^{c(\kappa)}$ where $c(\cdot)$ is a computable, polynomially-bounded function, the master authority $\mathcal{P}$ outputs master parameters *params* and a master secret key *msk*.
- In the Extract($\mathcal{P}(\text{params}, \text{msk}), \mathcal{U}(\text{params}, \text{id})) \to (\text{id}, sk_{id})$ protocol, an honest user $\mathcal{U}$ with identity $\text{id} \in \mathcal{I}$ obtains the corresponding secret key sk_{id} from the master authority $\mathcal{P}$ or outputs an error message. The master authority's output is **the identity** id or an error message.

- In the Encrypt($params, id, m$) algorithm, on input identity $id \in \mathcal{I}$ and message $m \in \mathcal{M}$, any party can output ciphertext C.
- In the Decrypt($params, id, sk_{id}, C$) algorithm, on input a ciphertext C, the user with sk_{id} outputs a message $m \in \mathcal{M}$ or the distinguished symbol ϕ.

Definition 1 (Selective-Identity Secure IBE (IND-sID-CPA) [15]**).** *Let κ be a security parameter, $c(\cdot)$ be a polynomially-bounded function, $|\mathcal{I}| \leq 2^{c(\kappa)}$ and $\mathcal{M}$ be the message space. An IBE is* IND-sID-CPA-*secure if every p.p.t. adversary $\mathcal{A}$ has an advantage negligible in κ for the following game: (1) $\mathcal{A}$ outputs a target identity $id^* \in \mathcal{I}$. (2) Run* Setup($1^\kappa, c(\kappa)$) *to obtain* ($params, msk$), *and give params to $\mathcal{A}$. (3) $\mathcal{A}$ may query an oracle $O_{params,msk}(\cdot)$ polynomially many times, where on any input $id \neq id^*$ in $\mathcal{I}$, the oracle returns sk_{id}, and on any other input, the oracle returns an error message. (4) $\mathcal{A}$ outputs two messages $m_0, m_1 \in \mathcal{M}$ where $|m_0| = |m_1|$. Select a random bit b and give $\mathcal{A}$ the challenge ciphertext $c^* \leftarrow$* Encrypt($params, id^*, m_b$)*. (5) $\mathcal{A}$ may continue to query oracle $O_{msk}(\cdot)$ under the same conditions as before. (6) $\mathcal{A}$ outputs $b' \in \{0, 1\}$. We define $\mathcal{A}$'s advantage in the above game as $|\Pr[b' = b] - 1/2|$.*

On stronger notions of ciphertext security for IBE. A stronger notion of ciphertext security for IBE schemes is adaptive-identity security (IND-ID-CPA) [6], which strengthens the IND-sID-CPA definition by allowing $\mathcal{A}$ to select the target identity id^* at the start of step (4) in the above game. In §3.1, we show blind IBE schemes satisfying both IND-sID-CPA and IND-ID-CPA security. Fortunately, our oblivious transfer applications in §4 require only IND-sID-CPA-security (because the "identities" will be fixed integers from 1 to poly(κ)), some additional applications in §5 require the stronger IND-ID-CPA-security.

Blind IBE. So far, we have only described traditional IBE schemes. A *blind IBE* scheme consists of the same players, together with the same algorithms Setup, Encrypt, Decrypt and yet we replace the protocol Extract with a new protocol BlindExtract which differs only in the authority's output:

- In the BlindExtract($\mathcal{P}(params, msk), \mathcal{U}(params, id)$) $\rightarrow$ (nothing, sk_{id}) protocol, an honest user $\mathcal{U}$ with identity $id \in \mathcal{I}$ obtains the corresponding secret key sk_{id} from the master authority $\mathcal{P}$ or outputs an error message. The master authority's output is **nothing** or an error message.

We now define security for blind IBE, which informally is any IND-sID-CPA-secure IBE scheme with a BlindExtract protocol that satisfies two properties:

1. **Leak-free Extract:** a potentially malicious user cannot learn anything by executing the BlindExtract protocol with an honest authority which she could not have learned by executing the Extract protocol with an honest authority; moreover, as in Extract, the user must know the identity for which she is extracting a key.
2. **Selective-failure Blindness:** a potentially malicious authority cannot learn anything about the user's choice of identity during the BlindExtract protocol; moreover, the authority cannot cause the BlindExtract protocol to fail in a manner dependent on the user's choice.

Of course, a protocol realizing the functionality BlindExtract (in a fashion that satisfies the properties above) is a special case of secure two-party computation [46,28,32]. However, using generic tools may be inefficient, so as in the case of blind signature protocols, we seek to optimize this specific computation. Let us now formally state these properties.

Definition 2 (Leak-Free Extract). *A protocol* BlindExtract $= (\mathcal{P}, \mathcal{U})$ *associated with an IBE scheme* $\Pi = (\mathsf{Setup}, \mathsf{Extract}, \mathsf{Encrypt}, \mathsf{Decrypt})$ *is leak free if for all efficient adversaries* $\mathcal{A}$, *there exists an efficient simulator* $\mathcal{S}$ *such that for every value* κ *and polynomial* $c(\cdot)$, *no efficient distinguisher* D *can distinguish whether* $\mathcal{A}$ *is playing Game Real or Game Ideal with non-negligible advantage:*

Game Real: *Run* $(params, msk) \leftarrow \mathsf{Setup}(1^\kappa, c(\kappa))$. *As many times as* D *wants,* $\mathcal{A}$ *chooses an identity id and executes the* BlindExtract *protocol with* $\mathcal{P}$: BlindExtract$(\mathcal{P}(params, msk), \mathcal{A}(params, id))$.

Game Ideal: *Run* $(params, msk) \leftarrow \mathsf{Setup}(1^\kappa, c(\kappa))$. *As many times as* D *wants,* $\mathcal{S}$ *chooses an identity id and queries a trusted party to obtain the output of* Extract$(params, msk, id)$, *if* $id \in \mathcal{I}$ *and* $\perp$ *otherwise.*

Here D *and* $\mathcal{A}$ *(or* $\mathcal{S}$) *may communicate at any time. Also, params defines* $\mathcal{I}$.

This definition implies that the identity *id* (for the key being extracted) is *extractable* from the BlindExtract protocol, since $\mathcal{S}$ must be able to interact with $\mathcal{A}$ to learn which identities to submit to the trusted party. We will make use of this observation later. Another nice property of this definition is that any key extraction protocol with leak-freeness (regardless of whether blindness holds or not) composes into the existing security definitions for IBE. (This would not necessarily be true of a blind signature protocol for the same type of signatures.) We state this formally below.

Lemma 1. *If* $\Pi = (\mathsf{Setup}, \mathsf{Extract}, \mathsf{Encrypt}, \mathsf{Decrypt})$ *is an* IND-sID-CPA-*secure (resp.,* IND-ID-CPA) *IBE scheme and* BlindExtract *associated with* Π *is leak-free, then* $\Pi' = (\mathsf{Setup}, \mathsf{BlindExtract}, \mathsf{Encrypt}, \mathsf{Decrypt})$ *is an* IND-sID-CPA-*secure (resp.,* IND-ID-CPA) *IBE scheme.*

Next, we define the second property of *blindness*. We use a strong notion of blindness called *selective-failure blindness* proposed recently by Camenisch et al. [12], ensuring that even a malicious authority is unable to induce BlindExtract protocol failures that are dependent on the identity being extracted.

Definition 3 (Selective-Failure Blindness (SFB) [12]). *A protocol* $P(\mathcal{A}(\cdot), \mathcal{U}(\cdot, \cdot))$ *is said to be selective-failure blind if every p.p.t. adversary* $\mathcal{A}$ *has a negligible advantage in the following game: First,* $\mathcal{A}$ *outputs params and a pair of identities* $id_0, id_1 \in \mathcal{I}$. *A random* $b \in \{0, 1\}$ *is chosen.* $\mathcal{A}$ *is given black-box access to two oracles* $\mathcal{U}(params, id_b)$ *and* $\mathcal{U}(params, id_{b-1})$. *The* $\mathcal{U}$ *algorithms produce local output* sk_b *and* sk_{b-1} *respectively. If* $sk_b \neq \perp$ *and* $sk_{b-1} \neq \perp$ *then* $\mathcal{A}$ *receives* (sk_0, sk_1). *If* $sk_b = \perp$ *and* $sk_{b-1} \neq \perp$ *then* $\mathcal{A}$ *receives* $(\perp, \varepsilon)$. *If* $sk_b \neq \perp$ *and* $sk_{b-1} = \perp$ *then* $\mathcal{A}$ *receives* $(\varepsilon, \perp)$. *If* $sk_b = \perp$ *and* $sk_{b-1} = \perp$ *then* $\mathcal{A}$ *receives* $(\perp, \perp)$. *Finally,* $\mathcal{A}$ *outputs its guess* b'. *We define* $\mathcal{A}$'s *advantage in the above game as* $|\Pr[b' = b] - 1/2|$.

We thus arrive at the following definition.

Definition 4 (Secure Blind IBE). *A* blind IBE Π = (Setup, BlindExtract, Encrypt, Decrypt) *is called* IND-sID-CPA-*secure (resp.* IND-ID-CPA*) if and only if: (1) Π is* IND-sID-CPA-*secure (resp.* IND-ID-CPA*), and (2)* BlindExtract *is leak free and selective-failure blind.*

3.1 IBE Schemes with Efficient BlindExtract Protocols

In this section, we describe efficient BlindExtract protocols for: (1) the IND-sID-CPA-secure IBE due to Boneh and Boyen [3] and (2) the IND-ID-CPA-secure IBE proposed independently by Naccache [34] and Chatterjee-Sarkar [17] which is a generalized version of Waters IBE [44]. Note that in §3.3 we will be adding some additional features to these IBE schemes; these will help us to construct oblivious transfer protocols in §4. Since all of these schemes share a similar structure, we'll begin by describing their common elements.

Setup($1^\kappa, c(k)$): Let $\gamma = (q, g, \mathbb{G}, \mathbb{G}_T, e)$ be the output of BMsetup(1^κ). Choose random elements $h, g_2 \in \mathbb{G}$ and a random value $\alpha \in \mathbb{Z}_q$. Set $g_1 = g^\alpha$. Finally, select a function $F : \mathcal{I} \to \mathbb{G}$ that maps identities to group elements. (The descriptions of F and $\mathcal{I}$ will be defined specific to the schemes below.) Output $params = (\gamma, g, g_1, g_2, h, F)$ and $msk = g_2^\alpha$.

Extract: Identity secret keys are of the form: $sk_{id} = (d_0, d_1) = (g_2^\alpha \cdot F(id)^r, g^r)$, where $r \in \mathbb{Z}_q$ is randomly chosen by the master authority. Note that the correctness of these keys can be publicly verified using a test described below.

Encrypt($params, id, M$): Given an identity $id \in \mathcal{I}$, and a message $M \in \mathbb{G}_T$, select a random $s \in \mathbb{Z}_q$ and output the ciphertext $C = (e(g_1, g_2)^s \cdot M, g^s, F(id)^s)$.

Decrypt($params, id, sk_{id}, c_{id}$): On input a decryption key $sk_{id} = (d_0, d_1) \in \mathbb{G}^2$ and a ciphertext $C = (X, Y, Z) \in \mathbb{G}_T \times \mathbb{G}^2$, output $M = X \cdot e(Z, d_1)/e(Y, d_0)$.

Next, we'll describe the precise format of the secret keys sk_{id} and corresponding BlindExtract protocols for particular IBEs.

A BlindExtract Protocol for an IND-sID-CPA-Secure IBE. In the Boneh-Boyen IBE [3], $\mathcal{I} \subseteq \mathbb{Z}_q$ and the function $F : \mathcal{I} \to \mathbb{G}$ is defined as $F(id) = h \cdot g_1^{id}$. A secret key for identity id, where $r \in \mathbb{Z}_q$ is random, is:

$$sk_{id} = (d_0, d_1) = (g_2^\alpha \cdot F(id)^r, g^r) = (g_2^\alpha \cdot (h \cdot g_1^{id})^r, g^r).$$

The protocol BlindExtract($\mathcal{P}(params, msk), \mathcal{U}(params, id)$) is described in Figure 1. Recall that $\mathcal{U}$ wants to obtain sk_{id} without revealing id, and $\mathcal{P}$ wants to reveal no more than sk_{id}. Let Π_1 be the blind IBE that combines algorithms Setup, Encrypt, Decrypt with the protocol BlindExtract in Figure 1.

Theorem 1. *Under the DBDH assumption, blind IBE Π_1 is secure (according to Definition 4); i.e.,* BlindExtract *is both leak-free and selective-failure blind.*

A proof of Theorem 1 is presented in the full version of this work [30].

$\mathcal{P}(params, msk)$	$\mathcal{U}(params, id)$
	1. Choose $y \xleftarrow{\$} \mathbb{Z}_q$.
	2. Compute $h' \leftarrow g^y g_1^{id}$ and send h' to $\mathcal{P}$.
	3. Execute $PoK\{(y, id) : h' = g^y g_1^{id}\}$.
4. If the proof fails to verify, abort.	
5. Choose $r \xleftarrow{\$} \mathbb{Z}_q$.	
6. Compute $d_0' \leftarrow g_2^\alpha \cdot (h'h)^r$.	
7. Compute $d_1' \leftarrow g^r$.	
8. Send (d_0', d_1') to $\mathcal{U}$.	
	9. Check that $e(g_1, g_2) \cdot e(d_1', h'h) = e(d_0', g)$.
	10. If the check passes, choose $z \xleftarrow{\$} \mathbb{Z}_q$; otherwise, output $\perp$ and abort.
	11. Compute $d_0 \leftarrow (d_0'/(d_1')^y) \cdot F(id)^z$ and $d_1 \leftarrow d_1' \cdot g^z$.
	12. Output $sk_{id} = (d_0, d_1)$.

Fig. 1. A BlindExtract protocol for the Boneh-Boyen IBE

A BlindExtract Protocol for an IND-ID-CPA-Secure IBE. In the generalized version of Waters IBE [44], proposed independently by Naccache [34] and Chatterjee and Sarkar [17], the identity space $\mathcal{I}$ is the set of bit strings of length N, where N is polynomial in κ, represented by n blocks of ℓ bits each. The function $F : \{0, 1\}^N \to \mathbb{G}$ is defined as $F(id) = h \cdot \prod_{j=1}^n u_j^{a_j}$, where each $u_j \in \mathbb{G}$ is randomly selected by the master authority and each a_j is an ℓ-bit segment of id. Naccache discusses practical IBE deployment with $N = 160$ and $\ell = 32$ [34]. A secret key for identity id, where $r \in \mathbb{Z}_q$ is random, is:

$$sk_{id} = (d_0, d_1) = (g_2^\alpha \cdot F(id)^r, g^r) = (g_2^\alpha \cdot (h \cdot \prod_{j=1}^n u_j^{a_j})^r, g^r).$$

The protocol BlindExtract($\mathcal{P}(params, msk), \mathcal{U}(params, id)$) is described in Figure 1, with the following alterations. Parse the identity as $id = (a_1, \ldots, a_n)$, where each a_i is ℓ bits. In line 2, compute h' as $g^y \cdot \prod_{j=1}^n u_j^{a_j}$. In line 3, execute the proof $PoK\{(y, a_1, \ldots, a_n) : h' = g^y \cdot \prod_{j=1}^n u_j^{a_j} \wedge 0 \leq a_i < 2^\ell$, for $i = 1$ to $n\}$. The range part of this proof (e.g., $0 \leq a_i < 2^\ell$) can be performed exactly or, by shortening each a_i by a few bits, can be done at almost no additional cost [16,11,8]. Follow the rest of the protocol as is. Let Π_2 be the blind IBE that combines Setup, Encrypt, Decrypt with the BlindExtract protocol described above.

Theorem 2. *Under the DBDH assumption, blind IBE Π_2 is secure (according to Definition 4); i.e., BlindExtract is both leak-free and selective-failure blind.*

A proof of Theorem 2 is presented in the full version of this paper [30].

3.2   On Other IBEs and HIBEs

Let us briefly summarize what we know about efficient BlindExtract protocols for other IBE schemes and hierarchical IBE (HIBE) schemes. First, random oracle based IBEs [6,22] appear to be less suited to developing efficient BlindExtract protocols than their standard model successors. This is in part due to the fact that the identity string is hashed into an element in $\mathbb{G}$ in these schemes, instead of represented as an integer exponent, which makes our proof of knowledge techniques unwieldy. We were not able to find BlindExtract protocols for the Boneh and Franklin [6], Cocks [22], or the recent Boneh-Gentry-Hamburg [7] IBEs with running time better than $O(|\mathcal{I}|)$, where $\mathcal{I}$ is the identity space. Additionally, we did not consider the efficient IBE of Gentry [27], as our focus was on schemes with *static* complexity assumptions.

We additionally considered hierarchical IBE schemes, such as those due to Boneh and Boyen [3], Waters [44] and Chatterjee and Sarkar [18]. For all of these HIBEs, the number of elements comprising an identity secret key grow with the depth of the hierarchy, but each piece is similar in format to the original keys and our same techniques would apply.

3.3   Additional Properties for a Blind IBE

In §4, we use blind IBE as a tool for constructing oblivious transfer protocols. We can use either of the efficient blind IBEs Π_1 and Π_2 defined above together with the following observations about efficient protocols relating to them.

First, in our OT constructions, we require an efficient zero-knowledge proof of knowledge protocol for the statement $PoK\{(msk) : (params, msk) \in \mathsf{Setup}(1^\kappa, c(\kappa))\}$. If efficiency were not critical, we could accomplish this proof using general techniques [46,28,32]. However, for the parameters used in Π_1, Π_2, this proof can be conducted efficiently in a number of ways; one technique is to set $msk = \alpha$ and conduct the equivalent $PoK\{(\alpha) : g_1 = g^\alpha\}$ using a standard Schnorr proof [42].

The second property that we require is more subtle. Note that in the schemes Π_1 and Π_2, there are many valid decryption keys for each identity. This may lead to a condition where some incorrectly-formed ciphertexts decrypt differently depending on which secret key is used. This can cause problems with the proofs of full-simulation security for our OT protocols (specifically, we may not be able to show Receiver security.) To address this condition in our OT protocols, we require that Π_1 and Π_2 possess a property similar to *committing encryption* [14]. Intuitively, this property ensures that for a ciphertext and identity (C, id): (1) running the honest decryption algorithm on C with respect to any valid secret key for identity id will result in the same unique value, or (2) if this is not so, then this fact can be publicly identified.

Let us define a public *ciphertext validity check* algorithm, which we denote by $\mathsf{IsValid}(params, id, C)$. In the case of blind IBE schemes Π_1 and Π_2, we implement this algorithm by first checking the group parameters γ are valid (see [20]), and verifying that for any *params* and $C = (X, Y, Z)$, all the values are in the correct groups and $e(Y, F(id)) = e(Z, g)$. The *correctness* property for the IsValid algorithm is that it outputs 1 for all honestly-generated parameters and ciphertexts. From the description of Π_1 and Π_2, it is easy to see that IsValid is correct. The algorithm's behavior in the case of maliciously-generated input is constrained insofar as it affects the following definition:

Definition 5 (Committing IBE). *An IBE scheme (resp., blind IBE) Π is committing if and only if: (1) it is* IND-sID-CPA*-secure (resp., secure in the sense of definition 4) and (2) every p.p.t. adversary $\mathcal{A}$ has an advantage negligible in κ for the following game: First, $\mathcal{A}$ outputs params, $id \in \mathcal{I}$ and a ciphertext C. If* IsValid$(params, id, C) \neq 1$ *then abort. Otherwise, the challenger, on input $(params, id)$, runs the* Extract *(resp.,* BlindExtract*) protocol with $\mathcal{A}$ twice to obtain purported keys sk_{id}, sk'_{id}. $\mathcal{A}$'s advantage is defined as:*

$$\left| \Pr \left[\text{Decrypt}(params, id, sk_{id}, C) \neq \text{Decrypt}(params, id, sk'_{id}, C) \right] \right|$$

In the full version of this work [30], we prove that both Π_1 and Π_2 are committing blind IBE schemes in the sense of definition 5.

4   Simulatable Oblivious Transfer

We now turn our attention to constructing efficient and fully-simulatable oblivious transfer protocols. We'll use any of the efficient blind IBEs presented in the previous section as a building block. In particular, we focus on building (non-adaptive) OT^N_k and (adaptive) $\mathsf{OT}^N_{k\times 1}$ protocols, in which a Sender and Receiver transfer up to k messages out of an N-message set. In the non-adaptive model [10,35], the Receiver requests all k messages simultaneously. In the adaptive model [36], the Receiver may request the messages one at a time, using the result of previous transfers to inform successive requests. Intuitively, the Receiver should learn only the messages it requests (and nothing about the remaining messages), while the Sender should gain no information about *which* messages the Receiver selected.

Full-simulation vs. half-simulation security. Security for oblivious transfer is defined via simulation. Informally, a protocol is secure if, for every real-world cheating Sender (resp., Receiver) we can describe an ideal-world counterpart who gains as much information from the ideal-world interaction as from the real protocol. Much of the oblivious transfer literature uses the simulation-based definition only to show *Sender* security, choosing to define Receiver security by a simpler game-based definition. Naor and Pinkas demonstrated that this weaker "half-simulation" approach permits *selective-failure* attacks, in which a malicious Sender induces transfer failures that are dependent on the message that the Receiver requests [36]. Recently, Camenisch et al. [12] proposed several practical $\mathsf{OT}^N_{k\times 1}$ protocols that are secure under a "full-simulation" definition, using adaptive (*e.g.*, q-PDDH) or interactive (*e.g.*, one-more-inversion RSA) assumptions. We now enhance their results by demonstrating efficient full-simulation OT^N_k and $\mathsf{OT}^N_{k\times 1}$ protocols secure under static complexity assumptions (*e.g.*, DBDH).

4.1   Definitions

Recall the definitions for both the non-adaptive and adaptive protocols. For consistency with earlier work, we use the notation from Camenisch *et al.* [12].

Definition 6 (k-**out-of-**N **Oblivious Transfer** (OT_k^N, $\mathsf{OT}_{k\times 1}^N$)). *An oblivious transfer scheme is a tuple of algorithms* ($\mathsf{S_I}, \mathsf{R_I}, \mathsf{S_T}, \mathsf{R_T}$). *During the initialization phase, the Sender and the Receiver run an interactive protocol, where the Sender runs* $\mathsf{S_I}(M_1, \ldots, M_N)$ *to obtain state value* S_0, *and the Receiver runs* $\mathsf{R_I}()$ *to obtain state value* R_0. *Next, during the transfer phase, the Sender and Receiver interactively execute* $\mathsf{S_T}, \mathsf{R_T}$, *respectively,* k *times as described below.*

Adaptive OT. In the adaptive $\mathsf{OT}_{k\times 1}^N$ *case, for* $1 \leq i \leq k$, *the* i^{th} *transfer proceeds as follows: the Sender runs* $\mathsf{S_T}(S_{i-1})$ *to obtain state value* S_i, *and the Receiver runs* $\mathsf{R_T}(R_{i-1}, \sigma_i)$ *where* $1 \leq \sigma_i \leq N$ *is the index of the message to be received. This produces state information* R_i *and the message* M_{σ_i}' *or* $\perp$ *indicating failure.*

Non-adaptive OT. In the non-adaptive OT_k^N *case the parties execute the protocol as above; however, for round* $i < k$ *the algorithm* $\mathsf{R_T}(R_{i-1}, \sigma_i)$ **does not** *output a message. At the end of the the the* k^{th} *transfer* $\mathsf{R_T}(R_{k-1}, \sigma_k)$ *outputs the messages* $(M_{\sigma_1}', \ldots, M_{\sigma_k}')$ *where for* $j = 1, \ldots, N$ *each* M_{σ_j}' *is a valid message or the symbol* $\perp$ *indicating protocol failure. (In a non-adaptive scheme, the* k *transfers do not necessarily require a corresponding number of communication rounds).*

Definition 7 (Full Simulation Security). *Security for oblivious transfer is defined according to a simulation-based definition.*

Real experiment. *In experiment* $\mathbf{Real}_{\hat{\mathsf{S}}, \hat{\mathsf{R}}}(N, k, M_1, \ldots, M_N, \Sigma)$ *the possibly cheating sender* $\hat{\mathsf{S}}$ *is given messages* $(M_1, \ldots, M_N)$ *as input and interacts with possibly cheating receiver* $\hat{\mathsf{R}}(\Sigma)$, *where* Σ *is a selection algorithm that on input messages* $(M_{\sigma_1}, \ldots, M_{\sigma_{i-1}})$ *outputs the index* σ_i *of the next message to be queried. At the beginning of the experiment, both* $\hat{\mathsf{S}}$ *and* $\hat{\mathsf{R}}$ *output initial states* (S_0, R_0). *In the adaptive case, for* $1 \leq i \leq k$ *the sender computes* $S_i \leftarrow \hat{\mathsf{S}}(S_{i-1})$, *and the receiver computes* $(R_i, M_i') \leftarrow \hat{\mathsf{R}}(R_{i-1})$, *where* M_i' *may or may not be equal to* M_i. *In the non-adaptive case, the Receiver obtains no messages until the* k^{th} *round, and therefore the selection strategy* Σ *must be non-adaptive. At the end of the* k^{th} *transfer the output of the experiment is* (S_k, R_k).

Ideal experiment. *In experiment* $\mathbf{Ideal}_{\hat{\mathsf{S}}', \hat{\mathsf{R}}'}(N, k, M_1, \ldots, M_N, \Sigma)$ *the possibly cheating sender algorithm* $\hat{\mathsf{S}}'$ *generates messages* $(M_1^*, \ldots, M_N^*)$ *and transmits them to a trusted party* T. *In the* i^{th} *round* $\hat{\mathsf{S}}'$ *sends a bit* b_i *to* T; *the possibly cheating receiver* $\hat{\mathsf{R}}'(\Sigma)$ *transmits* σ_i^* *to* T. *In the adaptive case, if* $b_i = 1$ *and* $\sigma_i^* \in (1, \ldots, N)$ *then* T *hands* $M_{\sigma_i^*}$ *to* $\hat{\mathsf{R}}'$. *If* $b_i = 0$ *then* T *hands* $\perp$ *to* $\hat{\mathsf{R}}'$. *Note that in the non-adaptive case,* T *does not give* $\hat{\mathsf{R}}'$ *any response until the* k^{th} *round. At the end of the* k^{th} *transfer the output of the experiment is* (S_k, R_k).

Sender Security. $OT_{k \times 1}^N$ *provides Sender security if for every real-world p.p.t. receiver* $\hat{R}$ *there exists a p.p.t. ideal-world receiver* $\hat{R}'$ *such that* $\forall N = \ell(\kappa)$, $k \in [1, N]$, $(M_1, \ldots, M_N)$, Σ, *and every p.p.t. distinguisher:*
$$\mathbf{Real}_{S, \hat{R}}(N, k, M_1, \ldots, M_N, \Sigma) \stackrel{c}{\approx} \mathbf{Ideal}_{S', \hat{R}'}(N, k, M_1, \ldots, M_N, \Sigma).$$

Receiver Security. $OT_{k \times 1}^N$ *provides Receiver security if for every real-world p.p.t. sender* $\hat{S}$ *there exists a p.p.t. ideal-world sender* $\hat{S}'$ *such that* $\forall N = \ell(\kappa)$, $k \in [1, N]$, $(M_1, \ldots, M_N)$, Σ, *and every p.p.t. distinguisher:*
$$\mathbf{Real}_{\hat{S}, R}(N, k, M_1, \ldots, M_N, \Sigma) \stackrel{c}{\approx} \mathbf{Ideal}_{\hat{S}', R'}(N, k, M_1, \ldots, M_N, \Sigma).$$

4.2 Constructions

Non-adaptive OT_k^N without Random Oracles. Given a committing blind IBE scheme Π, it is tempting to consider the following "intuitive" protocol: First, the Sender runs the IBE Setup algorithm and sends *params* to the Receiver. Next, for $i = 1, \ldots, N$ the Sender transmits an encryption of message M_i under identity "i". To obtain k messages, the Receiver extracts decryption keys for identities $(\sigma_1, \ldots, \sigma_k)$ via k distinct executions of BlindExtract, and uses these keys to decrypt the corresponding ciphertexts. If Π is a blind IBE secure in the sense of definition 4, then a cheating Receiver gains no information about the messages corresponding to secret keys he did not extract. Similarly, with additional precautions, a cheating Sender does not learn the identities extracted. However, it seems difficult to show this protocol is fully-simulatable, because the ideal Sender would have to form the N ciphertexts *before* learning the messages that k of them must decrypt to!

Fortunately, we are able to convert this simple idea into the fully-simulatable OT_k^N protocol shown in Figure 2. We require only the following modifications: first, we have the Sender prove knowledge of the value *msk* using appropriate zero-knowledge techniques.[1] Then, rather than transmitting the ciphertext vector during the first phase of the protocol, the Sender transmits only a *commitment* to a collision-resistant hash of the ciphertext vector, and sends the actual ciphertexts at the end of the kth round together with a proof that she can open the commitment to the hash of the ciphertexts. (She does *not* open the commitment; she only proves that she knows how to do so.)

Theorem 3 (Full-simulation Security of the OT_k^N Scheme). *If blind IBE* $\Pi \in \{\Pi_1, \Pi_2\}$ *with the IsValid as defined in §3.3 and* (CSetup, Commit, Decommit) *is a secure commitment scheme, then the* OT_k^N *protocol of figure 2 is sender-secure and receiver-secure in the full-simulation model under DBDH.*

We include a proof of Theorem 3 in the full version [30].

Adaptive $OT_{k \times 1}^N$ in the Random Oracle Model. While our first protocol is efficient and full-simulation secure, it permits only *non-adaptive* queries. For

---

[1] In §3.3, we describe how to conduct these proofs efficiently for the practical blind IBE constructions we consider.

$\mathsf{S}_\mathsf{I}(M_1,\ldots,M_N),\mathsf{S}_\mathsf{T}()$ $\mathsf{R}_\mathsf{I}(),\mathsf{R}_\mathsf{T}(\sigma_1,\ldots,\sigma_k)$

Sender and Receiver agree on parameters for a commitment scheme and
a collision-resistant hash function H.[a]

1. Generate $(params, msk) \leftarrow \mathsf{Setup}(1^\kappa, c(\kappa))$.
2. For $j = 1,\ldots,N$, set $C_j \leftarrow \mathsf{Encrypt}(params, j, M_j)$.
3. Compute $(\mathcal{C}, \mathcal{D}) \leftarrow \mathsf{Commit}(H(C_1,\ldots,C_N))$.
4. Send $(params, \mathcal{C})$ to Receiver.
5. Conduct $PoK\{(msk) : (params, msk) \in \mathsf{Setup}(1^\kappa, c(\kappa))\}$.
                           6. If the proof does not verify, abort.

For $i = 1, ..., k$, run $\mathsf{BlindExtract}$ on identity σ_i for Receiver to obtain sk_{σ_i}.

Following the kth extraction:
1. Send the ciphertexts $(C_1,\ldots,C_N)$ to the Receiver.
2. Conduct $PoK\{(\mathcal{D}) : \mathsf{Decommit}(H(C_1,\ldots,C_N),\mathcal{C},\mathcal{D}) = 1\}$.
                      3. If the proof does not verify, or for any i
                         $\mathsf{IsValid}(params, i, C_i) \neq 1$, abort and set
                         $M'_{\sigma_1},\ldots,M'_{\sigma_k} \leftarrow \perp$.
                      4. For $i = 1$ to k: If $\mathsf{BlindExtract}$ on σ_i failed,
                         set $M'_{\sigma_i} \leftarrow \perp$; else, set M'_{σ_i} to the value
                         $\mathsf{Decrypt}(params, \sigma_i, sk_{\sigma_i}, C_{\sigma_i})$.

Output S_k Output $R_k, (M'_{\sigma_1},\ldots,M'_{\sigma_k})$.

---

[a] In the case of Pedersen's commitment scheme, the parameters may be generated
by the Receiver. H may also be selected by the Receiver.

Fig. 2. OT^N_k from any of the committing blind IBEs in §3, with input messages
$M_1,\ldots,M_N \in \mathcal{M}$. We present the $\mathsf{S}_\mathsf{I}, \mathsf{R}_\mathsf{I}, \mathsf{S}_\mathsf{T}, \mathsf{R}_\mathsf{T}$ algorithms in a single protocol flow.

many practical applications (*e.g.*, oblivious retrieval from a large database), we
desire a protocol that supports an adaptive query pattern. We approach this
goal by first proposing an efficient $\mathsf{OT}^N_{k\times 1}$ protocol secure in the random oracle model. The protocol, which we present in Figure 3, requires an IBE scheme
with a super-polynomial message space (as in the constructions of §3.1), and
has approximately the same efficiency as the construction with random oracles
of Camenisch *et al.* [12]. However, their construction requires unique blind signatures and the two known options due to Chaum [19] and Boldyreva [2] both
require interactive complexity assumptions. By using the blind IBE schemes in
§3.1, our protocols can be based on the DBDH assumption.

Theorem 4 (Full-simulation Security of the $\mathsf{OT}^N_{k\times 1}$ Scheme). *If blind IBE*
$\Pi \in \{\Pi_1, \Pi_2\}$ *with the* $\mathsf{IsValid}$ *as defined in §3.3 and H is modeled as a random*

$\underline{S_I(M_1,\ldots,M_N)}$ $\underline{R_I()}$

1. Select $(params, msk) \leftarrow \mathsf{Setup}(1^\kappa, c(\kappa))$.
2. Select random $W_1,\ldots,W_N \in \mathcal{M}$, and for $j = 1,\ldots,N$ set:
  — $A_j \leftarrow \mathsf{Encrypt}(params, j, W_j)$
  — $B_j \leftarrow H(W_j) \oplus M_j$
  — $C_j = (A_j, B_j)$
3. Conduct $PoK\{(msk) : (params, msk) \in \mathsf{Setup}(1^\kappa, c(\kappa))\}$.
4. Send $(params, C_1,\ldots,C_N)$ to Receiver.

                                     5. If the proof fails to verify or for any i
                                          $\mathsf{IsValid}(params, i, C_i) \neq 1$, abort and
                                          set $M'_{\sigma_1},\ldots,M'_{\sigma_k} \leftarrow \bot$.

Output $S_0 = (params, msk)$ Output $R_0 = (params, C_1,\ldots,C_N)$

$\underline{S_T(S_{i-1})}$ $\underline{R_T(R_{i-1}, \sigma_i)}$

In the ith transfer, run $\mathsf{BlindExtract}$ on identity σ_i for Receiver to obtain sk_{σ_i}.

                                     1. If $\mathsf{BlindExtract}$ fails, then set M'_{σ_i} to $\bot$.
                                     2. Else set $t \leftarrow \mathsf{Decrypt}(params, \sigma_i, sk_{\sigma_i}, A_{\sigma_i})$
                                     and set $M'_{\sigma_i} \leftarrow B_{\sigma_i} \oplus H(t)$.

Output $S_i = S_{i-1}$ Output $R_i = (R_{i-1}, M'_{\sigma_i})$.

Fig. 3. Adaptive $\mathsf{OT}^N_{k \times 1}$ from any of the committing blind IBEs in §3, with $M_1,\ldots,M_N \in \{0,1\}^n$. Let hash $H : \mathcal{M} \to \{0,1\}^n$ be modeled as a random oracle.

oracle, then the $\mathsf{OT}^N_{k \times 1}$ protocol of figure 3 is sender-secure and receiver-secure in the full-simulation model under DBDH.

We include a proof of Theorem 4 in the full version [30].

Adaptive $\mathsf{OT}^N_{k \times 1}$ without Random Oracles. The random-oracle $\mathsf{OT}^N_{k \times 1}$ presented above is reasonably efficient both in terms of communication cost and round-efficiency. Ideally, we would like to construct a protocol of comparable efficiency in the standard model. We could construct an $\mathsf{OT}^N_{k \times 1}$ protocol by compiling k instances of the non-adaptive OT^N_k from §4.2. Each protocol round would consist of a 1-out-of-N instance of the protocol, with new IBE parameters and new a vector of ciphertexts $(C_1,\ldots,C_N)$. To ensure that each round is consistent with the previous rounds, the Sender would need to prove that the underlying plaintexts remain the same from round to round. This can be achieved using standard proof techniques, but is impractical for large values of k or N.

Alternatively, we could combine our scheme with the standard model $\mathsf{OT}^N_{k \times 1}$ of Camenisch *et al.* [12]. Their efficient $\mathsf{OT}^N_{k \times 1}$, for example, incurs only a constant cost per transfer phase. However, the protocol relies on the dynamic q-Strong

DH and q-Power Decisional DH assumptions, where large values of q require larger than normal security parameters [21]. Fortunately, one might be able to keep q small (on the order of k rather than N) by combining the Camenisch *et al.* scheme with ours as follows: in their initialization, the Sender releases N values corresponding to the messages that require $q = N$. Instead, we could use a blind IBE scheme to encrypt these N values during initialization, and then during the adaptive transfer phase, a Receiver could request the decryption key of his choice along with the information required in the Camenisch *et al.* scheme. Thus, reducing the values available to an adversary to $q = k$.

5   Other Applications of Blind IBE

Privacy-preserving delegated keyword search. Several works use IBE as a building-block for *public-key searchable encryption* [5,45]. These schemes permit a keyholder to delegate search capability to other parties. For example, Waters *et al.* [45] describe a searchable encrypted audit log in which a third party auditor is granted the ability to independently search the encrypted log for specific keywords. To enable this function, a central authority generates "trapdoors" for the keywords that the auditor wishes to search on. In this scenario, the trapdoor generation authority necessarily learns each of the search terms. This may be problematic in circumstances where the pattern of trapdoor requests reveals sensitive information (*e.g.*, the name of a user under suspicion). By using blind and partially-blind IBE, we permit the authority to generate trapdoors, yet learn no information (or only partial information) about the search terms.[2]

Blind and partially-blind signature schemes. Moni Naor observed that each adaptive-identity secure IBE implies an existentially unforgeable signature scheme [6]. By the same token, an adaptive-identity secure blind IBE scheme implies an unforgeable, selective-failure blind signature scheme. This result applies to the adaptive-identity secure Π_2 protocol of §3.1, and to the selective-identity secure protocol Π_1 when that scheme is instantiated with appropriately-sized parameters and a hash function (see §7 of [3]). The efficient BlindExtract protocol for the adaptive-identity secure Π_2 scheme can also be used to construct a *partially-blind* signature, by allowing the signer (the master authority) to supply a portion of the input string. Partially-blind signatures have many applications, such as document timestamping and electronic cash [33].

Temporary anonymous identities. In a typical IBE, the master authority can link users to identities. For some applications, users may wish to remain anonymous or pseudonymous. By employing (partially-)blind IBE, an authority can grant temporary credentials without linking identities to users or even learning which identities are in use.

---

[2] Boneh *et al.* [5] note that keyword search schemes can be constructed from any *key anonymous* IBE scheme. While the schemes of §3 are not key anonymous, Boyen and Waters remark that key anonymity in similar schemes might be acheived by implementing them in *asymmetric* bilinear groups [9].

Acknowledgments. Thanks to abhi shelat for helpful discussions, and to an anonymous reviewer for pointing out an issue regarding malformed ciphertexts.

References

1. Bellare, M., Micali, S.: Non-interactive oblivious transfer and applications. In: Brassard, G. (ed.) CRYPTO 1989. LNCS, vol. 435, pp. 547–557. Springer, Heidelberg (1990)
2. Boldyreva, A.: Threshold, Multisignature and Blind Signature Schemes Based on the Gap-Diffie-Hellman-Group Signature Scheme. In: Desmedt, Y.G. (ed.) PKC 2003. LNCS, vol. 2567, pp. 31–46. Springer, Heidelberg (2003)
3. Boneh, D., Boyen, X.: Efficient selective-ID secure Identity-Based Encryption without random oracles. In: Cachin, C., Camenisch, J.L. (eds.) EUROCRYPT 2004. LNCS, vol. 3027, pp. 223–238. Springer, Heidelberg (2004)
4. Boneh, D., Boyen, X.: Short signatures without random oracles. In: Cachin, C., Camenisch, J.L. (eds.) EUROCRYPT 2004. LNCS, vol. 3027, pp. 382–400. Springer, Heidelberg (2004)
5. Boneh, D., Di Crescenzo, G., Ostrovsky, R., Persiano, G.: Public key encryption with keyword search. In: Cachin, C., Camenisch, J.L. (eds.) EUROCRYPT 2004. LNCS, vol. 3027, pp. 506–522. Springer, Heidelberg (2004)
6. Boneh, D., Franklin, M.K.: Identity-based encryption from the Weil Pairing. In: Kilian, J. (ed.) CRYPTO 2001. LNCS, vol. 2139, pp. 213–229. Springer, Heidelberg (2001)
7. Boneh, D., Gentry, C., Hamburg, M.: Space-efficient identity based encryption without pairings. In: FOCS (to appear, 2007)
8. Boudot, F.: Efficient proofs that a committed number lies in an interval. In: Preneel, B. (ed.) EUROCRYPT 2000. LNCS, vol. 1807, pp. 431–444. Springer, Heidelberg (2000)
9. Boyen, X., Waters, B.: Anonymous hierarchical identity-based encryption (without random oracles. In: Dwork, C. (ed.) CRYPTO 2006. LNCS, vol. 4117, pp. 290–307. Springer, Heidelberg (2006)
10. Brassard, G., Crépeau, C., Robert, J.-M.: All-or-nothing disclosure of secrets. In: Odlyzko, A.M. (ed.) CRYPTO 1986. LNCS, vol. 263, pp. 234–238. Springer, Heidelberg (1987)
11. Camenisch, J., Michels, M.: Proving in zero-knowledge that a number n is the product of two safe primes. In: Stern, J. (ed.) EUROCRYPT 1999. LNCS, vol. 1592, pp. 107–122. Springer, Heidelberg (1999)
12. Camenisch, J., Neven, G., shelat, A.: Simulatable adaptive oblivious transfer. In: EUROCRYPT 2007. LNCS, vol. 4515, pp. 573–590. Springer, Heidelberg (2007)
13. Camenisch, J., Stadler, M.: Efficient group signature schemes for large groups. In: Kaliski Jr., B.S. (ed.) CRYPTO 1997. LNCS, vol. 1294, pp. 410–424. Springer, Heidelberg (1997)
14. Canetti, R., Feige, U., Goldreich, O., Naor, M.: Adaptively secure multi-party computation. In: Twenty-Eighth Annual ACM Symposium on the Theory of Computing, pp. 639–648 (1996)
15. Canetti, R., Halevi, S., Katz, J.: Chosen-ciphertext security from Identity Based Encryption. In: Cachin, C., Camenisch, J.L. (eds.) EUROCRYPT 2004. LNCS, vol. 3027, pp. 207–222. Springer, Heidelberg (2004)

16. Chan, A., Frankel, Y., Tsiounis, Y.: Easy come – easy go divisible cash. In: Nyberg, K. (ed.) EUROCRYPT 1998. LNCS, vol. 1403, pp. 561–575. Springer, Heidelberg (1998)

17. Chatterjee, S., Sarkar, P.: Trading time for space: Towards an efficient IBE scheme with short(er) public parameters in the standard model. In: Won, D.H., Kim, S. (eds.) ICISC 2005. LNCS, vol. 3935, pp. 424–440. Springer, Heidelberg (2006)

18. Chatterjee, S., Sarkar, P.: HIBE with Short Public Parameters without Random Oracle. In: Lai, X., Chen, K. (eds.) ASIACRYPT 2006. LNCS, vol. 4284, pp. 145–160. Springer, Heidelberg (2006)

19. Chaum, D.: Blind signatures for untraceable payments. In: CRYPTO 1982, pp. 199–203. Plenum Press (1982)

20. Chen, L., Cheng, Z., Smart, N.: Identity-based key agreement protocols from pairings. International Journal of Information Security 6, 213–241 (2007)

21. Cheon, J.H.: Security analysis of the strong Diffie-Hellman problem. In: Vaudenay, S. (ed.) EUROCRYPT 2006. LNCS, vol. 4004, pp. 1–11. Springer, Heidelberg (2006)

22. Cocks, C.: An identity based encryption scheme based on Quadratic Residues. In: Honary, B. (ed.) Cryptography and Coding. LNCS, vol. 2260, pp. 360–363. Springer, Heidelberg (2001)

23. Cramer, R., Damgård, I., Schoenmakers, B.: Proofs of partial knowledge and simplified design of witness hiding protocols. In: Desmedt, Y.G. (ed.) CRYPTO 1994. LNCS, vol. 839, pp. 174–187. Springer, Heidelberg (1994)

24. Ding, Y.Z., Harnik, D., Rosen, A., Shaltiel, R.: Constant-round oblivious transfer in the bounded storage model. In: Naor, M. (ed.) TCC 2004. LNCS, vol. 2951, pp. 446–472. Springer, Heidelberg (2004)

25. Even, S., Goldreich, O., Lempel, A.: A randomized protocol for signing contracts. In: CRYPTO 1982, pp. 205–210 (1982)

26. Fiat, A., Shamir, A.: How to prove yourself: Practical solutions to identification and signature problems. In: Odlyzko, A.M. (ed.) CRYPTO 1986. LNCS, vol. 263, pp. 186–194. Springer, Heidelberg (1987)

27. Gentry, C.: Practical identity-based encryption without random oracles. In: Vaudenay, S. (ed.) EUROCRYPT 2006. LNCS, vol. 4004, pp. 445–464. Springer, Heidelberg (2006)

28. Goldreich, O., Micali, S., Wigderson, A.: How to play any mental game or a completeness theorem for protocols with honest majority. In: STOC (1987)

29. Goyal, V.: Reducing trust in the PKG in identity based cryptosystems. In: CRYPTO 2007. LNCS, vol. 4622, pp. 430–447. Springer, Heidelberg (2007)

30. Green, M., Hohenberger, S.: Blind identity-based encryption and simulatable oblivious transfer. Cryptology ePrint Archive, Report 2007/235 (2007)

31. Kalai, Y.T.: Smooth projective hashing and two-message oblivious transfer. In: Cramer, R.J.F. (ed.) EUROCRYPT 2005. LNCS, vol. 3494, pp. 78–95. Springer, Heidelberg (2005)

32. Kilian, J.: Founding cryptography on oblivious transfer. In: STOC, pp. 20–31 (1988)

33. Miyazaki, S., Sakurai, K.: A more efficient untraceable e-cash system with partially blind signatures based on the discrete logarithm problem. In: Hirschfeld, R. (ed.) FC 1998. LNCS, vol. 1465, pp. 296–308. Springer, Heidelberg (1998)

34. Naccache, D.: Secure and practical identity-based encryption. Cryptology ePrint Archive, Report 2005/369 (2005), http://eprint.iacr.org/

35. Naor, M., Pinkas, B.: Oblivious transfer and polynomial evaluation. In: STOC 1999, pp. 245–254 (1999)

36. Naor, M., Pinkas, B.: Oblivious transfer with adaptive queries. In: Wiener, M.J. (ed.) CRYPTO 1999. LNCS, vol. 1666, pp. 573–590. Springer, Heidelberg (1999)
37. Naor, M., Pinkas, B.: Efficient oblivious transfer protocols. In: SODA 2001, pp. 448–457 (2001)
38. Ogata, W., Kurosawa, K.: Oblivious keyword search. Special issue on coding and cryptography Journal of Complexity 20(2-3), 356–371 (2004)
39. Okamoto, T.: Efficient blind and partially blind signatures without random oracles. In: Halevi, S., Rabin, T. (eds.) TCC 2006. LNCS, vol. 3876, pp. 80–99. Springer, Heidelberg (2006)
40. Pedersen, T.P.: Non-interactive and information-theoretic secure verifiable secret sharing. In: Feigenbaum, J. (ed.) CRYPTO 1991. LNCS, vol. 576, pp. 129–140. Springer, Heidelberg (1992)
41. Rabin, M.: How to exchange secrets by oblivious transfer. Technical Report TR-81, Aiken Computation Laboratory, Harvard University (1981)
42. Schnorr, C.-P.: Efficient signature generation for smart cards. Journal of Cryptology 4(3), 239–252 (1991)
43. Shamir, A.: Identity-based cryptosystems and signature schemes. In: Blakely, G.R., Chaum, D. (eds.) CRYPTO 1984. LNCS, vol. 196, pp. 47–53. Springer, Heidelberg (1985)
44. Waters, B.: Efficient Identity-Based Encryption without random oracles. In: Cramer, R.J.F. (ed.) EUROCRYPT 2005. LNCS, vol. 3494, pp. 114–127. Springer, Heidelberg (2005)
45. Waters, B.R., Balfanz, D., Durfee, G., Smetters, D.K.: Building an encrypted and searchable audit log. In: NDSS 2004 (2004)
46. Yao, A.: How to generate and exchange secrets. In: FOCS, pp. 162–167 (1986)

Multi-party Indirect Indexing and Applications

Matthew Franklin, Mark Gondree, and Payman Mohassel

Department of Computer Science
University of California, Davis
{franklin,gondree,mohassel}@cs.ucdavis.edu

Abstract. We develop a new multi-party generalization of Naor-Nissim indirect indexing, making it possible for many participants to simulate a RAM machine with only poly-logarithmic blow-up. Our most efficient instantiation (built from length-flexible additively homomorphic public key encryption) improves the communication complexity of secure multi-party computation for a number of problems in the literature. Underlying our approach is a new multi-party variant of oblivious transfer which may be of independent interest.

Keywords: communication complexity, oblivious RAM machine, privacy-preserving protocols, secure multiparty computation.

1 Introduction

Naor-Nissim indirect indexing [24] allows two parties to privately access an array at a shared index. We develop a multiparty generalization of Naor-Nissim indirect indexing, and show that our methods have many cryptographic applications. For example, we can transform any non-private multiparty protocol into a private one, in a manner that preserves its communication efficiency. Further, we can construct a multiparty generalization of Naor-Nissim circuits with look-up tables [24], enabling any number of parties to privately and obliviously simulate a RAM machine with only polylogarithmic overhead. The tools we build also yield automatic generalizations and efficiency improvements for several other protocols, including those for secure distributed constraint satisfaction [34,35,39,29] and private stable matching [18,11].

Underlying our techniques is a useful multiparty generalization of oblivious transfer (mOT), which may be of independent interest. In mOT, the role of the chooser is divided among many participants, each of whom holds a share of an input and receives a share of the output. We define this primitive and its related security notions, and provide two main constructions. Our first construction is generic, and can be built from black-box access to any ordinary two-party oblivious transfer. Our second construction is highly efficient and uses length-flexible additively homomorphic public key encryption [8,9].

The paper is organized as follows. In Section 2, we define our multiparty generalization of Naor-Nissim indirect indexing. In Section 3, we show how this tool yields multiparty generalizations of existing protocols and efficiency improvements in existent multiparty protocols. In Section 4, we reduce the construction of multiparty indirect indexing to that of a simpler protocol, which can be seen as a multiparty variant of the well-known oblivious transfer primitive. In Section 5, we provide an efficient construction for this new protocol.

K. Kurosawa (Ed.): ASIACRYPT 2007, LNCS 4833, pp. 283–297, 2007.
© International Association for Cryptology Research 2007

1.1   Background and Related Work

General secure multiparty computation (*e.g.*, see [14,15]) can be used to privately implement the functions of interest in our paper, though rather inefficiently. Particularly, the communication complexity of such a construction for our mOT function would be linear in the size of the database. We are most interested in protocols with sublinear communication complexity.

Ostrovsky and Shoup [31] design communication-efficient protocols for the case where the database is shared between k servers and the index to be accessed is held by a single chooser. Only the chooser will learn the element in this position. Our setting is more general, as the index and final output cannot be learned by any one party, and are instead shared. As a result, our protocols automatically give new constructions for the problem considered by Ostrovsky and Shoup. Their goal, however, is information-theoretic security, while we work in the computational setting.

Naor and Pinkas [26] introduce *distributed oblivious transfer* which distributes the task of the database among multiple servers to compute the standard oblivious transfer functionality. Unconditional security is guaranteed as long a limited number of these participants do not collude. Unlike our mLUT protocol, the database is not shared explicitly between the servers. Instead, the database sends these servers a "transfer function," which allows each to compute a value related to the original database. From these values, the chooser can compute the original desired value in the database.

Barkol and Ishai [2] design a communication-efficient secure multiparty protocol in which m parties share an input x, and all hold the same constant-depth circuit C. Parties then privately compute $C(x)$. Let $x = \sigma$ be an index shared between the parties and let circuit C hard-code elements of a database Δ and return the x-th element as its output. Our construction is different in the sense that the database and the final output are not known to any single party and are shared instead. These are crucial properties that we need in order to securely implement multiparty circuits with look-up tables.

Since its proposal by Rabin [33], oblivious transfer has been a widely studied primitive and many variants, reductions, and applications have been considered. Even, Goldreich and Lempel [10] formalized 1-out-of-2 OT as a generalization of Rabin's OT. This was further generalized by Brassard, Crépeau and Robert [4] into 1-out-of-n OT, under the name "all-or-nothing disclosure of secrets." We believe that the mOT primitive may be of independent interest. Goldreich and Vainish [17] and Killian [20] show that OT is a complete primitive in the sense that two parties can compute any circuit securely using only blackbox access to OT. Goldreich [15] provides a nice presentation of the completeness of OT using a linear (in the circuit size) number of invocations of 1-out-of-4 two-party OT. Our mOT primitive directly translates this result to the case of general multiparty computation in a straight-forward fashion, yielding a new proof of this result. It also leads to new proofs for other results in general secure multiparty computation such as, for example, given a secure two-party OT protocol, n parties can compute any function n-privately (*e.g.*, see [14]), given secure channels, n parties can compute any function t-privately (information theoretically) for $t < n/2$ (*e.g.*, see [3]), and similar results.

In concurrent and independent work, Ishai *et al.* [19] design an mOT protocol under the name "distributed OT." Both our protocol and theirs involve the use of efficient

PIR protocols, though in different ways. Thus, our work gives new constructions for the results in their paper. Comparing our two tools, our database performs $O(n)$ work where theirs performs $O(n^2)$, where n is the size of the database. While both tools are comparable in terms of communication efficiency, theirs is only efficient in this sense under some limitations on the number of parties m, since the size of the messages passed in their scheme is linear in m. The length of the messages passed in our protocol is independent of the number of parties, and thus we impose no limit on the number of parties involved in our protocols. Additionally, our protocol has a logarithmic (in n) round complexity, while theirs has a linear (in m) round complexity (the database's response is a $\log n$-iterated encryption in the former, and an $m - 1$-iterated encryption in the later).

1.2 Definitions and Notation

We use the following definitions and notations.

Notation 1. *We denote the negation of bit b by $\neg b$.*

Definition 2 (t-privacy). *A protocol is t-private if any set of at most t participants cannot compute after the protocol more then they could jointly compute solely from their set of private inputs and outputs.*

Notation 3 (Asymptotic notation). *We use the following asymptotic notation: $o(f)$ denotes that the asymptotic upper bound f is not tight; $\Omega(f)$ denotes that the asymptotic lower bound f is tight; and $\widetilde{O}(f)$ denotes the asymptotic upper bound $O(f)$, ignoring $\operatorname{polylog}(f)$ factors.*

Notation 4 (Share notation). *We let $([\delta]_1, [\delta]_2, \ldots, [\delta]_m)$ be the collection of the shares of δ split among m parties via some secret-sharing scheme, so that player i holds the share $[\delta]_i$. When the subscript can be determined from context, we abuse notation and omit the subscript for ease of exposition; thus, we may denote the share of player i as, simply, $[\delta]$.*

2   Secure Multiparty Computation with Look-Up Tables

Naor and Nissim [24] define and give a secure two-party protocol for circuits with look-up tables. In the computational model of *circuits with look-up tables*, gates of a circuit are represented by look-up tables (LUT). The LUT input wires define the table entries and an index, and the LUT output wires are set according to the value stored in the indexed position. The protocol for private LUT serves as a building block in a protocol for privately evaluating circuits with LUT (a variant of the garbled circuit transformation). Here, we extend the definition of the look-up table primitive to the multiparty case.

Definition 5 (Multiparty LUT). *In a multiparty LUT (mLUT) protocol, all the parties are both a chooser and a database holder. Each party i holds a share of the database Δ, and a share of the index σ. At the end of the protocol, each party learns a share of δ_σ,* *the element at position σ in database Δ. Let $\Delta = (\delta_0, \ldots, \delta_{n-1})$. Let party i's share of δ be denoted by $[\delta]_i$. Then, the mLUT protocol can be summarized by the following protocol Π.*

$$\Pi([\Delta]_1, [\sigma]_1; [\Delta]_2, [\sigma]_2; \ldots; [\Delta]_m, [\sigma]_m) \rightarrow ([\delta_\sigma]_1; [\delta_\sigma]_2; \ldots; [\delta_\sigma]_m)$$

Definition 6 (Private mLUT). *We call a mLUT protocol t-private if no coalition of up to t parties can learn any information about σ or any of the elements in Δ.*

Circuits with LUT amount to performing computations with tables as follows. (1) **Read operations:** The table values as well as the index specifying the location of the read item are either preset or the result of an intermediate computation. In particular, it is possible to perform any kind of indirect read. (2) **Write operations:** The value written to the table may be the result of an intermediate operation but the location should be predetermined. In other words, no indirect writes are allowed.

It follows that any computation on a RAM machine where write operations are oblivious, in the sense that the time and location of the write operations should not depend on the input and randomness, may be emulated by circuits with LUT.

Results of Pippenger and Ficher [32] imply that when considering circuits vs. Turing Machines there is no significant advantage to the latter since there exists a series of circuits of size comparable to the running time of the Turing Machine. Currently it is not known whether a similar result applies to circuits vs. RAM machines. Particularly, there is a potential gap between the two, *i.e.* a computation on a RAM machine may be much more efficient than any circuit family. But for circuits with LUT this gap is closed. Particularly, note that for any write-oblivious RAM machine M running in time $T(n)$, there exists a family of circuits with LUT of size $T(n)$ computing f_M. Now, all one needs to show is an efficient simulation of any RAM machine using a write-oblivious RAM machine. Such a simulation exists, with polylogarithmic blow-up [16,24]. Specifically, for any RAM machine M running in time $T(n)$ using space $S(n)$, there exist a series of circuits with LUT of size $T(n)\text{polylog}(S(n))$ computing f_M.

3   Applications

Although we have not yet provided a private protocol for multiparty LUT (mLUT), we show how such a protocol leads to immediate efficiency improvements for several privacy-preserving protocols in the literature and efficient multiparty generalizations of existing two-party protocols.

We note that by replacing the two-party private LUT of Naor and Nissim [24] with a private construction of mLUT, we generalize all the constructions given in that paper to the multiparty case. In Appendix A of the full version of this paper [12], we present a multiparty generalization of the communication complexity model and a transformation which makes any efficient, non-private protocol in this model into an efficient, private protocol with the same functionality. Also, a private mLUT protocol automatically yields the ability to simulate, as a multiparty computation, a private oblivious RAM machine with only a polylog (in size of the RAM) blowup in communication between the parties.

Furthermore, we believe our mLUT protocol to be useful in a variety of existing applications, such as private multiparty sampling protocols [19], distributing the function of an "auction issuer" in Naor-Pinkas-Sumner style auctions [27], private approximation protocols, and any setting where a global decision is privately computed using access to some of the inputs of several parties. In the remainder of this section, we discuss applying our tools to two such domains: protocols for distributed constraint satisfaction problems, and protocols for the stable matching problem.

3.1 Private DisCSPs

Distributed constraint satisfaction problems (DisCSPs) are composed of agents holding local variables, and a constraint network that restricts the legal assignments to agents' variables. A solution to a DisCSP is an assignment to variables that is in agreement with all the constraints ([38,36]). To achieve this goal, agents run a protocol where they check assignments to their and other agents' variables for consistency. Distributed CSPs are an elegant model for many every day combinatorial problems that are distributed by nature, such as meeting scheduling [13,23] in which agents attempt to schedule meetings according to their constrained personal schedule.

Nissim and Zivan [29] design new secure protocols for DisCSPs based on advanced search heuristics. The first protocol they design is a *centralized* protocol, where two of the agents collect "encrypted" data from all other parties, and obliviously perform a search algorithm. Their centralized algorithm avoids information leakage to all agents. their second protocol makes the first step toward a feasible *distributed* secured protocol for solving DisCSPs. They construct a network, whose nodes are small groups (*e.g.* pairs) of agents, from the original DisCSPs. Each node group obliviously performs the roles of all its members in the search algorithm. This protocol has the following disadvantages (1) it is *not fully distributed* and a small collusion of agents could learn information about the other participants' private inputs. (2) As mentioned in the paper, the protocol is not perfectly secure, *i.e.* the communication pattern in the protocol leaks information about the agents' private inputs.

Using our private construction for multiparty computation of circuits with LUT, we can securely extend the centralized protocol given in section 5 of [29] to a fully distributed one without adding any overhead in the communication or computation of their protocol. More specifically, the agents will collectively share the private data and obliviously perform the search algorithm. This leads to the first *fully distributed* and *completely secure* protocol for DisCSPs. For completeness, we include a brief description of our construction in Appendix B of the full version of this paper [12].

3.2 Private Stable Matching

Golle [18] initiated the study of privacy-preserving protocols for stable matching, arguing persuasively that such protocols could have great practical benefit. In Golle's framework, m "matching authorities" receive the encrypted preference lists from the participants and then perform a secure multiparty computation to return the stable matching to the participants. Franklin *et al.* [11] revisit Golle's work and design substantially more efficient protocols for private stable matching in this framework.

Naor, Pinkas, and Sumner [27] observe, in considering this problem as a possible domain for their paper's techniques, that the algorithm for solving the stable matching problem requires the power of indirect addressing of a RAM and, thus, its translation into a circuit is rather inefficient. Indeed, the stable matching algorithm of Franklin *et al.* [11] can be efficiently implemented as a circuit of size $O(n^2)$ with access to a RAM. More specifically, one can implement their algorithm [11, Section 5] in the multiparty setting[1] by implementing their array/matrix accesses using our mLUT protocol. In this way, we extend this (very efficient) construction of theirs from two-party to multiparty, yielding a protocol in the same framework as Golle and Franklin *et al.*, but a factor of n more efficient than previous private stable matching protocols. The following table compares our results with those of the previous work.

Protocol	Total Work	Total Communication	Round Complexity
Golle [18]	$O(n^5)$	$O(mn^5)$	$\tilde{O}(n^3)$
Franklin *et al.* [11]	$O(n^4\sqrt{\log n})$	$O(mn^3)$	$\tilde{O}(n^2)$
Ours	$O(n^4)$	$O(mn^2)$	$\tilde{O}(n^2)$

4   Protocols for Private mLUT

In this section, we reduce the problem of constructing a protocol for private mLUT to a subproblem we call "generalized multiparty oblivious transfer." First we define this subproblem, and then we show our construction for mLUT. Later, we define a related protocol we call "multiparty oblivious transfer" and draw connections between this new primitive and general multiparty computation. Finally, in Section 5, we give a construction for an efficient, private g-mOT protocol, completing our private mLUT construction.

4.1   A Construction for Private mLUT

Our construction for the private mLUT protocol invokes a protocol called *generalized multiparty oblivious transfer* (g-mOT) for each share of the database. Parties get their shares of the output for each run of the g-mOT protocol and combine their shares in the appropriate way to compute shares of the indexed position in the original database Δ. We define generalized mOT below, and then describe this protocol in more detail.

Definition 7 (Generalized multiparty oblivious transfer). *Generalized multiparty oblivious transfer (g-mOT) is a protocol involving m parties where: at the beginning of the protocol, each party holds a share of a secret index σ and one distinguished party holds a table of n bits, the database $\Delta = (\delta_0, \ldots, \delta_{n-1})$; at the end of the protocol,*

---

[1] Franklin *et al.* generalize this two-party protocol to the multiparty case, but the resulting protocol is only secure in a new security model where one considers collections of pairs of matching authorities, where each pair is honest-majority. Our generalization is secure in the standard passive adversary security model where up to a certain threshold of players may be corrupted.

each party holds a share of the database element δ_σ. In the terminology of oblivious transfer, every party is a chooser and one party is also the database. The protocol Π for $\binom{n}{1}$-g-mOT(m, t) can be summarized as:

$$\Pi(\Delta, [\sigma]; [\sigma]; \ldots; [\sigma]) \rightarrow ([\delta_\sigma]; [\delta_\sigma]; \ldots; [\delta_\sigma])$$

We give a full security description of g-mOT later but, for our mLUT construction, we only require that this protocol be t-private.

For simplicity, we assume that the outputs and database are shared using XOR sharing in the construction below. Any other sharing scheme would work fine, however, as the overhead for switching between different sharing methods does not effect the overall complexity of our protocols. Again, let m be the number of parties participating in the protocol. Let chooser i hold $\Delta^i = [\Delta]_i$, where $\oplus \Delta^i = \Delta$. The protocol is outlined below.

Inputs: Each party holds a share of the database $\Delta = (\delta_0, \ldots, \delta_{n-1})$ and a share of the index σ.
Output: Each party holds a share of δ_σ.

- For $i = 1$ to m:
  - Parties run
    g-mOT$(\Delta^i, [\sigma]; [\sigma]; [\sigma]; \ldots; [\sigma]) \rightarrow ([\delta^i_\sigma]; [\delta^i_\sigma]; \ldots; [\delta^i_\sigma])$.
- Participant i locally computes a share of δ_σ as $[\delta_\sigma] = \oplus [\delta^j_\sigma]$.

Claim. The complete protocol is a t-private multiparty LUT. The protocol has $O(k\ell \log^2 n \operatorname{poly}(m))$ communication complexity and $O(\log n)$ round complexity, where k is a security parameter, m is the total number of parties, and the database is composed of n strings of bit-length ℓ.

Proof (Sketch). Our mLUT protocol uses m invocations of a generalized mOT protocol. Thus, the communication complexity of our mLUT construction is simply m times that of the g-mOT protocol from Section 5.2. Since we can run the generalized mOT protocols in parallel, the round complexity of the mLUT protocol remains the same as that of the g-mOT protocol. The t-privacy of the mLUT protocol follows from general composition theorems [5,15] and the t-privacy of our g-mOT protocol.

4.2 Multiparty Oblivious Transfer

Before we give a construction for an efficient t-private generalized multiparty oblivious transfer protocol, we explore a related protocol we call multiparty oblivious transfer. We also give a detailed security definition for these protocols, as there may be interesting applications that require something stronger than t-privacy.

Multiparty oblivious transfer (mOT) is a protocol involving $m' + 1$ parties: m' choosers and a database. Each chooser holds a share of a secret index $\sigma \in [0, n-1]$. The database holds a table[2] of n bits, $\Delta' = (\delta_0, \ldots, \delta_{n-1})$. At the end of the protocol, each

---

[2] In Section 5.2, we consider a generalization of this definition, where the database is a table of n strings, each of length ℓ.

chooser holds a share of the database element δ_σ. The protocol Π for $\binom{n}{1}$–mOT(m', t) can be summarized as follows:

$$\Pi(\Delta'; [\sigma]_1; \ldots; [\sigma]_{m'}) \rightarrow (\emptyset; [\delta_\sigma]_1; \ldots; [\delta_\sigma]_{m'})$$

We consider mOT for its simplicity and because, in many scenarios, g-mOT reduces to mOT. For example, by letting $m = m' + 1$ it is clear that, when the inputs and outputs are XOR shares, there is a simple reduction of g-mOT to mOT. More specifically, the database in the g-mOT protocol can compute the database Δ' by permuting Δ according to x_0 (his share of the secret index) and blinding each entry by a random y_0 (his share of the output). Considering XOR shares, then, generalized mOT reduces to an invocation of the following mOT protocol Π.

$$\Pi(\Delta'; x_1, \ldots; x_{m'}) \rightarrow (\emptyset; y_1; \ldots; y_{m'}) \text{ where } \bigoplus_{i=0}^{m'} x_i = \sigma \text{ and } \bigoplus_{i=0}^{m'} y_i = \delta_\sigma$$

Definition 8 (Secure mOT). *Following Naor and Pinkas [26], we give a detailed, four-parameter security definition for this new variant of oblivious transfer. We relate this definition to the more common and intuitive security notion of t-privacy. We say the mOT protocol is (t_1, t_2, t_3, t_4)-secure if, when all the participants follow their steps properly (i.e., considering a passive adversary), the following properties are met:*

> input t_1-privacy: *no coalition of up to t_1 choosers should be able to learn any information about σ.*
> output t_2-privacy: *no coalition of up to t_2 choosers should be able to learn any information about δ_σ.*
> chooser t_3-privacy: *the database should not be able to learn any information about σ, even when colluding with up to t_3 other participants.*
> database t_4-privacy: *no coalition of up to t_4 non-database players should be able to learn any information about δ_j for $j \neq \sigma$.*

We could easily create information theoretic and computational variants of this definition by specifying the power of the adversary accordingly.

Remark 1. The following are automatic consequences.

- (t_1, t_2, t_3, t_4)-security implies $\min(t_1, t_2, t_3 + 1, t_4)$-privacy.
- It is necessary that $t_3 \leq \min(t_1, t_2)$. For g-mOT this becomes strict, $t_3 < \min(t_1, t_2)$.
- For g-mOT, since the database is a chooser, there is always a collusion of $t_3 + 1$ choosers who can learn σ, so $t_1 = t_3 + 1$. Furthermore, $t_1 = t_2$ because, for the database, learning σ implies learning δ_σ (and vice versa). Thus, for g-mOT, t-privacy implies $(t, t, t - 1, t_4)$-security, for some $t_4 \geq t$.
- If the players are computationally unbounded, it must be the case that $(m' + 1)/2 > \min(t_1, t_2, t_3 + 1, t_4)$, or else we contradict known results for the privacy of unconditionally secure multiparty computation.

5   Protocols for Private mOT and g-mOT

In this section, we give two constructions for multiparty oblivious transfer. The first mOT construction uses blackbox access to two-party oblivious transfer, showing that mOT can be constructed under a variety of complexity assumptions. The second is a construction of g-mOT which we rely on for our earlier applications, as it is efficient in terms of communication complexity. We leave open the problem of finding a fully black-box transformation of two-party oblivious transfer into multiparty oblivious transfer with sublinear (in size of the database) blowup in communication complexity.

5.1   A Generic Construction for 1-Out-of-2 mOT

Here, we describe a generic construction for a 1-out-of-2 mOT protocol, using blackbox access to a two-party oblivious transfer protocol. For this construction, we consider the case where the secret σ is shared among the m' choosers using XOR sharing. Let chooser i hold share b_i and $\oplus b_i = \sigma$.

---

1. The database chooses $2m'$ bits, $\{(r_0^1, r_1^1), (r_0^2, r_1^2), \ldots, (r_0^{m'}, r_1^{m'})\}$ uniformly at random, such that the bits satisfy the following condition:

$$\bigoplus_{i=1}^{m'} r_{b_i}^i = \delta_{\oplus b_i}$$

2. For all $1 \leq i \leq m'$
   Chooser i and the database run a two-party oblivious transfer protocol, where the chooser's private input is b_i and the database's private input is the two element "database" (r_0^i, r_1^i).
3. The output for chooser i is $r_{b_i}^i$ which, according to the previous condition, is an XOR share of $\delta_{\oplus b_i} = \delta_\sigma$.

It is clear that the values of the $2m'$ variables which satisfy the above condition are precisely the solutions to the following set of $m' + 1$ linear equations:

$$\left\{ r_1^i = \delta_0 \oplus \delta_1 \oplus r_0^i \mid i < m' \right\}, \; r_0^{m'} = \delta_0 \oplus \bigoplus_{i=1}^{m'-1} r_0^i \text{ and } r_1^{m'} = \delta_1 \oplus \bigoplus_{i=1}^{m'-1} r_1^i$$

In this form, it is easier to see that the database can find a random solution to the above system by simply choosing the values for variables $\{r_0^i \mid i < m'\}$ uniformly at random. The remaining values are uniquely defined.

When the two-party oblivious transfer protocol is private, the above mOT protocol is $(m' - 1)$-private. This construction is essentially the same as that of Crépeau and Kilian [6], though in a different context, and our proof of security follows directly from theirs.

This 1-out-of-2 mOT construction protocol can be turned into a 1-out-of-n mOT protocol using a variant of the Brassard-Crépeau-Robert transform [4] which constructs

1-out-of-n oblivious transfer from (a linear number of invocations of) the 1-out-of-2 variant. While these constructions are not particularly efficient, they do demonstrate that mOT protocols can be constructed under a variety of standard cryptographic assumptions and in the information-theoretic case. For example, given secure channels, each two-party OT protocol can be replaced with the distributed OT (dOT) protocol of Naor and Pinkas [26]. Briefly, in a (r, m, ℓ, t)-dOT protocol, the database sends messages to m servers[3] and the chooser contacts r of the servers to reconstruct δ_σ, where no coalition of less than t servers learns σ and no coalition of the chooser with less than ℓ servers can compute more than can be jointly computed from these participant's inputs and outputs. A straight-forward argument of Nikov *et al.* [28] shows that a necessary and sufficient condition for dOT is $r \geq t + \ell$. Thus, our mOT protocol based on dOT will be τ-private for $\tau < \min(\ell + 1, t)$. Since $r \leq m$, this condition implies our mOT protocol is τ-private for $\tau < (m + 1)/2$.

Using this construction for mOT instead of OT in a proof of the completeness of OT such as Goldreich's [15, §7.1.3.3] yields new proof that (given secure channels) n parties can compute any function τ-privately (information theoretically) for $\tau < n/2$. The original presentation of this result, due to Ben-Or, Goldwasser, and Wigderson [3], uses polynomial shares and requires a special, private polynomial degree-reduction technique to handle the degree growth during the interactive multiplication steps. This new proof avoids such complicated machinery. In fact, using a basic proof of the completeness of mOT while building mOT out of different tools (*e.g.*, secure channels, secure channels and one-way functions, two-party OT, etc) yields new proofs for a variety of interesting results in secure multiparty computation.

5.2   A Construction for 1-Out-of-n g-mOT

In this section, we describe a generic construction of a 1-out-of-n generalized multiparty oblivious transfer protocol. At a high level, the construction can be viewed as a non-black-box transformation from a two-party private information retrieval (PIR) protocol (see [30] for a recent survey). First, the two-party PIR protocol is converted into a two-party OT protocol. The owners of the secret sharing scheme engage in a multiparty computation, t-privately transforming their shares of σ into the messages $\bar{m}_0$ that would be sent to the database during the two-party OT protocol. A single chooser and the database then engage in the message passing of the original PIR protocol. The received messages $\bar{m}_1$ are then used as inputs to another multiparty computation, t-privately converting these messages into shares of δ_σ. In this construction, the sharing used for the inputs and outputs is some t-out-of-m linear secret sharing scheme with security parameter k, owned by an appropriate subset of the choosers.

One particularly efficient instantiation of our construction can be built using a two-round PIR protocol, the length-flexible additively homomorphic public key encryption [8,9] and design ideas of Aiello-Ishai-Reingold [1]. In the remainder of this section, we discuss this highly efficient instantiation. The steps of this protocol are assembled in order and summarized below.

---

[3] We note the database itself might play the role of a server, sending itself a message, causing dOT to be a protocol among $m + 1$ parties.

1. The choosers collaborate to create a (t-out-of-m) threshold, length-flexible, additively homomorphic) encryption system.
2. The choosers collaborate to compute the PIR scheme's first message $\bar{m}_0$, using their shares of σ (see Section 5.2).
3. The choosers send the public parameters, $E(\sigma)$, and $\bar{m}_0$ to the database.
4. The database uses $E(\sigma)$ to blind the database, according to the Aiello-Ishai-Reingold transform (see Section 5.2).
5. The database runs the PIR protocol as usual, using $\bar{m}_0$ and the blinded database (see Section 5.2).
6. The database sends its response $\bar{m}_1$ to the choosers.
7. The choosers collaborate to decrypt $\bar{m}_1$. In our case, they decrypt the response α times and then split the remaining ciphertext into shares (see Section 5.2).

Highly Efficient Two-Party PIR and OT. A highly efficient two-party PIR scheme can be built from length-flexible additively homomorphic public key encryption [8,9] using design ideas of Kushilevitz-Ostrovsky [21] (*e.g.*, following the presentation of Lipmaa [22]).

The database is composed of n ℓ-bit strings. The chooser takes her secret σ and constructs $\bar{q} = (q_1, \ldots, q_\alpha)$, the α-dimensional vector which indicates the position of σ in a $\lambda_1 \times \cdots \times \lambda_\alpha$ coordinate system. In this system, index $(i_1, \ldots, i_\alpha)$ is resolved in the following manner:

$$\Delta[(i_1, \ldots, i_\alpha)] = \Delta[i_1 \cdot \prod_{j=2}^{\alpha} \lambda_j + i_2 \cdot \prod_{j=3}^{\alpha} \lambda_j + \cdots + i_{\alpha-1} \cdot \lambda_\alpha + i_\alpha]$$

The first query sent to the database is the encryption of q_1 with the corresponding public key. The database uses this to construct $\Delta[q_1, i_2, \ldots, i_\alpha]$, a new database with $\alpha - 1$ dimensions. The next query is the encryption of q_2, the first coordinate of the same element in this new database. We iterate in this fashion α times. This is a standard trick, due to Kushilevitz and Ostrovsky [21] and is used in the PIR scheme of Stern [37]. In the final round, the database's response is the α times encryption of δ_i. In fact this process happens in one round, since the encryption of $\bar{q} = (q_1, \ldots, q_\alpha)$ can be sent in a single message. When encryption is achieved using a *length-flexible* additively homomorphic public-key cryptosystem, this PIR protocol has $\Theta(k \log^2 n + \ell \log n)$ communication complexity, as shown by Lipmaa [22].

A modification of this PIR scheme, using the Aiello-Ishai-Reingold transform, yields a highly efficient OT scheme. The chooser encrypts σ using a homomorphic encryption scheme and sends this to the database with the corresponding public-key. The database takes advantage of the homomorphic property of the ciphertext to compute a new database where each entry δ_j is represented by $E(r_j(\sigma - j) + \delta_j)$, for some random r_j. Thus, for all $j \neq \sigma$, the j-th element of the database is the encryption of a random element. The original Aiello-Ishai-Reingold transform suggests that the homomorphic encryption scheme generated for this step be verifiable, such as the El-Gamal scheme, so the database can verify the correctness of the public-key sent by the chooser.

As we consider only honest-but-curious adversaries, we can re-use the homomorphic encryption scheme used in the original PIR protocol and ignore the need for verifiable keys. The rest of the OT protocol proceeds just as in the original PIR protocol, but the database's response must now be decrypted $\alpha + 1$ times to recover δ_σ. This transformation increases the communication complexity by a term of $\ell + k(\log n + 1)$ bits, which does not effect the overall asymptotic complexity.

Input Share Conversion. In our g-mOT scheme, the choosers hold shares of σ using some linear secret sharing scheme. We describe below how the choosers can engage in an efficient t-private multiparty protocol to convert their shares of σ into an encryption of $\bar{q} = (\mathbf{q_1}, \ldots, \mathbf{q_\alpha})$. For simplicity, we represent the database as the $\alpha = \log n$-dimensional $2 \times \cdots \times 2$ system[4].

The choosers interact to define a t-out-of-m threshold version of the length-flexible homomorphic encryption scheme. In reality, $\mathbf{q_i}$ is a λ_i-length bit string of Hamming weight 1. Locally, the database uses $E(\mathbf{q_i})$, the bit-wise encryption of this value, to process the representation of the database at step i. In our simplified scenario (for all i, $\lambda_i = 2$) this bit string is simply $\mathbf{q_i} = (\neg b_i, b_i)$, where b_i is the i-th bit in the binary representation of σ. In other words, if we let Δ^j denote the $\alpha - j$-dimensional database constructed in round j of the PIR protocol, then

$$\Delta^{j+1}[i] = \neg \mathbf{q_j} \cdot \Delta^j[i] + \mathbf{q_j} \cdot \Delta^j[2^i + 1]$$

Since the encryption of the negation of a bit can be computed by the database, trivially, via the homomorphic property, it suffices to let $\mathbf{q_i} = b_i$. Damgård *et al.* [7] provide efficient, private constant-round multiparty protocols for computing shares of the binary representation of a secret, from shares of the secret. Using the homomorphic property, the choosers' shares are encrypted and combined, and $E(\mathbf{q})$, $E(\sigma)$, and the public key are sent to the database by a chooser. From this, the database can run its portion of the OT protocol, and send its response.

Output Conversion. The response from the database is jointly decrypted α times by the choosers to recover $E(\delta_\sigma)$, the desired element encrypted using the same t-threshold (length-flexible) additively homomorphic encryption scheme. This is already, in a sense, a share of δ_σ. Using the homomorphic property, this ciphertext can be split into additive shares for the choosers, or a different type of sharing if desired.

5.3 Analysis

Claim. The complete protocol of Section 5.2 has $O(k\ell \log^2 n \operatorname{poly}(m))$ communication complexity and $O(\log n)$ round complexity, where k is a security parameter, m is the total number of players, and the database is composed of n strings of bit-length ℓ.

---

[4] For efficiency in communication complexity when using this representation, we require the use of length-flexible additively homomorphic encryption. It is possible to use a generic additively homomorphic encryption system and achieve sublinear communication complexity by using a different representation, at the cost of increasing the round complexity (by a factor of $\log n$) during this pre-processing phase. Such a choice would not effect the efficiency of the complete protocol.

Proof (Sketch). The primitives used by the input share conversion protocol have $O(\text{poly}(m, \log q))$ communication complexity, where q is the size of the field in which σ lives. Since σ is a pointer into a table of size n, the communication complexity becomes, in our case, $O(\text{poly}(m, \log \log n)) = o(\text{poly}(m) \log n)$. Also, the messages passed between the database and the other parties are the same as those passed during the oblivious transfer protocol from Section 5.2, whose communication complexity is $\Theta(k \log^2 n + \ell \log n)$. Thus, our complete protocol has $O(m(k \log^2 n + \ell \log n) + \text{poly}(m) \log n) = O(k\ell \log^2 n \text{poly}(m))$ communication complexity and $O(\log n)$ round complexity.

Claim. The complete protocol of Section 5.2 is t-private, assuming the threshold length-flexible additively homomorphic public-key encryption scheme is IND-CPA secure.

Proof (Sketch). The above security claim follows from the security of the share conversion protocols, from general composition theorems [5,15], and from the same security arguments of [22] since (although we make use of the protocol in a non-blackbox manner) the transcript of the messages passed between the chooser and database in our protocol is identical.

More specifically, the g-mOT protocol is $(t, t, t - 1, m)$-secure, because the Aiello-Ishai-Reingold transform makes the OT scheme information-theoretically database-private. When the PIR protocol is converted into an OT protocol using a transformation that provides computational sender privacy, like the Naor-Pinkas transform [25], the resulting mOT protocol is $(t, t, t - 1, t)$-secure. The threshold, length-flexible homomorphic encryption scheme of Damgård and Jurik [9] is IND-CPA secure in the standard model, under the Paillier and composite DDH assumptions.

References

1. Aiello, B., Ishai, Y., Reingold, O.: Priced oblivious transfer: How to sell digital goods. In: Pfitzmann, B. (ed.) EUROCRYPT 2001. LNCS, vol. 2045, pp. 119–135. Springer, Heidelberg (2001)
2. Barkol, O., Ishai, Y.: Secure computation of constant-depth circuits with application to database search problems. In: Shoup, V. (ed.) CRYPTO 2005. LNCS, vol. 3621, Springer, Heidelberg (2005)
3. Ben-Or, M., Goldwasser, S., Wigderson, A.: Completeness theorems for non-cryptographic fault-tolerant disributed computation. In: Proc. of STOC 1988, pp. 1–10 (1988)
4. Brassard, G., Crépeau, C., Robert, J.-M.: Information theoretic reductions among disclosure problems. In: Proc. of FOCS, pp. 168–173 (1986)
5. Canetti, R.: Security and composition of multiparty cryptographic protocols. Journal of Cryptology 13, 143–202 (2000)
6. Crépeau, C., Kilian, J.: Achieving oblivious transfer using weakened security assumptions. In: Proc. of FOCS, pp. 42–52 (1988)
7. Damgård, I., Fitzi, M., Kiltz, E., Nielsen, J.B., Toft, T.: Unconditionally secure constant-rounds multi-party computation for equality, comparison, bits and exponentiation. In: Halevi, S., Rabin, T. (eds.) TCC 2006. LNCS, vol. 3876, pp. 285–304. Springer, Heidelberg (2006)

8. Damgård, I., Jurik, M.: A generalisation, a simplification and some applications of Paillier's probabilistic public-key system. In: Kim, K.-c. (ed.) PKC 2001. LNCS, vol. 1992, pp. 119–136. Springer, Heidelberg (2001)
9. Damgård, I., Jurik, M.: A length-flexible threshold cryptosystem with applications. In: Information Security and Privacy, pp. 350–364 (2003)
10. Even, S., Goldreich, O., Lempel, A.: A randomized protocol for signing contracts. Comm. of the ACM 28(6), 637–647 (1985)
11. Franklin, M., Gondree, M., Mohassel, P.: Improved efficiency for private stable matching. In: Proc. of CT-RSA (2007)
12. Franklin, M., Gondree, M., Mohassel, P.: Multi-party indirect indexing and applications. Cryptology ePrint Archive, Report 2007/341 (2007)
13. Freuder, E.C., Wallace, R.J.: Constraint-based multi-agent meeting scheduling: effects of agent heterogeneity on performance and privacy loss. In: Proc. of the 3rd Workshop on Distributed Constraint Reasoning (DCR 2002), pp. 176–182 (2002)
14. Goldreich, O., Micali, S., Wigderson, A.: How to play any mental game or a completeness theorem for protocols with honest majority. In: Proc. of STOC 1987, pp. 218–229 (1987)
15. Goldreich, O.: Foundations of Cryptography. Cambridge University Press, Cambridge (2001)
16. Goldreich, O., Ostrovsky, R.: Software protection and simulation on oblivious rams. Journal of the ACM 43(3), 431–473 (1996)
17. Goldreich, O., Vainish, R.: How to solve any protocol problem - an efficiency improvement. In: Pomerance, C. (ed.) CRYPTO 1987. LNCS, vol. 293, pp. 73–86. Springer, Heidelberg (1988)
18. Golle, P.: A private stable matching algorithm. In: Di Crescenzo, G., Rubin, A. (eds.) FC 2006. LNCS, vol. 4107, Springer, Heidelberg (2006)
19. Ishai, Y., Malkin, T., Strauss, M.J., Wright, R.N.: Private multiparty sampling and approximation of vector combinations. In: Proc. of International Colloquium on Automata, Languages and Programming (ICALP) (2007)
20. Kilian, J.: A general completeness theorem for 2-party games. In: Proc. of STOC 1991, pp. 553–560 (1991)
21. Kushilevitz, E., Ostrovsky, R.: Replication is not needed: Single database, computationally-private information retrieval. In: Proc. of FOCS, pp. 364–373 (1997)
22. Lipmaa, H.: Verifiable homomorphic oblivious transfer and private equality test. In: Laih, C.-S. (ed.) ASIACRYPT 2003. LNCS, vol. 2894, pp. 416–433. Springer, Heidelberg (2003)
23. Meisels, A., Lavee, O.: Using additional information in DisCSP search. In: Proc. of the 5th Workshop on Distributed Constraint Reasoning (DCR-04) (2004)
24. Naor, M., Nissim, K.: Communication preserving protocols for secure function evaluation. In: Proc. of STOC 2001, pp. 590–599 (2001)
25. Naor, M., Pinkas, B.: Oblivious transfer and polynomial evaluation. In: Proc. of STOC 1999, pp. 245–254 (1999)
26. Naor, M., Pinkas, B.: Distributed oblivious transfer. In: Okamoto, T. (ed.) ASIACRYPT 2000. LNCS, vol. 1976, pp. 205–219. Springer, Heidelberg (2000)
27. Naor, M., Pinkas, B., Sumner, R.: Privacy preserving auctions and mechanism design. In: EC 1999. Proc. of the 1st ACM conference on Electronic Commerce, pp. 129–139. ACM Press, New York (1999)
28. Nikov, V., Nikova, S., Preneel, B., Vandewalle, J.: On unconditionally secure distributed oblivious transfer. In: Menezes, A.J., Sarkar, P. (eds.) INDOCRYPT 2002. LNCS, vol. 2551, pp. 395–408. Springer, Heidelberg (2002)
29. Nissim, K., Zivan, R.: Secure DisCSP protocols - from centralized towards distributed solutions. In: Proc. of the 6th Workshop on Distributed Constraint Reasoning (DCR-05) (2005)
30. Ostrovsky, R., Skeith III, W.E.: A survey of single database PIR: Techniques and applications. Cryptology ePrint Archive, Report 2007/059 (2007)

31. Ostrovsky, R., Shoup, V.: Private information storage (extended abstract). In: Proc of STOC 1997, pp. 294–303 (1997)
32. Pippenger, N., Fischer, M.J.: Relations among complexity measures. Journal of the ACM 26(2), 361–381 (1979)
33. Rabin, M.O.: How to exchange secrets with oblivious transfer. Technical Report TR-81, Harvard University, available as the Cryptology ePrint Archive Report 2005/187 (1981), http://eprint.iacr.org/
34. Silaghi, M.-C.: Solving a distributed CSP with cryptographic multi-party computations, without revealing constraints and without involving trusted servers. In: Proc. of the 4th Workshop on Distributed Constraint Reasoning (DCR-03) (2003)
35. Silaghi, M.-C., Mitra, D.: Distributed constraint satisfaction and optimization with privacy enforcement. In: Proc. of the 3rd International Conference on Intelligence Agent Technology, pp. 531–535 (2004)
36. Solotorevsky, G., Gudes, E., Meisels, A.: Modeling and solving distributed constraint satisfaction problems (DCSPs). In: Constraint Processing-96, pp. 561–562 (1996)
37. Stern, J.P.: A new and efficient all-or-nothing disclosure of secrets protocol. In: Ohta, K., Pei, D. (eds.) ASIACRYPT 1998. LNCS, vol. 1514, pp. 357–371. Springer, Heidelberg (1998)
38. Yokoo, M.: Algorithms for distributed satisfaction problems: A review. In: Autonomous Agents and Multi-Agent Sys., pp. 198–212 (2000)
39. Yokoo, M., Suzuki, K., Hirayama, K.: Secure distributed constraint satisfaction: Reaching agreement without revealing private information. In: Artificial Intelligence, pp. 229–246 (2005)

Two-Party Computing with Encrypted Data

Seung Geol Choi[1], Ariel Elbaz[1], Ari Juels[2], Tal Malkin[1], and Moti Yung[1,3]

[1] Columbia University
{sgchoi,arielbaz,tal,moti}@cs.columbia.edu
[2] RSA Laboratories
ajuels@rsasecurity.com
[3] Google

Abstract. We consider a new model for online secure computation on encrypted inputs in the presence of malicious adversaries. The inputs are independent of the circuit computed in the sense that they can be contributed by separate third parties. The model attempts to emulate as closely as possible the model of "Computing with Encrypted Data" that was put forth in 1978 by Rivest, Adleman and Dertouzos which involved a single online message. In our model, two parties publish their public keys in an offline stage, after which any party (i.e., any of the two and any third party) can publish encryption of their local inputs. Then in an on-line stage, given any common input circuit C and its set of inputs from among the published encryptions, the first party sends a *single message* to the second party, who completes the computation.

Keywords: Computing with Encrypted Data, Secure Two-Party Computation, CryptoComputing, oblivious transfer.

1 Introduction

In "Computing with Encrypted Data", first a public key is published by one party, followed by collection of data encrypted under this key (potentially from various sources and independent of the actual computation). Later, in an online stage, a computing party who possesses a circuit of a function acts on the encrypted data, and sends the result (a single message) to the owner of the public key for output decryption. This wishful single message scenario for secure computation, was put forth as early as 1978 by Rivest, Adleman and Dertouzos [24]. This model is highly attractive since it represents the case where a database is first collected and maintained and only later a computation on it is decided upon and executed (i.e., data mining and statistical database computation done over the encrypted database). However, in its most general form (and the way [24] envisioned it), the model requires an encryption function that is homomorphic over a complete base (sometimes called doubly homomorphic encryption), which is a construction that we do not have (finding such a scheme is a long standing open problem and would have far reaching consequences); further, we have indications such a scheme cannot be highly secure [3].

In this paper we put forth a relaxation of the above model, that relies on two party secure computations, yet retains much of the desired properties of

K. Kurosawa (Ed.): ASIACRYPT 2007, LNCS 4833, pp. 298–314, 2007.

the original model, namely, it allows computing of any feasible functions over encrypted data, it further allows the data to come from various sources, and it employs a single online message as well. Our proposed relaxation is to allow two parties (rather than one) to publish a shared pubic key, and both parties hold shares of the private key and use their shares of the secret key to do computations on data encrypted with the public key. Once the public key is published, data contributors publish encrypted (committed) data as before (this is called the off-line stage). Then, in the on-line stage, one of the two parties (the compiler) is sending a **single message** to the second party (the cryptocomputer), that contains a circuit for a function to compute, and a garbled circuit of the same function, allowing the second party to compute the result securely (i.e., while keeping the inputs private, and gaining no computational advantage beyond what it can compute from the result and the inputs it knows). Note that because of its essentially non-interactive nature, our model is also particularly suitable for applications involving low-latency remote executions, such as for mobile agent applications [26].

We give two protocols in this model, which differ only in the cryptographic assumptions and the communication complexity. Both protocols are secure even against malicious parties, and both allow computing any polynomial function (or sequence of functions) by a single on-line message exchange, in a sense satisfying the original vision of [24] for computing with encrypted data.

If we limit the input contribution to the two parties involved, our model matches naturally the theory of general secure two party computation (see [17,32] and [20,21] for some of the earliest and the latest works in this area). While it may be possible to turn many of the works on two party computations to single message protocols (based on random oracle or non-interactive proofs), we have not seen this mentioned explicitly (the closest being [4]) or a proof of security given for it. To the best of our knowledge none of the previous garbled-circuit-based two party secure computation results allows for data contribution by third parties (an issue that was not even modeled earlier).

In the general two party computation setting, two parties Alice and Bob have private inputs x_A and x_B respectively, and wish to compute a function $f(x_A, x_B)$ securely, without leaking any further information. A particularly useful setting is where Alice and Bob have published commitments s_A, s_B on their inputs, which allows secure computation to proceed more efficiently. Applying our results to this setting, we can have Alice and Bob encrypt their input during the off-line stage (independently of any computation); then the subsequent secure computation (or "cryptocomputing" [27]) only requires a single message per function to be computed. A similar result was previously known only for functions of restricted complexity classes (e.g., [27] show how to securely compute functions in NC^1), while we provide a protocol for any function in P.

The idea of minimizing the on-line stage in cryptographic primitives goes back to the notion of Off-line On-line Signature of Even, Goldreich and Micali where they minimized the amount of computations of a signature at the on-line stage (after a message is given as an input) [12].

1.1   Our Model and Results

As outlined above, we propose the off-line/on-line model for crypto-computing using a single message (and thus optimal round complexity) for the on-line stage. For $k \geq 2$, there are parties $P_1, \ldots, P_k$. We name P_1 as Alice and P_2 as Bob. The model consists of the following four stages.

1. Alice and Bob publish prospective shares of the public key, y_A and y_B.
2. Separable Data Collection: Parties $P_1, \ldots, P_k$ publish their data, encrypted by a shared public key y.
3. Communication: Given an input circuit C with m designated inputs bits, Alice sends to Bob a single message containing a set of indexes to the published encrypted inputs $\{idx_i\}_{i=1}^m$, and a garbled circuit $\hat{C}$.
4. Computation: Bob decides if the message is consistent with the input circuit and its inputs, verifying that the indices to the encrypted inputs are valid, and that $\hat{C}$ is a garbled version of C. If all these tests succeed, Bob computes $\hat{C}$ on the committed inputs.

Note that since we deal with any polynomial-size function (or circuit), we can have some of the data encode circuits and the on-line circuit be a universal one [31].

We give two protocols that are secure within this model. The first is based on the traditional and quite minimal DDH assumption and uses ElGamal encryption, and the other is based on the DCR assumption and uses the simplified Camenisch-Shoup encryption scheme (introduced by [20]). The latter protocol achieves better communication complexity, at the price of using a stronger more recent assumption and encryption method.

We use non-interactive zero-knowledge proofs (NIZK) for the malicious case, which can be achieved either in the common reference string model or in the random oracle model. Under the common reference string model, the NIZK PoK of De Santis and Persiano [28] can be used, assuming dense secure public-key encryption scheme. Under the random oracle model, the well-known Fiat-Shamir technique [14] can be used.

A main primitive our work relies upon is a conditional exposure primitive we call $\mathcal{CODE}$ (Conditional Oblivious Decryption Exposure). $\mathcal{CODE}$ is a two-party non-interactive protocol, which allows Bob to learn the plaintext of a cyphertext c, if two other cyphertexts a, b encrypt the same value. Unlike other conditional exposure primitives (e.g. Gertner et al [16] and Aeillo et al [1]), in CODE the three cyphertexts a, b, c are encrypted with a shared public key, such that third parties can contribute them, and neither Alice nor Bob alone know anything else about the result of $\mathcal{CODE}$. The conditional exposure primitive of Aeillo et al. [1] is a natural translation of a logical 'if a equals b' to arithmetics on cyphertexts using encryption that is homomorphic in the plaintext. The $\mathcal{CODE}$ primitive uses homomorphic properties of the keys and of the plaintexts and gives more freedom to design protocols that include inputs shared among the parties.

This allows for oblivious yet secure "input directed navigation" in a garbled circuit based on a single trigger, given encrypted inputs. The technique also allows efficient combination with zero-knowledge proofs to assure robustness of the overall protocol.

We note that we concentrate on a single message computation and present the protocols with respect to the most efficient random oracle based proofs. Modifying the scheme to employ non-interactive proofs in the standard model and modifying the single message scheme to consider the universal composability model of security are possible as well.

1.2   Previous Work

As mentioned above, Rivest, Adleman, and Dertouzos [24] offer perhaps the first proposal for the study of blind computation on cyphertexts, considering them as a primitive for private data manipulation. Feigenbaum and Merritt [13] subsequently urged more focused investigation on cryptosystems with algebraic homomorphisms. The term "CryptoComputing" and the first non-trivial instantiation originated with Sander, Young, and Yung [27], who present a CryptoComuting protocol for functions f in NC^1. In their model, Alice does not publish her input s_A, but instead sends it (hides it) within her transcript, and information theoretic security is achieved with respect to Bob. This is to say that Bob learns no information whatever about s_A apart from the output of f. Beaver [2] extends [27] to accommodate any function in NLOGSPACE. Other reduced round secure computations (two message constructions, in fact) have been suggested by Naor, Pinkas, and Sumner [22] and by Cachin, Camenisch, Kilian, and Müller [4]. Their approaches are based on the two-party secure function evaluation scheme of Yao [32] and Goldreich, Micali, and Wigderson [17].

Recently the area of robust two-party computations in constant rounds has gained some attention. Specifically, the works of Jarecki and Shmatikov [20], Lindell and Pinkas [21] and Horvitz and Katz [19] gave protocols for two-party computation using Yao's garbled circuit that are secure against malicious adversaries. [20] uses a modified Camenisch-Shoup verifiable encryption scheme [6] to allow the party that sends the garbled circuit to prove its correctness. Our simplified-Camenisch-Shoup based protocol was devised by combining the ideas of our first protocol with those from [20], in order to satisfy our model with better communication complexity. Lindell and Pinkas [21] use a cut-and-choose approach to proving security of Yao's garbled circuit against malicious adversaries and their method is more generic yet requires a few more rounds. Horvitz and Katz [19] showed a UC-secure protocol in two rounds (four messages) using the DDH assumption. In their protocol, the two parties essentially run two instances of Yao's protocol simultaneously.

2   Preliminaries

In the primitives we describe below, as well as in our main protocol, we assume that Alice and Bob agree in advance on some groups over which the computation is being done.

Let ℓ be a security parameter. In the constructions below, it is generally appropriate to let $\ell = \log q$. We say that a function $f(l)$ is *negligible* if for any polynomial *poly*, there exists a value d such that for any $l \geq d$, we have $f(l) < 1/|poly(l)|$. To achieve non-interactive proofs in the malicious case, we also assume a random oracle for the underlying hash function.

2.1 ElGamal Cryptosystem

We employ the ElGamal cryptosystem [11] in our first construction. ElGamal encryption takes place over the group $\mathcal{G}_q$ over which it is hard to compute discrete logarithms. Typically, $\mathcal{G}_q$ is taken to be a subgroup of Z_p^*, where $q \mid p - 1$, for large primes p and q. We denote g as a published generator of $\mathcal{G}_q$.[1]

Let $y = g^x$ be the public key for the secret key x. The encryption of a message m (denoted $E_y(m)$) is $(g^r, m \cdot y^r)$ for $r \in_R [1, q]$. The decryption of a cyphertext (α, β) (denoted $D_x(\alpha, \beta)$ is β/α^x. The ElGamal cryptosystem is *semantically secure* [18] under the Decision Diffie-Hellman (DDH) assumption [10] over $\mathcal{G}_q$. We intensively use the multiplicative homomorphism of the ElGamal cryptosystem: $E_y(m_1) \cdot E_y(m_2) = E_y(m_1 \cdot m_2)$.

Our protocol makes use of a private/public keys $(x_A, y_A = g^{x_A})$ for Alice, as well as a private/public key $(x_B, y_B = g^{x_B})$ for Bob. We denote by y the shared public key $y_A \cdot y_B$, for which the corresponding private key is $x_A + x_B$. Note that y may be established implicitly by Alice on learning y_B and by Bob on learning y_A. In particular, there is no need for interaction between the parties to determine the shared key. Since the public keys are published, we assume all parties hold the joint public key y.

2.2 Simplified-Camenisch-Shoup Cryptosystem

For sCS cryptosystem, Alice and Bob work over $Z_{n^2}^*$ for $n = pq$, where $p = 2p' + 1$, $q = 2q' + 1$, and p, q, p', q' are all primes, and $|p| = |q|$. Let $n' = p'qp'$, and $h = (1 + n)$. The group $Z_{n^2}^*$ has unique (up to isomorphism) decomposition as the direct-product of four cyclic groups $Z_{n^2}^* = G_n \times G_{n'} \times G_2 \times T$, where G_n is generated by h and has order n, $G_{n'}$ has order n', and G_2 and T are of order 2. Let g' be a random element of $Z_{n^2}^*$. We know that the order of g' divides $\phi(n^2) = n \cdot \phi(n) = 4nn'$. With very high probability, the order of g' is a *multiple* of n', and $g = (g')^{2n}$ thus has order n' and is a generator of $G_{n'}$.

For the simplified-Camenisch-Shoup (as well as the original Camenisch-Shoup), all operations take place in $Z_{n^2}^*$. Note that h has order n and that $h^c = 1 + cn \pmod{n^2}$. The DCR assumption [23] is that given only n, random elements of $Z_{n^2}^*$ are hard to distinguish from random elements of P, which is the subgroup of $Z_{n^2}^*$ consisting of all nth powers of elements in $Z_{n^2}^*$.

---

[1] In the settings where $p = 2q + 1$ and $\mathcal{G}_q$ is the set of quadratic residues in Z_p^*, plaintexts not in $\mathcal{G}_q$ can be mapped onto $\mathcal{G}_q$ by appropriate forcing of the LeGendre symbol, e.g., through multiplication by a predetermined non-residue.

The sCS encryption scheme, introduced by [20] (and based on the CS scheme of [6]), is semantically secure under the DCR assumption.

Key generation. A private key is $x \in [0, \frac{n^2}{4}]$. A public key is (n, g, y) for $y = g^x$.

Encryption. We map the message m to an integer in $(-\frac{n}{2}, \frac{n}{2}]$. The encryption $E_{PK}(m)$ is a pair $(u, e) = (g^r, h^m y^r)$ for a random integer $r \in [0, \frac{n}{4}]$.

Decryption. Given a pair (u, e), if this is a valid cyphertext it is of the form $(g^r, h^m y^r)$. Let $\hat{m} = (\frac{e}{u^x})^2$. If $\hat{m}$ is valid, it is $(1+n)^m \equiv 1 + nm \pmod{n^2}$ for some m, so check that $n | \hat{m} - 1$ and reject otherwise. Else, let $m' = (\hat{m} - 1)/n$ (over the integers), let $m'' = m'/2 \pmod{n}$, and recover the message $m = m'' \text{ rem } n$, where $(a \text{ rem } b)$ is a if $a \leq b/2$ and otherwise it is $b - a$.

2.3 $\mathcal{CODE}$ (Conditional Oblivious Decryption Exposure)

The linchpin of our construction is a protocol that we newly introduce in this paper. We refer it to as *Conditional Oblivious Decryption Exposure*. One of the main differences between $\mathcal{CODE}$ and previously suggested conditional exposure primitives is that $\mathcal{CODE}$ allows for third parties to contribute encryptions using a public key, and then Alice and Bob, who share the private key can perform the conditional exposure.

Definition 1 (Conditional Oblivious Decryption Exposure). *Let (x_A, y_A) and (x_B, y_B) be two secret/public key pairs and E (resp. D) be the encryption (resp. decryption) function. Let c_1, c_2, c_3 be three cyphertexts encrypted under the joint key $y = y_A \cdot y_B$. The functionality $\mathcal{CODE}$ is defined by*

$$((c_1, c_2, c_3, x_A, y_B), (x_B, y_A)) \mapsto \begin{cases} (\bot, (c_1, c_2, c_3, D_x(c_3))) & \text{if } D_x(c_1) = D_x(c_2) \\ (\bot, (c_1, c_2, c_3, r)) & \text{otherwise.} \end{cases}$$

Where $x = x_A + x_B$ and $r \in_R \mathcal{G}_q$.

In this functionality, the decryption of c_3 is exposed to the second party conditioned on $c_1 \equiv c_2$ (i.e., if they encrypt the same message). Moreover the first party is oblivious of the outcome of the protocol.

We show protocols for secure implementations of $\mathcal{CODE}$ functionality using eitehr ElGamal and sCS encryptions. *impCODE* is a protocol for the $\mathcal{CODE}$ functionality secure in the honest-but-curious case.

impCODE. Let's call the first party Alice and the second party Bob. The $\mathcal{CODE}$ implementation consists of a single $\mathcal{CODE}$ transcript sent from Alice to Bob. Let $c_1 = (\alpha, \beta) = (g^{r_1}, m_1 y^{r_1})$, $c_2 = (\gamma, \delta) = (g^{r_2}, m_2 y^{r_2})$, and $c_3 = (\lambda, \mu) = (g^{r_3}, m_3 y^{r_3})$. Alice sends (ϵ, ζ, D) to Bob where

1. $\epsilon = (\alpha/\gamma)^e$ and $\zeta = (\beta/\delta)^e$, for $e \in_R Z_q$
2. $D = (\epsilon \lambda)^{x_A}$.

Bob computes $\tilde{m}_3 = \frac{\zeta\mu}{D \cdot D'}$ where $D' = (\epsilon \cdot \lambda)^{x_B}$ and outputs $(c_1, c_2, c_3, \tilde{m}_3)$. Note that

$$\tilde{m}_3 = \frac{\left(\frac{m_1 y^{r_1}}{m_2 y^{r_2}}\right)^e \cdot m_3 y^{r_3}}{\left(\left(\frac{g^{r_1}}{g^{r_2}}\right)^e \cdot g^{r_3}\right)^x} = \left(\frac{m_1}{m_2}\right)^e \cdot m_3$$

that is, if $m_1 = m_2$, then $\tilde{m}_3 = m_3$, as required.

Theorem 1. *The protocol impCODE securely implements the functionality CODE for the honest-but-curious two parties under DDH assumption.*

Proof. We show a simulator $S = (SIM_A, SIM_B)$ for impCODE. The case of corrupted Alice is easy; since Alice does not get any message from Bob, the simulator SIM_A is trivial. For a corrupted Bob, the simulator SIM_B has to simulate the view of Bob. Formally,

$$\{SIM_B((x_B, y_A), (c_1, c_2, c_3, d))\} \overset{c}{\approx} \{\text{view}_B((c_1, c_2, c_3, x_A, y_B), (x_B, y_A))\}$$

In other words, given the input and output of Bob, SIM_B has to simulate the impCODE transcript (ϵ, ζ, D) that Alice sends to Bob. The simulator SIM_B computes

$$e \in_R Z_q, \quad \epsilon = (\alpha/\gamma)^e, \quad \zeta = (\beta/\delta)^e, \quad D' = (\epsilon\lambda)^{x_B}, \quad D = \frac{\zeta\mu}{d \cdot D'},$$

and outputs (ϵ, ζ, D). The simulated (ϵ, ζ) have the same distribution as in the real protocol. Given (ϵ, ζ) and d, D is uniquely determined.

3   Honest-But-Curious Protocol

3.1   Intuition

In our one-message secure function evaluation scheme, Alice sends a garbled circuit to Bob, and Bob computes the function f using the garbled circuit. Let C be a circuit with gates $G_1, G_2, \ldots, G_m$ that computes the function f of interest, and let $T_1, T_2, \ldots, T_m$ be the corresponding truth tables. Sometimes we interchangeably use the term gates and tables.

First of all, Alice garbles each table by encrypting all the entries and then permuting the rows. See Figure 1 for example, where Alice garbled an AND gate with shuffling permutation (1 2 3).

As in Yao's garbled circuit, Bob's computation of a gate G_j depends on the computation of the two gates G_i, G_k associated with the inputs to G_j, where these gates' outputs are used in the decryption of the encrypted truth table T_j. One notable difference from Yao's technique, is that here we add another level of separation between these gates' (encrypted) outputs and the key for decrypting gate G_j - this is done using CODE. We thank the annonymous referee

T_i	I^L (left input)	I^R (right input)	O (output)
1	0	0	0
2	0	1	0
3	1	0	0
4	1	1	1

T_i^a	I^L	I^R	O
1	$E[1]$	$E[0]$	$E[0]$
2	$E[0]$	$E[0]$	$E[0]$
3	$E[0]$	$E[1]$	$E[0]$
4	$E[1]$	$E[1]$	$E[1]$

In case of ElGamal encryption scheme, $E[0]$ and $E[1]$ actually mean $E[g^0]$ and $E[g^1]$ respectively. We still use the notation $E[0]$ and $E[1]$ to handle both ElGamal and sCS encryption schemes.

Fig. 1. Alice Garbles an AND gate T_i with permutation $(1\ 2\ 3)$ and gets T_i^a

T_i^b	I^L	I^R	O	$\text{Plugs}_{[i \to j]}$
1	$E[1]$	$E[0]$	$E[0]$	(n,y,y,n)
2	$E[0]$	$E[0]$	$E[0]$	(n,y,y,n)
3	$E[0]$	$E[1]$	$E[0]$	(n,y,y,n)
4	$E[1]$	$E[1]$	$E[1]$	(y,n,n,y)

T_j^b	I^L	I^R	O	$\text{Plugs}_{[j \to \cdot]}$
1	$E[1]$	$E[0]$	$E[0]$	$\cdots$
2	$E[0]$	$E[0]$	$E[0]$	$\cdots$
3	$E[0]$	$E[1]$	$E[0]$	$\cdots$
4	$E[1]$	$E[1]$	$E[1]$	$\cdots$

Fig. 2. Plugs are now added

for commenting that indeed, in the honest-but-curious case, it is enough for us to use $\mathcal{CODE}$ only in the input gates (where Yao's protocol uses Oblivious Transfer), improving our construction's efficiency and readability. However, using $\mathcal{CODE}$ is still required for assuring security in the malicious case.

With only isolated garbled tables, however, Alice cannot have Bob compute the function. She needs to give to him 'wiring information' between a row of a table (output) and a row of an upper-level table (input). The wiring information is hereafter called a plug. See Figure 2 for example. Suppose that T_j^b is the upper-level table of T_i^b where T_i^b's output is propagated into T_j^b's left input. We denote the plugs in the v-th row of the table T_i^b by $\text{Plugs}_{[i \to j]}(v)$, and, more specifically, $\text{Plug}_{[i \to j]}(v, w)$ denotes the w-th element of $\text{Plugs}_{[i \to j]}(v)$. For example, $\text{Plugs}_{[i \to j]}(1) = (n, y, y, n)$ and $\text{Plug}_{[i \to j]}(1, 2) = y$. The plug $\text{Plug}_{[i \to j]}(1, 2) = y$ means that the output value on the first row of T_i^b is equal to the left-input value on the second row of T_j^b. On the other hand, from the plug $\text{Plug}_{[i \to j]}(1, 4) = n$, we know that the output value of the first row of T_i^b is different from the left-input value on the fourth row of T_j^b.

However, if Bob is honest-but-curious, he might be able to find out more than the output of the function by following other computation paths because all the plug information is exposed. For example, even if Bob determines that O_i is the correct output for table T_i^b, he can experiment and try computing another computation path using a different output O_i' on another row of the same table. Such an attack, if successful, can enable Bob to explore a rich set of different computational paths for f, potentially leaking information about the secret input.

The aim of our protocol is to restrict Bob's exploration exclusively to the correct computational path. Suppose that we have three tables T_i^b, T_j^b and T_k^b where the output of T_i^b and the left input of T_j^b are connected together and so are the output of T_k^b and the right input of T_j^b. Let O_{i,v_i} (resp. O_{k,v_k}) be the output for a given row v_i in T_i^b (resp. for a given row v_k in T_k^b), and I_{j,v_j}^L (resp. I_{j,v_j}^R) be the left (resp. right) input for a given row v_j in T_j^b. Now suppose that Bob has the plugs $\mathsf{Plug}_{[i \to j]}(v_i)$ and $\mathsf{Plug}_{[k \to j]}(v_k)$, and wants to retrieve plugs in the table T_j^b. We want to make sure that Bob obtains the plug for the v_j-th row of the T_j^b **only when** $O_{i,v_i} \equiv I_{j,v_j}^L$ and $O_{k,v_k} \equiv I_{j,v_j}^R$. Since the same will be true for all gates in C, Bob can only follow the correct computational path, and learns nothing about other paths.

In order to achieve our goal, for each row of a table Alice generates an encryption key pair (pk, sk), exposes the public key pk, and hides the secret key sk by encrypting it with the global encryption key (i.e., $y = y_A \cdot y_B$). She then encrypts the plug information with pk. She wants Bob to obtain the key sk and therefore get the plug information **only when** Bob follows correct computation path. The idea is using $\mathcal{CODE}$ transcript as a plug. Recall that $\mathcal{CODE}$, given three cyphertexts c_1, c_2 and c_3, outputs the decryption of c_3 when $c_1 \equiv c_2$. Here, c_1 and c_2 corresponds to O_{i,v_i} and I_{j,v_j}^L (or O_{k,v_k} and I_{j,v_j}^R), and and c_3 to the cyphertext of sk. Below, we describe our protocols in detail.

3.2   Protocol Details: Publication of Keys and Inputs

Alice and Bob publish their keys y_A and y_B. Input contributors encrypt input bits using the public key $y = y_A \cdot y_B$. Let s be an n-bit input string that is contributed by input contributors. Denote the i-th bit of s by s_i. When ElGamal encryption scheme is used, s is encrypted as $\{(g^{r_i}, g^{s_i} \cdot y^{r_i})\}_{i=1}^n$, where $r_i \in_R Z_q$. When sCS scheme is used, s is encrypted as $\{(g^{r_i}, h^{s_i} \cdot y^{r_i})\}_{i=1}^n$, where $r_i \in_R [0, n/4]$.

3.3   Protocol Details: Alice

Structure of the Table. Alice reads Bob's published key and input cyphertexts and computes $y = y_A y_B$. Now, in order to incorporate $\mathcal{CODE}$ we must extend the underlying table structure to incorporate plugs and associated keys. To do so, we append two columns to the basic table T_i^b, and denote the resulting expanded table by $\overline{T}_i$. See Figure 3.

Here, Bob obtains a key $k_{i,v1}$ (resp. $k_{i,v2}$) from the plug of the lower-level table when he makes a successful match against the left (resp. right) input on the row v.

Construction of the Overall Garbled Circuit. Alice has to construct three types of tables: input, output and intermediate gates. First, Alice constructs the set of intermediate tables $\{\overline{T}_i\}$ as follows.

1. Alice mixes each table T_i and encrypts all the entries to yield T_i^b.
2. For each table T_i^b and row v, Alice selects $k_{i,v1}, k_{i,v2} \in_R Z_q$ to construct two columns of K^L and K^R in $\overline{T}_i$.
3. Alice computes $\widehat{\mathsf{Plugs}}_{[i \to \cdot]}(v)$ for each row v.

$\overline{T}_i$	I^L	I^R	O	K^L (left key)	K^R (right key)	$\mathsf{Plugs}_{[i \to j]}$
1	$E_y(1)$	$E_y(0)$	$E_y(0)$	$E_y(k_{i,11}), g^{k_{i,11}}$	$E_y(k_{i,12}), g^{k_{i,12}}$	$E_{z_{i,1}}(\rho_{i,11}), \ldots, E_{z_{i,1}}(\rho_{i,14})$
2	$E_y(0)$	$E_y(0)$	$E_y(0)$	$E_y(k_{i,21}), g^{k_{i,21}}$	$E_y(k_{i,22}), g^{k_{i,22}}$	$E_{z_{i,2}}(\rho_{i,21}), \ldots, E_{z_{i,2}}(\rho_{i,24})$
3	$E_y(0)$	$E_y(1)$	$E_y(0)$	$E_y(k_{i,31}), g^{k_{i,31}}$	$E_y(k_{i,32}), g^{k_{i,32}}$	$E_{z_{i,3}}(\rho_{i,31}), \ldots, E_{z_{i,3}}(\rho_{i,34})$
4	$E_y(1)$	$E_y(1)$	$E_y(1)$	$E_y(k_{i,41}), g^{k_{i,41}}$	$E_y(k_{i,42}), g^{k_{i,42}}$	$E_{z_{i,4}}(\rho_{i,41}), \ldots, E_{z_{i,4}}(\rho_{i,44})$

1. The value $k_{i,vw}$ for $v \in [1,4]$, $w \in [1,2]$ is chosen randomly from Z_q.
2. The public key $z_{i,v} = g^{k_{i,v1}} \cdot g^{k_{i,v2}}$ for $v \in [1,4]$ is used to encrypt plugs of the v-th row.
3. When we want to emphasize on the abstract view of the plug $\rho_{i,vw}$ (resp. $E_{z_{i,v}}(\rho_{i,vw})$), we use the notation $\mathsf{Plug}_{[i \to j]}(v, w)$ (resp. $\widehat{\mathsf{Plug}}_{[i \to j]}(v, w)$).

Fig. 3. Schematic depiction of table $\overline{T}_i$

Inputs to the circuits are plugs connecting input ciphertexts and the first-level intermediate gates. Again, plugs are constructed using $\mathcal{CODE}$.

Output gates have much the same structure as intermediate gates. The only difference is in the last column. Rather than providing encrypted plugs to enable the computation to be continued, Alice provides encrypted output bits for the function f.

3.4 Protocol Details: Bob

Now let us consider how Bob evaluates the transcript sent by Alice. We assume, by recursion, that when Bob tries to evaluate the output of gate G_j, he has the plugs (i.e., $\mathsf{Plugs}_{[i \to j]}(v_i)$ and $\mathsf{Plugs}_{[k \to j]}(v_k)$) for these ciphertexts into $\overline{T}_j$.

1. For each $v \in \{1, 2, 3, 4\}$, Bob performs $impCODE$ with the two plugs $\mathsf{Plug}_{[i \to j]}(v_i, v)$ and $\mathsf{Plug}_{[k \to j]}(v_k, v)$ trying to obtain keys $k_{j,v1}$ and $k_{j,v2}$. If he fails (by checking if $g^\eta \overset{?}{=} g^{k_{j,v1}}$, where η is the output of $impCODE$), he tries the next row.
2. If he succeeds, he decrypts $\widehat{\mathsf{Plugs}}_{[j \to \cdot]}(v)$ with the decryption key $(k_{j,v1} + k_{j,v2})$ and gets the plug information $\mathsf{Plugs}_{[j \to \cdot]}(v)$. Note that $z_{j,v} = g^{k_{j,v1}+k_{j,v2}}$.
3. He proceeds with the computation using the obtained plugs.

When Bob has obtained all outputs from output gates, and so he learns the output of the circuit.

3.5   Communication Complexity in the Honest-But-Curious Case

Consider a single truth table; Each row of the table has 12 values of Z_p^* except the plugs. Plugs of each row has $4 \cdot 4 = 16$ values of Z_p^*. Therefore, each (output or intermediate) table contains $4 \cdot (12 + 16) = 112 = \mathcal{O}(1)$ values of Z_p^*. Each input plug has 5 values for Alice, and 3 values for Bob. Thus, we need $8n$ values of Z_p^* for inputs of Alice and Bob. We need another n bits for Bob to send the result of the function back to Alice. Summing all the above, it is clear that the total communication complexity is $\mathcal{O}((m + n) \log p)$ bits.

4   Full Protocol

4.1   Intuition

While the protocol described above is secure assuming honest-but-curious participants, it it not secure against active cheating on the part of Alice.

A corrupted party (either Alice or Bob) can publish a public key which is not chosen randomly. For example, Alice can wait for Bob to publish his public key y_B, pick a shared private key x of her choice, and send g^x / y_B as her public key y_B. This gives Alice knowledge of the shared private key and the power to decrypt any of the inputs (including Bobs: she just needs to re-encrypt Bob's input with y_B, and then she can decrypt them with x). To overcome this kind of attacks, the malicious case protocol requires that Alice and Bob publish non-malleable PoK for the knowledge of the discrete logs of their respective public keys, together with their public keys. We note that both in the common reference string model and in the random oracle model, adding non-malleability to NIZK PoK [28] is simple: In the CRS, we follow the technique of [25]; In the random oracle model, adding non-malleability to Fiat-Shamir style NIZK PoK [14] is simple: include the name of the publisher in hash function evalution.

A corrupt Alice may cheat in the construction of the gate. First, Alice may send encrypted truth tables that do not correspond to the gates of the circuit. In Section 4.2 we show how Alice can prove that the truth tables are correct. Second, Alice may fake the plugs. Specifically, Alice may use the fact that the plugs are encrypted, and encrypt random values instead of valid plugs at selected locations. If Bob does complete the protocol, Alice learns that these invalid plugs were not decrypted, thus learning about Bob's computation path.

Therefore, in our full protocol, Alice sends Bob not only the garbled circuit but also the proof of its correct construction. The proof comprises two parts: the proof of correct construction of basic gates, and the proof of correct construction of plugs.

4.2   Proof of Correct Construction of Basic Gates

In this section, we give a zero knowledge proof of knowledge for a correct construction of gates. We assume that the circuit consists of NAND gates.

Zero-knowledge Proof of Knowledge. Informally, a Proof of Knowledge is a proof for a relation R, in which the prover convinces the verifier that an instance is in the language, and also that *the prover knows a witness for this instance*, rather then just the existence of such a witness. In a (standard) proof of knowledge for the discrete log, the prover convinces the verifier that she knows the value of b, such that $a = g^b$, when a is known to both. We denote such proof by $PK\{b : a = g^b\}$. There are many variants on these proofs, such as in [30]. In this paper, we make use of variants in which Alice proves conjunctive statements, and statements regarding her knowledge of sets of discrete logs. See [9,29,5] for a description of how to achieve such variants in an efficient manner.

Proof of Boolean Plaintext. Let $\sigma^0 = 1$ and σ^1 represent boolean values 0 and 1, respectively. Specifically, we define $\sigma := g$ in ElGamal encryption while $\sigma := h$ in sCS encryption. Cramer et al. [8] showed how to prove that the plaintext of an ElGamal cyphertext $A = (\alpha, \beta)$ is Boolean, i.e.,

$$\mathsf{Bool}(A) \overset{def}{=} PK\{r : \alpha = g^r, (\beta = y^r \text{ or } \beta = \sigma \cdot y^r)\}.$$

Proof of Equality/Inequality of Boolean Plaintext. Using ZK PoK for the discrete log it is easy to prove equality/inequality of the plaintexts of two ElGamal/sCS cyphertexts. Given the two cyphertexts $A = (\alpha, \beta)$ and $A' = (\alpha', \beta')$, let $(\epsilon, \delta) = (\alpha/\alpha', \beta/\beta')$, and let $(\mu, \nu) = (\alpha\alpha', \beta\beta'/\sigma)$. To prove equality of $D_x(A) = D_x(A')$, we give $PK\{e : y = g^e, \delta = \epsilon^e\}$ and denote such proof by $\mathsf{Eq}(A, A')$. To prove inequality of $D_x(A) \neq D_x(A')$, we give $PK\{e : y = g^e, \mu = \nu^e\}$ and denote such proof by $\mathsf{Neq}(A, A')$.

Shuffling Lists of Cyphertexts. We adopt a protocol of [15] for non-interactively proving that two lists of cyphertexts are equivalent, and that one is a permutation of the other. We denote this protocol **Shuffle** and note that the length of the transcript of the protocol is linear with the number of cyphertexts. While the protocol of [15] is originally designed for ElGamal encryptions, it can be easily applied to sCS encryptions too.

I_L	I_R	O
A_1	B_1	C_1
A_2	B_2	C_2
A_3	B_3	C_3
A_4	B_4	C_4

I_L	I_R	O
A_1'	B_1'	C_1'
A_2'	B_2'	C_2'
A_3'	B_3'	C_3'
A_4'	B_4'	C_4'

I	O
A_1	B_1
A_2	B_2

Fig. 4. base NAND gate, NAND gate, and OUTPUT gate

Correct Construction of NAND Gate. For an NAND gate, we give a two-part proof; the first part shows the structure of the gate. However this part leaks information on the truth table, thus the second part shuffles and re-encrypts the

$\overline{T}_j$	I^L	I^R	O	K^L	K^R	$\text{Plugs}_{[j\to\cdot]}$
1	$(\alpha_{j,11},\beta_{j,11})$	$(\alpha_{j,12},\beta_{j,12})$	$(\gamma_{j,1},\delta_{j,1})$	$(\lambda_{j,11},\mu_{j,11}),\kappa_{j,11}$	$(\lambda_{j,12},\mu_{j,12}),\kappa_{j,12}$	$\text{Plugs}_{[j\to\cdot]}(1)$
2	$(\alpha_{j,21},\beta_{j,21})$	$(\alpha_{j,22},\beta_{j,22})$	$(\gamma_{j,2},\delta_{j,2})$	$(\lambda_{j,21},\mu_{j,21}),\kappa_{j,21}$	$(\lambda_{j,22},\mu_{j,22}),\kappa_{j,22}$	$\text{Plugs}_{[j\to\cdot]}(2)$
3	$(\alpha_{j,31},\beta_{j,31})$	$(\alpha_{j,32},\beta_{j,32})$	$(\gamma_{j,3},\delta_{j,3})$	$(\lambda_{j,31},\mu_{j,31}),\kappa_{j,31}$	$(\lambda_{j,32},\mu_{j,32}),\kappa_{j,32}$	$\text{Plugs}_{[j\to\cdot]}(3)$
4	$(\alpha_{j,41},\beta_{j,41})$	$(\alpha_{j,42},\beta_{j,42})$	$(\gamma_{j,4},\delta_{j,4})$	$(\lambda_{j,41},\mu_{j,41}),\kappa_{j,41}$	$(\lambda_{j,42},\mu_{j,42}),\kappa_{j,42}$	$\text{Plugs}_{[j\to\cdot]}(4)$

$\overline{T}_i$	I^L	I^R	O	K^L	K^R	$\text{Plugs}_{[i\to j]}$
1	$(\alpha_{i,11},\beta_{i,11})$	$(\alpha_{i,12},\beta_{i,12})$	$(\gamma_{i,1},\delta_{i,1})$	$(\lambda_{i,11},\mu_{i,11}),\kappa_{i,11}$	$(\lambda_{i,12},\mu_{i,12}),\kappa_{i,12}$	$\text{Plugs}_{[i\to j]}(1)$
2	$(\alpha_{i,21},\beta_{i,21})$	$(\alpha_{i,22},\beta_{i,22})$	$(\gamma_{i,2},\delta_{i,2})$	$(\lambda_{i,21},\mu_{i,21}),\kappa_{i,21}$	$(\lambda_{i,22},\mu_{i,22}),\kappa_{i,22}$	$\text{Plugs}_{[i\to j]}(2)$
3	$(\alpha_{i,31},\beta_{i,31})$	$(\alpha_{i,32},\beta_{i,32})$	$(\gamma_{i,3},\delta_{i,3})$	$(\lambda_{i,31},\mu_{i,31}),\kappa_{i,31}$	$(\lambda_{i,32},\mu_{i,32}),\kappa_{i,32}$	$\text{Plugs}_{[i\to j]}(3)$
4	$(\alpha_{i,41},\beta_{i,41})$	$(\alpha_{i,42},\beta_{i,42})$	$(\gamma_{i,4},\delta_{i,4})$	$(\lambda_{i,41},\mu_{i,41}),\kappa_{i,41}$	$(\lambda_{i,42},\mu_{i,42}),\kappa_{i,42}$	$\text{Plugs}_{[i\to j]}(4)$

Fig. 5. Variable-based representation of table $\overline{T}_i$ and $\overline{T}_j$

truth table entries. For two ElGamal/sCS cyphertexts $Y = (\alpha,\beta)$ and $Y' = (\alpha',\beta')$, denote $Y \oplus Y' = (\alpha\alpha',\beta\beta')$. Let $X = (1,1/\sigma^2)$ be a trivial encryption of $1/\sigma^2$. We use the following fact to construct the base gate:

$$c = a \text{ NAND } b \iff a + b + 2(c-1) \in \{0,1\}.$$

The base NAND gate:
1. $\text{Bool}(A_1),\ldots,\text{Bool}(C_4)$
2. $\text{Eq}(A_1,A_2)$, $\text{Eq}(A_3,A_4)$, $\text{Neq}(A_1,A_3)$
3. $\text{Eq}(B_1,B_3)$, $\text{Eq}(B_2,B_4)$, $\text{Neq}(B_1,B_2)$
4. $\text{Bool}(A_i \oplus B_i \oplus C_i \oplus C_i \oplus X)$ for $i \in \{1,\ldots,4\}$

The second and the third items show the input columns are valid. The last item shows the output columns are valid. Note that the proof in this step reveals some information such as equality of cyphertexts in the same column. Hence, the second part: $\text{Shuffle}(\langle A_i, B_i, C_i\rangle_{i=1}^4, \langle A_i', B_i', C_i'\rangle_{i=1}^4)$.

Correct Construction of an OUTPUT Gate. The proof for the correct construction is as follows:

The OUTPUT gate:
1. $\text{Bool}(A_1)$, $\text{Bool}(A_2)$, $\text{Bool}(B_1)$, $\text{Bool}(B_2)$
2. $\text{Neq}(A_1,A_2)$, $\text{Eq}(A_1,B_1)$, $\text{Eq}(A_2,B_2)$

4.3   Correct Construction of Plugs

Structure of the Plug. We modify the structure of $\widehat{\text{Plug}}_{[i\to j]}(v,w)$. a little bit in the full protocol. We assume that the output of the gate G_i and the left input of the gate G_j are connected together. See Figure 5 for the representation of the two tables $\overline{T}_i$ and $\overline{T}_j$. The plug is an encryption of *impCODE* transcript[2] for

---

[2] If the output of G_i were the right input of G_j, it would be $c_1 = (\alpha_{j,w2},\beta_{j,w2})$, $c_2 = (\gamma_{i,v},\delta_{i,v})$, $c_3 = (\lambda_{j,w2},\mu_{j,w2})$.

$c_1 = (\alpha_{j,w1}, \beta_{j,w1})$, $c_2 = (\gamma_{i,v}, \delta_{i,v})$, $c_3 = (\lambda_{j,w1}, \mu_{j,w1})$. The actual transcript will be of the following form $\mathsf{Plug}_{[i \to j]}(v,w) = \langle \epsilon, \zeta, D \rangle$, where

$$e \in_R Z_q, \quad \epsilon = \left(\frac{\alpha_{j,w1}}{\gamma_{i,v}} \right)^e, \quad \zeta = \left(\frac{\beta_{j,w1}}{\delta_{i,v}} \right)^e, \quad D = (\epsilon \cdot \lambda_{j,w1})^{x_A}.$$

Note that we don't have to encrypt ϵ or ζ; the exponent e for ϵ and ζ is already hard to find due to the hardness of DLP. So we only have to apply ElGamal encryption to D. The plug now looks as follows:

$$\widehat{\mathsf{Plug}}_{[i \to j]}(v,w) = \langle \epsilon, \; \zeta, \; (g^r, D \cdot z_{i,v}^r) \rangle, \quad \text{where } r \in_R Z_q.$$

We denote the $(g^r, D \cdot z_{i,v}^r)$ by $(\eta, \tilde{D})$.

When Bob obtains the (decrypted) plug $\mathsf{Plug}_{[i \to j]}(v,w)$, he executes imp-$CODE$ scheme and gets an output $\hat{k}$ by computing

$$\hat{k} = \frac{\zeta \cdot \mu_{j,w1}}{D \cdot D'}, \quad \text{where } D' = (\epsilon \cdot \lambda_{j,w1})^{x_B}.$$

He checks if $g^{\hat{k}} = \kappa_{j,w1}$ holds; if it holds, he decides that $(\alpha_{j,w1}, \beta_{j,w1}) \equiv (\gamma_{i,v}, \delta_{i,v})$.

ZKVerify: Proof of Correct Plug Construction. The goal of the ZKVerify proof is for Alice to prove that the encrypted $CODE$ transcripts are valid. Specifically we show how to generate the proof for the plug $\widehat{\mathsf{Plug}}_{[i \to j]}(v,w)$. The plug is encrypted using a key $z_{i,v} = \kappa_{i,v1} \cdot \kappa_{i,v2} = g^{k_{i,v1}} \cdot g^{k_{i,v2}}$ (See Figure 3 and 5 for notations), and the corresponding secret key is obtained by Bob only if he learns correctly $k_{i,v1}$ and $k_{j,v2}$ (this limits his computation to a single computational path in the circuit). ZKVerify proves two things: (1) given two *ciphertexts* $E_y(k_{i,v1}), E_y(k_{i,v2})$, the encrypted part of the plug, i.e., $(g^r, D \cdot z_{i,v}^r)$ is actually encrypted using the public key $z_{i,v}$; (2) she knows the discrete-log used in the rest part of the plug:

$$PK \left\{ e : \epsilon = \left(\frac{\alpha_{j,w1}}{\gamma_{i,v}} \right)^e, \zeta = \left(\frac{\beta_{j,w1}}{\delta_{i,v}} \right)^e \right\}.$$

In the ElGamal based construction, we assume that both p and q are safe primes such that $p = 2q + 1$ and $q = 2q' + 1$ (i.e., p is a double decker). It is claimed that there are infinitely many such tuples of primes, and they are easy to find. We let $k_{i,v1} = f^{\tau_1}$, and $k_{i,v2} = f^{\tau_2}$, where f is a generator in $\mathcal{G}_{q'}$. The proof ZKVerify $\left((\lambda_{i,v1}, \mu_{i,v1}, g^{\kappa_{i,v1}}), (\lambda_{i,v2}, \mu_{i,v2}, g^{\kappa_{i,v2}}), \widehat{\mathsf{Plugs}}_{[i \to j]}(v,w) \right)$ is as follows:

$$PK \Big\{ (r_1, \tau_1, r_2, \tau_2, e, r_3, x_A) : \lambda_{i,v1} = g^{r_1}, \; \mu_{i,v1} = f^{\tau_1} \cdot y^{r_1}, \; \kappa_{i,v1} = g^{f^{\tau_1}},$$

$$\lambda_{i,v2} = g^{r_2}, \; \mu_{i,v2} = f^{\tau_2} \cdot y^{r_2}, \; \kappa_{i,v2} = g^{f^{\tau_2}},$$

$$\epsilon = (\alpha_{j,w1}/\gamma_{i,v})^e, \; \zeta = (\beta_{j,w1}/\delta_{i,v})^e,$$

$$y_A = g^{x_A}, \; \eta = g^{r_3}, \; \tilde{D} = z_{i,v}^{r_3} \cdot (\epsilon \cdot \lambda_{j,w1})^{x_A} \Big\}.$$

The above proof uses proofs of knowledge of the double discrete log, which can be constructed by using Camenisch and Stadler [7]. They showed how to construct such proof in their paper, and this costs $\Theta(\ell)$ communication complexity (ℓ is security parameter).

For the sCS based protocol, ZKVerify is simpler, and we do not need to construct k_1, k_2 in a special form. The proof shows directly that $\kappa_{i,v1} = g^{k_{i,v1}}$. The proof ZKVerify is as follows:

$$
PK \Big\{ (r_1, \tau_1, r_2, \tau_2, e, r_3, x_A) : \; \lambda_{i,v1} = g^{r_1}, \; \mu_{i,v1} = h^{k_{i,v1}} \cdot y^{r_1}, \; \kappa_{i,v1} = g^{k_{i,v1}},
$$
$$
\lambda_{i,v2} = g^{r_2}, \; \mu_{i,v2} = h^{k_{i,v2}} \cdot y^{r_2}, \; \kappa_{i,v2} = g^{k_{i,v2}},
$$
$$
\epsilon = (\alpha_{j,w1}/\gamma_{i,v})^e, \; \zeta = (\beta_{j,w1}/\delta_{i,v})^e,
$$
$$
y_A = g^{x_A}, \; \eta = g^{r_3}, \; \tilde{D} = z_{i,v}^{r_3} \cdot (\epsilon \cdot \lambda_{j,w1})^{x_A} \Big\}.
$$

Note, in the sCS based protocol, the ZKVerify proof does not include a double discrete log proof.

4.4   Protocol Details: Input Contribution

The parties contibuting inputs might be malicious. For example, an input contributed may generate a committed input by mauling other committed input. To avoid this kind of attack, the input contributors add non-malleable zero-knowledge proofs of knowledge to each of their committed input bits. In addition, the parties who manage the public directory that stores the committed inputs check the committed inputs and reject any inputs that have the same proofs.

4.5   Protocol Details: Alice

Alice sends the tables as in the honest-but-curious case, and in addition, for each gate G_i, she sends a proof of correct construction of the gate and of the plugs ZKVerify $\Big((\lambda_{i,v1}, \; \mu_{i,v1}, \; g^{\kappa_{i,v1}}), \; (\lambda_{i,v2}, \; \mu_{i,v2}, \; g^{\kappa_{i,v2}}), \; \widehat{\text{Plugs}}_{[i \to j]}(v) \Big)$, where by $\widehat{\text{Plugs}}_{[i \to j]}(v)$ we mean the four encrypted pairs, one for each $\mathcal{CODE}$ transcript, which are all encrypted using $z_{i,v} = g^{\kappa_{i,v1} + \kappa_{i,v2}}$.

4.6   Protocol Details: Bob

In the full version of the protocol, Bob first verifies that all the proofs Alice sent are valid. That is, for each gate G_i Bob verifies that the proof of correct construction of the gate is valid. For each row v of table $\overline{T}_i$, Bob verifies that the proof for correct encryption of the plugs $\widehat{\text{Plugs}}_{[i \to j]}(v)$ is valid. If any of the proofs is invalid, Bob aborts the protocol. Otherwise (if all proofs are valid), Bob continues as described in Section 3.

4.7   Communication Complexity in the Malicious Case

In addition to the communication costs of the garbled circuit, the malicious case incurs the complexity of sending the additional proofs. When ElGamal encryption is used, the total communication complexity costs are $\mathcal{O}((m \cdot \ell + n) \log p$ bits mainly due to proof of double discrete log. When sCS encryption is used, the total communication complexity costs are $\mathcal{O}((m + n) \log p)$ bits.

References

1. Aiello, W., Ishai, Y., Reingold, O.: Priced oblivious transfer: How to sell digital goods. In: Pfitzmann, B. (ed.) EUROCRYPT 2001. LNCS, vol. 2045, pp. 119–135. Springer, Heidelberg (2001)
2. Beaver, D.: Minimal-latency secure function evaluation. In: Preneel, B. (ed.) EUROCRYPT 2000. LNCS, vol. 1807, pp. 335–350. Springer, Heidelberg (2000)
3. Boneh, D., Lipton, R.: Algorithms for black-box fields and their application to cryptography. In: Koblitz, N. (ed.) CRYPTO 1996. LNCS, vol. 1109, pp. 283–297. Springer, Heidelberg (1996)
4. Cachin, C., Camensich, J., Kilian, J., Müller, A.J.: One-round secure computation and secure autonomous mobile agents. In: Proc. 27th International Colloquium on Automata, Languages and Programming (ICALP) (2000)
5. Camenisch, J., Michels, M.: Proving that a number is the product of two safe primes. In: Stern, J. (ed.) EUROCRYPT 1999. LNCS, vol. 1592, pp. 107–122. Springer, Heidelberg (1999)
6. Camenisch, J., Shoup, V.: Practical verifiable encryption and decryption of discrete logarithms. In: Boneh, D. (ed.) CRYPTO 2003. LNCS, vol. 2729, pp. 126–144. Springer, Heidelberg (2003)
7. Camenisch, J., Stadler, M.: Efficient group signature schemes for large groups. In: Sommer, G., Daniilidis, K., Pauli, J. (eds.) CAIP 1997. LNCS, vol. 1296, pp. 410–424. Springer, Heidelberg (1997)
8. Cramer, R., Genaro, R., Schoenmakers, B.: A secure and optimally efficient multi-authority election scheme. In: Fumy, W. (ed.) EUROCRYPT 1997. LNCS, vol. 1233, pp. 103–118. Springer, Heidelberg (1997)
9. Cramer, R., Damgård, I., Schoenmakers, B.: Proofs of partial knowledge and simplified design of witness hiding protocols. In: Desmedt, Y.G. (ed.) CRYPTO 1994. LNCS, vol. 839, pp. 174–187. Springer, Heidelberg (1994)
10. Diffie, W., Hellman, M.E.: New directions in cryptography. IEEE Trans. on Information Theory, IT 22(6), 644–654 (1976)
11. ElGamal, T.: A public key cryptosystem and a signature scheme based on discrete logarithms. IEEE Transactions on Information Theory 31, 469–472 (1985)
12. Even, S., Goldreich, O., Micali, S.: On-line/off-line digital schemes. In: Brassard, G. (ed.) CRYPTO 1989. LNCS, vol. 435, pp. 263–275. Springer, Heidelberg (1990)
13. Feigenbaum, J., Merritt, M.: Open questions, talk abstracts, and summary of discussions. In: DIMACS. Series in Discrete Mathematics and Theoretical Computer Science, pp. 1–45 (1991)
14. Fiat, A., Shamir, A.: How to prove yourself: Practical solutions to identification and signature problems. In: Massey, J.L. (ed.) CRYPTO 1986. LNCS, vol. 263, pp. 186–194. Springer, Heidelberg (1987)
15. Furukawa, J., Sako, K.: An efficient scheme for proving a shuffle. In: Kilian, J. (ed.) CRYPTO 2001. LNCS, vol. 2139, pp. 368–387. Springer, Heidelberg (2001)
16. Gertner, Y., Ishai, Y., Kushilevitz, E., Malkin, T.: Protecting data privacy in private information retrieval schemes. In: Proceedings of the thirtieth annual ACM symposium on Theory of computing, pp. 151–160 (1998)

17. Goldreich, O., Micali, S., Wigderson, A.: How to play any mental game. In: Proc. 19th Annual ACM Symposium on Theory of Computing (STOC), pp. 218–229. ACM Press, New York (1987)
18. Goldwasser, S., Micali, S.: Probabilistic encryption. Journal of Computer and System Sciences 28(2), 270–299 (1984)
19. Horvitz, O., Katz, J.: Universally-composable two-party computation in two rounds. In: Advances in Cryptology — (CRYPTO 2007), pp. 111–129 (2007)
20. Jarecki, S., Shmatikov, V.: Efficient two-party secure computation on committed inputs. In: Advances in Cryptology — (EUROCRYPT 2007) (2007)
21. Lindell, Y., Pinkas, B.: An efficient protocol for secure two-party computation in the presence of malicious adversaries. In: Advances in Cryptology — (EUROCRYPT 2007) (2007)
22. Naor, M., Pinkas, B., Sumner, R.: Privacy preserving auctions and mechanism design. In: 1st ACM Conference on Electronic Commerce, ACM Press, New York (1999)
23. Paillier, P.: Public-key cryptosystems based on composite degree residuosity classes. In: Stern, J. (ed.) EUROCRYPT 1999. LNCS, vol. 1592, pp. 107–122. Springer, Heidelberg (1999)
24. Rivest, R., Adelman, L., Dertouzos, M.L.: On data banks and privacy homomorphisms. In: DeMillo, R.A., Dobkin, D.P., Jones, A.K., Lipto, R.J. (eds.) Foundations of Secure Computation, pp. 169–17. Academic Press, London (1978)
25. Sahai, A.: Non-malleable non-interactive zero knowledge and adaptive chosen-ciphertext security. In: Proc. 40th IEEE Symposium on Foundations of Computer Science (FOCS), pp. 543–553 (1999)
26. Sander, T., Tschudin, C.F.: Protecting mobile agents against malicious hosts. In: Vigna, G. (ed.) Mobile Agents and Security. LNCS, vol. 1419, pp. 44–61. Springer, Heidelberg (1998)
27. Sander, T., Young, A., Yung, M.: Non-interactive cryptocomputing for NC^1. In: Proc. 40th IEEE Symposium on Foundations of Computer Science (FOCS), pp. 554–567 (1999)
28. De Santis, A., Persiano, G.: Zero-knowledge proofs of knowledge without interaction. In: Proc. 33rd IEEE Symposium on Foundations of Computer Science (FOCS), pp. 427–437 (1992)
29. De Santis, A., Di Crescenzo, G., Persiano, G., Yung, M.: On monotone formula closure of SZK. In: Proc. 35th IEEE Symposium on Foundations of Computer Science (FOCS), pp. 454–465. IEEE Computer Society Press, Los Alamitos (1994)
30. Schnorr, C.P.: Efficient signature generation by smart cards. Journal of Cryptology 4, 161–174 (1991)
31. Valiant, L.: Universal circuits. In: Proc. 8th Annual ACM Symposium on Theory of Computing (STOC), pp. 196–203 (1976)
32. Yao, A.C.: How to generate an exchange secrets. In: Proc. 27th IEEE Symposium on Foundations of Computer Science (FOCS), pp. 162–167 (1986)

Known-Key Distinguishers for Some Block Ciphers[*]

Lars R. Knudsen[1] and Vincent Rijmen[2,**]

[1] Technical University of Denmark
Department of Mathematics
Building 303S, DK-2800 Lyngby, Denmark
www.ramkilde.com
[2] Graz University of Technology
Institute for Applied Information Processing and Communications
Inffeldgasse 16a, A-8010 Graz, Austria
Vincent.Rijmen@iaik.tugraz.at

Abstract. We present two block cipher distinguishers in a setting where the attacker *knows* the key. One is a distinguisher for AES reduced the seven rounds. The second is a distinguisher for a class of Feistel ciphers with seven rounds. This setting is quite different from traditional settings. We present an open problem: the definition of a new notion of security that covers attacks like the ones we present here, but not more.

Keywords: Block Cipher, Cryptanalysis, Distinguishing algorithms, AES, Feistel ciphers.

1 Introduction

The research leading to this paper was triggered by the following example. Consider an n-bit block cipher and a plaintext/ciphertext pair for which the least significant s bits in both n-bit strings are zeros. With $s < n/2$ such a pair can be found for any reasonable block cipher in time equivalent to approximately 2^s encryptions. Imagine a block cipher where if one is given any key k, one can find such a pair for k in time much less than 2^s, but where no efficient attacks are known in the traditional black-box model. Should we recommend the use of such a cipher? We don't think so!

In the next two sections we present two attacks —or rather distinguishers— for block cipher constructions, where the attacker knows the key. Section 2 presents

---

[*] The research described in this paper has been supported by the European Commission under grant number FP6-IST-033563 (Project SMEPP). The information in this document reflects only the authors' views, is provided as is and no guarantee or warranty is given that the information is fit for any particular purpose. The user thereof uses the information at its sole risk and liability.

[**] The second author's contribution was made during a stay with the Technical University of Denmark.

K. Kurosawa (Ed.): ASIACRYPT 2007, LNCS 4833, pp. 315–324, 2007.
© International Association for Cryptology Research 2007

a distinguisher on AES reduced to seven rounds; Section 3 presents distinguishers for a class of Feistel ciphers, also with seven rounds. At the first glance it might appear strange to consider attacks on a cipher where one is given the secret key. However, by studying this type of attacks, we might learn something about the security margin of a cipher. Intuitively, it seems clear that if one cannot find distinguishers for a block cipher when given the key, then one cannot find a distinguisher where the key is secret. Secondly, in some cases (mainly for block cipher based hashing) block ciphers are used with a key that is known to the attacker, and at least to a certain extent, the key is under the attacker's control. Our attacks are quite relevant to this case.

After introducing our two attacks, we discuss related work in Section 4. We present some thoughts on a new notion of security in Section 5. We conclude in Section 6.

2 Distinguishers for Reduced AES

In this section we present known-key distinguishers for AES [1] reduced to seven (out of ten) rounds. We shall use the so-called integrals [7] to do so.

AES is an iterated cipher where in each iteration the subfunctions SubBytes, ShiftRows, MixColumns, and AddRoundKey are employed, except for the last iteration where the function MixColumns is omitted. The reason for this is that it allows the decryption routine to be implemented in a similar style to the encryption routine.

Consider a collection of 256 texts, which have different values in one byte and equal values in each of the remaining fifteen bytes. It is well-known that after two rounds of encryption the texts take all 256 values in each of the sixteen bytes, and that after three rounds of encryption the sum of the 256 bytes in each position is zero [4]. Such a structure of 256 texts is called a 3-round integral.

2.1 Notation

We introduce some notation for integrals on AES. An integral with the terms $\mathcal{A}^i$ is a collection of 2^{8i} texts. Writing $\mathcal{A}^i_j$ in a byte position means that in the integral the (string) concatenation of all bytes with subscript j take all 2^{8i} $8i$-bit values exactly once. $\mathcal{A}^i$ means that in the integral the particular byte is balanced, that is, it takes all values exactly $2^{8(i-1)}$ times. $\mathcal{C}$ means that the values in the particular byte are constant, and $\mathcal{S}$ means for the particular byte the sum of all texts can be determined. For AES addition is defined by the exclusive-or operation. The special last round of AES in integral attacks has an interesting property, namely that the balance property of an integral is preserved through this round.

2.2 Integrals for AES

It is known that there is a 3-round integral for AES using 2^{32} texts [4,5]. The main observation is that one can choose 2^{32} plaintexts as a collection of 2^{24} 2-round

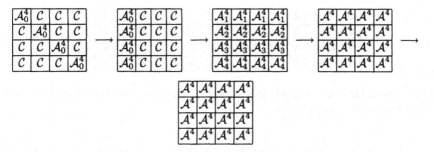

Fig. 1. An integral for 4-round AES with 2^{32} texts. The fourth round is a special round without MixColumns.

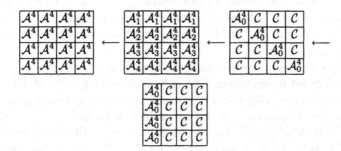

Fig. 2. A backwards integral for three (full) rounds of AES with 2^{32} texts

integrals described above (starting from the second round) each with 2^8 texts. Since the texts in each of these 2-round integrals take all values equally many times in any byte position after the third round, so does the set of all 2^{32} texts.

If we consider AES reduced to four rounds, that is, where the last round is of the special form described above, then one gets that all bytes of the ciphertexts are balanced in the 4-round integral. Figure 1 depicts this 4-round integral. Not surprisingly, one can also define integrals through the inverse cipher of AES. We present a backwards integral for three (full) rounds of AES in Figure 2. (Note the backward integral extended to four rounds does not preserve the balance property nor is it obvious to determine the sum of the texts).

The forward and backward integrals can be combined to integrals over more than four rounds of AES. One chooses a structure of 2^{56} texts which differ in seven bytes and which have constant values in the remaining nine bytes. One can view this as a collection of 2^{24} copies of the forward integral for 4-round AES, but also one can view this as a collection of 2^{24} copies of the backwards 3-round integral. Therefore, when one starts in the middle of the cipher one computes forwards and backwards for the two integrals. Next we show how to employ our findings in known-key distinguishers for AES reduced to seven rounds.

2.3 Known-Key Distinguishers for AES Reduced to Seven Rounds

Consider a variant of AES reduced to seven rounds, where MixColumns is omitted in the last round. Here one can specify the integral of Figure 3, which can

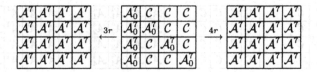

Fig. 3. An integral for 7-round AES with 2^{56} texts. The seventh round is a special round without MixColumns.

be used in an known-key distinguisher. This is constructed from the four-round integral in Figure 1 and the three-round integral of Figure 2.

The known-key distinguisher simply records the frequencies in each byte of the plaintexts and ciphertexts, checks whether the values in each byte of the plaintexts and in each byte of the ciphertexts occur equally often. The time complexity is similar to the time it takes to do 2^{56} 7-round AES encryptions and the memory needed is small.

The big question is of course, what the complexity is to find a similar structure for any 128-bit permutation. The only approach we know of, which comes close to an answer to this is the approach to solve the k-sum problem [10]. Given a function f on n bits, the k-sum problem is to find $x_1, \ldots, x_k$ such that $\sum_{i=1}^{k} f(x_i) = 0$. A solution to this problem is given in [10] with a running time of $\mathcal{O}(k2^{n/(1+\log_2 k)})$. In our case $n = 128$ and $k = 2^{56}$ indicating a running time of 2^{58} operations. However this is a very inaccurate estimation of the complexity we are looking for: the complexity estimate above is in the big $\mathcal{O}$ notation, thus ignoring smaller constants, the approach requires memory (more than for the AES distinguisher), but much more important, the k-sum problem does not give us the structure that we get for reduced AES, merely a collection of texts whose sum through the function f is zero with no conditions of balance on the values of x_i and $f(x_i)$. On the other hand, not much research has gone into finding efficient solutions for this problem. Nevertheless, we feel confident to conjecture that for a randomly chosen 128-bit permutation finding a collection of 2^{56} texts in similar time, using similar (little) memory and with similar properties as in the case of 7-round AES has a probability of succeeding which is very close to zero. Thus, we make the following claim.

Conjecture 1. There is a known-key distinguisher for AES reduced to seven rounds which uses 2^{56} texts.

We note that the above integrals might exist for a randomly chosen permutation but they are hard to find. The point we are making is that for the AES variants one finds the texts in the integrals much faster than for a randomly chosen permutation.

3 Distinguisher for a 7-Round Feistel Cipher

We present here a known-key distinguisher on an n-bit Feistel cipher with 7 rounds. The attack requires that the round function of the Feistel cipher consists of an XOR of the round key to the round function input, followed by an arbitrary key-independent transformation. An example of a Feistel cipher with such a round function is SEED [8], but note that SEED has 16, rather than 7, rounds.

3.1 Description

The distinguisher computes (in constant time) two plaintexts denoted by $p = (p_L, p_R)$ and $\tilde{p} = (\tilde{p}_L, \tilde{p}_R)$ which have a special property. Let the corresponding ciphertexts be denoted by $c = (c_L, c_R)$ and $\tilde{c} = (\tilde{c}_L, \tilde{c}_R)$, then the following equation will hold with probability 1:

$$p_R \oplus \tilde{p}_R \oplus c_R \oplus \tilde{c}_R. = 0. \tag{1}$$

Figure 4 gives the algorithm to compute the plaintexts p and $\tilde{p}$. Note that the algorithm works only if the round keys of the second and sixth rounds are not equal. For most key schedules, such an equality happens only for a negligible fraction of the keys.

For two randomly chosen plaintexts, (1) will be satisfied with probability only $2^{-n/2}$, so we can build a strong distinguisher in this case. Also, since x can be chosen arbitrarily one can find many such pairs, thereby increasing the advantage of the distinguisher.

3.2 Conditions on the Round Function f

If f is a bijection which is easy to invert, the computations of the pair of plaintexts is straightforward. Also, note that the subkeys can be independent or

---

Input:
The round function of the Feistel cipher, denoted by f.
The seven subkeys $k_1, \ldots, k_7$, with $k_2 \neq k_6$.

Algorithm:

1. Choose an arbitrary value for x.
2. Define the values γ, α, z as:

$$\gamma = k_2 \oplus k_6$$
$$\alpha = x \oplus f^{-1}(f(x) \oplus \gamma)$$
$$z = f^{-1}(k_3 \oplus k_5 \oplus \alpha)$$

3. Compute

$$p = (z \oplus f(x) \oplus k_4 \oplus f(p_R, k_1), x \oplus k_3 \oplus f(z \oplus f(x) \oplus k_4 \oplus k_2))$$
$$\tilde{p} = (z \oplus f(x) \oplus \gamma \oplus k_4 \oplus f(\tilde{p}_R, k_1), x \oplus \alpha \oplus k_3 \oplus f(z \oplus f(x) \oplus k_6 \oplus k_4)).$$

It follows that $p_R \oplus c_R = \alpha \oplus k_3 \oplus k_5 = f(z) = \tilde{p}_R \oplus \tilde{c}_R$, see Figure 5.
Consequently, $p_R \oplus \tilde{p}_R \oplus c_R \oplus \tilde{c}_R = 0$.

Fig. 4. Algorithm to compute the plaintexts p, $\tilde{p}$ satisfying (1)

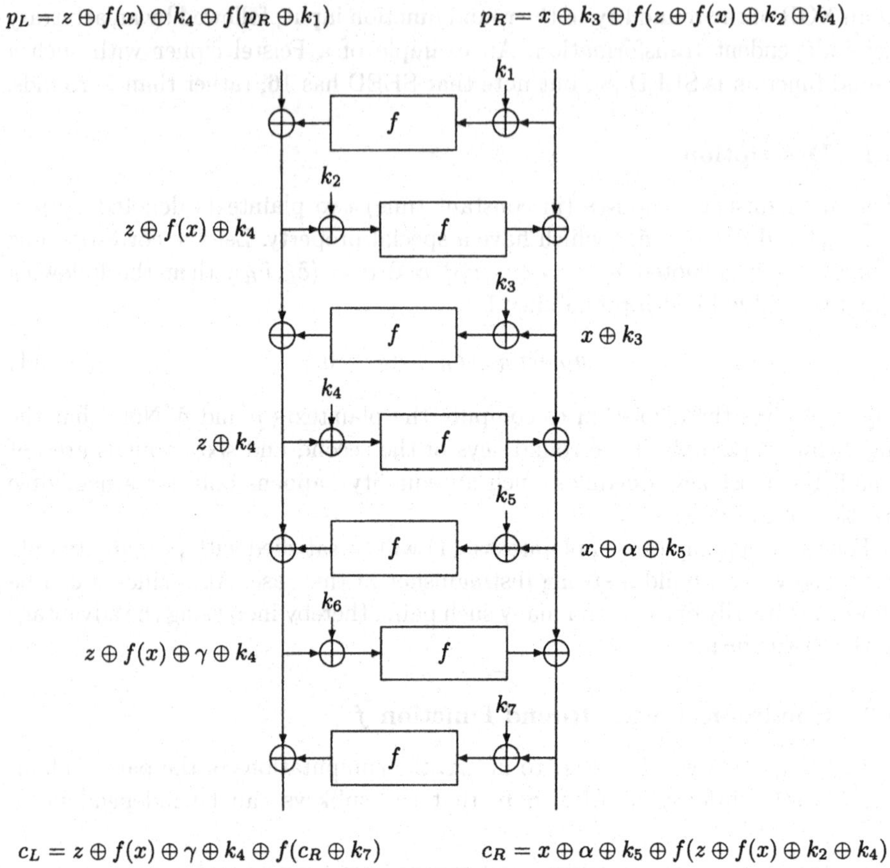

$p_L = z \oplus f(x) \oplus k_4 \oplus f(p_R \oplus k_1)$
$p_R = x \oplus k_3 \oplus f(z \oplus f(x) \oplus k_2 \oplus k_4)$
k_1
f
k_2
$z \oplus f(x) \oplus k_4$
k_3
$x \oplus k_3$
k_4
$z \oplus k_4$
k_5
$x \oplus \alpha \oplus k_5$
k_6
$z \oplus f(x) \oplus \gamma \oplus k_4$
k_7
$c_L = z \oplus f(x) \oplus \gamma \oplus k_4 \oplus f(c_R \oplus k_7)$
$c_R = x \oplus \alpha \oplus k_5 \oplus f(z \oplus f(x) \oplus k_2 \oplus k_4)$

Fig. 5. First encryption in 7-round Feistel cipher distinguisher. The second encryption is where x is replaced by $x \oplus \alpha$ and where $f(x)$ is replaced by $f(x) \oplus \gamma$. Notation: $\gamma = k_2 \oplus k_6$; $\alpha = x \oplus f^{-1}(f(x) \oplus \gamma)$; $z = f^{-1}(k_3 \oplus k_5 \oplus \alpha)$.

computed in a key-schedule, the only requirement we make above is that $k_2 \oplus k_6 \neq 0$. If f is not bijective, the method might still work, if inverting f is not too costly. One example is DES where given $f(w)$ is it relatively easy to find w', such $f(w) = f(w')$.

There is a variant of this attack which works for 7 rounds of Feistel ciphers where f is not bijective and where the following tasks should be "easy":

1. Find $x, y, \alpha \neq 0$ such that $f(x) = f(x \oplus \alpha) = y$,
2. Find z such that $f(z) = k_3 \oplus k_5$.

If one accomplishes these two tasks then one finds a pair of plaintexts such that (1) is satisfied. We omit the details here and refer to Appendix A.

3.3 Impact

To illustrate where the above findings could be exploited in practice consider the Matyas-Meyer-Oseas hashing mode, where the compression function is defined as

$$h(h_{i-1}, m_i) = F_{h_{i-1}}(m_i) \oplus m_i.$$

If F is a 7-round Feistel cipher construction where f is bijective, then one finds a pair of blocks which collide in half of the bits in the outputs of h doing only two encryptions.

4 Related Work

Distinguishing attacks on block ciphers where the key is known were introduced in [3] under the name *correlation intractability*. It was shown that no block cipher can be secure under this notion of security: for every block cipher, there exists a relation such that given the key, it is easy to find plaintext/ciphertext pairs satisfying this relation, but it is difficult to find them for a random permutation. The result is based on the observation that all implementable block ciphers (must) have a description, whereas a random oracle doesn't. The relation is constructed by putting the description of the block cipher in the plaintexts.

It can be argued however, that the relation of [3] is contrived. It is not clear at all how or whether such relation may lead to weaknesses in "reasonable" block-cipher based designs. Secondly, the relation is not interesting from a block cipher designer's point of view, because it applies to all implementable block ciphers. Hence, it gives no guidance on how to construct block ciphers that can be used for instance in block-cipher based hash function constructions, or in any other application where the key is known to the attacker or under her control.

5 Discussion of Known-Key Attacks

The discussion in the previous section suggests there might be a need for a new notion of security, under which the attacks presented in Section 2 and Section 3 count as valid attacks, but the general result of [3] doesn't. Indeed, the foremost idea in our mind, is to evaluate the security of specific, implementable block cipher designs and their suitability for applications which commonly use block ciphers as an underlying component.

However, it appears to be non-trivial to formalize a notion of security and at the same time avoid trivial attacks. A bullet-proof model is likely to be complicated and little transparent. Therefore, we present here some intuitions on what we think are essential elements of such a new notion of security. The introduction of the notion itself remains an open problem.

5.1 Intuitions for the Basic (Known-Key) Scenario

In this scenario, we would measure the security of the cipher against known-key attacks by computing the average advantage over all values of the key k.

A possible way to reduce the number of parasitical attacks in an informal model, would be to make the following thought exercise. Whenever we do a known-key analysis of one specific block cipher, we would rule out attacks which will succeed with approximately the same work effort on any block cipher. Hence such attacks would not change the relative ranking of the block ciphers we would examine.

5.2 Intuitions for Extended Scenarios

In a so-called *weak key* scenario, the attacker would know that the key would come out of a pre-specified subset of the whole key space. Such a scenario could reveal weak keys.

In a *related-key* scenario, we would consider scenarios where the attacker is given several different keys k_i which could have a known relation to one another. By loosening the relation between the k_is, we would eventually measure how well the block cipher would resemble a set of randomly selected permutations.

The above extensions can be illustrated using the block cipher DES. The differential attack on DES [2] uses a 13-round characteristic of average probability 2^{-47}, built from iterating a two-round characteristic of average probability $1/234$. However it is well-known that the exact probability for two rounds is either $1/146$ or $1/585$ depending on the value of one key bit. Thus by restricting ourselves to the subset of keys which provide the highest probabilities better results would be achieved. Also, if $y = DES_k(x)$ then it holds that $DES_{\overline{k}}(\overline{x}) = \overline{y}$ where $\overline{z}$ is the bitwise complemented value of z. This means that for a pair of keys (k_1, k_2), where k_1 is the bitwise complemented value of k_2 it is easy to distinguish the induced encryption functions from two randomly chosen permutations.

6 Conclusion

In this paper we presented two distinguishers for block ciphers, where the attacker is given the key. Although [3] already presented very strong results in this model, we tried to show that our attacks are still interesting from a practical security point of view, in particular when one considers block cipher applications where the key is indeed known to the attacker, e.g. block-cipher based hash functions.

Subsequently we argued that a suitable notion of security is still missing in the cryptographic literature and we presented some intuitions on how such a new notion could look like.

References

1. Specification for the Advanced Encryption Standard (AES), Federal Information Processing Standards Publication (FIPS) 197 (2001)
2. Biham, E., Shamir, A.: Differential cryptanalysis of DES-like cryptosystems. Journal of Cryptology 4(1), 3–72 (1991)
3. Canetti, R., Goldreich, O., Halevi, S.: The random oracle model, revisited. Journal of the ACM 51(4), 557–594 (2004)
4. Daemen, J., Knudsen, L., Rijmen, V.: The block cipher Square. In: Biham, E. (ed.) FSE 1997. LNCS, vol. 1267, pp. 149–165. Springer, Heidelberg (1997)
5. Ferguson, N., Kelsey, J., Lucks, S., Schneier, B., Stay, M., Wagner, D., Whiting, D.: Improved cryptanalysis of Rijndael. In: Schneier, B. (ed.) FSE 2000. LNCS, vol. 1978, pp. 213–230. Springer, Heidelberg (2001)
6. Knudsen, L.R.: DEAL - a 128-bit block cipher. Technical Report 151, Department of Informatics, University of Bergen, Norway, February 1998. Submitted as an AES candidate by Richard Outerbridge
7. Knudsen, L.R., Wagner, D.: Integral cryptanalysis. In: Daemen, J., Rijmen, V. (eds.) FSE 2002. LNCS, vol. 2365, pp. 112–127. Springer, Heidelberg (2002)
8. Lee, H.J., Lee, S.J., Yoon, J.H., Cheon, D.H., Lee, J.I.: The SEED encryption algorithm. RFC 4269 (2005)
9. Matyas, S.M., Meyer, C.H., Oseas, J.: Generating strong one-way functions with cryptographic algorithm. IBM Technical Disclosure Bulletin 27, 5658–5659 (1985)
10. Wagner, D.: A generalized birthday problem. In: Yung, M. (ed.) CRYPTO 2002. LNCS, vol. 2442, pp. 288–303. Springer, Heidelberg (2002)

A   Variant Attack on a 7-Round Feistel Cipher

We present here a variant on the statistical distinguisher presented in Section 3. It works only if the following conditions are met.

1. The round function f must map at least two inputs, denoted by $x, x + \alpha$, to the same output, denoted by y. It must be possible for the attacker to determine x, y and α.
2. For most outputs, it must be easy to construct an input mapping to that output.

The distinguisher can be seen as an extension of the 5-round impossible differential presented in [6]. The transcript consists now of the plaintexts (p_L, p_R), $(\tilde{p}_L, \tilde{p}_R)$ with

$$p_L = z \oplus y \oplus k_4 \oplus f(x \oplus k_3 \oplus f(z \oplus y \oplus k_4 \oplus k_2) \oplus k_1),$$
$$p_R = x \oplus k_3 \oplus f(z \oplus y \oplus k_4 \oplus k_2),$$
$$\tilde{p}_L = z \oplus y \oplus k_4 \oplus f(x \oplus \alpha \oplus k_3 \oplus f(z \oplus y \oplus k_4 \oplus k_2) \oplus k_1),$$
$$\tilde{p}_R = p_R \oplus \alpha,$$

and the corresponding ciphertexts. Here z is defined by $f(z) = k_3 \oplus k_5$. We discuss below what to do if no such z exists. The test is again: verify whether

$$p_R + \tilde{p}_R = c_R + \tilde{c}_R. \tag{2}$$

If it is not possible to find a z such that $f(z) = k_3 \oplus k_5$, then we can search for a z' such that $f(z') = k_3 \oplus k_5 \oplus \alpha$. We can then construct a plaintext pair such that in the first text the inputs to f in round three and five are x, respectively $x \oplus \alpha$, and in the second pair $x \oplus \alpha$, respectively x. This pair will also satisfy (2). Finally, if also this is not possible, there might be another difference α that can be used.

Generic Attacks on Unbalanced Feistel Schemes with Expanding Functions

Jacques Patarin[1], Valérie Nachef[2], and Côme Berbain[3]

[1] Université de Versailles
45 avenue des Etats-Unis, 78035 Versailles Cedex, France
[2] CNRS(UMR 8088) and Department of Mathematics
Université de Cergy-Pontoise
2 avenue Adolphe Chauvin, 95011 Cergy-Pontoise Cedex, France
[3] France Telecom Research and Development
38-40 rue du Général Leclerc, 92794 Issy-les-Moulineaux, France
`jacques.patarin@prism.uvsq.fr,`
`valerie.nachef@u-cergy.fr,`
`come.berbain@orange-ftgroup.com`

Abstract. Unbalanced Feistel schemes with expanding functions are used to construct pseudo-random permutations from kn bits to kn bits by using random functions from n bits to $(k-1)n$ bits. At each round, all the bits except n bits are changed by using a function that depends only on these n bits. Jutla [6] investigated such schemes, which he denotes by F_k^d, where d is the number of rounds. In this paper, we describe novel Known Plaintext Attacks (KPA) and Non-Adaptive Chosen Plaintext Attacks (CPA-1) against these schemes. With these attacks we will often be able to improve the results of Jutla.

Keywords: Unbalanced Feistel permutations, pseudo-random permutations, generic attacks on encryption schemes, Block ciphers.

1 Introduction

A Feistel scheme from $\{0,1\}^l$ to $\{0,1\}^l$ with d rounds is a permutation built from round functions $f_1, \ldots, f_d$. When these round functions are randomly chosen, we obtain what is called a "Random Feistel Scheme". The attacks on these "random Feistel schemes" are called "generic attacks" since these attacks are valid for most of the round functions $f_1, \ldots, f_d$.

When $l = 2n$ and when the f_i functions are from $\{0,1\}^n$ to $\{0,1\}^n$ we obtain the most classical Feistel schemes, also called "balanced" Feistel schemes. Since the famous paper of Luby and Rackoff [10], many results have been obtained on the security of such classical Feistel schemes (see [11] for an overview of these results). When the number of rounds is lower than 5, we know attacks with less than $2^l (= 2^{2n})$ operations: for 5 rounds, an attack in $O(2^n)$ operations is given in [14] and for 3 or 4 rounds an attack in $\sqrt{2^n}$ is given in [1,12]. When the functions are permutations, similar attacks for 5 rounds are given in [7,9]. Therefore, for

K. Kurosawa (Ed.): ASIACRYPT 2007, LNCS 4833, pp. 325–341, 2007.

security, at least 6 rounds are recommended, i.e. each bit will be changed at least 3 times.

When $l = kn$ and when the round functions are from $(k - 1)n$ bits to n bits, we obtain what is called an "Unbalanced Feistel Scheme with contracting functions". In [11] some security proofs are given for such schemes when for the first and the last rounds pairwise independent functions are used instead of random contracting functions. At Asiacrypt 2006 [15] generic attacks on such schemes have been studied.

When $l = kn$ and when the rounds functions are from n bits to $(k - 1)n$ bits, we obtain what is called an "Unbalanced Feistel Scheme with expanding functions", also called "complete target heavy unbalanced Feistel networks" [16]. Generic attacks on Unbalanced Feistel Schemes with expanding functions is the theme of this paper. One advantage of these schemes is that it requires much less memory to store a random function of n bits to $(k-1)n$ bits than a random function of $(k - 1)n$ bits to n bits. BEAR and LION [2] are two block ciphers which employ both expanding and contracting unbalanced Feistel networks. The AES-candidate MARS is also using a similar structure.

Attacks on Unbalanced Feistel Schemes with expanding functions have been previously studied by Jutla [6]. We will often be able to improve his attacks by attacking more rounds, or by using a smaller complexity. Moreover we will generalize these attacks by analyzing KPA (Known Plaintext Attacks), not only CPA-1 (non adaptive plaintext attacks) and by giving explicit formulas for the complexities. We will not introduce adaptive attacks, or chosen plaintext and chosen ciphertext attacks, since we have not found anything significantly better than CPA-1.

The paper is organized as follows. First, we give our notation. Then we describe the different families of attacks we have studied. We will have three families of attacks called "2-point attacks" (TWO), "rectangle attacks" (SQUARE, R1, R2, R3, R4) and "Multi-Rectangle attacks". In this paper, we will study in detail TWO and rectangle attacks, but we will give only a few comment on "Multi-Rectangle attacks" (Multi-Rectangle attacks are still under investigation). It can be noticed that $k = 2$ is very different from $k \geq 3$.

2   Notation

Our notation is very similar to [15]. An unbalanced Feistel scheme with expanding functions F_k^d is a Feistel scheme with d rounds. At each round j, we denote by f_j the round function from n bits to $(k - 1)n$ bits. f_j is defined as $f_j = (f_j^{(1)}, f_j^{(2)}, \ldots, f_j^{(k-1)})$, where each function $f_j^{(l)}$ is defined from $\{0,1\}^n$ to $\{0,1\}^n$. On some input $[I^1, I^2, \ldots, I^k]$ F_k^d produces an output denoted by $[S^1, S^2, \ldots, S^k]$ by going through d rounds. At round j, the first n bits of the round entry are used as an input to the round function f_j, which produces $(k - 1)n$ bits. Those bits are xored to the $(k - 1)n$ last bits of the round entry and the result is rotated by n bits. We introduce the internal variable X^j: it is the n-bit value produced by round j, which will be the input of next round function f_{j+1}. For example, we have:

$$X^1 = I^2 \oplus f_1^{(1)}(I^1)$$
$$X^2 = I^3 \oplus f_1^{(2)}(I^1) \oplus f_2^{(1)}(X^1)$$
$$X^3 = I^4 \oplus f_1^{(3)}(I^1) \oplus f_2^{(2)}(X^1) \oplus f_3^{(1)}(X^2)$$
$$\dots$$

The first round is represented on Figure 1 below:

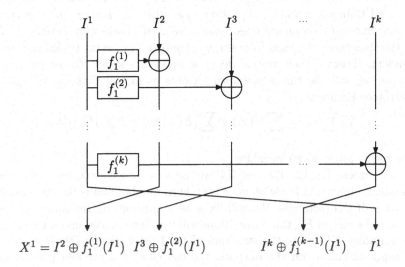

Fig. 1. First Round of F_k^d

After d rounds $(d \geq k + 1)$, the output $[S^1, S^2, \dots, S^k]$ can be expressed by using the introduced values X^j:

$$S^k = X^{d-1}$$
$$S^{k-1} = X^{d-2} \oplus f_d^{(k-1)}(X^{d-1})$$
$$S^{k-2} = X^{d-3} \oplus f_{d-1}^{(k-1)}(X^{d-2}) \oplus f_d^{(k-2)}(X^{d-1})$$
$$\dots$$

3   Overview of the Attacks

We investigated several attacks allowing to distinguish F_k^d from a random permutation. Depending on the values of k and d some attacks are more efficient than others. All our attacks are using sets of plaintext/ciphertext pairs : the sets can be simply couples (for attack TWO) or a rectangle structure with either four plaintext/ciphertext pairs (attack SQUARE) or more (attacks R1, R2, R3, and R4). Depending on the number of rounds, it is possible to find some relations between the input variables and output variables of the pairs of a set. Those relations can appear at random or due to equalities of some internal variables due to the structure of the Feistel scheme.

The TWO attack consists in using m plaintext/ciphertexts pairs and in counting the number $\mathcal{N}_{F_k^d}$ of couples of these pairs that satisfy the relations between the input and output variables. We then compare $\mathcal{N}_{F_k^d}$ with $\mathcal{N}_{perm}$ where $\mathcal{N}_{perm}$ is the number of couples of pairs for a random permutation instead of F_k^d. The attack is successful, i.e. we are able to distinguish F_k^d from a random permutation if the difference $|E(\mathcal{N}_{F_k^d}) - E(\mathcal{N}_{perm})|$ is much larger than the standard deviation σ_{perm} and than the standard deviation $\sigma_{F_k^d}$, where E denotes the expectancy function. In order to compute these values, we need to take into account the fact that the structures obtained from the m plaintext/ciphertext tuples are not independent. However their mutual dependence is very small. To compute σ_{perm} and $\sigma_{F_k^d}$, we will use this well-known formula as in [15] that we will call the "Covariance Formula":

$$V\left(\sum x_i\right) = \sum_i V(x_i) + \sum_{i<j} \left[E(x_i, x_j) - E(x_i)E(x_j)\right]$$

where the x_i are random variables.

In the attacks R1, R2, R3, and R4, we use a rectangle structure: we consider φ plaintext/ciphertext pairs where φ is an even number and is the total number of indexes of the rectangle. We will fix some conditions on the inputs of the φ pairs. On the case of F_k^d, those conditions will turn into conditions on the internal state variables X^j due to the structure of the Feistel scheme. These conditions will imply equations on the outputs. On the case of a random permutation, equations on the outputs will only appear at random. By counting the sets of φ pairs satisfying the conditions on inputs and outputs, we can distinguish between F_k^d and a random permutation, since in the case of F_k^d the equations on the outputs appear not only at random, but a part of them is due to the conditions we set. However, those attacks are not always able to distinguish between F_k^d and a random permutation, since it requires some internal collision to appear in the structure of the Feistel scheme. For some instances of F_k^d the desired collision will not exist and the attacks will fail. There exists a probability ϵ which is a strictly positive constant independent of n such that rectangle structures appear for F_k^d. How to compute this probability can be found in the extended version. Consequently, in order to verify that we are able to distinguish between the family of F_k^d permutations and the family of random permutations, we can apply our attacks on several randomly chosen instances of F_k^d or of random permutation, count the number of instances were the attack is working and compare this number for F_k^d and for a random permutation. Attacks R1, R2, R3, and R4 all share this principle but the conditions imposed on the plaintexts and ciphertexts are different.

The SQUARE attack is a special case of attack R1, when $\varphi = 4$. In the next sections, we will give more precise definitions of these attacks and examples for attack TWO and attack R1. Finally we will consider attacks with more than 2^{kn} computations, i.e. attacks against generators of pseudo-random permutations. All the results are summarized in Section 9.

For a fixed value of k, attack TWO is very efficient for small values of d. When d increases, first SQUARE, which is a variant of R1, then R1 will become the best known attack. Then, when d increases again, R2, R3 or R4 will become the best known attack. Finally, for very large d, TWO will become again the best known attack.

4   Attack "TWO"

In this section, we describe a family of attacks called "TWO". These attacks will use correlations on pairs of plaintext/ciphertext. Therefore, they can be called "2-point" attacks. When $k = 2$ i.e. on classical balanced Feistel Schemes, these attacks give the best known generic attacks [14]. However these attacks have not been studied in [6]. As we will see, TWO attacks are sometimes more efficient than the attacks of [6] for example when the number of rounds is very small.

The principle of attack TWO is to concentrate on one of the equations linking an output word S^i with some of the internal variables X^i. By fixing the first n-bit blocks of the input I we fix the value of some of the internal variables and a simple equality between the remaining input blocks and the output word becomes true assuming that a collision on some of the internal variable occurs. If the number of plaintext/ciphertext pairs is sufficiently large, this collision will appear and the attack succeeds.

In order to illustrate attack TWO, we now present the attack against F_k^d, $k + 2 \le d \le 2k - 1$. We will concentrate the attack on the equation:

$$S^{2k-d} = X^{k-1} \oplus \bigoplus_{i=k}^{d-1} f_{i+1}^{(2k-i-1)}(X^i)$$

The i-th pair is denoted by $[I^1(i), I^2(i), \ldots, I^k(i)]$ for the plaintext and by $[S^1(i), S^2(i), \ldots, S^k(i)]$ for the ciphertext. We will count the number $\mathcal{N}$ of (i, j) such that $I^1(i) = I^1(j), I^2(i) = I^2(j), \ldots, I^{k-1}(i) = I^{k-1}(j), S^k(i) = S^k(j)$, $S^{k-1}(i) = S^{k-1}(j), \ldots, S^{2k-d+1}(i) = S^{2k-d+1}(j)$ and $S^{2k-d}(i) \oplus S^{2k-d}(j) = I^k(i) \oplus I^k(j)$. For F_k^d, this last equation is a consequence of the other equations, i.e. of these $k - 1$ equations in I and $d - k$ equations in S. Therefore, the attack will succeed in KPA when $m^2 \ge 2^{(d-1)n}$, i.e. when $m \ge 2^{\frac{d-1}{2}n}$. In CPA-1, we will fix $I^1, I^2, \ldots, I^k$ to some values, and we will do this α times. The attack will succeed with $\alpha = 2^{(d-k-2)n}$ and the complexity in CPA-1 is $\alpha \cdot 2^n = 2^{(d-k-1)n}$.

5   "R1" Attack

5.1   Definition of R1

We now give a definition of attack R1. Let us consider φ plaintext/ciphertext pairs. We first set the following conditions on the input variables:

$$(I) = \begin{cases} I^1(1) = I^1(2), \ I^1(3) = I^1(4), \ I^1(5) = I^1(6), \dots, \ I^1(\varphi - 1) = I^1(\varphi) \\ \forall i, \ 2 \le i \le k, \ I^i(1) \oplus I^i(2) = I^i(3) \oplus I^i(4) = \dots = I^i(\varphi - 1) \oplus I^i(\varphi) \end{cases}$$

Conditions on the first block I^1 are here to cancel the impact of function f_1, while conditions on other blocks are used to obtain differential equations on the internal state variables. These equations will then propagate to other rounds with some probability until they turn to equations on the outputs, which then can be detected.

In order for the previous conditions to propagate with high probability, we need some extra conditions on the internal state variables. We have $d - 2$ internal state variables $X^1, X^2, \dots, X^{d-2}$ and $X^{d-1} = S^k$ is an output variable.

Let a be an integer, $1 \le a \le d - 1$. We will choose a values of $\{1, 2, \dots, d - k\}$. Let $\mathcal{E}$ be the set of these a values, and let $\mathcal{F}$ be the set of all integers i, $1 \le i \le d - 1$ such that $i \notin \mathcal{E}$. We have $|\mathcal{E}| = a$ and $|\mathcal{F}| = d - a - 1$. Let (X) be the set of the following equalities:

$$(X) = \begin{cases} \forall i \in \mathcal{E}, \ X^i(1) = X^i(3) = \dots = X^i(\varphi - 1) \\ \forall i \in \mathcal{F}, \ X^i(1) = X^i(2) \end{cases}$$

Between two different plaintext/ciphertext pairs i and j, $i \ne j$, we can have at most $k - 1$ successive equalities on the variables $I^1, X^1, X^2, \dots, X^{d-1}$. Otherwise from k successive equalities we would get $I^1(i) = I^1(j), I^2(i) = I^2(j), \dots, I^k(i) = I^k(j)$, so the two messages would be the same. Therefore we must have: $\lfloor \frac{d}{k} \rfloor \le a \le d - 1 - \lfloor \frac{d-1}{k} \rfloor$. For the same reason we must have $\{d - k\} \in \mathcal{E}$ since $d - 1$, $d - 2$, \dots, $d - k + 1$ are in $\mathcal{F}$.

From the conditions (I) and (X) and considering the equalities that we can derive from them with probability one, we will have:

$$(S) = \begin{cases} \forall i, \ 2 \le i \le k, \ S^i(1) = S^i(2), \ S^i(3) = S^i(4), \dots S^i(\varphi - 1) = S^i(\varphi) \\ S^1(1) \oplus S^1(2) = S^1(3) \oplus S^1(4) = \dots = S^1(\varphi - 1) \oplus S^1(\varphi) \end{cases}$$

Consequently the conditions (S) can appear by chance, or due to the conditions (X).

Our KPA attack consists in counting the number $\mathcal{N}$ of rectangle sets of plaintext/ciphertext pairs satisfying the conditions (I) and (S). The obtained number can be divided into two parts: either the conditions (I) and (S) appear completely at random, or conditions (I) appear and conditions (S) are satisfied because (X) happened.

Figure 2 illustrates one rectangle set of our attack. Plaintext/ciphertext pairs are denoted by $1, 2, \dots, \varphi$. Two points are joined by an edge if the values are equal (for example $I^1(1) = I^1(2)$). We draw a solid edge if the equality appears with probability $\frac{1}{2^n}$ and a dotted line if the equality follows conditionally with probability 1 from other imposed equalities.

5.2   "R1" Attack on F_3^7

Before studying the general properties of R1, we will illustrate this attack with an example. We will now describe our "R1" attack on F_3^7. As we will see, we

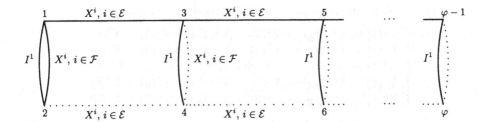

Fig. 2. Attack R1 on F_k^d

will obtain here a complexity in $O(2^{2n})$ in CPA-1 and in $O(2^{\frac{5n}{2}})$ in KPA. This is better than the $O(2^{3n})$ of the TWO attacks. In [6], Jutla shows that he can obtain on F_k^d attacks with complexity less than $O(2^{kn})$ when $d \leq 3k - 3$. For $d = 3$, this gives attacks up to only 6 rounds, unlike here where we will reach 7 rounds with the complexity less than 2^{3n}. We have $F_3^7[I^1, I^2, I^3] = [S^1, S^2, S^3]$.

Let $i_1, i_2, i_3, i_4, i_5, i_6$ be six indexes of messages (so these values are between 1 and m). We will denote by $[I^1(\alpha), I^2(\alpha), I^3(\alpha)]$ the plaintext of message i_α, and by $[S^1(\alpha), S^2(\alpha), S^3(\alpha)]$ the ciphertext of message i_α. (i.e. for simplicity we use the notation $I^1(\alpha)$ and $S^1(\alpha)$ instead of $I^1(i_\alpha)$ and $S^1(i_\alpha)$, $1 \leq \alpha \leq 6$). The idea of the attack is to count the number $\mathcal{N}$ of indexes $(i_1, i_2, i_3, i_4, i_5, i_6)$ such that:

$$
\begin{cases}
I^1(1) = I^1(2) \text{ and } I^1(3) = I^1(4) \text{ and } I^1(5) = I^1(6) \\
I^2(1) \oplus I^2(2) \;=\; I^2(3) \oplus I^2(4) \;=\; I^2(5) \oplus I^2(6) \\
I^3(1) \oplus I^3(2) \;=\; I^3(3) \oplus I^3(4) \;=\; I^3(5) \oplus I^3(6) \\
\qquad \text{and} \\
S^3(1) = S^3(2) \text{ and } S^3(3) = S^3(4) \text{ and } S^3(5) = S^3(6) \\
S^2(1) = S^2(2) \text{ and } S^2(3) = S^2(4) \text{ and } S^2(5) = S^2(6) \\
S^1(1) \oplus S^1(2) \;=\; S^1(3) \oplus S^1(4) \;=\; S^1(5) \oplus S^1(6)
\end{cases}
$$

We will call the 7 first equations the "input equations" and we will call the 8 last equations the "output equations".

KPA. If the messages are randomly chosen, for a random permutation we will have $E(\mathcal{N}_{perm}) \simeq \frac{m^6}{2^{15n}}$. For a F_3^7 permutation we will have about 2 times more solutions since the 8 output equations can occur at random, or due to the following 8 internal equations:

$$
\begin{cases}
X^1(1) = X^1(3) = X^1(5) \\
X^2(1) = X^2(2) \\
X^3(1) = X^3(2) \\
X^4(1) = X^4(3) = X^4(5) \\
X^5(1) = X^5(2) \\
X^6(1) = X^6(2)
\end{cases}
$$

We get the following conditions on the internal variables:

$$\begin{cases} X^2(1) = X^2(2) \text{ gives } X^2(3) = X^2(4) \text{ and } X^2(5) = X^2(6) \\ X^3(1) = X^3(2) \text{ gives } X^3(3) = X^2(4) \text{ and } X^3(5) = X^3(6) \\ X^4(1) = \ X^4(3) = X^4(5) \text{ gives } X^4(2) = X^4(4) = X^4(6) \\ X^5(1) = X^5(2) \text{ gives } X^5(3) = X^5(4) \text{ and } X^5(5) = X^5(6) \\ X^6(1) = X^6(2) \text{ gives } X^6(3) = X^6(4) \text{ and } X^6(5) = X^6(6) \end{cases}$$

Now since $S^3 = X^6$, $S^2 = X^5 \oplus f_7^{(2)}(X^6)$ and $S^1 = X^4 \oplus f_6^{(2)}(X^5) \oplus f_7^{(1)}(X^6)$, we get the 8 output equations written above. Therefore, in KPA, for a F_3^7 permutation, the expectancy of $\mathcal{N}_{F_3^7}$ is larger than for a random permutation by a value of about $\frac{m^6}{2^{15n}}$ (since we have 8 equations in X and 7 in I), i.e. we expect to have about 2 times more solutions for $\mathcal{N}$: $E(\mathcal{N}) \simeq \frac{2m^6}{2^{15n}}$ for F_3^7. So we will be able to distinguish with a high probability F_3^7 from a random permutation by counting $\mathcal{N}$ when $\mathcal{N} \neq 0$ with a high probability, i.e. when $m^6 \geq O(2^{15n})$, or $m \geq O(2^{\frac{5n}{2}})$. We have found here a KPA with $O(2^{\frac{5n}{2}})$ complexity and $O(2^{\frac{5n}{2}})$ messages. This is better than the $O(2^{3n})$ complexity of the attack TWO, and it shows that we can attack 7 rounds, not only 6 with a complexity less than 2^{3n}.

CPA-1. We can transform this KPA in CPA-1. We will choose only 3 fixed different values c_1, c_2, c_3 for I^1: $\frac{m}{3}$ plaintexts will have $I^1 = c_1$, $\frac{m}{3}$ plaintexts will have $I^1 = c_2$, and $\frac{m}{3}$ plaintexts will have $I^1 = c_3$. We will generate all (or almost all) possible messages $[I^1, I^2, I^3]$ with such I^1. Therefore, $m = 3 \cdot 2^{2n}$. We can derive from these m messages $\frac{2m^4}{27}$ tuples $(i_1, i_2, i_3, i_4, i_5, i_6)$ satisfying our 7 input equations. For a random permutation we will have $E(\mathcal{N}_{perm}) \simeq \frac{2m^4}{27 \cdot 2^{8n}}$ (since we have 8 output equations). For a permutation F_3^7, we will have $E(\mathcal{N}_{F_3^7}) \simeq \frac{4m^4}{27 \cdot 2^{8n}}$, i.e. about 2 times more solutions, since the 8 output equations can occur at random, or due to 8 internal equations in X as we have seen. So this CPA-1 will succeed when $\mathcal{N} \neq 0$ with a high probability, i.e. when $m^4 \geq O(2^{8n})$, or $m \geq O(2^{2n})$. Here we have $m \simeq 3 \cdot 2^{2n}$, the probability of success is not negligible. Moreover if it fails for some values (c_1, c_2, c_3) for I^1, we can start again with another (c_1, c_2, c_3). Therefore this CPA-1 is in $O(2^{2n})$ complexity and $O(2^{2n})$ messages. (This is better than the $O(2^{3n})$ we have found with the TWO attack).

5.3   Properties of R1

We now describe the general properties of R1. We will denote by n_I the number of equalities in (I), and by n_S the number of equalities in (S). Similarly, we will denote by n_X the number of equalities in (X). Therefore n_X is the number of independent equalities in the X^i variables needed in order to get (S) from (I) (in the previous example presented in Section 5.2, we have $n_I = 7$, $n_S = 8$ and $n_X = 8$). In this attack R1 we have:

$$\begin{cases} n_I = \frac{k\varphi}{2} - k + 1 \\ n_S = \frac{k\varphi}{2} - 1 \\ n_X = a(\frac{\varphi}{2} - 2) + d - 1 \end{cases}$$

The idea of R1 is to minimize the total number $n_I + n_X$ of needed equations in I and X. When this criteria is dominant, R1 will be the best attack.

The value $\mathcal{N}$ is expected to be larger for a F_k^d than for a random permutation due to the fact that (S) can come from random reasons or from (X) in F_k^d. Therefore, it is natural, in order to get necessary and sufficient condition of success for R1, to evaluate the expectancy and the standard deviation of $\mathcal{N}$ in the case of F_k^d and in the case of random permutations. This can be done (by using the covariance formula as in [15] or by using approximation as in [6]) and we have found that each time that R1 was better than TWO, we had $n_X \leq n_S$. However, when $n_X \leq n_S$ we can easily obtain sufficient condition of success for R1 without computing the standard deviations, since when $n_X \leq n_S$ we will have for most permutations about 2 times more (or more) solutions with F_k^d than with this random permutation. Therefore, a sufficient condition of success for R1 when $n_X \leq n_S$ is to have that (X) and (I) can be satisfied with a non-negligible probability. A sufficient condition for this is to have:

In KPA

Condition 1: $n_X \leq n_S$.
Condition 2: $m^\varphi \geq 2^{n(n_I + n_X)}$.
Condition 3: $m^2 \geq 2^{(d-a)n}$.
Condition 4: $m^3 \geq 2^{dn}$ and more generally $\forall i,\ 0 \leq i \leq \frac{\varphi}{2} - 1,\ m^{3+i} \geq 2^{(d+ia)n}$.
Condition 5: $m^4 \geq 2^{(d+k)n}$.

(Conditions 2, 3, 4, 5 are necessary. Conditions 1, 2, 3, 4, 5 are sufficient for success. Condition 1 is not necessary, but the computation of $\sigma(\mathcal{N})$ shows that R1 is not better than TWO when $n_X > n_S$.)

Condition 2 comes from the fact that we have about m^φ rectangles with φ points, and the probability that (I) and (X) are satisfied on one rectangle is $\frac{1}{2^{n(n_I + n_X)}}$.

Condition 3 comes from the fact that between points 1 and 2 we have $|\mathcal{F}|$ equations in X^i, and one equation in I^1. Therefore in KPA we must have $m^2 \geq 2^{(|\mathcal{F}|+1)n} = 2^{(d-a)n}$.

Condition 4 comes from the fact that between points 1, 2 and 3 we have $d - 1$ equations in X^i, and one equation in I^1. Therefore we must have $m^3 \geq 2^{dn}$. Similarly between the points 1, 2, 3, 5, we must have: $m^4 \geq 2^{(d+a)n}$. And similarly between the points 1, 2, 3, 5, 7, $\ldots$, $(\varphi - 1)$, we must have: $m^{\frac{\varphi}{2}+1} \geq 2^{(d+a(\frac{\varphi}{2}-2))n}$.

Condition 5 comes from the fact that between points 1, 2, 3, 4, we have $d - 1$ equations in X^i, 2 equations in I^1 and $(k - 1)$ in $I^2, I^3, \ldots, I^{k-1}$.

It is easy to see that the conditions on any points are consequences of these 5 conditions. Moreover, if $m \geq 2^{an}$ (we will often, but not always, choose a like this), condition 4 can be changed with only $m^3 \geq 2^{dn}$.

CPA-1. In CPA-1 the sufficient conditions when $m \leq 2^{(k-1)n}$ are:
Condition 1: $n_X \leq n_S$.
Condition 2: $m^{(\frac{\varphi}{2}+1)} \geq 2^{n \cdot n_X}$.

Condition 3: $m^2 \geq 2^{(d-a-1)n}$.

Condition 4 and Condition 5: $m^3 \geq 2^{(d-1)n}$.

From these conditions we can compute the best parameters a and φ for any d and k, when d and k are fixed.

Remark. If we choose $n_X < n_S$ (instead of $n_X \leq n_S$), the attacks are slightly less efficient but more spectacular since with a non-negligible probability (I) and (S) are satisfied with F_k^d and not with random permutations. Moreover with $n_X < n_S$ it is still possible (with R2) to attack $3k - 1$ rounds with less than 2^{kn} complexity.

6 "R2", "R3", "R4" Attacks for Any $k \geq 3$ with $d \geq k$

R2, R3, and R4 attacks are very similar to attack R1 but the conditions on the variables are not the same.

6.1 R2 Attacks

In the R2 attack, we will choose a values of $\{1, 2, \ldots, d - k\}$. Let $\mathcal{E}$ be the set of these a values, and let $\mathcal{F}$ be the set of all integers i, $1 \leq i \leq d - 1$ such that $i \notin \mathcal{E}$. We have $|\mathcal{E}| = a$, $|\mathcal{F}| = d - a - 1$, and $\mathcal{F}$ contains all the $k - 1$ values i, $d - k + 1 \leq i \leq d - 1$. For R2 we have:

$$(I) = \begin{cases} I^1(1) = I^1(3) = I^1(5) = \ldots = I^1(\varphi - 1) \\ I^1(2) = I^1(4) = I^1(6) = \ldots = I^1(\varphi) \\ \forall i, 2 \leq i \leq k, \; I^i(1) \oplus I^i(2) = I^i(3) \oplus I^i(4) = \ldots = I^i(\varphi - 1) \oplus I^i(\varphi) \end{cases}$$

$$(X) = \begin{cases} \forall i \in \mathcal{E}, \; X^i(1) = X^i(3) = \ldots = X^i(\varphi - 1) \\ \forall i \in \mathcal{F}, \; X^i(1) = X^i(2) \end{cases}$$

$$(S) = \begin{cases} \forall i, 2 \leq i \leq k, \; S^i(1) = S^i(2), \; S^i(3) = S^i(4), \ldots, S^i(\varphi - 1) = S^i(\varphi) \\ S^1(1) \oplus S^1(2) = S^1(3) \oplus S^1(4) = \ldots = S^1(\varphi - 1) \oplus S^1(\varphi) \end{cases}$$

The equations (X) have been chosen such that (S) is just a consequence of (I) and (X). Our attacks consist in counting the number $\mathcal{N}$ of rectangle sets of plaintext/ciphertext pairs satisfying the conditions (I) and (S). Figure 3 illustrates the equations for R2.

Between two different plaintext/ciphertext pairs i and j, $i \neq j$, we can have at most $k - 1$ successive equalities on the variables $I^1, X^1, \ldots, X^{d-1}$. Therefore, for R2, we have $\lfloor \frac{d-1}{k} \rfloor \leq a \leq d - 1 - \lfloor \frac{d}{k} \rfloor$, and

$$\begin{cases} n_I = \frac{k\varphi}{2} + \frac{\varphi}{2} - k - 1 \\ n_S = \frac{k\varphi}{2} - 1 \\ n_X = a(\frac{\varphi}{2} - 2) + d - 1 \end{cases}$$

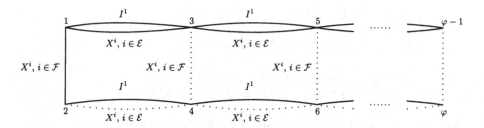

Fig. 3. Attack R2 on F_k^d

As we have explained for R1, sufficient conditions of success for R2 in KPA are the following 5 conditions:

Condition 1: $n_X \leq n_S$.

Condition 2: $m^\varphi \geq 2^{n(n_I + n_X)}$.

Condition 3: $m^3 \geq 2^{dn}$.

Condition 4: $m^2 \geq 2^{(d-a-1)n}$.

Condition 5: $m^4 \geq 2^{(d+k)n}$.

Example for R2. In the R2 attack on F_3^8, we have: $\varphi = 8$, $a = 2$, $n_I = 12$, $n_S = 11$ and $n_X = 11$. Details are in the extended version of the paper.

6.2 R3 Attack

In the R3 attack, we set the following conditions on the input variables:

$$(I) = \begin{cases} I^1(1) = I^1(2),\ I^1(3) = I^1(4),\ I^1(5) = I^1(6),\dots,\ I^1(\varphi-1) = I^1(\varphi) \\ \forall i,\ 2 \leq i \leq k,\ I^i(1) \oplus I^i(2) = I^i(3) \oplus I^i(4) = \dots = I^i(\varphi-1) \oplus I^i(\varphi) \end{cases}$$

Then the conditions on the internal variables (with $|\mathcal{E}| = d - a - 1$ and $|\mathcal{F}| = a$ and if $d - k + 2 \leq i \leq d - 1$ then $i \in \mathcal{F}$) are:

$$(X) = \begin{cases} \forall i \in \mathcal{E},\ X^i(1) = X^i(2) \\ \forall i \in \mathcal{F},\ X^i(1) = X^i(3) = \dots = X^i(\varphi-1) \end{cases}$$

Finally, the conditions on the output variables are given by:

$$(S) = \begin{cases} S^1(1) \oplus S^1(2) = S^1(3) \oplus S^1(4) = \dots = S^1(\varphi-1) \oplus S^1(\varphi) \\ S^2(1) \oplus S^2(2) = S^2(3) \oplus S^2(4) = \dots = S^2(\varphi-1) \oplus S^2(\varphi) \\ \forall i,\ 3 \leq i \leq k,\ S^1(1) = S^1(3) = S^1(5) = \dots = S^1(\varphi-1) \\ \forall i,\ 3 \leq i \leq k,\ S^1(2) = S^1(4) = S^1(6) = \dots = S^1(\varphi) \end{cases}$$

Then, the R3 attack proceeds exactly the same as R1 and R2 attacks.

6.3 R4 Attack

In the R4 attack, we have the following conditions on the input, internal and output variables:

$$(I) = \begin{cases} I^1(1) = I^1(3) = I^1(5) = \ldots = I^1(\varphi - 1) \\ I^1(2) = I^1(4) = I^1(6) = \ldots = I^1(\varphi) \\ \forall i, \ 2 \leq i \leq k, \ I^i(1) \oplus I^i(2) = I^i(3) \oplus I^i(4) = \ldots = I^i(\varphi - 1) \oplus I^i(\varphi) \end{cases}$$

$$(X) = \begin{cases} \forall i \in \mathcal{E}, \ X^i(1) = X^i(2) \\ \forall i \in \mathcal{F}, \ X^i(1) = X^i(3) = \ldots = X^i(\varphi - 1) \end{cases}$$

(with $|\mathcal{E}| = d - a - 1$ and $|\mathcal{F}| = a$ and if $d - k + 3 \leq i \leq d - 1$ then $i \in \mathcal{F}$)

$$(S) = \begin{cases} S^1(1) \oplus S^1(2) = S^1(3) \oplus S^1(4) = \ldots = S^1(\varphi - 1) \oplus S^1(\varphi) \\ S^2(1) \oplus S^2(2) = S^2(3) \oplus S^2(4) = \ldots = S^2(\varphi - 1) \oplus S^2(\varphi) \\ S^3(1) \oplus S^3(2) = S^3(3) \oplus S^3(4) = \ldots = S^3(\varphi - 1) \oplus S^3(\varphi) \\ \forall i, \ 4 \leq i \leq k, \ S^1(1) = S^1(3) = S^1(5) = \ldots = S^1(\varphi - 1) \\ \forall i, \ 4 \leq i \leq k, \ S^1(2) = S^1(4) = S^1(6) = \ldots = S^1(\varphi) \end{cases}$$

Example for R4. We will now present how to attack F_k^{3k-1} when $k \geq 5$ with a complexity less than 2^{kn}. This example is interesting since $3k - 1$ is the maximum number of rounds that we can attack with a complexity lower than 2^{kn} (for $d = 3k$ the complexity of the best known attacks become $O(2^{kn})$ and for $d \geq 3k + 1$ we need more than $O(2^{kn})$ computations). It is also interesting since in [6] Jutla was able to attack only $3k - 3$ rounds with a complexity less than 2^{kn}. We will present only the main ideas. We will use the attack R4 with $a = k - 1$, i.e. between 1 and 3 we have these $k - 1$ equations: $X^{d-1}, X^{d-2}, \ldots,$ X^{d-k+3}, plus X^k and X^{2k}.

Remark. With R2 (but not with R1) we can also attack F_k^{3k-1} (with $\varphi = 2k + 2$ and $a = k - 1$) with a complexity less than 2^{kn}, but the complexity of R4 will be slightly better.

In R4 with $a = k - 1$, we have:

$$\begin{cases} n_I = \frac{k\varphi}{2} + \frac{\varphi}{2} - k - 1 \\ n_S = k\varphi - \frac{3\varphi}{2} - 2k + 3 \\ n_X = \frac{k\varphi}{2} + d - 2k - \frac{\varphi}{2} + 1 \end{cases}$$

Therefore when $d = 3k - 1$, we have $n_X = \frac{k\varphi}{2} + k - \frac{\varphi}{2}$. $n_X \leq n_S$ gives $\varphi \geq 6 + \frac{6}{k-2}$. For $k \geq 5$, this means $\varphi \geq 8$ (φ is always even). Now if we look at all the 5 conditions for the complexity, these conditions give: $m \geq 2^{(k-\frac{1}{8})n}$ in KPA, and $m \geq 2^{(k-\frac{1}{2})n}$ in CPA-1. These complexities are less than 2^{kn} as claimed.

7   Experimental Results

We have implemented the CPA-1 attacks SQUARE and R1 against F_3^6, F_3^7, and F_3^8. The attack against F_3^6 uses 4 points and $2^{\frac{5n}{3}}$ plaintexts, the attack against F_3^7 uses 6 points and 2^{2n} plaintexts, and the attack against F_3^8 uses 8 points and $2^{2.5n}$ plaintexts. Our experiments confirm our ability to distinguish between F_3^6 or F_3^7 or F_3^8 and a random permutation. Our experiments were done as follows:

- choose randomly an instance of F_3^6 or F_3^7 or F_3^8
- choose randomly a permutation: for this we use classical balanced Feistel scheme with a large number of rounds (more than 20)
- launch the attack in CPA-1
- count the number of structures satisfying the input and output relations for the F_3^6 or F_3^7 or F_3^8 permutation and for the permutation
- if this number is higher or equal to a fixed threshold (generally 1 or 2), declare the function to be a F_3^6 or F_3^7 or F_3^8 permutation and otherwise a random permutation

All these procedures are iterated a large number of time (at least 1000 times) to evaluate the effectiveness of our distinguisher. We give the percentage of success, i.e. the number of F_3^6 or F_3^7 or F_3^8 that have been correctly distinguished and the percentage of false alarm, i.e. the number of random permutation that have incorrectly been declared as F_3^6 or F_3^7 or F_3^8.

Table 1. Experimental results for CPA-1 attacks

scheme	n	threshold	Percentage of success of the attack	Percentage of false alarm
F_3^6	8	2	54%	4%
F_3^7	6	1	33%	1%
F_3^8	6	1	38%	1%

We give some details in the F_3^7 case: here are the numbers of rectangles sets for 100 instances of F_3^7.

$2, 0, 25, 1, 0, 3, 1, 0, 0, 0, 0, 0, 1, 1, 0, 1, 0, 0, 2, 0, 0, 1, 0, 0, 0, 1, 0, 1, 0, 0, 12, 1, 4, 1,$

$0, 1, 4, 18, 0, 1, 1, 0, 0, 2, 0, 0, 0, 2, 0, 0, 0, 0, 1, 0, 0, 0, 3, 0, 0, 0, 0, 1, 0, 1, 13, 0, 1, 6, 0,$

$0, 0, 33, 0, 0, 0, 0, 4, 0, 0, 0, 0, 0, 1, 0, 3, 36, 1, 14, 0, 1, 0, 0, 0, 0, 0, 0, 0, 2, 0, 0$

The corresponding numbers for 100 random permutations are composed of 99 zero and a single one. This clearly shows that we can distinguish between the two cases.

Our experiments show that the distinguisher on F_3^6 is more efficient than the one on F_3^7 and than the one on F_3^8. But in all case they confirm our ability to distinguish.

8   Attack by the Signature

It can be proved that all the permutations F_k^d have an even signature. The proof of this result is quite similar to the proof in the case of a symmetric Feistel scheme [13]. Therefore, by computing the signature of F_k^d we are able to distinguish F_k^d from a random permutation with a non-negligible probability and $O(2^{kn})$ computations if all the 2^{kn} plaintext/ciphertext are known. However if we do not have access to the complex codebook of size 2^{kn}, or if we want to distinguish F_k^d from a random permutation with an even signature, this "attack" obviously fails.

9   Summary of the Results on F_k^d, $k \geq 3$, on TWO, SQUARE and Rectangle Attacks

The following table shows the results we have obtained with our different attacks.

Table 2. Results on F_k^d for $k = 3$, on TWO, SQUARE and Rectangle attacks (i.e. without Multi-rectangle attacks). CAUTION: Multi-Rectangle attacks may have sometimes better complexities.

	KPA	CPA-1
F_3^1	1	1
F_3^2	$2^{\frac{n}{2}}$, TWO	2
F_3^3	2^n, TWO	2
F_3^4	$2^{\frac{3}{2}n}$, TWO	$2^{\frac{n}{2}}$, TWO
F_3^5	2^{2n}, TWO	2^n, TWO
F_3^6	$2^{\frac{9}{4}n}$, SQUARE	$2^{\frac{5}{3}n}$, SQUARE
F_3^7	$2^{\frac{5}{2}n}$, M1, $\varphi = 6$	2^{2n}, M1, $\varphi = 6$
F_3^8	$2^{\frac{23}{8}n}$, R2, $\varphi = 8$	$2^{\frac{5}{2}n}$, R2, $\varphi = 8$
F_3^9	2^{3n}, R2, $\varphi \geq 10$	2^{3n}, R2, $\varphi \geq 10$
F_3^{10}	2^{7n}, TWO	2^{7n}, TWO
F_3^{11}	2^{8n}, TWO	2^{8n}, TWO
F_3^d, $d \geq 10$	$2^{(d-6+\lfloor \frac{d}{3} \rfloor)n}$, TWO	$2^{(d-6+\lfloor \frac{d}{3} \rfloor)n}$, TWO

10   Multi-rectangle Attacks

An interesting problem is to design better attacks than 2-point attacks, or rectangle attacks. We have tried attacks with different geometries of equations (hexagons instead of rectangles, multi-dimensional cubes instead of 2-dimension rectangles, etc...). So far the best new attacks that we have found are "Multi-Rectangle attacks", i.e. attacks where some "rectangles" in I equations are linked with S equations. We will present here only two examples. More details are given in the extended version of this paper. These new attacks are very promising asymptotically (i.e. when n becomes large) but their efficiency from a practical point of view and the design optimality are still under investigation.

Example 1. With a 2-rectangle attack (as in Figure 4 below), it seems that we can attack F_6^{18} with a complexity strictly less than 2^{6n}. Therefore this attack is expected to be better than rectangle attacks. However we have to use 2 rectangles of about 2×20 points. Consequently we will have a large constant in the complexity and therefore such a theoretical attack might be of no practical interest.

Example 2. It seems that we can attack F_k^d when $d \leq k^2 + k$ with a complexity less than $O(2^{kn})$ with a Multi-Rectangle attack when k is fixed (with a huge coefficient depending of k and not of n in the O). This attacks is based on arrays of $k + 1$ dimensional hypercubes. This attack is still under investigation.

Table 3. Results on F_k^d for $k > 3$, on TWO, SQUARE and Rectangle attacks (i.e. without Multi-rectangle attacks). CAUTION: Multi-Rectangle attacks may have sometimes better complexities.

	KPA	CPA-1
F_k^1	1	1
F_k^2	$2^{\frac{n}{2}}$, TWO	2
F_k^3	2^n, TWO	2
$F_k^d, 2 \leq d \leq k$	$2^{\frac{d-1}{2}n}$, TWO	2
F_k^{k+1}	$2^{\frac{k}{2}n}$, TWO	$2^{\frac{n}{2}}$, TWO
F_k^{k+2}	$2^{\frac{k+1}{2}n}$, TWO and SQUARE	2^n, TWO
F_k^{k+3}	$2^{\frac{2k+3}{4}n}$, SQUARE	2^{2n},TWO or $2^{\frac{k+2}{3}n}$, SQUARE
$F_k^d, k+2 \leq d \leq 2k$	$2^{\frac{d+k}{4}n}$, SQUARE	$2^{(d-k-1)n}$,TWO or $2^{\frac{d-1}{3}n}$, SQUARE
F_k^{2k}	$2^{\frac{3k}{4}n}$, SQUARE	$2^{\frac{2k-1}{3}n}$,SQUARE
$\vdots$	$\vdots$	$\vdots$
F_k^{3k-1}	$2^{(k-\frac{1}{8})n}$, R3 $k=4$, R4 $k \geq 5$	$2^{(k-\frac{1}{2})n}$, R2 $k=4$, R4 $k \geq 5$
F_k^{3k}	2^{kn}, R2	2^{kn}, R2
$F_k^d, 3k \leq d \leq k^2$	$2^{(d-2k)n}$, R2	$2^{(d-2k)n}$, R2

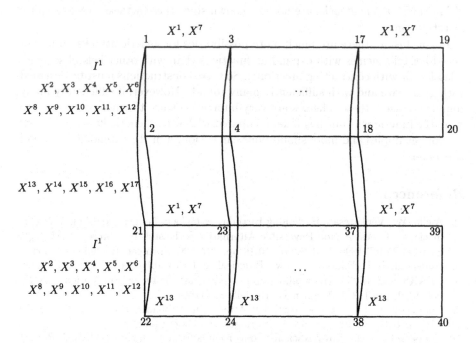

Fig. 4. Example of a multi-rectangle attack on F_6^{18}

Multi-Rectangle attacks are also of interest for less rounds, for example in order to attack F_k^{2k} with a smaller complexity than rectangle attacks.

11   Conclusion

In [6], Jutla has introduced "Rectangle attacks" against unbalanced Feistel schemes. To improve the attacks of Jutla, we have first made a systematic analysis of the different ways to optimize the parameters. We have obtained like this 5 different kinds of "rectangle attacks" that we have called SQUARE, R1, R2, R3 and R4. By computing the optimal parameters, we have shown that we can attack $3k-1$ rounds in KPA instead of $3k-3$ in CPA-1 for Jutla with a complexity strictly lower than 2^{kn} with these "Rectangle attacks" (This was confirmed with experimental simulations). Moreover, we have also described two other families of attacks that we have called TWO (for 2-point attacks) and "Multi-Rectangle attacks". We have shown that sometimes TWO attacks are the best, and sometimes it is SQUARE, R1, R2, R3, R4 or Multi-Rectangle attacks, depending of the choices of d and k. For example, for very small values of d, TWO attacks are the best. Multi-Rectangle attacks seem to be very promising from a theoretical point of view. For example, we may attack much more than $3k - 1$ rounds with a complexity strictly lower than 2^{kn}, and we may attack F_k^{2k} with a complexity better than with rectangle attacks. However the precise properties of Multi-Rectangle attacks are not yet known since these attacks are still under investigation.

In conclusion, there are much more possibilities for generic attacks on unbalanced Feistel schemes with expanding functions than with other Feistel schemes (classical or with contracting functions). So these constructions must be designed with great care and with sufficiently many rounds. However, if sufficiently many rounds are used, these schemes are very interesting since the memory needed to store the functions is much smaller compared with other generic Feistel schemes.

More examples and more simulations can be found in the extended version of this paper.

References

1. Aiello, W., Venkatesan, R.: Foiling Birthday Attacks in Length-Doubling Transformations - Benes: A Non-Reversible Alternative to Feistel. In: Maurer, U.M. (ed.) EUROCRYPT 1996. LNCS, vol. 1070, pp. 307–320. Springer, Heidelberg (1996)
2. Anderson, R.J., Biham, E.: Two Practical and Provably Secure Block Ciphers: BEARS and LION. In: Gollmann, D. (ed.) Fast Software Encryption. LNCS, vol. 1039, pp. 113–120. Springer, Heidelberg (1996)
3. Coppersmith, D.: Another Birthday Attack. In: Williams, H.C. (ed.) CRYPTO 1985. LNCS, vol. 218, pp. 14–17. Springer, Heidelberg (1986)
4. Coppersmith, D.: Luby-Rackoff: Four rounds is not enough.Technical Report RC20674, IBM Research Report (December 1996)
5. Girault, M., Cohen, R., Campana, M.: A Generalized Birthday Attack. In: Günther, C.G. (ed.) Advances in Cryptology – EUROCRYPT 1988. LNCS, vol. 330, pp. 129–156. Springer, Heidelberg (1988)

6. Jutla, C.S.: Generalized Birthday Attacks on Unbalanced Feistel Networks. In: Krawczyk, H. (ed.) CRYPTO 1998. LNCS, vol. 1462, pp. 186–199. Springer, Heidelberg (1998)
7. Knudsen, L.R.: DEAL - A 128-bit Block Cipher. Technical Report 151, University of Bergen, Department of Informatics, Norway (February 1998)
8. Knudsen, L.R., Lai, X., Preneel, B.: Attacks on Fast Double Block Length Hash Functions. J. Cryptology 11(1), 59–72 (1998)
9. Knudsen, L.R., Rijmen, V.: On the Decorrelated Fast Cipher (DFC) and Its Theory. In: Knudsen, L.R. (ed.) FSE 1999. LNCS, vol. 1636, pp. 81–94. Springer, Heidelberg (1999)
10. Luby, M., Rackoff, C.: How to Construct Pseudorandom Permutations from Pseudorandom Functions. SIAM J. Comput. 17(2), 373–386 (1988)
11. Naor, M., Reingold, O.: On the Construction of Pseudorandom Permutations: Luby-Rackoff Revisited.. J. Cryptology 12(1), 29–66 (1999)
12. Patarin, J.: New Results on Pseudorandom Permutation Generators Based on the DES Scheme. In: Feigenbaum, J. (ed.) CRYPTO 1991. LNCS, vol. 576, pp. 301–312. Springer, Heidelberg (1992)
13. Patarin, J.: Generic Attacks on Feistel Schemes. In: Boyd, C. (ed.) ASIACRYPT 2001. LNCS, vol. 2248, pp. 222–238. Springer, Heidelberg (2001)
14. Patarin, J.: Security of Random Feistel Schemes with 5 or More Rounds. In: Franklin, M.K. (ed.) CRYPTO 2004. LNCS, vol. 3152, pp. 106–122. Springer, Heidelberg (2004)
15. Patarin, J., Nachef, V., Berbain, C.: Generic Attacks on Unbalanced Feistel Schemes with Contracting Functions. In: Lai, X., Chen, K. (eds.) ASIACRYPT 2006. LNCS, vol. 4284, pp. 396–411. Springer, Heidelberg (2006)
16. Schneier, B., Kelsey, J.: Unbalanced Feistel Networks and Block Cipher Design. In: Gollmann, D. (ed.) Fast Software Encryption. LNCS, vol. 1039, pp. 121–144. Springer, Heidelberg (1996)

On Tweaking Luby-Rackoff Blockciphers

David Goldenberg[1], Susan Hohenberger[2,*], Moses Liskov[1],
Elizabeth Crump Schwartz[1], and Hakan Seyalioglu[1,**]

[1] The College of William and Mary
{dcgold,mliskov,eacrum}@cs.wm.edu, hakan.seyalioglu@gmail.com
[2] The Johns Hopkins University susan@cs.jhu.edu

Abstract. Tweakable blockciphers, first formalized by Liskov, Rivest, and Wagner [12], are blockciphers with an additional input, the *tweak*, which allows for variability. An open problem proposed by Liskov et al. is how to construct tweakable blockciphers without using a pre-existing blockcipher. There are many natural questions in this area: is it significantly more efficient to incorporate a tweak directly? How do direct constructions compare to existing techniques? Are these direct constructions *optimal* and for what levels of security? How large of a tweak can be securely added? In this work, we explore these questions for Luby-Rackoff blockciphers. We show that tweakable blockciphers can be created directly from Luby-Rackoff ciphers, and in some cases show that direct constructions of tweakable blockciphers are more efficient than previously known constructions.

1 Introduction

A *blockcipher*, also known as a *pseudorandom permutation*, is a pair of algorithms E and D. The encryption algorithm E takes two inputs – a key K and a message block M, and produces a ciphertext block C of the same length as M, while the decryption algorithm D reverses this process. A blockcipher is considered secure if, for a random secret key K, the cipher is indistinguishable from a random permutation.

A *tweakable blockcipher* takes an extra input, the *tweak*, (T), that is used only to provide variation and is not kept secret. Unlike changing the key, changing the tweak should involve minimal extra cost. A tweakable blockcipher is considered secure if it is indistinguishable from a family of random permutations indexed by the tweak. The Hasty Pudding Cipher by Schroeppel [21] was the first to introduce an auxiliary blockcipher input called a "spice" and Liskov, Rivest, and Wagner [12] later formalized the notion of tweakable blockciphers. Liskov et al. describe two levels of security: a secure (CPA) tweakable blockcipher is one that is indistinguishable from a random permutation family to any adversary

---

* Supported by an NDSEG Fellowship and NSF grant CT-0716142.
** Partially supported by a Monroe Grant and a Cummings Grant.

that may make chosen plaintext queries, while a strongly secure (CCA) tweakable blockcipher is pseudorandom even to an adversary that may also make chosen ciphertext queries.

Tweakable blockciphers have many practical applications. Liskov et al. describe how they can be used to implement secure symmetric encryption and authenticated encryption. Halevi and Rogaway [9,10] suggest an immediate application to private storage where the tweak is set to be the memory address of an enciphered block; and thus, the encryptions of two blocks with the same plaintext are not likely to look the same and yet decryption remains straightforward. Tweakable blockciphers have also been studied in a variety of other contexts [1,11,20,2].

Feistel Blockciphers. Feistel blockciphers [6] have been an actively studied class of constructions since Horst Feistel invented them in 1973. In particular, Luby and Rackoff showed how to construct a pseudorandom permutation from a pseudorandom function by composing three (or four in the case of CCA security) Feistel permutations [13]. We call this construction the Luby-Rackoff blockcipher. In 1996, Lucks [14] described an optimization for the secure 3-round version by replacing the first round with a universal hash function. Shortly afterwards, Naor and Reingold [15] provided the analogous optimization for the strongly secure 4-round cipher, replacing both the first and last rounds with a more general type of function. In 2001, Ramzan [18] formally studied many variations on the Luby-Rackoff cipher. Patarin gave proofs of security for certain constructions against unbounded adversaries with access to exponentially many queries, albeit assuming the individual round functions are random functions rather than pseudorandom. Specifically, Patarin proved security for 7 rounds against $q \ll 2^k$ queries, where the blockcipher input is of size $2k$ [16], and later improved this to show that 5 rounds is sufficient, both for chosen-plaintext and chosen-ciphertext attacks [17], which remains the best proven security level for Feistel ciphers. Dodis and Puniya recently provided a combinatorial understanding of Feistel networks when the round functions are *unpredictable* rather than pseudorandom [5].

Our Work. Liskov, Rivest, and Wagner [12] give two constructions for tweakable blockciphers, each one constructed from an underlying blockcipher. Subsequent work has also taken this approach; Halevi and Rogaway's EMD and EME modes [9,10] and Rogaway's XEX mode [20] were all blockcipher modes of operation. The only examples of specific tweakable blockciphers are the Hasty Pudding [21] and the Mercy [4] ciphers.

One open problem proposed by Liskov et al. was to study how to incorporate tweaks into existing blockciphers, or design tweakable blockciphers directly. In this work, we perform a systematic study of issues relating to directly tweaking Luby-Rackoff blockciphers. We analyze the approach of including a tweak by XOR-ing the tweak value into one or more places in the dataflow. This natural model for adding a tweak changes the cipher minimally. Also, approaches involving more direct cryptographic processing of the tweak (e.g. hashing the tweak) have a significant additional cost associated with changing the tweak.

Our Contributions. We present tweakable Luby-Rackoff blockciphers, for both CPA and CCA security, and against both polynomial-time adversaries, and against unbounded adversaries with $q \ll 2^k$ queries[1], where k is half the size of the input (matching the best result for ordinary blockciphers [17]). Specifically, we construct tweakable blockciphers:

- CPA-secure against polynomial adversaries in 4 rounds (Theorem 3)
- CCA-secure against polynomial adversaries in 6 rounds (Theorem 8)
- CPA-secure against $q \ll 2^k$ queries in 7 rounds (Theorem 4)
- CCA-secure against $q \ll 2^k$ queries in 10 rounds (Theorem 9)

Recall that for polynomial adversaries CPA-security requires 3 rounds whereas CCA-security requires 4. It is thus natural to wonder if our constructions are optimal. We prove our constructions against polynomial adversaries are indeed round-optimal in our model (Theorems 1 and 7). Furthermore, we show that any construction of 6 or fewer rounds in our model can be attacked with $O(2^{k/2})$ queries (Table 1), so our construction of Theorem 4 is also round-optimal. In addition, the attacks used to prove the round-optimality of our constructions, as well as our extension of the proof methods of Naor and Reingold, help to form the theoretical foundation necessary for the secure design of tweakable blockciphers regardless of construction, as well as shedding light on the difficulties in adding a tweak to Feistel-based blockciphers such as RC6 [19] and MARS [3].

We also explicitly address the problem of incorporating tweaks of arbitrary length, an important issue not addressed in the literature.[2] We show that our CPA-secure constructions can incorporate additional blocks of tweak at the cost of 1 round per block (Theorems 11 and 14), and that our CCA-secure constructions may be similarly extended at the cost of 2 rounds per block of tweak (Theorems 12 and 15).

2 Definitions

A *tweakable blockcipher* is a triple of algorithms $(\widetilde{G}, \widetilde{E}, \widetilde{D})$ for key generation, encryption, and decryption, respectively. We restrict our attention to tweakable blockciphers where $\widetilde{G}(\cdot)$, $\widetilde{E}_K(\cdot, \cdot)$, and $\widetilde{D}_K(\cdot, \cdot)$ are all efficiently computable algorithms; and where the correctness property holds; that is, for all M, T, and

---

[1] That is, any non-negative $q < 2^k$ such that $q2^{-k}$ is negligible.

[2] Using tweaks of arbitrary length has been considered for tweakable symmetric encryption [8], but not for one-block constructions. Certain applications require different, specific tweak sizes, and one may want to allow longer tweaks to include more information. Indeed, this was the motivation for Schroeppel to allow spice values of 512 bits in the Hasty Pudding Cipher [21].

for all keys $K \in \widetilde{G}(1^k)$, $\widetilde{D}_K(\widetilde{E}_K(M,T),T) = M$. We also generally assume that $\widetilde{G}(1^k)$ draws keys uniformly at random from $\{0,1\}^{p(k)}$ for some polynomial p.

We have two notions of security: (1) chosen-plaintext secure (CPA) and (2) chosen-ciphertext secure (CCA). Security is defined in terms of both a polynomial and an exponential adversary; polynomial adversaries are limited to a number of queries and computations polynomial in the message size, whereas an exponential adversary is allowed unlimited computation, but is bounded by an exponential number of queries relative to the message size.

Definition 1. *Over all adversaries with access to an encryption oracle, the maximum advantage is defined as:*

$$\mathsf{ADV\text{-}TBC}_K(\widetilde{E},\widetilde{D},q,t) = \max_{\mathcal{A}} : |\Pr[\mathcal{A}^{\widetilde{E}_K(\cdot,\cdot)}(1^k) = 1] - \Pr[\mathcal{A}^{\Pi}(1^k) = 1]|$$

where (1) for all k, K is generated by $\widetilde{G}(1^k)$, (2) Π is a random permutation family parameterized by its second input, and (3) $\mathcal{A}$ is allowed to run for t steps and make at most q oracle queries.

Definition 2. *Over all adversaries with access to an encryption and decryption oracle, the maximum advantage is defined as:*

$$\mathsf{ADV\text{-}STBC}_K(\widetilde{E},\widetilde{D},q,t) = \max_{\mathcal{A}} : |\Pr[\mathcal{A}^{\widetilde{E}_K(\cdot,\cdot),\widetilde{D}_K(\cdot,\cdot)}(1^k) = 1] - \Pr[\mathcal{A}^{\Pi,\Pi^{-1}}(1^k) = 1]|$$

where (1) for all k, K is generated by $\widetilde{G}(1^k)$, (2) Π, Π^{-1} are a pseudorandom permutation family and its inverse, and (3) $\mathcal{A}$ is allowed to run for t steps and make at most q oracle queries.

A tweakable blockcipher is CPA secure if for all k, for q queries and time t, $\mathsf{ADV\text{-}TBC}_K(\widetilde{E}, \widetilde{D}, q, t)$ is negligible in k. A tweakable cipher is said to be polynomially-secure if q and t are polynomial in k. If t is unspecified, then it may be unbounded. We define CCA security in the same manner.

3   The Feistel Blockcipher

Recall the formula for the Feistel blockcipher [6] on input $M = (L^0, R^0)$:

$$L^{i+1} = R^i$$
$$R^{i+1} = f_{i+1}(R^i) \oplus L^i$$

where the output after n rounds is (L^n, R^n), and each f_i is a pseudorandom function specified by the key. Further recall that the 3-round Feistel construction is secure against chosen plaintext attacks, and the 4-round construction is secure against chosen ciphertext attack [13].

3.1   Notation

In order to talk about where to add a tweak, we must first establish some notation. Unless otherwise specified, the tweaks we refer to are a *half-block* in length;

that is, on input M of size $2k$, the tweak is of size k. As we will later see, a blockcipher may allow for longer tweaks; we think of these as "multiple tweaks," as conceptually, the longer tweak can be thought of as being composed of multiple tweaks, each of the same size.

For an n-round Luby-Rackoff construction, a single half-block of tweak can conceivably be XOR-ed in at any of the following unique locations: $\mathcal{L}_0$, $\mathcal{L}_1$, ..., $\mathcal{L}_n$, $\mathcal{R}_0, \mathcal{R}_{0.5}$, $\mathcal{R}_1, \ldots, \mathcal{R}_{n-0.5}, \mathcal{R}_n$. Let this set be denoted by Λ_n. We illustrate the Λ_3 (3-round) locations in Figure 1.

Let T^λ be the XOR of all the tweaks used at location $\lambda \in \Lambda_n$. The formula for our construction is:

$$L^{i+1} = R^i \oplus T^{\mathcal{R}_i}$$
$$R^{i+1} = f_{i+1}(R^i \oplus T^{\mathcal{R}_i} \oplus T^{\mathcal{R}_{i+0.5}}) \oplus L^i \oplus T^{\mathcal{L}_i}$$

We use "$\mathcal{BC}(n, \lambda)$" to refer to the tweakable blockcipher construction where the number of Luby-Rackoff rounds is n and a tweak T^λ is XOR-ed in at some location $\lambda \in \Lambda_n$. To denote adding multiple tweaks, we write "$\mathcal{BC}(n, \lambda_1, \ldots, \lambda_t)$", where $T^{\lambda_i} = T_i$ is the tweak for location λ_i and different locations each have their own independent tweak. Thus, in such a construction, the tweak size is tk.

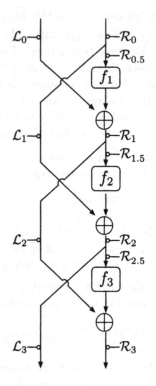

Fig. 1. An illustration of Λ_3; the locations at which to XOR a tweak of length $|M|/2$ for 3-round LR

We might also want to denote adding the *same* tweak value at two or more locations. We write this as "$\mathcal{BC}(n, \lambda_1 + \lambda_2)$", where the implication of using the *compound* location $\lambda_1 + \lambda_2$ is that $T^{\lambda_1} = T^{\lambda_2}$. Of course, we may also consider a construction with multiple tweaks, each of which may be a compound location; we use the obvious notation for this. We use the symbol Γ to denote a (possibly) compound tweak location.

In Λ_n, we have listed all tweaks at ".5" locations, i.e., $\mathcal{R}_{l+0.5}$ for some l. However, we do not have to consider these locations.

Lemma 1. *For all m, $\mathcal{R}_{m+0.5}$ is equivalent to $\mathcal{R}_m + \mathcal{L}_{m+1}$.*

Lemma 2. *For all $0 \le m < n$, $\mathcal{L}_m$ is equivalent to $\mathcal{R}_{m+1}$.*

Since $\mathcal{L}_m$ and $\mathcal{R}_{m+1}$ are equivalent, we will use them interchangeably. This starts us off with a reduced set of tweakable constructions to study including tweaks at locations $\mathcal{L}_n, \mathcal{R}_0, \ldots, \mathcal{R}_n$ and all combinations thereof.

4   Tweakable Blockciphers with CPA Security

In this section, we focus on achieving CPA security. In the next section, we will discuss the stronger CCA notion of security.

We begin by presenting some general results that hold for an arbitrary number of rounds. These results will help us to narrow down the possibilities for secure constructions and to prove the optimality of our final construction. As stated in Section 3, the set of possibly secure constructions includes those with tweaks at locations $\mathcal{L}_n$, $\mathcal{R}_0$, ..., $\mathcal{R}_n$ and all combinations thereof. However, we remark in Lemma 3 that we do not need to consider all possible locations, and that some locations can be simulated without directly tweaking the blockcipher; this important observation is used frequently throughout the paper.

Lemma 3. *For all n, without loss of generality, we can consider only constructions that never use the tweak locations $\mathcal{L}_n$ $\mathcal{R}_n$, $\mathcal{R}_0$, or $\mathcal{R}_1$, even in compound locations, and even when considering CCA security.*

Proof. We can simulate oracle queries with or without the tweaks in $\mathcal{L}_n$ $\mathcal{R}_n$, $\mathcal{R}_0$, or $\mathcal{R}_1$. To simulate a query $(L^0, R^0, T_1, \ldots, T_t)$ to a construction with these tweaks, we make a query $(L^0 \oplus T^{\mathcal{R}_1}, R^0 \oplus T^{\mathcal{R}_0}, T_1, \ldots, T_t)$ to the construction without these tweaks to obtain (L^n, R^n), and we return $(L^n \oplus T^{\mathcal{L}_n}, R^n \oplus T^{\mathcal{R}_n})$. Decryption queries can be simulated similarly. □

The set of tweak locations we need to consider is thus reduced to $\{\mathcal{R}_2 \ldots, \mathcal{R}_{n-1}\}$. From here on, we consider Λ_n to be $\{\mathcal{R}_2, \ldots, \mathcal{R}_{n-1}\}$.

Lemma 4. *For all n, $\mathcal{BC}(n, \mathcal{R}_{n-1})$ is not CPA-secure.*

Proof. We use a 2-query attack. If we query (L, R, T) to get (L_1^n, R_1^n), and then query (L, R, T') to get (L_2^n, R_2^n), then $L_1^n \oplus L_2^n = T \oplus T'$. □

Thus, we arrive at our first round-specific conclusion.

Theorem 1 (No Tweakable 3-Round Constructions). *For all $n < 4$ and all compound locations Γ of elements in Λ_n, $\mathcal{BC}(n, \Gamma)$ is not CPA-secure.*

Proof. This follows from Lemmas 3 and 4, and the set $\{\mathcal{R}_2, \ldots, \mathcal{R}_{n-2}\}$ being empty for $n = 3$. □

4.1   Secure Locations

We have reduced the set of possible secure single tweak locations to $\{\mathcal{R}_2, \ldots, \mathcal{R}_{n-2}\}$. We now show that each of these locations are secure for $n \geq 4$. However, first we must define $\epsilon - \mathsf{ARCU}_2$ hash functions and introduce some related work.

Definition 3. *An $\epsilon - \mathsf{ARCU}_2$ ("Almost Right-Collision-avoiding Universal") hash function family is a hash function family given a range of $\{0,1\}^{2k}$ with* the property that for all $x \neq y$, the probability that $h_R(x) = h_R(y)$ is at most $2^{-k} + \epsilon$, over the choice of h, where h_R denotes the right half of the output of h.

Naor and Reingold [15] create a secure blockcipher using two Luby-Rackoff rounds in combination with a potentially less expensive function.

Theorem 2 (Naor-Reingold). *If E denotes two Luby-Rackoff rounds with truly random round functions, and h is drawn from an $\epsilon - \text{ARCU}_2$ hash function family, then $E \circ h$ is indistinguishable (in a CPA attack) from a random function.*

Using Definition 3 and Theorem 2, we are able construct CPA-secure tweakable blockciphers.

Theorem 3 (Several Tweakable n-Round Constructions (for $n \geq 4$)). *For all $n \geq 4$ and $m \in \{2, \ldots, n-2\}$, $\mathcal{BC}(n, \mathcal{R}_m)$ is CPA-secure against polynomially bounded adversaries.*

Proof. We can capitalize on Theorem 2 as follows. We will prove that when we let $h(L, R, T) = (L \oplus f_{m-1}(R) \| R \oplus T \oplus f_m(L \oplus f_{m-1}(R)))$ over random choice of f_{m-1} and f_m, these conditions hold. Here, h is comprised of the last two rounds of the construction before the tweak, including the tweak. Once we prove this, the result will follow: the first $m - 2$ rounds are a permutation, so if h' is comprised of the first m rounds, it will be $\epsilon - \text{ARCU}_2$ if h is. Furthermore, since $m \leq n - 2$, there are at least 2 more rounds to follow; any further rounds are another permutation and pseudorandomness will be maintained.

Lemma 5. *The family $h(L, R, T) = (L \oplus f_1(R) \| R \oplus T \oplus f_2(L \oplus f_1(R)))$, where f_1 and f_2 are randomly chosen over the domain of all functions from k bits to k bits, is $\epsilon - \text{ARCU}_2$, for $\epsilon = 2^{-k} + 2^{-2k}$.*

Proof. Let $x = (L, R, T)$ and $y = (L', R', T')$, where $x \neq y$. Note that if $R \neq R'$ then the probability that $L \oplus f_1(R) = L' \oplus f_1(R')$ is the probability that $f_1(R) = L \oplus L' \oplus f_1(R')$ which is 2^{-k}. Similarly, if $R = R'$ but $L \neq L'$ then $L \oplus f_1(R) \neq L' \oplus f_1(R')$. In either case, the probability that $L \oplus f_1(R) = L' \oplus f_1(R')$ is at most 2^{-k}. Finally, if $R = R'$ and $L = L'$ then $T \neq T'$ so $h_R(L, R, T) = h_R(L, R, T') \oplus T \oplus T' \neq h_R(L, R, T')$.

The probability that $h_R(L, R, T) = h_R(L', R', T')$ given that $L \oplus f_1(R) \neq L' \oplus f_1(R')$ is the probability that $f_2(L \oplus f_1(R)) = R \oplus R' \oplus f_2(L' \oplus f_1(R'))$, which is 2^{-k}, so the probability we hit a collision is at most $(1-2^{-k})(2^{-k})+2^{-k} = 2^{-k} + 2^{-2k} + 2^{-k} = 2^{-k} + \epsilon$. □

From the Lemma, if all the round functions are random, then the h we are interested in is $\epsilon - \text{ARCU}_2$. By Theorem 2, $\mathcal{BC}(n, \mathcal{R}_m)$ is indistinguishable from a random function if all round functions are random. Therefore, $\mathcal{BC}(n, \mathcal{R}_m)$ must be CPA secure if its round functions are pseudorandom (since random functions are indistinguishable from random permutation families). This completes the proof of Theorem 3. □

Corollary 1 (CPA Security In 4 Rounds). $\mathcal{BC}(4, \mathcal{R}_2)$ *is CPA-secure and round-optimal.*

Proof. This follows directly from Theorems 1 and 3. □

4.2   Exponential Attacks

In this section, we investigate the security of tweakable blockcipher constructions against an adversary who is capable of making an exponential number of queries. We provide general attacks against several types of tweakable constructions built from Luby-Rackoff permutations. In this section, we assume all round functions are ideal, in other words, that they are uniform random functions.[3] We consider a construction secure against exponentially many queries if the probability of any computationally unbounded adversary allowed $q \ll 2^k$ queries to distinguish the construction from a random permutation family is negligible in k. These attacks appertain to constructions with both single and compound tweak locations (where the same tweak value is XOR-ed in multiple locations) and are used to prove that all constructions of less than 7 rounds can be distinguished from a random permutation family in $O(2^{\frac{k}{2}})$ queries.

Lemma 6. *For any* $0 \leq r < n$, $\mathcal{BC}(n, \mathcal{R}_{r+0.5})$ *is insecure against* $O(2^{\frac{k}{2}})$ *queries.*

Proof. The attack is as follows: fix the message and query with $2^{\frac{k}{2}}$ different tweaks. The probability that two different queries lead to the same output is negligible for a random permutation family. However, the probability that two queries lead to a collision in this construction is not negligible. On each query, the internal values stay constant until the input to f_{r+1}. Since we have made $2^{\frac{k}{2}}$ queries to an ideal round function, we can expect with non-negligible probability to get a collision on the output of f_{r+1} for two distinct queries. If we get such a collision, notice the entire output ciphertext will collide. □

Corollary 2. *For any* $0 \leq r < n$, $\mathcal{BC}(n, \mathcal{R}_{r+0.5} + \mathcal{R}_{r+1})$ *is insecure against* $O(2^{\frac{k}{2}})$ *queries.*

Proof. The attack is identical to that used in Lemma 6, except that instead of expecting a collision of the type $f_{r+1}(R^r \oplus T) = f_{r+1}(R^r \oplus T')$, we expect a collision of the type $f_{r+1}(\mathcal{R}^r \oplus T) \oplus T = f_{r+1}(\mathcal{R}^r \oplus T') \oplus T'$. □

Lemma 7. *For any* $0 \leq r < n$, $\mathcal{BC}(n, \mathcal{R}_{r+0.5} + \mathcal{R}_{n-1})$ *is insecure against* $O(2^{\frac{k}{2}})$ *queries.*

Proof. For this proof we will first need a result from probability.

Lemma 8 (Strong Birthday Lemma). *For all* $k > 1$, *there exists an* $m < 1.2 \times 2^{\frac{k}{2}}$ *such that if* p *is the probability of picking an element twice when selecting* m *elements from a* 2^k-*element set with replacement uniformly at random, then* p *and* $1 - p$ *are both non-negligible in* k.

---

[3] This is the standard assumption when we want to prove security in a setting where the adversary has beyond-polynomial capabilities [16,17].

Proof. For proof of the Strong Birthday Lemma, see full version [7].   □

The attack is as follows: Compute the m described in Lemma 8. Keep the message constant and query with m different tweaks. The probability that two ciphertexts are such that $L^n \oplus T = L'^n \oplus T'$ is significantly higher for the actual construction than for a random permutation family. Since $m \leq 1.2 \times 2^{\frac{k}{2}}$, this attack can be performed by an exponential adversary.

Notice that the internal values of any pair of queries are the same up to the input of f_{r+1}. For every query, f_{r+1} receives a different input (as the input is a fixed value XOR-ed by the tweak). Since the round functions are ideal, the event of getting a collision on two outputs of f_{r+1} with m different queries reduces to the event of picking the same element twice as described in Lemma 8; say that probability is p. Notice that if such a collision happens, we always get a collision of the type, $L^n \oplus T = L'^n \oplus T'$.

Assume that the outputs of f_{r+1} are distinct for each of the m queries. Notice that in order to have a collision of two R^{n-2} values, it must be true that the L^{n-2} values differ for both queries, because the intervening rounds act as a permutation. Therefore, we will get a collision on R^{n-2} if and only if we have a collision of the type:

$$f_{n-2}(L^{n-2}) \oplus L^{n-3} = f_{n-2}(L'^{n-2}) \oplus L'^{n-3}.$$

Since the probability of such a collision for any two queries is either 2^{-k} or 0 (in the case that the L^{n-2} values coincide), we can bound the probability of having such a collision above by $\frac{(1.2)^2 2^k}{2 \times 2^k} = .72$ since $m \leq 1.2 \times 2^{\frac{k}{2}}$. Therefore, in this case, with probability greater equal to $.28$, we can assume all R^{n-2} values are distinct. Notice:

$$L^n \oplus T = L'^n \oplus T' \Leftrightarrow f_{n-1}(R^{n-2}) \oplus L^{n-2} \oplus T = f_{n-1}(R'^{n-2}) \oplus L'^{n-2} \oplus T'.$$

The probability of such an event occurring over m queries with distinct R^{n-2} and ideal round functions is, again, p. Therefore, the overall probability of getting at least two ciphertexts with the described property is at least $p + (1-p)(.28p)$.

If the construction we are given is the random permutation family, the probability of getting the coincidence described is clearly p. Therefore the difference in probabilities of this event happening for the tweakable construction and the random permutation family is at least $p + .28p(1-p) - p = .28p(1-p)$. Since p and $1-p$ are non-negligible in k (by Lemma 8), this value is also non-negligible, and therefore our attack successfully distinguishes the two constructions.   □

Corollary 3. $\mathcal{BC}(n, \mathcal{R}_{r+0.5} + \mathcal{R}_{r+1} + \mathcal{R}_{n-1})$ *is insecure against* $O(2^{\frac{k}{2}})$ *queries.*

Proof. The generalization of Lemma 7 to Lemma 3 is identical to the extension of Lemma 6 to Lemma 2.   □

These four attacks can be used to attack every tweakable Luby-Rackoff blockcipher of 6 or fewer rounds. A rundown of which general attack applies for each construction can be found in Table 1. We do not include $\mathcal{L}_1, \mathcal{R}_1, \mathcal{L}_6$ or $\mathcal{R}_6$ in the possible locations, or their equivalent constructions of Table 1 since they can be simulated away by Lemma 3.

4.3 A Tweakable Construction Secure for $q \ll 2^k$ Queries

We now show a 7-round Luby - Rackoff construction that is secure against an adversary allowed $q \ll 2^k$ queries.

Theorem 4. $\mathcal{BC}(7, \mathcal{R}_3 + \mathcal{L}_3)$ is CPA-secure for $q \ll 2^k$ queries.

Proof. To prove that this construction is a secure tweakable blockcipher we utilize the following theorem from Patarin [16]:

Theorem 5 (Patarin). *Let F be a function from 2k bits to 2k bits. If F has the property that for $q \ll 2^k$ queries, the probability of having $l > O(k)$ indices such that $R_{i_1} = R_{i_2} = R_{i_3} = ...R_{i_l}$ is negligi-*

Table 1. All possible 6-round tweakable blockcipher constructions and the corresponding lemmas that prove the constructions are insecure

Tweak Locations		
Location	Equivalent	Attack
$\mathcal{R}_2$	$\mathcal{R}_{0.5}$	Lemma 6
$\mathcal{R}_3$	$\mathcal{R}_{1.5}$	Lemma 6
$\mathcal{R}_4$	$\mathcal{R}_{4.5}$	Lemma 6
$\mathcal{R}_5$	N/A	Lemma 4
$\mathcal{R}_2 + \mathcal{R}_3$	$\mathcal{R}_{1.5} + \mathcal{R}_2$	Corollary 2
$\mathcal{R}_2 + \mathcal{R}_4$	$\mathcal{R}_{2.5}$	Lemma 6
$\mathcal{R}_2 + \mathcal{R}_5$	$\mathcal{R}_{0.5} + \mathcal{R}_5$	Lemma 7
$\mathcal{R}_3 + \mathcal{R}_4$	$\mathcal{R}_{3.5} + \mathcal{R}_4 + \mathcal{R}_5$	Corollary 3
$\mathcal{R}_3 + \mathcal{R}_5$	$\mathcal{R}_{3.5}$	Lemma 6
$\mathcal{R}_4 + \mathcal{R}_5$	$\mathcal{R}_{4.5} + \mathcal{R}_5$	Corollary 2
$\mathcal{R}_2 + \mathcal{R}_3 + \mathcal{R}_4$	$\mathcal{R}_{2.5} + \mathcal{R}_3$	Corollary 2
$\mathcal{R}_2 + \mathcal{R}_3 + \mathcal{R}_5$	$\mathcal{R}_{1.5} + \mathcal{R}_2 + \mathcal{R}_5$	Corollary 3
$\mathcal{R}_2 + \mathcal{R}_4 + \mathcal{R}_5$	$\mathcal{R}_{2.5} + \mathcal{R}_5$	Lemma 7
$\mathcal{R}_3 + \mathcal{R}_4 + \mathcal{R}_5$	$\mathcal{R}_{3.5} + \mathcal{R}_4$	Corollary 2
$\mathcal{R}_2 + \mathcal{R}_3 + \mathcal{R}_4 + \mathcal{R}_5$	$\mathcal{R}_{2.5} + \mathcal{R}_3 + \mathcal{R}_5$	Corollary 3

ble, (where R_{i_j} is the right half of the j'th output of F), and on distinct inputs F has only a negligible probability of a full collision on its outputs, then $E \circ F$, (where E is a four-round Luby-Rackoff function), is indistinguishable from random for $q \ll 2^k$ input queries.

We decompose our 7-round construction into two functions, F and E, where F is the first three rounds, including the XOR-ed tweak at both $\mathcal{L}_3$ and $\mathcal{R}_3$,[4] and E is the last four rounds. It is obvious that E is a four-round Luby-Rackoff function. To prove that F has the properties enumerated in Theorem 5, we need to prove the following two properties about F.

Lemma 9. *F is such that for any two distinct queries, the probability of the outputs being equal is $O(2^{-2k})$ and the probability of the right halves of the outputs being equal is $O(2^{-k})$.*

---

[4] Although $\mathcal{L}_3$ is equivalent to $\mathcal{R}_4$, we think of this construction as using $\mathcal{L}_3$, so that we can conceptually split the function this way.

Proof. For proof see full version [7].   □

So long as the queries the adversary makes do not produce a full collision on F or a multi-collision on the right half of the output of F, the responses are indistinguishable from random. Therefore, the queries of the adversary are independent of the outputs of F so long as the required conditions hold. By Lemma 9, the probability of an overall collision in $q \ll 2^k$ queries is $O(q^2 2^{-2k})$ which is negligible. Similarly, the probability of an l-way multicollision on the right is $O(q^l 2^{-(l-1)k}) = O(2^k(q2^{-k})^l)$. Since $q < 2^{k(1-\epsilon)}$ for some ϵ, we know that $(q2^{-k})^l < (2^{-k\epsilon})^l = 2^{-kl\epsilon}$. If $l \geq k \geq 2/\epsilon$, which will be true for sufficiently large k, this probability is bounded by 2^{-k}. Thus, F satisfies the necessary properties with all but a negligible probability, which completes our proof of Theorem 4. □

5   Tweakable Blockciphers with CCA Security

In this section, we study the problem of achieving CCA security. An important observation to make in constructing a CCA-secure tweakable blockcipher is a distinguishing attack we will call the *four-message attack*, which is a type of Boomerang attack [22]. The attack can be performed by any adversary with access to encryption and decryption oracles, E and D respectively. To perform the attack, the adversary makes four queries:

1. For an arbitrary message M and tweak T, obtain $C = E(M, T)$.
2. For an arbitrary tweak $T' \neq T$, obtain $C' = E(M, T')$.
3. Obtain $M' = D(C', T)$.
4. Obtain $C'' = E(M', T')$. If $C = C''$; output 1, otherwise output 0.

A wide class of tweakable blockciphers fall to the four-message attack:

Theorem 6 (Four Message Attack). *Suppose that $g_1 : \{0,1\}^n \to \{0,1\}^l$ is an injective function that is invertible on its domain, that $g_2 : \{0,1\}^t \to \{0,1\}^l$ is any deterministic function, and that $g_3 : \{0,1\}^l \to \{0,1\}^n$ is a function such that for all C and T there exists a unique A such that $g_3(A \oplus g_2(T)) = C$. Then the construction $\widetilde{E}_K(M, T) = g_3(g_2(T) \oplus g_1(M))$ is not CCA-secure.*

Proof. Note that $C = g_3(g_2(T) \oplus g_1(M))$, $C' = g_3(g_2(T') \oplus g_1(M))$. Now if we decrypt C' with tweak T, we obtain $M' = g_1^{-1}(g_2(T') \oplus g_2(T) \oplus g_1(M))$. When we encrypt M' under tweak T', we get $C'' = g_3(g_2(T') \oplus g_1(g_1^{-1}(g_2(T') \oplus g_2(T) \oplus g_1(M)))) = g_3(g_2(T') \oplus g_2(T') \oplus g_2(T) \oplus g_1(M)) = g_3(g_2(T) \oplus g_1(M)) = C$.   □

Note in particular that if both g_1 and g_3 are permutations, the conditions are satisfied. This has immediate consequences:

Corollary 4. *For all $n, \mathcal{R}_m \in \Lambda_n$, both $\mathcal{BC}(n, \mathcal{R}_m)$ and $\mathcal{BC}(n, \mathcal{R}_m + \mathcal{R}_{m+1})$ are not CCA-secure.*

Proof. Here, g_1 is the permutation described by the m rounds of Luby-Rackoff before the tweak, $g_2(T) = 0^k \| T$ for $\mathcal{BC}(n, \mathcal{R}_m)$ and $g_2(T) = T \| T$ for $\mathcal{BC}(n, \mathcal{R}_m + \mathcal{R}_{m+1})$, and g_3 is the remaining $n - m$ rounds. Clearly g_1 and g_3 are permutations, so the four message attack applies.   □

This shows that if we are to be able to add a half-block of tweak to the construction anywhere, it must be used at multiple locations, and those locations must be separated by at least one round.[5] In fact, however, a one round distance will not suffice:

Lemma 10. *For all* $n, \mathcal{R}_m \in \Lambda_n$, $\mathcal{BC}(n, \mathcal{R}_m + \mathcal{R}_{m+2})$ *is not CCA-secure, and* $\mathcal{BC}(n, \mathcal{R}_m + \mathcal{R}_{m+1} + \mathcal{R}_{m+2})$ *is also not CCA-secure.*

Proof. To simplify, recall that $\mathcal{R}_m + \mathcal{R}_{m+2}$ is equivalent to $\mathcal{R}_{m+0.5}$ by Lemma 1. Noticing this makes it clear why this is unlikely to be secure, in light of the previous two corollaries, but we still have some work to do.

Here, we use the four-message attack again, but this time, suppose g_1 and g_3 are not permutations. Rather, if (L, R) is the output of the first m rounds of the Luby-Rackoff permutations, then $g_1(M)$ is the $3k$ bit response (L, R, R). Notice that $g_2(T)$ is $0^{2k}||T$, and $g_3(A, B, C)$ computes the remaining rounds, computing $L^{m+1} = B$ and $R^{m+1} = f_m(C) \oplus A$, and continuing from there. Note that $g_3(g_2(T) \oplus g_1(M))$ is the output we get from applying $\mathcal{BC}(n, \mathcal{R}_{m+0.5})$ to M with tweak T. For the $\mathcal{BC}(n, \mathcal{R}_m + \mathcal{R}_{m+1} + \mathcal{R}_{m+2})$ construction, this is just the same as $\mathcal{BC}(n, \mathcal{R}_{m+0.5} + \mathcal{L}_m)$, and change g_2 so that it produces $T||0^k||T$ rather than $0^{2k}||T$. Clearly g_1 is injective and invertible, and g_3 has unique inverses of the proper form, which we can find by inverting the tweakable blockcipher and noting the values in the proper place. Doing so requires the tweak T, but the answer is unique regardless, or we wouldn't have unique decryption. By Theorem 6, neither of these constructions are CCA-secure.   □

Theorem 7. *For all* $n < 6$ *and all compound locations* Γ *of elements in* Λ_n, $\mathcal{BC}(n, \Gamma)$ *is not CCA-secure.*

Proof. In order to construct a CCA-secure tweakable blockcipher, we must use the tweak at (minimally) $\mathcal{R}_m$ and $\mathcal{R}_{m+d}$ for some $d \geq 3$. And naturally, m and $m+d$ must be in the range $2, \ldots, n-1$ since all other locations can be simulated. For $n \leq 5$ no such pair of locations exists.   □

Therefore, the first construction that can be CCA-secure is $\mathcal{BC}(6, \mathcal{R}_2 + \mathcal{R}_5)$, and is in fact a secure construction!

Theorem 8. $\mathcal{BC}(6, \mathcal{R}_2 + \mathcal{R}_5)$ *is a CCA-secure tweakable blockcipher.*

Proof. For proof, see full version [7].   □

5.1   CCA Security Against Exponential Attacks

Theorem 9. $\mathcal{BC}(10, \mathcal{L}_3 + \mathcal{R}_3 + \mathcal{L}_7 + \mathcal{R}_7)$ *is CCA-secure for* $q \ll 2^k$ *queries.*

Proof. In order to construct a tweakable blockcipher secure against CCA exponential attacks, we use a theorem of Patarin [17]:

---

[5] This shows, along with Lemma 10, that an adversary making a CCA attack with XOR injection will be able to succeed, regardless of the location of the XOR.

Theorem 10 (Patarin). *Let F and F' be functions from $2k$ bits to $2k$ bits. If F and F'^{-1} each have the property that for $q \ll 2^k$ queries, the probability of having $l > O(k)$ indices such that $R_{i_1} = R_{i_2} = R_{i_3} = ...R_{i_l}$ is negligible, (where R_{i_j} is the right half of the j'th output of F or F'^{-1}), and on distinct inputs F (and F'^{-1}) has only a negligible probability of a full collision on its outputs, then $F' \circ E \circ F$, (where E is a four-round Luby-Rackoff function), is indistinguishable from random against chosen-ciphertext attack for $q \ll 2^k$ input queries.*

In our construction, the first three rounds, including the tweaks at $\mathcal{L}_3$ and $\mathcal{R}_3$, form F, and the last three rounds, including the tweaks at $\mathcal{L}_7$ and $\mathcal{R}_7$, form F'. F'^{-1} is just the same as F, except with distinct round functions. Both F and F'^{-1} meet the properties of Theorem 10, as we have shown in our proof of Lemma 9. $\mathcal{BC}(10, \mathcal{L}_3 + \mathcal{R}_3 + \mathcal{L}_7 + \mathcal{R}_7) = F' \circ E \circ F$, and is therefore CCA-secure against $q \ll 2^k$ queries. $\qquad\qquad\qquad\qquad\qquad\qquad\qquad\qquad\qquad\qquad\quad\square$

6   Allowing Longer Tweaks

In our previous results, all tweaks were assumed to be a half block in length. It may be desirable however, to have tweaks of arbitrary lengths. We can always lengthen a tweak that is less than a half block, by padding it in a deterministic way. However, increasing the length of a tweak beyond a half block in length does not follow easily. It may be useful to have constructions that are still secure with longer tweaks, as one usual way of choosing a tweak is to include data with it that makes it unique [21]. The longer the tweak, the more data can be included.

Tweakable Blockciphers with Longer Tweaks. For t half-blocks of tweak, we show how to construct a CPA-secure tweakable blockcipher in $t + 3$ rounds and a CCA-secure tweakble blockcipher in $2t + 4$ rounds.

Theorem 11. *For all n, one can use $n - 3$ half-blocks of tweak but no more. Specifically, $\mathcal{BC}(n, \mathcal{R}_2, ..., \mathcal{R}_{n-2})$ is secure, but any construction $\mathcal{BC}(n, \Gamma_1, ..., \Gamma_t)$ for $t > n - 3$ is not secure.*

Theorem 12. *For all n, the tweakable blockcipher $\mathcal{BC}(2n, \mathcal{R}_2 + \mathcal{R}_{2n-1}, \mathcal{R}_3 + \mathcal{R}_{2n-2}, ..., \mathcal{R}_{n-1} + \mathcal{R}_{n+2})$ is a CCA-secure tweakable blockcipher.*

Proof. For proof of Theorem 11 and Theorem 12 see full version [7].

Longer Tweaks with Exponential Security. Next, we focus on constructing Luby-Rackoff based tweakable blockciphers which are secure against an unbounded adversary with $q \ll 2^k$ queries. For t half-blocks of tweak, we show how to construct a CPA-secure tweakable blockcipher in $t+6$ rounds and give a CCA-secure tweakable blockcipher in $2t+8$ that meets this security goal. These constructions are based on a $t + 2$ round function F designed to meet the properties required by Patarin.

Theorem 13. *Let $\mu_i = \mathcal{L}_{i+2}$ if $i \equiv 1$ or $i \equiv 2 \bmod 4$, let $\mu_i = \mathcal{L}_{i+2} + \mathcal{L}_1$ if $i \equiv 3 \bmod 4$, and $\mu_i = \mathcal{L}_{i+2} + \mathcal{L}_2$ if $i \equiv 0 \bmod 4$. Let $\mu_i' = \mu_i + \mathcal{R}_i$ if $i \not\equiv 2 \bmod 4$, and $\mu_i' = \mu_i + \mathcal{R}_i + \mathcal{L}_1$ otherwise. Then let F be $\mathcal{BC}(n + 2, \mu_1, ..., \mu_{n-1}, \mu_n')$. F*

is a function such that for $q \ll 2^k$ queries, the probability of having $l = O(k)$ indices such that $R_{i_1} = R_{i_2} = R_{i_3} = ...R_{i_l}$ is negligible, (where R_{i_j} is the right half of the j'th output of F), and on q distinct inputs F has only a negligible probability of a full collision on its outputs.

Proof. For proof, see full paper [7]. □

Theorem 14. $E \circ F$ *is a tweakable blockcipher with t tweaks that is secure against any unbounded adversary with at most $q \ll 2^k$ queries, where E is a four-round Luby-Rackoff cipher.*

Proof. This follows from Theorem 13 and Theorem 5. Note that $E \circ F$ requires a total of $t + 6$ rounds.

Theorem 15. $F' \circ E \circ F$ *is a tweakable blockcipher with t tweaks that is CCA-secure against any unbounded adversary with at most $q \ll 2^k$ queries, where E is a four-round Luby-Rackoff cipher, F' is the inverse of the F described above, with new independent round functions.*

Proof. This follows from Theorem 13 and Theorem 10. Here, $F' \circ E \circ F$ requires $2(t + 2) + 4 = 2t + 8$ rounds.

7   Conclusion

Table 2 summarizes our constructions, compared to regular blockciphers and the second construction of Liskov et al. [12]. This table shows that our results are better for CPA constructions, equivalent for CCA against polynomial attacks, and worse for CCA against exponential ones.

Table 2. Number of rounds required for each construction. The prior tweakable construction we consider is $\widetilde{E}_{K,h}(M, T) = h(T) \oplus E_K(M \oplus h(T))$, where h is an $\epsilon-\text{AXU}_2$ hash function; subsequent constructions are similar. The natural way to realize the hash function would be to simply use two random functions on the tweak, one for each half of the data stream. Although Liskov et al. do not explicitly consider arbitrary tweak length, their construction and proof can be easily extended to do so.

Security Level	Blockciphers	Prior TBCs [12]	This paper
CPA with polynomial queries	3 rounds [13]	3 + 2 rounds/tweak	3 + 1 round/tweak
CPA with $\ll 2^k$ queries	5 rounds [17]	5 + 2 rounds/tweak	6 + 1 round/tweak
CCA with polynomial queries	4 rounds [13]	4 + 2 rounds/tweak	4 + 2 rounds/tweak
CCA with $\ll 2^k$ queries	5 rounds [17]	5 + 2 rounds/tweak	8 + 2 rounds/tweak

We conclude with some open problems: (1) incorporating tweaks securely into other blockcipher structures, (2) direct, specific design of tweakable blockciphers (Luby-Rackoff or otherwise) and (3) improving the provable level of security for tweakable blockciphers in general.

Acknowledgments. We thank Ronald L. Rivest and several anonymous reviewers for their helpful comments.

References

1. Bellare, M., Kohno, T.: A Theoretical Treatment of Related-Key Attacks: PKA-PRPs, RKA-PRFs, and Applications. In: Biham, E. (ed.) Advances in Cryptology – EUROCRPYT 2003. LNCS, vol. 2656, pp. 491–506. Springer, Heidelberg (2003)
2. Black, J., Cochran, M., Shrimpton, T.: On The Impossibility of Highly-Efficient Blockcipher-Based Hash Functions. In: Cramer, R.J.F. (ed.) EUROCRYPT 2005. LNCS, vol. 3494, pp. 526–541. Springer, Heidelberg (2005)
3. Burwick, C., Coppersmith, D., D'Avignon, E., Gennaro, R., Halevi, S., Jutla, C., Matyas Jr., S.M., O'Connor, L., Peyravian, M., Safford, D., Zunic, N.: MARS - A Candidate Cipher for AES. In: NIST AES proposal (June 1998)
4. Crowley, P.: Mercy: A Fast Large Block Cipher for Disk Sector Encryption. In: Schneier, B. (ed.) FSE 2000. LNCS, vol. 1978, pp. 49–63. Springer, Heidelberg (2001)
5. Dodis, Y., Puniya, P.: Feistel networks made public, and applications. In: EURO-CRYPT 2007. LNCS, vol. 4515, pp. 534–554. Springer, Heidelberg (2007)
6. Feistel, H.: Cryptography and Computer Privacy, pp. 15–23. Scientific American (1973)
7. Goldenberg, D., Hohenberger, S., Liskov, M., Crump Schwartz, E., Seyalioglu, H.: Full version of this paper, Cryptology ePrint Archive, Report 2007/350
8. Halevi, S.: EME*: Extending EME to Handle Arbitrary-Length Messages with Associated Data. In: Canteaut, A., Viswanathan, K. (eds.) INDOCRYPT 2004. LNCS, vol. 3348, pp. 315–327. Springer, Heidelberg (2004)
9. Halevi, S., Rogaway, P.: A Tweakable Enciphering Mode. In: Boneh, D. (ed.) CRYPTO 2003. LNCS, vol. 2729, pp. 482–499. Springer, Heidelberg (2003)
10. Halevi, S., Rogaway, P.: A Parallelizable Enciphering Mode. In: Okamoto, T. (ed.) CT-RSA 2004. LNCS, vol. 2964, pp. 292–304. Springer, Heidelberg (2004)
11. Joux, A.: Cryptanalysis of the EMD Mode of Operation. In: Biham, E. (ed.) Advances in Cryptology – EUROCRPYT 2003. LNCS, vol. 2656, pp. 1–16. Springer, Heidelberg (2003)
12. Liskov, M., Rivest, R., Wagner, D.: Tweakable Block Ciphers. In: Yung, M. (ed.) CRYPTO 2002. LNCS, vol. 2442, pp. 31–46. Springer, Heidelberg (2002)
13. Luby, M., Rackoff, C.: How To Construct Pseudorandom Permutations from Pseudorandom Functions. SIAM J. of Computing 17(2), 373–386 (1988)
14. Lucks, S.: Faster Luby-Rackoff Ciphers. In *Fast Software Encryption*. In: Gollmann, D. (ed.) FSE 1996. LNCS, vol. 1039, pp. 189–203. Springer, Heidelberg (1996)
15. Naor, M., Reingold, O.: On the Construction of Pseudorandom Permutations: Luby-Rackoff Revisited. Journal of Cryptology 12(1), 29–66 (1999)
16. Patarin, J.: Luby-Rackoff: 7 Rounds are Enough for $2^{n(1-\varepsilon)}$ Security. In: Boneh, D. (ed.) CRYPTO 2003. LNCS, vol. 2729, pp. 513–529. Springer, Heidelberg (2003)
17. Patarin, J.: Security of Random Feistel Schemes with 5 or More Rounds. In: Franklin, M. (ed.) CRYPTO 2004. LNCS, vol. 3152, pp. 106–122. Springer, Heidelberg (2004)
18. Ramzan, Z.: A Study of Luby-Rackoff Ciphers. PhD thesis, MIT (2001)
19. Rivest, R., Robshaw, M., Sidney, R., Yin, Y.L.: The RC6 Block Cipher. In: First AES conference (August 1998)
20. Rogaway, P.: Efficient Instantiations of Tweakable Blockciphers and Refinements to Mode OCB and PMAC. In: Lee, P.J. (ed.) ASIACRYPT 2004. LNCS, vol. 3329, pp. 16–31. Springer, Heidelberg (2004)
21. Schroeppel, R.: The Hasty Pudding Cipher. NIST AES proposal (1998), available http://www.cs.arizona.edu/~rcs/hpc
22. Wagner, D.: The Boomerang Attack. In: Knudsen, L.R. (ed.) FSE 1999. LNCS, vol. 1636, pp. 156–170. Springer, Heidelberg (1999)

Secure Protocols with Asymmetric Trust

Ivan Damgård[1], Yvo Desmedt[2], Matthias Fitzi[3], and Jesper Buus Nielsen[1]

[1] Aarhus University, Dept. of Computer Science, 8200 Aarhus N, Denmark
{ivan,buus}@daimi.au.dk
[2] University College London, Dept. of Computer Science, London WC1E 6BT,
United Kingdom
y.desmedt@cs.ucl.ac.uk
[3] ETH Zürich, Dept. of Computer Science, 8092 Zürich, Switzerland
fitzi@inf.ethz.ch

Abstract. In the standard general-adversary model for multi-party protocols, a global adversary structure is given, and every party must trust in this particular structure. We introduce a more general model, the *asymmetric-trust model*, wherein every party is allowed to trust in a different, personally customized adversary structure. We have two main contributions. First, we present non-trivial lower and upper bounds for broadcast, verifiable secret sharing, and general multi-party computation in different variations of this new model. The obtained bounds demonstrate that the new model is strictly more powerful than the standard general-adversary model. Second, we propose a framework for expressing and analyzing asymmetric trust in the usual simulation paradigm for defining security of protocols, and in particular show a general composition theorem for protocols with asymmetric trust.

1 Introduction

In the standard general-adversary model for multi-party computation (MPC) [13], an adversary structure is specified which basically lists all sets of parties that we expect the adversary might be able to corrupt. This model is *symmetric*: every party is required to trust in the same adversary structure $\mathcal{A}$. This is unnatural since there is no inherent reason why the parties should all have the same view on which adversary structure best models the given scenario. For instance, two parties may have completely contradictory beliefs on whether a third party can be corrupted or not. Also, insisting on one global adversary structure may imply that a party must consent to the fact that he himself is completely untrusted. In this paper, we introduce a more natural *asymmetric-trust* model where each party p_i is allowed to trust in his own adversary structure $\mathcal{A}_i$. We then explore the differences between this asymmetric model and the standard one.

Of course, a trivial approach is to try to build a protocol that will be secure even if any set from *any* $\mathcal{A}_i$ is corrupt. However, this may be impossible, namely if the union of all $\mathcal{A}_i$ violates known lower bounds for the symmetric model. Our

K. Kurosawa (Ed.): ASIACRYPT 2007, LNCS 4833, pp. 357–375, 2007.

main conclusion in this paper is that there are cases where the trivial symmetric solution does not work, but where nevertheless broadcast, verifiable secret sharing, or even general secure computation, are possible with asymmetric trust.

As an example, consider the three-party scenario where p_1 distrusts p_2, p_2 distrusts p_3, and p_3 distrusts p_1. In the standard model, MPC requires broadcast channels for this problem. In contrast, in the most natural one of our asymmetric-trust models, MPC does not require broadcast for the same scenario.

1.1   General Setting

We assume that n parties $\mathcal{P} = \{p_1, \ldots, p_n\}$ are given who are connected by a complete, synchronous network of pairwise channels. Also present is an adversary who may corrupt some subset of the parties.

We consider both *passive* and *active* corruption. We also consider both *computational* and *unconditional* security; where we may distinguish between *unconditional security with negligible error probability* or *perfect security*. When we do not state the type of security explicitly, positive results mean that the goal can be achieved with unconditional security, and negative results hold even w.r.t. to computational security.

A crucial point is whether the parties are additionally connected by *broadcast channels* and/or share a consistent *public-key infrastructure (PKI)*. In the active case, broadcast/PKI typically allow for more resilient protocols than in the setting with only pairwise channels. Note that a PKI can be set up with respect to an unconditional pseudo-signature scheme [2,17]. Therefore, in the PKI setting, the achievability of a computationally secure task typically implies its feasibility with unconditional security.

1.2   Contributions

General multi-party computation (MPC) [20,12] typically relies on the two fundamental building blocks *broadcast* [16] (BC, aka Byzantine agreement) and *(verifiable) secret-sharing* [4,19,7] ((V)SS). It is thus interesting to know to which extent these tasks can be achieved in a certain model.

We introduce different variants of the asymmetric-trust model and corresponding definitions for broadcast, VSS, and general MPC; and give feasibility and impossibility results for these cases. Most results demonstrate that protocols for the asymmetric model are able to tolerate a strictly stronger adversary than any protocol for the symmetric model. For broadcast and VSS, we come quite close to characterizing the difference between symmetric and asymmetric trust, while the situation is much more open for general MPC.

In addition we give a general framework for augmenting security models with asymmetric trust. For concreteness we describe how to extend the UC framework [5] with asymmetric trust. This seems to be the first simulation-based security model for reasoning about asymmetric trust. Finally, we explore the issue of when UC secure MPC is possible when the parties have asymmetric trust in the setup assumptions.

1.3 Symmetric-Trust Model

In the symmetric-trust model, a single **adversary structure** $\mathcal{A}$ is given which is a monotone subset of the power set of $\mathcal{P}$, $\mathcal{A} \subseteq 2^{\mathcal{P}}$. Monotone means that $A \in \mathcal{A}$ and $A' \subset A$ imply that $A' \in \mathcal{A}$.[1] The goal is to achieve secure MPC for the case that an adversary corrupts the parties in exactly one set in $\mathcal{A}$. However, if the adversary manages to corrupt a set $A \notin \mathcal{A}$ then no security is guaranteed. A set $A \in \mathcal{A}$ is called **maximal** if there is no set $A' \in \mathcal{A}$ that strictly contains A: $\nexists A' \in \mathcal{A} : A' \supset A$.

The tight bounds [13] for multi-party computation in the symmetric model are summarized in the following table where the second column indicates whether broadcast channels or a public-key infrastructure (PKI) are available.

STD	Broadcast/PKI	Unconditional	Computational
Passive	don't care	Q^2	Q^1
Active	available	Q^2	Q^2
Active	not available	Q^3	Q^3

$$Q^k \equiv \left(\forall A_1, \ldots, A_k \in \mathcal{A} : \bigcup_{i=1}^{k} A_i \neq \mathcal{P} \right)$$

1.4 Asymmetric-Trust Model

In the asymmetric-trust model, every party p_i has its own personalized adversary structure $\mathcal{A}_i \subseteq 2^{\mathcal{P}}$. We denote $\underline{\mathcal{A}} = (\mathcal{A}_1, \ldots, \mathcal{A}_n)$ as the **aggregate adversary structure** and define $\mathcal{A}^* := \bigcup_{i=1}^{n} \mathcal{A}_i$. We assume that each party p_i trusts itself, i.e., $A \in \mathcal{A}_i \Rightarrow p_i \notin A$. The set of corrupted parties is denoted by F.

We generally assume that all the adversary structures $\mathcal{A}_i$ are publicly known, so that we can use information on them in the code of our protocols. In other words, parties must make their beliefs public. Indeed, this seems necessary for our feasibility results and besides we do not believe this to be problematic: even if we were in the symmetric model and just wanted to agree on one global adversary structure, it would still seem necessary to discuss beliefs in public.

We now introduce some variants of the asymmetric-trust model. The presentation here is somewhat informal; we show later in the paper how to fully formalize it using a variant of the UC framework.

Via Symmetry. One approach is to define security for $(\mathcal{A}_1, \ldots, \mathcal{A}_n)$ via the usual symmetric notion. It is clear that if party p_i believes that the subsets $\mathcal{A}_i$ could be corrupted, then p_i would only be willing to participate in an $\mathcal{A}$-secure protocol π if $\mathcal{A}_i \subseteq \mathcal{A}$: if $\mathcal{A}_i \setminus \mathcal{A} \neq \emptyset$, then there exists a subset $F \subseteq \{p_1, \ldots, p_n\}$ which p_i thinks might be corrupted and which π might not tolerate being corrupted.

---

[1] However, we allow for the loose notation of non-monotone structures $\mathcal{A}$ in which case we actually mean the structure's monotone closure, e.g., $\mathcal{A} = \{\{p_1\}\}$ refers to the actual structure $\mathcal{A} = \{\{p_1\}, \emptyset\}$.

The definition going via symmetry insists on still giving a definition of security by specifying some subsets F against which the protocol should be secure. As argued above, to allow all parties to participate in π, any such definition would have to require π simply to tolerate the corruption structure $\mathcal{A}^* = \bigcup_{i=1}^{n} \mathcal{A}_i$. This of course gives no new views at asymmetric trust.

Via Allowed Consequences. A more interesting approach to trust is to say that in reality all subsets $F \subseteq \{p_1, \ldots, p_n\}$ can imaginably be corrupted. The party p_i having corruption structure $\mathcal{A}_i$ simply means that p_i thinks it very unlikely that a subset $A_i \notin \mathcal{A}_i$ will be corrupted. A reasonable security definition should therefore allow *any* corruption pattern $F \subseteq \{p_1, \ldots, p_n\}$ to occur. The goal is then (similarly to [15]) to specify for each $F \subseteq \{p_1, \ldots, p_n\}$ what consequences the corruption of F is allowed to have. These consequences should ideally be such that all p_i would be willing to participate in an $(\mathcal{A}_1, \ldots, \mathcal{A}_n)$-secure protocol.

STRICT. In the strict notion we take the standard security definitions for broadcast, VSS, and MPC, and require that no matter what subset $F \subseteq \{1, \ldots, n\}$ is corrupted, the protocol must provide full security to all uncorrupted parties. In terms of threshold security this corresponds to $t = n$ and is unattainable for most multi-party tasks. Two-party tasks like secure communication and zero-knowledge however have strictly secure implementations, possibly using setup assumptions.

FULLY RELAXED. At the other extreme from strict security we consider fully relaxed security. From the set $F \subseteq \{p_1, \ldots, p_n\}$ of corrupted parties we define three types of parties: corrupted, naïve, foreseeing. A corrupted party is a party from F. A naïve party p_i is honest (not from F) but it happens that $F \notin \mathcal{A}_i$. A foreseeing party p_i is honest and has $F \in \mathcal{A}_i$. A naïve party is called naïve as it believed it very unlikely that F would be corrupted, yet it was.

The fully relaxed model requires full security (in the usual sense) for the set of foreseeing parties but no security for the naïve parties. That is, a naïve party is treated like a corrupted party (although it is not controlled by the adversary).

If $(\mathcal{A}_1, \ldots, \mathcal{A}_n) = (\mathcal{A}, \ldots, \mathcal{A})$ for some common adversary structure $\mathcal{A}$, then all parties are foreseeing (and thus protected) as long as $F \in \mathcal{A}$ and all parties are naïve (and thus unprotected) as long as $F \notin \mathcal{A}$. In this sense fully relaxed security corresponds to usual $\mathcal{A}$-security.

SEMI-RELAXED. Strict security protects even naïve parties and fully relaxed security gives no security at all to naïve parties. There are different ways to define a semi-relaxed model in-between these extremes. In general, a semi-relaxed model requires full security for the set of foreseeing parties but still some partial security (to be defined) for naïve parties.

The main reason why we consider semi-relaxed models is that, in the fully relaxed model, composition of subprotocols is difficult. A naïve party may, for instance, not be able to consistently broadcast the message it wants although it follows the protocol. Extending some security constraints to the set of all honest parties thus allows to compose protocols more easily.

2   Broadcast, VSS, and MPC with Asymmetric Trust

In this section we focus on implementing broadcast, VSS, and MPC in the point-to-point model with asymmetric trust. A first observation is that in the passive case, as well as in the active case where broadcast or a PKI is given, the symmetric bounds (summarized in the table below[2]) still hold for any of the defined asymmetric-trust models:

Theorem 1. *In the passive case and in the active case with broadcast (or PKI), broadcast, VSS, and MPC in any asymmetric model are achievable with respect to an aggregate adversary structure $\underline{A} = (A_1, \ldots, A_n)$ if and only if they are achievable with respect to the structure $A^* = \bigcup_{i=1}^{n} A_i$ in the symmetric-trust model:*

	Passive	Active (BC/PKI)
Broadcast	Q^1	Q^1
(V)SS	Q^1	Q^2
MPC	Q^1 / Q^2	Q^2

Proof. The cases where there is a protocol for any structure are trivial. For all remaining cases $Q^2(A^*)$ is a tight bound in the symmetric model.

⇐ Trivially, if a task is achievable in the symmetric model for A^* then it is also achievable in any asymmetric model for aggregate structure $(A^*, \ldots, A^*)$ and thus for any $\underline{A} = (A_1, \ldots, A_n)$ such that $\bigcup_{i=1}^{n} A_i = A^*$.

⇒ Assume any protocol in the asymmetric model for some aggregate structure $\underline{A} = (A_1, \ldots, A_n)$ such that $\neg Q^2(A^*)$. Since each party trusts itself there must be two distinct parties p_i and p_j and adversary sets $A_i \in A_i$ and $A_j \in A_j$ such that $A_i \cup A_j = P$, and $p_i \in A_j$ and $p_j \in A_i$. From this, we can build a two-party protocol for the same task wherein the parties distrust each other. This is done by having one party simulate p_i (and the parties in A_j) and the other one p_j (and the parties in A_i), and then execute the asymmetric protocol we assumed exists.

For unconditionally secure MPC in the passive case this implies that two parties can securely compute the logical OR over their input bits, which is impossible [3,18].

For VSS (in the active case) this implies that a dealer can secret-share a value in the two-party setting such that the other party can reconstruct it during the reconstruction phase without the help of the dealer — but then it can also do so at any time after the sharing phase, which contradicts security.

---

[2] The only difference between computational and unconditional security occurs for MPC in the passive case where MPC for any structure is achievable with computational security but Q^2 is necessary for unconditional security.

For MPC (and secure function evaluation, in particular) in the active case this implies that two parties can flip a fair coin, which is impossible [8].   □

In view of this theorem, for the rest of this section, we concentrate on the case where the adversary is active and where BC/PKI are not assumed.

2.1 Broadcast

Definition 1 (Broadcast w/ full relaxation). *A protocol where sender $p_s \in \mathcal{P}$ inputs $x_s \in \mathcal{D}$, and all $p_i \in \mathcal{P}$ output $y_i \in \mathcal{D}$, achieves* **broadcast with full relaxation** *if:*

VALIDITY: *If p_s and p_i are honest and $F \in \mathcal{A}_s \cap \mathcal{A}_i$ then $y_i = x_s$.*
CONSISTENCY: *If p_i and p_j are honest and $F \in \mathcal{A}_i \cap \mathcal{A}_j$ then $y_i = y_j$.*   ◇

For the use as a subprotocol in MPC, a helpful additional property of broadcast is to demand validity independently of the sender's adversary structure. In that way, a naïve party can still consistently convey its view. We define semi-relaxed broadcast as broadcast with sender-independent validity in the following way — where we only state the different validity condition.

Definition 2 (Broadcast w/ sender-indep. validity (semi-relaxed)).

VALIDITY: *If p_s and p_i are honest and $F \in \mathcal{A}_i$ then $y_i = x_s$.*   ◇

The following theorem is proven in the full version of the paper.

Theorem 2. *Broadcast with sender-independent validity for every sender $p_s \in \mathcal{P}$ is (perfectly) achievable if and only if*

$$B^3(\underline{\mathcal{A}}) \equiv \forall \mathcal{A}_i, \mathcal{A}_j : \forall A_i \in \mathcal{A}_i, A_j \in \mathcal{A}_j, A_{ij} \in \mathcal{A}_i \cap \mathcal{A}_j : \ A_i \cup A_j \cup A_{ij} \neq \mathcal{P}.$$

Note that $B^3(\underline{\mathcal{A}})$ is a proper relaxation of $Q^3(\underline{\mathcal{A}})$, which is necessary and sufficient in the symmetric framework. In particular, $B^3(\underline{\mathcal{A}})$ is a condition on all pairs of parties, whereas $Q^3(\underline{\mathcal{A}})$ is the condition $\forall A_i \in \mathcal{A}_i, \forall A_j \in \mathcal{A}_j, \forall A_k \in \mathcal{A}_k : A_i \cup A_j \cup A_k \neq \mathcal{P}$ on all triples of parties. Trivially, any semi-relaxed version of broadcast implies broadcast with full relaxation. Achievability under $B^3(\underline{\mathcal{A}})$ thus follows for the fully relaxed case. However, the next two results show, first that $B^3(\underline{\mathcal{A}})$ is not necessary for fully relaxed broadcast, and second, a weaker but necessary condition.

Proposition 1. *There are aggregate structures $\underline{\mathcal{A}}$ such that $\neg B^3(\underline{\mathcal{A}})$ and broadcast with full relaxation is achievable for every selection of a sender $p_s \in \mathcal{P}$.*

Proof. Consider aggregate structure $\underline{\mathcal{A}} = (\{\{p_2\}, \{p_3\}\}, \{\{p_1\}, \{p_3\}\}, \emptyset)$ among $\mathcal{P} = \{p_1, p_2, p_3\}$. If the sender is p_1 or p_2 then it can simply multi-send its input value since, with respect to p_3, validity and consistency only have to hold if nobody is corrupted. If the sender is p_3 then p_3 can send its input value to p_1 who in turn sends it to p_2. Again, validity and consistency with respect to p_3 only have to hold if no party is corrupted; parties p_1 and p_2 are trivially consistent.   □

Theorem 3. *If there are structures $\mathcal{A}_i$, $\mathcal{A}_j$, and $\mathcal{A}_k$, and sets $A_{ij} \in \mathcal{A}_i \cap \mathcal{A}_j$, $A_{ik} \in \mathcal{A}_i \cap \mathcal{A}_k$, $A_{jk} \in \mathcal{A}_j \cap \mathcal{A}_k$, such that $A_{ij} \cup A_{ik} \cup A_{jk} = \mathcal{P}$ then broadcast with full relaxation is not achievable for any selection of a sender $p_s \in \mathcal{P}$.*

Proof. Along the lines of the lower-bound part of the proof of Theorem 2.   □

2.2 Verifiable Secret Sharing (VSS)

Definition 3 (VSS w/ full relaxation). *A pair of protocols* (Sh, Rec) *wherein dealer $p_d \in \mathcal{P}$ inputs secret s in protocol* Sh *and every $p_i \in \mathcal{P}$ outputs s_i in protocol* Rec *achieves VSS with full relaxation if:*

SECRECY: *If p_d is honest and $F \in \mathcal{A}_d$ then the adversary has no information about s as long as protocol* Rec *has not started yet.*
CORRECTNESS: *If p_d and p_i are honest and $F \in \mathcal{A}_d \cap \mathcal{A}_i$ then p_i computes output $s_i = s$ in protocol* Rec.
COMMITMENT: *If p_i and p_j (case $i = j$ included) are honest and $F \in \mathcal{A}_i \cap \mathcal{A}_j$ then, after termination of protocol* Sh, *there is a value $s' \in \mathbb{F}$ such that, in protocol* Rec, *p_i and p_j compute output $s_i = s_j = s'$.*   ◇

It may be tempting to believe that fully relaxed VSS could be obtained by just running a standard VSS protocol that is secure with respect to the dealer's adversary structure $\mathcal{A}_d$. But such a protocol provides no security at all if $F \notin \mathcal{A}_d$, and hence cannot in general guarantee that the commitment property is satisfied.

We define semi-relaxed VSS as VSS with dealer-independent correctness in the following way — where we only state the conditions different from the previous definition.

Definition 4 (VSS w/ dealer-indep. correctness (semi-relaxed)).

CORRECTNESS: *If p_d and p_i are honest and $F \in \mathcal{A}_i$ then p_i computes output $s_i = s$ in protocol* Rec.   ◇

We derive our VSS protocols from the VSS protocol in [14]. Note that, since we are not given full-fledged broadcast, additional measures have to be taken.

Theorem 4. *Perfectly secure VSS with full relaxation is achievable for every selection of a dealer $p_d \in \mathcal{P}$ if*

$$V^3(\underline{A}) \equiv \forall \mathcal{A}_i, \mathcal{A}_j : \forall A_i \in \mathcal{A}_i, \forall A_i' \in \mathcal{A}_i, \forall A_j \in \mathcal{A}_j : \quad A_i \cup A_i' \cup A_j \neq \mathcal{P}.$$

Proof. Follows from the protocol in Fig. 1 which is analyzed in Lemma 1.   □

Lemma 1. *For a given V^3-structure, the protocol in Fig. 1 achieves fully relaxed VSS with perfect security.*

Proof. SECRECY: If $F \in \mathcal{A}_d$ then the share s_k with $P_k = \mathcal{P} \setminus F \neq \emptyset$ being all honest does not get opened during the sharing phase by an honest dealer since it receives no complaints from within P_k with respect to this share (all broadcasts are valid with respect to p_d). Share s_k perfectly hides the secret.

Sharing Sh: For each maximal set $A_k \in \mathcal{A}_d$ the dealer p_d assigns a random share $s_k \in \mathbb{F}$ with the only restriction that $s = \sum_k s_k$. The dealer sends each s_k to all parties in $P_k = \mathcal{P} \setminus A_k$. Each party $p_i \in P_k$ stores s_k and $s'_k := s_k$.

For each s_k, the parties in P_k pairwisely compare their shares. If any inconsistency is detected by a party $p_i \in P_k$ it broadcasts (w/ sender-independent validity) a complaint to all parties in $\mathcal{P}$.

Now, if the dealer receives any complaint, it opens share s_k by broadcast (w/ sender-independent validity) towards $\mathcal{P}$. Party $p_i \in \mathcal{P}$ always adopts any opening by the dealer. If a party $p_i \in \mathcal{P}$ sent or received a complaint but does not see the dealer open s_k, it disqualifies the dealer and defines $s_k := 0$. Note that a party in P_k who disqualifies the dealer still stores the initial share s'_k it is holding — although, from now on, it uses $s_k = 0$ for its own computation.

A party $p_i \in A_k$ who, at this point, neither disqualified the dealer nor saw the dealer open share s_k, is called k-curious.

Reconstruction Rec: For each share s_k,

- All parties in P_k multi-send s'_k to the parties in A_k.
- All parties who are not k-curious accept s_k as the reconstructed share.
- All parties p_j who are k-curious wait for the parties $p_i \in P_k$ to send their shares. Then they search for a set $A_j \in \mathcal{A}_j$ such that all parties in $P_k \setminus A_j$ sent the same share $\hat{s}'_k$. Party p_j then accepts $s_k := \hat{s}'_k$.

Finally, all shares s_k are summed up in order to compute the reconstructed secret.

Fig. 1. Protocol VSS with full relaxation

CORRECTNESS: We show that when parties p_d and p_i are honest and $F \in \mathcal{A}_d \cap \mathcal{A}_i$ then, during reconstruction, p_i opens each share s_k (share with respect to $A_k \in \mathcal{A}$) correctly as distributed by p_d.

First, we observe that p_i does not disqualify the dealer p_d: disqualification implies a complaint sent or received by p_i — and thus also received by p_d. This forces p_d to open s_k, implying that p_i does not disqualify p_d. This implies that either p_d opened s_k during the sharing phase or that all honest parties in P_k agree on the same share $s'_k = s_k$. An opening during the sharing phase is correctly received by p_i (validity of broadcast). If p_i remains k-curious then there is the unique value $\hat{s}'_k = s_k$ such that there exists some $A_i \in \mathcal{A}_i$ with all parties in $P_k \setminus A_i$ opening the same share $\hat{s}'_k$ — since $A_d \cup A_i \cup A'_i \neq \mathcal{P}$.

COMMITMENT: Consider two honest parties p_i and p_j such that $F \in \mathcal{A}_i \cap \mathcal{A}_j$. All information that is broadcast is thus valid and consistent with respect to p_i and p_j. We distinguish three cases.

- $p_i, p_j \in P_k$. Because of broadcast consistency, both parties either disqualify the dealer ($s_k = 0$), or accept the same initial share, or adopt the same share being opened by the dealer.
- $p_i \in P_k$, $p_j \in A_k$. Because of broadcast consistency, p_i and p_j receive exactly the same values that are broadcast. Thus either both disqualify, or both adopt, or p_i stays with his initial share whereas p_j is k-curious. In the latter case, there was no complaint and thus no conflict among any honest parties in P_k — and thus all honest parties in P_k hold the

same share s'_k. As in the correctness argument, p_j thus finds the unique value $\hat{s}'_k = s_k$ such that there is some $A_j \in \mathcal{A}_j$ with all parties in $P_k \setminus A_j$ all opening the same share $\hat{s}'_k$ — which is identical to p_i's share. Thus, commitment is also guaranteed in the latter case.

- $p_i, p_j \in A_k$. The parties both either are k-curious, or adopt the same opening, or disqualify the dealer. If they are k-curious then no honest party in P_k broadcast a complaint and thus, again, all honest parties in P_k hold the same share s'_k. Since $F \in \mathcal{A}_i \cap \mathcal{A}_j$ both parties will determine a set $A_i \subseteq F$ (and $A_j \subseteq F$, respectively) such that the parties in $P_k \setminus A_i$ ($P_k \setminus A_j$) all open the same share $\hat{s}'_k = s'_k$.   □

Proposition 2. *There are aggregate structures $\underline{A}$ such that $\neg V^3(\underline{A})$ and VSS with full relaxation is achievable for every selection of a dealer $p_d \in \mathcal{P}$.*

Proof. Consider aggregate structure $\underline{A} = (\{\{p_2\}, \{p_3\}\}, \{\{p_1\}\}, \emptyset)$ among $\mathcal{P} = \{p_1, p_2, p_3\}$. The parties can run the preprocessing protocol from [10] trying to establish a PKI with unconditional security. If it succeeds then the players can simulate broadcast and thus use the VSS protocol for dishonest minorities in, e.g., [9]. If it fails then it suffices that the dealer always reconstructs his input value whereas the other parties reconstruct some default value.   □

The following theorem is proven in the full version of the paper.

Theorem 5. *Unconditionally secure VSS with dealer-independent correctness is achievable if $V^3(\underline{A})$. Additionally, secrecy with respect to any $F \in \mathcal{A}^*$ can be guaranteed.*

Theorem 6. *If $\neg V^3(\underline{A})$ then perfectly secure VSS with dealer-independent correctness is not achievable for every selection of a dealer $p_d \in \mathcal{P}$.*

Proof. If $n = 2$ then $\neg V^3(\underline{A})$ and self-trust imply $\neg Q^2(\mathcal{A}^*)$, and impossibility follows from Theorem 1. We can therefore assume that $n \geq 3$.

With $\neg V^3(\underline{A})$ there are structures $\mathcal{A}_i$ and $\mathcal{A}_j$, and sets $A_i, A'_i \in \mathcal{A}_i$ and $A_j \in \mathcal{A}_j$ with $A_i \cup A'_i \cup A_j = \mathcal{P}$. We show that there is no VSS with respect to dealer $p_d = p_j$. Note that $A_d \cup A_i \cup A'_i = \mathcal{P}$ and self-trust imply, wlog, that $p_d \in A_i$ and $p_i \in A_d$.

If such a VSS protocol existed then three parties p_δ, p_ι and p_κ could use it to simulate VSS among themselves with dealer p_δ where $(\mathcal{A}_\delta, \mathcal{A}_\iota, \mathcal{A}_\kappa) = \{\{p_\iota\}, \{\{p_\delta\}, \{p_\kappa\}\}, \emptyset\}$: p_δ simulates all parties in A_i, p_ι simulates all parties in A_d, and p_κ simulates all parties in A'_i. Now the share s_ι is not allowed to give any information about secret s but any triplet $(s_\delta, s_\iota, \cdot)$ perfectly reveals an honest dealer's correct secret and any triplet $(\cdot, s_\iota, s_\kappa)$ perfectly reveals the value a corrupted dealer was committed to. This is not possible.   □

Finally, note that impossibility of broadcast implies impossibility of VSS. Thus all impossibility results for broadcast naturally extend to VSS.

2.3   Multi-Party Computation (MPC)

We now argue informally that, also with respect to general MPC, the asymmetric-trust model allows to tolerate strictly more than in the symmetric case. We only consider fully relaxed security, i.e., privacy and correctness only hold for foreseeing parties. This notion of MPC security is formalized in the following section.

Theorem 7. *In the fully relaxed model, there exist infinite many aggregate structures $\underline{A} = (A_1, \ldots, A_n)$ with $\neg Q^3(A^*)$ for which unconditionally secure MPC is achievable.*

Proof. We construct an aggregate adversary structure A for $n = 3T$ parties, where each individual A_i is such that its maximal sets have size T, but where no set of size T occurs in more than one A_i. Clearly, for each n, there are several such structures and several of them are not Q^3. For such a structure, we can implement MPC by first running a preprocessing protocol from [11] that aims at establishing a PKI with unconditional security (as discussed earlier). This protocol in its most general form has parameters T and t, where $2T + t < n$; we choose $t = T - 1$. The protocol guarantees success if there are at most t corruptions. If there are at most T, there will be agreement on the result which is "success" or "failure." Our solution is that, if the preprocessing is successful, we run a standard MPC protocol secure against T corruptions based on the PKI constructed. If the preprocessing fails, each party computes its output locally using its own input and default values for the other parties. As for security, note first that if there are more than T corruptions, all parties are naïve or corrupted, and security is guaranteed. If there are at most $T - 1 = t$ corruptions, the preprocessing succeeds, and the protocol is secure. If there are T corruptions, either the preprocessing succeeds, in which case we are fine, as before. Otherwise, all honest parties agree that it failed. Since the corrupted set occurs in at most one of the A_i, at most one party is foreseeing, and it may securely compute its output locally since the fully relaxed requirement only forces foreseeing parties to be consistent. All other parties are naïve or corrupt.   □

Again, the impossibility results for broadcast naturally extend to MPC.

3   A Generic Framework for Asymmetric Trust

Until now we gave ad-hoc definitions of asymmetric security for VSS and broadcast. We now develop a general framework for augmenting security models with asymmetric trust. The asymmetric security notions introduced above can be derived as special cases. The exposition is meant as a framework for adding asymmetric trust to protocol security models phrased via ideal functionalities and corruptions. For concreteness we consider the UC framework.

3.1   Basic UC Framework

We consider protocols π for a party set $\mathcal{P} = \{p_1, \ldots, p_n\}$. A corruption pattern is a pair of subsets $\mathrm{PAT} = (\mathrm{ACT}, \mathrm{PAS})$, $\mathrm{ACT}, \mathrm{PAS} \subseteq \mathcal{P}$, where $\mathrm{ACT} \subseteq \mathrm{PAS}$; The interpretation is that the parties $p_i \in \mathrm{PAS}$ are passively corrupted and the parties $p_i \in \mathrm{ACT}$ actively corrupted. We write $(\mathrm{ACT}, \mathrm{PAS}) \subseteq (\mathrm{ACT}', \mathrm{PAS}')$ to mean $\mathrm{ACT} \subseteq \mathrm{ACT}'$ and $\mathrm{PAS} \subseteq \mathrm{PAS}'$. An adversary structure is a set $\mathcal{A} = \{(\mathrm{ACT}, \mathrm{PAS})\}$ of corruption patterns, where $\mathrm{PAT} \in \mathcal{A} \wedge \mathrm{PAT}' \subseteq \mathrm{PAT} \Rightarrow \mathrm{PAT}' \in \mathcal{A}$.

An ideal functionality is an ITM $\mathcal{F}$. It can receive inputs from each $p_i \in \mathcal{P}$ (p_i-inputs) and deliver outputs to each $p_i \in \mathcal{P}$ (p_i-outputs). Besides this, it can receive aux-inputs and deliver aux-outputs, thought of as inputs coming from the adversary respectively values leaked to the adversary. As an example an ideal functionality $\mathcal{F}_{\mathrm{COM}}$ for bit commitment can be phrased as follows: On p_i-input $(\mathtt{commit}, cid, p_i, p_j, m \in \{0,1\})$ produce aux-output $(\mathtt{commit}, cid, p_i, p_j)$; Here cid is a commitment identifier. On a later aux-input $(\mathtt{deliver}, cid, p_i, p_j)$, output $(\mathtt{receipt}, cid, p_i, p_j)$ to p_j. On p_i-input $(\mathtt{open}, cid, p_i, p_j)$ after receiving p_i-input $(\mathtt{commit}, cid, p_i, p_j, m)$, produce aux-output $(\mathtt{open}, cid, p_i, p_j, m)$. On a later aux-input $(\mathtt{open}, cid, p_i, p_j)$, output $(\mathtt{open}, cid, p_i, p_j, m)$ to p_j.

A protocol π consists of n parties $p_1, \ldots, p_n$ and some ideal functionalities $\mathcal{G}$, which might, e.g., model point-to-point lines or commitment. We write $\mathcal{G} \in \pi$ and $\pi[\mathcal{G}]$ to mean that π uses the ideal functionality $\mathcal{G}$. An environment $\mathcal{Z}$ for π is a ITM which gives inputs to the parties and gets outputs from the parties. We denote an **execution** of π in $\mathcal{Z}$ by $\mathrm{EXEC}_{\pi,\mathcal{Z}}$. The environment $\mathcal{Z}$ also corrupts parties.[3] For a corruption pattern $\mathrm{PAT} = (\mathrm{ACT}, \mathrm{PAS})$ the environment is allowed to see the internal state of $p_i \in \mathrm{PAS}$ and control $p_i \in \mathrm{ACT}$: When $p_i \in \mathrm{ACT}$, then in $\mathrm{EXEC}_{\pi,\mathcal{Z}}$ it is $\mathcal{Z}$ which determines all p_i-inputs to $\mathcal{G} \in \pi$ and receives all p_i-outputs from $\mathcal{G} \in \pi$. The party p_i is not run at all. Besides this, $\mathcal{Z}$ receives all aux-outputs from all $\mathcal{G} \in \pi$ and can give aux-inputs to all $\mathcal{G} \in \pi$. As an example, in $\mathrm{EXEC}_{\pi[\mathcal{F}_{\mathrm{COM}}],\mathcal{Z}}$ the environment sees when commitments are made and determines when to deliver receipts and openings.

The execution $\mathrm{EXEC}_{\pi,\mathcal{Z}}$ is compared to a simulation $\mathrm{SIM}_{\mathcal{F},\mathcal{S},\mathcal{Z}}$. Here the simulator $\mathcal{S}$ must simulate an execution of π. E.g., $\mathcal{S}$ simulates aux-outputs to $\mathcal{Z}$ from all $\mathcal{G} \in \pi$ and receives aux-inputs from $\mathcal{Z}$ to $\mathcal{G} \in \pi$. The simulator itself receives aux-outputs from $\mathcal{F}$ and gives aux-inputs to $\mathcal{F}$. When $\mathcal{Z}$ gives a p_i-input for $p_i \notin \mathrm{ACT}$, it is given to $\mathcal{F}$. The simulator gives all p_i-inputs to $\mathcal{F}$ for $p_i \in \mathrm{ACT}$. When $\mathcal{F}$ produces a p_i-output for $p_i \notin \mathrm{ACT}$, it is given to $\mathcal{Z}$, but when $\mathcal{F}$ produces a p_i-output for $p_i \in \mathrm{ACT}$, it is not given to $\mathcal{Z}$. When $\mathcal{Z}$ gives a p_i-input to $\mathcal{F}$ for $p_i \in \mathrm{PAS}$, it is shown to $\mathcal{S}$, and when $\mathcal{F}$ produces a p_i-output for $p_i \in \mathrm{PAS}$, it is shown to $\mathcal{S}$.

A protocol π is called a UC secure implementation of $\mathcal{F}$ if there exists a simulator $\mathcal{S}$ such that $\mathrm{SIM}_{\mathcal{F},\mathcal{S},\mathcal{Z}} \approx \mathrm{EXEC}_{\pi,\mathcal{Z}}$ for all $\mathcal{Z}$. It is possible to restrict $\mathcal{Z}$ to corrupting according to some $\mathrm{PAT} \in \mathcal{A}$, in which case we say that π is $\mathcal{A}$-secure (in the symmetric sense).

---

[3] We use the formulation of the UC framework without an explicit adversary, see full version of [5].

$\mathcal{F}^{(\mathrm{Xtn})}$ runs a copy of $\mathcal{F}$. When $\mathcal{F}$ produces aux-output z, $\mathcal{F}^{(\mathrm{Xtn})}$ produces aux-output z, and when $\mathcal{F}^{(\mathrm{Xtn})}$ receives aux-input z it gives $\mathcal{F}$ the aux-input z. When the (current) corruption pattern is PAT and Xtn(PAT) = (ACTIN, ACTOUT, PASIN, PASOUT), the remaining inputs and outputs are handled as follows:

- For $p_i \in$ PASIN: On p_i-input x, produce aux-output $(\mathbf{in}, p_i, x)$, and then give $\mathcal{F}$ the p_i-input x.
- For $p_i \in$ PASOUT: On p_i-output x from $\mathcal{F}$, produce aux-output $(\mathbf{out}, p_i, x)$, and then produce the p_i-output x.
- For $p_i \in$ ACTIN: Ignore all p_i-inputs, and on an aux-input $(\mathbf{in}, p_i, x)$, give $\mathcal{F}$ the p_i-input x.
- For $p_i \in$ ACTOUT: Ignore all p_i-outputs from $\mathcal{F}$, and on an aux-input $(\mathbf{out}, p_i, x)$, produce the p_i-output x.

Fig. 2. $\mathcal{F}^{(\mathrm{Xtn})}$

3.2 Modeling the Security Loss of Naïve Parties

To define asymmetric trust in the UC framework, we need to model the loss of security we will allow for a party who turns out to have been naïve. To express what we choose to allow, we introduce the concept of a corruption extension Xtn which is a function that maps a corruption pattern PAT to a tuple

$$\mathrm{Xtn}(\mathrm{PAT}) = (\mathrm{ACTIN}, \mathrm{ACTOUT}, \mathrm{PASIN}, \mathrm{PASOUT}),$$

of party subsets, where

$$\mathrm{PASIN}, \mathrm{PASOUT} \subseteq \mathcal{P} \setminus \mathrm{PAS} \text{ and } \mathrm{ACTIN}, \mathrm{ACTOUT} \subseteq \mathcal{P} \setminus \mathrm{ACT}.$$

These are subsets of parties who are not corrupt but nevertheless have their security violated in some way.

This is modeled in the simulation $\mathrm{SIM}_{\mathcal{F},\mathcal{S},\mathcal{Z}}$ by giving $\mathcal{S}$ the following extra power over $\mathcal{F}$: For the parties $p_i \in$ PASIN, respectively $p_i \in$ PASOUT, we show $\mathcal{S}$ the p_i-inputs to $\mathcal{F}$, respectively the p_i-outputs from $\mathcal{F}$. For the parties $p_i \in$ ACTIN, when $\mathcal{Z}$ gives a p_i-input to $\mathcal{F}$, it is not given to $\mathcal{F}$. Instead we allow $\mathcal{S}$ to specify these p_i-inputs. Finally, for the parties $p_i \in$ ACTOUT, when $\mathcal{F}$ produces a p_i-output to $\mathcal{Z}$, it is not given to $\mathcal{Z}$ but we allow $\mathcal{S}$ to specify these p_i-outputs.

Of course, a functionality $\mathcal{F}$ may also be used as an auxiliary functionality in a protocol. In this case the extra power is given to the environment (adversary), see more on this below.

In order to formally incorporate the above into the UC framework without making changes that require us to reprove the composition theorem, we define the following way to extend any ideal functionality: For a functionality $\mathcal{F}$ and any extension Xtn, let $\mathcal{F}^{(\mathrm{Xtn})}$ be the ideal functionality in Fig. 2. We say that π is an Xtn-secure implementation of $\mathcal{F}$ if π is a UC secure implementation of $\mathcal{F}^{(\mathrm{Xtn})}$ (tolerating environments corrupting any subset of parties).

Note that in $\text{SIM}_{\mathcal{F}^{(\text{Xtn})},\mathcal{Z}}$ it is $\mathcal{S}$ which has access to the aux-inputs and aux-outputs of $\mathcal{F}^{(\text{Xtn})}$, giving it exactly the desired extra power. Note also that $\mathcal{F}^{(\text{Xtn})}$ is allowed in the UC framework since it allows functionalities to know which parties are corrupted.

Note that in the above definition we do not restrict in any way how many parties the environment corrupts! We might however use Xtn to specify that for some corruptions $A \notin \mathcal{A}$ the simulator is allowed to corrupt all parties in the simulation. This allows to model that for corruptions $A \notin \mathcal{A}$ no security guarantees are given. The notion of corruption extensions therefore subsumes the normal notion of restricting the environment to certain corruption patterns $\mathcal{A}$.

As mentioned, extensions also apply to a functionality $\mathcal{G}$ used in protocol π. For this purpose we assume that π associates to each $\mathcal{G} \in \pi$ an extension $\text{Xtn}_{\mathcal{G}}$. We then let $\widehat{\pi}$ denote the protocol where each $\mathcal{G} \in \pi$ is replaced by $\mathcal{G}^{(\text{Xtn}_{\mathcal{G}})}$. In $\text{EXEC}_{\widehat{\pi},\mathcal{Z}}$ it is $\mathcal{Z}$ which has access to the aux-inputs and outputs of $\mathcal{G}^{(\text{Xtn}_{\mathcal{G}})}$, granting it extra power over $\mathcal{G}$ in the same way as we did for the simulator before.

Definition 5. *Let π be a protocol having an extension $\text{Xtn}_{\mathcal{G}}$ associated to each $\mathcal{G} \in \pi$, let Xtn be some extension and let $\mathcal{F}$ be some ideal functionality. We say that π is an Xtn-secure implementation of $\mathcal{F}$ if $\widehat{\pi}$ is a UC secure implementation of $\mathcal{F}^{(\text{Xtn})}$ (tolerating all corruption patterns).* ◇

We can prove a composition theorem for this notion of security. For a protocol $\pi = \pi[\mathcal{G}]$ and a protocol γ we use $\pi[\gamma/\mathcal{G}]$ to denote the protocol π where the use of $\mathcal{G}$ has been replaced by γ. Let Xtn^{π} (Xtn^{γ}) be the extensions π (γ) associates to its ideal functionalities. For $\mathcal{H} \in \pi[\gamma/\mathcal{G}]$ we associate the extension $\text{Xtn}(\mathcal{H}) = \text{Xtn}^{\pi}(\mathcal{H})$ when $\mathcal{H} \in \pi$ and $\text{Xtn}(\mathcal{H}) = \text{Xtn}^{\gamma}(\mathcal{H})$ when $\mathcal{H} \in \gamma$.

Theorem 8. *Assume that π is an Xtn-secure implementation of $\mathcal{F}$ and $\mathcal{G} \in \pi$ with $\text{Xtn}^{\pi}(\mathcal{G}) = \text{Xtn}_{\mathcal{G}}$. Assume furthermore that γ is an $\text{Xtn}_{\mathcal{G}}$-secure implementation of $\mathcal{G}$. Then $\pi[\gamma/\mathcal{G}]$ is an Xtn-secure implementation of $\mathcal{F}$.*

Proof. When $\text{Xtn}^{\pi}(\mathcal{G}) = \text{Xtn}_{\mathcal{G}}$ for $\mathcal{G} \in \pi$, then π being an Xtn-secure implementation of $\mathcal{F}$ implies that $\widehat{\pi}[\mathcal{G}^{(\text{Xtn}_{\mathcal{G}})}]$ is a UC secure implementation of $\mathcal{F}^{(\text{Xtn})}$. That γ is an $\text{Xtn}_{\mathcal{G}}$-secure implementation of $\mathcal{G}$ implies that $\widehat{\gamma}$ is a UC secure implementation of $\mathcal{G}^{(\text{Xtn}_{\mathcal{G}})}$. So, by the UC composition theorem, $\widehat{\pi}[\widehat{\gamma}/\mathcal{G}^{(\text{Xtn}_{\mathcal{G}})}]$ is a UC secure implementation of $\mathcal{F}^{(\text{Xtn})}$. Since $\widehat{\pi[\gamma/\mathcal{G}]} = \widehat{\pi}[\widehat{\gamma}/\mathcal{G}^{(\text{Xtn}_{\mathcal{G}})}]$ this implies that $\widehat{\pi[\gamma/\mathcal{G}]}$ is a UC secure implementation of $\mathcal{F}^{(\text{Xtn})}$ which by definition implies that $\pi[\gamma/\mathcal{G}]$ is an Xtn-secure implementation of $\mathcal{F}$. □

3.3 Asymmetric Trust

We now use Definition 5 to express asymmetric trust, formalizing the concepts we introduced in Section 1.4. To each p_i we associate an adversary structure $\mathcal{A}_i$ expressing that p_i trusts that only corruption patterns $\text{PAT} \in \mathcal{A}_i$ will actually occur. We call $\underline{\mathcal{A}} = (\mathcal{A}_1, \ldots, \mathcal{A}_n)$ an **aggregate adversary structure**. A symmetric adversary structure $\mathcal{A}$ corresponds to the aggregate adversary structure $\underline{\mathcal{A}}^n = (\mathcal{A}, \ldots, \mathcal{A})$. For an actually occurring corruption pattern $\text{PAT} =$

(ACT, PAS) we let FORESEEING$_A$(PAT) = $\{p_i \in \mathcal{P} \setminus \text{PAS}|\text{PAT} \in \mathcal{A}_i\}$ and we let NAÏVE$_A$(PAT) = $\{p_i \in \mathcal{P} \setminus \text{PAS}|\text{PAT} \notin \mathcal{A}_i\}$. We call $p_i \in$ FORESEEING$_A$(PAT) foreseeing and we call $p_i \in$ NAÏVE$_A$(PAT) naïve. We model asymmetric trust by treating the foreseeing honest parties as we normally treat the honest parties in UC security and treating the corrupted parties as we do normally. For the naïve parties we allow the simulator (environment) extra powers, using the concepts we defined earlier. Formally, we say that a corruption extension Xtn is an extension for $\mathcal{A} = (\mathcal{A}_1, \ldots, \mathcal{A}_n)$ if it holds for all PAT that Xtn(PAT) = (ACTIN, ACTOUT, PASIN, PASOUT) satisfies PASIN, PASOUT, ACTIN, ACTOUT $\subseteq$ NAÏVE$_A$(PAT). This gives a lot of granularity in how to treat the honest-but-naïve parties: PASIN specifies the naïve parties for which the inputs are allowed to leak to the adversary, PASOUT specifies the naïve parties for which the outputs are allowed to leak to the adversary, ACTIN specifies the naïve parties for which the inputs might be controlled by the adversary, and ACTOUT specifies the naïve parties for which the outputs might by controlled be the adversary.

To get some more structure, we name some special types of extensions, called `relaxed`, `semi-relaxed`, `strong`, `strict`, which are defined as follows:

- Xtn is of type `relaxed` if it is the extension of $\mathcal{A}$ that specifies ACTIN = ACTOUT = NAÏVE$_A$(PAT) for all PAT, i.e., there is no security for naïve parties.
- Xtn is of type `semi-relaxed` if it is the extension of $\mathcal{A}$ that specifies ACTIN = $\emptyset$, ACTOUT = NAÏVE $\setminus$ ACT, PASIN = NAÏVE $\setminus$ PAS, PASOUT = NAÏVE $\setminus$ PAS. I.e., the honest-but-naïve parties are guaranteed that their inputs are contributed correctly to the computation. They are however not guaranteed to receive correct outputs nor any privacy of their inputs or their outputs.
- Xtn is of type `strong` if it is the extension of $\mathcal{A}$ that specifies ACTIN = ACTOUT = $\emptyset$, PASIN = PASOUT = NAÏVE$_A$(PAT), i.e., naïve parties have no privacy but may contribute their inputs and get correct results.
- Xtn is of type `strict` if it is the extension of $\mathcal{A}$ that specifies Xtn$_G$(PAT) = $(\emptyset, \emptyset, \emptyset, \emptyset)$, i.e., there is full security for naïve parties.

If ATK is one of `relaxed`, `semi-relaxed`, `strong`, `strict`, we call π an ATK $\mathcal{A}$-secure implementation of $\mathcal{F}$ if π is an Xtn-secure implementation of $\mathcal{F}$ tolerating $\mathcal{A}$, where Xtn is the extension of $\mathcal{A}$ of type ATK. Also, if π makes use of functionality $\mathcal{G}$, we say that $\mathcal{G}$ is an ATK functionality if the extension π assigns to $\mathcal{G}$ is of type ATK.

The following composition theorem is an immediate corollary to Theorem 8.

Corollary 1. *Let* ATK, ATK$'$ $\in \{relaxed, semi\text{-}relaxed, strong, strict\}$. *If* π *is an* ATK $\mathcal{A}$-*secure implementation of* $\mathcal{F}$, *where* $\mathcal{G} \in \pi$ *is an* ATK$'$ *functionality, and* γ *is an* ATK$'$ $\mathcal{A}$-*secure implementation of* $\mathcal{G}$, *then* $\pi[\gamma/\mathcal{G}]$ *is an* ATK $\mathcal{A}$-*secure implementation of* $\mathcal{F}$.

Note that the notion of semi-relaxed security as defined here is equivalent to the notions sender-independent validity and dealer-independent correctness in Section 2. Indeed, defining broadcast and VSS by requiring a `semi-relaxed` secure implementation of a corresponding ideal functionality would define exactly these notions.

To see the connection between symmetric security and our notions of asymmetric security, let $\underline{A}$ be the aggregate adversary structure modeling that all parties trust that at most t parties will be corrupted, and let π be a protocol using only strict functionalities. In this case the simulator is given no extra corruption when at most t parties are corrupted, as all parties are foreseeing. So, as long as at most t parties are corrupted, relaxed, semi-relaxed, strong and strict $\underline{A}$-security are equivalent to the usual UC t-security. If however more than t parties are corrupted, then all honest parties are naïve, meaning e.g. that strong security allows the simulator to see the inputs and outputs of all parties, and relaxed security allows the simulator to specify the inputs and outputs of all parties. So, when more than t parties are corrupted, strong $\underline{A}$-security gives no guarantees on the privacy of any party but still guarantees correctness for the honest-but-naïve parties, and relaxed $\underline{A}$-security gives no guarantees at all. Note that giving no guarantees at all when more than t parties are corrupted is equivalent to normal t-security, where simulation is only required for environments corrupting at most t parties. Therefore relaxed security is a generalization of normal (symmetric) UC security, and strong security is a strengthening.

4   Multi-Party Computation in the UC Framework

In this section we first formalize the notion of secure multi-party computation in the UC framework where the parties have asymmetric trust in each other. In Section 2.3 we already informally looked at this case in the secure-channels model. In Section 4.2 we look at a setting where a number of certificate authorities (or common reference strings) are present and where the parties have asymmetric trust in these certificate authorities (or common reference strings).

4.1   Secure Function Evaluation

For simplicity we focus on secure function evaluation (SFE). SFE of $f(x_1, \ldots, x_n)$ can be expressed as securely evaluating the ideal functionality $\mathcal{F}_{\text{SFE}}^f$ for secure function evaluation of f. Essentially $\mathcal{F}_{\text{SFE}}^f$ takes an input x_i from each p_i, computes $(y_1, \ldots, y_n) = f(x_1, \ldots, x_n)$ and outputs y_i securely to p_i. We call π an $\underline{A}$ SFE w/ full relaxation of f if π is a relaxed $\underline{A}$-secure implementation of $\mathcal{F}_{\text{SFE}}^f$. We call π an $\underline{A}$ SFE w/ contributor-independent correctness of f if π is a semi-relaxed $\underline{A}$-secure implementation of $\mathcal{F}_{\text{SFE}}^f$. For concreteness we flesh out these notions below.

Definition 6 (SFE w/ full relaxation). *The simulator has the following extra powers:*

INPUT SECRECY: *If p_i is honest and $F \notin \mathcal{A}_i$ or p_i is corrupt, then the simulator sees x_i. If party p_i is honest and $F \in \mathcal{A}_i$ then the simulator is not shown x_i.*

INPUT CORRECTNESS: *If p_i is honest and $F \notin \mathcal{A}_i$ or p_i is corrupt, then the simulator can replace x_i by some x'_i. After this, the outputs $(y_1, \ldots, y_n) = f(x'_1, \ldots, x'_n)$ are computed, where $x'_i = x_i$ for all honest p_i with $F \in \mathcal{A}_i$.*

OUTPUT SECRECY: *If p_i is honest and $F \notin \mathcal{A}_i$ or p_i is corrupt, then the simulator sees y_i. If party p_i is honest and $F \in \mathcal{A}_i$ then the simulator is not shown y_i.*

OUTPUT CORRECTNESS: *If p_i is honest and $F \notin \mathcal{A}_i$ or p_i is corrupt, then the simulator can replace y_i by some y'_i. After this, $\mathcal{F}^f_{\text{SFE}}$ outputs y'_i on behalf of p_i, where $y'_i = y_i$ for all honest p_i with $F \in \mathcal{A}_i$.*

ROBUSTNESS: *Robustness is best expressed as a condition on the protocol (as opposed to the simulation), by requiring that all honest parties compute an output, i.e., no honest party aborts the protocol. Alternatively, one can require this only for the foreseeing parties, getting* **weak robustness**.   ◇

Definition 7 (SFE w/ contributor-independent correctness). *The simulator has the following extra powers (listing only differences from Definition 6):*

INPUT CORRECTNESS: *If p_i is corrupt, then the simulator can replace x_i by some x'_i. After this, the outputs $(y_1, \ldots, y_n) = f(x'_1, \ldots, x'_n)$ are computed, where $x'_i = x_i$ for all honest p_i.*   ◇

These notions can be generalized to MPC w/ full relaxation and MPC w/ contributor-independent correctness by requiring a `relaxed` (`semi-relaxed`) $\mathcal{A}$-secure implementation of a more general ideal functionality $\mathcal{F}$.

4.2   With Asymmetrically Trusted Setup

We now consider a setting where some setup is given. We focus on UC security, where setup is needed when there is no trust among the parties. We consider two setup assumptions which have been studied previously: common reference string (CRS) and key registration (KR), and we generalize the study to consider asymmetric trust. Here, we only cover the KR case whereas the CRS case is treated in the full version of the paper, using similar techniques.

Key Registration. In [1] Barak *et al.* gave a feasibility result for UC secure MPC in a network which had a key registration service $\mathcal{F}_{\text{KR}}$ which allows a user U_i to register a public key pk_i while checking that U_i knows a corresponding secret key. We extend this analysis of the power of key registration by analyzing a setting where there are several key registration services (KRS's) in which the users have different partial trust. For completeness we also assume that the users have different, partial trust in each other. We characterize the aggregate adversary structures which allow to securely compute any ideal functionality in this setting. We consider the same type of security as in [1,6]: polynomial time security and the protocol is only required to deliver outputs if all parties are honest. This is modeled by allowing the simulator to decide when and if honest outputs from $\mathcal{F}$ to $\mathcal{Z}$ are delivered in $\text{SIM}_{\mathcal{F},\mathcal{S},\mathcal{Z}}$.

We model the KRS's as parties $\mathcal{KR} = \{KR_k\}$. We then add n users $\mathcal{U} = \{U_1, \ldots, U_n\}$, making the party set $\mathcal{P} = \mathcal{KR} \cup \mathcal{U}$. The users are the parties which want to compute some ideal functionality $\mathcal{F}_\mathcal{U}$ among them.[4] We also add a strict functionality for authenticated, asynchronous point-to-point communication among the users and between the users and the KRS's, and we add a strict functionality for secure, asynchronous point-to-point communication among the users.[5] Finally we need that each user can give a proof of possession (PoP) of the secret key when it registers a public key. For this purpose we postulate an ideal functionality $\mathcal{POP}$. Let gen be the generator $pk = \text{gen}(r)$ used to generate public keys (we can wlog assume that the randomness r constitutes the private key). We assume that $\mathcal{POP}$ behaves as follows: On input (U_i, KR_k, r_i) from U_i, output $(U_i, KR_k, pk_i = \text{gen}(r_i))$ to KR_k. This models that U_i gives pk_i to KR_k and then somehow proves knowledge of r_i such that $pk_i = \text{gen}(r_i)$.

By U_i registering a public key at KR_k we then mean that U_i samples a random public key $pk_i \leftarrow \text{gen}(r_i)$ and inputs (U_i, KR_k, r_i) securely to $\mathcal{POP}$. The honest behavior of each KR_k is as follows: The first time it sees $\mathcal{POP}$ output (U_i, KR_k, pk_i) for U_i it sends (U_i, KR_k, pk_i) to all users U_j using authenticated point-to-point communication.

Since the behavior of KR_k is fixed and the behavior of $\mathcal{POP}$ is given by gen, we specify a protocol by $\pi = (\text{gen}, U_1, \ldots, U_n)$. For convenience we assume that each U_i starts the protocol by registering some $pk_{i,k}$ with each KR_k. Then U_i waits for each KR_k to send some $pk_{j,k}$ for each $U_j \in \mathcal{U}$ and stores all these keys. After this registration phase the users then proceed to run the actual protocol. We can therefore in the specification of p_i assume that it knows the keys $pk_{k,j}$. We call such a $\pi = (\text{gen}, U_1, \ldots, U_n)$ a KR-protocol.

As for trust, we consider only active corruptions, so that $\text{PAT} = (\text{ACT}, \text{ACT})$ for all patterns. We therefore write $\text{ACT} \in \mathcal{A}$ and consider $\mathcal{A} \in 2^\mathcal{P}$. We associate no trust to the KRS's. That is, we assume that $\mathcal{A}_{KR_k} = 2^\mathcal{P}$ for each KRS. To each U_i we associate a corruption structure $\mathcal{A}_i \subseteq 2^\mathcal{P}$. We call $(\mathcal{A}_1, \ldots, \mathcal{A}_n)$ complete for the KR setting if it allows to securely compute any efficient ideal functionality $\mathcal{F}_\mathcal{U}$ among the users using a KR protocol.

For $\text{ACT}_i \in \mathcal{A}_i$ we let $\text{ACT}_i^\mathcal{U} = \text{ACT}_i \cap \mathcal{U}$ and $\text{ACT}_i^{\mathcal{KR}} = \text{ACT}_i \cap \mathcal{KR}$. We say that two users $U_i \neq U_j$ are KR connected if it holds for all $\text{ACT}_i \in \mathcal{A}_i$ and $\text{ACT}_j \in \mathcal{A}_j$ that either $\text{ACT}_i^{\mathcal{KR}} \neq \mathcal{KR}$ or $\text{ACT}_j^{\mathcal{KR}} \neq \mathcal{KR}$ or $\text{ACT}_i^\mathcal{U} \cup \text{ACT}_j^\mathcal{U} \neq \mathcal{U}$. That is, together, U_i and U_j cannot imagine a scenario where both of them think that all KRS's might be corrupted and where together they think all users might be corrupted.

---

[4] We say that $\mathcal{F}_{\mathcal{P}'}$ is among $\mathcal{P}'$ if it ignores p_i-inputs for $\mathcal{P} \setminus \mathcal{P}'$ and gives no p_i-outputs for $\mathcal{P} \setminus \mathcal{P}'$.

[5] Since secure, asynchronous point-to-point communication has a normal UC secure implementation given authenticated channels and several standard complexity assumptions, this strict ideal functionality can be replaced with any such implementation to get an equivalent model with only authenticated communication, using Corollary 1.

Theorem 9. *An aggregate adversary structure* $\underline{A} = (\mathcal{A}_1, \ldots, \mathcal{A}_n)$ *is complete for the KR setting iff all pairs of distinct users are KR connected in* $\underline{A}$.

The proof of Theorem 9 is given in the full version of the paper. A special case of Theorem 9 is when the users have no trust in each other ($\mathcal{A}_i^{\mathcal{U}} = \mathcal{U}$ for all U_i) in which case the condition can be phrased as: There exists at most one user who thinks that all KRS's can be corrupted.

5 Conclusion

We proposed a notion of asymmetric trust in protocol security and gave a general definition of asymmetric secure MPC and gave specialized definitions of asymmetric secure broadcast, VSS, and SFE. We explored the feasibility of broadcast, VSS, and MPC in various models with asymmetric trust. A tight characterization of the feasibility of broadcast has been found for asymmetric trust, and nontrivial upper and lower bounds for VSS, and we have shown how to tolerate strictly stronger adversaries in MPC than with symmetric trust. It is an open problem to completely characterize the aggregate adversary structures that allow for MPC in the case with active adversaries and no set-up.

References

1. Barak, B., Canetti, R., Nielsen, J.B., Pass, R.: Universally composable protocols with relaxed set-up assumptions. In: 45th Annual Symposium on Foundations of Computer Science, pp. 186–195. IEEE, Los Alamitos (2004)
2. Baum-Waidner, B., Pfitzmann, B., Waidner, M.: Unconditional Byzantine agreement with good majority. In: 8th Annual Symposium on Theoretical Aspects of Computer Science. LNCS, vol. 480, Springer, Heidelberg (1991)
3. Ben-Or, M., Goldwasser, S., Wigderson, A.: Completeness theorems for non-cryptographic fault-tolerant distributed computation. In: 20th ACM Symposium on the Theory of Computing, pp. 1–10 (1988)
4. Blakley, G.R.: Safeguarding cryptographic keys. In: 1979 National Computer Conference. AFIPS Conference proceedings, vol. 48, AFIPS Press (1979)
5. Canetti, R.: Universally composable security: A new paradigm for cryptographic protocols. In: 42nd Annual Symposium on Foundations of Computer Science, pp. 136–145 (2001) Full version in IACR ePrint Archive 2000/067
6. Canetti, R., Lindell, Y., Ostrovsky, R., Sahai, A.: Universally composable two-party and multi-party secure computation. In: Proceedings of the Thirty-Fourth Annual ACM Symposium on the Theory of Computing, pp. 494–503 (2002)
7. Chor, B., Goldwasser, S., Micali, S., Awerbuch, B.: Verifiable secret sharing and achieving simultaneity in the presence of faults. In: 26th IEEE Symposium on the Foundations of Computer Science, pp. 383–395 (1985)
8. Cleve, R.: Limits on the security of coin flips when half the processors are faulty (extended abstract). In: 18th ACM Symposium on the Theory of Computing, pp. 364–369 (1986)
9. Cramer, R., Damgård, I., Dziembowski, S., Hirt, M., Rabin, T.: Efficient multi-party computations secure against an adaptive adversary. In: Stern, J. (ed.) EUROCRYPT 1999. LNCS, vol. 1592, Springer, Heidelberg (1999)

10. Fitzi, M., Gisin, N., Maurer, U., von Rotz, O.: Unconditional Byzantine agreement and multi-party computation secure against dishonest minorities from scratch. In: Knudsen, L.R. (ed.) EUROCRYPT 2002. LNCS, vol. 2332, pp. 482–501. Springer, Heidelberg (2002)
11. Fitzi, M., Gottesman, D., Hirt, M., Holenstein, T., Smith, A.: Detectable Byzantine agreement secure against faulty majorities. In: 21st ACM Symposium on Principles of Distributed Computing (PODC), pp. 118–126 (2002)
12. Goldreich, O., Micali, S., Wigderson, A.: How to play any mental game — a completeness theorem for protocols with honest majority. In: 19th ACM Symposium on the Theory of Computing, pp. 218–229 (1987)
13. Hirt, M., Maurer, U.: Player simulation and general adversary structures in perfect multiparty computation. Journal of Cryptology 13(1), 31–60 (2000)
14. Maurer, U.: Secure multi-party computation made simple. In: Cimato, S., Galdi, C., Persiano, G. (eds.) SCN 2002. LNCS, vol. 2576, pp. 14–28. Springer, Heidelberg (2003)
15. Maurer, U.: Towards a theory of consistency primitives. In: Guerraoui, R. (ed.) DISC 2004. LNCS, vol. 3274, pp. 379–389. Springer, Heidelberg (2004)
16. Pease, M., Shostak, R., Lamport, L.: Reaching agreement in the presence of faults. Journal of the ACM 27(2), 228–234 (1980)
17. Pfitzmann, B., Waidner, M.: Information-theoretic pseudosignatures and Byzantine agreement for $t >= n/3$. Technical Report RZ 2882 (#90830), IBM Research (1996)
18. Rabin, T., Ben-Or, M.: Verifiable secret sharing and multiparty protocols with honest majority. In: 21st ACM Symposium on the Theory of Computing, pp. 73–85 (1989)
19. Shamir, A.: How to share a secret. CACM 22, 612–613 (1979)
20. Yao, A.C.: Protocols for secure computations. In: 23rd IEEE Symposium on the Foundations of Computer Science, pp. 160–164. IEEE, Los Alamitos (1982)

Simple and Efficient Perfectly-Secure Asynchronous MPC⋆

Zuzana Beerliová-Trubíniová and Martin Hirt

ETH Zurich, Department of Computer Science,
CH-8092 Zurich
{bzuzana,hirt}@inf.ethz.ch

Abstract. Secure multi-party computation (MPC) allows a set of n players to securely compute an agreed function of their inputs, even when up to t players are under the control of an adversary. Known *asynchronous* MPC protocols require communication of at least $\Omega(n^3)$ (with cryptographic security), respectively $\Omega(n^4)$ (with information-theoretic security, but with error probability and non-optimal resilience) field elements per multiplication.

We present an asynchronous MPC protocol communicating $\mathcal{O}(n^3)$ field elements per multiplication. Our protocol provides perfect security against an active, adaptive adversary corrupting $t < n/4$ players, which is optimal. This communication complexity is to be compared with the most efficient previously known protocol for the same model, which requires $\Omega(n^5)$ field elements of communication (i.e., $\Omega(n^3)$ broadcasts). Our protocol is as efficient as the most efficient perfectly secure protocol for the synchronous model and the most efficient asynchronous protocol with cryptographic security.

Furthermore, we enhance our MPC protocol for a hybrid model. In the fully asynchronous model, up to t honest players might not be able to provide their input in the computation. In the hybrid model, all players are able to provide their input, given that the very first round of communication is synchronous. We provide an MPC protocol with communicating $\mathcal{O}(n^3)$ field elements per multiplication, where all players can provide their input if the first communication round turns out to be synchronous, and all but at most t players can provide their input if the communication is fully asynchronous. The protocol does not need to know whether or not the first communication round is synchronous, thus combining the advantages of the synchronous world and the asynchronous world. The proposed MPC protocol is the first protocol with this property.

Keywords: Multi-party computation, asynchronous, hybrid model, efficiency, perfect security.

⋆ This work was partially supported by the Zurich Information Security Center. It represents the views of the authors.

K. Kurosawa (Ed.): ASIACRYPT 2007, LNCS 4833, pp. 376–392, 2007.

1 Introduction

1.1 Secure Multi-Party Computation

Secure multi-party computation (MPC) enables a set of n players to securely evaluate an agreed function of their inputs even when t of the players are corrupted by a central adversary. A *passive adversary* can read the internal state of the corrupted players, trying to obtain information about the honest players' inputs. An *active adversary* can additionally make the corrupted players deviate from the protocol, trying to falsify the outcome of the computation.

The MPC problem dates back to Yao [Yao82]. The first generic solutions presented in [GMW87, CDG87, GHY87] (based on cryptographic intractability assumptions) and later [BGW88, CCD88, RB89, Bea91] (with information-theoretic security) assume the existence of a synchronous network. Synchronous networks assume that there is a global clock, and the delay of any message in the network is bounded by a constant. Such networks do not well model real-life networks like the internet.

1.2 Asynchronous Networks

In asynchronous networks, messages are delayed arbitrarily. As worst-case assumption, the adversary is given the power to schedule the delivery of messages. Asynchronous communication models real-world networks (like the Internet) much better than synchronous communication. However, protocols for asynchronous networks are much more involved than their synchronous counterparts. This comes from the fact that when a player does not receive an expected message, he cannot decide whether the sender is corrupted (and did not send the message at all) or the message is just delayed in the network.

This implies also that in fully asynchronous settings it is impossible to consider the inputs of *all* uncorrupted players. The inputs of up to t (potentially honest) players have to be ignored, because waiting for them could turn out to be endless.

For a good introduction to asynchronous protocols, see [Can95]. Due to its complexity, asynchronous MPC has attracted much less research than synchronous MPC. The most important results on asynchronous MPC are [BCG93, BKR94, SR00, PSR02, HNP05].

In the asynchronous setting perfect information-theoretic security against an active adversary is possible if and only if $t < n/4$ (whereas cryptographic and unconditional security are possible if and only if $t < n/3$).

1.3 Communication Complexity of MPC Protocols

The first proposed MPC protocols secure against active adversaries were very inefficient and so of theoretical relevance mainly. In the recent years lots of research concentrated on designing protocols with lower communication complexity (measured in bits sent by honest players). The currently most efficient MPC protocols for the synchronous model are [HMP00] (perfect security with $t < n/3$, $\mathcal{O}(n^3)$

communication per multiplication), [DN07] (information-theoretic security with $t < n/3$, $\mathcal{O}(n)$ communication per multiplication), [BH06] (information-theoretic security with $t < n/2$, communicating $\mathcal{O}(n^2)$ per multiplication), [HN06] (cryptographic security with $t < n/2$, communicating $\mathcal{O}(n)$ per multiplication).

However known MPC protocols for asynchronous networks still feature (impractically) high communication complexities. The most efficient asynchronous protocol is the one of [HNP05] communicating $\mathcal{O}(n^3)$ per multiplication while providing cryptographic security only. The most efficient information-theoretically secure protocols were proposed in [SR00, PSR02]. Both protocols are secure against an unbounded adversary corrupting up to $t < n/4$ players. The first one makes extensive use of the (communication-intensive) BA primitive – $\mathcal{O}(n^2)$ invocations per multiplication, which amounts to $\Omega(n^5)$[1] bits of communication per multiplication. The second one requires only $\mathcal{O}(n^2)$ invocations to BA in total, however, still communicates $\mathcal{O}(n^4)$ bits per multiplication, and provides unconditional security only (for which $t < n/4$ is not optimal).

1.4   Contributions

Known MPC protocols for the asynchronous setting suffer from two main disadvantages in contrast to their more restrictive synchronous counterparts, both significantly reducing their practicability: Asynchronous protocol tend to have substantially higher communication complexity, and they do not allow to take the inputs of all honest players. In this work, we propose a solution to both these problems.

First, we present an perfectly secure asynchronous MPC protocol that communicates only $\mathcal{O}(n^3)$ field elements per multiplication. This very same communication complexity is also required by the most efficient known perfectly secure protocol for the synchronous model [HMP00], as well as by the most efficient asynchronous protocol only secure against computationally bounded adversaries [HNP05]. The protocol provides perfect security against an unbounded adaptive active adversary corrupting up to $t < n/4$ players, which is optimal. In contrast to the previous asynchronous protocols, the new protocol is very simple.

Second, we extended the protocol for a hybrid communication model (with the same security properties and the same communication complexity), allowing all players to give input if the very first round of the communication is synchronous, and takes at least $n - t$ inputs in a fully asynchronous setting. It is well-known that fully asynchronous protocols cannot take the inputs of all players; however, we show that a single round of synchronous communication is sufficient to take all inputs. We stress that it is important that this round is the first round, because assuming the k-th round to be synchronous implies that all rounds up to k must also be synchronous. Furthermore, the protocol achieves the best of both worlds, i.e., takes the inputs of all players when indeed the first round is synchronous, and still takes the inputs of at least $n - t$ players even if the synchronity assumptions cannot be fulfilled. More precisely, the protocol takes

---

[1] The most efficient known asynchronous BA protocol requires $\Omega(n^3)$.

the inputs of at least $n - t$ players, and additionally, always takes the inputs of players whose first-round messages are delivered synchronously.

2 Preliminaries

2.1 Model

We consider a set $\mathcal{P}$ of n players, $\mathcal{P} = \{P_1, \ldots, P_n\}$, which are connected with a complete network of secure (private and authentic) asynchronous channels. The function to be computed is specified as an arithmetic circuit over a finite field $\mathcal{F} = \mathbb{Z}_p$ (with $p > n$), with input, addition, multiplication, random, and output gates. We denote the number of gates of each type by c_I, c_A, c_M, c_R, and c_O, respectively.

The faultiness of players is modeled in terms of a central adversary corrupting players. The adversary can corrupt up to t players for any fixed t with $t < n/4$, and make them deviate from the protocol in any desired manner. The adversary is computationally unbounded, active, adaptive, and rushing. Furthermore, in order to model the asynchronism of the network, the adversary can schedule the delivery of the messages in the network, i.e., she can delay any message arbitrarily. In particular, the order of the messages does not have to be preserved. However, every sent message will eventually be delivered.

The security of our protocols is perfect, i.e., information-theoretic without any error probability.

2.2 Design of Asynchronous MPC Protocols

Asynchronous protocols are executed in *steps*. Each step begins by the scheduler choosing one message (out of the queue) to be delivered to its designated recipient. The recipient is activated by receiving the message, he performs some (internal) computation and possibly sends messages on his outgoing channel (and waits for the next message).

The action to be taken by the recipient is defined by the relevant sub-protocol[2] consisting of a number of instructions what is to be done upon receiving a specified message. If the received message refers to a sub-protocol which is not yet "in execution", then the player keeps the message until the relevant sub-protocol is invoked.

2.3 Partial Termination

Many "asymmetric" tasks with a designated dealer (broadcast, secret-sharing) cannot be implemented with guaranteed termination in an asynchronous world; the players cannot distinguish whether the dealer is corrupted and does not start the protocol, or the dealer is correct but his messages are delayed in the network. Hence, these protocol are required to terminate only if the dealer is correct. However, we require that if such a sub-protocol terminated for one (correct) player, then it must eventually terminate for all correct players.

---

[2] We assume that for each message it is clear to which sub-protocol it belongs.

The issue with partial termination is typically attacked by invoking n instances of the protocol with partial termination in parallel, every player acting as dealer in one instance. Then, every player can wait till $n - t$ instances have terminated (from his point of view). In order to reach agreement on the set of terminated instances, a specialized sub-protocol is invoked, called agreement on a core-set. A player can only be contained in the core-set if his protocol instance has terminated for at least one honest player, and hence will eventually terminate for all honest players. The core-set contains at least $n - t$ players.

2.4 Input Provision

Providing input is an inherently asymmetric task, and it is not possible to distinguish between a corrupted input player who does not send any message and a correct input player whose messages are delayed in the network. For this reason, in a fully asynchronous world it is not possible to take the inputs of *all* players; up to t (possible correct) players cannot be waited for, as this waiting could turn out to be endless. Hence, the protocol waits only till $n - t$ of the players have achieved to provide input, and then goes on with the computation.

2.5 Byzantine Agreement

We need three flavors of Byzantine agreement, namely broadcast, consensus, and core-set agreement.

The broadcast (BC) primitive allows a sender to distribute a message among the players such that all players get the same message (even when the sender is corrupted), and the message they get is the sender's message if he is honest. As explained above, broadcast cannot be realized with complete termination; instead, termination of all (correct) players is required only when the sender is correct; however, as soon as at least one correct player terminates, all players must eventually terminate. Such a broadcast primitive can be realized rather easily [Bra84]. The required communication for broadcasting an ℓ-bit message is $\mathcal{O}(n^2\ell)$, where the hidden constant is small.

Consensus enables a set of players to agree on a value. If all honest players start the consensus protocol with the same input value v then all honest players will eventually terminate the protocol with the same value v as output. If they start with different input values, then they will eventually reach agreement on some value. All known i.t.-secure asynchronous consensus protocols start by having every player broadcast his input value, which results to communication complexity $\Omega(n^3\ell)$, where ℓ denotes the length of the inputs.

Agreement on a core set (ACS) is a primitive presented in [BCG93]. We use it to determine a set of at least $n - t$ players that correctly shared their values. More concretely, every player starts the ACS protocol with a accumulative set of players who from his point of view correctly shared one or more values (the share sub-protocol in which they acted as dealers terminated properly). The output of the protocol is a set of at least $n - t$ players, who really correctly shared their values, which means that every honest player will eventually get a share of every sharing dealt by a dealer from the core set. The communication cost of a ACS protocol are essentially the costs of n invocations to consensus (where the messages are index of players), i.e. $\Omega(n^4 \log n)$ bits.

2.6   Super-Invertible Matrices

We consider r-by-c matrices M over a field $\mathcal{F}$. When $r = c$, M is called *invertible* if all column-vectors are linearly independent. When $r \leq c$, M is called *super-invertible* if every subset of r column-vectors are linearly independent.

Formally, for an r-by-c matrix M and an index set $C \subseteq \{1, \ldots, c\}$, we denote by M_C the matrix consisting of the columns $i \in C$ of M. Then, M is super-invertible if for all C with $|C| = r$, M_C is invertible.

Super-invertible matrices over $\mathcal{F}$ can be constructed as follows: Fix c disjoint elements $\alpha_1, \ldots, \alpha_c \in \mathcal{F}$, and for $i = 1, \ldots, r$, let $f_i(\cdot)$ be a polynomial of degree at most $r - 1$ with $f_i(\alpha_i) = 1$ and $f_i(\alpha_j) = 0$ for $j \in \{1, \ldots, r\} \setminus \{i\}$. Then, $M = \{m_{i,j} = f_i(\alpha_j)\}$. M is super-invertible because $M_{\{1,\ldots,r\}}$ is invertible (it is the identity matrix), and any M_C for $C \subseteq \{1, \ldots, c\}$, $|C| = r$ can be mapped onto $M_{\{1,\ldots,r\}}$ using an invertible matrix given by Lagrange interpolation.

Super-invertible matrices are of great help to extract random elements from a set of some random and some non-random elements: Consider a vector $(x_1, \ldots, x_c)$ of elements, where for some $C \subseteq \{1, \ldots, c\}$ with $|C| = r$, the elements $\{x_i\}_{i \in C}$ are chosen uniformly at random (by honest players), and the elements $\{x_j\}_{j \notin C}$ are chosen maliciously (by corrupted players). Then, the vector $(y_1, \ldots, y_r) = M(x_1, \ldots, x_c)$ is uniformly random and unknown to the adversary.[3]

This means that given a super-invertible matrix and a set of c elements out of which at least r elements are chosen uniformly at random (and unknown to the adversary), we can generate r uniformly random elements (unknown to the adversary).

3   Protocol Overview

The new protocol proceeds in three phases: the preparation phase, the input phase and the computation phase. Every honest player will eventually complete every phase.

In the preparation phase many sharings of random values will be generated in parallel. For every multiplication gate, $3t + 1$ random sharing will be generated. For every random gate, one random sharing will be generated.

In the input phase the players share their inputs and agree on a core set of correctly shared inputs (every honest player will eventually get a share of every input from the core set).

In the computation phase, the actual circuit will be computed gate by gate, based on the core-set inputs. Due to the linearity of the used secret-sharing, the

---

[3] This follows from the observation that the $c - r$ maliciously chosen elements $\{x_j\}_{j \notin C}$ define a bijection from the r random elements $\{x_i\}_{i \in C}$ onto $(y_1, \ldots, y_r)$.

linear gates can be computed locally – without communication. Each multiplication gate will be evaluated with the help of $3t + 1$ of the prepared sharings.

4   Secret Sharing

4.1   Definitions and Notations

As secret-sharing scheme, we use the standard Shamir scheme [Sha79]: We say that a value s is d-*shared* if every correct player P_i is holding a share s_i of s, such that there exists a degree-d polynomial $p(x)$ with $p(0) = s$ and $p(i) = s_i$ for all $i = 1, \ldots, n$. We call the vector $(s_1, \ldots, s_n)$ of shares a d-sharing of s. A (possibly incomplete) set of shares is called d-*consistent* if these shares lie on a degree d polynomial.

Most of our Sharings will be t-sharings (where t denotes the maximum number of corrupted players). We denote a t-sharing of s by $[s]$. In the multiplication sub-protocol, we will also use $2t$-sharings, which will be denoted by $[[s]]$.

4.2   Share₁ and Recons — The Vanilla Protocols

In the following, we recap the Share₁ and Recons protocol of [BCG93].[4] Share₁ allows a dealer P_D to t-share a secret value $s \in \mathcal{F}$. Recons allows the players to reconstruct a d-sharing (for $d \leq 2t$) towards a receiver P_R. We stress that the protocol Share₁ does not necessarily terminate when the dealer P_D is corrupted. However, when it terminates for some correct player, then it eventually terminates for all players. The protocol Recons always terminates.

The intuition behind the protocol Share₁ is the following: In order to share a secret s, the dealer chooses a random two-dimensional polynomial $f(\cdot, \cdot)$ with $f(0, 0) = s$, and sends to every player P_i the polynomials $g_i(\cdot) = f(i, \cdot)$ and $h_i(\cdot) = f(\cdot, i)$. Then the players pairwisely check the consistency of the received polynomials, and publicly confirm successful checks. Once $n - t$ players are mutually consistent, the other players use the checking points received from these players to determine their respective polynomial $g_i(\cdot)$, and all players compute the share $s_i = g_i(0)$.

Protocol Share₁ (Dealer P_D, secret $s \in \mathcal{F}$)
- DISTRIBUTION — CODE FOR DEALER P_D: Choose a random two-dimensional degree-t polynomial $f(\cdot, \cdot)$ with $f(0, 0) = s$ and send to each player P_i the two degree-t polynomials $g_i(\cdot) = f(i, \cdot)$ and $h_i(\cdot) = f(\cdot, i)$.
- CONSISTENCY CHECKS — CODE FOR PLAYER P_i:
  1. Wait for $g_i(\cdot)$ and $h_i(\cdot)$ from P_D.
  2. To each player P_j send the share-share $s_{ji} = h_i(j)$.
  3. Upon receiving s_{ij} from P_j check whether $s_{ij} = g_i(j)$. If so broadcast (ok, i, j).

---

[4] We denote their sharing protocol by Share₁, as it allows to share only one single value.

- OUTPUT-COMPUTING — CODE FOR PLAYER P_i:
  1. Wait until there is a $(n - t)$-clique in the graph implicitly defined by the broadcasted confirmations.[5]
  2. Upon receiving at least $2t + 1$ t-consistent share-shares s_{ij} (for $j \in \{1, \ldots, n\}$) from the players in the clique, find the interpolation polynomial $\widetilde{g}_i(\cdot)$ and (re)compute your share $s_i = \widetilde{g}_i(0)$.[6]
  3. Output the share s_i.

Lemma 1. *For every coalition of up to t bad players and every scheduler, the protocol Share_1 achieves the following properties:*

- *Termination: If the dealer is correct, then every correct player will eventually complete Share_1, and if some correct player has completed Share_1, then all the correct players will eventually complete Share_1.*
- *Correctness: Once a correct player has completed Share_1, then there exists a unique value r which is t-shared among the players, where $r = s$ if the dealer is correct.*
- *Privacy: If the dealer is correct, then the adversary obtains no information about the shared secret.*

The communication complexity of Share_1 is $\mathcal{O}(n^2\kappa + n^2\mathcal{BC}(\kappa))$.

The intuition behind the protocol Recons is the following: Every player P_i sends his share s_i to P_R. The receiver waits until receiving at least $d+t+1$ d-consistent shares and outputs the value of their interpolation polynomial at 0. Note that corrupted players can send false shares to P_R, but for the latest when P_R has received the shares of all honest players, he has at least $n - t \geq d + t + 1$ t-consistent shares (for $t < n/4$ and $d \leq 2t$).

Protocol Recons (Receiver P_R, degree d, d-sharing of s)
- CODE FOR PLAYER P_i: Send s_i to P_R.
- CODE FOR RECEIVER P_R: Upon receiving at least $d + t + 1$ d-consistent shares s_i (and up to t inconsistent shares), interpolate the polynomial $p(\cdot)$ and output $s = p(0)$.

Lemma 2. *For any d-shared value s, where $d + 2t < n$, for every coalition of up to t bad players, and for every scheduler, the protocol Recons achieves the following properties:*

- *Termination: Every correct player will eventually complete Recons.*
- *Correctness: P_R will output s.*
- *Privacy: When P_R is honest, then the adversary obtains no information about the shared secret.*

The communication complexity of the protocol Recons is $\mathcal{O}(n\kappa)$.

Note that for $t < n/4$, Recons can be used to reconstruct t-sharings as well as $2t$-sharings. However, the protocol Share_1 can only generate t-sharings.

---

[5] The graph has n nodes representing the n players and there is an edge between i and j if and only if both (ok, i, j) and (ok, j, i) were broadcasted.

[6] If the dealer is correct or if P_i is a member of the clique $g_i(\cdot) = \widetilde{g}_i(\cdot)$.

Proofs of security as well as details on solving the clique-problem in $\mathsf{Share_1}$ (respectively, reducing it to a computationally simpler problem) and on finding (and interpolating) $d + t + 1$ d-consistent shares in Recons, can be found in [BCG93].

4.3 Share*: Sharing Many Values at Once

The following protocol $\mathsf{Share^*}$ extends the protocol $\mathsf{Share_1}$ in two ways: First, it allows the dealer to share a vector $(s^{(1)}, \ldots, s^{(\ell)})$ of ℓ secrets at once, substantially more efficient than ℓ independent invocations of $\mathsf{Share_1}$. Secondly, $\mathsf{Share^*}$ allows to share "empty" secrets, formally $s^{(k)} = \perp$, resulting in all shares of $s^{(k)}$ being $\perp$ as well. This will be used when a dealer should share an unknown value.

Protocol Share* (Dealer P_D, secrets $(s^{(1)}, \ldots, s^{(\ell)}) \in (\mathcal{F} \cup \{\perp\})^\ell$)

- DISTRIBUTION — CODE FOR DEALER P_D: For every $s^{(k)} \neq \perp$, choose a random two-dimensional degree-t polynomial $f^{(k)}(\cdot, \cdot)$ with $f^{(k)}(0,0) = s^{(k)}$. Send to every P_i the polynomials $(g_i^{(1)}, h_i^{(1)}, \ldots, g_i^{(\ell)}, h_i^{(\ell)})$, where $g_i^{(k)}(\cdot) = f^{(k)}(i, \cdot)$ and $h_i^{(k)}(\cdot) = f^{(k)}(\cdot, i)$ if $s^{(k)} \in \mathcal{F}$, and $g_i^{(k)} = h_i^{(k)} = \perp$ if $s^{(k)} = \perp$.

- CONSISTENCY CHECKS — CODE FOR PLAYER P_i:
  1. Wait for $(g_i^{(1)}, h_i^{(1)}, \ldots, g_i^{(\ell)}, h_i^{(\ell)})$ from P_D.
  2. To each P_j send $(s_{ji}^{(1)}, \ldots, s_{ji}^{(\ell)})$, where $s_{ji}^{(k)} = h_i^{(k)}(j)$, resp. $s_{ji}^{(k)} = \perp$ if $h_i^{(k)} = \perp$.
  3. Upon receiving $(s_{ij}^{(1)}, \ldots, s_{ij}^{(\ell)})$ from P_j, broadcast (ok, i, j) if for all $k = 1, \ldots, \ell$ it holds that $s_{ij}^{(k)} = g_i^{(k)}(j)$, resp. $s_{ij}^{(k)} = \perp = g_i^{(k)}$.

- OUTPUT-COMPUTING — CODE FOR PLAYER P_i:
  1. Wait until there is a $(n-t)$-clique in the graph defined by the broadcasted confirmations.
  2. For $k = 1, \ldots, \ell$, upon receiving at least $2t + 1$ t-consistent share-shares $s_{ij}^{(k)}$ (for $j \in \{1, \ldots, n\}$) from the players in the clique, find the interpolation polynomial $\widetilde{g}_i^{(k)}(\cdot)$ and (re)compute the share $s_i^{(k)} = \widetilde{g}_i^{(k)}(0)$. Upon receiving $2t + 1$ values $s_{ij}^{(k)} = \perp$ (for $j \in \{1, \ldots, n\}$), set $s_i^{(k)} = \perp$.
  3. Output the shares $(s_i^{(1)}, \ldots, s_i^{(\ell)})$.

Lemma 3. *The protocol* $\mathsf{Share^*}$ *allows* P_D *to share* ℓ *secrets from* $\mathcal{F} \cup \{\perp\}$ *at once, with the same security properties as required in Lemma 1. The communication complexity of* $\mathsf{Share^*}$ *is* $\mathcal{O}(\ell n^2 \kappa + n^2 \mathcal{BC}(\kappa))$.

5 Preparation Phase

The goal of the preparation phase is to generate t-sharings of ℓ uniformly random values $r^{(1)}, \ldots, r^{(\ell)}$, unknown to the adversary, where ℓ will be $c_M(3t + 1) + c_R$.

The idea of the protocol $\mathsf{PreparationPhase}$ is the following: First, every player acts as dealer in $\mathsf{Share^*}$ to share a vector of $\ell' = \lceil \ell/(n - 2t) \rceil$ random values.

Then the players agree on a core set of $n - t$ correct dealers (such that their Share* protocol was completed by at least one honest player). This results in $n - t$ vectors of ℓ' correct t-sharings, but up to t of these vectors may be known to the adversary (and may not be random). Then, these $n - t$ correct vectors are compressed to $n - 2t$ correct *random* vectors, unknown to the adversary, by using a $(n - 2t)$-by-$(n - t)$ super-invertible matrix (applied component-wise). This computation is linear, hence the players can compute their shares of the compressed sharings locally from their shares of the original sharings.

Protocol PreparationPhase (ℓ)
Code for player P_i:
- SECRET SHARING
  - Act as a dealer in Share* to share a vector of $\ell' = \lceil \ell/(n - 2t) \rceil$ random values $\left(s^{(i,1)}, \ldots, s^{(i,\ell')}\right)$.
  - For every $j = 1, \ldots, n$, take part in Share* with dealer P_j, resulting in the shares $\left(s_i^{(j,1)}, \ldots, s_i^{(j,\ell')}\right)$.
- AGREEMENT ON A CORE SET
  1. Create an accumulative set $C_i = \emptyset$.
  2. Upon completing Share* with dealer P_j, include P_j in C_i.
  3. Take part in ACS with the accumulative set C_i as input.
- COMPUTE OUTPUT (LOCAL COMPUTATION)
  1. Wait until ACS completes with output C. For simple notation, assume that $\{P_1, \ldots, P_{n-t}\} \subseteq C$.
  2. For every $k \in \{1, \ldots, \ell'\}$, the $(n - 2t)$ t-shared random values, unknown to the adversary, are defined as $\left(r^{(1,k)}, \ldots, r^{(n-2t,k)}\right) = M\left(s^{(1,k)}, \ldots, s^{(n-t,k)}\right)$, where M denotes a $(n - 2t)$-by-$(n - t)$ super-invertible matrix, e.g., constructed according to Section 2.6. Compute your shares $\left(r_i^{(1,k)}, \ldots, r_i^{(n-2t,k)}\right)$ accordingly. Denote the resulting $\ell'(n - 2t) \geq \ell$ sharings as $[r^{(1)}], \ldots, [r^{(\ell)}]$.

Lemma 4. PreparationPhase *(eventually) terminates for every honest player. It outputs independent random sharings of ℓ secret, independent, uniformly random values $r^(1), \ldots, r^{(\ell)}$. PreparationPhase communicates $\mathcal{O}(\ell n^2 \kappa + n^3 \mathcal{BC}(\kappa))$ bits and requires one invocation to ACS.*

6 Input Phase

In the InputPhase protocol every player P_i acts as a dealer in one Share* protocol in order to share his input s_i.[7] However the asynchrony of the network does not allow the players to wait for more than $n - t$ Share*-protocols to be completed. In order to agree on the players whose inputs will be taken into to computation one ACS protocol is run.

---

[7] s_i can be one value or an arbitrary long vector of values from $\mathcal{F}$.

Protocol InputPhase (Every P_i has input s_i)
Code for player P_i:
- SECRET SHARING
  - Share your secret input s_i with Share*.
  - For every $j = 1, \ldots, n$ take part in Share* with dealer P_j.
- AGREEMENT ON A CORE SET
  1. Create a accumulative set $C_i = \emptyset$.
  2. Upon completing Share* with dealer P_j, include P_j in C_i.
  3. Take part in ACS with your accumulative set C_i as your input.
  4. Output the agreed core set C and your outputs of the Share* protocols with dealers from C.

Lemma 5. *The* InputPhase *protocol will (eventually) terminate for every honest player. It enables the players to agree on a core set of at least $n - t$ players who correctly shared their inputs – every honest player will (eventually) complete the* Share* *protocol of every dealer from the core set (and get the correct shares of his shared input values).* InputPhase *communicates $\mathcal{O}(c_I n^2 \kappa + n^3 \mathcal{BC}(\kappa))$ bits and requires one invocation to* ACS.

7 Computation Phase

In the computation phase, the circuit is evaluated gate by gate, whereby all inputs and intermediate values are shared among the players. As soon as a player holds his shares of the input values of a gate, he joins the computation of the gate.

Due to the linearity of the secret-sharing scheme, linear gates can be computed locally simply by applying the linear function to the shares, i.e. for any linear function $f(\cdot, \cdot)$, a sharing $[c] = [f(a, b)]$ is computed by letting every player P_i compute $c_i = f(a_i, b_i)$. With every random gate, one random sharing (from the preparation phase) is associated, which is directly used as outcome of the random gate. With every multiplication gate, $3t + 1$ random sharings (from the preparation phase) are associated, which are used to compute a sharing of the product as described in the protocol Multiplication.

Protocol ComputationPhase ($(3t + 1)c_M + c_R$ random sharings $[r^{(1)}], \ldots, [r^{(\ell)}]$)
For every gate in the circuit — Code for player P_i:

1. Wait until you have shares of each of the inputs
2. Depending on the type of the gate, proceed as follows:
   - Linear gate $[c] = f([a], [b], \ldots)$: compute your share c_i as $c_i = f(a_i, b_i, \ldots)$.
   - Multiplication gate $[c] = [a][b]$: participate in protocol Multiplication($[a], [b], [r^{(0)}], \ldots, [r^{(3t+1)}]$), where $[r^{(0)}], \ldots, [r^{(3t+1)}]$ denote the $3t + 1$ associated random sharing.

- Random gate $[r]$: set your share $r_i = r_i^{(k)}$, where $[r^{(k)}]$ denotes the associated random sharing.
- Output gate $[a] \to P_R$: participate in $\mathsf{Recons}(P_R, d = t, [a])$.

In order to compute multiplication gates, we use the approach of of [DN07]: First, the players jointly generate a secret random value s, which is both t-shared (by $[s]$) and $2t$-shared (by $[[s]]$). These sharings can easily be generated based on the $3t + 1$ t-sharings associated with the multiplication gate. Then, every player locally multiplies his shares of a and b, resulting in a $2t$-sharing of the product $c = ab$, i.e., $[[c]]$. Then, the players compute and reconstruct $[[c - s]]$, resulting in every player knowing $d = c - s$, pick a default t-sharing $[d]$, and (locally) compute $[c] = [d] + [s]$, the correct product $[ab]$.

Protocol Multiplication $([a], [b], [r^{(0)}], \ldots, [r^{(3t+1)}])$
Code for player P_i:

1. PREPARE $[s]$: The degree-t polynomial $p(\cdot)$ to share s is defined by the shared coefficients $r^{(0)}, r^{(1)}, \ldots, r^{(t)}$. For every P_j, a sharing of his share $s_j = p(j)$ is defined as $[s_j] = [r^{(0)}] + [r^{(1)}]j + \ldots + [r^{(t)}]j^t$. Invoke $\mathsf{Recons}(P_j, d = t, [s_j])$ to let P_j learn his degree-t share s_j.

2. PREPARE $[[s]]$: The degree-$2t$ polynomial $p'(\cdot)$ to share s is defined by the shared coefficients $r^{(0)}, r^{(t+1)}, \ldots, r^{(3t)}$. For every P_j, a sharing of his share $s'_j = p'(j)$ is defined as $[s'_j] = [r^{(0)}] + [r^{(t+1)}]j + \ldots + [r^{(3t)}]j^{2t}$. Invoke $\mathsf{Recons}(P_j, d = t, [s'_j])$ to let P_j learn his degree-$2t$ share s'_j.

3. COMPUTE $[ab]$:

   1. Compute your degree-$2t$ share of $c = ab$ as $c_i = a_i b_i$, resulting in $[[c]]$.
   2. For every $j = 1, \ldots, n$, invoke $\mathsf{Recons}\ (P_j, d = 2t, ([[c]] - [[s]]))$, resulting in every P_j knowing $d = c - s$.
   3. Define $[d]$ as default sharing of d, e.g., the constant degree-0 polynomial.
   4. Compute $[c] = [d] + [s]$.

Lemma 6. *The protocol* Multiplication *(eventually) terminates for every honest player. Given correct sharings $[a], [b], [r^{(0)}], \ldots, [r^{(3t+1)}]$ as input, it outputs a correct sharing $[ab]$. The privacy is maintained when $([r^{(0)}], \ldots, [r^{(3t+1)}])$ are sharings of random values unknown to the adversary.* Multiplication *communicated $\mathcal{O}(n^2 \kappa)$ bits.*

Lemma 7. *The protocol* ComputationPhase *(eventually) terminates for every honest player. Given that the $\ell = (3t + 1)c_M + c_R$ sharings $[r^{(1)}], \ldots, [r^{(\ell)}]$ are correct t-sharings of random values, unknown to the adversary, it computes the outputs of the circuit correctly and privately, while communicating $\mathcal{O}(n^2 c_M + nc_O \kappa)$ bits (where c_M, c_R, and c_O denote the number of multiplication, random, and output gates in the circuit, respectively).*

8   The Asynchronous MPC Protocol

The following protocol allows the players to evaluate an agreed arithmetic circuit C of a finite field $\mathcal{F}$: Denote the number of input, multiplication, random and output gates as c_I, c_M, c_R, c_O, respectively.

Protocol AsyncMPC (C, c_I, c_M, c_R, c_O)
1. Invoke PreparationPhase to generate $\ell = c_M(3t + 1) + c_R$ random sharings.
2. Invoke InputPhase to let the players share their inputs.
3. Invoke ComputationPhase to evaluate the circuit (consisting of linear, multiplication, random, and output gates).

Theorem 1. *For every coalition of up to $t < n/4$ bad players and for every scheduler, the protocol AsyncMPC securely computes the circuit C. AsyncMPC communicates $\mathcal{O}\big((c_I n^2 + c_M n^3 + c_R n^2 + n c_O)\kappa + n^3 \mathcal{BC}(\kappa)\big)$ bits and requires 2 invocations to ACS,[8] (which requires $\mathcal{O}(n^2 \mathcal{BC}(\kappa))$).*

9   The Hybrid Model

9.1   Motivation

A big disadvantage of asynchronous networks is the fact that the inputs of up to t honest players cannot be considered in the computation. This restriction disqualifies fully asynchronous models for many real-world applications. Unfortunately, this drawback is intrinsic to the asynchronous model, no (what so ever clever) protocol can circumvent it. The only escape is to move to less general communication models, where at least some restriction on the scheduling of messages is given.

In [HNP05], an asynchronous (cryptographically secure) MPC protocol was presented in which all players can provide their inputs, given that one single round of communication is synchronous. However, this protocol has two serious drawbacks: First, the communication round which is required to be synchronous is round number 7 (we say that a message belongs to round k if it depends on a message received in round $k - 1$). This essentially means that *the first 7 rounds* must be synchronous, because if not, then the synchronous round can never be started (the players would have to wait until all messages of round 6 are delivered — an endless wait in an asynchronous network).

The second drawback of this protocol is that one must decide a priori the mode in which the protocol is to be executed, namely either in the hybrid mode (with the risk that the protocol fails when some message in the first 7 rounds is not delivered synchronously), or in the fully asynchronous mode (with the risk that up to t honest players cannot provide their input, even when the network is synchronous).

---

[8] The protocol can easily be modified to use only a single invocation to ACS, by invoking PreparationPhase and InputPhase in parallel, and invoking ACS to find those dealers who have both correctly shared their input(s) as well as correctly shared enough random values.

9.2 Our Hybrid Model

We follow the approach of [HNP05], but strengthen it in both mentioned directions: First, we require only *the very first round* to be synchronous, and second, we guarantee that even if some messages in the first round are not delivered synchronously, still at least $n - t$ inputs are provided — so to speak the best of both worlds. A bit more precisely, we provide a fully asynchronous input protocol with the following properties:

- For every scheduler, the inputs of at least $n - t$ players are taken.
- If all messages sent by P_i in the very first round of communication are delivered synchronously, then P_i's inputs are taken.

This means in particular that if the first round is fully synchronous, then the inputs of all honest players are taken, and if the network is fully asynchronous, then at least $n - t$ inputs are taken.

9.3 PrepareInputs and RestoreInput

We briefly describe the idea of the new input protocol (assuming, for the sake of simple notation, that every player gives exactly one input): In the first (supposedly synchronous) round, every player computes a degree-t Shamir-sharing of his input and sends one share to each player. Then, the players invoke the fully asynchronous input protocol, where the input of each player is a vector consisting of his real input, and his shares of the inputs of the other players. As result of the asynchronous input protocol, a core set C of at least $n - t$ players is found, whose input vectors are (eventually) t-shared among the players. For every player $P_i \in C$, the input is directly taken from his input vector. For every player $P_j \notin C$, the input is computed as follows: There are $n - t$ shares of his input, each t-shared as a component of the input vector of some player $P_i \in C$. Up to t of these players might be corrupted and have input a wrong share. Therefore, these t-shared shares are error-corrected and used as P_j's input. For error correction, $t + 1$ random t-sharings are used. These will be generated (additionally) in the preparation phase. Then, right before the computation phase, sharings of the missing inputs are computed.

In the following, we present a (trivial) sub-protocol PrepareInputs, which prepares the inputs of all players (to be invoked in the first, supposedly synchronous round), and a protocol RestoreInput, which restores the sharing of an input $s^{(k)}$ of a player not in the core set, if possible (to be invoked right before the computation phase). The protocol RestoreInput needs $t + 1$ t-sharings of random values, which must be generated in the preparation phase.

Protocol PrepareInputs (every P_i holding input $s^{(i)}$)
Code for player P_i:

1. Choose random degree-t polynomial $p(\cdot)$ with $p(0) = s^{(i)}$ and send to every P_j his share $s_j^{(i)} = p(j)$.

2. Collect shares $s_i^{(j)}$ (from P_j) till the first round is over. Then compose your new input $\tilde{s}^{(i)} = \left(s^{(i)}, s_i^{(1)}, \ldots, s_i^{(n)}\right)$, where $s_i^{(j)} = \bot$ if no share $s_i^{(j)}$ was received from P_j within the first round.

Protocol RestoreInput (Core Set C, Input Sharings $[\tilde{s}^{(i)}]$ of $P_i \in C$, $[r^{(0)}], \ldots, [r^{(t+1)}], k$)
Code for player P_i:

1. Define the blinding polynomial $b(x) = r^{(0} + r^{(1)}x + \ldots + r^{(t)}x^t$, and for every P_j, define $[b_j] = [b(j)] = [r^{(0)}] + [r^{(1)}]j + \ldots + [r^{(t)}]j^t$. Invoke Recons to reconstruct b_j towards P_j, for every P_j.

2. For every $P_j \in C$, denote by $[s_j^{(k)}]$ the sharing of P_j's share of P_k's input $s^{(k)}$. Note that $[s_j^{(k)}]$ is a part of the input vector $[\tilde{s}^{(j)}]$. If $[s_j^{(k)}] \neq \bot$, then compute $[d_j] = [s_j^{(k)}] + [b_j]$, and invoke Recons to reconstruct d_j towards every player.

3. If there exists a degree-t polynomial $p(\cdot)$ such that at least $2t + 1$ of the reconstructed values d_j lie on it, define $d_i' = p(i)$, and compute your share $s_i^{(k)}$ of P_k's input $s^{(k)}$ as $d_i' - b_i$. The sharing of input $[s^{(k)}]$ was successfully restored. If no such polynomial $p(\cdot)$ exists, then $[s^{(k)}]$ cannot be restored.

Lemma 8. *The protocol PrepareInputs and RestoreInput terminate for all players. When all messages of a player P_k in Step 1 of PrepareInputs are synchronously delivered, then a sharing of his input $s^{(k)}$ can be successfully restored in RestoreInput, by any core set C with $C \geq n - t$ (with up to t cheaters. When an input sharing $[s^{(k)}]$ of an honest player P_k is restored in RestoreInput, then the shared value is the correct input of P_k. Furthermore, both PrepareInputs and RestoreInput preserve the privacy of inputs of honest players.*

Proof (sketch). Termination and privacy are easy to verify. We focus on correctness. First assume that P_k is honest, and all his messages in Round 1 of PrepareInputs were synchronously delivered. Then every honest player P_i embeds the share $s_i^{(k)}$ in his input vector. There will be at least $n - t$ players in the core set, so at least $n - 2t$ honest players P_j. This means that there are at least $n - 2t$ t-consistent shares $s_j^{(k)}$, and hence, at least $n - 2t$ consistent shares d_j. For $t < n/4$, we have $n - 2t \geq 2t + 1$, and the result is a sharing of $d - b = (s^{(k)} + b) - b = s^{(k)}$. Then assume that P_k is honest, but not all his messages in Round 1 have been delivered synchronously. However, if there are $2t+1$ points on the polynomial $p(\cdot)$, at least $t+1$ of these points are from honest players, and hence the right input is restored.

9.4   The Hybrid MPC Protocol

The new main protocol for the hybrid model is as follows:

Protocol HybridMPC (C, c_I, c_M, c_R, c_O)
1. Invoke PrepareInputs to let every P_i with input $s^{(i)}$ Shamir share $s^{(i)}$ among all players.

2. Invoke PreparationPhase to generate $\ell = c_M(3t + 1) + c_R + c_I(t + 1)$ random sharings.
3. Invoke InputPhase (with P_i's input being the vector $\widetilde{s}^{(i)}$) to let the players share their input vectors.
4. Invoke RestoreInput to restore the inputs of every P_k not in the core set.
5. Invoke ComputationPhase to evaluate the circuit (consisting of linear, multiplication, random, and output gates).

Theorem 2. *For every coalition of up to $t < n/4$ bad players and for every scheduler, the protocol HybridMPC securely computes the circuit C, taking the inputs of all players (when the first round is synchronous), or taking the inputs of at least $n - t$ players (independently of any scheduling assumptions). AsyncMPC communicates $\mathcal{O}((c_I n^3 + c_M n^3 + c_R n^2 + n c_O)\kappa + n^3 \mathcal{BC}(\kappa))$ bits and requires 2 invocations to ACS (can be reduced to 1).*

10   Conclusions

We have presented an MPC protocol for the fully asynchronous model, which is perfectly secure against an active, adaptive adversary, corrupting up to $t < n/4$ players, what is optimal. The protocol communicates only $\mathcal{O}(n^3)$ field elements per multiplication. Even in the synchronous model, no perfectly secure MPC protocol with better communication complexity is known. Furthermore, the protocol is as efficient as the most efficient protocol for the asynchronous model, which provides only cryptographic security.

Furthermore, we have enhanced the protocol for a hybrid communication mode, where the inputs of all players can be taken under the only assumption that the very first communication round is synchronous. This assumption is very realistic, as anyway the players have to agree on set of involved players, on the circuit to be evaluated, etc. The proposed protocol combines best of both the hybrid model and the fully asynchronous model; it allows at least $n - t$ players provide their input (even when the communication is fully asynchronous), and additionally guarantees that the input of every player is taken, as long as his first-round messages are delivered synchronously.

Lastly, the proposed protocol is conceptually very simple. It uses neither player elimination nor repetition.

References

[BCG93]   Ben-Or, M., Canetti, R., Goldreich, O.: Asynchronous secure computation. In: Proc. 25th STOC, pp. 52–61 (1993)
[Bea91]   Beaver, D.: Secure multiparty protocols and zero-knowledge proof systems tolerating a faulty minority. Journal of Cryptology, 75–122 (1991)
[BGW88]   Ben-Or, M., Goldwasser, S., Wigderson, A.: Completeness theorems for non-cryptographic fault-tolerant distributed computation. In: Proc. 20th STOC, pp. 1–10 (1988)

[BH06]   Beerliova-Trubiniova, Z., Hirt, M.: Efficient multi-party computation with dispute control. In: Halevi, S., Rabin, T. (eds.) TCC 2006. LNCS, vol. 3876, pp. 305–328. Springer, Heidelberg (2006)

[BKR94]   Ben-Or, M., Kelmer, B., Rabin, T.: Asynchronous secure computations with optimal resilience (extended abstract). In: Proc. 13th PODC, pp. 183–192 (1994)

[Bra84]   Bracha, G.: An asynchronous $\lfloor(n-1)/3\rfloor$-resilient consensus protocol. In: Proc. 3rd PODC, pp. 154–162 (1984)

[Can95]   Canetti, R.: Studies in Secure Multiparty Computation and Applications. PhD thesis, Weizmann Institute, Israel (June 1995)

[CCD88]   Chaum, D., Crépeau, C., Damgård, I.: Multiparty unconditionally secure protocols (extended abstract). In: Proc. 20th STOC, pp. 11–19 (1988)

[CDG87]   Chaum, D., Damgård, I., van de Graaf, J.: Multiparty computations ensuring privacy of each party's input and correctness of the result. In: Pomerance, C. (ed.) CRYPTO 1987. LNCS, vol. 293, pp. 87–119. Springer, Heidelberg (1988)

[DN07]   Damgård, I., Nielsen, J.B.: Robust multiparty computation with linear communication complexity. In: CRYPTO 2007. LNCS, vol. 4622, Springer, Heidelberg (2007)

[GHY87]   Galil, Z., Haber, S., Yung, M.: Cryptographic computation: Secure fault-tolerant protocols and the public-key model. In: Pomerance, C. (ed.) CRYPTO 1987. LNCS, vol. 293, pp. 135–155. Springer, Heidelberg (1988)

[GMW87]   Goldreich, O., Micali, S., Wigderson, A.: How to play any mental game — a completeness theorem for protocols with honest majority. In: Proc. 19th STOC, pp. 218–229 (1987)

[HMP00]   Hirt, M., Maurer, U., Przydatek, B.: Efficient secure multi-party computation. In: Okamoto, T. (ed.) ASIACRYPT 2000. LNCS, vol. 1976, pp. 143–161. Springer, Heidelberg (2000)

[HN06]   Hirt, M., Nielsen, J.B.: Robust multiparty computation with linear communication complexity. In: Dwork, C. (ed.) CRYPTO 2006. LNCS, vol. 4117, pp. 463–482. Springer, Heidelberg (2006)

[HNP05]   Hirt, M., Nielsen, J.B., Przydatek, B.: Cryptographic asynchronous multiparty computation with optimal resilience. In: Cramer, R.J.F. (ed.) EUROCRYPT 2005. LNCS, vol. 3494, pp. 322–340. Springer, Heidelberg (2005)

[PSR02]   Prabhu, B., Srinathan, K., Rangan, C.P.: Asynchronous unconditionally secure computation: An efficiency improvement. In: Menezes, A.J., Sarkar, P. (eds.) INDOCRYPT 2002. LNCS, vol. 2551, Springer, Heidelberg (2002)

[RB89]   Rabin, T., Ben-Or, M.: Verifiable secret sharing and multiparty protocols with honest majority. In: Proc. 21st STOC, pp. 73–85 (1989)

[Sha79]   Shamir, A.: How to share a secret. Communications of the ACM 22, 612–613 (1979)

[SR00]   Srinathan, K., Rangan, C.P.: Efficient asynchronous secure multiparty distributed computation. In: Roy, B., Okamoto, E. (eds.) INDOCRYPT 2000. LNCS, vol. 1977, Springer, Heidelberg (2000)

[Yao82]   Yao, A.C.: Protocols for secure computations. In: Proc. 23rd FOCS, pp. 160–164 (1982)

Efficient Byzantine Agreement
with Faulty Minority[*]

Zuzana Beerliová-Trubíniová, Martin Hirt, and Micha Riser

ETH Zurich, Department of Computer Science
{bzuzana,hirt}@inf.ethz.ch, micha@povworld.org

Abstract. Byzantine Agreement (BA) among n players allows the players to agree on a value, even when up to t of the players are faulty.

In the broadcast variant of BA, one dedicated player holds a message, and all players shall learn this message. In the consensus variant of BA, every player holds (presumably the same) message, and the players shall agree on this message.

BA is the probably most important primitive in distributed protocols, hence its efficiency is of particular importance.

BA from scratch, i.e., without a trusted setup, is possible only for $t < n/3$. In this setting, the known BA protocols are highly efficient ($\mathcal{O}(n^2)$ bits of communication) and provide information-theoretic security.

When a trusted setup is available, then BA is possible for $t < n/2$ (consensus), respectively for $t < n$ (broadcast). In this setting, only computationally secure BA protocols are reasonably efficient ($\mathcal{O}(n^3\kappa)$ bits). When information-theoretic security is required, the most efficient known BA protocols require $\mathcal{O}(n^{17}\kappa)$ bits of communication per BA, where κ denotes a security parameter. The main reason for this huge communication is that in the information-theoretic world, parts of the setup are *consumed* with every invocation to BA, and hence the setup must be refreshed. This refresh operation is highly complex and communication-intensive.

In this paper we present BA protocols (both broadcast and consensus) with information-theoretic security for $t < n/2$, communicating $\mathcal{O}(n^5\kappa)$ bits per BA.

Keywords: Byzantine agreement, broadcast, consensus, information-theoretic security, multi-party computation, efficiency.

1 Introduction

1.1 Byzantine Agreement, Consensus, and Broadcast

The problem of Byzantine agreement (BA), as originally proposed by Pease, Shostak, and Lamport [PSL80], is the following: n players $P_1, \ldots, P_n$ want to

---

[*] This work was partially supported by the Zurich Information Security Center. It represents the views of the authors.

reach agreement on some message m, but up to t of them are faulty and try to prevent the others from reaching agreement. There are two flavors of the BA problem: In the broadcast problem, a designated player (the sender) holds an input message m, and all players should learn m and agree on it. In the consensus problem, every player P_i holds (supposedly the same) message m_i, and the players want to agree on this message.

More formally, a protocol with P_S giving input m is a *broadcast protocol*, when every honest P_i outputs the same message $m_i' = m'$ for some m' (*consistency*), and when $m' = m$, given that P_S is honest (*validity*). Analogously, a protocol with every player P_i giving input m_i is a *consensus protocol*, when every honest P_i outputs $m_i' = m'$ for some m' (*consistency*), and when $m' = m$, given that every honest P_i inputs the same message $m_i = m$ for some m (*validity*).

1.2   Models and Bounds

We assume that the players are connected with a complete synchronous network of secure channels. Complete means that each pair of players shares a channel. Synchronous means that all players share a common clock and that the message delay in the network is bounded by a constant.

The feasibility of broadcast and consensus depends on whether or not a trusted setup (e.g. a PKI setup) is available. When no trusted setup is available ("from scratch"), then consensus and broadcast are achievable if and only if at most $t < n/3$ players are corrupted. When a trusted setup is available, then consensus is achievable if and only if at most $t < n/2$ players are corrupted, and broadcast is achievable if and only if at most $t < n$ players are corrupted. All bounds can be achieved with information-theoretical security, and the bounds are tight even with respect to cryptographic security. We stress in particular that no broadcast protocol (even with cryptographic intractability assumptions) can exceed the $t < n/3$ bound unless it can rely on a trusted setup [FLM86, Fit03]. The main difference between protocols with information-theoretic security and those with cryptographic security is their efficiency.

1.3   Efficiency of Byzantine Agreement

We are interested in the communication complexity of BA protocols. The *bit complexity* of a protocol is defined as the number of bits transmitted by all honest players during the whole protocol, overall.

In the model without trusted setup, Byzantine agreement among n players is achievable for $t < n/3$ communicating $\mathcal{O}(n^2)$ bits [BGP92, CW92]. In the model with a trusted setup, the communication complexity of BA heavily depends on whether information-theoretic security is required or cryptographic security is sufficient. When cryptographic security is sufficient, then $\mathcal{O}(n^3 \kappa)$ bits are sufficient for reaching agreement, where κ denotes the security parameter [DS83]. When information-theoretic security is desired, then reaching agreement requires at least $\mathcal{O}(n^6 \kappa)$ bits of communication [BPW91, PW96, Fit03].

However, the latter result *consumes* the setup, i.e., a given setup can be used only for one single BA operation. Of course, one can start with a m times larger setup which supports m BA operations, but the number of BA operations is a priori fixed, and the size of the setup grows linearly with the number of intended BA operations. This diametrically contrasts the cryptographic scenario, where a fixed-size setup is sufficient for polynomially many BA operations. In [PW96], a method for *refreshing* the setup is shown: They start with a compact setup, use some part of the setup to perform the effective BA operation, and the remaining setup to generate a new, full-fledged setup. With this approach, a constant-size setup is sufficient for polynomially many BA invocations. However, with every BA invocation, the setup must be refreshed, which requires a communication of $\mathcal{O}(n^{17}\kappa)$ bits [PW96, Fit03]. Hence, when the initial setup should be compact, then the costs for a BA operation of [PW96] is as high as $\mathcal{O}(n^{17}\kappa)$ bits.

1.4   Contributions

We present a protocol for information-theoretically secure Byzantine agreement (both consensus and broadcast) which communicates $\mathcal{O}(n^4\kappa)$ bits when the setup may be consumed (i.e., the number of BA operations per setup is a priori fixed). This contrasts to the communication complexity of $\mathcal{O}(n^6\kappa)$ bits of previous information-theoretically secure BA protocols [BPW91, PW96].

More importantly, we present a refresh operation for our BA protocol, communicating only $\mathcal{O}(n^5\kappa)$ bits, contrasting the complexity of $\mathcal{O}(n^{17}\kappa)$ bits of previous refresh protocols [PW96]. This new results allows for polynomially many information-theoretically secure BA operations from a fixed-size setup, where each BA operations costs $\mathcal{O}(n^5\kappa)$ bits.

This substantial speed-up is primarily due to a new concept, namely that the refresh operation does not need to succeed all the time. Whenever the setup is to be refreshed, the players try to do so, but if they fail, they pick a fresh setup from an a priori prepared stock. Furthermore, using techniques from the player-elimination framework [HMP00], the number of failed refresh operations can be limited to t. Using algebraic information-theoretic pseudo-signatures [SHZI02] for appropriate parameters, the function to be computed in the refresh protocol becomes algebraic, more precisely a circuit over a finite field with multiplicative depth 1. Such a function is very well suited for efficient non-robust computation; in fact, it can be computed based on a simple one-dimensional Shamir-sharing, although $t < n/2$.[1] This allows a very simple refresh protocol with low communication overhead.

Compared to the refresh protocol of [PW96], our refresh protocol has the disadvantage that it requires $t < n/2$, whereas the protocol of [PW96] can cope with $t < n$. However, almost all applications using BA as sub-protocol (like voting, biding, multi-party computation, etc.) inherently require $t < n/2$, hence the limitation on our BA protocol is usually of theoretical relevance only.

---

[1] Note that general MPC protocols for this model need a three-level sharing, namely a two-dimensional Shamir sharing ameliorated with authentication tags [RB89, Bea91, BH06].

2 Preliminaries

2.1 Formal Model

We consider a set of n players $\mathcal{P} = \{P_1, \ldots, P_n\}$, communicating over pairwise secure synchronous channels. Many constructions require a finite field $\mathcal{F}$; we set this field to $\mathcal{F} = GF(2^\kappa)$ where κ is a security parameter (we allow a negligible error probability of $\mathcal{O}(2^{-\kappa})$). To every player $P_i \in \mathcal{P}$, a unique non-zero element $\alpha_i \in \mathcal{F} \setminus \{0\}$ is assigned. The faultiness of players is modeled by a central computationally unlimited adversary adaptively corrupting up to $t < n/2$ players and taking full control over them.

We assume that there is a trusted setup, i.e., before the protocol starts, a fixed probabilistic function $\mathsf{Init} : 1^\kappa \to (\mathsf{state}_1, \ldots, \mathsf{state}_n)$ is run by a trusted party, and every player $P_i \in \mathcal{P}$ secretly receives state_i as his initial state.

2.2 Information-Theoretically Secure Signatures

A classical (cryptographic) signature scheme consists of three algorithms: KeyGen, Sign, and Verify. KeyGen generates two keys, a *signing key* for the signer and a public *verification key*; Sign computes a signature for a given message and a given signing key; and Verify checks whether a signature matches a message for a given verification key. A secure signature scheme must satisfy that every signature created by Sign is accepted by Verify (with the corresponding signing/verification keys, completeness), and without the signing key it is infeasible to compute a signature which is accepted by Verify (unforgeability). Classical signature schemes provide cryptographic security only, i.e., an unbounded forger can always find an accepting signature for any given message, with exhaustive search, using Verify as test predicate.

As an information-theoretically secure signature scheme must be secure even with respect to a computationally unbounded adversary, every verifier must have a different verification key, and these verification keys must be kept private. Thus it cannot be automatically guaranteed that a signature is either valid for all verifiers or for no verifier (it might be valid for one verifier, but invalid for another one). Therefore, an additional property called *transferability* is required: It is impossible for a faulty signer to produce a signature which, with non-negligible probability, is valid for some honest verifier without being valid for some other honest verifier. We say that a signature scheme is information-theoretically secure if it is complete, unforgeable and transferable.

In [SHZI02], a so called (ψ, ψ')-secure signature scheme is presented, which allows the signer to sign a message $m \in \mathcal{F}$ such that any of the players in $\mathcal{P}$ can verify the validity of the signature. As long as the signer signs at most ψ messages and each verifier verifies at most ψ' signatures the success probability of attacks is less then $1/|\mathcal{F}| = 2^{-\kappa}$.

Here, we use a one-time signature scheme (i.e., one setup allows only for one single signature), where every verifier may verify up to $t + 2$ signatures (of the same signer). In context of [SHZI02], this means that we set $\psi = 1$ and $\psi' = t+2$.

By simplifying the notation (and by assuming that $2t + 1 \leq n$), we receive the following scheme:

KeyGen: Key generation takes as input the string 1^κ, and outputs the signing key sk to the signer P_S and the n verification keys $\mathsf{vk}_1, \ldots, \mathsf{vk}_n$ to the respective verifiers $P_1, \ldots, P_n$. The signing key is a random vector $\mathsf{sk} = (p_0, \ldots, p_{n+1}, q_0, \ldots, q_{n+1}) \in \mathcal{F}^{2(n+2)}$, defining the polynomial

$$F_{\mathsf{sk}}(V_1, \ldots, V_{n+1}, M) = \left(p_0 + \sum_{j=1}^{n+1} p_j V_j \right) + M \left(q_0 + \sum_{j=1}^{n+1} q_j V_j \right)$$

$$= p_0 + M q_0 + \sum_{j=1}^{n+1} (p_j + M q_j) V_j.$$

The verification key vk_i of each player $P_i \in \mathcal{P}$ is the vector $\mathsf{vk}_i = (v_{i,1}, \ldots, v_{i,n+1}, x_i, y_i)$, where the values $v_{i,1}, \ldots, v_{i,n+1}$ are chosen uniformly at random from $\mathcal{F}$, and the x_i- and y_i-values characterize the polynomial F_{sk}, when applied to $v_{i,1}, \ldots, v_{i,n+1}$, i.e., $x_i = p_0 + \sum_{j=1}^{n+1} p_j v_{i,j}$ and $y_i = q_0 + \sum_{j=1}^{n+1} q_j v_{i,j}$.

Sign: The signature σ of a message $m \in \mathcal{F}$ is a vector $\sigma = (\sigma_0, \ldots, \sigma_{n+1})$, characterizing the polynomial F_{sk} when applied to m, i.e., $\sigma_j = p_j + m q_j$ for $j = 0, \ldots, n+1$.

Verify: Given a message m, a signature $\sigma = (\sigma_0, \ldots, \sigma_{n+1})$, and the verification key $\mathsf{vk}_i = (v_{i,1}, \ldots, v_{i,n+1}, x_i, y_i)$ of player P_i, the verification algorithm checks whether

$$x_i + m y_i \stackrel{?}{=} \sigma_0 + \sum_{j=1}^{n+1} \sigma_j v_{i,j} \qquad \left(= F_{\mathsf{sk}}(v_{i,1}, \ldots, v_{i,n+1}, m) \right).$$

The protocol has the following sizes: Signing key: $(2n + 4)\kappa$ bits; verification key: $(n+3)\kappa$ bits; signature: $(n+2)\kappa$ bits. The total information distributed for one signature scheme (called *sig-setup*) consists of $(n^2 + 5n + 8)\kappa$ bits.

Note that a sig-setup for the player set $\mathcal{P}$ is trivially also a valid sig-setup for every player subset $\mathcal{P}' \subseteq \mathcal{P}$. We will need this observation later.

3   Protocol Overview

Basically, the new broadcast protocol is the protocol of [DS83], ameliorated with information-theoretically secure signatures [SHZI02]. Similarly to [PW96], we start with a compact (constant-size) setup, which allows only for few broadcasts, and use some of these broadcasts for broadcasting the payload, and some of them to refresh the remaining setup, resulting in a fresh, full-fledged setup.

We borrow ideas from the player-elimination framework [HMP00] to substantially speed-up the refresh protocol: The generation of the new setup is performed non-robustly, i.e., it may fail when an adversary is present, but then the failure is detected by (at least) one honest player. At the end of the refresh protocol, the players jointly decide (using one BA-Operation) whether the refresh has succeeded or not; if yes, they are happy to have generated a new setup. If it failed, they run a fault-handling procedure, which yields a set E of two players, (at least) one of them faulty. As originally the set $\mathcal{P}$ contains an honest majority, also the set $\mathcal{P} \setminus E$ contains an honest majority. So the player set is reduced to $\mathcal{P}' \leftarrow \mathcal{P} \setminus E$ (with at most $t' \leftarrow t - 1$ faulty players).

We are still missing the fresh setup; however, as with each fault-handling, one faulty player is eliminated from the actual player set, faults can occur only t times. For these t cases, we have a stock of t prepared setups, and with each fault, we take one out of this stock. This way it is ensured that at any point in the protocol, we have t' prepared setups on stock, where t' is the maximum number of faulty players in $\mathcal{P}'$. More precisely, the protocol runs as follows:

Initial Setup: The procedure Init generates $2 + 5t$ BA-setups[2]; one for the first BA operation, one for the first invocation of the refresh protocol, and t extra setups for the stock, each consisting of 2 BA-setups for replacing the failed refresh and 3 BA-setups for localizing the set $E \subseteq \mathcal{P}$ in the fault-handling procedure. The actual player set is set to $\mathcal{P}' = \mathcal{P}$ and the maximum number of faulty players in $\mathcal{P}'$ to $t' = t$.

Broadcast/Consensus: To perform a BA operation, the protocol Broadcast, resp. Consensus is invoked with the payload. In parallel, Refresh is invoked to refresh the reduced setup. If successful, Refresh produces two BA-setups using only one single BA operation. If Refresh fails, 5 BA-setups are taken from the stock, an elimination set $E \subseteq \mathcal{P}'$ is localized (using 3 BA's) and eliminated ($\mathcal{P}' \leftarrow \mathcal{P}' \setminus E$, $t' \leftarrow t' - 1$), and the two remaining BA-setups are kept as new state – for the next Broadcast/Consensus operation.

In our presentation, we ignore the fact that faulty players can sent *no* message (or a message in a wrong format) when they are expected to send a message to an honest player. As general rule, we assume that when an honest player does not receive an expected message, he behaves as if he had received the zero-message.

4   Broadcast and Consensus

We present the protocols for the actual broadcast and consensus operation.

Note that the Refresh protocol outputs correct BA setup for $\mathcal{P}'$ only (rather than $\mathcal{P}$). However, as $\mathcal{P} \setminus \mathcal{P}'$ might contain honest players we need to achieve BA in $\mathcal{P}$. We first present the BA protocols for $\mathcal{P}'$, then show how to realize BA in $\mathcal{P}$ using these protocols.

As [SHZI02] signatures can cope only with message in the field $\mathcal{F}$, also our BA protocols are limited to messages $m \in \mathcal{F}$. An extension to longer messages is sketched in Appendix A.

---

[2] Init invokes KeyGen $4 + 10t$ times in parallel for each signer $P_S \in \mathcal{P}$. As will become clear later, $2n$ sig-setups are equivalent to one BA-setup.

We first present a broadcast protocol that allows a sender $P_S \in \mathcal{P}'$ to consistently distribute a message $m \in \mathcal{F}$ to the players in $\mathcal{P}'$.[3] The protocol is essentially the protocol of [DS83], with a simplified description of [Fit03]. In addition, the protocol is modified such that in one protocol run every player verifies at most $\psi' = t+2$ signatures of each signer (as required by our signature scheme).

Every player maintains a set $\mathcal{A}$ of accepted messages, a set $\mathcal{N}$ of newly accepted messages, and (one or several) sets Σ_m of received signatures for a message m.

Protocol Broadcast'

  0. Sender P_S: Send m and the corresponding signature σ_S to all $P_i \in \mathcal{P}'$.

  1. $\forall P_i \in \mathcal{P}'$: If P_i received from the sender a message m together with a valid signature σ_S set $\mathcal{A} = \mathcal{N} = \{m\}$ and $\Sigma_m = \{\sigma_S\}$.

  k. In each Step $k = 2, \ldots, t' + 1$, execute the following sub-steps for every player $P_i \in \mathcal{P}' \setminus \{P_S\}$:

  k.1 For every message $m \in \mathcal{N}$, compute the signature σ_i on m, and send $(m, \Sigma_m \cup \{\sigma_i\})$ to all players in $\mathcal{P}'$. Set $\mathcal{N} = \{\}$.

  k.2 In turn, for every message (m, Σ_m) received in Sub-step $k.1$ do:
   - If $m \in \mathcal{A}$, or if $|\mathcal{A}| \geq 2$, ignore the message,
   - else if Σ_m contains valid signatures from at least k different players in $\mathcal{P}'$, including P_S, include m in $\mathcal{A}$ and in $\mathcal{N}$,
   - else ignore the received message (m, Σ_m) and all further messages from the player who has sent it.

  $t'+2$. $\forall P_i$: if $|\mathcal{A}| = 1$, then accept $m \in \mathcal{A}$ as the broadcasted value. Otherwise, the sender is faulty, and accept $m = \perp$ (or any fixed pre-agreed value from $\mathcal{F}$) as the broadcasted value.

One can easily verify that the protocol **Broadcast'** is as secure as the used signature scheme [DS83, Fit03] and that every player verifies at most $t+2$ signatures from the same signer. Furthermore, every signer P_i issues up to two signatures; however, the second one is for the sole goal of proving to other players that the sender P_S is faulty, and the secrecy of P_i's signing key is not required anymore. Hence, it is sufficient to use a one-time signature scheme, whose unforgeability property is broken once the signer issues two signatures.

To construct a consensus protocol in $\mathcal{P}'$, we use a trick of [Fit04]: Every player needs two sig-setups, a primary scheme for the same purpose as in the above protocol, and an alternative scheme for identifying the message (if there is any) originally held by the majority of the players. During the protocol execution, every player P_i additionally maintains (one or several) sets Σ'_m, containing alternative signatures σ'_j (issued by P_j) for m, where Σ'_m with $|\Sigma'_m| \geq n' - t'$ now "replaces" the sender's signature in the above broadcast protocol. Now we present the consensus protocol for $\mathcal{P}'$, each P_i holding a message $m_i \in \mathcal{F}$:

---

[3] Note that **Broadcast'** will not be used in the paper, it is presented only for the sake of clarity of the protocol **Consensus'**.

Protocol Consensus'

0. $\forall P_i \in \mathcal{P}'$: Send m_i and the corresponding (alternative) signature σ_i' to all players in $\mathcal{P}'$.

1. $\forall P_i \in \mathcal{P}'$: If there exists a message m received (together with a valid signature) from at least $n' - t'$ different players, let Σ_m' denote the set of all these signatures, and set $\mathcal{A} = \mathcal{N} = \{m\}$ and $\Sigma_m = \{\}$. If no such message exists, set $\mathcal{A} = \mathcal{N} = \{\}$.

k. In each Step $k = 2, \ldots, t' + 2$, execute the following sub-steps for every player $P_i \in \mathcal{P}'$:

    k.1 For every message $m \in \mathcal{N}$, compute the signature σ_i on m, and send $(m, \Sigma_m', \Sigma_m \cup \{\sigma_i\})$ to all players in $\mathcal{P}'$. Set $\mathcal{N} = \{\}$.

    k.2 In turn, for every message (m, Σ_m', Σ_m) received in Sub-step k.1 do:
- If $m \in \mathcal{A}$, or if $|\mathcal{A}| \geq 2$, ignore the message,
- else if Σ_m contains valid signatures in the primary scheme from at least $k - 1$ different players in $\mathcal{P}'$, and Σ_m' contains valid signatures in the alternative scheme from at least $n' - t'$ different players in $\mathcal{P}'$, then include m in $\mathcal{A}$ and in $\mathcal{N}$,
- else ignore the received message (m, Σ_m', Σ_m) and all further messages from the player who has sent it.

$t'+3$. $\forall P_i$: if $|\mathcal{A}| = 1$, accept $m \in \mathcal{A}$ as the agreed value, otherwise (there was no pre-agreement) accept $m = \perp$.

The security of the protocol **Consensus'** follows immediately from the security of the protocol **Broadcast'**, and the fact that every player issues at most one signature in the alternative scheme, and each such signature is verified at most $t + 1$ times. The communication complexity of BA in $\mathcal{P}'$ is at most $4n^3|\sigma| + 3n^2\kappa + n^2|\sigma| = (8n^4 + 26n^3 + 9n^2)\kappa$.

Broadcast and consensus in $\mathcal{P}$ can be constructed from consensus in $\mathcal{P}'$:

Protocol Broadcast

1. The sender $P_S \in \mathcal{P}$ sends the message m to every player $P_j \in \mathcal{P}'$.

2. Invoke **Consensus'** to reach agreement on m among $\mathcal{P}'$.

3. Every player $P_i \in \mathcal{P}'$ sends the agreed message m to every player $P_j \in \mathcal{P}$.

4. Every player $P_j \in \mathcal{P}$ accepts the message m which was received most often.

Protocol Consensus

1. Invoke **Consensus'** to reach agreement on m among $\mathcal{P}'$.

2. Every player $P_i \in \mathcal{P}'$ sends the agreed message m to every player $P_j \in \mathcal{P}$.

3. Every player $P_j \in \mathcal{P}$ accepts the message m which was received most often.

The security of these protocols follows from the security of **Consensus'** and from $t' < n'/2$ and $t < n/2$. The communication complexity of BA in $\mathcal{P}$ is at most $(8n^4 + 26n^3 + 11n^2)\kappa$.

5 Refreshing the Setup

5.1 Overview

To "refresh" the setup means to compute a new setup which allows for two BA operations, while this computation consumes only one BA-setup. The protocol Refresh generates the new setup with a special-purpose MPC among the players in $\mathcal{P}'$. This computation is performed *non-robustly*: Every sub-protocol either achieves its intended goal, or it fails. When it fails, then at least one honest player detects the failure. We do not require agreement on the fact whether or not a sub-protocol has failed. Only at the very end of Refresh, the players agree on whether or not a player has detected a failure during the computation (using consensus, thereby consuming one BA-setup). The computation takes only random values as input, so in case of failure, privacy is of no interest.

The computation of the verification keys will not only be non-robust, but even non-detectable, i.e., it might output wrong values without any (honest) player detecting the failure. However, once the verification keys are generated, their correctness is verified, and honest players can detect whether or not there was a failure.

We provide a fault-handling sub-protocol, to be invoked when Refresh fails, which localizes a set $E \subseteq \mathcal{P}'$ of two players, where (at least) one of them is faulty. This allows to reduce the actual player set, thereby reducing the maximum number of faulty players, thereby limiting the number of times Refresh can fail. In this fault-handling sub-protocol, every players sends to some designated player all messages he has received during the course of the protocol, as well as all random elements he sampled (which define the sent messages). Given this information, the designated player can help to compute the set E to eliminate.

In the sequel, we present the used sub-protocols (all of them non-robust), and finally the protocols Refresh and FaultHandling. The protocol Refresh invokes once the protocol Consensus', hence it consumes one valid BA-setup. The protocol FaultHandling invokes 3 times the protocol Broadcast; it requires enough BA-setups for that. However, the protocol FaultHandling is invoked only t times in total, so the required BA-setups can be prepared at beforehand.

For the sake of a simpler presentation, we give to every player P_i a flag fail_i, which is initialized to false, and is set to true once P_i has detected a failure. We say that a protocol *succeeds* when no player has detected a failure; otherwise, the protocol *fails*.

5.2 Secret Sharing

We use standard Shamir sharing [Sha79]. We say that a value a is t'-shared among the players $\mathcal{P}'$ if there exists a degree-t' polynomial $f(\cdot)$ with $f(0) = a$, and every (honest) player $P_i \in \mathcal{P}'$ holds a share $\langle a \rangle_i = f(\alpha_i)$, where α_i is the unique evaluation point assigned to P_i. We denote the collection of shares as $\langle a \rangle$. Observe that we can easily add up shared values, namely $\langle a + b \rangle = (\langle a \rangle_1 + \langle b \rangle_1, \ldots, \langle a \rangle_{n'} + \langle b \rangle_{n'})$. We write $\langle a \rangle + \langle b \rangle$ as a short hand.

In order to let a dealer $P_D \in \mathcal{P}'$ verifiably share a value a according to Shamir sharing, we employ the following (non-robust) protocol (based on the VSS protocol of [BGW88]).

Protocol Share

1. *(Distribution.)* P_D selects the coefficients $c_{0,1}, c_{1,0}, \ldots, c_{t',t'}$ at random, and sets $f(x,y) = a + c_{1,0}x + c_{0,1}y + c_{1,1}xy + \ldots + c_{t',t'}x^{t'}y^{t'}$. Then, to every $P_i \in \mathcal{P}'$, P_D computes and sends the polynomials $f_{i,*}(y) = f(\alpha_i, y)$ and $f_{*,i}(x) = f(x, \alpha_i)$.

2. *(Checking.)* For every pair $P_i, P_j \in \mathcal{P}'$, P_i sends $f_{i,*}(\alpha_j)$ to P_j, who compares the received value with $f_{*,j}(\alpha_i)$. P_j sets $\text{fail}_j = \text{true}$ if some difference is non-zero.

3. *(Output)* Every P_j outputs $\langle a \rangle_i = f_{i,*}(0)$.

Lemma 1. *The protocol Share has the following properties: (Completeness) If all players in $\mathcal{P}'$ correctly follow the protocol, then the protocol succeeds. (Correctness) If the protocol succeeds, then the outputs $(\langle a \rangle_1, \ldots, \langle a \rangle_{n'})$ define a degree-t' polynomial $f(\cdot)$. (Validity & Privacy) If the protocol succeeds and the dealer is honest with input a, then $f(0) = a$ and no subset of t' players obtains any information on a. (Complexity) The protocol communicates at most $(2n^2 - 2n)\kappa$ bits and requires at most $(\frac{1}{4}n^2 + \frac{1}{2}n - \frac{3}{4})\kappa$ random bits.*

The following protocol lets the players in $\mathcal{P}'$ reconstruct a correctly Shamir shared value a towards a designated player $P_R \in \mathcal{P}'$:

Protocol Recons

1. Every player $P_i \in \mathcal{P}'$ sends his share $\langle a \rangle_i$ to the recipient P_R.

2. P_R verifies whether $\langle a \rangle_1, \ldots, \langle a \rangle_{n'}$ lie on a degree-t' polynomial $f(\cdot)$ and outputs $a = f(0)$ if yes. Otherwise, P_R sets $\text{fail}_R = \text{true}$ and outputs $a = 0$.

Lemma 2. *The protocol Recons has the following properties: (Completeness) If all players in $\mathcal{P}'$ correctly follow the protocol, then the protocol succeeds. (Correctness) If the protocol succeeds, then P_R outputs the correct secret a. (Complexity) The protocol communicates at most $(n-1)\kappa$ bits and requires no randomness.*

5.3   Generating Random Values

We present a (trivial) protocol that allows the players to generate a random value $c \in_R \mathcal{F}$, known to all players in $\mathcal{P}'$.

Protocol GenerateRandom

1. $\forall P_i \in \{P_1, \ldots, P_{t'+1}\}$: select a random value $c_i \in_R \mathcal{F}$ and invoke Share to share c_i among $\mathcal{P}'$.

2. The players compute $\langle c \rangle = \sum_{i=1}^{t'+1} \langle c_i \rangle$.

3. $\forall P_k \in \mathcal{P}'$: invoke Recons to reconstruct $\langle c \rangle$ towards player P_k.

Lemma 3. *The protocol* GenerateRandom *has the following properties: (Completeness) If all players in $\mathcal{P}'$ correctly follow the protocol, then the protocol succeeds. (Correctness) If the protocol succeeds, then it generates a uniformly random value $c \in_R \mathcal{F}$, known to all players $P_j \in \mathcal{P}'$. (Complexity) The protocol communicates at most $(n^3 + n^2 - 2n)\kappa$ bits and requires at most $(\frac{1}{8}n^3 + \frac{3}{8}n^2 + \frac{3}{8}n - \frac{5}{8})\kappa$ random bits.*

Proof (sketch). Completeness and complexity follow from inspecting the protocol. We now focus on the case when the protocol succeeds. There is at least one honest player P_h in $\{P_1, \ldots, P_{t'+1}\}$, who chooses his value c_h uniformly at random. As in Step 1, the adversary does not obtain any information about c_h (privacy of Share), and as the values c_i of *every* player $P_i \in \mathcal{P}'$ are fixed after Step 1 (Correctness of Share), c_h is statistically independent of all other values c_j ($j \neq i$). Hence, the sum $c_1 + \ldots + c_{t'+1}$ is uniformly distributed. $\square$

5.4   Generating One Sig-Setup

Recall that a sig-setup for a designated signer P_S consists of the signing key $(p_0, \ldots, p_{n'+1}, q_0, \ldots, q_{n'+1})$, which should be random and known only to the signer P_S, and one verification key $(v_{i,1}, \ldots, v_{i,n'+1}, x_i, y_i)$ for each player $P_i \in \mathcal{P}'$, where the values $v_{i,1}, \ldots, v_{i,n'+1}$ should be random and known only to P_i,[4] and the values x_i and y_i are computed as $x_i = p_0 + \sum_{j=1}^{n'+1} p_j v_{i,j}$ and $y_i = q_0 + \sum_{j=1}^{n'+1} q_j v_{i,j}$, respectively. Table 1 summarizes the steps needed to compute these values.

Table 1. Preparing one sig-setup

Player	Inputs (rand.)			Intermediate (shared)			Outputs
P_S	p_0	$\cdots$	$p_{n'+1}$				
	q_0	$\cdots$	$q_{n'+1}$				
P_1	$v_{1,1}$	$\cdots$	$v_{1,n'+1}$	$p_1 v_{1,1}$	$\cdots\cdots$	$p_{n'+1} v_{1,n'+1}$	$x_1 = p_0 + \sum_k p_k v_{1,k}$
				$q_1 v_{1,1}$	$\cdots\cdots$	$q_{n'+1} v_{1,n'+1}$	$y_1 = q_0 + \sum_k q_k v_{1,k}$
$\cdots$	$\cdots$	$\cdots$	$\cdots$	$\cdots$	$\cdots$	$\cdots$	$\cdots\cdots$
$P_{n'}$	$v_{n',1}$	$\cdots$	$v_{n',n'+1}$	$p_1 v_{n',1}$	$\cdots\cdots$	$p_{n'+1} v_{n',n'+1}$	$x_{n'} = p_0 + \sum_k p_k v_{n',k}$
				$q_1 v_{n',1}$	$\cdots\cdots$	$q_{n'+1} v_{n',n'+1}$	$y_{n'} = q_0 + \sum_k q_k v_{n',k}$

In our protocol, first every player P_i chooses and secret-shares his verification key $(v_{i,1}, \ldots, v_{i,n'+1})$. Then, the players jointly generate three random vectors $(p_0, \ldots, p_{n'+1})$, $(q_0, \ldots, q_{n'+1})$, and $(r_0, \ldots, r_{n'+1})$. The first two of these vectors

---

[4] The randomness of $v_{i,1}, \ldots, v_{i,n'+1}$ is needed for the sole reason of protecting the verifier P_i, hence it must be guaranteed for honest verifiers only.

will serve as signing key, and the third will serve as blinding in the verification of the computation. Then, for each of these three vectors, the values $x_1, \ldots, x_{n'}$, respectively $y_1, \ldots, y_{n'}$ or $z_1, \ldots, z_{n'}$, are computed. This computation is not detectable: It might be that one of the x_i, y_i or z_i values is wrong, and still no honest player has detected a failure (however, when all players correctly follow the protocol, then all values will be correct). The correctness of these values is verified in an additional verification step: Two random challenges ρ and φ are generated, and the linearly combined (and blinded) signing vector $(\rho p_0 + \varphi q_0 + r_0, \ldots, \rho p_{n'+1} + \varphi q_{n'+1} + r_{n'+1})$ is computed, and (distributively) compared with the linearly combined verification keys. If all checks are successful, then (with overwhelming probability) all keys are correctly computed.

Protocol GenerateSignatureSetup

1. *(Generate $v_{i,k}$-values.)* Every $P_i \in \mathcal{P}'$ selects random $v_{i,1}, \ldots, v_{i,n'+1}$ and invokes **Share** to share them.

2. *(Generate p_k-values.)* Invoke **GenerateRandom** $n' + 1$ times to obtain shared $p_0, \ldots, p_{n'+1}$.

3. *(Compute x_i-values.)* For every x_i, execute the following steps:

   3.1 Every $P_j \in \mathcal{P}'$ (locally) computes $c_{i,j} = \sum_{k=1}^{n'+1} \langle p_k \rangle_j \langle v_{i,k} \rangle_j$ and invokes **Share** to share it.

   3.2 The players compute $\langle x_i \rangle = \langle p_0 \rangle + \sum_{j=1}^{n'} \lambda_j \langle c_{i,j} \rangle$, where λ_j denotes the j-th Lagrange coefficient[5].

4. *(Generate q_k/y_i-values.)* Generate $(q_0, \ldots, q_{n'+1})$ and $(y_1, \ldots, y_{n'})$ along the lines of Steps 2–3.

5. *(Generate r_k/z_i-values.)* Generate $(r_0, \ldots, r_{n'+1})$ and $(z_1, \ldots, z_{n'})$ along the lines of Steps 2–3.

6. *(Check correctness of the computed x_i/y_i-values)*

   6.1 Invoke **GenerateRandom** twice to generate random challenges ρ and φ.

   6.2 For $k = 1, \ldots, n' + 1$, compute and reconstruct towards every player $\langle s_k \rangle = \rho \langle p_k \rangle + \varphi \langle q_k \rangle + \langle r_k \rangle$.

   6.3 For $i = 1, \ldots, n'$, compute $\langle w_i \rangle = s_0 + \sum_{k=1}^{n'+1} s_k \langle v_{i,k} \rangle$.

   6.4 For $i = 1, \ldots, n'$, compute $\langle \widetilde{w}_i \rangle = \rho \langle x_i \rangle + \varphi \langle y_i \rangle + \langle z_i \rangle$.

   6.5 For $i = 1, \ldots, n'$, reconstruct to every player $\langle d_i \rangle = \langle w_i \rangle - \langle \widetilde{w}_i \rangle$.

   6.6 Every P_j checks whether $d_i \stackrel{?}{=} 0$ for $i = 1, \ldots, n'$, and sets $\mathsf{fail}_j = \mathsf{true}$ in case of any non-zero value.

7. *(Announce x_i/y_i-values.)* For every $P_i \in \mathcal{P}'$, invoke **Recons** to reconstruct $\langle x_i \rangle$ and $\langle y_i \rangle$ towards P_i.

Lemma 4. *The protocol GenerateSignatureSetup has the following properties: (Completeness) If all players in $\mathcal{P}'$ correctly follow the protocol, then the protocol succeeds. (Correctness) If the protocol succeeds, then (with overwhelming*

---

[5] The j-th Lagrange coefficient can be computed as $\lambda_j = \prod_{i=1, i \neq j}^{n'} \frac{-\alpha_i}{\alpha_j - \alpha_i}$.

probability) it generates a correct signature setup. (Privacy) If the protocol succeeds, then no subset of t' players obtains any information they are not allowed to obtain. (Complexity) The protocol communicates at most $(11n^4 + 4n^3 - 3n^2 - 13n)\kappa$ bits and requires at most $(2n^4 + 4n^3 + 2n^2 + 3)\kappa$ random bits.

Proof (sketch). (Completeness) We consider the case that all players follow the protocol, hence no sub-protocol fails. Observe that for every $i = 1, \ldots, n'$, the points $(\alpha_1, c_{i,1}), \ldots, (\alpha_{n'}, c_{i,n'})$ lie on a degree-$2t'$ polynomial $f_i(\cdot)$ with $f_i(0) = \sum_{k=1}^{n'+1} p_k v_{i,k}$. This polynomial is well defined because $n' > 2t'$, hence we can interpolate $f_i(0)$ with Lagrange's formula.[6] This interpolation is done distributively, i.e., every player P_j shares his $c_{i,j}$, then these sharings are combined using Lagrange's formula, and p_0 is distributively added, resulting in a sharing of $x_i = p_0 + \sum_{k=1}^{n'+1} p_k v_{i,k}$. Similarly, $y_i = q_0 + \sum_{k=1}^{n'+1} q_k v_{i,k}$ and $z_i = r_0 + \sum_{k=1}^{n'+1} r_k v_{i,k}$. Clearly, for any ρ and φ, $(\rho p_0 + \varphi q_0 + r_0) + \sum_{k=1}^{n'+1} (\rho p_k + \varphi q_k + r_k) v_{i,k} = \rho x_i + \varphi y_i + z_i$, hence $d_i = 0$, and no player detects a failure in Step 6.6.

(Correctness) We have to show that when the protocol succeeds, then for $i = 1, \ldots, n'$ holds $x_i = p_0 + \sum_{k=1}^{n'+1} p_k v_{i,k}$ and $y_i = p_0 + \sum_{k=1}^{n'+1} q_k v_{i,k}$. Observe that after Step 5, the values $v_{i,k}, p_k, q_k, r_k, x_i, y_i, z_i$ are fixed (they all are t'-shared). When x_i and y_i do no satisfy the required equation above, then only with negligible probability, for random ρ and φ they satisfy the equation $(\rho p_0 + \varphi q_0 + r_0) + \sum_{k=1}^{n'+1} (\rho p_k + \varphi q_k + r_k) v_{i,k} = \rho x_i + \varphi y_i + z_i$.

(Privacy) We have to show that when the protocol succeeds, every player learns only his respective key (plus some random data he could have generated himself with the same probability). First observe that in Steps 1–5, the only communication which takes place is by invocation of **Share**, which leaks no information to the adversary. In Step 6, the values $s_1, \ldots, s_{n'+1}$ and $d_1, \ldots, d_{n'}$ are reconstructed. Every value s_k is blinded with a random r_k (unknown to the adversary), so is uniformly random from the viewpoint of the adversary. The values d_i are either 0 (and hence the adversary can easily simulate them), or the protocol fails (and all computed values are discarded).

(Complexity) The complexity can be verified by inspecting the protocol. □

5.5   The Refresh-Protocol

In order to refresh a BA-setup, we need to generate two BA-setups, consuming only one BA-setup. Remember that one BA-setup consists of $2n'$ sig-setups (2 for every potential signer); hence, **Refresh** needs to generate $4n'$ sig-setups.

Protocol Refresh

0. $\forall P_i \in \mathcal{P}'$: set $\text{fail}_i = \text{false}$.

1. Invoke **GenerateSignatureSetup** $4n'$ times in parallel to generate 4 sig-setups for each signer $P_S \in \mathcal{P}'$.

---

[6] Note that $f_i(0)$ is arbitrary when a single player is incorrect — something we do not care for when arguing about completeness.

2. $\forall P_i \in \mathcal{P}'$: Send fail_i to every $P_j \in \mathcal{P}'$.

3. $\forall P_j \in \mathcal{P}'$: Set $\mathsf{fail}_j =$ true if any received bits $\mathsf{fail}_i =$ true.

4. Invoke Consensus' with P_j's input being fail_j'. Denote the output as fail.

5. $\forall P_i \in \mathcal{P}'$: send fail to every $P_j \in (\mathcal{P} \setminus \mathcal{P}')$.

6. $\forall P_j \in (\mathcal{P} \setminus \mathcal{P}')$: Set fail as the majority of the received bits.

It is easy to see that Refresh fails when any GenerateSignatureSetup failed for an honest player. On the other hand, when all players follow the protocol, then Refresh succeeds. Refresh communicates $\mathcal{O}(n^5)\kappa$ bits.

5.6   Fault Handling

The following fault-handling procedure is invoked only when Refresh has failed (i.e., the players agree on fail = true). The goal of FaultHandling is to localize a set $E \in \mathcal{P}'$ of two players, such that (at least) one of them is faulty.

FaultHandling exploits the fact that there is no need to maintain the secrecy of the failed Refresh protocol. Basically, in FaultHandling the whole transcript of Refresh is revealed and there will be a message from some player P_i to some player P_j, where P_i claims to have sent some other message than P_j claims to have received — hence either P_i or P_j is lying, and we can set $E = \{P_i, P_j\}$. Unfortunately, it would be too expensive to publicly reveal the whole transcript; instead, the transcript is revealed towards a selected player (e.g. $P_k \in \mathcal{P}'$ with the smallest index k), who searches for the fault and announces it.

We stress that the considered transcript not only contains the messages of all invocations of the protocol GenerateSignatureSetup, but also the messages of the protocol Refresh. This is important because it might be that no fault occurred in GenerateSignatureSetup, but still some (corrupted) player P_i claimed to have $\mathsf{fail}_i = true$.

Protocol FaultHandling

1. Every $P_i \in \mathcal{P}'$ sends to P_k all random values chosen during the course of the protocol Refresh (including all sub-protocols), as well as all values received during the course of Refresh.

2. P_k computes for every P_i the messages P_i should have sent (when being correct) during the course of Refresh; this can be done based on the random values and the received messages of P_i.

3. P_k searches for a message from some player $P_i \in \mathcal{P}'$ to some other player $P_j \in \mathcal{P}'$, where P_i should have sent a message x_i (according to his claimed randomness), but P_j claims to have received x_j, where $x_i \neq x_j$. Denote the index of this message by ℓ.

4. P_k invokes Broadcast to announce (i, j, ℓ, x_i, x_j).

5. P_i invokes Broadcast to announce whether he indeed sent x_i in the ℓ-th message.

6. P_j invokes Broadcast to announce whether he indeed received x_j in the ℓ-th message.

7. If Both P_i and P_j confirm to have sent x_i, respectively to have received x_j, then $E = \{P_i, P_j\}$. If P_i does not confirm to have sent x_i, then $E = \{P_k, P_i\}$. If P_j does not confirm to have received x_j, then $E = \{P_k, P_j\}$.

FaultHandling requires 3 BA invocations and communicates $O(n^5\kappa)$ bits.

6   Conclusions

We have presented a BA protocol for n players that achieves information-theoretic security against $t < n/2$ faulty players, communicating $\mathcal{O}(n^5\kappa)$ bits (for some security parameter κ). The protocol requires a compact constant-size setup, as all BA protocols that tolerate $t \geq n/3$ do (also those with cryptographic security only), and allows for polynomially many BA operations.

This result improves on the existential result of [PW96], which communicates $\mathcal{O}(n^{17}\kappa)$ bits per BA.

References

[Bea91]   Beaver, D.: Secure multiparty protocols and zero-knowledge proof systems tolerating a faulty minority. Journal of Cryptology, 75–122 (1991)

[BGP92]   Berman, P., Garay, J.A., Perry, K.J.: Bit optimal distributed consensus. Computer Science Research, 313–322 (1992)

[BGW88]   Ben-Or, M., Goldwasser, S., Wigderson, A.: Completeness theorems for non-cryptographic fault-tolerant distributed computation. In: Proc. 20th STOC, pp. 1–10 (1988)

[BH06]   Beerliova-Trubiniova, Z., Hirt, M.: Efficient multi-party computation with dispute control. In: Halevi, S., Rabin, T. (eds.) TCC 2006. LNCS, vol. 3876, pp. 305–328. Springer, Heidelberg (2006)

[BPW91]   Baum-Waidner, B., Pfitzmann, B., Waidner, M.: Unconditional Byzantine agreement with good majority. In: Jantzen, M., Choffrut, C. (eds.) STACS 1991. LNCS, vol. 480, pp. 285–295. Springer, Heidelberg (1991)

[CDD+99]   Cramer, R., Damgård, I., Dziembowski, S., Hirt, M., Rabin, T.: Efficient multiparty computations secure against an adaptive adversary. In: Stern, J. (ed.) EUROCRYPT 1999. LNCS, vol. 1592, pp. 311–326. Springer, Heidelberg (1999)

[CW79]   Carter, L., Wegman, M.N.: Universal classes of hash functions. JCSS 18(4), 143–154 (1979) (Preliminary version in Proc. 9st STOC, 1977)

[CW92]   Coan, B.A., Welch, J.L.: Modular construction of a Byzantine agreement protocol with optimal message bit complexity. Information and Computation 97(1), 61–85 (1992)

[DS83]   Dolev, D., Strong, H.R.: Authenticated algorithms for Byzantine agreement. SIAM Journal on Computing 12(4), 656–666 (1983) (Preliminary version in Proc. 14th STOC, 1982)

[Fit03]   Fitzi, M.: Generalized Communication and Security Models in Byzantine Agreement. PhD thesis, ETH Zurich (2003)

[Fit04]   Fitzi, M.: Personal communication (2004)

[FLM86]   Fischer, M.J., Lynch, N.A., Merritt, M.: Easy impossibility proofs for distributed consensus problems. Distributed Computing 1, 26–39 (1986)

[HMP00]   Hirt, M., Maurer, U., Przydatek, B.: Efficient secure multi-party compu-
          tation. In: Okamoto, T. (ed.) ASIACRYPT 2000. LNCS, vol. 1976, pp.
          143–161. Springer, Heidelberg (2000)
[PSL80]   Pease, M., Shostak, R., Lamport, L.: Reaching agreement in the presence
          of faults. Journal of the ACM 27(2), 228–234 (1980)
[PW96]   Pfitzmann, B., Waidner, M.: Information-theoretic pseudosignatures and
          Byzantine agreement for t >= n/3. Technical report, IBM Research (1996)
[RB89]   Rabin, T., Ben-Or, M.: Verifiable secret sharing and multiparty protocols
          with honest majority. In: Proc. 21st STOC, pp. 73–85 (1989)
[Sha79]   Shamir, A.: How to share a secret. Communications of the ACM 22, 612–
          613 (1979)
[SHZI02] Shikata, J., Hanaoka, G., Zheng, Y., Imai, H.: Security notions for uncondi-
          tionally secure signature schemes. In: Knudsen, L.R. (ed.) EUROCRYPT
          2002. LNCS, vol. 2332, pp. 434–449. Springer, Heidelberg (2002)

A   Long Messages

The proposed BA protocols only capture messages $m \in \mathcal{F}$, i.e., κ-bit messages. In order to reach BA on longer messages, one could invoke the according BA protocol several times (once for every κ bit block). However, this would blow up the communication complexity unnecessarily high: BA of a $\ell\kappa$ bit message would require a communication complexity of $\mathcal{O}(\ell n^5 \kappa)$ bits (as opposed to $\mathcal{O}(\ell\kappa n^2 + n^{17}\kappa)$ in [PW96]). In this section, we sketch a construction that allows BA of a $\ell\kappa$ bit message at costs of $\mathcal{O}(\ell\kappa n^2 + n^5\kappa)$ bits.

In order to achieve the stated complexity, we need to replace the protocol Consensus' by Consensus$_{\text{long}}$'. The basic idea of Consensus$_{\text{long}}$' is straight forward: Every player $P_i \in \mathcal{P}'$ sends his message m_i to every other player. Then, the players use Consensus' to reach agreement on a universal hash value. If agreement is achieved, all players output the message with the agreed hash value, otherwise they output $\perp$. The key for the universal hash function is assumed to be pre-shared among the players as part of the BA-setup, and only reconstructed when needed. We also explain how this sharing is prepared in the Refresh protocol.

A.1   Protocol Consensus$_{\text{long}}$'

In the following, we present the protocol Consensus$_{\text{long}}$' among the players in $\mathcal{P}'$, reaching agreement on a $\ell\kappa$ bit message m. The protocol makes use of universal hashing [CW79]. As universal hash with key $k \in \mathcal{F}$, we use the function $U_k : \mathcal{F}^\ell \to \mathcal{F}, (m^{(1)}, \dots, m^{(\ell)}) \mapsto m^{(1)} + m^{(2)}k + \dots + m^{(\ell)}k^{\ell-1}$. The probability that two different messages map to the same hash value for a uniformly chosen key is at most $\ell/|\mathcal{F}|$, which is negligible in our setting with $\mathcal{F} = GF(2^\kappa)$.

Protocol Consensus$_{\text{long}}$'
1. Every $P_i \in \mathcal{P}'$ sends his message m_i to every player $P_j \in \mathcal{P}'$.
2. The players reconstruct the random hash key $k \in \mathcal{F}$, which is part of the BA setup.

3. Every $P_i \in \mathcal{P}'$ computes (for his original message m_i) the universal hash $U_k(m_i)$.[7]

4. The players in $\mathcal{P}'$ invoke Consensus' to reach agreement on the hash value h.

5. If the above consensus fails (i.e., $h = \perp$), then every $P_i \in \mathcal{P}'$ outputs $\perp$. If it succeeds, then every $P_i \in \mathcal{P}'$ outputs that m_j received in Step 1 with $U_k(m_j) = h$.

One can easily see that the above protocol reaches consensus on m, and that it communicates $\mathcal{O}(\ell \kappa n^2)$ plus one invocations of Consensus', i.e., communicates $\mathcal{O}(\ell \kappa n^2 + n^4 \kappa)$ overall.

A.2   Generating the Hash Key

The protocol Consensus$_{long}$' needs a random hash key to be known to all players in $\mathcal{P}'$. We cannot afford to generate this hash key on-line (this would require several invocations of broadcast). Instead, we assume a robust sharing of a random field element to be part of every BA-setup. This sharing is then reconstructed when needed.

As robust sharing, we use the scheme of [CDD+99]. Essentially, this is a two-dimensional Shamir sharing, ameliorated with so called authentication tags. The sharing is constructed non-robustly; in the Share protocol, the players pairwisely check the consistency of the received shares, and fail in presence of faults. The sharing of the hash key is generated as sum of a sharing of each player in $\mathcal{P}'$. Such a sharing can be computed with communicating $\mathcal{O}(n^4 \kappa)$ bits (and without involving broadcast). When the hash key is needed, then the sharing of the actual BA setup is reconstructed towards every player in $\mathcal{P}'$. This is achieved by having every player sending his shares (including the authentication tags) to every other player; this involves a communication of $\mathcal{O}(n^3 \kappa)$ bits.

---

[7] In order to do so, the message m_i is split into blocks $m_i^{(1)}, \ldots, m_i^{(\ell)}$.

Information-Theoretic Security
Without an Honest Majority

Anne Broadbent and Alain Tapp

Université de Montréal
Département d'informatique et de recherche opérationnelle
C.P. 6128, Succ. Centre-Ville, Montréal (Québec), H3C 3J7, Canada
{broadbea,tappa}@iro.umontreal.ca

Abstract. We present six multiparty protocols with information-theoretic security that tolerate an arbitrary number of corrupt participants. All protocols assume pairwise authentic private channels and a broadcast channel (in a single case, we require a simultaneous broadcast channel). We give protocols for *veto, vote, anonymous bit transmission, collision detection, notification* and *anonymous message transmission.* Not assuming an honest majority, in most cases, a single corrupt participant can make the protocol abort. All protocols achieve functionality never obtained before without the use of either computational assumptions or of an honest majority.

Keywords: Multiparty computation, anonymous message transmission, election protocols, collision detection, dining cryptographers, information-theoretic security.

1 Introduction

In the most general case, *multiparty secure computation* enables n participants to collaborate to compute an n-input, n-output function (one per participant). Each participant only learns his private output which, depending on the function, can be the same for each participant. Assuming that private random keys are shared between each pair of participants, we known that every function can be securely computed in the presence of an active adversary if and only if less than $n/3$ participants are corrupt; this fundamental result is due to Michael Ben-Or, Shafi Goldwasser and Avi Wigderson [BGW88] and David Chaum, Claude Crépeau and Ivan Damgård [CCD88]. When a broadcast channel is available, the results of Tal Rabin and Michael Ben-Or [RB89] tell us that this proportion can be improved to $n/2$.

Here, we present six specific multiparty computation protocols that achieve correctness and privacy *without* any assumption on the number of corrupt participants. Naturally, we cannot always achieve the ideal functionality, for example in some cases, a single participant can make the protocol abort. This is the price to pay to tolerate an arbitrary number of corrupt participants and still provide information-theoretic privacy of the inputs.

K. Kurosawa (Ed.): ASIACRYPT 2007, LNCS 4833, pp. 410–426, 2007.

All protocols we propose have polynomial complexity in the number of participants and the security parameter. We always assume pairwise shared private random keys between each pair of participants, which allows pairwise private authentic channels. We also assume a broadcast channel and, even though it is a strong assumption, in some cases we need the broadcast to be simultaneous [CGMA85, HM05].

1.1 Summary of Results

Our main contributions are in the areas of elections (*vote*) and anonymity (*anonymous bit transmission* and *anonymous message transmission*). Each protocol is an astute combination of basic protocols, which are also of independent interest, and that implement *parity*, *veto*, *collision detection* and *notification*.

The main ingredient for our information-theoretically secure protocols is the dining cryptographers protocol [Cha88] (see also Section 2), to which we add the following simple yet powerful observation: if n participants each hold a private bit of an n-bit string with Hamming weight of parity p, then any single participant can randomize p by locally flipping his bit with a certain probability. It is impossible, however, for any participant to locally derandomize p. In the case of the anonymous message transmission, we also build on the dining cryptographers protocol by noting that a message that is sent can be ciphered with a one-time pad by having one participant (the receiver) broadcast a random bit. Any modification of the message can then be detected by the receiver with an *algebraic manipulation detection code* [CFP07].

Vote. Our *vote* protocol (Section 4) allows n participants to conduct an m-candidate election. The privacy is perfect but the protocol has the drawback that if it aborts (any corrupt participant can cause an abort), the participants can still learn information that would have been available had the protocol succeeded. For this protocol, we require a simultaneous broadcast channel. It would be particularly well-suited for a small group of voters that are unwilling to trust any third party and who have no advantage in making the protocol abort.

Previous work on information-theoretically secure voting protocols include [CFSY96], where a protocol is given in the context where many election authorities are present. To the best of our knowledge, our approach is fundamentally different from any other approaches for voting. It is the first to provide information-theoretic security without requiring or trusting any third party, while also providing ballot casting assurance (each participant is convinced that their input is correctly recorded [AN06]) and universal verifiability (each participant is conviced that only registered voters cast ballots and that the tally is correctly computed [SK95]).

Anonymity. Anonymity is the power to perform a task without identifying the participants that are involved. In the case of *anonymous message transmission*, it is simply the capacity of the sender to transmit a private message to a specific receiver of his choosing without revealing either his identity or the identity of the receiver. A number of protocols have been suggested for anonymous transmission. Many of these rely on trusted or semi-trusted third parties as well as computational assumptions (for instance, the MIX-net [Cha81]). Here, we do not make any such assumptions. The most notable protocol for anonymous transmission in our context is the dining cryptographers protocol [Cha88], which allows a single sender to anonymously broadcast a bit, and provides information-theoretical security against a passive adversary. We present the protocol in a version that implements the multiparty computation of the *parity* function in Section 2.

The case of multiple yet honest senders in the dining cryptographers protocol can be solved by time slot reservation techniques, as originally noted by Chaum [Cha88]. But nevertheless, any corrupt participant can jam the channel. Techniques offering computational security to this problem have been proposed [Cha88, WP89b]. Also, computational assumptions allow the removal of the reliance on a broadcast channel [WP89a].

In our implementation of *anonymous bit transmission* (Section 5), we elegantly deal with the case of multiple senders by allowing an unlimited amount of participants to act as anonymous senders. Each anonymous sender can target any number of participants and send them each a private bit of his choice. Thus, the outcome of the protocol is, for each participant, a private list indicating how many 0s and how many 1s were received. The anonymity of the sender and receiver and the privacy of all transmitted bits is always perfectly achieved, but any participant can cause the protocol to abort, in which case the participants may still learn some information about their own private lists.

We need a way for all participants to find out if the protocol has succeeded. This is done with the *veto* protocol (Section 3), which takes as input a single bit from each participant; the output of the protocol is the logical OR of the inputs. Our implementation differs from the ideal functionality since a participant that inputs 1 will learn if some other participant also input 1. We make use of this deviation from the ideal functionality in further protocols.

In our *fixed role anonymous message transmission* protocol (Section 8), we present a method which allows a single sender to communicate a message of arbitrary length to a single receiver. To the best of our knowledge, this is the first protocol ever to provide perfect anonymity, message privacy and integrity. For a fixed security parameter, the anonymous message transmission is asymptotically optimal.

Our final protocol for *anonymous message transmission* (Section 9) allows a sender to send a message of arbitrary length to a receiver of his choosing. While any participant can cause the protocol to abort, the anonymity of the sender and receiver is always perfectly achieved. The privacy of the message is preserved except with exponentially small probability. As far as we are aware, all previous proposed protocols for this task require either computational assumptions or a majority of honest participants. The protocol deals with the case of multiple senders by first executing the *collision detection* protocol (Section 6), in which each participant inputs a single bit. The outcome only indicates if the sum of the inputs is 0, 1 or more. Compared to similar protocols called *time slot reservation* [Cha88, WP89b], our protocol does not leak any additional information about the number of would-be senders. The final protocol also makes use of the *notification* protocol (Section 7) in which each participant chooses a list of other participants that are to be notified. The output privately reveals to each participant the logical OR of his received notifications. A special case of this protocol is when a single participant notifies another single participant; this is the version used in our final protocol to enable the sender to anonymously tell to the receiver to act accordingly.

1.2 Common Features to All Protocols

All protocols presented in the following sections share some common features, which we now describe. Our protocols are given in terms of multiparty computation with inputs and outputs and involve n participants, indexed by $i = 1, \ldots, n$. In the ideal functionality, the only information that the participants learn is their output (and what can be deduced from it). *Correctness* refers to the fact that the outputs are correctly computed, while *privacy* ensures that the inputs are never revealed.

The protocols ensure correctness and privacy even in the presence of an unlimited number of misbehaving participants. Two types of such behaviour are relevant: participants who collude (they follow the protocol but pool their information in order to violate the protocol's privacy), and participants who actively deviate from the protocol (in order to violate the protocol's correctness or privacy). Without loss of generality, these misbehaviours are modelled by assuming a central adversary that controls some participants, rendering them *corrupt*. The adversary is either *passive* (it learns all the information held by the corrupt participants), or *active* (it takes full control of the corrupt participants). We will deal only with the most general case of active adversaries, and require them to be *static* (the set of corrupt participants does not change). A participant that is not corrupt is called *honest*. Our protocols are such that if they do not abort, there exists inputs for the corrupt participants that would lead to the same output if they were to act honestly. If a protocol aborts, the participants do not learn any more information than they could have learned in an honest execution of the protocol. The input and output description applies only to honest participants.

We assume that each pair of participants shares a private, uniformly random string that can be used to implement an authentic private channel. The participants have access to a broadcast channel and in some cases, it is simultaneous. A *broadcast* channel is an authentic broadcast channel for which the sender is confident that all participants receive the same value and the receivers know the identity of the sender. A *simultaneous broadcast* channel is a collection of broadcast channels where the input of one participant cannot depend on the input of any other participant. This could be achieved if all participants *simultaneously* performed a broadcast. In order to distinguish between the two types of broadcast, we sometimes call the broadcast channel a *regular* broadcast. It is not uncommon in multiparty computation to allow additional resources, even if these resources cannot be implemented with the threshold on the honest participants (the results of [RB89] which combine a broadcast channel with $n/2$ honest participants being the most obvious example). Our work suggests that a simultaneous broadcast channel is an interesting primitive to study in this context.

In all protocols, the security parameter is s. Unfortunately, in many of our protocols, a single corrupt participant can cause the protocol to abort. All protocols run in polynomial time with respect to the number of participants, the security parameter and the input length. Although some of the protocols presented in this paper are efficient, our main focus here is in the *existence* of protocols for the described tasks. We leave for future work improvement of their efficiency. Finally, due to lack of space, we present only sketches of security proofs.

2 Parity

Protocol 1 implements the *parity* function and is essentially the same as the dining cryptographers protocol [Cha88], with the addition of a simultaneous broadcast channel. Note that if we used a broadcast channel instead, then the last participant to speak would have the unfair advantage of being able to adapt his input in order to fix the outcome of the protocol!

Protocol 1. Parity

Input: $x_i \in \{0, 1\}$
Output: $y_i = x_1 \oplus x_2 \oplus \cdots \oplus x_n$
Broadcast type: simultaneous broadcast
Achieved functionality:
1) (Correctness) If the protocol does not abort, the output is the same as in the ideal functionality.
2) (Privacy) No adversary can learn more than the output of the ideal functionality.

Each participant i does the following:
1. Select uniformly at random an n-bit string $r_i = r_i^1 r_i^2 \ldots r_i^n$ with Hamming weight of parity x_i.
2. Send r_i^j to participant j using the private channel; keep bit r_i^i to yourself.
3. Compute z_i, the parity of the sum of all the bits received, including r_i^i.
4. Use the simultaneous broadcast channel to announce z_i.
5. After the simultaneous broadcast is finished, compute $y_i = \bigoplus_{k=1}^{n} z_k$. This is the outcome of the protocol. If the simultaneous broadcast fails, abort the protocol.

Correctness and privacy follows from [Cha88]. Thus, any adversary can learn only what can be deduced from the corrupt participant's inputs and the outcome of the protocol. Note that this means that the adversary can deduce the parity of the inputs of the other participants. We will later use the two simple observations that there is no way to cheat except by refusing to broadcast and that any value that is broadcast is consistent with a choice of valid inputs. In the following protocols, we will adapt step 4 of the **parity** protocol to make it relevant to the scenario, this will allow us to remove the assumption of the simultaneous broadcast. We will also use the fact that if a single participant either does not broadcast, or broadcasts a random bit in step 4 then the value of the output of **parity** is known to this participant, but is perfectly hidden to all other participants.

3   Veto

In this section, we build on the **parity** protocol to give a protocol for the secure implementation of the *veto* function, which computes the logical OR of the participant's inputs (Protocol 2). As noted in Lemma 3, the protocol achieves a variant of the ideal functionality: any participant can passively learn the value of the logical OR of all other participants' inputs. This deviation from the ideal functionality is unavoidable since the two-participant ideal scenario is impossible to implement in our model. We will use this deviation in the **collision detection** protocol of Section 6.

Protocol 2. Veto

Input: $x_i \in \{0, 1\}$
Output: $y_i = x_1 \vee x_2 \vee \cdots \vee x_n$
Broadcast type: regular broadcast
Achieved functionality:
1) (Reliability) No participant can make the protocol abort.
2) (Correctness) The outcome of the protocol is the outcome of the ideal functionality.
3) (Privacy) Any adversary learns the logical OR of the other participants' inputs but nothing more.

The n participants agree on n orderings such that each ordering has a different last participant.
result $\leftarrow 0$
For each ordering,
　　Repeat s times:
　1. Each participant i sets the value of p_i in the following way: if $x_i = 0$ then $p_i = 0$; otherwise, $p_i = 1$ with probability $\frac{1}{2}$ and $p_i = 0$ with complimentary probability.
　2. The participants execute the **parity** protocol with inputs $p_1, p_2, \ldots p_n$, with the exception that the simultaneous broadcast is replaced by a regular broadcast with the participants broadcasting according to the current ordering (if any participant refuses to broadcast, set the value result $\leftarrow 1$). If the outcome of **parity** is 1, then set result $\leftarrow 1$.
Output the value result.

Lemma 1 *(Reliability). No participant can make the **veto** protocol abort.*

Proof. If a participant refuses to broadcast, it is assumed that the output of the protocol is 1.　　　　　　　　　　　　　　　　　　　　　　　　　　□

Lemma 2 *(Correctness).* *If all participants in the* **veto** *protocol have input* $x_i = 0$, *then the protocol achieves the ideal functionality with probability 1. If there exists a participant with input* $x_i = 1$ *then the protocol is correct with probability at least* $1 - 2^{-s}$.

Proof. The correctness follows by the properties of the **parity** protocol, with the difference that we now have a broadcast channel instead of a simultaneous broadcast channel. The case where all inputs are 0 is trivial. Let $x_i = 1$ and suppose that the protocol is executed until the ordering in which participant i speaks last. Then with probability at least $1 - 2^{-s}$, in step 2 of **veto**, the output of the protocol will be set to 1.   □

Lemma 3 *(Privacy).* *In the* **veto** *protocol, the most an adversary can learn is the logical OR of the other participants' inputs. Additionally, this information is revealed, even to a passive adversary, with probability at least* $1 - 2^{-s}$.

Proof. This follows from the properties of the **parity** protocol: for a given repetition, the adversary learns the parity of the honest participants' p_i's, but nothing else. Because of the way that the p_i's are chosen in step 1, if for any repetition, this parity is odd, the adversary concludes that at least one honest participant has input 1, and otherwise if all repetitions yield 0, then the adversary concludes that with probability at least $1 - 2^{-s}$, all the honest participant's inputs are 0. In all cases, this is the only information that is revealed; clearly, it is revealed to any passive adversary, except with exponentially small probability. Note that this information could be learned in the ideal functionality by assigning to all corrupt participants the input 0.   □

4   Vote

The participants now wish to conduct an m-candidate **vote**. The idea of Protocol 3 is simple. In the **veto** protocol, each participant with input 1 completely randomizes his input into the **parity** protocol, thus randomizing the output of **parity**. By flipping the output of **parity** with probability only $1/n$, the probability of the outcome being odd becomes a function of the number of such flips. Using repetition, this probability can be approximated to obtain the exact number of flips with exponentially small error probability. This can be used to compute the number of votes for each candidate. Unfortunately, a corrupt participant can randomize his bit with probability higher than $1/n$, enabling him to vote more than once. But since a participant cannot derandomize the parity, he cannot vote less than zero times. Verifying that the sum of the votes equals n ensures that all participants vote exactly once. Note that the protocol we present is polynomial in m and not in the length of m.

Lemma 4 *(Correctness).* *If the* **vote** *does not abort, then there exists an input for each corrupt participant such that the output of the honest participants equals the output of the ideal functionality, except with probability exponentially small in s.*

Protocol 3. Vote

Input: $x_i \in \{1, \ldots, m\}$
Output: for $k = 1$ to m, $y[k]_i = |\{x_j \mid x_j = k\}|$
Broadcast type: simultaneous broadcast
Achieved functionality:
1) (Correctness) If the protocol does not abort, then there exists an input x_i for each corrupt participant such that the protocol achieves the ideal functionality.
2) (Privacy) Even if the protocol aborts, no adversary can learn more that what it would have learned by setting in the ideal functionality $x_i = 1$ for all corrupt participants.

Phase A
For each candidate $k = 1$ to m,
    For $j = 1$ to s,
    1. Each participant i sets the value of p_i in the following way: if $x_i \neq k$, then $p_i = 0$; otherwise, $p_i = 1$ with probability $\frac{1}{n}$ and $p_i = 0$ with complimentary probability.
    2. The participants execute the **parity** protocol to compute the *parity* of $p_1, p_2, \ldots p_n$, but instead of broadcasting their output bit z_i, they store it as $z[k]_i^j$.

Phase B
All participants simultaneously broadcast $z[k]_i^j$ ($j = 1, 2, \ldots, s$). If the simultaneous broadcast is not successful, the protocol aborts.

Phase C
To compute the tally, $y[k]_i$, for each value $k = 1 \ldots m$, each participant sets: $p[k]_j = \bigoplus_{i=1}^n z[k]_i^j$, $\sigma[k]_i = \sum_{j=1}^s p[k]_j / s$ and if there exists an integer v such that $|\sigma[k]_i - p_v| < \frac{1}{2e^2 n}$,
where $p_v = \frac{1}{2} \left(\frac{n-2}{n}\right)^v \left(\left(\frac{n}{n-2}\right)^v - 1\right)$, then $y[k]_i = v$.
If for any k, no such value v exists, or if $\sum_{k=1}^m y[k]_i \neq n$, the protocol aborts.

Proof. If all participants are honest, the correctness of the protocol is derived from the Chernoff bound as explained in the Appendix. Assume now t corrupt participants. Since the **parity** protocol is perfect, the only place participant i can deviate from the protocol is by choosing p_i with an inappropriate probability. We first note that if the t corrupt participants actually transmit the correct number of private bits in **phase A** and broadcast the correct number of bits in **phase B**, then whatever they actually send is consistent with some global probability of flipping.

We use again the fact that it is possible to randomize the parity but not to derandomize it: if the corrupt participants altogether flip with a probability not consistent with an integer number of votes, either the statistics will be inconsistent, causing the protocol to abort, or we can interpret the results as being consistent with an integer amount of votes. If they flip with a probability consistent with an integer different than t, then each $y[k]_i$ will be assigned a value, but with probability exponentially close to 1, we will have $\sum_{k=1}^m y[k]_i \neq n$ and the protocol will abort.   □

Lemma 5 *(Privacy).* *In the **vote** protocol, no adversary can learn more than what it would have learned by assigning to all corrupt participants the input 1 in the ideal functionality, and this even if the protocol aborts.*

Proof. Assume that the first t participants are corrupt. No information is sent in **phase A** or **phase C**. We thus have to concentrate on **phase B** where the participants broadcast their information regarding each parity. For each execution of **parity**, the adversary learns the parity of the honest participant's values, $p_{t+1} \oplus p_{t+2} \oplus \ldots \oplus p_n$, but no information on these individual values is revealed. The adversary can thus only evaluate the probability with which the other participants have flipped the parity. But this information could be deduced from the output of the ideal functionality, for instance by fixing the corrupt participants' inputs to 1.   □

It is important to note that the above results do not exclude the possibility of an adversary causing the protocol to abort while still learning some information as stipulated in Lemma 5. This information could be used to adapt the behaviour of the adversary in a future execution of **vote**.

In addition to the above theorems, it follows from the use of the simultaneous broadcast channel that an adversary cannot act in a way that a corrupt participant's vote depends an honest participant's vote. In particular, it cannot *duplicate* an honest participant's vote. We claim that our protocol provides ballot casting assurance and universal verifiability. This is straightforward from the fact that participants do not entrust any computation to a third party: they provide their own inputs and can verify that the final outcome is computed correctly.

5   Anonymous Bit Transmission

The **anonymous bit transmission** protocol enables a sender to privately and anonymously transmit one bit to a receiver of his choice. Protocol 4 actually deals with the usually problematic scenario of multiple *anonymous senders* in an original way: it allows an arbitrary number participants to act as anonymous senders, each one targeting any number of participants and sending them each a chosen private bit. Each participant is also simultaneously a potential *receiver*: at the end of the protocol, each participant has a private account of how many anonymous senders sent the bit 0 and how many sent the bit 1. Note that in our formalism for multiparty computation, the *privacy* of the inputs implies the *anonymity* of the senders and receivers.

The security of the **anonymous bit transmission** protocol follows directly from the security of the **vote** and of the **veto**. Of course, the **anonymous bit transmission** also inherits the drawbacks of these protocols. More precisely we have the following:

Lemma 6 *(Correctness). The **anonymous bit transmission** protocol computes the correct output, except with exponentially small probability.*

Proof. If the protocol does not abort, by Lemmas 2 and 4, except with exponentially small probability, all bits are correctly transmitted.   □

Protocol 4. Anonymous Bit Transmission

Input: $x_i^j \in \{0, 1, \perp\}$, $(j = 1, 2, \ldots, n)$

Output: $y_i = (|\{x_j^i \mid x_j^i = 0\}|, |\{x_j^i \mid x_j^i = 1\}|)$

Broadcast type: regular broadcast

Achieved functionality:

1) (Correctness) If the protocol does not abort then the output of the protocol equals the output of the ideal functionality.

2) (Privacy) The privacy is the same as in the ideal functionality.

For each participant j,

1. Execute the **vote** protocol with $m = 3$ as modified below. The three choices are: 0, 1, or $\perp$ (*abstain*). Each participant i chooses his input to the **vote** according to x_i^j, his choice of message to be sent anonymously to participant j. The **vote** protocol is modified such that:

   (a) The output strings are sent to participant j through the private channel.

   (b) Participant j computes the tally as in the **vote** and if this computation succeeds, he finds out how many participants sent him a 0, how many sent him a 1 and how many abstained. If this occurs (and the results are consistent) he sets his success bit, s_j to 0. If the **vote** aborts, he sets s_j to 1.

Execute the **veto** protocol, using as inputs the success bits s_j. If the output of **veto** is 0, then the **anonymous bit transmission** succeeds. Otherwise, the protocol fails.

Lemma 7 *(Privacy). In the **anonymous bit transmission** protocol, the privacy is the same as in the ideal functionality.*

Proof. Each execution of the **vote** protocol provides perfect privacy, even if the protocol aborts. The final veto reveals some partial information about which honest participants have been targeted by corrupt participants, but this does not compromise the privacy of the protocol. $\square$

In Protocol 4, the use of the private channel in step (a) can be removed and replaced by a broadcast channel. Since participant j does not broadcast, the messages remain private. Another modification of the protocol makes it possible to send m possible messages instead of just two but note that the complexity is polynomial in m and not in the length of m. The transmission of arbitrarily long strings is discussed in Sections 8 and 9.

6   Collision Detection

The **collision detection** protocol (Protocol 5) enables the participants to verify whether or not there is a single sender in the group. This will be used as a procedure for the implementation of *anonymous message transmission* in Section 9. Ideally, a protocol to detect a collision would have as inputs only $x_i \in \{0, 1\}$, with outputs in $\{0, 1, 2\}$, depending on the sum of the inputs. Unfortunately we do not know how to achieve such a functionality; instead, we allow any participant to choose to force output 2, which in our description, corresponds to using input value 2.

Protocol 5. Collision Detection

Input: $x_i \in \{0, 1, 2\}$

Output: let $r = \sum_{i=1}^{n} x_i$ then $y_i = \min\{r, 2\}$

Broadcast type: regular broadcast

Achieved functionality:

1) (Reliability) No participant can make the protocol abort.

2) (Correctness) The output of the protocol equals the output of the ideal functionality.

3) (Privacy) An adversary cannot learn more than it could have learned by assigning to all corrupt participants the input 0 in the ideal functionality.

Veto A

All participants perform the **veto** protocol with inputs $\min\{x_i, 1\}$. As in Lemma 3, the participants note the value of the logical OR of the other participants' inputs.

Veto B

If the outcome of **veto A** is 0, skip this step. Otherwise, each participant with input 1 in **veto A** will set $b_i = 1$ if he detected in **veto A** that another participant had input 1, or if $x_i = 2$. All other participants set $b_i = 0$. Then all participants perform a second **veto** protocol with inputs b_i.

Output: $y_i = \begin{cases} 0 & \text{if the outcome of } \textbf{veto A} \text{ is } 0 \\ 1 & \text{if the outcome of } \textbf{veto A} \text{ is 1 and the outcome of } \textbf{veto B} \text{ is } 0 \\ 2 & \text{if the outcome of } \textbf{veto A} \text{ is 1 and the outcome of } \textbf{veto B} \text{ is } 1 \end{cases}$

Lemma 8 *(Reliability). No participant can make the **collision detection** protocol abort.*

Proof. This follows from the reliability of **veto**.   □

Lemma 9 *(Correctness). In the **collision detection** protocol, the output equals the output of the ideal functionality (except with exponentially small probability).*

Proof. This follows from the correctness of the **veto** protocol. There are only two ways a corrupt participant can deviate from the protocol. First, participant i can set $b_i = 0$ although $x_i \in \{0, 1\}$ and although in the first veto his input was 1 and a collision was detected. The outcome of **veto B** will still be 1 since another participant with input 1 in **veto A** will input 1 in **veto B**. This is consistent with input $x_i = 1$. Second, participant i can set $b_i = 1$ although $x_i = 0$. If **veto B** is executed, then we know that another participant has input 1 in **veto A**. This is consistent with input $x_i = 1$.   □

Note that we have raised a subtle deviation from the ideal protocol in the above proof: we showed how it is possible for a corrupt participant to set his input to 0 if all other participants have input 0 and to 1 otherwise. Fortunately, the protocol is still sufficiently good for the requirements of the following sections.

Lemma 10 *(Privacy). In the **collision detection** protocol, an adversary cannot learn more than it could have learned by assigning to all corrupt participants the input 0 in the ideal functionality.*

Proof. In each **veto**, an adversary can only learn whether or not there exists an honest participant with input 1. In all cases, this can be deduced from the outcome of the ideal functionality by setting the input to be 0 for all corrupt participants.   □

7   Notification

In the **notification** protocol (Protocol 6), each participant chooses a list of other participants to notify. The output privately reveals to each participant whether or not he was notified, but no information on the number or origin of such notifications is revealed. Because participants are notified one after another, our protocol does not exclude adaptive behaviours.

Protocol 6. Notification

Input: $\forall j \neq i, x_i^j \in \{0,1\}$
Output: $y_i = \bigvee_{j \neq i} x_j^i$
Broadcast type: regular broadcast
Achieved functionality:
1) (Correctness) If the protocol does not abort then the output of the protocol equals the output of the ideal functionality.
2) (Privacy) The privacy is the same as in the ideal functionality.

For each participant i:
    Participant i sets $y_i \leftarrow 0$.
    Repeat s times:
1. Each participant $j \neq i$ sets the value of p_j in the following way: if $x_j^i = 0$ then $p_j = 0$; otherwise, $p_j = 1$ with probability $\frac{1}{2}$ and $p_i = 0$ with complimentary probability. Let $p_i = 0$.
2. The participants execute the **parity** protocol with inputs $p_1, p_2, \ldots p_n$, with the exception that participant i does not broadcast his value, and the simultaneous broadcast is replaced by a regular broadcast (if any participant refuses to broadcast, abort).
3. Participant i computes the outcome of **parity**, and if it is 1, $y_i \leftarrow 1$.

Lemma 11. *The **notification** protocol achieves privacy and except with exponentially small probability, the correct output is computed.*

Proof. Privacy and correctness are trivially deduced from properties of the **parity** protocol.   □

8   Fixed Role Anonymous Message Transmission

In Section 5, we presented an **anonymous bit transmission** protocol. The protocol easily generalizes to m messages, but the complexity of the protocol becomes polynomial in m. It is not clear how to modify the protocol to transmit a string of arbitrary length, while still allowing multiple senders and receivers. However, in the context where a single sender S is allowed, it is possible to implement a secure protocol for S to anonymously transmit a message to a single receiver R, which we call **fixed role anonymous message transmission**

(Protocol 7). If the uniqueness condition on S and R is not satisfied, the protocol aborts. The protocol combines the use of the **parity** protocol with an *algebraic manipulation detection code* [CFP07], which we present as Theorem 1. Due to lack of space, the encoding and decoding algorithms, F and G, respectfully, are not repeated. For a less efficient algorithm that achieves a similar result, see [CPS02].

Theorem 1 ([CFP07]). *There exists an efficient probabilistic encoding algorithm F and decoding algorithm G, where $F : \{0,1\}^m \to \{0,1\}^{m+2(\log(m)+s}$ and $G : \{0,1\}^{m+2(\log(m)+s)} \to \{\perp, \{0,1\}^m\}$ such that for all w, $G(F(w)) = w$, and any fixed combination of bit flips applied to $w' = F(w)$ produces a w'' such that $G(w'') = \perp$, except with probability 2^{-s}.*

Protocol 7. Fixed Role Anonymous Message Transmission

Oracle: The sender S and receiver R know their identity
Input: S has input $w \in \{0,1\}^m$, all other players have no input
Output: R has output w, all other players have no output
Broadcast type: regular broadcast
Achieved functionality:
1) (Correctness) If the protocol does not abort, R obtains the correct message.
2) (Privacy) The only information that can be learned through the protocol is for R to learn w.
3) (Oracle) If the oracle conditions are not satisfied (in the sense that more than one honest participant believes to be the sender or the receiver), the protocol will abort.

---

1. S computes $w' = F(w)$
2. The participants execute $m + 2(\log(m) + s)$ rounds of the **parity** protocol, with participants using a broadcast instead of a simultaneous broadcast and using the following inputs:
   (a) S uses as input the bits of w'.
   (b) R uses as input the bits of a random m-bit string, r.
   (c) All other players use 0 as input for each round.
3. Let d be the output of the rounds of **parity**. R computes $w'' = d \oplus r$.
4. R computes $y = G(w'')$.
5. A **veto** is performed: all players input 0 except R who inputs 1 if $y = \perp$ and 0 otherwise.
   If the outcome of **veto** is 1, the protocol aborts. Otherwise, R sets his output to y.

Lemma 12 (Correctness, Privacy, Oracle). *In the **fixed role anonymous message transmission** protocol, the probability that R obtains as output a corrupt message is exponentially small. The protocol is perfectly private, and if the oracle conditions are not satisfied, it will abort (except with exponentially small probability).*

Proof. Because of the properties of **parity** and the fact that the receiver broadcasts a random bit, we have perfect privacy. Correctness is a direct consequence of Theorem 1. Finally, if more than one participant acts as a sender or receiver, then again by Theorem 1, the message will not be faithfully transmitted and the protocol will abort in step 5, except with exponentially small probability.   □

Theorem 2. *For a fixed security parameter, the **fixed role anonymous message transmission** protocol is asymptotically optimal.*

Proof. For any protocol to preserve the anonymity of the sender and the receiver, each player must sent at least one bit to every other player for each bit of the message. In the **fixed role anonymous message transmission** protocol, for a fixed s, each player actually sends $O(1)$ bits to each other player and therefore the protocol is asymptotically optimal.   □

9 Anonymous Message Transmission

Our final protocol allows a sender to anonymously transmit message to a receiver of his choosing. Contrary to the **fixed role anonymous message transmission** protocol of Section 8, **anonymous message transmission** (Protocol 8) does not suppose that there is a single sender, but instead, it deals with potential collisions (or lack of any sender at all) by producing the outputs COLLISION or NO TRANSMISSION. The only deviation from the ideal functionality in the protocol is that a single participant can force the COLLISION output. Note again that in this protocol, the privacy of the input implies anonymity of the sender and receiver.

Protocol 8. Anonymous Message Transmission

Input: $x_i = \perp$ or $x_i = (r, w)$ where $r \in \{1, \ldots, n\}$ and $w \in \{0, 1\}^m$
Output: If $|\{x_i \mid x_i \neq \perp\}| = 0$ then $y_i = $ NO TRANSMISSION and if $|\{x_i \mid x_i \neq \perp\}| > 1$ then $y_i = $ COLLISION. Otherwise let S be such that $x_S = (r, w)$ then all $y_i = \perp$ except $y_r = w$.
Broadcast type: regular broadcast
Achieved functionality:
1) (Correctness) The output equals the output of the ideal functionality except that a single participant can make the protocol produce the output COLLISION.
2) (Privacy) The privacy is the same as in the ideal functionality.

---

1. The participants execute the **collision detection** protocol; participants who have input $x_i = \perp$ use input 0 while all others use input 1. If the outcome of **collision detection** is 1, continue, otherwise output NO TRANSMISSION if the output is 0 and COLLISION if the output is 2.
2. Let the sender S be the unique participant with $x_S \neq \perp$. The participants execute the **notification** protocol, with S using input $x_S^r = 1$ and $x_S^j = 0$ otherwise. All other participants use the input bits 0. Let R be the participant who computes as output $y_R = 1$. If the **notification** protocol fails, abort.
3. The participants execute the **fixed role anonymous message transmission** protocol.

Lemma 13 *(Correctness)*. *In the **anonymous message transmission** protocol, the output equals the output of the ideal functionality except with* *exponentially small probability. The only exception is that a single participant can make the protocol produce the output* COLLISION.

Proof. This follows easily from the correctness of the **collision detection, notification** and **fixed role anonymous message transmission** protocols.   □

Lemma 14 *(Privacy). The anonymity of the sender and receiver are perfect. If the protocol succeeds, except with exponentially small probability, participant r is the only participant who knows w.*

Proof. Perfect anonymity follows from the privacy of the **collision detection, notification** and **anonymous message transmission** protocols. If the sender successfully notifies the receiver in step 2, then the privacy of w is perfect. But with exponentially small probability, the receiver will not be correctly notified, and an adversary acting as the receiver will receive the message w.   □

10   Conclusion

We have given six multiparty protocols that are information-theoretically secure without any assumption on the number of honest participants. It would be interesting to see if the techniques we used can be applied to other multiparty functions or in other contexts.

Our main goal was to prove the existence of several protocols in a model that does not make use of any strong hypotheses such as computational assumptions or an honest majority. This being said, all the presented protocols are reasonably efficient: they are all polynomial in terms of communication and computational complexity and in one case, asymptotically optimal.

Acknowledgements

The authors wish to thank Hugue Blier, Gilles Brassard, Serge Fehr and Sébastien Gambs. A. B. is supported by scholarships from the Canadian Federation of University Women, the Fonds Québecois de Recherche sur la Nature et les Technologies (FQRNT) and the Natural Sciences and Engineering Research Council of Canada (NSERC). A. T. is supported by the Canadian Institute for Advanced Research, FQRNT, the Mathematics of Information Technology and Complex Systems Network and NSERC.

References

[AN06]   Adida, B., Neff, C.A.: Ballot casting assurance. In: EVT 2006. Proceedings of the First Usenix/ACCURATE Electronic Voting Technology Workshop (2006)

[BGW88]   Ben-Or, M., Goldwasser, S., Wigderson, A.: Completeness theorems for non-cryptographic fault-tolerant distributed computation (extended abstract). In: Proceedings of the twentieth annual ACM Symposium on Theory of Computing (STOC), pp. 1–10. ACM Press, New York (1988)

[CCD88]   Chaum, D., Crépeau, C., Damgård, I.: Multiparty unconditionally secure protocols (extended abstract). In: Proceedings of the twentieth annual ACM Symposium on Theory of Computing (STOC), pp. 11–19. ACM Press, New York (1988)

[CFP07]   Cramer, R., Fehr, S., Padró, C.: Combinatorial codes for detection of algebraic manipulation and their applications. Manuscript (2007)

[CFSY96]   Cramer, R., Franklin, M., Schoenmakers, B., Yung, M.: Multi-authority secret ballot elections with linear work. In: Maurer, U.M. (ed.) EURO-CRYPT 1996. LNCS, vol. 1070, pp. 72–83. Springer, Heidelberg (1996)

[CGMA85]   Chor, B., Goldwasser, S., Micali, S., Awerbuch, B.: Verifiable secret sharing and achieving simultaneity in the presence of faults. In: Proceedings of the 26th Annual Symposium on Foundations of Computer Science (FOCS), pp. 383–395 (1985)

[Cha81]   Chaum, D.: Untraceable electronic mail, return addresses, and digital pseudonyms. Communications of the ACM 24, 84–88 (1981)

[Cha88]   Chaum, D.: The dining cryptographers problem: Unconditional sender and recipient untraceability. Journal of Cryptology 1, 65–75 (1988)

[CPS02]   Cabello, S., Padró, C., Sáez, G.: Secret sharing schemes with detection of cheaters for a general access structure. Designs, Codes and Cryptography 25, 175–188 (2002)

[HM05]   Hevia, A., Micciancio, D.: Simultaneous broadcast revisited. In: Proceedings of the twenty-fourth annual ACM symposium on Principles of distributed computing, pp. 324–333. ACM Press, New York (2005)

[RB89]   Rabin, T., Ben-Or, M.: Verifiable secret sharing and multiparty protocols with honest majority. In: Proceedings of the twenty-first annual ACM Symposium on Theory of Computing (STOC), pp. 73–85. ACM Press, New York (1989)

[SK95]   Sako, K., Kilian, J.: Receipt-free mix-type voting scheme — a practical solution to the implementation of a voting booth. In: Guillou, L.C., Quisquater, J.-J. (eds.) EUROCRYPT 1995. LNCS, vol. 921, pp. 393–403. Springer, Heidelberg (1995)

[WP89a]   Waidner, M., Pfitzmann, B.: The dining cryptographers in the disco: Unconditional sender and recipient untraceability with computationally secure serviceability. In: Quisquater, J.-J., Vandewalle, J. (eds.) EURO-CRYPT 1989. LNCS, vol. 434, p. 690. Springer, Heidelberg (1990)

[WP89b]   Waidner, M., Pfitzmann, B.: Unconditional sender and recipient untraceability in spite of active attacks — some remarks. Technical report, Universität Karlsruhe (1989)

A   Proof of Correctness for Protocol 3

Lemma 15 *(Correctness). If all participants are honest in Protocol 3 (vote), then the output is correct, except with probability exponentially small in s.*

Proof. We fix a value k and suppose that v participants have input $x_i = k$. Thus we need to show that in the **vote**, $y[k]_i = v$, except with probability exponentially small in s.

We now give the intuition behind **phase C** of the **vote**. Let p_v be the probability that $p[k]_j = \bigoplus_{i=1}^n z[k]_i^j = 1$. For $v \leq n$, we have $p_0 = 0$, $p_1 = \frac{1}{n}$ and $p_{v+1} = p_v \left(1 - \frac{1}{n}\right) + (1 - p_v)\frac{1}{n}$. Solving this recurrence, we get

$$p_v = \frac{1}{2}\left(\frac{n-2}{n}\right)^v\left(\left(\frac{n}{n-2}\right)^v - 1\right).$$
(1)

Thus, the idea of **phase C** of the **vote** is for the participants to approximate p_v by computing $\sigma[k]_i = \sum_{i=1}^{s} p[k]_j/s$. If the approximation is within $\frac{1}{2e^2n}$ of p_v, then the outcome is $y[k]_i = v$. We first show that if such a v exists, it is unique.

Clearly, for $v < n$, we have that $p_{v+1} > p_v$. We also have $\lim_{n\to\infty} p_n = \frac{1}{2} - \frac{1}{2e^2}$. Thus the difference between p_{v+1} and p_v is:

$$p_{v+1} - p_v = p_v\left(1 - \frac{1}{n}\right) + (1-p)\frac{1}{n} - p_v$$
(2)

$$= \frac{1 - 2p_v}{n} > \frac{1 - 2p_n}{n} > \frac{1}{e^2n}$$
(3)

Hence if such a v exists, it is unique. We now show that except with probability exponentially small in s, the correct v will be chosen. Let $X = \sum_{j=1}^{s} p[k]_j$ be the sum of the s executions of **parity**, with $\mu = sp_v$ the expected value of X. The participants have computed $\sigma[k]_i = X/s$.

By the Chernoff bound, for any $0 < \delta \le 1$,

$$\Pr[X \le (1-\delta)\mu] < \exp(-\mu\delta^2/2)$$
(4)

Let $\delta = \frac{1}{2e^2np_v}$. We have

$$\Pr[X \le \mu - \frac{s}{2e^2n}] < \exp(-\frac{s}{8e^4n^2p_v})$$
(5)

and so

$$\Pr[\sigma[k]_i - p_v \le \frac{-1}{2e^2n}] < \exp(-\frac{s}{8e^4n^2p_v})$$
(6)

Similarly, still by the Chernoff bound, for any $\delta < 2e - 1$,

$$\Pr[X > (1+\delta)\mu] < \exp(-\mu\delta^2/4)$$
(7)

Let $\delta = \frac{1}{2e^2np_v}$ and we get

$$\Pr[X > \mu + \frac{s}{2e^2n}] < \exp(\frac{-s}{16e^4n^2p_v})$$
(8)

and so

$$\Pr[\sigma[k]_i - p_v > \frac{1}{2e^2n}] < \exp(\frac{-s}{16e^4n^2p_v})$$
(9)

Hence the protocol produces the correct value for $y[k]_i$, except with probability exponentially small in s.   □

Black-Box Extension Fields and the Inexistence of Field-Homomorphic One-Way Permutations

Ueli Maurer and Dominik Raub

ETH Zurich, Department of Computer Science, CH-8092 Zurich, Switzerland
{maurer,raubd}@inf.ethz.ch

Abstract. The black-box field (BBF) extraction problem is, for a given field $\mathbb{F}$, to determine a secret field element hidden in a black-box which allows to add and multiply values in $\mathbb{F}$ in the box and which reports only equalities of elements in the box. This problem is of cryptographic interest for two reasons. First, for $\mathbb{F} = \mathbb{F}_p$ it corresponds to the generic reduction of the discrete logarithm problem to the computational Diffie-Hellman problem in a group of prime order p. Second, an efficient solution to the BBF extraction problem proves the inexistence of field-homomorphic one-way permutations whose realization is an interesting open problem in algebra-based cryptography. BBFs are also of independent interest in computational algebra.

In the previous literature BBFs had only been considered for the prime field case. In this paper we consider a generalization of the extraction problem to BBFs that are extension fields. More precisely we discuss the representation problem defined as follows: For given generators $g_1, \ldots, g_d$ algebraically generating a BBF and an additional element x, all hidden in a black-box, express x algebraically in terms of $g_1, \ldots, g_d$. We give an efficient algorithm for this representation problem and related problems for fields with small characteristic (e.g. $\mathbb{F} = \mathbb{F}_{2^n}$ for some n). We also consider extension fields of large characteristic and show how to reduce the representation problem to the extraction problem for the underlying prime field.

These results imply the inexistence of field-homomorphic (as opposed to only group-homomorphic, like RSA) one-way permutations for fields of small characteristic.

Keywords: Black-box fields, generic algorithms, homomorphic encryption, one-way permutations, computational algebra.

1 Introduction

1.1 Black-Boxes and Generic Algorithms

Algebraic structures like groups, rings, and fields, and algorithms on them, play a crucial role in cryptography. In order to compute in an algebraic structure one needs a representation of its elements, for instance as bitstrings. Algorithms that do not exploit any property of the representation are called *generic*. The concept

K. Kurosawa (Ed.): ASIACRYPT 2007, LNCS 4833, pp. 427–443, 2007.

of generic algorithms is of interest for two reasons. First, generic algorithms can be used no matter how the structure is represented, and second, this model allows for significant lower bound proofs for certain computational problems. For instance, Shoup [Sho97] proved a lower bound on the complexity of any generic algorithm for computing discrete logarithms in a finite cyclic group.

Representation-independent algorithms on a given algebraic structure S are best modeled by a *black-box* [BS84, BB99, Mau05], which initially contains some elements of S, describing an instance of the computational problem under consideration. The black-box accepts instructions to perform the operation(s) of S on the values stored in it. The (internal) values are stored in addressable registers and the result of an operation is stored in a new register. The values stored in the black-box are hidden and the only information about these values provided to the outside (an hence to the algorithm) are equalities of stored elements. This models that there is no (need for a) representation of values but that nevertheless one can compute on given values. The equality check provided by the black-box models the trivial property of any (unique) representation that equality is easily checked.[1]

A basic problem in this setting is the *extraction problem*: The black-box contains a secret value x (and possibly also some constants), and the task of the algorithm is to compute x (explicitly).

For example, a cyclic group of prime order p is modeled by a black-box where S is the additive group $\mathbb{Z}_p$ (and which can be assumed to contain the constants 0 and 1 corresponding to the neutral element and the generator, respectively). The discrete logarithm problem is the extraction problem for this black-box. Shoup's result implies that no algorithm can extract x (if uniformly chosen) with fewer than $O(\sqrt{p})$ expected operations. Actually, this many operations are required in expectation to provoke a single collision in the black-box, which is necessary for the algorithm to obtain any information about the content of the black-box. Both the baby-step giant-step algorithm and the Pohlig-Hellman algorithm are generic algorithm which can be described and analyzed in this model.

1.2   Black-Box Fields and Known Results

If one assumes in the above setting that the black-box not only allows *addition* but also *multiplication* of values modulo p, then this corresponds to a *black-box field* (BBF).

An efficient (non-uniform) algorithm for the extraction problem in $\mathbb{F}_p$ was proposed in [Mau94] (see also [MW99]), where non-uniform means that the algorithm depends on p or, equivalently, obtains a help-string that depends on p. Moreover, the existence of the help-string, which is actually the description of an elliptic curve of smooth order over $\mathbb{F}_p$, depends on a plausible but unproven number-theoretic conjecture.

---

[1] Note that this model is simpler than Shoup's model which assumes a random representation.

Boneh and Lipton [BL96] proposed a similar but *uniform* algorithm for the extraction problem in $\mathbb{F}_p$, but its running time is subexponential and the analysis also relies on a related unproven number-theoretic conjecture.

1.3   Black-Box Extention Fields

Prime fields differ significantly from extension fields, which is relevant in the context of this paper:

In contrast to an extension field $\mathbb{F}_{p^k}$ (for $k > 1$), a prime field $\mathbb{F}_p$ is generated by any non-zero element (for instance 1). Hence there is a unique isomorphism between any two instantiations of $\mathbb{F}_p$ that is given by mapping the 1 of the first instance to the 1 of the second. In particular, there is a unique isomorphism between a BBF over $\mathbb{F}_p$ and any explicit representation of $\mathbb{F}_p$. Therefore in an explicit representation there exists a unique element corresponding to a secret value x inside the black-box, and the extraction problem as stated above is well defined.

As an extension field $\mathbb{F}_{p^k}$ (for $k > 1$) contains non-zero elements that do *not* algebraically generate the entire field, it is not sufficient to give a secret value x inside the black box in order to describe an arbitrary extension field. Rather, the field must be given by a set of elements (generators) in the black-box algebraically generating the field. A vector space basis of $\mathbb{F}_{p^k}$ over $\mathbb{F}_p$ would be a natural choice, but our goal is to make no assumption whatsoever about how the given elements generate the field.

Furthermore, extension fields $\mathbb{F}_{p^k}$ (for $k > 1$) have non-trivial automorphisms, so there is *no unique* isomorphism between a black-box extension field and an explicit representation. Therefore the extraction problem as originally posed is not well defined for extension fields. We hence formulate a more general problem for extension fields, the *representation problem*: Write a secret x hidden inside the black-box as an algebraic expression in the other elements (generators) given in the black-box.

When an explicit representation of the field is given outside of the black-box (say in terms of an irreducible polynomial of degree k over $\mathbb{F}_p$), then one can also consider the problem of efficiently computing an isomorphism (and its inverse) between this explicitly given field and the BBF.

1.4   Contributions of This Paper

We present an efficient reduction of the representation problem for a finite black-box extension field to the extraction problem for the underlying prime field $\mathbb{F}_p$. If the characteristic p of the field in question is small, or if p is large but an efficient algorithm for the extraction problem for $\mathbb{F}_p$ exists, then this yields an efficient algorithm for the representation problem for the extension field. Under their respective number-theoretic assumptions one can also use the results of [Mau94, BL96, MW99].

Theorem 1 (informal). *The representation problem for the finite black-box extension field $\mathbb{F}_\mathbf{B}$ of characteristic p is efficiently reducible to the representation* *problem for* $\mathbb{F}_p$. *If the characteristic* p *is small (e.g.* $p = 2$*) then the representation problem for* $\mathbb{F}_{\mathbf{B}}$ *is efficiently solvable.*

Furthermore, our algorithms provide an efficiently computable isomorphism between the black-box field and an explicitly represented (outside the black-box) isomorphic copy. If we are given preimages of the generators inside the black-box under some isomorphism from an explicitly represented field into the black-box or if the black-box allows inserting elements from an explicitly represented field, we may even efficiently extract any element from the black-box field, i.e., we can find the element corresponding to an x inside the black-box in the explicit representation.

In particular, these results imply that any problem posed for a black-box field (of small characteristic) can efficiently be transformed into a problem for an explicit field and be solved there using unrestricted (representation-dependent) methods. For example, this implies that computing discrete logarithms in the multiplicative group over a finite field (of small characteristic) is not harder in the black-box setting than in the case where the field is given by an irreducible polynomial.

1.5   Cryptographic Significance of Black-Box Fields

A BBF $\mathbb{F}_p$ can be viewed as a black-box group of prime order p, where the multiplication operation of the field corresponds to a Diffie-Hellman oracle; therefore an efficient algorithm for the extraction problem for $\mathbb{F}_p$ corresponds to an efficient generic reduction of the discrete logarithm problem to the computational Diffie-Hellman problem in any group of prime order p (see [Mau94]). So an efficient algorithm for the extraction problem for $\mathbb{F}_p$ provides a security proof for the Diffie-Hellman key agreement protocol [DH76] in any group of order p for which the discrete logarithm problem is hard.[2]

Boneh and Lipton [BL96] gave a second reason why the extraction problem is of interest in cryptography, namely to prove the inexistence of certain field-homomorphic encryption schemes.

The RSA trapdoor one-way permutation defined by $x \mapsto x^e \pmod{n}$ is group-homomorphic: the product of two ciphertexts x^e and x'^e is the ciphertext for their product: $x^e \cdot x'^e = (x \cdot x')^e$. This algebraic property has proven enormously useful in many cryptographic protocols. However, this homomorphic property is only for one operation (i.e., for a group), and an open problem in cryptography is to devise a trapdoor one-way permutation that is field-homomorphic, i.e., for addition *and* for multiplication. Such a scheme would have applications in multiparty computation, computation with encrypted data (e.g. server-assisted computation), and possibly other areas in cryptography [SYY99, ALN87, Dom02].

---

[2] In this context it is not a problem that Maurer's efficient algorithm [Mau94] for the extraction problem for $\mathbb{F}_p$ is non-uniform, because one can construct a Diffie-Hellman group of order p together with the help-string and hence the equivalence really holds.

A solution to the extraction problem for $\mathbb{F}_p$ implies an equally efficient attack on any $\mathbb{F}_p$-homomorphic encryption scheme that permits checking the equality of two encrypted elements (which is for example true for any deterministic scheme). Indeed, a black-box field can be regarded as an idealized formulation of a field-homomorphic encryption scheme which allows for equality checks. Any algorithm that succeeds in recovering an "encrypted" element hidden inside the black-box will also break an encryption scheme that allows the same operations. In particular, an efficient algorithm for the extraction problem for $\mathbb{F}_p$ implies the inexistence of a secure $\mathbb{F}_p$-homomorphic one-way permutation.

This generalizes naturally to the extension field case yielding the following corollary to Theorem 1:

Corollary 1. *For fields of small characteristic p (in particular for $\mathbb{F}_{2^k}$) there are no secure field-homomorphic encryption schemes[3] that permit equality checks. In particular, there are no field-homomorphic one-way permutations over such fields.[4]*

The same holds even for large characteristic p if we admit non-uniform adversaries under the assumption of [Mau94, MW99].

Beyond its cryptographic significance, the representation problem for black-box extension fields is of independent mathematical interest. The representation problem for groups, in particular black-box groups, has been extensively studied [BB99, BS84], inciting interest in the representation problem for other algebraic black-box structures.

2   The Representation Problem for Finite Black-Box Fields

2.1   Preliminaries on Finite Fields

We assume that the reader is familiar with the basic algebraic concepts of groups, rings, fields, and vector spaces and we summarize a few basic facts about finite fields.

The cardinality of every finite field is a prime power, p^k, where p is called the *characteristic* and k the *extension degree*. There exists a finite field for every prime p and every k. Finite fields of equal cardinality are isomorphic, i.e., for each cardinality p^k there is up to isomorphism only one finite field, which allows one to refer to it just as $\mathbb{F}_{p^k}$.

---

[3] In the public-key case we can efficiently recover the encrypted field element, in the private-key case this is only possible up to isomorphism, as we may have no knowledge of the plaintext field.

[4] One may be led to believe that field-homomorphic one-way permutations cannot exist, since a finite field has only a small number of automorphisms, which can be enumerated exhaustively. However, we assume the target field to be given as a black-box without explicit representation of the elements. As such it is a priori not clear how to find the preimage of a random element.

Prime fields $\mathbb{F}_p$ (i.e., $k = 1$) are defined as $\mathbb{Z}_p = \{0, \ldots, p-1\}$ with addition and multiplication modulo p. An extension field $\mathbb{F}_{p^k}$ can be defined as the polynomial ring $\mathbb{F}_p[X]$ modulo an irreducible polynomial $m(X)$ of degree k over $\mathbb{F}_p$. It hence consists of all polynomials of degree at most $k - 1$ with coefficients in $\mathbb{F}_p$.

For every $x \in \mathbb{F}_{p^k}$, the p-fold sum of x (i.e., $x + x + \cdots + x$ with p terms), denoted px, is zero: $px = 0$. Moreover, $x^{p^k - 1} = 1$ for all $x \neq 0$, as $p^k - 1$ is the cardinality of the multiplicative group of $\mathbb{F}_{p^k}$, which is actually cyclic.

An extension field $\mathbb{F}_{p^k}$ is a vector space over $\mathbb{F}_p$ of dimension k. For appropriate $g \in \mathbb{F}_{p^k}$ there exist bases of the form $(1, g, g^2, \ldots, g^{k-1})$. The only automorphisms of a finite field $\mathbb{F}_{p^k}$ are the Frobenius automorphisms $x \mapsto x^{(p^i)}$ for $i = 0, \ldots, k-1$. In particular, a prime field has no non-trivial automorphisms.

For every ℓ dividing k, there is a subfield $\mathbb{F}_{p^\ell}$ of $\mathbb{F}_{p^k}$. The *trace function* $\mathrm{tr}_{\mathbb{F}_{p^k}/\mathbb{F}_{p^\ell}} : \mathbb{F}_{p^k} \to \mathbb{F}_{p^\ell}$, defined as

$$\mathrm{tr}_{\mathbb{F}_{p^k}/\mathbb{F}_{p^\ell}}(a) = \sum_{i=0}^{(k/\ell)-1} a^{(p^{i\ell})},$$

is a surjective and $\mathbb{F}_{p^\ell}$-linear function [LN97].

2.2   The Black-Box Model

We make use of the abstract model of computation from [Mau05]: A black-box field $\mathbb{F}_{\mathbf{B}}$ is characterized by a black-box $\mathbf{B}$ which can store an (unbounded number of) values from some finite field $\mathbb{F}_{p^k}$ of known characteristic p but not necessarily known extension degree in internal registers $V_0, V_1, V_2, \ldots$. The first $d + 1$ of these registers hold the initial state $I = [g_0, g_1, \ldots, g_d]$ of the black-box. We require the size $d+1$ of the initial state to be at most polynomial in $\log(|\mathbb{F}_{\mathbf{B}}|)$.

The black-box $\mathbf{B}$ provides the following interface: It takes as input a pair (i, j) of indices and a bit indicating whether addition or multiplication should be invoked. Then it performs the required operation on V_i and V_j, stores the result in the next free register, say V_ℓ, and reports all pairs of indices (m, n) such that $V_m = V_n$.[5]

Since we only allow performing the field operations $+$ and $\cdot$ on the values of the black-box, the black-box field $\mathbb{F}_{\mathbf{B}}$ is by definition the field $\mathbb{F}_{\mathbf{B}} = \mathbb{F}_p[g_0, g_1, \ldots, g_d]$ generated[6] by the elements $g_0, g_1, \ldots, g_d \in \mathbb{F}_{p^k}$ contained in the initial state $I = [g_0, g_1, \ldots, g_d]$ of the black-box.

A black-box field $\mathbb{F}_{\mathbf{B}}$ is thus completely characterized by the

- **public values:**   characteristic[7] p, size $d + 1$ of the initial state,
- **secret values:**   initial state $I = [g_0, g_1, \ldots, g_d]$ (hidden inside the black-box)

---

[5] Alternatively, equality checks could also be modeled as an explicit operation which must be called with two indices.

[6] By $\mathbb{F}_p[g_0, g_1, \ldots, g_d]$ we denote the field consisting of all polynomial expressions over $\mathbb{F}_p$ in the generators $g_0, g_1, \ldots, g_d$.

[7] If the characteristic p is small it need not be given but can be recovered in time $O(\sqrt{p})$ using a modified Baby-Step-Giant-Step algorithm [Mau05].

This is probably the most basic yet complete way of describing a finite field. Observe that the field $\mathbb{F}_{p^k}$, the elements of which the black-box can store, does not appear in the characterization. Since no algorithm can compute any value not expressible as an expression in the operators $+$ and $\cdot$, and the elements initially given inside the black-box, we can without loss of generality assume that k is such that $\mathbb{F}_{p^k} \cong \mathbb{F}_{\mathbf{B}}$, where k is unknown, but can be efficiently computed as we shall see later.

Also, the operations "additive inverse" and "multiplicative inverse" and the constants 0 and 1 need not be provided explicitly, since they can be computed efficiently given the characteristic p and the field size $|\mathbb{F}_{\mathbf{B}}| = p^k$: We can compute the additive inverse for an element $a \in \mathbb{F}_{\mathbf{B}}^*$ as $-a = (p-1)a$, and the multiplicative inverse is $a^{-1} = a^{p^k-2}$. Furthermore, $1 = a^{p^k-1}$ for any non-zero a and $0 = pa$ for any a. These expressions can be evaluated efficiently using square-and-multiply techniques.

When discussing the complexity of algorithms on black-box fields, we count each invocation of the black-box as one step. Additionally we will take into account the runtime of computations not directly involving the black-box.

We consider an algorithm to be *efficient* if it runs in time polynomial in the bit-size of a field element, $\log |\mathbb{F}_{\mathbf{B}}|$.[8]

2.3   The Representation Problem and Related Problems

We now turn to the problems we intend to solve. Let a characteristic p be given and let $\mathbf{B}$ be a black-box with initial state $I = [x, g_1, \ldots g_d]$ consisting of generators $g_1, \ldots g_d$ and a challenge x, where $\mathbb{F}_{\mathbf{B}} = \mathbb{F}_p[x, g_1, \ldots g_d]$. We then consider the following problems:

Definition 1 (Representability Problem, Representation Problem). *We call x representable (in the generators $g_1, \ldots g_d$) if $x \in \mathbb{F}_p[g_1, \ldots g_d]$. The problem of deciding whether $x \in \mathbb{F}_p[g_1, \ldots g_d]$ is called the* representability problem. *If x is representable, then finding a multi-variate polynomial $q \in \mathbb{F}_p[X_1, \ldots, X_d]$ such that $x = q(g_1, \ldots, g_d)$ is called the* representation problem.

We proceed to discuss two problems that are closely related to the representation problem. First, we state a generalization of the extraction problem, defined in [Mau05], that is applicable to all finite black-box fields. To do so, we need to specify an isomorphism ϕ from the black-box to some explicitly given field K. This is necessary for the extraction problem to be well-defined, because in contrast to prime fields there are many isomorphisms between two isomorphic extension fields.

Definition 2 (Extraction Problem). *Let K be an explicitly given field (e.g. by an irreducible polynomial) such that $K \cong \mathbb{F}_{\mathbf{B}}$. Let the images $\phi(g_1), \ldots, \phi(g_d)$*

---

[8] The requirement that the size $d+1$ of the initial state be at most polynomial in $\log(|\mathbb{F}_{\mathbf{B}}|)$ is imposed so that this makes sense.

of the generators $g_1, \ldots, g_d$ *under some isomorphism* $\phi : \mathbb{F_B} \to K$ *be given. The* extraction problem *is to compute* $\phi(x)$.[9]

Remark 1. Note that an efficient solution to the representation problem implies an efficient solution to the extraction problem. The expression $q(g_1, \ldots, g_d)$ returned as a solution to the representation problem can simply be evaluated over K, substituting $\phi(g_i)$ for g_i ($i = 1, \ldots, d$), which yields $\phi(x)$:

$$q(\phi(g_1), \ldots, \phi(g_d)) = \phi(q(g_1, \ldots, g_d)) = \phi(x).$$

Finally consider an efficient but representation-dependent algorithm A solving some problem Q on a finite field K (where the algorithm A requires for instance that the field K is given by an irreducible polynomial). We are interested if the existence of such an algorithm A generally implies the existence of a generic algorithm for the problem Q of comparable efficiency. More specifically, we are interested in algorithms Φ and Φ^{-1} efficiently computing an *arbitrary* isomorphism $\phi : \mathbb{F_B} \to K$ and its inverse ϕ^{-1}, yielding a generic solution $\Phi^{-1} \circ A \circ \Phi$ to the problem Q. That is the algorithm Φ maps an $x \in \mathbb{F_B}$ to K by solving the extraction problem with respect to ϕ. The inverse map Φ^{-1} on the other hand maps a field element $x' \in K$ into the black box field $\mathbb{F_B}$ by means of constructing $\phi^{-1}(x')$ from the generators inside the black-box using the field operations. These two algorithms can then be chained together with the original, representation dependent algorithm A, yielding a black-box, representation independent algorithm $\Phi^{-1} \circ A \circ \Phi$. Hence we consider the following problem:

Definition 3 (Isomorphism Problem). *Let K be an explicitly given field such that $K \cong \mathbb{F_B}$. The* isomorphism problem *consists of computing an (arbitrary but fixed) isomorphism $\phi : \mathbb{F_B} \to K$ and its inverse ϕ^{-1} for arbitrary elements of K and $\mathbb{F_B}$.*

In the following we will exhibit an efficient reduction from the representation problem for any finite field to the representation problem for the underlying prime field. Moreover, our solution to the representation problem will also yield an explicitly given field (by an irreducible polynomial) $\mathbb{F}_{p^k} \cong \mathbb{F_B}$ with an efficient solution to the isomorphism problem for $\mathbb{F}_{p^k}$ and $\mathbb{F_B}$. This allows to solve any problem posed on the black-box field $\mathbb{F_B}$ in the explicitly given field $\mathbb{F}_{p^k}$ using the corresponding algorithms.

2.4   The Representation Problem for $\mathbb{F}_p$

First, we shall see that the representation, extraction and isomorphism problems are equivalent when the black-box field $\mathbb{F_B}$ is isomorphic to some prime field $\mathbb{F}_p$:

---

[9] The extraction problem also makes sense if the isomorphism ϕ is given in another fashion. For example, the black-box might offer an operation that allows inserting elements from an explicitly given field K. This would for instance correspond to a field-homomorphic one-way permutation.

Lemma 1. *Let* $\mathbb{F}_\mathbf{B} \cong \mathbb{F}_p$ *be a BBF with initial state* $I = [x, g_1, \ldots, g_d]$. *Then the representation, extraction and isomorphism problems are efficiently reducible to one another.*

Proof. Note that there is a unique isomorphism $\phi : \mathbb{F}_\mathbf{B} \to \mathbb{F}_p$. Furthermore, as $\mathbb{F}_\mathbf{B} \cong \mathbb{F}_p$, there must be a $g_i \neq 0$ ($i \in \{1, \ldots, d\}$). This g_i can be efficiently found by checking the inequality $g_i + g_i \neq g_i$ and the constant 1 can be efficiently computed inside the black-box as g_i^{p-1} using square-and-multiply techniques.

Reduction extraction to representation: see Remark 1.

Reduction isomorphism to extraction: A solution to the extraction problem yields an efficient algorithm computing the isomorphism ϕ. The inverse ϕ^{-1} can be efficiently computed using square-and-multiply techniques, constructing $\phi^{-1}(a)$ for $a \in \mathbb{F}_p$ as a sum of 1s inside the black-box. This solves the isomorphism problem.

Reduction representation to isomorphism: A solution to the isomorphism problem yields an efficient algorithm computing the isomorphism ϕ. Then we have $\phi(x)g_i^{p-1}$ as a solution to the representation problem. $\square$

Note that solving the extraction problem for a black-box field $\mathbb{F}_\mathbf{B} \cong \mathbb{F}_p$ with initial state $V^1 = [x]$ amounts to solving the discrete logarithm problem for a group of order p (given as a black-box) for which a Diffie-Hellman oracle is given. The following results are known:

Lemma 2 ([Mau94]). *There exists a non-uniform algorithm that, under a (plausible) number-theoretic conjecture, solves the extraction (representation, isomorphism) problem for a black-box field* $\mathbb{F}_\mathbf{B} \cong \mathbb{F}_p$ *in time polynomial in* $\log(p)$, *and with a polynomial (in* $\log(p)$*) amount of advice depending on* p.

Lemma 3 ([BL96]). *There exists a (uniform) algorithm that, under a (plausible) number-theoretic conjecture, solves the extraction (representation, isomorphism) problem for a black-box field* $\mathbb{F}_\mathbf{B} \cong \mathbb{F}_p$ *in time subexponential in* $\log(p)$.

For the remainder of this work we will only concern ourselves with reducing other problems to the representation problem for $\mathbb{F}_p$. The reader may generally assume that p is small, such that the representation problem for $\mathbb{F}_p$ is easy to solve.

2.5   The Representation Problem for $\mathbb{F}_{p^k}$ for a Given $\mathbb{F}_p$-Basis

Before we proceed to the general case, we first investigate the simpler case where the initial state of the black-box $\mathbf{B}$ is $I = [x, b_1, \ldots, b_k]$, and $b_1, \ldots, b_k$ form a basis of $\mathbb{F}_\mathbf{B}$ as $\mathbb{F}_p$-vector space. We efficiently reduce this problem to the representation problem for $\mathbb{F}_p$ discussed in Section 2.4.

Lemma 4. *The representation problem for a black-box field* $\mathbb{F}_\mathbf{B}$ *of characteristic* p *with initial state* $I = [x, b_1, \ldots, b_k]$, *where* $b_1, \ldots, b_k$ *form an* $\mathbb{F}_p$-*basis of* $\mathbb{F}_\mathbf{B}$, *is efficiently reducible to the representation problem for* $\mathbb{F}_p$.

Proof. The proof relies on the well-known dual basis theorem (see e.g. [LN97]): For any $\mathbb{F}_p$-basis $\{b_1, \ldots, b_k\}$ of $\mathbb{F}_{p^k}$ there exists a dual basis $\{c_1, \ldots, c_k\}$ with the property that $\mathrm{tr}_{\mathbb{F}_{p^k}/\mathbb{F}_p}(c_i b_j) = \delta_{ij}$, where δ_{ij} designates the Kronecker-Delta. We calculate the dual basis $\{c_1, \ldots, c_k\}$ for the basis $\{b_1, \ldots, b_k\}$ inside the black-box. This can be done efficiently as follows:

We write the elements of the dual basis as $c_i = \sum_{l=1}^{k} \alpha_{il} b_l$. Furthermore, let $A = (\alpha_{il})_{i,l=1,\ldots,k}$ be the coefficient matrix, $B = (\mathrm{tr}_{\mathbb{F}_{p^k}/\mathbb{F}_p}(b_l b_j))_{l,j=1,\ldots,k}$ the trace matrix, and I_k the identity matrix. Then the definition of the dual basis yields a matrix equation $AB = I_k$. Traces can be computed efficiently inside the black-box using square-and-multiply techniques, so the trace matrix B can be efficiently computed inside the black-box. Since B always has full rank [LN97], the matrix equation $AB = I_k$ can be solved for the α_{il} using Gaussian elimination (inside the box **B**).

As the characteristic p and the exponent k are known, we can efficiently compute additive and multiplicative inverses (see Section 2.2). Solving for the k^2 unknowns in the matrix A using Gaussian elimination is efficient, and requires only field operations and equality checks. Hence it can be performed in the black-box and we can efficiently compute the dual basis elements c_i inside the black-box.

To represent the challenge x in the basis $\{b_1, \ldots, b_k\}$, we now calculate $\xi_i = \mathrm{tr}_{\mathbb{F}_{p^k}/\mathbb{F}_p}(c_i x) \in \mathbb{F}_p$ inside the black-box and have $x = \sum_{i=1}^{k} \xi_i b_i$ by the dual basis property. We use an oracle $\mathcal{O}$ that solves the representation problem for $\mathbb{F}_p$ (possibly instantiated according to Section 2.4) to extract the ξ_i from the black box, obtaining the required representation of x in the given generators (basis) $\{b_1, \ldots, b_k\}$.   □

3   The Representation Problem for $\mathbb{F}_{p^k}$ for Arbitrary Generating Sets

Now we turn to the general case, where a black-box field $\mathbb{F}_\mathbf{B}$ of characteristic p is not necessarily given by a basis, but by an arbitrary generating set $\{g_1, \ldots, g_d\}$ which generates $\mathbb{F}_\mathbf{B}$ as $\mathbb{F}_p$-algebra.

3.1   Main Theorem

Before we get to our main result, we first discuss the representability problem.

Lemma 5. *The representability problem for a black-box field $\mathbb{F}_\mathbf{B}$ of characteristic p with initial state $I = [x, g_1, \ldots, g_d]$ can be solved efficiently and the extension degree k such that $\mathbb{F}_\mathbf{B} \cong \mathbb{F}_{p^k}$ can be found efficiently.*

Proof. We need to determine efficiently whether x is representable in the generators $g_1, \ldots, g_d$ and then find k such that $\mathbb{F}_\mathbf{B} \cong \mathbb{F}_{p^k}$. To this end we first determine the size $k_i := k(g_i) := |\mathbb{F}_p[g_i]|$ of the subfield $\mathbb{F}_p[g_i] \leq \mathbb{F}_\mathbf{B}$ of the black-box field $\mathbb{F}_\mathbf{B}$ generated by g_i, for $i = 1, \ldots, d$. We have

$$k_i := k(g_i) = \min\{j \in \mathbb{N} : g_i = g_i^{p^j}\} \tag{1}$$

by the properties of the Frobenius homomorphism $y \mapsto y^p$ [LN97]. Eq. (1) can be evaluated efficiently using square-and-multiply.

Now the field element x is representable in the generators $g_1, \ldots, g_d$ if and only if $x \in \mathbb{F}_p[g_1, \ldots, g_d]$ or, equivalently, $\mathbb{F}_p[x] \leq \mathbb{F}_p[g_1, \ldots, g_d]$. But the field $\mathbb{F}_p[g_1, \ldots, g_d]$ generated by $g_1, \ldots, g_d$ is isomorphic to the smallest field $\mathbb{F}_{p^{k'}}$ where $k' = \mathrm{lcm}_{i=1}^{l}(k_i)$ that contains all the $\mathbb{F}_{p^{k_i}}$. Hence x is representable in the generators $g_1, \ldots, g_d$ if and only if $k(x) \mid k'$. Moreover, independently of the representability of x we have $k = \mathrm{lcm}(k(x), k')$. $\qquad\square$

We can now state our main result, an efficient reduction from the representation problem for an extension field to the representation problem for the underlying prime field:

Theorem 1. *The representation problem for the black-box field* $\mathbb{F}_\mathbf{B}$ *of characteristic p with initial state $I = [x, g_1, \ldots, g_d]$ (not necessarily a basis) such that x is representable in $g_1, \ldots, g_d$ is efficiently reducible to the representation problem for $\mathbb{F}_p$.*

We shall see later that from this theorem we can also obtain efficient reductions of the extraction and isomorphism problems to the representation problem for the underlying prime field $\mathbb{F}_p$.

3.2 Proof of Theorem 1

By assumption, the challenge x is representable in the generators $g_1, \ldots, g_d$. We will show how to efficiently generate a $\mathbb{F}_p$-power-basis $\{g^0, g^1, \ldots, g^{k-1}\}$ for $\mathbb{F}_\mathbf{B}$ inside the black-box. The representation problem can then be efficiently reduced to the representation problem for $\mathbb{F}_p$ using Lemma 4.[10]

Algorithm 1 returns an $\mathbb{F}_p$-power-basis for $\mathbb{F}_\mathbf{B}$ by computing an element $g \in \mathbb{F}_\mathbf{B}$ (a generator), such that $\mathbb{F}_p[g] = \mathbb{F}_{p^k}$. To this end Algorithm 1 iterates over the generators $g_1, \ldots, g_d$, checking if the current g_i is already contained in $\mathbb{F}_p[g]$ for the current g.[11] If not, Algorithm 1 invokes the algorithm combine_gen(g, g_i) to obtain a new g (which we call g' for now) such that $\mathbb{F}_p[g'] = \mathbb{F}_p[g, g_i]$. Clearly, $\mathbb{F}_p[g] = \mathbb{F}_p[g_1, \ldots, g_d]$ when the algorithm terminates, and hence $\{g^0, g^1, \ldots, g^{k-1}\}$ is a $\mathbb{F}_p$-power-basis for $\mathbb{F}_p[g_1, \ldots, g_d] = \mathbb{F}_\mathbf{B}$.

As g is computed inside the black-box from the initially given generators $g_1, \ldots, g_d$ using only field operations, a representation $q'(g_1, \ldots, g_d) = g$ of g

---

[10] One might suspect that the $\{g_i^j\}_{i=1,\ldots,d; j=1,\ldots,k}$ already generate $\mathbb{F}_\mathbf{B}$ as an $\mathbb{F}_p$-vector space. However, this is not the case. As an example, take $\mathbb{F}_{2^6}$. Then we can find generators $g_2 \in \mathbb{F}_{2^2} \subset \mathbb{F}_{2^6}$ and $g_3 \in \mathbb{F}_{2^3} \subset \mathbb{F}_{2^6}$ such that $\mathbb{F}_2[g_2, g_3] = \mathbb{F}_{2^6}$. But $g_i^j \in \mathbb{F}_{2^i}$, so the $\mathbb{F}_p$-vector space V generated by $\{g_i^j\}$ has dimension $\dim_{\mathbb{F}_2} V \leq \dim_{\mathbb{F}_2} \mathbb{F}_{2^2} + \dim_{\mathbb{F}_2} \mathbb{F}_{2^3} = 5 < 6 = \dim_{\mathbb{F}_2} \mathbb{F}_{2^6}$.

[11] Note that the number of generators g_i appearing in the representation of the generator g (and thereby the representation of x) could be reduced by considering only the generators g_i corresponding to the maximal elements in the lattice formed by the k_i under the divisibility relation (these suffice to generate the entire field $\mathbb{F}_\mathbf{B}$). For ease of exposition we do not do this.

Algorithm 1. Compute power-basis

1: $g := 1$
2: $m := 1$
3: **for** $i = 1$ to d **do**
4:    $k_i := k(g_i) := \min\{j \in \mathbb{N} : g_i = g_i^{p^j}\}$
5:    **if** $k_i \nmid m$ **then**
6:        $m := \mathrm{lcm}(m, k_i)$
7:        $g := \mathtt{combine\_gen}(g, g_i)$
8:    **end if**
9: **end for**
10: **return** power basis $\{g^0, g^1, \ldots, g^{k-1}\}$

(and therefore of all basis elements) in the generators $g_1, \ldots, g_d$ is known. Now Lemma 4 gives a representation $q''(g^0, g^1, \ldots, g^{k-1}) = x$ of the challenge x in the basis elements, so a representation $q(g_1, \ldots, g_d) = x$ of x in the generators $g_1, \ldots, g_d$ can be recovered by substitution:

$$q(g_1, \ldots, g_d) = q''(g^0, g^1, \ldots, g^{k-1})$$
$$= q''(q'(g_1, \ldots, g_d)^0, q'(g_1, \ldots, g_d)^1, \ldots, q'(g_1, \ldots, g_d)^{k-1})$$

Algorithm 1 is obviously efficient if the algorithm $\mathtt{combine\_gen}$ is efficient. So, to complete the proof of Theorem 1, we only need to provide an algorithm $\mathtt{combine\_gen}(a, b)$ that, given two elements $a, b \in \mathbb{F}_\mathbf{B}$, efficiently computes a generator g such that $\mathbb{F}_p[g] = \mathbb{F}_p[a, b]$.

Algorithm 2. $\mathtt{combine\_gen}(a, b)$

1: find k'_a, k'_b such that

- $k'_a \mid k(a)$, $k'_b \mid k(b)$,
- $\gcd(k'_a, k'_b) = 1$,
- $\mathrm{lcm}(k'_a, k'_b) = \mathrm{lcm}(k(a), k(b))$

2: find $a' \in \mathbb{F}_p[a]$ and $b' \in \mathbb{F}_p[b]$ such that $k(a') = k'_a$ and $k(b') = k'_b$
3: **return** $a' + b'$

Claim. Given two elements $a, b \in \mathbb{F}_\mathbf{B}$, the algorithm $\mathtt{combine\_gen}(a, b)$ efficiently computes a generator g such that $\mathbb{F}_p[g] = \mathbb{F}_p[a, b]$.

Proof. We analyze algorithm $\mathtt{combine\_gen}(a, b)$ step by step:

Step 1 can be performed in time polynomial in k (where $p^k = |\mathbb{F}_\mathbf{B}|$), and hence in $\log(|\mathbb{F}_\mathbf{B}|)$, by factoring $k(a)$ and $k(b)$ (which both divide k). [12]

Step 2 relies on the following lemma [Len05]:

---
[12] Bach and Shallit [BS96, Section 4.8] give a much more efficient algorithm for computing such values k'_a, k'_b of complexity $O((\log k(a)k(b))^2)$.

Lemma 6. *Let $M \geq L \geq K$ be a tower of finite fields and let $b_1, \ldots, b_n$ be a K-basis of M. Then $\{\mathrm{tr}_{M/L}(b_1), \ldots, \mathrm{tr}_{M/L}(b_n)\}$ contains a K-basis of L.*

Proof. From [LN97, 2.23(iii)] we know that $\mathrm{tr}_{M/L} : M \to L$ is L-linear and surjective. Hence for all $d \in L$ there exists an $c \in M$ such that $\mathrm{tr}_{M/L}(c) = d$. Since $b_1, \ldots, b_n$ form a K-basis of M, the element $c \in M$ can be expressed as $c = \sum_{i=1}^{n} \gamma_i b_i$ where $\gamma_i \in K$ $(i = 1, \ldots, n)$. Hence using the L-linearity of $\mathrm{tr}_{M/L}$ we have

$$d = \mathrm{tr}_{M/L}(c) = \mathrm{tr}_{M/L}\left(\sum_{i=1}^{n} \gamma_i b_i\right) = \sum_{i=1}^{n} \gamma_i \, \mathrm{tr}_{M/L}(b_i).$$

As we can represent every $d \in L$ by a K-linear combination in $\{\mathrm{tr}_{M/L}(b_1), \ldots, \mathrm{tr}_{M/L}(b_n)\}$, this set must contain a K-basis of L. $\quad\square$

As we know k'_a and $k(a)$ from Step 1, and using the fact that the elements $\{a^i : i = 0, \ldots, k(a) - 1\}$ form an $\mathbb{F}_p$-basis of $\mathbb{F}_p[a]$, we can compute the set $\{\mathrm{tr}_{\mathbb{F}_p[a]/\mathbb{F}_{p^{k'_a}}}(a^i) : i = 0, \ldots, k(a) - 1\}$ in time $O(k^3 \log(p))$, which contains by the lemma above an $\mathbb{F}_p$-basis of $\mathbb{F}_{p^{k'_a}}$.

The following claim is from [BvzGL01, Lemma 6.2]. For completeness we provide a short proof sketch.

Claim. Any $\mathbb{F}_p$-basis of an extension field $\mathbb{F}_{p^\ell}$ contains a basis element a' such that $\mathbb{F}_{p^\ell} = \mathbb{F}_p[a']$.

Proof (sketch). The $\mathbb{F}_p$-dimension of the span of all proper subfields of $\mathbb{F}_{p^\ell}$ can be computed by application of the inclusion-exclusion principle (first adding the dimensions of all maximal subfields, then subtracting the dimensions of their intersections, then adding the dimensions of the intersections of the intersections, and so on). Using the Möbius function μ and the Euler function φ we can hence write the $\mathbb{F}_p$-dimension of the span of all proper subfields of $\mathbb{F}_{p^\ell}$ as $-\sum_{d\mid\ell, d\neq\ell} \mu(\ell/d)d = \ell - \varphi(\ell) < \ell$. As the $\mathbb{F}_p$-dimension of the span of all proper subfields of $\mathbb{F}_{p^\ell}$ is smaller then the $\mathbb{F}_p$-dimension ℓ of $\mathbb{F}_{p^\ell}$, there must be a basis element a' which is not contained in any proper subfield of $\mathbb{F}_{p^\ell}$, and therefore $\mathbb{F}_{p^\ell} = \mathbb{F}_p[a']$. $\quad\square$

By the claim above there is a basis element a', that generates $\mathbb{F}_{p^{k'_a}}$, i.e. $\mathbb{F}_{p^{k'_a}} = \mathbb{F}_p[a']$:

$$\exists a' \in \{\mathrm{tr}_{\mathbb{F}_p[a]/\mathbb{F}_{p^{k'_a}}}(a^i) : i = 0, \ldots, k(a) - 1\} : \quad k(a') = k'_a.$$

By checking this property for all candidate elements in $\{\mathrm{tr}_{\mathbb{F}_p[a]/\mathbb{F}_{p^{k'_a}}}(a^i) : i = 0, \ldots, k(a) - 1\}$ we find the generator a' in time $O(k^3 \log(p))$. Analogously we may determine b' such that $k(b') = k'_b$.

Step 3. To complete the analysis of the algorithm $\mathtt{combine\_gen}(x, y)$, it remains to show that given a', b' from Step 2, we have $\mathbb{F}_p[a' + b'] = \mathbb{F}_p[a, b]$. Since $\mathrm{lcm}(k(a'), k(b')) = \mathrm{lcm}(k(a), k(b))$ by Step 1, we have $\mathbb{F}_p[a', b'] = \mathbb{F}_p[a, b]$, so it only remains to show that $\mathbb{F}_p[a' + b'] = \mathbb{F}_p[a', b']$. We have $\mathbb{F}_p[a', b'] = \mathbb{F}_p[a', a' + b'] = \mathbb{F}_p[a' + b', b']$ and $\gcd(k(a'), k(b')) = 1$, therefore

$$\mathrm{lcm}(k(a'), k(b')) = \mathrm{lcm}(k(a'), k(a' + b')) = \mathrm{lcm}(k(a' + b'), k(b')) = k(a')k(b').$$

It is easy to see that then $k(a' + b') = k(a')k(b')$ holds, and therefore $\mathbb{F}_p[a' + b'] = \mathbb{F}_p[a, b]$, as required. □

3.3   Implications of Theorem 1

From Theorem 1 and Remark 1 we obtain the following corollary:

Corollary 2. *The extraction problem for any BBF $\mathbb{F}_\mathbf{B}$ of characteristic p is efficiently reducible to the representation problem for $\mathbb{F}_p$.*

The extraction problem asks for the computation of an isomorphism $\phi : \mathbb{F}_\mathbf{B} \to K$. Note that the computation of ϕ^{-1} also reduces efficiently to the representation problem for $\mathbb{F}_p$, because we can efficiently obtain a power-basis $\{g^0, g^1, \ldots, g^{k-1}\}$ inside the black-box, as in the proof of Theorem 1. From this basis we can then compute the basis $\{\phi(g^0), \phi(g^1), \ldots, \phi(g^{k-1})\}$ for K. Hence the isomorphism ϕ^{-1} can be simply and efficiently computed by basis representation.

Corollary 3. *Let $\mathbb{F}_\mathbf{B}$ be a BBF of characteristic p and K some explicitly given field (in the sense of [Len91]) such that $K \cong \mathbb{F}_\mathbf{B}$. Then the isomorphism problem for $\mathbb{F}_\mathbf{B}$ and K can be efficiently reduced to the representation problem for $\mathbb{F}_p$.*

Proof. We show that it is possible to efficiently find a field $K' \cong \mathbb{F}_\mathbf{B}$ that is explicitly given by an irreducible polynomial, such that the isomorphism problem for $\mathbb{F}_\mathbf{B}$ and K' efficiently reduces to the representation problem for $\mathbb{F}_p$. The corollary then follows from [Len91], which states that the isomorphism problem for two explicitly given finite fields can be solved efficiently.

So, let an oracle $\mathcal{O}$ for the representation problem over $\mathbb{F}_p$ be given. As in the proof of Theorem 1 we efficiently compute a power-basis $\{g^0, g^1, \ldots, g^{k-1}\}$ inside the black-box. By Lemma 4 we compute a representation $q(g^0, g^1, \ldots, g^{k-1}) = g^k$ of g^k in the basis elements. Note that the minimal polynomial $f_g \in \mathbb{F}_p[X]$ of g over $\mathbb{F}_p$ is then exactly $f_g(X) = X^k - q(X^0, X^1, \ldots, X^{k-1})$. Let $K' = \mathbb{F}_p[X]/(f_g)$. Then the required isomorphisms ϕ and ϕ^{-1} are efficiently given by basis representation. □

4   Conclusion

We have shown that, given an efficient algorithm for the representation problem for $\mathbb{F}_p$, we can solve the representability, representation, extraction and isomorphism problems for a black-box extension field $\mathbb{F}_\mathbf{B} \cong \mathbb{F}_{p^k}$ in polynomial time.

We achieve this by efficiently constructing (in the generators) an $\mathbb{F}_p$-power-basis $\{g^0, g^1, \ldots, g^{k-1}\}$ for the black-box field $\mathbb{F}_{\mathbf{B}}$ inside the black-box, which is interesting in its own right.

For small characteristic p we can immediately solve the above problems efficiently, as in this case solving the representation problem for $\mathbb{F}_p$ (e.g. using Baby-Step-Giant-Step) is easy.

As a consequence, field-homomorphic one-way permutations over fields of small characteristic p, in particular over $\mathbb{F}_{2^k}$, do not exist, because such a function would constitute an instantiation of a black-box field[13] and could be efficiently inverted using the solution to the extraction problem given above. This implies that over fields of small characteristic there can be no field-homomorphic analogue to the group-homomorphic RSA encryption scheme, which constitutes a group-homomorphic trapdoor one-way permutation.

For the same reason, even probabilistic field-homomorphic encryption schemes (both private-[14] and public-key) over fields of small characteristic p, in particular over $\mathbb{F}_{2^k}$, cannot be realized, if they allow for checking the equality of elements. This is unfortunate because such schemes could have interesting applications in multi-party computation and computation with encrypted data (e.g. server-assisted computation) [SYY99, ALN87, Dom02]. For instance we might be interested in handing encrypted field elements to a computing facility and having it compute some (known) program on them. If the encryption permits equality checks, the computing facility can recover the field elements up to isomorphism.

Furthermore, a polynomial-time solution to the isomorphism problem implies that any problem posed on a black-box field (i.e., computing discrete logarithms over the multiplicative group) can be efficiently transferred to an explicitly represented field, and be solved there using possibly representation-dependent algorithms (e.g. the number field sieve). The solution can then efficiently be transferred back to the black-box field. So any representation-dependent algorithm for finite fields is applicable (in the case of small characteristic) to black-box fields. For example, computing discrete logarithms in the multiplicative group over a finite field is no harder in the black-box setting than if the field is given explicitly by an irreducible polynomial.

Of course these conclusions do apply not only to fields of small characteristic p, but to any scenario where we can efficiently solve the representation problem for the underlying prime field $\mathbb{F}_p$. Hence we obtain subexponential-time solutions to the above problems under a plausible number-theoretic conjecture applying the work of Boneh and Lipton [BL96] for solving the representation problem for $\mathbb{F}_p$. Furthermore we can, under a plausible number-theoretic conjecture, solve

---

[13] Instead of generators we have here the possibility to "insert" elements of an explicitly given field into the "black-box" of the image of the function.

[14] This result requires Theorem 1 whereas the results above already follow from Lemma 4. Also, note that in the private-key case it is only possible to recover encrypted field elements up to isomorphism, as we may have no knowledge of the plaintext field.

the problems above efficiently, even for large characteristic p, if we are willing to admit non-uniform solutions (solutions that require a polynomial amount of advice depending on the characteristic p) using an algorithm by Maurer [Mau94] for solving the representation problem for $\mathbb{F}_p$.

Compared to the case of small characteristic, the situation for fields of large characteristic is then more complex, because the only known efficient algorithm for solving the representation problem for $\mathbb{F}_p$ is non-uniform [Mau94, MW99], i.e. it requires a help-string that depends on p. When considering homomorphic encryption and homomorphic one-way permutations, this means that our impossibility results hold for cases where a malicious party may fix the characteristic p. In this case the attacker can generate p along with the required help-string to break the scheme. On the other hand our impossibility results do not apply if the characteristic p cannot be determined by the attacker, for instance because it is generated by a trusted party.

It remains an open problem to resolve this issue by providing an efficient *uniform* algorithm for the representation problem for $\mathbb{F}_p$, or by proving the inexistence thereof.

Acknowledgments

We thank Hendrik W. Lenstra, Jr. for insightful comments and discussions.

References

[ALN87]   Ahituv, N., Lapid, Y., Neumann, S.: Processing encrypted data. Communications of the ACM 30(9), 777–780 (1987)

[BB99]   Babai, L., Beals, R.: A polynomial-time theory of black box groups I. London Mathematical Society Lecture Note Series 260, 30–64 (1999)

[BL96]   Boneh, D., Lipton, R.J.: Algorithms for black-box fields and their application to cryptography (extended abstract). In: Koblitz, N. (ed.) CRYPTO 1996. LNCS, vol. 1109, pp. 283–297. Springer, Heidelberg (1996)

[BS84]   Babai, L., Szemerédi, E.: On the complexity of matrix group problems I. In: ó Babai, L. (ed.) 25th Annual Symposium on Foundations of Computer Science, pp. 229–240. IEEE Computer Society Press, Los Alamitos (1984)

[BS96]   Bach, E., Shallit, J.: Algorithmic Number Theory. Foundations of Computing 1 (1996)

[BvzGL01]   Bach, E., von zur Gathen, J., Lenstra Jr, H.W.: Factoring polynomials over special finite fields. Finite Fields and Their Applications 7, 5–28 (2001)

[DH76]   Diffie, W., Hellman, M.E.: New directions in cryptography. IEEE Transactions on Information Theory 22(5), 644–654 (1976)

[Dom02]   Domingo-Ferrer, J.: A provably secure additive and multiplicative privacy homomorphism. In: Chan, A.H., Gligor, V.D. (eds.) ISC 2002. LNCS, vol. 2433, pp. 471–483. Springer, Heidelberg (2002)

[Len91]   Lenstra Jr, H.W.: Finding isomorphisms between finite fields. Mathematics of Computation 56(193), 329–347 (1991)

[Len05]   Lenstra Jr, H.W.: Personal Communication (2005)

[LN97]   Lidl, R., Niederreiter, H.: Finite Fields. In: Encyclopedia of Mathemat-
           ics and its Applications, 2nd edn., vol. 20, Cambridge University Press,
           Cambridge (1997)
[Mau94]   Maurer, U.: Towards the equivalence of breaking the Diffie-Hellman proto-
           col and computing discrete logarithms. In: Desmedt, Y.G. (ed.) CRYPTO
           1994. LNCS, vol. 839, pp. 271–281. Springer, Heidelberg (1994)
[Mau05]   Maurer, U.: Abstract models of computation in cryptography. In: Smart,
           N.P. (ed.) Cryptography and Coding 2005. LNCS, vol. 3796, pp. 1–12.
           Springer, Heidelberg (2005)
[MW99]   Maurer, U., Wolf, S.: The relationship between breaking the Diffie-
           Hellman protocol and computing discrete logarithms. SIAM Journal on
           Computing 28(5), 1689–1721 (1999)
[Sho97]   Shoup, V.: Lower bounds for discrete logarithms and related problems.
           In: Fumy, W. (ed.) EUROCRYPT 1997. LNCS, vol. 1233, pp. 256–268.
           Springer, Heidelberg (1997)
[SYY99]   Sander, T., Young, A., Yung, M.: Non-interactive CryptoComputing for
           NC^1. In: Proceedings of the 40th Symposium on Foundations of Computer
           Science (FOCS), pp. 554–567. IEEE Computer Society Press, New York
           (1999)

Concurrent Statistical Zero-Knowledge Arguments for NP from One Way Functions

Vipul Goyal*, Ryan Moriarty**, Rafail Ostrovsky***, and Amit Sahai[†]

University of California, Los Angeles
{vipul,ryan,rafail,sahai}@cs.ucla.edu

Abstract. In this paper we show a general transformation from any honest verifier statistical zero-knowledge argument to a concurrent statistical zero-knowledge argument. Our transformation relies only on the existence of one-way functions. It is known that the existence of zero-knowledge systems for any non-trivial language implies one way functions. Hence our transformation *unconditionally* shows that concurrent statistical zero-knowledge arguments for a non-trivial language exist if and only if standalone secure statistical zero-knowledge arguments for that language exist.

Further, applying our transformation to the recent statistical zero-knowledge argument system of Nguyen et al (STOC'06) yields the first concurrent statistical zero-knowledge argument system for all languages in **NP** from any one way function.

1 Introduction

Zero-knowledge proof systems were introduced by Goldwasser, Micali and Rackoff [GMR89] and have the remarkable property that they yield nothing except the validity of assertion being proved. Such protocols involve a prover, who tries to prove some assertion, and a verifier, who is trying to decide if he believes the assertion. A cheating prover may act maliciously by trying to prove a false statement; a cheating verifier may try to learn more than the validity of the statement being proved. The property that the verifier learns nothing (except the validity of the statement) is formalized as the *zero-knowledge* condition and

---

* Research partially done while visiting IPAM. Supported in part by grants listed below.

** Research partially done while visiting IPAM. Supported in part by grants listed below.

*** Research partially done while visiting IPAM. This research was supported in part by IBM Faculty Award, Xerox Innovation Group Award, NSF Cybertrust grant no. 0430254, and U.C. MICRO grant.

[†] Research partially done while visiting IPAM. This research was supported in part by NSF ITR and Cybertrust programs (including grants 0627781, 0456717, and 0205594), a subgrant from SRI as part of the Army Cyber-TA program, an equipment grant from Intel, and an Alfred P. Sloan Foundation Research Fellowship.

the property that the prover cannot prove a false statement is formalized as the *soundness* condition.

Depending upon how strong we want the zero-knowledge property or the soundness property to be, we can define several different types of zero-knowledge systems. In *statistical zero-knowledge*, we require the zero-knowledge condition to hold even against an infinitely powerful cheating verifier. When we relax the zero-knowledge condition so that it need only hold against a probabilistic polynomial time cheating verifier, we get the so called *computational zero-knowledge*. Similarly, we can have zero-knowledge with either *statistical soundness* (known as zero-knowledge *proof systems*) or just *computational soundness* (known as zero-knowledge *argument systems*).

It would be desirable to construct statistical zero-knowledge proof systems for all languages in **NP**. Unfortunately it was shown that such systems can only be obtained for languages in **AM∩coAM** [BHZ87], and **AM∩coAM** cannot contain **NP** unless the polynomial hierarchy collapses. Thus if we want a zero-knowledge system for all language in **NP**, we can only have either statistical soundness or statistical zero-knowledge (but not both).

The original definition of zero-knowledge considers protocols running alone in isolation. That is, we have a single prover interacting with a single verifier. The concurrent setting was introduced by Dwork et al [DNS98] (see also [Fei90]) with a motivation to construct zero-knowledge protocols for more realistic settings (such as when the protocols are to be executed over the Internet). In the concurrent setting, many protocol executions are run at the same time with possibly a single prover simultaneously talking to many verifiers. The prover in this setting runs the risk of a coordinated attack from many different verifiers which interleave the execution of protocols and choose their responses to the prover based on each others' messages. If a zero-knowledge protocol maintains its zero-knowledge property even in the concurrent setting, it is said to be *concurrent zero-knowledge*.

Our Results. We give the first general transformation from any zero-knowledge system to concurrent zero-knowledge system that maintains the statistical zero-knowledge property of the system. Hence our compiler can be used to transform a computational zero-knowledge argument system into a concurrent computational zero-knowledge argument system as well as a statistical zero-knowledge argument system into a concurrent statistical zero-knowledge argument system. Our transformation only relies on the existence of one-way functions. Further, it does not require that the original protocol be public coin. These properties separate it from the compiler in [MP03], since the compiler in [MP03] was designed to maintain statistical soundness (whereas we deal with statistical zero-knowledge) and was designed to be very efficient (our transformation is polynomial time but we do not optimize for efficiency). Additionally, the compiler in [MP03] relies on specific number theoretic assumptions.

We would like to emphasize that our compiler only uses one-way functions. It is known that the existence of zero-knowledge systems for any non-trivial language implies one way functions [OW93]. Hence our transformation *unconditionally* shows that concurrent statistical zero-knowledge arguments for a non-trivial language exist if and only if standalone secure statistical zero-knowledge arguments for that language exist. This feature also allows us to achieve a main goal of ours: applying our transformation to the statistical zero-knowledge system from [NOV06], we get the first concurrent statistical zero-knowledge argument system for an **NP**-complete language from any one-way function.

Techniques. Here we describe our techniques at a high level. Our goal is to create a general compiler that will work for *honest verifier* statistical zero-knowledge arguments and turn them into concurrent statistical zero-knowledge arguments. We first use a modified version of the preamble from the concurrent zero knowledge protocol of [PRS02]. Using a preamble similar to [PRS02] enables us to have a verifier committed to his randomness for the run of the protocol and to give a strategy for a simulator that could extract that randomness in the concurrent setting. Thus we are be able to use a straight-line simulator after the preamble.

The main technical challenges are to adapt the preamble of [PRS02] to work with an all-powerful verifier and to base the preamble solely on one-way functions. The proof of soundness in [PRS02] relies on the verifier using statistically hiding commitments to commit to its randomness. However using statistically hiding commitments during the preamble does not seem plausible in our setting even though (independent of this work) they have recently been constructed from one way functions [HR07]. The main reason is that since we are dealing with statistical zero-knowledge, the verifier could potentially be all powerful. Thus all the commitments by the verifier to the prover should be statistically *binding*. Consequently, if the randomness of the verifier is not statistically hidden from the prover during the PRS preamble, it remains unclear how the proof of soundness would go through (even if the *prover* uses statistically hiding commitments).

To overcome this problem, the verifier commits using statistically binding commitments based on one-way functions as it appears essential in our setting. However, the verifier never actually opens the commitment. Instead the verifier gives a (standalone secure computational) zero-knowledge proof that his message are consistent with the randomness committed to in the PRS preamble. Note that it is important that we use a zero-knowledge *proof* here since the verifier is all powerful. This idea enables us to prove that our transformation preserves the soundness of the underlying proof system.

Furthermore, since we are transforming from an honest verifier statistical zero-knowledge argument into a concurrent statistical zero-knowledge argument, we need to find a way to relax the requirement that the verifier is honest. In order to achieve this goal, the randomness that the verifier uses is determined by a coin-flipping protocol between the prover and the verifier (instead of being chosen freely by the verifier alone). This is important for our proof of the zero-knowledge condition since our simulator for the underlying protocol will require verifier responses with correctly distributed randomness. Also, this technique combined with the trick of using zero-knowledge proofs from the verifier allows us to deal with *private-coin* protocols as well.

We are able to combine all of these ideas into a single compiler that lets us achieve our results.

1.1 Related Work

Statistical zero-knowledge arguments. In this paper, we will be examining statistical zero-knowledge arguments which were first introduced by [BCC88]. From the constructions of [GMW91, BCC88] it is clear that one main technique to construct statistical zero-knowledge arguments for any language in **NP** is to first construct statistically hiding commitments (and plug them into a standard protocol).

Early constructions of statistically hiding commitments were built on specific number theoretic assumptions [BCC88, BKK90]. In [GK96] it was shown how to construct statistically hiding commitments from claw-free permutations; this was further reduced to any family of collision-resistant hash functions in [NY89].

Naor et al [NOVY98] showed how to construct statistically hiding commitments from one way permutations. In [Ost91, OW93] it was shown that one could build a weak from of one-way functions from statistically hiding commitments. Thus one-way functions would be the minimal assumption needed to create statistically hiding commitments. Until recently, no further progress was made. Haitner et al [HHK+05] showed how to construct statistically hiding commitments from a one-way function that could approximate the pre-image size of points in the range.

In a recent breakthrough work, Nguyen et al [NOV06] were able to construct statistical zero-knowledge arguments from any one-way function for all languages in **NP**. They deviated from the traditional line of constructing statistically binding commitments from one way functions. Instead they created a relaxed variant of statistically binding commitments from one-way functions first introduced by Nguyen and Vadhan [NV06]. Building on [NOV06], Haitner and Reingold [HR07] recently constructed statistically hiding commitments from one way functions. We remark that [NOV06] serves as a critical component for our results.

Concurrent zero-knowledge. The notion of concurrent zero knowledge was introduced by [DNS98] (see also [Fei90]) who also gave a construction based on timing assumptions. Richardson and Kilian [RK99] exhibited a family of concurrent zero-knowledge protocols for all languages in **NP** in the plain model. The analysis of the their protocol required that the protocol have a polynomial number of rounds. This analysis was improved by Kilian and Petrank [KP01] who showed that the protocol only required a poly-logarithmic number of rounds. Prabhkaran, Rosen, and Sahai introduced a variant of the protocol and reduced the number of rounds further to $\omega(\log n)$ rounds in [PRS02]. This is the protocol we will mainly use in our general compiler.

In [MP03], Micciancio and Petrank give a general compiler to compile any public-coin honest verifier zero-knowledge proof system into a concurrent zero-knowledge proof system while incurring only an additional $\omega(\log n)$ rounds. This reduction is based on perfectly hiding commitment schemes (having some additional special properties) based on the Decisional Diffie-Hellman assumption. These reductions do not however maintain the statistical zero-knowledge property. In other words, even if the original protocol is statistical zero-knowledge, the resulting protocol may not be.

Concurrent statistical zero-knowledge. There has not been much work on concurrent statistical zero-knowledge. In [MOSV06], Micciancio et al show how to build concurrent statistical zero-knowledge proofs for a variety of problems *unconditionally*, that is, without making any unproven complexity assumptions. However since these were statistical zero-knowledge proofs, their results could not include proofs for all languages in **NP** (unless **NP** is in **AM∩coAM** and the polynomial hierarchy collapses).

2   Preliminaries

Statistical Difference. The *statistical difference* between two random variables X, Y taking values in a universe $\mathbb{U}$ is defined to be

$$\Delta(X, Y) \overset{def}{=} \max_{S \subseteq \mathbb{U}} \left| \Pr[X \in S] - \Pr[Y \in S] \right| = \frac{1}{2} \sum_{x \in \mathbb{U}} \left| \Pr[X = S] - \Pr[Y = S] \right|$$

We say two distributions are statistically close if $\Delta(X, Y)$ is negligible.

Definition 1 (Argument Systems ([Gol01])). *An interactive protocol* (P, V) *is an argument (or computationally sound proof system) for a language L if the following three conditions hold:*

1. *(Efficiency) P and V are computable in probabilistic polynomial time.*
2. *(Completeness) If $x \in L$, then V outputs* **accept** *with probability at least 2/3 after interacting with the honest prover P.*
3. *(Soundness) If $x \notin L$, then for every nonuniform PPT adversarial prover P^*, V outputs* **accept** *with probability at most 1/3.*

For an argument system (P, V), we define the following terms. If $x \in L$, then the value that lower bounds the probability of V outputting **accept** after interacting with the honest prover P is called the *completeness bound*. Similarly, If $x \notin L$, then the value that upper bounds the probability of V outputting **accept** after interacting with any nonuniform PPT adversarial prover P^* is called the *soundness error*.

We say that an argument system is public coin if all the messages sent by V are chosen uniformly at random, except for the final *accept/reject* message (which is computed as a deterministic function of the transcript).

Concurrent Zero-knowledge. We assume the conversation between the prover P and the verifiers $V_1 \ldots V_n$ is of the form $v_1, p_1, v_2, p_2, \ldots, v_t, p_t$ where each v_j is a messages sent to the prover from a verifier V_{i_j} and the provers' response is the message p_j. We assume that there is an adversary A which controls the verifiers and the verifiers' messages. The adversary will take as input the partial conversation so far, i.e., $v_1, p_1 \ldots v_k, p_k$ and output a pair (i, v) specifying that P will receive message v from verifier V_i. The view of the adversary on input x will include the verifiers' random tapes and all the messages exchanged between the prover and the verifiers. This view will be denoted by $(P, A)(x)$.

Definition 2. *We say that an argument system (P, V) for a language L is statistical (resp., computational) black box concurrent zero-knowledge if there exists a probabilistic polynomial time oracle machine S (the simulator) such that for any unbounded (resp., probabilistic polynomial time) adversary A, the distributions $(P, A)(x)$ and $S^A(x)$ are statistically close (resp., computationally indistinguishable) for every string x in L.*

We call the statistical difference of these distributions the *zero-knowledge error* of the protocol. If we are dealing with computational indistinguishability, the probability that a probabilistic polynomial time adversary can distinguish these distributions is called the zero-knowledge error of the protocol as well.

Honest Verifier. We say a proof system is an honest verifier proof system if the zero-knowledge property is guaranteed to hold only if the verifier acts according to the protocol.

Note on Notation. We will use $P(T, r)$ (resp., $V(T, r)$) to signify the correct next message of an honest P (resp., V) as per the protocol (P, V), given the random coins r and the interaction transcript T observed so far. Sometimes, the random coin r might be implicit (instead of being explicitly supplied as an input).

3   Compiler Parts

In this section, we give the different parts of the compiler in isolation before putting them together in the next section to give our full protocol.

3.1   Underlying Zero-Knowledge Protocol

We assume that as input to our compiler, we have an honest verifier statistical zero-knowledge argument system for some language L. This protocol will have a prover, a verifier, a completeness bound, a soundness error, a simulator, the number of rounds and a zero-knowledge error (denoted by P, V, e_c, e_s, S, t and e_z respectively). We let $p_1, \ldots p_t$ denote the messages of the prover and $v_1, \ldots v_t$ the messages of the verifier in a particular execution of the argument system.

3.2   Statistically Binding Commitments from Any OWF

In our protocol, we shall use statistically binding commitments from any OWF. Building on techniques from [HILL99], such commitments were constructed by Naor [Nao91].

We denote such a commitment scheme by COM. We denote the probability of an all powerful adversary breaking the binding property of the scheme as b_{com}. We denote the probability of a PPT adversary breaking the hiding property of the scheme as h_{com}.

3.3   Computational Zero-Knowledge Proof Based on Any OWF for All of *NP*

In our protocol, we shall use a computational zero-knowledge proof based on one-way functions for every language in **NP** with negligible soundness error and perfect completeness. One way to construct them is to create statistically binding commitments based on a OWF as stated earlier [HILL99, Nao91]. These commitments can then be used in the 3-colorability protocol of [GMW91] to give us a zero-knowledge proof for any language in **NP**. We can then repeat the protocol sequentially n^2 times (where n is the security parameter) to achieve negligible soundness error. We note that this protocol will also have perfect completeness. We denote the final protocol after the sequential repetitions as (P', V').

This protocol will have a prover, a verifier, a completeness bound, a statistical soundness error, a simulator, the number of rounds and a zero-knowledge error (denoted by $P', V', e'_c = 1, e'_s, S', t'$ and e'_z respectively).

3.4   Preamble from PRS [PRS02]

In this subsection, we describe the preamble from [PRS02] and give its useful properties for our context. We note that [RK99, KP01] also have similar preambles (with round complexity higher than [PRS02]) which could be used for our purpose.

The preamble of the PRS protocol is simple. Let n be the security parameter of the system and k be any super-logarithmic function in n. Let σ be the bit string we wish to commit to and γ be the length of σ. We break σ up into two random shares k^2 times. Let these shares be denoted by $\{\sigma_{i,\ell}^0\}_{i,\ell=1}^k$ and $\{\sigma_{i,\ell}^1\}_{i,\ell=1}^k$ with $\sigma_{i,\ell}^0 \oplus \sigma_{i,\ell}^1 = \sigma$ for every i, ℓ. The verifier will commit to these bits using COM with fresh randomness each time. The verifier then sends these k^2 commitments to the prover. This is then followed by k iterations where in the ℓth iteration, the prover sends a random k-bit string $b_\ell = b_{1,\ell}, \ldots, b_{k,\ell}$, and the verifier decommits to the commitments $\text{COM}(\sigma_{1,\ell}^{b_{1,\ell}}), \ldots, \text{COM}(\sigma_{k,\ell}^{b_{k,\ell}})$.

The goal of this protocol is to enable the simulator to be able to rewind and find the value σ with high probability by following a fixed strategy. Since the verifier commitments are set after the first round, once we rewind the verifier, the simulator will have the opportunity to have the verifier open both the σ^0

commitment and the σ^1 commitment. In the concurrent setting, rewinding a protocol can be difficult since one may rewind past the start of some other protocol in the system as observed by [DNS98]. The remarkable property of this protocol is that there is a fixed rewinding strategy the simulator can use to get the value of σ, for every concurrent cheating verifier strategy V^*, with high probability.

We will follow [MOSV06] in formalizing the properties of the PRS preamble we need. Without loss of generality, assume that there are Q concurrent sessions. Recall that k is the number of rounds of the PRS preamble.

We call the simulator for the PRS preamble CEC-Sim. CEC stands for concurrently-extractable commitments. CEC-Sim will have oracle access to V^* and will get the following inputs.

- Commitments schemes $\mathcal{COM} = COM_1, COM_2, \ldots, COM_Q$, where COM_s is the commitment scheme used for session s.
- Parameters γ, k, n and Q, all given in unary.

We also need to give the following definitions adapted from [MOSV06]:

Definition 3 (Major Decommitment). *A* major decommitment *is a reveal after the PRS preamble in which V^* reveals the opening of commitments* $\{COM(\sigma_{i,\ell}^0)\}_{i,\ell=1}^k$ *and* $\{COM(\sigma_{i,\ell}^1)\}_{i,\ell=1}^k$. *P only accepts the major decommitment if: (a) all these openings are valid openings to the commitments in the transcript, and, (b) there exists σ such that for all i, ℓ, $\sigma_{i,\ell}^0 \oplus \sigma_{i,\ell}^1 = \sigma$.*

Definition 4 (Valid Commit Phase). *For a transcript T of the commit phase interaction between P and V^*, let $T[s]$ denote the messages in session s. $T[s]$ is a valid commit phase transcript if there exists a major decommitment D such that $P(T[s], D) = accept$.*

Definition 5 *(Compatibility). Message $M = (\sigma, \sigma_{i,j}^0, \sigma_{i,j}^1)$ is compatible with $T[s]$ if*

1. $\sigma = \sigma_{i,j}^0 \oplus \sigma_{i,j}^1$
2. *There exist commitments $COM_s(\sigma_{i,j}^0)[s]$ and $COM_s(\sigma_{i,j}^1)[s]$ that are part of the transcript of the first message of $T[s]$.*

Observe that if a message $M = (\sigma, \sigma_{i,j}^0, \sigma_{i,j}^1)$ is compatible with the transcript $T[s]$, the cheating verifier can major-decommit to a message different from σ only with probability at most b_{com}. Thus we call σ the *extracted message*.

Definition 6. *A Simulator $CEC - Sim^{V^*}$ has the* concurrent extraction *property if for every interaction T it has with V^*, it also provides (on a separate output tape) an array of messages $(M_1, M_2, \ldots, M_Q)$ with the following property:*

For every session $s \in \{1, 2, \ldots, Q\}$, if $T[s]$ is a valid commit phase transcript, then M_s is compatible with $T[s]$.

A simulator that has the concurrently extractable property is also called a *concurrently-extractable simulator*.

Using the simulation and rewinding techniques in [PRS02], we can obtain a concurrently-extractable simulator for the PRS preamble. Let $\langle \mathbb{P}, V^* \rangle$ denote the output of V^* after concurrently interacting with $\mathbb{P}$. Recall that V^* is an unbounded adversary.

Lemma 1 *(implicit in [PRS02], adapted from [MOSV06]). There exists a PPT concurrently-extractable simulator CEC-Sim with a fixed strategy SIMULATE such that for $\mathcal{COM}$ and all concurrent adversaries V^*, for settings of parameters $\sigma = poly(n)$, $k = \tilde{O}(\log n)$, and $Q = poly(n)$, we have the ensembles*

$$\left\{ \text{CEC-Sim}^{V^*}(\mathcal{COM}, 1^\sigma, 1^k, 1^n, 1^Q) \right\}_{n \in \mathbb{N}} \quad and \quad \left\{ \langle \mathbb{P}, V^* \rangle(\mathcal{COM}, 1^\sigma, 1^k, 1^n, 1^Q) \right\}_{n \in \mathbb{N}}$$

have statistical difference ϵ, where ϵ is negligible.

4   The Compiler

In this section, we discuss the compiler in detail. It takes as input an honest verifier statistical zero knowledge argument system (P, V) and compiles it into a concurrent statistical zero knowledge argument system $(\mathbb{P}, \mathbb{V})$ assuming the existence of one way functions. The compiler uses statistically binding commitments and computational zero knowledge proofs as building blocks. Both of these can be constructed out of any one way function [HILL99, GMW91].

The compiler is presented formally in Figure 1. Let R denote the uniform distribution. The verifier $\mathbb{V}$ first generates a random string r (i.e., $r \xleftarrow{r} R$). $\mathbb{P}$ and $\mathbb{V}$ then carry out the PRS preamble [PRS02] where $\mathbb{V}$ sets σ to be r.

Instead of using statistically hiding commitments as in the PRS preamble, we will use statistically binding commitments based on one way functions. This however causes a problem in the PRS soundness proof [PRS02] since the statistical hiding property of the commitments is used in an essential manner in the soundness proof[1]. We resolve this problem later on.

Once $\mathbb{P}$ and $\mathbb{V}$ have finished the PRS preamble, $\mathbb{V}$ gives a computational zero knowledge proof acting as P' in the system (P', V') (constructed using a OWF as described in section 3). It proves that all the shares it committed to in the PRS preamble (first message) are "consistent" with r. In other words, $r_{i,\ell}^0 \oplus r_{i,\ell}^1 = r$ for every i, ℓ. The prover $\mathbb{P}$ then draws $r' \xleftarrow{r} R$ and sends it to $\mathbb{V}$. Now $\mathbb{P}$ and $\mathbb{V}$ will begin the supplied honest verifier statistical zero knowledge argument protocol (P, V) with some modifications. The random coins of the verifier V are fixed to be $r \oplus r' \overset{\text{def}}{=} r''$.

Let the protocol (P, V) have t rounds where one round involves a prover message followed by the verifier's response. P and V interact as follows. In the

---

[1] For example, if the verifier uses computationally hiding commitments, a cheating prover could potentially create dependencies between his own commitments and the verifier challenge.

Common Input to $\mathbb{P}$ and $\mathbb{V}$: $(P,V),(P',V'),x,$COM
Compiler:
1. $\mathbb{V} \to \mathbb{P}$: Generate $r \xleftarrow{r} R$. Using COM, commit to r and the shares $\{r_{i,\ell}^0\}_{i,\ell=1}^k, \{r_{i,\ell}^1\}_{i,\ell=1}^k$ such that $r_{i,\ell}^0 \oplus r_{i,\ell}^1 = r$ for every i,ℓ.
2. For $\ell = 1,\ldots k$:
   (a) $\mathbb{P} \to \mathbb{V}$: Send $b_{1,\ell},\ldots,b_{k,\ell} \xleftarrow{r} \{0,1\}^k$.
   (b) $\mathbb{V} \to \mathbb{P}$: Decommit to $r_{1,\ell}^{b_{1,\ell}},\ldots,r_{k,\ell}^{b_{k,\ell}}$.
3. $\mathbb{V} \leftrightarrow \mathbb{P}$: Zero-knowledge proof (P',V') where $\mathbb{V}$ acts as P' and proves to $\mathbb{P}$ that $r_{i,\ell}^0 \oplus r_{i,\ell}^1 = r$ for every i,ℓ and that there exist valid openings to the commitments in the PRS preamble to $r_{i,\ell}^0, r_{i,\ell}^1$. If $\mathbb{P}$ accepts the zero-knowledge proof, the transcript of the commit phase is guaranteed to be a *valid commit phase transcript*.
4. $\mathbb{P} \to \mathbb{V}$: send $r' \xleftarrow{r} R$.
5. $\mathbb{V}$ calculates $r'' \stackrel{\text{def}}{=} r \oplus r'$
6. For $j = 1,\ldots t$:
   (a) $\mathbb{P} \to \mathbb{V}$: send $P(T_j^P) = p_j$.
   (b) $\mathbb{V} \to \mathbb{P}$: send $V(T_j^V, r'') = v_j$.
   (c) $\mathbb{V} \leftrightarrow \mathbb{P}$: zero-knowledge proof (P',V') where $\mathbb{V}$ acts as P' and proves to $\mathbb{P}$ that there exist an r'' such that $r \oplus r' = r''$ and $V(T_j^V, r'') = v_j$.
7. $\mathbb{V} \to \mathbb{P}$: send $V(T,r'') =$ accept/reject.

Fig. 1. Compiler

jth round, $\mathbb{P}$ calculates the next message p_j of P on the transcript T_j^P of the interaction so far. Transcript T_j^P is defined to contain all the messages exchanged between P and V so far, i.e., $T_j^P = (p_1, v_1, \ldots, p_{j-1}, v_{j-1})$.

The verifier $\mathbb{V}$ receives p_j from $\mathbb{P}$. It will now calculate V's response in the protocol (P,V) using randomness r'' and V's transcript $T_j^V (= (T_j^P, p_j))$ of the interaction so far; we call this response v_j. Now $\mathbb{V}$ will act as the P' in the computational zero-knowledge proof system (P',V').

$\mathbb{V}$ will prove that his response is indeed consistent with V acting on input T_j^V and randomness r''. The statement being proven by $\mathbb{V}$ is in NP since it is possible to check the statement given the opening of the commitment to r. We are using the computational zero-knowledge proof here instead of just revealing the commitments to make our soundness proof go through. $\mathbb{P}$ acts as V' during this zero-knowledge proof. If the proof is accepted by V' then $\mathbb{P}$ accepts v_j.

Once these t rounds are complete, $\mathbb{V}$ accepts if and only if V would accept on the complete transcript $T (=(T_t^V, v_t))$.

4.1 Parameters of the Compiler

Let (P,V) be an honest verifier zero-knowledge argument system with t rounds, e_c completeness bound, e_s soundness error, and e_z zero-knowledge error. Let (P',V') be a computation zero-knowledge proof system with t' rounds, e_c' completeness bound, e_s' soundness error, and e_z' zero-knowledge error. Let ϵ be the value from Lemma 1 that represents the statistical difference of a simulated run of the PRS preamble using SIMULATE from a real run against an arbitrary unbounded concurrent verifier strategy. Let k be the number of rounds in the PRS preamble. Let e_p be the probability that the PRS preamble is accepted by the prover and the verifier if they are behaving honestly. Let COM be the commitment used in the PRS preamble. Let h_{com} be the probability of a PPT machine breaking the hiding property of COM and b_{com} be the probability of an all powerful adversary breaking the binding property of COM. Let S be the simulator for (P, V) and $\mathbb{S}$ be a simulator for $(\mathbb{P}, \mathbb{V})$.

We give the parameters that we obtain with our compiler in the following theorem.

Theorem 1. *Running the compiler given in Section 4 on the argument system* (P, V) *results in a system* $(\mathbb{P}, \mathbb{V})$ *with the following properties.*

- *The completeness bound of* $(\mathbb{P}, \mathbb{V})$ *is* $e_p e_c$.
- *The soundness error of* $(\mathbb{P}, \mathbb{V})$ *is* $e_s + (k^2 h_{com} + e_z')t$.
- *The zero-knowledge error of the protocol is:*
  $$\Delta((\mathbb{P}, \mathbb{V}^*)(x), \mathbb{S}^{V^*(x)}) = \epsilon + e_z + k^2 b_{com} + e_s' t$$

Proof. The proof of each of the above claims is given below individually.

Completeness. Suppose $x \in L$. Then the probability that the protocol is accepted by $\mathbb{V}$ is:

$$\Pr[(\text{PRS is accepted}) \wedge ((P, V) \text{ is accepted}) \wedge (\text{each execution of } (P', V') \text{ is accepted})] =$$

$$(e_p)(e_c)(e_c')^t$$

Note that e_c' is one since our protocol (P', V') has perfect correctness. Thus we get the probability that the transformed protocol is accepted is $(e_p)(e_c)$.

Soundness. Suppose $x \notin L$ and there exists an adversarial PPT prover $\mathbb{P}^*$ that can get $\mathbb{V}$ to accept with non-negligible probability ϕ. In other words, suppose $(\mathbb{P}, \mathbb{V})$ has non-negligible soundness error ϕ. We will show how to use $\mathbb{P}^*$ to build a machine D that breaks the soundness of the underlying zero-knowledge protocol (P, V). We give a formal description of D in Figure 2.

D will use $\mathbb{P}^*$ as follows. D runs $\mathbb{P}^*$ and executes the PRS preamble interacting with it setting σ to a random r. Now, D gives a computational zero knowledge proof to $\mathbb{P}^*$ and receives r' as shown in Figure 2. It then runs the honest verifier machine V acting a cheating prover P^* and trying to break the soundness of the system (P, V).

In the jth round, D receives p_j from $\mathbb{P}^*$ and sends it to V. V will respond to p_j with v_j. Now D wants to be able to give v_j as his response to $\mathbb{P}^*$ so as to be able to continue the protocol. However D needs his response to $\mathbb{P}^*$ to be generated using randomness $r \oplus r'$ as per the protocol (P, V). D has already committed to r with a statistically binding commitment and thus can not necessarily decommit to a r such that v_j is consistent with r, r' and (P, V).

Common Input to D and V: x

Auxiliary input to D: The cheating prover machine $\mathbb{P}^*$

Description of D, a cheating prover for (P, V)

    1. D runs a copy of $\mathbb{P}^*$, acting as the verifier itself.

    2. D generates $r \xleftarrow{r} R$. It then interacts with $\mathbb{P}^*$ to carry out the PRS preamble using r.

    3. D gives a zero knowledge proof (P', V') to $\mathbb{P}^*$ proving that all the shares it committed to in the PRS preamble are consistent with r.

    4. D receives r' from $\mathbb{P}^*$

    5. For $j = 1, \ldots t$:

       (a) D gets the message p_j from $\mathbb{P}^*$.

       (b) $D \rightarrow V$: p_j.

       (c) $V \rightarrow D$: v_j.

       (d) D uses the simulator S' of the system (P', V') and simulates a proof with $\mathbb{P}^*$ that $V(T_j^V, r \oplus r') = v_j$.

Fig. 2. D acting as a cheating prover for (P, V)

However D does not have to decommit to r, but only needs to give a zero-knowledge proof that he has committed to a randomness r such that v_j is consistent with r, r' and (P, V). He can use the simulator of (P', V') to do this. Hence, D sends v_j to $\mathbb{P}^*$ and simulates a zero knowledge proof of its correctness by rewinding $\mathbb{P}^*$. The probability that $\mathbb{P}^*$ can differentiate between such a simulated run and a real run can be analyzed using a simple hybrid argument. As we move from a real run to a simulated one, we construct the following hybrid. D acts as an honest V sending correct verifier messages v_j. However, instead of giving real zero knowledge proofs, D gives simulated proofs. In other words, although D would have the witness to the NP statement, it does not use it and instead simulates the zero knowledge proof. Clearly, the probability that $\mathbb{P}^*$ can distinguish this hybrid from a real run is bounded by the zero-knowledge error (see section 2) of (P', V'). Now, we move from the hybrid to the simulated run where, in the PRS preamble, D did not commit to a randomness which could explain his message v_j (but rather an unrelated randomness r). Hence, D would not necessarily possess the witness of his statement.

Using the above hybrid argument, it can be shown that:

$$\Pr[\mathbb{P}^* \text{ can distinguish this simulation from a real run}] \leq$$

$$\Pr[\mathbb{P}^* \text{can break the ZK condition of } (P', V')] +$$

$$\Pr[\mathbb{P}^* \text{can break any of the commitments during the PRS preamble}] \leq$$

$$k^2 h_{com} + e'_z$$

$\mathbb{P}^*$ will see t of these simulations from D. Thus we can use the union bound and get that the probability that $\mathbb{P}^*$ will be able to distinguish any of the simulation from a real run is $(k^2 h_{com} + e'_z)t$.

Now, $\mathbb{V}$ will only accept in the protocol if the internal V he is running accepts $p_1, v_1, \ldots, p_t, v_t$. Recall that the probability that $\mathbb{V}$ accepts when interacting with $\mathbb{P}^*$ is ϕ. Thus the probability that V will accept an interaction with D who is running $\mathbb{P}^*$ can be computed as follows:

$$\Pr[V \text{ accepts}] \geq$$

$$1 - \Pr[(\mathbb{P}^* \text{ does distinguish}) \vee (\mathbb{V} \text{ does not accept})] \geq$$

$$1 - \left(\Pr[\mathbb{P}^* \text{ does distinguish}] + \Pr[\mathbb{V} \text{ does not accept}]\right) \geq$$

$$1 - ((k^2 h_{com} + e'_z)t + (1 - \phi))$$

This value must be less than the soundness error of (P, V). Thus we get an upper bound on the soundness error of the compiled protocol

$$\phi \leq e_s + (k^2 h_{com} + e'_z)t$$

Note that if e_s, h_{com}, e'_z are all negligible and t, k are at most polynomial, the soundness error of the compiled protocol will be negligible.

Concurrent Statistical Zero-knowledge. Lets consider an arbitrary unbounded concurrent verifier strategy. Let $\mathbb{V}^*$ be one of the verifiers representing a session in the concurrent verifier strategy. Given S, the simulator for the underlying protocol (P, V), we show how to construct a simulator $\mathbb{S}$ for the protocol $(\mathbb{P}, \mathbb{V})$. $\mathbb{S}$ will output a simulated transcript from a distribution which is only a negligible statistical distance from the distribution of the transcript of a real interaction. The simulator $\mathbb{S}$ is described formally in Figure 3.

$\mathbb{S}$ will first run S, the simulator of the underlying protocol. $\mathbb{S}$ will act as the honest verifier oracle for S recording all the randomness that he uses as the oracle. After running S, $\mathbb{S}$ will have a transcript $\hat{p}_1, \hat{v}_1, \ldots \hat{p}_t, \hat{v}_t$ and the randomness $\hat{r}$ (used in creating the honest verifier responses $\hat{v}_1, \ldots \hat{v}_t$). This transcript $\hat{p}_1, \hat{v}_1, \ldots \hat{p}_t, \hat{v}_t$ will be statistically close to a real run of (P, V).

As shown in the figure, $\mathbb{S}$ then runs the concurrently extractable simulator CEC-Sim (or in other words, the PRS simulator) and recovers the committed randomness r^* with probability at least $(1 - \epsilon)$. Since the commitments that $\mathbb{V}^*$ used during the PRS preamble are statistically binding, even an all powerful $\mathbb{V}^*$ will not be able to change them except with negligible probability. We call this probability b_{com}. After finishing the preamble, $\mathbb{S}$ will be a straightline simulator and will not rewind $\mathbb{V}^*$ any further.

$\mathbb{S}$ will now give $\mathbb{V}^*$ a string r' such that $r^* \oplus r' = \hat{r}$. Note that the distribution of r' will look completely uniform to $\mathbb{V}^*$ since $\mathbb{V}^*$ has no information about $\hat{r}$.

Now for each round of the protocol, the simulator will proceed as follows. In round j, $\mathbb{S}$ will give $\hat{p}_j$ to $\mathbb{V}^*$. Since $\mathbb{V}^*$ has already committed to r^*, it will now be forced use randomness $r^* \oplus r'$ which is exactly $\hat{r}$, . It will therefore be forced to respond with $\hat{v}_j$, except of course with the probability that he can break either the binding property of the commitment or the soundness of the zero-knowledge proof (P', V'). Since we are using statistically binding commitments and a zero knowledge *proof*, the probability of an all powerful adversary

---

Input: V^*, one of the verifiers in an arbitrary unbounded concurrent verifier strategy.

The simulator $\mathbb{S}$

1. $\mathbb{S}$ acts as an honest verifier V and runs the simulator S of the argument system (P, V) on itself. $\mathbb{S}$ generates $\hat{r} \xleftarrow{r} R$ and uses it as randomness to interact with S. After the interaction, $\mathbb{S}$ gets as output the simulated transcript $\hat{p}_1, \hat{v}_1, \ldots \hat{p}_t \hat{v}_t$.
2. $\mathbb{S}$ runs a copy of V^*
3. $\mathbb{S}$ runs the concurrently extractable simulator CEC-Sim on V^*. CEC-Sim executes the PRS preamble with V^* and extracts its committed randomness r^*.
4. $\mathbb{S}$ carries out (P', V') with V^* in which V^* proves that all the shares it committed to in the PRS preamble are consistent with r^*.
5. $\mathbb{S}$ computes r' such that $r^* \oplus r' = \hat{r}$ and sends it to V^* .
6. For $j = 1, \ldots t$:
    (a) $\mathbb{S}$ sends $\hat{p}_j$ to V^* and receives V^*'s response $\hat{v}'_j$.
    (b) $\mathbb{S}$ carries out (P', V') with V^* in which V^* proves that its response $\hat{v}'_j = V(T_j^V, \hat{r})$. $\mathbb{S}$ aborts if $\hat{v}'_j \neq \hat{v}_j$.

Fig. 3. The simulator $\mathbb{S}$ for $(\mathbb{P}, V)$

breaking the binding property of the commitments or the soundness property of the (P', V') is negligible. Thus the randomness that V^* is forced to use will be $\hat{r}$ and his response will therefore be $\hat{v}_j$, exactly as in the transcript created by S. If this is not the case, $\mathbb{S}$ aborts.

We now analyze the probability of failure of the simulator $\mathbb{S}$. From a union bound, we can directly bound this probability by analyzing the probability of all the events which may cause $\mathbb{S}$ to fail. The failure probability is upper bounded by:

$$\Pr[\text{Output of } S \text{ is not identically distributed to } (P, V)] +$$

$$\Pr[\text{CEC-Sim is unsuccessful in recovering } r^*] +$$

$$\Pr[V^* \text{ breaks the binding property of any of the commitments}] +$$

$$\Pr[V^* \text{ breaks the soundness property of } (P', V') \text{ for any of the executions}]$$

$$= \epsilon + e_z + k^2 b_{\text{com}} + e'_s t$$

Thus $\Delta((\mathbb{P}, V^*)(x), \mathbb{S}^{V^*(x)}) = (\epsilon + e_z + k^2 b_{\text{com}} + e'_s t)$ as claimed.

Note that if $\epsilon, e_z, b_{\text{com}}, e'_s$ are all negligible and t, k are at most polynomial, the simulated transcript will have negligible statistical difference from a real run of the protocol. ∎

4.2 Concurrent Statistical Zero-Knowledge Arguments from Any One Way Function

In order to build concurrent statistical zero-knowledge arguments from a OWF, we need the following theorem implicit in [NOV06].

Theorem 2. *If one way functions exist, every language in* **NP** *has a public-coin statistical zero-knowledge argument system.*

We can now apply our compiler to the protocol of Nguyen et al [NOV06] to get the following corollary.

Corollary 1. *If one way functions exist, every language in* **NP** *has a concurrent statistical zero-knowledge argument system.*

References

[BCC88]   Brassard, G., Chaum, D., Crépeau, C.: Minimum disclosure proofs of knowledge. J. Comput. Syst. Sci. 37(2), 156–189 (1988)

[BHZ87]   Boppana, R.B., Håstad, J., Zachos, S.: Does co-np have short interactive proofs? Inf. Process. Lett. 25(2), 127–132 (1987)

[BKK90]   Boyar, J., Kurtz, S.A., Krentel, M.W.: A discrete logarithm implementation of perfect zero-knowledge blobs. J. Cryptology 2(2), 63–76 (1990)

[DNS98]   Dwork, C., Naor, M., Sahai, A.: Concurrent zero-knowledge. In: STOC, pp. 409–418 (1998)

[Fei90]   Feige, U.: Ph.d. thesis, alternative models for zero knowledge interactive proofs. Weizmann Institute of Science (1990)

[GK96]   Goldreich, O., Kahan, A.: How to construct constant-round zero-knowledge proof systems for np. J. Cryptology 9(3), 167–190 (1996)

[GMR89]   Goldwasser, S., Micali, S., Rackoff, C.: The knowledge complexity of interactive proof systems. SIAM J. Comput. 18(1), 186–208 (1989)

[GMW91]   Goldreich, O., Micali, S., Wigderson, A.: Proofs that yield nothing but their validity or all languages in np have zero-knowledge proof systems. J. ACM 38(3), 691–729 (1991)

[Gol01]   Goldreich, O.: Foundations of Cryptography - Basic Tools. Cambridge University Press, Cambridge (2001)

[HHK+05]   Haitner, I., Horvitz, O., Katz, J., Koo, C.-Y., Morselli, R., Shaltiel, R.: Reducing complexity assumptions for statistically-hiding commitment. In: Cramer, R.J.F. (ed.) EUROCRYPT 2005. LNCS, vol. 3494, pp. 58–77. Springer, Heidelberg (2005)

[HILL99]   Håstad, J., Impagliazzo, R., Levin, L.A., Luby, M.: A pseudorandom generator from any one-way function. SIAM J. Comput. 28(4), 1364–1396 (1999)

[HR07]   Haitner, I., Reingold, O.: Statistically-hiding commitment from any one-way function. In: Johnson, D.S., Feige, U. (eds.) STOC, pp. 1–10. ACM, New York (2007)

[KP01]   Kilian, J., Petrank, E.: Concurrent and resettable zero-knowledge in polyloalgorithm rounds. In: STOC, pp. 560–569 (2001)

[MOSV06]   Micciancio, D., Ong, S.J., Sahai, A., Vadhan, S.P.: Concurrent zero knowledge without complexity assumptions. In: Halevi, S., Rabin, T. (eds.) TCC 2006. LNCS, vol. 3876, pp. 1–20. Springer, Heidelberg (2006)

[MP03]   Micciancio, D., Petrank, E.: Simulatable commitments and efficient concurrent zero-knowledge. In: Biham, E. (ed.) Advances in Cryptology – EUROCRPYT 2003. LNCS, vol. 2656, pp. 140–159. Springer, Heidelberg (2003)

[Nao91]   Naor, M.: Bit commitment using pseudorandomness. J. Cryptology 4(2), 151–158 (1991)

[NOV06]   Nguyen, M.-H., Ong, S.J., Vadhan, S.P.: Statistical zero-knowledge arguments for np from any one-way function. In: FOCS, pp. 3–14. IEEE Computer Society, Los Alamitos (2006)

[NOVY98] Naor, M., Ostrovsky, R., Venkatesan, R., Yung, M.: Perfect zero-knowledge arguments for p using any one-way permutation. J. Cryptology 11(2), 87–108 (1998)

[NV06]   Nguyen, M.-H., Vadhan, S.P.: Zero knowledge with efficient provers. In: Proceedings of the 38th Annual ACM symposium on Theory of Computing, ACM Press, New York (2006)

[NY89]   Naor, M., Yung, M.: Universal one-way hash functions and their cryptographic applications. In: STOC, pp. 33–43 (1989)

[Ost91]   Ostrovsky, R.: One-way functions, hard on average problems, and statistical zero-knowledge proofs. In: Structure in Complexity Theory Conference, pp. 133–138 (1991)

[OW93]   Ostrovsky, R., Wigderson, A.: One-way fuctions are essential for nontrivial zero-knowledge. In: ISTCS, pp. 3–17 (1993)

[PRS02]   Prabhakaran, M., Rosen, A., Sahai, A.: Concurrent zero knowledge with logarithmic round-complexity. In: FOCS, pp. 366–375 (2002)

[RK99]   Richardson, R., Kilian, J.: On the concurrent composition of zero-knowledge proofs. In: Stern, J. (ed.) EUROCRYPT 1999. LNCS, vol. 1592, pp. 415–431. Springer, Heidelberg (1999)

Anonymous Quantum Communication

Gilles Brassard[1], Anne Broadbent[1], Joseph Fitzsimons[2], Sébastien Gambs[1], and Alain Tapp[1]

[1] Université de Montréal
Département d'informatique et de recherche opérationnelle
C.P. 6128, Succ. Centre-Ville, Montréal (Québec), H3C 3J7, Canada
{brassard,broadbea,gambsseb,tappa}@iro.umontreal.ca
[2] University of Oxford
Department of Materials
Parks Road, Oxford, OX1 3PH, United Kingdom
joe.fitzsimons@materials.ox.ac.uk

Abstract. We present the first protocol for the anonymous transmission of a quantum state that is information-theoretically secure against an active adversary, without any assumption on the number of corrupt participants. The anonymity of the sender and receiver, as well as the privacy of the quantum state, are perfectly protected except with exponentially small probability. Even though a single corrupt participant can cause the protocol to abort, the quantum state can only be destroyed with exponentially small probability: if the protocol succeeds, the state is transferred to the receiver and otherwise it remains in the hands of the sender (provided the receiver is honest).

Keywords: quantum cryptography, multiparty computation, anonymity, dining cryptographers.

1 Introduction

In David Chaum's classic dining cryptographers scenario [Cha88], a group of cryptographers is having dinner at a restaurant and it is the case that either one of them has anonymously paid the dinner bill or the NSA has paid. The task that the cryptographers wish to accomplish is to find out which of the two cases occurred, without revealing any additional information. The security of Chaum's protocol does not rely on any computational assumption, but only on the cryptographers having access to pairwise private channels and to a broadcast channel. A simple extension to this protocol allows a single participant, say Alice, to broadcast a message to all the other participants in such a way that Alice's identity is information-theoretically protected.

But what if Alice wishes to send a private message to Bob (who is also sitting at the dinner table), while ensuring the anonymity of both herself and of Bob? This task is called *anonymous message transmission*. As an instance of multiparty secure computation, such a protocol can be accomplished, assuming

K. Kurosawa (Ed.): ASIACRYPT 2007, LNCS 4833, pp. 460–473, 2007.

pairwise private channels and a broadcast channel, as long as a majority of participants are honest [RB89]. Recently, two of us [BT07] have given a protocol that requires pairwise private channels and a broadcast channel, and accomplishes anonymous message transmission *without* any assumption on the number of honest participants. The protocol, however, allows even a single corrupt participant to cause an abort.

Our main contribution is to give the first information-theoretically secure protocol for *quantum* anonymous transmission that tolerates any number of corrupt participants. That is, our protocol allows Alice to send a quantum message to Bob such that both Alice and Bob remain anonymous (no participant learns the identity of Alice—even if Bob is corrupt—and the identity of Bob remains known only to Alice), and the quantum message remains private (nothing about it leaks to participants other than Bob, unless of course Bob is corrupt). The anonymity of the sender and receiver, as well as the privacy of the quantum message, are perfect except with exponentially small probability, regardless of the behaviour of cheating parties, with no need to rely on any assumptions other than the availability of a classical broadcast channel as well as private authenticated quantum channels between each pair of participants. Our protocol has features similar to the anonymous (classical) message transmission protocol mentioned above: we can tolerate an arbitrary number of corrupt participants, but any single corrupt participant can cause the protocol to abort. However, no private information can be obtained by making the protocol abort.

Since Alice sends quantum information, we need to address a concern that did not exist in the context of classical anonymous message transmission: the state to be transmitted should never be destroyed *even if the protocol aborts* (unless the receiver is corrupt, since in that case he can follow honestly the protocol until the very end, and then destroy the successfully transmitted message!). Because of the no-cloning theorem [WZ82], the sender cannot generally keep a backup copy of the message before entering the protocol. Nevertheless, we accomplish this safeguard as part of the main protocol with a simple and novel notion called *fail-safe teleportation*. This notion ensures that if something went wrong with the transmission of the state, its integrity is never at stake because the receiver can always teleport it back to the sender in a way that does not compromise anonymity.

1.1 Anonymity

Anonymity is a basic cryptographic concept whose goal is to hide the identity of the sender or receiver of a message (or both). It is different from, but often complementary to *privacy*, which ensures the confidentiality of a message. Examples of anonymous tasks include sending an anonymous letter to one's love, using an email account with a pseudonym, accessing a web page through a trusted identity proxy server or blind reviewing of a conference paper. Three approaches to classical anonymity are generally considered. The first one requires the help of a trusted third party that forwards messages between participants without revealing the identity of the senders. Anonymizers [Boy97, GGK+99] belong to this class. The second approach uses chains of untrusted servers that randomize the ordering of messages. This reordering prevents an outside observer from linking the sender and the receiver of a particular message. The privacy of messages is generally assured by a public-key cryptosystem. Chaum's MixNets [Cha81] are an instance of techniques using this approach. The third and last approach offers information-theoretic security, assuming resources such as a broadcast channel and pairwise private channels. Chaum's dining cryptographers protocol [Cha88] is the archetypical example of a protocol in this category.

1.2   Model

In our model, we suppose that each pair of participants shares a *private authenticated quantum channel*, which means that a participant can send an authenticated private message (quantum or classical) to any other participant. Such a channel can be implemented if the participants share pairwise quantum channels as well as classical secret keys. An extra tool is given to the participants under the form of a (classical) *broadcast channel*. This channel guarantees that all participants receive the same message from a publicly known sender, and that the message is not modified while in transit.

Two security models are generally considered in secure multiparty computation: *honest-but-curious* and *malicious*. In the honest-but-curious model (also called *semi-honest*), the participants are assumed to follow the protocol (thus being honest) but at the same time record all the information they have seen during its execution (thus being curious). In this model, a protocol is said to be secure against a *collusion* of participants if, by pooling their data, these participants cannot learn more information than from their inputs and the output of the protocol alone. In the malicious model, participants may actively cheat and deviate from the original prescription of the protocol. Cheaters can for instance try to learn information about the input of honest participants or tamper with the output of the protocol. Formal definitions can be found in Chapter 7 of [Gol04]. Both these models are neatly encapsulated by considering a central entity called an *adversary*, which controls some of the participants, rendering them *corrupt*. The adversary is *passive* if the corrupt participants are honest-but-curious, and *active* if the corrupt participants are malicious. In this paper, we consider the case of an active adversary that chooses the set of corrupt participants before the execution of the protocol.

In the scenario that we consider, within a group of n participants, the anonymous sender communicates a private quantum message to an anonymous receiver. The sender is unknown to all participants and the receiver is unknown to all participants except to the sender. We give the following definitions:

Definition 1 (Sender Anonymity). *A protocol achieves* sender anonymity *if it does not reveal any information concerning the identity of the sender to any adversary. An exception concerns the receiver (or the adversary, if the receiver is corrupt), who may legitimately learn something about the identity of the sender by virtue of the contents of the transmitted message.*

Note that in particular, if the sender is corrupt, a protocol vacuously achieves sender anonymity, and that sender anonymity requires that no adversary can learn the identity of the sender, *even if the receiver is corrupt.*

Definition 2 (Receiver Anonymity). *A protocol achieves receiver anonymity if it does not reveal any information concerning the identity of the receiver to any adversary beyond what could be legitimately learned by knowing for each corrupt participant whether or not he is the receiver.*

Note that in particular, if the sender or receiver is corrupt, a protocol vacuously achieves receiver anonymity.

Definition 3 (Full Anonymity). *A protocol achieves full anonymity if it does not reveal any information about the relation between the identity of the sender and receiver to any adversary beyond what could be legitimately learned by knowing for each corrupt participant whether or not he is the receiver.*

Note that full anonymity implies sender and receiver anonymity and that if the sender is corrupt, a protocol vacuously achieves full anonymity.

Remark. *The asymmetry between the definitions of sender and receiver anonymity stems from the fact that, contrary to the sender, the receiver does not know at the onset of the protocol that such a role will be imparted upon him.*

In what follows, we are only interested in protocols that are unconditionally secure in the information-theoretic sense for the purpose of achieving full anonymity. We place no limit on the number of corrupt participants. However, our protocol could abort if even a single corrupt participant deviates from the prescribed protocol. Even if the protocol aborts, full anonymity as well as message privacy are never compromised, except with exponentially small probability. Note that if we had some sort of guarantee that a strict majority of participants is honest, then anonymous quantum message transmission could be implemented as a special case of quantum secure multiparty computation [BCG+06].

1.3 Anonymity in the Quantum World

The first protocol based on quantum mechanics that allows the anonymous communication of *classical* information was proposed by P. Oscar Boykin [Boy02]. In the case of a *quantum* message, Matthias Christandl and Stephanie Wehner were first to define the concept of *anonymous quantum message transmission* and to give an explicit protocol for solving this task [Weh04, CW05], but under the *deus ex machina* assumption that the n participants share ahead of time entangled state $|+_n\rangle = \frac{1}{\sqrt{2}}|0^n\rangle + \frac{1}{\sqrt{2}}|1^n\rangle$. (No mechanism is proposed to verify the validity of that state.) Under that assumption, their protocol is information-theoretically secure in terms of full anonymity, but malicious participants can alter the transmitted state in a way that will not be detected by the honest participants.

One key notion introduced in the paper of Christandl and Wehner is that of *anonymous entanglement*. Starting with the assumed n-party entangled state $|+_n\rangle$, the sender and the receiver end up sharing a two-party entangled state $|+_2\rangle$, better known as Bell State $|\Phi^+\rangle = \frac{1}{\sqrt{2}}|00\rangle + \frac{1}{\sqrt{2}}|11\rangle$, provided the other parties follow the protocol honestly. This entanglement is *anonymous* because the sender has chosen with which other party (the receiver) he shares it, but the receiver has no information concerning the party with which he is entangled. Moreover, the other parties have no information concerning who are the two entangled parties (assuming the entangled parties are not corrupt).

A first attempt to accomplish quantum message transmission in the presence of an unlimited number of corrupt participants *without* assuming that a trusted state $|+_n\rangle$ is shared between the participants before the onset of the protocol was made by Jan Bouda and Josef Šprojcar [BŠ07], but in a public-receiver model (the sender is anonymous but the receiver is public). The creation and distribution of a $|+_n\rangle$ state is an important part of their protocol. From there, they attempt to establish semi-anonymous entanglement (the identity of one of the entangled parties, the receiver, is public). However, careful analysis reveals that an active adversary can proceed in such a way that the probability that the protocol aborts becomes correlated with the identity of the sender, thus compromising his anonymity. If the protocol requires the receiver to stay quiet in order not to reveal whether or not the protocol has succeeded, it is true that the anonymity of the sender is preserved. However, this is very different from the model usually considered in secure multiparty computation, in which all the participants learn at the end of the protocol whether or not it has succeeded. More importantly, this approach makes it impossible to preserve the identity of the sender whenever the receiver is corrupt. Indeed, if we wanted to cope with a corrupt receiver and still preserve sender anonymity, this would require the need to hide from the receiver himself whether or not the protocol has succeeded. But if it were the case that the message itself (if received) did not convey any information on the success of the protocol, then it would mean that it is no more useful than a totally random state. Then, why bother send it at all?

Our own protocol is also based on the establishment of anonymous entanglement between the sender and the receiver. However, compared to the protocol of Christandl and Wehner, we do not need to assume an *a priori* shared $|+_n\rangle$ state and no malicious attempt at corrupting the intended final $|\Phi^+\rangle$ state between the sender and the receiver can succeed (except with exponentially small probability) without causing an abort. It follows that the intended state will be transmitted faithfully unless the protocol aborts, in which case it will end up intact at the sender's by virtue of fail-safe teleportation (unless the receiver is corrupt). Compared with the protocol of Bouda and Šprojcar, our receiver is anonymous and the identity of the sender and the receiver cannot be correlated with the probability that the protocol aborts, allowing us to achieve full anonymity according to Definition 3.

2   Toolbox

We now survey the classical and quantum tools that are used in our main protocol. Two of us recently developed several classical secure multiparty protocols [BT07]; we present below some of the relevant results, which will be used in the next section. All protocols assume pairwise authentic private classical channels and a broadcast channel. They offer information-theoretic security and have polynomial complexity in the number of participants as well as in a security parameter and, in the case of Theorem 4, in the number of bits in the transmitted message. In all cases, the expression "exponentially close to 1" or "exponentially small" means "exponentially in the security parameter". We also review a key result from [BCG+02].

Theorem 1 (Logical OR–[BT07]). *There exists a secure multiparty protocol to compute the logical OR of the participants' input bits (one bit per participant). If all participants are honest, the correct answer is computed with probability exponentially close to 1. Misbehaving participants cannot cause the protocol to abort. (Any refusal to participate when expected will cause the output to be 1.) The only information an active adversary can learn through the protocol is if at least one honest participant has input 1. No information about the number of such participants or their identity is revealed.*

Theorem 2 (Collision Detection–[BT07]). *There exists a collision detection protocol in which each participant inputs a bit. Let r denote the number of 1s among these input bits. The protocol has three possible outcomes corresponding to whether $r = 0$, $r = 1$ or $r \geq 2$. If all participants are honest, the correct value is computed with probability exponentially close to 1. No participant can make the protocol abort, and an adversary cannot learn more than it could have learned by assigning to all corrupt participants the input 0 and letting them follow the protocol faithfully. A single corrupt participant can cause the output corresponding to $r \geq 2$ regardless of the other inputs (even if all the other inputs are 0). Also, it is possible for a corrupt participant to set his input to 0 if all other participants have input 0 (producing an $r = 0$ output) and to 1 otherwise (producing an $r \geq 2$ output). No other form of cheating is possible.*

Although the collision detection protocol outlined above may look rather imperfect, it is actually just as useful as the ideal protocol for our purpose.

Theorem 3 (Notification–[BT07]). *There exists a notification protocol in which participants can notify other participants of their choosing. Each player's output is one private bit specifying if he has been notified at least once; this value is correctly computed with probability exponentially close to 1. This is the only information accessible through the protocol even in the case of an active adversary.*

According to [BT07], it is possible in general to invoke the notification protocol even if multiple senders want to notify several receivers. However, in the specific context of our use of this protocol for the purpose of anonymous quantum message transmission, we forbid any honest participant to engage in the above notification protocol without having previously caused output "$r = 1$" in the collision detection protocol (Theorem 2). Similarly, no honest participant S will ever engage in the anonymous message transmission protocol below unless he has initially caused output "$r = 1$" in the collision detection protocol *and* has notified a single other participant R.

Theorem 4 (Anonymous Message Transmission–[BT07]). *There exists an anonymous message transmission protocol in which a sender can transmit a classical message to a receiver such that even in the presence of an active adversary, full anonymity is achieved and the privacy of the message is perfect. If all participants are honest then the message is transmitted perfectly. Any attempt by a corrupt participant to modify the message will cause the protocol to abort, except with exponentially small probability.*

In 2002, Howard Barnum, Claude Crépeau, Daniel Gottesman and Alain Tapp presented a non-interactive scheme for the authentication of quantum messages [BCG+02]. The protocol also encrypts the quantum state to be transmitted and is information-theoretically secure.

Theorem 5 (Quantum Authentication–[BCG+02]). *There exists an information-theoretically secure quantum authentication scheme to authenticate an arbitrary quantum message $|\psi\rangle$ of length m with an encoding circuit (called authenticate) and a decoding circuit (called decode) of size polynomial in m, which uses a random private key of length $2m + 2s + 1$ and has authenticated message of length $m + s$. Let p the probability that the message is accepted. If the message is accepted then let q be the probability of obtaining outcome $|\psi\rangle$ when measuring in a basis containing $|\psi\rangle$. If the authenticated message is not modified, then $p = q = 1$. Otherwise, $pq + (1-p) > 1 - \frac{m+s}{s(2^s+1)}$. The protocol also perfectly preserves the privacy of the transmitted message.*

3   Protocol for Anonymous Quantum Message Transmission

In this section, we describe and analyse our protocol for anonymous quantum message transmission. Our protocol allows an anonymous sender S to transmit an m-qubit message $|\psi\rangle$ to an anonymous receiver R. We assume a broadcast channel as well as an information-theoretically secure private and authenticated quantum channel between each pair of participants (which can also be used, of course, to transmit classical information). Our protocol achieves full anonymity and message privacy, except with exponentially small probability. The security proof for the protocol makes no assumption on the number of corrupt participants, but a single corrupt participant can make the protocol abort. However, if the sender and the receiver are honest, the quantum message to be transmitted will only be lost with exponentially small probability.

Here is an informal description of the protocol. In the first step, the purely classical collision detection protocol of Theorem 2 is performed to establish that exactly one participant wants to send an anonymous quantum message. If this is not the case, the protocol aborts. In case it is found that more than one participant wants to speak, one might imagine alternative scenarios such as asking each one of them to decide at random whether or not to skip their turn and trying again the collision detection protocol until a single-sender occurrence occurs. This will reveal information on the number of honest would-be senders and may take too many trials if there are too many of them, so that more sophisticated solutions might need to be considered. (Further elaboration on this issue would go beyond the scope of this paper.)

In the next two steps, the participants collaborate to establish multiple instances of a shared state $|+_n\rangle = \frac{1}{\sqrt{2}}|0^n\rangle + \frac{1}{\sqrt{2}}|1^n\rangle$. Then, the sender designates a receiver by use of the notification protocol (Theorem 3).

If honest, the receiver will act differently from the other participants, but in a way that is indistinguishable, so that his anonymity is preserved. The shared instances of $|+_n\rangle$ are then used to create anonymous entanglement between the sender and the receiver. However, the anonymous entanglement could be imperfect if other participants misbehave. For this reason, the sender then creates a sufficient number of instances of Bell state $|\Phi^+\rangle$. The possibly imperfect anonymous entanglement is used to teleport [BBC+93] an authenticated version of half of each $|\Phi^+\rangle$. If this first teleportation is successful, the sender uses this newly established perfect anonymous entanglement to teleport the quantum message itself. Our fail-safe quantum teleportation protocol ensures that unless the receiver is corrupt, the quantum message is never destroyed, except with exponentially small probability: either it is safely transmitted to the receiver, or it comes back intact at the sender's.

In more detail, all classical communication from the sender to the receiver is performed anonymously using the anonymous message transmission protocol (Theorem 4). To create anonymous entanglement, all participants must be involved. One participant (who is chosen arbitrarily, for instance the first participant in lexicographic order) creates a state $|+_n\rangle$ and distributes one qubit to each participant, keeping one for himself. Of course, this participant could be corrupt, so that there is no guarantee that a proper $|+_n\rangle$ has been distributed. Moreover, a corrupt distributor could send different states to different honest participants, in the hope that the future evolution of the protocol may depend on who is the sender and who is the receiver. Foiling this threat constitutes a key contribution of our protocol. For this reason, all participants *verify* this state *without* destroying it in the next step. If the verification succeeds, the state shared amongst all participants is guaranteed to be invariant under permutation of the honest participants (Lemma 1), even though it could still not be a genuine $|+_n\rangle$ state. This ensures full anonymity. Furthermore, the behaviour of the state $|+_n\rangle$, when measured by all but two parties in the Hadamard basis, ensures correctness (unless it aborts) as shown in Theorems 6 and 8.

The full protocol is given as **Protocol 1**, where we denote by P the *conditional phase change* defined by $P|0\rangle = |0\rangle$ and $P|1\rangle = -|1\rangle$. Note that if two participants (such as the sender and the receiver) share an instance of Bell state $|\Phi^-\rangle = \frac{1}{\sqrt{2}}|00\rangle - \frac{1}{\sqrt{2}}|11\rangle$, a single participant (such as the sender) can convert this to a $|\Phi^+\rangle$ by locally applying the P operation. Note also that such a local operation (performed by the sender) has no detectable effect that could be measured by the other participants (in particular the receiver), which ensures that the anonymity of the sender is not compromised. It is easy to see that **Protocol 1** has polynomial complexity in n (the number of participants), s (the security parameter) and m (the length of the message).

Theorem 6 (Correctness). *Assume all participants are honest in **Protocol 1**. If more than one of them wishes to be a sender, this will be detected with probability exponentially close to 1 in the first step. Otherwise, the message is transmitted perfectly with probability exponentially close to 1, and the protocol can abort only with exponentially small probability.*

Proof. Even if all participants are honest, it is possible for collision detection or notification to produce an incorrect output (the notification protocol may also abort); however, this happens with exponentially small probability.

To ensure correctness of the protocol, we only have to verify that S and R share a sufficient number of proper Bell states $|\Phi^+\rangle$ at the end of step 5. It is clear

---

Protocol 1. Anonymous Quantum Message Transmission

Let s be the security parameter and m be the length of quantum message $|\psi\rangle$. All quantum communication is performed using the private authenticated quantum channels.

1. **Multiple Sender Detection**
    1.1 The collision detection protocol (Theorem 2) is used to determine if one and only one participant wants to be the sender. If not, the protocol aborts.
2. **Entanglement Distribution**
    2.1 One arbitrarily designated participant creates $2m+s$ instances of the state $|+_n\rangle$ and sends one qubit of each instance to each participant, keeping one qubit of each instance for himself.
3. **Entanglement Verification**
    For each of the $2m + s$ instances:
    3.1 Each participant makes $n-1$ *pseudo-copies* of his qubit by applying a control-not with it as the source and a qubit initialized to $|0\rangle$ as the target. One such pseudo-copy is sent to every other participant.
    3.2 Each participant verifies that all the n qubits in his possession are in the subspace spanned by $\{|0^n\rangle, |1^n\rangle\}$.
    3.3 Each participant broadcasts the outcome of the previous step. If any outcome is negative, the protocol aborts.
    3.4 Each participant *resets* $n-1$ of his qubits to $|0\rangle$ by performing $n-1$ control-not operations. These qubits are discarded and the one remaining is back to the state distributed at step 2.

Protocol 1. Anonymous Quantum Message Transmission (continued)

4. Receiver Notification

    4.1 The participants execute the notification protocol (Theorem 3) in which only S notifies a single R.

5. Anonymous Entanglement Generation

    For each of the $2m + s$ instances:

    5.1 All participants except S and R measure in the Hadamard basis the qubit that remains from step 3.

    5.2 Each participant broadcasts the result of his measurement (S and R broadcast two random dummy bits).

    5.3 S computes the parity of all the bits received during the previous step (except his own and that of R).

    5.4 If the parity is odd, S applies P, the conditional phase change, to his remaining qubit (the two qubits shared by S and R are now in Bell state $|\Phi^+\rangle$).

6. Perfect Anonymous Entanglement

    6.1 S creates $2m$ instances of Bell state $|\Phi^+\rangle$. He keeps the first qubit of each pair; let ρ be the rest of the pairs.

    6.2 S creates a random classical key k of length $4m + 2s + 1$, and computes $\rho' = $ authenticate(ρ, k).

    6.3 S performs a teleportation measurement on ρ' using the anonymous $|\Phi^+\rangle$ states generated during steps 2–5.

    6.4 S uses the anonymous message transmission protocol (Theorem 4) to send k and the teleportation bits to R.

    6.5 R completes the teleportation and computes $\rho = $ decode(ρ', k). If the decoding is successful, S and R share perfect anonymous entanglement (they share $2m$ instances of $|\Phi^+\rangle$).

    6.6 A logical OR is computed (Theorem 1): all players input 0 except R, who inputs 1 if the authentication failed and 0 otherwise. If the outcome is 1, the protocol aborts.

7. Fail-Safe Teleportation

    7.1 S teleports the state $|\psi\rangle$ to R using the first m pairs generated in the previous step. The teleportation bits are anonymously transmitted to R (Theorem 4). If the communication succeeds, R terminates the teleportation.

    7.2 A logical OR is performed (Theorem 1): all players input 0 except R, who inputs 1 if the communication of the teleportation bits failed. If the outcome is 0, the protocol succeeds. Otherwise, S and R do the following:

        7.2.1 R performs a teleportation measurement using the remaining perfect anonymous entanglement to teleport back to S the quantum state resulting from partially failed step 7.1.

        7.2.2 All participants broadcast $2m$ random bits, except R who broadcasts the teleportation bits from above. The protocol continues even if one of the participants refuses to broadcast.

        7.2.3 S reconstructs $|\psi\rangle$ from his own teleportation bits from step 7.1 and R's teleportation bits received from the broadcast. The protocol aborts.

that at the end of step 3, the participants share proper instances of state $|+_n\rangle$ (since we are assuming in this theorem that they are honest). When S computes the parity of the measurement outcomes in step 5, this corresponds to the parity of the measurement results in the Hadamard basis of the state $|+_n\rangle$, where all but two qubits are measured. If the parity is even, S and R share $|\Phi^+\rangle$ and otherwise $|\Phi^-\rangle$, which is corrected by the sender by the application of the conditional phase change P. $\qquad\qquad\qquad\qquad\qquad\qquad\qquad\qquad\qquad\qquad$ □

The following Lemma is necessary in the proof of anonymity and privacy (Theorem 7).

Lemma 1 (Invariance Under Permutation of Honest Participants).
In **Protocol 1,** *if step 3 succeeds, then the state of the system at the end of the step is:*

$$\alpha|00\ldots0\rangle_H|\psi_0\rangle_C + \beta|11\ldots1\rangle_H|\psi_1\rangle_C, \qquad (1)$$

where H denotes the honest participants' subsystem, C denotes the corrupt participants' subsystem, and $\alpha, \beta \in \mathbb{C}$ are such that $|\alpha|^2 + |\beta|^2 = 1$.

Proof. In the entanglement verification step, each honest participant sends a pseudo-copy of his state to every other honest participant. Therefore, after a single honest participant verifies that his qubits are in the subspace spanned by $\{|0^n\rangle, |1^n\rangle\}$, we are already ensured that if the entanglement verification succeeds, the state will be of the form given above. Note that the corrupt participants' subsystem C could span more than t qubits since they can bring arbitrary ancillas into their cheating strategy. $\qquad\qquad\qquad\qquad\qquad\qquad$ □

Theorem 7 (Anonymity and Privacy). *Regardless of the number of corrupt participants and except with exponentially small probability,* **Protocol 1** *achieves full anonymity and privacy of the transmitted message $|\psi\rangle$.*

Proof. We analyse the protocol step by step in order to prove the statement.

By virtue of Theorem 2, step 1 does not compromise the identity of the sender, and it involves neither the receiver nor the quantum state to be transmitted. Steps 2 and 3 are done without any reference to S or R and thus cannot compromise their anonymity either. Furthermore, the state obtained at the end of step 3 (if it does not abort) cannot be specifically correlated with any honest participant even if some other participants are corrupt. More precisely, by Lemma 1, the state is *invariant under any permutation of the honest participants.* This is crucial for the anonymity and privacy of the rest of the protocol. In particular, it guarantees that the probability that the protocol aborts does not depend on the identity of S or R, or any relationship between them. We prove this below in the analysis of step 6.

The security of step 4 follows directly from the unconditional security of the notification protocol (Theorem 3). However, if S fails to notify R in step 4 (this happens with exponentially small probability), an adversary can surreptitiously take over the role of the honest receiver in the rest of the protocol without being detected. In that case, the adversary will violate the secrecy of the transmitted state, yet without compromising the sender and receiver anonymity beyond what can be learned by inspecting the illegitimately received state.

In step 5, anonymous entanglement is generated. No information is revealed to the adversary in this step since all communication is done by honest participants broadcasting random bits.

For step 6, all communication is done using the **anonymous message trans-mission** protocol, which is secure according to Theorem 4, except in **logical OR** computation at the end, which reveals the success or failure of the authentica-tion part of the protocol. We now show that this last substep cannot reveal any information on the identity of S or R. This is because the success or failure of the authentication step is uncorrelated to the identity of S and R: by Lemma 1, as far as the qubits are concerned, all honest participants are identical under permutation. Thus the adversary has no strategy that would allow him to deter-mine any information about the identity of S or R, or even about any relation between them.

During step 7, all the bits sent from S to R are randomly and uniformly distributed because they are the classical bits resulting from the teleportation protocol, therefore they do not reveal any information about the identity of S. A similar observation about the bits broadcast by R in the case that the very last part of the protocol is executed ensures that R and S remain anonymous.

The privacy of the state $|\psi\rangle$ in the case that S successfully notified R in step 4 (which happens with probability exponentially close to 1) is guaranteed by the basic properties of teleportation. $\qquad\qquad\qquad\qquad\qquad\qquad\qquad\qquad\qquad\quad$ $\square$

Theorem 8 (Integrity). *At the end of* **Protocol 1**, *if R is honest then the state $|\psi\rangle$ is either in the possession of S or R, except with exponentially small probability. Furthermore, $|\psi\rangle$ can only stay with S if the protocol has aborted.*

Proof. If all participants are honest, then by Theorem 6, the state is in the pos-session of R except with exponentially small probability. Otherwise, the protocol might abort before step 7, in which case S still has $|\psi\rangle$. If the protocol reaches step 7, due to the **quantum authentication** of step 6, S and R share $2m$ perfect Bell states $|\Phi^+\rangle$ (with probability exponentially close to 1), which are used for teleportation in step 7. If the first step of the fail-safe teleportation fails, then S no longer has $|\psi\rangle$; however, the last three substeps of the protocol will always succeed and S will reconstruct $|\psi\rangle$ (provided R is honest). Furthermore, it fol-lows from the virtues of teleportation that if the protocol does not abort, the state is no longer with S. $\qquad\qquad\qquad\qquad\qquad\qquad\qquad\qquad\qquad\qquad\quad$ $\square$

The reason why we specify in Theorem 8 that R must be honest is that a corrupt R can destroy $|\psi\rangle$ by simply discarding it after having faithfully followed the entire protocol. There remains one subtlety to mention: a corrupt R could behave honestly until the last step. Then, he would input 1 in the **logical OR** computation to force S to accept the teleportation back of the state. At that point, the corrupt R could teleport back to S a fake state. As a result, S would be fooled into thinking he still has custody of the original quantum state when, in fact, that state is in the hands of R. (In general, there will be no way for S to know that this has happened).

4 Conclusion and Discussion

We have presented the first information-theoretically secure protocol for quantum communication between an anonymous sender and an anonymous receiver that tolerates an arbitrary number of corrupt participants. In particular, this means that no adversary can learn any information that will break the anonymity of the sender or receiver. Our protocol also provides perfect privacy for the quantum message and ensures that the quantum message is never destroyed, except with exponentially small probability. The drawback of our protocol is that any participant can disrupt the protocol and make it abort.

Acknowledgements

We are grateful to Patrick Hayden and Flavien Serge Mani Onana for insightful discussions. G. B. is supported in part by the Natural Sciences and Engineering Research Council of Canada (NSERC), the Canada Research Chair program and the Canadian Institute for Advanced Research (CIFAR). A. B. is supported in part by scholarships from the Canadian Federation of University Women and the Fonds Québecois de Recherche sur la Nature et les Technologies (FQRNT). J. F. is supported by a Helmore Award. S. G. is supported by NSERC. A. T. is supported in part by CIFAR, FQRNT, the Mathematics of Information Technology and Complex Systems Network, and NSERC. Furthermore, we acknowledge the support of the Quantum*Works* Network and of the Institut transdisciplinaire d'informatique quantique (INTRIQ).

References

[BBC+93]   Bennett, C.H., Brassard, G., Crépeau, C., Jozsa, R., Peres, A., Wootters, W.K.: Teleporting an unknown quantum state via dual classical and Einstein-Podolsky-Rosen channels. Physical Review Letters 70, 1895–1899 (1993)

[BCG+02]   Barnum, H., Crépeau, C., Gottesman, D., Smith, A., Tapp, A.: Authentication of quantum messages. In: Proceedings of the 43rd Annual IEEE Symposium on Foundations of Computer Science (FOCS 2002), p. 449. IEEE Computer Society Press, Los Alamitos (2002)

[BCG+06]   Ben-Or, M., Crépeau, C., Gottesman, D., Hassidim, A., Smith, A.: Secure multiparty quantum computation with (only) a strict honest majority. In: Proceedings of the 47th Annual IEEE Symposium on Foundations of Computer Science (FOCS 2006), pp. 249–260. IEEE Computer Society Press, Los Alamitos (2006)

[Boy97]   Boyan, J.: The Anonymizer: protecting user privacy on the Web. Computer-Mediated Communication Magazine 4(9) (1997)

[Boy02]   Boykin, P.O.: Information security and quantum mechanics: security of quantum protocols. PhD thesis, University of California, Los Angeles (2002)

[BŠ07]   Bouda, J., Šprojcar, J.: Anonymous transmission of quantum information.
           In: Proceedings of the First International Conference on Quantum, Nano,
           and Micro Technologies (ICQNM 2007) (2007)
[BT07]   Broadbent, A., Tapp, A.: Information-theoretic security without an honest
           majority. In: ASIACRYPT 2007. LNCS, vol. 4833, pp. 410–426. Springer,
           Heidelberg (2007)
[Cha81]   Chaum, D.: Untraceable electronic mail, return addresses, and digital
           pseudonyms. Communications of the ACM 24, 84–88 (1981)
[Cha88]   Chaum, D.: The dining cryptographers problem: Unconditional sender
           and recipient untraceability. Journal of Cryptology 1, 65–75 (1988)
[CW05]   Christandl, M., Wehner, S.: Quantum anonymous transmissions. In: Roy,
           B. (ed.) ASIACRYPT 2005. LNCS, vol. 3788, pp. 217–235. Springer, Hei-
           delberg (2005)
[GGK+99]   Gabber, E., Gibbons, P.B., Kristol, D.M., Matias, Y., Mayer, A.J.: Con-
           sistent, yet anonymous, Web access with LPWA. Communications of the
           ACM 42(2), 42–47 (1999)
[Gol04]   Goldreich, O.: The Foundations of Cryptography, vol. 2. Cambridge Uni-
           versity Press, Cambridge (2004)
[RB89]   Rabin, T., Ben-Or, M.: Verifiable secret sharing and multiparty protocols
           with honest majority. In: Proceedings of the twenty-first annual ACM
           Symposium on Theory of Computing (STOC), pp. 73–85. ACM Press,
           New York (1989)
[Weh04]   Wehner, S.: Quantum computation and privacy. Master's thesis, CWI Am-
           sterdam (2004)
[WZ82]   Wootters, W.K., Zurek, W.H.: A single quantum cannot be cloned. Na-
           ture 299, 802–803 (1982)

Authenticated Key Exchange and Key Encapsulation in the Standard Model

Tatsuaki Okamoto

NTT, Japan
okamoto.tatsuaki@lab.ntt.co.jp

Abstract. This paper introduces a new paradigm to realize various types of cryptographic primitives such as authenticated key exchange and key encapsulation in the standard model under three standard assumptions: the decisional Diffie-Hellman (DDH) assumption, target collision resistant (TCR) hash functions and pseudo-random functions (PRFs). We propose the first (PKI-based) two-pass authenticated key exchange (AKE) protocol that is comparably as efficient as the existing most efficient protocols like MQV and that is secure in the standard model (under these standard assumptions), while the existing efficient two-pass AKE protocols such as HMQV, NAXOS and CMQV are secure in the random oracle model. Our protocol is shown to be secure in the (currently) strongest security definition, the extended Canetti-Krawczyk (eCK) security definition introduced by LaMacchia, Lauter and Mityagin. This paper also proposes a CCA-secure key encapsulation mechanism (KEM) under these assumptions, which is almost as efficient as the Kurosawa-Desmedt KEM. This scheme is also secure in a stronger security notion, the chosen public-key and ciphertext attack (CPCA) security. The proposed schemes in this paper are redundancy-free (or validity-check-free) and the implication is that combining them with redundancy-free symmetric encryption (DEM) will yield redundancy-free (e.g., MAC-free) CCA-secure hybrid encryption.

1 Introduction

The most common paradigm to design practical public-key cryptosystems secure in the standard model is to combine a trapdoor function (e.g., Diffie-Hellman or RSA function) and target collision resistance (TCR) hash functions, where the security is proven under a trapdoor function assumption (e.g., DDH or SRSA assumption) and the TCR hash function assumption.

This paper introduces a new paradigm to design practical public-key cryptosystems, where a *pseudo-random function* (PRF) is employed in addition to a trapdoor function (DH) and target collision resistant (TCR) hash function.

The concept of a PRF was introduced by Goldreich, Goldwasser and Micali [4], and has been shown to exist if and only if a one-way function exists [4,5]. Therefore, the existence of a pseudo-random function is one of the weakest assumptions, and it is one of the most fundamental primitives in cryptography.

Since a target collision resistant (TCR) hash function (and the slightly bit more general concept, the universal one-way hash function) have also been shown to exist if and

K. Kurosawa (Ed.): ASIACRYPT 2007, LNCS 4833, pp. 474–484, 2007.

only if a one-way function exists [12,13], TCR hash function and PRF are the same level of (the most) fundamental primitives in cryptography. In practice, a well-designed efficient hash function can be assumed to be a TCR hash function, and such a hash function with a random seed as a part of the input (or a keyed hash function) can be assumed to be a PRF.

First, this paper presents a two-pass AKE protocol that offers the following properties:

1. Its efficiency is comparable to those of MQV [9], HMQV [6] and CMQV [14] (the message size of our scheme is that of MQV plus the size of two group elements, and the computational complexity for a session of our scheme is around 3.3 group exponentiations, while that of MQV is around 2.2 group exponentiations),
2. The assumption and model for its security proof are standard assumptions (DDH, TCR hash function and PRF) and standard model (not the random oracle model),
3. Its underlying security definition is (currently) the strongest one, the extended Canetti-Krawczyk (eCK) security definition introduced by LaMacchia, Lauter and Mityagin [8],
4. Its security proof reduction efficiency is better than those of previous protocols in the random oracle model.

This paper also proposes a *CCA-secure* key encapsulation mechanism (KEM) under these assumptions, which is almost as efficient as the Kurosawa-Desmedt KEM [7]. This scheme is also secure in a stronger security notion, the *chosen public-key and ciphertext attack (CPCA)* security, in which an adversary, given a target public key pk^* and ciphertext c^*, is allowed to query a pair of public key pk and ciphertext c to the decryption oracle, which answers the adversary with the decrypted result of c by the secret key of pk.

The proposed schemes in this paper are redundancy-free (or validity-check-free) and implies redundancy-free (e.g., MAC-free) CCA-secure hybrid encryption by combining with redundancy-free CCA-secure symmetric encryption (DEM).

2 Preliminaries

2.1 Notations

$\mathbb{N}$ is the set of natural numbers and $\overline{\mathbb{R}}$ is the set of real numbers. $\bot$ denotes a null string.

A function $f : \mathbb{N} \to \overline{\mathbb{R}}$ is *negligible* in k, if for every constant $c > 0$, there exists integer n such that $f(k) < k^{-c}$ for all $k > n$. Hereafter, we often use $f(k) < \epsilon(k)$ to mean that f is negligible in k.

When A is a probabilistic machine or algorithm, $A(x)$ denotes the random variable of A's output on input x. Then, $y \xleftarrow{R} A(x)$ denotes that y is randomly selected from $A(x)$ according to its distribution. When a is a value, $A(x) \to a$ denotes the event that A outputs a on input x. When A is a set, $y \xleftarrow{U} A$ denotes that y is uniformly selected from A. When A is a value, $y \leftarrow A$ denotes that y is set as A.

In this paper, we consider that the underlying machines are uniform Turing machines. But it is easy to extend our results to non-uniform Turing machines.

2.2 The DDH Assumption

Let k be a security parameter and $\mathbb{G}$ be a group with security parameter k, where the order of $\mathbb{G}$ is prime p and $|p| = k$. Let $\{\mathbb{G}\}_k$ be the set of group $\mathbb{G}$ with security parameter k.

For all $k \in \mathbb{N}$ we define the sets $\mathbb{D}$ and $\mathbb{R}$ as follows:

$$\mathbb{D}(k) \leftarrow \{(\mathbb{G}, g_1, g_2, g_1^x, g_2^x) \mid \mathbb{G} \overset{U}{\leftarrow} \{\mathbb{G}\}_k, (g_1, g_2) \overset{U}{\leftarrow} \mathbb{G}^2, x \overset{U}{\leftarrow} \mathbb{Z}_p\}$$
$$\mathbb{R}(k) \leftarrow \{(\mathbb{G}, g_1, g_2, y_1, y_2) \mid \mathbb{G} \overset{U}{\leftarrow} \{\mathbb{G}\}_k, (g_1, g_2, y_1, y_2) \overset{U}{\leftarrow} \mathbb{G}^4\}.$$

Let $\mathcal{A}$ be a probabilistic polynomial-time machine. For all $k \in \mathbb{N}$, we define the DDH advantage of $\mathcal{A}$ as

$$\mathsf{AdvDDH}_{\mathcal{A}}(k) \leftarrow |\Pr[\mathcal{A}(1^k, \rho) \rightarrow 1 \mid \rho \overset{U}{\leftarrow} \mathbb{D}(k)] - \Pr[\mathcal{A}(1^k, \rho) \rightarrow 1 \mid \rho \overset{U}{\leftarrow} \mathbb{R}(k)]|.$$

The DDH assumption for $\{\mathbb{G}\}_{k \in \mathbb{N}}$ is: For any probabilistic polynomial-time adversary $\mathcal{A}$, $\mathsf{AdvDDH}_{\mathcal{A}}(k)$ is negligible in k.

2.3 Pseudo-Random Function (PRF)

Let $k \in \mathbb{N}$ be a security parameter. A pseudo-random function (PRF) family F associated with $\{\mathsf{Seed}_k\}_{k \in \mathbb{N}}$, $\{\mathsf{Dom}_k\}_{k \in \mathbb{N}}$ and $\{\mathsf{Rng}_k\}_{k \in \mathbb{N}}$ specifies two items:

– A family of random seeds $\{\mathsf{Seed}_k\}_{k \in \mathbb{N}}$.
– A family of pseudo-random functions indexed by k, $\Sigma \overset{R}{\leftarrow} \mathsf{Seed}_k$, $\sigma \overset{U}{\leftarrow} \Sigma, \mathcal{D} \overset{R}{\leftarrow}$ Dom_k, and $\mathcal{R} \overset{R}{\leftarrow} \mathsf{Rng}_k$, where each such function $\mathsf{F}_\sigma^{k, \Sigma, \mathcal{D}, \mathcal{R}}$ maps an element of $\mathcal{D}$ to an element of $\mathcal{R}$. There must exist a deterministic polynomial-time algorithm that on input 1^k, σ and ρ, outputs $\mathsf{F}_\sigma^{k, \Sigma, \mathcal{D}, \mathcal{R}}(\rho)$.

Let $\mathcal{A}^O$ be a probabilistic polynomial-time machine with oracle access to O. For all k, we define

$$\mathsf{AdvPRF}_{\mathsf{F}, \mathcal{A}}(k) \leftarrow |\Pr[\mathcal{A}^F(1^k, \mathcal{D}, \mathcal{R}) \rightarrow 1] - \Pr[\mathcal{A}^{RF}(1^k, \mathcal{D}, \mathcal{R}) \rightarrow 1]|,$$

where $\Sigma \overset{R}{\leftarrow} \mathsf{Seed}_k$, $\sigma \overset{U}{\leftarrow} \Sigma, \mathcal{D} \overset{R}{\leftarrow} \mathsf{Dom}_k, \mathcal{R} \overset{R}{\leftarrow} \mathsf{Rng}_k$, $F \leftarrow \mathsf{F}_\sigma^{k, \Sigma, \mathcal{D}, \mathcal{R}}$, and $RF : \mathcal{D} \rightarrow$ $\mathcal{R}$ is a truly random function ($\forall \rho \in \mathcal{D}$ $RF(\rho) \overset{U}{\leftarrow} \mathcal{R}$).

F is a pseudo-random function (PRF) family if for any probabilistic polynomial-time adversary $\mathcal{A}$, $\mathsf{AdvPRF}_{\mathsf{F}, \mathcal{A}}(k)$ is negligible in k.

2.4 Target Collision Resistant (TCR) Hash Function

Let $k \in \mathbb{N}$ be a security parameter. A target collision resistant (TCR) hash function family H associated with $\{\mathsf{Dom}_k\}_{k \in \mathbb{N}}$ and $\{\mathsf{Rng}_k\}_{k \in \mathbb{N}}$ specifies two items:

– A family of key spaces indexed by k. Each such key space is a probability space on bit strings denoted by KH_k. There must exist a probabilistic polynomial-time algorithm whose output distribution on input 1^k is equal to KH_k.

- A family of hash functions indexed by k, $h \overset{R}{\leftarrow} KH_k$, $\mathcal{D} \overset{R}{\leftarrow} Dom_k$, and $\mathcal{R} \overset{R}{\leftarrow} Rng_k$, where each such function $H_h^{k,\mathcal{D},\mathcal{R}}$ maps an element of $\mathcal{D}$ to an element of $\mathcal{R}$. There must exist a deterministic polynomial-time algorithm that on input 1^k, h and ρ, outputs $H_h^{k,\mathcal{D},\mathcal{R}}(\rho)$.

Let $\mathcal{A}$ be a probabilistic polynomial-time machine. For all k, we define

$$AdvTCR_{H,\mathcal{A}}(k) \leftarrow$$

$$\Pr[\rho \in \mathcal{D} \wedge \rho \neq \rho^* \wedge H_h^{k,\mathcal{D},\mathcal{R}}(\rho) = H_h^{k,\mathcal{D},\mathcal{R}}(\rho^*) \mid \rho \overset{R}{\leftarrow} \mathcal{A}(1^k, \rho^*, h, \mathcal{D}, \mathcal{R})],$$

where $\mathcal{D} \overset{R}{\leftarrow} Dom_k$, $\mathcal{R} \overset{R}{\leftarrow} Rng_k$, $\rho^* \overset{U}{\leftarrow} \mathcal{D}$ and $h \overset{R}{\leftarrow} KH_k$. H is a target collision resistance (TCR) hash function family if for any probabilistic polynomial-time adversary $\mathcal{A}$, $AdvTCR_{H,\mathcal{A}}(k)$ is negligible in k.

2.5 PKI-Based Authenticated Key Exchange (AKE) and the Extended Canetti-Krawczyk (eCK) Security Definition

This section outlines the extended Canetti-Krawczyk (eCK) security definition for two pass PKI-based authenticated key exchange (AKE) protocols that was introduced by LaMacchia, Lauter and Mityagin [8], and follows the description in [14].

In the eCK definition, we suppose there are n parties which are modeled as probabilistic polynomial-time Turing machines. We assume that some agreement on the common parameters in the AKE protocol has been made among the parties before starting the protocol. The mechanism by which these parameters are selected is out of scope of the AKE protocol and the (eCK) security model.

Each party has a static public-private key pair together with a certificate that binds the public key to that party. $\hat{A}$ $(\hat{B})$ denotes the static public key A (B) of party $\mathcal{A}$ $(\mathcal{B})$ together with a certificate. We do not assume that the certifying authority (CA) requires parties to prove possession of their static private keys, but we require that the CA verifies that the static public key of a party belongs to the domain of public keys.

Here, two parties exchange static public keys A, B and ephemeral public keys X, Y; the session key is obtained by combining A, B, X, Y and possibly session identities. A party $\mathcal{A}$ can be activated to execute an instance of the protocol called a *session*. Activation is made via an incoming message that has one of the following forms: $(\hat{A}, \hat{B})$ or $(\hat{B}, \hat{A}, X)$. If $\mathcal{A}$ was activated with $(\hat{A}, \hat{B})$, then $\mathcal{A}$ is called the session initiator, otherwise the session responder. Session initiator $\mathcal{A}$ creates ephemeral public-private key pair, (X, x) and sends $(\hat{B}, \hat{A}, X)$ to session responder $\mathcal{B}$. $\mathcal{B}$ then creates ephemeral public-private key pair, (Y, y) and sends $(\hat{A}, \hat{B}, X, Y)$ to $\mathcal{A}$.

The session of initiator $\mathcal{A}$ with responder $\mathcal{B}$ is identified via session identifier $(\hat{A}, \hat{B}, X, Y)$, where $\mathcal{A}$ is said the owner of the session, and $\mathcal{B}$ the peer of the session. The session of responder $\mathcal{B}$ with initiator $\mathcal{A}$ is identified as $(\hat{B}, \hat{A}, Y, X)$, where $\mathcal{B}$ is the owner, and $\mathcal{A}$ is the peer. Session $(\hat{B}, \hat{A}, Y, X)$ is said a matching session of $(\hat{A}, \hat{B}, X, Y)$. We say that a session is completed if its owner computes a session key.

The adversary $\mathcal{M}$ is modeled as a probabilistic polynomial-time Turing machine and controls all communications. Parties submit outgoing messages to the adversary, who makes decisions about their delivery. The adversary presents parties with incoming messages via Send($message$), thereby controlling the activation of sessions. In order to capture possible leakage of private information, adversary $\mathcal{M}$ is allowed the following queries:

- EphemeralKeyReveal(sid): The adversary obtains the ephemeral private key associated with session sid.
- SessionKeyReveal(sid): The adversary obtains the session key for session sid, provided that the session holds a session key.
- StaticKeyReveal(pid): The adversary learns the static private key of party pid.
- EstablishParty(pid): This query allows the adversary to register a static public key on behalf of a party. In this way the adversary totally controls that party.

If a party pid is established by EstablishParty(pid) query issued by adversary $\mathcal{M}$, then we call the party *dishonest*. If a party is not dishonest, we call the party *honest*.

The aim of adversary $\mathcal{M}$ is to distinguish a session key from a random key. Formally, the adversary is allowed to make a special query Test(sid*), where sid* is called the *target session*. The adversary is then given with equal probability either the session key, K^*, held by sid* or a random key, $R^* \xleftarrow{U} \{0,1\}^{|K^*|}$. The adversary wins the game if he guesses correctly whether the key is random or not. To define the game, we need the notion of *fresh session* as follows:

Definition 1 *(fresh session).* *Let* sid *be the session identifier of a completed session, owned by an honest party* A *with peer* B, *who is also honest. Let* $\overline{\text{sid}}$ *be the session identifier of the matching session of* sid, *if it exists. Define session* sid *to be "fresh" if none of the following conditions hold:*

- $\mathcal{M}$ *issues a* SessionKeyReveal(sid) *query or a* SessionKeyReveal($\overline{\text{sid}}$) *query (if* $\overline{\text{sid}}$ *exists),*
- $\overline{\text{sid}}$ *exists and* $\mathcal{M}$ *makes either of the following queries:*
  both StaticKeyReveal(A) *and* EphemeralKeyReveal(sid), *or*
  both StaticKeyReveal(B) *and* EphemeralKeyReveal($\overline{\text{sid}}$),
- $\overline{\text{sid}}$ *does not exist and* $\mathcal{M}$ *makes either of the following queries:*
  both StaticKeyReveal(A) *and* EphemeralKeyReveal(sid), *or*
  StaticKeyReveal(B).

We are now ready to present the eCK security notion.

Definition 2 *(eCK security).* *Let* K^* *be a session key of the target session* sid* *that should be "fresh",* $R^* \xleftarrow{U} \{0,1\}^{|K^*|}$, *and* $b^* \xleftarrow{U} \{0,1\}$. *As a reply to* Test(sid*) *query by* $\mathcal{M}$, K^* *is given to* $\mathcal{M}$ *if* $b^* = 0$; R^* *is given otherwise. Finally* $\mathcal{M}$ *outputs* $b \in \{0,1\}$. *We define*

$$\text{AdvAKE}_{\mathcal{M}}(k) \leftarrow |\Pr[b = b^*] - 1/2|.$$

A key exchange protocol is secure if the following conditions hold:

- *If two honest parties complete matching sessions, then they both compute the same session key (or both output indication of protocol failure).*
- *For any probabilistic polynomial-time adversary $\mathcal{M}$, $\mathrm{AdvAKE}_{\mathcal{M}}(k)$ is negligible in k.*

This security definition is stronger than CK-security [2] and it simultaneously captures all the known desirable security properties for authenticated key exchange including resistance to key-compromise impersonation attacks, weak perfect forward secrecy, and resilience to the leakage of ephemeral private keys.

2.6 Key-Encapsulation Mechanism (KEM)

A key encapsulation mechanism (KEM) scheme is the triple of algorithms, $\Sigma = (\mathsf{K}, \mathsf{E}, \mathsf{D})$, where

1. K, the key generation algorithm, is a probabilistic polynomial time (PPT) algorithm that takes a security parameter $k \in \mathbb{N}$ (provided in unary) and returns a pair (pk, sk) of matching public and secret keys.
2. E, the key encryption algorithm, is a PPT algorithm that takes as input public key pk and outputs a key/ciphertext pair (K^*, C^*).
3. D, the decryption algorithm, is a deterministic polynomial time algorithm that takes as input secret key sk and ciphertext C^*, and outputs key K^* or $\perp$ ($\perp$ means that the ciphertext is invalid).

We require that for all (pk, sk) output by key generation algorithm K and for all (K^*, C^*) output by key encryption algorithm $\mathsf{E}(pk)$, $\mathsf{D}(sk, C^*) = K^*$ holds. Here, the length of the key, $|K^*|$, is specified by $l(k)$, where k is the security parameter.

Let $\mathcal{A}$ be an adversary. The attack game is defined in terms of an interactive computation between adversary $\mathcal{A}$ and its challenger, $\mathcal{C}$. The challenger $\mathcal{C}$ responds to the oracle queries made by $\mathcal{A}$. We now describe the attack game (IND-CCA2 game) used to define security against adaptive chosen ciphertext attacks (IND-CCA2).

1. The challenger $\mathcal{C}$ generates a pair of keys, $(pk, sk) \xleftarrow{\mathsf{R}} \mathsf{K}(1^k)$ and gives pk to adversary $\mathcal{A}$.
2. Repeat the following procedure $q_1(k)$ times, for $i = 1, \ldots, q_1(k)$, where $q_1(\cdot)$ is a polynomial. $\mathcal{A}$ submits string C_i to a decryption oracle, DO (in $\mathcal{C}$), and DO returns $\mathsf{D}_{sk}(C_i)$ to $\mathcal{A}$.
3. $\mathcal{A}$ submits the encryption query to $\mathcal{C}$. The encryption oracle, EO, in $\mathcal{C}$ selects $b^* \xleftarrow{\mathsf{U}} \{0,1\}$ and computes $(C^*, K^*) \leftarrow \mathsf{E}(pk)$ and returns (C^*, K^*) to $\mathcal{A}$ if $b^* = 0$ and (C^*, R^*) if $b^* = 1$, where $R^* \xleftarrow{\mathsf{U}} \{0,1\}^{|K^*|}$ (C^* is called "target ciphertext").
4. Repeat the following procedure $q_2(k)$ times, for $j = q_1(k) + 1, \ldots, q_1(k) + q_2(k)$, where $q_2(\cdot)$ is a polynomial. $\mathcal{A}$ submits string C_j to a decryption oracle, DO (in $\mathcal{C}$), subject only to the restriction that a submitted text C_j is not identical to C^*. DO returns $\mathsf{D}_{sk}(C_j)$ to $\mathcal{A}$.
5. $\mathcal{A}$ outputs $b \in \{0,1\}$.

We define the IND-CCA2 advantage of $\mathcal{A}$, $\mathsf{AdvKEM}_{\mathcal{A}}^{\mathsf{IND\text{-}CCA2}}(k) \leftarrow |\Pr[b = b^*] - 1/2|$ in the above attack game.

We say that a KEM scheme is IND-CCA2-secure (secure against adaptive chosen ciphertext attacks) if for any probabilistic polynomial-time (PPT) adversary $\mathcal{A}$, $\mathsf{AdvKEM}_{\mathcal{A}}^{\mathsf{IND\text{-}CCA2}}(k)$ is negligible in k.

3   The Proposed AKE Protocol

3.1   Protocol

Let $k \in \mathbb{N}$ be a security parameter, $\mathbb{G} \overset{\mathsf{U}}{\leftarrow} \{\mathbb{G}\}_k$ be a group with security parameter k, and $(g_1, g_2) \overset{\mathsf{U}}{\leftarrow} \mathbb{G}^2$, where the order of $\mathbb{G}$ is prime p and $|p| = k$. Let H be a TCR hash function family, and F, $\tilde{\mathsf{F}}$ and $\hat{\mathsf{F}}$ be PRF families. $(\mathbb{G}, g_1, g_2)$, H, F, $\tilde{\mathsf{F}}$ and $\hat{\mathsf{F}}$ are the system parameters common among all users of the proposed AKE protocol (although $\tilde{\mathsf{F}}$ and $\hat{\mathsf{F}}$ can be set privately by each party) We assume that the systems parameters are selected by a trusted third party.

Party $\mathcal{A}$'s static private key is $(a_1, a_2, a_3, a_4) \overset{\mathsf{U}}{\leftarrow} (\mathbb{Z}_p)^4$ and $\mathcal{A}$'s static public key is $A_1 \leftarrow g_1^{a_1} g_2^{a_2}$, $A_2 \leftarrow g_1^{a_3} g_2^{a_4}$. $h_A \overset{\mathsf{R}}{\leftarrow} \mathsf{KH}_k$ indexes a TCR hash function $H_A \leftarrow \mathsf{H}_{h_A}^{k, \mathcal{D}_H, \mathcal{R}_H}$, where $\mathcal{D}_H \leftarrow \Pi_k \times \mathbb{G}^4$, $\mathcal{R}_H \leftarrow \mathbb{Z}_p$ and Π_k denotes the space of possible certificates for static public keys.

Similarly, Party $\mathcal{B}$'s static private key is $(b_1, b_2, b_3, b_4) \overset{\mathsf{U}}{\leftarrow} (\mathbb{Z}_p)^4$ and $\mathcal{B}$'s static public key is $B_1 \leftarrow g_1^{b_1} g_2^{b_2}$, $B_2 \leftarrow g_1^{b_3} g_2^{b_4}$. $h_B \overset{\mathsf{R}}{\leftarrow} \mathsf{KH}_k$ indexes a TCR hash function $H_B \leftarrow \mathsf{H}_{h_B}^{k, \mathcal{D}_H, \mathcal{R}_H}$.

$\mathcal{A}$ and $\mathcal{B}$ set PRFs $F \leftarrow \mathsf{F}^{k, \Sigma_F, \mathcal{D}_F, \mathcal{R}_F}$, $\tilde{F} \leftarrow \tilde{\mathsf{F}}^{k, \Sigma_{\tilde{F}}, \mathcal{D}_{\tilde{F}}, \mathcal{R}_{\tilde{F}}}$ and $\hat{F} \leftarrow \hat{\mathsf{F}}^{k, \Sigma_{\hat{F}}, \mathcal{D}_{\hat{F}}, \mathcal{R}_{\hat{F}}}$, where $\Sigma_F \leftarrow \mathbb{G}$, $\mathcal{D}_F \leftarrow (\Pi_k)^2 \times \mathbb{G}^8$, $\mathcal{R}_F \leftarrow \{0,1\}^k$, $\Sigma_{\tilde{F}} \leftarrow (\mathbb{Z}_p)^4$, $\mathcal{D}_{\tilde{F}} \leftarrow \{0,1\}^k$, $\mathcal{R}_{\tilde{F}} \leftarrow \mathbb{Z}_p$, $\Sigma_{\hat{F}} \leftarrow \{0,1\}^k$, $\mathcal{D}_{\hat{F}} \leftarrow (\mathbb{Z}_p)^4$, and $\mathcal{R}_{\hat{F}} \leftarrow \mathbb{Z}_p$.

To establish a session key with party $\mathcal{B}$, party $\mathcal{A}$ performs the following procedure.

1. Select an ephemeral private key $\tilde{x} \overset{\mathsf{U}}{\leftarrow} \{0,1\}^k$.
2. Compute $x \leftarrow \hat{F}_{\tilde{x}}(a_1, a_2, a_3, a_4) + \tilde{F}_{(a_1, a_2, a_3, a_4)}(\tilde{x}) \bmod p$ and the ephemeral public key $(X_1 \leftarrow g_1^x, X_2 \leftarrow g_2^x)$.
3. Erase x.
4. Send $(\hat{B}, \hat{A}, X_1, X_2)$ to $\mathcal{B}$.

Upon receiving $(\hat{B}, \hat{A}, X_1, X_2)$, party $\mathcal{B}$ verifies that $(X_1, X_2) \in \mathbb{G}^2$. If so, perform the following procedure.

1. Select an ephemeral private key $\tilde{y} \overset{\mathsf{U}}{\leftarrow} \{0,1\}^k$.
2. Compute $y \leftarrow \hat{F}_{\tilde{y}}(b_1, b_2, b_3, b_4) + \tilde{F}_{(b_1, b_2, b_3, b_4)}(\tilde{y}) \bmod p$ and the ephemeral public key $(Y_1 \leftarrow g_1^y, Y_2 \leftarrow g_2^y)$.
3. Erase y.
4. Send $(\hat{A}, \hat{B}, X_1, X_2, Y_1, Y_2)$ to $\mathcal{A}$.

$\mathcal{A}$

$(a_1, a_2, a_3, a_4) \xleftarrow{\mathsf{U}} (\mathbb{Z}_p)^4$
$A_1 \leftarrow g_1^{a_1} g_2^{a_2}, A_2 \leftarrow g_1^{a_3} g_2^{a_4},$
h_A

$\tilde{x} \xleftarrow{\mathsf{U}} \{0, 1\}^k$
$x \leftarrow \hat{F}_{\tilde{x}}(a_1, a_2, a_3, a_4)$
$\qquad + \tilde{F}_{(a_1, a_2, a_3, a_4)}(\tilde{x}) \bmod p$
$X_1 \leftarrow g_1^x, X_2 \leftarrow g_2^x$

$\qquad\qquad\qquad\qquad \xrightarrow{\ (\hat{B}, \hat{A}, X_1, X_2)\ }$

$(Y_1, Y_2) \in \mathbb{G}^2?$
$c \leftarrow H_A(\hat{A}, Y_1, Y_2)$
$d \leftarrow H_B(\hat{B}, X_1, X_2)$
$\sigma \leftarrow Y_1^{a_1 + ca_3 + x} Y_2^{a_2 + ca_4 + x}.$
$\qquad B_1^x B_2^{dx}$
$K \leftarrow F_\sigma(\mathsf{sid})$

$\mathcal{B}$

$(b_1, b_2, b_3, b_4) \xleftarrow{\mathsf{U}} (\mathbb{Z}_p)^4$
$B_1 \leftarrow g_1^{b_1} g_2^{b_2}, B_2 \leftarrow g_1^{b_3} g_2^{b_4},$
h_B

$(X_1, X_2) \in \mathbb{G}^2?$
$\tilde{y} \xleftarrow{\mathsf{U}} \{0, 1\}^k$
$y \leftarrow \hat{F}_{\tilde{y}}(b_1, b_2, b_3, b_4)$
$\qquad + \tilde{F}_{(b_1, b_2, b_3, b_4)}(\tilde{y}) \bmod p$

$\xleftarrow{\ (\hat{A}, \hat{B}, X_1, X_2, Y_1, Y_2)\ } Y_1 \leftarrow g_1^y, Y_2 \leftarrow g_2^y$

$c \leftarrow H_A(\hat{A}, Y_1, Y_2)$
$d \leftarrow H_B(\hat{B}, X_1, X_2)$
$\sigma \leftarrow X_1^{b_1 + db_3 + y} X_2^{b_2 + db_4 + y}.$
$\qquad A_1^y A_2^{cy}$
$K \leftarrow F_\sigma(\mathsf{sid})$

Here, $\mathsf{sid} \leftarrow (\hat{A}, \hat{B}, X_1, X_2, Y_1, Y_2)$. Note that $(A_1, A_2, B_1, B_2) \in \mathbb{G}^4$ is confirmed indirectly through the certificates.

Fig. 1. The Proposed AKE

Upon receiving $(\hat{A}, \hat{B}, X_1, X_2, Y_1, Y_2)$, party $\mathcal{A}$ checks if he sent $(\hat{B}, \hat{A}, X_1, X_2)$ to $\mathcal{B}$. If so, $\mathcal{A}$ verifies that $(Y_1, Y_2) \in \mathbb{G}^2$.

To compute the session key, $\mathcal{A}$ computes $\sigma_A \leftarrow Y_1^{a_1 + ca_3 + x} Y_2^{a_2 + ca_4 + x} B_1^x B_2^{dx}$, and $\mathcal{B}$ computes $\sigma_B \leftarrow X_1^{b_1 + db_3 + y} X_2^{b_2 + db_4 + y} A_1^y A_2^{cy}$, where $c \leftarrow H_A(\hat{A}, Y_1, Y_2)$ and $d \leftarrow H_B(\hat{B}, X_1, X_2)$. If they are correctly computed, $\sigma \leftarrow \sigma_A (= \sigma_B)$. The session key is $K \leftarrow F_\sigma(\mathsf{sid})$, where $\mathsf{sid} \leftarrow (\hat{A}, \hat{B}, X_1, X_2, Y_1, Y_2)$.

3.2 Security

Theorem 1. *The proposed AKE protocol is secure (in the sense of Definition 2) if the DDH assumption holds for $\{\mathbb{G}\}_{k \in \mathbb{N}}$, H is a TCR hash function family, and F, $\tilde{F}$ and $\hat{F}$ are PRF families.*

The proof will be given in the full paper version of this paper.

4   The Proposed KEM Scheme

4.1   Scheme

In this section, we show a CCA secure KEM scheme.

Let $k \in \mathbb{N}$ be a security parameter, and let $\mathbb{G} \xleftarrow{U} \{\mathbb{G}\}_k$ be a group with security parameter k, where the order of $\mathbb{G}$ is prime p and $|p| = k$.

Let H be a TCR hash function family, and F be a PRF family.

Secret Key: The secret key is $sk \leftarrow (x_1, x_2, y_1, y_2) \xleftarrow{U} \mathbb{Z}_p^4$.

Public Key: $g_1 \xleftarrow{U} \mathbb{G}$, $g_2 \xleftarrow{U} \mathbb{G}$, $z \leftarrow g_1^{x_1} g_2^{x_2}$, $w \leftarrow g_1^{y_1} g_2^{y_2}$, $H \leftarrow \mathsf{H}_h^{k, \mathcal{D}_H, \mathcal{R}_H}$ and $F \leftarrow \mathsf{F}^{k, \Sigma_\mathsf{F}, \mathcal{D}_\mathsf{F}, \mathcal{R}_\mathsf{F}}$, where $h \xleftarrow{R} \mathsf{KH}_k$, $\mathcal{D}_H \leftarrow \{pk\} \times \mathbb{G}^2$ (pk is a possible public-key value), $\mathcal{R}_H \leftarrow \mathbb{Z}_p$, $\Sigma_\mathsf{F} \leftarrow \mathbb{G}$, $\mathcal{D}_\mathsf{F} \leftarrow \{pk\} \times \mathbb{G}^2$ and $\mathcal{R}_\mathsf{F} \leftarrow \{0, 1\}^k$.

The public key is $pk \leftarrow (\mathbb{G}, g_1, g_2, z, w, H, F)$.

Encryption: Choose $r \xleftarrow{U} \mathbb{Z}_p$ and compute

$$
\begin{aligned}
C_1 &\leftarrow g_1^r, \\
C_2 &\leftarrow g_2^r, \\
d &\leftarrow H(z, w, C_1, C_2) \\
\sigma &\leftarrow z^r w^{rd} \\
K &\leftarrow F_\sigma(pk, C_1, C_2).
\end{aligned}
$$

(C_1, C_2) is a ciphertext, and K is the secret key to be shared.

Decryption: Given (z, w, C_1, C_2), check whether

$$(z, w, C_1, C_2) \in \mathbb{G}^4.$$

If it holds, computes

$$
\begin{aligned}
d &\leftarrow H(z, w, C_1, C_2) \\
\sigma &\leftarrow C_1^{x_1 + dy_1} C_2^{x_2 + dy_2} \\
K &\leftarrow F_\sigma(pk, C_1, C_2).
\end{aligned}
$$

4.2   CCA Security

Theorem 2. *The proposed KEM scheme is IND-CCA2 secure if the DDH assumption holds for $\{\mathbb{G}\}_{k \in \mathbb{N}}$, H is a TCR hash function family, and F is a PRF family.*

The proof will be given in the full paper version of this paper.

4.3   CPCA Security

In this paper, we define a stronger security notion than the CCA security on KEM and PKE.

Here, we consider a trapdoor commitment, where committer (sender) S commits to x by sending $C \leftarrow \mathsf{E}_{pk}(x)$ to receiver $\mathcal{R}$, then S opens x by sending sk to $\mathcal{R}$, where (pk, sk) is a pair of public key and secret key, and $x = \mathsf{D}_{sk}(C)$. Using a trapdoor commitment, several committers, $S_1, \ldots, S_n$, commits to $x_1, \ldots, x_n$ respectively by sending $C_1 \leftarrow \mathsf{E}_{pk}(x_1), \ldots, C_n \leftarrow \mathsf{E}_{pk}(x_n)$ to receiver $\mathcal{R}$. Another party can open them simultaneously by sending sk to receiver $\mathcal{R}$. A possible malleable attack is as follows: after looking at pk and $C \leftarrow \mathsf{E}_{pk}(x)$ sent to receiver $\mathcal{R}$, adversary $\mathcal{A}$ computes pk', C', algorithm Conv and non-trivial relation Rel. $\mathcal{A}$ registers pk' and sends C' to $\mathcal{R}$ as a commitment to x' such that $\mathsf{Rel}(x, x')$. When sk is opened, $\mathcal{A}$ computes $sk' \leftarrow \mathsf{Conv}(sk)$ and sends sk' to $\mathcal{R}$ such that $x' = \mathsf{D}_{sk'}(C')$.

To capture the security against such malleable attacks, we now define the CPCA (Chosen Public-key and Ciphertext Attacks) security for KEM schemes.

Let $\Sigma = (\mathsf{K}, \mathsf{E}, \mathsf{D})$ be a KEM scheme. Let C^*, pk^* and sk^* be the target ciphertext, public key and secret key of KEM scheme Σ. In the CPCA security, an adversary $\mathcal{A}$, given pk^* and C^*, is allowed to submit a pair of a public key pk and a ciphertext C along with a polynomial-time algorithm Conv to the decryption oracle DO (with sk^*) under the condition that $(pk, C) \neq (pk^*, C^*)$. DO returns $\mathsf{D}_{sk}(C)$ to $\mathcal{A}$, where DO computes and confirms that $sk \leftarrow \mathsf{Conv}(sk^*, pk^*)$, $(c, k) \leftarrow \mathsf{E}_{pk}(1^k)$ and $k \leftarrow \mathsf{D}_{sk}(c)$. (Here, D_{sk} is equivalent to D_{sk^*} except for the difference of sk and sk^*).

We can define the advantage of $\mathcal{A}$ for the IND-CPCA game, $\mathsf{AdvKEM}_{\mathcal{A}}^{\text{IND-CPCA}}(k)$. We say that a KEM scheme is IND-CPCA-secure if for any probabilistic polynomial-time (PPT) adversary $\mathcal{A}$, $\mathsf{AdvKEM}_{\mathcal{A}}^{\text{IND-CPCA}}(k)$ is negligible in k.

We now show that the proposed KEM scheme is CPCA secure. To prove the security, we need a new requirement for a hash function family, the generalized TCR (GTCR) hash function family.

Let $k \in \mathbb{N}$ be a security parameter. Let $\mathbb{G}$ be a group with security parameter k, where the order of $\mathbb{G}$ is prime p and $|p| = k$, and $\{\mathbb{G}\}_k$ be the set of group $\mathbb{G}$ with security parameter k.

Let H be a TCR hash function family associated with $\mathsf{Dom}_k \leftarrow \{\mathbb{G}^4\}_k$, $\mathsf{Rng}_k \leftarrow \{\mathbb{G}\}_k$.

For all k, we define

$$\mathsf{AdvGTCR}_{\mathsf{H},\mathcal{A}}^{\mathsf{G}}(k) \leftarrow \Pr[\rho_3 \in \mathbb{G}^2 \wedge \rho^* \neq ((\rho_1^*)^u, (\rho_2^*)^v, \rho_3) \wedge$$
$$\mathsf{H}_h^{k,\mathbb{G}^4,\mathbb{G}}(\rho^*) = (v/u) \cdot \mathsf{H}_h^{k,\mathbb{G}^4,\mathbb{G}}((\rho_1^*)^u, (\rho_2^*)^v, \rho_3) \bmod p \mid$$
$$(u, v, \rho_3) \xleftarrow{\text{R}} \mathcal{A}(1^k, \rho^*, h, \mathbb{G})],$$

where $\mathbb{G} \xleftarrow{\text{U}} \{\mathbb{G}\}_k$, $\rho^* \leftarrow (\rho_1^*, \rho_2^*, \rho_3^*) \xleftarrow{\text{U}} \mathbb{G} \times \mathbb{G} \times \mathbb{G}^2$ and $h \xleftarrow{\text{R}} \mathsf{KH}_k$.

TCR hash function family H is a generalized target collision resistant (GTCR) hash function family associated with $\{\mathbb{G}\}_k$ if for any probabilistic polynomial-time adversary $\mathcal{A}$, $\mathsf{AdvGTCR}_{\mathsf{H},\mathcal{A}}^{\mathsf{G}}(k)$ is negligible in k.

Theorem 3. *The proposed KEM scheme is IND-CPCA secure, if the DDH assumption holds for* $\{\mathbb{G}\}_{k \in \mathbb{N}}$, H *is a GTCR hash function family, and* F *is a PRF family.*

The proof will be given in the full paper version of this paper.

Acknowledgments

The author would like to thank Masayuki Abe for his invaluable discussions and suggestions on the proposed paradigm, KEM and redundancy-free hybrid encryption. I also thank Alfred Menezes for his lectures on the AKE protocols and security models as well as insightful discussions and valuable comments. I am also grateful to David Pointcheval and Michel Abdalla for their valuable comments on a preliminary version of this manuscript. I would like to express my appreciation of Kaoru Kurosawa, the PC chair of Asiacrypt 2007, for giving me an opportunity to present this paper at the proceedings as an invited talk manuscript.

References

1. Abe, M., Gennaro, R., Kurosawa, K., Shoup, V., Tag-KEM/DEM, A.: New Framework for Hybrid Encryption and New Analysis of Kurosawa-Desmedt KEM, Adv. In: Cramer, R.J.F. (ed.) EUROCRYPT 2005. LNCS, vol. 3494, pp. 128–146. Springer, Heidelberg (2005)
2. Canetti, R., Krawczyk, H.: Analysis of key-exchange protocols and their use for building secure channels. In: Pfitzmann, B. (ed.) EUROCRYPT 2001. LNCS, vol. 2045, Springer, Heidelberg (2001), http://eprint.iacr.org/2001/040
3. Cramer, R., Shoup, V.: Design and analysis of practical public-key encryption schemes secure against adaptive chosen ciphertext attack. SIAM Journal on Computing 33(1), 167–226 (2003)
4. Goldreich, O., Goldwasser, S., Micali, S.: How to Construct Random Functions. Journal of the ACM 33(4), 792–807 (1986)
5. Hastad, J., Impagliazzo, R., Levin, L., Luby, M.: A Pseudorandom Generator from any One-way Function. SIAM Journal on Computing, 28(4), 1364–1396 (1999)
6. Krawczyk, H.: HMQV: A high-performance secure Diffie-Hellman protocol. In: Shoup, V. (ed.) CRYPTO 2005. LNCS, vol. 3621, Springer, Heidelberg (2005), http://eprint.iacr.org/2005/176
7. Kurosawa, K., Desmedt, Y.: A New Paradigm of Hybrid Encryption Scheme. In: Franklin, M. (ed.) CRYPTO 2004. LNCS, vol. 3152, pp. 426–442. Springer, Heidelberg (2004)
8. LaMacchia, B., Lauter, K., Mityagin, A.: Stronger security of authenticated key exchange, Cryptology ePrint Archive, Report, 2006/073 (2006), http://eprint.iacr.org/2006/073
9. Law, L., Menezes, A., Qu, M., Solinas, J., Van stone, S.: An efficient protocol for authenticated key agreement, Designs, Codes and Cryptography. 28, 119–134 (2003)
10. Menezes, A.: Another look at HMQV. Journal of Mathematical Cryptology 1, 148–175 (2007)
11. Matsumoto, T., Takashima, Y., Imai, H.: On Seeking Smart Public-key Distribution Systems. Transactions of the IECE of Japan E69, 99–106 (1986)
12. Naor, M., Yung, M.: Universal one-way hash functions and their cryptographic applications. In: Proceedings of the 21st Annual ACM Symposium on Theory of Computing, pp. 33–43. ACM Press, New York (1989)
13. Rompel, J.: One-way functions are necessary and sufficient for secure signatures. In: Proceedings of the 22nd Annual ACM Symposium on Theory of Computing, pp. 387–394. ACM Press, New York (1990)
14. Ustaoglu, B.: Obtaining a secure and efficient key agreement protocol from (H)MQV and NAXOS, Cryptology ePrint Archive, Report, 2007 /123 (2007), http://eprint.iacr.org/2007/123

Miniature CCA2 PK Encryption:
Tight Security Without Redundancy

Xavier Boyen

Voltage Inc.
xb@boyen.org

Abstract. We present a minimalist public-key cryptosystem, as compact as ElGamal, but with adaptive chosen-ciphertext security under the gap Diffie-Hellman assumption in the random oracle model. The novelty is a dual-hash device that provides tight redundancy-free implicit validation. Compared to previous constructions, ours features a tight security reduction, *both in efficacy and efficiency*, to a classic and essentially non-interactive complexity assumption, and without resorting to asymmetric/symmetric-key hybrid constructions. The system is very compact: on elliptic curves with 80-bit security, a 160-bit plaintext becomes a 320-bit ciphertext. It is also very simple and has a number of practical advantages, and we hope to see it adopted widely.

1 Introduction and Motivation

One of the major pursuits in cryptographic research has been to devise faster, nimbler, shorter, and stronger encryption systems that can be used in practice. In the realm of public-key cryptosystems, the lure of simplicity and efficiency has produced many a breakthrough and many more successive refinements, over the last three decades.

We propose one more such technical refinement, in the form of a CCA2-secure PK cryptosystem with the shortest ciphertext among Discrete-Log-based systems at any given *exact* security level. Our construction is simple and purely algebraic, and relies on a standard assumption in the random-oracle model of [2]. To obtain short ciphertexts, we eliminate all sources of redundancy, and limit the unavoidable randomness to a single element of the computational group. Furthermore, we ensure that no space is wasted in the encoding of that element, by shrinking the computational group itself to the smallest size that the birthday paradox will allow. The latter requirement is only possible with a *tight* reduction to the underlying security assumption, as we shall discuss momentarily. These properties taken together account for the scheme's compactness.

All comparable schemes that have been suggested over the years either have a non-tight security reduction, or are hybrid constructions with both an algebraic and a symmetric-key component, each bringing forth its own complexity assumption. (We note that all known redundancy-free systems depend either on some non-standard oracle assumption, or at least on the random-oracle model. Indeed, it remains a major open problem to withstand active attacks without

K. Kurosawa (Ed.): ASIACRYPT 2007, LNCS 4833, pp. 485–501, 2007.

redundancy and without relying on random oracles or some sort of interactive assumption).

By contrast, the scheme we propose can be proven tightly secure, in the random-oracle model, solely under the Gap Diffie-Hellman (Gap-DH) assumption [22], or even under the usual Computational Diffie-Hellman (CDH) assumption if the algebraic group admits an efficient bilinear pairing: This is because with a pairing one can instantiate the DDH oracle posited by the Gap-DH assumption, which then reduces to plain CDH. Pairing-friendly groups are easy to construct on certain types of elliptic curves; we refer the reader to the abundant literature on pairing-based cryptography. We emphasize that our scheme will be secure under CDH as soon as a pairing *exists* in the selected group, even though we never actually *use* it. In groups where no efficient pairing is known to exist, security still follows from the Gap-DH assumption.

1.1   On the Tightness of Reductions

The importance of a tight security reduction to a simple and well-studied assumption is crucial to the determination of the exact security of any cryptosystem. A security proof can be loose in two different ways: the final reduction may cause a loss of success probability, or the simulator can be slow and steal most of the computational time that should go to the attacker. The latter factor is too often ignored when a security proof is advertised as tight: it is often the case that a proof with tight efficacy probability-wise, would use an inefficient simulator whose running time is quadratic or worse, which can significantly hurt the security of the scheme in a real-world attack: the true security guarantee would *not* be tight if one accounted for all parameters, as one should. Accordingly, it is only by taking into account all intervening factors that a scheme's *true security* can be determined for a chosen *apparent security parameter*. Larger apparent security parameters will have to be selected to compensate for loose reductions (or strong assumptions), resulting in larger ciphertexts for the desired target security level.

In the random oracle model in particular, it is very important to pay close attention to the extent that a scheme's exact security deteriorates with the number of random oracle queries made by the adversary, because in reality the random oracle is instantiated as an algorithmic hash function that can be queried offline, limited only by the adversary's computational powers. Interactive assumptions that assume the existence of "fancy oracles" that have no actual instantiations (even imperfect ones) are even more troublesome, because there is no telling how a scheme that depends on such an oracle will fare in the real world: it might be completely insecure and it is not hard to find examples of such. Sensitivity to the number of decryption queries is less critical because in practice the decryption query rate is limited by various online processes, but it nevertheless remains an issue.

1.2   Our Contribution

For all of the reasons above, it is our purpose here to devise a compact encryption scheme based on plausible assumptions, and establish exact security bounds in function of the number of random-oracle and decryption queries made by the opponent. We seek to obtain a tight security bound that is quasi-independent of the number of those queries (as long as their number remains sub-exponential in the security parameter, which is an unavoidable requirement). Surely, eliminating the random oracle itself would be even more desirable, but it is an open problem whether that is even feasible at all if no redundancy whatsoever is tolerated.

Our main technical tool stems from the observation that a pair of sequential one-time pads, can, in the random-oracle model, give us an almost tight reduction from a mild assumption such as CDH or Gap-DH, without appealing to explicit ciphertext redundancy or a hybrid scheme. Whereas redundancy-free public-key schemes with a tight reduction have been proposed in the past, we view the dual-hash device and the simpler structure that it enables as our main contributions. As an added bonus, our system will support very efficient non-interactive threshold decryption.

2   Toward Active Security Without Redundancy

The most common threat to CCA2 security is that of a query on a malformed ciphertext causing the decryption oracle to leak damaging information, either about the private key, or about the plaintext (when the malformed ciphertext is a deformation of a legitimate one). For this reason, the most common way to construct a CCA-secure system from a CPA-secure one is to add some redundancy, thanks to which malformed or mauled ciphertexts can be safely rejected. Redundancy has also an utilitarian purpose in the security proofs: simulators use it to extract private knowledge about the ciphertext creation, which gives them a backdoor thanks to which decryption queries can be answered without knowledge of the decryption key. The two main ways that this backdoor is implemented are the NIZK and IBE approaches, briefly described below.

Redundancy can nevertheless be avoided provided that the decryption of malformed ciphertexts is made harmless, e.g., as will be the case if the decryption of bogus ciphertexts appears uniformly random to the adversary. Thus, as has been observed several times before, redundancy is not truly necessary in order to achieve chosen-ciphertext security (though randomness is always needed for semantic security). Technically, one must also ensure that the simulator is still able to answer the decryption queries in the absence of a redundancy backdoor: this is where idealized models such as the random oracle heuristic [2] must come into play, at least in our current state of knowledge.

Subject to the above limitations, there exists a rather extensive body of work on public-key encryption systems secure against active attacks. We now review the main proposals, concentrating on systems that are usable in practice. In order to depict a more complete landscape, we also discuss a number of redundant constructions, since they far outnumber the redundancy-free ones. Once again, if we insist on the lack of redundancy, no CCA2-secure public-key systems, not even conjectured ones, are known to exist in the standard model.

2.1   In the Standard Model

In the standard model, all known chosen-ciphertext-secure systems require some redundancy.

First of all, we mention the early theoretical work of Dolev, Dwork, and Naor [15], which achieves CCA-security using a bitwise construction which is too inefficient to be used in practice. More efficient constructions were to follow, based either on the so-called two-key paradigm, or, more recently, on identity-based encryption and related techniques.

The two-key (or double-encryption) framework for chosen-ciphertext security was first proposed by Naor and Yung [31], and perfected by Cramer and Shoup [12] who gave the first efficient CCA2-secure public-key scheme in the standard model. There were many subsequent improvements to the Cramer-Shoup system, and the current state of the art is due to Kurosawa and Desmedt [26]. The two-key paradigm consists in providing two independent encryptions of the same plaintext, along with a Non-Interactive Zero-Knowledge (NIZK) proof that the two plaintexts are the same. This provides the needed redundancy that allows the simulator to answer decryption queries. A drawback of this approach is that the redundancy cannot be checked until the complete ciphertext has been decrypted, which makes threshold decryption a complicated proposition [9,19,34].

The Identity-Based Encryption (IBE) approach was recently proposed by Canetti, Halevi, and Katz [10], and subsequently improved [7,8]. Here, the general idea is to encrypt a plaintext to an identity equal to a signature verification key, or some function of the ciphertext itself, that the recipient can use to authenticate the ciphertext. This is a different kind of redundancy that leads to a completely different type of simulation proof than in the two-key approach. Both methods are comparable in terms of efficiency. One advantage of the identity-based approach is that the integrity check can be done before decryption, which makes non-interactive threshold decryption easy [5]. The main disadvantage of the IBE approach is that it uses bilinear pairings, although it is possible to eliminate them entirely by making stronger assumptions [24].

Although reasonably efficient, all these constructions require at least two group elements' worth of ciphertext overhead. It is an open problem to achieve chosen-ciphertext security without redundancy in the standard model.

2.2   Using Random Oracles

In parallel to the above developments, researchers have sought to construct CCA2-secure systems with efficiency as the primary goal, even if that meant using the random oracle heuristic. One of the most significant works in this area is the RSA-OAEP padding scheme [3] and its subsequent improvements [4,33], which are widely deployed as a standard. However, the development of OAEP was tormented: the original redundancy-free design had to be scrapped in order to achieve provable chosen-ciphertext security, and it took several years until an RSA system with both properties was finally invented (see below).

In parallel, a powerful result by Fujisaki and Okamoto [17], subsequently improved by the same authors [18], shows that any CPA-secure encryption scheme can be generically transformed into a CCA2-secure one, in the random oracle model, simply by adding some judicious redundancy. One can thus assemble a very efficient CCA2-secure system simply by taking an elliptic-curve implementation of the ElGamal cryptosytem and applying the Fujisaki-Okamoto transformation. This does however introduce some redundancy.

2.3   From Interactive Hash Assumptions

Since random oracles alone did not seem sufficient to obtain redundancy-free chosen-ciphertext security, one had to appeal to more exotic and stronger assumptions. In general, these assumptions are interactive and involve at least a random function, very much like the random oracle model.

The first system to achieve redundancy-free chosen-ciphertext security, is that of Phan and Pointcheval [32]. The Phan-Pointcheval scheme can be thought of as an extension of RSA-OAEP that achieves adaptive security using the theoretical minimum amount of randomness and no redundancy, but under a strong non-standard interactive assumption. Roughly speaking, it combines a trapdoor permutation with an idealized random permutation; the CCA2 security proof then holds in the random permutation model. In practice, the system is instantiated using RSA and a Feistel network, which only requires a random oracle rather than a random permutation.

The second system in this category is DHIES [1], all of whose variants are based on a strong interactive assumption known as Oracle Diffie-Hellman. The DHIES system is a hybrid of ElGamal, a symmetric cipher, and a MAC, and is provably secure under the ODH assumption. Because of the MAC, the original DHIES system is not redundancy-free.

Kurosawa and Matsuo [27] subsequently gave an improvement to DHIES that eliminated the MAC from the ciphertext and thus the redundancy. This was done by means of a special "all-or-nothing" mode of operation for the symmetric cipher, such as CMC [20] and EME [21], which can be viewed as an analog to the pseudo-random permutation in the Phan-Pointcheval system. With this modification, DHIES no longer incurs any expansion, and thus the Kurosawa-Matsuo system is indeed free of redundancy. Since furthermore DHIES can be implemented on elliptic curves, unlike Phan-Pointcheval which uses integer arithmetic modulo a large RSA composite, Kurosawa-Matsuo can be made very compact. Indeed, their system currently holds the record for the most compact CCA2 public-key system for short messages.

Libert and Quisquater [28] later transposed the ideas of Kurosawa and Matsuo to the identity-based encryption setting, and in particular to the IBE system of Boneh and Franklin [6]. They show that CCA2 security can be obtained by using an expansion-less chosen-ciphertext-secure symmetric mode of operation (instead of the Fujisaki-Okamoto transformation as originally used in [6]). The Libert-Quisquater IBE system is in fact simpler than the Kurosawa-Matsuo PKE, but unfortunately, the security of the former rests (in the RO model) upon a very strong interactive assumption called Gap Bilinear Diffie-Hellman, which is not even falsifiable in our current state of knowledge since nobody knows how to construct a Gap-BDH challenger.

To conclude this tour, we now briefly review the main features of the Phan-Pointcheval and the Kurosawa-Matsuo systems, as these are the two schemes against our construction ought to be compared.

The Phan-Pointcheval System. Phan and Pointcheval [32] gave the first construction of a CCA2-secure public-key encryption system without redundancy. It is based on the RSA trapdoor permutation which is made non-malleable using a idealized random permutation instantiated as a Feistel network. The Phan-Pointcheval system incurs very little ciphertext expansion: for an *apparent* security parameter κ, the ciphertext is only κ bits longer than the message it encrypts. Without taking the security reduction efficiency into account, this is the smallest possible ciphertext expansion that can be achieved by any public-key encryption scheme at the $2^{-\kappa}$ security level.

In reality, Phan-Pointcheval is not quite as compact as we would like, for a couple of reasons: (1) its security reduction has tight efficacy but only quadratic efficiency in the Feistel network instantiation, which means that in practice its exact security could degrade significantly with the number of queries made by the adversary, which ought to be compensated by growing the modulus; (2) because the scheme is built around an RSA permutation, ciphertexts cannot be made smaller than 1024 bits at the 2^{-80} security level, or 15360 bits at the 2^{-256} security level, to guard against sub-exponential factorization attacks of complexity $L(1/3)$ using the number field sieve.

The Kurosawa-Matsuo System. To avoid the minimum size limitation associated with RSA groups, Kurosawa and Matsuo [27] have proposed a different construction of a CCA2-secure public-key cryptosystem, based not on RSA but on ElGamal. Since ElGamal can be implemented on elliptic curves, much fewer bits are in principle needed in order to achieve the same security. The Kurosawa-Matsuo construction is set in the KEM/DEM framework, where a CCA2-secure KEM is constructed simply by hashing an ElGamal session key, from which an expansion-less one-time chosen-ciphertext-secure DEM is used to encrypt the actual message. For an *apparent* security parameter κ, the ciphertext is 2κ bits longer than the message, which is the smallest possible expansion for a Discrete-Log-based cryptosystem, due to the birthday bound barrier associated with generic discrete-log attacks.

On the negative side, the security reduction of the Kurosawa-Matsuo system relies on the original DHIES construction, which is based on a very strong interactive assumption called the Oracle Diffie-Hellman assumption. Roughly speaking, the ODH problem asks us to distinguish (g, g^a, g^b, g^{ab}) from (g, g^a, g^b, g^r) given access to an oracle $\mathcal{O} : h \mapsto H(h^a)$, which can be thought of as the composition of the composition of a secret-power exponentiation with an ideal random hash function (also kept secret by default). We note however that Cramer and Shoup [14] later gave an alternative security proof of DHIES, replacing ODH with Gap-DH in the random oracle model. Their proof should also apply to the Kurosawa-Matsuo system.

Perhaps the main downside of the Kurosawa-Matsuo system is that it depends on rather complex modes of operation for block ciphers, such as the deterministic, redundancy-free, one-time chosen-ciphertext-secure modes given in [20,21]. Because of those extraneous components, the Kurosawa-Matsuo system may suffer from a larger implementation footprint than competing schemes. The complex modes of operation may also pose practical challenges for arbitrary-size plaintexts.

2.4 The New Construction

Here, we propose another efficient public-key encryption system without redundancy and with a tight adaptive chosen-ciphertext security proof. A feature of our scheme is its simple and self-contained algebraic structure. The security reduction is to the Gap Diffie-Hellman assumption in the random-oracle model. Gap-DH is a "decisional/computational gap" assumption [22], which simply posits that CDH is hard given a DDH oracle. Since Gap-DH itself reduces to the usual CDH in groups equipped with a bilinear map (which we know how to construct), our scheme belongs with the "plain" random-oracle schemes of Section 2.2, as opposed to the "fancy" interactive-assumption schemes of Section 2.3, which until now were the only ones known to avoid redundancy. Practically speaking, our system only uses hashing and generic group arithmetic (no block cipher and no complex mode of operation), and so its implementation should be straightforward in any programming language with a decent library.

The main idea of the scheme is to blind the message not once, but twice, using ElGamal one-time pads that are homomorphically related to the same secret decryption key. The resulting ciphertext has no explicit redundancy because the second key can be reconstructed from the first without having to include any information about it. In the random oracle model, this however gives us the implicit consistency check needed for chosen-ciphertext security. Furthermore we can simulate it in constant time and almost perfectly (i.e., with negligible security loss) against any polynomially bounded adversary, hence the tight security.

Security and Compacity. It should be mentioned that it does not seem feasible to achieve a better "ciphertext compacity vs. exact security" tradeoff without leaving the realm of Discrete-Log-based algebraic CCA2 PKE systems. Indeed, at the $2^{-\kappa}$ exact security level, the ciphertext overhead is a single group element, which takes as few as 2κ bits to represent; however, the randomness embedded in this element cannot be removed, and any attempt to reduce the entropy of that group element further will enable a generic discrete logarithm attack of relative complexity lower than $\sqrt{2^{2\kappa}} = 2^{\kappa}$.

However, one should not infer from this that shorter ciphertexts are not possible using different techniques. For example, with trapdoor permutations it is possible to reduce the overhead to the theoretical minimum of κ bits, as in the Phan-Pointcheval system; one problem with this approach is that RSA-based trapdoor permutations require much larger groups than elliptic curves for the same security (which is why Phan-Pointcheval ciphertexts remain large despite the very low overhead). Substituting a more compact trapdoor permutation for RSA in Phan-Pointcheval would be an excellent way to create a more compact scheme than the present proposal. Of course, constructing a compact trapdoor permutation in the first place, *e.g.*, whose inputs and outpus are no greater than 3κ bits at the $2^{-\kappa}$ security level, is another long-standing famous open problem in cryptography.

State of the Art. We do not claim that our construction constitutes a deep result, but merely a practical one that we hope will be adopted in practice. In retrospect, our construction and its security proof appear quite simple, indeed, as surely many other results of this sort have before it. However, the fact that with a simple trick we have improved upon the state of the art on an old problem is a compelling indication that there are still new insights to be gained in this area. Thus we hope that this contribution will be useful to security practitioners, and perhaps inspire new ideas to researchers in the field.

3   The Miniature CCA2 System

We are now almost ready to present the construction. Unlike Kurosawa and Matsuo, we seek to build an integrated encryption scheme without insisting on a separation between KEM and DEM. On the contrary, we look for an algebraic construction that avoids block ciphers and their complex modes of operations, and seek to base our scheme on a single mild and well-studied assumption.

3.1   Inching Toward a Solution

Before we present our construction, it is useful to try out a few approaches, to see what works and what does not. This will make it easier to understand the design of the final scheme.

1. To start, consider the hashed ElGamal system, whose ciphertext is $(c_1, c_2) = (M \oplus H(g_1^r), g_2^r)$ for random $r \in \mathbb{F}_p$. The public key is $(g_1, g_2) \in \mathbb{G}^2$, and the decryption key is $k = \operatorname{dlog}_{g_1}(g_2)$. The ciphertext is free of redundancy, but it is malleable and thus the scheme is only secure under passive attacks.
2. To make the scheme secure under active attacks, we can modify the ciphertext as follows: $(c_1, c_2) = (M \oplus H_1(g_1^r), g_2^r g_3^{r H_2(c_1)})$, where H_1 is viewed as a random oracle and H_2 is collision resistant. The public key is (g_1, g_2, g_3) and the secret key their discrete logs.

    Here, there is no obvious active attack, and in fact the scheme can be proven IND-CCA2 secure under the Gap-DH assumption in the random oracle model. Unfortunately, the reduction is not tight, and is in fact rather expensive because, for each decryption query, the DDH oracle must be tested against the inputs to all previous random-oracle queries.

3. The reduction in the previous scheme can be made more efficient, and thus the scheme more secure in the exact sense, by including more information inside the random-oracle input, as in: $(c_1, c_2) = (M \oplus H_1(g_1^r, g_2^r), g_2^r g_3^{r H_2(c_1)})$. We can also take $g_3 = g_1$ to make the key shorter.

   This simple modification greatly reduces the number of DDH oracle queries needed by the simulator (in a security reduction to Gap-DH), to the point that we now have proportionality between the adversary's and the simulator's use of their respective oracles, *i.e.*, one query to the DDH oracle for each random-oracle query. The resulting reduction is thus more efficient, and, indeed, public-key systems with this exact structure have been recently and independently suggested in at least two places [29,25], prior to the publication of this work.

   However, security still is not tight. For *every* decryption query, the simulator must perform a non-trivial group operation between c_2 and the input to *every* random oracle query made so far. Thus, if the adversary makes q_d decryption and q_H random-oracle queries, the simulator's running time will be at least the product of the two, *i.e.*, $\Omega(q_d q_H)$, which is clearly disproportionate (*i.e.*, super-linear) to the sum total of all of the adversary's queries.

   Hence, although the efficacy or succcess probability of the reduction may be tight, and the use of the DDH oracle parsimonious, the reduction algorithm remains inefficient due to an excess of bookeeping.

A general principle that emerges from these examples is how random oracles can be utilized to extract the information needed to answer decryption queries, when the ciphertext contains no redundancy that would let us do so in another way (as in the schemes mentioned in Section 2.1).

We can also see, in all these examples and analogous constructions based on a Gap assumption, that the simulator must try out all random oracle inputs to see if one works for every decryption query that it answers. This is not unrelated to the fact that our assumption (Gap-DH) only provides a decisional (yes/no) oracle to the simulator, and indeed, the Kurosawa-Matsuo scheme does not have this problem because its DHIES component relies on a stronger assumption.

However, the central reason for the schemes' reduction inefficiency is their use of a single random oracle for blinding the message (as in $M \oplus H(...)$). It turns out that a much more efficient simulator can be made if we had two random-oracle one-time pads to play with (as in $M \oplus H_1(...) \oplus H_2(...)$). Why this is so will become apparent when we construct a simulator in Section 3.4.

3.2   The Full Scheme

Our construction is based on some of the principles hinted to above. The main difficulty is to obtain a double one-time-pad blinding of the message without lengthening the ciphertext, and then to use this double blinding in the security proof to achieve a tight reduction.

We start with the construction, which uses two random oracles Φ and Ψ, and one collision-resistant function π which could be a simple injection.

Context: Let $\kappa \in \mathbb{N}$ be an arbitrary security parameter. Let $\mathbb{G} = \langle U \rangle$ be a cyclic prime-order group (written multiplicatively), generated by U, of prime order p, such that $2^{2\kappa-1} < p < 2^{2\kappa+1}$. Let $\mathbb{F}_p$ be the finite field of size p, and let $\mathbb{F}_p^{\times} = \mathbb{F}_p \setminus \{0\}$ denote its multiplicative group of order $p-1$. Let $\mathcal{M} = \{0,1\}^{\ell}$ be the set of all bit strings of length ℓ, for any fixed $\ell \geq 2\kappa$.

Let $\pi : \mathcal{M} \to \mathbb{F}_p^{\times}$ be an arbitrary injection or a collision-resistant hash function.

Let $\Phi : \mathbb{G} \times \mathbb{G} \to \mathcal{M}$ and $\Psi : \mathbb{G} \to \mathcal{M}$ be two cryptographic hash functions (viewed as RO).

Key generation: Draw a secret random exponent $s \in_{s} \mathbb{F}_p^{\times}$, and calculate $V = U^s$.

The public encryption key is $\mathsf{Pk} \leftarrow (U, V) \in \mathbb{G}^2$.
The private decryption key is $\mathsf{Sk} \leftarrow s \in \mathbb{F}_p^{\times}$.

Encryption: Given Pk and a plaintext $\mathsf{Msg} \in \mathcal{M}$, pick a randomizer $r \in_{s} \mathbb{F}_p^{\times}$, and let,

$$A \leftarrow V^r$$
$$B \leftarrow \Psi(A) \oplus \mathsf{Msg}$$
$$C \leftarrow V^{r/\pi(B)}$$
$$D \leftarrow U^{r/\pi(B)}$$
$$E \leftarrow \Phi(D, C) \oplus B$$

The ciphertext is $\mathsf{Ctx} = (D, E) \in \mathbb{G} \times \mathcal{M}$.

Decryption: Given Sk and a ciphertext $\mathsf{Ctx} = (\bar{D}, \bar{E})$, check that $1 \neq \bar{D} \in \mathbb{G}$, and let,

$$\bar{C} \leftarrow \bar{D}^{\mathsf{Sk}}$$
$$\bar{B} \leftarrow \bar{E} \oplus \Phi(\bar{D}, \bar{C})$$
$$\bar{A} \leftarrow \bar{C}^{\pi(\bar{B})}$$
$$\bar{M} \leftarrow \bar{B} \oplus \Psi(\bar{A})$$

The decrypted plaintext is $\bar{\mathsf{Msg}} = \bar{M} \in \mathcal{M}$.

3.3 Operational Efficiency

Encryption and decryption have essentially the same computational costs, which are dominated by the costs of two exponentiations in $\mathbb{G}$, plus (for long messages) two passes on a buffer whose size is that of the input string (resp. plaintext or ciphertext). In particular, we note the following:

- Encryption requires only two exponentiations (and not three), because most of the work done to compute V^r can be reused to compute $V^{r/\pi(B)}$, regardless of the exponentiation algorithm used (whether straight double-and-add, or one of the many efficient window methods; cf., e.g., [30]).
- Decryption can similarly be performed in about a single exponentiation (instead of two), by computing $\bar{C}^{\pi(\bar{B})}$ as $\bar{D}^{\pi(\bar{B}) \cdot \mathsf{Sk}}$, which uses the same generator as $\bar{D}^{\mathsf{Sk}}$ and thus shares the same intermediate powers.

- In both cases, only two passes on the buffer are needed (and not three): first on the input string Msg or $\bar{E}$, and then a second pass on the intermediate string B or $\bar{B}$ which must be stored temporarily. We do not need a separate pass to compute $\pi(B)$ or $\pi(\bar{B})$, since these values can be evaluated on-the-fly while computing B or $\bar{B}$. However, this really matters only for long inputs, where the benefits of redundancy-free encryption are less pronounced.

Any plaintext represented as a string of at least 2κ bits can be encrypted without requiring any special encoding, and without using any downstream symmetric-key cipher or other hybrid component. The ciphertext overhead is a single group element in $\mathbb{G}$.

3.4 Security Reduction

We prove the security of our scheme in the well-known and very standard sense of IND-CCA2 security, or indistinguishability under an adaptive chosen-ciphertext attack. The reduction will proceeds from an instance of the Gap-DH problem, in the random oracle model.

We recall that the Gap-DH problem is to solve the CDH problem given access to a DDH oracle. In a computational group $\mathbb{G}$, such an instance is a triple $(U, V, W) = (U, U^v, U^w) \in \mathbb{G}^3$, and the task is to compute the value $U^{vw} \in \mathbb{G}$, given repeated access to a decision oracle indicating whether an input tuple $(A, B, C, D) \in \mathbb{G}^4$ satisfies the relation $\mathrm{dlog}_A(B) = \mathrm{dlog}_C(D)$.

Theorem 1. *The miniature public-key cryptosystem is IND-CCA2 secure in the random oracle model, provided that the Gap Diffie-Hellman assumption holds in $\mathbb{G}$. The reduction is tight w.r.t. computational cost ("efficiency") and success probability ("efficacy") simultaneously.*

Proof. Suppose there is an adversary $\mathcal{A}$ that breaks the encryption scheme. We build from it an algorithm $\mathcal{B}$ that solves the Gap-DH problem by simulating an attack environment to such an adversary. During the course of the interaction, the simulator will record the answers it makes in response to all queries, and additionally maintain two separate "watch-lists" for Φ and Ψ.

Key generation. $\mathcal{B}$ is given access to a Decision Diffie-Hellman oracle $\mathcal{DDH}$: $\mathbb{G}^4 \to \{0, 1\}$; it receives a Diffie-Hellman instance $(U, V, W) = (U, U^v, U^w) \in \mathbb{G}^3$, and is to compute $U^{vw} \in \mathbb{G}$.

   To start the simulation, $\mathcal{B}$ gives to $\mathcal{A}$ the public key $\mathsf{Pk} = (U, V)$, implicitly letting $\mathsf{Sk} = v$.

Decryption queries. $\mathcal{A}$ makes adaptive decryption queries on any ciphertexts $(D_k, E_k) \in \mathbb{G} \times \mathcal{M}$.

   To respond, $\mathcal{B}$ sifts the query logs for a random oracle query $\Phi(D_j, C_j)$ such that $D_j = D_k$ and $C_j = D_k^{\mathsf{Sk}}$. To do this in constant time, $\mathcal{B}$ can maintain a hash-table of those oracle queries such that $\mathcal{DDH}(U, V, D_j, C_j) = 1$. Let thus (D_j, C_j) be the retrieved entry, if it exists.
- If it does, let $\phi_j = \Phi(D_k, C_j)$ be the previously assigned value; the simulator then computes $B_k \leftarrow E_k \oplus \phi_j$ and $A_k \leftarrow C_j^{\pi(B_k)}$, and returns $M_k \leftarrow B_k \oplus \Psi(A_k)$ as the plaintext.

– Otherwise, the simulator simply returns a random string $M_k \in_\$ \mathcal{M}$, while privately adding the triple (D_k, E_k, M_k) to the watch-list associated with Φ, for future use given below.

Hash-Φ queries. $\mathcal{A}$ adaptively queries the random oracle Φ on unique input pairs $(D_j, C_j) \in \mathbb{G}^2$.

To respond, $\mathcal{B}$ picks a random string $\phi_j \in_\$ \mathcal{M}$ which it returns as answer to the query. Additionally, it tests whether $\mathcal{DDH}(U, V, D_j, C_j) = 1$, in which case it pulls from the watch list associated with Φ all the triples (D_k, E_k, M_k) such that $D_k = D_j$. For all such triples, the simulator lets $B_k \leftarrow E_k \oplus \phi_j$, computes $A_k \leftarrow C_j^{\pi(B_k)}$, defines $\psi_k \leftarrow B_k \oplus M_k$, adds the pair (A_k, ψ_k) to the watch-list associated with Ψ, and deletes the triple from the list of Φ.

Observe that all E_k and thus all A_k are necessarily distinct, unless π collided, and that the work of the simulator is linear in the number of triples that were pulled from the watch-list. Later, we account for the small probability of getting a collision $A_{k_1} = A_{k_2}$ for $D_{k_1} \neq D_{k_2}$.

Hash-Ψ queries. $\mathcal{A}$ adaptively queries the random oracle Ψ on arbitrary unique inputs $A_i \in \mathbb{G}$.

To respond, $\mathcal{B}$ first determines whether the watch-list associated with Ψ contains a pair (A_k, ψ_k) with $A_k = A_i$. If there exists such a pair, the simulator removes it from the watch-list and returns the string ψ_k; otherwise, it returns a fresh random string $\psi_i \in_\$ \mathcal{M}$.

Challenge. $\mathcal{A}$ at some point outputs two messages M_1 and M_2 on which it wishes to be challenged.

To create the challenge, $\mathcal{B}$ picks a random string $E^* \in_\$ \mathcal{M}$, sets $D^* \leftarrow W$ from the Gap-DH instance, and declares the challenge ciphertext to be (D^*, E^*). It disregards M_1 and M_2.

Additional queries. $\mathcal{A}$ makes more adaptive decryption and random oracle queries on arbitrary inputs (but no decryption query on the challenge ciphertext), to which $\mathcal{B}$ responds as before.

As it services the queries, the simulator is now on the lookout for a query $\Phi(D^*, C^*)$ such that $D^* = W$ and $\mathcal{DDH}(U, V, W, C^*) = 1$. As soon as $\mathcal{A}$ makes this query, $\mathcal{B}$ terminates the simulation and outputs $C^* = U^{vw}$ as solution to the Gap-DH instance.

Outcome. If the adversary never asks for the value of $\Phi(W, U^{vw})$, its advantage must be zero, since then the simulation is perfect and the ciphertext is random. On the contrary, as soon as $\mathcal{A}$ makes this particular query, $\mathcal{B}$ obtains the solution it seeks without further interaction.

We now analyze the parameters of the reduction. We consider both *efficacy* (*i.e.*, the probability of success) and *efficiency* (*i.e.*, the computational overhead needed for a successful reduction).

Reduction Efficacy. It is easy to see that $\mathcal{B}$'s probability of solving Gap-DH is no less than $\mathcal{A}$'s advantage in the IND-CCA2 attack, minus a negligible loss $\Delta\epsilon$ that corresponds to the probability that the simulator made two conflicting random oracle assignments. A conflict can arise for $\Psi(A_k)$ due to a collision $A_{k_1} = C_{j_1}{}^{\pi(E_{k_1} \oplus \phi_{j_1})} = C_{j_2}{}^{\pi(E_{k_2} \oplus \phi_{j_2})} = A_{k_2}$ when $C_{j_1} \neq C_{j_2}$. Since the ϕ_j are jointly independent of the C_j and E_k, and since every troublesome C_j can be traced to a watch-list entry that in turn originates from a unique decryption query, the probability of such a collision over q_d decryption queries, which dictates the total efficacy loss of the system, is given by the birthday bound:

$$\Delta\epsilon = \epsilon(\mathcal{A}) - \epsilon(\mathcal{B}) \leq (q_d)^2/p \approx (q_d)^2\, 2^{-2\kappa} = \text{negl}(\kappa) \ .$$

Reduction Efficiency. To express $\mathcal{B}$'s running time of in terms of $\mathcal{A}$'s, let us assume that the adversary makes q_d decryption and q_Φ and q_Ψ hash queries, and that each exponentiation in $\mathbb{G}$ or $\mathcal{DDH}$ query costs the simulator one time unit. The simulation time overhead $\Delta\tau$ is then given by $\Delta\tau = \tau(\mathcal{B}) - \tau(\mathcal{A}) = \Theta(q_d + q_\Phi + q_\Psi)$, from which we deduce that the running times of $\mathcal{A}$ and $\mathcal{B}$ are within a constant factor $\gtrsim 1$ (1 being the best possible ratio):

$$\tau(\mathcal{B})/\tau(\mathcal{A}) = \Theta(1) \ .$$

It follows that the reduction is tight in all parameters, as long as the number of random oracle and decryption queries made by the adversary is sub-exponential in κ, as required.

3.5   Practical Extensions

We briefly describe two simple extensions to the basic scheme, which we expect to be useful in certain applications.

Adaptive Chosen-Ciphertext Security vs. Integrity. Most existing CCA2-secure cryptosystems to date, with or without random oracles, achieve security against active attacks by performing an integrity check during the decryption process, based on some amount of redundancy that is embedded in the ciphertext during encryption. Cryptosystems of this kind include Dolev-Dwork-Naor [15], Cramer-Shoup [12,13], Fujisaki-Okamoto [17,18], Kurosawa-Desmedt [26], and Canetti-Halevi-Katz [10], among many others. Most of the time the redundancy is secret, but it need not be.

By contrast, our scheme does *not* authenticate the ciphertext; it is similar in that respect to a few other systems such as Phan-Pointcheval [32] and Kurosawa-Matsuo [27] as already discussed. Indeed, without redundancy there cannot be a test to reject malformed ciphertexts, and thus the decryption process always succeeds. Hence there is no such thing as an "incorrect" ciphertext. (We remark, however, that because the IND-CCA2 security property implies PA-CCA2, or plaintext awareness, any ciphertext that was not created using the proper procedure will safely decrypt to an unpredictable and useless plaintext).

In some applications, it may be desirable to detect that a ciphertext has been tampered with. One solution is of course to use a "traditional" efficient CCA2-secure scheme, such as Fujisaki-Okamoto in the random oracle model or Kurosawa-Desmedt in the standard model. Another solution is to add a small amount of redundancy in the plaintext of our scheme, such as a few zeros. This approach might be more desirable in cases where a quick and inexpensive integrity test is desired but not required for the security of the larger system: in this case adding a few zeros to the plaintext of our scheme will be the cheapest and most effective solution.

Non-interactive Distributed Threshold Decryption. Recall that in a threshold public-key system, a number of distributed "partial decryption centers" compute partial decryptions from the ciphertext, or shares, which are then combined in a threshold manner by a single combiner to produce the final plaintext; cf., e.g., [19].

As mentioned earlier, CCA2-secure threshold cryptosystems are difficult to deploy based on the two-key paradigm, and also using the random-oracle-based Fujisaki-Okamoto transformation, because the decryption process will require the partial decryptors to communicate with each other in order to decide whether a ciphertext is valid or not. Essentially, this is because the redundancy in those schemes is secret [34], which makes it difficult to perform a validity test before the plaintext has been recovered. By contrast, the identity-based approach is much more conducive to secure threshold decryption under active attacks, because its redundancy is public and can be checked non-interactively by the decryption centers without costly inter-communications [5].

Our scheme turns out to be very easy to turn into a non-interactive CCA2-secure threshold system. The reasons for this are twofold. First, since the security of our scheme does not depend on any integrity check, the difficulty of conducting such a check in a threshold setting should have no ill effect. Second, the algebra of the scheme itself turns out to be very propitious to secret sharing, because the secret key Sk is only used once in the decryption process, to compute $\hat{C} \leftarrow \hat{D}^{\mathsf{Sk}}$.

Thus, our scheme can be used as a basis for a threshold scheme, by splitting the secret key Sk into a number of random shares $\mathsf{Sk}_1, ..., \mathsf{Sk}_n$ using Shamir's secret sharing. The partial decryption centers would use those shares to produce decryption shares $\hat{C}_i \leftarrow \hat{D}^{\mathsf{Sk}_i}$. With enough of those, the combiner can perform Lagrange interpolation "in the exponent" to recover the value of $\hat{C} = \prod_i \hat{C}_i^{\Lambda_i}$, where the Λ_i are publically computable Lagrange coefficients. Once it knows $\hat{C}$, the combiner can complete the decryption algorithm without further interaction with the decryption centers.

3.6   Implementation on Curves

Although our scheme generally relies on the Gap-DH assumption, it is possible to implement it in a computational group $\mathbb{G}$ where DDH is known to be easy (and CDH still believed to be hard): in this case the $\mathcal{DDH}$ oracle can actually be implemented, and Gap-DH reduces to the usual CDH assumption. In such groups, the security of the scheme thus follows from computational Diffie-Hellman, which has of course been studied extensively.

Elliptic curves equipped with an efficiently computable bilinear pairing are an obvious choice for the group $\mathbb{G}$, because the pairing lets us decide (but not compute) the Diffie-Hellman problem efficiently. (To be more precise, $\mathbb{G}$ will be a prime-order subgroup of the group of points on a pairing-friendly curve.) We refer to [6] and the abundant literature on pairings for details.

On pairing-friendly curves, and more generally in any computational group with a bilinear map, the mere fact that the $\mathcal{DDH}$ oracle *could* be implemented efficiently gives us a tight IND-CCA2 security reduction to the CDH assumption in the random-oracle model. In reality, we will never need to use or implement a pairing. Conceivably, an existential proof that an efficient pairing (or DDH) algorithm exists is all we need to relax Gap-DH into the weaker CDH assumption.

4 Summary

We have proposed a very simple public-key cryptosystem with the most compact ciphertext for a given level of exact CCA2 security, without relying on hybrid constructions. Earlier constructions with similarly compact ciphertexts required complex modes of operations for block ciphers and/or stronger assumptions. The ciphertext has no redundancy, and the scheme offers a tight security reduction (both efficacy-wise and efficiency-wise) to a classic complexity assumption (Gap-DH, or just CDH if the arithmetic is done on a pairing-friendly curve).

We have utilized a few new tricks to achieve "direct" tightness without redundancy. These tricks are set in the random oracle model, but we managed to avoid one of the problems associated with the random oracle methodology, namely, the fact that, once instantiated, the hash function can be queried offline a practically unlimited number of times. Since our scheme's security is not sensitive to the number of queries (below the birthday bound), exact security remains tight as long as the hash function is adequately modeled as a black box.

Of course, it would be nice to construct a redundancy-free CCA2-secure public-key encryption system in the standard model (even with a polynomially sloppy security reduction). However, this appears to be very difficult, because without redundancy, it is not clear how the simulator could extract the answer from the decryption queries. In this respect, our scheme represents another in a long series of *a priori* surprising results that crucially rely on the random oracle methodology [2,11,23,16].

We hope that our scheme will appeal to the practioners of cryptography. Ideal uses for it include bandwidth-contrained environments where active attacks are a concern, such as radio systems that frequently transmit short messages.

References

1. Abdalla, M., Bellare, M., Rogaway, P.: The oracle Diffie-Hellman assumption and an analysis of DHIES. In: Naccache, D. (ed.) CT-RSA 2001. LNCS, vol. 2020, pp. 143–158. Springer, Heidelberg (2001)
2. Bellare, M., Rogaway, P.: Random oracle are practical: A paradigm for designing efficient protocols. In: ACM Conference on Computer and Communications Security—CCS 2003, pp. 62–73. ACM Press, New York (1993)

3. Bellare, M., Rogaway, P.: Optimal asymmetric encryption - how to encrypt with RSA. In: De Santis, A. (ed.) EUROCRYPT 1994. LNCS, vol. 950, pp. 92–111. Springer, Heidelberg (1995)
4. Boneh, D.: Simplified OAEP for the RSA and Rabin functions. In: Kilian, J. (ed.) CRYPTO 2001. LNCS, vol. 2139, pp. 275–291. Springer, Heidelberg (2001)
5. Boneh, D., Boyen, X., Halevi, S.: Chosen ciphertext secure public key threshold encryption without random oracles. In: Pointcheval, D. (ed.) CT-RSA 2006. LNCS, vol. 3860, pp. 226–243. Springer, Heidelberg (2006)
6. Boneh, D., Franklin, M.: Identity-based encryption from the Weil pairing. In: Kilian, J. (ed.) CRYPTO 2001. LNCS, vol. 2139, pp. 213–229. Springer, Heidelberg (2001)
7. Boneh, D., Katz, J.: Improved efficiency for CCA-secure cryptosystems built using identity based encryption. In: Topics in Cryptology—RSA-CT 2005. LNCS, Springer, Heidelberg (2005)
8. Boyen, X., Mei, Q., Waters, B.: Direct chosen ciphertext security from identity-based techniques. In: ACM Conference on Computer and Communications Security—CCS 2005, pp. 320–329. ACM Press, New York (2005)
9. Canetti, R., Goldwasser, S.: An efficient threshold public key cryptosystem secure against adaptive chosen ciphertext attack. In: Stern, J. (ed.) EUROCRYPT 1999. LNCS, vol. 1592, pp. 90–106. Springer, Heidelberg (1999)
10. Canetti, R., Halevi, S., Katz, J.: Chosen-ciphertext security from identity-based encryption. In: Cachin, C., Camenisch, J.L. (eds.) EUROCRYPT 2004. LNCS, vol. 3027, pp. 207–222. Springer, Heidelberg (2004)
11. Coron, J.-S.: On the exact security of full-domain-hash. In: Bellare, M. (ed.) CRYPTO 2000. LNCS, vol. 1880, pp. 229–235. Springer, Heidelberg (2000)
12. Cramer, R., Shoup, V.: A practical public key cryptosystem provably secure against adaptive chosen ciphertext attack. In: Krawczyk, H. (ed.) CRYPTO 1998. LNCS, vol. 1462, Springer, Heidelberg (1998)
13. Cramer, R., Shoup, V.: Universal hash proofs and a paradigm for adaptive chosen ciphertext secure public-key encryption. In: Boneh, D. (ed.) CRYPTO 2003. LNCS, vol. 2729, pp. 45–64. Springer, Heidelberg (2003)
14. Cramer, R., Shoup, V.: Design and analysis of practical public-key encryption schemes secure against adaptive chosen ciphertext attack. SIAM Journal of Computing 33, 167–226 (2003)
15. Dolev, D., Dwork, C., Naor, M.: Non-malleable cryptography. In: ACM Symposium on Theory of Computing—STOC 1991, pp. 542–552. ACM Press, New York (1991)
16. Fischlin, M.: Communication-efficient non-interactive proofs of knowledge with online extractors. In: Shoup, V. (ed.) CRYPTO 2005. LNCS, vol. 3621, pp. 152–168. Springer, Heidelberg (2005)
17. Fujisaki, E., Okamoto, T.: Secure integration of asymmetric and symmetric encryption schemes. In: Wiener, M.J. (ed.) CRYPTO 1999. LNCS, vol. 1666, pp. 537–554. Springer, Heidelberg (1999)
18. Fujisaki, E., Okamoto, T.: How to enhance the security of public-key encryption at minimum cost. IEICE Transactions on Fundamentals E83-9(1), 24–32 (2000)
19. Gennaro, R., Rabin, T., Jarecki, S., Krawczyk, H.: Robust and efficient sharing of RSA functions. Journal of Cryptology 13(2), 273–300 (2000)
20. Halevi, S., Rogaway, P.: A tweakable enciphering mode. In: Boneh, D. (ed.) CRYPTO 2003. LNCS, vol. 2729, pp. 482–499. Springer, Heidelberg (2003)
21. Halevi, S., Rogaway, P.: A parallelizable enciphering mode. In: Okamoto, T. (ed.) CT-RSA 2004. LNCS, vol. 2964, pp. 292–304. Springer, Heidelberg (2004)

22. Joux, A., Nguyen, K.: Separating decision Diffie-Hellman from computational Diffie-Hellman in cryptographic groups. Journal of Cryptology 16(4), 239–247 (2003)
23. Katz, J., Wang, N.: Efficiency improvements for signature schemes with tight security reductions. In: ACM Conference on Computer and Communications Security—CCS 2003, pp. 155–164. ACM Press, New York (2003)
24. Kiltz, E.: Chosen-ciphertext secure key encapsulation based on hashed gap decisional Diffie-Hellman. In: Public Key Cryptography—PKC 2007. LNCS, vol. 4450, pp. 282–297. Springer, Heidelberg (2007)
25. Kiltz, E., Neven, G.: Hedging random oracles with generic groups. Unpublished manuscript (2007)
26. Kurosawa, K., Desmedt, Y.: A new paradigm of hybrid encryption scheme. In: Franklin, M. (ed.) CRYPTO 2004. LNCS, vol. 3152, pp. 426–442. Springer, Heidelberg (2004)
27. Kurosawa, K., Matsuo, T.: How to remove MAC from DHIES. In: Wang, H., Pieprzyk, J., Varadharajan, V. (eds.) ACISP 2004. LNCS, vol. 3108, pp. 236–247. Springer, Heidelberg (2004)
28. Libert, B., Quisquater, J.-J.: Identity based encryption without redundancy. In: Ioannidis, J., Keromytis, A.D., Yung, M. (eds.) ACNS 2005. LNCS, vol. 3531, pp. 285–300. Springer, Heidelberg (2005)
29. Lu, X., Lai, X., He, D.: Efficient chosen ciphertext secure PKE scheme with short ciphertext. Cryptology ePrint Archive, Report, 2007/210 (2007), http://eprint.iacr.org/
30. Menezes, A.J., Van Oorschot, P.C., Van stone, S.A.: Handbook of Applied Cryptography. CRC Press, Boca Raton, USA (1997)
31. Naor, M., Yung, M.: Public-key cryptosystems provably secure against chosen ciphertext attacks. In: ACM Symposium on Theory of Computing—STOC 1990, pp. 427–437. ACM Press, New York (1990)
32. Phan, D.H., Pointcheval, D.: Chosen-ciphertext security without redundancy. In: Laih, C.-S. (ed.) ASIACRYPT 2003. LNCS, vol. 2894, pp. 1–18. Springer, Heidelberg (2003)
33. Phan, D.H., Pointcheval, D.: OAEP 3-round: A generic and secure asymmetric encryption padding. In: Lee, P.J. (ed.) ASIACRYPT 2004. LNCS, vol. 3329, pp. 63–78. Springer, Heidelberg (2004)
34. Shoup, V., Gennaro, R.: Securing threshold cryptosystems against chosen ciphertext attack. Journal of Cryptology 15(2), 75–96 (2002)

Bounded CCA2-Secure Encryption

Ronald Cramer[1,2], Goichiro Hanaoka[3], Dennis Hofheinz[1], Hideki Imai[3,4],
Eike Kiltz[1], Rafael Pass[5], Abhi Shelat[6], and Vinod Vaikuntanathan[7]

[1] Centrum voor Wiskunde en Informatica (CWI), Amsterdam
[2] Leiden University
[3] National Institute of Advanced Industrial Science and Technology, Tokyo
[4] Chuo University
[5] Cornell University
[6] University of Virginia
[7] Massachusetts Institute of Technology

Abstract. Whereas encryption schemes withstanding passive chosen-plaintext attacks (CPA) can be constructed based on a variety of computational assumptions, only a few assumptions are known to imply the existence of encryption schemes withstanding adaptive chosen-ciphertext attacks (CCA2). Towards addressing this asymmetry, we consider a weakening of the CCA2 model — *bounded CCA2-security* — wherein security needs only hold against adversaries that make an a-priori bounded number of queries to the decryption oracle. Regarding this notion we show (without any further assumptions):

- For any polynomial q, a simple *black-box* construction of q-bounded *IND-CCA2-secure* encryption schemes, from any *IND-CPA-secure* encryption scheme. When instantiated with the Decisional Diffie-Hellman (DDH) assumption, this construction additionally yields encryption schemes with very short ciphertexts.
- For any polynomial q, a (non-black box) construction of q-bounded *NM-CCA2-secure* encryption schemes, from any *IND-CPA-secure* encryption scheme. Bounded-CCA2 non-malleability is the strongest notion of security yet known to be achievable assuming only the existence of IND-CPA secure encryption schemes.

Finally, we show that non-malleability and indistinguishability are *not equivalent* under bounded-CCA2 attacks (in contrast to general CCA2 attacks).

1 Introduction

Encryption is often compared to a 'secure envelope'. Though appealing as a metaphor, understanding encryption requires a more formal *definition of security* of the primitive. For this task, the notion of *semantic security against adaptive chosen-ciphertext attacks* (in short, IND-CCA2 security) captures the essential characteristics of secure envelopes.

Under adaptive chosen-ciphertext attacks (CCA2), whose study was pioneered by Naor and Yung [22], and Rackoff and Simon [26], security is required to hold

K. Kurosawa (Ed.): ASIACRYPT 2007, LNCS 4833, pp. 502–518, 2007.

with respect to adversaries that have access to a decryption oracle. This should be contrasted to the traditional type of chosen-plaintext attack (CPA), where the adversary is required to act on its own without any additional help [14].

While there are a number of candidate (practical) public-key encryption schemes known to be semantically secure against a CPA attack [13], designing ones that withstand a CCA2 attack is a delicate and difficult task. In the standard model, there are essentially three approaches known. The first approach, put forth by Naor and Yung [22] in the early 1990s, and subsequently extended by Dolev, Dwork and Naor [10], and later Sahai [28] and Lindell [20], is based on the use of non-interactive zero knowledge for NP. This leads to schemes based on quite general cryptographic assumptions. The second is due to Cramer and Shoup [6,7,8] and is based on hash-proof systems. This leads to quite practical schemes based on several concrete number-theoretic assumptions. The third and most recent approach is due to Canetti, Halevi and Katz [3] and relies on identity-based cryptography.

To sum up, all the above approaches make use of additional assumptions to construct CCA2-secure schemes (apart from the existence of CPA-secure encryption schemes). A fundamental open question is thus:

Can any CPA-secure encryption scheme be transformed into one that is also CCA2 secure, without making additional complexity-theoretic assumptions?

1.1   Our Results

Towards addressing this fundamental question, in this paper we introduce a weakening of the CCA2 attack which we call a *bounded-CCA2* attack. In such an attack, the adversary is restricted to making an *a-priori bounded* number of queries to the decryption oracle. This is indeed a reasonable model, since the use of encryption in many protocols (such as secure multiparty computation) can be upper-bounded to q decryptions. With this terminology, our main contributions are summarized below. Henceforth, unless otherwise mentioned, whenever we talk of CCA attacks, we mean adaptive chosen ciphertext attacks (CCA2), as opposed to the weaker lunch-time attacks (CCA1).

BOUNDED CCA2 SEMANTIC SECURITY. Our first result is a simple and efficient *black-box* construction of a public-key encryption (PKE) scheme that is semantically secure against a q-bounded CCA2 attack (technically termed IND-q-CCA-secure), starting from any CPA-secure encryption scheme. Technically, this result combines techniques from [3,9]. However, it appears that the implications for black-box constructions of chosen ciphertext secure encryption from semantically secure encryption, as we deduce them here, have not been reported before.

Theorem 1 (Informal). *For any polynomial q, there exists a black-box construction of an IND-q-CCA-secure encryption scheme from any CPA-secure encryption scheme.*

The key size and the ciphertext size of this construction are quadratic in q and thus quite large; nevertheless, it demonstrates the *feasibility* of black-box constructions of bounded-CCA2-secure encryption schemes from any CPA-secure scheme. Interestingly, this result stands in sharp contrast to the recent results of Gertner, Malkin and Myers [12] showing that "such" black-box constructions are impossible when considering standard (unbounded) CCA2-secure encryption. (The black-box separation result from [12] only holds for constructions where the *decryption* function of the CCA2 secure scheme does not make calls to the *encryption* function of the CPA secure scheme. Our black-box construction of q-bounded CCA2 secure encryption falls into this category).

We additionally show that if the underlying CPA-secure PKE scheme has certain homomorphic properties, then we can construct a q-bounded CCA2-secure PKE scheme with very short ciphertexts. In particular, in groups where the DDH assumption holds, we can give a q-bounded CCA2 secure PKE scheme with only one group element of ciphertext expansion. In contrast, the best known DDH-based schemes such as the one by Kurosawa and Desmedt [18] which achieve full CCA2 security have two group elements plus a MAC. The length of the public keys in this construction are, however, still quadratic in q.

BOUNDED CCA2 NON-MALLEABILITY. A q-bounded-CCA2 non-malleable (in technical terms, NME-q-CCA-secure) encryption scheme is one that is "non-malleable" with respect to an adversary making at most q decryption queries. For this notion, we are able to show:

Theorem 2 (Informal). *Assuming CPA-secure public-key encryption schemes exist, for any polynomial q, there exists an* NME-q-CCA-*secure encryption scheme.*

As far as we know, the notion of bounded-CCA2 non-malleability is the strongest notion of security for encryption schemes known to be achievable under only the assumption of CPA-secure encryption schemes. Furthermore, the length of both the the public-key and the ciphertexts grows *linearly* with q (instead of quadratically as in our previous construction). However, this second construction makes a *non-black-box* use of the underlying CPA secure encryption scheme. In particular, we use a proof that several ciphertexts are encryptions of the same message, and this may require analyzing the encryption circuit to form a theorem statement. (On the other hand, even though our construction uses ZK proofs and thus costly $\mathcal{NP}$ reductions, in many cases, there exist efficient proofs — Σ protocols [4], for example — for the type of theorems we encounter).

RELATION BETWEEN SEMANTIC SECURITY AND NON-MALLEABILITY AGAINST BOUNDED CCA2 ATTACKS. It is known that under a CCA2 attack, the otherwise weaker notion of semantic security in fact implies also non-malleability [1]. In the case of bounded-CCA2 security, however, we show that this equivalence does not hold. In particular, we show that q-bounded-CCA2 security for any (fixed) q does not even imply non-malleability under the simple CPA attack.

Theorem 3 (Informal). *Assume CPA-secure public-key encryption schemes exist. Then, for every q, there exists an encryption scheme that is q-bounded CCA2-secure, but is not non-malleable (even under a CPA attack).*

This separation of notions highlights the importance of directly proving non-malleability of our second scheme (which slightly complicates the analysis).

1.2 Importance of These Results

The notion of *bounded* CCA2 security which we present is a weakening of the traditional notion of CCA2 security. Since it is possible to achieve CCA2 security, one may then wonder why it is important to consider this notion. There are in fact two simple reasons:

1. There are many hardness assumptions (such as computational-Diffie-Hellman and many lattice-based hardness assumptions) for which we can only construct CPA-secure encryption schemes. Our results show how to transform those schemes into ones with much stronger security properties. Since no one knows how to achieve full (unbounded) CCA2 security under these assumptions, our result represents the state-of-the-art for encryption in that area.
2. Being a weaker notion, bounded-CCA2 security may allow for more efficient constructions. Indeed, under the DDH assumption, we present a bounded-CCA2 scheme which is less than half the size of the smallest full-CCA2 secure scheme. For certain low-bandwidth applications in which the size of the ciphertext is critical, this may be the best construction to use.

ORGANIZATION. After fixing some notation in §2, we formally define the notion of q-bounded CCA2 security. Section §3 contains a black-box construction of a q-bounded IND-CCA-secure encryption scheme, and Section §4 contains an optimized instantiation under the DDH assumption. Section §5 contains a non-black-box construction of a q-bounded NME-CCA-secure encryption scheme. Finally, in Section §6, we present a separation between the definitions of semantic security and non-malleability under q-bounded attacks.

PUBLICATION INFO. This paper is a merge of three independent preprints [5,15,23].

2   Preliminaries and Definitions

If S is a set then $s \xleftarrow{\$} S$ denotes the operation of picking an element s of S uniformly at random. We write $\mathcal{A}(x, y, \dots)$ to indicate that $\mathcal{A}$ is an algorithm with inputs $x, y, \dots$ and by $z \xleftarrow{\$} \mathcal{A}(x, y, \dots)$ we denote the operation of running $\mathcal{A}$ with inputs $(x, y, \dots)$ and letting z be the output. We write $\mathcal{A}^{\mathcal{O}_1, \mathcal{O}_2, \dots}(x, y, \dots)$ to indicate that $\mathcal{A}$ is an algorithm with inputs $x, y, \dots$ and black-box access to oracles $\mathcal{O}_1, \mathcal{O}_2, \dots$. If $\mathcal{A}$ is a randomized algorithm, the notation $\mathcal{A}(x; r)$ means running $\mathcal{A}$ with input x and randomness r.

Definition 1 (Encryption scheme). *A triple* PKE $=$ (Gen, Enc, Dec) *is a public key encryption scheme, if (1)* Gen *and* Enc *are p.p.t. algorithms and* Dec *is a deterministic polynomial-time algorithm, (2)* Gen *on input* 1^k *produces a pair* (pk, sk), *where* pk *is the public-key and* sk *is the secret-key, (3)*

Enc : $pk \times \{0,1\}^* \rightarrow \{0,1\}^*$ *runs on input a public key pk and a message* $m \in \{0,1\}^*$ *and produces a ciphertext c, (4)* Dec : $sk \times \{0,1\}^* \rightarrow \{0,1\}^* \cup \{\perp\}$ *runs on input (sk, c) and produces either a message* $m \in \{0,1\}^*$ *or a special symbol* $\perp$, *(5)(Perfect Correctness) There exists a polynomial p(k) and a negligible function* $\mu(k)$ *such that for* every *message m, and* every *random tape* r_e,

$$\Pr[(pk, sk) \leftarrow \mathsf{Gen}(1^k; r_g) : \exists r_e, m \ s.t \ \mathsf{Dec}_{sk}(\mathsf{Enc}_{pk}(m; r_e)) \neq m] \leq \mu(k).$$

where the probability is over the random choice of r_g. *That is, with high probability over the keys generated by* Gen, *all valid ciphertexts decrypt correctly.*

Next, we define the notions of IND-q-CCA-security and NME-q-CCA-security.

Definition 2 (IND-q-CCA security). *For a function* $q(k) : \mathbb{N} \rightarrow \mathbb{N}$, *we define the security notion of indistinguishability against q-bounded CCA adversaries* (IND-q-CCA). *For an adversary* $\mathcal{A} = (\mathcal{A}_1, \mathcal{A}_2)$ *we define the advantage function*

$$\mathbf{Adv}_{\mathsf{PKE},\mathcal{A}}^{\mathsf{IND}\text{-}q\text{-}\mathsf{CCA}}(k) = \left| \Pr[\mathbf{Exp}_{\mathsf{PKE},\mathcal{A}}^{\mathsf{IND}\text{-}q\text{-}\mathsf{CCA}\text{-}1}(k) = 1] - \Pr[\mathbf{Exp}_{\mathsf{PKE},\mathcal{A}}^{\mathsf{IND}\text{-}q\text{-}\mathsf{CCA}\text{-}0}(k) = 1] \right|$$

where, for $b \in \{0,1\}$, $\mathbf{Exp}_{\mathsf{PKE},\mathcal{A}}^{\mathsf{IND}\text{-}q\text{-}\mathsf{CCA}\text{-}b}$ *is defined by the following experiment.*

> **Experiment** $\mathbf{Exp}_{\mathsf{PKE},\mathcal{A}}^{\mathsf{IND}\text{-}q\text{-}\mathsf{CCA}\text{-}b}(k)$
>
> $(pk, sk) \xleftarrow{\$} \mathsf{Gen}(1^k)$
> $(M_0, M_1, St_1) \xleftarrow{\$} \mathcal{A}_1^{\mathsf{Dec}(sk,\cdot)}(pk)$ s.t. $|M_0| = |M_1|$
> $c^* \xleftarrow{\$} \mathsf{Enc}(pk, M_b)$
> $b' \xleftarrow{\$} \mathcal{A}_2^{\mathsf{Dec}(sk,\cdot)}(c^*, St_1)$
> Return b'

The adversary $(\mathcal{A}_1, \mathcal{A}_2)$ *is restricted to ask at most* $q(k)$ *queries to the decryption oracle* Dec *in total in each run of the experiment, and none of the queries of* $\mathcal{A}_2$ *may contain* c^*. *The scheme* PKE *is said to be indistinguishable against q-bounded chosen-ciphertext attacks (*IND-q-CCA-*secure, in short) if the advantage function* $\mathbf{Adv}_{\mathsf{PKE},\mathcal{A}}^{\mathsf{IND}\text{-}q\text{-}\mathsf{CCA}}(k)$ *is negligible in k for all adversaries* $\mathcal{A} = (\mathcal{A}_1, \mathcal{A}_2)$.

We have the following relation to the standard security definitions for PKE schemes. Scheme PKE is said to be (1) indistinguishable against chosen-plaintext attacks [14] (CPA), denoted IND-CPA, if it is IND-0-CCA-secure, and (2) indistinguishable against chosen-ciphertext attacks [26] (CCA2), denoted IND-CCA, if it is IND-q-CCA-secure for *any* polynomial $q(k)$.

  As was done above with indistinguishability, we extend the definition of non-malleability presented in [24] to consider $q(k)$-bounded adversaries.

Definition 3 (NME-q-CCA security). *Let* PKE $=$ (Gen, Enc, Dec) *be an encryption scheme and let the random variable* NME-q-CCA$_b$(Π, A, k, ℓ) *where* $b \in \{0,1\}$, $\mathcal{A} = (\mathcal{A}_1, \mathcal{A}_2)$ *and* $k, \ell \in \mathbb{N}$ *denote the result of the following probabilistic experiment:*

$\text{NME-}q\text{-CCA}_b(\text{PKE}, \mathcal{A}, \mathsf{k}, \ell):$

$\quad (pk, sk) \leftarrow \text{Gen}(1^k)$

$\quad (m_0, m_1, \text{STATE}_\mathcal{A}) \leftarrow \mathcal{A}_1^{\text{Dec}(sk, \cdot)}(pk) \; s.t. \; |m_0| = |m_1|$

$\quad y \leftarrow \text{Enc}_{pk}(m_b)$

$\quad (c_1, \ldots, c_\ell) \leftarrow \mathcal{A}_2^{\text{Dec}(sk, \cdot)}(y, \text{STATE}_\mathcal{A})$

$\quad Output \; (d_1, \ldots, d_\ell) \; where \; d_i = \begin{cases} \text{COPY} & if \; c_i = y \\ \text{Dec}_{sk}(c_i) & otherwise \end{cases}$

PKE $=$ (Gen, Enc, Dec) *is* NME-q-CCA-*secure for a function* $q(k) : \mathbb{N} \to \mathbb{N}$ *if,* $\forall$ *p.p.t. algorithms* $\mathcal{A} = (\mathcal{A}_1, \mathcal{A}_2)$ *which make* $q(k)$ *total queries to the oracles and for any polynomial* $p(k)$, *the following two ensembles are computationally indistinguishable:*

$$\Big\{ \text{NME-}q\text{-CCA}_0(\text{PKE}, \mathcal{A}, \mathsf{k}, \mathsf{p}(k)) \Big\}_{k \in \mathbb{N}} \overset{c}{\approx} \Big\{ \text{NME-}q\text{-CCA}_1(\text{PKE}, \mathcal{A}, \mathsf{k}, \mathsf{p}(k)) \Big\}_{k \in \mathbb{N}}$$

If $q(k) = 0$, then the encryption scheme is said to be NME-CPA-*secure*.

3   Construction of Bounded IND-CCA Secure Encryption

In this section, we present a black-box construction of an IND-q-CCA-secure encryption scheme. The general outline of our construction is as follows.

First, as demonstrated by Canetti, Halevi and Katz [3], every identity-based encryption scheme can be transformed into a fully chosen-ciphertext secure encryption scheme. Second, an IND-CPA secure encryption scheme implies a "q-resilient" identity-based encryption scheme. (The notion of q-resilient security in the context of identity-based encryption [16] means that the scheme guarantees security as long as at most q private keys are established). The latter result is only implicitly contained in a paper about key-insulated public-key cryptosystems by Dodis, Katz, Xu, and Yung [9]. A closer observation of the combination of the two results already reveals the construction of our IND-q-CCA-secure encryption scheme. Since both transformations are black-box, our main result can be obtained. However, it appears that the implications for black-box constructions of IND-q-CCA-secure encryption from IND-CPA-secure encryption as we deduce them here have not been reported before.

Stateful versus Stateless Encryption. When one only considers stateful encryption, the problem of constructing black-box IND-q-CCA-secure encryption becomes trivial: the receiver's public-key contains q independent public-keys pk_i of the IND-CPA-secure scheme. For $1 \le j \le q$, to encrypt the jth message, a sender uses the jth public-key pk_j as a "one-time key" for the IND-CPA-secure encryption scheme, the state being j that is incremented after each encryption. However, this construction requires *all participants* to share and update the dynamic state information j. (This is in contrast to signature schemes where the signer may maintain a private state).

We circumvent this unrealistic state update assumption by "load-balancing" the use of instances of the IND-CPA-secure base scheme. The general outline of our construction is as follows. We use the q-resilient identity-based encryption construction implicitly given in [9] based on any IND-CPA-secure PKE scheme. Using a transformation from [3], this q-resilient identity-based encryption scheme can be transformed into a PKE scheme. As we will see, the resulting PKE scheme is secure against q-bounded chosen-ciphertext adversaries.

Theorem 4. *For any fixed polynomial q, there exists a black-box construction that, given any IND-CPA-secure scheme (kg, enc, dec), builds an IND-q-CCA-secure public-key encryption scheme (Gen^{kg}, Enc$^{\text{kg,enc}}$, Dec$^{\text{kg,dec}}$).*

Here we give a direct proof of this theorem that bypasses the notion of identity-based encryption altogether. We furthermore note that there are some technical problems with the security proof of the implicitly contained q-resilient IBE scheme from [9] that we fix in this note.[1]

3.1 Building Blocks

COVER-FREE FAMILIES. If S, T are sets, we say that S does not cover T if $S \not\supseteq T$. Let d, q, s be positive integers, and let $F = (F_i)_{1 \leq i \leq s}$ be a family of subsets of $\{1, \ldots, d\}$. We say that family F is q-cover-free over $\{1, \ldots, d\}$, if for each subset $F_i \in F$ and each S that is the union of at most q sets in $(F_1, \ldots, F_{i-1}, F_{i+1}, \ldots, F_s)$, it is the case that S does not cover F_i. Furthermore, we say that F is l-uniform if all subsets in the family have size l. We use the following fact [11,17]: there is a deterministic polynomial time algorithm that on input integers s, q returns l, d, F where $F = (F_i)_{1 \leq i \leq s}$ is a l-uniform q-cover-free family over $\{1, \ldots, d\}$, for $l = d/4q$ and $d \leq 16q^2 \log(s)$. In the following we let SUB denote the resulting deterministic polynomial-time algorithm that on input s, q, i returns F_i. We call $F_i = \text{SUB}(s(k), q(k), i)$ the subset associated to index $i \in \{1, \ldots, s(k)\}$.

For our construction we will need a cover-free family with the parameters

$$s(k) = 2^k, \quad d(k) = 16kq^2(k), \quad l(k) = 4kq(k) . \tag{1}$$

ONE-TIME SIGNATURES. In our construction, we need a strong one-time signature scheme OTS = (Sigkg, Sign, Verify) (see [19]). We assume that the verification keys which are part of the output by Sigkg are bit strings of size k which we interpret as natural numbers in $\{1, \ldots, 2^k\}$. Strong one-time signature schemes can be constructed from (the key-generation algorithm of) any IND-CPA-secure encryption scheme via a black-box reduction (since a one-way function can be constructed from the key-generation algorithm, and one-way functions imply strong signature schemes [19,27]).

---

[1] The problem in the proof of Theorem 2 in [9] (only contained in the full version) is that their simulator (simulating the view of an adversary attacking the IBE scheme) sometimes is forced to abort. However, this forced abort is *not* independent of the adversary's view in this simulation. This dependence could be exploited by an adversary that has a higher chance in breaking the IBE scheme only if the simulator aborts. We give a different simulation to overcome this problem.

3.2 The Construction

Let $q(k) : \mathbb{N} \to \mathbb{N}$ be a function. Our construction of the IND-q-CCA encryption scheme (Gen, Enc, Dec) with black-box access to the IND-CPA-secure encryption scheme (kg, enc, dec) is depicted in Fig. 1. In general we can also use any computationally secure all-or-nothing transform (e.g., the black-box construction from [2] based on one-way functions) to decrease ciphertext size.

Public and secret keys have size polynomial (quadratic) in the maximal number of decryption queries $q(k)$. Also note that the upper bound $q(k)$ must be known in advance as a parameter of the construction.

$\mathsf{Gen}^{\mathsf{kg}}(1^k)$: Define $s(k) = 2^k, d(k) = 16kq^2(k), l(k) = 4kq(k)$ as in Equation (1). For $i = 1, \dots, d(k)$ run $(pk_i, sk_i) \xleftarrow{\$} \mathsf{kg}(1^k)$. Output $PK = (pk_1, \dots, pk_{d(k)})$ and $SK = (sk_1, \dots, sk_{d(k)})$.

$\mathsf{Enc}^{\mathsf{kg,enc}}(PK, M)$: Create a random pair of one-time signing keys $(vk, sigsk) \xleftarrow{\$} \mathsf{Sigkg}^{\mathsf{kg}}(1^k)$. Let $F_{vk} = \{s_1, \dots, s_{l(k)}\}$ be the subset associated to verification key vk. Pick random $M_1, \dots, M_{l(k)}$ subject to $M = M_1 \oplus \dots \oplus M_{l(k)}$ and run $c_j \xleftarrow{\$} \mathsf{enc}(pk_{s_j}, M_j)$, for $j = 1, \dots, l(k)$. Sign the ciphertexts $c = (c_1, \dots, c_{l(k)})$ with $sigsk$ by running $\sigma \leftarrow \mathsf{Sign}^{\mathsf{kg}}(sigsk, c)$ and output $C = (c, vk, \sigma)$.

$\mathsf{Dec}^{\mathsf{kg,dec}}(SK, (c = (c_1, \dots, c_{l(k)}), vk, \sigma))$: If $\mathsf{Verify}^{\mathsf{kg}}(vk, c, \sigma)$ rejects, return *reject*. Let $F_{vk} = \{s_1, \dots, s_{l(k)}\}$ be the subset associated to vk. For $j = 1, \dots, l(k)$ run $M_j \leftarrow \mathsf{dec}(sk_{s_j}, c_j)$ and output $M = M_1 \oplus \dots \oplus M_{l(k)}$.

Fig. 1. Black-box construction of an IND-q-CCA secure encryption scheme (Gen, Enc, Dec) from any IND-CPA-secure scheme (kg, enc, dec)

The following proves our main result, Theorem 4.

Lemma 1. *If* (kg, enc, dec) *is* IND-CPA *secure then* $(\mathsf{Gen}^{\mathsf{kg}}, \mathsf{Enc}^{\mathsf{kg,enc}}, \mathsf{Dec}^{\mathsf{kg,dec}})$ *as described in Fig. 1 is* IND-q-CCA *secure.*

Proof. For any PPT adversary $\mathcal{A}$ against the IND-q-CCA security of $(\mathsf{Gen}^{\mathsf{kg}}, \mathsf{Enc}^{\mathsf{kg,enc}}, \mathsf{Dec}^{\mathsf{kg,dec}})$, we show, via a game-based proof, that $\mathcal{A}$'s advantage in the IND-q-CCA game is negligible.

Let **Game 0** be the IND-q-CCA game with adversary $\mathcal{A}$ and uniformly chosen experiment bit b. Let X_0 denote the event that $\mathcal{A}$'s final guess is correct (i.e., X_0 denotes that $b' = b$). For later games, let X_i $(i > 0)$ be defined analogously.

$$\frac{1}{2}\mathbf{Adv}_{\mathsf{PKE},\mathcal{A}}^{\mathsf{IND\text{-}q\text{-}CCA}}(k) = \left| \Pr[X_0] - \frac{1}{2} \right|.$$

Game 1 is identical to **Game 0**, except that the verification key vk^* for the challenge ciphertext is *initially* chosen, and all decryption queries with $vk = vk^*$ are rejected.

By reduction on the security of the signature scheme OTS, one can show that

$$|\Pr[X_1] - \Pr[X_0]| \leq \mathbf{Adv}_{\text{OTS},\mathcal{F}}^{ots\text{-}ex\text{-}for}(k),$$

for a suitable adversary $\mathcal{F}$, where $\mathbf{Adv}_{\text{OTS},\mathcal{F}}^{ots\text{-}ex\text{-}for}(k)$ is the probability that $\mathcal{F}$ breaks the existential unforgeability of the one-time signature scheme.

Game 2 proceeds like **Game 1**, but we introduce some notation useful for later. Denote by $C^{(i)} = (c^{(i)}, vk^{(i)}, \sigma^{(i)})$ the i-th decryption request of $\mathcal{A}$. Define

$$Q := \bigcup_{vk^{(i)} \neq vk^*} F_{vk^{(i)}}$$

for the sets $F_{vk^{(i)}}$ of PKE keypairs associated with the respective i-th query. We know that $F_{vk^*} \not\subseteq Q$, so we can define $j := \min(F_{vk^*} \setminus Q)$. Additionally, we choose (this can be done at the beginning of the game, right after vk^* is fixed) uniformly and independently $i \in F_{vk^*}$. Call FAIL the event that $i \neq j$. Note that

$$\Pr[\text{FAIL} \mid X_2] = \frac{l-1}{l} = \Pr[\text{FAIL}],$$

so the events X_2 and FAIL are independent, and in particular, $\Pr[X_2] = \Pr[X_2 \mid \neg\text{FAIL}]$. Since we did not actually change anything, $\Pr[X_2] = \Pr[X_1]$.

In **Game 3**, we substitute $\mathcal{A}$'s output b' with a random bit whenever FAIL occurs. Obviously,

$$\Pr[X_3 \mid \neg\text{FAIL}] = \Pr[X_2 \mid \neg\text{FAIL}] \text{ and } \Pr[X_3 \mid \text{FAIL}] = \frac{1}{2}.$$

Since $\Pr[\text{FAIL}] = (l-1)/l$ in Game 3 as well, we can establish that

$$\Pr[X_3] - \frac{1}{2} = \frac{\Pr[X_2] - \frac{1}{2}}{l}.$$

In **Game 4**, we immediately stop the experiment and set FAIL to true (hence immediately taking a random bit for $\mathcal{A}$'s output) as soon as $\mathcal{A}$ asks for a decryption of a ciphertext with a verification key $vk \neq vk^*$ such that $i \in F_{vk}$. Note that already in Game 3, such a query would have implied $j \neq i$ and hence FAIL. Consequently,

$$\Pr[X_4] = \Pr[X_3].$$

Note that Game 4 can be run without knowledge of the secret key sk_i.

In **Game 5**, the challenge ciphertext is prepared as follows. For encrypting the challenge message M_b with PKE, we first choose uniformly PKE plaintexts $M_1^*, \ldots, M_{i-1}^*, M_{i+1}^*, \ldots, M_l^*$ and *then* the suitable

$$M_i^* := M_b \oplus \bigoplus_{r \neq i} M_r^*.$$

Note that then, only the plaintext M_i^* depends on the experiment bit b. This does not change the distribution of the whole vector $M_1^*, \ldots, M_l^*$, and we have

$$\Pr[X_5] = \Pr[X_4].$$

On the other hand, Game 5 can be directly mapped to an adversary $\mathcal{B}$ on the IND-CPA security of PKE. More concretely, $\mathcal{B}$ simulates Game 5, but substitutes pk_i with its own challenge public key, and submits as challenge plaintexts

$$\hat{M}_0 := M_0 \oplus \bigoplus_{r \neq i} M_r^* \text{ and } \hat{M}_1 := M_1 \oplus \bigoplus_{r \neq i} M_r^*.$$

Then, $\Pr[X_5]$ is precisely the success probability of $\mathcal{B}$ in the IND-CPA experiment

$$\left|\Pr[X_5] - \frac{1}{2}\right| = \frac{1}{2}\mathbf{Adv}_{\text{PKE},\mathcal{B}}^{\text{IND-CPA}}(k).$$

Collecting probabilities shows that

$$\mathbf{Adv}_{\text{PKE},\mathcal{A}}^{\text{IND-}q\text{-CCA}}(k) \leq l(k) \cdot \mathbf{Adv}_{\text{PKE},\mathcal{B}}^{\text{IND-CPA}}(k) + 2 \cdot \mathbf{Adv}_{\text{OTS},\mathcal{F}}^{ots\text{-}ex\text{-}for}(k).$$

Since $\mathbf{Adv}_{\text{PKE},\mathcal{B}}^{\text{IND-CPA}}$ and $\mathbf{Adv}_{\text{OTS},\mathcal{F}}^{ots\text{-}ex\text{-}for}$ are negligible, this shows the claim. □

Remark 1. We stress that it is important for our construction that the number of subsets $s(k)$ is super-polynomial in k. One could try to trivially build $q(k)$-bounded CCA secure encryption PKE from CPA secure PKE using a public/secret key vector of size $q(k)$ and defining the subsets F_i as $\{i\}$, for $1 \leq i \leq s(k) := q(k)$. For encryption, a message gets encrypted using pk_{vk}, where $vk \in \{1, \ldots, q(k)\}$ is one of the $q(k)$ distinct public keys of PKE, and vk is a random verification key of the signature scheme. However, since there are only $q(k)$ many possible choices of verification keys, one can break the scheme with probability $\frac{1}{q(k)}$ by (trivially) breaking the signature scheme with probability $\frac{1}{q(k)}$.

Remark 2. It might be interesting to explore what (additional) security properties PKE satisfies once invoked with a scheme PKE that itself is not only IND-CPA-secure, but, say, NME-CPA-secure. Unfortunately, we cannot hope that PKE is NME-CPA-secure, independently of PKE's security: say that adversary $\mathcal{A}$ receives a challenge ciphertext $C^* = (c^*, vk^*, \sigma^*)$ with $c^* = (c_1, \ldots, c_l)$ and $F_{vk^*} = \{s_1^*, \ldots, s_l^*\}$. Then $\mathcal{A}$ may be able to construct $l(k)$ ciphertexts $C^{(1)}, \ldots, C^{(l)}$ such that $C^{(i)}$ is associated with a subset $F^{(i)}$ with $s_i^* \in F^{(i)} \neq F_{\text{verk}}$, and the vector $c^{(i)}$ consists only of 0-encryptions except for c_i^*. The XOR of the decryptions of $C^{(i)}$ is precisely the challenge plaintext, hence this is a successful malleability attack.

We note that if we assume the IND-CCA1 security of PKE, this proof also shows that the resulting scheme PKE is secure against IND-CCA attackers who have full access to a decryption oracle before receiving the challenge ciphertext, but only limited access (q queries) to it in the second attack phase.

4   Bounded IND-CCA-Secure Encryption from DDH

In this section we propose a construction of IND-q-CCA-secure encryption based on the Decisional Diffie Hellman (DDH) assumption. The construction follows the approach from the previous section; we make use of cover-free sets and (with the same parameters as in Section 3) set up $d(k)$ independent instances of the (semantically secure) El-Gamal encryption scheme. We encrypt a message using a subset of the $d(k)$ keys, where the subset is determined by cover-free sets. Certain homomorphic properties of El-Gamal encryption are exploited to shrink the ciphertext size down to one group element. (This stands in contrast to Cramer-Shoup encryption which requires 4 group elements, and the Kurosawa-Desmedt one which requires 2 group elements and a MAC). The main contribution of this section is to demonstrate the existence of such limited $q(k)$-bounded CCA secure schemes with such an optimal ciphertext size.

To instantiate our scheme we need the following building blocks:

- A cyclic group $\mathbb{G}$ of prime-order p where the DDH assumption is believed to hold, i.e, the two distributions (g, g^x, g^y, g^{xy}) and (g, g^x, g^y, g^z) are computationally indistinguishable, for random $g \in \mathbb{G}$, and random $x, y, z \in \mathbb{Z}_p$.
- A redundancy-free symmetric-key encryption scheme (E, D) which is secure against chosen-ciphertext attacks [8]. Such schemes can be constructed based on strong pseudorandom permutations [25]. For simplicity, we assume that the key space of (E, D) is $\mathbb{G}$. (In practice, we can convert $K \in \mathbb{G}$ into a random binary string by using key derivation functions [8]).
- A hash function $\mathsf{TCR} : \mathbb{G} \to \{0, 1\}^k$ that is assumed to be target collision-resistant [21].

Let $\mathbb{G}$ be a prime order group and g a random generator of $\mathbb{G}$. The construction is given in Fig. 2. Correctness is easy to verify. Public and secret keys have quadratic size in the maximal number of decryption queries $q(k)$. The ciphertext overhead of the scheme (i.e., the difference between ciphertext and plaintext size) is only one group element $c \in \mathbb{G}$. The ciphertext length of our scheme is considered optimal since it is the same as that of the CPA secure (original) El-Gamal encryption.

Theorem 5. *Assume* TCR *is a target collision-resistant hash function,* $\mathbb{G}$ *is a group where the DDH assumption holds, and* (E, D) *is a symmetric encryption scheme that is secure against chosen-ciphertext attacks. Then* PKE *as described in Fig. 2 satisfies* IND-q-CCA *security.*

The proof of this theorem is very similar to the one of Lemma 1 and is omitted here. The idea is to prove that the underlying key encapsulation mechanism (KEM) is IND-q-CCA-secure under the DDH assumption. Using the KEM/DEM composition theorem [8], this implies the result. Intuitively, we can explain $q(k)$-bounded CCA security of the KEM part as follows: Given $(g, g^x, g^y, h) \in \mathbb{G}^4$, an algorithm $\mathcal{B}$ against the DDH problem randomly picks α from F_{t^*} where $t^* = \mathsf{TCR}(g^y)$, and sets $X_\alpha \leftarrow g^x$. For all $i \in \{1, \ldots, d(k)\} \backslash \{\alpha\}$, $\mathcal{B}$ computes

---

$\mathsf{Gen}(1^k)$: Define $s(k) = 2^k, d(k) = 16kq^2(k), l(k) = 4kq(k)$. For $i = 1, \ldots, d(k)$
  compute $X_i = g^{x_i}$ for random $x_i \in \mathbb{Z}_p$. Output $PK = (X_1, \ldots, X_{d(k)})$ and
  $SK = (x_1, \ldots, x_{d(k)})$.

$\mathsf{Enc}(PK, M)$: Compute $c = g^r$ for random $r \in \mathbb{Z}_p$. Let F_t be the subset associated
  to $t = \mathsf{TCR}(c)$. Use symmetric key $K = (\prod_{i \in F_t} X_i)^r$ to encrypt message M to
  $\psi \leftarrow \mathsf{E}_K(M)$. Output $C = (c, \psi)$.

$\mathsf{Dec}(SK, C = (c, \psi))$: Let F_t be the subset associated to $t = \mathsf{TCR}(c)$. Reconstruct
  the symmetric key as $K = c^{\sum_{i \in F_t} x_i}$ and decrypt ψ to $M \leftarrow \mathsf{D}_K(\psi)$.

Fig. 2. An IND-q-CCA-secure PKE scheme based on DDH

$x_i \xleftarrow{\$} \mathbb{Z}_p^*$ and $X_i \leftarrow g^{x_i}$, and gives $PK = (X_1, \ldots, X_{d(k)})$ to another adversary $\mathcal{A}$ against the IND-q-CCA security of the KEM part. $\mathcal{B}$ also sets (c^*, K^*) as a challenge which will be given to $\mathcal{A}$, where $c^* = g^y$, and $K^* = h \cdot \prod_{i \in F_{t^*} \setminus \{\alpha\}} (g^y)^{x_i}$. $\mathcal{B}$ outputs "$h = g^{xy}$" if $\mathcal{A}$ outputs "real key", or "$h \neq g^{xy}$" otherwise. It is clear that for any query c, $\mathcal{B}$ can respond $K = c^{\sum_{i \in F_t} x_i}$ unless $\alpha \in F_t$ where $t = \mathsf{TCR}(c)$. Then, by a similar argument to that in Lemma 1, we can show that $\mathcal{B}$ breaks the DDH assumption.

5   Construction of Bounded NME-CCA-Secure Encryption

In this section, we construct an NME-q-CCA-secure encryption scheme using any semantically secure (IND-CPA-secure) encryption scheme. The construction is *the same* as the DDN construction [10] and the construction of Pass, Shelat and Vaikuntanathan [24], except that the NIZK proof used is a "designated-verifier" NIZK proof (DV-NIZK) with "q-bounded strong soundness". Informally, a designated-verifier NIZK proof is one where the verifier has some secret information that enables him to check the validity of a proof. A DV-NIZK proof is q-bounded sound, if soundness holds even against an adversary who can query the verifier on at most q proofs and learn if the proofs are valid or not. We refer the reader to the full version for definitions and constructions of such designated verifier NIZK (relying on the construction from [24]).[2]

Because the security proof for this construction is so similar to the one from [24], we merely summarize the differences necessary to take care of the additional decryption oracle available to a q-CCA adversary. For a full proof, refer to the full version of this paper.

Theorem 6. *Assume there exists an IND-CPA-secure scheme. Then, for every polynomial q, there exists an encryption scheme that is NME-q-CCA-secure.*

Proof idea: Recall that an encryption of a message m from the construction in [24] is of the form $(\mathbf{c}, \pi, vk, \sigma)$, where $vk := v_1 \ldots v_k$ is a k-bit verification-key

---

[2] For technical reasons we also require to slightly strengthen the zero-knowledge property of designated verifier NIZK of [24].

for a strong one-time signature scheme, $\mathbf{c} = (c_1, \ldots, c_k)$ is a vector of encryptions of m where c_i is an encryption of m under the IND-CPA public-key pk_{v_i}, π is a DV-NIZK proof that all the encryptions in $\mathbf{c}$ are encryptions of the same message, and σ is a signature of $(\mathbf{c}, \pi)$ under a signing key corresponding to vk.

The proof in [24] proceeds by defining hybrid experiments $\mathsf{NME}_b^{(1)}$ and $\mathsf{NME}_b^{(2)}$ and proceeding to show that the experiments are indistinguishable, and that if an adversary succeeds in breaking $\mathsf{NME}_b^{(2)}$, it breaks the semantic security of the underlying encryption scheme.

We will proceed in a completely analogous way, by defining experiments $\mathsf{NME\text{-}q\text{-}CCA}_b^{(1)}$ and $\mathsf{NME\text{-}q\text{-}CCA}_b^{(2)}$ for $b \in \{0, 1\}$. The experiment $\mathsf{NME\text{-}q\text{-}CCA}_b^{(1)}$ proceeds like $\mathsf{NME\text{-}q\text{-}CCA}_b$ except that the DVNIZK proof in the challenge ciphertext is generated by the zero-knowledge simulator for the DVNIZK proof system. To answer the decryption queries, notice that each experiment itself knows all the secret keys, including the DV-NIZK key SP that is required to check the validity of a proof.

If the two experiments are distinguishable, we can construct an adversary that breaks the adaptive zero-knowledge of the DVNIZK. Slightly more precisely, a theorem-chooser/distinguisher pair $(\mathcal{A}_{\mathsf{zk}}, \mathcal{D}_{\mathsf{zk}})$ on the DV-NIZK is constructed such that $\mathcal{A}_{\mathsf{zk}}$ internally simulates the first stage (up to the generation of the challenge ciphertext) of the NME_b experiment, and $\mathcal{D}_{\mathsf{zk}}$ internally simulates the second stage. $\mathcal{A}_{\mathsf{zk}}$ generates all encryption and signature keypairs on its own, but takes the DV-NIZK public key PP from the adaptive zero-knowledge experiment. Since we assume a DV-NIZK with a *strong* adaptive zero-knowledge property, in the corresponding reduction already $\mathcal{A}_{\mathsf{zk}}$ knows SP and can thus answer decryption queries before the challenge ciphertext is known. This is the only difference from the proof of Claim 1 in [24].

In Claim 2 of [24], the probability for the event $\textsc{BadNizk}(\mathsf{Expt})$ that the adversary breaks the soundness of the DV-NIZK (in $\mathsf{Expt} \in \{\mathsf{NME}_b, \mathsf{NME}_b^{(1)}, \mathsf{NME}_b^{(2)}\}$) must be shown negligible. For $\mathsf{Expt} = \mathsf{NME}_b$, this is done by constructing an adversary $\mathcal{A}_s$ on the soundness property of the DV-NIZK. Here, $\mathcal{A}_s$ internally simulates the complete NME_b experiment (except for the final decryption of the forged ciphertext vector) and generates all keypairs *except* the DV-NIZK key on its own. The DV-NIZK public key PP is taken from the soundness experiment; since in the [24] CPA setting, no decryptions are necessary, this is sufficient. However, in our q-CCA setting, $\mathcal{A}_s$ might need to answer up to q decryption queries in the NME-q-CCA experiment, and thus needs to check the validity of up to q DV-NIZK proofs. Fortunately, this is exactly what an adversary against the assumed q-adaptive soundness property can do by using the "verifier-oracle" that checks the validity of proofs at most q times.

Then, $\Pr\left[\mathsf{NME\text{-}q\text{-}CCA}_b^{(1)}\right] \approx \Pr\left[\mathsf{NME\text{-}q\text{-}CCA}_b\right]$, follows similarly (only now by a reduction on the *strong* adaptive zero-knowledge property as before).

The experiment $\mathsf{NME\text{-}q\text{-}CCA}_b^{(2)}$ is defined similarly to [24]. However, we cannot show $\Pr\left[\mathsf{NME\text{-}q\text{-}CCA}_b^{(1)}\right] = \Pr\left[\mathsf{NME\text{-}q\text{-}CCA}_b^{(2)}\right]$, but *can* only show

$\Pr\left[\mathsf{NME\text{-}q\text{-}CCA}_b^{(1)}\right] \approx \Pr\left[\mathsf{NME\text{-}q\text{-}CCA}_b^{(2)}\right]$, which sufficient for the further argument. The reason that we cannot show equality is that the view of an adversary in the $\Pr\left[\mathsf{NME\text{-}q\text{-}CCA}_b^{(i)}\right]$ experiments is identical for $i = 1, 2$ only under the condition that the answers to CCA decryption queries do not differ (for $i = 1, 2$; note that in experiment $\mathsf{NME\text{-}q\text{-}CCA}_b^{(2)}$, decryption is performed differently than in $\mathsf{NME\text{-}q\text{-}CCA}_b^{(1)}$). However, such decryption queries are answered differently only if event BADNIZK happens or if the adversary successfully forged a signature. The probability that one of these events occurs in $\mathsf{NME\text{-}q\text{-}CCA}_b^{(1)}$ is negligible, and thus $\Pr\left[\mathsf{NME\text{-}q\text{-}CCA}_b^{(1)}\right] \approx \Pr\left[\mathsf{NME\text{-}q\text{-}CCA}_b^{(2)}\right]$ follows.

If the adversary succeeds in $\mathsf{NME\text{-}q\text{-}CCA}_b^{(2)}$, we can construct another adversary that breaks the semantic security of the underlying cryptosystem. The rest of the proof is completely analogous to that in [24].

6   Separating NME-CPA from IND-q-CCA

In this section, we show that under bounded chosen ciphertext attacks, non-malleability of the encryption scheme is not immediately implied by indistinguishability. In particular, for any polynomial q, we exhibit an encryption scheme that is IND-q-CCA-secure but is *not non-malleable* under even a chosen plaintext attack (i.e., a malleability attack where the adversary makes no decryption queries). In contrast, it has been shown that unbounded IND-CCA security implies non-malleability (even against unbounded CCA attacks) [10,1].

$\mathsf{Gen}'(1^k)$: Run $\mathsf{Gen}(1^k)$ and get a pair of keys (pk, sk). Suppose sk is an ℓ-bit string. Choose a random degree-q polynomial $p(x) = p_q x^q + \cdots + p_1 x + sk$ with coefficients in $GF(2^\ell)$ and whose constant term is sk. Output $pk' = pk$ and $sk' = (sk, p)$.

$\mathsf{Enc}'(pk, m)$: Get $c \leftarrow \mathsf{Enc}(pk, m)$ and output $(0, c)$.

$\mathsf{Dec}'(sk, c)$: Parse c as (c_1, c_2). If $c_1 = 0$, output $\mathsf{Dec}(sk, c_2)$. Else, if $c_2 > 0$, output $p(c_2)$ and otherwise return 0.

Fig. 3. An IND-q-CCA-secure PKE scheme PKE' which is malleable

Theorem 7. *If there exists an* IND-q-CCA *secure cryptosystem* PKE, *then there exists another* IND-q-CCA *secure cryptosystem* PKE' *that is not* NME-CPA-*secure.*

REMARK. Theorem 4 shows that the existence of a semantically-secure cryptosystem implies the existence of an IND-q-CCA cryptosystem. Therefore, the "if" clause of the above theorem can be simplified. However, we choose to present it as above to highlight the point that IND-CCA does not imply NME-CPA.

Proof. Assume that there exists an encryption scheme PKE = (Gen, Enc, Dec) that iss IND-q-CCA-secure. Then, we construct an encryption scheme PKE' = (Gen', Enc', Dec') (given in Figure 6) that is also IND-q-CCA-secure, but is not NME-CPA-secure. The proof follows from the two claims shown below.

Claim. (Gen', Enc', Dec') is IND-q-CCA-secure.

Proof. Suppose that the claim does not hold. We use the adversary $\mathcal{A}$ that breaks the security of PKE' = (Gen', Enc', Dec') to construct a q-bounded IND-q-CCA attack against PKE = (Gen, Enc, Dec). The new adversary $\mathcal{A}'$, on input pk, simply runs $\mathcal{A}(pk)$. When asked to decrypt a ciphertext $(0, c)$, it forwards the query to its own decryption oracle. When asked to decrypt a ciphertext of the form $(1, c_2)$, it returns either 0 if $c_2 = 0$ or a random value. Since $\mathcal{A}$ makes at most q queries, then $\mathcal{A}'$ will be able to answer all queries. The simulation is perfect because the degree-q polynomial $p(\cdot)$ is q-wise independent. This adversary $\mathcal{A}'$ succeeds with the same probability as $\mathcal{A}$, which contradicts the assumption that PKE is q-bounded secure.   □

Claim. (Gen', Enc', Dec') is not NME-CPA-secure.

Proof. Without loss of generality, assume that the message space of PKE include the bits 0 and 1. On input a public key pk, the adversary submits as a message pair, 0 and 1.

Upon receiving a ciphertext c, the attacker first computes $\alpha = \mathsf{Enc}(pk, c)$. It then returns the vector $(\alpha, \beta_1, \ldots, \beta_{q+1})$ where $\beta_i = (1, i)$.

Notice that the output of the experiment is the vector $(c, p(1), \ldots, p(q+1))$. The distinguisher D now works as follows. It first uses $p(1), \ldots, p(q+1)$ to interpolate the secret key sk, and then runs $\mathsf{Dec}(sk, c)$ and prints the result as its output.

The distinguisher's output in the NME_0 experiment will therefore be 0 and its output in the NME_1 will be 1, which shows that PKE' is not even NME-CPA-secure.

As one final point, it may be that the message space of PKE does not include the ciphertext — for example, the size of the ciphertext may be too big. This is easily handled. The adversary can simply encode c in a bit-by-bit fashion over many ciphertexts, and the distinguisher can simply reconstruct c to perform its test.   □

Acknowledgments

We thank Ivan Damgård, Tal Malkin, and Moti Yung for their comments.

References

1. Bellare, M., Desai, A., Pointcheval, D., Rogaway, P.: Relations among notions of security for public-key encryption schemes. In: Krawczyk, H. (ed.) CRYPTO 1998. LNCS, vol. 1462, pp. 26–45. Springer, Heidelberg (1998)

2. Canetti, R., Dodis, Y., Halevi, S., Kushilevitz, E., Sahai, A.: Exposure-resilient functions and all-or-nothing transforms. In: Preneel, B. (ed.) EUROCRYPT 2000. LNCS, vol. 1807, pp. 453–469. Springer, Heidelberg (2000)
3. Canetti, R., Halevi, S., Katz, J.: Chosen-ciphertext security from identity-based encryption. In: Cachin, C., Camenisch, J.L. (eds.) EUROCRYPT 2004. LNCS, vol. 3027, pp. 207–222. Springer, Heidelberg (2004)
4. Cramer, R., Damgård, I., Schoenmakers, B.: Proofs of partial knowledge and simplified design of witness hiding protocols. In: Desmedt, Y.G. (ed.) CRYPTO 1994. LNCS, vol. 839, pp. 174–187. Springer, Heidelberg (1994)
5. Cramer, R., Hofheinz, D., Kiltz, E.: A note on bounded chosen ciphertext security from black-box semantical security. Cryptology ePrint Archive, Report 2006/391 (2006), http://eprint.iacr.org/
6. Cramer, R., Shoup, V.: A practical public key cryptosystem provably secure against adaptive chosen ciphertext attack. In: Krawczyk, H. (ed.) CRYPTO 1998. LNCS, vol. 1462, pp. 13–25. Springer, Heidelberg (1998)
7. Cramer, R., Shoup, V.: Universal hash proofs and a paradigm for adaptive chosen ciphertext secure public-key encryption. In: Knudsen, L.R. (ed.) EUROCRYPT 2002. LNCS, vol. 2332, pp. 45–64. Springer, Heidelberg (2002)
8. Cramer, R., Shoup, V.: Design and analysis of practical public-key encryption schemes secure against adaptive chosen ciphertext attack. SIAM Journal on Computing 33(1), 167–226 (2003)
9. Dodis, Y., Katz, J., Xu, S., Yung, M.: Key-insulated public key cryptosystems. In: Knudsen, L.R. (ed.) EUROCRYPT 2002. LNCS, vol. 2332, Springer, Heidelberg (2002)
10. Dolev, D., Dwork, C., Naor, M.: Nonmalleable cryptography. SIAM Journal on Computing 30(2), 391–437 (2000)
11. Erdös, P., Frankel, P., Furedi, Z.: Families of finite sets in which no set is covered by the union of r others. Israeli Journal of Mathematics 51, 79–89 (1985)
12. Gertner, Y., Malkin, T., Myers, S.: Towards a separation of semantic and CCA security for public key encryption. In: Vadhan, S.P. (ed.) TCC 2007. LNCS, vol. 4392, pp. 434–455. Springer, Heidelberg (2007)
13. Goldreich, O.: Foundations of Cryptography: Basic Applications, vol. 2. Cambridge University Press, Cambridge, UK (2004)
14. Goldwasser, S., Micali, S.: Probabilistic encryption. Journal of Computer and System Sciences 28(2), 270–299 (1984)
15. Hanaoka, G., Imai, H.: A generic construction of CCA-secure cryptosystems without NIZKP for a bounded number of decryption queries. Cryptology ePrint Archive, Report, 2006/408 (2006), http://eprint.iacr.org/
16. Heng, S.-H., Kurosawa, K.: k-resilient identity-based encryption in the standard model. In: Okamoto, T. (ed.) CT-RSA 2004. LNCS, vol. 2964, pp. 67–80. Springer, Heidelberg (2004)
17. Kumar, R., Rajagopalan, S., Sahai, A.: Coding constructions for blacklisting problems without computational assumptions. In: Wiener, M.J. (ed.) CRYPTO 1999. LNCS, vol. 1666, pp. 609–623. Springer, Heidelberg (1999)
18. Kurosawa, K., Desmedt, Y.: A new paradigm of hybrid encryption scheme. In: Franklin, M. (ed.) CRYPTO 2004. LNCS, vol. 3152, pp. 426–442. Springer, Heidelberg (2004)
19. Lamport, L.: Constructing digital signatures from a one-way function. Technical Report CSL-98, SRI International (October 1979)
20. Lindell, Y.: A simpler construction of CCA2-secure public-key encryption under general assumptions. Journal of Cryptology 19(3), 359–377 (2006)

21. Naor, M., Yung, M.: Universal one-way hash functions and their cryptographic applications. In: STOC 1989, pp. 33–43. ACM Press, New York (1989)
22. Naor, M., Yung, M.: Public-key cryptosystems provably secure against chosen ciphertext attacks. In: STOC 1990, ACM Press, New York (1990)
23. Pass, R., Shelat, A., Vaikuntanathan, V.: Bounded-CCA secure non-malleable encryption. MIT CSAIL Technical Report TR-2006-081 (December 2006)
24. Pass, R., Shelat, A., Vaikuntanathan, V.: Construction of a non-malleable encryption scheme from any semantically secure one. In: Dwork, C. (ed.) CRYPTO 2006. LNCS, vol. 4117, pp. 271–289. Springer, Heidelberg (2006)
25. Phan, D.H., Pointcheval, D.: About the security of ciphers (semantic security and pseudo-random permutations). In: Handschuh, H., Hasan, M.A. (eds.) SAC 2004. LNCS, vol. 3357, pp. 182–197. Springer, Heidelberg (2004)
26. Rackoff, C., Simon, D.R.: Non-interactive zero-knowledge proof of knowledge and chosen ciphertext attack. In: Feigenbaum, J. (ed.) CRYPTO 1991. LNCS, vol. 576, pp. 433–444. Springer, Heidelberg (1992)
27. Rompel, J.: One-way Functions are necessary and sufficient for secure signatures. In: STOC 1990, pp. 387–394
28. Sahai, A.: Non-malleable non-interactive zero knowledge and adaptive chosen-ciphertext security. In: FOCS 1999, pp. 543–553. IEEE Computer Society Press, Los Alamitos (1999)

Relations Among Notions of Non-malleability for Encryption

Rafael Pass[1], Abhi Shelat[2], and Vinod Vaikuntanathan[3]

[1] Cornell
[2] U. Virginia
[3] MIT

Abstract. Since its introduction in the early 90's, the notion of non-malleability for encryption schemes has been formalized using a number of conceptually different definitional approaches—most notably, the "pragmatic" indistinguishability-based approach and the "semantical" simulation-based approach. We provide a full characterization of these approaches and consider their robustness under composition.

Keywords: Public-key Encryption, Non-malleability.

1 Introduction

The basic goal of an encryption scheme is to guarantee the *privacy* of data. A good formalization of privacy is the notion of *semantic security* as defined by Goldwasser and Micali [GM84]. Intuitively, semantic security guarantees that "whatever a polynomial-time machine can learn about a message given its encryption, it can learn even without seeing the encryption."

When encryption schemes are deployed in more complex environments, the demands for security of encryption grow beyond just the basic privacy requirement. Motivated by practical security requirements, the seminal work of Dolev, Dwork and Naor [DDN00] defined the notion of *non-malleability*—a qualitatively stronger notion of security for encryption schemes. In addition to the normal "privacy" guarantee, non-malleability ensures that it is infeasible for an adversary to *modify* a vector of ciphertexts $\alpha_1, \ldots, \alpha_n$ into other ciphertexts of messages which are related to the decryption of $\alpha_1, \ldots, \alpha_n$. This stronger notion of security is critical for many practical applications.

Two Formalizations. The notion of non-malleability for encryption schemes has been formalized using two different approaches:

- **The "Semantical" Simulation-based Approach.** The definition presented in the original work of [DDN00] is a so-called "simulation-based" one. The main idea is to capture the requirement that an adversary having access to ciphertexts (and potentially a decryption oracle in case of CCA1/CCA2 attacks), will not be able to "cause more harm" than a simple adversary

K. Kurosawa (Ed.): ASIACRYPT 2007, LNCS 4833, pp. 519–535, 2007.

that does not see any ciphertexts and does not have access to a decryption oracle. This simulation-based definition of non-malleability is denoted SIM-NME, and like semantic security, the goal of this definition is to capture the "meaning" of non-malleability. As a result, it is often harder to directly prove that a scheme meets the simulation-based definition.

– **The "Pragmatic" Indistinguishability-based Approach.** Bellare et.al. present a "comparison-based" formalization of non-malleability [BDPR98]. This notion does away with the "simulator" used in [DDN00] and instead captures non-malleability through an indistinguishability-style definition. Other indistinguishability-based definitions appear in [BS99, PSV06]. We denote by IND-NME the indistinguishability-based approach to defining non-malleability. The goal of this indistinguishability-based approach is to provide definitions that are easier to "work with."

Just as Goldwasser and Micali [GM84] show equivalence between simulation-based and indistinguishability-based definitions of secrecy, Bellare and Sahai [BS06] (clarifying [BS99]) show an equivalence between the simulation-based and the indistinguishability-based approach to defining non-malleability. As we discuss later, their proof however makes certain implicit assumptions on the type of encryption schemes used. As far as we know, equivalences for general encryption schemes are not known.

Composition and Invalid Ciphertexts. In practice, encryption schemes must guarantee security also when an adversary receives encryptions of *multiple* messages. It is well known that for the traditional definition of secrecy, "single-message" security implies "multi-message" security – we say that the definition is *closed under composition.* It would be desirable to have a definition of non-malleability that composes (i.e., for which non-malleability for a single message implies non-malleability for multiple messages).

It turns out that this property is highly sensitive to the way non-malleability is formalized. As pointed out by Pass, shelat and Vaikuntanathan [PSV06], there is some ambiguity in the original work of Dolev, Dwork and Naor [DDN00] about how to treat an adversary that sometimes produces *invalid* ciphertexts as part of its output. Whereas the intuitive description of the "spirit" of non-malleability considers an adversary successful if it is able to output ciphertexts that are related to the ciphertexts it receives, the formal definition does not consider an adversary who outputs an invalid ciphertext (even if this event is correlated with the input ciphertexts it receives). It is shown in [PSV06] that for the case of *chosen-plaintext* attacks, this (seemingly minor) issue becomes critical in certain (traditional) applications, and is also essential for proving composability of non-malleability. In both situations a stronger definition, which does not automatically fail an adversary which outputs an invalid ciphertext, is sufficient, whereas the weaker (traditional one) is not. We denote by SIM-NME', IND-NME' these stronger variants of SIM-NME, IND-NME (which are in-line with the definitions of [PSV06, BS06]).

1.1   Our Results

We may thus broadly categorize definitions of non-malleability into two major groups: "simulation-based" and "indistinguishability-based," and each with two sub-groups: "invalid-allowing" and "invalid-prohibiting." In this paper we first fully characterize the relationship among the different definitional approaches outlined above. Secondly, we consider the robustness of each of the definitions under a natural (and highly desirable) notion of composition. Our motivation is to clarify the definitional imbroglio surrounding the notions. To so do, we present a unified way of defining non-malleability according the above-mentioned different approaches. We furthermore believe that our definitions provide the simplest and cleanest way to formalize non-malleability according to these approaches.

Relations Between Definitions. Our results are as follows.

1. *The Case of Invalid-Allowing Definitions* For the case of invalid-allowing definitions, we obtain a separation between the simulation-based definition of non-malleability, SIM-NME′, and indistinguishability-based definition, IND-NME′. In particular, under CCA1 or CCA2 attacks, SIM-NME′ is *strictly* stronger than IND-NME′, whereas under CPA attacks they are equivalent.
2. *The Case of Invalid-Prohibiting Definitions* For the case of invalid-prohibiting definitions, the simulation-based definition, SIM-NME is *equivalent* to the indistinguishability-based definition IND-NME, under all attacks (i.e., CPA, CCA1 and CCA2).
3. *The Relation between Invalid-Allowing and -Prohibiting Definitions* The first approach to defining non-malleability is *strictly* stronger than the second one. In fact, this holds under all attacks in the simulation-based notion, and under CCA1 and CPA attacks for the indistinguishability-based notion.

A full characterization of the different definitions is summarized in the table below. The starred results appear in either [DDN00] and/or [BDPR98].

ATTACK	RELATIONSHIPS
CCA2	SIM-NME′ > IND-NME′ = SIM-NME =* IND-NME =* IND
CCA1	SIM-NME′ > IND-NME′ > SIM-NME = IND-NME >* IND
CPA	SIM-NME′ = IND-NME′ > SIM-NME = IND-NME >* IND

Results Concerning Practical Schemes and Restricted Message Spaces. Many practical and efficient encryption schemes only work for *restricted message spaces*. For example, the El Gamal and Cramer-Shoup schemes work for messages that are elements of some finite group. While it seems natural for the above equivalences to also hold for this special class of encryption schemes, we show in §5 that this intuition is not true. In particular, we show that also for the case of CCA2 attacks, SIM-NME is strictly stronger than IND-NME. Thus, somewhat surprisingly,

> *For restricted message spaces, "simple"* IND-CCA2 *security does not imply*
> *the original semantical (simulation-based) definition of non-malleability.*

This stands in sharp contrast to the result of [DDN00, BDPR98] showing that IND-CCA2 indeed is equivalent SIM-NME for the case of full messages spaces.

Why Simulation-Based Non-malleability Is Desirable. Many practical system attacks such as buffer overflows rely on creating a situation in which a process is fed unexpected input. With this in mind, consider an encryption scheme which has been dutifully designed so that an adversary cannot produce a ciphertexts which decrypt to a certain output value (say $\bot$). A system designer might employ this scheme in a process, and rely on the fact that such inputs cannot be produced by the decrypting algorithm for the correctness of the process.

Now suppose that the adversary might have a way to implement a CCA2 attack. A cryptographer may be content to prove that their encryption scheme is IND-CCA2-secure. However, the systems' practitioner may require something more. She would like the guarantee that even if the adversary has a decryption oracle, the adversary will be unable to "do any more harm" than if the adversary did not have the decryption oracle. In other words, the adversary will be unable to produce unexpected outputs in this case as well—and so the practitioner's original assumptions are still valid. In essence, the situation calls for simulation-based security.

Remarks. As shown by Canetti [Can01], a Universally Composable (UC) implementation of an "idealized" encryption functionality $\mathcal{F}_{pke}$ is equivalent to IND-CCA2-secure encryption. Furthermore, the UC definition of security is a semantical notion which provides security under arbitrary concurrent executions; in particular UC security provides security with respect to man-in-the-middle attacks. However, the definition of $\mathcal{F}_{pke}$ allows a corrupted sender to make an honest receiver decrypt a ciphertext to any arbitrary string (and not only those in the domain of the encryption function) *even if this was not possible in a stand-alone setting*; as such UC encryption does not satisfy the above desiderata. We also mention that Goldreich [Gol04] presents a similar semantical (simulation-based) definition of non-malleability, which is equivalent to (simple) indistinguishability under CCA2 attacks; this definition too does not prevent a corrupted sender from making an honest receiver decrypt a ciphertext to any arbitrary string.[1]

Additional Equivalences. To further clarify the semantical relation between the various notions, we present additional equivalences for certain restricted encryption schemes: Concisely, a scheme which is IND-NME secure and for which it is possible to efficiently produce a ciphertext which decrypts to every output in

---

[1] On a high-level, the difference between SIM-NME and the definition of [Gol04] is that in the latter, the simulator is required to output *plaintexts* that are indistinguishable from the messages the adversary encrypts, whereas in the former the simulator must do the same as the adversary and output ciphertexts.

the range of the decryption function is also (multi-message) SIM-NME' secure.[2] Thus, for encryption schemes satisfying certain technical conditions all the above notions are equivalent. In light of this our separation results might seem "artificial".[3] Note, however, that although these restriction are not implausible, they are far from being satisfied all "practical" encryption schemes. Indeed, whereas RSA-OAEP satisfies them (at the cost of "truncating" the message space), other schemes such as CS1 from [CS98] does not.

Composability of Definitions. The table below summarizes new and known results regarding the composability of of the various definitional approaches. A $\sqrt{}$-mark indicates that the definitions composes, **X**-mark indicates it does not, and ? indicates that the status is unknown. Pass, shelat, and Vaikuntanathan [PSV06] show the * result. Gennaro and Lindell [GL03] show the † result. All other results are new in this paper. These new results show that, contrary to folklore belief, *indistinguishability*-based definitions of encryption do *not* necessarily compose in the context of non-malleability.

	SIM-NME'	IND-NME'	SIM-NME	IND-NME
CCA2	?	$\sqrt{}$	$\sqrt{}$	$\sqrt{}$
CCA1	?	$\sqrt{}$	**X**	**X**
CPA	$\sqrt{}$	$\sqrt{}^*$	**X**†	**X**

Related Work. The work of [BS06] (clarifying the original work of [BS99]) provided a comprehensive study of equivalence between indistinguishability-based and simulation-based definitions. Their main results show such an equivalence for the case of *invalid-allowing* definitions. We here note that their result implicitly makes the assumption that the encryption schemes considered have the property that it is "easy" (i.e., there is a prescribed polynomial-time algorithm) to generate invalid ciphertexts. In contrast, we consider general encryption schemes (i.e., without any such restriction). Interestingly, we show that the notions no longer are equivalent when doing so (furthermore, when considering restricted messages spaces, equivalence does not hold even if there exists a prescribed polynomial-time algorithm for generating invalid ciphertexts).

Nevertheless, we emphasize that proof techniques from [BS99, BS06] are useful also when considering general encryption schemes. Indeed, our equivalence proof for the case of *invalid-prohibiting* definitions (i.e., showing that SIM-NME = IND-NME) borrows from their original proof.[4]

---

[2] This result generalizes the earlier results by [BS06]. See Section 1.1 for more details.

[3] In a sense all separation results can be called either "artificial" or "trivial"—if they are satisfied by known schemes then they are trivial, otherwise they are "artificial".

[4] The original published version of their results [BS99] claimed an equivalence between SIM-NME and an indistinguishability-based definition of non-malleability due to [BDPR98]. This claim was later retracted in the new version [BS06] (due to subtleties pointed out by Lindell). We mention, however, that our definition of IND-NME is (seemingly) different from the indistinguishability-based definition of [BDPR98].

We also mention that various other definitions of non-malleability for encryption schemes have been proposed (e.g [BDPR98, BS06, Gol04]). Our goal is not to fully characterize the relative strength of all variants of non-malleability. Rather, we highlight the differences between certain natural definitional approaches (i.e., simulation v.s. indistinguishability, and invalid-allowing v.s. invalid-prohibiting).

2   Definitions

Oracles. In a chosen-plaintext attack (CPA), the oracles O_1, O_2 return the empty string. In a CCA1 attack, the oracle $O_1(\text{PK}, \cdot)$ returns the decryption of its input under public key PK (which is implicit by context). Finally, in a CCA2 attack, both oracles return decryptions with the exception that $O_2(\text{PK}, \boldsymbol{y}, \cdot)$ returns $\perp$ when queried on a ciphertext contained in $\boldsymbol{y}$.

Comparing Definitions. If D1, D2 are two definitions, the notation D1 > D2 means that: "Every scheme Π which satisfies D1 also satisfies D2, and if there exists a scheme Π which satisfies D2, then there exists a scheme Π' which also satisfies D2 but does not satisfy D1." We say that D1 = D2 if the set of schemes that satisfy D1 is identical to the set of schemes that satisfy D2.

2.1   Simulation-Based Definitions of Non-malleable Encryption

Definition 1 (SIM-NME' Security). *Define the following two experiments.*

SIM-NME'(Π, A, k, ℓ, r)
  $(\text{PK}, \text{SK}) \leftarrow \text{Gen}(1^k)$
  $(M, s) \leftarrow A_1^{O_1}(\text{PK})$
  $(m_1, \ldots, m_\ell) \xleftarrow{\$} M(1^k)$
  $\boldsymbol{y} \leftarrow \text{Enc}(\text{PK}, \boldsymbol{m})$
  $((c_1, \ldots, c_r), \sigma) \leftarrow A_2^{O_2}(\boldsymbol{y}, h(\boldsymbol{m}), s)$
  $d_i = \begin{cases} \text{COPY} & \text{if } c_i \in \boldsymbol{y} \\ \text{Dec}(\text{SK}, c_i) & \text{o.w.} \end{cases}$
  Output $(M, \boldsymbol{m}, (d_1, \ldots, d_r), \sigma)$

SIM-NME'(Π, S, k, ℓ, r)
  $(\text{PK}, \text{SK}) \leftarrow \text{Gen}(1^k)$
  $\boxed{(M, s) \leftarrow S_1(\text{PK})}$
  $(m_1, \ldots, m_\ell) \xleftarrow{\$} M(1^k)$

  $\boxed{((c_1, \ldots, c_r), \sigma) \leftarrow S_2(h(\boldsymbol{m}), s)}$
  $d_i = \begin{cases} \text{COPY} & \text{if } c_i = \text{COPY} \\ \text{Dec}(\text{SK}, c_i) & \text{o.w.} \end{cases}$
  Output $(M, \boldsymbol{m}, (d_1, \ldots, d_r), \sigma)$

Here M is a Turing machine that samples a vector of $\ell(k)$ messages from a distribution. We say that M is an (p, ℓ)-valid message-sampler if 1) the running-time of $M(1^k)$ is bounded by $p(k)$, and 2) there exists polynomials $l_1, l_2, .., l_\ell$ such that $M(1^k)$ always outputs message sequences $(m_1, \ldots, m_{\ell(k)})$ such that $|m_i| = l_i(1^k)$ for all $1 \leq i \leq \ell(k)$.

An encryption scheme $\Pi = (\text{Gen}, \text{Enc}, \text{Dec})$ is SIM-NME'-secure if for polynomials $\ell(k)$, $r(k)$ and $p(k)$, every polynomial-time computable history function $h(\cdot)$, every p.p.t. adversary $A = (A_1, A_2)$ which runs in time $p(k)$ and always outputs a (p, ℓ)-valid message sampler, there exists a p.p.t. algorithm $S = (S_1, S_2)$

that always outputs a (p, ℓ)-valid message sampler, such that the following two distributions are computationally indistinguishable:

$$\left\{\mathsf{SIM\text{-}NME'}(\Pi, A, k, \ell(k), r(k))\right\}_k \stackrel{c}{\approx} \left\{\overline{\mathsf{SIM\text{-}NME'}}(\Pi, S, k, \ell(k), r(k))\right\}_k \quad (1)$$

We also define a weaker notion of this definition named SIM-NME by requiring that the outputs of the two experiments are indistinguishable only for a certain "restricted" set of adversaries A. Define the following two types of adversaries:

1. *non-copying adversaries:* $A = (A_1, A_2)$ is said to be non-copying if in the above experiment A_2 never outputs a ciphertext c_i, s.t., $c_i \in \boldsymbol{y}$.
2. *valid adversaries*[5]: A is said to be valid if in the above experiment A only outputs ciphertexts that are in the range of the encryption function (on input PK), i.e., it holds that for all c_i, there exists an d_i such that $c_i \in \mathsf{Enc}(\mathrm{PK}, d_i)$.

Definition 2 (SIM-NME Security). *An encryption scheme $\Pi = (\mathsf{Gen}, \mathsf{Enc}, \mathsf{Dec})$ is SIM-NME-secure if for polynomials $\ell(k)$, $r(k)$ and $p(k)$, every polynomial-time computable history function $h(\cdot)$, every **non-copying, valid** p.p.t. adversary $A = (A_1, A_2)$ which runs in time $p(k)$ and always outputs a (p, ℓ)-valid message sampler, there exists a p.p.t. algorithm $S = (S_1, S_2)$ that always outputs a (p, ℓ)-valid message sampler, such that the ensembles in equation (1) are indistinguishable to any p.p.t. distinguisher D.*

Single-Message Versus Many-Message Security. We have presented definitions which allow the adversary to see a sequence of encrypted messages. Forboth the above definitions of non-malleability, a scheme satisfying the definition in the case when $\ell(k) = 1$ (but $r(k)$ is still arbitrary), is said to be *single-message* secure. The question of whether any single-message secure scheme is also (many-message) secure is the question of composability of the definition.

Remarks. Single-message SIM-NME security is a rewriting of the original DDN simulation-based definition of non-malleability. The main difference between our definition and definition of DDN is that we dispense with the relation R and instead use the notion of indistinguishability of the outputs. This difference is inconsequential (since any p.p.t distinguisher can be described as a p.p.t relation and vice versa); however, this draws a parallel to the (upcoming) indistinguishability-based definition of non-malleability, which we term IND-NME. In this way, we emphasize the meaning of this definition: neither a ciphertext of a chosen message or a decryption oracle can substantially alter an adversaries ultimate "behavior." Given this interpretation, it is also intuitive to see why the valid-adversary is somehow artificial. Moreover this restriction prevents the definition from composing—i.e., it is possible for a scheme to be single-message SIM-NME secure, but not SIM-NME secure. We also remark that our definition of single-message SIM-NME' security is syntactically equivalent to the SNM definition of non-malleability from [BS06].

---

[5] This interpretation comes from [DDN00] where they write "A produces...ciphertexts $(f_1, \ldots)$...with $f_i \in \mathsf{Enc}(\beta_i)$...".

2.2 Indistinguishablility-Based Definitions

The following definition of non-malleability was introduced in [PSV06] and is syntactically very close to the definition of [BS99, BS06].

Definition 3 (IND-NME′ Security [PSV06]). *Let* $\Pi = (\mathsf{Gen}, \mathsf{Enc}, \mathsf{Dec})$ *be an encryption scheme and let the random variable* $\mathsf{IND\text{-}NME}_b(\Pi, A, k, \ell, r)$ *where* $b \in \{0, 1\}$, $A = (A_1, A_2)$ *and* $k, \ell, r \in \mathbb{N}$ *denote the result of the following probabilistic experiment:*

> $\mathsf{IND\text{-}NME}'_b(\Pi, A, k, \ell, r):$
> $(\mathrm{PK}, \mathrm{SK}) \leftarrow \mathsf{Gen}(1^k)$
> $((m_{0,1}, \ldots, m_{0,\ell}), (m_{1,1}, \ldots, m_{1,\ell}), s) \leftarrow A_1^{O_1}(\mathrm{PK}) \ s.t. \ |m_{0,i}| = |m_{1,i}|$
> $y_i \leftarrow \mathsf{Enc}(\mathrm{PK}, m_{b,i}) \ for \ i \in [1, \ell]$
> $(c_1, \ldots, c_r) \leftarrow A_2^{O_2}(\boldsymbol{y}, s)$
> $Output \ (d_1, \ldots, d_r) \ where \ d_i = \begin{cases} \text{COPY} & if \ c_i \in \boldsymbol{y} \\ \mathsf{Dec}(\mathrm{SK}, c_i) & otherwise \end{cases}$

$(\mathsf{Gen}, \mathsf{Enc}, \mathsf{Dec})$ *is* $\mathsf{IND\text{-}NME}'$*-secure if* $\forall$ *p.p.t. algorithms* $A = (A_1, A_2)$ *and for any polynomials* $\ell(k)$ *and* $r(k)$, *the following two ensembles are computationally indistinguishable:*

$$\left\{ \mathsf{IND\text{-}NME}'_0(\Pi, A, k, \ell(k), r(k)) \right\}_k \overset{c}{\approx} \left\{ \mathsf{IND\text{-}NME}'_1(\Pi, A, k, \ell(k), r(k)) \right\}_k \quad (2)$$

We also introduce a weaker version of this definition, IND-NME, in which, as in the previous section, (2) need only hold for non-copying, valid adversaries A.

Definition 4 (IND-NME Security). *An encryption scheme* $(\mathsf{Gen}, \mathsf{Enc}, \mathsf{Dec})$ *is* IND-NME*-secure if* $\forall$ **non-copying, valid** *p.p.t. algorithms* $A = (A_1, A_2)$ *and for any polynomials* $\ell(k)$ *and* $r(k)$, *the ensembles in the equation (2) are computationally indistinguishable.*

Single-Message Security. For both the above indistinguishability-based definitions, we obtain the weaker notion of *single-message* security by restriction attention to the case when $\ell(k) = 1$. We also note that our definition of single-message IND-NME′ security is a syntactical rewriting of (and thus equivalent to) the definition of IND-PAX of [BS06].

3 Equivalences Between Definitions

Theorem 1. SIM-NME = IND-NME *for all attacks.*

The equivalence proof for this theorem uses ideas from Bellare and Sahai [BS99]. Note however that it does not show that SIM-NME′ = IND-NME′ (as was the goal in Bellare and Sahai's revised paper [BS06]). Let us briefly recall the subtle issue in the original proof in [BS99] (the same issue appears in the revised proof that SIM-NME′ = IND-NME′ in [BS06]). In one step of the equivalence proof, the SIM-NME simulator must re-encrypt a vector of ciphertexts which the adversary has produced. If an "aborting" adversary has produced an invalid ciphertext, it is not clear whether the simulator can proceed—in particular, the encryption scheme Π *might not provide* an efficient method available to produce an invalid ciphertext (as was the case in the previous section). The proof does hold, however, for a valid adversary who always produces ciphertexts that are in the range of the Enc function.

In the full version, we present a direct equivalence proof for SIM-NME and IND-NME which is simple and extends to the case of many-message security. Moreover, the proof also leads to the following corollary relating SIM-NME' and IND-NME' used in Theorem 4:

Corollary 1. *If* Π *is* SIM-NME'*-secure, then* Π *is also* IND-NME' *secure.*

For completeness, we present a proof of the following theorem in the full version which has been partially shown by Dolev, Dwork, and Naor [DDN00].

Theorem 2. IND-NME'-CCA2 = IND-NME-CCA2 = IND-CCA2.

In the weaker CPA attack, we show that the simulation and indistinguishability definitions for invalid ciphertext-producing adversaries are also equivalent by adapting a simpler version of Thm. 1. This implies that the construction from [PSV06] meets the strongest notion of non-malleability for the CPA attack. The proof appears in the full version.

Theorem 3. *Under a CPA attack,* SIM-NME' = IND-NME'.

4   Separating the SIM-NME' and IND-NME' Definitions

Theorem 4 (Main Separation). *Under* CCA1 *or* CCA2 *attacks,* SIM-NME' > IND-NME' *even for single-message security.*

Corollary 1 shows that SIM-NME' implies IND-NME'. Thus, the main idea for this separation is to design an encryption scheme in which the set of messages for which a ciphertext can be efficiently computed and the range of the decryption function *differ*. As one concrete example below, we design an IND-NME' scheme in which it is nearly impossible for an adversary to produce a ciphertext which decrypts to $\bot$ (i.e., an invalid ciphertext) *unless* it has adaptive access to a decryption oracle. [6] We show the scheme so constructed meets the IND-NME' definition. However, it does not meet the SIM-NME' definition under a CCA1 or CCA2 attack, because an adversary (with access to a decryption oracle) is able to produce a ciphertext that decrypts to $\bot$ whereas a simulator (without access to a decryption oracle) is unable. Thus, the outputs of the SIM-NME' and SIM-NME' experiments will be trivially distinguishable. The general idea behind these type of arguments first appears in [DDN00] and is also used in [BDPR98] to show other separations.

---

[6] Another example would be a finite message space, i.e., a message space which includes all strings in $\{0,1\}^k$ and a scheme in which the range of the decryption function includes one k^2 bit string. We discuss this later in §5.

Proof. Let $\Pi = (\mathsf{Gen}, \mathsf{Enc}, \mathsf{Dec})$ be an encryption scheme that satisfies IND-NME′ under a CCA attack. Consider encryption scheme Π' defined in the figure below. The key property of Π' is that Dec′ never outputs $\perp$ unless it is queried with

---

ENCRYPTION SCHEME Π'

$\mathsf{Gen}'(1^k)$: Run $(\mathrm{PK}, \mathrm{SK}) \leftarrow \mathsf{Gen}(1^k)$. Pick random k-bit string α and set $\mathrm{SK}' \leftarrow (\mathrm{SK}, \alpha)$.

$\mathsf{Enc}'(\mathrm{PK}', m)$: Run $c \leftarrow \mathsf{Enc}(\mathrm{PK}, m)$. Output $(1, 0^k, c)$ as ciphertext.

$\mathsf{Dec}'(\mathrm{SK}', c')$: Parse c' as (b, β, c) where b is a bit, β is a k-bit string.

    1. If $b = 0$ and $\beta = 1^k$, then output α.
    2. If $b = 0$ and $\beta = \alpha$, then output $\perp$.
    3. If $b = 1$ and $\beta = 0^k$, run $m \leftarrow \mathsf{Dec}(\mathrm{SK}, c)$. If the output is $\perp$, output 0. Otherwise, output m.
    4. Otherwise, output 0.

---

the special "open sesame" string α, and a decryption oracle is necessary to learn the "open sesame" string.

It is easy to see that Π' syntactically is an encryption scheme. The only issue is to argue that Π' is perfectly correct, which follows because perfect correctness only applies to decryption of honestly encrypted messages (which are never invalid ciphertexts).

Claim. $\Pi' = (\mathsf{Gen}', \mathsf{Enc}', \mathsf{Dec}')$ meets the IND-NME′-CCA definition.

Proof. Suppose there exists an adversary A' which breaks the IND-NME′-CCA definition for Π'. Such an adversary can be used to construct an adversary A which breaks the IND-NME′-CCA definition for Π as follows:

The new adversary A simulates $(\mathsf{Gen}', \mathsf{Enc}', \mathsf{Dec}')$ for A' by picking α itself and using the oracles for Dec to answer queries. More precisely, on input a public key PK, A generates a k-bit string α and feeds PK to A'. When A' asks decryption queries, A simulates the Dec′ algorithm by using α as the second component of SK′ and the decryption oracle in order to compute $\mathsf{Dec}(c, \mathrm{SK})$. When A' produces two challenge messages, A forwards these messages along, and when it receives a challenge ciphertext y, A feeds $(1, 0^k, y)$ to A'. In the case of a CCA2 attack, A again simulates the Dec′ function, and when A' finally returns an answer, A echoes it. A perfectly simulates the IND-NME′-CCA game for A', and thus succeeds with exactly the same probability as A'.

Claim. Π' does not meet the SIM-NME′-CCA definition.

Proof. Consider the relation $R(x, \boldsymbol{x}, M, s)$ which is 1 if x is $\perp$ and 0 otherwise.

A CCA1 adversary with access to a decryption oracle can satisfy R by making a decryption query on the message $(0, 1^k, 0)$ to get the value α, and then by outputting the ciphertext $(0, \alpha, 0)$.

However, it is not possible for a simulator S without access to the decryption oracle to satisfy R. Such a simulator only has an exponentially small chance of guessing the correct α string necessary to produce $\bot$. Thus, Π' will not satisfy SIM-NME'-CCA1.

4.1   More Separations for CCA1 and CPA Attacks

We now show that IND-NME' is stronger than IND-NME *when considering weaker CPA and CCA1 attacks.* Recall that IND-NME' and IND-NME are different only in that the former protects against all PPT adversaries, whereas the latter protects against only valid PPT adversaries.[7] By combining the equivalence from Theorem 1, we also get a separation between IND-NME' and SIM-NME. For CCA2 attacks, they become equivalent (See Thm. 2).

Theorem 5. IND-NME' > IND-NME *for CCA1 and CPA attacks even for single-message security.*

Corollary 2. IND-NME' > SIM-NME *for CCA1 and CPA attacks even for single-message security.*

Proof. (Of Corollary 2.) By Theorem 5, IND-NME' > IND-NME for CCA1 and CPA attacks and by Theorem 1, SIM-NME = IND-NME under all attacks.

The main idea for the proof of Theorem 5 is to use the *DDN-lite* transformation [Dwo99, Nao04] to transform an IND-NME-secure encryption scheme into one that remains IND-NME-secure (Claim 4.1), but is vulnerable to an IND-NME' attack (Claim 4.1).

We actually prove a stronger statement which gives us a way to transform an IND-CPA-secure encryption scheme into one that is IND-NME-secure. While this result has been claimed in [Dwo99, Nao04], as far as the authors know, a proof has never been printed. Our proof also shows that the construction also transforms an IND-CCA1 scheme into an IND-NME-CCA1 scheme. The IND-NME'-attack against this scheme is an adaptation of the attack against DDN-lite, given in [PSV06].

Proof. (of Theorem 5) Let $\Pi = (\mathsf{Gen}, \mathsf{Enc}, \mathsf{Dec})$ be an encryption scheme that is IND-CPA-secure (respectively, IND-CCA1-secure). Let $\Sigma = (\mathsf{Gen}_{sig}, \mathsf{Sign}, \mathsf{Ver})$ be a strongly unforgeable one-time signature scheme. Such a signature scheme can be constructed from one-way functions (The existence of one-way functions, in turn, is implied by the existence of a IND-CPA-secure encryption scheme). We construct a new encryption scheme Π_{L} from Π and show that Π_{L} satisfies the IND-NME definition but does does not satisfy IND-NME'.

Claim. Π_{L} meets the IND-NME definition.

---

[7] We say that an invalid ciphertext "decrypts" to $\bot$ (Bot) and hence the title of the subsection.

ENCRYPTION SCHEME Π_L

$\mathsf{Gen}'(1^k)$: Run $\mathsf{Gen}(1^k)$ $2k$ times with independent random coins to produce $2k$ pairs of keys $(\text{PK}_b^i, \text{SK}_b^i)$ for $i \in [1, k]$ and $b \in \{0, 1\}$. Let $\text{PK}' = \left[\text{PK}_b^i\right]_{i \in [k], b \in \{0,1\}}$ and $\text{SK}' = \left[\text{SK}_b^i\right]_{i \in [k], b \in \{0,1\}}$

$\mathsf{Enc}'(m, \text{PK}')$: Run $\mathsf{Gen}_{sig}(1^k)$ to generate a key-pair $(\text{VKSIG}, \text{SKSIG})$ for the signature scheme. Let VKSIG a k-bit string, and let the ith bit of VKSIG be denoted VKSIG_i.

Run $c_i \leftarrow \mathsf{Enc}(\text{PK}_i^{\text{VKSIG}_i}, m)$ for $i \in [1, k]$.

Let $\sigma \leftarrow \mathsf{Sign}(\text{SKSIG}, (c_1, c_2, \ldots, c_k))$.

Output $[(c_1, \ldots, c_k), \text{VKSIG}, \sigma]$ as the ciphertext.

$\mathsf{Dec}'(c', \text{SK}')$: Parse c' as $((c_1, \ldots, c_k), \text{VKSIG}, \sigma)$.

If $\mathsf{Ver}(\text{VKSIG}, (c_1, \ldots, c_k), \sigma) = \text{REJECT}$, output $\perp$.

Otherwise, decrypt the c_i's with the corresponding secret-keys to get corresponding messages m_i. If all m_i's are equal, output m_1, else output $\perp$.

Proof. First, we show that an encryption scheme $\widetilde{\Pi}$, constructed from Π in the following way, meets the IND-CPA (respectively, IND-CCA1) definition (Proposition 1). $\widetilde{\Pi} = (\widetilde{\mathsf{Gen}}, \widetilde{\mathsf{Enc}}, \widetilde{\mathsf{Dec}})$ is constructed as follows:

1. $\widetilde{\mathsf{Gen}}$ runs k copies of Gen to generate public-keys $\widetilde{\text{PK}} = (\text{PK}_1, \text{PK}_2, \ldots, \text{PK}_k)$ and corresponding secret-keys $\widetilde{\text{SK}} = (\text{SK}_1, \text{SK}_2, \ldots, \text{SK}_k)$.
2. $\widetilde{\mathsf{Enc}}(m, \widetilde{\text{PK}})$ runs $\mathsf{Enc}(m, \text{PK}_i)$ for all $i \in [k]$, with independently chosen randomness, and outputs the vector of k encryptions $[c_1, c_2, \ldots, c_k]$.
3. $\widetilde{\mathsf{Dec}}(c, \widetilde{\text{SK}})$ parses c as $[c_1, c_2, \ldots, c_k]$. Let $m_i = \mathsf{Dec}(c_i, \text{SK}_i)$. If all the m_i are the same, output m_1. Otherwise, output $\perp$.

Secondly, in Proposition 2, we show that if $\widetilde{\Pi}$ is IND-CPA-secure (respectively, IND-CCA1-secure), then Π' is IND-NME-CPA-secure (resp., IND-NME-CCA1-secure). This proof appears in the full version.

Proposition 1. *If Π is IND-CPA-secure (or IND-CCA1-secure), then so is $\widetilde{\Pi}$.*

Proof. The proof is a straightforward hybrid argument. The only complication stems from the simulation of the oracle in the CCA1 case. When the adversary asks to decrypt a ciphertext $\hat{c} = (\hat{c}_1, \hat{c}_2, \ldots, \hat{c}_k)$, decrypt c_j using the secret-key SK_j (if $j \neq i$) and using the decryption oracle for PK_i (if $j = i$).

Proposition 2. *If $\widetilde{\Pi}$ is IND-CPA-secure (respectively, IND-CCA1-secure), then Π_L is IND-NME-secure (respectively, IND-NME-CCA1-secure).*

Claim. Π_L is not IND-NME'-secure under CPA and CCA1 single-message attacks.

Proof. We specify an adversary $A = (A_1, A_2)$ and a distinguisher D such that D distinguishes between $\{\text{IND-NME}_0'(\Pi, A, k, 1)\}$ and $\{\text{IND-NME}_1'(\Pi, A, k, 1)\}$. A works as follows:

1. A_1 outputs two arbitrary messages (m_0, m_1) and no state information.
2. On input ciphertext $c = [(e_1, \ldots, e_k), \text{VKSIG}, \sigma]$, let $\text{VKSIG} := b_1 b_2 \ldots b_k$. A_2 produces a new ciphertext c' as follows: A_2 generates a new signing key $(\text{SKSIG}', \text{VKSIG}')$. Let $\text{VKSIG}' := b'_1 b'_2 \ldots b'_k$. A_2 outputs ciphertext $c' = ((x_1, \ldots, x_k), \text{VKSIG}', \sigma')$ where

$$x_i = \begin{cases} e_i & \text{if } b'_i = b_i \\ E_{\text{PK}_i^{b'_i}}(m_0) & \text{otherwise} \end{cases}$$

and σ' is the signature of $(x_1, \ldots, x_k)$ under the signing key SKSIG'.

Notice that $\text{NME}_0(\Pi, A, k, 1) = m_0$ and $\text{NME}_1(\Pi, A, k, 1) = \perp$ which can be easily distinguished by a distinguisher D that outputs 0 on m_0 and 1 on $\perp$.

5   Additional Separations with Finite Message Spaces

Many encryption schemes such as El Gamal, RSA, Cramer-Shoup, and the league of schemes based on elliptic curves and bilinear maps only process messages from a finite message space such as the elements of some group G. In order to capture the security of such systems, Cramer and Shoup [CS98] redefine the encryption primitive to incorporate (a) a key-dependent message space M_{PK} and (b) a p.p.t. message tester algorithm $\mathcal{M}$ that on input 1^k, PK, α, determines whether α is an element of the message-space for the security parameter 1^k and the public key PK. The encryption algorithm $\text{Enc} : M_{\text{PK}} \rightarrow \{0, 1\}^*$ now takes an input message from M_{PK} and produces general bit strings, and the decryption algorithm maps $\{0, 1\}^*$ to $M_{\text{PK}} \cup \perp$. The correctness property is only required to hold over the message space.

In this section, however, we note that if the message space is finite, then the previously proven equivalence relationship between the weaker notions of SIM-NME and IND-NME no longer holds. While the particular counter-example that we use for the separation may seem contrived, this separation has practical significance since it runs against our "intuition" about IND-CCA2 security.

The idea behind this separation is as follows. We construct an encryption scheme whose message space includes three elements, $\{0, 1, \chi\}$ where χ is related to the public key PK. Moreover, we make it difficult for an adversary to learn χ unless it has a decryption oracle (notice, the definition for finite message space only requires the message space to be easily decidable, but does not require it to be enumerable.[8]) From this point, the argument is the same. Namely, an adversary with an oracle can produce a (valid) ciphertext decrypting to χ (therefore it is a valid adversary), whereas the simulator can only produce ciphertexts decrypting to 0 or 1. The subtle difference between this argument and

---

[8] One could require enumerability of the message space. However, it is unclear such a restriction helps; and it is clear that it needlessly prevents us from using more exotic algebraic structures for encryption.

the one from §4 is that in this one, it is not the simulator's inability to produce a ciphertext which decrypts to ⊥, but rather its inability to *learn a special
message in the message space* which provides the separation. In the full message
case, there are *no* such special messages since any string can be encrypted. This
is the reason that the separation can be extended to valid adversaries.

Let (Gen, Enc, Dec) be an IND-NME-secure encryption scheme for general message spaces, and let f be a one-way permutation.[9]

FINITE MESSAGE SPACE ENCRYPTION SCHEME Γ

$\mathsf{Gen}'(1^k)$: Run $\mathsf{Gen}(1^k)$ to generate a key pair (PK, SK). Pick k-bit random string
α and compute $\beta = f(\alpha)$. Set SK$' = ($SK$, \alpha)$ and PK$' = ($PK$, \beta)$. The message
tester $\mathcal{M}(m)$ works as follows: if $m \in \{0, 1\}$ or if $f(m) = \beta$, then return 1.
Otherwise, return 0. (The messages space consists of $\{0, 1, \alpha\}$.)

$\mathsf{Enc}'(m, PK')$: if $\mathcal{M}(m) = 0$, return an error. Otherwise, run $c \leftarrow \mathsf{Enc}(PK, m)$ and
return $(1, c)$.

$\mathsf{Dec}'(c', SK')$: Parse c' as (b, c), and SK$'$ as (SK, α). If $b = 0$ then output α. Otherwise, output $m \leftarrow \mathsf{Dec}(SK, c)$.

IND-NME security of the above finite-message space encryption scheme directly follows from the security of (Gen, Enc, Dec). In order to violate SIM-NME,
the adversary B must be non-aborting. Therefore, the final ciphertext it produces
must be in the range of the Enc function (i.e., of the form $(1, c)$). Combined with
the one-wayness of f, a simulator not having access to a decryption oracle will
not be able to construct a *valid* encryption to the message α.

However, a CCA1 attacker can easily do so by first querying $(0, 0)$ to find α
(notice that the attacker can *query* the oracle on invalid ciphertexts, but cannot
produce them as final output), and then honestly encrypting α.

6   Special Cases for Equivalence

The separation between SIM-NME$'$ and IND-NME$'$ hinged on the fact that the
set of messages for which one can efficiently compute a ciphertext and the range
of the decryption procedure differ. When these two sets are made to coincide, a
scheme that is IND-NME$'$ secure is also SIM-NME$'$-secure. Thus, we provide an
easy way to prove that a scheme meets the strongest notion of non-malleability.
As a corollary, we get that the main construction of [DDN00] achieves the
strongest form of security – that is SIM-NME$'$-security against CCA2 attacks.

Theorem 6. *Any (finite message-space) encryption scheme Π which meets the
IND-NME definition and for which there is an efficient algorithm F, which on
input (PK, d) where d is a string in the range of Dec, produces a ciphertext c
such that $d \leftarrow \mathsf{Dec}(SK, c)$, also meets the SIM-NME$'$ definition.*

---

[9] In fact a one-way function would suffice. We only use a permutation for ease of
exposition.

This restriction could easily be added to many schemes by taking the message space to be some set $\{0,1\}^{\ell(k)}$ for all keys generated by $\mathsf{Gen}(1^k)$ (and by making it easy to generate invalid ciphertext). We note that the RSA-OAEP padding scheme does exactly this.

7   Composition: Many Message Security

In [PSV06], the authors show that IND-NME' security under CPA attacks composes. That is, if an encryption scheme is IND-NME'-secure when the adversary receives one encryption, it will also be IND-NME'-secure in a situation in which the adversary receives many encryptions.

A natural question is whether the same phenomena occurs under stronger CCA1 and CCA2 attacks. In this section, we answer affirmatively as described in the following theorem.

Theorem 7. *A scheme Π meets IND-NME' under attack ATK iff it meets single-message IND-NME' under attack ATK.*

Proof Sketch: The forward implication follows directly. For the reverse direction, we present a routine hybrid argument that uses an adversary $(A_1, A_2), D$ with advantage ϵ to construct a new adversary $(A_1', A_2'), D$ which breaks the single-message security with advantage η/ℓ^2.

Define a new experiment $\mathsf{IND\text{-}NME}'_{(b_1,\ldots,b_\ell)}(\Pi, A, k, \ell)$ indexed by an ℓ-bit string $(b_1, \ldots, b_\ell)$ which is the same as $\mathsf{IND\text{-}NME}'_0(\Pi, A, k, \ell)$ except in the fourth line (change is underlined): $y_i \leftarrow \mathsf{Enc}(\underline{\mathrm{PK}, m_{b_i,i}})$ for $i \in [1, \ell]$. Define

$$B(i) = (\overbrace{0,\ldots,0}^{l-i}, \overbrace{1,\ldots,1}^{i})$$

and note that $\mathsf{IND\text{-}NME}'_0 = \mathsf{IND\text{-}NME}'_{B(0)}$ and $\mathsf{IND\text{-}NME}'_1 = \mathsf{IND\text{-}NME}'_{B(\ell)}$. Because D distinguishes $\mathsf{IND\text{-}NME}'_0$ from $\mathsf{IND\text{-}NME}'_1$, there exists some $g^* \in [1, \ell]$ such that D distinguishes $\mathsf{IND\text{-}NME}'_{B(g^*)}$ from $\mathsf{IND\text{-}NME}'_{B(g^*+1)}$ with advantage η/ℓ. This suggests the following adversary: $A_1'^O(\mathrm{PK})$ guesses value $g \in [1, \ell]$ and runs $A_1(\mathrm{PK})$—answering any decryption queries by using its own decryption oracle—and waits to receive the two vector of messages $(m_{0,1}, \ldots, m_{0,\ell})$ and $(m_{1,1}, \ldots, m_{1,\ell})$. Finally, A' outputs $(m_{0,g}, m_{1,g})$ as its challenge pair and outputs state information containing g and m_0, m_1.

Adversary $A_2'^O(y, \mathrm{STATE}')$, on input an encryption y, first executes the replaced line 4 of experiment $\mathsf{IND\text{-}NME}'_{B(g)}$ (described above) with the exception that it uses y for the $(g+1)$th encryption: $y_{g+1} \leftarrow y$. This is possible because it receives the messages vectors m_0 and m_1 in STATE'.

It then feeds the resulting vector of ciphertexts y to A_2 to produce another vector of ciphertexts $(c_1, \ldots, c_\ell)$ and uses this vector as its own output. To answer any oracle query c from A_2, A_2' uses the following procedure: If $c = y_j$ for any $j \in [1, \ell]$, then return $\perp$. Otherwise, it uses its own decryption oracle to decrypt c and answers with the returned message.

Notice that $\mathsf{IND\text{-}NME}'_0(A'_1, A'_2)$ and $\mathsf{IND\text{-}NME}'_{B(g^*)}(A_1, A_2)$ are *syntactically* the same, as are $\mathsf{IND\text{-}NME}'_1(A'_1, A'_2)$ and $\mathsf{IND\text{-}NME}'_{B(g^*+1)}(A_1, A_2)$. Because A' guesses g^* correctly with probability $1/\ell$, D's overall advantage in breaking the single-message non-malleability is η/ℓ^2. $\qquad\qquad\square$

One can see here the importance of removing the "valid adversary" restriction for the hybrid argument to work. This follows because the reduction feeds a hybrid distribution to A_2 and, *even if A_2 is itself a valid adversary* for the multi-message experiment, A_2 may produce invalid ciphertexts when it is fed a *hybrid* distribution. Moreover, these $\perp$ values may form the basis for distinguishability in the hybrid experiment. Thus, one cannot guarantee that valid adversaries for the multi-message experiment can be transformed into valid adversaries for the single-message experiment. The separation in Claim 4.1 exploits this issue.[10]

SIM-NME and IND-NME Do Not Compose Against CCA1 or CPA Attacks

We now show that (if there exist SIM-NME-secure encryption schemes) there is an encryption scheme Π' that is SIM-NME or IND-NME-secure when the adversary is given *one* ciphertext as the challenge, but there is an adversary A' that completely breaks the IND-NME-security of Π' when given *polynomially many* ciphertexts as challenge.

The encryption scheme Π' is simply the encryption scheme constructed in the proof of Thm. 5 (relying on the DDNLite construction). Thm. 5 showed that Π_L is 1-message IND-NME-secure (and therefore 1-message SIM-NME-secure). The many-message attack against Π' is a simple *covering attack*. (We mention that Gennaro and Lindell [GL03] pointed out that the DDNLite encryption scheme is not secure under under many messages. Although they did not include a description of the attack, we believe they had a similar attack in mind.)

Recall that an encryption of a message m under Π' consists of many encryptions of m with respect to a randomly chosen set of k (out of $2k$) public-keys. Given many (roughly $k \log k$) independent encryptions of m, the one can essentially recover an encryption of m under *all* the $2k$ public-keys. This will enable us to construct a completely new encryption of m, and thus break IND-NME' security.

Theorem 8. *Let* atk $\in \{\mathsf{CPA}, \mathsf{CCA1}\}$. *If there exists an encryption scheme that is* IND-atk *secure, then there exists another encryption scheme Π' that is 1-message* IND-NME-atk-*secure (respectively* SIM-NME-atk-*secure), but is not even* IND-NME-CPA-*secure (respectively,* SIM-NME-CPA-*secure).*

Proof. Omitted

---

[10] This argument also applies to a different interpretation of "valid adversary" in which one forces the single-message experiment to return 0 when invalid ciphertexts are produced. In this case, when A_2 produces invalid ciphertexts in the hybrid experiments, the value of both hybrid experiments ($b = 0, 1$) will be 0 and the weaker definition will thus be met *even though* there might still be a distinguisher which could have distinguished the output of A'_2.

SIM-NME and IND-NME Compose Under CCA2 Attacks

Theorem 9. *If an encryption scheme Π is 1-message* IND-NME-CCA2-*secure, then it is many-message* IND-NME-CCA2-*secure.*

The proof of this theorem follows from Theorem 2, which shows that under CCA2 attacks, IND-NME and SIM-NME definitions coincide with the IND-NME' definition, and Theorem 7 which shows that IND-NME' composes under a many-message attack.

Acknowledgments. We would like to thank one of the anonymous Crypto referees for thorough and helpful comments.

References

[BDPR98] Bellare, M., Desai, A., Pointcheval, D., Rogaway, P.: Relations among notions of security for public key encryption schemes. In: Krawczyk, H. (ed.) CRYPTO 1998. LNCS, vol. 1462, Springer, Heidelberg (1998)

[BS99] Bellare, M., Sahai, A.: Non-malleable encryption: Equivalence between two notions, and an indistinguishability-based characterization. In: Wiener, M.J. (ed.) CRYPTO 1999. LNCS, vol. 1666, pp. 519–536. Springer, Heidelberg (1999)

[BS06] Bellare, M., Sahai, A.: Non-malleable encryption: Equivalence between two notions, and an indistinguishability-based characterization (2006), http://eprint.iacr.org/2006/228

[Can01] Canetti, R.: Universally composable security: A new paradigm for cryptographic protocols. In: FOCS, pp. 136–145 (2001)

[CS98] Cramer, R., Shoup, V.: A practical public key cryptosystem provably secure against adaptive chosen ciphertext attack. In: Krawczyk, H. (ed.) CRYPTO 1998. LNCS, vol. 1462, pp. 13–25. Springer, Heidelberg (1998)

[DDN00] Dolev, D., Dwork, C., Naor, M.: Nonmalleable cryptography. SIAM J. Comput. 30(2), 391–437 (2000)

[Dwo99] Dwork, C.: The non-malleability lectures. Course notes for Stanford CS 359 (1999), http://theory.stanford.edu/~{g}durf/cs359-s99/

[GL03] Gennaro, R., Lindell, Y.: A framework for password-based authenticated key exchange. In: Biham, E. (ed.) Advances in Cryptology – EUROCRPYT 2003. LNCS, vol. 2656, pp. 524–543. Springer, Heidelberg (2003)

[GM84] Goldwasser, S., Micali, S.: Probabilistic encryption. J. Comput. Syst. Sci. 28(2), 270–299 (1984)

[Gol04] Goldreich, O.: Foundations of Cryptography, vol. 2. Cambridge University Press, Cambridge (2004)

[Nao04] Naor, M.: A taxonomy of encryption scheme security (2004)

[PSV06] Pass, R., Shelat, A., Vaikuntanathan, V.: Construction of a non-malleable encryption scheme from a any semantically secure one. In: Dwork, C. (ed.) CRYPTO 2006. LNCS, vol. 4117, Springer, Heidelberg (2006)

Cryptanalysis of the Tiger Hash Function[*]

Florian Mendel and Vincent Rijmen

Institute for Applied Information Processing and Communications (IAIK),
Graz University of Technology, Inffeldgasse 16a, A-8010 Graz, Austria
{Florian.Mendel,Vincent.Rijmen}@iaik.tugraz.at

Abstract. Tiger is a cryptographic hash function with a 192-bit hash
value. It was proposed by Anderson and Biham in 1996. Recently, weaknesses have been shown in round-reduced variants of the Tiger hash
function. First, at FSE 2006, Kelsey and Lucks presented a collision
attack on Tiger reduced to 16 and 17 (out of 24) rounds with a complexity of about 2^{44} and a pseudo-near-collision for Tiger reduced to 20
rounds. Later, Mendel *et al.* extended this attack to a collision attack on
Tiger reduced to 19 rounds with a complexity of about 2^{62}. Furthermore,
they show a pseudo-near-collision for Tiger reduced to 22 rounds with
a complexity of about 2^{44}. No attack is known for the full Tiger hash
function.

In this article, we show a pseudo-near-collision for the full Tiger hash
function with a complexity of about 2^{47} hash computations and a pseudo-
collision (free-start-collision) for Tiger reduced to 23 rounds with the
same complexity.

Keywords: Cryptanalysis, hash functions, differential attack, collision,
near-collision, pseudo-collision, pseudo-near-collision.

1   Introduction

Tiger is a cryptographic iterated hash function that processes 512-bit blocks and
produces a 192-bit hash value. It was proposed by Anderson and Biham in 1996.
Recent results in the cryptanalysis of Tiger show weaknesses in round-reduced
variants of the hash function. At FSE 2006, Kelsey and Lucks presented a collision attack on 16 and 17 (out of 24) rounds of Tiger. The attack has a complexity
of about 2^{44} evaluations of the compression function. Furthermore, they present
a pseudo-near-collision for a variant of Tiger reduced to 20 rounds with a complexity of about 2^{48}. These results were later improved by Mendel *et al.* in [3].
They show that a collision can be found for Tiger reduced to 19 rounds with a
complexity of about 2^{62} evaluations of the compression function. Furthermore,
they present a pseudo-near-collision for Tiger reduced to 22 rounds with a complexity of about 2^{44}. However, so far no attack is known for the full Tiger hash
function.

[*] The work in this paper has been supported by the Austrian Science Fund (FWF),
project P18138.

K. Kurosawa (Ed.): ASIACRYPT 2007, LNCS 4833, pp. 536–550, 2007.

In this article, we present a 1-bit circular pseudo-near-collision for the full Tiger hash function with a complexity of about 2^{47} hash computations and a pseudo-collision (free-start-collision) for a variant of Tiger reduced to 23 rounds with the same complexity. The attack is based on previous attacks presented in [2] and [3]. Note that in the attacks of Kelsey and Lucks and Mendel *et al.* on round-reduced variants of Tiger, the S-boxes of the hash function are addressed wrongly (big endian instead of little endian). However, this error can be fixed easily, because there is really a large amount of freedom in these attacks on round-reduced variants of Tiger.

The remainder of this article is structured as follows. A description of the Tiger hash function is given in Section 2. In Section 3, we describe the basic attack strategy on Tiger based on the work of Kelsey and Lucks on round-reduced Tiger. We follow this attack strategy in Section 4 to construct a 1-bit circular pseudo-near-collision for Tiger with a complexity of about 2^{47}. In Section 5, we show a pseudo-collision for Tiger reduced to 23 rounds with the same complexity. Finally, we present conclusions in Section 6.

2   Description of the Hash Function Tiger

Tiger is a cryptographic hash function that was designed by Anderson and Biham in 1996 [1]. It is an iterative hash function that processes 512-bit input message blocks and produces a 192-bit hash value. In the following, we briefly describe the hash function. It basically consists of two parts: the key schedule and the state update transformation. A detailed description of the hash function is given in [1]. For the remainder of this article, we will follow the notation given in Table 1.

Table 1. Notation

Notation	Meaning
$A \boxplus B$	addition of A and B modulo 2^{64}
$A \boxminus B$	subtraction of A and B modulo 2^{64}
$A \boxtimes B$	multiplication of A and B modulo 2^{64}
$A \oplus B$	bit-wise XOR-operation of A and B
$\neg A$	bit-wise NOT-operation of A
$A \ll n$	bit-shift of A by n positions to the left
$A \gg n$	bit-shift of A by n positions to the right
X_i	message word i (64 bits)
$X_i[\text{even}]$	the even bytes of message word X_i (32 bits)
$X_i[\text{odd}]$	the odd bytes of message word X_i (32 bits)

2.1   State Update Transformation

The state update transformation of Tiger starts from a (fixed) initial value IV of three 64-bit words and updates them in three passes of eight rounds each. In each round one 64-bit word X is used to update the three state variables A, B and C as follows:

$$C = C \oplus X$$
$$A = A \boxminus \mathbf{even}(C)$$
$$B = B \boxplus \mathbf{odd}(C)$$
$$B = B \boxtimes \mathtt{mult}$$

The results are then shifted such that A, B, C become B, C, A. Fig. 1 shows one round of the state update transformation of Tiger.

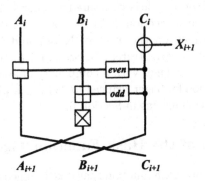

Fig. 1. The round function of Tiger

The non-linear functions **even** and **odd** used in each round are defined as follows:

$$\mathbf{even}(C) = T_1[c_0] \oplus T_2[c_2] \oplus T_3[c_4] \oplus T_4[c_6]$$
$$\mathbf{odd}(C) = T_4[c_1] \oplus T_3[c_3] \oplus T_2[c_5] \oplus T_1[c_7]$$

where state variable C is split into eight bytes $c_7, \ldots, c_0$ with c_7 is the most significant byte (and not c_0). Four S-boxes $T_1, \ldots, T_4 : \{0,1\}^8 \to \{0,1\}^{64}$ are used to compute the output of the non-linear functions **even** and **odd**. For the definition of the S-boxes we refer to [1]. Note that state variable B is multiplied with the constant $\mathtt{mult} \in \{5,7,9\}$ at the end of each round. The value of the constant is different in each pass of the Tiger hash function.

After the last round of the state update transformation, the initial values A_{-1}, B_{-1}, C_{-1} and the output values of the last round A_{23}, B_{23}, C_{23} are combined, resulting in the final value of one iteration (feed forward). The result is the final hash value or the initial value for the next message block.

$$A_{24} = A_{-1} \oplus A_{23}$$
$$B_{24} = B_{-1} \boxminus B_{23}$$
$$C_{24} = C_{-1} \boxplus C_{23}$$

2.2   Key Schedule

The key schedule is an invertible function which ensures that changing a small number of bits in the message will affect a lot of bits in the next pass. While the message words $X_0, \ldots, X_7$ are used in the first pass to update the state variables, the remaining 16 message words, 8 for the second pass and 8 for the third pass, are generated by applying the key schedule as follows:

$$(X_8, \ldots, X_{15}) = \text{KeySchedule}(X_0, \ldots, X_7)$$
$$(X_{16}, \ldots, X_{23}) = \text{KeySchedule}(X_8, \ldots, X_{15})$$

The key schedule modifies the inputs $(Y_0, \ldots, Y_7)$ in two steps:

first step

$$Y_0 = Y_0 \boxminus (Y_7 \oplus \text{A5A5A5A5A5A5A5A5})$$
$$Y_1 = Y_1 \oplus Y_0$$
$$Y_2 = Y_2 \boxplus Y_1$$
$$Y_3 = Y_3 \boxminus (Y_2 \oplus ((\neg Y_1) \ll 19))$$
$$Y_4 = Y_4 \oplus Y_3$$
$$Y_5 = Y_5 \boxplus Y_4$$
$$Y_6 = Y_6 \boxminus (Y_5 \oplus ((\neg Y_4) \gg 23))$$
$$Y_7 = Y_7 \oplus Y_6$$

second step

$$Y_0 = Y_0 \boxplus Y_7$$
$$Y_1 = Y_1 \boxminus (Y_0 \oplus ((\neg Y_7) \ll 19))$$
$$Y_2 = Y_2 \oplus Y_1$$
$$Y_3 = Y_3 \boxplus Y_2$$
$$Y_4 = Y_4 \boxminus (Y_3 \oplus ((\neg Y_2) \gg 23))$$
$$Y_5 = Y_5 \oplus Y_4$$
$$Y_6 = Y_6 \boxplus Y_5$$
$$Y_7 = Y_7 \boxminus (Y_6 \oplus \text{0123456789ABCDEF})$$

The final values $(Y_0, \ldots, Y_7)$ are the output of the key schedule and the message words for the next pass.

3   Basic Attack Strategy

In this section, we briefly describe the attack strategy of Kelsey and Lucks to attack round-reduced variants of the Tiger hash function. A detailed description of the attack is given in [2]. For a good understanding of our attack it is recommended to study it carefully. The attack can be summarized as follows.

1. Find a characteristic for the key schedule of Tiger which holds with high probability. In the ideal case this probability is 1.
2. Use a kind of message modification technique developed for Tiger to construct certain differences in the state variables, which can then be canceled by the differences of the message words in the following rounds.

These two steps of the attack are described in detail in the following sections.

3.1   Finding a Good Characteristic for the Key Schedule of Tiger

To find a good characteristic for the key schedule of Tiger, we use a linearized model of the key schedule. Therefore, we replace all modular additions and subtractions by an XOR operation resulting in a linear code over $GF(2)$. Finding a characteristic in the linear code is not difficult, since it depends only on the differences in the message words. The probability that the characteristic holds in the original key schedule of Tiger is related to the Hamming weight of the characteristic. In general, a characteristic with low Hamming weight has a higher probability than one with a high Hamming weight.

For finding a characteristic with high probability (low Hamming weight), we use probabilistic algorithms from coding theory. It has been shown in the past (cryptanalysis of SHA-1 [4]) that these algorithms work quite well. Furthermore, we can impose additional restrictions on the characteristic by forcing certain bits/words to zero. Note that this is needed to find suitable characteristics for the key schedule of Tiger. For an attack on the Tiger hash function we need many zeros in the first and last rounds of the hash function.

3.2   Message Modification by Meet-in-the-Middle

In order to construct a collision in Tiger reduced to 16 rounds, Kelsey and Lucks use a message modification technique developed for Tiger. The idea of message modification in general is to use the degree of freedom one has in the choice of the message words to fulfill conditions on the state variables. In the attack on Tiger this method is used to construct a certain differential pattern in the state variables, which can then be canceled by the differences of the message words in the following rounds. This leads to a collision in a round reduced variant of Tiger. In the following we will briefly describe this message modification technique according to Fig. 2.

Assume, we are given A_{i-1}, B_{i-1}, C_{i-1} and A_{i-1}^*, B_{i-1}^*, C_{i-1}^* as well as $\Delta^\oplus(X_i)$ and $\Delta^\oplus(X_{i+1})$. Then the modular difference $\Delta^\boxplus(C_{i+1})$ can be forced to be any difference δ with a probability of 2^{-1} by using a birthday attack. We try out all 2^{32} possibilities for $X_{i-1}[\text{odd}]$ to generate 2^{32} candidates for $\Delta^\boxplus(\text{odd}(B_i))$. Similarly, we try out all $X_i[\text{even}]$ to generate 2^{32} candidates for $\Delta^\boxplus(\text{even}(B_{i+1}))$. Subsequently, we use a meet-in-the-middle approach to solve the following equation:

$$\Delta^\boxplus(C_{i+1}) = \texttt{mult} \boxtimes [\Delta^\boxplus(B_{i-1}) \boxplus \Delta^\boxplus(\text{odd}(B_i))] \boxminus \Delta^\boxplus(\text{even}(B_{i+1})) = \delta \ . \quad (1)$$

The method can be summarized as follows:

1. Store the 2^{32} candidates for $\Delta^\boxplus(\text{odd}(B_i))$ in a table.
2. For all 2^{32} candidates for $\Delta^\boxplus(\text{even}(B_{i+1}))$, test if some $\Delta^\boxplus(\text{odd}(B_i))$ exists in the table with

$$\Delta^\boxplus(\text{odd}(B_i)) = (\Delta^\boxplus(\text{even}(B_{i+1})) \boxplus \delta) \boxtimes \texttt{mult}^{-1} \boxminus \Delta^\boxplus(B_{i-1}) \ .$$

This technique needs about 2^{36} bytes of storage and takes 2^{33} evaluations of each of the functions **odd** and **even**. This is equivalent to about 2^{29} evaluations of the compression function of Tiger.

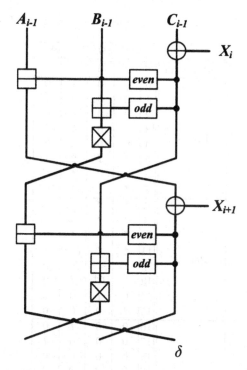

Fig. 2. Message Modification by Meet-in-the-Middle

4   A Pseudo-near-collision for Tiger

In this section, we will present a 1-bit circular pseudo-near-collision for the Tiger hash function. Note that the difference in the final hash value is the same as in the initial value. In other words, we have a pseudo-collision in the compression function of Tiger after 24 rounds, but due to the feed forward the collision after 24 rounds is destroyed, resulting in a 1-bit pseudo-near-collision for the Tiger hash function. The attack has a complexity of about 2^{47} evaluations of the compression function. In the attack, we extend techniques invented by Kelsey and Lucks in the attack on round-reduced variants of Tiger.

We use the characteristic given below for the key schedule of Tiger to construct the pseudo-near-collision in the hash function. This characteristic holds with a probability of 2^{-1} which facilitates the attack.

$$(0, I, 0, 0, 0, I, I', 0) \rightarrow (0, I, 0, I, 0, 0, 0, 0) \rightarrow (0, I, 0, 0, 0, 0, 0, 0) \quad (2)$$

I denotes a difference in the MSB of the message word and $I' := I \gg 23$. Note that the XOR-difference (denoted by $\Delta^{\oplus}$) equals I if and only if the modular difference (denoted by $\Delta^{\boxplus}$) equals I.

In order to have a pseudo-collision in the compression function of Tiger after 24 rounds, it is required that there is a pseudo-collision after round 17. Hence,

Table 2. Characteristic for a 1-bit pseudo-near-collision in the Tiger hash function

	i	ΔA_i	ΔB_i	ΔC_i	ΔX_i
initial value	-1	I	0	0	
	0	0	0	I	0
	1	0	0	0	I
	2	0	0	0	0
Pass 1	3	0	0	0	0
	4	0	0	0	0
	5	*	I	0	I
	6	*	I'	*	I'
	7	*	*	*	0
	8	*	*	*	0
	9	*	*	*	I
	10	*	*	*	0
Pass 2	11	*	*	$K^\oplus$	I
	12	*	K^+	$L^\oplus$	0
	13	0	L^+	I	0
	14	0	I	0	0
	15	I	0	0	0
	16	0	0	I	0
	17	0	0	0	I
	18	0	0	0	0
Pass 3	19	0	0	0	0
	20	0	0	0	0
	21	0	0	0	0
	22	0	0	0	0
	23	0	0	0	0
feed forward	24	I	0	0	

the following differences are needed in the state variables for round 14 of Tiger (see Table 2).

$$\Delta^\oplus(A_{14}) = 0, \quad \Delta^\oplus(B_{14}) = I, \quad \Delta^\oplus(C_{14}) = 0 \tag{3}$$

Constructing these differences in the state variables for round 14 is the most difficult part of the attack. We use the message modification technique described in Section 3.2 for this. In the following sections, we will describe all steps of the attack in detail.

4.1   Precomputation

The precomputation step basically consists of 2 parts. First, we have to find a set $\mathcal{L}$ of *possible* modular differences L^+ which are consistent to a low weight XOR-difference $L^\oplus$. A modular difference L^+ is consistent to $L^\oplus$ if there exist p and p^* such that $p^* \oplus p = L^\oplus$ and $p^* \boxminus p = L^+$. Let $\mathcal{L}'$ be the set of modular differences L^+ which are consistent to the XOR-difference $L^\oplus$ then we define the set $\mathcal{L}$ of *possible* modular differences as follows:

$$\mathcal{L} = \{L^+ \in \mathcal{L}' :\ L^+ = \mathbf{odd}(B_{14} \oplus I) \boxminus \mathbf{odd}(B_{14})\}$$

Note that the size of the set $\mathcal{L}'$ is related to the Hamming weight of $L^\oplus$, namely $|\mathcal{L}'| = 2^{\mathrm{HW}(L^\oplus)}$. In order to optimize the complexity of the meet-in-the-middle step used in the attack, we need an $L^\oplus$ with low Hamming weight. In [2], the authors assume that an $L^\oplus$ with Hamming weight of 8 exists. However, the best Hamming weight we found for $L^\oplus$ is 10.

$$L^\oplus = \mathtt{02201080A4020104} \tag{4}$$

In total we found $502 = |\mathcal{L}|$ *possible* modular differences (out of $1024 = |\mathcal{L}'|$) which are consistent to the XOR-difference $L^\oplus$ given above. This facilitates the attack in the following steps.

Second, we need a set $\mathcal{K}$ of *possible* modular differences K^+ which are consistent to a low weight XOR-difference $K^\oplus$.

$$\mathcal{K} = \{K^+ \in \mathcal{K}' :\ K^+ = \mathbf{odd}(B_{13} \oplus L^\oplus) \boxminus \mathbf{odd}(B_{13})\}$$

where $\mathcal{K}'$ is the set of modular differences K^+ which are consistent to the XOR-difference $K^\oplus$. Of course, the choice of $L^\oplus$ and the number of possible modular differences $L^+ \in \mathcal{L}$ restricts our choices for $B_{13}[\mathbf{odd}]$. Nevertheless, we found $2 = |\mathcal{K}|$ possible modular differences K^+ (out of $256 = |\mathcal{K}'|$) which are consistent to the XOR-difference $K^\oplus$ given below.

$$K^\oplus = \mathtt{0880020019000900} \tag{5}$$

Note that the precomputation step of the attack has to be done only once. It has a complexity of about $2 \cdot 2^{32}$ round computations of Tiger. This is approximately about $2^{28.5}$ evaluations of the compression function of Tiger.

4.2   Compute B_9, C_9, and C_{10}

In this step of the attack, we have to compute B_9, C_9 and C_{10}. Therefore, we first choose random values for B_4 and B_5 and compute $A_5 = (B_4 \boxplus \mathbf{odd}(B_5)) \boxtimes \mathbf{mult}$. Since there is a difference in the MSB of X_5 and no differences in B_4 and C_4, we also get $\Delta^\boxplus(B_5) = I$ and $\Delta^\boxplus(A_5) = A_5^* \boxminus A_5$. Note that there is no difference in C_5, since there are no differences in A_4 and $B_5[\mathbf{even}]$.

Second, we choose a random value for B_6. Since there is a difference in $\Delta^\oplus(X_6) = I'$ and no difference in C_5, we also know the modular difference of $\Delta^\boxplus(B_6) = (B_6 \oplus I') \boxminus B_6$. Once we know B_6 and $B_6^* = B_6 \boxplus \Delta^\boxplus(B_6)$, we can calculate B_9, C_9, C_{10} (and B_9^*, C_9^*, C_{10}^*) by choosing random values for $X_7, \ldots, X_9$ and $X_{10}[\mathbf{even}]$. This step of the attack has a complexity of about 12 round computations of Tiger and fixes the message words $X_7, \ldots, X_9$ and $X_{10}[\mathbf{even}]$.

4.3   Constructing the XOR-Difference $\Delta^\oplus(C_{11}) = K^\oplus$

To construct the XOR-difference $K^\oplus$ in round 11, we use the message modification technique described in Section 3.2. For all modular differences $K^+ \in \mathcal{K}'$, we do a message modification step and check if $\Delta^\oplus(C_{11}) = K^\oplus$. Since the Hamming weight of $K^\oplus$ is 8, this holds with a probability of 2^{-8}. Furthermore, the message modification step has a probability of 2^{-1}. Hence, this step of the attack succeeds with a probability of $2^{-8} \cdot 2^{-1} \cdot |\mathcal{K}'| = 2^{-1}$ and determines the message words $X_{10}[\text{odd}]$ and $X_{11}[\text{even}]$.

Finishing this step of the attack has a complexity of about $(12 + 2^{32} + 2^8 \cdot 2^{32}) \cdot 2 \approx 2^{41}$ round computations of Tiger. This is approximately about $2^{36.5}$ evaluations of the compression function of Tiger.

4.4   Constructing the XOR-Difference $\Delta^\oplus(C_{12}) = L^\oplus$

Once we have fixed $X_{10}[\text{odd}]$ and $X_{11}[\text{even}]$, we can calculate the state variables B_{10}, C_{10}, C_{11} (and B_{10}^*, C_{10}^*, C_{11}^*). To construct $L^\oplus$ in round 12, we use the same method as described before. For all modular differences $L^+ \in \mathcal{L}'$, we do a message modification step and check if $\Delta^\oplus(C_{12}) = L^\oplus$. Since the Hamming weight of $L^\oplus$ is 10, this equation holds with a probability of 2^{-10}. Hence, this step of the attack has a probability of $2^{-10} \cdot 2^{-1} \cdot |\mathcal{L}'| = 2^{-1}$ and determines the message words $X_{11}[\text{odd}]$ and $X_{12}[\text{even}]$. Finishing this step of the attack has a complexity of about $(2^{41} + (2^{32} + 2^{32} \cdot 2^{10})) \cdot 2 \approx 2^{43.6}$ round computations of Tiger. This is approximately about 2^{39} evaluations of the compression function of Tiger.

4.5   Constructing the XOR-Difference $\Delta^\oplus(C_{13}) = I$

Once we have fixed $X_{11}[\text{odd}]$ and $X_{12}[\text{even}]$, we can compute B_{11}, C_{11} and C_{12} as well as the according modular differences. In order to construct the needed difference $\Delta^\oplus(A_{13}) = I$ in round 13, we apply again a message modification step. Since the XOR-difference and the modular difference is the same for differences in the MSB, we do not need to compute the list of modular differences that are consistent to the XOR-difference I for the message modification step. This step of the attack succeeds with a probability of 2^{-1} and determines the message words $X_{12}[\text{odd}]$ and $X_{13}[\text{even}]$.

Once we have fixed the message words, we can compute B_{12}, C_{12} and C_{13} as well as the according modular differences. In order to guarantee that $\Delta^\boxplus(B_{12})$ can be canceled by $\Delta^\boxplus(\text{odd}(B_{13}))$, we need that $\Delta^\boxplus(B_{12}) \in \mathcal{K}$. Since the number of modular differences $\Delta^\boxplus(B_{12}) = K^+$ consistent to $K^\oplus$ is $|\mathcal{K}'| = 2^8$ and $|\mathcal{K}| = 2$, the probability that $\Delta^\boxplus(B_{12}) \in \mathcal{K}$ is 2^{-7}. Hence, we have to repeat the attack about $2 \cdot 2^7$ times to finish this step of the attack. This determines the message words $X_{12}[\text{odd}]$, $X_{13}[\text{even}]$ and $X_{13}[\text{odd}]$ and has a complexity of about $(2^{43.6} + (2^{32} + 2^{32})) \cdot 2^8 \approx 2^{51.6}$ round computations of Tiger. This is about 2^{47} evaluations of the compression function of Tiger.

Once we have fixed $X_{13}[\text{odd}]$ and X_{13}, we can compute A_{13}, B_{13} and C_{13} as well as the according modular differences. In order to guarantee that $\Delta^\boxplus(B_{13})$ can be canceled in round 14 by $\Delta^\boxplus(\text{odd}(B_{14}))$, we need that $\Delta^\boxplus(B_{13}) \in \mathcal{L}$. Due to the choice of $L^\oplus$ and $K^\oplus$ in the precomputation step this holds with probability 1.

Hence, we can construct a pseudo-collision in the compression function of Tiger after 17 rounds, respectively after 24 rounds with a complexity close to 2^{47} evaluations of the compression function of Tiger.

4.6 Computing the Message Words $X_0, \ldots, X_7$

The attack fixes the message words $X_7, \ldots, X_{13}$ and $X_{14}[\text{odd}]$. To compute the message words $X_0, \ldots, X_7$ we use the inverse key schedule of Tiger. Therefore, we choose a random value for $X_{14}[\text{even}]$ and compute X_{15} as follows:

$$X_{15} = (X_7 \oplus (X_{14} \boxminus X_{13})) \boxminus (X_{14} \oplus \text{0123456789ABCDEF})$$

This guarantees that X_7 is correct after computing the key schedule backward.

Since the characteristic we use for the key schedule of Tiger has a probability 2^{-1} to hold, we expect that we have to repeat this step of the attack (for a different value of $X_{14}[\text{even}]$) about two times such that the characteristic holds in the key schedule of Tiger. This adds negligible cost to the attack complexity.

4.7 Computing the Initial Value IV

Once we have computed the message words $X_0, \ldots, X_7$, we can run the rounds $6, 5, \ldots, 0$ backwards to get the initial value IV. Since there is a difference I induced in round 1 by X_1, we have to inject the same difference in the initial value to cancel it out, namely

$$\Delta^{\oplus}(A_{-1}) = I .$$

Since the difference is in the MSB, this happens with probability 1. Of course, the feed forward destroys the pseudo-collision. After the feed forward we get the same output differences as in the initial values.

$$\Delta^{\oplus}(A_{24}) = \Delta^{\oplus}(A_{-1} \oplus A_{23}) = I$$

Hence, we get a 1-bit circular pseudo-near-collision for the Tiger hash function with a complexity of about 2^{47} evaluations of the compression function of Tiger. Note that for an ideal hash function with a hash value of 192-bit one would expect a complexity of about 2^{90} to construct a pseudo-near-collision with a 1-bit difference.

5   A Pseudo-collision for 23 Rounds of Tiger

In a similar way as we construct the pseudo-near-collision for the full Tiger hash function, we can also construct a pseudo-collision (free-start-collision) for Tiger reduced to 23 rounds by using another characteristic for the key schedule. For the attack we use the key schedule differences given below. It holds with probability 1.

$$(0, 0, 0, I, 0, 0, 0, I) \rightarrow (0, I, 0, 0, 0, 0, 0, I) \rightarrow (0, 0, 0, 0, 0, 0, 0, I) \qquad (6)$$

This characteristic for the key schedule of Tiger can be used in a similar way (as in the pseudo-near-collision for the full Tiger hash function) to construct a pseudo-collision in Tiger reduced to 23 rounds. The attack has a complexity of about 2^{47} evaluations of the compression of Tiger. It can be summarized as follows:

0. Precomputation: First, find a set of possible modular differences L^+ with a low Hamming weight XOR-difference $L^{\oplus}$ which can be canceled by a suitable choice for B_{12}. Second, we have to find a set of possible modular differences K^+ with a low Hamming weight XOR-difference $K^{\oplus}$ which can be canceled out by a suitable choice for B_{11}. Note that we use in the attack the same value for $L^{\oplus}$ and $K^{\oplus}$ as in the pseudo-near-collision attack on the full Tiger hash function. This step of the attack has a complexity of about $2^{28.5}$ evaluations of the compression function of Tiger.
1. Choose random values for A_2, B_2, C_2 and $X_3, \ldots, X_7$ and $X_8[\text{even}]$ to compute B_7, C_7 and C_8. This step of the attack has a complexity of about 12 round computations of Tiger.
2. Apply a message modification step to construct the XOR-difference $K^{\oplus}$ in round 9. This has a complexity of about $2^{36.5}$ and determines the message words $X_8[\text{odd}]$ and $X_9[\text{even}]$.
3. Apply another message modification step to construct the XOR-difference $L^{\oplus}$ in round 10. Finishing this step of the attack has a complexity of about 2^{39} and determines the message words $X_9[\text{odd}]$ and $X_{10}[\text{even}]$.
4. To construct the XOR-difference I in round 11, we apply again a message modification step. This step has a complexity of about 2^{40} and determines the message words $X_{10}[\text{odd}]$ and $X_{11}[\text{even}]$.
5. Once we have fixed the message words, we can compute B_{10}, C_{10} and C_{11} as well as the according modular differences. Since the difference in B_{10} can be cancel out with a probability close to 2^{-7} (*cf.* Section 4.5), we have to repeat the attack about 2^7 times. Hence, finishing this step of the attack has a complexity of about 2^{47} hash computations.
6. Determine $X_{11}[\text{odd}]$ and $X_{12}[\text{odd}]$ according to the result of the precomputation step. This adds no additional cost to the attack complexity.
7. To compute the message words $X_0, \ldots, X_7$, we have to choose suitable values for $X_{12}[\text{even}]$ and $X_{13}, \ldots, X_{15}$ such that X_5, X_6 and X_7 are correct after computing the key schedule backward. Note that X_3 and X_4 can be chosen freely, because we can modify C_2 and C_3 such that $C_2 \oplus X_3$ and $C_3 \oplus X_4$ stay constant. In detail, we choose arbitrary values for X_{13}, X_{14}, X_{15} and calculate $X_{13}, \ldots, X_{15}$ as follows.

$$X_{13} = (X_5 + (X_{12} + (X_{11} \oplus (\neg X_{10} \gg 23)))) \oplus X_{12}$$
$$X_{14} = (X_6 - (X_{13} \oplus X_{12} \oplus (\neg(X_{12} + (X_{11} \oplus (\neg X_{10} \gg 23))) \gg 23))) + X_{13}$$
$$X_{15} = (X_7 \oplus (X_{14} - X_{13})) - (X_{14} \oplus \text{0123456789ABCDEF})$$

This adds negligible cost to the attack complexity and guarantees that X_5, X_6 and X_7 are always correct after computing the key schedule backward.

8. To compute the initial chaining values A_{-1}, B_{-1} and C_{-1} run the rounds 2, 1, and 0 backwards.

Hence, we can construct a pseudo-collision (free-start-collision) for Tiger reduced to 23 rounds with a complexity of about 2^{47} applications of the compression function.

6   Conclusion

In this article, we have shown a 1-bit circular pseudo-near-collision for the full Tiger hash function with a complexity of about 2^{47} evaluations of the compression function of Tiger. This is the first attack on the full Tiger hash function. Furthermore, we show a pseudo-collision for Tiger reduced to 23 (out of 24) rounds with the same complexity. Our attack is based on the attack of Kelsey and Lucks on round-reduced variants of the Tiger hash function. This work shows that the security margins of the Tiger hash function are not as good as one would expect.

Acknowledgement

The authors wish to thank Sebastiaan Indesteege, and the anonymous referees for useful comments and discussions.

References

1. Anderson, R.J., Biham, E.: TIGER: A Fast New Hash Function. In: Gollmann, D. (ed.) Fast Software Encryption. LNCS, vol. 1039, pp. 89–97. Springer, Heidelberg (1996)
2. Kelsey, J., Lucks, S.: Collisions and Near-Collisions for Reduced-Round Tiger. In: Robshaw, M. (ed.) FSE 2006. LNCS, vol. 4047, pp. 111–125. Springer, Heidelberg (2006)
3. Mendel, F., Preneel, B., Rijmen, V., Yoshida, H., Watanabe, D.: Update on Tiger. In: Barua, R., Lange, T. (eds.) INDOCRYPT 2006. LNCS, vol. 4329, pp. 63–79. Springer, Heidelberg (2006)
4. Pramstaller, N., Rechberger, C., Rijmen, V.: Exploiting Coding Theory for Collision Attacks on SHA-1. In: Smart, N.P. (ed.) Cryptography and Coding. LNCS, vol. 3796, pp. 78–95. Springer, Heidelberg (2005)

A   Collision Attack on Tiger Reduced to 16 Rounds

In this section, we briefly describe the attack of Kelsey and Lucks on Tiger reduced to 16 rounds. Note that in the original description of the attack the wrong S-boxes are addressed. However, the attack can be easily modified to work with the correct S-boxes as well. Note that the modified attack has a slightly worse complexity, namely about 2^{47} instead of 2^{44} hash computations. For the attack the same characteristic is used for the key schedule of Tiger as in the original attack. The characteristic is shown below.

$$(I, I, I, I, 0, 0, 0, 0) \rightarrow (I, I, 0, 0, 0, 0, 0, 0) \tag{7}$$

It has a probability of 1 to hold in the key schedule of Tiger, which facilitates the attack. The attack can be summarized as follows.

0. Precomputation: Like in the pseudo-near-collision attack on Tiger described before, we have to find a set of possible modular differences L^+ with a low Hamming weight XOR-difference $L^\oplus$ which can be canceled out by a suitable choice for B_6.

$$\mathcal{L} = \{L^+ \in \mathcal{L}' : L^+ = \mathbf{odd}(B_6 \oplus I) \boxminus \mathbf{odd}(B_6)\}$$

Second, we have to find a set of possible modular differences K^+ with a low Hamming weight XOR-difference $K^\oplus$ which can be canceled out by a suitable choice for B_7.

$$\mathcal{K} = \{K^+ \in \mathcal{K}' : K^+ = \mathbf{odd}(B_5 \oplus L^\oplus) \boxminus \mathbf{odd}(B_5)\}$$

Note that we assume in the attack that we can find a XOR-difference $L^\oplus$ with Hamming weight of 10 and a XOR-difference $K^\oplus$ with Hamming weight of 8 (as in the pseudo-near-collision attack on the full Tiger hash function). The precomputation step of the attack has a complexity of about $2^{28.5}$ evaluations of the compression function of Tiger.

1. Choose random values for $X_0, \dots, X_1$ and $X_2[\mathbf{even}]$ to compute B_1, C_1 and C_2. This step of the attack has a complexity of about 6 round computations of Tiger.

2. Apply a message modification step to construct the XOR-difference $K^\oplus$ in round 3. This step has a complexity of about $2^{36.5}$ hash computations and determines the message words $X_2[\mathbf{odd}]$ and $X_3[\mathbf{even}]$.

3. Apply a second message modification step to construct the XOR-difference $L^\oplus$ in round 4. Finishing this step of the attack has a complexity of about 2^{39} and determines the message words $X_3[\mathbf{odd}]$ and $X_4[\mathbf{even}]$.

4. To construct the XOR-difference I in round 5, we apply again a message modification step. Finishing this step has a complexity of about 2^{40} and determines the message words $X_4[\mathbf{odd}]$ and $X_5[\mathbf{even}]$.

5. Once we have fixed the message words, we can compute B_4, C_4 and C_5 as well as the according modular differences. To cancel the difference in B_4 we need that $\Delta^{\boxplus}(B_4) \in \mathcal{K}$. Since we assume that the Hamming weight of $K^\oplus$ is 8, this has (in the worst case) a probability of 2^{-7}.

   In order to guarantee that the difference in B_5 is canceled, we need that $\Delta^{\boxplus}(B_5) \in \mathcal{L}$. Since $L^\oplus$ has a Hamming weight of 10, this has a probability (in the worst case) of 2^{-9}. Hence, we expect that we have to repeat the attack about 2^{16} to finish this step. However, by choosing $L^\oplus$ and $K^\oplus$ carefully this can be improved. Form our analysis (for the pseudo-near-collision for the full Tiger hash function), we expect that this probability can be improved by a factor of 2^9, resulting in an attack complexity of about 2^{47} hash computations.

6. Determine $X_5[\text{odd}]$ and $X_6[\text{odd}]$ according to the results of the precomputation step. This adds no additional cost to the attack complexity.

Hence, a collision can be constructed in Tiger reduced to 16 rounds with a complexity close to 2^{47} evaluations of the compression function. Note that the other attacks on round-reduced variants of Tiger can be adjusted in a similar way.

B   Collision Attack on Tiger Reduced to 19 Rounds

In this section, we show how the collision attack on Tiger-19 presented in [3] has to be modified to work with the correct S-boxes. The complexity of the attack is close to 2^{62} evaluations of the compression function of Tiger. To construct a collision in Tiger-19 the key schedule difference given in (8) is used. It has probability 1 to hold in the key schedule of Tiger which facilitates the attack.

$$(0,0,0,I,I,I,I,0) \rightarrow (0,0,0,I,I,0,0,0) \rightarrow (0,0,0,I,I,I,I,I) \qquad (8)$$

Since the key schedule difference from round 3 to 18 is the 16-round difference used in the attack on Tiger-16, the same attack strategy can be used for the collision attack on Tiger-19 as well. The attack can be summarized as follows:

1. Choose arbitrary values for $X_0, \dots, X_4$ and compute the state variables A_3, B_3, and B_4.
2. Employ the attack on 16 rounds of Tiger, to find the message words $X_5, \dots,$ X_7 and $X_8, X_9[\text{odd}]$ such that the output after round 18 collides.
3. To guarantee that $X_8, X_9[\text{odd}]$ are correct after applying the key schedule, we use the degrees of freedom we have in the choice of $X_0, \dots, X_4$. Note that for any difference injected in X_0 and X_1 one can adjust X_2, X_3, X_4 accordingly such that A_3, $B_3 = C_2 \oplus X_3$ and $B_4 = C_3 \oplus X_4$ stay constant. Furthermore, we get the following equations for X_8 and X_9 from the key schedule of Tiger.

$$X_8 = Y_0 \boxplus Y_7$$
$$X_9 = Y_1 \boxminus (X_8 \oplus (\neg Y_7 \lll 19))$$

where

$$Y_0 = X_0 \boxminus (X_7 \oplus \text{A5A5A5A5A5A5A5A5})$$
$$Y_1 = X_1 \oplus Y_0$$
$$Y_2 = X_2 \boxplus Y_1$$
$$Y_3 = X_3 \boxminus (Y_2 \oplus (\neg Y_1 \lll 19))$$
$$Y_4 = X_4 \oplus Y_3$$
$$Y_5 = X_5 \boxplus Y_4$$
$$Y_6 = X_6 \boxminus (Y_5 \oplus (\neg Y_4 \ggg 23))$$
$$Y_7 = X_7 \oplus Y_6$$

To solve these equations the following method is used:

(a) Choose a random value for Y_0. This determines Y_7 and X_0.
(b) Choose a random value for $X_9[\mathbf{even}]$. This determines X_1.
(c) Adjust X_2, X_3, X_4 accordingly such that A_3, $B_3 = C_2 \oplus X_3$ and $B_4 = C_3 \oplus X_4$ stay constant.
(d) Once we have fixed X_2, X_3, and X_4, we have to check if Y_7 is correct (this holds with a probability of 2^{-64}). After repeating the method about 2^{64} times for different values of Y_0, we expect to find a match.

Hence, this step of the attack has a complexity of at about 2^{64} key schedule computations and $4 \cdot 2^{64}$ round computations of Tiger. This is equivalent to about 2^{62} evaluations of the compression function of Tiger.

Thus, we can construct a collision in Tiger reduced to 19 rounds with a complexity of about $2^{62} + 2^{47} \approx 2^{62}$ evaluations of the compression function of Tiger.

Cryptanalysis of GRINDAHL

Thomas Peyrin*

France Télécom R&D, Issy-les-Moulineaux, France
AIST, Tokyo, Japan
University of Versailles, France
thomas.peyrin@orange-ftgroup.com

Abstract. Due to recent breakthroughs in hash functions cryptanalysis, some new hash schemes have been proposed. GRINDAHL is a novel hash function, designed by Knudsen, Rechberger and Thomsen and published at FSE 2007. It has the particularity that it follows the RIJNDAEL design strategy, with an efficiency comparable to SHA-256. This paper provides the first cryptanalytic work on this new scheme. We show that the 256-bit version of GRINDAHL is not collision resistant. With a work effort of approximatively 2^{112} hash computations, one can generate a collision.

Keywords: GRINDAHL, hash functions, RIJNDAEL.

1 Introduction

Hash functions are one of the most utilized primitives in cryptography. Basically, a hash function H is a function that maps an input of variable size to a fixed length output value. A cryptographic hash function has the additional feature that it must satisfy some security properties such as preimage resistance, second preimage resistance and collision resistance. For an ideal hash function with an n-bit output, one expects that compromising these properties should require 2^n, 2^n and $2^{n/2}$ operations respectively [12].

A possible way of building a hash function has been introduced by the pioneering work of Merkle and Damgård [22,10], using an iterative process: at each iteration, a fixed-length input function h (the compression function) updates an internal state called *chaining variable* with some part of the message. With some appropriate padding of the message to be hashed, the problem of building a collision-resistant hash function H is then reduced to the problem of building a collision-resistant compression function h. However, due to recent attacks [16,18,17,14] against this iterative process, other hash domain extensions have been introduced [2,5].

Almost all the proposed hash functions define a compression function to be used with any hash domain extension algorithm. There are basically three different ways of building a compression function. First, one can relate the security of h to a hard problem, such as factorisation [9], finding small vectors in lattices [3], syndrome decoding [1] or solving multivariate quadratic equations [6]. The usually bad efficiency

---

* The author is supported by the Japan Society for Promotion of Science and the French RNRT SAPHIR project (http://www.crypto-hash.fr).

of these schemes is compensated by the proofs of security they provide. Another very active domain is the construction of secure compression functions based on block ciphers. The problem of building a secure n-bit compression function from an ideal n-bit block cipher is more or less resolved [27,28,7] and due to a need of bigger output size the cryptographic community is now concentrated on the problem of building a secure $(k \times n)$-bit compression function from an ideal n-bit block cipher [13,26,30]. Finally, the most common and efficient way of building a compression function is from scratch, for example the well known and standardized SHA-1 [25] or MD5 [29]. However, almost all of this type of hash functions have been broken by novel cryptanalysis results [31,32,33,34,8].

To anticipate further improvements of the attacks, the NIST is initiating an effort [24] to develop one or more additional hash algorithms through a public competition, similar to the development process for the Advanced Encryption Standard [23]. In parallel, new hash functions have been published very recently, such as FORK-256 [15] (broken in [21]), RADIO-GATÙN [4] or GRINDAHL [20]. We show here that for the GRINDAHL hash function one can find a collision (resp. a second preimage) with a work effort of 2^{112} (resp. 2^{224}) hash computations approximatively, whereas $2^{n/2}$ (resp. 2^n) is expected for an ideal hash function. Note that the conceptors of GRINDAHL only claimed a (second) preimage security of $2^{n/2}$ operations, already providing an attack requiring lower than 2^n operations.

The paper is organized as follows. In Section 2 we quickly recall the specification of the GRINDAHL hash function and in Section 3 we begin the analysis with various observations on the scheme and the general methodology that allows us to build a differential path. Then, in Section 4, we provide the first collision attack on GRINDAHL. Finally, we discuss possible patches in Section 5 and we conclude in Section 6.

2 Description of GRINDAHL

GRINDAHL is a family of hash functions based on the so-called *Concatenate-Permute-Truncate* strategy, where in our case the permutation uses the design principles of RIJNDAEL [11], well known for being the winning candidate of the Advanced Encryption Standard (AES) process [23]. Two algorithms are defined, a version with a 256-bit output and a 512-bit one. Also, a compression function mode is given, taking only fixed-length inputs, to be used with any hash domain extension algorithm. We give in this section a quick description of the GRINDAHL hash function with a 256-bit output. For a more detailed specification of the algorithm, we refer to [20].

Let $n = 256$ be the number of output bits of the hash function H, with an *internal state s* of 48 bytes (384 bits), and let M be the message (appropriately padded) to be hashed. M is split into m blocks $M_1, \ldots, M_m$ of 4 bytes each (32 bits). At each iteration k, the message block M_k will be used to update the internal state s_{k-1}. We call *extended internal state $\hat{s}_k$* the concatenation of the message block M_{k+1} and the internal state s_k, i.e. $\hat{s}_k = M_{k+1}||s_k$. We thus have $|\hat{s}_k| = (4 + 48) \times 8 = 416$ bits. We denote by $trunc_t(x)$ the least significant t bits of x. Let $P : \{0,1\}^{416} \longmapsto \{0,1\}^{416}$ be a non-linear permutation, and let s_0 be the *initial internal state* defined by $s_0 = \{0\}^{384}$.

Then, for each iteration k with $0 < k < m$, we have $s_k = trunc_{384}(P(\hat{s}_{k-1}))$. For the last iteration, the truncation is omitted: $\hat{s}_m = P(\hat{s}_{m-1})$. Finally, we apply eight *blank rounds* $\hat{s}_k = P(\hat{s}_{k-1})$, for $m < k \leq m + 8$, and the output of the hash function is $trunc_{256}(\hat{s}_{m+8})$.

The description is not complete since P has not yet been defined. This permutation follows the design principle of RIJNDAEL (the reader is expected to be familiar with the transformation defined in the RIJNDAEL specifications) and thus the extended state $\hat{s}$ is viewed as a matrix of bytes. However, instead of a $(4, 4)$ bytes matrix, we have a matrix α of 4 rows and 13 columns in the case of the 256-bit version of GRINDAHL. The entry of the matrix α located at the i-th row and the j-th column is a byte denoted by $\alpha_{i,j}$. Thus, we have:

$$\alpha = \begin{pmatrix} \alpha_{0,0} & \alpha_{0,1} & \cdots & \alpha_{0,12} \\ \alpha_{1,0} & \alpha_{1,1} & \cdots & \alpha_{1,12} \\ \alpha_{2,0} & \alpha_{2,1} & \cdots & \alpha_{2,12} \\ \alpha_{3,0} & \alpha_{3,1} & \cdots & \alpha_{3,12} \end{pmatrix}.$$

By splitting the extended internal state $\hat{s}$ into 52 8-bit chunks $x_0, \ldots, x_{51}$, we can define the conversion from $\hat{s}$ to α by $\alpha_{i,j} = x_{i+4\times j}$. This mapping has a natural inverse. Basically, before each iteration, the first column of α is overwritten with the incoming message block. Finally, the permutation P is defined as

$$P(\alpha) = \text{MixColumns} \circ \text{ShiftRows} \circ \text{SubBytes} \circ \text{AddConstant}(\alpha).$$

MixColumns. This transformation is defined as in the RIJNDAEL specifications.

ShiftRows. This transformation cyclically shifts bytes a number of positions along each row. Thus, the i-th row is rotated by ρ_i positions to the right, with $\rho_0 = 1$, $\rho_1 = 2$, $\rho_2 = 4$ and $\rho_3 = 10$.

SubBytes. The only non-linear part of the permutation, exactly defined as the SubBytes function of RIJNDAEL.

AddConstant. This function is simply defined by $\alpha_{3,12} \longleftarrow \alpha_{3,12} \oplus 01$, where 01 is the byte-wise hexadecimal value of 1.

Note that the 512-bit version of GRINDAHL is based on the same principle as the 256-bit version, but the extended internal state is bigger (8 rows instead of 4). The compression function mode for GRINDAHL-256 (without optional input) simply consists in hashing 40 4-byte message blocks for each compression function call.

3   Overall Analysis

In this section, we study possible ways of finding a good differential path for the 256-bit version of GRINDAHL. More precisely, we look for a trail of k iterations starting from s_0 and so that with two different messages M and M' we have the same hash output, i.e. $trunc_{256}(\hat{s}_{m+8}) = trunc_{256}(\hat{s}_{m'+8})$. Thus, we only care about collision and second preimage resistance. Finding a differential path including the blank rounds seems hard since no message block is inserted during this last operation and thus we have very few control on this part. However, the problem looks much easier when trying to find an internal collision: a differential path excluding the blank rounds, i.e. $\hat{s}_m = \hat{s}_{m'}$. Here, we explain how to find such a path, with the constraint that we want this path to have a good probability of success.

3.1   A Known Potential Attack and the Truncated-Differences

In the original paper from FSE 2007, a section explains a potential attack method, pointed out by an anonymous reviewer. This method seems quite natural: the attacker does not look at the actual values of differences inserted in the bytes of the internal state, but only checks if there is a difference or not (this greatly simplifies the analysis). We call this kind of zero or non-zero differences *truncated-differences* in reference to the very similar truncated differences used by Knudsen in [19]. Then, a chain of truncated-differences in which in every round the number of actives bytes (bytes with a non-zero truncated-difference) is low must be found. In this differential path, the truncated-differences can only be erased during two stages of an iteration: during a MixColumns transformation or during the truncation at the end of the iteration. In other words, the number of truncated-differences in a column can be reduced and their position changed by a clever use of the MixColumns transformation (note however that one can never erase all the truncated-differences of a column at a time). Otherwise, a truncated-difference is deleted if it goes to the first column of α at the end of the iteration, due to the truncation. Since at this stage of the attack the differential trail is already settled, one can not force anything for the truncation but one can play with the message blocks inserted at each iteration, in order to force a good behavior in the MixColumns processes (see Section 3.2). In fact, the message bytes act as *active/passive bits* in the sense that new input bytes do not affect some parts of the internal state for a limited number of rounds (see Section 3.3). The feasibility of this method was left as an open problem, and we argue in Section 3.4 that there is a better way of finding a collision on GRINDAHL.

3.2   Analysis of Differences Propagation in MixColumns

The MixColumns transformation used in GRINDAHL is the same as in RIJNDAEL, and its MDS property ensures maximal difference propagation. More precisely, the sum of the number of active bytes of the input and the output is greater or equal to 5. In other words, the number of non-zero truncated-differences of the input and the output of MixColumns is greater or equal to 5.

More formally, let $V = (A, B, C, D)$ be an input vector of four bytes A, B, C and D; and let $W = (A', B', C', D')$ be an output vector of four bytes A', B', C' and D'. We denote the function MixColumns by $MC : V \longmapsto W$ or $MC : (A, B, C, D) \longmapsto (A', B', C', D')$. We also denote by $D_i(V_1, V_2)$ the function returning 1 if the i-th byte of the 4-byte vectors V_1 and V_2 are different, and 0 otherwise. Finally, $ND(V_1, V_2)$

Table 1. Approximate probability that two 4-byte input words with D_I different bytes on predefined positions maps to two 4-byte output words with D_O different bytes on predefined positions through MixColumns. The values are base 2 logarithms.

D_I \ D_O	0	1	2	3	4
0	0	$-\infty$	$-\infty$	$-\infty$	$-\infty$
1	$-\infty$	$-\infty$	$-\infty$	$-\infty$	0
2	$-\infty$	$-\infty$	$-\infty$	-8	0
3	$-\infty$	$-\infty$	-16	-8	0
4	$-\infty$	-24	-16	-8	0

returns the number of such differences, i.e. $ND(V_1, V_2) = \#\{i \mid D_i(V_1, V_2) = 1\}$. We thus have that if $W_1 = MC(V_1)$ and $W_2 = MC(V_2)$ with $V_1 \neq V_2$, then

$$ND(V_1, V_2) + ND(W_1, W_2) \geq 5.$$

Another interesting property is that any input byte of MixColumns defines a permutation for any output byte. Thus, with $W_1 = MC(V_1)$, $W_2 = MC(V_2)$ and $V_1 \neq V_2$ drawn uniformly and randomly in $\{0, 1\}^{4 \times 8}$, we have for any $1 \leq i \leq 4$:

$$P_D = P[D_i(W_1, W_2) = 0] = \frac{256^3 - 1}{256^4 - 1} \simeq 2^{-8}, \tag{1}$$

$$\overline{P_D} = P[D_i(W_1, W_2) = 1] = 1 - P_D \simeq 1 - 2^{-8}. \tag{2}$$

Our goal is to compute the probability that a fixed mask of input truncated-differences maps to a fixed mask of output truncated-differences (later this will be often utilized in order to compute the probability of success of the differential path). For example, we want to be able to know the probability that given two input words V_1 and V_2 distinct on their 2 first bytes give two output words different on their 3 first bytes through MixColumns (note that this is slightly different from the event that any 2-byte difference input maps to any 3-byte difference output). We can compute those probabilities in two ways, formally or empirically by testing exhaustively all the input values: since MixColumns is linear, dealing with differences or values is the same (during the test, instead of looking for differences or non-differences, we checked for zero values or non-zero values). We give in Table 1 an approximation of those probabilities.

3.3 Existence of Control Bytes

Modifying some message bytes will obviously modify quite quickly the internal state, but not necessarily immediately. For each modified byte of the message M_k, we give in Table 2 the columns of s (in its matrix representation α) affected by this modification after 1, 2 and 3 iterations. Note that for more than 3 iterations, any message byte affect all the internal state. This *active/passive bytes* feature will allow us to attack different columns of different iterations independently. More precisely, we will control independently the behaviour of some MixColumns transitions thanks to the active/passive bytes.

Table 2. Influences on the columns of the extended internal states for a modification of a byte of the message block $M_k = (A_k, B_k, C_k, D_k)$ incoming at iteration k. We denote by ✓ if the column is affected (or active) and void if not. The first table shows influences on s_{k-1}, the second on s_k and the third on s_{k+1}.

	0	1	2	3	4	5	6	7	8	9	10	11	12
A_k		✓											
B_k			✓										
C_k					✓								
D_k											✓		

	0	1	2	3	4	5	6	7	8	9	10	11	12
A_k			✓	✓		✓						✓	
B_k				✓	✓		✓						✓
C_k		✓				✓	✓		✓				
D_k		✓						✓				✓	✓

	0	1	2	3	4	5	6	7	8	9	10	11	12
A_k	✓		✓	✓	✓	✓	✓	✓	✓	✓			✓
B_k	✓	✓		✓	✓	✓	✓	✓	✓	✓	✓		
C_k			✓	✓		✓	✓	✓	✓	✓	✓	✓	✓
D_k	✓	✓	✓	✓	✓	✓			✓	✓		✓	✓

3.4   General Strategy

We now have all the necessary tools in order to build a truncated-differential path and evaluate its probability of success. But how to actually find one ? The natural intuition one would have (as the anonymous reviewer suggested) is to always maintain a low number of truncated-differences along the path (to increase the probability). However, finding one such path seems really difficult as one can convince oneself with Property 1 from the original paper:

Property 1. An internal collision for GRINDAHL-256 requires at least 5 iterations. Moreover, any characteristic starting or ending in the extended state with no difference contains at least on round where at least half the extended state bytes (excluding the first column) are active.

This property can be verified with a meet-in-the-middle exhaustive search, as explained in the original paper. However, with a small speed improvement of this algorithm, one can check that an internal collision for GRINDAHL-256 requires at least 6 iterations. Another observation is that by introducing differences in the state, after a few iterations we quickly come to an "all-difference" pair of extended states. Moreover, this "all-difference" pair of extended states is almost stable: the probability that an all-difference pair of columns remains an all-difference pair of columns through MixColumns is approximatively $P_A = (1 - 2^{-8})^4$, so for the twelve columns of the extended state (excepted the first column) we have a probability of $P_A^{12} \simeq 2^{-0.27}$. Thus, our first idea is to not search for a path starting from a zero difference but from an all-difference pair of extended states (which is very easy to get). The overwhelming probability P_A^{12} allows us to start with as much valid starting states as we want.

3.5 Finding a Truncated Differential Path

Searching for a differential path starting from an all-difference pair of extended internal states is quite easy. One method is to go backward almost exhaustively. Indeed, in GRINDAHL the truncated differences propagate in the forward direction as quickly as in the backward direction. More precisely, if we look for a collision at the end of iteration k, we try all the possible truncated difference masks for the message blocks inserted at iterations k, $k - 1$, etc. and all the possible transitions of truncated differences through MixColumns, until we come to an all-difference pair of extended states. This algorithm can be greatly improved with an early-abort strategy: we compute a lower bound on the cost of the current trail we are building (taking in account the control provided by the active/passive bytes, see Section 4) and we stop the search branch if the complexity of the attack is already greater or equal to 2^{128} operations. We also stop the search if we go too far in terms of number of iterations[1].

Obviously, by always adding truncated differences to all the message blocks inserted is the fastest way to reach this goal. However, we will use the message bytes inserted as *control bytes* to attack some parts of the differential path independently and thus increase the probability of success. Thus, it may be better not to go too fast on adding truncated differences in order to increase the total number of iterations during the differential path. This will increase the total number of message blocks inserted and therefore provide more control bytes. For example, we can find a path starting from an all-difference pair of extended internal states and requiring only 4 iterations to get a collision, with a probability of success of approximatively 2^{-312}. However, another path requiring 8 iterations to get a collision, with a probability of success of approximatively 2^{-440} may be better. Indeed, in the latter case, even if the probability of success has been divided by a factor 2^{138}, we have inserted 8 message word pairs instead of only 4 in the former case. Thus, we get roughly $2 \times 4 \times 4 \times 8 = 256$ degrees of freedom compared to the former case (4 pairs of message of 4 bytes each). Thus, we obtained more degrees of freedom than what we paid for the probability drop. Obviously, a limit exists: at some point, adding more iterations does not improve things anymore.

---

[1] In some particular cases, the overall complexity of the attack can remain stable even if the number of iterations of the differential path increases.

4   Finding a Collision

In this Section, from the previous observations, we give a complete collision attack for the 256-bit version of GRINDAHL.

4.1   The Differential Path

Before describing the collision attack, we give in Figure 1 the differential path used and which has been generated thanks to a program implementing the previously explained technique (see Section 3.5). This trail is the best found (among other possible candidates leading to the same complexity). Several candidates were possible and we kept the one providing the best collision attack. We denote by k the number of the last iteration of our differential path, i.e. the last line of Figure 1. First, one can check that all the MixColumns transitions are valid. This differential path has a probability of success of approximatively $2^{-55\times 8} = 2^{-440}$, but we will see that we also have a lot of message blocks inserted allowing to attack some parts independently.

Our aim is to find a pair of messages following the expected differential trail. For this, we don't take care of each iteration one by one, but we deal with each of the 4-byte message words inserted one by one. Said in other words, we will fix the four bytes of a message word pair and check that the newly imposed MixColumns differential transitions are the ones expected in the truncated-differential path. If so, we continue to the next message word pair until we get a collision.

In Table 3, we give all the dependencies of the MixColumns transitions with the message blocks inserted, used as control bytes during the differential path from Figure 1. The cost of all the transitions are given (see Section 3.2) also with the number of control bytes inserted at each iteration (see Section 3.3). The second column of the Table gives the position of the columns of the state in which we force a differential transition during a MixColumns transformation, and the first column indicates in which iteration this event occurs. For each transition, we give in the third column its cost in terms of number of bytes (i.e. for a cost c, the transition has a probability of $2^{-c\times 8}$). Then, each of the seven other columns of the table represents a pair of message words that will be used as control bytes (the letters a or A, b or B, c or C and d or D represent respectively the first, second, third and fourth byte of the 4-byte message inserted). Capital letters means that we have 2 control bytes (we insert a difference for this block) and small letters means that we only have 1 control byte (no difference inserted for this message block). In the core of the table a dash or a cross represents the fact that the MixColumns transition indicated by the corresponding line is affected by the control byte indicated by the corresponding column. We divided those dependencies for the sake of simplicity, the crosses are the dependencies that will be used for the attack: they represent for each MixColumns transition the dependencies of the last involved message word. Finally, the last line gives the cost of each message word insertion in terms of number of bytes (the sum gives the total complexity of the attack).

Note that a lot of the inserted message bytes provide two one-byte degrees of freedom (capital letters) in the case where we introduce a difference for this message block (we can make independently both messages of the pair vary). From Table 3, one can check

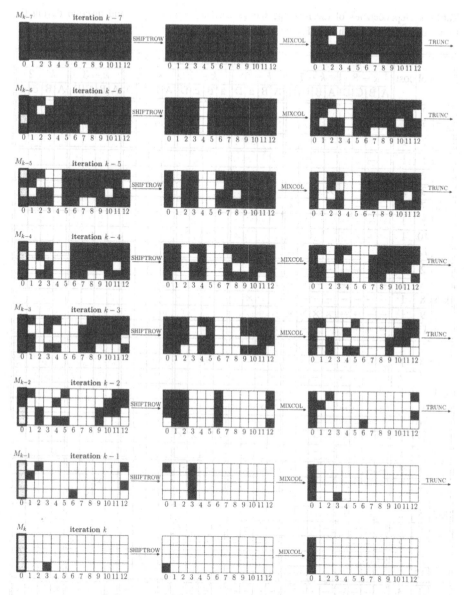

Fig. 1. Truncated-differential path in 8 iterations starting from an all-difference pair of states. The dark cells mean that we have a non-zero difference for this byte, and the light cells stand for no difference. Each row represents an iteration. The first column gives the differences in the state just after its update with the 4-byte message word, and the second column gives the same state after application of the ShiftRows transformation. Finally, the third column represents the internal state just after application of the MixColumns function. Note that the AddConstant and SubBytes functions have no effect on the differential path, thus they are omitted here. Each first 4-byte column of the first column states represents the message words inserted at each iteration, that will later be used as control bytes. The first 4-byte column of the state after every MixColumns transition can have whatever difference mask since those bytes will be immediately truncated.

Table 3. Dependencies of the message blocks used as control bytes and inserted during the truncated-differential path from Figure 1, for a collision at the end of iteration k

message blocks inserted

it	col	cost	k−8 A	B	C	D	k−7 A	B	C	D	k−6 A	B	c	D	k−5 a	B	c	D	k−4 A	b	C	D	k−3 A	B	C	D	k−2 A	B	c	d
k-7	2	1	−				×																							
	3	1	×	×																										
	7	1				×																								
k-6	1	1	−		−				−	−	×																			
	2	1	−				−	−	−			×																		
	3	2	−	−	−	−	×	×																						
	7	1	−	−	−								×																	
	8	1	−	−	−			×																						
	10	1	−	−										×																
	12	1	−		−	−	×		×																					
k-5	2	1	−	−	−	−	−		−	−	−					×														
	3	1	−	−	−	−	−	−	−	−	×	×																		
	8	1	−	−	−	−	−	−	−	−			×																	
	9	1	−	−	−	−	×	×	×	×																				
	11	1	−	−	−	−			−	−	×		×	×																
k-4	1	1	−	−	−	−	−	−	−	−					−		−	−	×											
	3	1	−	−	−	−	−	−	−	−	−	−	−	−	×	×														
	4	2	−	−	−	−	−	−	−	−	−	−	−	−		×														
	7	1	−	−	−	−	−	−	−	−	−	−	−	−			×													
	9	1	−	−	−	−	−	−	−	−	−	−	−	−	×	×	×	×												
	10	1	−	−	−	−	−	−	−	−	−	−	−	−		×														
	11	1	−	−	−	−	−	−	−	−	−	−	−	−	×		×	×												
	12	1	−	−	−	−	−	−	−	−	−	−	−	−	×		×													
k-3	1	3	−	−	−	−	−	−	−	−	−	−	−	−	−		−	−	−	−	×									
	2	2	−	−	−	−	−	−	−	−	−	−	−	−	−	−	−	−	−	−	−	−	×							
	4	2	−	−	−	−	−	−	−	−	−	−	−	−	−	−	−	−	−	−	−	−		×						
	5	2	−	−	−	−	−	−	−	−	−	−	−	−	−	−	−	−	×		×									
	9	2	−	−	−	−	−	−	−	−	−	−	−	−	−	−	−	−	×	×	×	×								
	10	2	−	−	−	−	−	−	−	−	−	−	−	−	−	−	−	−	−	−	−	−			×					
	11	1	−	−	−	−	−	−	−	−	−	−	−	−	−	−	−	−	×		×	×								
	12	2	−	−	−	−	−	−	−	−	−	−	−	−	−	−	−	−		×	×									
k-2	1	3	−	−	−	−	−	−	−	−	−	−	−	−	−	−	−	−	−	−	−	−			−	−	×			
	2	3	−	−	−	−	−	−	−	−	−	−	−	−	−	−	−	−	−	−	−	−	−	−	−	−		×		
	6	3	−	−	−	−	−	−	−	−	−	−	−	−	−	−	−	−	−	−	−	−	−	−	×	×				
	12	2	−	−	−	−	−	−	−	−	−	−	−	−	−	−	−	−	−	−	−	−	−		×	−	×			
k-1	3	3	−	−	−	−	−	−	−	−	−	−	−	−	−	−	−	−	−	−	−	−	−	−	−	−	×	×		
COST			0				0				0				1				2				6				5			

that we need to test $2^{14 \times 8} = 2^{112}$ all-difference pairs of internal state in order to have a good probability of obtaining a collision. More precisely, the collision attack is as follows.

4.2   The Collision Attack

First step: start with the predefined initial value and compute some iterations with lots of truncated-differences in the incoming message blocks in order to quickly come to an all-difference pair of states denoted A after a few iterations. This step is omitted in the complexity analysis since very largely negligible.

Second step: from this pair of states A, generate $2^{14*8} = 2^{112}$ all-difference pairs of states $A_1, \ldots, A_{2^{112}}$. This step requires $2^{112} \times 2^{0,27} = 2^{112,27}$ iterations computations.

Third step: we continue the attack by fixing the control bytes iteration per iteration: for the message blocks inserted at the beginning of iterations $k - 8$, $k - 7$, $k - 6$ of our truncated-differential path from Table 3, we have more control bytes incoming than necessary. Indeed, we have for the messages inserted at iterations $k - 8$, $k - 7$ and $k - 6$, 8, 8 and 7 control bytes available respectively, whereas we only require 2, 7 and 7 bytes of degrees of freedom respectively. More precisely, for each pair of message words (M_{k-i}, M'_{k-i}) inserted, its bytes are used in order to adjust the behavior of the MixColumns transitions where crosses appear at column M_{k-i} in Table 3 [2]. For each step, the total cost is equal to the sum of the costs of all the MixColumns transitions involved, minus the number of control bytes available from M_{k-i}. Thus, at this point of the attack, we maintain 2^{112} pairs of messages and states following the differential trail. For the message words inserted at iteration $k - 5$, we have 6 control bytes for 7 bytes of conditions, thus we only keep 1 out of 2^8 message pairs and we go to the $(k - 4)$-th message word with 2^{104} valid pairs. We continue in the same way for the three lasting message words $k - 4$, $k - 3$ and $k - 2$, having 7, 8 and 4 control bytes respectively [3] and requiring 9, 14 and 9 bytes of conditions respectively. We thus expect to have one pair of messages following the differential trail with a good probability by starting with $2^{14\times8} = 2^{112}$ all-difference pairs of states.

Fourth step: add a $(k + 1)$-th message block without truncated-difference in order to force a truncation after the last iteration k of the differential trail (the final blank rounds are done without truncation).

4.3   Discussion on the Attack

For the sake of clarity, we explain more precisely how to deal with the control bytes by giving an example. Let set ourselves when the attacker has to fix the message pair incoming at step $k - 5$ (seventh column in Table 3). The previous message words have already been fixed during the attack, thus we only have to deal with the crosses in Table 3. Some MixColumns differential transitions have to behave as required by the

---

[2] Since in Table 3 the crosses represent the last message word involved for the transition, the previous dependencies (represented by a dash) are already fixed at this point.

[3] For the $k - 2$ case, we only have 4 control bytes and not 6 as indicated in Table 3. Indeed, since c and d are not involved in any MixColumns transition, they can not be considered as control bytes.

truncated-differential path, and this has a cost. For example, at the second column of the $(k - 5)$-th iteration, we need a 4-truncated-differences to 3-truncated-differences transition and this will happen with probability 2^{-8}, thus with a cost of 1 byte. However, to make this event occur, we can use the message word inserted at iteration $k - 5$ (more precisely its second byte) in order to randomize the instantiation of the transition. Note that there are several ways of doing this step, and this is discussed below. We actually have a good probability to find 2^8 valid pairs of message bytes for this transition: two control bytes for one byte of condition. We do the same process for the seventh column transition of iteration $k - 4$ with the fourth byte of the message word: again two control bytes for one byte of condition. Then we identify the subset of the cross product of the two sets of 2^8 byte pairs such that the twelfth column transitions of iteration $k - 4$ is verified (depending only on the two previously fixed pairs of message bytes), which costs one byte of condition. So, we maintain 2^8 valid possibilities. Then, we fix the first byte of the message word to deal with the third column transition of iteration $k - 4$: since this costs one control byte for one byte of condition, we still maintain 2^8 valid possibilities. Finally, with the lasting byte of the message word (the third), we look for a good transition for the ninth column of iteration $k - 3$: this costs one control byte for two bytes of conditions but we had maintained 2^8 valid possibilities before. Thus, in the end, we have a good probability to find a valid message word for all the transitions cited. However, we didn't take care of the eleventh column of iteration $k - 4$, which costs us one byte of condition. To summarize, this whole step will cost us 2^8 tries because we had a total of six control bytes for a total of seven bytes of conditions. Repeating this reasoning for all the message words inserted at each iteration of the differential path explains the 2^{112} tries cost for the whole collision attack.

One may argue that we indeed need to try 2^{112} all-difference pairs of states but the basic operation is costly when playing with the control bytes. Indeed, with the previous example, some steps require to pass through 2^8 or 2^{16} values of message words, each requiring only a SubBytes computation on a whole column, or one or two iteration processes (depending on which column of the state the transition occur). Even if it is still an attack, the complexity would be a slightly higher. This argument is true if the attacker uses a naive search method. However, unexpensive precomputations allow to reduce the computational cost of the search table lookups. For example, with as few as 2^{32} precomputation time and memory, one can generate all the informations needed to quickly execute the search needed during the third step of the collision search. Only a few table lookups would then be required. One might also wonder why we did not count the complexity of the few 4-truncated-differences to 4-truncated-differences transitions. Such transitions always have a great probability to happen $P_A = (1 - 2^{-8})^4 \simeq 2^{-0,02}$. Therefore they have very little effect on the complexity of the attack. This operation is clearly less costly than doing a whole iteration process. Moreover, the compression function mode performs 40 iterations for one compression call. Thus our attack actually runs in less than 2^{112} hash computations, all the complexity coming from the generation of 2^{112} all-difference pairs of states.

Note that we checked that this kind of attack also works with a complexity of at most 2^{120} hash computations for all the rotation constants providing the best diffusion, which seems to indicate that the internal state of GRINDAHL is not big enough.

We provide in Appendix the extension of this technique for the second preimage case applied to the 256-bit version of GRINDAHL. However, note that the GRINDAHL conceptors only claimed a 128-bit security for (second) preimage resistance, showing that (second) preimages can be found in less than 2^{256} operations.

5   Discussion on the Attack and Possible Patches

Most of the difficulty of the presented attack is to actually find a good differential path, and this is possible by letting the differences totally spread and start from an all-difference pair of states. Moreover, even if better differential trails may be found by maintaining a low weight of differences (which is hard to find), we think that the complexity will not drastically decrease compared to our attack. Indeed, the complexity cost grows quickly due to the last iterations of the differential trail (where very few control bytes are available), and these steps will remain very costly whatever the differential trail used. Said in other words, we can compute a lower bound on the complexity of an attack using any truncated-differential path and control bytes. For example, a short program gives us that a similar truncated-differential attack for the 256-bit version of GRINDAHL requires at least 2^{104} operations (whatever the truncated-differential path). Note that this does not mean that such an attack exists.

Thus it would be very interesting to think of a new version of GRINDAHL (with a comparable efficiency) that resists the presented attack but also any attack dealing with truncated-differences and control bytes. Thus, one wants the lower bound on the complexity of an attack using truncated-differential path and control bytes to be greater or equal to 2^{128} operations, and even greater for a good security margin. If this is possible, an attacker that wants to find a collision would have to first find a differential trail and then to deal with the actual values of differences in order to lower the complexity. The SubBytes transformation would therefore discourage this kind of attack and we would obtain a hash function with a strong security argument. A new GRINDAHL version with such a property and a reasonable efficiency could be designed by adding some more columns in the states. The question of the number of the columns to be added or other possible patches is left open for future researches.

6   Conclusion

We showed in this work that the 256-bit version of GRINDAHL is not collision resistant. By introducing a non-intuitive technique in order to find a good differential path and with a careful use of the control bytes available, we presented an attack finding collisions with no more than 2^{112} hash computations. We believe that such a reasoning would apply for the 512-bit version of GRINDAHL, even if the search space for a differential path in this case would be much bigger. Finally, we provided possible patches for the 256-bit version of GRINDAHL that may lead to new versions with stronger security arguments.

Acknowledgements

The author would like to thank the conceptors of GRINDAHL (Lars Knudsen, Christian Rechberger, Søren Thomsen) and Henri Gilbert, Olivier Billet and Yannick Seurin for their valuable remarks on the attack and discussions on the GRINDAHL design.

References

1. Augot, D., Finiasz, M., Sendrier, N.: A Family of Fast Syndrome Based Cryptographic Hash Functions. In: Dawson, E., Vaudenay, S. (eds.) Mycrypt 2005. LNCS, vol. 3715, pp. 64–83. Springer, Heidelberg (2005)
2. Bellare, M., Ristenpart, T.: Multi-Property-Preserving Hash Domain Extension and the EMD Transform. In: Lai, X., Chen, K. (eds.) ASIACRYPT 2006. LNCS, vol. 4284, pp. 299–314. Springer, Heidelberg (2006)
3. Bentahar, K., Page, D., Saarinen, M.-J.O., Silverman, J.H., Smart, N.P.: LASH. In: Proceedings of Second NIST Cryptographic Hash Workshop (2006). Available from: www.csrc.nist.gov/pki/HashWorkshop/2006/program_2006.htm
4. Bertoni, G., Daemen, J., Peeters, M., Van Assche, G.: RadioGatun, a Belt-and-Mill Hash Function. In: Proceedings of Second NIST Cryptographic Hash Workshop (2006). Available from: www.csrc.nist.gov/pki/HashWorkshop/2006/program_2006.htm
5. Biham, E., Dunkelman, O.: A Framework for Iterative Hash Functions: HAIFA. In: Proceedings of Second NIST Cryptographic Hash Workshop (2006). Available from: www.csrc.nist.gov/pki/HashWorkshop/2006/program_2006.htm
6. Billet, O., Robshaw, M.J.B., Peyrin, T.: On Building Hash Functions From Multivariate Quadratic Equations. In: Pieprzyk, J. (ed.) Information Security and Privacy – ACISP 2007. LNCS, Springer, Heidelberg (2007)
7. Black, J., Rogaway, P., Shrimpton, T.: Black-Box Analysis of the Block-Cipher-Based Hash-Function Constructions from PGV. In: Yung, M. (ed.) CRYPTO 2002. LNCS, vol. 2442, pp. 320–335. Springer, Heidelberg (2002)
8. De Cannière, C., Rechberger, C.: Finding SHA-1 Characteristics: General Results and Applications. In: Lai, X., Chen, K. (eds.) ASIACRYPT 2006. LNCS, vol. 4284, pp. 1–20. Springer, Heidelberg (2006)
9. Contini, S., Lenstra, A.K., Steinfeld, R.: VSH, an Efficient and Provable Collision-Resistant Hash Function. In: Vaudenay, S. (ed.) EUROCRYPT 2006. LNCS, vol. 4004, pp. 165–182. Springer, Heidelberg (2006)
10. Damgård, I.: A Design Principle for Hash Functions. In: Brassard, G. (ed.) CRYPTO 1989. LNCS, vol. 435, pp. 416–427. Springer, Heidelberg (1990)
11. Daemen, J., Rijmen, V.: The Design of Rijndael. Springer, Heidelberg (2002)
12. Menezes, A.J., Vanstone, S.A., Van Oorschot, P.C.: Handbook of Applied Cryptography. CRC Press, Boca Raton, FL, USA (1996)
13. Hirose, S.: Some Plausible Constructions of Double-Block-Length Hash Functions. In: Robshaw, M. (ed.) FSE 2006. LNCS, vol. 4047, pp. 210–225. Springer, Heidelberg (2006)
14. Hoch, J.J., Shamir, A.: Breaking the ICE - Finding Multicollisions in Iterated Concatenated and Expanded (ICE) Hash Functions. In: Robshaw, M.J.B. (ed.) FSE 2006. LNCS, vol. 4047, pp. 179–194. Springer, Heidelberg (2006)
15. Hong, D., Chang, D., Sung, J., Lee, S., Hong, S., Lee, J., Moon, D., Chee, S.: Dedicated 256-Bit Hash Function: FORK-256. In: Robshaw, M. (ed.) FSE 2006. LNCS, vol. 4047, pp. 195–209. Springer, Heidelberg (2006)

16. Joux, A.: Multi-collisions in Iterated Hash Functions. In: Franklin, M. (ed.) CRYPTO 2004. LNCS, vol. 3152, pp. 306–316. Springer, Heidelberg (2004)
17. Kelsey, J., Kohno, T.: Herding Hash Functions and the Nostradamus Attack. In: Vaudenay, S. (ed.) EUROCRYPT 2006. LNCS, vol. 4004, pp. 183–200. Springer, Heidelberg (2006)
18. Kelsey, J., Schneier, B.: Second Preimages on n-bit Hash Functions for Much Less Than 2^n Work. In: Cramer, R.J.F. (ed.) EUROCRYPT 2005. LNCS, vol. 3494, pp. 474–490. Springer, Heidelberg (2005)
19. Knudsen, L.R.: Truncated and Higher Order Differentials. In: Preneel, B. (ed.) Fast Software Encryption. LNCS, vol. 1008, pp. 196–211. Springer, Heidelberg (1995)
20. Knudsen, L.R., Rechberger, C., Thomsen, S.S.: Grindahl - A family of hash functions. In: Biryukov, A. (ed.) Fast Software Encryption – FSE 2007. LNCS, Springer, Heidelberg (2007)
21. Matusiewicz, K., Peyrin, T., Billet, O., Contini, S., Pieprzyk, J.: Cryptanalysis of FORK-256. In: Biryukov, A. (ed.) Fast Software Encryption – FSE 2007. LNCS, Springer, Heidelberg (2007)
22. Merkle, R.C.: One Way Hash Functions and DES. In: Brassard, G. (ed.) CRYPTO 1989. LNCS, vol. 435, pp. 428–446. Springer, Heidelberg (1990)
23. National Institute of Standards and Technology. FIPS 197: Advanced Encryption Standard, November 2001. Available from: www.csrc.nist.gov
24. National Institute of Standards and Technology. Advanced Hash Standard. Available from: www.csrc.nist.gov/pki/HashWorkshop/index.html
25. National Institute of Standards and Technology. FIPS 180-2: Secure Hash Standard (August 2002). Available from: www.csrc.nist.gov.
26. Peyrin, T., Gilbert, H., Muller, F., Robshaw, M.J.B.: Combining Compression Functions and Block Cipher-Based Hash Functions. In: Lai, X., Chen, K. (eds.) ASIACRYPT 2006. LNCS, vol. 4284, pp. 315–331. Springer, Heidelberg (2006)
27. Preneel, B.: Analysis and Design of Cryptographic Hash Functions. PhD thesis, Katholieke Universiteit Leuven (1993)
28. Preneel, B., Govaerts, R., Vandewalle, J.: Hash Functions Based on Block Ciphers: A Synthetic Approach. In: Stinson, D.R. (ed.) CRYPTO 1993. LNCS, vol. 773, pp. 368–378. Springer, Heidelberg (1994)
29. Rivest, R.L.: RFC 1321: The MD5 Message-Digest Algorithm (April 1992). Available from, www.ietf.org/rfc/rfc1321.txt
30. Seurin, Y., Peyrin, T.: Security Analysis of Constructions Combining FIL Random Oracles. In: Biryukov, A. (ed.) Fast Software Encryption – FSE 2007. LNCS, Springer, Heidelberg (2007)
31. Wang, X., Lai, X., Feng, D., Chen, H., Yu, X.: Cryptanalysis of the Hash Functions MD4 and RIPEMD. In: Cramer, R.J.F. (ed.) EUROCRYPT 2005. LNCS, vol. 3494, pp. 1–18. Springer, Heidelberg (2005)
32. Wang, X., Yin, Y.L., Yu, H.: Finding Collisions in the Full SHA-1. In: Shoup, V. (ed.) CRYPTO 2005. LNCS, vol. 3621, pp. 17–36. Springer, Heidelberg (2005)
33. Wang, X., Yu, H.: How to Break MD5 and Other Hash Functions. In: Cramer, R.J.F. (ed.) EUROCRYPT 2005. LNCS, vol. 3494, pp. 19–35. Springer, Heidelberg (2005)
34. Wang, X., Yu, H., Yin, Y.L.: Efficient Collision Search Attacks on SHA-0. In: Shoup, V. (ed.) CRYPTO 2005. LNCS, vol. 3621, pp. 1–16. Springer, Heidelberg (2005)

Appendix

Extending the Collision Attack to Second Preimage Resistance. Our previously explained collision attack has a nice feature for an attacker: one does not care about the

566   T. Peyrin

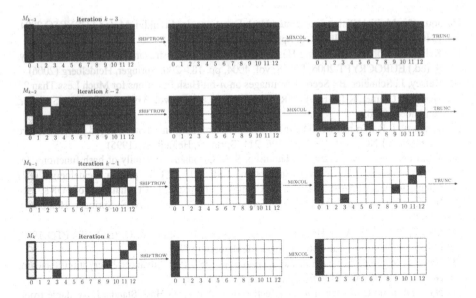

Fig. 2. Truncated-differential path in 4 iterations starting from an all-difference pair of states, to be used for a second preimage attack

actual values of the differences. Thus, we have very few constraints during the differential path. This remark allows us to extend our collision attack to second preimage resistance if the second preimage challenge has a reasonable number of message blocks. For example, let us look at the differential path from Figure 2. If one wants to find a second preimage using this path, only the number of control bytes will change as compared with the collision attack case: when we previously had two control bytes because of the insertion of a non-zero truncated-difference (capital letters in Table 3), we only get one control byte since the first message block is fixed by the challenge. For the same reason, when a zero truncated-difference is inserted, we have one control byte for the collision case (small letters in Table 3) and we have no more control byte in the second preimage case.

Using exactly the same techniques as for the collision attack, one can find a second preimage in approximatively $2^{28\times 8} = 2^{224}$ hash computations whereas 2^{256} hash computations should be required for an ideal 256-bit hash function. The drawback of this method is that we require the challenge to contain enough message blocks in order to have enough iterations to follow our differential path (around 8 iterations: 3 to reach an all-difference pair of states, 4 to follow the path from Figure 2 and 1 to force the truncation at the end of our differential trail). Moreover, we need approximatively 7 more iterations if we also take in account that we need to generate 2^{224} all-difference pairs of internal state to pass the differential trail. Thus, our attack works for a challenge of at least 15 message words.

Note that the GRINDAHL designers only claimed a 2^{128} security for their 256-bit version, and provided in their original paper a (second) preimage algorithm requiring 2^{176} operations and memory with a meet-in-the-middle reasoning on the internal state size.

Table 4. Dependencies of the message blocks used as control bytes and inserted during the truncated-differential path from Figure 2 in a second preimage attack, for an internal collision at the end of iteration k. Note that for the pairs of message words that will be used as control bytes, since we set ourselves in the second preimage attack case, capital letters means that we have one control byte (we insert a difference for this block) and small letters means that we have no control byte (no difference inserted for this message block).

it	col	cost	message blocks inserted											
			$k-4$				$k-3$				$k-2$			
			A	B	C	D	A	B	C	D	A	B	c	D
k-3	2	1					×							
	3	1	×	×										
	7	1				×								
k-2	1	2		—		—			—	—	×			
	2	2	—		—	—	—					×		
	3	3	—	—	—	—		×	×					
	5	3	—	—	—	—	—	×		×				
	6	3	—	—	—			×	×					
	7	2	—	—	—					×				
	8	2	—	—	—	—		×						
	9	2	×	×	×	×	×							
	10	2	—	—										×
	11	2			—	—	×		×	×				
	12	1	—		—	—		×		×				
k-1	3	3	—	—	—	—	—	—	—	—	×	×		
	9	3	—	—	—	—	×	×	×	×				
	11	3	—	—	—	—			—	—	×		×	×
	12	3	—	—	—	—	—		—	—	×			×
COST			**0**				**16**				**12**			

A Key Recovery Attack on Edon80

Martin Hell and Thomas Johansson

Dept. of Electrical and Information Technology, Lund University,
P.O. Box 118, 221 00 Lund, Sweden
{martin,thomas}@eit.lth.se

Abstract. Edon80 is a recent stream cipher design that has advanced to the third and last phase of the eSTREAM project. It has remained unbroken and untweaked since it was designed and submitted to eS-TREAM. It is now one of the 8 final hardware candidates. In this paper we cryptanalyze the cipher by describing a key recovery attack. The complexity of the attack is around 2^{69} simple operations for a keystream of similar length.

1 Introduction

Edon80 is a recent stream cipher design, described in [1], that was submitted to the eSTREAM project. It uses a novel approach in stream cipher design, concatenating 80 basic building blocks derived from 4 different quasigroups of order 4. A quasigroup is basically a Latin square, a very simple combinatorial object.

The design has received a lot of attention and much work has been done based on Edon80. Regarding security, Hong observed in [2] that with some small probability, the period of the keystream sequence could be quite small. This was further studied by the designers themselves in [3] and later also in the paper [4]. However, this property could not be exploited in any kind of attack. A theoretical treatment of the quasigroups used in Edon80 is given in [5]. Finally, from an implementations point of view, it was shown in [6] that Edon80 can be implemented using less than 3000 gates. Even though the eSTREAM project has allowed tweaks, the Edon80 construction has remained untweaked since it was designed and submitted to eSTREAM. However, due to the probability of short periods, the designers has introduced a limitation in the number of keystream bits that can be produced per key/IV pair. This limitation is 2^{48} bits and was proposed in [7], when entering the second phase of eSTREAM.

The small implementation and the fact that the construction has remained untweaked are the main reasons for the success of Edon80 in eSTREAM – its advancement to the third and last phase phase of the eSTREAM project. It is now one of the 8 final hardware candidates.

In this paper we cryptanalyze the cipher by describing a key recovery attack. The complexity of the attack is around 2^{69} for a keystream of similar length. The design philosophy is not completely broken. A design using, say, 160 concatenated quasigroup operations would be out of scope of the new attack. On the other hand, such a change of the design would double the implementation cost, making such a design much less interesting.

The new attack to be presented is based on exploiting some periodicity inside the generator. Using the fact that some elements will repeat with large probability, we can build a kind of test to find out the correct value of the key bits used at the end of the concatenation. This leads to a key recovery attack, where we may vary some parameters and obtain a trade-off between required length of the received key stream and the computational complexity.

The paper is organized as follows. In Section 2 we describe in more detail the stream cipher design Edon80. In Section 3 we summarize some previous work relating to the security of Edon80. In Section 4 we then give the basic ideas of the new attack, followed by a more detailed analysis in Section 5. In Section 6 we discuss how the attack can be efficiently implemented. In Section 7 we verify some of the claims by presenting simulation results. Finally, in Section 8 we derive some possible attack complexities and then we conclude.

2   Description of Edon80

In this section we give a description of the Edon80 stream cipher. An additive synchronous stream cipher is built around a keystream generator. A generator takes a key K and an IV value (nonce) IV as its input and produces an arbitrary long keystream sequence $Z = z_1, z_2, z_3, \ldots$. The keystream is then added to the plaintext in the encryption phase.

The sizes of the key and IV in Edon80 are 80 bits and 64 bits, respectively. The design of Edon80 is based on string transformation using 4 quasigroups of order 4 denoted $(Q, \bullet_j)$ $(0 \leq j \leq 3)$. The internal updated state consists of 80 memory cells of two bits each. Each memory cell, referred to as an e-transformer $*_i$ $(0 \leq i \leq 79)$, holds 2 bits representing a value between 0 and 3. The 80 e-transformers are connected in series and the result from $*_i$ is used as input to $*_{i+1}$.

The 80 bit key K is divided into 40 2-bit values $K = K_0 K_1 \ldots K_{39}$ each represented as a value $0 \leq K_i \leq 3$. The quasigroup $(Q, *_i)$, $(0 \leq i \leq 79)$ used by e-transformer $*_i$ is given by

$$(Q, *_i) \leftarrow \begin{cases} (Q, \bullet_{K_i}) & 0 \leq i \leq 39, \\ (Q, \bullet_{K_{i-40}}) & 40 \leq i \leq 79. \end{cases}$$

The quasigroups used in Edon80 are given in Figure 1.

Let the value in $*_i$ at time t be denoted $a_{i,t}$. Then the values are updated as

$$\begin{cases} a_{0,0} = a_0 *_0 0, \\ a_{0,j} = a_{0,j-1} *_0 (j \mod 4), & 1 \leq j, \\ a_{i,0} = a_i *_i a_{i-1,0}, & 1 \leq i \leq 79, \\ a_{i,j} = a_{i,j-1} *_i a_{i-1,j}, & 1 \leq i \leq 79, \ 1 \leq j, \end{cases}$$

where a_i denotes the initial value of $*_i$ for $1 \leq i \leq 79$ at the beginning of the keystream generation phase.

$\bullet_0$	0 1 2 3	$\bullet_1$	0 1 2 3	$\bullet_2$	0 1 2 3	$\bullet_3$	0 1 2 3
0	0 2 1 3	0	1 3 0 2	0	2 1 0 3	0	3 2 1 0
1	2 1 3 0	1	0 1 2 3	1	1 2 3 0	1	1 0 3 2
2	1 3 0 2	2	2 0 3 1	2	3 0 2 1	2	0 3 2 1
3	3 0 2 1	3	3 2 1 0	3	0 3 1 2	3	2 1 0 3

Fig. 1. The 4 quasigroups used in Edon80

Summarizing, the infinite period 4 string $0, 1, 2, 3, 0, 1, 2, 3, 0, \ldots$ is transformed by $*_0$ and the resulting string is transformed by $*_1$ etc. The keystream is obtained by taking every second value produced by $*_{79}$, see Figure 2.

$*_i$		0	1	2	3	0	1	2	3	0
$*_0$	a_0	$a_{0,0}$	$a_{0,1}$	$a_{0,2}$	$a_{0,3}$	$a_{0,4}$	$a_{0,5}$	$a_{0,6}$	$a_{0,7}$	$a_{0,8}$
$*_1$	a_1	$a_{1,0}$	$a_{1,1}$	$a_{1,2}$	$a_{1,3}$	$a_{1,4}$	$a_{1,5}$	$a_{1,6}$	$a_{1,7}$	$a_{1,8}$
$\vdots$	$\vdots$	$\vdots$	$\vdots$	$\vdots$	$\vdots$	$\vdots$	$\vdots$	$\vdots$	$\vdots$	$\vdots$
$*_{79}$	a_{79}	$a_{79,0}$	$a_{79,1}$	$a_{79,2}$	$a_{79,3}$	$a_{79,4}$	$a_{79,5}$	$a_{79,6}$	$a_{79,7}$	$a_{79,8}$

Fig. 2. The quasigroup string e-transformation in keystream generation mode

For simplicity, we adopt the notation $Z = z_1, z_3, z_5, \ldots$ as the received keystream, where

$$z_t = a_{79,t} \quad t \geq 0, \quad t \text{ odd}.$$

A schematic picture of Edon80 is given in Figure 3. Remember that only every second output is used in the keystream.

$0, 1, 2, 3, 0, \ldots \to \boxed{*_0} \to \boxed{*_1} \to \boxed{*_2} \to \quad \to \boxed{*_{76}} \to \boxed{*_{77}} \to \boxed{*_{78}} \to \boxed{*_{79}} \to$ keystream

Fig. 3. The keystream generator Edon80

The initial state of Edon80, $(a_0, a_1, \ldots, a_{79})$, is determined by the key K and the IV through an IV setup process. Exactly how this is done is not relevant in our analysis and we refer to the design document [1] for a detailed description of the IV setup. We can assume that the mapping from the 80-bit key and the 64-bit IV to the initial state $a_0, a_1, \ldots, a_{79}$ is a random mapping. However, the attack will still be applicable even if the mapping would be shown to suffer from some nonrandomness.

Edon80 is designed to be a hardware efficient stream cipher. The hardware description is slightly different from the algorithmic description given above. In order to output 1 bit/clock, the implementation uses a second 2-bit memory cell in $*_i$ which stores the output from $*_{i-1}$. Though, in [6] the authors demonstrated an implementation which does not use this extra memory cell. The implementation required only a gate count of about 3000 but the output was decreased to 1/80 bit/clock resulting in a throughput of just a few Mbit/s. However, this small implementation cost shows that Edon80 is a very interesting candidate for a stream cipher suitable for constrained environments.

3   Previous Analysis of Edon80

In this section we review the previous results and known properties of Edon80 that will be used in our cryptanalysis. The most important property that will be exploited in the attack is the relatively short period of Edon80. In the design document [1] it was stated that the expected average period of the keystream is about 2^{103}. In [2], Hong argued that there are many key/IV pairs that produce a keystream with undesirably short period. Referring to Figure 2, using exhaustive search all d-row key/state pairs of period $p = 4, 8$ and 16 was found. Extrapolating the results to 40 rows, and then repeating the same key for the lower 40 rows, it was concluded that there are many key/IV pairs that produce a keystream with relatively short period. As an example, it was claimed that there is a 2^{-75} probability that a key/IV pair generates a keystream with period 2^{61}. In response to these results, the designers claimed in [3] that the values given by Hong was actually underestimated and that the probability of generating a keystream with period less than 2^{61} was $2^{-18.62}$. Thus, with a total of $2^{79.62}$ bits we can expect to find a sequence with period less than 2^{61}. Further, it was concluded that the average period of Edon80 is 2^{91}. A more detailed investigation of the periods was given in [4]. Each e-transformer increases the period of the incoming string by a factor 1, 2, 3 or 4. Let X_i denote the factor by which e-transformer $*_i$ increases the period. Considering several consecutive e-transformers, it was shown that the probability distribution for X_i converges to the stationary distribution

$$X = \begin{pmatrix} 1 & 2 & 3 & 4 \\ \frac{1}{4} & \frac{1}{4} & \frac{11}{32} & \frac{5}{32} \end{pmatrix},$$

with expected value $E(X) = \frac{77}{32}$ and variance $\sigma^2 = V(X) = \frac{1079}{1024}$. Furthermore, let $2m$ be the total number of e-transformers and let P_{2m} be a random variable for the period after $2m$ e-transformers. Then when $m \to \infty$, probability density function (pdf) $f_{P_{2m}}$ can be approximated by the continuous function [4, section 2]

$$f_{P_{2m}}(s) = \frac{1}{0.701658s\sqrt{2\pi m}} \exp\left(-\frac{(\ln(s) - 1.535086m)^2}{0.984648m}\right), \quad 0 < s < \infty. \quad (1)$$

We refer to [4] for more details. Despite the relatively high probability of short periods, it has until now been unclear how to use this to obtain information about the key.

4   A Key Recovery Attack – Basic Ideas

In this section we give the ideas behind our key recovery attack on Edon80. The details are then given in Section 5. We assume a known plaintext scenario i.e., the keystream sequence $Z = z_1, z_3, z_5, \ldots$ is known to the adversary. The basic ideas behind the attack are based on the following properties of the cipher,

- The quasigroup $(Q, \bullet_j)$ $(0 \le j \le 3)$ used in e-transformer $*_i$ $(0 \le i \le 79)$ is completely determined by the key. For example, if we know which quasigroup is used in the last e-transformer, we also know 2 key bits.
- The period of the string produced by $*_i$ can be expected to be moderately small for small i. In fact, some internal values (output from e-transformers) will repeat with large probability due to the periodicity.

We visualize the attack in Figure 4 by considering a matrix with elements $a_{i,j}$, $(0 \le i \le 79, t \le j \le t + u + v)$, u, v to be defined later. Every column here corresponds to one specific time instance t. Also, the ith row corresponds to the ith e-transformer. Thus we have 80 rows in the Edon80 description. A restriction to the first B rows simply corresponds to an Edon instance with only B e-transformers.

Looking at a specific value $a_{i,j}$, this value is calculated from its neighbours to the left and above. I.e., the value at position (i, j) will depend on all values at

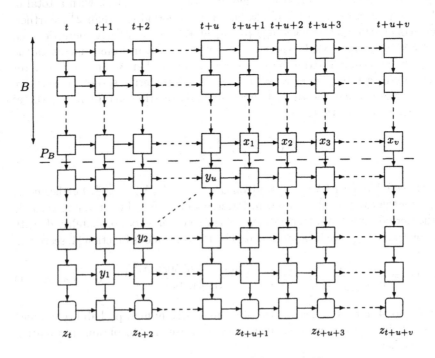

Fig. 4. Visualization of the attack idea

positions (i', j') for $i' < i$ and $j' < j$, i.e., all values above and to the left in the matrix.

In order to set up the attack, we select the B top rows as one part (upper part) and the remaining rows below as a second part (lower part) of the e-transformers. Consider two vectors, X and Y of length $v = |X|$ and $u = |Y|$ respectively,

$$X = (x_1, x_2, \ldots, x_v),$$
$$Y = (y_1, y_2, \ldots, y_u),$$

$x_i, y_j \in \{0, 1, 2, 3\}, i = 1, 2, \ldots v; j = 1, 2, \ldots, u$, with the values located as shown in Figure 4. For Edon80, we then have $B = 80 - u - 1$. As can be seen, the $X = (x_1, x_2, \ldots, x_v)$ vector is simply v symbols coming out of the chain of B e-transformers starting from some predetermined time. The $Y = (y_1, y_2, \ldots, y_u)$ can be characterized as the values needed to compute the internal state of the second part of the e-transformers.

Each quasigroup transformation will increase the period of the initial string by a factor of 1, 2, 3 or 4. Thus the period, denoted P_i, of the sequence produced by $*_i$ is given by

$$P_i = 2^{\mu_1} 3^{\mu_2}, \tag{2}$$

for some $\mu_1, \mu_2 \in \mathbb{Z}$. Let P_B be the period of the sequence produced by the upper part of the e-transformers, giving output corresponding to the vector $X = (x_1, x_2, \ldots, x_v)$. Then, the matrix corresponding to time instance t and time instance $t + kP_B$, $k = 0, 1, 2, \ldots$ will have the same values in the e-transformers $*_i$ for $i \leq B$. More specifically, and which will be used in the attack, *the vector X will have the same value in all considered time instances.*

Assume for a moment that the key bits used to determine the quasigroups in the second part are known. With in total $u + v$ values in the vectors X and Y, we consider the $(u + v)/2$ known keystream symbols that are directly below X and Y, see Figure 4 again. Using the knowledge of these keystream symbols, the number of possible combinations of the two vectors X, Y will be reduced from 4^{u+v} to roughly 2^{u+v}. The idea is to choose u and v such that $v > u$. This means that not all X vectors will be possible in the set of possible X, Y pairs. Thus, the outcome of this part is a set Γ_k such that

$$\Gamma_k = \{X : \text{there exists } (X, Y) \text{ matching } z_{t+kP_B}, z_{t+kP_B+2}, \ldots z_{t+kP_B+u+v}\}.$$

Finally, we combine this with the fact that the vector $X = (x_1, x_2, \ldots, x_v)$ will be the same at time instances t and $t + kP_B$. This means that X must appear in all sets Γ_k and hence in the intersection of them. The procedure should now be clear.

For each choice of the $2u + 2$ key bits used to define the quasigroups in the lower part, we determine the sets Γ_k, for $k = 0, 1, 2, \ldots$. We take the intersection between the sets obtained so far, and continue until the intersection is empty. If we eventually receive an empty intersection, the chosen value of the key bits is discarded. On the other hand, if at the end there is only one vector X in the intersection, then we assume that we found the correct key bits. The number of key bits that are guessed in this attack is $2u + 2$. When we know these key bits, the remaining part of the key could be exhaustively searched.

5   A More Detailed Analysis of the Attack

In this section we give a more detailed analysis of the different parts and parameters used in the attack. The parameters that will be covered are

- Guessing the correct period P_B.
- The length of the vectors X and Y.
- The number of time instances that has to be considered in order to discard a wrong key candidate.

5.1   The Period P_B

As stated in (2), the period of the sequence after B e-transformers have the form $P_B = 2^{\mu_1} 3^{\mu_2}$ for some μ_1, μ_2. It is clear that the X vector will repeat the same values if the distance between two matrices as described in Figure 4 is a multiple of the period. So we will assume a distance P_B' and the repetition of the value for the X vectors will be true if the actual period is a factor, i.e., if $P_B | P_B'$. We denote the probability that $P_B | P_B'$ by $\alpha_{P_B'}$. This value is, according to [4], approximately calculated as

$$\alpha_{P_B'} = \int_0^{P_B'} f_{P_{2m}}(s)\,ds, \tag{3}$$

where $f_{P_{2m}}(s)$ is defined in (1).

Recall that X_i denoted the factor by which e-transformer $*_i$ increases the period. In Section 3 we saw that the probability distribution for X_i converges to the distribution

$$X = \begin{pmatrix} 1 & 2 & 3 & 4 \\ \frac{1}{4} & \frac{1}{4} & \frac{11}{32} & \frac{5}{32} \end{pmatrix}.$$

This gives us a rough idea of the expected period. For example, if $B = 64$ we can expect around 16 of the factors being 1, around the same number being 2, around 22 factors being 3, and around 10 factors being 4. So for $B = 64$ we can set $P_B' = 2^{36} \cdot 3^{22}$ and there is a fairly large chance that $P_B | P_B'$. The actual probability for different values of the period deviated slightly from the above since the probabilities are not as the asymptotic ones for low values of i. However, it can all be computed numerically.

5.2   The Length of Vectors X and Y

Assuming that we have chosen a value $B = 80 - u - 1$ and an assumed period P_B' such that $P_B | P_B'$, we now consider the choice of v. In order to create a set Γ_k where not all X vectors appear we need to choose $v > u$. We denote the difference by d, hence

$$v = u + d.$$

The simplest approach is then to start at time t and move forward. We assign all 4^2 possible values to y_1, y_2. We can then calculate everything below these positions in Figure 4. As we already know the value of z_{t+2}, only 4 of the possible candidates for y_1, y_2 will survive. For each surviving value of y_1, y_2, we assign all possible values for y_3, y_4, compute the values below and check against the known value of z_{t+4}. We will have 16 possibilities for the (y_1, y_2, y_3, y_4) vector. After finishing the Y vector we just continue in this fashion with $x_i, i = 1, \ldots x_v$. The set of possible assignments of (Y, X) is then 2^{u+v}. The complexity of calculating this set in this basic way is then roughly 2^{u+v}. Finally, the Y values are stripped off and the result is the set Γ_k. In an actual implementation we can make the constant factor in the algorithm very small. This will be described in more detail in Section 6.

5.3   The Number of Intersections Needed to Discard a Key Candidate

The total number of possible X vectors is 4^v. However, in the algorithm, using the knowledge of the keystream z_t, the vector X can only take 2^{u+v} values. Thus, using $v = u + d$, only a fraction $1/2^d$ of all values will be possible. Actually, in practice it is slightly less because some X vectors may appear twice (for different Y vectors). If we put

$$4^v \cdot \left(\frac{1}{2^d}\right)^K \approx 1,$$

we see that we need about $K \approx \frac{2v}{d}$ sets $\Gamma_k, k = 0, 1, \ldots, K - 1$ to get an empty intersection. At least, the average number is around $2v/d$. As an example, for the choice $v = u + 2$ $(d = 2)$ there can be at most 25% of all the X vectors in Γ_k. Since the number of possible X vectors is 4^v we expect that we do not need much more than v sets.

In general, a higher value of d will increase the computational complexity but since the reduction of possible X values in an intersection is much higher, it will lead to a smaller number of required intersections and hence a shorter required keystream length.

5.4   Computational Complexity

Let us summarize the computational complexity of the attack. We assume first a value $B = 80 - u - 1$ and P'_B such that $P_B | P'_B$. There is an error probability, $1 - \alpha_{P'_B}$ that this assumption is not true.

Then we guess $2u + 2$ key bits corresponding to the last $u + 1$ quasigroups used. For each such key the complexity of checking it is then roughly $2^{u+v} \cdot K$. Since $v = u + d$ this results in a total complexity of about

$$2^{4u+d+3} \cdot \frac{u+d}{d}.$$

After recovering $2u + 2$ key bits one can either reconstruct the sequence after B e-transformers and apply the same attack again, now with much less complexity; or simply do an exhaustive key search on the remaining key bits.

6   Algorithmic Aspects

In this section we describe some algorithmic aspects of the attack and show that the complexity is based on very simple operations, much faster than the operation of verifying a key candidate in exhaustive key search. The considerations here relate to the part of the attack that calculates the Γ_k sets.

Let $(a_{B+1,t}, a_{B+2,t}, \ldots, a_{79,t})$ be the state of the lower part of Edon80 at time t and denoted S_t. In Figure 4 this corresponds to a column starting below an x_i value.

In a straight forward algorithm we save all possible states S_t and the corresponding X vector. Each time a new $a_{79,t}$ (t even) is introduced, each state S_t with corresponding X vector will produce 4 new states. Each new state will have a corresponding X vector with 2 additional entries. Thus, at the end of the algorithm, we will have 2^{u+v} possible states and X vectors. We can note that the last step is the most expensive step. It will cost $C \cdot 2^{u+v}$ where C is the cost for making $2u + 2$ table lookups. This constant can be significantly reduced by using a slightly different algorithm.

We can take advantage of the following observation. Since the length of the state vector S_t is $u + 1$ there are in general 4^{u+1} possible values for the state of the lower part of Edon80 at any time. However, looking at the attack as illustrated in Figure 4, where we have a given keystream sequence $z_t, z_{t+2}, \ldots$, we observe that at any time instance (with a received keystream symbol) only $2^{2\lceil u/2 \rceil}$ different states of the second part of Edon80 are possible.

This property comes from the fact that we know every second of the values $z_t = a_{79,t}$. Knowing $a_{79,t}$ and $a_{79,t+2}$ and allowing 4 possible values for $a_{79,t+1}$ will give 4 possibilities for the pair $(a_{77,t+2}, a_{78,t+2})$. Knowing $a_{79,t}$, $a_{79,t+2}$ and $a_{79,t+4}$ and allowing 16 possibilities for $(a_{79,t+1}, a_{79,t+3})$ gives 16 possibilities for the vector $(a_{75,t+4}, a_{76,t+4}, a_{77,t+4}, a_{78,t+4})$ etc.

We can from the known keystream compute all 2^u possible states for times $t+u+1, t+u+3, \ldots$. We can then obtain a trellis by including all possible state transitions from time $t + u + 1$ to $t + u + 3$ and so on. A state transition from time $t + u + 1$ to $t + u + 3$ can be labelled by the values of (x_1, x_2) giving rise to that transition. This way of modelling the lower part of Edon80 is useful when we implement the algorithm for computing the Γ_k sets for a given choice of key bits.

We can divide the X vector in two equally sized parts, $X = (X_1, X_2)$, where $X_1 = (x_1, x_2, \ldots, x_{v/2})$ and $X_2 = (x_{v/2+1}, x_{v/2+2}, \ldots, x_v)$. We first assign Y and compute possible values of Y as before. This is actually equivalent to computing the state of the second part of Edon80 at time $t + u$, so when we continue we do not keep the value of Y but instead we keep the state S_t at the time we are considering. We continue as before, but only over the X_1 vector. This results in a set of possible X_1 vectors and their ending states $S_{t+u+v/2}$. The complexity of calculating this set is then $C \cdot 2^{u+v/2}$. Next, for every choice of the 2^u possible states $S_{t+u+v/2}$ at time $t + u + v/2$, we assign all possible values for $x_{v/2+1}, x_{v/2+2}, \ldots$, and create a second set of all possible X_2 vectors and their starting states $S_{t+u+v/2}$. The complexity of calculating this second set is also

$C \cdot 2^{u+v/2}$. Thus, calculating the two sets is much faster than finding Γ_k in the straight forward algorithm.

The bottle neck in this algorithm is to create Γ_k from the two sets. This is done by selecting all possible combinations of X_1 and X_2 where the ending state of X_1 and the starting state of X_2 are the same. With the two sets sorted according to the states $S_{t+u+v/2}$, the set Γ_k is easily obtained. Since the size of Γ_k is about 2^{u+v} this does not change the asymptotic complexity but the constant term in the complexity is very small. Each operation consists of just concatenating X_1 and X_2, a very simple operation.

The memory requirement in the algorithm is moderately small. We need about 2^{u+v} words, where each word represents an X vector.

7   Simulation Results

In order to verify the attack, it has been simulated on a reduced version of Edon80. We have produced a keystream exactly as in Edon80 with the modification that only 24 e-transformers was used, i.e., a variant logically denoted Edon24. We have investigated the case when the assumed period P'_B is such that $P_B | P'_B$. The simulations target the number of possible values for the vector X that are still possible after intersecting the k' sets Γ_k, $k = 0, 1, \ldots, k'$. Table 1 shows the average number of remaining elements for different values of k' when $v = u + 2$, i.e., when $d = 2$. As stated in Section 5.3 we expect that we need about v intersections of sets Γ_k. For all simulated values of u we have in average only 0.1 possible value for the X vector left in Γ_k after $v = u + 2$ intersections. This verifies our claim. Table 2 shows the average number of remaining elements when $d = 6$. As expected, the intersections produce an empty set with much fewer sets Γ_k than in the case with $d = 2$.

Table 1. The average number of possible values for X left in the intersection of $\Gamma_k, k = 0, 1, \ldots, k'$ sets for different choice of u, when $d = 2$

k'	$|Y| = u$					
	4	5	6	7	8	9
0	909.3	3597.7	14534.2	57953.3	232281.4	927796.6
1	201.6	788.9	3226.0	12823.0	51486.9	205105.3
2	45.8	172.3	716.5	2837.0	11407.7	45379.9
3	10.1	37.7	159.0	626.2	2526.2	10033.2
4	2.3	8.3	35.2	138.4	558.9	2223.5
5	0.5	1.9	7.8	30.6	124.2	493.0
6	0.1	0.4	1.7	6.8	27.7	109.2
7	0.0	0.1	0.4	1.5	6.1	23.9
8	0.0	0.0	0.1	0.3	1.3	5.4
9	0.0	0.0	0.0	0.1	0.3	1.1
10	0.0	0.0	0.0	0.0	0.1	0.2
11	0.0	0.0	0.0	0.0	0.0	0.1
12	0.0	0.0	0.0	0.0	0.0	0.0

Table 2. The average number of possible values for X left in the intersection of Γ_k, $k = 0, 1, \ldots, k'$ sets for different choice of u, when $d = 6$

	$|Y| = u$			
k'	4	5	6	7
0	16265.1	64310.8	260222.9	1040318.8
1	253.0	983.8	4036.7	16164.6
2	3.8	15.2	62.9	250.0
3	0.1	0.2	0.9	4.1
4	0.0	0.0	0.0	0.1
5	0.0	0.0	0.0	0.0

Moreover, our implementation also always found the correct key and discarded all false key candidates using our algorithm.

8   Estimating the Attack Complexity

As explained before, we have several parameters that we can choose, giving different parameters for the attack. Basically, there is a trade-off between the required length of the received keystream and computational complexity of the key recovery part. For example, choose $d = 2$ and $u = 9$ as simulated above, i.e. $B = 70$ in the Edon80 case, and an assumed period of $P'_B = 2^{40} \cdot 3^{24}$. Then the computational complexity is low, roughly 2^{44} but the required keystream is large, roughly $2^{78} \cdot 11$, where the factor 11 comes from the fact that we need to intersect at most $11 + 1$ sets Γ_k. With the low computational complexity we can of course increase the d parameter and reduce the required keystream to roughly 2^{78}. Finally, we must include the error probability. An error occurs if P'_B is not a multiple of the true period P_B. We simply use (3) to estimate this probability. A numerical calculation gives that the period is below 2^{78} with probability more than $1/2$. There may be some possible periods below 2^{78} which does not divide P'_B. On the other hand, we can try out different (the most probable) forms of P'_B in our attack with only a slight increase in complexity. So here we can assume that the error probability is about $1 - \alpha_{P'_B} \approx 1/2$.

Clearly, such a long received keystream sequence as 2^{78} is not desirable, even if the computational complexity is low. We also see that allowing the error probability to be quite close to 1 might be beneficial. We will then repeat the attack $\alpha_{P'_B}^{-1}$ times and the requirement is now to receive $\alpha_{P'_B}^{-1}$ different keystreams (obtained from different IV values). The computational complexity, T, grows to

$$T = \alpha_{P'_B}^{-1} \cdot 2^{4u+d+3} \cdot \frac{u+d}{d}.$$

Though in average we only need slightly less than K intersections, there will be key candidates that need more intersections before they can be discarded. On the other hand, it is not crucial that *all* wrong key candidates are discarded. If we end up with a set up possible keys then these keys can be tested individually at the end. This will not affect the computational complexity. With $P'_B \cdot K$ keystream bits, we will have $K + 1$ sets Γ_k, $k = 0, 1, \ldots, K$ to intersect. This will keep the probability of false alarm low. Thus, the number of keystream bits, D_{IV}, that are needed from each IV is given by

$$D_{IV} = P'_B \cdot \frac{2u + 2d}{d}.$$

The total number of keystream bits, D_{tot}, is given by

$$D_{tot} = \alpha_{P'_B}^{-1} \cdot P'_B \cdot \frac{2u + 2d}{d}.$$

The trade-off parameters in the attack are u, d and P'_B. The attack complexities are all functions of these values. We consider two cases.

I There is no restriction on the amount keystream that can be generated by one key/IV pair.
II We respect the limitation given in [7], i.e., only 2^{48} keystream bits can be generated before reinitialization with a new IV.

In Table 3 we tabulate some possible values of T, D_{IV} and D_{tot} for the two different cases. With no restriction on the keystream per key/IV pair the parameter choice $u = 13$, $d = 4$ and $P'_B = 2^{58}$ gives about 2^{69} for both computational complexity and total amount of keystream. We conclude that we have an attack requiring a total of 2^{69} received keystream bits and 2^{69} simple operations to recover the key.

If we respect the 2^{48} limit, choosing parameters $u = 9$, $d = 6$ and $P'_B = 2^{45}$ will allow us to recover the key with in total $2^{72.4}$ keystream bits and $2^{71.4}$ simple operations. In many situations it is difficult to argue that we can have a computational complexity that is lower than the number of keystream bits.

Table 3. Attack complexity for various parameter choices

Case	u	d	P'_B	$\alpha_{P'_B}$	D_{IV}	D_{tot}	T
	9	6	2^{60}	$2^{-9.18}$	$2^{62.3}$	$2^{71.5}$	$2^{55.5}$
I	13	2	2^{54}	$2^{-10.9}$	$2^{57.9}$	$2^{68.8}$	$2^{70.8}$
	13	4	2^{58}	$2^{-7.72}$	$2^{61.1}$	$2^{68.8}$	$2^{68.8}$
	15	2	2^{56}	$2^{-7.73}$	$2^{60.1}$	$2^{67.8}$	$2^{75.8}$
	7	10	2^{46}	$2^{-26.1}$	$2^{47.8}$	$2^{73.9}$	$2^{67.9}$
II	9	6	2^{45}	$2^{-25.1}$	$2^{47.3}$	$2^{72.4}$	$2^{71.4}$
	9	8	2^{45}	$2^{-25.1}$	$2^{47.1}$	$2^{72.2}$	$2^{73.2}$
	11	4	2^{45}	$2^{-22.7}$	$2^{47.9}$	$2^{70.6}$	$2^{75.6}$

An adversary observing the keystream is likely to need at least one operation per observed keystream bit. On the other hand, only very few keystream bits are actually used in the attack. If the adversary can randomly access keystream bits, the computational complexity can be allowed to be much smaller than the keystream.

Comparing the attack to an exhaustive key search, we can note that an exhaustive key search would require computing the key/IV setup consisting of 160 cycles and then additionally 80 cycles to get the 80 first output bits. Every cycle must compute 80 quasigroup operations. So a software implementation would require $240 \cdot 80$ quasigroup operations, i.e., more than 2^{14} operations to test one key. Thus, our attack requiring roughly 2^{69} simple operations is about 2^{25} times faster than a software implemented exhaustive key search.

9   Conclusion

An attack on Edon80 has been presented. It takes advantage of the relatively short period inside the state of the cipher. By knowing that some values in the internal state will repeat with high probability after a certain amount of state updates, it was possible to determine several key bits used in the update of the last part of the state. The required number of keystream bits as well as the total complexity is around 2^{69}, if we allow each key/IV pair to generate about 2^{61} keystream bits. If we consider the restriction put by the designers i.e., only 2^{48} keystream bits can be produced by each key/IV pair, then the total complexity is about 2^{72} simple operations with about 2^{47} bits from each key/IV pair.

Adding just a few more quasigroup operations to the chain of 80 is not enough to counter the attack, but doubling this number to 160 would be sufficient to resist the attack. However, such a modification comes at the cost of doubling the hardware (and the gate count).

We do not exclude the possibility of improving this attack by for example finding more efficient ways of computing the intersection of Γ_k sets. Since we are guessing a lot of key bits, there might be a possibility to do something more efficient. Some minor improvements to the described attack have already been found, and will be described in the full version of this paper.

References

1. Gligoroski, D., Markovski, S., Kocarev, L., Gusev, M.: Edon80. eSTREAM, ECRYPT Stream Cipher Project, Report 2005/007 (2005)
   http://www.ecrypt.eu.org/stream
2. Hong, J.: Period of streamcipher Edon80. In: Maitra, S., Madhavan, C.E.V., Venkatesan, R. (eds.) INDOCRYPT 2005. LNCS, vol. 3797, pp. 23–34. Springer, Heidelberg (2005)
3. Gligoroski, D., Markovski, S., Kocarev, L., Gusev, M.: Understanding periods in edon80. eSTREAM, ECRYPT Stream Cipher Project, Report 2005/054 (2005)
   http://www.ecrypt.eu.org/stream

4. Gligoroski, D., Markovski, S., Knapskog, S.J.: On periods of Edon-(2m, 2k) family of stream ciphers. The State of the Art of Stream Ciphers, Workshop Record, SASC 2006, Leuven, Belgium (2006)

5. Kasper, M., Kumar, S., Lemke-Rust, K., Paar, C.: A note on algebraic properties of quasigroups in Edon80. eSTREAM, ECRYPT Stream Cipher Project, Report 2007/032 (2007), *http://www.ecrypt.eu.org/stream*

6. Kasper, M., Kumar, S., Lemke-Rust, K., Paar, C.: A compact implementation of Edon80. eSTREAM, ECRYPT Stream Cipher Project, Report 2006/057 (2006), *http://www.ecrypt.eu.org/stream*

7. Gligoroski, D., Markovski, S., Kocarev, L., Gusev, M.: Status of Edon80 in the second phase of eSTREAM. eSTREAM, ECRYPT Stream Cipher Project (2006) *http://www.ecrypt.eu.org/stream/p2ciphers/edon80/edon80_p2note.pdf*

Author Index

Lecture Notes in Computer Science

Sublibrary 4: Security and Cryptology

Vol. 4237: H. Leitold, E.P. Markatos (Eds.), Communications and Multimedia Security. XII, 253 pages. 2006.

Vol. 4236: L. Breveglieri, I. Koren, D. Naccache, J.-P. Seifert (Eds.), Fault Diagnosis and Tolerance in Cryptography. XIII, 253 pages. 2006.

Vol. 4219: D. Zamboni, C. Krügel (Eds.), Recent Advances in Intrusion Detection. XII, 331 pages. 2006.

Vol. 4189: D. Gollmann, J. Meier, A. Sabelfeld (Eds.), Computer Security – ESORICS 2006. XI, 548 pages. 2006.

Vol. 4176: S.K. Katsikas, J. López, M. Backes, S. Gritzalis, B. Preneel (Eds.), Information Security. XIV, 548 pages. 2006.

Vol. 4117: C. Dwork (Ed.), Advances in Cryptology - CRYPTO 2006. XIII, 621 pages. 2006.

Vol. 4116: R. De Prisco, M. Yung (Eds.), Security and Cryptography for Networks. XI, 366 pages. 2006.

Vol. 4107: G. Di Crescenzo, A. Rubin (Eds.), Financial Cryptography and Data Security. XI, 327 pages. 2006.

Vol. 4083: S. Fischer-Hübner, S. Furnell, C. Lambrinoudakis (Eds.), Trust and Privacy in Digital Business. XIII, 243 pages. 2006.

Vol. 4064: R. Büschkes, P. Laskov (Eds.), Detection of Intrusions and Malware & Vulnerability Assessment. X, 195 pages. 2006.

Vol. 4058: L.M. Batten, R. Safavi-Naini (Eds.), Information Security and Privacy. XII, 446 pages. 2006.

Vol. 4047: M.J.B. Robshaw (Ed.), Fast Software Encryption. XI, 434 pages. 2006.

Vol. 4043: A.S. Atzeni, A. Lioy (Eds.), Public Key Infrastructure. XI, 261 pages. 2006.

Vol. 4004: S. Vaudenay (Ed.), Advances in Cryptology - EUROCRYPT 2006. XIV, 613 pages. 2006.

Vol. 3995: G. Müller (Ed.), Emerging Trends in Information and Communication Security. XX, 524 pages. 2006.

Vol. 3989: J. Zhou, M. Yung, F. Bao (Eds.), Applied Cryptography and Network Security. XIV, 488 pages. 2006.

Vol. 3969: Ø. Ytrehus (Ed.), Coding and Cryptography. XI, 443 pages. 2006.

Vol. 3958: M. Yung, Y. Dodis, A. Kiayias, T.G. Malkin (Eds.), Public Key Cryptography - PKC 2006. XIV, 543 pages. 2006.

Vol. 3957: B. Christianson, B. Crispo, J.A. Malcolm, M. Roe (Eds.), Security Protocols. IX, 325 pages. 2006.

Vol. 3956: G. Barthe, B. Grégoire, M. Huisman, J.-L. Lanet (Eds.), Construction and Analysis of Safe, Secure, and Interoperable Smart Devices. IX, 175 pages. 2006.

Vol. 3935: D.H. Won, S. Kim (Eds.), Information Security and Cryptology - ICISC 2005. XIV, 458 pages. 2006.

Vol. 3934: J.A. Clark, R.F. Paige, F.A.C. Polack, P.J. Brooke (Eds.), Security in Pervasive Computing. X, 243 pages. 2006.

Vol. 3928: J. Domingo-Ferrer, J. Posegga, D. Schreckling (Eds.), Smart Card Research and Advanced Applications. XI, 359 pages. 2006.

Vol. 3919: R. Safavi-Naini, M. Yung (Eds.), Digital Rights Management. XI, 357 pages. 2006.

Vol. 3903: K. Chen, R. Deng, X. Lai, J. Zhou (Eds.), Information Security Practice and Experience. XIV, 392 pages. 2006.

Vol. 3897: B. Preneel, S. Tavares (Eds.), Selected Areas in Cryptography. XI, 371 pages. 2006.

Vol. 3876: S. Halevi, T. Rabin (Eds.), Theory of Cryptography. XI, 617 pages. 2006.

Vol. 3866: T. Dimitrakos, F. Martinelli, P.Y.A. Ryan, S. Schneider (Eds.), Formal Aspects in Security and Trust. X, 259 pages. 2006.

Vol. 3860: D. Pointcheval (Ed.), Topics in Cryptology - CT-RSA 2006. XI, 365 pages. 2006.

Vol. 3858: A. Valdes, D. Zamboni (Eds.), Recent Advances in Intrusion Detection. X, 351 pages. 2006.

Vol. 3856: G. Danezis, D. Martin (Eds.), Privacy Enhancing Technologies. VIII, 273 pages. 2006.

Vol. 3786: J.-S. Song, T. Kwon, M. Yung (Eds.), Information Security Applications. XI, 378 pages. 2006.

Vol. 3108: H. Wang, J. Pieprzyk, V. Varadharajan (Eds.), Information Security and Privacy. XII, 494 pages. 2004.

Vol. 2951: M. Naor (Ed.), Theory of Cryptography. XI, 523 pages. 2004.

Vol. 2742: R.N. Wright (Ed.), Financial Cryptography. VIII, 321 pages. 2003.